LEARNING EMPLOYMENT LAW

▪ ▪ ▪

Francis J. Mootz III

Professor of Law
McGeorge School of Law
University of the Pacific

Leticia M. Saucedo

Professor of Law
School of Law
University of California, Davis

Michael P. Maslanka

Assistant Professor of Law
College of Law
University of North Texas, Dallas

LEARNING SERIES

WEST ACADEMIC PUBLISHING

444 Cedar Street, Suite 700
St. Paul, MN 55101
1-877-888-1330

Printed in the United States of America

ISBN: 978-0-314-27869-2

To my parents, Lois and Pete Mootz,
who taught me the importance and dignity of hard work.
—FJM III

To my mother, Veronica, from whom I inherited
the ability to find joy in my work.
—LMS

To my parents, Dorothy and Frank Maslanka,
and to their parents, whose hard work made
these contributions possible.
—MPM

PREFACE

Employment law is a diverse, challenging, and fascinating practice area. This book provides contemporary materials that address the most important questions in the field today. Each Lesson is self-contained to enable you to focus on specific learning objectives for each class period. We use brief textual introductions to frame the issues, provide Restatement provisions to clarify the elements of various rules, offer short and clear examples of the issues, and then challenge your understanding with problems. The Lessons include contemporary cases, statutes, and other sources of law that have been carefully edited to ensure that you focus on the salient questions.

Employment law touches a vital part of most people's lives, and the labor market is a critical aspect of our economy. We focus on practical lawyering skills, but not at the expense of ignoring the broader questions that drive contemporary practice. It is difficult to understand employment law without appreciating its history and the theories used to define the issues and propose solutions. This text provides a bridge between the broader context and the specific problems that arise in practice.

This course covers a variety of topics, but does not provide in-depth treatment of labor law or anti-discrimination law, both of which are generally covered in a separate course. You may review Lesson 2 for an overview of these other legal frameworks that address workplace law.

We deeply appreciate the hard work of our research assistants on this project. Professor Mootz would like to thank Simone Leighty (McGeorge School of Law '20) for her extensive work, and also Meghan Shiner (McGeorge School of Law '20), Jessica Gandara (McGeorge School of Law '19), and Michael Hopkins (McGeorge School of Law '19). Professor Saucedo would like to thank Angela Breining (U.C. Davis School of Law '19), Tanairi Alcaraz (U.C. Davis School of Law '18), Mayra Sandoval (U.C. Davis School of Law '19), Gymmel Garcia Carmona (U.C. Davis School of Law '19), and Gloria Chong (U.C. Davis School of Law '19) for their work and dedication to this project. Professor Maslanka would like to thank Linda Sulik (UNT Dallas College of Law '19) and Stewart A. Caton, Law Librarian Research (UNT Dallas College of Law) for their invaluable research and editing help, and former Academic Dean Ellen Pryor (UNT Dallas College of Law) for her encouragement.

We hope that our casebook helps you to learn and appreciate employment law. If you have any comments or suggestions, we would love to hear from you.

Francis J. Mootz III
Sacramento, CA

Leticia M. Saucedo
Davis, CA

Michael P. Maslanka
Dallas, TX

November 2018

ACKNOWLEDGMENTS

The authors would like to thank the following for use of their materials:

ABA Model Rules of Professional Conduct, Rules 1.1, 1.3, 1.6, 1.7, 1.9, 1.10, 4.1, 5.6, 7.1, 8.4, © 2016 by the American Bar Association. Permission for use has been granted by the American Bar Association. All rights reserved. This information or any or portion thereof may not be copied or disseminated in any form or by any means or stored in an electronic database or retrieval system without the express written consent of the American Bar Association.

Flora Gill, *The Meaning of Work: Lessons from Sociology, Psychology, and Political Theory*, J. of Socio-Economics 28:725–43 (1999).

THE FISSURED WORKPLACE: WHY WORK BECAME SO BAD FOR SO MANY AND WHAT CAN BE DONE TO IMPROVE IT by David Weil, Cambridge, Mass.: Harvard University Press, Copyright © 2014 by the President and Fellows of Harvard College.

Excerpt from *Working: People Talk About What They Do All Day and How They Feel About What They Do*—Copyright © 1996 by Studs Terkel. Reprinted by permission of The New Press. www.thenewpress.com.

"Corporate Securities Lawyer," "Slaughterhouse Human Resources Director," and "Poultry Factory Worker" from GIG: AMERICANS TALK ABOUT THEIR JOBS AT THE TURN OF THE MILLENNIUM edited by John Bowe, Marisa Bowe, & Sabin Streeter, with Daron Murphy and Rose Kernochan, copyright © 2000, 2001 by John Bowe, Marisa Bowe, and Sabin Streeter. Used by permission of Crown Books, an imprint of Random House, a division of Penguin Random House LLC. All rights reserved.

Thomas Kohler, *Individualism and Communitarianism At Work*, 1993 B.Y.U. L. Rev. 727 (January 1993).

Colorable Claims: The Continuing Significance of Color Under Title VII Forty Years After Its Passage, Cynthia E. Nance © 2005 by the Regents of the University of California Reprinted from the Berkeley Journal of Employment & Labor Law—26 Berkeley J. Emp. & Lab. L. 435 (2005) By permission of the Regents of the University of California.

NAT'L CTR FOR LESBIAN RIGHTS & CALIFORNIA RURAL LEGAL ASSISTANCE, *Tips for Legal Advocates Working with Lesbian, Gay, Bisexual, & Transgender Clients*, http://www.nclrights.org/wp-content/uploads/2013/07/Proyecto_Poderoso_Flyer_cd.pdf.

Jatrine Bentsi-Enchill, *Client Communication: Measuring Your Cross-Cultural Competence, The Canadian Bar Association* (September 29, 2014). Reprinted with permission from the Canadian Bar Association (CBA). The views are the opinion of the author and do not necessarily reflect the views of the CBA.

Matt Bodie, *Participation as a Theory of Employment*, Vol. 89 NOTRE DAME LAW REVIEW 684–88 (2013). Reprinted with permission. © Notre Dame Law Review, University of Notre Dame. The Notre Dame Law Review is not responsible for any errors that have occurred in editing or reprinting this piece.

Seth D. Harris and Alan B. Krueger, *A Proposal for Modernizing Labor Laws for Twenty-First Century Work: The "Independent Worker"*, The Hamilton Project Discussion Paper 2015–10 (December 2015), Brookings.

James Gray Pope, "A Brief History of United States Labor and Employment Law," in The Oxford International Encyclopedia of Legal History 477–86 (Stanley N. Katz ed., 2009). Reproduced with permission of the Licensor through PLSclear.

Jay M. Feinman, *The Development of the Employment at Will Rule*, by permission of Oxford University Press and the American Journal of Legal History, 20 issue 2 118 (1976).

Deborah A. Ballam, *The Development of the Employment at Will Rule Revisited: A Challenge to its Origins as Based in the Development of Advanced Capitalism*, 13 Hofstra Lab. And Employment L. J. 75 (1995).

Bill Taylor, *Trust Your Employees, Not Your Rule Book*, Harv. Bus. Rev. Apr. 2017.

'Bro-culture' at Google Led to Sexual Harassment and Violence, Lawsuit Alleges, Ethan Baron, Mercury News, February 24, 2018. Used with permission of Mercury News Copyright© 2019. All rights reserved.

Sarah Trotto, *Fatigue and worker safety: Experts say employers play a role in tackling the issue*, 195 *Safety+Health* magazine 2, February 26, 2017.

Jia Tolentino, *The Gig Economy Celebrates Working Yourself to Death*, The New Yorker (c) Conde Nast, Mar 22, 2017.

Eric J. Conn & Kate M. McMahon, *The OSHA Defense Report: OSHA Updates from Conn Maciel Carey's OSHA Practice Group: OSHA Criminal Cases on the Rise*, Conn Maciel Carey LLP (Jan. 22, 2016) https://oshadefensereport.com/.

Patricia A. Patrick, *Be Prepared Before You Blow the Whistle: Protection Under State Whistle-blowing Laws*, Fraud Magazine 24: 28–31 (2010). Fraud Magazine, a publication of the Association of Certified Fraud Examiners of Austin, Texas.

Thoughts on the Deadly Boston Trench Collapse (October 26, 2016) Mark Garfinkel/Pictureboston.com/ for the Boston Herald.

Leticia M. Saucedo, *States of Desire: How Immigration Law Allows States to Attract Desired Immigrants*, 52 U.C. Davis L. Rev. 471 (2018).

SUMMARY OF CONTENTS

TABLE OF CONTENTS

TABLE OF CASES

The principle cases are in bold type.

LEARNING EMPLOYMENT LAW

1

Introduction

Key Concepts

- Work is extremely significant on a personal level, and is vital to modern societies.
- Legal regulation often seeks to balance the protection of individual interests with the needs of the economic system.
- Regulation has been piecemeal, accomplished through various common law developments and the enactment of statutes that address discrete issues.
- This book does not cover labor law or anti-discrimination law because these topics merit a separate course.

Lesson 1:
The Personal and Social Meaning of Work

Objectives and Expected Learning Outcomes

In this first Lesson, you will develop an appreciation of the personal significance and social importance of work. This Lesson provides an important foundation that will allow you to better understand *how* and *why* employment law has developed. You will be a more effective lawyer if you understand the broader context in which legal doctrine operates, rather than just studying the doctrine.

We begin the course by considering the nature of work. It is easy to assume that work is a simple, utilitarian effort that is not central to our lives. The familiar phrase, "it's just a job," captures this sentiment. However, if you reflect for a moment, you will recognize that work is a very important part of human life. Freud's famous quotation, "Love and work are the cornerstones of our humanness," captures the deep significance that work holds for individuals. By regulating the work relationship, then, employment law addresses a foundational aspect of our humanity. The matcrials that follow will make the most sense if you understand that employment law is not just a regulation of an anonymous economic exchange.

The personal significance of work to our lives does not mean that the economic view of work is completely misplaced. Work is one of the primary ways in which individuals participate in the social realm. Advanced capitalist economies are founded on individuals exchanging their labor for money, and then using that money for later economic exchanges. You should remember that this is a recent development in the history of work. For much of human history, including the early history of the United States, work has been performed by slaves, indentured servants, peonage labor and conscripted workers. One of the great advances of modern civilization has been to acknowledge the dignity of work and the right of the worker to the value of her labor.

This course will consider contemporary regulation of work through various legal means (common law, statutes, regulations, etc.), but it is important to begin the course with a solid understanding of the deep significance of work to the workers and to the society in which they live. This first Lesson covers no legal doctrine, but it is an important part of the course because we will refer back to our discussions of the nature of work as the semester progresses.

1. The Personal Significance of Work

On a day-to-day basis we think of work instrumentally: it is the exchange of labor for money that provides the worker with the means to survive. Few people in our society are fortunate enough to perform work that is immediately, intrinsically and completely satisfying to them. Work is labor; it is not undertaken for its own sake. Despite its largely instrumental character, however, work also has a deeply personal significance. Employees spend most of their waking hours in the workplace setting, so their accomplishments and their relationships with co-workers play a very large role in their lives. It should be intuitive that an employee who is fired from a job may suffer personal emotional distress above and beyond the effect of losing his wages, even though the employee would have gladly quit his position upon winning the lottery. Work is more than an economic means to an end for most persons. To understand the legal regulation of the workplace, it is important to appreciate the non-economic factors that give work its personal significance.

Consider the following overview of the importance of non-economic factors in the workplace, and the personal significance of work beyond the economic exchange that takes place between employer and employee.

Flora Gill, *The Meaning of Work: Lessons from Sociology, Psychology, and Political Theory*

J. of Socio-Economics 28: 725–43 (1999).

Economics stands alone in describing the positive aspect of paid work simply as the opportunity to make money. Economics is also unique in emphasizing just one negative, the loss of leisure. In contrast, psychology (both individual and social) and sociology emphasize the centrality of work, per se, to individual well-being. These academic disciplines do not play down the critical role played by purchasing power as a need essential to well-being, but they emphasize the critical role played by the nonpecuniary aspects of the work experience. These include not only the features of the job itself, but also the general character of the physical and human environment at the workplace. The pecuniary and the nonpecuniary aspects are fundamentally seen as two vital determinants of well-being that cannot simply be treated as substitutes for each other.

. . . .

These issues have been the focus of a large body of literature ranging from Marxist scholarship through political science to the more recent developments in feminist scholarship. This diverse body of literature points to a range of factors that assign privilege to select groups of individuals—power is possessed by virtue of affiliation with a privilege group. Whereas the Marxist literature emphasizes class, other discourses have drawn attention to the categories of race, ethnicity, sex, and gender. The emphasis on class tends to focus on power exercised vertically down the managerial hierarchy at the workplace. The feminist and ethnographic scholarships, in contrast, draw attention to power currents running not only vertically but also horizontally, setting apart individuals working alongside each other in objectively identical productive capacities according on gender and ethnicity.

Yet, another category of people can be described as comprising a socially privileged group. These are people with temperament and personal ethics such that in a given socioeconomic structure they naturally wield power.

This is reflected in a common workplace scenario where less assertive individuals find themselves dominated by the more powerful. Here power is exerted not only across the gender and ethnic divides, but also within each of these groups.

. . . .

In summary, the thrust of the literature surveyed in this section is that the design of job content and the structure of human relationships governing social interaction in the workplace are governed by specific business goals and a culture that allows management to exercise power over others without necessarily being aware of it. These goals, this literature clearly suggests, do not necessarily satisfy the psychological needs of workers. The literature also cogently argues that the specific set of social values that guide management strategies tends to favor select social groups, while rendering the merits of other groups of individuals invisible. This, I propose, has implications for both economic science's notion of optimal allocation of social resources and for modern society's image of itself as a community that adheres to fundamental democratic tenets and secures a reasonable degree of social justice.

. . . .

Our society has entrusted the bulk of our human resources in the hands of those who legally own workplaces. The design of jobs, physical environment, and the core structure of human relations at the workplace are largely the domain of managers guided by their own cultural outlook, operating as the agents of the shareholders. True, in most advanced industrial societies the owners of workplaces are required to abide by certain socially prescribed principles that set certain obligatory minimum standards, and to this extent workers are recognized as *stakeholders* in the workplace. However, the requirements address only a few of the variables that influence workers' welfare, and hence, represent only minimal recognition of workers as stakeholders with legitimate claims on the design of jobs and the workplace environment. This, in turn, suggests that there are strong grounds to believe that our deployment of our human resources in the workplace falls short of a social optimum. The supporting argument is threefold:

First, if we accept that the mental and emotional well-being of workers is a substantial element of society's social welfare, then social welfare is suboptimal because this aspect of it is systematically undervalued in the design of work and the workplace. Second, although shareholders' (or business) goals are recognized as legitimate goals of the business enterprise as a whole, the quest for power, per se, and the significant role played by social and cultural preconception must operate as natural brakes on the capacity of the enterprise to realize its own long-term profits. Third, the thrust of the disciplinary discourse surveyed in earlier sections of this paper is that the allocation of resources may well violate certain fundamental social concerns. In terms of the economic vernacular, this requires expansion of our notion of "social-welfare" function to include society's concerns about social justice, basic democratic tenets, and economic preconditions for genuine citizenship. This conclusion follows from the very notion of "efficiency" because efficiency, strictly speaking, means meeting an objective, whatever it may be, at the lowest possible resource cost. Once we expand the concept of resources to include workers' physical and psychological well-being, expand the notion of social objective to include maximization not just of the value of purchased goods and services, but also the quality of social interaction, social justice, and compliance with democratic tenets, we come up with a very different efficient allocation of resources.

Economics, however, does not readily accommodate the proposition that the market and the manner in which we assign property rights at the workplace places too little weight on the worker's mental and emotional well-being.

QUESTIONS

1. Think about your own experience: how important are the nonpecuniary aspects of a job compared to the pecuniary aspects?
2. Do you agree that the "design of work and the workplace" systematically undervalues the mental and emotional well-being of workers in favor of their pecuniary interests? If so, how might this problem be corrected? Should it be corrected?
3. Take a few minutes to write about an important experience or observation in a workplace that might be relevant to our discussion of the personal significance of work.

2. The Social and Economic Significance of Work

Work is not only important to the individual; it is also the cornerstone of the social and economic structures of society. It is helpful to think about the historical development of work as a social and economic structure. In the following subsections, we consider the Marxist critique of wage labor in the mid-nineteenth century when employment law was virtually absent, more contemporary critiques of the government regulation of advanced capitalist economies, and a description of the fundamental economic changes in today's workplace. The purpose of the following excerpts is not to provide a "true" account, but instead to provide a sense of the history leading to modern employment law and the need to take a broad view (whether Marxist, libertarian, etc.) in order to gain perspective on the specifics of the legal regulation of work.

A. Marx's Critique of the Industrial Revolution

We begin with excerpts from Karl Marx's famous pamphlet, *The Communist Manifesto.* He traces the history of the development of the modern working class (proletariat) and predicts increasing economic crisis and confrontation. When this tract was published there was a great deal of economic unrest around the world. As you read the excerpt, consider whether Marx accurately diagnoses the conditions around him, and how the subsequent development of labor and employment law has altered the conditions he describes.

Karl Marx and Frederick Engels,
Manifesto of the Communist Party

(1848).

The history of all hitherto existing society is the history of class struggles.

Freeman and slave, patrician and plebeian, lord and serf, guild-master and journeyman, in a word, oppressor and oppressed, stood in constant opposition to one another, carried on an uninterrupted, now hidden, now open fight, a fight that each time ended, either in a revolutionary re-constitution of society at large, or in the common ruin of the contending classes.

In the earlier epochs of history, we find almost everywhere a complicated arrangement of society into various orders, a manifold gradation of social rank. In ancient Rome we have patricians, knights, plebeians, slaves; in the

Middle Ages, feudal lords, vassals, guild-masters, journeymen, apprentices, serfs; in almost all of these class, again, subordinate gradations.

The modern bourgeois society that has sprouted from the ruins of feudal society has not done away with class antagonisms. It has but established new classes, new conditions of oppression, and new forms of struggle in place of the old ones.

Our epoch, the epoch of the bourgeoisie, possesses, however, this distinctive feature: it has simplified the class antagonisms. Society as a whole is more and more splitting up into two great hostile camps, into two great classes directly facing each other: Bourgeoisie and Proletariat.

. . . .

. . . Modern bourgeois society with its relations of production, of exchange and of property, a society that has conjured up such gigantic means of production and of exchange, is like the sorcerer, who is no longer able to control the powers of the nether world whom he has called up by his spells. For many a decade past the history of industry and commerce is but the history of the revolt of modern productive forces against modern conditions of production, against the property relations that are the conditions for the existence of the bourgeoisie and of its rule. It is enough to mention the commercial crises that by their periodical return put on its trial, each time more threateningly, the existence of the entire bourgeois society. In these crises a great part not only of the existing products, but also of the previously created productive forces, are periodically destroyed. In these crises there breaks out an epidemic that, in all earlier epochs, would have seemed an absurdity—the epidemic of over-production. Society suddenly finds itself put back into a state of momentary barbarism; it appears as if a famine, a universal war of devastation had cut off the supply of every means of subsistence; industry and commerce seem to be destroyed; and why? Because there is too much civilization, too much means of subsistence, too much industry, too much commerce. The productive forces at the disposal of society no longer tend to further the development of the conditions of bourgeois property; on the contrary, they have become too powerful for these conditions, by which they are fettered, and so soon as they overcome these fetters, they bring disorder into the whole of bourgeois society, endanger the existence of bourgeois property. The conditions of bourgeois society are too narrow to comprise the wealth created by them. And how does the bourgeoisie get over these crises? On the one hand, by enforced destruction of a mass of productive forces; on the other, by the conquest of new markets, and by the more thorough exploitation of the old ones. That is to say, by paving the way for more extensive and more destructive crises, and by diminishing the means whereby crises are prevented.

The weapons with which the bourgeoisie felled feudalism to the ground are now turned against the bourgeoisie itself.

. . . .

In place of the old bourgeois society, with its classes and class antagonisms, we shall have an association, in which the free development of each is the condition for the free development of all.

. . . .

The Communists disdain to conceal their views and aims. They openly declare that their ends can be attained only by the forcible overthrow of all existing social conditions. Let the ruling classes tremble at a Communistic revolution. The proletarians have nothing to lose but their chains. They have a world to win.

WORKING MEN OF ALL COUNTRIES, UNITE!

B. Contemporary Marxist Critiques of Advanced Capitalism

Marx's deterministic theory of historical materialism is not widely embraced today. First, socialist economies have tended to be inefficient and oppressive. Second, capitalist economies have proven resilient to the predicted proletariat revolution. Why did the proletariat revolution fail to materialize? Supporters of capitalism argue that economic development has successfully improved the lives of all members of society rather than degenerating into an opposition of oppressed workers and oppressive employers. Under this "conservative" or "libertarian" view, government intervention into the economy generally, and into employment relations specifically, threatens to undermine the beneficial effects of the capitalist economy. Others argue that the capitalism of the nineteenth century was indeed headed for collapse until the federal and state governments intervened in the economy to offset its harsh effects. Under this "liberal" view, the Great Depression was the culmination of an increasingly harsh and unstable business economy, which was overcome only through the massive intervention of government in the form of the "New Deal," massive defense spending during World War II, and subsequently by the adoption of Keynesian economic policy. Under both the conservative and liberal views, one thing is certain: viewed as a collective body of law, modern employment law represents an ongoing response to broader political, social, and economic trends.

A neo-Marxist interpretation of twentieth-century capitalist development is less comforting. According to this perspective, government intervention in the economy neither threatens (without entirely thwarting) economic efficiency and progress, nor does it save the economic system from ruin. Instead, government intervention in the form of the modern "welfare state" serves only to transfer the economic crisis of capitalism to the political system. Jürgen Habermas, certainly one of the most influential living sociologists and philosophers, advances this neo-Marxist analysis by describing the resulting "legitimation crisis" of "advanced capitalist societies." Think about how the public now reacts to high unemployment rates: they demand that the government adopt policies to promote job creation, and the government loses legitimacy if it fails to do so. Even those who argue that "the free market" should be unleashed from government control require a government that enforces contracts and property rights to permit economic growth to occur.

Take a few minutes to write down the extent of government intervention into the workplace that you believe is desirable, and why. We will be asking this same question in every Lesson.

C. The Contemporary Labor Economy of the "Fissured Workplace"

The Marxist critique of "advanced capitalism" may seem old-fashioned at this point in history, when the labor economy is undergoing profound disruption. The name of the car service, "Uber," has become a shorthand nickname for the new "on demand" economy that relies on networks rather than formal employment relationships. Some argue that the shift to the "on demand" economy will provide as significant a challenge to work regulation as the transition from liberal capitalism to advanced capitalism. Consider the following description of the challenges that the increasingly "fissured workplaces" in the contemporary economy present for owner, workers, and society.

David Weil, The Fissured Workplace: Why Work Became So Bad for So Many and What Can Be Done to Improve It

1–26 (Harvard University Press 2014).

Part 1: Vignettes from the Modern Workplace

A maid works at the San Francisco Marriott on Fisherman's Wharf. The hotel property is owned by Host Hotels and Resorts Inc., a lodging real estate company. The maid, however, is evaluated and supervised daily and her hours and payroll managed by Crestline Hotels and Resorts Inc., a national third-party hotel management company. Yet she follows daily procedures (and risks losing her job for failure to accomplish them) regarding cleaning, room set-up, overall pace, and quality standards established by Marriott, whose name the property bears.

A cable installer in Dayton, Ohio, works as an independent contractor (in essence a self-employed business provider), paid on a job-by-job basis by Cascom Inc., a cable installation company. Cascom's primary client is the international media giant Time Warner, which owns cable systems across the United States. The cable installer is paid solely on the basis of the job completed and is entitled to no protections normally afforded employees. Yet all installation contracts are supplied solely by Cascom, which also sets the price for jobs and collects payment for them. The installer must wear a shirt with the Cascom logo and can be removed as a contractor at will for not meeting minimum quotas or quality standards, or at the will of the company.

. . . .

In an earlier era, Marriott, Time Warner, . . . as well as other large employers that produced well-known products and services, would likely have directly employed the workers in the above vignettes. Not so now. As major companies have consciously invested in building brands and devoted customers as the cornerstone of their business strategy, they have also shed their role as the direct employer of the people responsible for providing those products and services.

In all of the above cases, the jobs shifted away to be done by separate employers who pay low wages; provide limited or often no health care, pension, or other benefits; and offer tenuous job security. Moreover, workers in each case received pay or faced workplace conditions that violated one or more workplace laws. . . .

The cases are not exceptional, but rather indicative of practices found in the varied industries depicted above as well as in a growing number of other sectors and occupations. Yet these working conditions are not an inevitable result of the nature of those jobs or of amorphous forces like globalization. They result from a fundamental restructuring of employment in many parts of the economy.

. . . .

By shedding direct employment, lead business enterprises select from among multiple providers of those activities and services formerly done inside the organization, thereby substantially reducing costs and dispatching the many responsibilities connected to being the employer of record. Information and communication technologies have enabled this hidden transformation of work, since they allow lead companies to promulgate and enforce product and quality standards key to their business strategies, thereby maintaining the carefully created reputation of their goods and services and reaping price premiums from their loyal customer base.

The new organization of the workplace also undermines the mechanisms that once led to the workforce sharing part of the value created by their large corporate employers. By shedding employment to other parties, lead companies change a wage-setting problem into a contracting decision. The result is stagnation of real wages for many of the jobs formerly done inside.

Laws originally intended to ensure basic labor standards and to protect workers from health and safety risks now enable these changes by focusing regulatory attention on the wrong parties. Core federal and state laws that regulate employment, often dating back to the first half of the twentieth century, often assume simple and direct employee/employer relationships. They make presumptions about responsibility and liability similar to those we make as customers, presumptions that ignore the transformation that has occurred under the hood of many business enterprises. Traditional approaches to enforcing those laws similarly ignore the myriad new relationships that lie below the surface of the workplace. As a result, the laws crafted to safeguard basic standards, to reduce health and safety risks, and to cushion displacement from injury or economic downturn often fail to do so.

In essence, private strategies and public policies allow major companies to simultaneously profit from the core activities that create value in the eyes of customers and the capital markets and shed the actual production of goods and services. In so doing, they have their cake and eat it too.

. . . .

As the fissured workplace has deepened and spread across the economy, work that once provided middle-class wages and benefits has declined. Jobs that once resided inside lead businesses providing decent earnings and stability now reside with employers who set wages under far more competitive conditions. Where lead companies once shared gains with their internal workforce fissuring leads to growing inequality in how the value created in the economy is distributed.

Laws that protect workers have not kept pace with the new boundaries of the fissured workplace. Americans' commitment to providing safety and health and decent conditions at the workplace has not changed. But relentless subcontracting can blur responsibility for safety and workers in harm's way. Outsourcing management to third parties can lead to violation of minimum wage laws. And franchising, an often unrecognized form of fissured employment, can create incentives that simultaneously demand adherence to product quality and create incentives for franchisees to violate laws.

Even the business cycle may be affected by the spread of fissuring. Historically, hiring by large businesses led economic recoveries: as aggregate demand recovered, large firms directly increased employment. Now, employment decisions in many industries are mediated by fissured structures. Not only does this mean that the timing of recoveries may be slowed, since they must flow through multiple layers of fissured relationships: but the composition of jobs added also will reflect those relationships. Seen in this light, it is not surprising that the first jobs to be added following the Great Recession were predominantly at the low end of the wage distribution.

. . . .

Although the fissured workplace plays out in different ways across industries, its consequences for workplace conditions are similar. By shifting the provision of service or parts of production to other employers, lead businesses create markets for services that are usually very competitive, thereby creating downward pressure on the marginal price for them. This means that the employers competing for that work face significant pressures on the wages and conditions they can offer their workforce, particularly in industries where there is an elastic supply of labor, skill requirements are relatively low, and labor costs represent a significant part of overall costs.

There is abundant evidence that the majority of workers in the United States face an increasingly difficult workplace—and did so even before the Great Recession of 2007–2009. Falling real wages, declining benefits, reduced employment security, and a stifled ability to complain about problems describe a growing part of the employment landscape. Trends in the labor market (particularly in the low-wage segment), studies of workplace compliance, and the findings of government regulators paint a picture of a worsening workplace and more vulnerable workers in recent decades. Consider:

- Real wages for median workers (those at the 50th percentile of the wage distribution) grew by only 0.5% between 2000 and 2012. Median hourly compensation (wages plus benefits) grew by only 4%. Yet productivity (measured as output of goods and services per hour worked) rose by 23% over the same period.

- Fewer and fewer workers have pensions: the proportion of private sector workers with some form of pension fell from 51% in 1979 to 43% in 2009. Of those workers who have them, the vast majority now have defined contribution plans that shift the risk of retirement income onto the worker.

- Among low-wage workers, the U.S. Bureau of Labor Statistics in its 2007 National Compensation Survey reported that only 24% in the bottom quintile of the wage distribution had employer-provided health coverage, compared to 62% of workers in the middle-wage quintile.

- In 2012 the U.S. Department of Labor recovered a record level of back wages from employers—representing the difference between wages workers received and what the law says their employers are responsible for paying.

Many of the industries where researchers in recent years have found high rates of violations of basic labor standards and worsening employment conditions coincide with industries where fissuring is most advanced. These include restaurant and hospitality sectors, janitorial services, many segments of manufacturing, residential construction, and home health care. But fissuring also is present in retailing, telecommunication and IT sectors, hospitals, public schools, auto supply, transportation, and logistics/distribution services. Accounts of fissuring of paralegal and legal jobs, accounting, journalism, and professional services are also increasingly common. In fact, employment fissuring represents an organizational format that has been adopted across many sectors of the economy, assuming many different forms.

There are three reasons we should worry about the social consequences of the fissured workplace. First, it often undermines compliance with basic labor standards. Second, chopping employment into pieces makes production coordination harder and results in a problem economists call externalities that can result in accidents, injuries, and fatalities. Third, there are distributional consequences of the fissured workplace, shifting surplus generated by businesses away from the workforce and to investors.

Mending the Fissured Workplace

An examination of fissured employment puts the question of the boundaries of employment responsibility center stage. Most employment laws in the United States at the state and federal level define "employee" according to stated objectives of the individual statute. This has led to varied—and highly contested—debates on who is or is not an employee. Common law defines an employer as a party who has the right to "direct and control" the performance of an employee as he or she undertakes a set of compensated activities. Courts apply a long list of factors used to determine if such control exists in a given situation, such as control of the work, product, determination of the time and place of work, and the provision of tools and materials.

Federal workplace laws define employees and employers. The problem is that each law does so differently. Take two examples. The Fair Labor Standards Act, which sets minimum wage and overtime standards and regulates child labor, defines an employee as "any individual who is employed by an employer" and states that "employ included to suffer or permit to work." To help clarify this vague definition, courts apply an economic realities test to evaluate the particular employment situation surrounding a worker and an employer. This potentially gives the agency responsible for enforcement the latitude to adjust to changing employment conditions on the ground.

. . . .

But as the vignettes opening Part I also make clear, fissured employment further muddies these already murky waters. Although most laws look to the owner of the enterprise as the party ultimately responsible, in many cases the owners are only nominally involved in the setting of employment policies or their implementation. In hotels, for example, the pace and nuances of work are set by the brand (for example, Hilton); day-to-day human resource functions and oversight of the workforce are handled by an independent hotel operating company (for example, Tharaldson Lodging); and the employee may receive her paycheck from a staffing company hired by the hotel operator, rendering the owners of the property little more than the ultimate wallet from which pay is dispensed. Employment therefore bears little resemblance to the dyadic relationship often assumed in how we think about and administer our core workplace regulations.

. . . .

Addressing the problems of working conditions, wages, and employment over the next decades will require wrestling with the consequences of the fissured organization and the public's willingness to balance its benefits to some consumers and shareholders against its consequences to those whose workplaces have been fundamentally altered by it. Although the fissured organization raises a raft of new questions and challenges, and understanding of its origins, operation, and implications opens a range of opportunities to address its consequences.

QUESTIONS

1. The "fissured" workplace is subject to legal rules based on the model of employer and employee. How should the government deal with the rise of the "1099 economy," in which many workers are treated as independent contractors who are outside the scope of employment regulation?
2. Who is the "boss" in the "fissured workplace?" Who has obligations to the employee under employment laws?

3. Putting the Analysis Together: Workers in Their Own Voices

The way in which workers describe their jobs provides concrete insight into how the personal significance of work intersects with larger social and economic forces. The following excerpts provide short segments from interviews with workers in the modern economy. The first excerpts are from Studs Terkel's pathbreaking oral history of workers taken during the late 1960s and early 1970s. This reflects a certain era of work in American history. The later excerpts follow in Terkel's tradition by providing oral histories of workers in the new century.

Studs Terkel, Working: People Talk About What They Do All Day and How They Feel About What They Do

xxxi–xxxv, 164–66 (The New Press 1972).

Mike Lefevre (Steelworker in Cicero, Illinois)

I'm a dying breed. A laborer. Strictly muscle work . . . picks it up, put it down, pick it up, and put it down. We handle between forty and fifty thousand pounds of steel a day. (Laughs) I know this is hard to believe—from four hundred pounds to three- and four-pound pieces. It's dying.

You can't take pride any more. You remember when a guy could point to a house he built, how many logs he stacked. He built it and he was proud of it. . . .

It's hard to take pride in a bridge you're never going to cross, in a door you're never gonna open. You're mass-producing things and you never see the end result of it. (Muses) I worked for a trucker one time. And I got this tiny satisfaction when I loaded a truck. At least I could see the truck depart loaded. In a steel mill, forget it. You don't see where nothing goes.

I got chewed out by my foreman once. He said, "Mike, you're a good worker but you have a bad attitude." My attitude is that I don't get excited about my job. I do my work but I don't say whoopee-doo. The day I get excited about my job is the day I go to a head shrinker. How are you gonna get excited about pullin' steel? How are you gonna get excited when you're tired and want to sit down?

It's not just the work. Somebody built the pyramids. Somebody's going to build something. Pyramids, Empire State Building—these things just don't happen. There's hard work behind it. I would like to see a building, say, the Empire State, I would like to see on one side of it a foot-wide strip from top to bottom with the name of every bricklayer, the name of every electrician, with all the names. So when a guy walked by, he could take his son and say, "See, that's me over there on the forty-fifth floor. I put the steel beam in." Picasso can point to a painting. What can I point to? A writer can point to a book. Everybody should have something to point to.

. . . .

You're doing this manual labor and you know that technology can do it. (Laughs). Let's face it, a machine can do the work of a man; otherwise they wouldn't have space probes. Why can we send a rocket ship that's unmanned and yet send a man in a steel mill to do a mule's work?

Automation? Depends how it's applied. It frightens me if it puts me out on the street. It doesn't frighten me if it shortens my work week. You read that little thing: what are you going to do when this computer replaces you? Blow up computers. (Laughs) Really. Blow up computers. I'll be goddamned if a computer is gonna eat before I do! I want milk for my kids and beer for me. Machines can either liberate man or enslave 'im, because they're pretty neutral. It's man who has the bias to put the thing one place or another.

. . . .

It isn't that the average working guy is dumb. He's tired, that's all. I picked up a book on chess one time. That thing laid in the drawer for two or three weeks, you're too tired.

. . . .

If I were to put you in front of a dock and I pulled up a skid in front of you with fifty hundred-pound sacks of potatoes and there are fifty more skids just like it, and this is what you're gonna do all day, what would you think about—potatoes? Unless a guy's a nut, he never thinks about work or talks about it. Maybe about baseball or about getting drunk the other night or he got laid or he didn't get laid. I'd say one out of a hundred will actually get excited about work.

Why is it that the communists always say they're for the workingman, and as soon as they set up a country, you got guys singing to tractors? They're singing about how they love the factory. That's where I couldn't buy communism. It's the intellectuals' utopia, not mine. I cannot picture myself singing to a tractor, I just can't (Laughs) Or singing to steel. (singsongs) Oh whoop-dee-doo, I'm at the bonderizer, oh how I love this heavy steel. No thanks. Never happen.

. . . .

Jim Grayson (spot-welder outside Chicago, Illinois; part-time student)

Ford keeps its overhead down. If I had to go a few feet to get some stock, that would be the time I'm not working. So Ford has everything set up. If you run out, the truck'll come blowin' carbon monoxide all over your face. But it's making sure you'll never run out of work. I mean you're *really* tied down to the job. (Laughs) You stand on your feet and you run on your feet. (Laughs)

We get forty-eight minutes of break—thirty minutes in the morning and the other eighteen in the evening. You always go to the bathroom first. (Laughs) It's three flights up. You come down, you walk to another part of the plant, and you walk up another three flights to get a bite to eat. On the line, you don't go to the washroom when you have to go. You learn to adjust your physical . . . (Laughs) For new workers this is quite hard. I haven't gotten used to it yet. I've been here since 1968.

The part of the automobile I work on is before it gets all the pretties. There's no paint. The basic car. There's a conveyorlike . . . Mr. Ford's given credit for inventing this little . . . (Laughs) There is no letup, the line is always running. It's not like . . . if you lift something, carry it for a little while, lay it down, and go back—while you're going back, you're actually catching a breather. Ford has a better idea. (Laughs) You hear the slogan: They have a better idea. They have better ideas of getting all the work possible out of your worn body for eight hours.

You can work next to a guy for months without even knowing his name. One thing, you're too busy to talk. Can't hear. (Laughs) You have to holler in his ear. They got these little guys comin' around in white shirts and if they see you runnin' your mouth, they say, "This guy needs more work." Man, he's got no time to talk.

A lot of guys who've been in jail, they say you don't work as hard in jail. (Laughs) They say, "Man, jail ain't never been this bad." (Laughs) That's the way I feel. I'm serving a life sentence till I graduate from college. So I got six more months in jail. Then I'll do something else, probably at a reduction in pay.

If it was up to these ignorant foremen, they'd never get a car out. But they have these professional people, engineering time study. They're always sneakin' around with their little cameras. I can smell 'em a mile away. These people stay awake nights thinking of ways to get more work out of you.

Last night I heard one of the guys say we did 391 cars. How many welds are we supposed to put in a car? They have governmental regulations for consumer protection. We just put what we think ought to be in there and then let it go. (Laughs) There are specifications, which we pay very little attention to.

. . . .

Everyone has a station. You're supposed to get your work completed within a certain area, usually around ten, maybe fifteen feet. If you get behind, you're in the hole. When you get in the hole, you're bumping into the next worker. Man, sometimes you get in the hole and you run down. The next worker up from you, he can't do his job until you get finished. If you're slowin' up, that starts a chain reaction all the way up the line.

Ford is a great believer in the specialization of labor, brings about more efficiency. Actually, I can be thinking about economics, politics, anything while I am doing this work. Lotta times my mind is on schoolwork. There's no way I could do that job and think about what I'm doin', cause it's just impossible for me. The work is just too boring. Especially someone like myself, who is going to school and has a lot of other things on my mind.

Gig: Americans Talk About Their Jobs

(John Bowe, Marisa Bowe, and Sabin Streeter, eds.) (Three Rivers Press 2000).

John Hart (Corporate Securities Lawyer in a BigLaw firm)

[After graduating law school] I took a position with a midsized southeastern law firm. It turned out to be a very difficult, basically horrible experience. The firm, in fact, was breaking up—and later broke up—with partners literally going at each other's throats. I actually once stood by and watched two partners grab each other and try to strangle each other in the hallway.

. . .

So I realized, after a little more than a year at that firm, that I'd made a very bad and possibly disastrous choice and that I had to get out. A friend of mine from law school knew about an opening in this particular office where I am now. They needed someone who had some securities experience, and I had done enough securities law that this friend of mine said, you know, "Talk to them." And that's how it worked out. I've now been in this position for almost six years. So more by chance than by design, I've become a securities lawyer.

This isn't exactly the stimulation I'd hoped for when I signed up for law school. [Laughs] Securities law deals with the legal aspects of raising funds for corporations, partnerships, all types of business entities. It involves looking at and crunching a lot of numbers, oftentimes at very late hours of the night, and also being able to take the numbers and translate them into meaningful, logical, readable documents. . . .

It pays well, and it's challenging—it's very challenging—which can be very rewarding, but I'd say at least half of the time I can barely tolerate it, because in a nutshell, basically, I have no quality of life.

. . . .

I'm at my desk at least thirteen, fourteen hours a day. Sometimes it's much more. I usually get into work around eight a.m. and already have three to four voice-mail messages and sometimes as many as fifteen emails, some of which were generated by partners in the other office as late as midnight or one o'clock in the morning. And these aren't "Hi, how are you?" emails—they address complicated problems, things our clients want done, and I have to start immediately dealing with them as if they were crises. Which they often are.

Securities law is a very stressful place to be right now. When the stock market is doing well like it has been for most of the last few years, everything is insane, everything is damn the torpedoes, full speed ahead, had to have been done yesterday. A lot of money's being made, and clients and other lawyers do not like to hear it when somebody says, "Wait a minute." There's been lots of instances where people will get right into my face and yell at me, and in some cases—more than one—I've had people grab me and try to shake me or, you know, hit me, and I've basically had to take my arms and push them away and say, "You don't want to do this to me." It's not as bad as it was at my first firm, but it's pretty damned awful.

Every day is full of extreme, extreme stress. . . .

. . . .

Basically, the reason I keep at it, and this is going to sound kind of strange, is that my wife is from this area, she is very happy to be here, and this is the only firm of its type here that does the kind of law that I have now trained for and worked in over the last seven years of my life. It would be very difficult to break out. It would be impossible to break out and do this at another firm in town, so I find myself basically saying, "Well, as long as I can do this to keep the family together, that's what I'm going to do." That does not, however, keep me from looking around, including trying to convince my wife we need to move away.

It's a deal with the devil. And it's eating me up. I used to be the kind of person who believed that even though bad things happened, and there were bad people, that most people were generally positive. That most people, given the right circumstances, usually would do the right thing. Now I'm not so sure. I think people are a lot more self-interested than I used to think they were, I've just seen too much.

I had a client track me down at the hospital and curse me out when my wife was about to give birth. I told him what was going on, you know, "I'm at the hospital, my wife, you know, a baby—can I call you later?" And he wouldn't stop. What kind of person does that?

I'm not a happy guy. I'm much more short-tempered than I was seven years ago. I find I have a lot less patience in dealing with general mundane situations after you've been working twenty-plus hours a day. A *lot* less patience. I don't think it's helped my family life, dealing with my wife and my child—or my friends for that matter. But the family's the big problem. There's an awful lot of lip service that's given by a lot of big law firms to family time and quality of life, and family values and all that, but I see very little really being done to make a difference with people who either have families or would like to have families. As a result, I think a lot of lawyers' families are really struggling.

The only thing I really feel like I totally enjoy at this point in my life is running. . . .

The area I live in is pretty quiet at night, it's safe. So I just run around, sometimes, for as long as it takes to feel okay. And sometimes that's a really long time.

Sandy Wilkins (Cattle Slaughterhouse Human Resources Director)

I'm the director of the plant's human resources department. It's a multi-tasked position, but mostly I hire and train our employees—the people who process the cows and do the slaughter. I'd hoped that I would come in here and use some of my background. My master's degree is in counseling and guidance, and I thought I'd be able to take care of the employees if they had any problems and write safety policies and make sure everything was going smooth. And I do write policies a bit, but really, the job is a lot more basic than that. It's all about getting people in the door, getting workers. We just need bodies in this place. We're desperate. Because even though we pay a very decent wage, the working conditions are terrible. It's not a job that normal people want anymore. It's just very tough.

There are many different kinds of beef-processing plants: we're at the tail end of them. Your better plants deal with what are called "fat cattle," those are your best cows and that product is usually sold to the higher-end restaurants and markets. We process "caners and cutters," that means the ol' rickety cows. Kind of second-rate cows. We have some contracts with restaurants and markets, but lesser places. Mostly, we have a lot of government contracts. We sell a lot to schools for school lunches.

What happens here is the cows come into the kill department—that's where they do the slaughter—they lead them in the chute, take them, and they stun them first with a stun gun, then they swing them up with hydraulics, about twenty feet up into the air. These are full-blown cows hanging up there. And while they're still stunned, they slit their throats. The floor is usually a couple of inches deep in blood.

The dead cows go around the room on a hydraulic pulley system so people can do different procedures to them. For instance, they take the hide off. That's the hide-puller's job. Someone else takes out the intestines. They split the middle and all the intestines fall out. There's other people who clean the cheek meat off the head. Then they take the tongues and box them separately because we send most of that meat overseas. A lot of places overseas get the specialty parts. Like the Vietnamese—they like to have the intestines and the stomach linings.

Every part of the cow is used. If they find a fetus, they take the blood out of it and send it to universities for research. And they take the fetus's hide—that's used for very fine purses. They even reuse the magnets found in the cow's stomachs. The poor old dumb cows will eat anything, including barbed wire, which rips out stomach lining unless it gets hooked to something, so the farmers feed the cows magnets and they collect all of the metal parts the cows eat, and those magnets, we wash and save them.

. . . .

It's a big operation. We need to have at least two hundred and seventy workers every day to run the plant. And, like I said, we're just desperate for workers. Last month, I hired eighty-five people and ninety-two left. That's not uncommon. We're bleeding people. I hire them and they leave. No matter how I sell them on the job, they go down there and find it not exactly to their liking. Some people will quit fifteen minutes after they get on the floor because it's so ugly to them. It's a special person who wants to work in a meat processing plant.

Another problem is that there is never a set schedule. I wish there would be. The employees work from eight to twelve hours a day, but nobody knows if they'll be working those twelve-hour days until noon because that's when the orders come in. And we often have temporary workers, so my job is a lot of just making sure they're in the number that I've been asked for and that they're going to the right spots in the plant, never mind if they understand their schedule. That makes people pretty frustrated sometimes. There's been a lot of angry situations.

But the biggest problem is the simple fact that nobody wants to kill cows. Not here, anyway. The recruitment, boy, I use every tactic to get people to work in this place. . . .

Basically, if you just look like a fairly decent person, I'll hire you. We don't do any reference checking or anything because we need people so badly. We need people to start tomorrow. I'm serious. We don't have the normal steps used for hiring.

The only thing that would stop us from hiring a person are immigration problems. We have to check their green cards. We watch those like hawks. We take photos of IDs—we require two forms—we check all of their numbers on their green cards. A few years before I got here, Immigration came to the plant and found illegal aliens and we were fined eighty thousand dollars. So there's no more of that.

Unfortunately, and I hate to say this, but I think the only people who would do this job willingly anymore are those illegal aliens—people who can't turn down work.

. . . .

We see about a hundred injuries a year and I'm amazed that there aren't more. The main causes are inexperience and repetition. And drugs. There's no drug testing so some, not many, people come in high. But repetition is the biggest, I'd say. Everybody works so fast that there's a lot of repetitive injuries. People work the same job all the time and they stop thinking. Workers in a plant like this need to be moved around, but that would require more training and we can barely give what we give now.

. . . .

I'm going to end up walking out. I have nothing left to give. It's like someone pounding on your head eleven to twelve hours a day. For years. Some mornings I wake up, I can't move.

. . . .

I don't know why I've stayed here so long. Maybe it's because I'm able to separate the job a little bit when I get home, because of my counseling degree. But I bring home my exhaustion. My husband and I have a little trailer where we go and relax on the weekends. Lately, when we go there, I just sleep. There's nothing left of me to do the things I want to do. I like to cook, read, play around with my family, but I'm just worn out. I don't bring my job home with me, but the exhaustion—you can't escape that.

Javier Lopez (Poultry Factory Worker)
{translated from the Spanish by Sonia Bowe-Gutman}

I sort chicken parts in a factory in Duplin County, North Carolina. There's a lot of poultry in this area. I don't want to say the name of the company I work for, but you can use my real name because I'm not legally here in this country anyway. No one knows I'm here.

I work the night shift. The second shift. It starts at ten-thirty p.m. It's supposed to go until eight a.m. but sometimes we can go on till nine or ten. Sometimes till noon. It depends on whether we get our chickens done.

. . . .

I work in Department 20 with about a thousand other people. It's equally divided between men and women. Our job is to separate the wings, legs, and breasts. We also do some deboning. After we separate, another department packages the chickens and sorts them by weight. Then another department labels them and packs them in crates and stamps them for shipping. I don't know where it goes when it leaves here. I think supermarkets, restaurants, maybe.

. . . .

You have to be careful with the knives and the machines, because everything is so slippery. A lot of fat falls on the machines and the floor. There's fat everywhere. Everything's greasy. So, especially when you cut the wings, you know, there's a disk cutter with a rotating blade, so your fingers are in danger. And if you cut yourself, you're going to get very contaminated from bacteria in the chickens because, before you cook them, the raw chickens are full of bacteria.

I work very fast, and I'm not always checking what I'm doing, even while I'm doing dangerous work like deboning with the disk saws. We are slaves. They don't care. If we are not done with the truck full of chickens, we cannot leave work at the end of our shift. Sometimes it's because of mechanical breakdowns, machinery malfunctions—nothing that we did, but it doesn't matter. We can't leave. They don't care how long you work. You just have to be very fast. So you're not always working safely because you have to keep up with the production line. The managers always want more production in less time.

. . . .

The company wants everything for themselves, and nothing for the workers. You have to buy your boots, aprons, and gloves. Boots are ten dollars. Gloves cost fifty cents and aprons cost four dollars and fifty cents. That's a lot when you're only making six twenty-five per hour. Why should they make us buy this equipment?

I have heard that some of the poultry plants are better. This is apparently one of the worst ones. If you want to go to the bathroom, it's very difficult. Even if you need to go, you have to wait for break time and there are only two breaks per shift, and you have to eat during them. And the breaks last for half an hour each, but in reality they are less than twenty-five minutes because you have to dress and undress the gloves and things like that. They take this time away, and it's important because if you are going to eat, and go to the cafeteria, you still want to washup before you go. But for the men there are only two toilets, so you have to wait in line. It takes at least five minutes to get into the bathroom just to wash your hands. And it is completely dirty and disgusting. There's so much chlorine all over the place it stings. It hurts your skin, your eyes burn.

Then there is the food. The "cafeteria"—and I call it that between quotes—is disgusting. They feed you chicken, chicken, chicken. It's no good or clean there. Where you eat, it is unfortunately dark, smoky. People complain, but with everything else, there is no discipline about cleanliness. Smoking should be done outside because the cafeteria is for eating. But there is no discipline, no respect. Nothing.

Another thing—racism. The large majority of the workers here are illegal Hispanics, like me. There's also some legal Hispanics, some Haitians and black gringos. But most of us are illegal Hispanics. The bosses know we're illegal, and it's illegal for them to hire us, but we're the cheapest, so they don't care. We probably wouldn't work such a bad job if we had documents. And they always yell at us Hispanics. With the others they are more flexible, more lenient. The others come in late sometimes, they talk on the phone. And they can get away with it. The black gringos that work here have more flexibility, they speak English. The blacks talk back, and they can argue because they speak English.

QUESTION

1. Do the workers' stories focus on the pecuniary or nonpecuniary aspects of their jobs? Can we draw a sharp distinction between these aspects?

Conclusion

The first Lesson has provided you with ample materials to begin thinking about the personal meaning and social significance of work. We will refer back to the material in this first Lesson during the course as a means of putting the legal doctrine into context. Work is the cornerstone of our economy, but it is not simply an economic transaction. We have tried to focus your attention on why the workplace is a potential site of conflict, but we end with an uplifting perspective on the dignity of all work.

Martin Luther King, Jr., All Labor Has Dignity

171–72 (Michael K. Honey, ed.) (2011).

[Editor's Note: Martin Luther King, Jr. delivered a speech in Memphis, Tennessee in support of striking sanitation workers on March 18, 1968. The workers were protesting dangerous and humiliating work conditions. The transcript includes the chants of his audience in parentheses. Dr. King was assassinated seventeen days after this speech.]

You are doing many things here in this struggle. You are demanding that this city will respect the dignity of labor. So often we overlook the work and the significance of those who are not in professional jobs, (Yeah) of those who are not in the so-called big jobs. But let me say to you tonight, that whenever you are engaged in work that serves humanity and is for the building of humanity, it has dignity, and it has worth. (Applause) One day our society must come to see this. One day our society will come to respect the sanitation worker if it is to survive, for the person who picks up our garbage, in the final analysis, is as significant as the physician, for if he doesn't do his job, diseases are rampant. (Applause) All labor (All labor) has dignity. (Yes!)

Lesson 2:
An Overview of Workplace Law: Labor Law and Anti-Discrimination

Objectives and Expected Learning Outcomes

This casebook does not cover labor law or anti-discrimination law, both of which generally are taught as separate courses. However, in this Lesson, you will develop an understanding of the historical forces that led to the labor movement and laws prohibiting employment discrimination. This overview will reveal the tension between the communal good and individual rights that subtends most employment law. We will explore how effectively these older laws are addressing the new cultural, sexual, and demographic changes rapidly altering the United States. Finally, you will develop a sensitivity on how to practice employment law in our increasingly multi-cultural and diverse country.

In this Lesson, we briefly explore labor law and anti-discrimination law as an important backdrop for the employment law that you will be studying this semester. We begin with an overview of the labor law movement, followed by a discussion of the adoption of Title VII as the paradigm of anti-discrimination law. We will explore some of the contemporary themes and issues under Title VII, as a way to introduce you to the statute and as a means of considering the importance of cultural competence in the American workplace.

1. The Union Movement: Private and Public Employees

Early in the previous century the United States experimented with a communal approach to workplace regulation. In 1935, Congress enacted the National Labor Relations Act, which promoted the recognition of unions and collective bargaining over the terms and conditions of employment. A union may be certified to represent the employees if they request a vote conducted by the National Labor Relations Board, and the employees vote in favor of the union. The employer must then negotiate in good faith with the union, and the terms and conditions are reduced to a "collective bargaining agreement." The NLRA was enacted in the wake of what its drafters called a "procession of bloody and costly strikes." When employees banded together to demand higher wages and better working conditions, employers often responded with violence. The NLRA changed this dynamic by providing a structured way for employees to organize a union, for employee self-determination through an election process, and for all employees to engage in protected concerted activity regardless of union organizing. We will discuss the right of employees to engage in concerted activity in Lesson 36.

The union model was premised on a communal approach to workplace issues. At its heart, the collective bargaining agreement represented a "one for all, all for one" paradigm. At the peak of the union movement in 1979, there were an estimated 21 million employees covered by a collective bargaining agreement. Measured as a percentage of employed workers, union membership peaked in 1954 at 28.3%. However, membership in unions has dramatically declined over the past few decades. In 2017, the Bureau of Labor Statistics estimated that only 10.7% of workers were covered by collective bargaining agreements. The decline is, in part, caused by the employment law protections that we will be studying in this course. Statutes such as the Occupational Safety and Health Act reduced the need for unions to protect the health and welfare of employees. Additionally, the labor laws developed in ways that favored the employer. The Taft-Hartley Act of 1947 prevented unions and employers from entering into a collective bargaining agreement that required employees to become dues paying members of the union in order to keep their jobs. This resulted in "right-to-work" laws that were enacted in 28 states. Without compulsory union dues, unions faced a free-rider problem because employees could benefit from union activities without paying the cost of those activities.

Much of the decrease in union membership has occurred among private employers. However, public employee unions are also facing challenges. Public union employees include police, teachers, and firefighters. Union growth in the public sector has remained relatively strong. In 2017, the union membership rate for public sector employees was 34.4%. In particular, nearly 20% of African American adults work for a government agency, many of whom are in a public union. However, the steady growth of public unions may soon come to an end as a result of cutbacks in the government workforce, combined with increasing disincentives for employees to join. There are no "right-to-work" laws for public employers. Instead, 21 states have "fair-share" laws requiring workers to pay a certain amount to the union (even if they decline to join the union and pay dues) for services such as negotiating the collective bargaining agreements or adjusting workplace grievances. These laws reduced the risk of the free-riding problem, and were premised on the assumption that all employees benefit from the union's role as their representative. However, this was abruptly upset by the 2018 United States Supreme Court decision in

Janus v. AFSCME, in which the Court struck down "fair share" agreements for violating the First Amendment rights of employees who did not wish to join the union. In *Janus*, the plaintiff disagreed with the union's bargaining position with the State because it was asking for increased pension benefits at a time when the state was facing a budget crisis. The Court held that the plaintiff could refuse to pay a "fair share" of union expenses, because the mandatory payment amounted to compelled speech that violated his First Amendment right. The expected result is simple: reduced funding for the union means decreased financial support for union activities, which results in less union influence.

The following excerpt describes the waxing and waning of communitarian impulses over the past century of union activity.

Thomas Kohler, *Individualism And Communitarianism At Work*

1993 B.Y.U. L. Rev. 727 (January 1993).

II. WORK-LIFE IN THE UNITED STATES

. . . . In the United States, the term collective bargaining is virtually synonymous with the NLRA. The core goal of the statute is to protect and enhance individuals' status through the defense and maintenance of freely formed and autonomous employee groups. This feature defines the statute and characterizes the unique position the Act holds in American law. It represents the only place in our otherwise highly individualistically-oriented jurisprudence where the law has encouraged the formation of mediating bodies through which to promote individual empowerment and to foster self-determination. In the final analysis, the Wagner Act rests on a distinctly different idea of the character of our personhood than that which typically informs American law. The transformations that have occurred in our culture since the time of the Act's passage, however, appear to have left the statute's basic purpose and meaning increasingly opaque to us.

Congress enacted the (NLRA) in 1935. In so doing, and in sharp contrast to the course taken by the rest of the industrialized world, Congress deliberately opted for a system that would involve minimal state intervention in the employment relationship. In the United States context, collective bargaining can be best and most thoroughly understood as a private law-making system. Thus, the United States Supreme Court has described the collective bargaining agreement as not just a contract, but "a generalized code" that represents "an effort to erect a system of industrial self-government" through which the employment relationship can be "governed by an agreed-upon rule of law."

The promulgation and administration of this law largely is the responsibility of the affected parties alone. Consequently, American collective bargaining agreements typically erect a private dispute resolution system—the grievance arbitration process—that the employer and union jointly administer. These systems generally have jurisdiction over nearly every sort of dispute that might arise concerning the employment relationship. The presence of an arbitration system normally precludes the courts or other arms of the state from adjudicating matters that come within the parties' dispute resolution scheme.

The so-called "exclusivity principle" bottoms the American model of collective bargaining. It also marks one of the starkest differences between the American and Continental industrial-relations systems. The exclusivity principle rests on the idea of the majority rule. The principle establishes the association formed by most employees in the affected workplace unit as the exclusive representative of them all. The principle prohibits an employer from attempting to bypass the majority-designated representative by unilaterally changing the terms or conditions of employment, or by dealing with individuals or groups of employees independently of the union. The preferred status the majority representative enjoys in this scheme carries with it the legally enforceable obligation to represent all employees fairly and even-handedly, regardless of their support for or membership in the union.

The exclusivity doctrine prevents the fragmentation and dissolution of the strength employees achieve through collective action. It thereby acts to protect the principles of majoritarianism that underpins the Act's scheme. The exclusivity principle reflects the fact that American workers generally organize and bargain on a workplace or employer basis, and not at an industry-wide or national level. To a substantial degree, the principle is a function of the emphasis in American-style collective bargaining on local, "bottoms-up" law-making. The centrality of exclusivity to the Act's scheme reveals the statute's preoccupation with the removal of impediments to the free formation of autonomous, self-organized employee associations.

In considering the statute, it is important to note that Congress did not "invent" collective bargaining. Rather, Congress through the [NLRA] adopted a scheme whose characteristics and practices jointly had been developed over time by workers and employers. Congress in passing the Act intended to institute a comprehensive, uniform, and flexible system through which the employment relationship could be ordered. Hence, rather than attempting to adjust specific problems legislatively, the Act left it to the parties themselves to identify and resolve matters of mutual concern. The chief significance of the American collective bargaining scheme lies in the opportunity it provides to involve people in making and administering the law that most directly determines the details of their daily lives. The process both permits and requires people to decide for themselves the kind of people they will be, and to explain and justify those choices to one another. . . .

The decline in private-sector unionization constitutes one of the most pronounced changes that has occurred in the United States work-life sphere during the past thirty years. . . .

Significantly, the decline of unions began at roughly the same time that families, neighborhoods, religious congregations, service and fraternal groups, local political clubs, and the other institutions that characterized American democracy began to unravel. This is no mere coincidence. No single "mediating body," whether in the form of families, churches, civic, political and service organizations, or unions, is likely to survive in the absence of the others. All of them require, and can instill, the same sorts of habits: decision, commitment, self-rule, and direct responsibility. No single institution on its own can inculcate or sustain these characteristics. The existence and decline of all these bodies is mutually conditioning; the collapse or deformation of any of them affects the rest.

So, what is to become of what Tocqueville called "the nation of joiners"? Recent survey data indicates that Americans remain eager participants in the activities of voluntary associations. Yet, the same data suggests that during the past thirty years, much of that participation has been limited to clipping a coupon in a magazine and returning it with a small financial contribution to an association like the Sierra Club, Common Cause, or the American Association of Retired Persons (which is now the largest voluntary association in the U.S.). The smaller, local bodies that directly mediate the relationship between individuals and the large institutions of public life—and which involve people in the often messy business of actually associating with each other—are faring less well.

The American work-life sphere has not been insulated from the trends toward fragmentation that have affected the other institutions of civil life, along with the decline of unions and other mediating bodies has come a significant loosening in the employment bond itself. So-called "contingent employment arrangements" (part-time, temporary, and contract-based) are on the rise, and are expected to double over the next few years. One well-known observer of labor market trends characterized these arrangements as "just-in-time" employment. As American industry seeks to become more competitive, she predicted, "all employment relationships are going to become more fluid." It may be that instability increasingly characterizes many of the significant relationships among Americans: employment relationships in the U.S. now last an average of 4.5 years, while the average marriage lasts but seven. Trends are not wholly clear, but the average length of both may be on the way down.

Consistent with these developments is the fact that increasingly the workplace itself is less one "place." Thus, for example, ten percent of the Chicago area employees of American Telephone and Telegraph now work at locations other than company facilities—many of them at home. Despite concerns about the impact of employee isolation, such "telecommuter" arrangements are on the rise.

Our legal culture also has influenced our prevailing views about the desirability of a system that promotes private ordering through groups. In short, it has taught us to apply what Paul Ricoeur calls the "hermeneutic of suspicion" towards groups, and to see in them an ever-present threat to personal liberties and the unfettered exercise of individual choice. . . .

So, what has replaced collective bargaining? Like nature, law abhors a vacuum. Thus, the piecemeal and ad hoc regulation of the employment relationship markedly has increased as the practice of collective bargaining has declined. Common law courts have entered the area by developing various contract, tort, and public policy-based restrictions of an employer's ability to discharge or discipline employees. Congress and state legislatures also have become very active in enacting a wide variety of legislation addressed to specific workplace problems. This thrust away from private ordering has left parties with a contracting boundary within which to regulate the terms of their relationship through collective bargaining.

QUESTIONS

1. Do you agree with Professor Kohler's conclusion that Americans are becoming much less communal and, thus, the model set out by the NLRA is antiquated? Do you agree with the arguments that we are suspicious of groups and their dynamics?
2. Would you consider voting for a union in your workplace? Would you prefer to negotiate your own conditions of employment? Would your answer change if you were a factory worker making minimum wage rather than a law student preparing for a professional career?

---

2. Title VII of the Civil Rights Act of 1964

Like the NLRA, Title VII of the Civil Rights Act of 1964 was the product of turbulent times. *Brown v. Board of Education*, desegregating public schools, was decided in 1954. Progress towards implementing its mandate was painfully slow. In the late 1950s, President Eisenhower was forced to use federal troops to enforce desegregating a high school in Little Rock, Arkansas. In the early 1960s, Governor George Wallace of Alabama stood dramatically in front of the University of Alabama to protest court ordered desegregation, yelling "Segregation now. Segregation forever." This was not just the fringe speaking. Governor Wallace ran for president in 1968 as an independent candidate, receiving thirteen percent of the total popular vote and earning the electoral votes of five southern states. At this time, an employer could deny employment to a black applicant or terminate a black employee because of his or her race.

In 1963 the quest for civil rights was energized, but it encountered a violent backlash. Birmingham police, under the direction of police safety commissioner Eugene ("Bull") Connor, turned fire hoses and police dogs on citizens peacefully protesting discrimination against blacks. With this violence shown across the country on the evening news, President Kennedy appeared on national television and announced that civil rights was a national priority. On the night of President Kennedy's address, civil rights leader Medgar Evers was shot and killed by a member of the Ku Klux Klan. One week later, on June 19, 1963, Evers was buried in Arlington National Cemetery. That same day, the Kennedy Administration sent a civil rights bill to Congress.

President Johnson continued the push for passage of the bill after President Kennedy's death in November 1963. Members of Congress from many Southern states opposed the bill. Historians recount that their strategy was that delaying passage of the bill would frustrate black citizens and generate violent protests, thereby justifying a backlash among white citizens. Additionally, conservative members introduced a "poison pill" amendment that added "sex" as a protected classification. Liberals were concerned that this might derail the legislation, but women in Congress then pushed the amendment. At a pivotal moment, Congresswoman Martha Griffiths took to the House floor and argued that deletion of "sex" would mean "you are going to have white men in one bracket, you are going to try to take colored men and colored women and give them equal employment rights, and down at the bottom of the list is going to be a white woman with no rights at all." Supporters of the bill ended their opposition to the amendment to, as stated by Minority Leader Senator Everett Dirksen, "avoid the wrath of the women." For an incisive account of the passage of Title VII, see Louis Menand, *The Sex Amendment*, *The New Yorker*, (July 21, 2014), http://www.newyorker.com/magazine/2014/07/21/sex-amendment.

With this strange twist, Title VII was enacted with protected classifications of race, color, religion, national origin, and sex. Employers were given until July 2, 1965 to adapt their practices to the new law. Then began the process of interpreting the meaning of "discrimination" in the workplace, a discussion which continues today.

QUESTIONS

1. Do we still need laws that outlaw discrimination in employment? Won't the marketplace in our global economy ensure that discrimination ends, given that discriminating against employees based on sex or race when they are well-qualified would hurt the employer's competitive position?
2. It is uncommon for an employer to confess to unlawful discrimination. While there are occasional smoking gun admissions such as "this position isn't right for a woman," or "our customers won't purchase from black sales representatives," many discrimination claims are premised on a failure to follow company procedures or inconsistency of treatment under similar circumstances. Does this mean that the problem is not overt discrimination, but rather poor human resources management? Should it matter?

It is interesting to note the changes in the charges of discrimination filed with the Equal Employment Opportunity Commission under Title VII. Consider the following statistics comparing the percentage of claims for each protected class over time.

	FY 1997	FY 2002	FY 2007	FY 2012	FY 2017
Total Charges	80,680	84,442	82,792	99,412	84,254
Race	29,199	29,910	30,510	33,512	28,528
	36.2%	35.4%	37.0%	33.7%	33.9%
Sex	24,728	25,536	24,826	30,356	25,605
	30.7%	30.2%	30.1%	30.5%	30.4%
National Origin	6,712	9,046	9,396	10,883	8,299
	8.3%	10.7%	11.4%	10.9%	9.8%
Religion	1,709	2,572	2,880	3,811	3,436
	2.1%	3.0%	3.5%	3.8%	4.1%
Color	762	1,381	1,735	2,662	3,240
	0.9%	1.6%	2.1%	2.7%	3.8%

3. Contemporary Issues Under Title VII

We will consider contemporary issues under Title VII as a means of understanding how the statute works. The statutory language is brief and direct: an employer may not discriminate against an applicant or employee "because of" race, color, religion, sex, or national origin with respect to the "terms, conditions or privileges of employment." We will explore current controversies under these protected classes.

A. Discrimination Because of Sex

Because "sex" was added to the bill as a protected class at the last minute, there was little in the way of legislative history to guide the courts. One of the key developments was the Supreme Court's recognition that a work environment that is hostile to women is a form of sex discrimination. *See Meritor Savings Bank, FSB v. Vinson*, 477 U.S. 57 (1986). More recently, courts have addressed whether discrimination based on sexual orientation is "discrimination because of sex" under Title VII. Recall that in 1964, discrimination against gay men and women was not on the table for public debate. Same-sex relations were criminalized in almost every state.

In 1964, the American Psychiatric Association and the American Psychological Association classified homosexuality as a mental illness.

Oncale v. Sundowner Offshore Svcs., Inc.

523 U.S. 75 (1998).

Justice Scalia delivered the opinion of the Court.

This case presents the question whether workplace harassment can violate Title VII's prohibition against "discriminat[ion] . . . because of . . . sex," 42 U.S.C. § 2000e–2(a)(1), when the harasser and the harassed employee are of the same sex. . . .

[Editor's Note: The plaintiff, a male roustabout on an offshore oil rig, complained that male co-workers harassed him by sex-related comments, threats and conduct.]

. . . .[W]e hold today that nothing in Title VII necessarily bars a claim of discrimination "because of . . . sex" merely because the plaintiff and the defendant (or the person charged with acting on behalf of the defendant) are of the same sex.

. . . .We see no justification in the statutory language or our precedents for a categorical rule excluding same-sex harassment claims from the coverage of Title VII. As some courts have observed, male-on-male sexual harassment in the workplace was assuredly not the principal evil Congress was concerned with when it enacted Title VII. But statutory prohibitions often go beyond the principal evil to cover reasonably comparable evils, and it is ultimately the provisions of our laws rather than the principal concerns of our legislators by which we are governed. Title VII prohibits "discrimination . . . because of . . . sex" in the "terms" or "conditions" of employment. Our holding that this includes sexual harassment must extend to sexual harassment of any kind that meets the statutory requirements.

Oncale established that men may sue for sex discrimination for behavior that was not driven by sexual desire but that was more broadly "because of" sex. Consider how *Oncale* has now set the stage for considering whether discrimination on the basis of one's sexual orientation is a violation of Title VII.

Zarda v. Altitude Express, Inc.

883 F.3d 100 (2nd Cir. en banc, 2018).

Katzmann, Chief Judge:

Donald Zarda, a skydiving instructor, brought a sex discrimination claim under Title VII of the Civil Rights Act of 1964 ("Title VII") alleging that he was fired from his job at Altitude Express, Inc., because he failed to conform to male sex stereotypes by referring to his sexual orientation. Although it is well-settled that gender stereotyping violates Title VII's prohibition on discrimination "because of . . . sex," we have previously held that sexual orientation discrimination claims, including claims that being gay or lesbian constitutes nonconformity with a gender stereotype, are not cognizable under Title VII.

> *[Editor's Note: The court then decides to conduct an en banc review of its precedent.]*

In the summer of 2010, Donald Zarda, a gay man, worked as a sky-diving instructor at Altitude Express. As part of his job, he regularly participated in tandem skydives, strapped hip-to-hip and shoulder-to-shoulder with clients. In an environment where close physical proximity was common, Zarda's co-workers routinely referenced sexual orientation or made sexual jokes around clients, and Zarda sometimes told female clients about his sexual orientation to assuage any concern they might have about being strapped to a man for a tandem skydive. That June, Zarda told a female client with whom he was preparing for a tandem skydive that he was gay "and ha[d] an ex-husband to prove it." Although he later said this disclosure was intended simply to preempt any discomfort the client may have felt in being strapped to the body of an unfamiliar man, the client alleged that Zarda inappropriately touched her and disclosed his sexual orientation to excuse his behavior. After the jump was successfully completed, the client told her boyfriend about Zarda's alleged behavior and reference to his sexual orientation; the boyfriend in turn told Zarda's boss, who fired Zarda shortly thereafter. Zarda denied inappropriately touching the client and insisted he was fired solely because of his reference to his sexual orientation.

. . . .

While Zarda's remaining claims were still pending, the Equal Employment Opportunity Commission (EEOC) [decided a case before it and held] that "allegations of discrimination on the basis of sexual orientation necessarily state a claim of discrimination on the basis of sex." The Commission identified three ways to illustrate what it described as the "inescapable link between allegations of sexual orientation discrimination and sex discrimination." First, sexual orientation discrimination, such as suspending a lesbian employee for displaying a photo of her female spouse on her desk while not suspending a man for displaying a photo of his female spouse, "is sex discrimination because it necessarily entails treating an employee less favorably because of the employee's sex." Second, it is "associational discrimination" because "an employee alleging discrimination on the basis of sexual orientation is alleging that his or her employer took his or her sex into account by treating him or her differently for associating with a person of the same sex." Lastly, sexual orientation discrimination "necessarily involves discrimination based on gender stereotypes," most commonly "heterosexually defined gender norms."

. . . .

II. Sexual Orientation Discrimination

. . . .[We] have stated that "Title VII should be interpreted broadly to achieve equal employment opportunity." *Huntington Branch, N.A.A.C.P. v. Town of Huntington*, 844 F.2d 926, 935 (2d Cir. 1988) (citing *Griggs v. Duke Power Co.*, 401 U.S. 424, 429–36 (1971)).

In deciding whether Title VII prohibits sexual orientation discrimination, we are guided, as always, by the text and, in particular, by the phrase "because of . . . sex." However, in interpreting this language, we do not write on a blank slate. Instead, we must construe the text in light of the entirety of the statute as well as relevant precedent. As defined by Title VII, an employer has engaged in "impermissible consideration of . . . sex . . . in employment practices" when "sex . . . was a motivating factor for any employment practice," irrespective of whether the employer was also motivated by "other factors." 42 U.S.C. § 2000e–2(m). Accordingly, the critical inquiry for a court assessing whether an employment practice is "because of . . . sex" is whether sex was "a motivating factor."

Recognizing that Congress intended to make sex "irrelevant" to employment decisions, *Griggs*, 401 U.S. at 436, the Supreme Court has held that Title VII prohibits not just discrimination based on sex itself, but also discrimination based on traits that are a function of sex, such as life expectancy and non-conformity with gender norms. As this Court has recognized, "any meaningful regime of antidiscrimination law must encompass such claims" because, if an employer is " '[f]ree to add non-sex factors, the rankest sort of discrimination' " could be worked against employees by using traits that are associated with sex as a proxy for sex. *Back v. Hastings On Hudson Union Free Sch. Dist.*, 365 F.3d 107, 119 n.9 (2d Cir. 2004) (quoting *Phillips v. Martin Marietta Corp.*, 416 F.2d 1257, 1260 (5th Cir. 1969) (Brown, C.J., dissenting from denial of rehearing en banc)). Applying Title VII to traits that are a function of sex is consistent with the Supreme Court's view that Title VII covers not just "the principal evil[s] Congress was concerned with when it enacted" the statute in 1964, but also "reasonably comparable evils" that meet the statutory requirements. *Oncale v. Sundowner Offshore Servs., Inc.*, 523 U.S. 75, 79 (1998).

With this understanding in mind, the question before us is whether an employee's sex is necessarily a motivating factor in discrimination based on sexual orientation. If it is, then sexual orientation discrimination is properly understood as "a subset of actions taken on the basis of sex."

B. Sexual Orientation Discrimination as a Subset of Sex Discrimination

We now conclude that sexual orientation discrimination is motivated, at least in part, by sex and is thus a subset of sex discrimination. Looking first to the text of Title VII, the most natural reading of the statute's prohibition on discrimination "because of . . . sex" is that it extends to sexual orientation discrimination because sex is necessarily a factor in sexual orientation. This statutory reading is reinforced by considering the question from the perspective of sex stereotyping because sexual orientation discrimination is predicated on assumptions about how persons of a certain sex can or should be, which is an impermissible basis for adverse employment actions. In addition, looking at the question from the perspective of associational discrimination, sexual orientation discrimination—which is motivated by an employer's opposition to romantic association between particular sexes—is discrimination based on the employee's own sex.

1. Sexual Orientation as a Function of Sex

a. "Because of . . . sex"

We begin by considering the nature of sexual orientation discrimination. The term "sexual orientation" refers to "[a] person's predisposition or inclination toward sexual activity or behavior with other males or females" and is commonly categorized as "heterosexuality, homosexuality, or bisexuality." See *Sexual Orientation*, BLACK'S LAW DICTIONARY (10th ed. 2014). To take one example, "homosexuality" is "characterized by sexual desire for a person of the same sex." *Homosexual, id.*; see also *Heterosexual, id.* ("Of, relating to, or characterized by sexual desire for a person of the opposite sex."); *Bisexual, id.* ("Of, relating to, or characterized by sexual desire for both males and females."). To operationalize this definition and identify the sexual orientation of a particular person, we need to know the sex of the person and that of the people to whom he or she is attracted. *Hively*, 853 F.3d at 358 (Flaum, J., concurring) ("One cannot consider a person's homosexuality without also accounting for their sex: doing so would render 'same' [sex] . . . meaningless."). Because one cannot fully define a person's sexual orientation without identifying his or her sex, sexual orientation is a function of sex. Indeed sexual orientation is doubly delineated by sex because it is a function of both a person's sex and the sex of those to whom he or she is attracted. Logically, because sexual orientation is a function of sex and sex is a protected characteristic under Title VII, it follows that sexual orientation is also protected. See *id.* ("[D]iscriminating against [an] employee because they are homosexual constitutes discriminating against an employee because of (A) the employee's sex, *and* (B) their sexual attraction to individuals of the same sex.")

. . . .

The argument has also been made that it is not "even remotely plausible that in 1964, when Title VII was adopted, a reasonable person competent in the English language would have understood that a law banning employment discrimination 'because of sex' also banned discrimination because of sexual orientation[.]". . . .

. . . . As Judge Goldberg, one of the early proponents of hostile work environment claims, explained in a case involving national origin discrimination,

> [Title VII's] language evinces a Congressional intention to define discrimination in the broadest possible terms. Congress chose neither to enumerate specific discriminatory practices, nor to elucidate in extenso the parameter of such nefarious activities. Rather, it pursued the path of wisdom by being unconstrictive, knowing that constant change is the order of our day and that the seemingly reasonable practices of the present can easily become the injustices of the morrow.

Rogers v. E.E.O.C., 454 F.2d 234, 238 (5th Cir. 1971). . . .

The Supreme Court gave voice to this principle of construction when it held that Title VII barred male-on-male sexual harassment, which "was assuredly not the principal evil Congress was concerned with when it enacted Title VII," *Oncale*, 523 U.S. at 79–80, and which few people in 1964 would likely have understood to be covered by the statutory text. But the Court was untroubled by these facts. "[S]tatutory prohibitions," it explained, "often go beyond the principal evil to cover reasonably comparable evils, and it is ultimately the provisions of our laws rather than the principal concerns of our legislators by which we are governed." *Id.* Applying this reasoning to the question at hand, the fact that Congress might not have contemplated that discrimination "because of . . . sex" would encompass sexual orientation discrimination does not limit the reach of the statute.

. . . .We take no position on the substance of the dissent's discussion of the legislative history or the zeitgeist of the 1960s, but we respectfully disagree with its approach to interpreting Title VII as well as its conclusion that sexual orientation discrimination is not a "reasonably comparable evil," *Oncale*, 523 U.S. at 79, to sexual harassment and male-on-male harassment. Although legislative history most certainly has its uses, in ascertaining statutory meaning in a Title VII case, *Oncale* specifically rejects reliance on "the principal concerns of our legislators," *id.* at 79–80—the centerpiece of the dissent's statutory analysis. Rather, *Oncale* instructs that the text is the lodestar of statutory interpretation, emphasizing that we are governed "by the provisions of our laws." *Id.* The text before us uses broad language, prohibiting discrimination "because of . . . sex," which Congress defined as making sex "a motivating factor." 42 U.S.C. §§ 2000e–2(a)(1), 2000e–2(m). We give these words their full scope and conclude that, because sexual orientation discrimination is a function of sex, and is comparable to sexual harassment, gender stereotyping, and other evils long recognized as violating Title VII, the statute must prohibit it.

QUESTION

1. In recent years, bills have been introduced in Congress to prohibit employment discrimination based on sexual orientation. However, no legislation has been enacted. Should this fact matter in deciding whether "discrimination because of sex" encompasses sexual orientation discrimination?

Problem 2-1

You work at a law firm representing plaintiffs in employment discrimination cases. A prospective client named Laura comes to see you. She explains that she works as an assistant manager of a small and exclusive boutique hotel. Most of her work is done in the "back of the house," which means that she has little interaction with guests. Recently, Laura applied for the position of manager when it opened, but the hotel owner discouraged her from applying. He told her, "I'd like to consider you for the manager position, but the job entails much more guest interaction and, candidly, I do not think you have the right look for our guests. You have short hair, dress like Ellen DeGeneres, and wear no makeup. If you'd change your look to be more 'feminine,' maybe I would consider you for the position. I do not care if you are a lesbian. Hey, my daughter is lesbian, but I can't have you representing the hotel." How would you develop a claim for Laura under Title VII?

Problem 2-2

Steve Henry was designated as male at birth. Steve joined a Funeral Home as an apprentice on October 1, 2007, and served as a Funeral Director/Embalmer at the Funeral Home from April 2008 until August 2013. Although she goes by the name Sophie in her personal life, during her employment at the Funeral Home she presented as a man under her then-legal name, Steve Henry. On July 31, 2013, Steve delivered a letter to the owner of the Funeral Home, Rick, stating that she has struggled with gender identity her entire life, and informing Rick that she has decided to transition to a woman with sex reassignment surgery. The letter explained that the first step is to live and work as a woman for one year. To that end, Steve stated that she would return from her vacation on August 26, 2013, as her true self, Sophie Henry, in appropriate business attire. Rick went to Sophie and said "this is not going to work out," and offered her a severance agreement if she agreed to leave quietly. Instead, Sophie sued for a violation of Title VII. Rick testified that he fired Sophie because she was no longer going to present herself as a man, and his clientele are often distraught and emotional and would likely have difficulties if they interacted with Sophie. Analyze how you would build a case on behalf of Sophie, and how the Funeral Home should respond.

B. Discrimination Because of Color

Title VII prohibits discrimination based upon color, as well as race. As the United States becomes more multi-cultural, there are increasing numbers of employees of differing skin tones. While so far case law is scant, courts have allowed cases to go forward in which a plaintiff claims that he was discriminated against by a supervisor who had a different skin tone. Some scholars posit that skin tone discrimination goes back to the days of slavery when lighter skinned blacks were assigned to easier tasks, often in the home of the slave owners. Even today, the "brown paper bag" test—in which a sorority or fraternity refuses admittance to any student whose skin color is darker than a brown paper bag—is the subject of study. Consider your own experiences as you read the following selection.

Cynthia E. Nance, *Colorable Claims: The Continuing Significance of Color under Title VII Forty Years after Its Passage*

26 Berkeley J. of Emp.& L. Law 435 (Sept. 2005).

. . . .

"When people see me, they invariably look past the person and see my color."[1]

---

1 Yolanda Adams, *Don't Want to be Black Anymore (Dark-Skinned African American Feels More Comfortable with Caucasians)*, ESSENCE, Aug. 1999, at 54.

To prevail in a Title VII disparate treatment claim, a plaintiff alleging color discrimination must show that she was subjected to an adverse employment action based on her color. As might be imagined, there will rarely be a "smoking gun" situation in color discrimination cases, making it difficult for a plaintiff to prove the employer's bias, or intent. Social science research might be used to substantiate the existence of color discrimination and to bolster the claim of the employee who is trying to raise an inference of discrimination as it could provide evidence of the continued prevalence of colorist attitudes.

The studies presented immediately below provide data on blacks, skin color, stereotyping and the socioeconomic impact of colorism. The first study from Tufts University looks at the attitudes of both whites and blacks towards skin color variations among blacks by having the participants assign traits to blacks of varying skin tones. The second study examines the socioeconomic impact of skin color. The final study presented below looks at how skin color impacts voters' choices.

In the Tufts University 2002 study of both intraracial and interracial colorism, researchers asked participants to watch a simulated interaction among six men discussing what activity they would perform on a particular day. Statements were randomly attributed to each of the six speakers. One group of participants watched a discussion among six Black men and the other group observed a discussion among three white and three Black men.

The skin color of the men in the Black group was digitally manipulated. Later, the participants were asked to match the speaker to the statement. The results of the study showed that all participants in the study used race and skin color to organize the discussion. The results supported the hypothesis that "perceivers do notice skin tone and can use it as an organizing cue, suggesting that skin tone is a basis of categorization among both Black and White perceivers."

Noting that skin tone perception is a precursor to skin tone-based stereotypes, the researchers then tested previous findings that dark-skinned Blacks were more closely aligned with negative cultural stereotypes. The researchers had participants complete questionnaires that purported to "examine both their knowledge and cultural beliefs about various racial and ethnic groups." Each page of the questionnaire listed a specific social group, followed by directions to list positive, negative, and neutral traits associated with each group.

What the researchers found confirmed earlier studies. Although the finding that "White participants associated a greater number of positive compared to negative traits to light-skinned male targets" was not statistically significant, the finding that these same individuals assigned more negative attributes to dark-skinned men was statistically significant. The data also showed that both racial groups were aware of cultural distinctions between light and dark-skinned Blacks. According to the researchers, "this procedure tapped into common aspects of a predominantly negative cultural stereotype of Blacks that appears to be closely associated to Blacks with dark skin. Participants described dark-skinned Blacks using more negative and stereotypic traits, whereas light-skinned Blacks were described with more positive and counter stereotypic traits." The study also found that in looking at individual trait assignments, "in each case where a reliable difference was found, it was always in the direction describing dark-skinned Blacks as more closely aligned with the traditionally negative stereotype of Blacks."

While the Tufts University study reveals underlying attitudes towards skin color, another examines the socioeconomic impact of colorism. The results of this second study support the idea that not only does American society hold negative perceptions based on skin color, but these stereotypes lead to reduced opportunities for those perceived as dark. Hill tested two competing theories used to explain socioeconomic differences between dark and light-skinned Blacks. The first theory, social origin, posits that "color stratification stems from historical advantages passed down from privileged white and mixed-race ancestors to their descendants." The second theory, colorism, is based on "social stigmatization of dark skin and physical traits associated with African Ancestry."

To test the two theories, the researcher used longitudinal data from the census to examine the socioeconomic attainment of Black men classified as Black or mulatto. The results of the study confirmed previous findings that document the skin color advantage for light-skinned Blacks. "[M]en identified as mulatto enjoyed a modestly higher socioeconomic attainment compared with men identified as Black," which lent support to the colorism theory. The data, however, did not strongly support the social origin theory. According to Hill, "These results give prima facie support to the importance of color bias as an explanation of color-based stratification among African-Americans and are consistent with the assertion that African Americans who approximate European standards of physical attractiveness are viewed as more competent than their darker peers." This finding provides support for the idea that perceptions of competency play a direct role in determining which of two candidates most deserves a promotion or raise.

In a third study, Terkildsen examined colorism in the political process by determining the effect of black skin color on voters. The study found that the "darker-skinned Black candidate was evaluated much more harshly than his lighter-skinned peer. Racially intolerant whites were particularly brutal in their evaluations of the darker-skinned candidate." The author concludes,

> Regrettably, if voters continue to base their evaluations on candidate race and subtle skin color differences, two infamously unreliable criteria for determining individual qualities and job suitability, the elective future of African Americans is pessimistic. Such findings seem to indicate that no amount of structural reforms can compensate for the deeply held racial beliefs and physically supported misconceptions white voters hold about black politicians.

C. Discrimination Because of Religion

A more multicultural society includes diversity of religious beliefs, as well as persons of different race, color, and national origin. Do you think that Congress had the following scenario in mind when it enacted Title VII?

Adeyeye v. Heartland Sweeteners, LLC

721 F.3d 444 (7th Cir. 2013).

Hamilton, Circuit Judge.

Title VII of the Civil Rights Act of 1964 prohibits discrimination in employment on the basis of religion. Among other consequences, the law requires a covered employer to provide a reasonable accommodation for an employee's request to participate in a religious observance or practice if an accommodation would not cause the employer undue hardship. Plaintiff Sikiru Adeyeye made such a request to his former employer, defendant Heartland Sweeteners, LLC, after his father's death. Adeyeye is a native of Nigeria who moved to the United States in 2008. He requested several weeks of unpaid leave so he could travel to Nigeria to lead his father's burial rites. He explained to Heartland that his participation in the funeral ceremonies was "compulsory" and that if he failed to lead the burial rites, he and his family members would suffer at least spiritual death. Heartland denied Adeyeye's request, but he traveled to Nigeria for the ceremonies anyway. He was fired when he returned and reported to work

. . . .

United States v. Seeger provides a helpful definition of religion: The test "is whether a given belief that is sincere and meaningful occupies a place in the life of its possessor parallel to that filled by the orthodox belief in God." 380 U.S. 163, 165–66 (1965). . . .

Thus, a genuinely held belief that involves matters of the afterlife, spirituality, or the soul, among other possibilities, qualifies as religion under Title VII. *See Kaufman v. McCaughtry*, 419 F.3d 678, 681 (7th Cir. 2005) ("[W]hen a person sincerely holds beliefs dealing with issues of ultimate concern that for her occupy a place parallel to that filled by God in traditionally religious persons, those beliefs represent her religion.") (internal quotations and ellipses omitted). There are three factors to consider when determining whether a belief is in fact religious for purposes of Title VII: (1) the belief necessitating the accommodation must actually be religious, (2) that religious belief must be sincerely held, and (3) accommodation of the employee's sincerely held religious beliefs must not impose an undue hardship on the employer.

. . . .

. . . . Let's look at Adeyeye's first written request for leave, dated July 19, 2010:

> I hereby request for five weeks leave in order to attend funeral ceremony of my father. This is very important for me to be there in order to participate in the funeral rite according to our custom and tradition. The ceremony usually cover from three to four weeks and is two weeks after the burial, there is certain rite[s] that all of the children must participate. And after the third week, my mother will not come out until after one month when I have to be there to encourage her, and I have to [k]ill five goats, then she can now come out. This is done compulsory for the children so that the death will not come or take away any of the children's life. I will appreciate if this request is approved.

After this request was denied, Adeyeye wrote a second request dated September 15, 2010, in which he reduced his request from five weeks of unpaid leave to one week of (already earned) vacation and three weeks of unpaid leave:

> I hereby request for my one week vacation and three weeks leave in order to attend the funeral ceremony of my father in my country, Nigeria—Africa, which is taking place by October next month. This is the second time I will inform you and request for this travelling trip from the company but no reply to this matter. Nevertheless, the burial will be taking place by October next month and I have to be there and involved totally in this burial ceremony being the first child and the only son of the family. I therefore request for this period stated above for this trip and back to my work by November 4th, 2010. Your help towards this matter will highly be appreciated.

These requests to Heartland would allow a reasonable jury to find that Adeyeye gave sufficient notice of the religious nature of his request for unpaid leave. His first request referred to a "funeral ceremony," a "funeral rite," and animal sacrifice. He explained that participation in the funeral ceremonies was "compulsory" and that the spiritual consequence of his absence would be his own and family members' deaths. A reasonable jury could certainly find that the letter's multiple references to spiritual activities and the potential consequences in the afterlife provided sufficient notice to Heartland that Adeyeye was making a religious request. The second request was not as specific as the first, but referred to a funeral ceremony and burial ceremony and the importance of his attendance as the first child and only son. At least when read with the first letter in mind, it also conveyed a religious request with sufficient clarity to preclude summary judgment on the issue.

We recognize, of course, that the religious beliefs and practices Adeyeye referred to are not as familiar as beliefs and practices closer to the modern American mainstream. But the protections of Title VII are not limited to familiar religions. *See Redmond*, 574 F.2d at 900–01 (Title VII protects conduct that is "religiously motivated" and includes "all forms and aspects of religion, however eccentric"), quoting *Cooper v. General Dynamics*, 533 F.2d 163, 168 (5th Cir. 1976). If the managers who considered the request had questions about whether the request was religious, nothing would have prevented them from asking Adeyeye to explain a little more about the nature of his request without risking the sort of hostility to an employee's religion that was at issue in *Venters v. City of Delphi*, 123 F.3d 956, 972 (7th Cir. 1997) (reversing summary judgment for employer where supervisor made clear his expectations that employee needed to share supervisor's religious beliefs and values), or *Shapolia v. Los Alamos Nat'l Lab.*, 992 F.2d 1033, 1037 (10th Cir. 1993) (affirming summary judgment for employer; employee failed to show supervisors' hostility to his religion motivated decision to fire him). The law leaves ample room for dialogue on these matters. The district court erred by granting summary judgment on the question of notice.

. . . .

In our view, the issue is Adeyeye's sincerity, but that does not require a deep analysis of his conscious and/or subconscious reasons or motives for holding his beliefs. As Adeyeye's counsel aptly noted in oral argument, the prospect that courts would begin to inquire into the personal reasons an individual has for holding a religious belief would create a slippery slope we have no desire to descend. Has the plaintiff had a true conversion experience? Is he following religious practices that are embedded in his culture and family upbringing? Is he making Pascal's coldly rational wager to believe in God based on his self-interest? These questions are simply not an appropriate or necessary line of inquiry for courts. We are not and should not be in the business of deciding whether a person holds religious beliefs for the "proper" reasons. We thus restrict our inquiry to whether or not the religious belief system is sincerely held; we do not review the motives or reasons for holding the belief in the first place.

Adeyeye was born in Nigeria and lived there until he moved to the United States as a legal permanent resident in 2008. In his deposition testimony and declaration, Adeyeye explained that his family's religion is a blend of Christianity and customs, traditions, and ceremonial rites developed in his Nigerian village. As a part of this religion, the specific dictates of each family's religious practice are identified, determined, and required by the father or male head of the household. Thus, participating in the rites and traditions identified by his father is a necessary part of Adeyeye's religious observance. Adeyeye explained this in his deposition: "I have to go to Nigeria to go to perform my rites. Being my rites—what I mean by rite, we have a customary rite, our whole culture. So being the main child of the family, so I have to go there and perform a rite."

Adeyeye identified these religious rites in his letters requesting unpaid leave, quoted above, as well as in his deposition and declaration. They included leading an extended procession through the village, animal sacrifice in the form of killing five goats, and cutting off his mother's hair and anointing her head twice with snail oil while she remained secluded in her home for one month of mourning until Adeyeye coaxed her to exit her home and to reenter society. . . .

Problem 2-3

Sean is a factory foreman. He is white and he belongs to the Church of the White Light. The Church's central beliefs are that people of color are the "mud people" who are inferior to the Caucasian race and should be prevented from procreating. Another belief is that the Holocaust did not occur, but rather was a fiction created by a worldwide Jewish conspiracy to foster the creation of the State of Israel. Sean's supervisor learns about his beliefs and questions him about them. He tells the company that his beliefs are very important to him and provide a central structure and meaning to his life. He asserts that he does not believe in an afterlife.

After a careful review, the supervisor discovers no indication that any employees of color have been subjected to racial discrimination in the workplace by Sean. Nonetheless, the company fires Sean and states in his severance letter that "your beliefs are inconsistent with our company's commitment to equal opportunity regardless of sex or race or color. At present we know of no evidence that you have engaged in race discrimination, but the possibility exists and, therefore, we believe that your termination is necessary to prevent such discrimination from occurring."

What do you tell Sean when he comes to your office seeking your advice?

D. Discrimination Because of National Origin

Title VII did not define the term "national origin." In November 2016, the EEOC issued an Enforcement Guidance Memorandum in which it gave an expansive definition of national origin that included "discrimination because of an individual's, or his or her ancestor's, place of origin. The place of origin may be a country (e.g., Mexico, China, Syria) or a former country (e.g., Yugoslavia). The place of origin may be the United States. Finally, it may be a geographic region, including a region that never was a country but nevertheless is closely associated with a particular national origin group, for example, Kurdistan or Acadia." The timing of the EEOC Enforcement Guidance was likely not happenstance. The United States Census for 2010 records that there were 40,000,000 million foreign-born individuals living in the United States, making up 12.9% of the population. The breakdown by country of origin of the foreign-born population in 2010 who came to live in the United States in 2005 or later are telling: India (29%); China (23%); the Philippines (17%); (Mexico 14%); and Vietnam (13%).

In the era of travel bans and heightened sensitivity to threats coming from certain regions or countries, we might expect that this influx of persons may lead to an increase in Title VII claims on the basis of national origin.

QUESTION

1. Do you think these immigration trends will continue? What impact will this trend line have on workplace issues?

E. Pregnancy Discrimination Act (PDA)

The courts do not always extend statutory language to meet unforeseen situations. The Supreme Court found that discrimination because of sex did not include discrimination against a person (admittedly, always a woman) who was pregnant. *General Electric Co. v. Gilbert*, 429 U.S. 125 (1976). Congress responded promptly by amending Title VII with the Pregnancy Discrimination Act of 1978. The Act is broadly worded to cover medical procedures related to pregnancy, as the following case illustrates.

Turic v. Holland Hospitality, Inc.

85 F.3d 1211 (6th Cir. 1996).

Krupansky, Circuit Judge.

Defendant-Appellant, Holland Hospitality, Inc. ("Holland Hospitality"), appealed the district court's award of compensatory damages, punitive damages and backpay to plaintiff, a former restaurant busser and room service attendant at its Holiday Inn in Holland, Michigan, under Title VII of the Civil Rights Act of 1964, 42 U.S.C. § 2000e–2(a)(1) (1991), as amended by the Pregnancy Discrimination Act ("PDA"). The court found that Holland Hospitality discharged Turic because she had become the subject of controversy among the hotel staff as a result of her perpended abortion. The court concluded, as a matter of law, that Turic's termination for the stated reason constituted gender-based discrimination which violated Title VII. Holland Hospitality appealed, asserting Turic's termination resulted from her failure to perform her assigned responsibilities. Holland Hospitality also appealed the court's legal conclusions that Title VII and the broad language of 42 U.S.C. § 2000e–2(a)(1) extend equal protection to contemplated abortions and permit the award of compensatory damages, punitive damages and backpay.

. . . . In 1978, Congress enacted the Pregnancy Discrimination Act ("PDA"), an amendment to Title VII, to ensure that discrimination against women because of pregnancy was covered by Title VII. Section 2000e(k) states:

> The terms 'because of sex' or 'on the basis of sex' include, but are not limited to, because of or on the basis of pregnancy, childbirth, or related medical conditions; and women affected by pregnancy, childbirth, or related medical conditions shall be treated the same for all employment-related purposes, including receipt of benefits under fringe benefit programs, as other persons not so affected but similar in their ability or inability to work, and nothing in section 2000e–2(h) of this title shall be interpreted to permit otherwise. . . .

42 U.S.C. § 2000e(k). The lower court concluded that pregnancy "related medical conditions" included the right to an abortion. The EEOC guidelines interpreting this section, which are entitled to a high degree of deference under *Griggs v. Duke Power*, 401 U.S. 424, 433–34 (1971), expressly state that an abortion is covered by Title VII:

> The basic principle of the [PDA] is that women affected by pregnancy and related conditions must be treated the same as other applicants and employees on the basis of their ability or inability to work. A woman is therefore protected against such practices as being fired . . . merely because she is pregnant *or has had an abortion.*

Appendix 29 C.F.R. 1604 (1986) (emphasis added). Similarly, the legislative history of section 2000e(k) provides:

> Because [the PDA] applies to all situations in which women are "affected by pregnancy, childbirth, and related medical conditions," its basic language covers women who chose to terminate their pregnancies. Thus, no employer may, for example, fire or refuse to hire a woman simply because she has exercised *her right to have an abortion.*

H.R.Conf.Rep. No. 95–1786, 95th Cong., 2d Sess. 4, reprinted in 1978 U.S.C.C.A.N. pp. 4749, 4765–66 (emphasis added). Thus, the plain language of the statute, the legislative history and the EEOC guidelines clearly indicate that an employer may not discriminate against a woman employee because "she has exercised her right to have an abortion." Additionally, the Supreme Court has already considered the impact of the PDA in broadening the scope of prohibited sex discrimination under Title VII. In *International Union v. Johnson Controls, Inc.*, 499 U.S. 187 (1991), the Court held that Title VII, as amended by the PDA, "prohibit[s] an employer from discriminating against a woman because of her capacity to become pregnant unless her reproductive potential prevents her from performing the duties of her job." *Id.* at 206. In light of the plain language of the statute, the legislative history of the PDA, the EEOC guidelines, and the principles of Johnson Controls, the panel concludes that an employer who discriminates against a female employee because she has "exercised her right to have an abortion" violates Title VII.

Turic, however, did not claim, nor did the district court find, that she was terminated because she had exercised her right to have an abortion. (In fact, Turic did not terminate her pregnancy, but carried it to term.) Rather, Turic's claim, and the district court's conclusion, was that she was fired because she contemplated having an abortion. The panel concludes, however, that this distinction has no effect on its result. A woman's right to have an abortion encompasses more than simply the act of having an abortion; it includes the contemplation of an abortion, as well. Since an employer cannot take adverse employment action against a female employee for her decision to have an abortion, it follows that the same employer also cannot take adverse employment action against a female employee for merely thinking about what she has a right to do. As a result, the district court's legal conclusion that Title VII, as amended by the PDA, applies to the action of Holland Hospitality in discharging Turic, is affirmed.

Problem 2-4

Roger accompanied his wife, Chris, to her firm's annual holiday party. They were engaged in conversation about New Year's resolutions and shared that they are seeking to start a family. A manager was notified after the party, and Chris was fired on January 15. At that time, she was not pregnant, although she later did become pregnant. You are advising the firm. Are they exposed to liability?

Problem 2-5

Charisse is having difficulty becoming pregnant and so she begins in-vitro treatments. This requires her to miss time at work. Her employer learns that this may continue for some time, and subsequently fired Charisse. The company's president said that both men and women can be infertile and have related medical treatments, and so this was not a violation of the Pregnancy Discrimination Act. Is the president correct?

Problem 2-6

Gloria has been on maternity leave and is preparing to return to work. She calls her supervisor and tells him that she will need a private area to express milk when she returns. Her supervisor says that this is not welcome activity and fires her. Does Gloria have a claim under the PDA?

Mastery Problem 2-1

Practicing Employment Law in a Multicultural and Sexually Diverse World

The expansion of rights means that employment lawyers must work with and deal with new and different clients. As you read the following excerpts, consider your own interactions with those of different cultures and sexual orientations. While many of you have grown up in diverse cultures, there is still a skillset that you will need to develop when dealing professionally with a diverse client base. Read the following materials and think about how you will address dealing with a diverse group of clients.

Sexual Orientation

Nat'l Ctr For Lesbian Rights & California Rural Legal Assistance, *Tips for Legal Advocates Working with Lesbian, Gay, Bisexual, & Transgender Clients*, http://www.nclrights.org/wp-content/uploads/2013/07/Proyecto_Poderoso_Flyer_cd.pdf.

1. Become comfortable with the issues. Historically, society has been intolerant of lesbian, gay, bisexual, and transgender (LGBT) people and these negative attitudes may affect how we think about LGBT people. It is important for advocates to understand LGBT people and the issues they face. One can become a compassionate advocate by building relationships with local LGBT organizations and activists, attending trainings, visiting educational websites, and reading articles and books or watching movies with positive portrayals of LGBT people.

2. Make your office space friendly to LGBT people. Often, LGBT people will assume that a lawyer's office is unfriendly to LGBT people until he or she receives a clear indication otherwise. Use visual cues to indicate that your office is a safe and welcoming space for LGBT people. Put up posters or stickers that have positive messages about LGBT people and make sure your resource display includes materials specifically for LGBT people. When possible, hire LGBT people as staff members in your organization.

3. With all clients, use language that does not implicitly assume the client's sexual orientation or gender. Using inclusive language that does not assume the gender of your client or your client's significant other sends a message that it is safe for your client to talk to you about his or her sexual orientation or gender identity. It is important to use this inclusive language with all clients, not just the ones who you think may be LGBT. For example, ask "are you in a relationship?" instead of "do you have a boyfriend?"

4. Be aware of assumptions you may have based on a client's sexual orientation or gender identity. We all make assumptions about others based on our own background and experience. The important thing is to be aware so that you do not unconsciously make decisions based on your assumptions about people who are LGBT rather than on your client's unique situation. For example, a gay male client does not necessarily appreciate sexual advances from other male coworkers, and he may have a sexual harassment claim.

5. Use the name and pronoun that conforms to the client's gender identity consistently in all your interactions with the client, as well as in all correspondence and court documents. It is important to be respectful of your client's gender identity by using the name and pronoun that he or she prefers and by asking co-workers, opposing counsel, judges, and court staff to do so. If you are unsure what name or pronoun to use, ask. Court documents may need a footnote explaining that you will use to the client's current name and gender.

6. An LGBT client's legal problems may not be directly related to his or her sexual orientation or gender identity. LGBT clients face the same types of legal identity problems that non-LGBT clients face. An LGBT client's legal problems will not inevitably involve sexual orientation or gender identity discrimination. For example, an LGBT client may come to the legal aid office because his or her landlord has failed to fix an unsafe condition, and that failure may be unrelated to the client's sexual orientation or gender identity.

7. Be prepared to address hostile attitudes and irrelevant arguments. An LGBT client may face hostility from the legal system, even if the case does not relate directly to his or her sexual orientation or gender identity. For example, in a custody case between different-sex parents where one parent is LGBT, the other parent may argue that the LGBT parent shouldn't have custody because of his or her sexual orientation or gender identity.

8. Reach out to LGBT organizations and attorneys who have experience working with LGBT legal issues. The laws affecting LGBT people are complicated and constantly changing. Organizations and attorneys experienced with LGBT legal issues can help you identify the most effective strategies and may be able to provide legal research and information on these issues.

Jatrine Bentsi-Enchill, *Client Communication: Measuring Your Cross-Cultural Competence*

The Canadian Bar Association (September 29, 2014).

Cross-Cultural Communication and Cultural Competence

So what is cultural competence? For individuals, cultural competence is the ability to function effectively in the context of cultural difference and the capacity to effectively adapt, accept and interpret culturally relevant behavior. . . .

The most effective way to determine your level of cultural competence is to take an assessment. Dr. Milton Bennett, developer of the Developmental Model of Intercultural Sensitivity, provides a good starting point to review current perspectives around culture and difference.

His model outlines [several] stages that provide insight into an individual's level of intercultural sensitivity and cultural competence:

Denial

In this stage, lawyers are unaware of cultural difference.

The prevailing attitude is likely to be: "Business is business the world over" or "Everyone would respond this way." Lawyers in this stage of development might be so intent on the tasks at hand that they fail to notice the cultural aspects of business relationships with clients and colleagues. In this stage, there is a general lack of awareness about difference.

However, awareness is a key element in cross-cultural communication. Effective cross-cultural communication requires that individuals have some awareness and appreciation of difference. A lawyer in denial would be completely insensitive to their client's cultural taboos, expectations, family norms, communication, and conflict styles.

While in the denial stage, lawyers will be ineffective in establishing trust and good client relations with clients from a different culture. The failure to understand the significance of cultural differences may lead lawyers to implement ineffective case strategies due to the misinterpretation of client behavior.

For lawyers in this stage, unnecessary conflicts and misunderstandings, along with an overall lack of understanding of the importance of cross-cultural communication, are common.

Defense

Lawyers in this stage will recognize some cultural differences and view such differences negatively.

Instead of striving to understand or interpret the patterns of conduct or communication that differ from their own culture, lawyers in defense are likely to mislabel such conduct as "wrong", "unintelligent", "dishonest", etc. In this stage, the greater the difference, the more negatively it is perceived.

A criminal defense lawyer in the denial stage will most likely be frustrated by a female murder defendant from China, who is more committed to preserving family honor than asserting a claim of self defense in the murder of her husband. (For many in China, issues of honor, shame and commitment to family take precedence over individual goals and objectives.) How effectively could a lawyer in the denial stage represent this client? How might the difference in cultural worldviews and behaviors affect the lawyer's relationship with her client?

Clearly, lawyers in this stage will struggle to communicate and work effectively with clients they perceive as different. This perception may cause otherwise well-meaning lawyers to misjudge or stereotype a client. Negative attitudes and perceptions held about people from other cultures serve to diminish cross-cultural understanding and communication, ultimately undermining a lawyer's ability to establish a healthy and respectful relationship with his or her client.

Minimization of Difference

It is common for lawyers in this stage to avoid stereotypes and appreciate differences in language and culture. However, many will still view their own values as universal and superior, rather than viewing them simply as part of their own ethnicity and culture.

As a result, it is common for lawyers in minimization to believe that everyone else shares their ideals, goals, and values with regard to family, work, professionalism, humor, communication, etc. In dealing with clients, the lawyer is likely to misinterpret the client's behavior, opinions, and reactions because the lawyer will misperceive that the client shares his or her cultural values.

For example, in American culture when assessing credibility, lawyers may read a client's or a witnesses' failure to maintain eye contact as a sign of dishonesty. However, in many cultures, averting the eyes is a sign of respect to someone in authority. How will an inaccurate read on behavior impact the lawyer's ability to make an accurate assessment of the credibility of a client or witness?

Lawyers in this stage focus on minimizing difference and in so doing they misread relevant behavioral and communication cues that are based on culture. Assuming similarity when none exists serves as a barrier to successful cross-cultural communication.

Acceptance of Difference

It is important for lawyers to have the ability to properly analyze and respond to clients as a basis for establishing effective lawyer-client relations.

The following is a real situation described by an immigration lawyer. It provides a great example of effective cross-cultural communication and lawyering:

> The lawyer was representing a client eager to obtain his permanent resident status, so he could take a long-awaited trip home to visit family and friends.
>
> During a discussion about timeframes for the permanent resident process, the lawyer gently explained to the client that his expectations regarding processing timelines were unreasonable and simply impossible to meet. In an attempt to "expedite" the process, the client responded by offering the lawyer a bribe.
>
> In this situation, the lawyer was aware of his client's cultural background, and as such, was aware that in his client's culture, it is customary to pay officials bribes in order to expedite certain processes; in fact, such bribes were often expected.
>
> The immigration lawyer's awareness of his client's background allowed him to respond in an appropriately sensitive and informative manner. Additionally, since the lawyer approached the

situation with understanding instead of judgment, the lawyer-client relationship was preserved.

This example speaks to the heart of the significance of cultural awareness and competence required to develop and sustain successful attorney-client relationships. . . .

Tips for Improving Cross-Cultural Communication

Although training and coaching interventions are the most effective methods of improving cross-cultural communication skills and cultural competence, the following are some things that lawyers can begin doing to improve cross-cultural communication skills:

1. *Gain awareness.* Become aware that although a gesture, word or response may mean something in your culture; it may mean something totally different to someone from another culture.

2. *Take a look at your own culture.* Understanding how your worldview and culture impacts your perception of others will help you identify instances where you may tend to use biases or stereotypes when interacting with those whom you may perceive as different.

3. *Try a little understanding.* In trying to better understand your clients and their motivations, understand the impact that culture plays on their values, perspectives, and behavior.

4. *Listen closely and pay attention.* Try to focus on verbal as well as non-verbal cues and the behavior of your client. If the client seems distracted, confused, or ill at ease, ask questions.

5. *Suspend judgment as much as possible.* Approaching people from other cultures in a judgmental manner will hinder your ability to gain a clear understanding of the situation.

6. *Be flexible.* Flexibility, adaptability, and open-mindedness are critical to effective cross-cultural communication. Understanding, embracing, and addressing cultural differences will lead to better lines of communication, client-service, and lawyering.

Conclusion

This Lesson provided an overview of labor law and anti-discrimination law. You learned that unions are decreasing in importance due to a shift from communal interests to individual rights. You also studied some of the cutting edge issues in anti-discrimination law, as courts define the broad terms of the statute. Keep these areas of law in mind as the backdrop for our study of employment law.

2

The Parties

Key Concepts

- Employment law imposes obligations on, and provides protections to, "employees" and "employers." Unfortunately, these key definitions are indeterminate.
- The definition of "employee" is generally resolved through application of a multi-factor "control test," derived from agency law, that focuses on the employer's right to control the completion of the work involved. However, an older approach is still used to interpret the Fair Labor Standards Act and Family Medical Leave Act in light of the "economic realities" of the relationship and the remedial purpose of the statutes.
- Recently, courts have focused on the "entrepreneurial opportunities" afforded by the relationship, perhaps suggesting a revival of the "economic realities" approach.
- A new approach, "the ABC test" has just been endorsed by California for wage claims, suggesting that a presumption of "employee" status might be emerging.
- Defining "employer" is also difficult, especially with regard to the liability of individuals as the "employer" and the doctrine of joint employment.
- The definitions of "employee" and "employer" do not work well in today's dynamic platform economy.
- Particular complexities arise with immigrant workers, who may or may not have work authorization.

Lesson 3:
Who Is an Employee? The "Multi-Factor" Tests

Objectives and Expected Learning Outcomes

In this Lesson, you will learn the different principal tests for "employee" status, and you will apply these tests to different factual scenarios. The traditional distinction between an "employee" and an "independent contractor" is becoming more difficult in the modern economy, which has moved away from the traditional employment relationship.

1. The Multi-Factor "Right of Control" Test

The duties and benefits of employment law are imposed only when there is an employment relationship. Only those persons who have the status of an "employee" are able to utilize the protections of employment law. Unfortunately, employment statutes tend to be hopelessly circular in their definitions of employee. For example, the National Labor Relations Act (29 U.S.C. § 152(3)) provides that the term "employee . . . shall include any employee, and shall not be limited to the employees of a particular employer, . . . and shall include any individual whose work has ceased as a consequence of, or in connection with, any current labor dispute or because of any unfair labor practice." Similarly, the Fair Labor Standards Act (Sec. 29 U.S.C. § 203(e)(1)) and the Employee Retirement Income Security Act (29 U.S.C. § 1002(6)) both define the term employee as "any individual employed by an employer."

To add detail to these definitions, the Supreme Court has borrowed from the common law definitions of employee under agency law. In *Community for Creative Non-Violence v. Reid*, 490 U.S. 730 (1989) the Court explained the multi-factor control test that it derived from the Restatement of Agency 2d, § 220(1):

> In determining whether a hired party is an employee under the general common law of agency, we consider the hiring party's right to control the manner and means by which the product is accomplished. Among the other factors relevant to this inquiry are the skill required; the source of the instrumentalities and tools; the location of the work; the duration of the relationship between the parties; whether the hiring party has the right to assign additional projects to the hired party; the extent of the

> hired party's discretion over when and how long to work; the method of payment; the hired party's role in hiring and paying assistants; whether the work is part of the regular business of the hiring party; whether the hiring party is in business; the provision of employee benefits; and the tax treatment of the hired party.

490 U. S. at 751–752. The Court has since reaffirmed this approach in the context of defining "employee" for purposes of various statutory schemes. See, e.g., *Nationwide Mutual Ins. Co. v. Darden*, 503 U.S. 318 (1992) (Employment Retirement Income Security Act) and *Clackamas Gastroenterology Assocs., P.C. v. Wells*, 538 U.S. 440, 448 (2003) (Americans with Disabilities Act). Consequently, for purposes of defining "employee" under federal statutes and the common law, we turn to the definition of a master-servant relationship under the Restatement (Second) of Agency.

Restatement (Second) of Agency

§ 220(1). Definition of Servant

(1) A servant [employee] is a person employed to perform services in the affairs of another and who[,] with respect to the physical conduct in the performance of the services[,] is subject to the other's control or right to control.

(2) In determining whether one acting for another is a servant or an independent contractor, the following matters of fact, among others, are considered:

- (a) the extent of control which, by the agreement, the master may exercise over the details of the work;
- (b) whether or not the one employed is engaged in a distinct occupation or business;
- (c) the kind of occupation, with reference to whether, in the locality, the work is usually done under the direction of the employer or by a specialist without supervision;
- (d) the skill required in the particular occupation;
- (e) whether the employer or the workman supplies the instrumentalities, tools, and the places of work for the person doing work;
- (f) the length of time for which the person is employed;
- (g) the method of payment, whether by the time or by the job;

(h) whether or not the work is a part of the regular business of the employer;

(i) whether or not the parties believe they are creating the relation of master and servant; and

(j) whether the principal is or is not in business.

Example 3-1

Shane Wilson has built a business cleaning homes in his neighborhood. He meets with the homeowner to determine what they want him to do and how often, and he schedules them accordingly. He currently cleans 14 homes on a weekly basis. Shane brings all the tools and supplies he requires to the job, and he cleans the home at times that the owners are away. He charges for the job according to an agreed upon price, and he files taxes as a sole proprietor. Shane is not an employee of any of the homeowners.

Example 3-2

Shane Wilson applied to Housecleaners, a franchise that provides cleaning services in town. Shane wears a Housecleaners uniform and is assigned houses to clean by the Housecleaners front office. He was required to take a four hour course on how to clean a house in the manner promised by Housecleaners, and his work is reviewed every quarter. Shane is not permitted to communicate directly with the homeowners regarding the work to be performed, and he is required to be on call during the week if new customers are signed by Housecleaners. Consequently, Shane depends on Housecleaners for his income, although he occasionally drives an hour or two for Uber when he is not cleaning houses. Shane is an employee of Housecleaners.

A recent district court opinion provides a good example of the multi-factor control test. In *Lawson v. Grubhub, Inc.,* 302 F. Supp. 3d 1071 (N.D. Cal. 2018), the Court determined that Grubhub had met its burden of showing that Lawson, one of their drivers, was properly classified as an independent contractor. Although some elements of the test pointed toward employee status, Grubhub's lack of all necessary control over his work, including whether he performed deliveries, how long he was available to accept deliveries and how he performed the actual deliveries, established his status as an independent contractor.

Grubhub is an internet-based application that connects diners seeking food delivery to a variety of local restaurants. Customers order food and Grubhub transmits the order to the restaurant and arranges for a delivery driver if the restaurant does not have its own driver. Grubhub operates in 1,200 markets in the United States, with 250 in California alone. As of June, 2016, there were 4,000 Grubhub delivery drivers in California.

Once per week, Grubhub posted a schedule of available shifts, or "blocks," to its drivers, and drivers selected their blocks on a first-come-first-served basis. No drivers were assigned mandatory blocks, nor were they required to sign up for a minimal number of blocks. Nearly 40% of persons who sign up on the Grubhub app to be a delivery driver never follow through by signing up for a block and performing work. However, drivers who performed especially well were given "priority scheduling" rights, and so there were advantages to making oneself available. Drivers were paid a per-order-delivered payment plus any tips offered by customers, and a nominal amount for mileage. However, Grubhub ensured a minimum hourly compensation if the driver accepted at least 85% of the deliveries offered to him during a block.

When Lawson began a block he would move the Grubhub driver app to the "available" setting. Grubhub then used a computer algorithm to offer deliveries to the available drivers, and the driver would then accept or reject the delivery. If the delivery was rejected, the algorithm would move to the next available driver without removing the first driver from the block. In the event that customers outnumbered available drivers, Grubhub would send a market-wide message to all drivers asking them if they wished to be available for assignment.

The court analyzed Grubhub's right to control the manner and means of Lawson's performance of duties as follows:

> Grubhub exercised little control over the details of Mr. Lawson's work during the four months he performed delivery services for Grubhub. Grubhub did not control how he made the deliveries—whether by car, motorcycle, scooter or bicycle. Nor did it control the condition of the mode of transportation Mr. Lawson chose. Grubhub never inspected or even saw a photograph of Mr. Lawson's vehicle. Grubhub did ensure that Mr. Lawson's chosen vehicle was registered and insured, and that he had a valid driver's license. But given that he could not legally drive

the car without these conditions being satisfied, Grubhub's oversight in this respect does not weight in favor of employee status. *See Linton*, 15 Ca.App.5th at 1223 ("A putative employer does not exercise any degree of control merely by imposing requirements mandated by government regulation").

Grubhub also did not control Mr. Lawson's appearance while he was making Grubhub deliveries. While Mr. Lawson could wear a Grubhub shirt and hat, he was not required to do so and did not always do so. . . .

Grubhub did not require Mr. Lawson to undergo any particular training or orientation. He was not provided with a script for how to interact with restaurants or customers. He was not told what supplies, if any, he had to have with him, whether condiments, straws or extra napkins. No Grubhub employee ever performed a ride along with Mr. Lawson; indeed, no Grubhub employee ever met Mr. Lawson in person before this lawsuit.

Grubhub did not control who could be with Mr. Lawson in his vehicle, or even accompany him into a restaurant to pick up an order or to a customer's door to make a delivery. . . .

Mr. Lawson could decide not to work a block he signed up for right up to the time the block started. Mr. Lawson even had the right to reject any order offered during his scheduled block; in other words, he had no obligation to perform any delivery offered to him by Grubhub even though he had signed up to work a particular block. . . .

Thus, at bottom, Mr. Lawson had complete control of his work schedule: Grubhub could not make him work and could not count on him to work. . . . .

Grubhub also did not control how and when Mr. Lawson delivered the restaurant orders he chose to accept. The Agreement did not specify an amount of time in which a driver had to reach a restaurant to pick up an order; nor did it specify how quickly the driver had to complete the delivery. Mr. Lawson picked his own route; indeed, he could make as many stops as he desired and even make a delivery for another company while delivering for Grubhub, and on many occasions he made deliveries for Grubhub's restaurant delivery competitors while working a Grubhub scheduled block. . . .

> Grubhub also did not prepare performance evaluations of Mr. Lawson. While for a time drivers whom Grubhub in its sole discretion determined were its top performers were offered priority scheduling, failing to qualify as a top performer did not jeopardize Mr. Lawson's contract with Grubhub. No one at Grubhub was Mr. Lawson's boss or supervisor. . . .
>
> Grubhub did control some aspects of Mr. Lawson's work. Grubhub determined the rates Mr. Lawson would be paid and the fee customers would pay for delivery services. . . . The Court finds that Mr. Lawson could not negotiate his pay in any meaningful way and therefore this fact weighs in favor of an employment relationship.

Lawson, 302 F. Supp. 3d, at 1084–1086.

The court found that the fact that most suggested employment status was the ability to terminate the Agreement at-will. However, the at-will status was completely mutual: Lawson never was required to sign up for a block, or even to complete deliveries during a block for which he had signed up. Moreover, he was not in a vulnerable position because he did not have to invest in any special equipment or supplies. He merely had to use his existing vehicle and cell phone.

The court then assessed the secondary factors. First, it found that "Mr. Lawson was not engaged in a distinct occupation or business. He did not run a delivery business of which Grubhub was simply one client." *Id.* at 1089. Additionally, it found that the work required little skill, *id.*, was essentially compensated on an hourly basis, *id.* at 1090, and that the work performed was part of Grubhub's regular business, *id.* All these factors augured in favor of employee status. On the other hand, the work was not performed under Grubhub's supervision, *id.* at 1089, Mr. Lawson provided all necessary tools and equipment, *id.*, and the Agreement did not last for a stated period of time, *id.* at 1089–90. These factors augured in favor of independent contractor status.

The court concluded that the last factor, the parties' intent, was neutral. On one hand, the express Agreement provides that Mr. Lawson agreed to independent contractor status. On the other hand, it was a take-it-or-leave-it offer. *Id.* at 1091. On balance, the court concluded that Mr. Lawson was an independent contractor.

> The *Borello* [multi-factor control test] factors "cannot be applied mechanically as separate tests; they are intertwined and their weight depends often on particular combinations." *Alexander*, 765 F.3d at 989. Here, some secondary factors favor an employee/employer relationship: namely,

> Mr. Lawson's delivery work was part of Grubhub's regular business in Los Angeles; the work was low-skilled; Mr. Lawson was not engaged in a distinct delivery business of which Grubhub was just one client; and, slightly less, Grubhub's method of payment. The other factors, however, favor a finding that Mr. Lawson was an independent contractor. Of primary significance, Grubhub did not control the manner or means of Mr. Lawson's work, including whether he worked at all or for how long or how often, or even whether he performed deliveries for Grubhub's competitors at the same time he had agreed to delivery for Grubhub. Grubhub also did not provide Mr. Lawson with any of the tools for his work (other than a downloadable mobile app) and neither Grubhub nor Mr. Lawson con templated the work to be long term or regular, but rather episodic at Mr. Lawson's sole convenience. And while Grubhub had the right to terminate the Agreement at will upon 14 days' notice, under the specific circumstances of this case, this right did not allow Grubhub to exert control over Mr. Lawson's work. After considering all the facts, and the caselaw regarding the status of delivery drivers, the Court finds that all the factors weighed and considered as a whole establish that Mr. Lawson was an independent contractor and not an employee.
>
> . . . .
>
> Under California law whether an individual performing services for another is an employee or an independent contractor is an all-or-nothing proposition. If Mr. Lawson is an employee, he has rights to minimum wage, overtime, expense reimbursement and workers compensation benefits. If he is not, he gets none. With the advent of the gig economy, and the creation of a low wage workforce performing low skill but highly flexible episodic jobs, the legislature may want to address this stark dichotomy. In the meantime the Court must answer the question one way or the other. Based on what the Court observed at trial and the facts found, and after applying the *Borello* [multi-factor control] test, the Court finds that during the four months Mr. Lawson performed delivery services for Grubhub he was an independent contractor. Since he was not an employee, he cannot prevail on his . . . claims. Accordingly, judgment must be entered in favor of Grubhub and against Mr. Lawson.

Id. at 1091–1093.

QUESTIONS

1. Should the rights and benefits of employment law be an "all-or-nothing" proposition?
2. Does the judge explain how she balanced the conflicting evidence under the multi-factor test to come to her conclusion? Is it possible for a judge to provide an account of multi-factor decisionmaking?

---

2. The Economic Realities Test: An Earlier Alternative to the Control Test

Early on, courts sometimes went beyond the strict common law test to ensure that the remedial employment law statutory schemes were applied broadly to fulfill their purpose of protecting workers. However, through statutory amendment Congress restricted the scope of employment in several major acts to the traditional common law "control" test. One exception is the expansive definition of employee under the Fair Labor Standards Act. Professor Matt Bodie explains this development of the (now limited) economic realities test.

Matt Bodie, *Participation as a Theory of Employment*

89 Notre Dame L. Rev. 661, 684–688 (2013).

The primary alternative to the control test, particularly in the realm of employment law, is the "economic realities" or "economic dependence" test. It is generally interpreted to provide a more expansive definition to the term "employee," one that covers more vulnerable workers who may have some aspects of separation from the firm but lack true economic independence. It has its roots in the interpretation of critical New Deal statutes soon after their passage. While clearly rejecting the common law control test, these cases did not craft a specific and readily cognizable alternative. Instead, they looked to the purpose of the statutes and attempted to glean an approach that harmonized with that purpose. Interpreting the NLRA, the Court noted that it was "not necessary in this case to make a completely definitive limitation around the term 'employee.' " But the Court did distinguish between the traditional common law definition and a broader perspective based on the ills at which the statute was directed. In other words, the term "employee" was "to be determined broadly, in doubtful situations, by underlying economic facts rather than technically and exclusively by previously established legal classifications." That reference to "economic facts" became "economic reality" in later cases defining the category of "employee" in the context of the Social Security Act and the Fair Labor Standards Act. This test—lacking any factors or even specific doctrinal definition—was something of a gestalt or eyeball standard, designed to look at the overall economic relationship and determine whether Congress intended such a relationship to come under the purview of the particular statutory scheme.

Although the Court's "economic reality" definition was overturned by statutory amendments to both the NLRA and the Social Security Act, it has remained in place with regard to the FLSA. That statute's definition of employee is the circular one found in many statutes: "the term 'employee' means any individual employed by an employer." However, the Act also defines "employ" to include "suffer or permit to work." Because employ is defined differently and more broadly, the Supreme Court has recognized that the FLSA may extend to cover workers beyond the reach of the common law agency test. The definition of "employee" under the FMLA incorporates the standard from the FLSA by reference, and thus courts have applied the same "economic realities" test. Outside of these contexts, however, the Supreme Court has made it clear that the "control" test is to apply as the default rule.

According to the "economic realities" test, "employees are those who as a matter of economic reality are dependent upon the business to which they render service." Courts have generally looked to a number of factors in calculating coverage under the "economic realities" test. One popular test, developed in *Bonnette v. California Health & Welfare Agency*, asks whether the employer: "(1) had the power to hire and fire the employee; (2) supervised and controlled employee work schedules or conditions of employment; (3) determined the rate and method of payment; and (4) maintained employment records." Other circuits have more closely mirrored the control test. But in recognition of the FLSA's broader coverage, courts have either implicitly or explicitly looked to the "reality" of the worker's dependence on the putative employer. Such dependence is often manifested through the economic weakness of the workers, and the focus on economic reality is meant to cut through formalistic trappings to get at the heart of the relationship. In *Secretary of Labor v. Lauritzen*, for example, the court held that migrant workers on a pickle farm were employees because they "depend on the [employer's] land, crops, agricultural expertise, equipment, and marketing skills."

Some commentators have argued that the economic realities test should replace the control test, because its focus on economic dependence provides more protection to vulnerable workers. However, in the United States the test has thus far remained limited to the FLSA and FMLA. The concept of dependency has been more successful in foreign jurisdictions, which have adopted concepts such as "dependent contractors" and "employee-like" persons in certain worker-protection regimes. In the United Kingdom, for example, several employment law regimes have expanded to include those working relationships "whereby the individual undertakes to do or perform personally any work or services for another party to the contract whose status is not by virtue of the contract that of a client or customer of any profession or business undertaking carried on by the individual." At present, the extended protections include minimum wage requirements, overtime limitations, grievance processes, and restrictions on wage deductions. However, the definition of "worker" has only extended these protections to an additional set of laborers; it has not replaced the concept of "cmployee" in the law.

Example 3-3

In *Perez v. SuperMaid, LLC*, 55 F. Supp. 3d 1065 (N.D. Ill. 2014), the court determined that workers at SuperMaid were employees for FLSA purposes (minimum wage and overtime). The employees were substantially controlled by the business: they were provided with vehicles, uniforms, cleaning supplies and tools; they were trained how to clean houses, and their performance was monitored; and their work was scheduled by the office, and they did not manage their own workflow. However, the court also emphasized that the economic realities test under the broad definition of FLSA provided strong support for the holding:

> Opportunity for Profit and Loss. "An independent contractor risks loss of an investment and has the opportunity to increase profits through managerial discretion." *E.E.O.C. v. Century Broadcasting Corp.*, No. 89 C 5842, 1990 WL 43286, at *4 (N.D.Ill. Mar. 23, 1990) (citing *Lauritzen*, 835 F.2d at 1536).

> Strict prearranged pay scales and situations that do not afford workers "managerial discretion" to adjust their hours or work more efficiently eliminate the opportunity for those workers to realize increased profits by adjusting their own performance. *See Int'l Detective*, 819 F.Supp.2d at 748; *Skokie Maid*, 2013 WL 3506149 at *8. In *Skokie Maid*, compensating workers on a per-house basis and strict enforcement of permitted work hours weighed in favor of employee status. With Supermaid, workers are similarly not allowed to vary their start and end times, even if they are able to complete their work more efficiently than scheduled; their ability to perform more effectively does not increase their ability to increase their personal pay or profits. The defendants have made no showing, and the Court sees no basis in the record to find, that the maids in this case have any autonomy to increase their earning rate through managerial discretion, again weighing in favor of employee classification.

Perez, 55 F. Supp. at 1077.

---

3. Contemporary Applications of the Multi-Factor Test: Emphasizing "Entrepreneurial Opportunity for Gain or Loss" Rather than "Control"

The first factor in the common law test, *the right of control*, is generally regarded as the central question to determine the scope of employment law statutes. In recent years, the element of the right to control has been criticized for being out of step with the evolving characteristics of the modern workplace. As an alternative, some courts have suggested that the more appropriate factor would be to focus on the "entrepreneurial opportunity for gain or loss." The test focuses on the economic reality of the relationship rather than formal characteristics of "control" over the work.

The struggle over defining employee status has been pronounced in certain industries where corporations seek to maintain a flexible workforce to adjust to rapidly changing circumstances and demands. For example, the shipping company, FedEx, began hiring drivers as independent contractors who were not subject to the full control of FedEx in carrying out their detailed obligations. On one hand, FedEx regarded them as contractors hired to assist with its variable delivery demands. On the other hand, the independent drivers were dependent on FedEx in many ways and subject to detailed rules and regulations. The following opinion was notable for its effort to recast the test of employment status.

FedEx Home Delivery v. NLRB

563 F.3d 492 (D.C. Cir. 2009).

Brown, Circuit Judge:

FedEx Ground Package System, Inc. ("FedEx"), a company that provides small package delivery throughout the country, seeks review of the determination of the National Labor Relations Board ("Board") that FedEx committed an unfair labor practice by refusing to bargain with the union certified as the collective bargaining representative of its Wilmington, Massachusetts drivers. The Board cross-applies for enforcement of its order. Because the drivers are independent contractors and not employees, we grant FedEx's petition, vacate the order, and deny the cross-application for enforcement

I.

. . . .

In July 2006, the International Brotherhood of Teamsters, Local Union 25, filed two petitions with the NLRB seeking representation elections at the Jewel Drive and Ballardvale Street terminals in Wilmington, neither of which boasts many contractors. The Union won the elections, prevailing by a vote of 14 to 6 at Jewel Drive and 10 to 2 at Ballardvale Street, and was certified as the collective bargaining representative at both. FedEx refused to bargain with the Union. The company did not contest the vote count; instead, FedEx disputed the preliminary finding that its single-route drivers are "employees" within the meaning of Section 2(3) of the National Labor Relations Act, 29 U.S.C. § 152(3).

. . . .

II.

To determine whether a worker should be classified as an employee or an independent contractor, the Board and this court apply the common-law agency test, a requirement that reflects clear congressional will. While this seems simple enough, the Restatement's non-exhaustive ten-factor test is not especially amenable to any sort of bright-line rule, a long-recognized rub. Thus, "there is no shorthand formula or magic phrase that can be applied to find the answer, but all of the incidents of the relationship must be assessed and weighed with no one factor being decisive," always bearing in mind the "legal distinction between 'employees' . . . and 'independent contractors' . . . is permeated at the fringes by conclusions drawn from the factual setting of the particular industrial dispute." *North Am. Van Lines, Inc. v. NLRB*, 869 F.2d 596, 599 (D.C.Cir.1989) ("NAVL").

This potential uncertainty is particularly problematic because the line between worker and independent contractor is jurisdictional—the Board has no authority whatsoever over independent contractors.

. . . .

For a time, when applying this common law test, we spoke in terms of an employer's right to exercise control, making the extent of actual supervision of the means and manner of the worker's performance a key consideration in the totality of the circumstances assessment. Though all the common law factors were considered, the meta-question, as it were, focused on the sorts of controls employers could use without transforming a contractor into an employee. . . .

Gradually, however, a verbal formulation emerged that sought to identify the essential quantum of independence that separates a contractor from an employee . . . .

In any event, the process that seems implicit in those cases became explicit—indeed, as explicit as words can be—in *Corporate Express Delivery Systems v. NLRB*, 292 F.3d 777 (D.C.Cir. 2002). In that case, both this court and the Board, while retaining all of the common law factors, "shift[ed the] emphasis" away from the unwieldy control inquiry in favor of a more accurate proxy: whether the "putative independent contractors have 'significant entrepreneurial opportunity for gain or loss.' " *Id.* at 780 (quoting *Corp. Express Delivery Sys.*, 332 N.L.R.B. No. 144, at 6 (Dec. 19, 2000)). This subtle refinement was done at the Board's urging in light of a comment to the Restatement that explains a " 'full-time cook is regarded as a servant,' "—and not "an independent contractor"—" 'although it is understood that the employer will exercise no control over the cooking.' " *Id.* (quoting Restatement (Second) of Agency § 220(1) cmt. d). Thus, while all the considerations at common law remain in play, an important animating principle by which to evaluate those factors in cases where some factors cut one way and some the other is whether the position presents the opportunities and risks inherent in entrepreneurialism.

. . . .

This struggle to capture and articulate what is meant by abstractions like "independence" and "control" also seems to play a part in the Board's own cases, though we readily concede the Board's language has not been as unambiguous as this court's binding statement in *Corporate Express.* For instance, in the latest but far from only statement of the principle, the Board held that where carriers sign an independent contractor agreement; own, maintain, and control their own vehicles; hire full-time substitutes and control the substitutes' terms and conditions of employment; are permitted to hold contracts on multiple routes; select the delivery sequence; and are not subject to the employer's progressive discipline system, the evidence establishes that the carriers are independent contractors. Importantly, the Board, noting many drivers had "multiple routes" and could deliver newspapers for another publisher, also concluded significant entrepreneurial opportunity existed, even if most failed to make the extra effort. "[T]he fact that many carriers choose not to take advantage of this opportunity to increase their income does not mean that they do not have the entrepreneurial potential to do so."

The record here shares many of the same characteristics of entrepreneurial potential. In the underlying representation decision, the Regional Director found the contractors sign a Standard Contractor Operating Agreement that specifies the contractor is not an employee of FedEx "for any purpose" and confirms the "manner and means of reaching mutual business objectives" is within the contractor's discretion, and FedEx "may not prescribe hours of work, whether or when the contractors take breaks, what routes they follow, or other details of performance"; "contractors are not subject to reprimands or other discipline"; contractors must provide their own vehicles, although the vehicles must be compliant with government regulations and other safety requirements; and "contractors are responsible for all the costs associated with operating and maintaining their vehicles." *FedEx Home Delivery and Local 25*, N.L.R.B. Case Nos. 1–RC–22034, 22035, slip op. at 10–14 (First Region, Sept. 20, 2006) ("*Representation Decision*"). They may use the vehicles "for other commercial or personal purposes . . . so long as they remove or mask all FedEx Home logos and markings," and, even on this limited record, some do use them for personal uses like moving family members, and in the past "Alan Douglas[ ] used his FedEx truck for his 'Douglas Delivery' delivery service, in which he delivered items such as lawn mowers for a repair company." *Id.* at 14, 15. Contractors can independently incorporate, and at least two in Wilmington have done so. At least one contractor has negotiated with FedEx for higher fees. *Id.* at 20.

Tellingly, contractors may contract to serve multiple routes or hire their own employees for their single routes; more than twenty-five percent of contractors have hired their own employees at some point. "The multiple route contractors have sole authority to hire and dismiss their drivers"; they are responsible for the "drivers' wages" and "all expenses associated with hiring drivers, such as the cost of training, physical exams, drug screening, employment taxes, and work accident insurance." *Representation Decision*, slip op. at 27. The drivers' pay and benefits, as well as responsibility for fuel costs and the like, are negotiated "between the contractors and their drivers." In addition, "both multiple and single route contractors may hire drivers" as "temporary" replacements on their own routes; though they can use FedEx's "Time Off Program" to find replacement drivers when they are ill or away, they need not use this program, and not all do. Thus, contrary to the dissent's depiction, contractors do not need to show up at work every day (or ever, for that matter); instead, at their discretion, they can take a day, a week, a month, or more off, so long as they hire another to be there. "FedEx [also] is not involved in a contractor's decision to hire or terminate a substitute driver, and contractors do not even have to tell FedEx [ ] they have hired a replacement driver, as long as the driver is 'qualified.' " *Representation Decision*, slip op. at 29. "Contractors may also choose to hire helpers" without notifying FedEx at all; at least six contractors in Wilmington have done so. *Id.* at 29–30. This ability to hire "others to do the Company's work" is no small thing in evaluating "entrepreneurial opportunity." *Corp. Express*, 292 F.3d at 780–81; *see also St. Joseph News Press*, 345 N.L.R.B. at 479 ("Most importantly, the carriers can hire full-time substitutes. . . .").

Another aspect of the Operating Agreement is significant, and is novel under our precedent. Contractors can assign at law their contractual rights to their routes, without FedEx's permission. The logical result is they can sell, trade, give, or even bequeath their routes, an unusual feature for an employer-employee relationship. In fact, the amount of consideration for the sale of a route is negotiated "strictly between the seller and the buyer," with no FedEx involvement at all other than the new route owner must also be "qualified" under the Operating Agreement, *Representation Decision*, slip op. at 30, with "qualified" merely meaning the new owner of the route also satisfies Department of Transportation ("DOT") regulations, *see id.* at 8–10. Although FedEx assigns routes without nominal charge, the record contains evidence, as the Regional Director expressly found, that at least two contractors were able to sell routes for a profit ranging from $3,000 to nearly $16,000. *See id.* at 30–32, 38–39.

. . . .

The Regional Director . . . thought FedEx's business model distinguishable from those where the Board had concluded the drivers were independent contractors. For example, FedEx requires: contractors to wear a recognizable uniform and conform to grooming standards; vehicles of particular color (white) and within a specific size range; and vehicles to display FedEx's logo in a way larger than that required by DOT regulations. The company insists drivers complete a driving course (or have a year of commercial driving experience, which need not be with FedEx) and be insured, and it "conducts two customer service rides per year" to audit performance. FedEx provides incentive pay (as well as fuel reimbursements in limited instances) and vehicle availability allotments, and requires contractors have a vehicle and driver available for deliveries Tuesday through Saturday. *Id.* at 508–14. Moreover, FedEx can reconfigure routes if a contractor cannot provide adequate service, though the contractor has five days to prove otherwise, and is entitled to monetary compensation for the diminished value of the route. *Id.* at 512. These aspects of FedEx's operation are distinguishable from the business models in *Dial-A-Mattress*, 326 N.L.R.B. 884 (contractors arranged their own training, could decline work, did not wear uniforms, could use any vehicle, and were provided no subsidies or minimum compensation) and *Argix Direct, Inc.*, 343 N.L.R.B. 1017 (2004) (contractors could decline work, delivered to major retailers using any vehicle, and had no guaranteed income).

But those distinctions, though not irrelevant, reflect differences in the type of service the contractors are providing rather than differences in the employment relationship. In other words, the distinctions are significant but not sufficient. FedEx Home's business model is somewhat unique. The service is delivering small packages, mostly to residential customers. Unlike some trucking companies, its drivers are not delivering goods that FedEx sells or manufacturers, nor does FedEx move freight for a limited number of large clients. Instead, it is an intermediary between a diffuse group of senders and a broadly diverse group of recipients. With this model comes certain customer demands, including safety. As the Internal Revenue Service ("IRS") persuasively notes, and ordinary experience confirms, a uniform requirement often at least in part "is intended to ensure customer security rather than to control the [driver]." INTERNAL REVENUE SERVICE, EMPLOYMENT TAX GUIDELINES: CLASSIFYING CERTAIN VAN OPERATORS IN THE MOVING INDUSTRY 23, http://www.irs.gov/pub/irs-utl/van-ops.pdf (last visited April 3, 2009). And once a driver wears FedEx's logo, FedEx has an interest in making sure her conduct reflects favorably on that logo, for instance by her being a safe and insured driver—which is required by DOT regulations in any event. *See Representation Decision*, slip op. at 8–9, 14, 24.

We have held that constraints imposed by customer demands and government regulations do not determine the employment relationship. *See C.C. Eastern*, 60 F.3d at 859 ("[W]here a company's control over an aspect of the workers' performance is motivated by a concern for customer service, that control does not suggest an employment relationship."); *NAVL*, 869 F.2d at 599 ("[E]mployer efforts to monitor, evaluate, and improve the results of ends of the worker's performance do not make the worker an employee."); *id.* ("[R]estrictions upon a worker's manner and means of performance that spring from government regulation . . . do not necessarily support a conclusion of employment status" because the company "is not controlling the driver," the law is.). As our "emphasis [shifts] to entrepreneurialism," *Corp. Express*, 292 F.3d at 780, these precedents apply a fortiori.

Likewise, "an incentive system designed `to ensure that the drivers' overall performance meets the company standards' . . . is fully consistent with an independent contractor relationship." *C.C. Eastern*, 60 F.3d at 860 (quoting *NAVL*, 869 F.2d at 603). At the same time, a contractual willingness to share a small part of the risk—for instance, by providing fuel reimbursements when prices jump sharply, or by guaranteeing a certain minimum amount of income for making a vehicle available—does not an employee make. *See Argix Direct, Inc.*, 343 N.L.R.B. at 1019 (contractors were independent even though the "[e]mployer also pays the owner-operators a fuel surcharge when the price of fuel surpasses a preset average").

The Regional Director also emphasized that these "contractors perform a function that is a regular and essential part of FedEx Home's normal operations, the delivery of packages," and that few have seized any of the alleged entrepreneurial opportunities. *Representation Decision*, slip op. at 34, 38. While the essential nature of a worker's role is a legitimate consideration, it is not determinative in the face of more compelling countervailing factors, otherwise companies like FedEx could never hire delivery drivers who are independent contractors, a consequence contrary to precedent. And both the Board and this court have found the failure to take advantage of an opportunity is beside the point. *See C.C. Eastern*, 60 F.3d at 860 (opportunities cannot be ignored unless they are the sort workers "cannot realistically take," and even "one instance" of a driver using such an opportunity can be sufficient to "show[ ] there is no unwritten rule or invisible barrier preventing other drivers from likewise exercising their contractual right"); *Arizona Republic*, 349 N.L.R.B. at 1045. Instead, "it is the worker's retention of the right to engage in entrepreneurial activity rather than his regular exercise of that right that is most relevant for the purpose of determining whether he is an independent contractor." *C.C. Eastern*, 60 F.3d at 860.

III.

. . . .

The dissent . . . argues that emphasizing entrepreneurialism has only truly begun with this case, and suggests we are doing so here for reasons apart from allegiance to precedent. Lest any be confused, we again quote *Corporate Express*: "[W]e uphold as reasonable the Board's decision, at the urging of the General Counsel, to focus not upon the employer's control of the means and manner of the work but instead upon whether the putative independent contractors have a 'significant entrepreneurial opportunity for gain or loss.' " 292 F.3d at 780. We explicitly "agree[d] with the Board's suggestion that the latter factor better captures the distinction between an employee and an independent contractor," because, as reflected by the Restatement's comment, it is not "the degree of supervision under which [one] labors but . . . the degree to which [one] functions as an entrepreneur—that is, takes economic risk and has the corresponding opportunity to profit from working smarter, not just harder," that better illuminates one's status. We retained the common law test (as is required by the Court's decision in *United Insurance*), but merely "shift[ed our] emphasis to entrepreneurialism," using this "emphasis" to evaluate common law factors such as whether the contractor "supplies his own equipment." *Corporate Express* is thus doctrinally consistent with *United Insurance* and the Restatement.

. . . .

IV.

We have considered all the common law factors, and, on balance, are compelled to conclude they favor independent contractor status. The ability to operate multiple routes, hire additional drivers (including drivers who substitute for the contractor) and helpers, and to sell routes without permission, as well as the parties' intent expressed in the contract, augurs strongly in favor of independent contractor status. Because the indicia favoring a finding the contractors are employees are clearly outweighed by evidence of entrepreneurial opportunity, the Board cannot be said to have made a choice between two fairly conflicting views. Though evidence can be marshaled and debater's points scored on both sides, the evidence supporting independent contractor status is more compelling under our precedent. The evidence might have been stronger still had not the Regional Director erroneously excluded the national data. But even as the record stands, the Board's determination was legally erroneous.

Accordingly, we grant the petition, vacate the Board's order, and deny the cross-application for enforcement.

So ordered.

The NLRB Administrative Response

Prior to the DC Circuit Court of Appeals ruling in *FedEx Home Delivery*, the National Labor Relations Board had also determined that drivers in Hartford, Connecticut who operated under virtually the same conditions as the drivers in that case were employees within the meaning of The National Labor Relations Act. After the Court of Appeals ruling, the Board vacated its decision in the Hartford case and undertook a new review. The Board granted summary judgment to the union, ruling that the drivers were employees under Section 2(3) of the NLRA and that FedEx violated Sections 8(a)(5) and (1) of the NLRA by refusing to recognize and bargain with the union as those drivers' representative.

The majority of the Board noted that the Supreme Court has relied on an independent contractor test from the Restatement (Second) of Agency § 220, but rejected the conclusion that any particular factor is decisive. In

Roadway Package System, 326 N.L.R.B. 842 (1998), the Board explained how it evaluates a worker's status under the common law test: all factors must be assessed and weighed; no one factor is decisive; other relevant factors may be considered; and the weight to be given to a particular factor depends on the facts of each case. Within this structure, the Board has considered whether the worker has had significant entrepreneurial opportunity for gain or loss by considering several factors, such as whether the worker: has the ability to work for other companies; can hire his own employees; and has a proprietary interest in his work.

The Board insisted that the DC Circuit improperly concluded that entrepreneurial opportunity is a key factor in its independent contractor assessment. In the FedEx case the shift in focus results in a broader exclusion of workers from NLRA coverage than Congress intended. The Board then sought to clarify the independent contractor status test by subsuming the entrepreneurial opportunity factors collectively into the multi-factor test, and by giving weight to entrepreneurial opportunities that purported contractors actually seized, rather than opportunities that were merely theoretical. Additionally, the Board evaluated the constraints imposed by the company on the worker's ability to pursue an entrepreneurial opportunity.

Under this revised approach, the Board weighed each of the Restatement factors and determined that the Hartford FedEx drivers were employees. The dissent argued that the Board's decision in effect resurrected the "economic realities" or "economic dependence" standard that had been applied until Congress amended the NLRA in 1947 to exclude independent contractors as determined under the common-law test.

Critics immediately seized on the uncertainty that would result from the Board's new approach of distinguishing "actual" from "theoretical" entrepreneurial opportunities. If a contracting structure affords entrepreneurial opportunities to workers, but the Board ignores those opportunities unless they are actualized, then the new standard may create a paradox where different workers performing the exact same functions could be found to be independent contractors or employees based on evidence of their personal initiative, willingness to take economic risks and attempts to build personal enterprises. The dissent also noted that the majority failed to provide a benchmark for what qualifies as an actual entrepreneurial opportunity.

On March 3, 2017, the DC Circuit reviewed the Board's decision. The Court concluded that the case involved the same parties and presented nearly the same factual question as *FedEx Home Delivery v. NLRB,* 563 F.3d 492 (D.C. Cir. 2009). Consequently, the Court vacated the Board's election and unfair labor practice orders, holding that its 2009 decision had established the law of the case. *FedEx Home Delivery v. NLRB*, 849 F.3d 1123 (D.C. Cir. 2017). Because the court ruled that the case had already been decided, it did not address the nuances of the Board's newly announced approach to the independent contractor status which shifted the focus from "theoretical" opportunities to "actual" opportunities.

QUESTIONS

1. In *FedEx Home Delivery,* the Court of Appeals for the D.C. Circuit held that the NLRB had no jurisdiction over drivers because they had entrepreneurial opportunities available to them despite the high level of control exercised by FedEx. Does this approach effectively ignore Supreme Court precedent that the common law control test should be used to determine the scope of the NLRA?
2. How could the court better articulate the "entrepreneurial opportunity for gain or loss" test in order to avoid the criticisms leveled by the NLRB?

---

4. The Restatement Approach to "Restating" This Complex Doctrine

The Restatement of Employment Law recognizes the evolving debate over the centrality of the factors in the control test. The right to control continues to play the principal role in defining the employment relationship, but the Restatement also acknowledges that the opportunity for entrepreneurial gain or loss is also a factor to be considered.

Restatement of Employment Law

§ 1.01. Conditions for Existence of Employment Relationship

(a) Except as provided in §§ 1.02 and 1.03, an individual renders services as an employee of an employer if:

(1) the individual acts, at least in part, to serve the interests of the employer;

(2) the employer consents to receive the individual's services; and

(3) the employer controls the manner and means by which the individual renders services, or the employer otherwise effectively prevents the individual from rendering those services as an independent businessperson.

(b) An individual renders services as an independent businessperson and not as an employee when the individual in his or her own interest exercises entrepreneurial control over important business decisions, including whether to hire and where to assign assistants, whether to purchase and where to deploy equipment, and whether and when to provide service to other customers.

QUESTION

1. Does the Restatement frame the "entrepreneur" test differently than the FedEx case and the NLRB?

Conclusion

The foundation of Employment Law is the "employment" relationship. However, determining who is an "employee" is difficult because courts focus on a number of factors with an emphasis on the "control" over the worker. The basis for recognizing employee status in the caselaw is often imprecise, and sometimes absolutely contradictory. In the next Lesson, we will consider efforts to move beyond the current approach to defining "employees."

Lesson 4:
Who Is an Employee? Current Developments

Objectives and Expected Learning Outcomes

In this Lesson, we will explore efforts by courts to move beyond the multi-factor definitions of employment and to address the special concerns in the gig economy.

1. An Emerging Alternative to the "Multi-Factor" Tests: The "ABC Test"

In response to the complexity of applying the multi-factor common law agency test, several jurisdictions have embraced a simpler approach when interpreting state laws. Under this approach, the court presumes that a worker is an employee for purposes of state law, unless the putative employer can meet the burden of proving (a) that the worker is free from control and direction of the worker's performance, both under the work agreement and in fact; (b) that the work is outside the scope of the usual course of business of the putative employer; AND (c) that the worker customarily engages in an independent trade, occupation, or business. If the putative employer cannot prove all three elements, the worker is an employee.

The ABC test was recently employed by the California Supreme Court for purposes of wage claims under California State Law that uses the broad "suffers or permits to work" language of the FLSA. Read the following case carefully, determine how the various tests would be applied, and describe the effect that California adopting the ABC standard has on the result.

Dynamex Operations West, Inc. v. Superior Court

4 Cal. 5th 903 (2018).

Under both California and federal law, the question whether an individual worker should properly be classified as an employee or, instead, as an independent contractor has considerable significance for workers, businesses, and the public generally. On the one hand, if a worker should properly be classified as an employee, the hiring business bears the responsibility of paying federal Social Security and payroll taxes, unemployment insurance taxes and state employment taxes, providing workers' compensation insurance, and, most relevant for the present case, complying with numerous state and federal statutes and regulations governing the wages, hours, and working conditions of employees. The worker then obtains the protection of the applicable labor laws and regulations. On the other hand, if a worker should properly be classified as an independent contractor, the business does not bear any of those costs or responsibilities, the worker obtains none of the numerous labor law benefits, and the public may be required under applicable laws to assume additional financial burdens with respect to such workers and their families.

Although in some circumstances classification as an independent contractor may be advantageous to workers as well as to businesses, the risk that workers who should be treated as employees may be improperly misclassified as independent contractors is significant in light of the potentially substantial economic incentives that a business may have in mischaracterizing some workers as independent contractors. Such incentives include the unfair competitive advantage the business may obtain over competitors that properly classify similar workers as employees and that thereby assume the fiscal and other responsibilities and burdens that an employer owes to its employees. In recent years, the relevant regulatory agencies of both the federal and state governments have declared that the misclassification of workers as independent contractors rather than employees is a very serious problem, depriving federal and state governments of billions of dollars in tax revenue and millions of workers of the labor law protections to which they are entitled.

Issue

The issue in this case relates to the resolution of the employee or independent contractor question in one specific context. Here we must decide what standard applies, under California law, in determining whether workers should be classified as employees or as independent contractors *for purposes of California wage orders*, which impose obligations relating to the minimum wages, maximum hours, and a limited number of very basic working conditions (such as minimally required meal and rest breaks) of California employees.

. . . .

I. Facts and Proceedings Below

We summarize the facts as set forth in the prior Court of Appeal opinions in this matter, supplemented by additional facts set forth in the record.

Dynamex is a nationwide same-day courier and delivery service that operates a number of business centers in California. Dynamex offers on-demand, same-day pickup and delivery services to the public generally and also has a number of large business customers—including Office Depot and Home Depot—for whom it delivers purchased goods and picks up returns on a regular basis. Prior to 2004, Dynamex classified its California drivers as employees and compensated them pursuant to this state's wage and hour laws. In 2004, Dynamex converted all of its drivers to independent contractors after management concluded that such a conversion would generate economic savings for the company. Under the current policy, all drivers are treated as independent contractors and are required to provide their own vehicles and pay for all of their transportation expenses, including fuel, tolls, vehicle maintenance, and vehicle liability insurance, as well as all taxes and workers' compensation insurance.

Dynamex obtains its own customers and sets the rates to be charged to those customers for its delivery services. It also negotiates the amount to be paid to drivers on an individual basis. For drivers who are assigned to a dedicated fleet or scheduled route by Dynamex, drivers are paid either a flat fee or an amount based on a percentage of the delivery fee Dynamex receives from the customer. For those who deliver on-demand, drivers are generally paid either a percentage of the delivery fee paid by the customer on a per delivery basis or a flat fee basis per item delivered.

Drivers are generally free to set their own schedule but must notify Dynamex of the days they intend to work for Dynamex. Drivers performing on-demand work are required to obtain and pay for a Nextel cellular telephone through which the drivers maintain contact with Dynamex. On-demand drivers are assigned deliveries by Dynamex dispatchers at Dynamex's sole discretion; drivers have no guarantee of the number or type of deliveries they will be offered. Although drivers are not required to make all of the deliveries they are assigned, they must promptly notify Dynamex if they intend to reject an offered delivery so that Dynamex can quickly contact another driver; drivers are liable for any loss Dynamex incurs if they fail to do so. Drivers make pickups and deliveries using their own vehicles, but are generally expected to wear Dynamex shirts and badges when making deliveries for Dynamex, and, pursuant to Dynamex's agreement with some customers, drivers are sometimes required to attach Dynamex and/or the customer's decals to their vehicles when making deliveries for the customer. Drivers purchase Dynamex shirts and other Dynamex items with their own funds.

In the absence of any special arrangement between Dynamex and a customer, drivers are generally free to choose the sequence in which they will make deliveries and the routes they will take, but are required to complete all assigned deliveries on the day of assignment. If a customer requests, however, drivers must comply with a customer's requirements regarding delivery times and sequence of stops.

Drivers hired by Dynamex are permitted to hire other persons to make deliveries assigned by Dynamex. Further, when they are not making pickups or deliveries for Dynamex, drivers are permitted to make deliveries for another delivery company, including the driver's own personal delivery business. Drivers are prohibited, however, from diverting any delivery order received through or on behalf of Dynamex to a competitive delivery service.

Drivers are ordinarily hired for an indefinite period of time but Dynamex retains the authority to terminate its agreement with any driver without cause, on three days' notice. And, as noted, Dynamex reserves the right, throughout the contract period, to control the number and nature of deliveries that it offers to its on-demand drivers.

. . . .

II. Relevant Wage Order Provisions

We begin with a brief review of the relevant provisions of the wage order that applies to the transportation industry. (See Cal. Code Regs., tit. 8, § 11090.)

In describing its scope, the transportation wage order initially provides in subdivision 1: "This order shall apply to all persons employed in the transportation industry, whether paid on a time, piece rate, commission, or other basis," except for persons employed in administrative, executive, or professional capacities, who are exempt from most of the wage order's provisions. (Cal. Code Regs., tit. 8, § 11090, subd. 1.)

Subdivision 2 of the order, which sets forth the definitions of terms as used in the order, contains the following relevant definitions:

> "(D) 'Employ' means to engage, suffer, or permit to work."
>
> "(E) 'Employee' means any person employed by an employer."
>
> "(F) 'Employer' means any person as defined in Section 18 of the Labor Code, who directly or indirectly, or through an agent or

> any other person, employs or exercises control over the wages, hours, or working conditions of any person." (Cal. Code Regs., tit. 8, § 11090, subd. 2(D)–(F).)

Thereafter, the additional substantive provisions of the wage order that establish protections for workers or impose obligations on hiring entities relating to minimum wages, maximum hours, and specified basic working conditions (such as meal and rest breaks) are, by their terms, made applicable to "employees" or "employers." (See, e.g., Cal. Code Regs., tit. 8, § 11090, subds. 3 [Hours and Days of Work], 4 [Minimum Wages], 7 [Records], 11 [Meal Periods], 12 [Rest Periods].)

. . . .

III. Background of Relevant California Judicial Decisions

We next summarize the most relevant California judicial decisions, providing a historical review of the treatment of the employee or independent contractor distinction under California law.

The difficulty that courts in all jurisdictions have experienced in devising an acceptable general test or standard that properly distinguishes employees from independent contractors is well documented. As the United States Supreme Court observed in *Board v. Hearst Publications* (1944) 322 U.S. 111, 121: "Few problems in the law have given greater variety of application and conflict in results than the cases arising in the borderland between what is clearly an employer-employee relationship and what is clearly one of independent, entrepreneurial dealing. This is true within the limited field of determining vicarious liability in tort. It becomes more so when the field is expanded to include all of the possible applications of the distinction." (Fn. omitted.)

As the above quotation suggests, at common law the problem of determining whether a worker should be classified as an employee or an independent contractor initially arose in the tort context—in deciding whether the hirer of the worker should be held vicariously liable for an injury that resulted from the worker's actions. In the vicarious liability context, the hirer's right to supervise and control the details of the worker's actions was reasonably viewed as crucial, because " '[t]he extent to which the employer had a right to control [the details of the service] activities was . . . highly relevant to the question whether the employer ought to be legally liable for them . . . .' "

(*Borello, supra*, 48 Cal.3d 341, 350.) For this reason, the question whether the hirer controlled the details of the worker's activities became the primary common law standard for determining whether a worker was considered to be an employee or an independent contractor.

> *[Editor's Note: The Court engaged in an extensive review of the precedents for defining "employee." The foundational case for analysis—*S.G. Borello & Sons, Inc. v. Dept. of Industrial Relations, 48 Cal. 3d 341 (1989)*—held that farmworkers were employees for purposes of the workers' compensation statutes. The Court used the "control" test, but gave deference to the remedial nature of the statutes in question. Thus,* Borello *attended to the intended scope and purpose of protecting workers. The Court then discussed* Martinez v. Combs, 49 Cal. 4th 35 (2010), *which analyzed the meaning of employment under California wage orders.]*

. . . .

The adoption of the exceptionally broad suffer or permit to work standard in California wage orders finds its justification in the fundamental purposes and necessity of the minimum wage and maximum hour legislation in which the standard has traditionally been embodied. Wage and hour statutes and wage orders were adopted in recognition of the fact that individual workers generally possess less bargaining power than a hiring business and that workers' fundamental need to earn income for their families' survival may lead them to accept work for substandard wages or working conditions. The basic objective of wage and hour legislation and wage orders is to ensure that such workers are provided at least the minimal wages and working conditions that are necessary to enable them to obtain a subsistence standard of living and to protect the workers' health and welfare. . . .

Given the intended expansive reach of the suffer or permit to work standard as reflected by its history, along with the more general principle that wage orders are the type of remedial legislation that must be liberally construed in a manner that serves its remedial purposes (see, e.g., *Industrial Welf. Com.*, *supra*, 27 Cal.3d at p. 702), as our decision in *Martinez* recognized, the suffer or permit to work standard must be interpreted and applied broadly to include within the covered "employee" category *all* individual workers who can reasonably be viewed as *"working in the [hiring entity's] business."* (*Martinez, supra*, 49 Cal.4th at p. 69, italics added ["A proprietor who knows that persons are *working in his or her business* without having been formally hired, or while being paid less than the minimum wage, clearly suffers or permits that work by failing to prevent it, while having the power to do so" (italics added)].) Under the suffer or permit to work standard, an individual worker who has been hired by a company can properly be viewed as the type of independent contractor to which the wage order was not intended to apply only if the worker is the type of traditional independent contractor—such as an independent plumber or electrician—who would *not* reasonably have been viewed as working *in the hiring business.* Such an individual would have been realistically understood, instead, as *working only in his or her own independent business.* (See, e.g., *Allen v. Hayward* (Q.B. 1845) 115 Eng.Rep. 749, 755 [describing independent contractor as "a person carrying on an independent business . . . to perform works which [the hiring local officials] could not execute for themselves, and who was known to all the world as performing them"]; *Enforcing Fair Labor Standards, supra,* 46 UCLA L.Rev. at pp. 1143–1144.)

The federal courts, in applying the suffer or permit to work standard set forth in the FLSA, have recognized that the standard was intended to be broader and more inclusive than the preexisting common law test for distinguishing employees from independent contractors, but at the same time, does not purport to render every individual worker an employee rather than an independent contractor. (See *Rutherford Food, supra,* 331 U.S. 722, 728–729.) As noted above (*ante,* pp. 56–58, fn. 20), the federal courts have developed what is generally described as the "economic reality" test for determining whether a worker should be considered an employee or independent contractor for purposes of the FLSA—namely, whether, as a matter of economic reality, the worker is economically dependent upon and makes a living in another's business (in which case he or she is considered to be a covered employee) or, instead is in business for himself or herself (and may properly be considered an excluded independent contractor). (See, e.g., *Whitaker House Co-op, supra,* 366 U.S. 28, 33; *Alamo Foundation, supra,* 471 U.S. 290, 301.) In applying the economic reality test, federal courts have looked to a list of factors that is briefer than, but somewhat comparable to, the list of factors considered in the pre-*Borello* California decisions and in *Borello* itself. (See, e.g., *Superior Care, supra,* 840 F.2d at p. 1059; *Lauritzen, supra,* 835 F.2d at pp. 1534–1535.) Furthermore, like *Borello,* federal FLSA decisions applying the economic reality standard have held that no one factor is determinative and that the ultimate decision whether a worker is to be found to be an employee or independent contractor for purposes of the FLSA should be based on all the circumstances. (*Rutherford Food, supra*, 331 U.S. at p. 730; *Scantland*, *supra*, 721 F.3d at pp. 1312–1313; *Real v. Driscoll Strawberry Associates, Inc.* (1979) 603 F.3d 748, 754–755; see generally Annot., *supra*, 51 A.L.R.Fed. 702.)

A multifactor standard—like the economic reality standard or the *Borello* standard—that calls for consideration of all potentially relevant factual distinctions in different employment arrangements on a case-by-case, totality-of-the-circumstances basis has its advantages. A number of state courts, administrative agencies and academic commentators have observed, however, that such a wide-ranging and flexible test for evaluating whether a worker should be considered an employee or an independent contractor has significant disadvantages, particularly when applied in the wage and hour context.

. . . .

As already noted . . . a number of jurisdictions have adopted a simpler, more structured test for distinguishing between employees and independent contractors—the so-called "ABC" test—that minimizes these disadvantages. The ABC test presumptively considers all workers to be employees, and permits workers to be classified as independent contractors only if the hiring business demonstrates that the worker in question satisfies *each* of three conditions: (a) that the worker is free from the control and direction of the hirer in connection with the performance of the work, both under the contract for the performance of the work and in fact; *and* (b) that the worker performs work that is outside the usual course of the hiring entity's business; *and* (c) that the worker is customarily engaged in an independently established trade, occupation, or business of the same nature as that involved in the work performed.[23]

---

23 The wording of the ABC test varies in some respects from jurisdiction to jurisdiction. (See *ABC on the Books, supra*, 18 U.Pa. J.L. & Soc. Change, at pp. 67–71.) The version we have set forth in text (and which we adopt hereafter (*post*, pp. 66–77)) tracks the Massachusetts version of the ABC test. (See Mass.G.L., ch. 149, § 148B; see also Del. Code Ann., tit. 19, §§ 3501(a)(7), 3503(c).) Unlike some other versions, which provide that a hiring entity may satisfy part B by establishing *either* (1) that the work provided is outside the usual course of the business for which the work is performed, *or* (2) that the work performed is outside all the places of business of the hiring entity (see, e.g., N.J. Stat. Ann. § 43:21–19(i)(6)(A–C)), the Massachusetts version permits the hiring entity to satisfy part B only if it establishes that the work is outside the usual course of the business of the hiring entity. In light of contemporary work practices, in which many employees telecommute or work from their homes, we conclude the Massachusetts version of part B provides the alternative that is more consistent with the intended broad reach of the suffer or permit to work definition in California wage orders.

Many jurisdictions that have adopted the ABC test use the standard only in the unemployment insurance context, but other jurisdictions use the ABC test more generally in determining the employee or independent contractor question with respect to a variety of employee-protective labor statutes. (See, e.g., Mass.G.L. ch. 149, § 148B; Del.

Unlike a number of our sister states that included the suffer-or-permit-to-work standard in their wage and hour laws or regulations *after* the FLSA had been enacted and had been interpreted to incorporate the economic reality test, California's adoption of the suffer or permit to work standard predated the enactment of the FLSA. (See *Martinez, supra*, 40 Cal.4th at pp. 57–59.) Thus, as a matter of legislative intent, the IWC's adoption of the suffer or permit to work standard in California wage orders was not intended to embrace the federal economic reality test. Furthermore, prior California cases have declined to interpret California wage orders as governed by the federal economic reality standard and instead have indicated that the California wage orders are intended to provide broader protection than that accorded workers under the federal standard.

We find merit in the concerns noted above regarding the disadvantages, particularly in the wage and hour context, inherent in relying upon a multifactor, all the circumstances standard for distinguishing between employees and independent contractors. As a consequence, we conclude it is appropriate, and most consistent with the history and purpose of the suffer or permit to work standard in California's wage orders, to interpret that standard as: (1) placing the burden on the hiring entity to establish that the worker is an independent contractor who was not intended to be included within the wage order's coverage; and (2) requiring the hiring entity, in order to meet this burden, to establish *each* of the three factors embodied in the ABC test—namely (A) that the worker is free from the control and direction of the hiring entity in connection with the performance of the work, both under the contract for the performance of the work and in fact; *and* (B) that the worker performs work that is outside the usual course of the hiring entity's business; *and* (C) that the worker is customarily engaged in an independently established trade, occupation, or business of the same nature as the work performed. (Accord *Hargrove, supra*, 106 A.3d at pp. 463–464; see also Weil, The Fissured Workplace (2014) pp. 204–205 [recommending adoption of the ABC test]; *ABC on the Books, supra*, 18 U.Pa. J.L. & Soc. Change at pp. 61, 82–84, 101–102.)

> *[Editor's Note: The Court then applied the three factors to the case. The Court found that the workers were subject to control. It also found that the workers provided the key service offered by the employer, unlike a retail store that might hire a plumber to come in and fix a*

Code Ann., tit. 19, §§ 3501(a)(7), 3503(c); *Hargrove, supra*, 106 A.3d at pp. 462–465; see generally *ABC on the Books, supra*, 18 U.Pa. J.L. & Soc. Change, at pp. 65–72 [discussing numerous state statutes and judicial decisions].)

leaking sink. Finally, the Court found that the employees were not engaged in an independent business.]

. . . .

In sum, we conclude that unless the hiring entity establishes (A) that the worker is free from the control and direction of the hiring entity in connection with the performance of the work, both under the contract for the performance of the work and in fact, (B) that the worker performs work that is outside the usual course of the hiring entity's business, and (C) that the worker is customarily engaged in an independently established trade, occupation, or business, the worker should be considered an employee and the hiring business an employer under the suffer or permit to work standard in wage orders. The hiring entity's failure to prove any one of these three prerequisites will be sufficient in itself to establish that the worker is an included employee, rather than an excluded independent contractor, for purposes of the wage order.

In our view, this interpretation of the suffer or permit to work standard is faithful to its history and to the fundamental purpose of the wage orders and will provide greater clarity and consistency, and less opportunity for manipulation, than a test or standard that invariably requires the consideration and weighing of a significant number of disparate factors on a case-by-case basis.

. . . .

We now turn to application of the suffer or permit to work standard in this case. As Dynamex points out, the trial court, in applying the suffer or permit to work definition in its class certification order, appears to have adopted a literal interpretation of the suffer or permit to work language that, if applied generally, could potentially encompass the type of traditional independent contractor—like an independent plumber or electrician—who could not reasonably have been viewed as the hiring business's employee. We agree with Dynamex that the trial court's view of the suffer or permit to work standard was too broad. For the reasons discussed below, however, we nonetheless conclude, for two independently sufficient reasons, that under a proper interpretation of the suffer or permit to work standard, the trial court's ultimate determination that there is a sufficient commonality of interest to support certification of the proposed class is correct and should be upheld.

First, with respect to part B of the ABC test, it is quite clear that there is a sufficient commonality of interest with regard to the question whether the work provided by the delivery drivers within the certified class is outside the usual course of the hiring entity's business to permit plaintiffs' claim of misclassification to be resolved on a class basis. In the present case, Dynamex's entire business is that of a delivery service. Unlike other types of businesses in which the delivery of a product may or may not be viewed as within the usual course of the hiring company's business, here the hiring entity is a delivery company and the question whether the work performed by the delivery drivers within the certified class is outside the usual course of its business is clearly amenable to determination on a class basis. As a general matter, Dynamex obtains the customers for its deliveries, sets the rate that the customers will be charged, notifies the drivers where to pick up and deliver the packages, tracks the packages, and requires the drivers to utilize its tracking and recordkeeping system. As such, there is a sufficient commonality of interest regarding whether the work performed by the certified class of drivers who pick up and deliver packages and documents from and to Dynamex customers on an ongoing basis is outside the usual course of Dynamex's business to permit that question to be resolved on a class basis.

Because each part of the ABC test may be independently determinative of the employee or independent contractor question, our conclusion that there is a sufficient commonality of interest under part B of the ABC test is sufficient in itself to support the trial court's class certification order. Nonetheless, for guidance we go on to discuss whether there is a sufficient commonality of interest under part C of the ABC test to support class treatment of the relevant question under that part of the ABC test as well.

Second, with regard to part C of the ABC test, it is equally clear from the record that there is a sufficient commonality of interest as to whether the drivers in the certified class are customarily engaged in an independently established trade, occupation, or business to permit resolution of that issue on a class basis. As discussed above, prior to 2004 Dynamex classified the drivers who picked up and delivered the packages and documents from Dynamex customers as employees rather than independent contractors. In 2004, Dynamex adopted a new business structure under which it required all of its drivers to enter into a contractual agreement that specified the driver's status as an independent contractor. Here the class of drivers certified by the trial court is limited to drivers who, during the relevant time periods, performed delivery services only for Dynamex. The class excludes drivers who performed delivery services for another delivery service or for the driver's own personal customers; the class also excludes drivers who had employees of their own. With respect to the class of included drivers, there is no indication in the record that there is a lack of commonality of interest regarding the question whether these drivers are customarily engaged in an independently established trade, occupation, or business. For this class of drivers, the pertinent question under part C of the ABC test is amenable to resolution on a class basis.

For the foregoing reasons, we conclude that under a proper understanding of the suffer or permit to work standard there is, as a matter of law, a sufficient commonality of interest within the certified class to permit the question whether such drivers are employees or independent contractors for purposes of the wage order to be litigated on a class basis. Accordingly, we conclude that with respect to the causes of action that are based on alleged violations of the obligations imposed by the wage order, the trial court did not abuse its discretion in certifying the class and in denying Dynamex's motion to decertify the class.

QUESTIONS

1. Assess the court's defense of the ABC test when compared with the *Borello* multi-factor test that previously was applied to wage claims in California.
2. Will the adoption of the ABC test undermine decisions such as *Lawson v. Grubhub* in the previous Lesson?

---

2. Employees and Independent Contractors in the Gig Economy

The gig economy has spawned policy debates and criticisms of the limited utility of carving the work world into only two realms: employees and independent contractors. Assess the following proposal by former U.S. Secretary of Labor, Seth Harris, and Princeton economics professor, Alan Krueger. We have not yet studied the various employment law regimes they discuss, but you should be able to follow the logic of their argument based on your general knowledge.

Seth D. Harris and Alan B. Krueger, *A Proposal for Modernizing Labor Laws for Twenty-First Century Work: The "Independent Worker"*[1]

New and emerging work relationships arising in the "online gig economy" do not fit the existing legal definitions of "employee" and "independent contractor" status. These definitions determine which workers are required to receive certain protections and benefits from their employers. Under the current legal framework, the workers and intermediaries with whom they work in these emerging relationships face unnecessary and excessive uncertainty regarding a range of legal protections and benefits that employees receive. Legal uncertainty creates inefficiencies for all parties concerned. In addition, work-related benefits that could prove valuable to both workers and businesses—such as intermediaries using their size and pooling advantages to purchase low-cost life insurance for the independent workers they engage—are sometimes eschewed to reduce the risk that the law will impose an employment relationship and the corresponding legal obligations because of the provision of these benefits. As a result, the emergence of new forms of work that could benefit workers, businesses, and consumers could be slowed, or even stopped, by a legal regime for classifying workers that does not accommodate these innovative arrangements. A further concern with the current legal framework is that companies working online and offline to match workers to final customers could organize work in such a way as to classify jobs that were traditionally performed by employees into independent contractor relationships to avoid providing employees with benefits that are a crucial part of the social compact.

To address these problems, we propose a new legal category of workers, which we call "independent workers," who occupy a middle ground between traditional employees and independent contractors. An archetypal example of independent workers is for-hire drivers who work on the Lyft or Uber platforms. We refer to these companies, and others like them, as "intermediaries" because they are the intermediary between the independent worker and the ultimate customer. These independent worker arrangements bear some similarities to independent contractors and some similarities to traditional employees. On the one hand, the drivers can choose when and whether to

1 *See* The Hamilton Project Discussion Paper 2015–10 (December 2015), *available at* http://www.hamiltonproject.org/assets/files/modernizing_labor_laws_for_twenty_first_century_work_krueger_harris.pdf.

work, similar to independent contractors, but on the other hand, drivers face restrictions that are imposed by the intermediary on how much they charge customers. Other online intermediaries that utilize a similar model include TaskRabbit (for a variety of tasks) and Mechanical Turk (for tasks completed online).

Technology is creating exciting new opportunities to link workers who provide services directly to customers, with potentially large gains in the quality, speed, and efficiency of service. From an economic and societal perspective, however, it is important that, if these new intermediaries are to succeed and expand, it is a result of their superior technology, efficiency, or service, not because their technology or business model enables regulatory arbitrage. For example, if an intermediary succeeds by displacing traditional employers who offer the same service because the intermediary gains a cost advantage by avoiding provision of certain legally mandated benefits and protections, then welfare is reduced by the innovation.

Below, we propose that Congress and, where appropriate, state legislatures, enact legislation to define and establish a third legal category of workers: independent workers. This legislation would clearly define the protections and benefits that intermediaries would be required to provide to the workers with whom they conduct business. These protections and benefits would approximate the social compact guaranteed to employees, albeit with important differences that reflect the substantive distinctions between employment relationships and independent worker-intermediary relationships. In crafting this legislation, Congress should abide by a set of governing principles to identify these workers; we describe those principles below. We also provide an analysis of the size, growth, and business models used by an emerging set of online intermediaries.

. . . .

INDEPENDENT WORKERS

. . . .

We propose the following reforms.

<u>Freedom to Organize and Collectively Bargain.</u> [The authors recommend an amendment to antitrust laws that would allow an "independent workers exemption" to antitrust laws that currently prohibit nonemployees from organizing or collective bargaining].

Ability to Pool. Intermediaries could use their scale and pooling opportunities to offer independent workers a range of insurance services, tax preparation assistance, and financial services. Products and services that likely would be offered include auto insurance, disability insurance, health insurance and health care, banking and savings products, retirement products, and liability insurance. Currently, however, intermediaries are loath to take advantage of pooling efficiencies because offering benefits to workers would raise the risk that their work relationships would be adjudged employment by a court or administrative agency. To overcome this inefficient predicament, we propose that intermediaries be covered by a safe harbor provision such that pooling independent workers for purposes of providing benefits would not be legally interpreted as an indication of employee status.

Civil Rights Protections. The most obvious and straightforward solution to inadequate antidiscrimination protections for independent workers would be to include them within the protections of the federal employment discrimination laws. This approach ensures neutrality between employment relationships and independent worker relationships while providing more-expansive protection against inefficient discriminatory acts in the workplace and labor market.

Tax Withholding and Federal Insurance Contributions Act. Tax withholding by intermediaries would reduce workers' administrative burden of paying income and social insurance taxes. Given economies of scale, withholding services provided by intermediaries would also be economically efficient and improve compliance with tax laws. We propose that intermediaries would be required to provide withholding services for income and social insurance taxes owed by all independent workers with whom they work. Tax withholding by intermediaries would support the principle of neutrality between employment status and independent worker status since most employees benefit when their employers withhold state and federal income and payroll taxes.

In addition, to maintain neutrality with employees, we propose that intermediaries pay half of independent workers' contributions toward the Federal Insurance Contributions Act (FICA) payroll taxes for Social Security and Medicare. Although in the long run, intermediaries are likely to shift the ultimate burden of paying for FICA contributions to workers through fee adjustments, . . . the assignment of legal tax liability can potentially affect tax incidence in some cases. In addition, tax shifting can take place for employees as well, so requiring intermediaries to contribute half of FICA contributions will make it easier for employees and independent workers to compare their compensation, because they will be on more-equal footing.

Our principles that guide the creation of an independent worker status lead us to suggest a more nuanced approach to some other benefits, such as allowing intermediaries to opt into workers' compensation insurance. We conclude that it would not be efficient or feasible to require intermediaries to provide this class of workers with other protections and benefits, such as overtime protection or unemployment insurance.

. . . .

Conclusion

The online gig economy represents a small but rapidly growing segment of the workforce, especially in the ride-sharing and food-delivery sectors. This new and emerging sector has the potential to provide many new opportunities for workers and customers but raises serious challenges to the administration of existing employment, labor, and tax law. In particular, the workers who utilize intermediaries to identify customers to deliver services, such as car rides, do not fit neatly into existing legal categories of independent contractors and employees. We have sought to craft a new employment status that we call "independent workers," to fill this void and improve the efficiency and fairness of the labor market, and reduce legal uncertainty. Many workers in the "offline economy" who are currently classified as independent contractors, such as taxi drivers, would also fit into this new category.

Independent workers would receive some protections and benefits of employees, such as the right to organize and the requirement that intermediaries contribute half of Social Security and Medicare payroll taxes, but not others, such as time-and-a-half for overtime hours. Most importantly, we think that reforms along the lines that we propose would help to protect and extend the hard-earned social compact that has protected workers and improved living standards over the past century, reduce uncertainty, and enhance the efficient operation of the labor market.

QUESTIONS

1. Is the Harris-Krueger proposal for protections and benefits for independent workers sufficient to cover today's expanding forms of employment arrangements?
2. Can you think of other forms of labor arrangements that would not be covered by an independent worker, employee, or independent contractor category?
3. Would their approach capture workers such as Grubhub drivers that were discussed in the *Lawson* case in the previous Lesson?

Mastery Problem 4-1

UberLaw is a new online platform that advertises itself as a site where providers of affordable legal services of all kinds can connect with potential clients. For example, a person who requires a simple will can obtain standard forms from UberLaw and then connect with a lawyer who will review the documents once they are personalized. Numerous services are available, including reviewing a draft contract, obtaining an immigration visa, and incorporating a small business.

UberLaw contracts with thousands of attorneys across the country who wish to be promoted on the site. UberLaw has approximately 30 attorneys on staff in its San Francisco headquarters who operate as in-house counsel. These counsels oversee the work of the contract attorneys to ensure that UberLaw contract attorneys provide sufficiently high quality legal services for the prices being charged. In particular, in-house counsel provides technical assistance and conducts annual audits to ensure that contract attorneys are fulfilling their professional responsibilities to their UberLaw clients.

UberLaw has adopted the following "Attorney Work Policies" that apply to all attorneys in the organization, whether they are in-house counsel or contract attorneys:

1. Employment with UberLaw is at-will, unless otherwise specified in a written contract. You are free to resign at any time, for any reason, with or without notice. Likewise, UberLaw is free to end the relationship at any time, with or without cause, and with or without prior notice.

2. In the course of your work with UberLaw, you may have access to confidential information, including but not limited to, business strategies, plans for the future, financial information, client information, personnel information, and information that UberLaw considers proprietary and confidential. You must protect the confidentiality of this information by using it only for business purposes and only when authorized to do so. This duty of confidentiality applies on or off-duty and even at the end of your work for the Company. If you establish a client relationship through UberLaw, you are expected to maintain that relationship through UberLaw while you are employed with the company.

Everyone must sign an acknowledgment of receipt and acceptance of UberLaw's "Attorney Contract Policies" upon beginning work. The acknowledgment provides in part: "I understand and agree that the policies described in the handbook are intended as a guide only and do not constitute a contract for ongoing employment. The employment-at-will relationship may not be modified except by a specific written agreement between me and an authorized representative of the company."

Samantha is an employee of UberLaw who works in the San Francisco office. She monitors the work of contract attorneys across the country who are working on employment disputes and contracts. She enjoys her position, especially because she no longer has the hassle of running her own solo practice as an employment lawyer. Samantha signed the acknowledgement and has no other written agreement with UberLaw.

John is an UberLaw contract attorney who works in Los Angeles. Samantha and John went to law school together, and Samantha recruited John to quit his job and to work for UberLaw out of his home. The vast majority of his legal work comes from the UberLaw app, and John is happy with the freedom and flexibility he has under the arrangement. Most of John's work referrals involve general contracts, employment contracts, and employment disputes. John did not sign a written contract with UberLaw, but he did sign the UberLaw employee policy acknowledgment form.

In discussions with Samantha, John learned that the contract attorneys are not paid at the same rates as the in-house counsel. He wants to organize the contract attorneys to seek better pay, better benefits, and a pension by forming a union. John approaches you to seek advice. Is he an employee of UberLaw, entitled to rights under the National Labor Relations Act?

Conclusion

Employment law generally applies to relationships between employers and employees. However, traditional work relationships have eroded, and the economy increasingly is shifting to an "independent contractor" model. Critics have charged that this will undermine the law's protections for vulnerable actors, whereas proponents celebrate the entrepreneurial opportunities opened for workers in the emerging gig economy.

Lesson 5:
Who Is an Employer?

Objectives and Expected Learning Outcomes

In this Lesson, we will build on the definition of employee from the previous two Lessons to focus on defining who is an employee. In the modern economy there are a number of situations where it is problematic to determine which entity is liable as an employer. Under the control test, the key factor is determining who retains control over the employee's work. Controlling owners of a business are the prime example of employers. You will learn that a controlling owner is defined as one who has control over economic and operational decisions and holds a significant ownership interest. You will develop your problem-solving skills by focusing on a number of novel and complex fact patterns concerning what constitutes control and who qualifies as an employer.

The employer and employee have a contractual relationship that is valuable to both parties. In many cases they may want to share the benefits of the relationship. An employee is not limited to working for a single employer, and so may be considered an employee of two entities for the purpose of employment law protections. The law makes accommodation for these situations called "joint employment." The existence of joint employment neither negates an employer's obligations, nor does it inherently diminish the employee's protections, subject to any modifications by legislation.

When the employment statute in question does not resolve the issue, the Restatement of Employment Law describes the framework generally used by courts to determine whether a party is an employer. The analysis is a twofold inquiry regarding control and ownership.

Restatement of Employment Law

§ 1.03. Controlling Owners Are Not Employees

An individual is not an employee of an enterprise if the individual through an ownership interest controls all or a part of the enterprise.

§ 1.04. Employees of Two or More Employers

(a) An individual is an employee of two or more separate employers if (i) the individual renders services to each of the employers on a separate basis during a given day, week, or other time period and (ii) during such time period is subject solely to that employer's control or supervision as provided in § 1.01(a)(3).

(b) An individual is an employee of two or more joint employers if (i) the individual renders services to at least one of the employers and (ii) that employer and the other joint employers each control or supervise such rendering of services as provided in § 1.01(a)(3).

We will explore these definitions by focusing first on how one defines a "controlling owner," and then by determining when an employee is an employee of "joint employers."

1. Controlling Owner

As a general principle of blackletter law, courts define a controlling owner as anyone who: 1) is not an employee of an enterprise, 2) has an ownership interest in the enterprise, and 3) through this ownership interest controls all or part of the enterprise. Generally, a person controls all or part of the enterprise if she manages the enterprise, can hire and fire employees, can assign tasks to employees and supervises their performance, and decides how the profits and losses of the business are distributed. *Clackamas Gastroenterology Associates, P.C. v. Wells*, 538 U.S. 440, 450 (2003). It is not critical that a controlling owner have a particular title—such as partner, director, or vice president—because the inquiry is whether the person exercises the authority of a partner, officer, member of a board of directors, or major shareholder.

We turn to the Supreme Court's consideration of whether the shareholders and directors of professional corporations should always be considered controlling owners, or whether on certain facts they should be treated as employees.

Clackamas Gastroenterology Assoc., P. C. v. Wells

538 U.S. 440 (2003).

Justice Stevens delivered the opinion of the Court.

The Americans with Disabilities Act of 1990 (ADA or Act), 104 Stat. 327, as amended, 42 U.S.C. § 12101 et seq., like other federal antidiscrimination legislation, is inapplicable to very small businesses. Under the ADA an "employer" is not covered unless its work force includes "15 or more employees for each working day in each of 20 or more calendar weeks in the current or preceding calendar year." § 12111(5). The question in this case is whether four physicians actively engaged in medical practice as shareholders and directors of a professional corporation should be counted as "employees."

I

Petitioner, Clackamas Gastroenterology Associates, P. C., is a medical clinic in Oregon. It employed respondent, Deborah Anne Wells, as a bookkeeper from 1986 until 1997. After her termination, she brought this action against the clinic alleging unlawful discrimination on the basis of disability under Title I of the ADA. Petitioner denied that it was covered by the Act and moved for summary judgment, asserting that it did not have 15 or more employees for the 20 weeks required by the statute. It is undisputed that the accuracy of that assertion depends on whether the four physician-shareholders who own the professional corporation and constitute its board of directors are counted as employees.

The District Court, adopting the Magistrate Judge's findings and recommendation, granted the motion. Relying on an "economic realities" test adopted by the Seventh Circuit in *EEOC v. Dowd & Dowd, Ltd.*, 736 F.2d 1177, 1178 (1984), the District Court concluded that the four doctors were "more analogous to partners in a partnership than to shareholders in a general corporation" and therefore were "not employees for purposes of the federal antidiscrimination laws."

A divided panel of the Court of Appeals for the Ninth Circuit reversed. Noting that the Second Circuit had rejected the economic realities approach, the majority held that the use of any corporation, including a professional corporation, " 'precludes any examination designed to determine whether the entity is in fact a partnership.' " It saw "no reason to permit a professional corporation to secure the 'best of both possible worlds' by allowing it both to assert its corporate status in order to reap the tax and civil liability advantages and to argue that it is like a partnership in order to avoid liability for unlawful employment discrimination." The dissenting judge stressed the differences between an Oregon physicians' professional corporation and an ordinary business corporation, and argued that Congress' reasons for exempting small employers from the coverage of the Act should apply to petitioner.

We granted certiorari to resolve the conflict in the Circuits, which extends beyond the Seventh and the Second Circuits.

II

"We have often been asked to construe the meaning of 'employee' where the statute containing the term does not helpfully define it." *Nationwide Mut. Ins. Co. v. Darden*, 503 U.S. 318, 322 (1992). The definition of the term in the ADA simply states that an "employee" is "an individual employed by an employer." 42 U.S.C. § 12111(4). That surely qualifies as a mere "nominal definition" that is "completely circular and explains nothing." *Darden*, 503 U.S. at 323. As we explained in *Darden*, our cases construing similar language give us guidance on how best to fill the gap in the statutory text.

In *Darden* we were faced with the question whether an insurance salesman was an independent contractor or an "employee" covered by the Employee Retirement Income Security Act of 1974 (ERISA). Because ERISA's definition of "employee" was "completely circular," we adopted a common-law test for determining who qualifies as an "employee" under ERISA. [W]e explained that " 'when Congress has used the term "employee" without defining it, we have concluded that Congress intended to describe the conventional master-servant relationship as understood by common-law agency doctrine.' "

. . . .

. . . At common law the relevant factors defining the master-servant relationship focus on the master's control over the servant. The general definition of the term "servant" in the Restatement (Second) of Agency § 2(2) (1957), for example, refers to a person whose work is "controlled or is subject to the right to control by the master." In addition, the Restatement's more specific definition of the term "servant" lists factors to be considered when distinguishing between servants and independent contractors, the first of which is "the extent of control" that one may exercise over the details of the work of the other. We think that the common-law element of control is the principal guidepost that should be followed in this case.

This is the position that is advocated by the Equal Employment Opportunity Commission (EEOC), the agency that has special enforcement responsibilities under the ADA and other federal statutes containing similar threshold issues for determining coverage. . . .

Specific EEOC guidelines discuss both the broad question of who is an "employee" and the narrower question of when partners, officers, members of boards of directors, and major shareholders qualify as employees. With respect to the broad question, the guidelines list 16 factors—taken from *Darden*—that may be relevant to "whether the employer controls the means and manner of the worker's work performance." The guidelines list six factors to be considered in answering the narrower question, which they frame as "whether the individual acts independently and participates in managing the organization, or whether the individual is subject to the organization's control."

We are persuaded by the EEOC's focus on the common-law touchstone of control, and specifically by its submission that each of the following six factors is relevant to the inquiry whether a shareholder-director is an employee:

Employer test

> Whether the organization can hire or fire the individual or set the rules and regulations of the individual's work;
>
> Whether and, if so, to what extent the organization supervises the individual's work;
>
> Whether the individual reports to someone higher in the organization;
>
> Whether and, if so, to what extent the individual is able to influence the organization;
>
> Whether the parties intended that the individual be an employee, as expressed in written agreements or contract;
>
> Whether the individual shares in the profits, losses, and liabilities of the organization.

EEOC Compliance Manual § 605:0009.

As the EEOC's standard reflects, an employer is the person, or group of persons, who owns and manages the enterprise. The employer can hire and fire employees, can assign tasks to employees and supervise their performance, and can decide how the profits and losses of the business are to be distributed. The mere fact that a person has a particular title—such as partner, director, or vice president—should not necessarily be used to determine whether he or she is an employee or a proprietor. Nor should the mere existence of a document styled "employment agreement" lead inexorably to the conclusion that either party is an employee. Rather, as was true in applying common-law rules to the independent-contractor-versus-employee issue confronted in *Darden*, the answer to whether a shareholder-director is an employee depends on " 'all of the incidents of the relationship . . . with no one factor being decisive.' "

III

Some of the District Court's findings—when considered in light of the EEOC's standard—appear to weigh in favor of a conclusion that the four director-shareholder physicians in this case are not employees of the clinic. For example, they apparently control the operation of their clinic, they share the profits, and they are personally liable for malpractice claims. There may, however, be evidence in the record that would contradict those findings or support a contrary conclusion under the EEOC's standard that we endorse today. Accordingly, as we did in *Darden*, we reverse the judgment of the Court of Appeals and remand the case to that court for further proceedings consistent with this opinion.

JUSTICE GINSBURG, with whom JUSTICE BREYER joins, dissenting.

"There is nothing inherently inconsistent between the coexistence of a proprietary and an employment relationship." *Goldberg v. Whitaker House Cooperative, Inc.*, 366 U.S. 28, 32 (1961). As doctors performing the everyday work of petitioner Clackamas Gastroenterology Associates, P. C., the physician-shareholders function in several respects as common-law employees, a designation they embrace for various purposes under federal and state law. Classifying as employees all doctors daily engaged as caregivers on Clackamas' premises, moreover, serves the animating purpose of the Americans with Disabilities Act of 1990. Seeing no cause to shelter Clackamas from the governance of the ADA, I would affirm the judgment of the Court of Appeals.

The issue of an owner also being an employee has arisen in multiple contexts involving a variety of ownership structures. In addition to shareholders of a corporation, cases have considered the status of members of cooperatives, non-shareholding managers, and other individuals who have status within the entity but also are workers.

In *Goldberg v. Whitaker House Co-op., Inc.*, 366 U.S. 28, 32 (1961), the Supreme Court held that members of a co-op can be both members and employees of a co-op. Because members of the co-op are not self-employed, the sale of their products on the market is governed by the co-op, and they are not free to sell their products for whatever price they can command, the co-op functioned as an employer and members were employees.

In *Smith v. Castaways Family Diner*, 453 F.3d 971, 978, 981 (7th Cir. 2006) the court held that the *Clackamas* test is inapposite to managers who have no ownership interest. The inquiry into whether an individual is an employer must take into account not only whether they control or have the right to control an enterprise but also the source of that authority. The court *must* consider whether an individual exercises control by right, or whether they exercise this control by delegation from those who ultimately do possess the right to control the enterprise. Managers are like other employees in the fundamental sense that they lack the right to control the enterprise.

In *Mariotti v. Mariotti Bldg. Products, Inc.*, 714 F.3d 761, 767 (3d Cir. 2013) the court held that the *Clackamas* test applies to close corporations as well as to professional corporations. The Court noted that the *Clackamas* factors address the extent of an individual's control but also the source of the individual's authority to control. An individual who is entitled to participate in the management, development, and governance of the enterprise by sitting on the board of directors and/or serving as a corporate officer participates in making fundamental decisions of the business and cannot be considered an employee. *Exclusive* control over an enterprise is only one attribute of the employment relationship and its absence does not compel a conclusion that an individual who lacks it is an employee.

You now have sufficient familiarity with the basic blackletter rules to refine your knowledge by solving a variety of problems.

Problem 5-1

Al, Betty, Carl, and Diane, all licensed accountants, form a professional corporation. Accounting Firm ("AF") was formed under the governing laws of the state in which they work. AF rents a building to house the offices and conference rooms of the accountants. AF also hires an office manager, assistants, janitorial staff, a receptionist, and a clerical worker. Al, Betty, Carl, and Diane are the only members of the board of directors and the only shareholders of AF. They agree to share the profits based on the level of fees garnered from the services they render to clients. The board discusses and jointly sets some practice protocols, but each accountant is responsible for bringing in their own clients, setting their own fees, and does not have work reviewed by any of the other accountants. The office manager has no power to control or review the professional activity of the accountants, fire them, or alter their fee structure. If Diane seeks protection under federal law as an employee, will she be successful?

Problem 5-2

Assume the same facts as in Problem 5-1. Al, Betty, Carl, and Diane decide to issue shares of AF to another accountant, Eddie. Eddie receives half as many shares as each of the other four accountants and is told that, for the first two years of his association with AF, he will be assigned clients, his fees will be set by the other four accountants, and his work will be reviewed weekly by them. Determine whether Eddie is a "controlling owner," or whether he is an employee.

Problem 5-3

Finn, Gael, and Holt form a law partnership, LP. They hire three associates, three secretaries, one legal assistant, a paralegal, a receptionist and a clerical worker. Five years later their partnership has grown to include Iris, Jane, Kendrick, and Lee as partners. The seven partners employ ten associates, an office manager, seven secretaries, three legal assistants, three paralegals and a receptionist. The seven partners, each of whom control a share of the partnership, meet monthly to set managerial policies, including how the partners share the time of the associates, legal assistants, and paralegals. No partner is required to work under anyone's supervision, even though two or more partners often work together on the same case. Each partner's compensation is proportional to the percentage of the fees from the cases that partner brings to the firm and manages. Are Finn, Gael, and Holt employees of LP? Are Iris, Jane, Kendrick, and Lee employees of LP? If Iris, Jane, Kendrick, and Lee were required to work under the supervision of Finn, Gael, and Holt would they be employees?

Problem 5-4

Alexandra Roberts owns "Gilligan's Island," a small family restaurant on the California coast. Because she works full-time in the health care industry, her husband, Robert, and her mother, Felicia, manage the restaurant on a day-to-day basis. Alexandra does not require them to keep a set schedule, and she does not control their hours. Robert is the restaurant chef, and is in charge of the menu and managing the kitchen staff. Felicia manages the restaurant's finances, and she supervises the restaurant's wait staff. They both have the authority to issue checks on behalf of the restaurant. Both Robert and Felicia together develop the restaurant's employee policies and they have the power to hire, discipline, and fire employees without consulting Alexandra. Both Robert and Felicia are on the restaurant's payroll, and they also share in the restaurant's profits and losses. Alexandra relies completely on Robert and Felicia to run the restaurant, and she considers them her partners even though she is the sole owner of the restaurant.

Elizabeth Jones worked part-time as a waitress at the restaurant for a period of approximately four months. Shortly after she began work, two co-workers, a line cook and a waiter began to sexually harass her. They made lewd remarks and they propositioned her several times. She spoke to both Robert and Felicia, but the harassment continued. Elizabeth quit and soon filed a sex discrimination complaint with the Equal Employment Opportunity Commission (EEOC). Because the EEOC's jurisdiction covers only employers who employ fifteen employees or more, the number of employees at Gilligan's Island is a threshold question. If Robert and Felicia are considered employers rather than employees, the EEOC does not have jurisdiction over the restaurant. Does the *Clackamas* test apply to Robert and Felicia? Are they controlling owners or employees? If Alexandra applied for a small business loan available only to women and minorities who own a majority of the company in order to start the restaurant, would this fact make a difference in determining whether Robert and Felicia are employers?

2. Joint Employers

A worker might be an employee of two entities when performing her work. Joint employer status has important consequences. Both of the joint employers would owe duties under employment law, and they both would be vicariously liable for injuries caused by the employee in the course and scope of their employment (we will study the principle of *respondeat superior* in Lesson 14). The baseline rule as articulated in the Restatement is that an individual is considered an employee of two or more joint employers if the individual renders services to at least one of the employers, and that employer and the other joint employer each control or supervise such rendering of services. Even when there are two or more employers involved, the question remains whether each has control over the means and manner of the employee's performance. *Nationwide Mut. Ins. Co. v. Darden*, 503 U.S. 318, 323 (1992).

The issue of joint employers often arises in the context of the Fair Labor Standards Act (FLSA). In Lessons 23–25 you will learn about the FLSA, which is principally known for requiring overtime pay and a minimum wage. The FLSA defines an employer as "any person acting directly or indirectly in the interest of an employer in relation to an employee." 29 U.S.C. § 203(d). Given this exceptionally broad language, most courts of appeals have adopted the "economic realities test" to determine who should be treated as an employer under the FLSA. The "economic realities" test takes into account whether the alleged employer: (1) possessed the power to hire and fire the employees, (2) supervised and controlled employee work schedules or conditions of employment, (3) determined the rate and method of payment, and (4) maintained employment records. *Gray v. Powers*, 673 F.3d 352, 354–355 (5th Cir. 2012). Rather than a formal or definitional analysis, the economic realities test focuses on the vulnerability of the worker to the putative employer. Because the FLSA's purpose is to provide a remedy to workers for labor and employment violations, courts "define 'employer' more broadly than the term would be interpreted in traditional common law applications." *McLaughlin v. Seafood, Inc.*, 867 F.2d 875, 877 (5th Cir.1989).

A particularly difficult question arises when employees seek to hold individual owners or officers of corporate employers liable as joint employers under the FLSA for violations by the corporation. The following case addresses these factual questions in the detail required under the multi-factor test.

IRIZARRY V. CATSIMATIDIS

722 F.3d 99 (2d Cir. 2013).

WESLEY, CIRCUIT JUDGE.

After the failure of a settlement in a wage-and-hour case brought by a group of employees of Gristede's supermarkets, the plaintiff employees moved for partial summary judgment on the issue of whether John Catsimatidis, the chairman and CEO of Gristede's Foods, Inc., could be held personally liable for damages. The case turns on whether Catsimatidis is an "employer" under the Fair Labor Standards Act ("FLSA"), 29 U.S.C. § 203(d) . . . .

Catsimatidis is the chairman, president, and CEO of Gristede's Foods, Inc., which operates between 30 and 35 stores in the New York City metro area and has approximately 1700 employees. . . .

In 2004, a group of then-current and former employees of Gristede's supermarkets sued several companies involved in operating the stores. The employees also sued three individual defendants: Catsimatidis, Gristede's District Manager James Monos, and Gristede's Vice President Gallo Balseca. The district court certified a class composed of "[a]ll persons employed by defendants as Department Managers or Co-Managers who were not paid proper overtime premium compensation for all hours that they worked in excess of forty in a workweek any time between April 30, 1998 and the date of final judgment in this matter (the 'class period')." *Torres v. Gristede's Operating Corp.*, No. 04 Civ. 3316(PAC), 2006 WL 2819730, at *11 (S.D.N.Y. Sept. 29, 2006) ("*Torres I*") (quotation marks omitted). In this decision, the court noted that the parties disputed the duties of co-managers and department managers, though the scope of plaintiffs' duties is not at issue in this appeal.

After two-and-a-half years of litigation, the district court granted summary judgment for the plaintiffs on their FLSA . . . claims, which concerned reduction of hours, withholding of overtime, misclassification as exempt employees, and retaliation. *See Torres v. Gristede's Operating Corp.*, 628 F.Supp.2d 447, 461–63, 475 (S.D.N.Y.2008) ("*Torres II*"). The court held that plaintiffs were entitled to liquidated damages, the amount of which would be determined in future proceedings. *Id.* at 462 n. 14, 465. Plaintiffs reserved the right to move separately for a determination that the individual defendants were individually liable as joint employers. *Id.* at 453 n. 2.

Following the summary judgment order, the parties reached a settlement agreement, which the district court approved. The corporate defendants later defaulted on their payment obligations under the agreement. Defendants sought to modify the settlement, but the district court denied their request. Plaintiffs then moved for partial summary judgment on Catsimatidis's personal liability as an employer.

The district court granted the motion for reasons both stated on the record at the conclusion of oral argument on the motion, *see* Special App'x at 43–46, and memorialized in a written decision, *see Torres III.* The reasons included the fact that Catsimatidis "hired managerial employees," "signed all paychecks to the class members," had the "power to close or sell Gristede's stores," and "routinely review[ed] financial reports, work[ed] at his office in Gristede's corporate office and generally preside[d] over the day to day operations of the company." *Torres III,* 2011 WL 4571792, at *2. According to the district court, "[f]or the purposes of applying the total circumstances test, it does not matter that Mr. Catsimatidis has delegated powers to others [; w]hat is critical is that Mr. Catsimatidis has those powers to delegate." *Id.* The court concluded that "[t]here is no area of Gristede's which is not subject to [Catsimatidis's] control, whether [or not] he chooses to exercise it," and that, therefore, Catsimatidis "had operational control and, as such, [ ] may be held to be an employer." *Id.* at *3.

Discussion

I. Definition of "employer" under the FLSA

> *[Editor's Note: The court discussed the broad definition of "employer" under the FLSA, and the corresponding use of the "economic realities test."]*

. . . .

The Second Circuit "has treated employment for FLSA purposes as a flexible concept to be determined on a case-by-case basis by review of the totality of the circumstances"; we have "identified different sets of relevant factors based on the factual challenges posed by particular cases." *Barfield,* 537 F.3d at 141–42.

In *Carter v. Dutchess Community College,* 735 F.2d 8 (2d Cir.1984), we identified factors that are likely to be relevant to the question of whether a defendant is an "employer." In that case, prison inmates teaching classes in a program that was managed by a college claimed the college was their employer. The district court rejected this assertion because "the college had only qualified control over the inmate instructors; the Department of Correctional Services always maintained ultimate control." *Barfield,* 537 F.3d at 142 (describing *Carter*) (quotation marks omitted). This Court, however, concluded that the "ultimate control" rule "would not comport with the 'remedial' purpose of the FLSA, which Congress intended to 'have the widest possible impact in the national economy.' " *Id.* (quoting *Carter,* 735 F.2d at 12). Instead, we established four factors to determine the "economic reality" of an employment relationship: "whether the alleged employer (1) had the power to hire and fire the employees, (2) supervised and controlled employee work schedules or conditions of employment, (3) determined the rate and method of payment, and (4) maintained employment records." *Id.* (quoting *Carter,* 735 F.2d at 12).

Barfield also discusses the factors this court has used "to distinguish between independent contractors and employees," 537 F.3d at 143 (citing *Brock v. Superior Care, Inc.,* 840 F.2d 1054, 1058–59 (2d Cir.1988)), and "to assess whether an entity that lacked formal control nevertheless exercised functional control over a worker," *id.* (citing *Zheng v. Liberty Apparel Co.,* 355 F.3d 61, 72 (2d Cir.2003)). None of the factors used in any of these cases, however, comprise a "rigid rule for the identification of an FLSA employer." *Id.* "To the contrary, . . . they provide 'a nonexclusive and overlapping set of factors' to ensure that the economic realities test mandated by the Supreme Court is sufficiently comprehensive and flexible to give proper effect to the broad language of the FLSA." *Id.* (quoting *Zheng,* 355 F.3d at 75–76).

a. Individual liability

None of the cases above dealt specifically with the question we confront here: whether an individual within a company that undisputedly employs a worker is personally liable for damages as that worker's "employer." The only case from our Circuit to confront the question squarely is *RSR,* 172 F.3d 132. RSR provided guards, pre-employment screening, and other security services. It was sued for FLSA violations with regard to its security guards. Its chairman of the board, Portnoy, was found by the district court after a bench trial to be an "employer" under the statute. We affirmed, in a decision that both applied the four-factor test from *Carter* and noted other factors bearing upon the "overarching concern [of] whether the alleged employer possessed the power to control the workers in question." *Id.* at 139.

As background, we noted that "[a]lthough Portnoy exercised broad authority over RSR operations . . ., he was not directly involved in the daily supervision of the security guards." *Id.* at 136. Nonetheless, because "he was the only principal who had bank credit, he exercised financial control over the company." *Id.* "Thus, he had authority over" the operations manager, who directly supervised the guards. *Id.* "Portnoy kept himself apprised of RSR operations by receiving periodic reports [including] work orders, memos, investigation reports, and invoices concerning the business operations, as well as weekly timesheets of [a manager's] duties." *Id.* at 137. He also "referred a few individuals to RSR as potential security guard employees," "assigned guards to cover specific clients, sometimes set the rates clients were charged for those services, gave [a manager] instructions about guard operations, and forwarded complaints about guards to" a manager. *Id.*

Portnoy also "signed payroll checks on at least three occasions" and "established a payment system by which clients who wanted undercover operatives would pay" Portnoy's separate labor-relations firm. *Id.* Additionally, Portnoy "represented himself to outside parties as" being "the 'boss' of RSR" by "allowing his name to be used in sales literature, by representing to potential clients that he was a principal with control over company operations . . . and by giving [a manager] instructions with respect to [ ] clients' security needs." *Id.*

We determined that at least three of the four *Carter* factors applied. First, Portnoy had hired employees, and although this "involved mainly managerial staff, the fact that he hired individuals who were in charge of the guards [was] a strong indication of control." *Id.* at 140. Second, Portnoy had, "on occasion, supervised and controlled employee work schedules and the conditions of employment." *Id.* Third, he had "participate[d] in the method of pay[ing]" the guards, even though he was not involved in determining their salaries, because he had previously "ordered a stop to the illegal pay practice of including security guards on 1099 forms as independent contractors," and he "had the authority to sign paychecks throughout the relevant period." *Id.* Although there was no evidence that Portnoy had been involved in maintaining employment records, we confirmed that the fact that "this fourth factor is not met is not dispositive." *Id.* The " 'economic reality' test encompasses the totality of circumstances, no one of which is exclusive." *Id.* at 139. In sum, we determined that Portnoy was "not only a 50 percent stockowner; he had direct involvement with the security guard operations from time to time and was generally involved with all of RSR's operations." *Id.* at 141.

RSR also highlighted two legal questions relevant here. The first concerns the scope of an individual's authority or "operational control" over a company—at what level of a corporate hierarchy, and in what relationship with plaintiff employees, must an individual possess power in order to be covered by the FLSA? The second inquiry, related but distinct, concerns hypothetical versus actual power: to what extent and with what frequency must an individual actually use the power he or she possesses over employees to be considered an employer?

i. Operational control

In addition to applying the *Carter* test, *RSR* noted the district court's recognition that Portnoy exercised direct authority over the two persons most responsible for managing the security guards, as well as the fact that "[b]ecause [Portnoy] controlled the company financially, it was no idle threat when he testified that he *could have* dissolved the company if [one of the managers] had not followed his directions." *Id.* at 140 (emphasis added). Accordingly, we emphasized that we rejected Portnoy's argument "that evidence showing his authority over management, supervision, and oversight of RSR's affairs in general is irrelevant, and that only evidence indicating his direct control over the guards should be considered." *Id.* We concluded that this formulation "ignores the relevance of the totality of the circumstances in determining Portnoy's operational control of RSR's employment of the guards." *Id.* We also noted that "operational control" had been cited as relevant by other circuits considering the question of individual liability under the FLSA. *See id.*

"Operational control" is at the heart of this case. Catsimatidis's core argument is that he was a high-level employee who made symbolic or, at most, general corporate decisions that only affected the lives of the plaintiffs through an attenuated chain of but-for causation. Although Catsimatidis undisputedly possessed broad control over Gristede's corporate strategy, including the power to decide to take the company public, to open stores, and to carry certain types of merchandise, he contends that a FLSA "employer" must exercise decision-making in a "day-to-day" capacity. Appellant's Br. at 3. By this, he appears to mean decisions about individual store-level operations, close to, if not actually including, the particular working conditions and compensation practices of the employees themselves. Plaintiffs counter that many cases have found individuals with "operational control" on a more general level to be employers. Appellees' Br. at 28–31.

Most circuits to confront this issue have acknowledged—and plaintiffs do not dispute—that a company owner, president, or stockholder must have at least some degree of involvement in the way the company interacts with employees to be a FLSA "employer." . . .

. . . .

These cases reaffirm the logic behind our holding in *RSR,* which focused on defendant Portnoy's "operational control *of RSR's employment of the guards,*" *see RSR,* 172 F.3d at 140 (emphasis added), rather than simply operational control of the company. Evidence that an individual is an owner or officer of a company, or otherwise makes corporate decisions that have nothing to do with an employee's function, is insufficient to demonstrate "employer" status. Instead, to be an "employer," an individual defendant must possess control over a company's actual "operations" in a manner that relates to a plaintiff's employment. It is appropriate, as we implicitly recognized in *RSR,* to require some degree of individual involvement in a company in a manner that affects employment-related factors such as workplace conditions and operations, personnel, or compensation—even if this appears to establish a higher threshold for individual liability than for corporate "employer" status.

The fundamental concern in the initial cases construing the FLSA was preventing a business entity from causing workers to engage in work without the protections of the statute. . . .

Even in the individual-liability context, however, "the remedial nature of the [FLSA] . . . warrants an expansive interpretation of its provisions so that they will have 'the widest possible impact in the national economy.' " *RSR,* 172 F.3d at 139 (quoting *Carter,* 735 F.2d at 12). Nothing in *RSR,* or in the FLSA itself, requires an individual to have been personally complicit in FLSA violations; the broad remedial purposes behind the statute counsel against such a requirement. The statute provides an empty guarantee absent a financial incentive for individuals with control, even in the form of delegated authority, to comply with the law, and courts have continually emphasized the extraordinarily generous interpretation the statute is to be given. Nor is "only evidence indicating [an individual's] direct control over the [plaintiff employees] [to] be considered." *RSR,* 172 F.3d at 140. Instead, "evidence showing [an individual's] authority over management, supervision, and oversight of [a company's] affairs in general" is relevant to "the totality of the circumstances in determining [the individual's] operational control of [the company's] employment of [the plaintiff employees]." *Id.*

A person exercises operational control over employees if his or her role within the company, and the decisions it entails, directly affect the nature or conditions of the employees' employment. Although this does not mean that the individual "employer" must be responsible for managing plaintiff employees—or, indeed, that he or she must have directly come into contact with the plaintiffs, their workplaces, or their schedules—the relationship between the individual's operational function and the plaintiffs' employment must be closer in degree than simple but—for causation. Although the answer in any particular case will depend, of course, on the totality of the circumstances, the analyses in the cases discussed above, as well as the responsibilities enumerated in the *Carter* factors, provide guidance for courts determining when an individual's actions rise to this level.

ii. Potential power

In *RSR,* we noted that "operational control" need not be exercised constantly for an individual to be liable under the FLSA:

> [Employer] status does not require continuous monitoring of employees, looking over their shoulders at all times, or any sort of absolute control of one's employees. Control may be restricted, or exercised only occasionally, without removing the employment relationship from the protections of the FLSA, since such limitations on control do not diminish the significance of its existence.

172 F.3d at 139 (quotation marks and alteration omitted). The district court in this case appears to have relied on this language in stating that "[w]hat is critical is that Mr. Catsimatidis has [certain] powers to delegate" and that "[t]here is no area of Gristede's which is not subject to his control, whether [or not] he chooses to exercise it." *Torres III,* 2011 WL 4571792, at *2–3. The parties also dispute the importance of evidence indicating that Catsimatidis only rarely exercised much of the power he possessed.

Employer power that is "restricted or exercised only occasionally" does not mean "never exercised." In *Donovan v. Janitorial Services, Inc.,* 672 F.2d 528, 531 (5th Cir.1982), the Fifth Circuit noted that the company owner's "considerable investment in the company gives him ultimate, if latent, authority over its affairs," and the fact that he had "exercised that authority only occasionally, through firing one employee, reprimanding others, and engaging in some direct supervision of Johnson Disposal drivers, does not diminish the significance of its existence." . . .

II. Catsimatidis as "employer"

"Using this 'economic reality' test, we must decide whether [Catsimatidis] is an employer under the FLSA." *See RSR,* 172 F.3d at 140. Is there "evidence showing his authority over management, supervision, and oversight of [Gristede's] affairs in general," *see id.,* as well as evidence under the *Carter* framework or any other factors that reflect Catsimatidis's exercise of direct control over the plaintiff employees?

a. Catsimatidis's overall authority

. . . .

In general, employees agreed, as Executive Vice President Robert Zorn testified, that Catsimatidis "has whatever privileges an owner of a company has" to "make ultimate decisions as to how the company is run," and that there was "no reason to believe that if he chose to make a decision anybody there has the power to override him." *Id.* at 1329. They also agreed that Catsimatidis has the power to "shut down a store" or "sell a store if he felt that was the appropriate thing to do." *Id.* at 1370.

b. Involvement with stores

Although Catsimatidis did not exercise managerial control in stores on the day-to-day level of a manager, the evidence demonstrates that he exercised influence in specific stores on multiple occasions. For example, he made suggestions regarding how products are displayed in stores. In general, he testified that he focused on "driv[ing] sales, driv[ing] product, get[ting] more sales out of the stores" through techniques such as "buying a Coca-Cola at [the] right price, and [ ] put[ting] it on a front end display at the right price." *Id.* at 1819.

Catsimatidis testified specifically that "when [he] used to go around the stores, [he] used to make comments to the store managers about displays," telling them, for example, "if you put up this product, you might sell $100 a week." *Id.* at 1828. He would make visits to "five or ten" stores on Saturday mornings, staying about ten minutes in each one. *Id.* He referred to these as "just [ ] goodwill visit[s], merchandising, sales, what are we doing right, what are we doing wrong, what can we do better." *Id.* at 1831–32. His deposition also contained the following exchange:

Q: Why did you want to visit every store?

A: To check the merchandising.

Q: Can't the store managers take care of that themselves?

A: If the store managers did it perfectly, then I wouldn't have to visit the stores.

Q: But you have a level of trust in the store managers, right?

A: You hope so, yes.

Q: Why do you think it was necessary for the president of the company to go around to all these stores?

A: For the same reason Sam Walton went and visited his stores.

Q: What reason is that?

A: You just get a better feeling for merchandising. Sam Walton was a great merchandiser.

Q: On the Saturday morning visits to the stores, what did you do?

A: I walked in, introduced myself to the manager, most of them I knew, and just we would talk about merchandising. I would say is this selling, is this not selling, are you missing any products that you think you should have? And I would—I felt I would get input from store managers on merchandising problems.

Id. at 1829–30.

. . . .

Additionally, Catsimatidis testified that the company's system automatically forwards him copies of any consumer complaints, which he then forwards by email "to the responsible parties . . . with a comment of 'What the hell is happening?' " *Id.* at 1821. For example, he might forward a complaint about a store being dirty, and he sent a complaint about lids not fitting coffee cups to the deli director. *Id.* He testified, "I figured if they think I know about the problem, they'll work harder towards fixing it." *Id.* at 1822. When asked why this was, he said, "I guess they want to keep the boss happy, and I want to keep the consumers happy," and that "one of my jobs is how to get the consumers in our stores, and how to keep them in our stores." *Id.* at 1823. He has directed similar complaints to store managers. *Id.* at 1825.

. . . .

c. The *Carter* factors

The first element of the *Carter* test considers whether the individual defendant "had the power to hire and fire employees." *Barfield,* 537 F.3d at 142 (quotation marks omitted). The evidence demonstrates that Catsimatidis possesses, but rarely exercises, the power to hire or fire anyone he chooses. He testified, "I guess I can fire the people that directly report to me," which he said would include "only maybe four or five" employees such as the COO and CFO. Joint App'x 1863. He testified in 2005 that he could not remember having fired anyone in five or six years. *Id.* at 1862. In *RSR,* we emphasized that the hiring and firing of "individuals who were in charge of [the plaintiff employees] is a strong indication of control." *RSR,* 172 F.3d at 140.

Zorn testified that Catsimatidis had hired him and "obviously would" have the authority to hire and fire others, "but he doesn't get involved in that." Joint App'x 1338. For example, when Zorn was "involved in letting go long-time employees for various reasons," he let Catsimatidis know "as a courtesy" and fired the employees even if Catsimatidis "wasn't happy about it." *Id.* at 1343. On one occasion when both Zorn and Catsimatidis interviewed a potential manager, Catsimatidis "was in favor of it but he left the decision to" Zorn. *Id.* at 1342. Catsimatidis promoted Deborah Clusan from director of payroll to director of payroll and human resources. *Id.* at 476. He promoted Moore to store manager from night manager. Moore testified that Catsimatidis "came to speak with me, asked me what my background was, . . . and then the next day the vice president called me, and told me that I would be starting in the Store 504 the next day." *Id.* at 1412, 1415. Moore, like other employees, indicated that he "view[ed] Mr. Catsimatidis as [his] boss" and that Catsimatidis would have the power to fire a store employee. *Id.* at 1425–26.

The second *Carter* factor asks whether the individual defendant "supervised and controlled employee work schedules or conditions of employment." *Barfield,* 537 F.3d at 142 (quotation marks omitted). Plaintiffs overstate the importance of the two pieces of evidence on which they rely for this factor. Although they state in their brief that Catsimatidis said he "has handled complaints from Gristede's workers' union representatives 'every week for as long as I could remember,' " Appellees' Br. at 39, this mischaracterizes Catsimatidis's testimony; he stated that he had not been personally involved in union negotiations or discussions of problems, *see* Joint App'x 1802–03,

1812, 1876. Plaintiffs also assert that Catsimatidis "authorized an application for wage subsidies and tax credits on behalf of Gristede's employees." Appellees' Br. at 39. The evidence reflects only that Catsimatidis signed the application for tax credits to which Gristede's was entitled for employing people "coming off of Social Services, off of welfare." Joint App'x at 482–83. Moreover, plaintiffs do not indicate how this affected their "work schedules or conditions of employment." Although Catsimatidis's involvement in the company and the stores as discussed above demonstrates some exercise of operational control, it does not appear to relate closely to this factor of the *Carter* test.

The third factor asks whether the individual defendant "determined the rate and method of payment." *Barfield,* 537 F.3d at 142 (quotation marks omitted). The district court and plaintiffs emphasize the fact that Catsimatidis's electronic signature appears on paychecks. This—like all factors—is not dispositive. *See Gray,* 673 F.3d at 354. Nonetheless, we held in *RSR* that "[t]he key question is whether [the defendant] had the authority to sign paychecks throughout the relevant period, and he did." *RSR,* 172 F.3d at 140.

RSR also focused on the fact that the defendant "controlled the company financially." *Id.* It is clear that Catsimatidis possessed a similar degree of control. He testified that he keeps track of "payroll" as "a line item on accounting" and "a part of profit and loss," to know what percentage of Gristede's sales and expenses payroll comprises, but he does not get involved with individual salaries or schedules. Joint App'x at 1834–35. Although he did not speak to his managers "about people getting paid," *id.* at 1834, he knew that employees were paid on time "[b]ecause the unions would have come down on us real hard" if there was a problem. *Id.* at 1852. Catsimatidis explained that he might also learn about a problem "[i]f I walked down the aisle, and the employee saw me, they might complain," although the official procedure for such complaints involved the employees' union and store manager. *Id.* at 1866–67. Catsimatidis set up a meeting between lower-level managers and an outside payroll company, *id.* at 1452–53, and although he did not know specifically "if George Santiago in the store got a paycheck that week," his "rules are if somebody works, they get paid," *id.* at 469. The district court also noted that Catsimatidis stated "in open Court in this proceeding that he could shut down the business, declare bankruptcy, as well as provide the personal signature necessary for a bank letter of credit to be issued in favor of Gristede's," *Torres III,* 2011 WL 4571792, at *1, which further demonstrates the kind of financial control emphasized in *RSR.*

The fourth *Carter* factor asks whether the individual defendant "maintained employment records." *Barfield,* 537 F.3d at 142 (quotation marks omitted). Plaintiffs offer only that "Catsimatidis works in the same office where employment records are kept" and promoted the payroll director, Appellees' Br. at 41, essentially admitting that Catsimatidis did not meet this factor. In sum, the evidence—much of it Catsimatidis's own testimony—indicates that Catsimatidis meets the first and third *Carter* factors.

d. Totality of the circumstances

There is no question that Gristede's was the plaintiffs' employer, and no question that Catsimatidis had functional control over the enterprise as a whole. His involvement in the company's daily operations merits far more than the symbolic or ceremonial characterization he urges us to apply. Unlike the defendant in *Wirtz,* who visited his company's facilities only a few times a year, Catsimatidis was active in running Gristede's, including contact with individual stores, employees, vendors, and customers. Catsimatidis dealt with customer complaints, in-store displays and merchandising, and the promotion of store personnel. That he may have done so "only occasionally" does not mean that these actions are irrelevant, *see RSR,* 172 F.3d at 139, especially when considered in the context of his overall control of the company.

Although there is no evidence that he was responsible for the FLSA violations—or that he ever directly managed or otherwise interacted with the plaintiffs in this case—Catsimatidis satisfied two of the *Carter* factors in ways that we particularly emphasized in *RSR:* the hiring of managerial employees, and overall financial control of the company. *See id.* at 136–37, 140 (finding that the individual defendant "exercised financial control over the company" and "frequently" gave instructions to subordinate managers); *see also Donovan v. Grim Hotel Co.,* 747 F.2d 966, 972 (5th Cir.1984) (noting that the individual defendant was the " 'top man' " in a hotel company who "held [the hotels'] purse-strings and guided their policies" and that the hotels "speaking pragmatically, . . . functioned for the profit of his family"). This involvement meant that Catsimatidis possessed, and exercised, "operational control" over the plaintiffs' employment in much more than a "but-for" sense. His decisions affected not only Gristede's bottom line but individual stores, and the personnel and products therein.

We recognize that the facts here make for a close case, but we are guided by the principles behind the liquidated damages provision of the FLSA in resolving the impact of the totality of the circumstances described herein. The Supreme Court has noted that "liquidated damages as authorized by the FLSA are not penalties but rather compensatory damages 'for the retention of a workman's pay which might result in damages too obscure and difficult of proof for estimate other than by liquidated damages.' " *Republic Franklin Ins. Co. v. Albemarle County Sch. Bd.,* 670 F.3d 563, 568 (4th Cir.2012) (quoting *Brooklyn Sav. Bank v. O'Neil,* 324 U.S. 697, 707, 65 S.Ct. 895, 89 L.Ed. 1296 (1945)); *see also Marshall v. Brunner,* 668 F.2d 748, 753 (3d Cir.1982) (noting that liquidated damages "are compensatory, not punitive in nature").

As counsel for *amicus curiae* the Secretary of Labor explained at oral argument, the purpose of the FLSA is not to punish an employer but to remunerate aggrieved employees. Considered in the context of the expansive interpretation that courts have afforded the statute, this policy reasoning particularly counsels in favor of finding that Catsimatidis was an "employer" given the failure of the settlement between the corporate defendants and the plaintiff employees. Catsimatidis was not personally responsible for the FLSA violations that led to this lawsuit, but he nonetheless profited from them. And although the Gristede's Supermarkets business entity appears to have been larger than other businesses discussed in the cases that have considered this question, the company was not so large as to render Catsimatidis's involvement company is not public. Its stores actively exercised his influence, City metropolitan area, as are the where he worked almost daily. In sum, as the district court concluded, "it is pellucidly clear that he is the one person who is in charge of the corporate defendant." *Torres III,* 2011 WL 4571792, at *3.

Although we must be mindful, when considering an individual defendant, to ascertain that the individual was engaged in the culpable company's affairs to a degree that it is logical to find him liable to plaintiff employees, we conclude that this standard has been met here. Catsimatidis's actions and responsibilities—particularly as demonstrated by his active exercise of overall control over the company, his ultimate responsibility for the plaintiffs' wages, his supervision of managerial employees, and his actions in individual stores—demonstrate that he was an "employer" for purposes of the FLSA.

The issue of joint employers under the FLSA comes up frequently in the context of franchises. The franchisor-franchisee relationship is often regarded as a quintessential example of joint employers because the manner of work is controlled both by the local owner and also by the franchisor seeking to protect its brand. For example, because the McDonald's corporation exercises substantial control over the work environment in individual stores, it might be considered a joint employer with the store owner.

The economic realities test has also been applied in the agricultural sector, where labor contractors employ farmworkers and then contract with large growers to provide a workforce. Some courts have found that the seasonal relationship lacks permanency and duration and that some of the activities are not an integral part of the company's business, concluding that the grower is not a joint employer. *Martinez-Mendoza v. Champion International Corp.*, 340 F.3d 1200 (11th Cir.2003). Other courts, using a seven-factor version of the economic realities test, have found that both growers and labor contractors are employers under both the Migrant and Seasonal Agricultural Worker Protection Act (AWPA), 29 U.S.C. § 1823, and the FLSA, because they have the power to control the work and determine compensation. *Antenor v. D & S Farms*, 88 F.3d 925, 938 (11th Cir. 1996).

Garment workers in New York present a similar scenario. Courts have found that garment manufacturers who hire contractors to provide workers to stitch and finish pieces of clothing are "joint employers" within the meaning of the FLSA. *Zheng v. Liberty Apparel Co., Inc.*, 355 F.3d 61, 70 (2d Cir. 2003) (an entity can be a joint employer under the FLSA even when it does not hire and fire its joint employees, directly dictate their hours, or pay them, if the entity exercises the prerogatives of an employer).

Finally, courts have recognized joint employer status beyond the FLSA context. In 2015, the National Labor Relations Board decided that a franchisor could, under some circumstances, be considered a joint employer for purposes of labor law. In *Browning-Ferris Industries of California, Inc.*, 362 N.L.R.B. No. 186 (2015), the NLRB established that a franchisor would be liable as a joint employer of a franchisee's employees if it exercises, or reserves the authority to exercise, control over employees' terms and conditions of employment. Indirect or unexercised control, such as through an intermediary, may be sufficient to establish joint employer status. In response to the NLRB ruling, fourteen states have passed laws either explicitly excluding franchisors from the definition of employer or protecting them from liability. In December 2017, the National Labor Relations Board overruled the Board's 2015 Browning-Ferris decision and returned to the pre-Browning Ferris standard that governed joint-employer liability. According to the NLRB, in all pending or future joint employer cases, "two or more entities will be deemed joint employers under the National Labor Relations Act (NLRA) if there is proof that one entity has exercised control over essential employment terms of another entity's employees (rather than merely having reserved the right to exercise control) and has done so directly and immediately (rather than indirectly) in a manner that is not limited and routine."

Courts have also applied the FLSA's general joint employer criteria to statutes that were modeled on the FLSA, such as the Family and Medical Leave Act (FMLA). In *Moreau v. Air France*, 356 F.3d 942, 945 (9th Cir. 2004), the question was whether Air France should be considered a joint employer of contracted service workers under the FMLA. The court found that Air France did not share in the control of the means and manner of work or the compensation of the servers because the supervision and control by Air France was minimal, and this consideration was outweighed by other factors. *Id.* at 951. In contrast, in *Grace v. USCAR*, 521 F.3d 655, 667 (6th Cir. 2008), the court found that there was a joint-employer relationship under the FMLA because one employer controlled the worker's wages while the other controlled and supervised the work.

Finally, state courts have extended the joint employer doctrine for the purpose of establishing liability for workers' compensation claims. *Beaver v. Jacuzzi Bros., Inc.*, 454 F.2d 284, 285 (8th Cir. 1972) ("an employee may be employed by more than one employer even while doing the same work" and pursue a workers' compensation claim against either).

Problem 5-5

Erica works as a masseuse for Starz, a luxury spa. Starz requires Erica to report for work each day at 10 a.m. She is obligated to provide all scheduled massages for that day, and to take walk-ins. Erica normally completes her work by 3 p.m., but sometimes she works an additional hour or two because of walk-ins or the scheduling needs of regular clients. Erica is paid by the hour. Erica also works a half-shift at a local restaurant, Rainforest, for which Erica is paid an hourly wage. Is Erica an employee of Starz and Rainforest? Are they joint employers?

Problem 5-6

Now assume that Starz is owned by a franchisee. The franchisor is Constellation. Constellation does not have the power to hire or fire Starz employees. Constellation reserves the right to set general policies for its franchisees, but has no authority implement its policies except by dealing with

Starz. Constellation provides its franchisees with an employee handbook that includes disciplinary procedures, but Starz implements the policies. Starz creates the business records relating to its business, but periodically provides copies to Constellation. Constellation sets a floor for payment of masseuses, but does not directly control the rate or method of payment. Starz has sole control over scheduling employees and the conditions of employment. Is Erica an employee of Constellation?

Problem 5-7

Jorge is a seasonal worker employed by a farm labor contractor (FuCo) during the harvest season to pick the grapes at Vex vineyards. Vex contracts with FuCo to provide grape pickers for the harvest season. Vex notifies FuCo how many acres of grapes will need to be picked but does not dictate how many workers to hire nor does Vex get involved in establishing the working conditions. FuCo has sole control over hiring and firing. FuCo has sole control over the worker's schedule and sets the rate of pay. Is Jorge an employee of Vex?

Problem 5-8

Sharon works for Garment as a seamstress. Sharon works almost exclusively to assemble garments to be delivered to a department store, Doran's. Doran's provides an approved-vendors list from which Garment can purchase fabric and other materials to create the garments. Doran's provides guidelines and specifications for the making of the garment, and specifies the time for delivery by Garment. Doran's pays for the costs of the fabric and a set rate for each design. Garment has sole authority to hire and fire Sharon, to set her pay rate, and to establish workplace conditions. Is Sharon an employee of Doran's?

Conclusion

Under the control test, controlling owners of a business are the paradigm of who is an employer. A controlling owner is defined as one who has control over economic and operational decisions and holds a significant ownership interest. Additionally, parties may operate as joint employers of an employee. In the FLSA context, an individual may be held personally responsible for violations, along with the entity that is nominally the employer.

Lesson 6:
Work-Authorized Immigrants

Objectives and Expected Learning Outcomes

In this Lesson, we will consider the significance of immigration status for employment related issues. You will learn how the federal government enforces immigration law in the workplace. You will learn the complexities that arise in the employment setting, given the extensive federal regulation of immigration.

1. The Intersection of Immigration Policy and Employment Law

The Federal Government has authority over immigration matters, including the vital roles of determining who may enter the country and how long they may remain. On the other hand, federal, state, and local governments regulate the workplace through common law and statutory provisions that are keyed to broad definitions of "employer" and "employee." You might assume that immigration and employment are parallel universes without much overlap. There are, however, close connections between the two regimes. Immigration regulation originally was part of the Federal Bureau of Labor, reflecting the fact that immigration policy was closely connected to economic policy. In particular, the INS regulated the entry of contract laborers from other countries who were authorized to work in certain industries where there were identified labor shortages. For example, the *Bracero* program of the 1940s–1960s was specifically designed to provide laborers in agricultural industries by permitting temporary immigrants to enter the country and work.

In 1965, Congress amended the Immigration and Nationality Act ("INA"). The Act replaced long-imposed national origin quotas for those seeking to immigrate with more broadly defined hemispheric quotas. For the first time, immigrants from the Western hemisphere were regulated, resulting in a backlog of visa applications by persons from Mexico and the rest of Latin America. Given these backlogs, significant numbers of persons chose to enter the country without documentation and seek work. The population of undocumented persons has only grown since Congress made changes to immigration law in 1965. Undocumented workers fill jobs throughout the economy, but immigrants are particularly overrepresented in industries such as agriculture, food processing, and service. Although not documented, these workers are clearly within the very broad definition of "employee" under various state and federal laws, and so they would seemingly be entitled to the protections of employment law.

In 1986 Congress passed the Immigration Reform and Control Act (IRCA). For the first time in history, the worksite became a focus for enforcing immigration regulation. Congress incorporated an employer sanctions provision into the IRCA. Under § 274A of the Act it is unlawful for an employer "to hire, or to recruit or refer for a fee, for employment in the United States an alien knowing the alien is an unauthorized alien (as defined in subsection (h)(3)) with respect to such employment." An "authorized alien" under the Act is "either (A) an alien lawfully admitted for permanent residence, or (B) authorized to be so employed by this Act or by the Attorney General." The regulations promulgated under this section authorize several categories of immigrants, in addition to lawful permanent residents, to work, including asylees and refugees, several categories of nonimmigrants in the U.S. temporarily, persons granted temporary protected status and persons granted deferred action from removal. The most famous example of deferred action status is the Obama administration's Deferred Action for Childhood Arrivals (DACA). Almost one million people who were brought to the United States as children were allowed relief from removal proceedings and were granted work authorization under the program. The DACA recipient is the classic example of a person who is in the United States without authorization, and yet has authorization to work. The DACA program was the target of a lawsuit by several states that argued the Obama administration overstepped its authority when it implemented the program. It has also been the target of the Trump administration which threatened to end it by March 2018. At the time of this writing, the courts have not resolved the issue.

The employer sanctions provisions require employers to have every prospective employee complete an I-9 form, which permits the employers to verify their identity and work authorization status. Sanctions for unauthorized work are imposed on the employers and not the immigrant employees. Congress explicitly decided not to sanction undocumented employees because the threat of punishment would threaten to create an underclass of undocumented workers who then would be completely vulnerable to exploitation by their employer. In effect, the law locates the harm in the employer's action of hiring a non-work-authorized immigrant rather than in the immigrant's attempt to work. The Supreme Court reiterated that Congress intended to sanction employers and not employees when it struck down the State of Arizona's attempts to punish employees for unauthorized employment. See *Arizona v. United States*, 567 U.S. 387 (2012). However, Congress did add sanctions for those who create, use, and disseminate false or fraudulent I-9 documents. Additionally, an immigrant who signs an I-9 form is subject to penalties of perjury for providing false information on such documents.

Employer sanctions can be substantial. An employer is subject to civil monetary penalties up to $2,000 for every unauthorized worker hired, recruited, or referred for employment. The penalty can be as high as $5,000 per worker if the employer has committed previous violations. Employers with a pattern and practice of hiring undocumented workers are subject to criminal penalties. Employers are also subject to criminal violations for harboring undocumented employees for profit. The following sentencing memorandum for a former manager of the meatpacking plant Agriprocessors in Iowa illustrates the charges brought against employers for hiring and harboring undocumented workers.

IN THE UNITED STATES DISTRICT COURT FOR THE NORTHERN DISTRICT OF IOWA EASTERN DIVISION

UNITED STATES OF AMERICA, Plaintiff,

vs.

BRENT BEEBE,

Defendant.

No. 08–CR–1324–LRR

SENTENCING MEMORANDUM

I. INTRODUCTION

The matter before the court is the sentencing of Defendant Brent Beebe.

II. RELEVANT PRIOR PROCEEDINGS

On July 16, 2009, a grand jury returned a 163-count Seventh Superseding Indictment against Defendant and four co-defendants. Count 1 charged Defendant with Conspiracy to Harbor Undocumented Aliens for Profit, in violation of 8 U.S.C. § 1324(a)(1)(A)(v)(I) and 1324(a)(1)(B)(i). Counts 57 through 70 charged Defendant with Harboring Undocumented Aliens for Profit, in violation of 8 U.S.C. § 1324(a)(1)(A)(iii), 1324(a)(1)(A)(iv), 1324(a)(1)(A)(v)(II) and 1324(a)(1)(B)(i). Count 71 charged Defendant with Conspiracy to Commit Document Fraud, in violation of 18 U.S.C. § 371.

On January 11, 2010, Defendant appeared before United States Magistrate Judge Jon S. Scoles and pled guilty to Count 71 of the Seventh Superseding Indictment. On January 26, 2010, the undersigned accepted Defendant's guilty plea.

* * * *

STIPULATED FACTS

* * * Defendant worked for Agriprocessors, Inc. ("Agriprocessors"). Agriprocessors owned and operated a slaughterhouse and meatpacking plant in Postville, Iowa. Defendant was employed as an Operations Manager. His responsibilities at Agriprocessors included managing the "beef kill" department and generally overseeing beef production at the plant.

On or about May 8, 2008, beef department supervisor Juan Carlos Guerrero-Espinoza met with Defendant to discuss the social security numbers of employees in the beef department. Defendant and Guerrero-Espinoza were aware that a number of employees were working under social security numbers that did not match their identities. Defendant and Guerrero-Espinoza discussed the problem and agreed to help these employees. Defendant requested that Guerrero-Espinoza determine the best way to resolve the problem. Guerrero-Espinoza and another employee in the beef department ("beef employee") met with the employees at issue that same day.

After the meeting, Guerrero-Espinoza reported to Defendant that the employees needed approximately $4,500 to resolve the social security problem by obtaining new fraudulent identification documents. Defendant knew that this money would aid approximately nineteen employees.

Later that day, Defendant and Guerrero-Espinoza met with Agriprocessors' vice president, co-defendant Sholom Rubashkin. Defendant and Guerrero-Espinoza told Rubashkin that they needed $4,500 to procure fraudulent identification documents for employees in the beef department. Rubashkin agreed to loan the money to these employees. Rubashkin suggested that Defendant and Guerrero-Espinoza should consider providing assistance to other employees. Defendant refused to provide any further assistance.

On May 9, 2008, Guerrero-Espinoza met with the beef employee and other employees in the beef department. The employees provided money, photographs, false names, and birth dates to the beef employee to enable the beef employee to obtain new false identification documents. Guerrero-Espinoza loaned a portion of the $4,500 to the employees.

That same date, Rubashkin asked Agriprocessors Human Resources employee, Laura Althouse, to report to work on May 11, 2008 to process new employee and applicant paperwork. On or about May 10 and 11, 2008, the beef employee obtained false documents for a number of Agriprocessors employees under Guerrero-Espinoza's supervision, as well as other Agriprocessors employees.

On May 11, 2008, Rubashkin inspected the new fraudulent documents Guerrero-Espinoza had procured and indicated that Agriprocessors should hire the individuals who possessed these new identification documents. Althouse assisted the employees in completing application paperwork for these employees, even though she knew that the identification documents were fraudulent. Guerrero-Espinoza assisted. Defendant copied blank employment packets and delivered them to the Human Resources Department.

* * *

Defendant concedes that the offense involved 6 to 24 documents or passports, and that his base offense level should be increased by **3** levels. USSG § 2L2.1(a)(2)(A). Defendant states that he "agreed to jointly undertake obtaining a loan for the [nineteen] undocumented employees that worked on the beef side, [but that he] affirmatively declined to expand his criminal conduct when invited to do so by [Rubashkin]." Def. Sent. Memo at 6.

In ascertaining the amount of documents involved in the offense, the court looks to the doctrine of relevant conduct. This doctrine is described in USSG § 1B1.3. "The Guidelines include as relevant conduct in the case of a jointly undertaken criminal activity all (1) 'reasonably foreseeable acts and omissions of others' (2) 'in furtherance of' (3) 'the jointly undertaken criminal activity.' " *United States v. Spotted Elk*, 548 F.3d 641, 673 (8th Cir. 2008) (quoting USSG § 1B1.3(a)(1)(B)). Although these elements closely mirror the requirements for conspiracy liability, "the commentary to USSG § 1B1.3 explains that the concepts of relevant conduct under the Guidelines, on the one hand, and conspiracy liability, on the other, are not the same[.]" *Id.* The commentary "shows that while the emphasis in substantive conspiracy liability is the scope of the *entire conspiracy* and foreseeability in light of that scope, the emphasis under § 1B1.3 is the scope of the *individual defendant's* undertaking and foreseeability in light of that undertaking, rather than the scope of the conspiracy as a whole[.]" *Id.* at 673–74 (emphasis in the original).

In this case, Defendant undertook to aid approximately nineteen individuals in obtaining fraudulent documents. In light of that undertaking, it was reasonably foreseeable to Defendant that nineteen individuals would receive fake documents. Defendant's conduct was limited to those nineteen documents. There is no evidence that Defendant's undertaking and foreseeability extended beyond these nineteen individuals. Indeed, Defendant expressly declined to assist additional employees in obtaining new false documents even though his boss suggested that he do so. When Rubashkin asked Defendant to aid additional individuals seeking employment identification documents, Defendant refused to participate. Accordingly, the court finds that the government failed to prove by a preponderance of the evidence that Defendant's offense involved 100 or more documents. The court finds that the offense involved 6 to 24 documents and thus, Defendant's base offense level should be increased by **3** levels. USSG § 2L2.1(a)(2)(A). This brings Defendants base offense level to **11**.

B. Role in the Offense

USSG § 3B1.1(b) provides that, "[i]f the defendant was a manager or supervisor (but not an organizer or leader) and the criminal activity involved five or more participants or was otherwise extensive, increase by **3** levels."

* * * *

In assessing whether to apply this enhancement, the court should consider:

> the exercise of decision making authority, the nature of participation in the commission of the offense, the recruitment of accomplices, the claimed right to a larger share of the fruits of the crime, the degree of participation in planning or organizing the offense, the nature and scope of the illegal activity, and the degree of control and authority exercised over others.

USSG § 3B1.1(b) cmt. (n.4). "In the document fraud context, the Eighth Circuit Court of Appeals held that a defendant was entitled to a three-level increase because 'she was one of the core members of the conspiracy and chiefly responsible for the manufacture and distribution of many of the fraudulent documents.' " *United States v. Elmardoudi*, 611 F. Supp. 2d 879,

894 (N.D. Iowa 2008) (Reade, C.J.) (quoting *United States v. Telemaque*, 934 F.2d 169, 171 (8th Cir. 1991)).

The court declines to apply the three-level enhancement. The court agrees with Defendant that, "[a]lthough [he] was a supervisor of Guerrero-Espinoza within the beef division at Agriprocessors, it does not follow that he was a supervisor for obtaining the fake documents." Def. Sent. Memo at 8. The evidence cited by the government in support of its argument for the enhancement is more reflective of Defendant's role as a supervisor at the plant—not as a supervisor of the illegal activity. For instance, the government argues that Defendant "instructed Guerrero-Espinoza that the employees 'should remain at the same pay level' after being rehired under their new identities." Gov. Sent. Memo at 8. The court agrees with Defendant that he made this instruction in the scope of his employment, not in the scope of the illegal activity.

Defendant was not "one of the core members of the conspiracy." *Telemaque*, 934 F.2d at 171. He was not "chiefly responsible for the manufacture and distribution of many of the fraudulent documents." *Id.* Defendant simply obtained a loan to buy documents and made copies of blank application forms. He did not exercise significant decision-making with respect to the conspiracy, nor did he recruit accomplices or claim a larger fruit of the crime than others. USSG § 3B1.1(b) cmt. (n.4). Accordingly, the court declines to apply the role enhancement.

VI. CALCULATION OF ADVISORY SENTENCING GUIDELINES RANGE

After all the applicable adjustments, Defendant's adjusted offense level is **9**. Defendant is **Criminal History Category I**. His advisory guidelines range, prior to any departure or variance, is **4 to 10 months of imprisonment.**

* * *

IT IS SO ORDERED.

DATED this 24th day of May, 2010.

LINDA R. READE
CHIEF JUDGE, U.S. DISTRICT COURT
NORTHERN DISTRICT OF IOWA

As this Sentencing Memorandum makes clear, IRCA's employer sanctions were designed to punish employers and to stop the "pull" of undocumented workers into the workplace by essentially extending the border to the workplace where employers act as enforcers of federal immigration policy.

QUESTIONS

1. Why do you think the supervisor assists in the production of fraudulent documents, given the monetary and criminal penalties at stake?
2. What are the primary assumptions made by the federal government to support the focus on worksite enforcement and to punish the employer rather than the immigrant?

---

2. IRCA's Non-Discrimination Provisions

Congress understood the potential for widespread discrimination if employers faced sanctions for hiring undocumented workers. Consequently, IRCA amended the INA to include an anti-discrimination provision that prohibits discrimination on the basis of citizenship status or national origin in hiring, firing, or recruitment or referral for a fee; document abuse or unfair documentary practices during the verification of employment eligibility; and retaliation against workers asserting their rights. The statute specifically states that U.S. citizens, recent permanent residents, temporary residents, asylees, and refugees are all protected from citizenship status discrimination. For these employees, employers are prohibited from requiring different documents than the statute requires to verify employment eligibility.

The provision is enforced by the Office of Special Counsel for Immigration-Related Unfair Employment Practices of the Department of Justice (OSC). The immigration statute also protects those who file charges, cooperate with an OSC investigation, who complain of unfair documentary practices, or who assert their rights under the INA's anti-discrimination provision from intimidation, threats, coercion, and retaliation.

Problem 6-1

The Home of Goods, a California-based home goods store, seeks to hire a salesclerk for its Sacramento location. The manager interviews several candidates and is impressed with Joel Solis, a recent graduate of U.C. Berkeley. The manager offers Joel a job. As required by federal law, the manager requests that Joel submit an I-9 form that establishes his ability to work. As a recipient of Deferred Action for Childhood Arrivals (DACA), Joel has received work authorization from the federal government. Joel's work authorization card has an expiration date of December 31 of this year. When the manager sees that the work authorization card will expire within a few months, he rescinds his offer to hire Joel. Consider the claim that Joel might make for this refusal to hire, and how the employer would respond.

---

3. Temporary Work Programs and Work Authorization

The INA contains several provisions allowing for both permanent and temporary migration to the United States for work. Prospective employees can seek employment-based visas for outstanding or extraordinary achievements, for high skill work requiring advanced degrees, for low-skill work, or for investing in entrepreneurial activities that generate employment for U.S. workers. These visas allow for permanent residency, and, eventually, citizenship status. The INA and its regulations govern important aspects of the terms and conditions of employment for these workers, including the conditions under which one can obtain a visa, the terms of pay, and even lodging for low-skill workers.

The INA contains several provisions permitting workers to come to the United States temporarily for work or business. See, e.g., INA § 101(a)(15)(B), (H), (L), (O), (P). One set of visas, the H visas, are reserved for guest workers, hired to work temporarily in the United States and to fill the temporary needs of employers. In general, employers must demonstrate there are no qualified, willing, and available U.S. workers in the region before they can seek foreign guest workers. The H-1B visas are reserved for specialized fields, typically requiring a bachelor's degree or higher. Many of these visas are used in high tech fields and in areas of labor shortage, such as Silicon Valley. The H-2 visas are reserved for agricultural and low-skill guest workers. Employers include those in agricultural, forestry, service, and some food processing industries. Guest workers typically spend up to ten months on these visas, and they perform seasonal work or work that fulfills a specific temporary purpose. These visas are limited in number, and there is a high demand among employers for guest workers. Every year Congress entertains proposals to expand the categories and increase the number of visas available for guest workers.

Mastery Problem 6-1

A proposed Agricultural Guestworker Act of 2017 was introduced in Congress in response to the food industry's concerns over labor shortages. The shortage exists, according to the industry, because Americans do not want to take menial jobs in the food processing industry. The Act proposes to expand the current guestworker program, which is limited to traditional farm labor in agricultural fields and in low-skilled labor.

The proposed legislation would create a new category of guest worker, the H-2C worker. It would dramatically increase the number of visas available to food industry workers to 450,000 visas per year; would target visas for jobs in the food processing industry; and would lengthen the period allowed for temporary employment from ten months to three years. To ensure that employers are not vulnerable to labor shortages, the proposed legislation would allow employers to seek additional visas, should the cap be reached in any given year.

The proposed new H-2C program would be available to employers in aquaculture operations, dairies, raw (including meat and poultry) food processors, and forestry-related industries. Unlike the current H-2A program, the H-2C program would not require employers to provide free transportation and housing for workers. Under the H-2C program, wages would be calculated off the minimum wage, rather than the higher prevailing wage, or the adverse effect wage rate, required under the current H-2 programs. Thus, the wages offered to H-2C workers would be lower than those currently offered to guest workers. One study suggests that guest workers under this program could make less than $9/hour, compared to the $13/hour that dairy workers now earn.

The H-2C program would redefine at-will employment by allowing the employer to terminate a worker, but not allowing a worker to quit a job without losing legal status. A worker who leaves a job before the termination of a contract term is considered having abandoned the job under the proposed legislation.

The proposed Act would circumscribe the methods by which this category of workers could complain or grieve their working conditions. First, the legislation would require that H-2C workers seek mediation before filing a civil action against an employer. Second, mandatory binding arbitration would be a condition of employment. Moreover, the statute would require workers to share the costs of mediation or arbitration of an employment-related dispute. Finally, workers would be barred from using federal legal aid for filing complaints against employers.

The Act would limit the federal benefits available to these workers. H-2C workers would not be eligible for earned income, child tax, or health care premium credits. More importantly, while H-2C workers would not be eligible for insurance under the Affordable Care Act, they would nonetheless be required to obtain their own health insurance as a condition of employment. Finally, employers would also withhold 10 percent of a worker's wages and deposit them into a fund only available in a US embassy or consulate in the worker's home country, as a way to guarantee that workers return home.

You are a staffer to a member of the House of Representatives who is thinking of being actively involved in the consideration of this bill. She asks you to prepare a memorandum that provides a policy assessment. You should include the following elements in your analysis:

1. What are the underlying values that this Act promotes?
2. If enacted, would this law have any effect on the working conditions of employees in the general U.S. labor market?
3. What values would you introduce to this legislation to make it more U.S.-worker friendly, and how would you implement those values through statutory language?

Conclusion

Although conceptually distinct, federal immigration policy and employment law are now deeply connected. Employers face penalties for hiring undocumented persons, and yet there are millions of undocumented workers in the United States. We discuss the employment law remedies available to these workers in Lesson 38.

3

Defining the Relationship

Key Concepts

- The historical common law rule is that an employment relationship is presumed to be at-will, which means it can be terminated by either party at any time and for any reason, or no reason at all.
- The employment relationship is fundamentally contractual in nature, and so the at-will rule can be overcome by agreement of the parties.
- In the modern workplace, the employer's handbook is an important organizing tool that can sometimes bind the employer to promises made.
- Many employment relationships include mandatory arbitration agreements as a means of settling disputes.

Lesson 7:
The At-Will Rule and Its History

Objectives and Expected Learning Outcomes

In this Lesson, you will learn about the emergence of the at-will rule in employment law, set against a longer history of regulation designed to ensure an adequate and efficient workforce. In modern American law, the at-will rule is the foundation of the employment relationship. Most developments in the common law and statutes regarding employee rights against discharge can be understood as exceptions to the general at-will rule.

1. The History of the At-Will Rule

Work has always been performed against the backdrop of a combination of familial, social, economic, and legal structures. Modern labor law in England is traced to the Ordinance of Labourers (issued by King Edward III in 1349) and the Statute of Labourers (enacted by Parliament in 1351). After the Black Death decimated the agricultural workforce, the government stepped in to stabilize the labor economy by requiring every person, man and woman, under the age of 60 to work; by limiting wages to pre-plague levels despite the shortage of laborers; by prohibiting the hiring of excess workers; and by regulating the prices of food to prevent excess profit. These efforts largely failed and ultimately led to revolts by peasants against the austere conditions. The modern era of workplace regulation, and a struggle in response, had begun.

The feudal agrarian economy had been defined by the lord-serf relationship. As wage labor began to develop, the law recognized what it termed the "master-servant" relationship that was regarded as a bond of reciprocal duties. The master-servant relationship was certainly an improvement on serfdom, as it converted the relationship to one between two free people. However, it remained a very hierarchical relationship. The following excerpt provides a brief synopsis of the history of workplace regulation in the United States through the master-servant phase.

James Gray Pope, "A Brief History of United States Labor and Employment Law," in The Oxford International Encyclopedia of Legal History

477–86 (Stanley N. Katz, ed.) (2009).

Before the American Revolution, there was no field of labor or employment law. The legal organization of labor centered on the family. Heads of households—male, unless there was no qualified adult male present—exercised plenary authority over the labor of spouses, children, hired servants, bound servants, and slaves. The American law governing servants generally followed the English pattern, but it was legislated and administered at the level of the individual colony or locality, and not by Parliament. . . .

[Editor's Note: More than half of the white immigrants to America were able to finance the cost of their journey only by agreeing to be bound to work for a term of years. Bound, or indentured, servants were treated as personal property for the period of their indenture.]

The typical indenture bound the servant to provide "such service and employments as the master shall there employ him according to the Custom of the County" and obliged the master to provide "meat drink apparel and lodging with other necessarys during the said term."

. . . .

Unlike bound servants, hired workers were not considered to be chattels. As in England, however, American colonists who entered into labor contracts were subject to criminal punishment for desertion or absence during the contract term. In addition, courts made the remedy of specific performance (a court order compelling labor) available to employers enforcing labor contracts. The typical labor contract ran for six months or more.

> *[Editor's Note: The slave trade was the source of a large number of workers until the Civil War ended slavery in the United States.]*

. . . .

After the American Revolution, European travelers remarked that even domestic workers in the new nation refused to accept the label "servant." At least in theory, employers and workers were equals in the eyes of the law. Terms and conditions of employment were said to result not from a hierarchical status relationship, but from the voluntary agreement of freely contracting individuals. In practice, however, employment contracts left many terms unspecified. When disputes arose, judges filled the gaps. They turned to the common-law relationship of master and servant, which endowed the former with paternalistic authority over the latter. Although the master-servant law had grown out of the close, interpersonal setting of the household, courts did not hesitate to extend it even to textile mills employing hundreds of operators.

The authority of the master was reflected in numerous rules. For example, courts presumed that the master enjoyed the right to control the servant's labor. When workers contested employer directives (for example to work on Sunday or to work at an excessive pace), they forfeited their rights under the contract—including for wages already performed. Courts also delegated rulemaking authority to employers. Many employers drew up codes regulating employee conduct. Courts took from juries the power to determine the effect of these codes and held as a matter of law both that the rules were part of the employment contract and that workers effectively consented to them by showing up at work with a general knowledge of their existence.

The parties remained free to negotiate contract terms that departed from the courts' master-servant model, but few workers possessed the legal knowledge, confidence and bargaining power necessary to do so. Workers and their attorneys urged courts to recognize and respond to this imbalance lest workers be denied republican "liberty and independence" and find themselves reduced to "a species of slavery." But the judiciary was not receptive to these arguments. By the 1840s, the terms "master and servant" had become synonymous with "employer and employee" in the professional language of law.

Legal historians debate the particulars regarding the transition from the traditional master-servant rules inherited from England to the contemporary at-will contract rule, under which an employment relationship is terminable at the will of either party, with or without notice or reason. In an influential article, Professor Jay Feinman argues that English precedents, grounded in the reality of the agricultural economy, presumed that the duration of employment was one year. As other sectors of work opened, the courts transitioned to a rule that permitted termination with adequate notice, based on the context and customs in the particular industry. The situation in America, however, was less orderly. As Professor Feinman explains below, the at-will rule emerged suddenly and without careful consideration.

Jay M. Feinman, *The Development of the Employment at Will Rule*

20 Am. J. Legal Hist. 118 (1976).

While English law followed a relatively clear path, American law at the same time exhibited a confusion of principles and rules. Through the middle of the nineteenth century, American courts and lawyers relied heavily on English precedents but often came to different results.

In colonial times, some hirings, such as of day laborers, were conventionally terminable at will. Agricultural and domestic service relations often followed the English rule of yearly hirings. In the nineteenth century, however, whatever consensus existed about the state of the law dissolved. For example, Tapping Reeve's pioneering domestic relations treatise at mid-century stated the English presumption of yearly hiring but noted that no such rule existed in Connecticut. But, in the same year that Reeve's second edition was published, the New York Court of Appeals held that the English rule of yearly hiring was still in effect in New York, even giving Blackstone's "benefit of the seasons" rationale. Shortly thereafter Charles Manly Smith's treatise on master and servant, the first devoted solely to the subject in the United States, was published in Philadelphia. Covering English law with reference to American cases, Smith's treatise had significant impact for that reason. Smith stated a presumption that a general hiring was a yearly hiring for all servants, the presumption was rebuttable by custom or other evidence, and, in spite of yearly hiring, the relations was terminable on notice where that was customary.

The confusion over the nature of the field of master and servant law contributed to the confusion over the duration of service contracts issues. Master and servant law was originally classed as a domestic relation. The master-servant relation was personal, often familial; servants were described as "menial" not derogatorily but because they resided *intra moenia*, within the walls of the master's house. As the nineteenth century progressed, however, the true master-servant relationship became overshadowed by the number of employees whose relationship to their employers was essentially commercial and therefore did not fit the pattern. The resulting tension influenced the direction of the law, with the earlier perception acting as a force delaying accommodations to new economic conditions.

> *[Editor's Note: Feinman describes how, unlike in England, American courts did not utilize the concept of "reasonable notice" as a means of meeting the reasonable expectations of the parties as the presumption of yearly hiring no longer matched economic reality.]*

Thus, the time was ripe for a sure resolution of the problem; it was achieved by an Albany lawyer and prolific treatise writer named Horace Gray Wood. Wood sliced through the confusion and stated the employment at will doctrine in absolutely certain terms:

> With us the rule is inflexible, that a general or indefinite hiring is prima facie a hiring at will, and if the servant seeks to make it out a yearly hiring, the burden is upon him to establish it by proof. . . . [I]t is an indefinite hiring and is determinable at the will of either party, and in this respect there is no distinction between domestic and other servants.

The puzzling question is what impelled Wood to state the rule that has since become identified with his name. Wood's master and servant treatise, like his other works, won him acclaim for his painstaking scholarship, but that comprehensiveness and concern for detail were absent in his treatment of the duration of service contracts. First, the four American cases he cited in direct support of the rule were in fact far off the mark. Second, his scholarly disingenuity was extraordinary; he stated incorrectly that no American courts in recent years had approved the English rule, that the employment at will rule was inflexibly applied in the United States, and that the English rule was only for a yearly hiring, making no mention of notice. Third, in the absence of valid legal support, Wood offered no policy grounds for the rule he proclaimed.

Whatever its origin and the inadequacies of its explanation, Wood's rule spread across the nation until it was generally adopted.

[Editor's Note: Feinman goes on to argue that the sudden emergence of the rule served the need for capitalists to have maximum flexibility over their mid-level managers to ensure profitability. Feinman argues that the at will rule guaranteed the "capitalist's authority over the worker. . . If employees could be dismissed on a moment's notice, obviously they could not claim a voice in the determination of the conditions of work or the use of the product of their labor."]

Legal historian Deborah Ballam criticizes Feinman's thesis, arguing that New York law amply supported Wood's rule, even though Wood did not provide accurate citations. However, Ballam agrees that the new rule in America was grounded in the economic realities of a developing economy.

Deborah A. Ballam, *The Development of the Employment At Will Rule Revisited: A Challenge to its Origins as Based in the Development of Advanced Capitalism*

13 Hofstra Lab. and Employment L. J. 75 (1995).

An examination of New York law, from colonial times to the nineteenth century, and historical evidence regarding working relationships in the dominant types of labor illustrates that New York has always followed the employment at will doctrine. Further, the doctrine was not the creation of a late-nineteenth century judiciary intent on creating a favorable legal climate for business development. However, to conclude that employment at will was not the creation of the judiciary does not negate this article's opening quote, that "legal doctrine . . . is strongly influenced by economic conditions." . . . Economic conditions in the North American British colonies were very different from those in England that gave rise to the annual hiring rule. While early nineteenth century England was characterized by a labor surplus and a shortage of land, the colonies were characterized by a labor shortage and an abundant supply of cheap land. English employees benefitted from the rule for the reverse reason; employers would not be able to hire them for the busy season and cast them off during the slack times. English communities also benefitted from the rule. Because of the English poor laws, discharged employees, who could not easily obtain other jobs or land of their own because of the shortage of property, became charges on their community and the communities bore the brunt of supporting them. The annual hiring rule, then, served a number of interests in England.

However, these same factors were not in operation in the colonies. Discharged employees easily found other jobs due to the labor shortage, and the abundance of free land also made it much easier for the colonists to become property owners. In addition, due to the high wages attributable to the labor shortage, employers did not want to make long-term commitments to their employees unless they were lower-cost indentured servants or slaves who basically worked for room and board.

Class Exercise 7-1

Wood did not justify his rule by proper precedent or policy reason. Work in a small group to develop rationales for adopting the at-will rule in employment, both with regard to legal arguments and policy arguments. Pay particular attention to the competing economic explanations offered by Professors Feinman and Ballam, and consider whether we are now in a new economic era in which the baseline rules of employment law should change.

2. The At-Will Rule

The Restatement of Employment recognizes that the at-will rule is the "default rule" in all but one state. In Comment b the reporters explain the scope of this default rule.

> *b. Rebuttable presumption of at-will employment.* At its core, employment is a contractual relationship. The law of contracts rests on a series of default rules that provide starting points for bargaining between the parties. These default rules control in the event neither the parties' agreement nor the applicable law prescribe different rules. The high courts in 49 states and the District of Columbia recognize as the default rule the principle that employment is presumptively an at-will relationship. (The sole exception is Montana, which by statute requires "good cause" for an employer's termination of a non-probationary employee.)
>
> The at-will presumption states a default rule that applies when the agreement between the parties or other binding employer promise or employer policy statement under § 2.02 does not provide for a definite term or contain a limit on the employer's power to terminate the relationship. The default rule is also subject to contrary statute, law, or public policy.

Restatement of Employment Law § 2.01, c. b.

The California Supreme Court recently defined the at-will rule in rather stark terms:

> Labor Code section 2922 establishes the presumption that an employer may terminate its employees at will, for any or no reason. A fortiori, the employer may act peremptorily, arbitrarily, or inconsistently, without providing specific protections such as prior warning, fair procedures, objective evaluation, or preferential reassignment. Because the employment relationship is "fundamentally contractual" *[Editor's note: quoting the* Foley *case below]* limitations on these employer prerogatives are a matter of the parties' specific agreement, express or implied in fact. The mere existence of an employment relationship affords no expectation, protectable by law, that employment will continue, or will end only on certain conditions, unless the parties have actually adopted such terms. Thus if the employer's termination decisions, however arbitrary, do not breach such a substantive contract provision, they are not precluded by the covenant [of good faith and fair dealing that is implied in every contractual relationship].

Guz v. Bechtel National, Inc., 24 Cal. 4th 317 (2000).

Example 7-1

Ted Wilson is the owner of a car dealership, and he suffers from severe mood swings. None of his employees work under an express contract of employment. Every six months or so, Ted will randomly fire an employee without offering any basis for his decision and without any apparent cause for doing so. Ted may not be held accountable for wrongful termination under the at-will rule.

Example 7-2

Suzanne Blue is an ardent fan of Duke University basketball. She is employed in the tax division at an accounting firm in Chicago, Illinois. Her office is decorated exclusively with photos and other memorabilia celebrating Duke basketball. In October, Gregory Heel is hired as the new supervisor for the tax division. On his first day in the office, Gregory drops by Suzanne's office and notices the décor. He asks if she is a fan of Duke basketball, and when she responds affirmatively he tells her that as a North Carolina basketball fan he doesn't think that he can work with her. He terminated her employment on the spot. Gregory may not be held accountable for wrongful termination under the at-will rule.

Class Exercise 7-2

Should the California Supreme Court acknowledge any exceptions to the at-will rule as stated in *Guz*? Is it realistic to permit an employer to act arbitrarily, without fair procedure and without objective basis and never face consequences? Think about potential exceptions to this stark rule and how they might be framed so as not to completely undermine the at-will rule. You will work together in small groups to formulate potential exceptions.

---

3. Contemporary Challenges to the At-Will Rule

Modern employment law addresses a number of topics: safety in the workplace, worker privacy, adequate compensation, and many others. However, efforts by legislatures and courts to eliminate or modify the at-will rule have been some of the most important developments. Numerous statutes prohibit termination of employment under certain circumstances, such as discrimination, and many courts have created some common law exceptions that we will study later in the course. In some states, however, the courts have refused to modify the at-will rule to any extent, leaving the matter solely to the legislature. Consider the following case from the New York Court of Appeals, which adopts a famously stark position.

MURPHY V. AMERICAN HOME PRODUCTS CORP.

58 N.Y.2d 293 (Ct. App. N.Y. 1983).

JONES, JUDGE.

This court has not and does not now recognize a cause of action in tort for abusive or wrongful discharge of an employee; such recognition must await action of the Legislature. . . .

Plaintiff, Joseph Murphy, was first employed by defendant, American Home Products Corp., in 1957. He thereafter served in various accounting positions, eventually attaining the office of assistant treasurer, but he never had a formal contract of employment. On April 18, 1980, when he was 59 years old, he was discharged.

Plaintiff claims that he was fired for two reasons: because of his disclosure to top management of alleged accounting improprieties on the part of corporate personnel and because of his age. As to the first ground, plaintiff asserts that his firing was in retaliation for his revelation to officers and directors of defendant corporation that he had uncovered at least $50 million in illegal account manipulations of secret pension reserves which improperly inflated the company's growth in income and allowed high-ranking officers to reap unwarranted bonuses from a management incentive plan, as well as in retaliation for his own refusal to engage in the alleged accounting improprieties. He contends that the company's internal regulations required him to make the disclosure that he did. He also alleges that his termination was carried out in a humiliating manner.

As to the second basis for his termination, plaintiff claims that defendant's top financial officer told him on various occasions that he wished he could fire plaintiff but that, because to do so would be illegal due to plaintiff's age, he would make sure by confining him to routine work that plaintiff did not advance in the company. Plaintiff also asserts that a contributing factor to his dismissal was that he was over 50 years of age.

> *[Editor's Note: Plaintiff filed a multi-count complaint, using a number of theories that we will consider in subsequent chapters as exceptions to the at-will rule. The defendant argues that the plaintiff was an at-will employee who could be discharged at any time, and that none of the exceptions should be recognized as a basis for recovery.]*

. . . .

With respect to his first cause of action, plaintiff urges that the time has come when the courts of New York should recognize the tort of abusive or wrongful discharge of an at-will employee. To do so would alter our long-settled rule that where an employment is for an indefinite term it is presumed to be a hiring at will which may be freely terminated by either party at any time for any reason or even for no reason (see *Martin v. New York Life Ins. Co.,* 148 N.Y. 117, 42 N.E. 416; *Parker v. Borock,* 5 N.Y.2d 156, 182 N.Y.S.2d 577, 156 N.E.2d 297). Plaintiff argues that a trend has emerged in the courts of other States to temper what is perceived as the unfairness of the traditional rule by allowing a cause of action in tort to redress abusive discharges. He accurately points out that this tort has elsewhere been recognized to hold employers liable for dismissal of employees in retaliation for employee conduct that is protected by public policy. . . . Plaintiff would have this court adopt this emerging view. We decline his invitation, being of the opinion that such a significant change in our law is best left to the Legislature.

Holding

Those jurisdictions that have modified the traditional at-will rule appear to have been motivated by conclusions that the freedom of contract underpinnings of the rule have become outdated, that individual employees in the modern work force do not have the bargaining power to negotiate security for the jobs on which they have grown to rely, and that the rule yields harsh results for those employees who do not enjoy the benefits of express contractual limitations on the power of dismissal. Whether these conclusions are supportable or whether for other compelling reasons employers should, as a matter of policy, be held liable to at-will employees discharged in circumstances for which no liability has existed at common law, are issues better left to resolution at the hands of the Legislature. In addition to the fundamental question whether such liability should be recognized in New

York, of no less practical importance is the definition of its configuration if it is to be recognized.

Both of these aspects of the issue, involving perception and declaration of relevant public policy (the underlying determinative consideration with respect to tort liability in general, see, e.g., *Pulka v. Edelman,* 40 N.Y.2d 781, 390 N.Y.S.2d 393, 358 N.E.2d 1019; Prosser, Torts [4th ed], § 3, pp 14–16) are best and more appropriately explored and resolved by the legislative branch of our government. The Legislature has infinitely greater resources and procedural means to discern the public will, to examine the variety of pertinent considerations, to elicit the views of the various segments of the community that would be directly affected and in any event critically interested, and to investigate and anticipate the impact of imposition of such liability. Standards should doubtless be established applicable to the multifarious types of employment and the various circumstances of discharge. If the rule of nonliability for termination of at-will employment is to be tempered, it should be accomplished through a principled statutory scheme, adopted after opportunity for public ventilation, rather than in consequence of judicial resolution of the partisan arguments of individual adversarial litigants.

Additionally, if the rights and obligations under a relationship forged, perhaps some time ago, between employer and employee in reliance on existing legal principles are to be significantly altered, a fitting accommodation of the competing interests to be affected may well dictate that any change should be given prospective effect only, or at least so the Legislature might conclude.

For all the reasons stated, we conclude that recognition in New York State of tort liability for what has become known as abusive or wrongful discharge should await legislative action.

[Editor's Note: The court permitted the claim for age discrimination to proceed.]

MEYER, JUDGE (dissenting in part).

The harshness of a rule which permits an employer to discharge with impunity a 30-year employee one day before his pension vests (see *United Steelworkers of Amer., Local No. 1617 v. General Fireproofing Co.,* 464 F.2d 726 (6th Cir.1972); and *Savodnick v. Korvettes, Inc.,* 488 F.Supp. 822) or for no other reason than that he filed a compensation claim (2A Larson, Workmen's

Compensation Law, § 68.36), the bizarre origin of the termination-at-will rule,[1] the change of economic and constitutional philosophy that has occurred since its adoption, the exclusion of a substantial segment of the working community from its effects through "just cause" limitations upon the right to fire resulting from collective bargaining, and the inconsistency of the rule not only with the common law of England and with earlier New York decisions but also with the law of most industrial countries of the world, have caused an outpouring of judicial and scholarly writings intended to ameliorate, if not abolish, the rule. I agree with the majority that we should not now adopt the tort remedies proposed in those writings, because such remedies are essentially grounded in public policy, the declaration of which is a function of both the Legislature and the courts, because the New York Legislature has not been reticent in the area, and because of the difficulty encountered by the courts adopting such remedies in articulating the exact nature of the public policy which will bring them into play.

. . . . I cannot, however, accept the majority's refusal to follow precedent decisional law recognizing an implied-in-law obligation on the part of the employer not to discharge an employee for doing that which the employment contract obligated him to do or to differentiate between that existing contract obligation and the public policy laden tort of abusive discharge. Plaintiff's complaint alleges that "defendant's internal regulations . . . required that plaintiff report any deviation from proper accounting practice to defendant's top management" and that he was dismissed as a result of his doing just that. Because those allegations sufficiently state a cause of action for breach of contract not only under decisions of other States but as a matter of New York law as well, I dissent from the majority's affirmance of the dismissal of the fourth cause of action. . . .

---

1 *Martin v. New York Life Ins. Co.*, 148 N.Y. 117, 121 accepted as correct the rule stated in section 136 of *Wood, Master and Servant* (2d Ed) that "the fact that the compensation is measured at so much a day, month or year does not necessarily make such hiring a hiring for a day, month or year, but that in all such cases the contract may be put an end to by either party at any time, unless the time is fixed". Though later stated to have been "deliberately adopted, all the judges concurring, to settle the differences of opinion which had prevailed in the lower courts" (*Watson v. Guguino*, 204 N.Y. 535, 541–42), *Martin*'s adoption of the rule may fairly be characterized as bizarre in light of (1) Wood's concession that "In England it is held that a general hiring, or a hiring by the terms of which no time is fixed, is a hiring by the year", (2) the contrary statement of the rule in *Adams v. Fitzpatrick*, 125 N.Y. 124 in reliance upon the English cases cited at pages 128 and 130 and the New York cases cited at page 130, . . . the fact, documented in the Annotation at 11 A.L.R. 469, 476, and in a number of the articles referred to in footnote 4 below, that Wood's rule was not supported by any of the cases cited by him, and (4) the logical inconsistency of a rule the ultimate statement of which is that "permanent employment means nothing more than that the employment is to continue indefinitely and until one or the other of the parties wishes for some good reason to sever the relation" *Arentz v. Morse Dry Dock & Repair Co.*, 249 N.Y. 439, 444.

QUESTIONS

1. The majority concludes that only the legislature can alter the long-established at-will rule. If the courts created the at-will rule based on Woods' treatise, why should the courts shy away from altering or rejecting the rule? Is the majority just concerned with reversing the at-will presumption, or are other factors at play in its decision to defer to the legislature?
2. Does the dissenting opinion provide a persuasive argument for the court to reject the at-will rule entirely, or does it just seek some form of exception? If the court were to reject the at-will rule, what presumptive rule would replace it?
3. Articulate the dissent's basis for permitting the plaintiff to recover for his discharge even if the at-will rule is not overturned.
4. Given that the plaintiff was able to proceed with his lawsuit for age discrimination, and that there are many statutory protections against certain kinds of wrongful discharge, is the at-will rule really problematic anymore?

In contrast to the New York courts, California courts have been very aggressive in cutting back on the scope of the at-will rule. Later we will study how the implied promise of good faith and fair dealing in every contract has been used by some jurisdictions to temper the at-will rule. In California, employee advocates had pushed for a "bad faith" termination to result in tort damages, effectively eliminating the contract-based at-will rule. The *Foley* case was much anticipated by the employment bar, as it offered the opportunity for the Court to employ a tort-based "bad faith" approach to wrongful termination. In the end, though, the California Supreme Court pulled back. In *Foley*, the Court reaffirmed that the employment relationship was a contractual relationship with ordinary contract rules, and that at-will termination remained the baseline rule.

FOLEY V. INTERACTIVE DATA CORPORATION

765 P.2d 373 (Cal. 1988).

LUCAS, CHIEF JUSTICE.

After Interactive Data Corporation (defendant) fired plaintiff Daniel D. Foley, an executive employee, he filed this action seeking compensatory and punitive damages for wrongful discharge.

[Editor's Note: Foley alleged a number of causes of action, including a claim for tort damages for termination of employment in bad faith.]

. . . .

We will hold . . . that the covenant of good faith and fair dealing applies to employment contracts and that breach of the covenant may give rise to contract but not tort damages.

FACTS

Because this appeal arose from a judgment entered after the trial court sustained defendant's demurrer, "we must, under established principles, assume the truth of all properly pleaded material allegations of the complaint in evaluating the validity" of the decision below.

According to the complaint, plaintiff is a former employee of defendant, a wholly owned subsidiary of Chase Manhattan Bank that markets computer-based decision-support services. Defendant hired plaintiff in June 1976 as an assistant product manager at a starting salary of $18,500. As a condition of employment defendant required plaintiff to sign a "Confidential and Proprietary Information Agreement" whereby he promised not to engage in certain competition with defendant for one year after the termination of his employment for any reason. The agreement also contained a "Disclosure and Assignment of Information" provision that obliged plaintiff to disclose to defendant all computer-related information known to him, including any innovations, inventions or developments pertaining to the computer field for a period of one year following his termination. Finally, the agreement imposed on plaintiff a continuing obligation to assign to defendant all rights to his computer-related inventions or innovations for one year following termination. It did not state any limitation on the grounds for which plaintiff's employment could be terminated.

Over the next six years and nine months, plaintiff received a steady series of salary increases, promotions, bonuses, awards and superior performance evaluations. In 1979 defendant named him consultant manager of the year and in 1981 promoted him to branch manager of its Los Angeles office. His annual salary rose to $56,164 and he received an additional $6,762 merit bonus two days before his discharge in March 1983. He alleges defendant's officers made repeated oral assurances of job security so long as his performance remained adequate.

Plaintiff also alleged that during his employment, defendant maintained written "Termination Guidelines" that set forth express grounds for discharge and a mandatory seven-step pretermination procedure. Plaintiff understood that these guidelines applied not only to employees under plaintiff's supervision, but to him as well. On the basis of these representations, plaintiff alleged that he reasonably believed defendant would not discharge him except for good cause, and therefore he refrained from accepting or pursuing other job opportunities.

The event that led to plaintiff's discharge was a private conversation in January 1983 with his former supervisor, vice president Richard Earnest. During the previous year defendant had hired Robert Kuhne and subsequently named Kuhne to replace Earnest as plaintiff's immediate supervisor. Plaintiff learned that Kuhne was currently under investigation by the Federal Bureau of Investigation for embezzlement from his former employer, Bank of America.[1] Plaintiff reported what he knew about Kuhne to Earnest, because he was "worried about working for Kuhne and having him in a supervisory position . . ., in view of Kuhne's suspected criminal conduct." Plaintiff asserted he "made this disclosure in the interest and for the benefit of his employer," allegedly because he believed that because defendant and its parent do business with the financial community on a confidential basis, the company would have a legitimate interest in knowing about a high executive's alleged prior criminal conduct.

In response, Earnest allegedly told plaintiff not to discuss "rumors" and to "forget what he heard" about Kuhne's past. In early March, Kuhne informed plaintiff that defendant had decided to replace him for "performance reasons" and that he could transfer to a position in another division in Waltham, Massachusetts. Plaintiff was told that if he did not accept a transfer, he might be demoted but not fired. One week later, in Waltham, Earnest informed plaintiff he was not doing a good job, and six days later, he notified plaintiff he could continue as branch manager if he "agreed to go on a 'performance plan.' Plaintiff asserts he agreed to consider such an arrangement." The next day, when Kuhne met with plaintiff, purportedly to present him with a written "performance plan" proposal, Kuhne instead informed plaintiff he had the choice of resigning or being fired. Kuhne offered neither a performance plan nor an option to transfer to another position.

1 In September 1983, after plaintiff's discharge, Kuhne pleaded guilty in federal court to a felony count of embezzlement.

. . . .

III. BREACH OF THE IMPLIED COVENANT OF GOOD FAITH AND FAIR DEALING

We turn now to plaintiff's cause of action for tortious breach of the implied covenant of good faith and fair dealing. Relying on *Cleary,* and subsequent Court of Appeal cases, plaintiff asserts we should recognize tort remedies for such a breach in the context of employment termination.

The distinction between tort and contract is well grounded in common law, and divergent objectives underlie the remedies created in the two areas. Whereas contract actions are created to enforce the intentions of the parties to the agreement, tort law is primarily designed to vindicate "social policy." (Prosser, Law of Torts (4th ed. 1971) p. 613.) The covenant of good faith and fair dealing was developed in the contract arena and is aimed at making effective the agreement's promises. Plaintiff asks that we find that the breach of the implied covenant in employment contracts also gives rise to an action seeking an award of tort damages.

In this instance, where an extension of tort remedies is sought for a duty whose breach previously has been compensable by contractual remedies, it is helpful to consider certain principles relevant to contract law. First, predictability about the cost of contractual relationships plays an important role in our commercial system. . . . Moreover, "Courts traditionally have awarded damages for breach of contract to compensate the aggrieved party rather than to punish the breaching party." (Note, *"Contort": Tortious Breach of the Implied Covenant of Good Faith and Fair Dealing in Noninsurance, Commercial Contracts—Its Existence and Desirability* (1985) 60 Notre Dame L.Rev. 510, 526, & fn. 94, citing Rest.2d Contracts, § 355, com. a ["The purpose[ ] of awarding contract damages is to compensate the injured party"].) With these concepts in mind, we turn to analyze the role of the implied covenant of good faith and fair dealing and the propriety of the extension of remedies urged by plaintiff.

"Every contract imposes upon each party a duty of good faith and fair dealing in its performance and its enforcement." (Rest.2d Contracts, § 205.) This duty has been recognized in the majority of American jurisdictions, the Restatement, and the Uniform Commercial Code. Because the covenant is a contract term, however, compensation for its breach has almost always been limited to contract rather than tort remedies. As to the scope of the covenant, " '[t]he precise nature and extent of the duty imposed by such an implied promise will depend on the contractual purposes.' " (*Egan v. Mutual of Omaha Ins. Co.* (1979) 24 Cal.3d 809, 818, 169 Cal.Rptr. 691, 620 P.2d 141.) Initially, the concept of a duty of good faith developed in contract law as "a kind of 'safety valve' to which judges may turn to fill gaps and qualify or limit rights and duties otherwise arising under rules of law and specific contract language." (Summers, *The General Duty of Good Faith—Its Recognition and Conceptualization* (1982) 67 Cornell L.Rev. 810, 812, fn. omitted; see also Burton, supra, 94 Harv.L.Rev. 369, 371 ["the courts employ the good faith doctrine to effectuate the intentions of parties, or to protect their reasonable expectations" (fn. omitted)].) As a contract concept, breach of the duty led to imposition of contract damages determined by the nature of the breach and standard contract principles.

An exception to this general rule has developed in the context of insurance contracts where, for a variety of policy reasons, courts have held that breach of the implied covenant will provide the basis for an action in tort. California has a well-developed judicial history addressing this exception. In *Comunale v. Traders & General Ins. Co.* (1958) 50 Cal.2d 654, 658, 328 P.2d 198, we stated, "There is an implied covenant of good faith and fair dealing in every contract that neither party will do anything which will injure the right of the other to receive the benefits of the agreement." (See also *Egan v. Mutual of Omaha Ins. Co.*, supra, 24 Cal.3d 809, 818, 169 Cal. Rptr. 691, 620 P.2d 141.) Thereafter, in *Crisci v. Security Ins. Co.* (1967) 66 Cal.2d 425, 58 Cal.Rptr. 13, 426 P.2d 173, for the first time we permitted an insured to recover in tort for emotional damages caused by the insurer's breach of the implied covenant. We explained in *Gruenberg v. Aetna Ins. Co.* (1973) 9 Cal.3d 566, 108 Cal.Rptr. 480, 510 P.2d 1032, that "[t]he duty [to comport with the implied covenant of good faith and fair dealing] is immanent in the contract whether the company is attending [on the insured's behalf] to the claims of third persons against the insured or the claims of the insured itself. Accordingly, when the insurer unreasonably and in bad faith withholds payment of the claim of its insured, it is subject to liability in tort." (*Id.*, at p. 575, 108 Cal.Rptr. 480, 510 P.2d 1032.)

In *Egan v. Mutual of Omaha Ins. Co.*, supra, 24 Cal.3d 809, 169 Cal.Rptr. 691, 620 P.2d 141, we described some of the bases for permitting tort recovery for breach of the implied covenant in the insurance context. "The insured in a contract like the one before us does not seek to obtain a commercial advantage by purchasing the policy—rather, he seeks protection against calamity." (*Id.*, at p. 819, 169 Cal.Rptr. 691, 620 P.2d 141.) Thus, "As one commentary has noted, 'The insurers' obligations are . . . rooted in their status as purveyors of a vital service labeled quasi-public in nature. Suppliers of services affected with a public interest must take the public's interest seriously, where necessary placing it before their interest in maximizing gains and limiting disbursements. . . . [A]s a supplier of a public service rather than a manufactured product, the obligations of insurers go beyond meeting reasonable expectations of coverage. The obligations of good faith and fair dealing encompass qualities of decency and humanity inherent in the responsibilities of a fiduciary.' . . . (Goodman & Seaton, *Foreword: Ripe for Decision, Internal Workings and Current Concerns of the California Supreme Court* (1974) 62 Cal.L.Rev. 309, 346–347.)" (24 Cal.3d at p. 820, 169 Cal.Rptr. 691, 620 P.2d 141.)

In addition, the *Egan* court emphasized that "the relationship of insurer and insured is inherently unbalanced: the adhesive nature of insurance contracts places the insurer in a superior bargaining position." (24 Cal.3d at p. 820, 169 Cal.Rptr. 691, 620 P.2d 141.) This emphasis on the "special relationship" of insurer and insured has been echoed in arguments and analysis in subsequent scholarly commentary and cases which urge the availability of tort remedies in the employment context.

The first California appellate case to permit tort recovery in the employment context was *Cleary,* supra, 111 Cal.App.3d 443, 168 Cal.Rptr. 722. To support its holding that tort as well as contract damages were appropriate to compensate for a breach of the implied covenant, the *Cleary* court relied on insurance cases without engaging in comparative analysis of insurance and employment relationships and without inquiring into whether the insurance cases' departure from established principles of contract law should generally be subject to expansion.

. . . .

In fact, although Justice Broussard asserts that the weight of authority is in favor of granting a tort remedy, the clear majority of jurisdictions have either expressly rejected the notion of tort damages for breach of the implied covenant in employment cases or impliedly done so by rejecting any application of the covenant in such a context.

. . . .

In our view, the underlying problem in the line of cases relied on by plaintiff lies in the decisions' uncritical incorporation of the insurance model into the employment context, without careful consideration of the fundamental policies underlying the development of tort and contract law in general or of significant differences between the insurer/insured and employer/employee relationships. When a court enforces the implied covenant it is in essence acting to protect "the interest in having promises performed" (Prosser, Law of Torts (4th ed. 1971) p. 613)—the traditional realm of a contract action—rather than to protect some general duty to society which the law places on an employer without regard to the substance of its contractual obligations to its employee. Thus, in *Tameny,* 27 Cal.3d 167, 175–176, 164 Cal.Rptr. 839, 610 P.2d 1330, as we have explained, the court was careful to draw a distinction between "ex delicto" and "ex contractu" obligations. (See, ante, at p. 216 of 254 Cal.Rptr., at p. 378 of 765 P.2d.) An allegation of breach of the implied covenant of good faith and fair dealing is an allegation of breach of an "ex contractu" obligation, namely one arising out of the contract itself. The covenant of good faith is read into contracts in order to protect the express covenants or promises of the contract, not to protect some general public policy interest not directly tied to the contract's purposes. The insurance cases thus were a major departure from traditional principles of contract law. We must, therefore, consider with great care claims that extension of the exceptional approach taken in those cases is automatically appropriate if certain hallmarks and similarities can be adduced in another contract setting. With this emphasis on the historical purposes of the covenant of good faith and fair dealing in mind, we turn to consider the bases upon which extension of the insurance model to the employment sphere has been urged.

The "special relationship" test gleaned from the insurance context has been suggested as a model for determining the appropriateness of permitting tort remedies for breach of the implied covenant of the employment context. One commentary has observed, "[j]ust as the law of contracts fails to provide adequate principles for construing the terms of an insurance policy, the substantial body of law uniquely applicable to insurance contracts is practically irrelevant to commercially oriented contracts.... These [unique] features characteristic of the insurance contract make it particularly susceptible to public policy considerations." (Louderback & Jurika, *Standards for Limiting the Tort of Bad Faith Breach of Contract* (1982) 16 U.S.F.L.Rev. 187, 200–201, fns. omitted.) These commentators assert that tort remedies for breach of the covenant should not be extended across the board in the commercial context, but that, nonetheless, public policy considerations suggest extending the tort remedy if certain salient factors are present. (*Id.*, at pp. 216–218.) "The tort of bad faith should be applied to commercial contracts only if four of the features characteristic of insurance bad faith actions are present. The features are: (1) one of the parties to the contract enjoys a superior bargaining position to the extent that it is able to dictate the terms of the contract; (2) the purpose of the weaker party in entering into the contract is not primarily to profit but rather to secure an essential service or product, financial security or peace of mind; (3) the relationship of the parties is such that the weaker party places its trust and confidence in the larger entity; and (4) there is conduct on the part of the defendant indicating an intent to frustrate the weaker party's enjoyment of the contract rights." (*Id.*, at p. 227.) The discussion of these elements includes an assumption that a tort remedy should be recognized in employment relationships within the stated limitations.

Others argue that the employment context is not sufficiently analogous to that of insurance to warrant recognition of the right to tort recovery. (See, e.g., *Miller & Estes*, supra, 16 U.C. Davis L.Rev. 65, 90–91; Note, *Defining Torts,* supra, 34 Stan.L.Rev. at pp. 164–167.) They contend that (1) inequality in bargaining power is not a universal characteristic of employment contracts, standardized forms are often not used, and there is often room for bargaining as to special conditions; (2) employers do not owe similar fiduciary duties to employees who are themselves agents of the employer and obligated to act in the employer's interests; and (3) unlike insurance companies, employers are not "quasi-public entities" and they "seldom have government-like functions, and do not serve primarily, if at all, to spread losses across society." (Note, *Defining Torts,* supra, 34 Stan.L.Rev. at pp. 165–167; *Miller & Estes*, supra, 16 U.C.Davis L.Rev. at p. 91.)

In contrast to those concentrating on the match between insurance and employment relationships, yet another article suggests, "The fundamental flaw in the 'special relationship' test is that it is illusory. It provides a label to hang on a result but not a principled basis for decision. . . . The qualifying contracts cannot be identified until the issue has been litigated, which is too late." (*Putz & Klippen*, supra, 21 U.S.F.L.Rev. at p. 478–479.) The authors assert that " 'public interest, adhesion and fiduciary responsibility,' are not sufficiently precise to provide a basis for reliable prediction." (*Id.*, at p. 479, fn. omitted.) Instead, they assert that, "While the 'special relationship' test purports to be only a modest extension of the tort of bad faith beyond insurance and employment, it opens the way for pleading a tort cause of action in nearly every contract case, leaving it ultimately to a jury to decide whether or not the parties had a 'special relationship.' " (*Id.*, at p. 480, fn. omitted.) Extension of the test to employment cases would similarly leave the door open to such a claim in every termination case, and readers are cautioned not to infer "that the authors support extension of tort liability beyond insurance through use of the 'special relationship' test." (*Id.*, at p. 461, fn. 163.)

Similarly, another commentary argues that the special relationship model fails because (1) it does not explain why it "justifies tort liability" for otherwise legal conduct, or for conduct which may give rise to contract remedies (Comment, *Reconstructing Breach,* supra, 73 Cal.L.Rev. at p. 1299, fn. omitted), (2) use of the concept "is inadequate to define the scope and application of a tort duty of good faith and fair dealing" (*id.*, at p. 1300), (3) use of the model "fails to distinguish between breach of the implied covenant of good faith and fair dealing and 'bad faith breach of contract' " (*ibid.*, fn. omitted), and (4) the model does not provide justification for imposition of punitive damages and thus "might serve to unfairly chill legitimate conduct" (*id.*, at p. 1301).

After review of the various commentators, and independent consideration of the similarities between the two areas, we are not convinced that a "special relationship" analogous to that between insurer and insured should be deemed to exist in the usual employment relationship which would warrant recognition of a tort action for breach of the implied covenant. Even if we were to assume that the special relationship model is an appropriate one to follow in determining whether to expand tort recovery, a breach in the employment context does not place the employee in the same economic dilemma that an insured faces when an insurer in bad faith refuses to pay a claim or to accept a settlement offer within policy limits. When an insurer takes such actions, the insured cannot turn to the marketplace to find another insurance company willing to pay for the loss already incurred. The wrongfully terminated employee, on the other hand, can (and must, in order to mitigate damages, make reasonable efforts to seek alternative employment. Moreover, the role of the employer differs from that of the "quasi-public" insurance company with whom individuals contract specifically in order to obtain protection from potential specified economic harm. The employer does not similarly "sell" protection to its employees; it is not providing a public service. Nor do we find convincing the idea that the employee is necessarily seeking a different kind of financial security than those entering a typical commercial contract. If a small dealer contracts for goods from a large supplier, and those goods are vital to the small dealer's business, a breach by the supplier may have financial significance for individuals employed by the dealer or to the dealer himself. Permitting only contract damages in such a situation has ramifications no different from a similar limitation in the direct employer-employee relationship.

Finally, there is a fundamental difference between insurance and employment relationships. In the insurance relationship, the insurer's and insured's interest are financially at odds. If the insurer pays a claim, it diminishes its fiscal resources. The insured of course has paid for protection and expects to have its losses recompensed. When a claim is paid, money shifts from insurer to insured, or, if appropriate, to a third party claimant.

Putting aside already specifically barred improper motives for termination which may be based on both economic and noneconomic considerations, as a general rule it is to the employer's economic benefit to retain good employees. The interests of employer and employee are most frequently in alignment. If there is a job to be done, the employer must still pay someone to do it. This is not to say that there may never be a "bad motive" for discharge not otherwise covered by law. Nevertheless, in terms of abstract employment relationships as contrasted with abstract insurance relationships, there is less inherent relevant tension between the interests of employers and employees than exists between that of insurers and insureds. Thus the need to place disincentives on an employer's conduct in addition to those already imposed by law simply does not rise to the same level as that created by the conflicting interests at stake in the insurance context. Nor is this to say that the Legislature would have no basis for affording employees additional protections. It is, however, to say that the need to extend the special relationship model in the form of judicially created relief of the kind sought here is less compelling.

We therefore conclude that the employment relationship is not sufficiently similar to that of insurer and insured to warrant judicial extension of the proposed additional tort remedies in view of the countervailing concerns about economic policy and stability, the traditional separation of tort and contract law, and finally, the numerous protections against improper terminations already afforded employees.

. . . .

It cannot be disputed that legislation at both the state and national level has profoundly affected the scope of at-will terminations. As noted, regulation of employment ranging from workers' compensation laws to antidiscrimination enactments, fair labor standards, minimum compensation, regulation of hours, etc., all have significantly impinged on the laissez-faire underpinnings of the at-will rule. Moreover, unionization of a portion of the domestic workforce has substantial implications for the judicial development of employment termination law because the rights of such workers when terminated are often governed exclusively by the terms of applicable collective bargaining agreements. The slate we write on thus is far from clean.

. . . .

. . . These various approaches on the one hand suggest a widespread perception that present compensation is inadequate, but on the other hand vividly demonstrate substantial disagreement about the propriety or even the potential form of tort remedies for breaches of contractual duties of covenants. The multiplicity of solutions advanced underscores the caution with which any attempts to extend such relief must be viewed.

As we have reiterated, the employment relationship is fundamentally contractual, and several factors combine to persuade us that in the absence of legislative direction to the contrary contractual remedies should remain the sole available relief for breaches of the implied covenant of good faith and fair dealing in the employment context. Initially, predictability of the consequences of actions related to employment contracts is important to commercial stability. In order to achieve such stability, it is also important that employers not be unduly deprived of discretion to dismiss an employee by the fear that doing so will give rise to potential tort recovery in every case.

Moreover, it would be difficult if not impossible to formulate a rule that would assure that only "deserving" cases give rise to tort relief. . . . In a tort action based on an employee's discharge, it is highly likely that each case would involve a dispute as to material facts regarding the subjective intentions of the employer. As a result, these actions could rarely be disposed of at the demurrer or summary judgment stage.

. . . .

We are not unmindful of the legitimate concerns of employees who fear arbitrary and improper discharges that may have a devastating effect on their economic and social status. Nor are we unaware of or unsympathetic to claims that contract remedies for breaches of contract are insufficient because they do not fully compensate due to their failure to include attorney fees and their restrictions on foreseeable damages. These defects, however, exist generally in contract situations. As discussed above, the variety of possible courses to remedy the problem is well demonstrated in the literature and include increased contract damages, provision for award of attorney fees, establishment of arbitration or other speedier and less expensive dispute resolution, or the tort remedies (the scope of which is also subject to dispute) sought by plaintiff here.

Broussard, Justice, concurring and dissenting.

. . . I respectfully dissent to part III of the majority opinion. Although written in conservative tones of deference to legislative action, it is in fact a radical attempt to rewrite California law in a manner which, as the majority themselves acknowledge, will leave the wrongfully discharged worker without an adequate remedy. The majority opinion does not preserve the status quo, leaving it to the Legislature to adopt innovative solutions. It uproots the status quo, leaving it to the Legislature to remedy the problems the opinion creates.

I.

. . . .

As a general rule, damages recoverable in contract actions have been limited to those within the contemplation of the parties at the time of the contract. Since the ordinary commercial contract does not contemplate damages for mental or emotional distress, this rule has led to the maxim that damages for mental suffering are generally not recoverable in an action for breach of contract. But it has always been clear that this maxim is subject to the obvious exception: if the contracting parties *did* contemplate that breach of the contract would cause emotional distress, damages for that injury are recoverable.

In *Allen v. Jones, supra,* 104 Cal.App.3d 207, 163 Cal.Rptr. 445, for example, defendant funeral home breached a contract to transport the cremated remains of plaintiff's brother. Because it was reasonably foreseeable that such breach would cause mental anguish to plaintiff, the court upheld a cause of action for mental distress. (*Id.* at pp. 214–215, 163 Cal.Rptr. 445.) In *Ross v. Forest Lawn Memorial Park* (1984) 153 Cal.App.3d 988, 995, 203 Cal.Rptr. 468, the court upheld a claim for mental distress occasioned by breach of a contract to protect a grave from vandalism. In *Wynn v. Monterey Club* (1980) 111 Cal.App.3d 789, 799–800, 168 Cal.Rptr. 878, plaintiff claimed that defendants' breach of a contract to bar plaintiff's wife from their gaming tables led to the breakup of his marriage; the court found a triable issue of fact whether damages for mental suffering were reasonably foreseeable and within the contemplation of the contracting parties. *Windeler v. Scheers Jewelers* (1970) 8 Cal.App.3d 844, 88 Cal.Rptr. 39 upheld recovery for emotional distress when defendant, in breach of a contract of bailment, lost jewelry of great sentimental value.

These precedents have not yet been applied to wrongful discharge. But a review of the facts of the Court of Appeal cases overruled by the majority in part III of their opinion, and similar cases pending before this court, makes it clear that in many cases the employer is aware at the time of the contract that bad faith discharge will create great mental and emotional distress. In such cases, the application of existing precedent could serve to provide some redress for that injury.

II.

The majority's discussion of the cause of action for wrongful discharge transposes the positions of plaintiffs and defendants, asserting, incorrectly, that plaintiffs seek to change established law. . . . I maintain that we should retain the well-recognized tort cause of action for bad faith discharge. To demonstrate the point, I propose to show (1) that a tort cause of action for bad faith discharge is an established feature of California common law; (2) that the analogy between the insurance cases, in which a tort cause of action has long been recognized, justifies tort recovery for bad faith discharge; (3) that the existence of a cause of action in contract for discharge in breach of contract does not exclude a tort action for bad faith; and (4) that it is fundamentally illogical to abolish a tort cause of action on the ground that radical change in existing remedies should be left to legislative action.

. . . .

2. *Analogy to the cases upholding a tort cause of action for bad faith breach of a contract of insurance justifies a tort action for bad faith discharge of an employee.*

The majority deride the prior cases for their uncritical incorporation of the insurance model into the employment context without considering the significant differences between the insurer-insured and employer-employee relationships. But when we consider the differences noted by the majority, we find that they are not significant at all.

The majority finds one fundamental difference between insurance and employment relationships: "[i]f an insurer pays a claim, it diminishes its fiscal resources . . . [while] as a general rule it is to the employer's economic benefit to retain good employees." But their comparison is not between insurers and employers, but between short-sighted insurers and far-sighted employers. In the short run, the insurer saves money by not paying claims, and the employer by not paying wages. (If the work cannot be deferred, he can hire less experienced but cheaper help.) In the long run, an insurer that never paid claims would be out of business, and an employer that always fired experienced help would not be much better off. Thus if we examine insurers and employers with the same lens, the difference the majority find fundamental simply disappears.

But the majority's analysis leaves a lingering trace, for it betrays their misunderstanding of the problem. We need not be concerned about insurers that never pay claims or employers that fire all experienced help—the marketplace will take care of them. The concern is with the insurer or employer that acts arbitrarily some of the time—and can get away with it unless threatened with damages that, unlike traditional contract damages, exceed the short-term profit.

The majority also point to some nonfundamental distinctions between the insurer-insured and the employer-employee relationships. They argue that the discharged employee may be able to mitigate damages while the insured generally cannot. But as we all know, in many cases the discharged worker cannot mitigate damages. As Justice Kaufman asks, "What market is there for the factory worker laid-off after 25 years of labor in the same plant, or for the middle-aged executive fired after 25 years with the same firm?" The ability of some persons to mitigate damages is no reason to deny a cause of action to those unable to mitigate them.

It is next suggested that the employer, unlike the insurer, is not performing a "public service." I fail to understand the significance of the statement. Employment is even more important to the community than insurance; most people value their jobs more than their insurance policies. The public interest in deterring arbitrary breach of employment contracts is, I suggest, at least equal to that in deterring arbitrary breach of insurance contracts.

Finally, the majority reject the idea that an employee is like an insured because both contract for financial security. A business, they point out, may also seek financial security. They put the case of a business contracting to secure a reliable source of supply. But what emerges from the majority's analysis is three propositions: a) that insureds *generally* buy insurance policies for financial security; (b) that employees *generally* seek financial security in their employment; (c) that businesses *occasionally* contract for financial security. These propositions should lead the majority to conclude that the employment contract is more analogous to an insurance contract than to a commercial contract.

The majority are focusing upon the exceptions, not upon the general rule. If we must argue analogies, the question is not whether the employment contract differs from an insurance contract in one particular respect, or resembles a commercial contract in another. It is whether, as a whole, the contract of employment more closely resembles an insurance contract or an ordinary commercial contract. The answer is clear. The principal reason we permit tort damages for breach of the covenant of good faith and fair dealing in an insurance contract is that persons do not generally purchase insurance to obtain a commercial advantage, but to secure the peace of mind and security it will provide in protecting against accidental loss. That reason applies equally to the employer-employee relationship. A man or a woman usually does not enter into employment solely for the money; a job is status, reputation, a way of defining one's self-worth and worth in the community. It is also essential to financial security, offering assurance of future income needed to repay present debts and meet future obligations. Without a secure job a worker frequently cannot obtain a retirement pension, and often lacks access to affordable medical insurance. In short, "in a modern industrialized economy employment is central to one's existence and dignity." (Gould, *The Idea of the Job as Property in Contemporary America: The Legal and Collective Bargaining Framework,* 1986 B.Y.U.L.Rev. 885, 892.)

Because workers value their jobs as more than merely a source of money, contract damages, if limited to loss of income, are inadequate. Again the analogy to the insurance cases is close. Explaining the basis for tort damages in insurance cases, *Wallis v. Superior Court, supra,* 160 Cal.App.3d 1109, 1118, 207 Cal.Rptr. 123, said that "[m]oney damages paid pursuant to a judgment years after . . . do not remedy the harm suffered . . ., namely the immediate inability to support oneself and its attendant horrors"—language which applies equally to a suit for wrongful discharge. As summarized in

Miller & Estes, *Recent Judicial Limitations On the Right to Discharge: A California Trilogy* (1982) 16 U.C. Davis L.Rev. 65, 90–91, insureds and employees both depend on the contracts "for their security, well-being, and peace of mind. If insurance companies or employers act in bad faith, the consequences can be very severe, indeed much greater than those that result from a breach of contract."

In contrast, commercial contracts, generally speaking, are negotiated between parties of more nearly equal bargaining strength, and are entered into for purpose of profit. Breach entails only lost profits, and often a market exists in which the damaged party can cover its loss. I conclude that past decisions were justified in analogizing the relationship between employer and employee to that between insurer and insured, and in distinguishing both from commercial contracts for the sale of goods and services.

. . . .

QUESTION

1. Many jurisdictions join California in providing a tort action to policyholders who suffer loss at the refusal of their insurer to comply with the policy. Foley addressed a simple question: are employees vulnerable to employers in ways that are similar to how policyholders are vulnerable to insurance carriers, and should the common law therefore protect employees with a tort action for bad faith termination of employment? Be prepared to discuss this question in depth.

---

4. The "Just Cause" Standard Under Collective Bargaining Agreements

When debating the at-will rule, many employee advocates have argued that the enforcement of a "just cause" standard under collective bargaining agreements between employers and unions provides a model of an alternative baseline rule. They emphasize that no real value is gained by permitting employers to act arbitrarily and without just cause. Employer advocates respond by asserting that there will be significant transaction costs as parties and the courts struggle to define the contours of "just cause" in each individual case.

Over time, labor arbitrators have articulated basic principles of just cause. Famously, arbitrator Carroll Daugherty devised a seven-part test for "just cause" in an arbitration decision he issued. *See In re Enterprise Wire Co. and Enterprise Independent Union*, 46 LA 359 (March 28, 1966). These often-cited factors can be viewed as ensuring that fair procedures have resulted in appropriate reasons for the employer's action. As to procedural justice, the tests include (1) giving fair notice to the employee that certain actions could result in discipline, (2) conducting an investigation before taking action, (3) ensuring that the investigation is fair and objective, and (4) treating like cases alike. On the substantive side, the tests include (1) ensuring that the rule in question is reasonably related to the employer's interests, (2) requiring proof that employee violated the rule, and (3) that the discipline administered was reasonably related to the employee's previous record and the seriousness of the violation in question.

Through numerous arbitrations in the union context, this seven part test for "just cause" discipline has been developed in detail. Some observers argue that actual decision-making goes beyond these simple factors, and that the assessment of "just cause" by an adjudicator is always contextual and based on a balancing of many factors. The question is whether this just cause approach can be successfully used to replace the at-will rule, or whether at this stage the courts will defer to the legislature on this larger question.

Conclusion

This Lesson has focused your attention on the history and justification of the at-will rule. It appears highly unlikely that states will move to a just cause standard for discipline or termination, as is used in the union context. Much of this course will focus on contemporary regulation of the workplace that modifies, but does not eliminate, the default rule that employment is terminable at-will.

Lesson 8:
Contract Law

Objectives and Expected Learning Outcomes

In this Lesson, we will discuss the elements of a contract of employment, which can displace the at-will default rule regarding the duration and termination of the relationship. You will learn that ordinary contract principles may be used differently in the context of a strong presumption of at-will employment. We will analyze express contracts, implied contracts and liability premised on promissory estoppel as potential avenues of recovery for a former employee.

The at-will rule is a default rule, which means that the parties are able to enter a contract that limits the right of one or both parties to terminate the relationship. This can be accomplished by an express contract, in which the parties conclude a binding agreement, either orally or in writing, regarding the duration of the employment and the permitted grounds for termination. Alternatively, the parties may create an implied-in-fact contract through their actions and communications, when these are sufficient to give rise to reasonable expectations regarding the terms of the employment relationship. Finally, in the absence of an express or implied contract, an employee might be able to recover under principles of promissory estoppel if the employer makes a promise that leads the employee to act or forebear from acting in reliance on the promise.

Example 8-1

A professional football team has numerous employees with varying employment contracts. A member of the football team is a member of a union and subject to an express collective bargaining agreement regarding many terms of the relationship, but the member also engages an agent to negotiate terms that pertain only to the individual player. The head coach is not a member of the union, but has an express written contract that governs the duration and terms of the employment relationship. An assistant coach might not have an express contract, but the communications between the parties, the past practices and other evidence may support an implied contract that the assistant coach would be given at least six months of notice before termination (or six months of severance payment). Finally, a marketing executive who was lured away from another team for a position without a contract may have a cause of action for certain promises made to her during the recruitment under the principle of promissory estoppel.

We will cover three primary topics in this Lesson. Employees alleging an oral or implied contract that alters the at-will default rule face challenges. First, the statute of frauds generally precludes enforcement of a contract that cannot be completed within one year of its making without a writing that contains the material terms of the agreement. For parties who allege a contractual agreement that the employment could be terminated only for good cause, this may present a hurdle. Second, if the parties have executed a writing that is at least a partial integration of the terms of the employment relationship, the employee would have to satisfy the terms of the parol evidence rule if the question of duration and termination is not addressed in the writing. Third, if the parties have not created a binding contract, the at-will rule might be altered if the employer made promises that can be enforced under the doctrine of promissory estoppel. You should recall from your contracts class that the remedy for reliance on a promise may be limited to the cost of reliance rather than full expectation damages, if justice requires.

1. Contracting out of the At-Will Rule

Parties are able to contract out of the at-will rule, either by express contracting or by means of a contract implied from the facts and circumstances. As is often the case, California and Texas have adopted different approaches to this employment law question. Read the following two cases and then work through the questions and problems relating to the creation of a contract and the implications of the statute of frauds for enforcement.

Foley v. Interactive Data Corp.

47 Cal. 3d 654 (Cal. In Bank 1988).

Lucas, Chief Justice.

After Interactive Data Corporation (defendant) fired plaintiff Daniel D. Foley, an executive employee, he filed this action seeking compensatory and punitive damages for wrongful discharge. In his second amended complaint, plaintiff asserted . . . (2) a contract cause of action for breach of an implied-in-fact promise to discharge for good cause only (e.g., *Pugh v. See's Candies, Inc.* (1981) 116 Cal.App.3d 311, 171 Cal.Rptr. 917 [all references are to this case rather than the 1988 post-trial decision appearing at 203 Cal.App.3d 743, 250 Cal.Rptr. 195]) . . . The trial court sustained a demurrer without leave to amend, and entered judgment for defendant.

. . . .

. . . We . . . conclude . . . that plaintiff has sufficiently alleged a breach of an "oral" or "implied-in-fact" contract, and that the statute of frauds does not bar his claim so that he may pursue his action in this regard. . . .

FACTS

. . . .

According to the complaint, plaintiff is a former employee of defendant, a wholly owned subsidiary of Chase Manhattan Bank that markets computer-based decision-support services. Defendant hired plaintiff in June 1976 as an assistant product manager at a starting salary of $18,500. As a condition of employment defendant required plaintiff to sign a "Confidential and Proprietary Information Agreement" whereby he promised not to engage in certain competition with defendant for one year after the termination of his employment for any reason. The agreement also contained a "Disclosure and Assignment of Information" provision that obliged plaintiff to disclose to defendant all computer-related information known to him, including any innovations, inventions or developments pertaining to the computer field for a period of one year following his termination. Finally, the agreement imposed on plaintiff a continuing obligation to assign to defendant all rights to his computer-related inventions or innovations for one year following termination. It did not state any limitation on the grounds for which plaintiff's employment could be terminated.

Over the next six years and nine months, plaintiff received a steady series of salary increases, promotions, bonuses, awards and superior performance evaluations. In 1979 defendant named him consultant manager of the year and in 1981 promoted him to branch manager of its Los Angeles office. His annual salary rose to $56,164 and he received an additional $6,762 merit bonus two days before his discharge in March 1983. He alleges defendant's officers made repeated oral assurances of job security so long as his performance remained adequate.

. . . .

The event that led to plaintiff's discharge was a private conversation in January 1983 with his former supervisor, vice president Richard Earnest. During the previous year, defendant had hired Robert Kuhne and subsequently named Kuhne to replace Earnest as plaintiff's immediate supervisor. Plaintiff learned that Kuhne was currently under investigation by the Federal Bureau of Investigation for embezzlement from his former employer, Bank of America. Plaintiff reported what he knew about Kuhne to Earnest, because he was "worried about working for Kuhne and having him in a supervisory position . . ., in view of Kuhne's suspected criminal conduct." Plaintiff asserted he "made this disclosure in the interest and for the benefit of his employer," allegedly because he believed that because defendant and its parent do business with the financial community on a confidential basis, the company would have a legitimate interest in knowing about a high executive's alleged prior criminal conduct.

In response, Earnest allegedly told plaintiff not to discuss "rumors" and to "forget what he heard" about Kuhne's past. In early March, Kuhne informed plaintiff that defendant had decided to replace him for "performance reasons" and that he could transfer to a position in another division in Waltham, Massachusetts. Plaintiff was told that if he did not accept a transfer, he might be demoted but not fired. One week later, in Waltham, Earnest informed plaintiff he was not doing a good job, and six days later, he notified plaintiff he could continue as branch manager if he "agreed to go on a 'performance plan.' Plaintiff asserts he agreed to consider such an arrangement." The next day, when Kuhne met with plaintiff, purportedly to present him with a written "performance plan" proposal, Kuhne instead informed plaintiff he had the choice of resigning or being fired. Kuhne offered neither a performance plan nor an option to transfer to another position.

no alternative options

. . . .

II. BREACH OF EMPLOYMENT CONTRACT

Plaintiff's second cause of action alleged that over the course of his nearly seven years of employment with defendant, the company's own conduct and personnel policies gave rise to an "oral contract" not to fire him without good cause. The trial court sustained a demurrer without leave to amend on two grounds: that the complaint did not state facts sufficient to give rise to such contract, and that enforcement of any such contract would be barred by the statute of frauds. The Court of Appeal affirmed, relying on the latter ground alone. We consider both grounds, discussing the statute of frauds issue first.

A. *Statute of Frauds Defense*

Civil Code section 1624, subdivision (a), invalidates "[a]n agreement that by its terms is not to be performed within a year from the making thereof" unless the contract "or some note or memorandum thereof, [is] in writing and subscribed by the party to be charged or by the party's agent...." In *White Lighting Co. v. Wolfson* (1968) 68 Cal.2d 336, 66 Cal.Rptr. 697, 438 P.2d 345, we held that this portion of the statute of frauds "applies only to those contracts which, by their terms, cannot possibly be performed within one year." (*Id.*, at p. 343, 66 Cal.Rptr. 697, 438 P.2d 345.) In that case the employee alleged the breach of an express oral agreement whereby the defendant promised to employ him on a "permanent" basis and pay him a fixed commission on an "annual basis." We concluded that the trial court erroneously sustained the defendant's demurrer because, although the agreement contemplated employment on a "permanent" basis, the statute does not apply to an employment contract of indefinite duration "unless its terms foreclose the employee's completion of the performance of the contract within one year...." (*Id.*, at p. 341, 66 Cal.Rptr. 697, 438 P.2d 345.)

Relying exclusively on its own decision in *Newfield v. Insurance Co. of the West* (1984) 156 Cal.App.3d 440, 203 Cal.Rptr. 9, the Court of Appeal here nevertheless held that plaintiff's alleged employment contract, if modified to include a promise to discharge him for cause only, is barred by the statute of frauds. Neither *Newfield* nor the opinion below distinguishes, or even cites, the rule in *White Lighting*, supra, 68 Cal.2d 336, 66 Cal.Rptr. 697, 438 P.2d 345. The rationale of both opinions is summed up in the following passage from *Newfield*: "[A]llegedly only [employee] had the right to terminate the contract. Equality or justice between the parties would no longer exist in this alleged kind of oral contract.[14] Appellant cannot have it both ways.

---

14 We observe there is nothing intrinsically unfair or uncommon about a contract that permits the employee to leave at will, but limits the employer's right of discharge. As explained in *Pugh*, supra, 116 Cal. App. 3d 311, 325, 171 Cal. Rptr. 917, "A contract which limits the power of the employer with respect to the reasons for termination is no less enforceable because it places no equivalent limits upon the power of the employee to quit his employment. 'If the

Either his employment relationship was a contract in which both parties had equal rights to terminate at will (in which case it was not in violation of the statute of frauds), or it was a contract where the employer did not have the right to terminate at will, and there was a reasonable expectation of employment for more than one year (in which case the statute of frauds does apply, barring this action)." (156 Cal.App.3d at p. 446, 203 Cal.Rptr. 9.)

Newfield is irreconcilable with the rule in *White Lighting*. Even if the original oral agreement had expressly promised plaintiff "permanent" employment terminable only on the condition of his subsequent poor performance or other good cause, such an agreement, if for no specified term, *could* possibly be completed within one year. (See *White Lighting*, supra, 68 Cal.2d at pp. 343–344, 66 Cal.Rptr. 697, 438 P.2d 345.) Because the employee can quit or the employer can discharge for cause, even an agreement that strictly defines appropriate grounds for discharge can be completely performed within one year—or within one day for that matter.

Our courts have consistently held that such contracts are not within the statute of frauds. Decisions from other states uniformly hold that a good-cause termination clause does not render an employment agreement unenforceable under the statute of frauds. These authorities support the general rule that if a condition terminating a contract may occur within one year of its making, then the contract is performable within a year and does not fall within the scope of the statute of frauds. This is true even though performance of the contract may extend for longer than one year if the condition does not occur.

Other courts have pointed out that within a year an employee such as plaintiff could have (1) been discharged for cause; (2) retired, died or voluntarily left employment; or (3) been terminated if declining profitability compelled a general lay-off or cessation of business altogether. "Interpreting the allegations of the complaint liberally, as we must, we cannot say as a matter of law that the contract . . . could not be performed within a year." (*Plumlee v. Poag*, supra, 150 Cal.App.3d 541, 549, 198 Cal.Rptr. 66.)

. . . .

requirement of consideration is met, there is no additional requirement of . . . equivalence in the values exchanged, or "mutuality of obligation." ' . . . As we shall discuss further in the next portion of the opinion, there is no reason why standard contract principles should not apply in the employment context.

B. *Sufficiency of the Allegations of Oral or Implied Contract*

Although plaintiff describes his cause of action as one for breach of an oral contract, he does not allege explicit words by which the parties agreed that he would not be terminated without good cause. Instead he alleges that a course of conduct, including various oral representations, created a reasonable expectation to that effect. Thus, his cause of action is more properly described as one for breach of an implied-in-fact contract.[20]

As noted, the Court of Appeal did not reach the question of the sufficiency of plaintiff's allegations to state a cause of action for breach of an implied-in-fact contract term not to discharge except for good cause, because it disposed of the issue by erroneously applying the statute of frauds. Nonetheless, the court extensively criticized the reasoning of *Pugh*, supra, 116 Cal.App.3d 311, 171 Cal.Rptr. 917, stating that it "destroys the centuries-old solid and settled principle of vast and demonstrated value to employer and employee, to the world of commerce and to the public of a contract which either can terminate at will." Before this court, defendant urges that we disapprove precedent permitting a cause of action for wrongful discharge founded on an implied-in-fact contract and require instead an express contract provision requiring good cause for termination, supported by independent consideration. Alternatively, defendant requests that we distinguish *Pugh* and its progeny from the present case. We conclude, however, that *Pugh* correctly applied basic contract principles in the employment context, and that these principles are applicable to plaintiff's agreement with defendant.

The plaintiff in *Pugh* had been employed by the defendant for 32 years, during which time he worked his way up the corporate ladder from dishwasher to vice president. (116 Cal.App.3d at p. 315, 171 Cal.Rptr. 917.) When hired, he had been assured that "if you are loyal . . . and do a good job, your future is secure." (*Id.*, at p. 317, 171 Cal.Rptr. 917.) During his long employment, the plaintiff received numerous commendations and promotions, and no significant criticism of his work. Throughout this period the company maintained a practice of not terminating administrative personnel without good cause. On this evidence, the Court of Appeal concluded that the jury could determine the existence of an implied promise that the

20 Plaintiff alleges defendant maintained written "Guidelines for Termination" that required good cause for discharge of an employee, and that plaintiff understood these guidelines applied to him. If he had further alleged that the parties expressly agreed that these guidelines governed his employment, he could state a cause of action for breach of an express oral contract. He has made no such allegation.

employer would not arbitrarily terminate the plaintiff's employment. (*Id.*, at p. 329, 171 Cal.Rptr. 917.)

Pugh has been followed in numerous decisions in this state. A review of other jurisdictions also reveals a strong trend in favor of recognizing implied contract terms that modify the power of an employer to discharge an employee at will. Thus the rule defendant asks us to disapprove is one that has achieved widespread acceptance in recent years.

We begin by acknowledging the fundamental principle of freedom of contract: employer and employee are free to agree to a contract terminable at will or subject to limitations. Their agreement will be enforced so long as it does not violate legal strictures external to the contract, such as laws affecting union membership and activity, prohibitions on indentured servitude, or the many other legal restrictions already described which place certain restraints on the employment arrangement. As we have discussed, Labor Code section 2922 establishes a presumption of at-will employment if the parties have made no express oral or written agreement specifying the length of employment or the grounds for termination. This presumption may, however, be overcome by evidence that despite the absence of a specified term, the parties agreed that the employer's power to terminate would be limited in some way, e.g., by a requirement that termination be based only on "good cause."

The absence of an express written or oral contract term concerning termination of employment does not necessarily indicate that the employment is actually intended by the parties to be "at will," because the presumption of at-will employment may be overcome by evidence of contrary intent. Generally, courts seek to enforce the actual understanding of the parties to a contract, and in so doing may inquire into the parties' conduct to determine if it demonstrates an implied contract. "[I]t must be determined, as a question of fact, whether the parties acted in such a manner as to provide the necessary foundation for [an implied contract], and evidence may be introduced to rebut the inferences and show that there is another explanation for the conduct." *Silva v. Providence Hosp. of Oakland* (1939) 14 Cal.2d 762, 774, 97 P.2d 798; . . . Such implied-in-fact contract terms ordinarily stand on equal footing with express terms. (Rest.2d Contracts, supra, §§ 4, 19.) At issue here is whether the foregoing principles apply to contract terms establishing employment security, so that the presumption of Labor Code section 2922 may be overcome by evidence of contrary implied terms, or whether such agreements are subject to special substantive or evidentiary limitations.

Defendant contends that courts should not enforce employment security agreements in the absence of evidence of independent consideration and an express manifestation of mutual assent. Although, as explained below, there may be some historical basis for imposing such limitations, any such basis has been eroded by the development of modern contract law and, accordingly, we conclude that defendant's suggested limitations are inappropriate in the modern employment context. We discern no basis for departing from otherwise applicable general contract principles.

The doctrine that special limitations should be placed on the enforceability of employment security agreements arose during the late 19th century in the context of interpretation of contracts which promised "permanent" employment to the employee. In *Lord v. Goldberg* (1889) 81 Cal. 596, 601–602, 22 P. 1126, we held that language promising "permanent" employment created employment of no particular duration terminable only "for some good reason." Later cases developed the rule that "a contract for permanent employment, for life employment, for so long as the employee chooses, or for other terms indicating permanent employment, is interpreted as a contract for an indefinite period terminable at the will of either party. . . ." (See, e.g., *Ruinello v. Murray* (1951) 36 Cal.2d 687, 689, 227 P.2d 251; *Speegle v. Board of Fire Underwriters* (1946) 29 Cal.2d 34, 39, 172 P.2d 867; *Shuler v. Corl* (1918) 39 Cal.App. 195, 198, 178 Cal.Rptr. 535.) This rule was not a substantive limitation on the parties' right to contract, but rather a rule of construction that could be overcome by a showing that the employment security term of the contract was supported by consideration other than the services to be rendered or by "other terms indicating a contrary intention." (*Ruinello v. Murray*, supra, 36 Cal.2d at p. 690, 227 P.2d 251; *Drzewiecki v. H & R Block, Inc.*, supra, 24 Cal.App.3d at p. 704, 101 Cal.Rptr. 169.)

As the *Pugh* court explained, a rule imposing a requirement of separate consideration as a substantive limitation on an enforceable employee security agreement would be "contrary to the general contract principle that courts should not inquire into the adequacy of consideration. (See Calamari & Perillo, Contract (2d ed. 1977) § 4–3, p. 136.) 'A single and undivided consideration may be bargained for and given as the agreed equivalent of one promise or of two promises or of many promises.' (1 Corbin on Contracts (1963) § 125, pp. 535–536.) Thus there is no analytical reason why an employee's promise to render services, or his actual rendition of services over time, may not support an employer's promise both to pay a particular wage (for example) and to refrain from arbitrary dismissal.

The limitations on employment security terms on which defendant relies were developed during a period when courts were generally reluctant to look beyond explicit promises of the parties to a contract. "The court-imposed presumption that the employment contract is terminable at will relies upon the formalistic approach to contract interpretation predominant in late nineteenth century legal thought: manifestations of assent must be evidenced by definite, express terms if promises are to be enforceable." (Note, *Protecting At Will Employees*, supra, 93 Harv.L.Rev. at p. 1825, fns. omitted.) In the intervening decades, however, courts increasingly demonstrated their willingness to examine the entire relationship of the parties to commercial contracts to ascertain their actual intent, and this trend has been reflected in the body of law guiding contract interpretation. (See, Goetz & Scott, *The Limits of Expanded Choice: An Analysis of the Interactions Between Express and Implied Contract Terms* (1985) 73 Cal.L.Rev. 261, 273–276 ["The (Uniform Commercial) Code, now joined by the Second Restatement of Contracts, effectively reverses the common law presumption that the parties' writing and the official law of contract are the definitive elements of the agreement. Evidence derived from experience and practice can now trigger the incorporation of additional, implied terms"].)

Similarly, 20 years ago, Professor Blumrosen observed that during the decades preceding his analysis, courts had demonstrated an increasing willingness to "consider the entire relationship of the parties, and to find that facts and circumstances establish a contract which cannot be terminated by the employer without cause." (Blumrosen, *Settlement of Disputes Concerning the Exercise of Employer Disciplinary Power: United States Re supra*, 18 Rutgers L.Rev. at p. 432, fn. omitted.) "This approach has been recognized as consistent with customary interpretation techniques of commercial contracts permitting 'gap filling' by implication of reasonable terms." (Miller & Estes, *Recent Judicial Limitations on the Right to Discharge: A California Trilogy* (1982) 16 U.C.Davis L.Rev. 65, 101, fn. omitted; see also, McCarthy, Punitive Damages in Wrongful Discharge Cases (Lawpress 1985) §§ 3.55–3.56, pp. 206–207.)

In the employment context, factors apart from consideration and express terms may be used to ascertain the existence and content of an employment agreement, including "the personnel policies or practices of the employer, the employee's longevity of service, actions or communications by the employer reflecting assurances of continued employment, and the practices of the industry in which the employee is engaged." (*Pugh*, supra, 116 Cal. App.3d at p. 327, 171 Cal.Rptr. 917; see Note, *Implied Contract Rights to Job Security* (1974) 26 Stan.L.Rev. 335, 350–366 [reviewing factors courts have used in implied contract analyses].) Pursuant to Labor Code section 2922, if the parties reach no express or implied agreement to the contrary, the relationship is terminable at any time without cause. But when the parties have enforceable expectations concerning either the term of employment or the grounds or manner of termination, Labor Code section 2922 does not diminish the force of such contractual or legal obligations.[23] The presumption that an employment relationship of indefinite duration is intended to be terminable at will is therefore "subject, like any presumption, to contrary evidence. This may take the form of an agreement, express or implied, that . . . the employment relationship will continue indefinitely, pending the occurrence of some event such as the employer's dissatisfaction with the employee's services or the existence of some 'cause' for termination." *Pugh, supra.*

Finally, we do not agree with the Court of Appeal that employment security agreements are so inherently harmful or unfair to employers, who do not receive equivalent guarantees of continued service, as to merit treatment different from that accorded other contracts. On the contrary, employers may benefit from the increased loyalty and productivity that such agreements may inspire. (See *Mauk*, supra, 21 Idaho L.Rev. 201, 217.) Permitting proof of and reliance on implied-in-fact contract terms does not nullify the at-will rule, it merely treats such contracts in a manner in keeping with general contract law. (See Note, *Defining Public Policy Torts in At-Will Dismissals* (1981) 34 Stan.L.Rev. 153, 154–155 [hereafter *Defining Torts*] ["While the implied contract approach reflects a movement away from the harshness of the at-will rule, it by no means represents a rejection of the rule, since

23 A few recent cases, including *Shapiro v. Wells Fargo Realty Advisors*, supra, 152 Cal.App.3d 467, 199 Cal.Rptr. 613, can be interpreted to preclude enforcement of an implied-in-fact modification of an on-going employment agreement when some express written provision insists on the employee's at-will status. (See also *Crain v. Burroughs Corp.* (C.D.Cal.1983) 560 F.Supp. 849 [applying Cal. law]; *Crossen v. Foremost-McKesson, Inc.* (N.D.Cal.1982) 537 F.Supp. 107 [same].) This, however, is not such a case. The only two writings revealed by plaintiff's complaint—an agreement barring plaintiff's employment with a competitor, and one requiring his assignment of all computer-related information and innovations for one year after termination—are silent on permissible bases for discharge and arguably are consistent with both a promise not to terminate except for good cause under defendant's termination guidelines and defendant's acceptance of independent consideration to support such a promise.

it merely allows employees to rebut more easily the presumption that their employment is terminable at will" (fn. omitted)].) We see no sound reason to exempt the employment relationship from the ordinary rules of contract interpretation which permit proof of implied terms.

MONTGOMERY COUNTY HOSPITAL DISTRICT v. BROWN

965 S.W.2d 501 (Texas 1998).

HECHT, JUSTICE.

The principal issue before us is whether at-will employment can be modified by nothing more than an employer's oral assurances that an employee whose work is satisfactory will not be terminated without good cause. We hold that an employer's oral statements do not modify an employee's at-will status absent a definite, stated intention to the contrary. We conclude that the court of appeals improperly reversed the summary judgment for the employer in this case.

For ten years Valarie Brown was employed by the Montgomery County Hospital District as laboratory systems manager for Medical Center Hospital. After her employment terminated, Brown brought this action against the District and its president and vice president (collectively, "the District") for breach of oral and written contracts of employment and deprivation of property and liberty interests protected by the Texas Constitution. The district court granted summary judgment for the District. The circumstances surrounding the termination of Brown's employment, vigorously disputed by the parties, are largely irrelevant to the contract issues before us. Given the conflict in the summary judgment record, we accept as true Brown's assertion that she did not voluntarily resign but was fired without good cause. We assume that Brown is not estopped by acceptance of her severance pay to assert that she was wrongfully terminated. And we take Brown's word that:

> At the time I was hired as well as during my employment, I was told by [the Hospital administrator] that I would be able to keep my job at the Hospital as long as I was doing my job and that I would not be fired unless there was a good reason or good cause to fire me. This representation was important to me since I was

> going to have to relocate from Houston to the Conroe area if I accepted the position with the Hospital.

The court of appeals held . . . that fact questions subsisted concerning the existence of an oral employment contract, based on the hospital administrator's alleged assurances, that precluded summary judgment. The court also held that such a contract was not, as a matter of law, barred by the Statute of Frauds, Tex. Bus. & Com. Code § 26.01. Because the effect of an employer's oral assurances on at-will employment is an important and recurring issue, we granted the District's application for writ of error.

For well over a century, the general rule in this State, as in most American jurisdictions, has been that absent a specific agreement to the contrary, employment may be terminated by the employer or the employee at will, for good cause, bad cause, or no cause at all. The District argues that its assurances to Brown were too indefinite to constitute an agreement limiting the District's right to discharge Brown at will. We agree.

A promise, acceptance of which will form a contract, "is a manifestation of intention to act or refrain from acting in a specified way, so made as to justify a promisee in understanding that a commitment has been made." Restatement (Second) of Contracts § 2(1) (1981). General statements like those made to Brown simply do not justify the conclusion that the speaker intends by them to make a binding contract of employment. For such a contract to exist, the employer must unequivocally indicate a definite intent to be bound not to terminate the employee except under clearly specified circumstances. General comments that an employee will not be discharged as long as his work is satisfactory do not in themselves manifest such an intent. Neither do statements that an employee will be discharged only for "good reason" or "good cause" when there is no agreement on what those terms encompass. Without such agreement the employee cannot reasonably expect to limit the employer's right to terminate him. An employee who has no formal agreement with his employer cannot construct one out of indefinite comments, encouragements, or assurances.

. . . .

The District also argues that oral promises modifying employment at will are unenforceable under the Statute of Frauds. The District is correct only if the promises cannot be performed within one year. An employment contract for an indefinite term is considered performable within one year. It would be unusual, however, for oral assurances of employment for an indefinite term to be sufficiently specific and definite to modify an at-will relationship.

The concurring opinion "would imply a term of working-life duration into the District's alleged oral commitment to provide Brown job security, a period that clearly exceeded one year." *Post*, at 505. The record, however, does not support such an implication. Perhaps Brown, like most employees, hoped to work for the District as long as she wanted, and much longer than a year, but the concurrence cites no evidentiary support for the assertion that "the 'tenor and understanding' between the parties, if any, was that Brown would have many years of job security." *Post*, at 504. Even if a term can be supplied by implication, there is no basis for doing so in this case. The concurrence's reliance on *Schroeder v. Texas Iron Works, Inc.*, 813 S.W.2d 483, 489 (Tex.1991), to justify an implication is misplaced. In that case we simply accepted as true the plaintiff's allegations that his contract was to remain in effect for eight to ten years.

. . . .

Accordingly, the judgment of the court of appeals is reversed and judgment is rendered for the District.

GONZALEZ, JUSTICE, concurring.

The Court decides this case on the basis of lack of specificity and definiteness; however, the Court chooses to leave open the issue of whether more specific statements assuring job security can modify at-will contracts. Because the terms "good reason" and "good cause" lack a standardized meaning, but can mean different things in different contexts, I concur with the Court's judgment. Definiteness is but one element of contract formation that will be helpful in determining whether an agreement is sufficient to rebut the strong presumption of at-will employment. But even assuming that Brown's job assurances were specific and emphatic enough to show that the parties had the mutual intent and understanding necessary to create a contract, I would hold the contract void under the Statute of Frauds. *See* Tex. Bus. & Com. Code § 26.01 (making unenforceable an oral "agreement which is not to be performed within one year from the date of making the agreement"). This would more fully resolve whether oral statements of job security can ever trump the presumption that employment is at-will.

The Court holds that Brown's job assurances are not subject to the Statute of Frauds . . . . I disagree. While the *general* rule is that "where no period of performance is stated . . . the statute is inapplicable," this is true only if "there is nothing in the agreement itself to show that it cannot be performed within a year *according to the tenor and the understanding of the parties.*" *Bratcher*, 346 S.W.2d at 796; *Miller*, 517 S.W.2d at 776 (emphasis added). Our inquiry should not end simply because the contract was for an indefinite term. We should examine the understanding of the parties and the nature of the performance expected before deciding whether the agreement can be performed within a year.

The fact that the parties do not expressly state the term of performance is not determinative. It is settled law in this state that "where an oral contract omits the performance term, duration may properly be implied from extrinsic evidence." *Niday v. Niday*, 643 S.W.2d 919, 920 (Tex.1982) (per curiam); *see also Hall v. Hall*, 158 Tex. 95, 308 S.W.2d 12, 16 (1957) ("When the parties omit an express stipulation as to time, it is in accord with human experience and accepted standards of law for us to assume that they meant whatever term of days or years might be reasonable in the light of the circumstances before them at the date of the contract."). For summary judgment purposes, Brown's reliance upon the District's alleged assurances establishes that the "tenor and understanding" between the parties, if any, was that Brown would have many years of job security. Brown asserts an entitlement to her job that must be objectively understood as extending until she retired, quit, or died, provided there was no good reason or good cause to fire her.

This Court implied a term of working-life duration into a similar oral contract for job security. *See Schroeder v. Texas Iron Works, Inc.*, 813 S.W.2d 483 (Tex.1991). Schroeder sought assurances of job security from his supervisor because he was "about to build his home and 'did not want to just get it built or just moved in and get laid-off.' " *Id.* at 484. The supervisor assured him: "No, don't worry about that, go ahead and build it." *Id.* There was no mention in this oral exchange of any definite period of time. Nevertheless, we did not hesitate to imply a definite term of eight to ten years into this job security agreement, since Schroeder was 57 years old and hoped to live out his eventual retirement in the house he was building. *Id.* at 489. Because Schroeder expected more than one year of job security, we held that these oral assurances were void under the Statute of Frauds. *Id.*

In *Texas Iron Works*, we recognized Schroeder's expectation of long-term job security by noticing his residential concerns; likewise, Brown's residential concerns reveal that she had similar expectations of long-term job-security. Brown explains that "[t]his representation was important to me since I was going to have to relocate from Houston to the Conroe area if I accepted the position with the Hospital." Moreover, there is no evidence that Brown believed that the District's promise of job security was for one year or less. Consistent with *Schroeder*, I would imply a term of working-life duration into the District's alleged oral commitment to provide Brown job security, a period that clearly exceeded one year.

There were three contingencies which could have terminated Brown's employment within one year: Brown could have (1) died; (2) breached the contract by *not* performing at the level of a person of ordinary prudence; or (3) quit. However, none of these three contingencies removes the alleged contract from the operation of the Statute of Frauds.

In *Gilliam v. Kouchoucos*, 161 Tex. 299, 340 S.W.2d 27 (1960), this Court held that a provision of an oral contract of employment terminating the contract upon the death of the employee did not remove the contract from the operation of the Statute of Frauds. We noted that the Statute of Frauds "has application only to contracts which are terminated *by performance*, and does not apply to contracts which may be terminated within a year by some means other than performance." *Id.* at 28. Death, we explained, is not performance, but instead excusable nonperformance. *Id.* at 29.

This reasoning is equally applicable to termination by breach. Although it was possible for Brown to discontinue "doing her job" within one year of the alleged agreement, such a contingency would constitute nonperformance and would not save the contract from the operation of the Statute of Frauds. *See Collins v. Allied Pharmacy Mgt., Inc.*, 871 S.W.2d 929, 934 (Tex. App.—Houston [14th Dist.] 1994, no writ) ("[F]or a contract to fall outside the statute of frauds, *performance* must be possible within one year; termination for cause is not equivalent to *performance* of the contract.").

Likewise, it was possible for Brown to quit her job within one year of the alleged agreement; but by quitting, Brown would have simply exercised her unilateral right to discharge the District of its obligation to retain her. Quitting constitutes a *release*, not a *performance* of an employment contract. As we explained in *Gilliam*, "[c]ontracts for service for more than a year [terminable] at the election of a party upon the happening of some event, or even at the mere will of a party, have generally been held to be within the statute." 340 S.W.2d at 29 (quoting *Marble v. Clinton*, 298 Mass. 87, 9 N.E.2d 522, 524 (1937)).

Although the Court held that the Statute of Frauds did not apply to the oral employment contracts in both *Miller* and *Bratcher*, those cases concerned the enforcement of oral compensation agreements, not promises of future job security. In both cases the employer was free to terminate the employee at any time and for any reason, provided it compensated the employee for work done up until the time of termination. Accordingly, in both cases the employer and employee were capable of completely performing their respective obligations within a year, and therefore *Miller* and *Bratcher* do not apply to Brown's alleged agreement.

In summary, I would hold that even if the District's alleged oral agreement with Brown formed a contract, it would be subject to the Statute of Frauds. This would settle the issue we left open in *Goodyear Tire and Rubber Co. v. Portilla*, 879 S.W.2d 47, 52 n. 8 (Tex.1994), of whether oral statements assuring job security can modify employment-at-will contracts. Because a promise not to terminate employment except for good cause cannot be performed within one year, but can only be terminated by the promisee's death, breach, or release, the promise is not enforceable unless it is in writing.

QUESTIONS

1. Compare the different approaches taken in *Foley* and *Brown* regarding the statute of frauds issue. Which approach is more persuasive?
2. What does the majority in *Brown* mean when it says, "It would be unusual, however, for oral assurances of employment for an indefinite term to be sufficiently specific and definite to modify an at-will relationship."?
3. In *Brown,* the concurring judge argues that an oral agreement regarding compensation is not within the statute of frauds, but an oral agreement providing for a "just cause" termination of employment is within the statute. Does this distinction make sense?

Problem 8-1

Pat Grun worked for BNI for 14 years. During this time she received stellar reviews by her supervisors, was constantly assured that she would continue to rise in the organization, and the firm followed progressive discipline guidelines issued by the Human Resources department. In November, BNI announced a series of layoffs related to a general economic downturn and a drop in demand for its products. Grun sued, arguing that her dismissal was contrary to an implied-in-fact contract that she would be judged on her merits.

The trial judge found that Grun's longevity, promotions, raises, and favorable performance reviews, together with BNI's written progressive discipline policy and BNI officials' statement of company practices, raised a triable issue that Grun had an implied-in-fact contract to be dismissed only for good cause. Grun offered some evidence that BNI closed several departments on the false ground of declining demand, when in fact it wished to avoid applying the company's procedures to each individual employee.

The question presented on appeal is whether long, successful service, standing alone, can demonstrate an implied-in-fact contract right not to be terminated at-will. Grun claims no particular actions or communications by BNI that altered the at-will rule. Develop the arguments in support of Grun and anticipate the objections.

2. Using Express Contracts to Reinforce the At-Will Rule

As contract theories developed for overcoming the at-will rule, employers began creating express contracts as a way to ensure that the relationship was at-will. The following case reveals how employers use written contracts and the parol evidence rule, to avoid claims that the at-will presumption has been overcome through express promises or by implication.

Broyles v. J.P. Morgan Chase & Co.

2010 WL 815123 (S.D.N.Y. 2010).

William H. Pauley III, District Judge.

BACKGROUND

On September 20, 2007, Foster Smith ("Smith"), the managing director of JPMorgan's global commodities group, offered Broyles a position as a commodities trader on the natural gas desk. Broyles claims that Smith's offer included a bonus based on a percentage of Broyles' trading profits. Memorializing his offer, Smith emailed Human Resources noting that he "communicated E[xecutive] D[irector] title w/ 150k base. No guarantee." (56.1 Stmt. Ex. 4: Email from Foster J. Smith to Patricia Dever dated Sept. 20, 2007.)

JPMorgan sent a formal offer letter to Broyles which he signed, dated, and returned (the "Offer Letter"). The Offer Letter provided that Broyles's annual salary would be $150,000, and included the following conditions:

> This letter contains the entire understanding of the parties with respect to the terms and conditions of the offer of employment and supersedes any prior verbal or written communication. This offer may only be modified in a document signed by the parties referring specifically to this offer.
>
> You will be eligible to participate in the current Investment Bank Incentive Plan . . . while in effect, or any applicable successor Incentive Plan then in effect. The payment and amount of any incentive compensation award under the Incentive Plan is in the complete discretion of the firm. Subject to your being actively employed as of the date of payout, you will be eligible under the Incentive Plan to receive an annual incentive bonus which is intended to motivate future performance, and which may be based on individual achievement, business unit and overall corporate results and awarded under the terms of the Plan and in our sole discretion.
>
> You must be actively employed by the firm on the date that annual incentive compensation is awarded to be eligible for any incentive compensation. If your employment terminates for any

> reason before the award date, whether the termination is initiated by you or the firm you will not earn or receive any award. . . . No employee or officer of the firm is authorized to make any oral promises to you about an incentive compensation award.
>
> Your offer of employment is subject to the terms and conditions outlined in the accompanying Attachment of the same date (which is incorporated into and made part of this offer letter) and all policies and procedures of JPMorgan, including but not limited to the Code of Conduct and the "employment at-will" doctrine.

On December 31, 2007, Broyles's trading profits exceeded $23 million. However, beginning January 2, 2008, his portfolio experienced significant losses. In the three trading days that week, Broyles lost $3.6 million. His portfolio's losses accelerated the following week. On Wednesday, January 9, Broyles lost nearly $2.2 million, twice as much as on January 8. As the losses mounted, Smith tried to reach Broyles on the morning of January 10. However, Broyles did not arrive at the office until after noon time and his portfolio lost more than $5.2 million that day. During the week of January 7, Broyles' portfolio lost more than $12.6 million.

On January 16, Broyles endeavored to explain his late arrival on January 10 and his attempts to mitigate the losses. The next day, Smith advised Broyles that his employment would be terminated if he did not resign and that, in any event, he would not receive an incentive compensation award for 2007. On January 18, Broyles advised Smith that he would "resign but . . . effectively consider this a termination." Between January 14 and January 16, Broyles's portfolio lost an additional $6.9 million. JPMorgan did not pay Broyles any incentive compensation for 2007.

DISCUSSION

. . . .

II. *Contract Claims*

The four elements of a breach of contract claim are: (1) the existence of a valid contract, (2) plaintiff's performance of the contract, (3) defendant's material breach of the contract, and (4) resulting damages. Under New York law, "when the parties to a contract have memorialized their agreement in a writing which purports to be a complete and accurate integration, i.e., which embodies all of the mutual rights and obligations of the parties, the

Court will exclude evidence of prior or contemporaneous agreements which would vary the terms of the written instrument."

Broyles claims breach of an oral contract. However, the Offer Letter states that it "contains the entire understanding of the parties with respect to the terms and conditions of the offer of employment and supersedes any prior verbal or written communication." If the Offer Letter is valid, it precludes any claim for breach of an oral agreement.

. . . .

The terms of the Offer Letter are clear. They constitute "the entire understanding of the parties with respect to the terms and conditions of the offer of employment and supersede [ ] any prior verbal or written communication." Even if an oral understanding had been reached during the September 20 conversation, the Offer Letter—signed by Broyles a few days later—superseded it. Moreover, Broyles does not allege that he received any written commitment from JPMorgan regarding a 2007 incentive award. Consequently, the breach of an oral agreement claim must be dismissed.

III. *Quasi-Contract Claims*

"The existence of a valid and enforceable written contract governing a particular subject matter ordinarily precludes recovery in quasi contract for events arising out of the same subject matter. . . . A 'quasi contract' only applies in the absence of an express agreement, and is not really a contract at all, but rather a legal obligation imposed in order to prevent a party's unjust enrichment. . . ." *Clark-Fitzpatrick, Inc. v. Long Island R.R. Co.*, 70 N.Y.2d 382, 388 (N.Y.1987): *see also Beth Israel Med. Ctr. v. Horizon Blue Cross & Blue Shield of N.J., Inc.*, 448 F.3d 573, 587 (2d Cir.2006) ("It is impermissible . . . to seek damages in an action sounding in quasi contract where the suing party has fully performed on a valid written agreement, the existence of which is undisputed, and the scope of which clearly covers the dispute between the parties."); *BroadVision Inc. v. Gen. Elec. Co.*, No. 08 Civ. 1478(WHP), 2009 WL 2603145, at *3 (S.D .N.Y. Aug. 13, 2009) (("[a] contract cannot be implied in fact where there is an express contract covering the subject matter involved.") (citing *Julien J. Studley, Inc. v. N.Y. News, Inc.*, 512 N.E.2d 300, 301 (N.Y.1987)). Here, a valid written agreement governed the relationship between JPMorgan and Broyles. That contract disposes of Broyles's quasi-contract claims of *quantum meruit*, unjust enrichment, implied-in-fact contract, and promissory estoppel.

. . . .

For the foregoing reasons, JPMorgan's motion for summary judgment is granted, and this action is dismissed.

QUESTIONS

1. Would the result change if the employer had not issued the Offer Letter?
2. Would you advise your employer clients always to enter into an express written contract with their employees in order to reaffirm the right to terminate at-will? What problems might this cause? Are there other terms of the relationship that employers may want to memorialize in an express written contract?

---

3. Promissory Estoppel

In the absence of a contract, whether express or implied, an employee can assert that the employer made a promise that induced a reasonable action or forbearance on the part of the employee. One interesting scenario occurs when an employer makes a promise of employment but then rescinds before the employee can begin work. Consider the following case as a basis to think through the use of promissory estoppel when the promised relationship is at-will.

Goff-Hamel v. Obstetricians & Gynecologists, P.C.

588 N.W.2d 798 (Neb. 1999).

Wright, J.

NATURE OF CASE

Julie Goff-Hamel brought this action against Obstetricians & Gynecologists, P.C. (Obstetricians), seeking damages for breach of an alleged oral employment contract or, in the alternative, damages for detrimental reliance on a promise of employment. The trial court granted summary judgment in favor of Obstetricians, and Goff-Hamel appeals.

. . . .

FACTS

Goff-Hamel worked for Hastings Family Planning for 11 years. Prior to leaving Hastings Family Planning, Goff-Hamel was earning $24,000 plus the following benefits: 6 weeks' paid maternity leave, 6 weeks' vacation, 12 paid holidays, 12 sick days, an educational reimbursement, and medical and dental insurance coverage.

In July 1993, Goff-Hamel met with representatives of Obstetricians regarding the possibility of employment. Present at the meeting were Janet Quackenbush, the office manager; Dr. George Adam, a part owner of Obstetricians; and Larry Draper, a consultant of Obstetricians involved in personnel decisions. Adam had approached Goff-Hamel in June 1993 about working for him as a patient relations and outreach coordinator at Obstetricians. Goff-Hamel initially declined the offer, explaining that she had made commitments to do some training in the fall and to hire and help train a new bookkeeper. Adam spoke to Goff-Hamel approximately 1 month later, asking her to reconsider and whether she was ready to "jump ship and come work for him." Goff-Hamel told Adam she would be interested in hearing some details, and an interview was set for July 27 at Adam's office.

At the meeting, Adam represented to Goff-Hamel that the position would be full time and would start at a salary of $10 per hour and that she would be provided 2 weeks' paid vacation, three or four paid holidays, uniforms, and an educational stipend. A retirement plan would start after the end of the second year, retroactive to the end of the first year. The job would not provide health insurance.

Goff-Hamel was offered a job with Obstetricians during the July 27, 1993, meeting, and she accepted the job offer at that time. She expressed concern that she be given time to finish some projects at Hastings Family Planning, and it was agreed that she would start her employment on October 4. Goff-Hamel gave notice to Hastings Family Planning in August, informing them that she would be resigning to take a job with Obstetricians.

Subsequently, Goff-Hamel went to Obstetricians' office and was provided with uniforms for her job. She was given a copy of her schedule for the first week of work, but did not receive a copy of the employee handbook.

On October 3, 1993, Goff-Hamel was told by Draper that she should not report to work the next morning as had been planned. Draper told her that Janel Foote, the wife of a part owner of Obstetricians, Dr. Terry Foote, opposed the hiring of Goff-Hamel.

The trial court found that there were no facts in dispute and that Goff-Hamel had not turned down any other employment opportunities between July and October 1993. The court found that she had terminated her employment at Hastings Family Planning in reliance on an offer of employment from Obstetricians; however, the prospective employment agreement was not for a specific term of employment. The court noted that Goff-Hamel sought replacement employment, but was unable to obtain employment until April 1995, when she was employed part time at the rate of $11 per hour.

The trial court concluded that since Goff-Hamel was to be employed at will, her employment could be terminated at any time, including before she began working. The court concluded that under either contract law or promissory estoppel, Obstetricians was entitled to a judgment as a matter of law.

. . . .

ANALYSIS

In sustaining Obstetricians' motion for summary judgment, the trial court concluded as a matter of law that since Goff-Hamel's employment could have been terminated after 1 day without Obstetricians incurring liability, logic dictated that her employment could also be terminated before it started without liability.

It is undisputed that on July 27, 1993, Obstetricians offered Goff-Hamel employment and that she accepted. The oral agreement did not specify that the employment was for a definite period. We have consistently held that when employment is not for a definite term and there are no contractual, statutory, or constitutional restrictions upon the right of discharge, an employer may lawfully discharge an employee whenever and for whatever cause it chooses. Therefore, the trial court correctly determined as a matter of law that Goff-Hamel could not bring a claim for breach of an employment contract.

Goff-Hamel's second cause of action was based upon promissory estoppel. " '[T]he development of the law of promissory estoppel "is an attempt by the courts to keep remedies abreast of increased moral consciousness of honesty and fair representations in all business dealings." ' " *Rosnick v. Dinsmore*, 235 Neb. 738, 751, 457 N.W.2d 793, 801 (1990).

Promissory estoppel provides for damages as justice requires and does not attempt to provide the plaintiff damages based upon the benefit of the bargain. *Id.* It requires only that reliance be reasonable and foreseeable. It does not impose the requirement that the promise giving rise to the cause of action must be so comprehensive in scope as to meet the requirements of an offer that would ripen into a contract if accepted by the promisee.

We have not specifically addressed whether promissory estoppel may be asserted as the basis for a cause of action for detrimental reliance upon a promise of at-will employment. In *Merrick v. Thomas*, 246 Neb. 658, 522 N.W.2d 402 (1994), the employee was terminated from her job approximately 4 months after she had been hired. We determined that because the employee had worked for a time, the employer had kept his promise to employ the plaintiff and that promissory estoppel was not available. We did not consider whether a cause of action based upon promissory estoppel could be stated by a prospective at-will employee who had been induced to leave previous gainful employment based upon the promise of other employment, but who did not commence employment at the new job.

Other jurisdictions which have addressed the question of whether a cause of action for promissory estoppel can be stated in the context of a prospective at-will employee are split on the issue. Some have held that an employee can recover damages incurred as a result of resigning from the former at-will employment in reliance on a promise of other at-will employment. They have determined that when a prospective employer knows or should know that a promise of employment will induce an employee to leave his or her current job, such employer shall be liable for the reliant's damages. Recognizing that both the prospective new employer and the prior employer could have fired the employee without cause at any time, they have concluded that the employee would have continued to work in his or her prior employment if it were not for the offer by the prospective employer. Although damages have not been allowed for wages lost from the prospective at-will employment, damages have been allowed based upon wages from the prior employment and other damages incurred in reliance on the job offer.

In contrast, other jurisdictions have held as a matter of law that a prospective employee cannot recover damages incurred in reliance on an unfulfilled promise of at-will employment, concluding that reliance on a promise consisting solely of at-will employment is unreasonable as a matter of law because the employee should know that the promised employment could be terminated by the employer at any time for any reason without liability. These courts have stated that an anomalous result occurs when recovery is allowed for an employee who has not begun work, when the same employee's job could be terminated without liability 1 day after beginning work.

. . . .

Holding

Having reviewed and considered decisions from other jurisdictions, we conclude under the facts of this case that promissory estoppel can be asserted in connection with the offer of at-will employment and that the trial court erred in granting Obstetricians summary judgment. A cause of action for promissory estoppel is based upon a promise which the promisor should reasonably expect to induce action or forbearance on the part of the promisee which does in fact induce such action or forbearance. Here, promissory estoppel is appropriate where Goff-Hamel acted to her detriment in order to avail herself of the promised employment.

. . . .

Stephan, J., dissenting.

I respectfully dissent. In my opinion, the district court correctly determined as a matter of law that Goff-Hamel could not proceed under either a breach of contract or a promissory estoppel theory of recovery. I cannot reconcile the result reached by the majority or its rationale with our firmly established legal principles governing at-will employment. As succinctly and, in my view, correctly stated by the district court: "Since plaintiff could have been terminated after one day's employment without the defendant incurring liability, logic dictates she could also be terminated before the employment started."

. . . .

. . . Suppose plaintiff in this case had not been told not to report to work. Instead, suppose plaintiff packed his belongings, sold his house, and moved himself and his family to a new location to commence employment with defendant. After working one day, plaintiff is discharged. The plaintiff in this example would be denied recovery altogether, although he incurred considerably more "reliance" damages than were alleged by the plaintiff in the case at bar, who, under *Bower*, would be allowed to recover.

. . . .

The conflict between the court's decision today and the law of at-will employment is further demonstrated by the manner in which the majority addresses the issue of damages. Goff-Hamel's damage claim is based entirely upon her allegation that after learning on October 3, 1993, that appellee had withdrawn its offer of employment, she was unable to find "comparable" full-time employment until May 15, 1995. The majority acknowledges that under the theory of recovery which it recognizes in this case, damages cannot be "based upon the wages the employee would have earned in the prospective employment because the employment was terminable at will." Following the same logic, damages based upon wage loss during any *interval* between withdrawal of a promise of at-will employment and the securing of "comparable" employment would not be recoverable, because the promised employment could have been terminated by either party at any time after it had begun. Thus, the record reflects no factual basis upon which damages claimed by Goff-Hamel could be awarded under the remedy which the majority recognizes.

I would follow what I consider to be the better reasoned view, that promissory estoppel may not be utilized to remedy an unfulfilled promise of at-will employment. I acknowledge that this reasoning would produce a seemingly harsh result from the perspective of Goff-Hamel under the facts of this case, but to some degree, this is inherent in the concept of at-will employment. For example, in *Hamersky v. Nicholson Supply Co.*, 246 Neb. 156, 158, 517 N.W.2d 382, 385 (1994), a 22-year employee was discharged " 'without any notification, cause or reason,' " and although this action may seem harsh, we held that it was permissible where there was no contractual provision for employment of specific duration. Similarly, an employer which has made a significant expenditure in training an at-will employee may feel harshly treated if, upon completing the training, the employee immediately utilizes his or her newly acquired skills to secure more remunerative employment with a competitor. If the law of at-will employment were regularly bent to circumvent what some may consider a harsh result in a particular case, its path would soon become hopelessly circuitous and impossible to follow.

Employment for a specific duration imposes certain benefits and burdens upon each party to the relationship. Under our established law, parties wishing to create such a relationship must do so by contract. Where, as in this case, the parties have not chosen to impose contractual obligations upon themselves, it is my view that a court should not utilize the principle of promissory estoppel to impose the subjective expectations of either party upon the other. I agree with the view that in the context of an employment relationship, promissory estoppel "should be construed 'in such a way that it compl[e]ments, rather than undermines, traditional contract principles.' " *White v. Roche Biomedical Laboratories, Inc.*, 807 F.Supp. at 1220, quoting *Blanton Enterprises, Inc. v. Burger King Corp.*, 680 F.Supp. 753 (D.S.C.1988). In my opinion, the majority has done just the opposite in this case.

For these reasons, I would affirm the judgment of the district court.

QUESTION

1. Is the dissenting judge necessarily correct that there could be no recovery if the plaintiff arrived in town and worked for one day before she was fired? Develop the argument that promissory estoppel can protect the plaintiff in such a situation.

Mastery Problem 8-1

Don Ohlms began working for Value Rent-a-Car Boston office in 1997. He was promoted to Area Manager, then District Manager in New York, and ultimately to Northwest Regional Manager based in San Francisco. His region consistently outperformed other regions and he received stellar performance reviews. In 2010, the Northeast Region was underperforming significantly, and the CEO asked Ohlms to move back to New York to serve as the Regional Manager for the Northeast.

Ohlms was reluctant to move for several reasons. First, he had built a very cohesive team. Second, he and his family enjoyed living in the Bay Area. Third, he was wary of the brutal politics in the Northeast Region. The CEO repeatedly called Ohlms to make his case. He assured Ohlms that if the switch didn't work out he could return to his position in San Francisco, and that Ohlms would always have a place at Value as long as he didn't "completely screw up," given his long track record of success. While Ohlms was considering the deal, the CEO promised to pay Ohlms a six month severance package if things didn't work out for any reason.

After he moved to New York, Ohlms received a form from Human Resources that he was required to sign before receiving his relocation expense reimbursement. He completed the blanks on the form and signed it. The reimbursement form signed by Ohlms included the following among a page of "standard terms."

> I also acknowledge that nothing contained herein or in connection with the change in my position at Value shall be deemed to constitute an obligation on the part of Value to employee me for any period of time, and both Value and I can terminate my employment at will.
>
> There are no other agreements or understandings with respect to my change in position with Value or the moving of my residence except as is set forth herein, and these undertakings cannot be modified or altered except by a writing signed by me and Value.

Ohlms does not recall reading the form, and assumed that the written terms simply referred to the details of his relocation reimbursement.

After eight months, Ohlms decided that he had made a mistake. He requested a transfer back to the Northwest Region. When the CEO indicated that would not be possible, Ohlms demanded that he be permitted to move back and refused to stay in the Northeast. One month later he was terminated without any severance pay. After a year, he was able to secure employment for another rental car company at an annual compensation package that was $30,000 less per year than with Value. Ohlms seeks lost wages for the rest of his working career. Develop the arguments that support his claim, and anticipate the responses.

Conclusion

The at-will rule is a default provision that can be displaced by express or implied agreements, or with theories of unjust enrichment (quantum meruit) or promissory estoppel. Employers often choose to use express contracts to carefully define the employment relationship and to avoid implication that the at-will rule has been altered.

Lesson 9:
The Handbook

Objectives and Expected Learning Outcomes

In this Lesson, you will learn about the legal effects of employer handbooks in the workplace. Using ordinary contract principles, courts have found that the employer is contractually obligated to follow the policies it sets forth in its handbook, including termination provisions that appear to modify the at-will rule. Finally, we will consider the proper role of handbooks in the contemporary workplace.

Employee handbooks are a fixture of the American workplace. Employers use them as an efficient way to describe the employee's terms and conditions of employment, and for convenient reference by both managers and workers. Handbooks also are used as a means of communicating the employer's philosophy, goals, and vision. Handbooks became prevalent as the increasing number of employment-related laws required employers to arrange the workplace in certain ways and to ensure uniform, non-discriminatory procedures are followed.

In the 1970s and 1980s, plaintiffs lawyers sought a means of ameliorating the harsh effects of the at-will rule in cases where employees claimed they were terminated unfairly. Because many employee handbooks at the time included provisions that provided for progressive discipline and some manner of due process before termination of employment, creative lawyers argued that handbook terms were binding, contractual commitments by the employer that displaced the at-will rule. Courts were receptive to these arguments, and started subscribing to the growing trend to question the at-will rule. Juries, too, were receptive and began returning verdicts for breach of contract in cases where the terminations did not adhere strictly to the procedures and principles described in the handbook regarding when an employee could be terminated.

These issues are all the more important in the digital age. Employee handbooks are rarely paper documents, but instead are made accessible on an intranet as digital documents. Additionally, the employer can now communicate with employees as a group in many ways: email, texting, websites, etc. You should pay particular attention to how the legal principles we discuss will play out in the digital age.

We begin by considering the application of contract doctrine to employee handbooks, the response by employers to this encroachment on the at-will rule, and then finally consider the role of handbooks in the modern workplace. Should employers primarily use handbooks to limit their potential obligations to employees, or are there countervailing purposes that can be served?

QUESTION

1. Recall the various jobs you have held. Did the employer provide you with access to a handbook? Was it a paper document or an electronic document? Did you read the handbook? Did you ever refer to the handbook? Why did your employer provide a handbook?

---

1. Employee Handbooks as Contracts

The at-will rule is a default rule. Employers are free to agree to displace the at-will rule through contract. After termination of their employment, employees began to argue that failure of the employer to adhere to the procedures and standards outlined in the handbook constituted a breach of contract. You will recall the basic requirements of a contract: offer, acceptance, and consideration. Does the distribution of an employee handbook to the workforce meet this test?

Woolley v. Hoffman-La Roche, Inc.

491 A.2d 1257 (N.J. 1983).

Wilentz, C.J.

[Editor's Note: After Woolley was fired he sued Hoffman, alleging that it failed to follow the procedures for termination that were in the Hoffman employment handbook.]

The at-will rule has come under severe criticism from commentators who argue that the economic justifications for the development of the rule have changed dramatically and no longer support its harshness. . .

. . . .

Commentators have questioned the compatibility of the traditional at will doctrine with the realities of modern economics and employment practices. . . . The common law rule has been modified by the enactment of labor relations legislation. . . . The National Labor Relations Act and other labor legislation illustrate the governmental policy of preventing employers from using the right of discharge as a means of oppression. . . . Consistent with this policy, many states have recognized the need to protect employees who are not parties to a collective bargaining agreement or other contract from abusive practices by the employer.

. . . .

This Court has long recognized the capacity of the common law to develop and adapt to current needs. . . . The interests of employees, employers, and the public lead to the conclusion that the common law of New Jersey should limit the right of an employer to fire an employee at will.

. . . .

In recognizing a cause of action to provide a remedy for employees who are wrongfully discharged, we must balance the interests of the employee, the employer, and the public. Employees have an interest in knowing they will not be discharged for exercising their legal rights. Employers have an interest in knowing that they can run their businesses as they see fit as long as their conduct is consistent with public policy. The public has an interest in employment stability and in discouraging frivolous lawsuits by dissatisfied employees.

The spirit of this language foreshadows a different approach to these questions. No longer is there the unquestioned deference to the interests of the employer and the almost invariable dismissal of the contentions of the employee. Instead, as Justice Pollock so effectively demonstrated, this Court was no longer willing to decide these questions without examining the underlying interests involved, both the employer's and the employees', as well as the public interest, and the extent to which our deference to one or the other served or disserved the needs of society as presently understood.

In the last century, the common law developed in a laissez-faire climate that encouraged industrial growth and approved the right of an employer to control his own business, including the right to fire without cause an employee at will. . . . The twentieth century has witnessed significant changes in socioeconomic values that have led to reassessment of the common law rule. Businesses have evolved from small and medium size firms to gigantic corporations in which ownership is separate from management. Formerly there was a clear delineation between employers, who frequently were owners of their own businesses, and employees. The employer in the old sense has been replaced by a superior in the corporate hierarchy who is himself an employee. We are a nation of employees. Growth in the number of employees has been accompanied by increasing recognition of the need for stability in labor relations.

. . . .

What is before us in this case is not a special contract with a particular employee, but a general agreement covering all employees. There is no reason to treat such a document with hostility.

. . . .

A policy manual that provides for job security grants an important, fundamental protection for workers. . . . If such a commitment is indeed made, obviously an employer should be required to honor it. When such a document, purporting to give job security, is distributed by the employer to a workforce, substantial injustice may result if that promise is broken.

We do not believe that Hoffmann-La Roche was attempting to renege on its promise when it fired Woolley. On the contrary, the record strongly suggests that even though it believed its manual did not create any contractually binding agreements, Hoffmann-La Roche nevertheless almost invariably honored it. In effect, it gave employees more than it believed the law required. Its position taken before us is one of principle: while contending it treated Woolley fairly, it maintains it had no legal obligation to do so.

Given the facts before us and the common law of contracts interpreted in the light of sound policy applicable to this modern setting, we conclude that the termination clauses of this company's Personnel Policy Manual, including the procedure required before termination occurs, could be found to be contractually enforceable. Furthermore, we conclude that when an employer of a substantial number of employees circulates a manual that, when fairly read, provides that certain benefits are an incident of the employment (including, especially, job security provisions), the judiciary, instead of "grudgingly" conceding the enforceability of those provisions,

. . . should construe them in accordance with the reasonable expectations of the employees.

The employer's contention here is that the distribution of the manual was simply an expression of the company's "philosophy" and therefore free of any possible contractual consequences. The former employee claims it could reasonably be read as an explicit statement of company policies intended to be followed by the company in the same manner as if they were expressed in an agreement signed by both employer and employees. From the analysis that follows we conclude that a jury, properly instructed, could find, in strict contract terms, that the manual constituted an offer; put differently, it could find that this portion of the manual (concerning job security) set forth terms and conditions of employment.

In determining the manual's meaning and effect, we must consider the probable context in which it was disseminated and the environment surrounding its continued existence. The manual, though apparently not distributed to all employees ("in general, distribution will be provided to supervisory personnel . . ."), covers all of them. Its terms are of such importance to all employees that in the absence of contradicting evidence, it would seem clear that it was intended by Hoffmann-La Roche that all employees be advised of the benefits it confers.

We take judicial notice of the fact that Hoffmann-La Roche is a substantial company with many employees in New Jersey. The record permits the conclusion that the policy manual represents the most reliable statement of the terms of their employment. At oral argument counsel conceded that it is rare for any employee, except one on the medical staff, to have a special contract. Without minimizing the importance of its specific provisions, the context of the manual's preparation and distribution is, to us, the most persuasive proof that it would be almost inevitable for an employee to regard it as a binding commitment, legally enforceable, concerning the terms and conditions of his employment. Having been employed, like hundreds of his co-employees, without any individual employment contract, by an employer whose good reputation made it so attractive, the employee is given this one document that purports to set forth the terms and conditions of his employment, a document obviously carefully prepared by the company with all of the appearances of corporate legitimacy that one could imagine. If there were any doubt about it (and there would be none in the mind of most employees), the name of the manual dispels it, for it is nothing short of the official policy of the company, it is the Personnel Policy Manual. As every employee knows, when superiors tell you "it's company policy," they mean business.

The mere fact of the manual's distribution suggests its importance. Its changeability—the uncontroverted ability of management to change its terms—is argued as supporting its non-binding quality, but one might as easily conclude that, given its importance, the employer wanted to keep it up to date, especially to make certain, given this employer's good reputation in labor relations, that the benefits conferred were sufficiently competitive with those available from other employers, including benefits found in collective bargaining agreements. The record suggests that the changes actually made almost always favored the employees.

Given that background, then, unless the language contained in the manual were such that no one could reasonably have thought it was intended to create legally binding obligations, the termination provisions of the policy manual would have to be regarded as an obligation undertaken by the employer. It will not do now for the company to say it did not mean the things it said in its manual to be binding. Our courts will not allow an employer to offer attractive inducements and benefits to the workforce and then withdraw them when it chooses, no matter how sincere its belief that they are not enforceable.

Whatever else the manual may deal with (as noted above, we do not have the entire manual before us), one of its major provisions deals with the single most important objective of the workforce: job security. The reasons for giving such provisions binding force are particularly persuasive. Wages, promotions, conditions of work, hours of work, all of those take second place to job security, for without that all other benefits are vulnerable.

We are dependent upon others for our means of livelihood, and most of our people have become completely dependent upon wages. If they lose their jobs they lose every resource, except for the relief supplied by the various forms of social security. Such dependence of the mass of the people upon others for all of their income is something new in the world. For our generation, the substance of life is in another man's hands.

Job security is the assurance that one's livelihood, one's family's future, will not be destroyed arbitrarily; it can be cut off only "for good cause," fairly determined. Hoffmann-La Roche's commitment here was to what working men and women regard as their most basic advance. It was a commitment that gave workers protection against arbitrary termination.

Many of these workers undoubtedly know little about contracts, and many probably would be unable to analyze the language and terms of the manual. Whatever Hoffmann-La Roche may have intended, that which was read by its employees was a promise not to fire them except for cause.

. . . .

Having concluded that a jury could find the Personnel Policy Manual to constitute an offer, we deal with what most cases deem the major obstacle to construction of the terms as constituting a binding agreement, namely, the requirement under contract law that consideration must be given in exchange for the employer's offer in order to convert that offer into a binding agreement. The cases on this subject deal with such issues as whether there was a promise in return for the employer's promise (the offer contained in the manual constituting, in effect, a promise), or whether there was some benefit or detriment bargained for and in fact conferred or suffered, sufficient to create a unilateral contract; whether the action or inaction, the benefit or the detriment, was done or not done in reliance on the employer's offer or promise; whether the alleged agreement was so lacking in "mutuality" as to be insufficient for contractual purposes—in other words, whether the fundamental requirements of a contract have been met.

We conclude that these job security provisions contained in a personnel policy manual widely distributed among a large workforce are supported by consideration and may therefore be enforced as a binding commitment of the employer. Holding

In order for an offer in the form of a promise to become enforceable, it must be accepted. Acceptance will depend on what the promisor bargained for: he may have bargained for a return promise that, if given, would result in a bilateral contract, both promises becoming enforceable. Or he may have bargained for some action or nonaction that, if given or withheld, would render his promise enforceable as a unilateral contract. In most of the cases involving an employer's personnel policy manual, the document is prepared without any negotiations and is voluntarily distributed to the workforce by the employer. It seeks no return promise from the employees. It is reasonable to interpret it as seeking continued work from the employees, who, in most cases, are free to quit since they are almost always employees at will, not simply in the sense that the employer can fire them without cause, but in the sense that they can quit without breaching any obligation. Thus analyzed, the manual is an offer that seeks the formation of a unilateral contract—the employees' bargained-for action needed to make the offer binding being their continued work when they have no obligation to continue.

The unilateral contract analysis is perfectly adequate for that employee who was aware of the manual and who continued to work intending that continuation to be the action in exchange for the employer's promise; it is even more helpful in support of that conclusion if, but for the employer's policy manual, the employee would have quit. See generally M. Petit, "*Modern Unilateral Contracts*," 63 B.U.L.Rev. 551 (1983) (judicial use of unilateral contract analysis in employment cases is widespread).

Those solutions seem to be technically correct. Among the cases holding that the document in question satisfied technical contractual requirements are *Toussaint, supra*, 408 Mich. 579, 292 N.W.2d 880. . . . In *Toussaint* one main issue was the contractual force of an oral assurance given to the employee when he was hired that he would not be discharged so long as he was "doing his job." In addition to that assurance, Toussaint was at the same time handed a manual, which provided that an employee would not be discharged without cause and without following certain procedures. The court noted in dictum that the oral assurance was not necessary to its holding. The court's discussion of the effect of distributing a manual is worth noting:

> While an employer need not establish personnel policies or practices, where an employer chooses to establish such policies and practices and makes them known to its employees, the employment relationship is presumably enhanced. The employer secures an orderly, cooperative and loyal work force, and the employee the peace of mind associated with job security and the conviction that he will be treated fairly. No pre-employment negotiations need take place and the parties' minds need not meet on the subject; nor does it matter that the employee knows nothing of the particulars of the employer's policies and practices or that the employer may change them unilaterally. It is enough that the employer chooses, presumably in its own interest, to create an environment in which the employee believes that, whatever, the personnel policies and practices, they are established and official

> at any given time, purport to be fair, and are applied consistently and uniformly to each employee. The employer has then created a situation "instinct with an obligation."

. . . .

Defendant expresses some concern that our interpretation will encourage lawsuits by disgruntled employees. As we view it, however, if the employer has in fact agreed to provide job security, plaintiffs in lawsuits to enforce that agreement should not be regarded as disgruntled employees, but rather as employees pursuing what is rightfully theirs. The solution is not deprivation of the employees' claim, but enforcement of the employer's agreement. The defendant further contends that its future plans and proposed projects are premised on continuance of the at-will employment status of its workforce. We find this argument unpersuasive. There are many companies whose employees have job security who are quite able to plan their future and implement those plans. If, however, the at-will employment status of the workforce was so important, the employer should not have circulated a document so likely to lead employees into believing they had job security.

. . . .

Our opinion need not make employers reluctant to prepare and distribute company policy manuals. Such manuals can be very helpful tools in labor relations, helpful both to employer and employees, and we would regret it if the consequence of this decision were that the constructive aspects of these manuals were in any way diminished. We do not believe that they will, or at least we certainly do not believe that that constructive aspect *should* be diminished as a result of this opinion.

All that this opinion requires of an employer is that it be fair. It would be unfair to allow an employer to distribute a policy manual that makes the workforce believe that certain promises have been made and then to allow the employer to renege on those promises. What is sought here is basic honesty: if the employer, for whatever reason, does not want the manual to be capable of being construed by the court as a binding contract, there are simple ways to attain that goal. All that need be done is the inclusion in a very prominent position of an appropriate statement that there is no promise of any kind by the employer contained in the manual; that regardless of what the manual says or provides, the employer promises nothing and remains free to change wages and all other working conditions without having to consult anyone and without anyone's agreement; and that the employer continues to have the absolute power to fire anyone with or without good cause.

Reversed and remanded for trial.

QUESTIONS

1. Does the *Hoffman* court undermine the at-will rule? Would the court be better advised to wait for the legislature to determine whether employees can be terminated only for cause?
2. Should an employer agree to negotiate terms of the handbook with an employee if there is a particular provision that offends the employee? What problems would the employer face?
3. Will the gig economy lead back to individual negotiations between company and worker, eliminating the need for handbooks in this growing sector of the economy?

Problem 9-1

You are an associate attorney at a mid-sized employment firm in New Jersey in 1983. The *Hoffman* case has just been decided, and industry newsletters are describing the case as a potential catastrophe for employers in the state. A senior partner at the firm asks you to prepare a presentation to be made to the firm's largest clients regarding the potential impact of the *Hoffman* decision and how the clients can best respond. The partner advises you that she is receiving the following questions, and asks for your counsel.

(1) What if the worker is hired but never reads the handbook? After all, isn't knowledge of an offer a condition precedent to acceptance?

(2) What if the handbook is indefinite and vague? Can there still be a contract? Why or why not?

(3) What about provisions in the handbook that relate to matters other than termination? Can an employee sue, arguing that the employer wrongfully calculated benefits or commissions owed based on the

handbook? How can employers protect themselves from these commitments?

---

2. The Empire Strikes Back: Disclaimers

After courts began construing handbooks as binding employment contracts, employers responded by attempting to disclaim contractual liability. As employers changed the language of their handbooks to achieve this goal, courts monitored whether they were successful. The question is whether a reasonable employee would conclude that the employer has not assented to be bound by the provisions contained in the handbook. Consider the next case, which addresses the question of whether it is reasonable for an employee who has never read the handbook to rely on its terms.

Anderson v. Douglas & Lomason Co.

540 N.W.2d 277 (Iowa 1995).

Ternus, Justice.

Defendant, Douglas & Lomason Company (DLC), discharged plaintiff, Terry Anderson, for taking a box of pencils. Anderson responded with a breach-of-contract action claiming DLC failed to follow progressive discipline policies contained in the employee handbook. The district court granted DLC's motion for summary judgment, which argued, in part, that the handbook did not constitute a contract. Anderson appealed.

Although we conclude progressive discipline policies meeting the requirements for a unilateral contract are enforceable, a disclaimer in the handbook given to Anderson prevented the policies from constituting a contract. Therefore, we affirm the district court's grant of summary judgment.

On Anderson's first day of work at DLC he attended a six hour orientation session for new employees. He was informed that DLC had a progressive discipline policy and he was given a fifty-three page employee handbook which included these policies. Anderson read only the first few pages of the handbook; he admits he never read the provisions on progressive discipline.

DLC fired Anderson after three years of employment. His termination was based on an incident which occurred as he was leaving the plant one day. Company personnel stopped his pickup and asked to search it. Anderson gave permission and the workers found a box of company pencils. As a result, they also asked to search his home and garage. Anderson consented and a subsequent search revealed no company property. However, that same day, DLC asked Anderson to resign. He refused and was immediately fired.

Anderson responded by filing this breach-of-contract action against DLC. He claims DLC did not follow the progressive discipline policies outlined in its handbook for unauthorized possession of company property. These progressive discipline policies require a written warning for the first offense, a three-day suspension without pay for the second offense, and discharge for the third offense. Because this was not Anderson's third offense, he claims DLC could not fire him.

DLC filed a motion for summary judgment claiming the handbook did not constitute a contract and therefore Anderson was employed at-will. First, DLC contended the handbook was never communicated to or accepted by Anderson because he did not read it. Second, DLC argued the handbook was not definite enough to constitute an offer. DLC cited two reasons for its vagueness claim: the handbook contains no written guarantees that discharge will occur only for cause or under certain conditions—the rules are mere guidance; and the manual contains a written disclaimer. The district court granted the employer's summary judgment motion without explanation in a calendar entry.

. . . .

When considering whether a handbook creates a contract we utilize unilateral contract theory. A unilateral contract consists of an offeror making a promise and an offeree rendering some performance as acceptance. An employee handbook is a unilateral contract when three elements are present: (1) the handbook is sufficiently definite in its terms to create an offer; (2) the handbook is communicated to and accepted by the employee so as to constitute acceptance; and (3) the employee provides consideration.

As with any contract, the party who seeks recovery on the basis of a unilateral contract has the burden to prove the existence of a contract. Therefore, Anderson has the burden to prove DLC's handbook created an enforceable contract. We begin our analysis with a discussion of the communication aspect of the acceptance element of Anderson's claim.

Anderson read only a few pages of the employee manual; he did not read the provisions on progressive discipline. DLC contends that under these circumstances, there can be no acceptance. We disagree. DLC distributed its employee handbook to new employees. We think Anderson's receipt of the handbook is sufficient communication.

Under traditional contract analysis, an offer is not effective until it reaches the offeree. . . .

The most common illustration of the application of this rule is the general offer of a reward. The reward-giver, or offeror, bargains for performance, not a reciprocal promise; sometimes the performance is rendered without knowledge of the offer. Some courts resolve this issue using the traditional law of contracts: there can be no contract unless the claimant when giving the desired information knew of the offer of the reward and acted with the intention of accepting such offer; otherwise the claimant gives the information not in the expectation of receiving a reward but rather out of a sense of public duty or other motive unconnected with the reward.

. . . .

It is probable, indeed, that the chief reason for enforcing a promise is that it has induced the promisee to act in reliance upon it. One who has rendered a service without knowledge of an offered promise has not so acted. But the chief reason is not necessarily the only reason for enforcing a promise. If it seems fair to the courts to enforce a promise when the promisor has received the desired equivalent, even though the one rendering it knew nothing of the promise and rendered the service from other motives, there is no sufficient reason for refusing to call that enforceable promise a contract.

. . . .

Where a contract is based upon an employee handbook distributed to all employees, the contract is not an individually negotiated agreement; it is a standardized agreement between the employer and a class of employees. We analogize to the interpretation of standardized contracts: "A standardized agreement 'is interpreted wherever reasonable as treating alike all those similarly situated, without regard to their knowledge or understanding of the standard terms of the writing.' " *Kinoshita v. Canadian P. Airlines, Ltd.*,

68 Haw. 594, 724 P.2d 110, 116–17 (1986) (quoting Restatement (Second) of Contracts § 211(2) (1981)).

Therefore, we hold it unnecessary that the particular employee seeking to enforce a promise made in an employee manual have knowledge of the promise. Although this holding is a departure from traditional 'bargain-theory' contract analysis, we think it produces "the salutary result that all employees, those who read the handbook and those who did not, are treated alike." E. Allan Farnsworth, *Developments in Contract Law During the 1980's: The Top Ten*, 41 Case W.Res.L.Rev. 203, 209 (1990). Moreover, our deviation from traditional contract theory is consistent with the spirit of the judicially created at-will presumption: It is a common law presumption created in response to statutory and societal demands.

. . . .

We now consider whether DLC's handbook constituted an offer to Anderson to utilize progressive disciplinary procedures. We believe this aspect of the analysis should be conducted according to traditional contract theory.

. . . .

DLC asserts the handbook was not definite enough to constitute an offer for two reasons: It claims there are no guarantees that the company will always follow the progressive discipline procedures, and the handbook includes a written disclaimer that expressly states there is no intent to create a contract. Therefore, DLC contends no offer existed for Anderson to accept.

When considering whether a handbook is objectively definite to create a contract we consider its language and context. Our analysis of case law reveals [two] factors to guide this highly fact-intensive inquiry: (1) Is the handbook in general and the progressive disciplinary procedures in particular mere guidelines or a statement of policy, or are they directives? (2) Is the language of the disciplinary procedures detailed and definite or general and vague? . . .

Here, the text of the disciplinary procedures contains language of command: "The following action is prohibited, and the penalties for violation of these Shop Rules *shall* be as follows [progressive discipline steps are then listed]." (Emphasis added.) However, the introduction to the section of the handbook containing the disciplinary procedures states twice that the rules "have been designed for the *information and guidance* of all employees." (Emphasis added.) Second, the procedures themselves are fairly specific.

There are four categories that describe in detail the offenses included in each category. In addition, the discipline for each category is also specific: for unauthorized possession of company property, the first offense requires a written warning, the second offense a three day unpaid suspension and the third offense results in discharge. Finally, DLC retained the power to alter the procedures at will. We need not decide whether these factors alone result in a sufficiently definite offer, however, because we must also consider the effect of DLC's disclaimer.

A disclaimer can prevent the formation of a contract by clarifying the intent of the employer not to make an offer. Befort Article, 13 Indus.Rel.L.J. at 349; Chagares Article, 17 Hofstra L.Rev. at 378. "In the context of employee handbooks, the essential purpose of a disclaimer is to claim at-will status for the employment relationship by repudiating or denying liability for statements expressed in the handbook." Befort Article, 13 Indus.Rel.L.J. at 349. Although in theory disclaimers protect employers, many courts have imposed requirements that make it more difficult to give effect to them. *Id.*

For example, many jurisdictions require the disclaimer be "clear and conspicuous" to be enforceable and negate any contractual relationship between an employer and employee. While we have never considered whether a disclaimer in an employee handbook must be clear and conspicuous, our court of appeals has implicitly endorsed a conspicuous requirement by holding a disclaimer "[p]rominently displayed in the first page" of a handbook prevented the formation of a contract. *Palmer v. Women's Christian Ass'n*, 485 N.W.2d 93, 95–96 (Iowa App.1992).

The requirement that a disclaimer be conspicuous has given rise to much litigation. . . .

We think such uncertainty is unnecessary. A disclaimer should be considered in the same manner as any other language in the handbook to ascertain its impact on our search for the employer's intent. Therefore, we reject any special requirements for disclaimers; we simply examine the language and context of the disclaimer to decide whether a reasonable employee, reading the disclaimer, would understand it to mean that the employer has not assented to be bound by the handbook's provisions. Cf. *Bolling*, 484 N.E.2d at 1373 ("the employees . . . must be justified 'in understanding that a commitment has been made.' ") (citations omitted); *Payne v. Sunnyside Community Hosp.*, 78 Wash.App. 34, 894 P.2d 1379, 1384 (1995) ("crucial question is whether the employee has a reasonable expectation the employer will follow the discipline procedure, based upon the language used").

Similar to our consideration of handbook language in general, we believe two factors guide our inquiry. First, is the disclaimer clear in its terms: does the disclaimer state that the handbook does not create any rights, or does not alter the at-will employment status? Second, is the coverage of the disclaimer unambiguous: what is the scope of its applicability? Here the disclaimer appears on page fifty-three, the last page of the handbook, two inches below the preceding paragraph:

> This Employee Handbook is not intended to create any contractual rights in favor of you or the Company. The Company reserves the right to change the terms of this handbook at any time.

When examining the disclaimer we first consider the text employed. In no uncertain terms DLC's disclaimer states the handbook "is not intended to create any contractual rights." (Emphasis added.) . . . We believe DLC's disclaimer is clear in its disavowal of any intent to create a contract.

Second, we examine the scope of the disclaimer. There is nothing about the location of DLC's disclaimer or the language used to suggest that the disclaimer does not apply to the progressive discipline policies. The disclaimer is found in the handbook itself and unequivocally applies to the entire employee handbook.

We think a reasonable person reading the handbook could not believe that DLC has assented to be bound to the provisions contained in the manual. Thus, we hold DLC's handbook is not sufficiently definite to constitute a valid offer.

We hold as a matter of law no contract existed between Anderson and DLC. Anderson was employed at-will. Therefore, the trial court correctly granted summary judgment to DLC.

AFFIRMED.

QUESTIONS

1. Do you agree with the court's analysis that an employee can accept the terms of the handbook without having read the handbook? Will this rule affect how employers draft and publicize their handbook?
2. How would you draft an "iron clad" disclaimer under the rule in *Anderson*?

Read the following case with this question in mind: "If I were an employer in Vermont, would I feel that the state Supreme Court was engaged in a convoluted game of cat and mouse with me?"

Dillon v. Champion Jogbra, Inc.

819 A.2d 703 (Vt. 2002).

Morse, J.

> *[Editor's Note: Linda Dillon appealed from a summary judgment in favor of her employer, arguing that the trial court erroneously concluded as a matter of law that Dillon's at-will employment status had not been modified by Jogbra's employment manual and employment practices.]*

. . . .

The first page of the manual states the following in capitalized print:

> The policies and procedures contained in this manual constitute guidelines only. They do not constitute part of an employment contract, nor are they intended to make any commitment to any employee concerning how individual employment action can, should, or will be handled. Champion Jogbra offers no employment contracts nor does it guarantee any minimum length of employment. Champion Jogbra reserves the right to terminate any employee at any time "at will," with or without cause.

During the period from 1996 to 1997, however, Jogbra developed what it termed a "Corrective Action Procedure." This procedure established a progressive discipline system for employees and different categories of disciplinary infractions. It states that it applies to all employees and will be carried out in "a fair and consistent manner." Much of the language in the section is mandatory in tone.

. . . .

Additionally, it must be remembered when analyzing Dillon's argument that principles of contract law govern such determinations. . . . "The rule imposes no substantive limitation on the right of contracting parties to modify terms of their arrangement or to specify other terms that supersede the terminable-at-will [arrangement]." *Foote*, 158 Vt. at 570, 613 A.2d at 1279. Additionally, an employer may modify an at-will employment agreement unilaterally. *Id.* at 571, 613 A.2d at 1279–80. When determining whether an employer has done so, we look to both the employer's written policies and its practices. An employer not only may implicitly bind itself to terminating only for cause through its manual and practices, but may also be bound by a commitment to use only certain procedures in doing so.

At least one court has interpreted our case law to hold that the interpretation of employment manuals is always a question for the jury. A closer reading of our case law, however, demonstrates that only when the terms of the manual are ambiguous should the question be submitted to the jury.

We have not abrogated, in the employment context, the long-standing law of contract that the interpretation of unambiguous writings is a matter of law for the court . . . .

When the terms of a manual are ambiguous, however, or send mixed messages regarding an employee's status, the question of whether the presumptive at-will status has been modified is properly left to the jury. This may be the case even if there is a disclaimer stating employment is at-will, as the presence of such a disclaimer is not dispositive in the determination. See *Farnum*, 164 Vt. at 494, 671 A.2d at 1254 ("The mere inclusion of boilerplate language providing that the employee relationship is at will cannot negate any implied contract and procedural protections created by an employee handbook."). Furthermore, an employer's practices can provide context for and help inform the determination.

The question of whether a written manual is ambiguous is a determination of law that we review de novo. In this case, we cannot agree with the trial court that the terms of Jogbra's manual are unambiguous such that, as a matter of law, Dillon's status was not modified, especially considered in light of the conflicting record before the court regarding Jogbra's employment practices.

Notwithstanding the disclaimer contained on the first page of the manual quoted above, the manual goes on to establish in Policy No. 720 an elaborate system governing employee discipline and discharge. It states as its purpose: "To establish Champion Jogbra policy for all employees." It states that actions will be carried out "in a fair and *consistent* manner." (Emphasis added.) It provides that "[t]he Corrective Action Policy *requires* management to use training and employee counseling to achieve the desired actions of employees." (Emphasis added.) It establishes three categories of violations of company policy and corresponding actions to be generally taken in each case. It delineates progressive steps to be taken for certain types of cases, including "[u]nsatisfactory quality of work," and time periods governing things such as how long a reprimand is considered "active." All of these terms are inconsistent with the disclaimer at the beginning of the manual, in effect sending mixed messages to employees. Furthermore, these terms appear to be inconsistent with an at-will employment relationship, its classic formulation being that an employer can fire an employee "for good cause or for no cause, or even for bad cause."

With respect to the record before the court on Jogbra's employment practices, Dillon herself was aware of at least one employee whose termination was carried out pursuant to the terms set forth in the manual. She also testified in her deposition to conversations with the human resources manager, with whom she was friendly, in which the manager had described certain procedures used for firing employees. She stated that the manager had told her that Jogbra could not "just get rid of" people, but instead had to follow procedures. The human resources manager herself testified that, although the progressive discipline system was not generally applied to salaried employees, it was "historically" used for nonsalaried employees. She could only recall two instances in which the portion of the manual providing for documentation of progressive action was not followed, one of which resulted in a legal claim against the company and the other of which involved an employee stealing from the company. In fact, the manual specifically provides that stealing "will normally result in *discharge on the first offense*." (Emphasis in original.) Thus, it is not clear how that discharge deviated from the provisions of the manual.

In conclusion, the manual itself is at the very least ambiguous regarding employees' status, and Jogbra's employment practices appear from the record to be both consistent with the manual and inconsistent with an at-will employment arrangement. Therefore, summary judgment was not proper on Dillon's breach of implied contract claim.

Amestoy, C.J., dissenting.

. . . I disagree that the trial court erred in granting employer summary judgment on employee's breach of implied contract claim. I therefore respectfully dissent.

The salient question in this case is whether the following language of the employment manual is ambiguous:

> THE POLICIES AND PROCEDURES CONTAINED IN THIS MANUAL CONSTITUTE GUIDELINES ONLY. THEY DO NOT CONSTITUTE PART OF AN EMPLOYMENT CONTRACT, NOR ARE THEY INTENDED TO MAKE ANY COMMITMENT TO ANY EMPLOYEE CONCERNING HOW INDIVIDUAL EMPLOYMENT ACTION CAN, SHOULD, OR WILL BE HANDLED. CHAMPION JOGBRA OFFERS NO EMPLOYMENT CONTRACTS NOR DOES IT GUARANTEE ANY MINIMUM LENGTH OF EMPLOYMENT. CHAMPION JOGBRA RESERVES THE RIGHT TO TERMINATE ANY EMPLOYEE AT ANY TIME "AT WILL," WITH OR WITHOUT CAUSE.

The majority offers two explanations as to why the employer's extraordinarily direct statement that it "reserves the right to terminate any employee at any time 'at will,' with or without cause" should be construed to mean exactly the opposite of what it says. I disagree with each.

First, the majority concludes that additional language contained within the manual setting forth progressive steps to be taken for certain types of cases sends a "mixed message" to employees about their employee status. But the manual carefully reiterates the employer's unambiguous initial message that the discipline system is intended only as a guideline, and specifically reserves the right of managers to deviate from said guidelines in individual cases.

We have previously noted that "disciplinary procedures are not inconsistent or in conflict with the at-will doctrine." *Ross v. Times Mirror, Inc.*, 164 Vt. 13,

21, 665 A.2d 580, 585 (1995). A policy that expressly leaves the disciplinary sanction to the employer's discretion does not create an enforceable promise to terminate for cause. *Id.* at 21, 665 A.2d at 585. Moreover, even a statement which expressly or impliedly includes a promise to an employee for specific treatment in specific situations will not bind an employer "if it conspicuously and effectively states that the policy is not intended to be part of the employment relationship." *Id.* at 20–21, 665 A.2d at 584 (citing *Thompson v. St. Regis Paper Co.*, 102 Wash.2d 219, 685 P.2d 1081, 1088 (1984)). As noted above, the employment manual contained the following statement in capital letters: "THE POLICIES AND PROCEDURES CONTAINED IN THIS MANUAL CONSTITUTE GUIDELINES ONLY. THEY DO NOT CONSTITUTE PART OF AN EMPLOYMENT CONTRACT." If the majority considers this statement to be insufficient, then it is difficult to imagine the language an employer could use in order to conspicuously state that the policy is not intended to be part of the employment relationship.

I do not believe that the manual at issue in this case can reasonably be construed as ambiguous. The "mixed message" the majority discerns more accurately describes the message conveyed by an opinion which observes that "at-will employment relationships have fallen into disfavor," when recently this Court cautioned against interpretations that "irreconcilably conflict[ ] with the employment at-will doctrine . . . and result[ ] in unreasonable judicial interference into what is a private relationship." *Ross*, 164 Vt. at 23, 665 A.2d at 586 (internal citations omitted). The trial court correctly determined that the terms of the employer's manual are unambiguous as a matter of law.

Nor do I agree with the majority's second justification that the record before the court of employer's practices created ambiguity. In support of employee's contention that employer's practices were at odds with an at-will policy, employee cites to her own deposition, wherein she claimed to have known of other employees who received progressive discipline prior to termination. When pressed, however, employee admitted that, of the three employees with whose discharge she was familiar, she could state with certainty that only one received progressive discipline. Moreover, employee stated that she was unfamiliar with the manner in which the other two employees' cases were handled prior to their discharge. While her own experience is relevant, it does not by itself suggest a definitive companywide practice. Hearsay statements about what employee "had heard" is insufficient to raise a genuine issue. I would affirm the trial court's grant of summary judgment. I am authorized to state that Justice Skoglund joins in this dissent.

QUESTIONS

1. Your firm represented Jogbra in the litigation. Given the court's holding, you have been asked to rewrite the handbook to provide protection to Jogbra. Describe your strategy.
2. Do the majority and dissent apply different legal rules, or come to different conclusions on the facts?

---

3. Should an Employer Have a Rulebook, a Handbook, or Something Else?

Employers reacted swiftly to cases that construed handbooks as binding contracts, using increasingly clear, stark, and conspicuous language to disclaim any contract liability. This wasn't necessarily the best business response, as handbooks became much more lawyerly and less inspirational.

Mastery Problem 9-1

You are the Vice-President for Human Resources at a large manufacturing company that has more than 600 blue-collar and white-collar employees. You gather with your staff (some of whom are lawyers, most of whom are human resources professionals with other training) to develop a strategy for revamping your employee handbook and other digital communications to employees about workplace matters. Read the following article and then report to the class on your team's strategy.

Bill Taylor, *Trust Your Employees, Not Your Rule Book*

Harv. Bus. Rev. (Apr. 2017).

[Editor's Note: On April 9, 2017, United needed to bump four passengers from a full plane to transport a flight crew to Louisville. No passengers accepted the $400 coupon, and so the airline selected four passengers to evict from the plane. David Dao protested and screamed as police officers pulled him out of his seat, and his face hit an armrest during the struggle. Officers then dragged him, apparently unconscious, by his arms on his back along the aircraft aisle past rows of onlooking passengers, some of whom were filming and then posted the incident.]

Here's the good news: The big airlines are revising their rules for booking and boarding flights—rules that led to one of the great business fiascos in recent history, United Express Flight 3411. Here's the bad news: If the long-term lesson that leaders of the airline business (or any other business) take away from this episode is that it's time to rewrite policies and practices, to fine-tune bureaucratic procedures, then they will have missed a huge, perhaps even historic, learning opportunity.

The truly important lesson is one that applies to companies in all sorts of fields. It has to do with the grave shortcomings of an approach to business, culture, and customer service that relies on rules and procedures at the expense of letting flesh-and-blood human beings solve problems and make sound decisions. It's time for leaders to toss out their rule books and trust their people.

The Wall Street Journal published an in-depth analysis of the "recipe for the disastrous decision" that triggered a front-page crisis at Chicago O'Hare International Airport. Its conclusion? The problem wasn't with United's employees, but with a "rules-based culture" in which 85,000 people are "reluctant to make choices" that are not in the "tomes of rule books" and "giant manuals" that govern life at the airline. In other words, employees at every level did what they were supposed to do—*they followed the rules*—yet the result was a total failure.

When I read the Journal analysis, I couldn't help but think about another famous service organization, the retail giant Nordstrom, and the long-standing handbook that defines life at this 72,500-person company. The entirety of the Nordstrom Employee Handbook fits on a single 5×8 card and involves exactly one rule. Here is Rule #1: "Use best judgment in all situations. There will be no additional rules."

No wonder Nordstrom's image and brand is built on heroic stories of above-and-beyond service and problem solving. Sometimes those stories even involve the airlines. In one case, an employee discovered that a customer had left her luggage (along with her flight itinerary) in the parking lot of a Nordstrom store in Connecticut. So he hopped in his car, drove her luggage to JFK, and reached her before the flight left. There's no rule that can foresee that kind of problem or response!

Truth be told, life inside most giant organizations is much closer to the rules-obsessed culture of the big airline than the common-sense freedoms of a high-end retailer. Have you ever tried to explain your special family circumstances to a health insurance provider? Or hoped for satisfaction during a painfully robotic conversation with a cellphone company or internet service provider? Or asked for a common-sense exception to established policies and procedures from a financial services conglomerate?

Good luck with that! As leaders, we've become so obsessed with efficiency, productivity, and consistency that we've designed cultures that can't handle the exceptions to the rules that real life invariably demands. And yet it's how we handle these exceptions, for good or for ill, that increasingly defines how we're perceived by our customers, especially in a world where social media captures and amplifies everyone's behavior.

Mark White, a business theorist who studies what he calls "adaptive organizations," makes an intriguing distinction between companies that are based on Roman law principles of governance and decision making and those based on common-law principles. In Roman law, White explains, anything that is not expressly permitted is forbidden. So Roman law companies rely on formal policies and bureaucratic procedures, on predetermined rules and established practices. In common law, anything that is not expressly forbidden is permitted. So common law organizations rely on fast action, nimble reactions, good judgment, and common sense. Not surprisingly, when it comes to service, empathy, and the capacity to do the right things in difficult situations, common-law organizations trump Roman law organizations, even though the biggest, most-established companies remain stuck in the Roman law mindset.

One of my favorite financial services companies is a young, fast-growing bank in the UK called Metro Bank. Metro is the ultimate challenger brand, the first new major retail bank chartered in the UK since 1835. One big reason why it's growing so fast and generating such buzz is that it has built a culture around nimble, creative, common-sense approaches to solving customer problems—a huge difference from the bureaucratic, rules-based cultures of the UK's Big Five established banks.

One of the few formal rules at Metro is known as "one to say yes, two to say no." Translation: If a customer has a special request or a difficult problem, every frontline employee is authorized to solve the problem (to say "yes") on the spot, without permission from above. If, however, a frontline employee thinks the situation should not be resolved to the customer's satisfaction (if the answer is "no"), then that employee must receive permission from above to reject the request.

Imagine if *that* rule had been in force at Chicago O'Hare last week. So as you reflect on leadership and culture after United 3411, don't just look for opportunities to fine-tune your procedures and update your employee manuals. Give your people the chance to think for themselves, to do what makes sense, to break the rules when they confront situations where the existing rules make no sense. Rome may not have been built in a day, but the days of Roman law organizations feel like they're numbered.

Mastery Problem 9-2

You are working on a client's handbook revisions. A fellow associate suggests the provisions below. Explain your decision as to whether you will incorporate these provisions.

> "As an integral part of its corporate purpose, the company will deal fairly with all groups that it works with, including employees. You can expect fair treatment, the opportunity to grow and to be paid according to standards for the area, and to be rewarded for outstanding performance."
>
> "In determining whether you will be terminated in a reduction in force, due consideration is given to your seniority, your length of employment with the company, your re-election for promotion or for additional

> training, or in making previous personnel reductions or transfers where necessary because of a decline in work requirements."

Mastery Problem 9-3

An employee is provided access to a handbook at the commencement of employment. It states, "This personnel policy is designed to provide employees with a clear set of guidelines for taking action in situations that develop in the workplace. This manual is not a contract; rather, it is a statement of the company's intention in matters covered by the policies contained herein." The handbook further states, "The contents of the manual are presented as a matter of 'information only' and are not to be understood or construed as a promise or contract between the company and its employees."

The manual contains a progressive disciplinary process which provides that "informal counseling will occur when a supervisor recognizes unsatisfactory work performance"; that "formal counseling will occur after a repeated infraction"; that "a final warning will then be administered as the next step"; and that "except in cases of gross misconduct or negligence, a discharge will be preceded by a final warning." This progressive discipline section is preceded by this statement: "It is the company's intention to adhere to an established protocol to ensure fair and consistent treatment of employee's disciplinary actions." Other provisions of the manual provide that employees "shall" receive certain benefits, such as double time for working on a holiday.

An employee was terminated for a first offense that was stipulated not to be either gross misconduct nor gross negligence. The progressive discipline policy was not followed. He brings a breach of contract lawsuit. You are clerking for the judge. She asks that you prepare a memo on the issues she must address and for you to provide a recommendation on how she must rule.

Conclusion

In this Lesson, you learned that employees began to be successful in arguing that the employer should be bound to the terms of its handbook, leading employers to begin using very broad disclaimers. Employers now must walk a fine line between publishing policies that provide direction to their workforce without committing themselves contractually. This is a balance between having an effective handbook and having flexibility to address employee matters.

Lesson 10:
Arbitration Agreements

Objectives and Expected Learning Outcomes

Arbitration agreements are now an integral part of the practice of employment law. In this Lesson, you will learn how enforceable agreements to arbitrate are formed, the necessity of ensuring that the employee has proper notice of the agreement's existence, how the agreement applies to the employee, and the ways in which the enforceability of the agreement can be challenged. In addition, you will assess the pros and cons of arbitration for both parties.

Arbitration is a way to resolve legal disputes privately, bypassing a judicial system financed by and open to the public. Arbitrators are empowered to issue binding decisions, called Awards, following some manner of evidentiary hearing or other form of fact-finding. In the typical scenario, the employer and employee agree that any work-related claim by either party, such as discrimination or breach of contract, must be submitted to binding arbitration. To be enforceable, the agreement to arbitrate must meet the requirements of a contract. In short, the agreement must be supported by consideration (it may not be an "illusory bargain") and the terms of the agreement must not be unconscionable (with regard to both the prescribed procedures and the substantive provisions). Both parties are bound by the Award, which may be set aside by a court only on very limited grounds.

The Federal Arbitration Act, interpreted expansively by the Courts, governs arbitration agreements in the employment setting. We begin with the relevant statutory provisions.

The Federal Arbitration Act

9 U.S.C. § 2. Validity, irrevocability, and enforcement of agreements to arbitrate

A written provision in any maritime transaction or a contract evidencing a transaction involving commerce to settle by arbitration a controversy thereafter arising out of such contract or transaction, or the refusal to perform the whole or any part thereof, or an agreement in writing to submit to arbitration an existing controversy arising out of such a contract, transaction, or refusal, shall be valid, irrevocable, and enforceable, save upon such grounds as exist at law or in equity for the revocation of any contract.

9 U.S.C. § 3. Stay of proceedings where issue therein referable to arbitration

If any suit or proceeding be brought in any of the courts of the United States upon any issue referable to arbitration under an agreement in writing for such arbitration, the court in which such suit is pending, upon being satisfied that the issue involved in such suit or proceeding is referable to arbitration under such an agreement, shall on application of one of the parties stay the trial of the action until such arbitration has been had in accordance with the terms of the agreement, providing the applicant for the stay is not in default in proceeding with such arbitration.

9 U.S.C. § 5. Appointment of arbitrators or umpire

If in the agreement provision be made for a method of naming or appointing an arbitrator or arbitrators or an umpire, such method shall be followed; but if no method be provided therein, or if a method be provided and any party thereto shall fail to avail himself of such method, or if for any other reason there shall be a lapse in the naming of an arbitrator or arbitrators or umpire, or in filling a vacancy, then upon the application of either party to the controversy the court shall designate and appoint an arbitrator or arbitrators or umpire, as the case may require, who shall act under the said agreement with the same force and effect as if he or they had been specifically named therein; and unless otherwise provided in the agreement the arbitration shall be by a single arbitrator.

9 U.S.C. § 10. Same; vacation; grounds; rehearing

(a) In any of the following cases the United States court in and for the district wherein the award was made may make an order vacating the award upon the application of any party to the arbitration—

(1) where the award was procured by corruption, fraud, or undue means;

(2) where there was evident partiality or corruption in the arbitrators, or either of them;

(3) where the arbitrators were guilty of misconduct in refusing to postpone the hearing, upon sufficient cause shown, or in refusing to hear evidence pertinent and material to the controversy; or of any other misbehavior by which the rights of any party have been prejudiced; or

> (4) where the arbitrators exceeded their powers, or so imperfectly executed them that a mutual, final, and definite award upon the subject matter submitted was not made.
>
> (b) If an award is vacated and the time within which the agreement required the award to be made has not expired, the court may, in its discretion, direct a rehearing by the arbitrators.
>
> (c) The United States district court for the district wherein an award was made that was issued pursuant to section 580 of title 5 may make an order vacating the award upon the application of a person, other than a party to the arbitration, who is adversely affected or aggrieved by the award, if the use of arbitration or the award is clearly inconsistent with the factors set forth in section 572 of title 5.

1. The Development and Growth of Arbitration in the Employment Setting

Courts historically disfavored arbitration. They had deep suspicions about the private resolution of disputes outside of the public judicial system. In response to state courts refusing to enforce agreements to arbitrate, Congress enacted the Federal Arbitration Act (FAA) in 1925. This statute empowered the federal courts to compel the parties to a written arbitration agreement to honor their contractual commitment and to stay any ongoing proceedings to permit the arbitration of the dispute to proceed. The existence of an enforceable agreement to arbitrate remained a matter of state contract law; however, the FAA provided that state courts could not disfavor agreements to arbitrate by treating them differently from other contracts. Like other business owners, employers began using agreements to arbitrate as a way to avoid lengthy and expensive litigation costs. Most states enacted arbitration acts modeled on the FAA that provided the applicable procedures.

Two major developments in the law have now led to an explosion in the use of arbitration in the employment setting. First, in *Gilmer v. Interstate/Johnson Lane Corp.*, 500 U.S. 20 (1991), the United States Supreme Court held that an employee's claim under a federal anti-discrimination statute could be submitted to binding arbitration. Two dissenting Justices emphasized that an employer could compel employees to agree to disadvantageous arbitration terms, and that the role of the federal courts in combatting discrimination with broad injunctive relief would be sacrificed to a commercial resolution of specific disputes. *Id.* at 41–42 (Stevens, J., dissenting). Following this opinion, employers aggressively embraced arbitration agreements to secure private adjudication outside the glare of public scrutiny and pursuant to procedures that favored their interests, such as shorter statute of limitations, limitations on damages, and extremely limited discovery. In a slight retrenchment, in *EEOC v. Waffle House, Inc.*, 534 U.S. 279 (2002), the Supreme Court later held that the EEOC could sue an employer and seek victim-specific relief despite the existence of an arbitration agreement, but the practical effect of this holding is limited due to the small number of cases that the EEOC can bring.

The second major development occurred in 2001, when the Supreme Court held that employment claims that did not invoke a federal statute nevertheless were within the scope of the FAA, which had been interpreted much more liberally than state statutory schemes governing arbitration. In *Circuit City Stores, Inc. v. Adams*, 523 U.S. 105 (2001), the Court determined that Congress intended the jurisdictional requirement of "a transaction involving commerce" to invoke its full powers under the commerce clause. The Court held that the district court properly stayed an action in state court brought pursuant to a state statute and compelled the parties to arbitrate. It was now clear that employers could apply to federal courts under the FAA to compel arbitration of any employment-related disputes. This fueled a rush of employer-sponsored arbitration agreements in the employment setting.

Employers anticipated that they would benefit from resolving employee claims in arbitration, and the facts have borne out this hope. Professor Alexander J. S. Colvin conducted an empirical study of arbitrations in California during a four-year period.[1] His findings were striking. Employees prevailed in arbitration only 21.4% of the time, and when they prevailed they received substantially less money than the amounts awarded in court litigation. Arbitrations also proved to be more efficient, with the average time between filing a demand and settlement being 284.4 days, and the average time between filing an arbitration demand and an Award being 361.5 days. These facts serve as powerful motivators for employers. In a later study conducted for the Economic Policy Institute and published in 2017,[2] Professor Colvin determined that 56.2% of employers used mandatory arbitration provisions, covering more than 60 million workers. Large employers were more likely to use arbitration, with 65% of employers with more than 1,000 employees requiring mandatory arbitration.

1 Alexander J. S. Colven, "An Empirical Study of Employment Arbitration: Case Outcomes and Processes," 8 J.of Empirical Stud. 1–23 (2011).

2 Alexander J. S. Colven, "The Growing Use of Mandatory Arbitration," Economic Policy Institute (September 27, 2017) (available at epi.org/135056).

With employers embracing mandatory arbitration and the courts enforcing federal policy in support of arbitration, employees are left with only several strategies to avoid arbitration or to limit its effects. We will discuss four primary lines of attack for employees: (1) Whether the issue that has been submitted to arbitration is within the scope of the arbitration clause, (2) Whether the employee's agreement to arbitrate is supported by consideration and is not an illusory agreement, (3) Whether the employee received sufficient notice of the arbitration agreement to be bound, and (4) Whether the arbitration agreement is procedurally or substantively unconscionable. We will consider each issue in turn.

2. Determining the Scope of the Agreement to Arbitrate

Arbitration is a creation of contract. The agreement to arbitrate, then, only extends as far as the parties have agreed. The first step in determining whether a party is required to arbitrate is to assess whether the claim falls within the scope of the arbitration clause. Generally, employers seek to have every potential claim by an employee subject to mandatory arbitration. In this case, they use very broad language to describe the scope of the arbitration clause, such as "any and all claims arising out of, or related to, your employment or the termination of your employment shall be subject to arbitration as provided below." If a broad clause is used, courts will respect the parties' agreement.

Sometimes, however, an employer might find that a broad arbitration clause backfires. One of the important benefits of an arbitration clause is that it presumably forestalls class action lawsuits by requiring every claimant to arbitrate her case individually. In *Oxford Health Plans LLC v. Sutter*, 569 U.S. 564 (2013), the Supreme Court held that the arbitrator's broad authority under the arbitration clause, coupled with the very limited bases for overturning an arbitrator's decision, permitted the arbitrator to conduct a class arbitration. In *Oxford,* a physician filed a class action suit on behalf of all New Jersey physicians who worked under a contract for reimbursement for treating Oxford's policyholders. The Court stayed the class action and compelled arbitration. The arbitrator then considered whether a class arbitration should proceed, and decided that it should, given the very broad scope of the arbitration provision, which provided that no "civil actions concerning any dispute arising under this Agreement shall be instituted before any court, and all such disputes shall be submitted to final and binding arbitration." The arbitrator reasoned that "all such disputes" meant any disputes that could be brought in court, including class actions, because the clause did not suggest any exceptions.

The Supreme Court's opinion emphasized the interplay between a very broad arbitration clause and the very limited grounds upon which an arbitrator's decision may be reversed by the courts.

> Here, Oxford invokes § 10(a)(4) of the [FAA], which authorizes a federal court to set aside an arbitral award "where the arbitrator[ ] exceeded [his] powers." A party seeking relief under that provision bears a heavy burden. "It is not enough . . . to show that the [arbitrator] committed an error—or even a serious error." *Stolt-Nielsen*, 559 U.S., at 671, 130 S.Ct. 1758. Because the parties "bargained for the arbitrator's construction of their agreement," an arbitral decision "even arguably construing or applying the contract" must stand, regardless of a court's view of its (de)merits. *Eastern Associated Coal Corp. v. Mine Workers*, 531 U.S. 57, 62 (2000) (quoting *Steelworkers v. Enterprise Wheel & Car Corp.*, 363 U.S. 593, 599 (1960); *Paperworkers v. Misco, Inc.*, 484 U.S. 29, 38, 108 S.Ct. 364, 98 L.Ed.2d 286 (1987); internal quotation marks omitted). Only if "the arbitrator act[s] outside the scope of his contractually delegated authority"—issuing an award that "simply reflect[s] [his] own notions of [economic] justice" rather than "draw[ing] its essence from the contract"—may a court overturn his determination. *Eastern Associated Coal*, 531 U.S., at 62 (quoting *Misco*, 484 U.S., at 38). So the sole question for us is whether the arbitrator (even arguably) interpreted the parties' contract, not whether he got its meaning right or wrong.
>
> And we have already all but answered that question just by summarizing the arbitrator's decisions, see *supra*, at 2071–2072; they are, through and through, interpretations of the parties' agreement. The arbitrator's first ruling recited the "question of construction" the parties had submitted to him: "whether [their] Agreement allows for class action arbitration." App. 29–30. To resolve that matter, the arbitrator focused on the arbitration clause's text, analyzing (whether correctly or not makes no difference) the scope of both what it barred from court and what it sent to arbitration. The arbitrator concluded, based on that textual exegesis, that the clause "on its face . . . expresses the parties' intent that class action arbitration can be maintained." *Id.*, at 32. When Oxford requested reconsideration in light of Stolt-Nielsen, the arbitrator explained that his prior decision was "concerned solely with the parties' intent as evidenced by the words of the arbitration clause itself." App. 69. He then ran through his textual analysis again, and reiterated his conclusion: "[T]he text of the clause itself authorizes" class arbitration.

> *Id.*, at 73. Twice, then, the arbitrator did what the parties had asked: He considered their contract and decided whether it reflected an agreement to permit class proceedings. That suffices to show that the arbitrator did not "exceed[ ] [his] powers." § 10(a)(4).

Oxford Health Plans LLC, 569 U.S. at 569–70.

3. Creating an Enforceable Agreement to Arbitrate

Agreements to arbitrate are measured according to the standard requirements for all contracts. You will recall that a contract must be supported by consideration, which is satisfied when the parties exchange promises. If the employer does not promise anything in exchange, the agreement will be deemed illusory and therefore unenforceable.

Lizalde v. Vista Quality Markets

746 F.3d 222 (5th Cir. 2014).

E. Grady Jolly, Judge.

The defendant, Vista Quality Markets ("Vista"), the employer of the plaintiff, appeals the judgment of the district court denying Vista's motion to compel arbitration of this on-the-job injury claim. The district court denied the motion, agreeing with the plaintiff, Jorge Lizalde, that the Mutual Agreement to Arbitrate Claims (the "Arbitration Agreement") between him and Vista is illusory because, as the district court interpreted the Arbitration Agreement, it provided Vista the unrestrained right to unilaterally terminate the Arbitration Agreement. We hold that the Arbitration Agreement is not illusory under Texas law. We therefore REVERSE the judgment of the district court and REMAND for the entry of an order compelling arbitration.

Lizalde works for Vista as a meat-cutter. Pursuant to this employment, Lizalde and Vista entered into two agreements that are relevant to this appeal: the Arbitration Agreement, and the Employment Injury Benefit Plan (the "Benefit Plan").

In the Arbitration Agreement, the parties agreed to submit to an arbitrator all claims which arise from "[a]ny injury suffered by Claimant while in the Course and Scope of Claimant's employment with Company." The Arbitration Agreement is terminable by Vista, but this termination ability has some constraints. "Company shall have the right to prospectively terminate [the Arbitration Agreement]. Termination is not effective for Covered Claims which accrued or occurred prior to the date of the termination. Termination is also not effective until ten (10) days after reasonable notice is given to Claimant." So by the terms of this termination provision in the Arbitration Agreement, a termination by Vista is only effective ten days after notice has been given to an employee and only as to prospective claims. Finally, the Arbitration Agreement also contains a provision recognizing its connection with the Benefit Plan. Specifically, the Arbitration Agreement states, "this Agreement is presented in connection with Company's [Benefit Plan]. Payments made under [the Benefit Plan] also constitute consideration for this Agreement."

As relevant to this appeal, the Benefit Plan itself also contains a termination provision providing that Vista "may terminate [the Benefit Plan] by executing and delivering to the Plan Administrator a notice of termination specifying the date of termination." Notably, this termination power under the Benefit Plan is completely unconstrained. These two different termination clauses present one of the complexities of this appeal.

Finally, Lizalde signed a document in which he acknowledged that upon employment, he had received and read both the Arbitration Agreement and the Benefit Plan.

. . . .

In ruling on the motion, the district court agreed with Lizalde that the Arbitration Agreement was illusory. . . .

. . . .

On appeal, Vista challenges the district court's holding that the Arbitration Agreement was illusory. First, Vista argues that the two agreements—the Arbitration Agreement and the Benefit Plan—are not properly read as a single contract, so the unconstrained termination provision in the Benefit Plan does not apply to the Arbitration Agreement. Alternatively, Vista argues that even if the Arbitration Agreement and the Benefit Plan are read as one contract, the Benefit Plan termination provision still does not apply to the Arbitration Agreement, which has its own properly constrained termination provision. We agree with Vista that even if the two agreements are read as one contract, the Arbitration Agreement cannot be terminated without following the established procedural requirements, and consequently is not illusory. We therefore need not decide the first issue because we will assume, as Lizalde urges, that the two agreements are properly construed as a single contract and move on to interpreting that contract.

. . . .

Both parties agree that Texas law governs the contract in this case. Under Texas law, "[a]n agreement to arbitrate, like other contracts, must also be supported by consideration." . . . Thus, "when a purported bilateral contract is supported only by illusory promises, there is no contract." . . . As it relates specifically to arbitration agreements, the "[m]utual agreement to arbitrate claims provides sufficient consideration to support an arbitration agreement." Where one party has the unrestrained unilateral authority to terminate its obligation to arbitrate, however, the agreement understandably is illusory. This is not to say that if a party retains any ability to terminate the agreement, the agreement is illusory. Instead, retaining termination power does not make an agreement illusory so long as that power 1) extends only to prospective claims, 2) applies equally to both the employer's and employee's claims, and 3) so long as advance notice to the employee is required before termination is effective.

. . . .

Looking at the two agreements in this case, we see no indication that the parties intended the broader termination provision found in the Benefit Plan to also apply to the Arbitration Agreement. . . .

. . . .

This view is further supported by the plain language of the two termination provisions. The termination provision found in the Arbitration Agreement explicitly states that Vista "shall have the right to prospectively terminate *this Agreement*" (emphasis added) . . . .

To summarize, the parties included a termination provision in the Arbitration Agreement that constrained Vista's power to terminate the agreement . . . . Because Vista's power to terminate the Arbitration Agreement is properly constrained, the Arbitration Agreement is not illusory and is enforceable under Texas law.

> . . . .
>
> Accordingly, the Arbitration Agreement is not illusory. We therefore REVERSE the decision of the district court, and REMAND the case for the district court to enter an order compelling arbitration.
>
> REVERSED and REMANDED.

Problem 10-1

The following clause is included in an employment application that is signed by prospective employees.

> As a condition for considering you for employment, and if employed, (Company) and the Applicant/Employee designated below mutually agree to arbitrate claims relating to his/her being considered for employment and subsequent employment . . . The Company and Applicant/Employee each voluntarily promise and agree to submit any claim covered by this agreement to binding arbitration. We further agree that arbitration pursuant to this agreement shall be the sole and exclusive remedy for resolving any such claims or disputes . . . It is mutually agreed that this document shall govern and apply to the resolution of all claims and/or disputes among applicant/employee . . . concerning any federal, state, or local laws, regulations, or statutes prohibiting discrimination . . . This agreement is issued with the authority of the Company and is binding on the Company. The agreement may not be altered except by consent of the company, and any such alterations shall be immediately effective upon notice to Applicant/Employee of its terms, regardless of whether it is signed by either agreeing party. Any change to this agreement will only be effective upon notice to Applicant/Employee and shall apply only prospectively.

Does this clause create a binding agreement to arbitrate? If you were asked by your employer client to review the clause, would you suggest any changes?

Problem 10-2

Bannon Enterprises has developed an "Alternate Dispute Resolution Policy" that is printed in its employee handbook. Under the Policy, mandatory arbitration is required for all employment-related disputes as a condition of employment. Additionally, the Policy provides that Bannon will also forgo its right to sue the employee for any claims that it has against the employee. A former employer of Bannon comes to your office and describes a potential discrimination claim that she wishes to file. Will the claim have to be arbitrated? Describe what other provisions of the handbook you may want to review to determine if the agreement is enforceable.

Problem 10-3

Klaus is hired by Spinner Realty. When he began work, Klaus was given a one-page document entitled "Dispute Policy" and an employee handbook. The Policy provides that both parties waive their right to bring a civil court action for any claims arising out of, or relating to, the employment relationship. The Policy specifically provides that claims of unlawful discrimination, among other claims, will be decided by mandatory arbitration. The Policy provides that the procedures and details of the arbitration agreement are set out in the employee handbook, as it may be revised from time to time. The first page of the employee handbook includes the following provision in bold letters: "You are an at will employee. This means that you may resign at any time, with or without prior notice to Spinner; likewise, Spinner may terminate your employment at any time, with or without prior notice. Spinner reserves the right to revise, delete, and add to any provision of this handbook." Klaus believes that he has an age discrimination claim against Spinner. Will his claim have to be arbitrated?

---

4. Providing Sufficient Notice of the Agreement to Arbitrate

Even if the employer has prepared an arbitration provision that is enforceable, it will be enforced against a particular employee only if the employee received sufficient notice of the employer's policy. One might expect that technology can solve the problem of notice easily, but as the following case demonstrates, it can also complicate matters, even for a sophisticated employer such as a law firm.

Alexander Dubose Jefferson & Townsend LLP v. Vance

2017 WL 2241538 (W.D. Tex. 2017).

Robert Pitman, United States District Judge.

Plaintiff Alexander Dubose Jefferson & Townsend LLP ("Plaintiff" or "ADJT") is a law firm specializing in appellate representation. Defendant Susan Vance ("Defendant" or "Ms. Vance") was a non-equity partner at ADJT until her employment was terminated on November 16, 2016. On February 22, 2017, ADJT filed suit against Ms. Vance pursuant to the Computer Fraud and Abuse Act, the Texas Uniform Trade Secrets Act, and the Texas Theft Liability Act. On March 15, 2017, Ms. Vance filed an Original Answer and Counterclaims, advancing claims for conversion, negligence, breach of contract, and violations of the anti-discrimination and anti-retaliation provisions of Title VII of the Civil Rights Act of 1964 and the Age Discrimination in Employment Act.

ADJT filed the instant motion, which seeks to compel all claims in this matter to arbitration and to stay or dismiss this proceeding, on April 19, 2017. On May 3, 2017, Ms. Vance filed a Response and Request for Pre-Arbitration Discovery, contending—among other things—that ADJT "has failed to show the existence of a valid arbitration agreement." She subsequently filed a Motion to Permit Discovery, seeking a court order permitting her to conduct "limited pre-arbitration discovery" regarding (1) whether the arbitration provision in question is procedurally unconscionable, is substantively unconscionable, was fraudulently obtained, or rests on an illusory promise; and (2) whether ADJT has waived its right to arbitrate.

The Federal Arbitration Act ("FAA" or "the Act") permits an aggrieved party to file a motion to compel arbitration when an opposing party has "failed, neglected, or refused to comply with an arbitration agreement." The Act represents a "liberal federal policy favoring arbitration agreements."

A court's consideration of a motion to compel arbitration pursuant to the FAA is subject to a two-step inquiry. The Court must first determine whether the parties agreed to arbitrate the dispute. That determination involves two questions: (1) whether there is a valid agreement to arbitrate between the parties; and (2) whether the dispute in question falls within the scope of that arbitration agreement. The Court must then determine whether any legal constraints foreclose arbitration of those claims.

. . . .According to state law, "[a]n employer may enforce an arbitration agreement entered into during an at-will employment relationship if the employer establishes that the employee received notice of its arbitration policy and accepted it." "If the employee receives notice and continues working with the knowledge of the modified employment terms, the employee accepts them as a matter of law."

III. DISCUSSION

The arbitration provision at issue in this case, which the parties refer to as the ADJT Dispute Resolution Program ("the Dispute Resolution Program"), states that it "govern[s] all disputes that may arise between employees and ADJT." The Dispute Resolution Program also states that "[a]ll legal disputes directly or indirectly arising out of or relating to the employment relationship . . . not otherwise resolved through negotiation or mediation, shall be submitted by ADJT or by the employee for final, binding arbitration . . . ."

To evaluate the parties' respective arguments regarding the enforceability of the Dispute Resolution Program, the Court must first consider whether there is a valid agreement to arbitrate between the parties. Central to that inquiry is whether ADJT has established that Ms. Vance received notice of the arbitration policy and accepted its terms. Actual notice can be express or implied. The Court will thus first consider whether ADJT has established that Ms. Vance received express notice; if necessary, it will then turn to whether Ms. Vance received implied notice.

A. Express Notice

Here, employees were first informed of the Dispute Resolution Program in an October 13, 2016 email. That email, entitled "Firm Policies," explained that "management [was] in the process of organizing, updating, and supplementing the firm's employee and practice policies." After giving instructions on how to access the "Employee Handbook" folder on the firm's computer system, the email listed a series of existing policies included in the folder. It then noted that a "new policy," the "ADJT Dispute Resolution Program," was available in the Employee Handbook folder and would take effect on November 12, 2016. The email did not include any substantive information regarding the Dispute Resolution Program; indeed, it did not even use the word "arbitration." As a result, Ms. Vance contends that no valid agreement to arbitrate exists. ADJT disagrees, arguing both that it provided Ms. Vance with sufficient notice and that she had a duty to make further inquiry after receiving the October 13, 2016 email.

. . . .

Here, ADJT has not established that it provided direct notice of the arbitration agreement to Ms. Vance. While the firm informed employees, including Ms. Vance, of a "dispute resolution program" via email and provided instructions on how to access the policy, it did not attach the policy to the email or otherwise directly inform Ms. Vance of the policy's substance.

. . . .

. . . . [Our] Court, however, must apply Texas law, and at least one Texas court has deemed an analogous distinction dispositive. That court found that an employer provided insufficient notice of its arbitration policy despite the fact that (1) the employer posted the policy on the company intranet site; (2) the employer informed the employee in question about the intranet site; (3) the employee acknowledged that she could access the employer's policies on the intranet site; (4) the employer instructed the employee that she was responsible for reviewing and familiarizing herself with the policies; and (5) the employee acknowledged that she had received "orientation" on "Problem solving/Grievance Procedures." [*Doe v. Columbia N. Hills Hosp. Subsidiary, L.P.*, 2017 WL 1089694, at *5 (Tex. App.—Fort Worth, Mar. 23, 2017)]

B. Implied Notice

Whether ADJT provided sufficient notice to Ms. Vance therefore depends on whether notice may be implied because Ms. Vance had a duty to make further inquiry. "A duty to make further inquiry 'extends only to those matters that are fairly suggested by the facts really known.' " . . . .

ADJT's email informing employees about the upcoming implementation of a "dispute resolution program" and providing information on how to electronically access a copy of that policy fairly suggested that (1) ADJT's policies were in electronic format and available for review; and (2) ADJT was implementing a dispute resolution program that would become effective on November 12, 2016. It did not, however, fairly suggest to employees that the firm was implementing a mandatory, binding arbitration policy . . . .

. . . Here, Ms. Vance received an email noting that a new "Dispute Resolution Program" would take effect the following month. Applying the *Columbia* court's reasoning to the facts of this case, the Court reaches a similar conclusion. ADJT's email to Ms. Vance did not fairly suggest that the firm was implementing a binding arbitration policy and that her continued employment would constitute her acquiescence to that policy. She cannot, therefore, be held to have had a duty to further investigate the terms of that policy.

The Court therefore concludes that ADJT has failed to establish that Ms. Vance received sufficient notice—whether express or implied—to create a valid agreement to arbitrate. Plaintiff's Motion to Compel Arbitration must therefore be denied.

. . . .

QUESTION

1. Courts routinely hold that employees must receive notice of an agreement to arbitrate for it to be enforceable against them. Why don't courts require that the employee sign a copy of the policy? Reach back to your first year of contracts to help you.

Problem 10-4

Payne University has experienced a number of employee grievances recently. As a result, the President sent an email to all employees with the subject line: "Important Notice to all Employees: New Dispute Resolution Procedure." In the text of the email, the message states that the University is committed to "open, forthright, and honest communication." The message then states that all workplace disputes involving statutory claims must be resolved by arbitration. There are two embedded links in the main text of the email that redirect the employee to the Dispute Resolution Procedure and also to a one-page document that summarizes and explains the binding nature of arbitration. The email urged all employees to read these "important documents that have important consequences for your employment rights." The University tracked whether an employee opened the email, but did not track whether the employee opened one or both of the links.

Later in the year, an employee brings suit against the University for allegedly violating the Americans with Disabilities Act. Your firm has just been hired to represent Payne, and you have been asked to file a motion to stay the court action and to compel the employee to submit to arbitration. What investigation will you conduct in order to support the motion? What advice would you give to the University for improving their distribution of important policies via email?

---

5. Ensuring That the Arbitration Agreement Is Not Unconscionable

Arbitration agreements are contracts, and so all defenses to contract formation are available to attack the enforceability of an agreement. If an agreement to arbitrate is secured through fraud or duress, for example, it will not be enforceable. Because employers write the policies to protect their interests, unconscionability has been one of the leading defenses raised by employees. The following case is a notorious example of an employer that went far beyond the pale and paid the price.

HOOTERS OF AMERICA, INC. v. PHILLIPS

173 F.3d 933 (4th Cir. 1999).

WILKINSON, CHIEF JUDGE:

Annette R. Phillips alleges that she was sexually harassed while working at a Hooters restaurant. After quitting her job, Phillips threatened to sue Hooters in court. Alleging that Phillips agreed to arbitrate employment-related disputes, Hooters preemptively filed suit to compel arbitration under the Federal Arbitration Act, 9 U.S.C. § 4. Because Hooters set up a dispute resolution process utterly lacking in the rudiments of even-handedness, we hold that Hooters breached its agreement to arbitrate. Thus, we affirm the district court's refusal to compel arbitration.

Appellee Annette R. Phillips worked as a bartender at a Hooters restaurant in Myrtle Beach, South Carolina. She was employed since 1989 by appellant Hooters of Myrtle Beach (HOMB), a franchisee of appellant Hooters of America (collectively Hooters).

Phillips alleges that in June 1996, Gerald Brooks, a Hooters official and the brother of HOMB's principal owner, sexually harassed her by grabbing and slapping her buttocks. After appealing to her manager for help and being told to "let it go," she quit her job. Phillips then contacted Hooters through an attorney claiming that the attack and the restaurant's failure to address it violated her Title VII rights. Hooters responded that she was required to submit her claims to arbitration according to a binding agreement to arbitrate between the parties.

This agreement arose in 1994 during the implementation of Hooters' alternative dispute resolution program. As part of that program, the company conditioned eligibility for raises, transfers, and promotions upon an employee signing an "Agreement to arbitrate employment-related disputes." The agreement provides that Hooters and the employee each agree to arbitrate all disputes arising out of employment, including "any claim of discrimination, sexual harassment, retaliation, or wrongful discharge, whether arising under federal or state law." The agreement further states that

> the employee and the company agree to resolve any claims pursuant to the company's rules and procedures for alternative resolution of employment-related disputes, as promulgated by the company from time to time ("the rules"). Company will make available or provide a copy of the rules upon written request of the employee.

The employees of HOMB were initially given a copy of this agreement at an all-staff meeting held on November 20, 1994. HOMB's general manager, Gene Fulcher, told the employees to review the agreement for five days and that they would then be asked to accept or reject the agreement. No employee, however, was given a copy of Hooters' arbitration rules and procedures. Phillips signed the agreement on November 25, 1994. When her personnel file was updated in April 1995, Phillips again signed the agreement.

After Phillips quit her job in June 1996, Hooters sent to her attorney a copy of the Hooters rules then in effect. Phillips refused to arbitrate the dispute.

Hooters filed suit in November 1996 to compel arbitration under 9 U.S.C. § 4. Phillips defended on the grounds that the agreement to arbitrate was unenforceable. Phillips also asserted individual and class counterclaims against Hooters for violations of Title VII and for a declaration that the arbitration agreements were unenforceable against the class. In response, Hooters requested that the district court stay the proceedings on the counterclaims until after arbitration, 9 U.S.C. § 3.

. . . .

In support of arbitration, Congress passed the Federal Arbitration Act (FAA), ch. 213, 43 Stat. 883 (1925) (codified as amended at 9 U.S.C. § 1 *et seq.*). "Its purpose was to reverse the longstanding judicial hostility to arbitration agreements that had existed at English common law and had been adopted by American courts, and to place arbitration agreements upon the same footing as other contracts." The FAA manifests "a liberal federal policy favoring arbitration agreements." When a valid agreement to arbitrate exists between the parties and covers the matter in dispute, the FAA commands the federal courts to stay any ongoing judicial proceedings, 9 U.S.C. § 3, and to compel arbitration, *id.* § 4.

The threshold question is whether claims such as Phillips' are even arbitrable. The EEOC as amicus curiae contends that employees cannot agree to arbitrate Title VII claims in predispute agreements. We disagree.

> *[Editor's Note: The court held that federal discrimination claims under Title VII are arbitrable, an extension of the Supreme Court's landmark ruling in* Gilmer *that claims under the ADA are arbitrable.]*

. . . .

Hooters argues that Phillips gave her assent to a bilateral agreement to arbitrate. That contract provided for the resolution by arbitration of all employment-related disputes, including claims arising under Title VII. Hooters claims the agreement to arbitrate is valid because Phillips twice signed it voluntarily. Thus, it argues the courts are bound to enforce it and compel arbitration.

We disagree. The judicial inquiry, while highly circumscribed, is not focused solely on an examination for contractual formation defects such as lack of mutual assent and want of consideration. Courts also can investigate the existence of "such grounds as exist at law or in equity for the revocation of any contract." 9 U.S.C. § 2 . . . . In this case, the challenge goes to the validity of the arbitration agreement itself. Hooters materially breached the arbitration agreement by promulgating rules so egregiously unfair as to constitute a complete default of its contractual obligation to draft arbitration rules and to do so in good faith.

. . . .

The Hooters rules when taken as a whole, however, are so one-sided that their only possible purpose is to undermine the neutrality of the proceeding. The rules require the employee to provide the company notice of her claim at the outset, including "the nature of the Claim" and "the specific act(s) or omissions(s) which are the basis of the Claim." Rule 6–2(1), (2). Hooters, on the other hand, is not required to file any responsive pleadings or to notice its defenses. Additionally, at the time of filing this notice, the employee must provide the company with a list of all fact witnesses with a brief summary of the facts known to each. Rule 6–2(5). The company, however, is not required to reciprocate.

The Hooters rules also provide a mechanism for selecting a panel of three arbitrators that is crafted to ensure a biased decisionmaker. Rule 8. The employee and Hooters each select an arbitrator, and the two arbitrators in turn select a third. Good enough, except that the employee's arbitrator and the third arbitrator must be selected from a list of arbitrators created exclusively by Hooters. This gives Hooters control over the entire panel and places no limits whatsoever on whom Hooters can put on the list. Under the rules, Hooters is free to devise lists of partial arbitrators who have existing relationships, financial or familial, with Hooters and its management. In fact, the rules do not even prohibit Hooters from placing its managers themselves on the list. Further, nothing in the rules restricts Hooters from punishing arbitrators who rule against the company by removing them from the list. Given the unrestricted control that one party (Hooters) has over the panel, the selection of an impartial decision maker would be a surprising result.

Nor is fairness to be found once the proceedings are begun. Although Hooters may expand the scope of arbitration to any matter, "whether related or not to the Employee's Claim," the employee cannot raise "any matter not included in the Notice of Claim." Rules 4–2, 8–9. Similarly, Hooters is permitted to move for summary dismissal of employee claims before a hearing is held whereas the employee is not permitted to seek summary judgment. Rule 14–4. Hooters, but not the employee, may record the arbitration hearing "by audio or videotaping or by verbatim transcription." Rule 18–1. The rules also grant Hooters the right to bring suit in court to vacate or modify an arbitral award when it can show, by a preponderance of the evidence, that the panel exceeded its authority. Rule 21–4. No such right is granted to the employee.

. . . .

If by odd chance the unfairness of these rules were not apparent on their face, leading arbitration experts have decried their one-sidedness. George Friedman, senior vice president of the American Arbitration Association (AAA), testified that the system established by the Hooters rules so deviated from minimum due process standards that the Association would refuse to arbitrate under those rules. George Nicolau, former president of both the National Academy of Arbitrators and the International Society of Professionals in Dispute Resolution, attested that the Hooters rules "are inconsistent with the concept of fair and impartial arbitration." He also testified that he was "certain that reputable designating agencies, such as the AAA and Jams/Endispute, would refuse to administer a program so unfair and one-sided as this one." Additionally, Dennis Nolan, professor of labor law at the University of South Carolina, declared that the Hooters rules "do not satisfy the minimum requirements of a fair arbitration system." He found that the "most serious flaw" was that the "mechanism [for selecting arbitrators] violates the most fundamental aspect of justice, namely an impartial decision maker." Finally, Lewis Maltby, member of the Board of Directors of the AAA, testified that "This is without a doubt the most unfair arbitration program I have ever encountered."

In a similar vein, two major arbitration associations have filed amicus briefs with this court. The National Academy of Arbitrators stated that the Hooters rules "violate fundamental concepts of fairness . . . and the integrity of the arbitration process." Likewise, the Society of Professionals in Dispute Resolution noted that "[i]t would be hard to imagine a more unfair method of selecting a panel of arbitrators." It characterized the Hooters arbitration system as "deficient to the point of illegitimacy" and "so one sided, it is hard to believe that it was even intended to be fair."

We hold that the promulgation of so many biased rules—especially the scheme whereby one party to the proceeding so controls the arbitral panel—breaches the contract entered into by the parties. The parties agreed to submit their claims to arbitration—a system whereby disputes are fairly resolved by an impartial third party. Hooters by contract took on the obligation of establishing such a system. By creating a sham system unworthy even of the name of arbitration, Hooters completely failed in performing its contractual duty.

Moreover, Hooters had a duty to perform its obligations in good faith. *See Restatement (Second) of Contracts* § 205 (1981) ("Every contract imposes upon each party a duty of good faith and fair dealing in its performance and its enforcement."). Good faith "emphasizes faithfulness to an agreed common purpose and consistency with the justified expectations of the other party." *Restatement (Second) of Contracts* § 205 cmt. a. Bad faith includes the "evasion of the spirit of the bargain" and an "abuse of a power to specify terms." *Id.* § 205 cmt. d. By agreeing to settle disputes in arbitration, Phillips agreed to the prompt and economical resolution of her claims. She could legitimately expect that arbitration would not entail procedures so wholly one-sided as to present a stacked deck. Thus we conclude that the Hooters rules also violate the contractual obligation of good faith.

Given Hooters' breaches of the arbitration agreement and Phillips' desire not to be bound by it, we hold that rescission is the proper remedy . . . .

We respect fully the Supreme Court's pronouncement that "questions of arbitrability must be addressed with a healthy regard for the federal policy favoring arbitration." *Moses H. Cone*, 460 U.S. at 24. Our decision should not be misread: We are not holding that the agreement before us is unenforceable because the arbitral proceedings are too abbreviated. An arbitral forum need not replicate the judicial forum. "[W]e are well past the time when judicial suspicion of the desirability of arbitration and of the competence of arbitral tribunals inhibited the development of arbitration as an alternative means of dispute resolution." *Mitsubishi Motors*, 473 U.S. at 626–27.

. . . .

By promulgating this system of warped rules, Hooters so skewed the process in its favor that Phillips has been denied arbitration in any meaningful sense of the word. To uphold the promulgation of this aberrational scheme under the heading of arbitration would undermine, not advance, the federal policy favoring alternative dispute resolution. This we refuse to do.

The judgment of the district court is affirmed, and the case is remanded for further proceedings consistent with this opinion.

AFFIRMED AND REMANDED.

Baltazar v. Forever 21, Inc., et al.

62 Cal.4th 1237 (Cal. 2016).

Kruger, J.

In this case, we are once again asked to determine the enforceability of an arbitration agreement under the law of unconscionability. As a condition of her employment with defendants, plaintiff Maribel Baltazar signed an agreement to resolve any employment-related disputes by means of arbitration. The agreement provides that, in the event a claim proceeds to arbitration, the parties are authorized to seek preliminary injunctive relief in the superior court. The primary question before us is whether this clause renders the arbitration agreement unconscionable, and therefore unenforceable, because it unreasonably favors the employer. We conclude that the clause, which does no more than restate existing law (see Code Civ. Proc., § 1281.8, subd. (b) (section 1281.8(b))), does not render the agreement unconscionable. Finding no other basis to support Baltazar's claim of unconscionability, we affirm the judgment of the Court of Appeal.

In November 2007, Baltazar was invited to a job interview at a Los Angeles warehouse operated by Forever 21, a clothing retail merchandiser. When she arrived for the interview, she was asked to fill out an 11-page employment application. Pages 8 and 9 of the application consisted of an arbitration agreement. Several blank spaces on the application were highlighted in yellow, indicating places where Baltazar should sign. Although Baltazar signed all other portions of the application, she initially refused to sign the arbitration agreement. A Forever 21 employee told Baltazar, "[S]ign it or no job." Baltazar then signed the arbitration agreement and was hired.

The agreement provides that the parties "mutually agree" to arbitrate "any claim or action arising out of or in any way related to the hire, employment, remuneration, separation or termination of Employee." The agreement specifies that the disputes subject to arbitration "include but are not limited to: claims for wages or other compensation due; claims for breach of any employment contract or covenant (express or implied); claims for unlawful discrimination, retaliation or harassment . . ., and Disputes arising out of or relating to the termination of the employment relationship between the parties, whether based on common law or statute, regulation, or ordinance." In the event the parties proceed to arbitration, the agreement provides that either party may seek provisional relief: "Pursuant to California Code of

Civil Procedure [section] 1281.8 either party hereto may apply to a California court for any provisional remedy, including a temporary restraining order or preliminary injunction." The agreement also contains a confidentiality provision: "Both parties agree that the Company has valuable trade secrets and proprietary and confidential information. Both parties agree that in the course of any arbitration proceeding all necessary steps will be taken to protect from public disclosure such trade secrets and proprietary and confidential information." And finally, as relevant here, the agreement provides that if a court determines that "the parties['] agreement to arbitrate under the Model Rules for Arbitration of Employment Disputes of the American Arbitration Association is not enforceable," then the parties will arbitrate the dispute under the California Arbitration Act (CAA) (Code Civ. Proc., § 1280 et seq.).

Baltazar resigned from Forever 21 in January 2011. Later that year, she filed a complaint against defendants in the superior court. Her complaint alleges that during the course of her employment at Forever 21, she suffered verbal and physical harassment, race and sex discrimination, and retaliation, all in violation of California law. Defendants filed a motion to compel arbitration under the terms of the agreement that Baltazar had signed. Baltazar opposed the motion, arguing that the arbitration agreement was unconscionable and therefore unenforceable. Agreeing with Baltazar, the trial court denied the motion to compel arbitration. The trial court found that the agreement was procedurally unconscionable because of the parties' unequal bargaining power. It explained that Forever 21 had required Baltazar to sign the agreement, without modification, as a condition of receiving employment. The trial court also found that the agreement was substantively unconscionable because (1) it lists only employee claims as illustrative examples of the types of disputes to which it applies, (2) it gives Forever 21 the right to protect trade secrets and other confidential information, and (3) it still requires arbitration even if a court finds the agreement to be unenforceable insofar as it requires arbitration under the model rules of the American Arbitration Association (AAA).

The Court of Appeal reversed. It agreed with the trial court's conclusion that the agreement was "oppressive and procedurally unconscionable" because Baltazar "was required to sign the Agreement as a condition of employment, was unable to negotiate the terms of the Agreement, and had no meaningful choice in the matter." But the Court of Appeal disagreed with the trial court's conclusion that the agreement was substantively unconscionable.

The court rejected Baltazar's argument that the clause of the arbitration agreement permitting either party to seek provisional relief in superior court was substantively unconscionable because such relief more often serves the interests of employers than employees. . . .

As a starting point for our analysis, we review general principles of unconscionability. " 'One common formulation of unconscionability is that it refers to " 'an absence of meaningful choice on the part of one of the parties together with contract terms which are unreasonably favorable to the other party.' " As that formulation implicitly recognizes, the doctrine of unconscionability has both a procedural and a substantive element, the former focusing on oppression or surprise due to unequal bargaining power, the latter on overly harsh or one-sided results.' "

" 'The prevailing view is that [procedural and substantive unconscionability] must both be present in order for a court to exercise its discretion to refuse to enforce a contract or clause under the doctrine of unconscionability.' But they need not be present in the same degree. 'Essentially a sliding scale is invoked which disregards the regularity of the procedural process of the contract formation, that creates the terms, in proportion to the greater harshness or unreasonableness of the substantive terms themselves.' In other words, the more substantively oppressive the contract term, the less evidence of procedural unconscionability is required to come to the conclusion that the term is unenforceable, and vice versa."

"[A] finding of procedural unconscionability does not mean that a contract will not be enforced, but rather that courts will scrutinize the substantive terms of the contract to ensure they are not manifestly unfair or one-sided." . . . [T]here are degrees of procedural unconscionability. At one end of the spectrum are contracts that have been freely negotiated by roughly equal parties, in which there is no procedural unconscionability. . . . Contracts of adhesion that involve surprise or other sharp practices lie on the other end of the spectrum. Ordinary contracts of adhesion, although they are indispensable facts of modern life that are generally enforced, contain a degree of procedural unconscionability even without any notable surprises, and 'bear within them the clear danger of oppression and overreaching.' We have instructed that courts must be "particularly attuned" to this danger in the employment setting, where "economic pressure exerted by employers on all but the most sought-after employees may be particularly acute."

. . . .

. . . '[C]ourts, including ours, have used various nonexclusive formulations to capture the notion that unconscionability requires a substantial degree of unfairness beyond "a simple old-fashioned bad bargain." ' This latter qualification is important. Commerce depends on the enforceability, in most instances, of a duly executed written contract. A party cannot avoid a contractual obligation merely by complaining that the deal, in retrospect, was unfair or a bad bargain. Not all one-sided contract provisions are unconscionable; hence the various intensifiers in our formulations: 'overly harsh,' 'unduly oppressive,' 'unreasonably favorable.' The ultimate issue in every case is whether the terms of the contract are sufficiently unfair, in view of all relevant circumstances, that a court should withhold enforcement."

Here, the trial court concluded that the arbitration agreement was procedurally unconscionable because it was written on a preprinted form and offered on a take-it-or-leave-it basis, thus making it a contract of adhesion. The Court of Appeal agreed. The Court of Appeal noted, however, that while the contract was adhesive in nature, there was no element of surprise. Baltazar not only knew about the arbitration agreement, but initially sought to avoid it, ultimately deciding to accept it because Forever 21 was not willing to offer the job on other terms. Nor was there any oppression or sharp practices on the part of Forever 21. Baltazar was not lied to, placed under duress, or otherwise manipulated into signing the arbitration agreement. The adhesive nature of the employment contract requires us to be "particularly attuned" to her claim of unconscionability, but we do not subject the contract to the same degree of scrutiny as "[c]ontracts of adhesion that involve surprise or other sharp practices"

. . . .

. . . Baltazar argues that the arbitration agreement at issue is unfairly one-sided because it lists only employee claims as examples of the types of claims that are subject to arbitration. As noted, the arbitration agreement states that the parties mutually agree to arbitrate "any claim or action arising out of or in any way related to the hire, employment, remuneration, separation or termination of Employee," and it further provides that the disputes subject to arbitration "include but are not limited to: claims for wages or other compensation due; claims for breach of any employment contract or covenant (express or implied); claims for unlawful discrimination, retaliation or harassment . . ., and Disputes arising out of or relating to the termination of the employment relationship between the parties, whether based on common law or statute, regulation, or ordinance." In Baltazar's view, this provision makes clear that the kinds of claims typically brought by employees are all subject to arbitration, but it leaves in doubt whether the kinds of claims employers typically bring are also subject to arbitration, thus allowing the employer to litigate that issue when it brings a claim.

We disagree. The arbitration agreement at issue here makes clear that the parties mutually agree to arbitrate all employment-related claims: that is, "any claim or action arising out of or in any way related to the hire, employment, remuneration, separation or termination of Employee." That provision clearly covers claims an employer might bring as well as those an employee might bring. The illustrative list of claims subject to the agreement is just that . . . .

. . . Baltazar [also] argues that the arbitration agreement here is unduly one-sided because it provides that, in the course of arbitration, "all necessary steps will be taken to protect from public disclosure [Forever 21's] trade secrets and proprietary and confidential information." Baltazar contends that because the agreement neither defines "all necessary steps" nor specifies what constitutes "proprietary and confidential information," the agreement unfairly demands that employees take whatever steps the employer deems "necessary" to protect whatever information the employer claims to be "proprietary and confidential."

Baltazar misreads the confidentiality provision. Nothing in the agreement indicates that an employee must accede to any and all demands Forever 21 might make for the protection of confidential and proprietary information. As defendants explain: "This provision contemplates that if trade secret, confidential and proprietary information need[s] to be introduced into the arbitration that the parties [will] work with the arbitrator to make sure that such information is not disclosed to the public." The agreement does not restrict the use of such information in the proceeding, nor does it pretermit any determination of whether a particular piece of information is a trade secret or otherwise qualifies as proprietary and confidential. Agreements to protect sensitive information are a regular feature of modern litigation, and they carry with them no inherent unfairness.

To the extent that Baltazar's complaint is instead that the agreement calls for the protection of an employer's confidential information without similarly calling for the protection of the confidential information of employees, we disagree with the suggestion that this omission renders the arbitration agreement unduly harsh or one-sided. As we have stated . . . "[A] contract can provide a "margin of safety" that provides the party with superior bargaining strength a type of extra protection for which it has a legitimate commercial need without being unconscionable." Here, the basis for the extra measure of protection is a legitimate commercial need to protect Forever 21's "valuable trade secrets and proprietary and confidential information" from public disclosure. Although Baltazar may dislike the wording of the confidentiality provision, she does not dispute that it is based on a legitimate commercial need. Moreover, nothing in the agreement precludes employees from seeking comparable protection for their personal information during arbitration proceedings, as circumstances may warrant.

We conclude that the parties' arbitration agreement is not unconscionable. Accordingly, we affirm the judgment of the Court of Appeal.

QUESTIONS

1. In ordinary business negotiations is it unethical for the party with a stronger bargaining position to insist that its demands be met—the so-called "take it or leave it offer?" If so, should this rule be applied differently in the employment context?
2. Consider your role as an attorney if your client is pushing to have the arbitration agreement as one-sided as possible. Is it ethical for you to draft an unenforceable agreement, knowing that most employees will not challenge the provision?
3. Is there a way to draft the arbitration clause to remedy any specific findings of unconscionability in later litigation?
4. What if an arbitration provision specified that the parties could each conduct only one deposition for no longer than two hours. Would it potentially be unconscionable? What if the arbitration provision precluded any discovery?
5. After learning that you passed the bar exam, you are offered a job with a mid-sized law firm. The firm requires you to sign an arbitration agreement as a condition of employment that provides that all disputes between you and the firm would be resolved by mandatory arbitration. Would you sign it?

Mastery Problem 10-1

Your firm has been hired by a company to develop a comprehensive alternative dispute resolution program. The company wants employees to agree to the program on a truly voluntary basis, but they do want most employees to agree. The senior partner in your firm comes to you and says, "Develop a promotional piece to be given to the employees. We get a bonus for every employee who signs up. Don't let us down!"

Mastery Problem 10-2

Your firm has been hired by a new client to develop an aggressive arbitration policy. The client had read a pro-arbitration article in a trade magazine extolling the virtues of mandatory arbitration. The client emails you: "Finally, a way to manage my risk and deal with these whining employees! I want you to stick it to them, so that these expensive cases stop draining my company. Limit my exposure and do what it takes for me to win these cases. If I lose these cases, then make sure that I don't pay through the nose." Prepare an outline of the conversation you will need to have with your senior partner, considering the Rules of Professional Conduct.

Conclusion

Employers increasingly use arbitration clauses to reduce the costs of employment-related litigation and to thwart class actions. The Federal Arbitration Act has been interpreted by the Supreme Court very liberally, resulting in the enforcement of broadly worded arbitration clauses. Employers are held to certain basic procedural standards, such as ensuring that employees have sufficient notice of the policy, and also to minimal substantive standards under the doctrine of unconscionability.

4

Third Party Obligations to Employees and Employers

Key Concepts

- The employment relationship is valuable to both the employer and employee, and third parties who improperly interfere with this relationship are liable in tort.
- An employer cannot interfere with a relationship to which it is a party, but an agent of the employer acting outside the scope of agency might incur personal liability.

Lesson 11:
Tortious Interference with Contract or Prospective Advantage

Objectives and Expected Learning Outcomes

In this Lesson, we address how the law protects the employment relationship from interference by third parties. A third party will be liable in tort only if the interference is "wrongful," which is the key element to analyze in most cases. You will further develop your problem-solving skills by addressing novel and complex fact patterns relating to what amounts to "wrongful" behavior, and who qualifies as a "third party."

The employer and employee have a contractual relationship that is valuable to both parties. If a third party interferes with this relationship, that party might be liable in tort for the resulting losses. The parties need not have an express, formal employment contract in place to have a protected interest. A "prospective business relation" is also protected from tortious interference by third parties. In this chapter we explore the rights of the employer and employee to be free of tortious interference with their relationship.

The Restatement of Torts provides the blackletter framework generally used by courts to determine whether a third party has tortiously interfered with an employment relationship. As with most torts, the analysis requires a balancing of factors.

Restatement (Second) Torts

§ 766. Intentional Interference with Performance of Contract by Third Person

One who intentionally and improperly interferes with the performance of a contract (except a contract to marry) between another and a third person by inducing or otherwise causing the third person not to perform the contract, is subject to liability to the other from the failure of the third person to perform the contract.

§ 766A. Intentional Interference with Another's Performance of His Own Contract

One who intentionally and improperly interferes with the performance of a contract (except a contract to marry) between another and a third person, by preventing the other from performing the contract or causing his performance to be more expensive or burdensome, is subject to liability to the other for the pecuniary loss resulting to him.

§ 766B. Intentional Interference with Prospective Contractual Relation

One who intentionally and improperly interferes with another's prospective contractual relation (except a contract to marry) is subject to liability to the other for the pecuniary harm resulting from loss of the benefits of the relation, whether the interference consists of

(a) inducing or otherwise causing a third person not to enter into or continue the prospective relation or

(b) preventing the other from acquiring or continuing the prospective relation.

The Restatement test structures the analysis of liability in terms of two primary distinctions. First, these provisions distinguish between "contract" and "prospective contractual relation" as the object of the interference. Second, they distinguish between interference that causes the other to terminate the relationship with the plaintiff and interference that impairs the ability of the plaintiff to perform under the relationship, leading to termination of the agreement. Additionally, there are two other key elements to the claim: the interference in question must be "wrongful," and it must be caused by a "third person." We explore these four doctrinal distinctions in turn.

1. The Nature of the Relationship

The first issue is to determine the nature of the employment relationship. An employment contract for a term of years is clearly a "contract" that is protected from tortious interference, but courts sometimes have struggled to determine how to characterize an ongoing at-will relationship. This relationship may be conceptualized in one of two ways. First, although the at-will relationship is terminable by either party, at any time, with or without reason, it still constitutes an existing contractual relationship between the parties. The gravamen of the tort is the improper interference, and not the ability of one party to compel the other to continue their contract relationship into the future. Second, courts have considered an at-will relationship to be similar to a prospective contractual relationship. It is no less harmful for a third party to improperly prevent a party from continuing an advantageous relationship even if the party does not have a contractual right to continue the relationship. The subtleties raised by the at-will nature of the employment relationship are summarized in Comment g to Restatement (Second) Torts § 766: "Until he has so terminated [a contract terminable at-will], the contract is valid and subsisting, and the defendant may not improperly interfere with it. The fact that the contract is terminable at-will, however, is to be taken into account in determining the damages that the plaintiff has suffered by reason of its breach."

QUESTIONS

1. What does an at-will employee lose if a third party interferes with the employee's relationship with the employer?
2. How would you prove damages if you represented an at-will employee who is suing a third party for interfering with the employee's at-will employment relationship?
3. What does an employer lose if a third party interferes with an at-will employee's relationship with the employer?

4. How would you prove damages if you represented an employer who is suing a third party for interfering with the employer's at-will employment relationship with an employee?

---

2. Nature of the Interference

The typical case of tortious interference in the employment setting involves a claim by the employer or employee that a third party has interfered with their relationship by contracting with one of the parties. The gravamen of the tort is that interfering with one party's performance caused the other party to suffer a loss.

Example 11-1

Samantha is a commissioned salesperson for a pharmaceutical distribution firm. She signed a five-year exclusive contract two years ago. Droog Distribution knows that Samantha is under contract, but nevertheless offers her a position as a commissioned salesperson with its firm. By knowingly hiring Samantha despite an express contract forbidding her to work for another firm, Droog is wrongfully interfering with the employee's performance to the detriment of the employer.

Another form of actionable interference occurs when the third party prevents one of the parties to the relationship from performing its obligations. The gravamen of the tort in such a case is that interfering with a party's performance under an existing contract causes them to lose the benefits of the contract. This scenario is less common in the employment context, but there are situations when this type of interference may occur.

Example 11-2

Samantha is an at-will commissioned salesperson for a pharmaceutical distribution firm. David used to work for the same firm, but was fired one year ago. David believes that Samantha caused him to be fired, so David begins spreading lies about Samantha to her customers. As a result of David's actions, Samantha cannot meet her sales quotas and receives less compensation than usual. Ultimately, she is terminated for poor performance. By knowingly seeking to make Samantha's performance of her contract more difficult, David is wrongfully interfering with Samantha's ability to perform her work, thereby causing her injury.

---

3. Defining "Improper Interference"

Whether the object of interference is a contract or prospective business relation, the key issue is whether the defendant's behavior amounts to "improper" interference. The traditional common law rule used a complicated burden-shifting approach, in which the plaintiff first made a *prima facie* showing of interference, the defendant provided justification for the interference, and then the plaintiff had the burden of vitiating the justification by proving "malice." As is often the case with common law rules, the term "malice" was articulated on a case-by-case basis and was not a helpful guide to parties and courts. The Restatement utilizes what appears to be a much cleaner approach by listing the factors to be balanced in determining whether the interference is "improper."

Restatement (Second) Torts

§ 767. Factors in Determining Whether Interference is Improper

In determining whether an actor's conduct in intentionally interfering with a contract or a prospective contractual relation of another is improper or not, consideration is given to the following factors:

(a) the nature of the actor's conduct,

(b) the actor's motive,

(c) the interests of the other with which the actor's conduct interferes,

(d) the interests sought to be advanced by the actor,

(e) the social interests in protecting the freedom of action of the actor and the contractual interests of the other,

(f) the proximity or remoteness of the actor's conduct to the interference and

(g) the relations between the parties.

§ 768. Competition as Proper or Improper Interference

(1) One who intentionally causes a third person not to enter into a prospective contractual relation with another who is his competitor or not

to continue an existing contract terminable at will does not interfere improperly with the other's relation if

(a) the relation concerns a matter involved in the competition between the actor and the other and

(b) the actor does not employ wrongful means and

(c) his action does not create or continue an unlawful restraint of trade and

(d) his purpose is at least in part to advance his interest in competing with the other.

(2) The fact that one is a competitor of another for the business of a third person does not prevent his causing a breach of an existing contract with the other from being an improper interference if the contract is not terminable at will.

Take the time to diagram these rules, and especially to determine when a party is insulated from liability because that party's actions are motivated by competition with the plaintiff. If not motivated by "competition," is the only other option that the party is motivated by "malice?"

Example 11-3

Jon is a teacher at a private grade school, but he has taught history to high school students in the past. He signed an express written contract in July for a 9-month term at the grade school, covering the upcoming school year. In October, Jon is approached by a private high school to replace a history teacher who has become ill. The high school cannot find a suitable replacement, and implores Jon to accept their position immediately with a 20% increase in pay so that the high school students have a qualified teacher. The high school advised Jon that it is much easier for grade schools to find replacement teachers. If Jon breaches his contract, the high school will be liable to the grade school for interference with contract. It is irrelevant that the high school is pursuing its legitimate interests and not seeking to harm the grade school. The high school has intentionally interfered with an express contract.

Mastery Problem 11-1

Catherine Smith is a prominent litigation associate at one of the largest private law firms in your city—Freed, Santos (FS). She feels that she is underpaid and undervalued, despite being one of the firm's most successful lawyers. FS has told her that she will not be considered for early partnership, but that they fully plan to make her an equity partner with a superb compensation package.

Another large law firm in town—Wisniewski, Palmer (WP)—decides that Smith would make a great addition to their litigation team and probably would bring some very good clients with her. Additionally, FS has received a great deal of negative press about personnel shakeups at the firm, and the partners at WP are convinced that WP will gain tremendous prestige at the expense of FS if they are successful in convincing Smith to join them. FS and WP wage a constant public relations campaign against each other to assert their status as the most prominent law firm in the city. WP offers Smith a 20% increase in her salary and early consideration for partnership, and they successfully induce her resignation from FS. FS immediately sues WP. During discovery, FS learns that before courting Smith WP had decided to place a moratorium on new full equity partnerships due to reduced revenues, but that they still planned to make top associates partial-equity partners in the firm.

Is WP liable to FS for tortious interference? If so, how would FS prove its damages? How would your analysis change if Smith were in the second year of a five-year written employment agreement?

---

4. Who Is a Third Party?

It is clear that a party to a contract or prospective business advantage is not a "third person" to the relationship. If an employer fires an employee in violation of an employment contract, the employer is liable for a breach of contract, but not for "interfering" with a contract. Sometimes, however, the analysis of who is a third party can be complicated. This is especially the case when the party accused of interference is not the employer itself, but rather an agent of the employer. Recall that an agent's tortious acts are attributed to the principal under the principle of *respondeat superior*, because of the agency relationship. However, if the agent acts outside the scope of employment the agent might be directly liable for her actions.

Consider the following articulation of the black letter principles regarding the "third party" status of an agent.

Frierson v. University of Chicago

2015 Ill. App. (1st) 151176–U, 2015 WL 7771030 (December 2, 2015) (Unpublished opinion).

[Editor's Note: Frierson was employed as the Director of Financial Aid at the University's medical school. Her supervisor, Robertson, gave her a negative evaluation and recommended termination. Frierson was then fired. Frierson sued the University for defamation, based on Robertson's performance evaluation. Frierson later added Robertson as a defendant and alleged that Robertson interfered with her employment relationship.]

ANALYSIS

A [motion for summary judgment] tests the legal sufficiency of the complaint. The motion requires the trial court to accept all well-pled facts, as well as inferences reasonably drawn from those facts, as true. We review the dismissal of Frierson's second amended complaint . . . *de novo.*

The sole count in Frierson's second amended complaint is tortious interference with prospective economic advantage, pled against the University of Chicago and Sylvia Robertson. . . .

In order to state a cause of action for tortious interference, the plaintiff must allege that the defendant purposefully interfered with and defeated plaintiff's legitimate expectation of entering or continuing a valid business relationship, causing plaintiff damages. Ordinarily, the defendant's interference must be directed towards a third party: an employer cannot interfere with its own business relationship with its employee.

There is an exception, however, where a corporate officer interferes with an employee's employment with the corporation. Specifically, where the officer acts "solely for their own gain or solely for the purpose of harming plaintiff," the officer's conduct may support a tortious interference claim, "since such conduct is not undertaken to further the corporation's interest." *Mittelman v. Witous,* 135 Ill.2d 220, 249 (1989). "To be tortious, a corporate officer's action must be done without justification or maliciously." *Id.*

It is this exception Frierson relies on here, arguing that Robertson's performance review was unjustified and malicious. But Frierson offers no facts supporting her claim that Robertson acted maliciously or solely for Robertson's own gain. Indeed, there is nothing in the complaint that suggests Robertson benefitted from Frierson's termination. Instead, Frierson merely disputes the accuracy of Robertson's statements in her performance evaluation and baldly describes them as "without justification" and "maliciously based." Such conclusory allegations are insufficient to state a claim for tortious interference. See *Willcutts v. Galesburg Clinic Association,* 201 Ill.App.3d 847, 851 (1990) (dismissal of pleading upheld where plaintiff failed to allege specific actions by defendants directed at third parties but instead presented "broad, conclusory allegations"); see also *Alpha School Bus Co., Inc. v. Wagner,* 391 Ill.App.3d 722, 735 (2009) ("[A] pleading that merely paraphrases the elements of a cause of action in conclusory terms is insufficient.").

Because Frierson fails to allege specific acts of malice, she likewise cannot overcome the qualified privilege attached to Robertson's statements. It is well settled that corporate officers are privileged against claims that their activities interfered in a third party's relationships with their principals. Of course, that privilege may be defeated by a showing that the officer's acts were unjustified or malicious. But allegations of malice must be pleaded with specificity, and Frierson's failure to so plead is fatal to her claim.

Even assuming *arguendo* that Frierson had sufficiently alleged that Robertson was acting "solely in her own interest," as she contends, this, too, dooms her cause of action against the university, as it is premised on a *respondeat superior* theory of liability. While an employer may be liable even for malicious acts of its employees provided they are committed within the scope of the employment, the employer is *not* liable where the acts were committed solely for the benefit of the employee. And because Frierson explicitly argues that Robertson acted "solely for the purpose of hurting plaintiff," it follows that the university cannot be liable for Robertson's actions.

In sum, Frierson has pled herself out of court: no cause of action against the university lies regardless of whether Frierson has successfully alleged tortious interference against Robertson.

QUESTIONS

1. If you represented Frierson, is there any way to avoid "pleading her out of court" and yet still maintain an action against the University for *respondeat superior* liability, and an action against Robertson for tortious interference?
2. If you were given the opportunity to file an amended complaint on behalf of Frierson, what kind of factual allegations would be sufficient to meet the court's test?
3. Does the Restatement of Employment Law capture the *Frierson* rule, or does it propose a different test?

Restatement of Employment Law

§ 6.04. Employer Does Not Wrongfully Interfere with Its Own Employment Relationship

(a) An employer is not subject to liability for wrongful interference with the employer's own present or prospective employment relationships.

(b) An employee may be subject to liability for wrongful interference with another employee's employment relationship with the interfering employee's employer only if the employer does not authorize or ratify the interfering employee's actions and those actions are not within the scope of the employee's employment.

Example 11-4

Gerry is a supervisor in a mass-marketing call center. He had an altercation with another supervisory employee, Louis, in a bar downtown. Gerry was so angry that he decided to make life miserable for Louis so that Louis would quit. Gerry began harassing Louis both at the worksite and offsite, urging him to find a new job. Louis complains to Gerry's boss, but no action was taken. Louis then complained to the company president, but again no action was taken. Ultimately, Gerry's boss told Louis that Gerry was a very good supervisor, and so the company would not take any action against him for "interpersonal problems" with other employees. Louis then quits his job and sues Gerry personally for interfering with his employment.

Louis cannot prevail because the employer ratified Gerry's actions toward Louis. These actions were within Gerry's conduct as an employee because they were accepted as such.

Example 11-5

Kirk worked for Sierra Environmental Consultants (SEC), which is a wholly owned subsidiary of The Sierra Group (SG). Kirk was assigned to serve as general manager of a joint venture formed by SEC and a Saudi corporation to bid for projects with the Saudi government. Kirk discovered that the minister with authority to grant contracts, Prince Surki, was also an investor in SG. Believing this to be a potential violation of the Foreign Corrupt Practices Act, Kirk reported it to his boss at SG. Kirk was recalled to the United States and interviewed about the situation by the General Counsel of SG. Kirk was fired by SEC two months later and told there were no positions available within SG for him.

Kirk sued SEC for wrongful discharge in violation of public policy, and he sued SG for tortuously interfering with his employment relationship with SEC. As to the latter claim, Kirk alleged that SG authorities requested that SEC terminate his employment.

Kirk most likely cannot prevail on his claim against SG for tortious interference with his employment at SEC. As a general rule, because the economic interests of a parent company and its subsidiary are closely aligned, the parent company is not a true "third party" to the subsidiary's employment relationships. There may be limited exceptions to this rule, but in this case it appears that SEC and SG were in fact completely aligned in acting on their shared economic interests.

Mastery Problem 11-2

Assume that you are a judge ruling on a Motion to Dismiss in the following scenario, and that *Frierson* is precedent in your jurisdiction.

Sharon Williams was hired as the warden of the Pacific County Correctional Facility under a 5-year contract. The Pacific County Prison Board supervised her employment. Donald Drake was the Chairman of the 5-member Board. Williams was appointed to a second 5-year term, after receiving very positive reviews of her work. Two years later she suffered an illness and underwent a series of medical procedures. She was placed on medical leave. After several months she returned to work, but requested accommodations for her medical condition, including the ability to work from home.

Williams alleges that Drake immediately began to badger her about being on-site for at least 8 hours per day. Williams reminded Drake of her accommodations, but he stated that he didn't believe employees should be paid when they are just "gaming the system." After a series of increasingly angry interactions, Williams reiterated her request that the Board grant her medical accommodations. Shortly thereafter, Williams was terminated for breach of contract by a vote of 3–2.

Williams sues Pacific County for retaliating against her for asserting her rights under the Family Medical Leave Act. Williams also sues Drake personally, alleging that he acted out of malice towards her and obtained her termination by falsely claiming to other Board members that she was "taking advantage" and "malingering." Specifically, Williams alleges that he "acted maliciously to interfere with her employment by Pacific County with no purpose other than to cause her harm, as a result of his disdain for her request for accommodations. He did so for his own purposes, and not for the benefit of Pacific County."

Should this case proceed to discovery?

Does the analysis change when the employee is suing co-employees for tortious interference rather than a supervisor? Consider the following case and develop the arguments for and against the court's decision to permit liability against co-workers for tortious interference.

ESERHUT V. HEISTER

762 P.2d 6 (Wash. Ct. App. 1988).

Leonard Eserhut appeals the trial court's decision that his former co-employees, Steve Heister, Tom Weist and Gary Venn (hereinafter co-employees), are not liable for the tort of intentional interference with a business relationship. . . .

Facts

Eserhut was employed as a design engineer by Utility Vault from 1979 to October 1983. Heister and Weist were design engineers and worked in the same office as Eserhut. Venn was employed as a salesman and his desk was located in another part of the office building.

During 1980 and 1981, Eserhut and the co-employees worked together on standard engineering projects, and their relationship was good. During 1982, however, the co-employees became jealous of Eserhut when he began working with company management on a special project. On occasion, Eserhut referred to some of the co-employees in "unfortunate language terms." These comments, together with personality conflicts and the co-employees' jealousy, led to a deterioration in Eserhut's relationship with them.

After the special project was completed in January 1983, Eserhut was required to work and interact with the co-employees once again on standard projects. However, as a group, they isolated Eserhut by not communicating with and socially ostracizing him. These actions interfered with Eserhut's work, and he experienced sleeplessness, depression, and indigestion.

On several occasions, Eserhut solicited help from management, who advised the co-employees that their actions were harmful to the company and encouraged them to get along with Eserhut. However, nothing changed.

In mid-October 1983, Eserhut felt he had no reasonable alternative but to resign his employment. He communicated his intention to the company president, who asked him to delay his decision until that afternoon. Later, the president called Eserhut and informed him that the three co-employees had "voted him out." This was only a figurative expression; no actual vote took place, and the co-employees had no authority to hire or fire other employees. The president then acquiesced in Eserhut's decision to leave.

Initially, Eserhut brought this suit against the co-employees only. Later, Utility Vault was joined on the theory that it had ratified the co-employees' actions. The trial court found in favor of all defendants. With regard to the co-employees, the trial court concluded that the effect of their actions on Eserhut was to interfere with his work, that it was unlikely anyone would have been comfortable in the same situation, that their actions had caused Eserhut to terminate his employment relationship, and that Eserhut's damages were in the amount of $48,500. However, the trial court decided that the co-employees could not be held liable for the tort of intentional interference because their actions had focused on Eserhut, rather than on Utility Vault, and because the actions did not cause Utility Vault to terminate Eserhut.

Appeal

Eserhut contends that the trial court failed to apply the correct rule of law when it determined that Eserhut's co-employees could not be held liable for the tort at issue. We agree.

Washington law has defined the elements of intentional interference with a business relationship as

> (1) The existence of a valid contractual relationship or business expectancy; (2) knowledge of the relationship or expectancy by the alleged interfering party; (3) intentional interference inducing or causing a breach or termination of the relationship or expectancy; and (4) resultant damage.

The defendant's actions may focus on either party to the contract. For example, liability may be imposed when the defendant has intentionally interfered with a *third person's performance* of his existing contract with the plaintiff. *See F.D. Hill & Co. v. Wallerich,* 67 Wash.2d 409, 414, 407 P.2d 956 (1965) (defendant-buyer promised seller of land that he would "take care of" plaintiff-broker's sales commission, but failed to do so); Restatement (Second) of Torts § 766 (1979). In addition, liability may be imposed when the defendant has intentionally interfered with the *plaintiff's performance* of his own contract with a third person. *See Pacific TypeSetting Co. v. International Typographical Union,* 125 Wash. 273, 216 P. 358 (1923) (defendant-union coerced employees to strike in order to render it impossible for plaintiff employer to complete its printing contracts with other companies); *see* Restatement (Second) of Torts § 766A. The same analysis applies when the contractual relations are prospective, *i.e.,* not yet reduced to contract.

Applying the foregoing analysis to the facts of the present case, it becomes clear that if the elements of the tort are otherwise met, then the co-employees can be held liable for intentionally interfering with Eserhut's employment with Utility Vault. Other jurisdictions have reached the same conclusion under similar facts. *See Lewis v. Oregon Beauty Supply Co.,* 302 Or. 616, 733 P.2d 430 (1987) (defendant-son of employer held liable to plaintiff-employee who quit as a result of defendant's harassment); *Kyriazi v. Western Electric*

Co., 461 F.Supp. 894 (D.N.J.1978) (defendant-employees who harassed plaintiff-employee held liable).

Although we have found that the trial court applied the wrong standard of law, we cannot reverse the decision because the trial court's findings on intent, the third element of the cause of action, are ambiguous. Finding of fact 10 states that "the actions of the individual defendants were intentional." However, finding of fact 19 states that "[n]one of the acts or omissions complained of . . . or omitted by the individual defendants . . . was done with deliberate intention within the meaning of RCW [51.24.020]." Because this is a fact question, we cannot resolve it and, therefore, remand for clearer findings and application of the correct rule of law.

QUESTIONS

1. If you represented Eserhut, what facts would you seek to prove on remand to establish your case?
2. From a policy perspective, how does this case compare with *Frierson*? Is liability more justified on these facts?
3. On remand the plaintiff prevailed, and the defendant again appealed. In *Eserhut II*, the Court of Appeals revised its earlier ruling on the applicable legal standard by carefully re-reading the precedents from other jurisdictions it had cited. The majority opinion concluded:

   > Fairly read, these cases stand for no more than the proposition that when coemployees intentionally, directly, and substantially interfere with the performance of the plaintiff's work responsibilities, knowing that the plaintiff's termination is a substantially certain consequence thereof, they risk liability for intentional interference with a business relationship.
   >
   > Far less has been proven in this case. The trial court noted in its oral ruling that the defendants' conduct amounted to social ostracism. It did not constitute the tort of outrage, and it did not focus on the employer-employee relationship directly.
   >
   > Thus, we hold that the defendants cannot be held liable here, since the evidence did not show that they acted with the intent and result of directly interfering with the performance of plaintiff's work responsibilities. We therefore reverse the judgment in favor of Eserhut.

Eserhut v. Heister, 62 Wash. App. 10, 15–16 (1991) (*Eserhut II*). In a concurring opinion, Judge Forrest provided a rationale for the Court's cautious approach:

> There is no constitutional, statutory, or common law duty requiring an employee to be socially friendly with his or her co-employees. Conversely, an employee does not have any "right" to social friendship from his co-employees. Eserhut makes no claim to come within any statutory protection. Here, there is no claim or proof that Eserhut was prevented from performing his duties by lack of cooperation by co-employees. Indeed, his employer was satisfied with his work and would like for him to have continued. This is not a case where Eserhut was physically or economically prevented from performing his contract, but merely a case where he was unhappy with his treatment by his co-employees. Such purely subjective unhappiness would be an insufficient basis to justify his breach of a contract with his employer and is likewise an insufficient basis for asserting tortious interference with his employment contract. Such a cause of action would not only spawn work place litigation between co-employees but would have other ramifications which are impossible to forecast.

Eserhut II at 16–17. Does this criticism suggest that co-employees could never be found liable for tortious interference?

4. What if Eserhut was mercilessly teased and subjected to vicious taunts by his coworkers in the workplace, despite the employer's honest effort to prevent the behavior? If Eserhut suffered emotional distress and quit his job as a result, could he have a plausible case for damages against his coworkers?
5. How might the legal system address the claims in *Eserhut* other than by imposing tort liability? Is this matter better left to non-legal social norms? Should the matter be left to an employer's decision about the kind of workplace it wishes to maintain?

Mastery Problem 11-3

Professor David Yamada has led an effort to develop a legislative response to the problem of workplace bullying. Noting that the tort of Intentional Interference is not well-suited to address workplace bullying,[1] Yamada has proposed a model

1 David C. Yamada, *The Phenomenon of "Workplace Bullying" and the Need for Status-Blind Hostile Work Environment Protection*, 88 Geo. L.J. 475, 489–90 (2000).

statute—The Healthy Workplace Bill—to address the problem.[2] The proposed Bill subjects employers to vicarious liability for an "abusive work environment" unless they take reasonable steps to prevent the abuse and the affected employee fails to take advantage of the employer's preventive or corrective opportunities, and also subjects co-employees to personal liability for their wrongful acts in creating an "abusive work environment." The proposed Bill defines an "abusive work environment" as follows:

> (A) Abusive work environment. An abusive work environment exists when an employer or one or more of its employees, acting with intent to cause pain or distress to an employee, subjects that employee to abusive conduct that causes physical harm, psychological harm, or both.
>
> (1) Abusive conduct. Abusive conduct includes, acts, omissions, or both, that a reasonable person would find abusive, based on the severity, nature, and frequency of the conduct. Abusive conduct may include, but is not limited to: repeated verbal abuse such as the use of derogatory remarks, insults, and epithets; verbal, non-verbal, or physical conduct of a threatening, intimidating, or humiliating nature; or the sabotage or undermining of an employee's work performance. It shall be considered an aggravating factor that the conduct exploited an employee's known psychological or physical illness or disability. A single act normally will not constitute abusive conduct, but an especially severe and egregious act may meet this standard.
>
> . . . .
>
> (B) Adverse employment action. An adverse employment action includes, but is not limited to, a termination, demotion, unfavorable reassignment, failure to promote, disciplinary action, or reduction in compensation.
>
> (C) Constructive discharge. A constructive discharge shall be considered a termination, and, therefore, an adverse employment action within the meaning of the Chapter. A constructive discharge for purposes of the Chapter exists where: (1) the employee reasonably believed he or she was subjected to an abusive work environment; (2) the employee resigned because of that conduct; and, (3) the employer was aware of the abusive conduct prior to the resignation and failed to stop it.

---

2 David C. Yamada, *Emerging American Legal Responses to Workplace Bullying*, 22 Temple Pol. & Civil Rights L. Rev. 333–38, 350–54 (2013).

Assume that you work for an industry trade group that is opposing the Healthy Workplace Bill, which has been introduced in your state legislature. What arguments would you make against the Bill? What arguments do you anticipate proponents will make, and how will you respond to those arguments?

Conclusion

Employers and employees can protect their relationship from wrongful interference by third parties by suing in tort. An agent of the employer might be treated as a third party to the employer-employee relationship, but only if the agent acts outside the scope of its agency and the employer does not ratify the wrongful action.

5

Obligations Owed by Employers to Third Parties

Key Concepts

- The employment relationship provides the basis for various obligations owed by an employer to third parties.
- Employees can be agents of the employer. An agency relationship empowers the employee to bind the employer to contracts with third parties.
- Employers may be directly liable to third parties for their tortious behavior in hiring or retaining an employee who causes harm, or for negligently providing a reference to a subsequent employer.
- Under the common law doctrine of *respondeat superior*, an employer may be vicariously responsible for the tortious behavior of an employee that occurs during the course of the employee's duties.

Lesson 12:
Direct Contract Liability for Acts of Agents

Objectives and Expected Learning Outcomes

In this Lesson, you will learn when an employee has the power to bind its employer contractually to third parties. There are different types of agency relationships that might apply to an employee. An employer has a strong interest in defining its relationships with its employees carefully to ensure that an employee can contractually bind it only when the employer desires this result.

You will recall from Lesson 3 that an important distinction exists between an employee and an independent contractor. Employees have duties and rights under employment law, whereas an independent contractor's relationship with the hiring entity is defined by contract. In this Lesson, we will explore the employer's direct contract liability for acts of its agents. An independent contractor may serve as an agent of the hiring entity, and so may an employee.

Example 12-1

Terra Excavation performs site work at construction projects. Terra has a team of contract specialists who prepare bids and review proposed contract language. The Vice-President for Operations signs all agreements with general contractors as part of her duties. On these facts alone, the contract specialist employees would not be agents capable of binding Terra contractually, but the Vice-President for Operations would be considered an employee who has agency power to bind the company contractually.

Example 12-2

George is an attorney specializing in employment law. George represents Sarah in a wrongful discharge action against her former employer. George is not an employee of Sarah, but rather is an independent contractor who also has fiduciary obligations to Sarah given the nature of the attorney-client relationship. Under their written retention agreement, Sarah granted George the authority to settle the claim on her behalf, subject to her further direction. George is suffering financial distress and is aggressively trying to settle cases to generate contingency fee income. George advises Sarah that the court has scheduled a settlement conference and that he must be empowered to settle the case during that session. Sarah agrees that George may settle the case for no less than $150,000, based on his judgment. George settles the claim for $150,000 quickly, despite evidence that the claim was worth as much as $200,000. On these facts alone, because George has actual authority to settle the claim, the claim by Sarah against her former employer has been settled and may not be reopened. However, Sarah may sue George for breach of his fiduciary obligations as her attorney.

---

1. The Nature of the Agency Relationship

An agency relationship is a fiduciary relationship that is created when one person (the "principal") manifests assent that another person (the "agent") may act on the principal's behalf and subject to the principal's control, and the agent manifests assent or otherwise consents. The agency relationship may be manifested through written or spoken words, or other conduct. There are different ways in which an agency relationship may be created. An agent has "actual authority" when the employer has expressly manifested this result, or it may be implied from the employer's manifestations. The agent has "apparent authority" if a third party has a reasonable belief that an agency relationship exists based on some manifestation made by the principal. Finally, an agent has "inherent authority" to bind the principal if the agent is acting within the scope of the powers established by the employment relationship. We will address these doctrines in turn.

2. Agents with Actual Authority

Actual authority may be given by a principal to an agent, either expressly or through implication. In both cases, the authority must be manifested by the principal in somc manner.

Restatement (Third) of Agency

§ 2.01. Actual Authority

An agent acts with actual authority when, at the time of taking action that has legal consequences for the principal, the agent reasonably believes, in accordance with the principal's manifestations to the agent, that the principal wishes the agent so to act.

"Express actual authority" occurs when an employer instructs an agent to do some particular thing. For example, if an employer instructs an employee to execute contracts with suppliers to provide the raw materials for the employer's business, the employee has express actual authority to act as the employer's agent in this regard. Express actual authority is generally easy to determine on the facts because the principal must manifest the granting of authority in some manner.

"Implied actual authority" arises when the employer gives an employee the authority to accomplish a task, and there are subsidiary acts required to accomplish the task. For example, an employee who is given the express actual authority to purchase real estate for her employer would likely have the implied authority to retain a commercial real estate agent to act on the employer's behalf to assist in the purchase. In some circumstances, it can be difficult to determine if agency authority may properly be implied. Consider the following case.

Ruffin v. Temple Church of God in Christ, Inc.

749 A.2d 719 (D.C. Ct. App. 2000).

Steadman, Associate Judge:

[Editor's Note: Attorney Thomas Ruffin sued for breach of contract when he was not paid for providing legal services, and a jury found in his favor. The trial judge entered judgment as a matter of law for the defendant, finding that a dispute between the pastor and the church precluded a finding that the pastor had authority to bind the church.]

I.

The evidence at trial, viewed in the light most favorable to appellant, revealed the following situation. From 1923 until the appointment of Frank Morris as pastor in 1992, appellee Temple Church of God in Christ ("the Church") had a long history of pastorship under a single man—the founder of the Church, Samuel Kelsey. While Kelsey had run the Church with the help of a board of trustees, during his tenure Kelsey also entered into a number of significant contracts on behalf of the Church without specific approval. In 1992, a bishop of the Church publicly, in the presence of the board of trustees and the Church congregation, including [attorney Thomas] Ruffin, appointed Morris as co-pastor without objection, to take over for the ailing Kelsey. The bishop gave what Morris thought was "full authority to run the church." Shortly after the appointment, a conflict began to arise between the Church's board and Morris with regard to aspects of fiscal responsibility and powers of appointment within the Church.

In early 1993, Ruffin was contacted by Morris to help reconcile the internal dispute, and Ruffin entered an oral contract with Morris to perform legal services on behalf of the Church. Between January 4 and March 11, 1993, Ruffin worked on drafting new by-laws for the Church and engaged in other activities designed to alleviate the rift. However, when Ruffin presented the Church with his bill of about $8,000, payment was refused. The Church asserted that as a non-profit organization, its board of trustees had sole authority to contract, and that the board did not authorize or reasonably appear to authorize Morris to enter into the contract for Ruffin's legal services. Ruffin brought suit to recover his fees.

At the close of Ruffin's case-in-chief, the Church moved for a directed verdict. The motion was denied by the trial court because, according to the trial judge,

> a reasonable juror could decide . . . based on the testimony . . . that there was a course of conduct over time in which the board of trustees had essentially delegated to the pastor the business end of running the church, and that that had not been formally rescinded at the time in January of '93 when Mr. Ruffin and the pastor entered into their contract. . . . [O]n that ground alone, the motion should be . . . denied. Whether the pastor did or did not have authority, a reasonable juror could conclude that the course of conduct over those years established the pastor's authority.

During the defendant's case-in chief no evidence was introduced to demonstrate that the board expressly rescinded any and all contractual authority of the pastor.

The jury was instructed that under the law, the Church's board of trustees had ultimate control of the Church. However, the jury was also instructed, under the doctrines of implied and apparent authority, that if either Morris or Ruffin reasonably believed authority existed for Morris to enter into the contract on behalf of the Church, the Church would be liable on the contract. The jury returned a verdict in favor of Ruffin. . . .

II.

> *[Editor's Note: The standard of review to affirm a judgment as a matter of law is that no reasonable person viewing all the evidence in the light most favorable to the prevailing party, could reach a verdict in favor of that party.]*

. . . .

As with our standard of review, the doctrine of implied authority has been defined by this court.

> Implied authority is actual authority inferred from the circumstances, such as the relationship between the parties and conduct of the principal toward the agent manifesting the principal's consent to have the agent act for him." *Lewis v. Washington Metro. Area Transit Auth.*, 463 A.2d 666, 669 (D.C.1983). Implied authority, therefore, exists when the act of "the servant or agent is incidental to authorized conduct and furthers the master's business. A servant or agent is authorized to do anything which is reasonably regarded as incidental to the work specifically directed or which is usually done in connection with such work." *Presley* [*v. Commercial Credit Corp.*, 177 A.2d 916, 918 (D.C.Mun.App.1962)].

Sigal Const. Corp. v. Stanbury, 586 A.2d 1204, 1217–18 (D.C.1991).

At trial, plaintiff introduced evidence intended to show that, although there was a dispute between the Church's board of trustees and the newly-appointed Pastor Morris, there were reasonable grounds for the pastor and Ruffin to believe that authority to enter into this particular contract existed. Ruffin produced testimony that reflected Morris' belief, based on past practice and the bishop's public statements, that Morris "would have the authority to run the church." Morris also testified regarding specific evidence of the prior pattern and practice of the pastor, exercised by Pastor Kelsey during his seventy-year tenure, to make contracts of reasonable size without explicit prior board approval. Thomas Ruffin, Sr., appellant's father and a former member of the board of trustees, also testified regarding the pastor's authority within the Church, as reflected by prior practices. In addition, the appellant testified and introduced evidence which revealed that during his employment period under the contract, he had held himself out to the board of trustees, and the public' as an "attorney for the Temple Church of God in Christ," without objection by the board.

Evidence was also admitted that tended to show that the pastors of the Church, including Pastor Morris, were considered "chief executive officers" of the Church, having the "right to execute that office as [the pastor] sees fit." The general implications of that role was significant and supportive to a claim of implied authority. As we have previously stated:

> Where a person is appointed to a recognized position such as the president or manager of a corporation, or the cashier of a bank, or is given a specific authority in general terms . . . he [or she]

> is thereby given authority to do the various matters which by business custom such persons normally have. . . .

Sigal, supra, 586 A.2d at 1218 (quoting W. SEAVEY, AGENCY, § 8, at 12–13 (1964)). That a chief executive officer would "normally" have the authority to contract with an attorney to assist the corporation in resolving internal management issues is well within the permissible understanding of a juror, if not uncontestable on its face.

Despite the view of the trial court and the argument of the Church to the contrary, we must conclude that the mere fact that a "power struggle" between the board and the pastor was underway does not, in and of itself, necessarily defeat the implication of authority grounded in seven decades of prior practice with respect to the specific contract at issue here. The focus on the narrow time frame just prior to Ruffin's engagement ignores both the import of this long background relationship between the Church and its pastor, and the lack of any explicit revocation of the authority to contract. Because of the history of the pastoral authority and the testimony of Morris and Ruffin, the jury could have reasonably concluded that authority to contract had been delegated to the pastor of the Church, and that Morris' appointment did nothing to alter the arrangement.

The defendants offered no evidence demonstrating any clear revocation of all such authority.[8] . . . Had the Board of Trustees intended to exclude the specific authority to contract from the scope of the pastor's authority, they had every right and opportunity to do so under its control concededly granted by D.C.Code § 29–518. Their silence on this issue, both before and during Ruffin's contract, permitted the inference that the authority once held by Pastor Kelsey continued, at least to some extent, in Pastor Morris.[9]

This is not to say that the known dispute between the pastor and the board would have no bearing on the extent to which the pastor could reasonably

---

8 The Church introduced a resolution by the board, passed in December, 1992, which ostensibly vested sole signatory authority over accounts and investments in the board. However, such evidence did not compel the jury to find that all implied authority of Morris to *contract* had been revoked. The powers are distinct. *See, e.g., Hausam v. Schnabl*, 126 Idaho 569, 887 P.2d 1076, 1078–79 (Idaho App.1994) (although agent had authority to run business, including "the authority to hire and fire employees, to seek . . . contracts and to assign jobs," agent's execution of a promissory note was invalid because principal did not grant authority to agent to write checks or withdraw money).

9 This should not be confused with a conclusion of liability based on specific acquiescence or ratification—theories not presented to the jury. Rather the board's relative silence in the face of Ruffin's asserted representation of the Church speaks to the failure of the board to effectively rescind all contractual authority previously granted to the pastor, whether that prior grant was explicit or implied through acquiescence itself.

conclude that he continued to possess the full implied authority vested in his predecessor. Certainly that was not true as to signatory authority. See *supra,* note 1. Furthermore, it could be questioned whether the pastor could consider that he had the continued right to bind the Church on, say, significant contracts for church acquisitions or remodeling or the like. The present focus, however, must be on the specific contract in question here: one in which the pastor of a church, seeking to reconcile differences with the board of trustees over their respective areas of authority, responsibility and control, seeks to employ an attorney under a contract of relatively minimal cost to further the process of bringing the church, its board, and its pastor into harmony again. We think a jury could reasonably find, on the evidence presented here, that the pastor could conclude that he retained implied authority to execute such a contract on behalf of the Church.

[For the foregoing reasons we reverse the trial court's grant of judgment as a matter of law and reinstate the jury verdict.]

QUESTIONS

1. The Court of Appeals reversed the judgment as a matter of law by the trial judge. If the jury had found in favor of the Church rather than for the pastor, would the Court of Appeals have supported entry of judgment as a matter of law by the trial judge?
2. The court discusses the reasonable expectations of the pastor and his lawyer. Do the lawyer's reasonable expectations play any role in the court's analysis? Why does the court reference the lawyer's expectations?

---

3. Agents with Apparent Authority

Even in cases when there is no actual authority (express or implied), a person may have the "apparent authority" to bind a principal. Apparent authority exists when an employer leads a third person to believe that it has empowered the agent with actual authority. The third party must act reasonably. The key factor in most cases is determining whether the employer has in some manner "clothed" the employee with authority through its actions.

Example 12-3

In the construction trade in a particular location, it is customary for the procurement manager to enter into contracts with suppliers on behalf of an employer. If an employer hires Samantha but expressly withholds her authority to enter into contracts with suppliers, Samantha might still have the apparent authority to bind the employer if she is given the title of "procurement manager" and provided with business cards and stationery that reflect this title. However, if a supplier knows that Samantha lacks actual authority, the supplier cannot prevail under a theory of apparent authority.

Example 12-4

Will visits a furniture store, looking to purchase a sofa. He is met at the door by a man wearing a suit who asks if he may assist. The man leads Will around the store and helps with the selection of a new sofa. The man then advises Will that the sofa must be ordered, and that he must pay a 20% deposit for the order to be placed. Will presents his credit card, and the man runs a charge on his cell phone plug-in device. Four weeks later Will goes to the store to check on his order, only to find that the company has no record of the purchase. It appears that the man who helped him was running a scam, and cannot be located. It is unlikely that the store would be bound by the contract for purchase because the store did not "clothe" the man with authority in any manner. However, Will might be able to sue the store for negligence in failing to discover and prevent the scam. In some jurisdictions this tort action would be fashioned as an "agency by estoppel."

HARKNESS v. PLATTEN

359 Or. 715 (2016).

BALDWIN, J.

[Editor's Note: The plaintiffs sued Kantor, a loan officer, for robbing them through a fraudulent investment scheme. They also sued Kantor's successive employers, Sunset Mortgage (Sunset) and Directors Mortgage, Inc. (Directors), seeking to hold them liable for Kantor's

actions under agency theory. The trial court entered a directed verdict for the corporate defendants, finding that there was insufficient evidence in the record to support the finding of an agency relationship. The Court of Appeals affirmed, and the plaintiffs appealed to the Supreme Court.]

The facts as stated by the Court of Appeals, which we adopt, are as follows:

"Plaintiffs * * * were interested in using the equity in their home to invest when [Mr. Harkness] saw a homemade flyer for various businesses at work. The flyer included a photocopy of Kantor's business card that indicated Kantor was a loan officer with Sunset. After [Mr. Harkness] spoke with a coworker who had worked with Kantor to purchase an apartment complex, plaintiffs set up and attended a meeting with Kantor at her Sunset office. Kantor proposed that plaintiffs borrow money from Sunset, using the equity in their house as collateral, and then she would invest those proceeds in short-term, high-interest loans to developers and building contractors (hard-money loans). She told plaintiffs that those hard-money loans would be secured by first or second liens on real property with 'lots' of equity. Kantor explained that she and Sunset would get paid from the commission on plaintiffs' conventional loan on their house and from the conventional construction loans that Sunset would do for the builders.

"After meeting with Kantor at Sunset again, plaintiffs agreed to the proposal, took out a conventional loan from Sunset, and turned over the loan proceeds to Kantor. Kantor did use those proceeds to make hard-money loans to several people and prepared certain documentation on Sunset letterhead. For the first of those loans, which was not funded from the Sunset loan proceeds turned over to Kantor, [Mrs. Harkness] gave Kantor a cashier's check made out to Sunset. [Mrs. Harkness] always met with Kantor at her Sunset office to learn about additional hard-money loan opportunities and to receive copies of notes for the loans Kantor made, which were always closed outside of plaintiffs' presence.

"Kantor later went to work as a loan officer at Directors. Plaintiffs continued their same investment relationship with Kantor at Directors and met with her at her Directors' office in the same manner as when Kantor was at Sunset. Plaintiffs also took out an additional loan from Directors, using their rental house as collateral, the proceeds of which were paid directly to Kantor to make hard-money loans to people Kantor found. Kantor's assistant at Directors was knowledgeable about all of plaintiffs' hard-money loans and would assist plaintiffs with information on those matters.

"Plaintiffs did not get loan payments directly from borrowers and did not know how borrowers made payments, but Kantor arranged deposits into plaintiffs' bank account to service plaintiffs' personal loans. [Mrs. Harkness] testified that certain notes directed payments to be made at addresses that corresponded to Sunset's or Directors' office address. Plaintiffs did not receive the proceeds from some of the note payoffs; instead, when a note was paid off or came due but not paid off, Kantor would recommend that plaintiffs immediately invest payoffs into new loans or roll over unpaid loans into a new loan to the same borrower, which plaintiffs would then do.

"[Mrs. Harkness] testified that she would not have dealt with Kantor if she were not working through Sunset. She also testified that she would not have continued working with Kantor if Kantor had not been at Directors. [Mrs. Harkness] believed that Kantor was a representative of Sunset, and then Directors, and was acting within the scope of her employment in all her dealings with plaintiffs. However, it was undisputed that Kantor, in fact, was not performing duties for which she was hired as a loan officer with regard to the investment scheme and hard-money loan arrangements—that type of transaction was not part of the business of either Sunset or Directors—and neither Sunset nor Directors received any fees or commissions from the hard-money loans. There also was no evidence that the control persons at Sunset or Directors were aware of Kantor's arrangement with plaintiffs.

"After about two years of investing with Kantor, plaintiffs were contacted by an attorney for one of the borrowers on a hard-money loan financed by plaintiffs. Kantor told [Mrs. Harkness] that she just had forgotten to record a lien, so [Mrs. Harkness] accompanied Kantor to record the lien. The borrower then sued plaintiffs. At the end of that lawsuit, plaintiffs learned that Kan-

> tor had forged the documents for at least that loan, and, for other loans, Kantor had not recorded any liens, or had recorded a lien in third position behind a lien Kantor had placed in favor of Directors on the property. Kantor also had been running all the money through her personal accounts. At the conclusion of that lawsuit, plaintiffs held notes to five outstanding loans, including the one deemed a forgery by the court, that totaled approximately $980,000, and at least one of the borrowers had already filed bankruptcy.
>
> . . . .

. . . [P]laintiffs proceeded on a theory that Kantor had apparent authority from Sunset and Directors to bind those companies to the oral contract that was the basis for Kantor's investment scheme with plaintiffs—loaning funds to plaintiffs based on the equity in their different properties and then facilitating the lending of those funds to other borrowers for plaintiffs' investment purposes. . . .

> *[Editor's Note: The trial court entered a directed verdict in favor of Sunset and Directors.]*

The Court of Appeals affirmed the trial court's ruling that plaintiffs had not presented sufficient evidence of apparent authority to survive defendant's directed-verdict motion: "Plaintiffs presented no evidence that Kantor had the apparent authority to give investment advice on behalf of either company, engage in the proposed investment scheme, or, for the contract claim, bind Sunset or Directors to the oral terms of that scheme." In reaching that conclusion, the court disregarded the evidence related to Kantor arranging for plaintiffs to take out a conventional loan from Sunset and Directors and to those companies receiving a commission on those loans, "because those acts were within Kantor's actual authority as a loan officer for Sunset and Directors and are not evidence that Kantor had apparent authority to do more than just that." The court then considered the remaining evidence and concluded that "[i]t was not objectively reasonable for plaintiffs to believe that that type of investment scheme [in which Kantor had engaged] was part of Kantor's job as a 'loan officer,' nor did Sunset or Directors provide any information to plaintiffs, whether directly or indirectly, that such a scheme or financial advice was part of Kantor's job." *Id.* at 273, 348 P.3d 1145. The court also concluded that "[p]laintiffs' reliance on *Badger* to make their case is misplaced."

. . . .

We begin with a brief discussion of Oregon law relating to the doctrine of apparent authority. This court recently summarized the legal principles applicable to a determination of when "a putative principal can be held responsible for the acts of another on an apparent agency theory" in *Eads v. Borman*, 351 Or. 729, 277 P.3d 503 (2012):

> "Classically, an agency relationship 'results from the manifestation of consent by one person to another that the other shall act on behalf and subject to his control, and consent by the other so to act.' *Vaughn v. First Transit, Inc.*, 346 Or. 128, 135, 206 P.3d 181 (2009) (emphasis in *Vaughn* omitted) * * *. The agency relationship can arise either from actual consent (express or implied) or from the appearance of such consent. *See generally Taylor v. Ramsay-Gerding Construction Co.*, 345 Or. 403, 410, 196 P.3d 532 (2008) (so discussing). In either circumstance, the principal is bound by or otherwise responsible for the actual or apparent agent's acts only if the acts are within the scope of what the agent is actually or apparently authorized to do. *Id.*; *see also Beeson v. Hegstad*, 199 Or. 325, 330, 261 P.2d 381 (1953) (one cannot hold principal liable for an act that does not fall within the scope of agent's real or apparent authority).
>
> " * * *. Under this court's settled cases, '[a]pparent authority to do any particular act can be created only by some conduct of the principal which, when reasonably interpreted, causes a third party to believe that the principal consents to have the apparent agent act for him on that matter.' *Jones v. Nunley*, 274 Or. 591, 595, 547 P.2d 616 (1976). There accordingly are two keys to the analysis: (1) the principal's representations; and (2) a third party's reasonable reliance on those representations."

Id. at 735–37, 277 P.3d 503 (internal quotation marks omitted).

This court also observed in *Eads* that the test in Oregon to determine when a principal is bound by an actor under an apparent authority theory is consistent with the rule stated in the *Restatement (Third) of Agency* section 2.03 (2006):

> " 'Apparent authority is the power held by an agent or other actor to affect a principal's legal relations with third parties when a third party reasonably believes the actor has authority to act on behalf of the principal and that belief is traceable to the principal's manifestations.' "

351 Or. at 737 n. 5, 277 P.3d 503 (quoting *Restatement (Third)* § 2.03). That test is applicable both "to determine when a principal is bound by actors who appear to be agents but are not, as well as actors who act beyond the scope of their actual authority." *Id.* (citing *Restatement (Third)* § 2.03 comment a).

Regarding the first element of the apparent authority test—a putative principal's representation that an agent is authorized to act on its behalf—an agent's actions, standing alone, will not give rise to apparent authority. *Id.* at 737, 277 P.3d 503 (citing *Taylor*, 345 Or. at 410, 196 P.3d 532). Instead, the principal "must take some affirmative step in creating the appearance of authority, one that the principal either intended to cause or 'should realize' likely would cause a third party to believe that the putative agent has authority to act on the principal's behalf." *Id.* (ultimately quoting *Restatement (Second) of Agency* § 27 comment a (1958)). The principal's words, conduct, or other representation need not be made directly to or witnessed directly by the third party for the principal to be liable under a theory of apparent authority; rather, the representation of authority need only be *traceable* to the principal. *Id.*; *see Taylor*, 345 Or. at 411, 196 P.3d 532 (indirect information attributed to principal's conduct "can be used to support apparent agency, as long as that information can be traced back to the principal"); *see also Restatement (Third)* § 1.03 comment b (although "the presence of actual authority depends upon whether the principal has made a manifestation to the agent," by contrast, "a manifestation sufficient to establish apparent authority may, but need not necessarily be, directed toward an identified person as its audience").[3]

3 The *Restatement (Third)* describes a "manifestation" of authority by a putative principal in similarly broad terms. Section 1.03 notes that "[a] person manifests assent or intention through written or spoken words or other conduct," and the commentary to section 1.03 explains that "[a] manifestation is conduct by a person, observable by others, that expresses meaning. It is a broader concept than communication." *Id.* § 1.03 comment b; see *State v. Sines*, 359 Or. 41, 55–56, 379 P.3d 1023, 2016 WL 1459146 (2016) (citing section 1.03 and observing that "in determining whether agency exists, the emphasis is on 'manifestations' that can be assessed objectively").

The *Restatement (Third)* commentary further explains that "an organization manifests its assent to be bound by the acts of individuals through the observable connections between the individual and the organization. An organization manifests assent to an individual by appointing that person to a position defined by the organization." *Id.* § 1.03 comment c. Moreover, the commentary emphasizes that the significance of manifestations by a putative principal must be understood in context:

Further, when a principal cloaks an agent with actual authority to perform certain tasks, that actual authority may create the appearance of authority to perform other, related tasks. *Taylor*, 345 Or. at 411, 196 P.3d 532; *see Badger*, 311 Or. at 26, 803 P.2d 1178 (sales representatives' actual authority to sell approved securities lent weight to sales representatives' apparent authority to sell unregistered securities). Additionally, when a principal appoints an agent to a position that carries "generally recognized duties," a principal may create apparent authority to perform those duties. *Badger*, 311 Or. at 24–25 n. 9, 803 P.2d 1178 (quoting *Restatement (Second)* § 27 comment a).

Regarding the second element of the apparent authority test—the third party's reasonable reliance—the third party must in fact rely on the principal's representation in dealing with the apparent agent, and that reliance must be objectively reasonable. *Eads*, 351 Or. at 737, 277 P.3d 503 (citing *Jones*, 274 Or. at 595–96, 547 P.2d 616; *Badger*, 311 Or. at 26, 803 P.2d 1178). In assessing the reasonableness of the third party's reliance, a court must consider what is customary and usual for certain positions or within certain professions. *Eads*, 351 Or. at 737 n. 5, 277 P.3d 503 ("Apparent authority also includes concepts of 'usual authority' and 'customary authority' in determining whether 'a substantial basis for a third party's belief' exists that the person with whom the third party dealt was acting as an agent for a principal in a particular circumstance.") (quoting *Restatement (Third)* § 2.03 comment b).

We now turn to the Court of Appeals' analysis of whether a factfinder could reasonably infer that Kantor had apparent authority to bind Sunset and Directors to the loan transactions between plaintiffs and third parties. As noted, the court focused almost entirely on the nature of the "investment scheme"[4] perpetrated by Kantor as precluding a factfinder from drawing an inference of apparent authority, because "[i]t was not objectively reason-

---

> "A manifestation does not occur in a vacuum, and the meaning that may reasonably be inferred from it will reflect the context in which the manifestation is made. Assent and intention may be expressed explicitly, but often they are inferred from surrounding facts and circumstances. For example, if an organization hires a person as its purchasing manager, the organization's act expresses assent that the person undertake the manager's role as defined by the organization."

Id. at comment e; *see Peoples Heritage Sav. Bank v. Pease*, 2002 ME 82, ¶¶ 20–21, 797 A.2d 1270, 1276 (2002) (genuine issue of material fact whether mortgagee's employee acted within apparent authority in negotiating terms with mortgagors to pay off loans).

4 Although the court referred to Kantor's fraudulent scheme as an "investment scheme," we note that that scheme could just as accurately be referred to as a "loan scheme," or an "investment and loan scheme." Kantor advised plaintiffs that they could use the equity in their home to obtain "loans" from Sunset and Directors that could be "invested" by plaintiffs by making secure "loans" to developers and contractors.

able for plaintiffs to believe that that type of investment scheme was part of Kantor's job as a 'loan officer[.]' " However, in so narrowing its inquiry, the court disregarded, as irrelevant, the evidence concerning the actual authority with which Sunset and Directors had cloaked Kantor. Having disregarded that evidence, the court readily distinguished *Badger*, a case in which this court concluded that—under the circumstances presented—sales representatives with actual authority to sell approved securities were apparent agents with authority to sell unregistered securities.

. . . .

We conclude, however, that the Court of Appeals made two missteps in determining that Sunset and Directors had made no manifestations from which plaintiffs could reasonably have concluded that Kantor was authorized to perform the acts constituting the fraudulent scheme. First, the court disregarded evidence concerning the actual authority with which Sunset and Directors clothed Kantor. Second, the court does not appear to have considered evidence in the record relating to the usual or customary authority of a loan officer for a mortgage company.

As to the first misstep, this court's case law makes clear that the appearance of authority may, at least in part, be based on conduct relating to an agent's actual authority. *Taylor*, 345 Or. at 411, 196 P.3d 532 ("[W]hen a principal clothes an agent with actual authority to perform certain tasks, the principal might create apparent authority to perform other, related tasks."); *Badger*, 311 Or. at 26, 803 P.2d 1178 (sales representatives had apparent authority to sell unregistered securities when they had actual authority to sell approved securities). That is so because, as noted, the rationale for the doctrine of apparent authority is that a principal must be held accountable for the results of reasonable third-party beliefs about an actor's authority to act as an agent based on manifestations that are traceable to the principal. One such manifestation is the actual authority with which the principal has cloaked an agent. Indeed, much of the commentary to section 1.03 and section 2.03 of the *Restatement (Third)* contemplates situations where an actor for a putative principal is an agent for the principal for other purposes. *See, e.g., Restatement (Third)* § 2.03 comment d ("[A] third party should assess what is observed of the agent in light of the agent's position as a fiduciary with a duty to use authority on behalf of the principal."). Thus, evidence of an agent's actual authority to perform certain tasks is relevant to determining whether the agent was apparently authorized to perform other, related tasks, and the Court of Appeals erred in disregarding that evidence in this case.

As to the second misstep, the Court of Appeals does not appear to have considered the evidence in the record concerning the role of a loan officer for a mortgage company in the local industry. That evidence included excerpts from a deposition of Todd Johnson, Sunset's president, in which Johnson indicated that Sunset was a "mortgage finance provider" and a "mortgage broker" that used its own money and the money of others to make real estate loans and that Kantor was employed on a commission basis as a loan officer to originate loans. Johnson also testified that there could be "a time that a hard money loan would be a benefit" as part of his "creative approach" to making loans, that a good loan officer could tell clients to utilize the equity in their real property to make money, and that his loan officers were encouraged to go out and find business. As we stated in *Eads*, apparent authority "includes concepts of 'usual authority' and 'customary authority' in determining whether 'a substantial basis for a third party's belief' exists that the person with whom the third party dealt was acting as an agent for a principal in a particular circumstance." 351 Or. at 738 n. 5, 277 P.3d 503 (citing *Restatement (Third)* § 2.03 comment b); *see also Taylor*, 345 Or. at 413, 196 P.3d 532 (reasonable reliance on apparent authority where owner's general contractor testified that it was customary to obtain warranties in writing). Accordingly, evidence relating to Kantor's usual or customary role as a loan officer was relevant to the determination whether plaintiffs reasonably believed that Kantor had apparent authority, and that evidence should not have been disregarded by the Court of Appeals.

. . . .

Viewing [the] evidence in the light most favorable to plaintiffs, we conclude that a reasonable factfinder could infer that Sunset and Directors manifested their assent to be bound by the acts of Kantor through the observable connections between Kantor and those organizations. *Restatement (Third)* § 1.03 comment c. As we have explained, a factfinder in this case could consider all of the relevant conduct of Sunset and Directors in the context of those organizations having hired Kantor as a "loan officer," given Kantor actual authority to perform the tasks of a loan officer, and placed her in their offices without notice to customers of any limitation on her authority or fiduciary duties as a loan officer. Under those circumstances, a factfinder could infer that Sunset and Directors manifested their assent to be bound to the loan transactions between plaintiffs and third parties arranged by Kantor. *Taylor*, 345 Or. at 410–11, 196 P.3d 532; *Badger*, 311 Or. at 24–25, 803 P.2d 1178; *Restatement (Third)* § 2.03.[5]

We further conclude that a reasonable factfinder could infer from the evidence that it was reasonable for plaintiffs to believe that Kantor was authorized—as a loan officer for Sunset and Directors—to engage in the investment and loan scheme on behalf of those companies. In particular, a factfinder could infer that plaintiffs reasonably believed that Kantor's actions were part of her usual or customary authority as a loan officer hired by Sunset and Directors to make and arrange loans on behalf of the mortgage companies. *See Eads*, 351 Or. at 738 n. 5, 277 P.3d 503 (concepts of "usual authority" and "customary authority" help inform determination whether third party's reliance was reasonable).

Additionally, we find the *Restatement (Third)* commentary instructive on the question of the reasonableness of plaintiffs' belief. Comment d to section 2.03 notes that, where "a third party knows that the actor in question is an agent and knows the identity of the principal, the third party should assess what is observed of the agent in light of the agent's position as a fiduciary with a duty to use authority on behalf of the principal." *Restatement (Third)* § 2.03 at comment d. With respect to particular transactions, such as the loan transactions in this case, a third party should consider whether it appears to be reasonably related to the principal's known business. *Id.* "Absent circumstances that should raise questions in the mind of a reasonable third party, as a general matter there is no requirement that the third party inquire into the scope of an agent's authority." *Id.* Here, plaintiffs knew that Kantor was an agent of Sunset and Directors and observed Kantor in light of her position as a fiduciary with a duty to use authority on behalf of Sunset and Directors. Under the circumstances described above, plaintiffs could reasonably have believed that all the loans were reasonably related to Sunset's and Directors' business, and that Kantor was acting within her fiduciary duty as a "loan officer."

. . . .

5 Defendant's argument that Sunset and Directors did nothing to create the appearance of authority for Kantor to act "as a financial advisor and propose, and then carry out, an investment scheme involving the placement of private loans" misses the mark. Plaintiffs do not seek to hold Sunset and Directors liable under an apparent authority theory for Kantor's financial advice. Rather, plaintiffs seek to bind Sunset and Directors to the loan transactions arranged by Kantor. The evidence that we have recited provides a basis for a factfinder to draw an inference that Kantor—as a "loan officer" hired by Sunset and Directors—was authorized to facilitate the receipt of loans to plaintiffs from those companies and to arrange for plaintiffs to make loans to third parties.

QUESTIONS

1. What might explain why the Supreme Court of Oregon quoted the facts from the Appeals Court opinion rather than restating them?
2. Is the court persuasive in its analysis that the conferring of actual authority can also constitute a manifestation of apparent authority beyond the actual authority? How can an employer protect itself in these circumstances?

Problem 12-1

Jose decided to sell his car to his sister, Marie. They agreed that Jose could still use the car if he needed to do so. On the day that they transferred title, Jose called the customer service number for his automobile insurer, and a representative answered the call. Jose asked if his current policy would continue to provide coverage even though he had transferred title, since he would still be driving the car. Jose testified that the representative stated that the coverage would continue. Three weeks later the car was totaled when Jose was driving it, and the insurer denied coverage because he was no longer the owner of the vehicle, which ultimately voided his policy. Argue on behalf of Jose that the customer service representative bound the insurer to continue his prepaid coverage.

Mastery Problem 12-1

Gloria owned a retail store specializing in Asian antique furniture, and Brendan worked for her as the store manager. Gloria did not use a corporate form, but instead owned the store as a sole proprietor. Gloria decided to close the store in 2018 and to move to Illinois to be near her ailing mother. Brendan supervised the final sale of merchandise, and the store was closed. Gloria called a moving company to determine the cost to move the remaining stock from the previous store in California to Illinois. Mega Van Lines provided an oral estimate based on her description of the pieces of furniture. Gloria emphasized that she wished to insure her property for full replacement value, estimated to be $50,000. Mega then sent an employee to the closed store to conduct a walk-through and provide a written estimate for the move. Gloria arranged for Brendan to meet the Mega employee at the store and to provide access.

Mega emailed a written estimate, which Gloria signed and returned. The estimate indicated in boilerplate language that Gloria must affirm the actual declared value of the property at the time of loading, and declare this value on the Bill of Lading. On the day scheduled for the move, Gloria asked Brendan to go to the store and to give access to the movers, which he did. While the movers were loading the truck, Brendan signed the bill of lading on a line that indicated that he was Gloria's authorized agent. The bill of lading limited damages to $.80 per pound in the boilerplate terms. Brendan did not declare a higher value, nor did he purchase optional insurance for a higher value.

The moving van was destroyed on the trip to Illinois, and the entire cargo was lost. When Gloria sought payment of $50,000 for the full value of her possessions, Mega produced the signed Bill of Lading that provided for limited recovery. Gloria expressed shock that she was not given this document to sign, and she rejected the idea that Brendan had authority to do anything other than open the store to provide access.

Did Brendan's signature on the Bill of Lading bind Gloria to the $.80 per pound limit?

Mastery Problem 12-2

Jane Wilson owns Sierra Pet Supplies ("Sierra"), a retailer specializing in high end products for house pets. She saw an article in Whole Dog Journal for Blue Star dog food, claiming it was one of the best dry dog foods in the country. Jane called the 800 number for Blue Star that was provided in the article, and the customer service representative connected her with Arnie Scher. Jane discussed her desire to be an exclusive retailer in her area for Blue Star, and she and Scher had four or five subsequent telephone conversations.

At all relevant times, Scher was CEO of California Wholesalers ("CW"), which sells pet products throughout the state for a number of producers, including Blue Star. Scher sent various documents to Jane, all of which bore the CW logo. One brochure was captioned, "CW wants you on the Blue Star team!," included an official price list for Blue Star products that was prepared by Blue Star, and included such statements as "CW is looking for Blue Star retailers in your region!" Jane completed a "Distributor Agreement" form, which she believed entitled her to be the sole retailer of Blue Star in her area. The Agreement was countersigned by Scher on behalf of CW. The document referenced Blue Star products, but there was no signature of any official from Blue Star.

Jane later discovers that another retailer is selling Blue Star products through a different wholesaler than CW. The competitor is charging a lower price, apparently based on better volume discounts through its wholesaler. Jane contacted the Blue Star corporate office to complain about the cancellation of her exclusive distributorship. A Blue Star official replied, "We don't have an agreement with you. You might have an agreement with Scher but that's between the two of you." Does Jane have a contract with Blue Star?

4. Agents with Inherent Authority

Inherent authority exists when an agent is clearly acting beyond her actual authority, but is acting within her scope of power. When determining if the acts in question are attributable to the employer under a theory of inherent agency, the employer's manifestations and the third party's reliance are both irrelevant. The sole question is the *scope* of the actual agency. For example, while a general agent may do what it deems "best", the primary question revolves around the nature of the agency. Thus, an employee who serves as a general agent of the employer may bind the employer even if the employer expressly withholds actual authority for a particular transaction that ordinarily would be within the scope of a general agent's duties.

Local Joint Exec. Bd. v. Nationwide Downtowner Motor Inns

229 F. Supp. 413 (W.D. Mo. 1964).

[Editor's Note: A union sued for specific performance of a bargaining agreement. The defendant's general manager, John Nichols, Jr., signed a green contract (a labor agreement on a form commonly used between the plaintiff and the area's hotel association). Defendant claimed that it was not bound by the agreement because Nichols lacked the authority to sign the contract on its behalf.]

GIBSON, CHIEF JUDGE.

. . . .

Although the evidence amply demonstrates that Mr. Baker, vice president of defendant, informed Nichols after Nichols had signed the green contract that Nichols did not have the authority to sign such an agreement, there is also evidence that prior to the time that Nichols signed the contract that he had been informed that he could pay union scale wages, and that he could join the Hotel Association on behalf of the [defendant] Downtowner. From this evidence it could be inferred that Nichols had implied authority to enter into a collective bargaining agreement, however, the Court is of the opinion that there existed both apparent authority and inherent agency power to enter into the contract, and that the question of implied authority need not be reached. Defendant employed Nichols as its general manager at the Kansas City Downtowner continuously from March 1, 1962, until January 1963. The employment of Nichols as general manager from March 1, 1962, until the time the green contract was signed by him in May 1962, was a manifestation by Downtowner to third persons of the authority of Nichols to bind Downtowner, and the Court is of the opinion that a collective bargaining agreement would not be such an unusual or extraordinary contract that it would be outside the scope of the apparent authority of Nichols. It is the further opinion of the Court that Nichols, through his employment as general manager, had inherent agency power to bind his principal to the contract, even if he was specifically informed that he had no authority to enter a contract of the type here involved. Nichols' duties as a general manager involved placing the Downtowner in operation as soon as the physical plant was completed; thus, necessitating the hiring and securing of some experienced personnel to operate the business. In such a situation a labor contract could be a favorable factor in securing personnel and acquiring experienced help. Whether the signing of a contract for representation was in the best interest of the Downtowner was a matter of judgment that would have to be considered and resolved before opening the Downtowner to the public and thus certainly was within the ambit of a general manager's inherent authority as well as apparent authority to manage, conduct and operate the business.

. . . .

For the foregoing reasons the Court finds that a valid contract was entered into between plaintiff and defendant on or about May 1, 1962, and that such agreement continued in effect until June 16, 1963. Defendant is liable under the terms of the agreement for any dues and initiation fees which should have been checked off, and is also liable for any insurance payments under Section 42 of the green contract which should have been made in the period from May 1, 1962 to June 16, 1963. . . .

QUESTION

1. Describe the facts that would support the allegation that Nichols had apparent authority to sign the contract.

---

5. Ratification

Even if an employee lacks all manner of authority to bind her employer, the employer may assume liability for the actions of the employee by ratifying those actions. For example, a prospective employee might negotiate for extended disability benefits with a hiring supervisor who lacks any manner of authority to grant these additional benefits. If the employment letter signed by the President of the company recognizes these additional benefits, the action by the hiring supervisor might be deemed ratified by an employer who does have authority.

Conclusion

In this Lesson, we covered several ways in which an employee may be an agent of the employer, able to bind the employer in contract. As a means of reviewing the doctrines, consider the facts in the *Ruffin* case and analyze how the other types of agency might be established through additional fact discovery.

Lesson 13:
Direct Tort Liability for Negligent Hiring, Retention, Supervision and Referral

Objectives and Expected Learning Outcomes

In this Lesson, you will learn how an employer may be directly liable for torts committed by its employees if the employer acts negligently in hiring, retaining or supervising the employee. Additionally, an employer that negligently refers a former employee to a prospective employer may be liable for injuries suffered by the employer. This liability is founded on ordinary negligence principles, and so you will be able to refine your skills in formulating theories of tort liability. In Lesson 13, you will learn that the employer is vicariously liable for tortious acts committed within the scope of an employee's duties. When the employer is directly negligent, however, it is liable for *all* foreseeable harms, and not just those that are caused by actions committed within the scope of employment.

We will address two forms of liability in this Lesson. First, we cover the situation in which the employer's negligence places one of its employees in a position to cause injury. Second, we address the situation in which a current employer sues a former employer for negligently providing a reference that places the employee in a position with the new employer to cause harm. For example, the new employer might be liable under principles of *respondeat superior* for the torts of the employee who was hired based on a negligent reference.

1. Negligent Hiring, Retention, and Supervision

As with most general tort duties, the rule for employers is stated in simple terms: If an employer acts negligently, it will be liable for the foreseeable harms that result. There is one significant exception to this rule: in most situations, employers are not responsible in tort for negligent conduct by an employee that results in harm to other employees. You will learn in Lesson 26 that workers' compensation statutory programs provide payments to injured workers on a no-fault basis, in exchange for absolving the employer of direct tort liability. In recognition of this general exception, this Lesson addresses only cases in which the harm is not to a fellow employee. The Restatement of Employment Law expressly recognizes the workers' compensation exception to liability, and the Restatement of Agency sets out the elements of the employer's liability generally.

Restatement of Employment Law

§ 4.04. Employer's Duty to Exercise Care in Selecting, Retaining, and Supervising Employees or Agents

Except to the extent precluded by a workers' compensation statute or other law, an employer is subject to liability for the harm caused by an employee by negligence in selecting, retaining, or supervising employees or agents whose tortious acts resulted in the harm.

Restatement (Third) of Agency

§ 7.05. Principal's Negligence in Conducting Activity Through Agent; Principal's Special Relationship with Another Person

(1) A principal who conducts an activity through an agent is subject to liability for harm to a third party caused by the agent's conduct if the harm was caused by the principal's negligence in selecting, training, retaining, supervising, or otherwise controlling the agent.

(2) When a principal has a special relationship with another person, the principal owes that person a duty of reasonable care with regard to risks arising out of the relationship, including the risk that agents of the principal will harm the person with whom the principal has such a special relationship.

An employer that negligently hires or retains an employee who poses an unreasonable risk to other parties is liable for any harm that foreseeably results. The imposition of tort liability has the practical effect of requiring employers to investigate prospective employees to ensure that they pose no unreasonable risk, and to monitor their performance after they are hired. If an employer knows or should have known that an employee has been engaging in risky conduct in the workplace, the employer is under a duty to take corrective action, such as training the employee, changing the employee's job duties, or terminating the employment.

There are countervailing policies, however, that often are set forth in statutes. For example, many employers would be hesitant to hire a prospective employee with a criminal record, or to retain an employee who has been arrested, for fear that doing so would be judged as negligent behavior. However, social "policies seeking to promote the reentry into society of those with criminal convictions and to prevent discrimination against individuals erroneously accused of criminal conduct may limit employer liability for hiring or retaining employees with criminal records." RESTATEMENT OF EMPLOYMENT LAW § 4.04 comment c.

In this part, we explore the factors that determine when an employee presents an unreasonable risk to others, and therefore should not have been employed. Then, we review the actions that employers must take to avoid an unreasonable risk of harm. In particular, we analyze the balancing of issues regarding using criminal records to assess prospective employees. Finally, we study when the employer's negligence is regarded as the proximate cause of the injury suffered by a third person.

A. When Employees Pose an Unreasonable Risk of Harm

The first element of the tort is that the employee was unfit in some manner, such that the employee posed an unreasonable risk of harm to third persons. In some situations, an employee is plainly unfit for the position. For example, if a taxi company hired a driver with an extensive record of traffic offenses involving risks to third persons, it would be easy to conclude that the employee is unfit for that position. On the other hand, one might be tempted to regard the employee as unfit by definition if the employee has in fact caused harm to a third person, using 20-20 hindsight. The question presented is whether the employer is fairly charged with the knowledge that the employee is unfit. The following case presents all of these issues.

BRYANT V. LIVIGNI

619 N.E.2d 550 (Ill. App. 1993).

JUSTICE MAAG delivered the opinion of the court:

FACTS

In 1970, Mark Livigni was a 16-year-old high school student. He was hired by National Super Markets, Inc., as a bagger and continued to work for National after graduating from high school. Livigni worked himself up to a management position, and in 1985 he was made manager of the National store in Cahokia. Livigni was evaluated on a regular basis by National with respect to his ability to relate to customers and employees. The record reflects that he always received good evaluations while employed at National.

On March 18, 1987, while off duty, Livigni stopped by the Cahokia National store. As manager, he was authorized to check and supervise the operation of the store even during off-duty hours. He was intoxicated at the time of this visit, which was a violation of National rules. Livigni observed a young man urinating on the store wall outside the east exit doors. He hollered at the young man and followed the fleeing youth to the parked vehicle of Diana Bryant.

Livigni pulled four-year-old Farris Bryant from the automobile. Farris, however, was not the boy who had been urinating. The boy Livigni had followed was Donya Jackson, age 10, who was also in the back seat of the Bryant automobile. Livigni shouted racial epithets and profanity at Diana Bryant and the children, and he attacked four-year-old Farris, throwing the child through the air.

Farris was taken to Centreville Township Hospital's emergency room for medical treatment. Farris was admitted to the hospital and was released after four days. He was released from all medical treatment approximately one month after the battery.

In a multicount complaint, Farris Bryant and Diana Bryant sued both Livigni and his employer, National. Mark Livigni was accused of committing battery and invasion of privacy. National was alleged to be liable based upon theories of *respondeat superior* (for Livigni's actions), negligent retention of Livigni as an employee, and willful and wanton retention of Livigni as an employee.

At trial, Livigni's supervisor testified that during Livigni's 17-year tenure with National, Livigni had been a good employee. This supervisor never received any reports from customers or employees that Livigni had "violent-related" problems, although he was aware of a report that Livigni threw an empty milk crate which struck a coworker.

Evidence was offered of two batteries committed by Livigni prior to his attack of Farris. In 1980, Livigni had a disagreement with a subordinate employee resulting in Livigni throwing an empty milk crate at the employee striking him on the arm and necessitating medical treatment. At the time of this battery, Livigni was an assistant store manager. A workers' compensation claim was filed against National by the injured employee. A short time after the workers' compensation claim was resolved, Livigni was promoted to store manager by National in spite of this incident.

The second battery occurred in 1985 when Livigni, while disciplining his 13-year-old son, threw the boy into a bed causing the boy to sustain a broken collar bone. In June 1986 Livigni pleaded guilty to aggravated battery to a child and was sentenced to two years' probation. He was still on probation at the time he attacked Farris.

Livigni testified at trial that he had not told any of his supervisors at National about the battery of his son. He admitted to telling employees of equal or lesser positions than himself about the battery. He considered these people to be his friends.

. . . .

I

National first contends that the trial court erred in denying its motion for a directed verdict and further erred in refusing to grant its motion for a judgment notwithstanding verdict on the claims of both Farris and Diana Bryant (counts V and IX) which alleged National was negligent in retaining Mark Livigni as an employee. This allegation of error is premised on the proposition that insufficient evidence was presented to show that National knew or should have known that Livigni was not fit to serve as a store manager. National also argues that there was no showing that its retention of Livigni was a proximate cause of the plaintiff's injuries.

In considering this issue, we must remain cognizant of the relief sought by National. National is not seeking a new trial. Rather the only relief requested is a judgment notwithstanding the verdict. The standard of review in such a case is that set forth in *Pedrick v. Peoria & Eastern R.R. Co.* (1967), 37 Ill.2d 494, 510, 229 N.E.2d 504, 513–14:

> "verdicts ought to be directed and judgments *n.o.v.* entered only in those cases in which all of the evidence, when viewed in its aspect most favorable to the opponent, so overwhelmingly favors movant that no contrary verdict based on that evidence could ever stand."

According to National, there was no evidence that it knew or had reason to know that Livigni was anything other than "an excellent store manager, fit for his position." To support this argument, National claims that there was conflicting evidence regarding the 1980 incident where Livigni threw a milk crate at a coworker causing injury. It argues that the 1980 incident was of uncertain origin since differing versions of the incident and its cause were presented in the evidence. It asserts that due to this conflicting evidence the incident could not form the basis for a negligent retention claim.

We find this argument to be unpersuasive. Under the *Pedrick* standard, we must refrain from resolving conflicts in the testimony. That is the function of the jury. Our charge is to view the evidence in the light most favorable to the party which prevailed below. In doing so, we believe that the evidence regarding this incident was sufficient to present an issue for the jury to resolve on the question of whether National was negligent in retaining Livigni in its employ.

Rather than disciplining Livigni after he injured a subordinate employee in an unprovoked attack, National promoted him following the resolution of the injured employee's workers' compensation claim.

National further argues that it had no knowledge of the incident involving Livigni's son that resulted in Livigni's felony conviction for aggravated battery of a child. Relying upon *Campen v. Executive House Hotel, Inc.* (1982), 105 Ill.App.3d 576, 61 Ill.Dec. 358, 434 N.E.2d 511, National points to the general rule which states that to impute knowledge of this occurrence to National a showing was required that an agent or employee of National had notice or knowledge of the incident and that the knowledge concerned a matter within the scope of the agent's authority. According to National, evidence of such knowledge was lacking.

This claimed ignorance of the facts is premised upon several different bases. Each will be considered in order.

National first admits that Livigni told employees of equal or lesser rank within the corporation about the battery involving his son. However, it claims that this is insufficient notice to the corporation. It argues that the people Livigni told were his "friends" and that as mere "coworkers" of equal or subordinate position no notice could legally be imputed to National. We disagree.

The issue is not whether these persons were Livigni's friends. The law does not recognize a "friendship privilege". Being his friends did not diminish the duty of loyalty owed to the corporation (Restatement (Second) of Agency sec. 39, at 130 (1958)), nor did this friendship relieve them of the duty to act in the best interest of the corporation. The duty is clearly set forth in comment *a* to section 39 of the Restatement as follows: "Authority is conferred to carry out the purposes of the principal and not those of someone else. These purposes, as manifested to the agent, constitute the benefit for which, as the agent should realize, the agency is created. In business enterprises, an agent normally has no authority . . . to conduct his principal's business with a mind to the benefit of others." Restatement (Second) of Agency, sec. 39, comment *a*, at 130 (1958).

The friendship enjoyed by Livigni and his coworkers does not constitute a reason to ignore the information admittedly learned by these coworkers, nor does it constitute a reason to forego imputing this information to National.

Assuming for the sake of discussion that no National employees in a position to supervise Livigni knew he had battered his son, we believe that the knowledge admittedly held by the coworkers must still be imputed to National. *St. Paul Mercury Insurance Co. v. Statistical Tabulating Corp.* (1987), 155 Ill. App.3d 545, 550, 108 Ill.Dec. 272, 275, 508 N.E.2d 433, 436.

There is no rule which requires this knowledge held by coworkers to be disregarded unless the coworker possessing the knowledge "outranks" the employee in question. To the contrary, whether the agent obtaining the knowledge is in a subordinate or a superior position in the corporation, that knowledge is still chargeable to the corporation if the information concerns a matter within the scope of the agent's authority. *St. Paul Mercury Insurance Co.*, 155 Ill.App.3d at 550, 108 Ill.Dec. at 275, 508 N.E.2d at 436.

In this case, the defendant tendered, as its instruction No. 2, IPI No. 50.06 (Illinois Pattern Jury Instruction, Civil, No. 50.06 (2d ed. 1971)), and it was given by the court. The instruction explained to the jury the concept of agency and what was required for the jury to conclude that a matter was within the scope of an agent's authority. Viewing the evidence in the light most favorable to the plaintiff (*Pedrick*), we believe that a reasonable jury could have concluded that the information concerning the battery of Livigni's son, learned by these coworkers, was within the scope of their authority to act upon. Whether reported to higher authorities or not, the information still constitutes "corporate knowledge." (*Campen*, 105 Ill.App.3d at 586,

61 Ill.Dec. at 364, 434 N.E.2d at 517.) In such a case, their knowledge is chargeable to National.

. . . .

III

[Editor's Note: The court then found that the jury verdict premised on National's vicarious liability for Livigni's behavior within the course and scope of employment was supported by the evidence. We will discuss this doctrine—known as "respondeat superior"*—in the next Lesson.]*

Justice Welch, concurring in part and dissenting in part:

I concur with the majority's opinion with respect to, and would affirm the judgment of the circuit court on the jury verdict against National Food Stores on, the *respondeat superior* counts of plaintiffs' complaint. With respect to the majority's opinion concerning the judgment against National on the negligent and wilful and wanton retention counts of plaintiffs' complaint, however, I must respectfully dissent.

A cause of action for negligent hiring or retention must establish that a "particular unfitness" of an applicant or employee creates a danger of harm to third parties of which the employer knew, or should have known, when he hired, placed, or continued the person in employment where he could injure others. (*Huber v. Seaton* (1989), 186 Ill.App.3d 503, 508, 134 Ill.Dec. 285, 288, 542 N.E.2d 464, 467.) Under plaintiffs' complaint alleging wilful and wanton retention, plaintiffs were further required to show a deliberate intention to harm or an utter indifference to or conscious disregard for the safety of others in the retention of defendant Livigni as an employee. (*Gregor v. Kleiser* (1982), 111 Ill.App.3d 333, 336, 67 Ill.Dec. 38, 41, 443 N.E.2d 1162, 1165.) In the instant case, plaintiffs failed to establish by the two incidents occurring, respectively, two and seven years earlier that defendant Livigni had a violent propensity that could manifest itself in Livigni's dealings with those persons in the zone of foreseeable risk created by Livigni's employment.

As the majority notes, Livigni had been employed at National for 17 years at the time of the incident and was a good employee; National had never received any reports from customers or employees that Livigni had any violence-related problems. The 1980 incident in which a subordinate employee was struck by an empty milk crate thrown by Livigni and the 1985 incident in which he injured his 13-year-old son while disciplining him involved persons over whom Livigni was trying to assert authority, not the general public. As such, National was not put on notice by these two incidents that Livigni's continued employment created a danger of harm to the store customers or others with whom Livigni, as store manager, would have come in contact. In order to prove the negligent and the wilful and wanton retention counts of the complaint to the jury, plaintiffs were required to establish a causal relationship between the particular unfitness and the negligent act of the agent. (*Huber*, 186 Ill.App.3d at 508, 134 Ill.Dec. at 288, 542 N.E.2d at 467.) In my opinion, plaintiffs failed to show a connection between the nature of Livigni's prior acts of violence and the conduct of Livigni towards the plaintiffs in the instant case.

From a practical standpoint, the majority's opinion sends a message to all employers that in order to insulate themselves from liability for negligent or wilful and wanton retention any employee who has ever had an altercation on or off the workplace premises must be fired. Moreover, the majority opinion places an unreasonable investigative burden upon the employer by forcing the employer to discover, retain, and analyze the criminal records of its employees. Is not the majority's opinion then at cross-purposes with the established public policy and laws of Illinois protecting the privacy of citizens and promoting the education and rehabilitation of criminal offenders? See Ill.Rev.Stat.1991, ch. 68, par. 2–103 (making it a civil rights violation to ask a job applicant about an arrest record); see also Ill.Rev.Stat.1991, ch. 38, par. 1003–12–1 *et seq.* (concerning correctional employment programs whose function is to teach marketable skills and work habits and responsibility to Illinois prisoners).

I would have granted defendant National Food Stores' motion for judgment *non obstante veredicto* on the negligent retention count of plaintiffs' complaint, because "no contrary verdict based on that evidence could ever stand" (*Pedrick*, 37 Ill.2d at 510, 229 N.E.2d at 514), in that plaintiffs failed to sustain their burden of proof. Similarly, since the theory of negligence was not proved, plaintiffs also failed to prove that the alleged conduct or omission showed a deliberate intention to harm or an utter indifference or conscious disregard for the safety of others. Accordingly, I would have also granted defendant National's motion for judgment *non obstante veredicto* on the wilful and wanton retention count of plaintiff's complaint.

Class Exercise 13-1

You represent a large employer with multiple retail stores. Your client reads about the *Bryant* case in the news, and asks you to provide an overview of what characteristics make an employee "unfit" for employment in a retail setting. Work with classmates to develop a response to your client.

B. Employer's Duty to Prevent an Unreasonable Risk of Harm

The fact that an employee is unfit is not the end of the analysis. The employer will be held liable only if it knew or should have known that the employee was unfit. In the *Bryant* case, the court attributed knowledge of co-workers to the employer. As the following case emphasizes, whether an employer should have conducted some manner of investigation is a highly contextual question that depends on the nature of the job and the ability of the employer to determine the employee's fitness.

SMITH V. ORKIN EXTERMINATING CO., INC.

540 So. 2d 363 (La. App. 1989).

EDWARDS, JUDGE.

This is an appeal by defendant, Orkin Exterminating Company, Inc., in a personal injury suit arising out of injuries sustained in a sexual assault conducted by one of Orkin's employees. For reasons stated herein, we affirm.

FACTS AND PROCEDURAL HISTORY

The facts of this case are not in dispute and the issues are only of law. Plaintiff, Ms. Smith, hired the defendant, Orkin Exterminating Company, Inc., to provide exterminating services for her home. In the process of providing those services, Orkin sent into plaintiff's home one of its employees, Mr. Vincent Johnson.

Mr. Johnson had been hired as a service representative of Orkin in March of 1977. As part of the security measures that Orkin had established to protect its customers and itself, Mr. Johnson had to undergo vigorous screening prior to being hired. That screening included the taking of a mandatory polygraph examination as well as a background investigation. During the initial polygraph examination, Mr. Johnson was extensively questioned as to any criminal activity in his past. Mr. Johnson passed the polygraph and was hired.

As an additional protective measure for its customers and itself, all Orkin employees were required to submit to yearly polygraph examinations as a continuing security monitor. Mr. Johnson took such a security polygraph on February 21, 1982, and was allowed to continue his employment duties entering customers' homes for pest control services. Prior to this polygraph, Mr. Johnson had been arrested for burglary and had raped another Orkin customer. On May 13, 1983, Mr. Johnson, while in the performance of his exterminating duties, formulated and began carrying out the assault which became the subject of this suit. While spraying plaintiff's home, Mr. Johnson unlocked a window to ensure he would have access upon his return to assault plaintiff. On May 15, 1983, Mr. Johnson returned and raped the plaintiff. After filing suit, the trial judge, on submitted briefs, memorandum, and argument found Orkin liable and this appeal followed.

LAW

We note at the outset that this is an ordinary negligence suit based upon Orkin's duty as a provider of services carried out in a customer's home. Whether negligence is actionable in Louisiana is determined by a duty-risk analysis.

The pertinent inquiries are: I. Whether the conduct of which plaintiff complains was a cause-in-fact of the harm; II. Whether there was a duty on the part of the defendant which was imposed to protect against the risk involved; III. Whether there was a breach of that duty; and IV. Damages.

CAUSE-IN-FACT

The first inquiry is whether the negligence of Orkin was the cause-in-fact of plaintiff's injuries. The trial judge, in his reasons for judgment states, in relevant portion:

> The main basis of the case, as the Court sees it, is that the employee had been arrested in Vidalia, Louisiana a few days before he was given his yearly polygraph test. The plaintiff takes the position that *if the polygraph test had been administered properly that there would probably have been a determination that this employee had recently been arrested for the crime of burglary and that therefore,*

> *the employer should have taken the necessary steps to prevent him from going into homes as a result of his employment.*

and further:

> The Court feels that a preponderance of the evidence indicates that Orkin did not do everything that it could do under the circumstances. *The court is of the opinion that the polygraph test should have been fine-tuned a little bit more, particularly in this instance.* Therefore, the Court finds liability on the part of Orkin. (Emphasis added).

Hence, the trial judge found that but for defendant's negligent administration of the polygraph, plaintiff would not have been injured. The cause-in-fact of plaintiff's injuries was the negligent administration of Orkin's own chosen method of protecting itself and its customers. The findings of fact of the trial judge are to be given great deference. Cause-in-fact is usually enunciated as whether the defendant's conduct was a "substantial factor" in bringing about the harm.

Here, Orkin had recently given a polygraph examination to Mr. Johnson which was calculated to screen illegal activity of any of its employees. Its failure to ask the proper questions allowed Mr. Johnson to continue in his employment. The continued employment gained him access to plaintiff's home where he unlocked her window. "But-for" Orkin's failure to properly screen its employee, the plaintiff would not have been raped.

The defendant cannot escape liability for an intentional tort if its negligence led to that tort. *Harris*, 455 So.2d at 1371. The questions asked of Mr. Johnson in his regular yearly security check were different than the questions asked in his pre-employment screening polygraph. In the regular security polygraph given yearly there were seventy-four questions asked, with only six concerning the employee's relationship with customers. No questions were asked about prior arrests or assaults and the vast majority of the questions were targeted to protect Orkin rather than its customers. This, despite the fact that the initial screening did contain questions about prior criminal activity. The trial judge found this failure to properly screen was the cause-in-fact of plaintiff's injuries, and we find no error in that determination.

DUTY

Duty is a question of law. Generally there is no duty to protect others from the criminal activity of third persons. However, when a duty to protect others against such criminal conduct has been assumed, liability may be created by the negligent breach of that duty. Moreover, when an employer hires an employee who in the performance of his duties will have a unique opportunity to commit a crime against a third party, he has a duty to exercise reasonable care in the selection of that employee. Under the unique circumstances of Orkin's business, we also believe that there is a continuing duty to exercise reasonable care in the retention of its employees.

. . . .

Orkin's business is somewhat unique in that the service it renders requires that it send its employees directly into customers' homes. For this service Orkin is compensated and earns profits. Orkin's duty in these situations is to exercise reasonable care in the hiring and retention of those individuals it chooses to send into customers' homes. Orkin has recognized these duties and instituted security measures to prevent harm to itself and to its customers. Orkin's routine method of carrying out that duty was to have its employees take a yearly polygraph examination.

While *Harris* and cases cited therein deal mostly with a retail establishment's premises, all of them recognize a reasonable standard of care for the protection of their patrons. It would seem to this court that the duty to protect patrons against criminal activity in a business which maintains its own premises would be lower than that duty which is expected of a business which sends its employees into a private home to perform regular services for profit.

Defendant cites *Lou-Con, Inc.* for the proposition that even if it had the duty, it carried out that duty in a reasonable fashion. Orkin maintains that it would have no reason to suspect a rape even had the polygraph examination asked the questions which would have revealed Johnson's prior arrest. In this we believe defendant is in error.

Lou-Con, Inc. involved a case of arson in plaintiff's building set by an employee of defendant who had been sent to perform janitorial duties in plaintiff's building. The employee set fire to plaintiff's structure to hide a theft which he had perpetrated. While the court refused to impose liability on defendants on the negligence issue, they refused to do so because the steps taken to protect the plaintiff were reasonable. One of the steps taken in *Lou-Con, Inc.* was a routine police check of its employee's arrest record. Had Orkin performed this check, it would have found out about Mr. Johnson's arrest record. *Lou-Con, Inc.* does not protect the defendant from the high standard of duty required of those in this type of business.

BREACH

Orkin breached its duty to the plaintiff by failing to properly administer its own chosen method of providing security with due care. Of the seventy-four questions asked during the polygraph examination all but six of the questions were aimed at protecting Orkin and had little to do with preventing harm to its customers. The six questions asked Mr. Johnson were only calculated to find out if he had stolen or if he was a drug abuser. In contrast to these six questions, Orkin asked sixty-eight questions covering all aspects of Mr. Johnson's relationship with Orkin.

Orkin's lack of care in administering the polygraph is demonstrated by the fact that a thief and a rapist could pass. Previous to the test, Mr. Johnson had been arrested for burglary and had twice raped another female customer of Orkin. Orkin's customer-related questions were so sparse and incomplete that a rapist, who was using his job to further his criminal activities, could tell the truth and still pass the exam.

Orkin's duty was to take reasonable steps to protect its customers from a predictable risk of criminal activity by its employees. Orkin recognized such a duty in the instruction manuals given to its managers which provide the guidelines for the hiring and retention of employees. Additionally, Orkin's preface to its yearly security polygraph provides:

> 1. Orkin's working environment requires that all branch employees *hold a position of responsibility and trust: Our employees go unsupervised into our customer's homes,* handle potentially harmful chemicals, operate motor vehicles and collect or account for monies due to Orkin. *In order to protect our customers,* employees and company, a "Security" type polygraph examination is requested of all branch employees. *The security polygraph is designed to identify those few individuals who violate the responsibility and trust delegated to them.* (Emphasis added).

The breach of this duty produced results reasonably associated with the risk it was provided to protect, and we so hold.

. . . .

CONCLUSION

Orkin is in a unique business that as a matter of course sends employees into the homes of its customers to perform services for which it charges and earns a profit. Orkin's place of business is essentially a customer's home. Because Orkin sends employees into homes, it is subjected to a higher standard of duty to protect against intentional torts than is a regular business. Orkin recognized this duty and provided measures to meet this requirement. The measures it chose were carried out in a negligent fashion. This negligent attempt at compliance with its duty constituted a breach which allowed the harm reasonably calculated to be within the risk attempted to be prevented by the duty. It was, therefore, the cause in fact of plaintiff's injuries. Because we believe that Orkin was negligent, we affirm. All costs of this appeal to be borne by the appellant.

AFFIRMED.

QUESTIONS

1. Would the result in the case be different if Orkin did not administer polygraphs after an employee's probationary period of one year expires?
2. Would the result in the case be different if Orkin's polygraph questioning led it to discover that Johnson had been arrested after a scuffle in a bar regarding which football game would be shown on the big screen TV, but nevertheless did not terminate Johnson's employment?

Problem 13-1

Edward applied to be a long-haul truck driver with Crystal Trucking. The employment application asked whether Edward had any vehicular offenses, and separately asked about any other criminal convictions. Edward answered "no" to both questions. Crystal verified that he had a clean driving record, but did not verify his negative answer regarding other criminal convictions. In fact, Edward had a history of convictions for violent sex-related crimes. Edward had been arrested the year prior to his employment with Crystal for aggravated sexual assault of two teenage hitchhikers while driving for another employer. Upon being hired by Crystal, Edward was given written instructions and regulations, including a strict prohibition against picking up hitchhikers in his Crystal truck. The truck was furnished with a sleeping compartment so that Edward did not have to stop at a motel during long trips.

Four months after he was hired, Edward picked up a 17-year-old hitchhiker at a truck stop plaza. He repeatedly assaulted her and viciously beat her in the sleeping compartment of his truck on the side of the highway. Edward was arrested, convicted, and sentenced to 50 years with no opportunity for parole. The hitchhiker sued Crystal for compensatory and punitive damages for its negligence. Develop a strategy on behalf of the plaintiff for asserting that Crystal was negligent. Also, develop a strategy for Crystal to defend itself from liability.

C. Using Criminal Records to Assess Prospective Employees

Most states recognize a public policy in favor of rehabilitation of those who are convicted of crimes and have served their time. However, the existence of a conviction is also considered relevant to the employer's decision to hire an employee and place him in contact with the public. As you might expect, this leads many employers to be very cautious about hiring convicted criminals. A separate issue arises regarding arrest records. If a person has been arrested for a serious crime, but has been acquitted or the charges subsequently were dropped, an employer might be concerned about potential liability if the person is hired and subsequently injures a customer of the employer. In this case, states have made the policy determination that arrest records are not relevant to the employee's fitness and may not be utilized by the employer. Consider the California provision below.

California Labor Code

§ 432.7. Disclosure of arrest or detention not resulting in conviction, or information concerning referral or participation in diversion programs, or conviction judicially dismissed or sealed; disclosure of information related to arrest, detention, processing, diversion, supervision, adjudication, or court disposition while subject to juvenile court law; violations; remedies; exception; health facility applicants; prospective concessionaires

(a)(1) No employer, whether a public agency or private individual or corporation, shall ask an applicant for employment to disclose, through any written form or verbally, information concerning an arrest or detention that did not result in conviction, or information concerning a referral to, and participation in, any pretrial or posttrial diversion program, or concerning a conviction that has been judicially dismissed or ordered sealed pursuant to law, including, but not limited to, Sections 1203.4, 1203.4a, 1203.45, and 1210.1 of the Penal Code, nor shall any employer seek from any source whatsoever, or utilize, as a factor in determining any condition of employment including hiring, promotion, termination, or any apprenticeship training program or any other training program leading to employment, any record of arrest or detention that did not result in conviction, or any record regarding a referral to, and participation in, any pretrial or posttrial diversion program, or concerning a conviction that has been judicially dismissed or ordered sealed pursuant to law, including, but not limited to, Sections 1203.4, 1203.4a, 1203.45, and 1210.1 of the Penal Code. As used in this section, a conviction shall include a plea, verdict, or finding of guilt regardless of whether sentence is imposed by the court. Nothing in this section shall prevent an employer from asking an employee or applicant for employment about an arrest for which the employee or applicant is out on bail or on his or her own recognizance pending trial.

exception for arrest still pending

D. Employer's Negligence as the Proximate Cause of Injury

If the employee is found unfit for the position, the employer will not be held liable for any and all injury caused by the employee. The employer's negligence must in some relatively direct manner result in an injury; in tort law this is often described as the requirement that the negligence is the "proximate cause" of the injury. In the following case, the court discusses causation in terms of the specific requirements that the injury occur on the employer's property or through the use of the employer's personal property (chattels), but also in terms of a general proximate cause analysis given the horrific and intentional violent behavior by the employee.

ANICICH V. HOME DEPOT U.S.A., INC.

852 F.3d 643 (7th Cir. 2017).

HAMILTON, CIRCUIT JUDGE.

This tragic case tests the scope of Illinois employers' tort liability for intentional torts committed by their supervisory employees against other employees where the employer has been negligent. Plaintiff's complaint alleges that the defendants jointly employed as a supervisor a man with a known history of sexually harassing, verbally abusing, and physically intimidating his female subordinates. The complaint also alleges that the joint employers failed to take reasonable steps in response to female employees' complaints and to misbehavior that more senior managers observed.

The supervisor's treatment of one subordinate, Alisha Bromfield, included verbally abusing her while throwing things, controlling and monitoring her both during and outside her work hours, and requiring her to come with him on business trips. After five years of that treatment, he used his supervisory authority to require Alisha to come on a personal trip with him—to an out-of-state family wedding—by threatening to fire her or cut her hours if she refused. She went. After the wedding, he killed and raped her.

Alisha's mother, acting as the administrator of the estates of Alisha and Alisha's unborn daughter, has sued the employers. The defendant-employers persuaded the district court that they had no duty to control this supervisor's behavior. We respectfully disagree. Illinois law permits recovery from employers whose negligent hiring, supervision, or retention of their employees causes injury. The unusually detailed complaint plausibly states such claims. We believe the Illinois courts would apply this general principle to the claims arising from Alisha's murder.

I. *Factual and Procedural Background*

The defendant-employers moved to dismiss under Federal Rule of Civil Procedure 12(b)(6) for failure to state a claim upon which relief can be granted. By that strategic choice, they have asked us to treat the allegations in the complaint as true and to give the plaintiff the benefit of any reasonable and favorable inferences from those allegations. *Reynolds v. CB Sports Bar, Inc.*, 623 F.3d 1143, 1146 (7th Cir. 2010). In its general outline, the complaint's story is all too familiar: defendants employed as a supervisor a man with a history of sexually harassing his young female subordinates. He fixated on one. He began making advances on her and calling her his girlfriend. His behavior escalated over time, from such inappropriate comments to verbal abuse, public outbursts, throwing and slamming objects, and finally, to deadly violence.

In its specifics, the complaint's story is tragic, ending in the deaths of Alisha and her unborn daughter at the hands of Brian Cooper, a regional manager for the defendant-employers. The three defendants are Home Depot U.S.A., Inc., Grand Service, LLC, and Grand Flower Growers, Inc., which managed garden centers for Home Depot stores. All three defendants jointly employed Brian Cooper as a regional manager.

Cooper had a history of sexually harassing his young female subordinates. He fixated for a while on a recent high school graduate named Jessica. He would introduce her as his girlfriend, make comments about his genitals to her, and rub himself against her. He once required her to ride alone with him from Joliet to Chicago while he made such comments. Jessica complained to her group leader, who told her that other employees had complained about Cooper and that even the group leader herself felt uncomfortable working with him. Cooper became increasingly loud and abusive with Jessica, yelling and swearing at her. Ultimately, Jessica quit her job.

Cooper then shifted his attention to Alisha Bromfield. Alisha was a teenager when she began working for the defendants in 2006, and she worked seasonally for them until her death in 2012. Cooper's behavior toward her at first resembled his behavior towards Jessica. He would call her his girlfriend. He started swearing and yelling at her, calling her names like "bitch," "slut," and "whore" in front of customers. These outbursts came to include throwing and slamming things.

Cooper became increasingly controlling of Alisha's time away from work. If she was going to spend a lunch break with a man, he sometimes denied her lunch breaks. Once, when she asked him for a day off, he called her a "whore." He started calling and texting her outside of work, pretending he wanted to talk about a work-related issue in order to get her attention, to monitor her, and to pressure her to spend time with him alone. And he required Alisha to come with him on business trips, once insisting that they share a hotel room. In her last year working for the defendants, and the last year of her life, Alisha became pregnant. Cooper reacted angrily.

Cooper's behavior toward female subordinates in general and Alisha in particular was known to more senior management. Throughout her time working for the defendants, Alisha complained repeatedly about Cooper to other supervisors and managers in the defendants' hierarchies. She told her group leader that she did not want to be left alone with him. One Home Depot manager saw Alisha crying after Cooper denied her a break. Another sent Cooper home after he called Alisha a "slut" and a "whore" in front of customers. Grand ordered him to take anger management classes, but he did not complete the course. He confronted his human resources manager about the requirement, and was ordered to attend additional anger management classes, but neither employer followed up to make sure he did so. Defendants' managers told Alisha that they knew about Cooper's behavior. Yet he remained Alisha's supervisor.

In 2012, when Alisha was about seven months pregnant, Cooper began asking her to go to his sister's wedding in Wisconsin with him. She refused. Then, invoking the authority the defendants had entrusted to him as a supervisor, he told her he would fire her or reduce her hours if she did not go. She went. After the wedding, Cooper took Alisha to the hotel room he had rented for the two of them. He asked her, again, to be in a relationship with him. She refused, again. Cooper strangled her to death. He then raped her corpse.

. . . .

II. *Analysis*

We review *de novo* the district court's decision to dismiss, "construe [the complaint] in the light most favorable to the nonmoving party, accept well-pleaded facts as true, and draw all inferences in [that party's] favor." *Reynolds*, 623 F.3d at 1146, quoting *Reger Development, LLC v. National City Bank*, 592 F.3d 759, 763 (7th Cir. 2010). Applying that standard, we reverse.

. . . .

The general rule in Illinois tort law is that one person has no duty to prevent the criminal acts of another. *Simmons v. Homatas*, 236 Ill.2d 459, 338 Ill.Dec. 883, 925 N.E.2d 1089, 1099 (2010). But Illinois courts recognize several exceptions that limit the general rule. We focus on one: employers have a duty to act reasonably in hiring, supervising, and retaining their employees.

Van Horne v. Muller, 185 Ill.2d 299, 235 Ill.Dec. 715, 705 N.E.2d 898, 904 (1998) ("Illinois law recognizes a cause of action against an employer for negligently hiring, or retaining in its employment, an employee it knew, or should have known, was unfit for the job so as to create a danger of harm to third persons."); *Platson v. NSM, America, Inc.*, 322 Ill.App.3d 138, 255 Ill.Dec. 208, 748 N.E.2d 1278, 1284 (2001) ("[P]laintiff has alleged sufficient facts to establish a possibility of recovery for negligent supervision.").

To recover for a breach of that duty, a plaintiff must prove that: (1) the defendant-employer knew or should have known that an employee had a particular unfitness for his position so as to create a danger of harm to third persons; (2) that such particular unfitness was known or should have been known at the time of the hiring, retention, or failure to supervise; and (3) that this particular unfitness proximately caused the plaintiff's injury. *Van Horne*, 235 Ill.Dec. 715, 705 N.E.2d at 904; *Platson*, 255 Ill.Dec. 208, 748 N.E.2d at 1284. The proximate causation element is satisfied when the employee's particular unfitness "rendered the plaintiff's injury foreseeable to a person of ordinary prudence in the employer's position." *Platson*, 255 Ill.Dec. 208, 748 N.E.2d at 1284.

> *[Editor's Note: The Court addressed the foreseeability question in two steps. First, it considered the rule that negligence could lie only when the employee commits the act on the employer's premises or by using the employer's chattels. Second, it considered general principals of foreseeability of harm.]*

. . . .

The Restatement (Second) of Torts provides that employers have "a duty to exercise reasonable care" to control employees who are acting outside the scope of their employment if the employees are on the employers' premises or using the employers' chattels. Restatement (Second) of Torts § 317(a) (Am. Law Inst. 1965). (As examples of chattels that could be used in such torts, consider motor vehicles, power tools, or weapons.)

Illinois has adopted that rule and has used it to limit employers' liability for negligent hiring, supervision, or retention. The requirement is intended not to be arbitrary or formalistic but to limit recovery to injuries which "occurred by virtue of the servant's employment." *Doe v. Boy Scouts of America*, 378 Ill.Dec. 667, 4 N.E.3d 550, 561 (2014), quoting *Carter v.*

Skokie Valley Detective Agency, Ltd., 256 Ill.App.3d 77, 195 Ill.Dec. 138, 628 N.E.2d 602, 604 (1993).

In particular, Illinois applies this rule to avoid holding an employer liable simply because the tortfeasor and the victim know each other through work. See *MacDonald v. Hinton*, 361 Ill.App.3d 378, 297 Ill.Dec. 162, 836 N.E.2d 893, 901–02 (2005) (premises requirement not met where murderer befriended victim through work); see also *Carter*, 195 Ill.Dec. 138, 628 N.E.2d at 605–06 (murderer's negligent employment not the cause of victim's death, even though victim let him into her car because "she trusted him because she knew him from work"). In *Escobar*, for example, the defendant employed as a foreman a carpenter with a history of verbal abuse and violent confrontation, both on and off the defendant's worksites. 168 Ill.Dec. 238, 589 N.E.2d at 638. One night, the carpenter got into a fight with a co-worker in a bar; the next morning, he shot the co-worker. *Id.* at 638–39. The Illinois appellate court affirmed summary judgment for the employer, reasoning that the employment and the assault were not sufficiently connected. *Id.* at 639. The tortfeasor "was not on Madsen's job site, not doing Madsen's work, and not using Madsen's gun." *Id.* at 640. The employment only "provided a condition" for the attack. *Id.* at 639.

Cooper was not on the defendants' premises when he killed Alisha, nor did he use their chattels. But he used something else the defendants gave him: supervisory authority over Alisha. He threatened to fire her or reduce her hours if she did not go with him to his sister's wedding. He thus threatened to take what the Supreme Court calls "tangible employment actions." *Ellerth*, 524 U.S. at 761, 118 S.Ct. 2257. He could do that only because the defendants made him Alisha's supervisor. See *id.* at 762, 118 S.Ct. 2257 ("Tangible employment actions fall within the special province of the supervisor.").

We believe that § 317(a) should be satisfied by a tortfeasor's use of supervisory authority. We predict that the Illinois Supreme Court would agree . . . because supervisory authority is in this respect analogous to a chattel . . . .

We see no principled reason to hold employers liable for the tortious abuse of their chattels but not for the tortious abuse of supervisory authority. Defendants' argument asks us to predict that Illinois courts would treat entrustment with keys or with a truck as more serious than entrustment with control over others' livelihoods. Cf. *Carter*, 195 Ill.Dec. 138, 628 N.E.2d at 605 (claim for willful and wanton hiring supported where security guard used his passkey to enter plaintiff's apartment and assault her), discussing

Easley v. Apollo Detective Agency, Inc., 69 Ill.App.3d 920, 26 Ill.Dec. 313, 387 N.E.2d 1241, 1243 (1979); *Malorney v. B & L Motor Freight, Inc.*, 146 Ill.App.3d 265, 100 Ill.Dec. 21, 496 N.E.2d 1086, 1088–89 (1986) (question of fact for the jury existed in negligent hiring case, where employer equipped driver with truck in which he raped hitchhiker).

Formalistic adherence to the literal terms of § 317(a) would also produce odd, even arbitrary, results. In *Kigin v. Woodmen of the World Ins. Co.*, 185 Ill.App.3d 400, 133 Ill.Dec. 524, 541 N.E.2d 735, 737 (1989), for example, an Illinois appellate court held that the plaintiff stated a claim against the operator of a youth camp for the actions of a camp counselor. The counselor, a 41-year-old man, gave alcohol to a 15-year-old female camper, took her to a remote area of the campground, and sexually molested her. *Id.* at 736. The *Kigin* court noted that the attack took place on the defendant's premises, bringing it within the terms of § 317(a). *Id.* We think it unlikely that the result would have been different if the attacker had taken his victim across the property line of the campground. The employer knew that the counselor had gone "off into the woods at 11:30 at night alone with [a] 15-year-old girl[ ] after plying" her with alcohol. *Id.* at 737. The employer's obligation to act on that information surely does not change depending on whether the counselor crossed a property line when he took his victim away.

Both entrustment with a chattel and entrustment with supervisory authority set employees apart from the general public. Both can enable tortious conduct. In both situations, employers have the ability and incentive to consider and monitor the employees whom they are trusting and how that trust is used. Injuries caused by using a chattel and injuries caused by abusing supervisory authority both occur "by virtue of the [tortfeasor's] employment," and not because the tortfeasor and victim merely know each other through their work. *Doe*, 378 Ill.Dec. 667, 4 N.E.3d at 561.

. . . .

C. Foreseeability

To succeed on a claim for negligent hiring, supervision, or retention, the plaintiff must demonstrate that the employee's "particular unfitness . . . rendered the plaintiff's injury foreseeable to a person of ordinary prudence in the employer's position." *Van Horne*, 235 Ill.Dec. 715, 705 N.E.2d at 906. In this context, foreseeability is ordinarily a question of fact for a jury to decide. *Platson*, 255 Ill.Dec. 208, 748 N.E.2d at 1284, citing *Nowak v. Coghill*, 296 Ill.App.3d 886, 231 Ill.Dec. 15, 695 N.E.2d 532, 537 (1998).

Cooper's "particular unfitness" was his harassing, controlling, and aggressive behavior toward his female subordinates. Defendants suggest two reasons why Alisha's injuries were not foreseeable from that conduct. First, Cooper's violent attack on Alisha was a radical break from even his most offensive prior behavior: even if a reasonable employer could have foreseen violence, they argue, they could not have foreseen murder. Second, a reasonable employer could not have predicted violence at all since Cooper had not made explicit threats and had not yet hit anyone. We conclude that both arguments present factual issues that cannot be decided on a Rule 12(b)(6) motion to dismiss.

Q of fact

"In order to satisfy the foreseeability component, it is not necessary that a defendant must have foreseen the precise nature of the harm or the exact manner of occurrence; it is sufficient if, at the time of the defendant's action or inaction, some harm could have been reasonably foreseen." *Regions Bank v. Joyce Meyer Ministries, Inc.*, 383 Ill.Dec. 767, 15 N.E.3d 545, 552 (2014); see also *Rowe v. State Bank of Lombard*, 125 Ill.2d 203, 126 Ill.Dec. 519, 531 N.E.2d 1358, 1369 (1988) ("[W]here a plaintiff's injury results from the same risk, the existence of which required the exercise of greater care, unforeseeability of what exactly could develop and the extent of the injury or loss will not limit liability."). Illinois courts can and have applied that rule to find foreseeable harms disproportionate to more predictable harms.

In *Platson*, for example, an employee assaulted an intern—he grabbed her, pulled her to the floor, and forced himself on top of her before she escaped. The complaint alleged that the employer knew its employee "would rub and massage plaintiff's shoulders and intentionally brush his body against hers." 255 Ill.Dec. 208, 748 N.E.2d at 1282, 1284. The court reversed dismissal of the complaint.

And in *Rowe*, the court determined that the plaintiff's evidence presented a genuine issue of material fact: the landlord in that case knew that master keys to the property were missing and that burglaries without forced entry had been committed. 126 Ill.Dec. 519, 531 N.E.2d at 1369. Based on that knowledge, an ex-employee obtaining a key, entering the property, and shooting two people—killing one—was foreseeable. *Id.* at 1360, 1369. The magnitude of the harm Cooper inflicted on Alisha does not by itself render the harm unforeseeable.

We are left with the question whether "some harm" was foreseeable to a person of ordinary prudence. The district court said that as a matter of law the answer is no. In reviewing that decision, we reiterate that this is a question of fact; judgment calls made from the perspective of ordinary, prudent people are jury questions. We are therefore skeptical at the outset of the district court's effort to resolve this point as a matter of law. We ultimately disagree with and reverse that decision. If the plaintiff can prove her allegations at trial, a reasonable jury could find that "some harm" was foreseeable.[5]

The plaintiff's amended complaint is unusually detailed—much more detailed than required by Federal Rule of Civil Procedure 8. The amended complaint recounts how Cooper's behavior escalated: from private inappropriate comments and touching, to workplace retaliation, to continual harassment and monitoring, and finally to public outbursts, verbal abuse, and physical intimidation. Hearing such evidence, a reasonable jury could easily find that the employers could and should have foreseen that Cooper would take the small further step to violence.

The defendants and the district court emphasize that Cooper never made explicit threats and never physically harmed anyone before his fatal attack on Alisha. The district court's opinion all but requires such a history to support an inference of reasonable foreseeability. See *Anicich*, 2016 WL 930655, at *5 ("[T]here are no allegations of a prior pattern of violence from which it can be inferred that Cooper's attack was reasonably foreseeable to defendants."). We find no support in Illinois law for such a bright-line rule on this issue of fact. Cf. *Platson*, 255 Ill.Dec. 208, 748 N.E.2d at 1286 (employee's assault on plaintiff was foreseeable where employer knew plaintiff was the "object" of "inappropriate physical advances").

The defendants' argument also assumes that none of Cooper's alleged behavior was implicitly threatening. That is incorrect. Anyone who saw Cooper, for example, "throwing and slamming items in the garden center and . . . parking lot while screaming obscenities," could have easily concluded that

5 The district court appears to have believed the issue was a question of law. That view is understandable. Reasonable foreseeability must be proved as a matter of fact on a claim to recover for negligent hiring, supervision, or retention, but reasonable foreseeability is one of the factors in deciding whether a defendant has a duty to a plaintiff, and duty is treated as a question of law. See *Simpkins*, 358 Ill.Dec. 613, 965 N.E.2d at 1096–97. Some of the plaintiff's theories of recovery, and the defendants' responses, required considering the latter question. But the plaintiff's theory of negligent hiring, supervision, or retention does not. An employer's duty to exercise reasonable care to control his employee under certain conditions is well-established in Illinois law. See, e.g., *Kigin*, 133 Ill.Dec. 524, 541 N.E.2d at 736 ("Even when an employee is acting outside the scope of his employment, his employer may still have a duty to exercise reasonable care to control him . . . under certain conditions.").

Cooper either was dangerous because he had lost control of himself or was trying to frighten Alisha.[7]

Every life lost to brutality is unique, each family's hell a private one. We do not diminish that truth when we repeat that Alisha's story is an old story that has been told too many times. Its ending is both shocking and predictable. Alisha's family is entitled to try to prove its truth.

Holding

For these reasons, we REVERSE the judgment of the district court in favor of defendants and REMAND for further proceedings consistent with this opinion.

QUESTIONS

1. Would the result in the case be different if Cooper and Alisha were co-workers at the same level in the organization chart, rather than supervisor and subordinate?
2. Would the result have been different if Cooper and Alisha were in an abusive relationship?

---

2. Former Employer Liability for Failure to Warn Prospective Employer

As a general rule, courts find that an employer does not have an affirmative obligation to warn the prospective employer about the unfitness of one of its former employees. However, if an employer speaks about the characteristics of a former employee, it must do so in a manner that is accurate and not misleading. Moreover, as we will learn in Lesson 34, an employer may be liable for defamation if it publishes a false statement about an employee. It should be immediately apparent that this legal regime incentivizes employers to remain silent about their former employees, rather than to risk liability if their reference is deemed incomplete or

7 In what might be described generously as excessive zeal by advocates, Grand's brief minimizes Cooper's behavior as "rude" and "mean to inanimate objects," Grand Br. 22, and even characterizes Cooper's final and fatal trip with Alisha as a "date." *Id.* at 17. Home Depot told the district court that Cooper had "made a few mistakes." See *Anicich* 2016 WL 930655, at *4 n.5.

inaccurate. Often, employers will only agree to confirm the fact of employment and its duration, providing confirmation of the former employee's resume.

Example 13-1

Refer back to *Bryant v. Livigni*. Assume that National Supermarkets accepts the resignation of Mark Livigni after the lawsuit. Subsequently, a greeting card chain contacts National because Livigni has applied to be a manager of a retail store for one of their chains. If National responds to the inquiry by stating that Livigni worked for National from 1970–87, it has little chance for legal exposure if these dates are correctly reported. However, if National responds that Livigni was very punctual, organized and responsible in his managerial position, it would be exposed to a tort lawsuit for misrepresentation because it didn't reveal the act of violence that occurred in the course of his employment duties. On the other hand, if National responds by reporting that Livigni had anger management problems and had violent tendencies, it may be exposed to a tort lawsuit for defamation.

These rules are dependent on state law. In California, the courts have placed a duty on a former employer to fully report the former employee's record or be subject to a suit for negligent misrepresentation. In *Randi W. v. Muroc Jt. Unified Sch. Dist.*, 929 P.2d 582 (Cal. 1997) the court held that a former employer was subject to suit for negligent misrepresentation when it provided recommendation letters that did not mention sexual misconduct complaints against the former employee. Previous cases had required that a special relationship exist between the former employer and the injured party before imposing liability, but the court extended liability in the case because of the deceptive nature of the reference letters.

> . . . the plaintiff argues convincingly that, under the facts pleaded in this case, defendants indeed made "positive assertion[s]" regarding Gadams's character, assertions deceptively incomplete because defendants knowingly concealed material facts regarding Gadams's sexual misconduct with students. Thus, defendant . . . allegedly extolled Gadams's "genuine concern" for and "outstanding rapport" with students, knowing that Gadams had engaged in inappropriate physical conduct with them. [The former employer] declared in the letter that he "wouldn't hesitate to recommend Mr. Gadams for any position!"

. . . .

> We conclude that these letters, essentially recommending Gadams for any position without reservation or qualification, constituted affirmative representations that strongly implied Gadams was fit to interact appropriately and safely with female students. These representations were false and misleading in light of defendants' alleged knowledge of charges of Gadams's repeated sexual improprieties. We also conclude that plaintiff's complaint adequately alleged misleading half-truths that could invoke an exception to the general rule excluding liability for mere nondisclosure or other failure to act.

Id. at 1083–84.

In contrast, in *Richland Sch. Dist. v. Mabton Sch. Dist.*, 45 P.3d 580 (Wash. Ct. App. 2002) the court found that the former employer, Mabton, was not subject to liability despite providing recommendation letters that did not reference sexual misconduct complaints against the former employee. Mr. Caballero was charged with child molestation while working as a custodian for the defendant school district. Ultimately, the State agreed to dismiss the case if Caballero agreed to resign from Mabton. The defendant wrote a number of reference letters praising Caballero's work as a custodian without any qualification, and Caballero was hired by Richland, a different school district. Richland dismissed him two years later after learning of the criminal charges that had been filed against him, and was required to pay him approximately $100,000 in front and back wages on account of this dismissal. The court found that Mabton's letters of recommendation were not actionable because they failed to reference only minor reprimands in Caballero's file. The court found that Mabton had no duty to advise prospective employers of the criminal charges that had been dismissed.

> Even if this court found a duty of care under [principles of negligent misrepresentation,] Richland cannot show that Mabton's alleged misrepresentations presented a substantial, foreseeable risk of physical injury or that any person suffered physical harm [citing *Randi W*]. None of the reprimands involved risks of physical harm, merely inappropriate, somewhat adolescent, comments to students. The charges of child molestation apparently were not confirmed by the police investigation and were dismissed, albeit with the proviso that Mr. Caballero agree to resign from the school district. Mabton officials, with some personal knowledge of the parties involved in the allegations, decided that the charges were baseless. A reasonable person would not foresee that a

> person with Mr. Caballero's record of questionable accusations and minor discipline problems posed a risk of physical harm to students.
>
> . . . .
>
> When the declarant and the recipient have a common interest in the subject matter of the communication and the recipient is reasonably entitled to know the information, the declarant has no liability in tort if the communication is slanderous. . . . Assuming a common interest between Mabton and Richland (the safety of each district's school children, for instance), the qualified privilege would protect Mabton from liability to Mr. Caballero for any defamatory statements Mabton might make in Mr. Caballero's letter of recommendation. But the privilege does not create a duty to disclose potentially defamatory information to Richland. The privilege operates as a shield in cases involving slander, not as a sword as urged here. Consequently, Mabton's duty to disclose cannot be predicated on the common interest privilege.

Id. at 389–90.

Mastery Problem 13-1

Adam worked as a custodian at a Minnesota grade school from 1962–1969. In 1969, Adam was arrested and charged with lewd touching of a minor. The alleged incident involved a neighborhood child who complained that Adam lured her into his house. Upon being arrested Adam immediately quit his job, although he proclaimed his innocence. The case against Adam ultimately was dismissed before trial due to lack of evidence. In the course of the investigation, several children at the school claimed that Adam had acted in a strange manner toward them over the years, but no criminal acts were alleged to the satisfaction of the prosecution.

In 1970, Adam moved to California and obtained a job with Clean, Inc., cleaning downtown office buildings. In 1972, he obtained his custodial position with the Oakland Unified School District with a favorable recommendation from Clean, Inc. The Minnesota school district refused to comment extensively on Adam's work history when it was contacted, other than confirming the dates of his employment and stating that Adam resigned his position and was not discharged for cause.

Adam had a good employment record at the school until he viciously attacked an 11-year old student in 1977. Adam followed the student as she walked home from school one day, and attacked her in an abandoned building off of the school premises.

Analyze whether the Oakland School District might be liable to the student, whether the Minnesota School District might be liable to the student, and whether the Minnesota School District might be liable to the Oakland School District.

Conclusion

Employers have a duty to hire, retain and supervise employees who do not pose an unreasonable risk of harm to third parties. Negligently performing this duty subjects the employer to direct tort liability. Concerns about hiring unfit workers may clash with public policies regarding discrimination against those who have an arrest record.

Lesson 14:
Vicarious Liability (*Respondeat Superior*)

Objectives and Expected Learning Outcomes

In this Lesson, we cover the situations in which an employer may be held vicariously liable for the tortuous act of an employee, under the common law doctrine of *respondeat superior*. Generally, the employer is liable only for the actions of an employee acting within the scope of the employment relationship. The distinction between an employee and an independent contractor is critical for this analysis, although there are exceptions when an employer can be held liable for the actions of an independent contractor.

In this Chapter, we have already covered the ways in which an employer may be bound to a contract by an employee with agency authority, as well as the employer's direct liability for its negligence in hiring or retaining an employee who causes harm to third persons. In this Lesson, we explore the common law doctrine of *respondeat superior*. *Respondeat superior* is a kind of bounded "strict liability" that is imposed on the employer by virtue of the employment relationship; generally, this is called "vicarious" liability because there need not be a showing of fault on the part of the employer. The simple rule is stated in the Restatement.

Restatement (Third) of Agency

§ 2.04. Respondeat Superior

An employer is subject to liability for torts committed by employees while acting within the scope of their employment.

There are two seemingly simple criteria for holding the employer vicariously liable for another's tort: first, the wrongdoer must be an employee; second, the wrongdoer must be acting within the scope of her employment.

Example 14-1

Joan owns a jewelry store. She has retained a transportation firm to pick up and deliver merchandise to her store. The transportation firm has numerous clients, and it determines how to staff Joan's transportation needs. An employee of the transportation firm negligently drove the van while carrying some of Joan's inventory, causing injury to a pedestrian. Joan is not liable to the pedestrian under the doctrine of *respondeat superior* because the wrongdoer is not Joan's employee.

Example 14-2

Joan employs Fred, a longtime sales manager of the jewelry store. Fred assists customers in selecting appropriate pieces of jewelry. While shopping at a mall on his day off, Fred observes a past customer who was particularly difficult to deal with. Fred and the customer exchange heated words, and Fred then commits a battery against the customer. Joan is not liable to the customer under the doctrine of *respondeat superior* because Fred is acting outside the scope and course of his employment.

Problem 14-1

Analyze the two examples above, assuming that you represent the injured person in each case. What theories of liability might you apply to Joan, and how would you investigate the likelihood of success?

We will explore the doctrine of *respondeat superior* by considering the two elements in turn: whether the wrongdoer is an employee, and whether the wrongdoing occurred during the scope and course of employment.

1. Vicarious Liability for Acts of an Employee

A. General Rule: The Wrongdoer Must Be an Employee

We begin by recalling the important distinction made between an employee and an independent contractor.

Restatement (Third) of Employment Law

§ 1.01. Conditions for Existence of Employment Relationship

(a) [A]n individual renders services as an employee of an employer if:

(1) the individual acts, at least in part, to serve the interests of the employer;

(2) the employer consents to receive the individual's services; and

(3) the employer controls the manner and means by which the individual renders services, or the employer otherwise effectively prevents the individual from rendering those services as an independent businessperson.

(b) An individual renders services as an independent businessperson and not as an employee when the individual in his or her own interest exercises entrepreneurial control over important business decisions, including whether to hire and where to assign assistants, whether to purchase and where to deploy equipment, and whether and when to provide service to other customers.

QUESTIONS

1. In light of the definition of "employee," what are the policy reasons for imposing vicarious liability on an employer for the torts of his employee?
2. Does it make sense to insulate employers from vicarious liability for the torts of independent contractors, given the increasing use of independent contractors? Consider a Marriott hotel that contracts with a service company to provide maid service. A maid wearing a Marriott uniform and cleaning rooms is found to have assaulted a guest of the hotel. Wouldn't the guest reasonably expect that Marriott would be vicariously liable?

Formal job descriptions or contracts adopted by the parties are not controlling. A worker's status as an employee is based on the nature of the relationship rather than a determination made by the parties. Consider the following illustration from the Restatement.

Restatement (Third) of Employment Law

§ 1.01. Conditions for Existence of Employment Relationship

Illustration 19

P, a producer of computer software, and A, a programmer, contract to have A help P's regular programmers complete certain projects. A's contract with P provides that A is "self-employed as an independent contractor" and "is not in an employment relationship" with P. A is paid through P's accounts-payable department rather than through its regular payroll. A is required to work on the projects with P's regular employees during the same hours and under the same level of supervision from P's managers.

The language of A's contract with P is not controlling. Whether A is an employee of P depends on whether P's control over the scheduling and detail of A's work for P effectively prevents A from servicing P as an independent business.

BOISSONNAULT v. BRISTOL FEDERATED CHURCH

642 A.2d 328 (N.H. 1994).

[Editor's Note: A certified public accountant, Elizabeth Seeler, was performing services as a volunteer worker for the defendant church. Seeler was delivering church financial records to the church's treasurer when Seeler collided with the plaintiff. The plaintiff sued the church on the basis of vicarious liability and claimed that Seeler was an employee of the church.]

. . . .

Whether Seeler was acting in a capacity and manner that would necessarily invoke vicarious liability based upon the doctrine of respondeat superior is the question before us. The law in this area has developed around the issue of control. There was a period in our jurisprudence when the courts required the employer to have the right to control the manner and the means of the performance of the work in order for the doctrine to come into play. *McCarthy v. Souther,* 83 N.H. 29, 36–38, 137 A. 445, 449–50 (1927). A more expansive view of the relationship and its determination was adopted by this court in *Hunter v. R.G. Watkins & Son, Inc.,* 110 N.H. 243, 265 A.2d 15 (1970). In *Hunter,* we adopted what is now referred to as the "totality of the circumstances test," requiring consideration of many factors, including the criteria set forth in Restatement (Second) of Agency § 220 (1958). Noting that the control factor has been overemphasized in judicial reasoning, we concluded that our concern will usually be "whether on all the facts the community would consider the person an employee." *Hunter,* 110 N.H. at 246, 265 A.2d at 17. The issue here is whether *Hunter* applies to volunteer service.

The rule that arises from *Hunter* is based in common sense and an appreciation of what takes place in the market place on a day to day basis, whether the activity is that of commercial enterprise or charitable service. The only factor which volunteer status adds to the *Hunter* equation is that vicarious liability may arise from the activities of one acting without hope of material reward or other compensation. Because we live in a society where the law requires us to pay for what we break when we are at legal fault, it is merely an extension of the underlying common sense principles of tort law to judge the volunteer's activities by the standards we use in cases where the activity giving rise to the claim is performed with hope or expectation of reward.

The plaintiffs rely upon Restatement (Second) of Agency § 225, which states: "One who volunteers services without an agreement for or expectation of reward may be a servant of the one accepting such services." Their reliance is not well taken, however, because the section merely indicates that in appropriate circumstances, a servant relationship may arise from a volunteer activity. The *Hunter* test must still be satisfied.

The trial judge rendered a detailed order on the motion for summary judgment in which consideration was given to each of the criteria set forth in the Restatement (Second) of Agency § 220. Particularly, the judge found that although the church may have had control over the tasks assigned to Seeler, it had no right to control the physical performance or the details of the accounting services she performed. To carry the plaintiffs' argument to its logical conclusion could result in a client of a certified public accountant being liable for the accountant's negligent driving while delivering the client's tax return.

The Restatement (Third) of Employment Law § 1.02 provides that an "individual is a volunteer and not an employee if the individual renders uncoerced services to a principal without being offered a material inducement." However, in Comment a, the Restatement notes that this rule does not govern questions of vicarious liability, and offers the following illustration.

> 1. A, a high-school student, tells the principal of his high school that he would be happy to serve as a host for students from a Canadian high school who are visiting under an exchange program sponsored by A's school. As part of his duties as a host, A drives the Canadian students around the town in which the high school is located. During one drive, A negligently speeds through a red light, hits another car, and injures that car's driver, D.
>
> Although the school may be vicariously liable to D for the negligence of A, A is not an employee of the school for purposes of employment laws.

QUESTIONS

1. How do you reconcile the *Boissannault* case and the rule of the Restatement (Third) of Employment Law?
2. What additional facts might render the church liable for the car accident by its volunteer?
3. What additional facts might absolve the high school of liability for the acts of the driver?

B. Exceptions: Vicarious Liability for Acts of Independent Contractors

Some jurisdictions have created exceptions to the general rule that *respondeat superior* liability attaches only if the wrongdoer is an employee. Given the increasing use of independent contractors in the modern economy, there may be important policy reasons for broadening the scope of *respondeat superior* liability. We consider two prominent exceptions. First, courts will impose vicarious liability on an entity if it has hired an independent contractor to perform a "non-delegable" arising out of a duty owed to the public. In other words, a party cannot avoid responsibility for a duty imposed on it, simply by hiring an independent contractor to perform that duty. Second, courts have held that "inherently dangerous" activity, or activity of a "personal character" performed by an independent contractor may give rise to vicarious liability. This is essentially a particular instance of the "non-delegable duty" exception, with courts finding that it is against public policy for a party to shield itself from liability for inherently dangerous activities by hiring a contractor.

KLEEMAN v. RHEINGOLD

614 N.E.2d 712 (N.Y. Ct. App. 1993).

TITONE, J.

[Editor's Note: Plaintiff hired defendant law firm to file a lawsuit, and the defendant hired a process server to deliver service. Because of the process server's negligence, the statute of limitations on the action ran. The plaintiff sued the defendant for the negligence of the process server.]

. . . .

The general rule is that a party who retains an independent contractor, as distinguished from a mere employee or servant, is not liable for the independent contractor's negligent acts. Although several justifications have been offered in support of this rule, the most commonly accepted rationale is based on the premise that one who employs an independent contractor has no right to control the manner in which the work is to be done and, thus, the risk of loss is more sensibly placed on the contractor.

Despite the courts' frequent recitation of the general rule against vicarious liability, the common law has produced a wide variety of so-called "exceptions." Indeed, it has been observed that the general rule "is now primarily important as a preamble to the catalog of its exceptions" (*Pacific Fire Ins. Co. v. Kenny Boiler & Mfg. Co.*, 201 Minn. 500, 503, 277 N.W. 226, 228; *accord, La Count v. Hensel Phelps Constr. Co.*, 79 Cal.App.3d 754, 145 Cal. Rptr. 244 [general rule of nonliability applies only where no good reason can be found for departing from it]; Restatement, *op. cit.*, § 409, comment *b*, at 370 [same]). These exceptions, most of which are derived from various public policy concerns fall roughly into three basic categories: negligence of the employer in selecting, instructing or supervising the contractor;[1] employment for work that is especially or "inherently" dangerous; and, finally, instances in which the employer is under a specific nondelegable duty.

The exception that concerns us here—the exception for nondelegable duties—has been defined as one that "requires the person upon whom it is imposed to answer for it that care is exercised by anyone, even though

1 Notably, although often classified as an "exception," this category may not be a true exception to the general rule, since it concerns the employer's liability for its own acts or omissions rather than its vicarious liability for the acts and omissions of the contractor.

he be an independent contractor, to whom the performance of the duty is entrusted" (Restatement, *op. cit.,* ch 15, topic 2, Introductory Note, at 394, quoted in *Feliberty v. Damon, supra,* 72 N.Y.2d at 118–119, 531 N.Y.S.2d 778, 527 N.E.2d 261). The exception is often invoked where the particular duty in question is one that is imposed by regulation or statute. However, the class of duties considered "nondelegable" is not limited to statutorily imposed duties. To the contrary, examples of nondelegable common-law duties abound.

There are no clearly defined criteria for identifying duties that are nondelegable. Indeed, whether a particular duty is properly categorized as "nondelegable" necessarily entails a *sui generis* inquiry, since the conclusion ultimately rests on policy considerations.

The most often cited formulation is that a duty will be deemed nondelegable when " 'the responsibility is so important to the community that the employer should not be permitted to transfer it to another' " (*id.,* at 119, 531 N.Y.S.2d 778, 527 N.E.2d 261, quoting Prosser and Keeton, *op. cit.,* at 512). This flexible formula recognizes that the "privilege to farm out [work] has its limits" and that those limits are best defined by reference to the gravity of the public policies that are implicated (5 Harper, James and Gray, Torts § 26.11, at 73 [2d ed.]; *see also, id.,* at 76–77).

Viewed in the light of these principles, the duty at issue here—that owed by an attorney to his or her client to exercise care in the service of process—fits squarely and neatly within the category of obligations that the law regards as "nondelegable." Manifestly, when an individual retains an attorney to commence an action, timely and accurate service of process is an integral part of the task that the attorney undertakes (*see,* 5 Harper, James and Gray, *op. cit.,* at 76–77; *cf., Feliberty v. Damon, supra,* at 120, 531 N.Y.S.2d 778, 527 N.E.2d 261). Furthermore, proper service of process is a particularly critical component of a lawyer's over-all responsibility for commencing a client's lawsuit, since a mistake or oversight in this area can deprive the client of his or her day in court regardless of how meritorious the client's claim may be. Given the central importance of this duty, our State's attorneys cannot be allowed to evade responsibility for its careful performance by the simple expedient of "farming out" the task to independent contractors.

The existence of an extensive and comprehensive Code of Professional Responsibility that governs the obligations of attorneys to their clients reinforces our conclusion. Under the Code, a lawyer may not "seek, by contract or other means, to limit prospectively the lawyer's individual liability to a client for malpractice" (DR 6–102, 22 NYCRR 1200.31). Moreover, the Code forbids lawyers from "[n]eglect[ing] legal matter[s] entrusted to [them]" (DR 6–101[a][3], 22 NYCRR 1200.30[a][3]), enjoins them to assist in "secur[ing] and protect[ing] available legal rights" (EC 7–1) and requires them to represent their clients as zealously as the "bounds of the law" permit (Canon 7). All of the latter ethical and disciplinary considerations are implicated when a client's lawsuit is undermined—or even defeated—as a consequence of carelessness in the service of process.

Our conclusion is also supported by the perceptions of the lay public and the average client, who may reasonably assume that *all* of the tasks associated with the commencement of an action, including its formal initiation through service of process, will be performed either by the attorney or someone acting under the attorney's direction. While it may be a common practice among attorneys to retain outside agencies like Fischer's to assist them in effecting service, that custom is not necessarily one of which the general public is aware. Even where a client is expressly made aware that a process serving agency will be retained, it is unlikely that the client will understand or appreciate that the process serving agency's legal status as an "independent contractor" could render the retained attorney immune from liability for the agency's negligence. Under established principles, the client's reasonable expectations and beliefs about who will render a particular service are a significant factor in identifying duties that should be deemed to be "nondelegable" (*see,* Restatement, *op. cit.,* § 429; *see also, Feliberty v. Damon, supra,* at 120, 531 N.Y.S.2d 778, 527 N.E.2d 261).

Finally, we conclude that permitting lawyers to transfer their duty of care to process servers would be contrary to sound public policy. In this State, licensed attorneys have been granted an exclusive franchise to practice law, with the understanding that they have both the specialized knowledge and the character required to represent clients in a competent, diligent and careful manner. Under this system, lawyers are authorized to hold themselves out as being uniquely qualified to manage their clients' legal affairs, a task that unquestionably includes the commencement of lawsuits. While it is true that the State also licenses nonlawyers to perform certain discrete, law-related tasks such as service of process (*see,* General Business Law art. 8), the existence of that licensing system certainly does not evince a governmental intent to relieve attorneys of the responsibilities implicit in their franchise. To the contrary, the purpose of the licensing system for process servers is to "combat a continuing and pervasive problem of unscrupulous service practices" in order to protect *defendants* who might otherwise be deprived of their day in court or be victimized by "fraudulent default judgments" (*Matter of Barr v. Department of Consumer Affairs,* 70 N.Y.2d 821, 822, 523 N.Y.S.2d 435, 517 N.E.2d 1321; *accord,* Givens, Practice Commentary, McKinney's Cons. Laws of N.Y., Book 19, General Business Law art. 8, at 128–130). That purpose is obviously unrelated to the entirely separate goal of assuring clients who are would-be *plaintiffs* that their process will be timely served in a manner that complies with the complex requirements of CPLR articles 2 and 3, as well as with the numerous other statutory provisions relating to commencement of actions (*see, e.g.,* Business Corporation Law §§ 304–308) and the formidable body of case law illuminating those statutes. The responsibility for achieving that goal—and the liability for negligent failures to achieve it—must remain squarely on the shoulders of trained and licensed attorneys who, as members of a "learned profession," alone have the necessary knowledge and experience to protect their clients' rights (*cf., Feliberty v. Damon, supra,* 72 N.Y.2d at 120, 531 N.Y.S.2d 778, 527 N.E.2d 261 [refusing to impose nondelegable duty to provide competent defense on insurers, because "insurer necessarily must rely on independent counsel to conduct the litigation" and is, in fact, barred from interfering with independent counsel's "professional judgment"]).

Before closing, we note that, contrary to the concurrer's suggestion that our ruling has a far broader application, the nondelegable duty of care that we have recognized in this case is limited to the discrete and unique function of commencing an action through service of process. Furthermore, the duty extends only to clients who have retained an attorney for the purpose of commencing a lawsuit. We do not decide here the entirely separate question of an attorney's liability for the wrongs that a retained process server may commit against a potential defendant or another third party. Nor do we consider the right of an attorney who has been held liable for the negligence of a retained process server to pursue whatever contractual or tort remedies that the attorney may have against that process server. We hold only that an attorney has a nondelegable duty to his or her clients to exercise due care in the service of process and that, accordingly, an attorney may be held liable to the client for negligent service of process, even though the task may have been "farmed out" to an independent contractor.[3]

3 Contrary to the concurrer's concern about the practical implications of our holding, we find nothing untoward or "unrealistic" about a rule that holds practicing attorneys responsible to their clients for the negligence of the

. . . .

BELLACOSA, JUDGE (concurring).

While I agree with the Court's result, I am unable to join in the broad rationale upon which it is premised. This case should be more prudently resolved on the narrower ground that questions of fact exist as to whether the defendant law firm was negligent in choosing its process server . . . .

. . . .

The Court's result is reached instead by classifying service of process, for the first time, as a nondelegable duty of the attorney. This rationale opens up an unrealistic and undue liability channel not only with respect to the relationship of attorneys to process servers but, by analogous extension, also to many other relationships in which attorneys retain specialists and experts in the discharge of their professional obligations to clients.

This broad new rule requires, in effect, that an attorney inquire beyond any facially sufficient affidavit of service of process to verify personally the facts that underlie it. This contradicts the justification and practicality for the long-standing practice of utilizing and relying on independent process servers. For practical purposes, it will compel attorneys to assume the role of process servers themselves. While many large firms already have such in-house operatives, attorneys practicing in small firms and solo practitioners may now also have no choice but to hire in-house process servers so that the lawyers can always maintain direct supervision and control over them. No other way is left to avoid potential liability to disgruntled or harmed clients. Since the ordinary question-of-fact path is available through which plaintiff's cause may proceed beyond summary judgment, I see no justification or necessity for paving this boulevard route to that same result.

Notably, the rule that would make an attorney liable for the acts of an outside process server on the basis announced in this case also conflicts with the useful teachings of several of our lower courts and at least one sibling State. They continue the classification of "outside" process servers as independent contractors. This approach is prudent because attorneys in these situations have no effective control over the particular manner in which selected

process servers they choose to retain. Further, we see no sound reason for permitting attorneys who happen to use outside process servers to escape liability while attorneys who use in-house staff to perform the same functions can be held liable under ordinary principles of respondeat superior.

process servers do their jobs. The long-standing classification of process servers as independent contractors should be retained, with the result that attorneys would not be liable to plaintiff on a respondeat superior basis for the negligent acts of process servers.

Accordingly, I would modify to deny defendants' motion for summary judgment but on the more narrowly expressed basis.

QUESTIONS

1. If the process server ran over a pedestrian while racing to make a filing before the court closed, could the law firm be held vicariously liable to the injured pedestrian?
2. How would you state the rule of the case, after reading both the majority and concurring opinions? Is there a way to conclude that both opinions are stating the same rule differently?

Rosenberg v. Equitable Life Assurance Society

595 N.E.2d 840 (N.Y. Ct. App., 1992).

Simons, J.

[Editor's Note: As part of its underwriting, a life insurer required an applicant for insurance to take a stress electrocardiogram exam. The exam life insurer contracts with several physicians in the area to perform required medical exams. The applicant was referred to a private physician. The patient was 51 years old, diabetic, had a history of heart disease, and had suffered a heart attack seven years earlier. During the stress exam, the applicant suffered cardiac failure and died. The applicant's estate alleged that the life insurer was vicariously liable for the death.]

. . . .

The general rule is that an employer who hires an independent contractor is not liable for the independent contractor's negligent acts. There are exceptions, however. For reasons of public policy, the employer's duty is sometimes held to be nondelegable and, though blameless, it is liable for the independent contractor's negligence. The exceptions generally recognized involve situations where the employer (1) is under a statutory duty to perform or control the work, (2) has assumed a specific duty by contract, (3) is under a duty to keep premises safe, or (4) has assigned work to an independent contractor which the employer knows or has reason to know involves special dangers inherent in the work or dangers which should have been anticipated by the employer.

In such instances, the employer cannot insulate itself from liability by claiming that it was not negligent: the employer is vicariously liable for the fault of the independent contractor because a legal duty is imposed on it which cannot be delegated. We are concerned in this case with the fourth exception involving "inherently dangerous" work.

The trial court instructed the jury that Dr. Arora was an independent contractor and that, generally, an employer is not liable for the acts of an independent contractor. It also told the jury of the exception to that general rule fixing liability on the employer "when danger to others is inherent in the acts." The jury was instructed that if it found that defendant should have anticipated the consequences of the negligent acts performed by Dr. Arora, then it could consider defendant responsible for those acts. Although these instructions accurately reflect the rules of vicarious liability when inherently dangerous work is delegated to an independent contractor, we conclude the issue should not have been submitted to the jury in this case but should have been decided as a question of law.

The nature of those acts qualifying as "inherently dangerous" has been stated in a number of ways, not always with perfect consistency. The Restatement explains the rule and the acts within it as follows:

> One who employs an independent contractor to do work involving a special danger to others which the employer knows or has reason to know to be inherent in or normal to the work, or which he contemplates or has reason to contemplate when making the contract, is subject to liability for physical harm caused to such others by the contractor's failure to take reasonable precautions against such danger.

(Restatement [Second] of Torts § 427; *see also, McDonald v Shell Oil Co.,* 20 NY2d 160, 166, *supra; Rohlfs v Weil,* 271 NY 444, 448.)

Thus, before the exception applies, it must appear not only that the work involves a risk of harm inherent in the nature of the work itself, but also that the employer recognizes, or should recognize, that risk in advance of the contract. Prosser and Keeton illustrate the exception with two illustrations. First, they consider the employment of a trucker to haul goods. If the trucker drives at excessive speed, he presents a danger to others, but the danger is not one that is inherent in the nature of the contract work and there is no vicarious liability on the part of the employer for the trucker's negligence. If an owner hires an independent contractor to excavate an area next to a thoroughfare, however, the work obviously presents inherent dangers to those who must use the thoroughfare. The employer of the independent contractor retained for such work cannot avoid vicarious liability for the contractor's negligence because the work was performed by another *(see generally,* Prosser and Keeton, Torts § 71, at 514–515 [5th ed 1984]). The exception has been applied similarly in a variety of circumstances *(see, e.g., Wright v Tudor City Twelfth Unit,* 276 NY 303 [employer liable where danger to pedestrians inherent in work involving placing mats on sidewalk and cleaning them with soap and water]; *Rohlfs v Weil,* 271 NY 444, supra. [work of independent contractor performing work on scaffolding on outside of building inherently dangerous when warning signs are not placed on sidewalk below]; *Besner v Central Trust Co.,* 230 NY 357, supra. [employer liable for negligence of contractor's employee because it was inherently dangerous to request independent contractor to install fireproof doors to elevator shaft while elevator was still being used by tenants]; *State of New York v Schenectady Chems.,* 103 AD2d 33, 38 [disposal of hazardous waste may be considered as inherently dangerous]). Whether the work is inherently dangerous is normally a question of fact to be determined by the jury.

The Appellate Division affirmed the jury's determination here, concluding that the inherently dangerous exception applied "in light of evidence that the doctor was mandated to follow defendant's strict protocol" (169 AD2d 533, 534). Although the record supports the finding that defendant requested Dr. Arora to perform the test, defendant could not have "mandated" him to do so because Dr. Arora had not assumed any contractual obligation to do as it bid. In the form letter which was presumably sent to the doctor, it was stated that a stress EKG was required to complete decedent's application for life insurance. However, the letter also stated: "If you cannot complete the test according to our protocol, please return this letter immediately to enable us to make alternate arrangements." More to the point, however, the issue here is not the degree of control exercised over Dr. Arora but whether the act involved was inherently dangerous.

Generally speaking, performing an EKG is not an inherently dangerous activity and plaintiff's evidence that certain dangers accompanied performance of a stress EKG under the circumstances presented was not sufficient to take the case to the jury. Although the stress EKG was ordered for a person with serious heart problems, performance of it, as a matter of law, did not constitute an inherently dangerous activity because defendant's independent contractor was a medical professional under no duty to perform the examination in a manner contrary to his legal and professional responsibilities. That being so, there were no apparent risks involved in defendant requesting him to do so.

Stated another way, the inherently dangerous exception cannot be applied unless a risk inherent in the nature of the procedures is apparent or contemplated by the employer. Dr. Arora, in addition to his professional responsibility embodied in the Hippocratic Oath "to do no harm," had a legal duty common to both New York and New Jersey authority to disclose to his patients inherent risks to them and to perform dangerous procedures only with the patient's consent. . . Defendant could not reasonably anticipate that Dr. Arora would disregard these responsibilities and administer a stress EKG to decedent if decedent's condition foreclosed doing so safely and it could reasonably expect that the potential risks posed by a stress EKG would be explained to decedent and that he would either give his informed consent or decline to undergo the test. Under the circumstances, the inherent danger exception does not apply and the employer could not be answerable for the negligence of the independent contractor.

It is also worth emphasizing that these exceptions imposing vicarious liability on an employer are grounded on public policy and should have no role when public policy is not served by applying them. In this case, plaintiffs seek to hold defendant liable for requiring Dr. Arora to conduct a stress EKG. However, no medical doctor can be *required* to render services which, in the doctor's professional judgment, are dangerous or contraindicated and public policy is not served by imposing liability for the doctor's fault in doing so on the insurer. High risk life insurance is an integral part of personal and commercial financial planning. When applicants seek such coverage, insurers must be free, before issuing a policy, to test them in a manner calculated to evaluate the risk presented. In the process, they necessarily rely on members of the medical profession, not only to provide the information required but, also, to perform their duty by refusing to conduct dangerous tests unless the patient is fully apprised of the risks and consents to their administration.

QUESTIONS

1. The applicant for insurance clearly suffered from significant health problems, and the insurer did not want to issue a policy without a stress test that indicated the strength of the applicant's heart. How can this not be an "inherently dangerous" test required by the insurer?
2. If the insurer were held responsible under the "inherently dangerous" exception, what public policy arguments would support its claim that this ruling would prove to be detrimental to life insurance applicants rather than protective of them?
3. The court appears to place full responsibility on the doctor who was hired as an independent contractor. Does the *Kleeman* case provide support for this approach, even if in an indirect manner?

Mastery Problem 14-1

Hank owns a bar and nightclub called "The Bourbon Cowboy." It is known for having a boisterous crowd. Hank hires Sagebrush Security to provide security services at the Bourbon Cowboy, including monitoring who enters the club, ejecting unruly or obviously intoxicated customers, and monitoring activities in the parking lot. Sagebrush hires and trains its security personnel, makes all assignments to the various bars that retain its services, and pays its security personnel as employees. One evening, three customers showed up at the Bourbon Cowboy already intoxicated. Two employees of Sagebrush refused them entry. Allegedly, when the customers became loud and rowdy, the Sagebrush employees beat them and expelled them from the property. The injured customers have sued Hank, alleging that he is vicariously liable for their injuries. Assess the strength of their various theories of recovery.

---

2. Vicarious Liability for Wrongful Acts Within the Course and Scope of Employment

An employer is not vicariously liable for all torts committed by its employees. Liability is limited to tortuous acts committed with the scope of the employment relationship and in the course of that relationship. This corresponds with the policy basis for imposing liability. If an employer has control over the activities of the employee, then the employer should be liable for harm that results from activities under its control. Determining the scope of the employment relationship is not simple, because an employer rarely, if ever, defines the employment relationship to include committing tortious acts against third parties.

Alma W. v. Oakland Unified School Dist.

176 Cal.Rptr. 287 (Cal. Ct. App. 1981).

Miller, J.

[Editor's Note: Appellant, an 11 year old elementary school student, was raped by A.B., the custodian at her school. The attack was on school grounds, in A.B.'s office on a Friday afternoon. Appellant sued the school district under the doctrine of respondeat superior.*]*

. . . .

The general rule of respondeat superior at common law for nongovernmental employers is the same as that set forth in the Government Code for public employers: An employer is vicariously liable for the torts of employees committed within the course or scope of their employment. Accordingly, we look to the interpretation given the phrase "scope of employment" at common law to guide us in resolving the issue of whether the actions of a public employee fall within the scope of his employment.

Our division recently articulated the test for determining whether an employee's wrongful act falls within the course or scope of employment. "The determination as to whether an employee committed a tort during the course of his employment turns on whether or not: 1) the act performed was either required or 'incident to his duties', or 2) the employee's misconduct could be reasonably foreseen by the employer in any event." (*Clark Equipment Co. v. Wheat* (1979) 92 Cal.App.3d 503, 520 [154 Cal.Rptr. 874].) If an employee's actions fall within the range of actions covered by either part of this two-prong test, the employer will be liable for the wrong, even though the employee has acted maliciously and intentionally. (*Id.*, at p. 521.)

In assessing whether an employee's wrongful act was required by or incidental to his duties, the law defines occupational duties broadly. The fact that an employee is not engaged in the ultimate object of his employment at the time of his wrongful act does not preclude attribution of liability to an employer. For example, acts necessary to the comfort, convenience, health, and welfare of the employee while at work, though strictly personal to himself and not acts of service, do not take him outside the scope of his employment. However, that is not to say, that employers are strictly liable for all actions of their employees during working hours. If an employee substantially deviates from his duties for personal purposes, the employer is not vicariously liable for the employee's actions.

This case presents us with a factual situation where the connection between the employee's duties and the employee's wrongful action has become so attenuated that the law will not hold the employer vicariously liable. Sexual molestation is in no way related to mopping floors, cleaning rooms, or any of the other tasks that are required of a school custodian. Though there may be those cases where personal motivations so mingle with the employee's pursuit of occupational duties that it is arguable whether the employee's action is incidental to his duties, this is not such a case. A. B.'s action, prompted by wholly personal motivations, was clearly not required or incidental to his duties as a school custodian.

Appellant's undisputed allegations that A. B. used school facilities in the commission of his offense do not convince us that A. B.'s action may have been incidental to his custodial duties. Where an employee pursues his own ends, the use of property or facilities entrusted to him by the principal is an inadequate basis for imputing liability to the employer. For example, the fact that a dry cleaning operation affords an employee a unique opportunity to pilfer items inadvertently left in customer's clothing does not render the dry cleaning company vicariously liable for the employee's theft. (*Copelin v. Berlin Dye Works etc. Co.* (1914) 168 Cal. 715, 719 [144 P. 961].) Similarly, the custodian's use of the janitor's office, which arguably furnished a unique opportunity for A. B.'s action, does not impute liability to the school district. The mere fact that an employee has the opportunity to abuse facilities necessary to the performance of his duties does not render an employer vicariously liable for the abuse.

Nor does the fact that the offense occurred during working hours make A. B.'s action incidental to his employment. Although appellant strenuously argues that the janitor's presence at his workplace and his attendance to his duties immediately before and immediately after the offense is a determinative factor in resolving the issue of scope of employment, he is unable to cite any authority for that proposition. In fact, mere presence at the place of employment before, during, or after the commission of the offense has not been a decisive factor in resolving the scope of employment issue. If an employee's tort is personal in nature, mere presence at the place of employment and attendance to occupational duties prior or subsequent to the offense will not give rise to a cause of action against the employer under the doctrine of respondeat superior.

In attempting to establish a nexus between A. B.'s janitorial duties and his act of sexual molestation, appellant places considerable reliance on a number of decisions holding employers vicariously liable for their employees' tortious assaults on third parties: *Carr v. Wm. C. Crowell Co., supra.*, 28 Cal.2d 652 (construction employee threw hammer during dispute over construction procedure); *Fields v. Sanders* (1947) 29 Cal.2d 834 [180 P.2d 684, 172 A.L.R. 525] (employee truck driver assaulted third party driver during dispute over truck driver's performance of his driving duties); *Hiroshima v. Pacific Gas & Elec. Co.* (1936) 18 Cal.App.2d 24 [63 P.2d 340] (dispute over employee's collection of employer's bill); *Pritchard v. Gilbert* (1951) 107 Cal.App.2d 1 [236 P.2d 412] (dispute between traveling salesman and passing motorist over near accident) and *Rodgers v. Kemper Constr. Co.* (1975) *supra.*, 50 Cal. App.3d 608 (dispute over employee's right to use employer's equipment). None of the cases alluded to provides any support for the proposition that a sexual assault by a janitor at a public school is incidental to the janitor's duties. In each of these cases, a work-related dispute preceded the assault. While it is clear from this line of cases that an employer can be vicariously liable for an agent's intentional torts, it is equally clear from the same cases that the acts leading up to the tort must bear some relation to the employee's duties. The fundamental issue is whether the wrongful act was committed "*in the course of* a series of acts of the agent which were authorized by the principal. Of course, where the agent, for however brief a space of time, has ceased to serve his principal, he alone is responsible for his acts during the period of such cessation." (*Fields v. Sanders, supra.*, 29 Cal.2d 834 at P. 839, italics added.) A. B.'s act of rape was not an integral part of a course of action on behalf of his employer, but rather an independent, self-serving pursuit wholly unrelated to his custodial duties.

We now turn to the second part of our inquiry: Whether the employee's misconduct was foreseeable in any event. Appellant cites the broad foreseeability test articulated in *Rodgers v. Kemper Constr. Co., supra.*, as support for her argument that the rape occurred within the scope of employment. The *Rodgers* test reads as follows: "One way to determine whether a risk is inherent in, or created by, an enterprise is to ask whether the actual occurrence was a generally foreseeable consequence of the activity. However, 'foreseeability' in this context must be distinguished from 'foreseeability' as a test for negligence. In the latter sense 'foreseeable' means a level of probability which would lead a prudent person to take effective precautions whereas 'foreseeability' as a test for *respondeat superior* merely means that in the context of the particular enterprise an employee's conduct is not so unusual or startling that it would seem unfair to include the loss resulting from it among other costs of the employer's business. In other words, where the question is one of vicarious liability, the inquiry should be whether the risk was one 'that may fairly be regarded as typical of or broadly incidental' to the enterprise undertaken by the employer." (*Rodgers v. Kemper Constr. Co., supra.*, 50 Cal.App.3d 608, 618–619.) Appellant reasons as follows from the *Rodgers* decision: Given the enormity of the state educational enterprise, some employees will inevitably step aside from their duties to commit a sexual assault. Further, appellant argues, the Legislature anticipated such an eventuality in drafting Education Code sections 44425 and 45123, which attempt through screening mechanisms to safeguard the school system against those with a history of sexual offenses. Appellant concludes that the code is a tacit acknowledgement by the Legislature of the foreseeability of sexual assaults by public school employees on public school children. We believe appellant's argument stretches the *Rodgers* foreseeability standard far beyond its logical limits. While *Rodgers* establishes that the foreseeability test for respondeat superior is broader than that for negligence, the decision also limits liability to those torts which "may fairly be said to be characteristic" of the enterprise's activities. (50 Cal.App.3d at p. 618.) A quarrel among employees over the use of equipment at a construction site might fairly be considered characteristic of the construction industry. But it defies every notion of fairness to say that rape is characteristic of a school district's activities.

Nor does appellant's reference to the Education Code redeem her argument. Efforts by the California Legislature to guard against sexual assaults on public school students hardly prove that the state Legislature believed sexual molestation to be characteristic of public school employees. The fact that the Legislature has taken the action it has in no way alters the fact that sexual molestation is an *aberrational* act. Although appellant argues that the Legislature's anticipation of such an eventuality proves that sexual molestation was foreseeable, the legislative action does not in itself meet the foreseeability test that is the law of this state. The test is not whether it is foreseeable that one or more employees might at some time act in such a way as to give rise to civil liability, but rather, whether the employee's act is foreseeable *in light of the duties* the employee is hired to perform. (Rest.2d Agency (1957) § 245.) Thus, while it might be foreseeable for a school custodian to become involved in a dispute over the manner in which he swept the floors or cleaned a classroom and for the dispute to end in someone being hit with a mop, the same statement cannot be made with reference to rape. There is no aspect of a janitor's duties that would make sexual assault anything other than highly unusual and very startling.

Reference to California's workers' compensation law lends added support to our decision today. Although the rationale underlying respondeat superior and workers' compensation are not identical, courts have frequently been guided by workers' compensation decisions in determining whether a particular act was within the scope of employment: "Under the modern rationale for *respondeat superior*, the test for determining whether an employer is vicariously liable for the tortious conduct of his employee is closely related to the test applied in workers' compensation cases for determining whether an injury arose out of or in the course of employment. This must necessarily be so because the theoretical basis for placing the loss on the employer in both the tort and workers' compensation fields is the allocation of the economic cost of an injury resulting from a risk incident to the enterprise. Consequently, our high court has on many occasions relied upon workers' compensation cases in tort cases." (*Rodgers v. Kemper Constr. Co., supra.*, 50 Cal.App.3d 608, 619.) In looking to workers' compensation law, we are essentially asking whether any injuries A. B. might have incurred while engaged in the sexual molestation and rape would be compensable under workers' compensation. Necessarily, if A. B.'s conduct were within the "course and scope" of his employment as a custodian, then any injury to A. B. which occurred while these acts were in progress would be a compensable injury for workers' compensation purposes. However, to assert that A. B. would be entitled to workers' compensation benefits had he, for example, injured his back in perpetrating a rape is totally absurd. If A. B. had been injured, it would clearly not be compensable because the alleged misconduct is ipso facto not within the "course and scope of his employment." It necessarily follows that such conduct would be outside the scope of his employment under a respondeat superior analysis since the latter test is *more restrictive* than the workers' compensation standard. (*Church v. Arko* (1977) 75 Cal. App.3d 291, 298 [142 Cal.Rptr. 92].)

Distilled to its essence, appellant's argument is little more than that the risk of loss from an employee's sexual assault should fall on the school district as a means of spreading the risk to the community at large. Appellant is leaning on a slender reed. The "spread the risk" concept underlying the doctrine of respondeat superior does not mean that attribution of liability to an employer is merely a legal artifice invoked to reach a deep pocket or that it is based on an elaborate theory of optimal resource allocation. (*Rodgers v. Kemper Constr. Co., supra.*, 50 Cal.App.3d 608, 618.) Rather, the concept of spreading the risk is simply another way of saying that an enterprise should be charged with the cost of those accidents directly attributable to its activities. (See *Clark Equipment Co. v. Wheat, supra.*, 92 Cal.App.3d 503, 520; *Rodgers v. Kemper Constr. Co., supra.*, 50 Cal.App.3d 608, 618.) As our Supreme Court explained in *Hinman v. Westinghouse*: " '[T]he modern justification for vicarious liability is a rule of policy, a deliberate allocation of a risk. The losses caused by the torts of employees, *which as a practical matter are sure to occur* in the conduct of the employer's enterprise, are placed upon that enterprise itself, as a required cost of doing business. They are placed upon the employer because, having engaged in an enterprise which will, on the basis of past experience, involve harm to others through the torts of employees, and sought to profit by it, it is just that he, rather than the innocent injured plaintiff, should bear them; and because he is better able to absorb them, and to distribute them, through prices, rates or liability insurance, to the public, and so to shift them to society, to the community at large." ' (2 Cal.3d 956, 959–960, italics added.) Even assuming that schools are equipped, as are businesses, to absorb the costs of employees' torts in that schools are able indirectly to absorb and distribute the costs through taxation to the community at large, the rationale for vicarious liability does not justify allocating the risk of sexual assaults by a school employee to the community at large. Under the express terms of the *Hinman* rule, we invoke the doctrine of respondeat superior to indemnify only those losses which as a practical matter are sure to occur in the conduct of the employer's business. A sexual assault simply does not fall within the range of risks allocable to an employer.

As we have stated, the act of rape is not attributable to the school district because it is neither a required or incidental duty of a school employee, nor is it a reasonably foreseeable consequence of the educational enterprise. We will not depart from settled precedent to establish a rule that would divert limited educational funds to create a new compulsory insurance fund which would cover virtually all torts of an employee occurring during working hours at the place of employment, regardless of the extremity or personal nature of the act. The facts, construed most favorably for the appellant, will admit of no inference other than that in his rape of the appellant, A. B. stepped outside the scope of his employment.

QUESTIONS

1. The result in *Alma W.* seems almost obvious. How could rape ever be considered to occur within the scope of employment? Does the case stand for the proposition that an employer will never be held vicariously liable for sexual assault?
2. Clearly there is a vital public policy in favor of deterring sexual assaults and ensuring compensation for those who are attacked. If *respondeat superior* is not applicable, how can this public policy be implemented?

Problem 14-2

A temporary staffing company hired Theresa to work as a medical assistant. After several other placements, Theresa was assigned to work at a clinic, which was shorthanded due to an employee taking family leave. After engaging in an argument with an employee of the clinic, Theresa responded by putting acid in the employee's water bottle during work hours, causing severe injury. The clinic worker sued the staffing company that placed Theresa in the workplace, under the doctrine of *respondeat superior*. Will the plaintiff prevail?

Problem 14-3

Clive is employed by a bar to check identification and manage admission to the club. With a long line outside the door, Clive began giving priority entrance to persons he recognized. Several customers complained that Clive was acting unfairly. Clive responded by striking them with his flashlight. Can the customers prevail in an action against the bar under the doctrine of *respondeat superior*?

Problem 14-4

Carolyn was a cashier at Filco Pet Supplies. During a paid break, Carolyn drove to a convenience store to buy cookies for herself and another employee. Carolyn was not required to notify a supervisor before leaving the work site on break, even though she was on the clock. On her way to the store, Shinn collided with the plaintiff car. The plaintiff sued Filco for his injuries on the basis of *respondeat superior*. Will the plaintiff prevail?

Conclusion

By hiring an employee, the employer undertakes obligations to the employee, but also to third parties. An employer will be liable for torts committed by its employees within the course and scope of their employment. A party may also be liable for the tortious acts of its independent contractor if the wrongful acts concern a duty that it non-delegable by the entity, or if the activity is inherently dangerous. These doctrinal lines are drawn on the basis of public policy, in an effort to balance the rights of third parties who suffer injury as a result of the employee's actions, and the employer's right to be protected from liability for purely personal activities by its employees.

6

Obligations Owed by Employers to Employees During the Relationship

A. Privacy Interests

Key Concepts

- Generally, people enjoy the ability to keep their personal affairs private. However, the employer may have an interest in one's private life if it affects the employer's legitimate business interests.
- Public employees do not sacrifice their constitutional rights against the government, but the government is given some latitude to act as an employer. A person's right to privacy may be overcome by an employer's reasonable investigation of an employment matter.
- Non-government employees have recourse to common law protections of privacy that prohibit offensive intrusions on the employee.
- In the contemporary workplace, privacy of electronic information and communications is of particular concern for employers and employees.
- Testing employees for use of illegal substances that may affect their performance at work brings a heightened clash of interests generally addressed by statute.

Lesson 15:
Expectation of Privacy in Public Employment

Objectives and Expected Learning Outcomes

In this Lesson, you will explore the right of privacy extended to public sector workers by the Fourth Amendment to the Constitution, which places limits on the government. The Fourth Amendment protects against unreasonable searches and seizures by the government. The constitutional standard for searches and other intrusions is "reasonableness." Reasonableness is measured both by societal standards and expectations employers establish in the workplace. In the public workplace, a Fourth Amendment analysis considers the extent to which employees have a reasonable expectation of privacy at work. Reasonableness is contextual, and so the government is given some latitude when it is acting as an employer. You will learn how to balance the reasonableness of the government's intrusions in its capacity as an employer. Once an individual's reasonable expectation of privacy has been established, courts will weigh the nature and quality of employer intrusion against the government's need for supervision, control, and the efficient operation of the workplace.

Americans tend to place a high value on their privacy, resulting in a strong desire to be free from unwelcome intrusions. This interest is at its strongest in one's home, but most people expect to retain a reasonable degree of privacy and autonomy with regard to personal matters even when they are in the workplace. An employee has a reasonable expectation of privacy that must be balanced with the employer's interest in providing a safe and productive workplace. This balancing is a matter of constitutional law when the employer is an arm of the government.

Public employers are state actors, and therefore they are constrained by the Fourth Amendment. The Fourth Amendment provides that Americans shall be "secure in their persons, houses, papers, and effects against unreasonable searches and seizures." Ordinarily, when the government conducts a search it must obtain a warrant supported by probable cause. However, as the next case explains, there is no probable cause requirement when the search is work-related and conducted by a government in its role as an employer. The question becomes whether the search is reasonable, which the court says is determined by considering: (1) whether the employee maintained a reasonable expectation of privacy over the item searched,

(2) whether the employer had justification to conduct the search, and (3) whether the search as conducted was reasonably related in scope to the circumstances which justified it in the first place.

O'CONNOR v. ORTEGA

480 U.S. 709 (1987).

JUSTICE O'CONNOR announced the judgment of the Court and delivered an opinion in which THE CHIEF JUSTICE, JUSTICE WHITE, and JUSTICE POWELL join.

This suit under 42 U. S. C. § 1983 presents two issues concerning the Fourth Amendment rights of public employees. First, we must determine whether the respondent, a public employee, had a reasonable expectation of privacy in his office, desk, and file cabinets at his place of work. Second, we must address the appropriate Fourth Amendment standard for a search conducted by a public employer in areas in which a public employee is found to have a reasonable expectation of privacy.

I

Dr. Magno Ortega, a physician and psychiatrist, held the position of Chief of Professional Education at Napa State Hospital (Hospital) for 17 years, until his dismissal from that position in 1981. As Chief of Professional Education, Dr. Ortega had primary responsibility for training young physicians in psychiatric residency programs.

In July 1981, Hospital officials, including Dr. Dennis O'Connor, the Executive Director of the Hospital, became concerned about possible improprieties in Dr. Ortega's management of the residency program. . . .

On July 30, 1981, Dr. O'Connor requested that Dr. Ortega take paid administrative leave during an investigation of these charges. At Dr. Ortega's request, Dr. O'Connor agreed to allow Dr. Ortega to take two weeks' vacation instead of administrative leave. Dr. Ortega, however, was requested to stay off Hospital grounds for the duration of the investigation. On August 14, 1981, Dr. O'Connor informed Dr. Ortega that the investigation had not yet been completed, and that he was being placed on paid administrative leave. Dr. Ortega remained on administrative leave until the Hospital terminated his employment on September 22, 1981.

Dr. O'Connor selected several Hospital personnel to conduct the investigation, including an accountant, a physician, and a Hospital security officer. Richard Friday, the Hospital Administrator, led this "investigative team." At some point during the investigation, Mr. Friday made the decision to enter Dr. Ortega's office. The specific reason for the entry into Dr. Ortega's office is unclear from the record. At the time of the search, however, the Hospital had not yet terminated Dr. Ortega's employment; Dr. Ortega was still on administrative leave. [T]here was no policy of inventorying the offices of those on administrative leave. Before the search had been initiated, however, petitioners had become aware that Dr. Ortega had taken the computer to his home. Dr. Ortega contends that the purpose of the search was to secure evidence for use against him in administrative disciplinary proceedings.

The resulting search of Dr. Ortega's office was quite thorough. The investigators entered the office a number of times and seized several items from Dr. Ortega's desk and file cabinets, including a Valentine's Day card, a photograph, and a book of poetry all sent to Dr. Ortega by a former resident physician. These items were later used in a proceeding before a hearing officer of the California State Personnel Board to impeach the credibility of the former resident, who testified on Dr. Ortega's behalf. The investigators also seized billing documentation of one of Dr. Ortega's private patients under the California Medicaid program. The investigators did not otherwise separate Dr. Ortega's property from state property. . . Thus, no formal inventory of the property in the office was ever made. Instead, all the papers in Dr. Ortega's office were merely placed in boxes, and put in storage for Dr. Ortega to retrieve.

Dr. Ortega commenced this action against petitioners in Federal District Court under 42 U. S. C. § 1983, alleging that the search of his office violated the Fourth Amendment. On cross-motions for summary judgment, the District Court granted petitioners' motion for summary judgment. The District Court concluded that the search was proper because there was a need to secure state property in the office. The Court of Appeals for the Ninth Circuit affirmed in part and reversed in part concluding that Dr. Ortega had a reasonable expectation of privacy in his office. While the Hospital had a procedure for office inventories, these inventories were reserved for employees who were departing or were terminated. The Court of Appeals also concluded—albeit without explanation—that the search violated the Fourth Amendment. The Court of Appeals held that the record justified a grant of partial summary judgment for Dr. Ortega on the issue of liability for an unlawful search, and it remanded the case to the District Court for a determination of damages.

We granted certiorari and now reverse and remand.

II

The strictures of the Fourth Amendment, applied to the States through the Fourteenth Amendment, have been applied to the conduct of governmental officials in various civil activities. Thus, we have held in the past that the Fourth Amendment governs the conduct of school officials, building inspectors and Occupational Safety and Health Act inspectors. Searches and seizures by government employers or supervisors of the private property of their employees, therefore, are subject to the restraints of the Fourth Amendment.

The Fourth Amendment protects the "right of the people to be secure in their persons, houses, papers, and effects, against unreasonable searches and seizures . . . ." Our cases establish that Dr. Ortega's Fourth Amendment rights are implicated only if the conduct of the Hospital officials at issue in this case infringed "an expectation of privacy that society is prepared to consider reasonable." [T]he Court [g]ives weight to such factors as the intention of the Framers of the Fourth Amendment, the uses to which the individual has put a location, and our societal understanding that certain areas deserve the most scrupulous protection from government invasion.

Because the reasonableness of an expectation of privacy, as well as the appropriate standard for a search, is understood to differ according to context, it is essential first to delineate the boundaries of the workplace context. The workplace includes those areas and items that are related to work and are generally within the employer's control. At a hospital, for example, the hallways, cafeteria, offices, desks, and file cabinets, among other areas, are all part of the workplace. These areas remain part of the workplace context even if the employee has placed personal items in them, such as a photograph placed in a desk or a letter posted on an employee bulletin board.

Not everything that passes through the confines of the business address can be considered part of the workplace context, however. An employee may bring closed luggage to the office prior to leaving on a trip, or a handbag or briefcase each workday. While whatever expectation of privacy the employee has in the existence and the outward appearance of the luggage is affected by its presence in the workplace, the employee's expectation of privacy in the *contents* of the luggage is not affected in the same way. The appropriate standard for a workplace search does not necessarily apply to a piece of closed personal luggage, a handbag, or a briefcase that happens to be within the employer's business address.

Within the workplace context, this Court has recognized that employees may have a reasonable expectation of privacy against intrusions by police. As with the expectation of privacy in one's home, such an expectation in one's place of work is "based upon societal expectations that have deep roots in the history of the Amendment." . . . .

. . . .Public employees' expectations of privacy in their offices, desks, and file cabinets, like similar expectations of employees in the private sector, may be reduced by virtue of actual office practices and procedures, or by legitimate regulation. The employee's expectation of privacy must be assessed in the context of the employment relation. An office is seldom a private enclave free from entry by supervisors, other employees, and business and personal invitees. Instead, in many cases offices are continually entered by fellow employees and other visitors during the workday for conferences, consultations, and other work-related visits. Simply put, it is the nature of government offices that others—such as fellow employees, supervisors, consensual visitors, and the general public—may have frequent access to an individual's office. We agree with JUSTICE SCALIA that "[constitutional] protection against *unreasonable* searches by the government does not disappear merely because the government has the right to make reasonable intrusions in its capacity as employer," but some government offices may be so open to fellow employees or the public that no expectation of privacy is reasonable. Given the great variety of work environments in the public sector, the question whether an employee has a reasonable expectation of privacy must be addressed on a case-by-case basis.

The Court of Appeals concluded that Dr. Ortega had a reasonable expectation of privacy in his office, and five Members of this Court agree with that determination. Because the record does not reveal the extent to which Hospital officials may have had work-related reasons to enter Dr. Ortega's office, we think the Court of Appeals should have remanded the matter to the District Court for its further determination. But regardless of any legitimate right of access the Hospital staff may have had to the office as such, we recognize that the undisputed evidence suggests that Dr. Ortega had a reasonable expectation of privacy in his desk and file cabinets. The undisputed evidence discloses that Dr. Ortega did not share his desk or file cabinets with any other employees. Dr. Ortega had occupied the office for 17 years and he kept materials in his office, which included personal correspondence, medical files, correspondence from private patients unconnected to the Hospital, personal financial records, teaching aids and notes, and personal gifts and mementos. The files on physicians in residency training were kept outside Dr. Ortega's office. Indeed, the only items found by the investigators were apparently personal items because, with the exception of the items seized for use in the administrative hearings, all the papers and effects found in the office were simply placed in boxes and made available to Dr. Ortega. Finally, we note that there was no evidence that the Hospital had established any reasonable regulation or policy discouraging employees such as Dr. Ortega from storing personal papers and effects in their desks or file cabinets, although the absence of such a policy does not create an expectation of privacy where it would not otherwise exist.

On the basis of this undisputed evidence, we accept the conclusion of the Court of Appeals that Dr. Ortega had a reasonable expectation of privacy at least in his desk and file cabinets.

III

Having determined that Dr. Ortega had a reasonable expectation of privacy in his office. . .we must determine the appropriate standard of reasonableness applicable to the search. A determination of the standard of reasonableness applicable to a particular class of searches requires "[balancing] the nature and quality of the intrusion on the individual's Fourth Amendment interests against the importance of the governmental interests alleged to justify the intrusion." In the case of searches conducted by a public employer, we must balance the invasion of the employees' legitimate expectations of privacy against the government's need for supervision, control, and the efficient operation of the workplace.

"[It] is settled . . . that 'except in certain carefully defined classes of cases, a search of private property without proper consent is "unreasonable" unless it has been authorized by a valid search warrant.' There are some circumstances, however, in which we have recognized that a warrant requirement is unsuitable. In particular, a warrant requirement is not appropriate when "the burden of obtaining a warrant is likely to frustrate the governmental purpose behind the search." Or, as JUSTICE BLACKMUN stated in *T. L. O.*, "[only] in those exceptional circumstances in which special needs, beyond the normal need for law enforcement, make the warrant and probable-cause requirement impracticable." . . . .

. . . .

The legitimate privacy interests of public employees in the private objects they bring to the workplace may be substantial. Against these privacy interests, however, must be balanced the realities of the workplace, which strongly suggest that a warrant requirement would be unworkable. While police, and even administrative enforcement personnel, conduct searches for the primary purpose of obtaining evidence for use in criminal or other enforcement proceedings, employers most frequently need to enter the offices and desks of their employees for legitimate work-related reasons wholly unrelated to illegal conduct. Employers and supervisors are focused primarily on the need to complete the government agency's work in a prompt and efficient manner. An employer may have need for correspondence, or a file or report available only in an employee's office while the employee is away from the office. Or, as is alleged to have been the case here, employers may need to safeguard or identify state property or records in an office in connection with a pending investigation into suspected employee misfeasance.

In our view, requiring an employer to obtain a warrant whenever the employer wished to enter an employee's office, desk, or file cabinets for a work-related purpose would seriously disrupt the routine conduct of business and would be unduly burdensome. Imposing unwieldy warrant procedures in such cases upon supervisors, who would otherwise have no reason to be familiar with such procedures, is simply unreasonable. In contrast to other circumstances in which we have required warrants, supervisors in offices such as at the Hospital are hardly in the business of investigating the violation of criminal laws. Rather, work-related searches are merely incident to the primary business of the agency. Under these circumstances, the imposition of a warrant requirement would conflict with "the common-sense realization that government offices could not function if every employment decision became a constitutional matter."

Whether probable cause is an inappropriate standard for public employer searches of their employees' offices presents a more difficult issue. For the most part, we have required that a search be based upon probable cause, but . . ."[the] fundamental command of the Fourth Amendment is that searches and seizures be reasonable, and although 'both the concept of probable cause and the requirement of a warrant bear on the reasonableness of a search, . . . in certain limited circumstances neither is required.' " Thus, "[where] a careful balancing of governmental and private interests suggests that the public interest is best served by a Fourth Amendment standard of reasonableness that stops short of probable cause, we have not hesitated to adopt such a standard." We have concluded, for example, that the appropriate standard for administrative searches is not probable cause in its traditional meaning. Instead, an administrative warrant can be obtained if there is a showing that reasonable legislative or administrative standards for conducting an inspection are satisfied.

As an initial matter, it is important to recognize the plethora of contexts in which employers will have an occasion to intrude to some extent on an employee's expectation of privacy. Because the parties in this case have alleged that the search was either a noninvestigatory work-related intrusion or an investigatory search for evidence of suspected work-related employee misfeasance, we undertake to determine the appropriate Fourth Amendment standard of reasonableness *only* for these two types of employer intrusions and leave for another day inquiry into other circumstances.

The governmental interest justifying work-related intrusions by public employers is the efficient and proper operation of the workplace. Government agencies provide myriad services to the public, and the work of these agencies would suffer if employers were required to have probable cause before they entered an employee's desk for the purpose of finding a file or piece of office correspondence. Indeed, it is difficult to give the concept of probable cause, rooted as it is in the criminal investigatory context, much meaning when the purpose of a search is to retrieve a file for work-related reasons. Similarly, the concept of probable cause has little meaning for a routine inventory conducted by public employers for the purpose of securing state property. To ensure the efficient and proper operation of the agency, therefore, public employers must be given wide latitude to enter employee offices for work-related, noninvestigatory reasons.

We come to a similar conclusion for searches conducted pursuant to an investigation of work-related employee misconduct. Even when employers conduct an investigation, they have an interest substantially different from "the normal need for law enforcement." Public employers have an interest in ensuring that their agencies operate in an effective and efficient manner, and the work of these agencies inevitably suffers from the inefficiency, incompetence, mismanagement, or other work-related misfeasance of its employees. Indeed, in many cases, public employees are entrusted with tremendous responsibility, and the consequences of their misconduct or incompetence to both the agency and the public interest can be severe. In contrast to law enforcement officials, therefore, public employers are not enforcers of the criminal law; instead, public employers have a direct and overriding interest in ensuring that the work of the agency is conducted in a proper and efficient manner. In our view, therefore, a probable cause requirement for searches of the type at issue here would impose intolerable burdens on public employers. The delay in correcting the employee misconduct caused by the need for probable cause rather than reasonable suspicion will be translated into tangible and often irreparable damage to the agency's work, and ultimately to the public interest. Additionally, while law enforcement officials are expected to "[school] themselves in the niceties of probable cause," no such expectation is generally applicable to public employers, at least when the search is not used to gather evidence of a criminal offense. It is simply unrealistic to expect supervisors in most government agencies to learn the subtleties of the probable cause standard. As JUSTICE BLACKMUN observed "[a] teacher has neither the training nor the day-to-day experience in the complexities of probable cause that a law enforcement officer possesses, and is ill-equipped to make a quick judgment about the existence of probable cause." We believe that this observation is an equally apt description of the public employer and supervisors at the Hospital, and we conclude that a reasonableness standard will permit regulation of the employer's conduct "according to the dictates of reason and common sense."

Balanced against the substantial government interests in the efficient and proper operation of the workplace are the privacy interests of government employees in their place of work which, while not insubstantial, are far less than those found at home or in some other contexts. As with the building inspections in *Camara*, the employer intrusions at issue here "involve a relatively limited invasion" of employee privacy. 387 U.S. at 537. Government offices are provided to employees for the sole purpose of facilitating the work of an agency. The employee may avoid exposing personal belongings at work by simply leaving them at home.

In sum, we conclude that the "special needs, beyond the normal need for law enforcement make the . . . probable-cause requirement impracticable," 469 U.S. at 351 (BLACKMUN, J., concurring in judgment), for legitimate work-related, noninvestigatory intrusions as well as investigations of work-related misconduct. A standard of reasonableness will neither unduly burden the efforts of government employers to ensure the efficient and proper operation of the workplace, nor authorize arbitrary intrusions upon the privacy of public employees. We hold, therefore, that public employer intrusions on the constitutionally protected privacy interests of government employees for noninvestigatory, work-related purposes, as well as for investigations of work-related misconduct, should be judged by the standard of reasonableness under all the circumstances. Under this reasonableness standard, both the inception and the scope of the intrusion must be reasonable:

> Determining the reasonableness of any search involves a twofold inquiry: first, one must consider 'whether the . . . action was justified at its inception,' *Terry* v. *Ohio*, 392 U.S., at 20; second, one must determine whether the search as actually conducted 'was reasonably related in scope to the circumstances which justified the interference in the first place,' *ibid.*

New Jersey v. *T. L. O., supra*, at 341.

Ordinarily, a search of an employee's office by a supervisor will be "justified at its inception" when there are reasonable grounds for suspecting that the search will turn up evidence that the employee is guilty of work-related misconduct, or that the search is necessary for a noninvestigatory work-related purpose such as to retrieve a needed file. Because petitioners had an "individualized suspicion" of misconduct by Dr. Ortega, we need not decide whether individualized suspicion is an essential element of the standard of reasonableness that we adopt today. The search will be permissible in its scope when "the measures adopted are reasonably related to the objectives of the search and not excessively intrusive in light of . . . the nature of the [misconduct]."

Accordingly, the judgment of the Court of Appeals is reversed, and the case is remanded to that court for further proceedings consistent with this opinion.

It is so ordered.

The test created by the plurality in *O'Connor* is expressly fact-intensive and case-specific. The Court returned to the test in a case involving modern communication devices.

City of Ontario v. Quon

560 U.S. 746 (2010).

Justice Kennedy delivered the opinion of the Court.

This case involves the assertion by a government employer of the right, in circumstances to be described, to read text messages sent and received on a pager the employer owned and issued to an employee. The employee contends that the privacy of the messages is protected by the ban on "unreasonable searches and seizures" found in the Fourth Amendment to the United States Constitution, made applicable to the States by the Due Process Clause of the Fourteenth Amendment. . . .

I

A

The city of Ontario (City) is a political subdivision of the State of California. . . .[I]n October 2001, the City acquired 20 alphanumeric pagers capable of sending and receiving text messages. Arch Wireless Operating Company provided wireless service for the pagers. Under the City's service contract with Arch Wireless, each pager was allotted a limited number of characters sent or received each month. Usage in excess of that amount would result in an additional fee. The City issued pagers to Quon and other SWAT Team members in order to help the SWAT Team mobilize and respond to emergency situations.

Before acquiring the pagers, the City announced a "Computer Usage, Internet and E-Mail Policy" (Computer Policy) that applied to all employees. Among other provisions, it specified that the City "reserves the right to monitor and log all network activity including e-mail and Internet use, with or without notice. Users should have no expectation of privacy or confidentiality when using these resources." In March 2000, Quon signed a statement acknowledging that he had read and understood the Computer Policy.

The Computer Policy did not apply, on its face, to text messaging. Text messages share similarities with e-mails, but the two differ in an important way. In this case, for instance, an e-mail sent on a City computer was transmitted through the City's own data servers, but a text message sent on one of the City's pagers was transmitted using wireless radio frequencies from an individual pager to a receiving station owned by Arch Wireless. It was routed through Arch Wireless' computer network, where it remained until the recipient's pager or cellular telephone was ready to receive the message, at which point Arch Wireless transmitted the message from the transmitting station nearest to the recipient. After delivery, Arch Wireless retained a copy on its computer servers. The message did not pass through computers owned by the City.

Although the Computer Policy did not cover text messages by its explicit terms, the City made clear to employees, including Quon, that the City would treat text messages the same way as it treated e-mails. At an April 18, 2002, staff meeting at which Quon was present, Lieutenant Steven Duke, the OPD officer responsible for the City's contract with Arch Wireless, told officers that messages sent on the pagers "are considered e-mail messages. This means that [text] messages would fall under the City's policy as public information and [would be] eligible for auditing." Duke's comments were put in writing in a memorandum sent on April 29, 2002, by Chief Scharf to Quon and other City personnel.

Within the first or second billing cycle after the pagers were distributed, Quon exceeded his monthly text message character allotment. Duke told Quon about the overage, and reminded him that messages sent on the pagers were "considered e-mail and could be audited." Duke said, however, that "it was not his intent to audit [an] employee's text messages to see if the overage [was] due to work related transmissions." Duke suggested that Quon could reimburse the City for the overage fee rather than have Duke audit the messages. Quon wrote a check to the City for the overage. Duke offered the same arrangement to other employees who incurred overage fees.

Over the next few months, Quon exceeded his character limit three or four times. Each time he reimbursed the City. Quon and another officer again incurred overage fees for their pager usage in August 2002. At a meeting in October, Duke told Scharf that he had become " 'tired of being a bill collector.' " Scharf decided to determine whether the existing character limit was too low—that is, whether officers such as Quon were having to pay fees for sending work-related messages—or if the overages were for personal messages. Scharf told Duke to request transcripts of text messages sent in August and September by Quon and the other employee who had exceeded the character allowance.

At Duke's request, an administrative assistant employed by OPD contacted Arch Wireless. After verifying that the City was the subscriber on the accounts, Arch Wireless provided the desired transcripts. Duke reviewed the transcripts and discovered that many of the messages sent and received on Quon's pager were not work related, and some were sexually explicit. Duke reported his findings to Scharf, who, along with Quon's immediate supervisor, reviewed the transcripts himself. After his review, Scharf referred the matter to OPD's internal affairs division for an investigation into whether Quon was violating OPD rules by pursuing personal matters while on duty.

The officer in charge of the internal affairs review was Sergeant Patrick McMahon. Before conducting a review, McMahon used Quon's work schedule to redact the transcripts in order to eliminate any messages Quon sent while off duty. He then reviewed the content of the messages Quon sent during work hours. McMahon's report noted that Quon sent or received 456 messages during work hours in the month of August 2002, of which no more than 57 were work related; he sent as many as 80 messages during a single day at work; and on an average workday, Quon sent or received 28 messages, of which only 3 were related to police business. The report concluded that Quon had violated OPD rules. Quon was allegedly disciplined.

B

. . . .

The District Court held a jury trial to determine the purpose of the audit. The jury concluded that Scharf ordered the audit to determine the efficacy of the character limits. The District Court accordingly held that petitioners did not violate the Fourth Amendment. It entered judgment in their favor.

The United States Court of Appeals for the Ninth Circuit reversed in part. The panel agreed with the District Court that Jeff Quon had a reasonable expectation of privacy in his text messages but disagreed with the District Court about whether the search was reasonable. Even though the search was conducted for "a legitimate work-related rationale," the Court of Appeals concluded, it "was not reasonable in scope." The panel disagreed with the District Court's observation that "there were no less-intrusive means" that Chief Scharf could have used "to verify the efficacy of the 25,000 character limit . . . without intruding on [respondents'] Fourth Amendment rights.". . . .

The Ninth Circuit denied a petition for rehearing en banc. . . .This Court granted the petition for certiorari filed by the City, OPD, and Chief Scharf challenging the Court of Appeals' holding that they violated the Fourth Amendment.

II

The Fourth Amendment states: "The right of the people to be secure in their persons, houses, papers, and effects, against unreasonable searches and seizures, shall not be violated . . . ." It is well settled that the Fourth Amendment's protection extends beyond the sphere of criminal investigations. "The Amendment guarantees the privacy, dignity, and security of persons against certain arbitrary and invasive acts by officers of the Government," without regard to whether the government actor is investigating crime or performing another function. The Fourth Amendment applies as well when the acts in its capacity as an employer.

The Court discussed this principle in *O'Connor*. [A]ll Members of the Court agreed with the general principle that "[i]ndividuals do not lose Fourth Amendment rights merely because they work for the government instead of a private employer." A majority of the Court further agreed that " 'special needs, beyond the normal need for law enforcement,' " make the warrant and probable-cause requirement impracticable for government employers.

The O'Connor Court disagree[d] on the proper analytical framework for Fourth Amendment claims against government employers. A four-Justice plurality concluded that the correct analysis has two steps. First, because "some government offices may be so open to fellow employees or the public that no expectation of privacy is reasonable," a court must consider "[t]he operational realities of the workplace" in order to determine whether an employee's Fourth Amendment rights are implicated. On this view, "the question whether an employee has a reasonable expectation of privacy must be addressed on a case-by-case basis." Next, where an employee has a legitimate privacy expectation, an employer's intrusion on that expectation "for noninvestigatory, work-related purposes, as well as for investigations of work-related misconduct, should be judged by the standard of reasonableness under all the circumstances."

Justice Scalia, concurring in the judgment, outlined a different approach. His opinion would have dispensed with an inquiry into "operational realities" and would conclude "that the offices of government employees . . . are covered by Fourth Amendment protections as a general matter." But he would also have held "that government searches to retrieve work-related materials or to investigate violations of workplace rules—searches of the sort that are regarded as reasonable and normal in the private-employer context—do not violate the Fourth Amendment."

. . . .[I]n the two decades since *O'Connor*, however, the threshold test for determining the scope of an employee's Fourth Amendment rights has not been clarified further. Here, though they disagree on whether Quon had a reasonable expectation of privacy, both petitioners and respondents start from the premise that the *O'Connor* plurality controls. It is not necessary to resolve whether that premise is correct. The case can be decided by determining that the search was reasonable even assuming Quon had a reasonable expectation of privacy. The two *O'Connor* approaches—the plurality's and Justice Scalia's—therefore lead to the same result here.

III

A

Before turning to the reasonableness of the search, it is instructive to note the parties' disagreement over whether Quon had a reasonable expectation of privacy. . . .

. . . .

. . . . For present purposes we assume several propositions, arguendo: First, Quon had a reasonable expectation of privacy in the text messages sent on the pager provided to him by the City; second, petitioners' review of the transcript constituted a search within the meaning of the Fourth Amendment; and third, the principles applicable to a government employer's search of an employee's physical office apply with at least the same force when the employer intrudes on the employee's privacy in the electronic sphere.

B

Even if Quon had a reasonable expectation of privacy in his text messages, petitioners did not necessarily violate the Fourth Amendment by obtaining and reviewing the transcripts. Although as a general matter, warrantless searches "are per se unreasonable under the Fourth Amendment," there are "a few specifically established and well-delineated exceptions" to that general rule. The Court has held that the " 'special needs' " of the workplace justify one such exception.

Under the approach of the *O'Connor* plurality, when conducted for a "noninvestigatory, work-related purpos[e]" or for the "investigatio[n] of work-related misconduct," a government employer's warrantless search is reasonable if it is " 'justified at its inception' " and if " 'the measures adopted are reasonably related to the objectives of the search and not excessively intrusive in light of' " the circumstances giving rise to the search. The search here satisfied the standard of the *O'Connor* plurality and was reasonable under that approach.

The search was justified at its inception because there were "reasonable grounds for suspecting that the search [was] necessary for a noninvestigatory work-related purpose. "As a jury found, Chief Scharf ordered the search in order to determine whether the character limit on the City's contract with Arch Wireless was sufficient to meet the City's needs. This was, as the Ninth Circuit noted, a "legitimate work-related rationale." The City and OPD had a legitimate interest in ensuring that employees were not being forced to pay out of their own pockets for work-related expenses, or on the other hand that City was not paying for extensive personal communications.

As for the scope of the search, reviewing the transcripts was reasonable because it was an efficient and expedient way to determine whether Quon's overages were the result of work-related messaging or personal use. The review was also not " 'excessively intrusive.' Although Quon had gone over his monthly allotment a number of times, OPD requested transcripts for only the months of August and September 2002. While it may have been reasonable as well for OPD to review transcripts of all the months in which Quon exceeded his allowance, it was certainly reasonable for OPD to review messages for just two months in order to obtain a large enough sample to decide whether the character limits were efficacious. And it is worth noting that during his internal affairs investigation, McMahon redacted all messages Quon sent while off duty, a measure which reduced the intrusiveness of any further review of the transcripts.

Furthermore, and again on the assumption that Quon had a reasonable expectation of privacy in the contents of his messages, the extent of an expectation is relevant to assessing whether the search was too intrusive.

. . . .

From OPD's perspective, the fact that Quon likely had only a limited privacy expectation, with boundaries that we need not here explore, lessened the risk that the review would intrude on highly private details of Quon's life. OPD's audit of messages on Quon's employer-provided pager was not nearly as intrusive as a search of his personal e-mail account or pager, or a wiretap on his home phone line, would have been. That the search did reveal intimate details of Quon's life does not make it unreasonable, for under the circumstances a reasonable employer would not expect that such a review would intrude on such matters. The search was permissible in its scope.

The Court of Appeals erred in finding the search unreasonable. It pointed to a "host of simple ways to verify the efficacy of the 25,000 character limit . . . without intruding on [respondents'] Fourth Amendment rights." The panel suggested that Scharf "could have warned Quon that for the month of September he was forbidden from using his pager for personal communications, and that the contents of all of his messages would be reviewed to ensure the pager was used only for work-related purposes during that timeframe. Alternatively, if [OPD] wanted to review past usage, it could have asked Quon to count the characters himself, or asked him to redact personal messages and grant permission to [OPD] to review the redacted transcript."

This approach was inconsistent with controlling precedents. This Court has "repeatedly refused to declare that only the 'least intrusive' search practicable can be reasonable under the Fourth Amendment." That rationale "could raise insuperable barriers to the exercise of virtually all search-and-seizure powers," because "judges engaged in post hoc evaluations of government conduct can almost always imagine some alternative means by which the objectives of the government might have been accomplished." The analytic errors of the Court of Appeals in this case illustrate the necessity of this principle. Even assuming there were ways that OPD could have performed the search that would have been intrusive, it does not follow that the search as conducted was unreasonable.

Because the search was motivated by a legitimate work-related purpose, and because it was not excessive in scope, the search was reasonable under the approach of the *O'Connor* plurality. For these same reasons—that the employer had a legitimate reason for the search, and that the search was not excessively intrusive in light of that justification—the Court also concludes that the search would be "regarded as reasonable and normal in the private-employer context" and would satisfy the approach of Justice Scalia's concurrence. The search was reasonable, and the Court of Appeals erred by holding to the contrary. Petitioners did not violate Quon's Fourth Amendment rights.

C

. . . .

Because the search was reasonable, petitioners did not violate respondents' Fourth Amendment rights, and the court below erred by concluding otherwise. The judgment of the Court of Appeals for the Ninth Circuit is reversed, and the case is remanded for further proceedings consistent with this opinion.

It is so ordered.

QUESTIONS

1. In *Quon*, the scope of the search was reasonable because the search was an efficient and expedient way to determine whether Quon's overages were the result of work-related messaging or personal use. In *O'Connor*, the inquiry is limited to whether scope of the intrusion was itself reasonable in light of its justification. Is there a distinction between the two?
2. How should a court determine whether an employee has a reasonable expectation of privacy?
3. How can an employer establish a practice of what is within the scope of a reasonable expectation of privacy?
4. What weight should a court give to a public employer's mandate to provide services to the public in an efficient and adequate manner?

Problem 15-1

A draft California Highway Patrol employee handbook contains the following provision:

> The CHP provides computers, tablets, and smart phones to employees for their convenience. Employees should be aware that the information transmitted through these devices belongs

> to CHP, and CHP has the right to access such information at all times.

The CHP installed key-logger software on all devices it distributed to its employees. The software periodically sent information to CHP managers who could use the information to figure out passwords to accounts, including personal email accounts. Karina, a CHP employee, confronted managers about the practice, asking them to stop. In response, Karina was fired. Develop the arguments on behalf of Karina that she has a reasonable expectation of privacy in the information that she shared through CHP's computers, tablets, and smart phones. How should CHP respond?

Problem 15-2

Jim works in the Sacramento CHP office as an analyst. Jim spends most of his time on the computer. Jim is a shopaholic and he spends countless hours perusing online clothing store sites. CHP managers were able to calculate how much time he was spending on clothing sites by monitoring the addresses of the sites he visited. You represent the CHP. Develop the arguments that Jim does not have a reasonable expectation of privacy with regard to his computer searches on his work computer. How should Jim respond?

Problem 15-3

CHP has also installed an app called "Xora" on all communication devices that it distributes to its employees. Xora permits CHP to track the location of the device 24 hours a day, 7 days a week. When Bettina asked her manager to remove the app because it interfered with her privacy, he refused. Can Bettina establish that Xora violates the rights of CHP employees?

Conclusion

In this Lesson, you learned that public sector employees are protected from unreasonable search and seizures by their governmental employer, which is subject to the Fourth Amendment. The courts balance the employee's reasonable expectation of privacy against the government's need to have some latitude as an employer to ensure an efficient workplace.

Lesson 16:
Common Law Privacy Protections

Objectives and Expected Learning Outcomes

In this Lesson, we will explore an employee's right to privacy as developed in tort law. An employer may be subject to liability in tort for violating an employee's privacy interests if the nature of the intrusion is highly offensive under the circumstances. Tort causes of action include intrusion upon seclusion, publicizing private matters, casting another in a false light, and appropriating another's name or likeness.

Unlike public employees who enjoy constitutional protections because their employer is the government, the privacy protections afforded to private sector employees stem primarily from the common law. Most generally, the right to privacy is the interest in being left alone. The Restatement articulates this right in more detail, and provides the organization for this Lesson.

Restatement of Employment Law

§ 7.02. Protected Employee Privacy Interests

Protected employee privacy interests include:

(a) the privacy of the employee's person (including aspects of his physical person, bodily functions, and personal possessions) as well as the privacy of the physical and electronic locations, including work locations provided by the employer, as to which the employee has a reasonable expectation of privacy (as provided in § 7.03);

(b) the privacy of the employee's information of a personal nature (as provided in § 7.04); and

(c) the privacy of the employee's information of a personal nature disclosed in confidence to the employer (as provided in § 7.05).

1. Intrusion upon Seclusion

Employees enjoy a zone of privacy with respect to their bodies, personal property and physical locations. This right of privacy is balanced against the employer's interest in controlling its workplace and having the flexibility to manage its workforce. The tort of "intrusion upon seclusion" is recognized by 41 states and the District of Columbia. Five of the remaining nine states have some form of statutory privacy protection. The general tort is defined by the Restatement of Torts.

Restatement (Second) of Torts

§ 652B. Intrusion Upon Seclusion

One who intentionally intrudes, physically or otherwise, upon the solitude or seclusion of another or his private affairs or concerns, is subject to liability to the other for invasion of his privacy, if the intrusion would be highly offensive to a reasonable person.

This intentional tort is defined in the context of employment law by the Restatement of Employment Law, which articulates the scope of the employee's protected interests in some detail.

Restatement of Employment Law

§ 7.03. Protected Employee Privacy Interests in the Employee's Physical Person and in Physical and Electronic Locations

(a) An employee has a protected privacy interest against employer intrusion into:

(1) the employee's physical person, bodily functions, and personal possessions; and

(2) physical and electronic locations, including employer-provided locations, as to which the employee has a reasonable expectation of privacy.

(b) An employee has a reasonable expectation in the privacy of a physical or electronic work location provided by the employer if:

(1) the employer has provided notice that the location or aspects of the location are private for employees; or

(2) the employer has acted in a manner that treats the location or aspects of the location as private for employees, the type of location is customarily treated as private for employees, and the employee has made reasonable efforts to keep the employee's activities in that location private.

(c) An employer intrudes upon an employee's protected privacy interest under this Section by such means as an examination, search, or surveillance into the locations discussed in subsection (a).

As is always the case with a tort, it is necessary to explore the definition in a particular factual context. The following case explores the elements of the intrusion upon seclusion claim with regard to the employee's expectation of privacy in her personal property that is brought into the workplace.

K-Mart Corp. Store No. 7441 v. Trotti

677 S.W.2d 632 (Tex. App. 1984).

K-Mart Corporation appeals from a judgment awarding the appellee, Trotti, $8,000.00 in actual damages and $100,000.00 in exemplary damages for invasion of privacy.

The appellee was an employee in the hosiery department at the appellants' store number 7441. Her supervisors had never indicated any dissatisfaction with her work nor any suspicion of her honesty.

The appellants provided their employees with lockers for the storage of personal effects during working hours. There was no assignment of any given locker to any individual employee. The employees could, on request, receive locks for the lockers from the appellants, and if the appellants provided the lock to an employee they would keep either a copy of the lock's combination or a master key for padlocks. Testimony indicated that there was some problem in providing a sufficient number of locks to employees, and, as a result, the store's administrative personnel permitted employees to purchase and use their own locks on the lockers, but in these instances, the appellants did not require the employee to provide the manager with either a combination or duplicate key. The appellee, with appellants' knowledge, used one of these lockers and provided her own combination lock.

On October 31, 1981, the appellee placed her purse in her locker when she arrived for work. She testified that she snapped the lock closed and then pulled on it to make sure it was locked. When she returned to her locker during her afternoon break, she discovered the lock hanging open. Searching through her locker, the appellee further discovered her personal items in her purse in considerable disorder. Nothing was missing from either the locker or the purse. The store manager testified that, in the company of three junior administrators at the store, he had that afternoon searched the lockers because of a suspicion raised by the appellants' security personnel that an unidentified employee, not the appellee, had stolen a watch. The manager and his assistants were also searching for missing price-marking guns. The appellee further testified that, as she left the employee's locker area after discovering her locker open, she heard the manager suggest to his assistants, "Let's get busy again." The manager testified that none of the parties searched through employees' personal effects.

The appellee approached the manager later that day and asked if he had searched employees' lockers and/or her purse. The manager initially denied either kind of search and maintained this denial for approximately one month. At that time, the manager then admitted having searched the employees' lockers and further mentioned that they had, in fact, searched the appellee's purse, later saying that he meant that they had searched only her locker and not her purse.

The manager testified that during the initial hiring interviews, all prospective employees received verbal notification from personnel supervisors that it was the appellants' policy to conduct ingress-egress searches of employees and also to conduct unannounced searches of lockers. A personnel supervisor and an assistant manager, however, testified that, although locker searches did regularly occur, the personnel supervisors did not apprise prospective employees of this policy.

. . . .

The fundamental and basic right to be left alone constitutes the essence of the right to privacy.

The right of privacy has been defined as the right of an individual to be left alone, to live a life of seclusion, to be free from unwarranted publicity. This right to privacy is so important that the United States Supreme Court has repeatedly deemed it to stem implicitly from the Bill of Rights. Our State courts have long recognized a civil cause of action for the invasion of the right to privacy and have defined such an invasion in many ways: As an intentional intrusion upon the solitude or seclusion of another that is highly offensive to a reasonable person, and as the right to be free from the wrongful intrusion into one's private activities in such manner as to outrage or cause mental suffering, shame or humiliation to a person of ordinary sensibilities.

The appellants requested the trial court to define an "invasion of privacy" as "the intentional intrusion upon the solitude or seclusion of another that is highly offensive to a reasonable person". . .The court refused to include the part of the requested instruction, ". . . that is highly offensive to a reasonable person." The appellants argue that this refusal constituted an abuse of discretion because the Rules of Civil Procedure require such an instruction. The appellee alleges that the record establishes that the intrusion was highly offensive as a matter of law, and that, therefore, the instruction was unnecessary.

. . . .In deciding whether there has been an abuse of such discretion, this court may not substitute its judgment for that of the trial court, and instead must decide only whether the trial court's action was arbitrary or unreasonable. Therefore, we must determine if the omitted part of the requested explanation was so important to a fair determination of a crucial issue that the trial court's refusal to include that part was arbitrary or unreasonable.

The definition of "invasion of privacy" that the appellant requested is one widely and repeatedly accepted. Although the Texas Supreme Court has not adopted a verbatim rendition of this definition, it is clear that, in Texas, an actionable invasion of privacy by intrusion must consist of an unjustified intrusion of the plaintiff's solitude or seclusion of such magnitude as to cause an ordinary individual to feel severely offended, humiliated, or outraged.

The appellants correctly point out that no Texas case yet reported has ever declined to include a requirement that the intrusion complained of be highly offensive to a reasonable person, and the appellee agrees with this statement. Nevertheless, the appellee urges that since the facts of this case established the highly objectionable nature of the intrusion as a matter of law, the requested instruction was unnecessary, and thus the trial court properly refused to include it.

We disagree with the appellee's contention. The record does indicate the appellee's outrage upon discovering the appellants' activities but fails to demonstrate that there could be no dispute as to the severity of the offensiveness of the intrusion, thereby making it impossible for us to conclude that the facts established the disputed portion of the instruction as a matter of law.

Moreover, we note that the result of accepting this contention would be to raise the legal theory of invasion of privacy from the realm of intentional torts into the sphere of strict liability. It would make any wrongful intrusion actionable, requiring a plaintiff to establish merely that the intrusion occurred and that the plaintiff did not consent to it. Because of the stern form of liability which already stems from an invasion of privacy, discussed, accepting a definition of invasion of privacy which lacked a standard of high offensiveness would result in fundamentally unfair assessments against defendants who offended unreasonably sensitive plaintiffs, but whose transgressions would not realistically fill either an ordinary person or the general society with any sense of outrage. A business executive, for example, could find himself liable for entering an associate's office without express permission; so could a beautician who opened a co-worker's drawer in order to find some supplies needed for a customer.

We hold that the element of a highly offensive intrusion is a fundamental part of the definition of an invasion of privacy, and that the term "invasion of privacy" is a highly technical, legal term, requiring, under Rule 277, an explanation to the jury. In the instant case, the definition of an invasion of privacy necessarily required the inclusion of the requested standard of offensiveness.

. . . .

The lockers undisputably were the appellants' property, and in their unlocked state, a jury could reasonably infer that those lockers were subject to legitimate, reasonable searches by the appellants. This would also be true where the employee used a lock provided by the appellants, because in retaining the lock's combination or master key, it could be inferred that the appellants manifested an interest both in maintaining control over the locker and in conducting legitimate, reasonable searches. Where, as in the instant case, however, the employee purchases and uses his own lock on the lockers, with the employer's knowledge, the fact finder is justified in concluding that the employee manifested, and the employer recognized, an expectation that the locker and its contents would be free from intrusion and interference.

In the present case, there is evidence that the appellee locked the locker with her own lock; that when the appellee returned from a break, the lock was lying open; that upon searching her locker, the appellee discovered that someone had rifled her purse; that the appellants' managerial personnel initially denied making the search but subsequently admitted searching her locker and her purse. We find this is far more evidence than a "mere scintilla," and we hold that there is some evidence to support the jury's finding.

As to the "insufficiency" point, after examining the record as a whole, we find it indicates all of the above. The appellee remembers having locked the locker and having seen the lock closed before starting work that day. The record indicates that the searching personnel denied having gone through any employee's purses, yet nothing in the record directly challenges the appellee's testimony as to the disruption of her personal effects inside her purse, and, therefore, the jury could make a reasonable inference that the managerial personnel had, in fact, gone through her personal effects. The record also establishes that other employees knew these searches were going on. The store manager testified that all employees received notification of these sporadic searches during their hiring interviews; however, two administrators, including a former personnel supervisor, denied that employees ever received this notification. We hold that the weight of the evidence indicates that the appellants' employees came upon a locker with a lock provided by an employee, disregarded the appellee's demonstration of her expectation of privacy, opened and searched the locker, and probably opened and searched her purse as well; and, in so holding, we consider it is immaterial whether the appellee actually securely locked her locker or not. It is sufficient that an employee in this situation, by having placed a lock on the locker at the employee's own expense and with the appellants' consent, has demonstrated a legitimate expectation to a right of privacy in both the locker itself and those personal effects within it. . . .

. . . .

The basis of a cause of action for invasion of privacy is that the defendant has violated the plaintiff's rights to be left alone. This intrusion itself is actionable, and the plaintiff can receive at least nominal damages for that actionable intrusion without demonstrating physical detriment. The appellants' improper intrusion of an area where the appellee had manifested an expectation of privacy alone raised her right to recover. . . .

. . . .

The appellants intentionally intruded upon an area where the appellee had a legitimate expectation of privacy. The evidence supports a further finding that the appellants wrongfully intruded upon the appellee's personal property. The conduct of this inspection, and the appellants' subsequent denial and ultimate admission support the conclusion that they were aware that their actions constituted a covert intrusion. The appellants clearly made this wrongful intrusion with neither the appellee's permission nor justifiable suspicion that the appellee had stolen any store inventory. Sufficient factors exist to enable this court to conclude that the jury's award of exemplary damages was the result of proper motivations. We disagree with the appellant that any set ratio of exemplary to actual damages constitutes a ceiling beyond which a greater award would be excessive, and even were we to agree with appellants, we do not find that the exemplary damages in the instant case exceed that ceiling.

. . . .

The judgment is reversed, and the case is remanded for new trial.

QUESTIONS

1. As a matter of constitutional law, the Fourth Amendment does not apply to private employers. Why isn't the common law interpreted to provide similar protections that prevent the employer from engaging in "unreasonable searches and seizures?"
2. A woman's purse is obviously personal property, but is the court persuasive in holding that the employee had a reasonable expectation of privacy when the purse is left in an employee locker that is not assigned exclusively to the employee?

Problem 16-1

Jasmine worked for Best Cars, an automotive dealership. While assisting a customer, she slipped on a wet sidewalk outside the carwash area, injuring her back. Jasmine requested disability leave on the basis that her back injury prevented her from standing for long periods of time. Jasmine's doctor certified that her back injury caused her to be disabled. Jasmine's supervisor, Jim, did not believe that Jasmine was unable to work. Jim told Jasmine that he was opening an investigation on behalf of the company. Jim hired Blue Moon Investigations to surveil Jasmine. Blue Moon confirmed Jim's suspicions. Blue Moon observed Jasmine working in her garden, carrying gardening supplies, and standing for an extended period of time to fix a fence around the garden. Blue Moon provided Jim with a video of Jasmine in her garden. Jim fired Jasmine immediately, and she responded by suing Best Cars for invasion of privacy by intruding upon her seclusion. Make the best case for Jasmine, and anticipate the response by Best Cars.

Problem 16-2

The Valley View School voted to install surveillance cameras in its high school. The surveillance cameras were installed in classrooms, in hallways, in the faculty break room, and in public areas of the sports locker rooms. Adrianne Long, a teacher and coach at Valley View High, is disturbed by what she considers a serious invasion of her privacy. Does Adrianne have a reasonable expectation of privacy in the classroom? The break room? The locker rooms?

Problem 16-3

Veronica works as an accountant at a small bookkeeping and accounting firm. Betty owns the firm, and is considering firing Veronica because she is disappointed with her work product. Betty discusses the matter with two of Veronica's co-workers, who agreed that Betty should fire Veronica. Betty summoned Veronica to her office, with the two co-workers still there, and fired her. Veronica was humiliated and believes she should never have been fired in front of her co-workers. Veronica sues Betty for invasion of privacy, on an intrusion on seclusion theory. Does Veronica have a valid claim?

---

2. Publicizing Private Matters

Privacy is not limited to security from unwanted intrusions, it also includes the ability to keep certain matters private. Employees provide their employer with personal data with the expectation that this information will be kept confidential. In addition, employers are in a position to learn about their employees' private lives as an outgrowth of the close working relationships that tend to form in workplaces. The Restatement of Torts describes the elements of the tort of publicizing private matters.

Restatement (Second) of Torts

§ 652D. Publicity Given to Private Life

One who gives publicity to a matter concerning the private life of another is subject to liability to the other for invasion of his privacy, if the matter publicized is of a kind that (a) would be highly offensive to a reasonable person, and (b) is not of legitimate concern to the public.

Sharp v. Whitman Council, Inc.

2007 WL 2874058 (E.D. Pa 2007).

Joyner, J.

. . . .[T]his case arises out of the plaintiff, Janet DeGiovanni Sharp's employment with the Whitman Council, where she has been employed as the Executive Director since September, 1991. Whitman Council, Inc. ("Whitman") is a Pennsylvania Non-Profit Corporation which is funded as a Neighborhood Advisory Committee organization ("NAC") by the City of Philadelphia's Office of Housing and Community Development ("OHCD") and which provides services to the Whitman section of South Philadelphia. Whitman is governed by a Board of Directors composed of up to thirteen elected Class "A" members and up to three Class "B" Directors who are chosen by the Class "A" members. Four of the thirteen Class "A" Board members serve as the President, Vice-President, Secretary and Treasurer of the Board. The Board of Directors supervises the Executive Director. Each year, Whitman enters into a contract, known as an NAC Provider Agreement with OHCD, pursuant to which Whitman agrees to provide housing and community development services and activities for Whitman area residents and OHCD agrees to provide the funding necessary to allow Whitman to provide those services.

Prior to August 2004, one of the Whitman "A" Board Members was a local Catholic pastor. At that time, the pastor "made the difficult decision to leave the active ministry of priesthood and because he moved from the area, he was no longer eligible to be a member of the Whitman Board." Plaintiff "formed a deep friendship with the former pastor and they ultimately married in June, 2005." Plaintiff's relationship with the former priest apparently generated some controversy in the Whitman community as it was shortly after he left the church that the defendants began the pattern of activities which prompted Plaintiff's complaint in this case including: (1) questioning the plaintiff about her personal relationship with the former priest, ostensibly so as to discern whether or not the plaintiff had been the victim of sexual harassment or had violated Whitman's personnel policies; (2) contacting the Director of Neighborhood Coordination for OHCD about Plaintiff's relationship in an effort to find grounds to terminate her; (3) questioning community members and church authorities about the matter; (4) forming a special investigating committee and appropriating $ 2,000 of Whitman's funding to conduct an investigation; (5) threatening Plaintiff with termination for insubordination if she refused to answer questions regarding her relationship.

Shortly after Plaintiff and her new husband were married, a church reunion gathering was held in Wildwood, NJ at which some of the attendees purportedly wore badges and T-shirts mocking the Sharps. Despite the defendants' threats, however, Ms. DeGiovanni Sharp continues in her employment as the Whitman Council Executive Director to this day. On August 11, 2005, after exhausting her administrative remedies with the EEOC and the PHRC, Plaintiff instituted this lawsuit for having been "subjected to rumor and innuendo," "held up to public ridicule," suffering a loss of "professional status and reputation" as well as of "pay, benefits and other employee remunerations," and "emotional distress, humiliation and loss of life's pleasures. Ms. DeGiovanni Sharp sought relief [claiming several causes of action, including invasion of privacy] under . . . the common law theories of publication of private information. . .

. . . .

C. Invasion of Privacy by Publication of Private Facts

It is axiomatic that one who gives publicity to a matter which concerns the private life of another is subject to liability to the other for invasion of privacy if the matter published is of a kind that (a) would be highly offensive to a reasonable person, and (b) is not of legitimate concern to the public. Stated otherwise, in order to make out a claim of publicity to private life, a plaintiff must establish that (1) a private fact was (2) publicized and (3) that such fact was of a type highly offensive to a reasonable person and (4) not of legitimate concern to the public.

A private fact is one that has not already been made public. Publicity requires that the matter is made public, by communicating it to the public at large or to so many persons that it must be regarded as "substantially certain to become one of public knowledge.

In application of the preceding principles to the matter at hand, we find that sufficient evidence exists on this record that the defendants did, indeed, communicate and discuss with various members of the Whitman/Our Lady of Mt. Carmel communities the fact that the plaintiff was engaged in a personal relationship with and eventually married, the former Father Sharp. It further appears that the defendants also made public that they were of the opinion that the Sharps' relationship was violative of, among other things, Whitman Council's personnel policies, that money was missing from both the Mt. Carmel church and the Whitman Council, and that they were formally investigating Ms. DeGiovanni-Sharp and this relationship. . . [W]e find that the issue of whether the plaintiff did nor did not have an intimate relationship with a former board member who happened to be a Catholic priest is a truly private matter in which we can discern no legitimate public interest." . . . .

. . . .

For all of the foregoing reasons, the defendants' motions for summary judgment are denied pursuant to the attached order.

QUESTIONS

1. Is there any legitimate reason for employers to be interested in the personal relationships of its employees?
2. If you were counsel for the employer in this case, would you have advised your client to ignore the innuendo and to refrain from discussing the matter with the plaintiff? If you did give this advice, is there a risk that your client could face difficulties or legal liability for not being interested in the matter?

Problem 16-4

Marty is an aerobics instructor at 24/7 Fitness. After he was fired, he applied for work at area fitness centers but was unsuccessful. Marty assumed that his former supervisors at 24/7 Fitness must be giving him bad recommendations. As he investigated, he discovered that a manager had posted the following message on the 24/7 Fitness's Facebook page:

> For those commenting and speculating about our group fitness/coordinator who isn't there anymore—first, shame on you for gossiping about a man's career, and the decisions of his supervisors on an open forum. Second, my understanding as one peripherally aware of the decision, it had nothing to do with his abilities as an instructor. That wasn't the extent of his job though, and some serious HR/Administrative issues arose surrounding his other responsibilities and parting was the decision. That is all that needs to be said.

Marty sued 24/7 Fitness for invasion of privacy, on the ground that they had publicized a private matter. Describe your strategy on behalf of Marty, and anticipate the responses of 24/7 Fitness.

Problem 16-5

Lakeview Express Motor delivers packages throughout the country. It employs over 500 truckers, and it has a human resources department that maintains records for all of its employees. Sara, a human resources employee, mistakenly sent the names, addresses and social security numbers of 200 truckers to district managers as part of a records check. When the human resources department realized Sara's mistake, it sent a notice to its employees, and assured them that the company had directed its district managers to destroy the records. Nonetheless, a group of truckers sued the company claiming the dissemination of the Social Security numbers constituted a violation of the truckers' right to privacy. Do the truckers have a viable claim based on a theory of publicity to private life?

3. Publicity That Places a Person in a False Light

The right to privacy extends beyond protecting against intrusion into one's private affairs. It is an invasion of privacy if a person publicizes matters that present another person in a false light to the public. In this case, privacy is the right to be free from unwanted negative publicity that is premised on falsehoods. The elements of the general tort emphasize that the publicity must be highly offensive to a reasonable person in order to recover, which again leads to a balancing test within the context of the employment relationship.

Restatement (Second) of Torts (1979)

§ 652E. Publicity Placing a Person in False Light

One who gives publicity to a matter concerning another that places the other before the public in a false light is subject to liability to the other for invasion of his privacy, if

(a) the false light in which the other was placed would be highly offensive to a reasonable person, and

(b) the actor had knowledge of or acted in reckless disregard as to the falsity of the publicized matter and the false light in which the other would be placed.

Hogan v. Winder

762 F.3d 1096 (10th Cir. 2014).

Tymkovich, Circuit Judge.

Chris Hogan lost his job with the Utah Telecommunications Open Infrastructure Agency, or "UTOPIA," a state agency charged with upgrading high-speed internet access. Claiming he was fired for revealing a conflict of interest in contract awards, he threatened to sue the agency for wrongful termination. Shortly after making this threat, he was subject to several unflattering media articles about his job performance and his termination dispute with the agency's leaders. Several of the stories claimed his threats to sue the agency amounted to extortion or blackmail. It turns out the first of these stories was written pseudonymously by Michael Winder, who was the mayor of West Valley City, where UTOPIA did much of its business.

Hogan sued UTOPIA, the mayor, the City, and a number of other persons he believes were involved in the publication of the articles. He claims the articles constitute . . . false light invasion of privacy. . .

. . . .

False Light Invasion of Privacy

Hogan. . . contends the articles invaded his privacy and cast him in false light.

In Utah, the tort of false light invasion of privacy requires the plaintiff to show four elements: 1) "giving publicity to a matter concerning another"; 2) "that places the other before the public in a false light"; 3) the false light would be "highly offensive to a reasonable person" and 4) the defendant "has knowledge of or acted in reckless disregard as to the falsity of the publicized matter and the false light in which the other would be placed." Like defamation claims, claims of "false light invasion of privacy provide legal redress for uninvited notoriety grounded in falsehoods caused by the defendant."

This district court dismissed Hogan's false light claim, concluding that, if a statement is not defamatory, it does not cast the plaintiff in a false light. While true to a large extent, Utah's false light law does not apply only to defamatory statements. The tort of "false light invasion of privacy protects a different interest than defamation[.] . . . An actionable portrayal of a person in a false light may or may not include the communication of defamatory information about the victim." . . . .

Thus, the Utah Supreme Court has recognized the "possibility that a false light invasion of privacy claim may turn on operative facts that do not include defamation." The court's example of a non-defamatory statement that would still give rise to a false light claim was "dissemination of praiseworthy but untrue information about that person," if a reasonable person would find the information highly objectionable. Although not defamatory because it does not impeach an individual's reputation, a statement could still cast a person in a false and objectionable light.

Hogan contends his claim can go forward even though we have concluded the articles were not defamatory. But even as the KSL and Fierce Telecom articles cannot give rise to a defamation claim, they do not place Hogan in a false light when read in context because none of the statements can be construed as false. The articles accurately report the statements or documents as part of an ongoing employment dispute, or as we discussed above, are simply too vague and nonspecific to sustain a false impression that would be highly objectionable to a reasonable person.

QUESTIONS

1. Claims of false light publicity are very similar to defamation claims, which we will discuss in Lesson 34. How does the court distinguish these two torts?
2. Under the case, can an employer publicize truthful information regarding an employment investigation with impunity, even if the disclosure is highly offensive?

Problem 16-6

Joanna, a Wall Financial Management (WFM) employee, requested temporary leave from work under the Family Medical Leave Act to care for her husband who suffered a heart attack. Joanna is a very private person, and she emphasized that she wanted this information kept completely confidential. The Human Resources director was annoyed because the request came at the busiest time of the year for WFM, but he granted her request. Chip asked a security guard to escort Joanna out of the building before the workday ended and in full view of the office. He then sent an email to all employees of WFM advising them that Joanna was taking an extended leave at the request of management and that she should not be permitted on the premises without the permission of a manager. Upset at this treatment, Joanna decided to resign. She sued WFM for false light publicity. Assess whether Joanna has a viable claim.

---

4. Appropriation of Another's Likeness

It is an invasion of privacy to appropriate another person's likeness for profit. This principle is easily understood in the context of endorsements. A company cannot use the image of LeBron James to sell its products without reaching an agreement with LeBron, because he has an interest in controlling the integrity of his image.

This tort is less applicable in the typical employment setting, but it can arise. Consider the elements of the tort as expressed in the Restatement, and analyze why it doesn't provide a viable cause of action in the following case.

Restatement (Second) of Torts

§ 652C. Appropriation of Name or Likeness

One who appropriates to his own use or benefit the name or likeness of another is subject to liability to the other for invasion of his privacy.

STIEN V. MARRIOTT OWNERSHIP RESORTS

944 P.2d 374 (Utah Ct. App. 1997).

ORME, JUDGE:

At the center of this case is a videotape for which defendants are responsible, in which seventeen employees of defendant Marriott Ownership Resorts, Inc. (Marriott), whose properties include Summit Watch in Park City, describe in detail a household chore they hate doing. The video includes appearances by nine men and eight women, including plaintiff's husband, Brad Bauman. The video does not identify any of the employees by name, job title, or employment task.

Unbeknownst to Mr. Bauman, and apparently unbeknownst to the other sixteen participants, the videotape was edited to make it appear as if the employees were answering the question, "What's sex like with your partner?" The video, about five minutes and twenty seconds long, was then shown at a formal company Christmas party for the amusement of some 200 Marriott employees and their guests, including Bauman and plaintiff.

The video opens with a closeup of a picturesque pond, with classical music playing in the background. After a second or two, a female voice serenely states: "Recently, we asked a collection of people what they thought and felt about having sex with their partner. Let's listen to their comments."

Following this introduction, the video presents edited clips of the employees' earlier descriptions of a household chore. Each employee-participant appearing in the video is seated in a chair behind what appears to be a conference room table. A caption appears for the first few minutes at the side of the participant, reading: "What's sex like with your partner?" The first employee appearing on the video is male and comments: "Having to carry this huge thing down some stairs; and it's heavy and it smells real bad." Similarly, another male employee states that he "hates doing it because it involves so much time and energy." A female employee states that "it's one of those greasy grimy things that you just have to do at least once a year whether you want to or not." Still another female employee states that she "hates something that has to be done every day." Not all of the comments were negative. For instance, one female employee stated that she was "very tall" and therefore was "good at it."

Interspersed throughout the video are comments made by Bauman. His statements and descriptions are as follows:

> The smell. The smell, the smell. And then you go with the goggles. You have to put on the goggles. And then you get the smell through the nose. And as you get into it things start flying all over the place. And the smell. And you get covered in these things.
>
> . . . .
>
> And you have to do it and you have to enjoy doing it. And you cannot—you can't—get into the idea that this is something that you don't want to do.
>
> . . . .
>
> But the smell gets worse and then it gets worse and then it gets worse.
>
> . . . .
>
> And then your biggest problem is you forget to remove this smell from the house and then you leave it there and then you come back and your wife uncovers the smell.
>
> . . . .
>
> But I've found that the goggles work very well because eye protection is a very important item.

Once the employees' comments are concluded, the video returns to the scenic pond and accompanying background music which opened the video. The same female voice from the introduction concludes the video by stating: "So remember, we at Summit Watch are concerned about you achieving balance in your life. So let's make tonight the start of a productive and balanced new year."

Plaintiff did not appear in the video, nor is she ever mentioned by name, either by her husband, Mr. Bauman, or by any other participant. Nonetheless, plaintiff was not amused by the video. She and Bauman filed this lawsuit against Marriott and various individuals who had a hand in making the video, alleging that her privacy was invaded. Specifically, plaintiff alleged that defendants intruded upon her seclusion, appropriated her name and likeness for the benefit of Marriott, publicized private facts regarding plaintiff, and placed her in a false light. All defendants subsequently moved for summary judgment, which the court granted. In so doing, the trial court ruled, as a matter of law, that the elements constituting the four distinct torts of invasion of privacy could not be established by plaintiff. This appeal, pursued by plaintiff Cassedy Stien only, followed.

On appeal, plaintiff contends the trial court erred in ruling, as a matter of law, that the [appropriation of name or likeness] privacy tort[ ] could not be established by plaintiff given the undisputed facts. . .

. . . .

[A]ppropriation of name or likeness for the benefit of another. . .requires the plaintiff to establish three elements: (1) appropriation, (2) of another's name or likeness that has some "intrinsic value," (3) for the use or benefit of another.

In this case, plaintiff concedes that neither her name or likeness appeared in the video. Nonetheless, plaintiff argues that anybody that knew her husband, whose likeness was presented on the video, knew automatically to whom the reference concerning his sex life was made. Plaintiff argues further that a rule requiring plaintiff's actual name to be used would do nothing but exalt form over substance. Plaintiff also argues that her identity as Bauman's wife was used to create entertainment for corporate purposes.

It is axiomatic that "the interest protected by the [appropriation tort] . . . is the interest of the individual in the exclusive use of his own identity, in so far as it is represented by his *name or likeness*, and in so far as the use may be of benefit to him or to others." In order to invoke this protection, plaintiff must be able to establish that her identity in the video was represented by her name or likeness. In this case, there is absolutely no reference in the video to plaintiff's name or likeness. Although Mr. Bauman referred to his wife coming home and uncovering a smell, this passing reference is wholly insufficient to establish an appropriation claim. Therefore, the trial court was correct in ruling that plaintiff's name or likeness was not appropriated by defendants. . .

Plaintiff's invasion of privacy claims fails as a matter of law. . .because plaintiff did not appear in the video by name or likeness. . .

QUESTION

1. Why didn't the plaintiff sue for false light invasion of privacy?

Mastery Problem 16-1

After suffering a spinal cord injury, Nancy uses a wheelchair to maintain her mobility and her active lifestyle. Nancy works for a large law firm that specializes in representing management in employment law disputes. The firm competes with other large law firms for the top law graduates in the country, and it spends considerable sums on marketing materials used to attract candidates to the firm. The firm's marketing manager directs their photographer to take candid shots of associates in the workplace. The final brochure contains a large picture of Nancy, above a caption that touts the firm's commitment to diversity. Can Nancy sue the firm for invasion of privacy?

Mastery Problem 16-2

The Teamsters Union is seeking to unionize the Marin Plant. The Teamsters organize off-site meetings for employees to explain the benefits of a union. The local police department engaged in surveillance of the plaintiffs and other employees of Marin near the off-site meetings and recorded license plate numbers and the identity of persons attending the meetings. The police subsequently traced the license plate numbers to automobile registrations and then provided the identities of the persons to Marin. The Teamsters obtained an injunction against the practice because it qualified as an unfair labor practice under the National Labor Relations Act. The employees sue Marin for invading their privacy before the issuance of the injunction. Analyze whether the employees can make a case for false light, misappropriation, public disclosure of private facts, or intrusion upon seclusion.

Conclusion

In this Lesson, you have learned the elements of the general torts involving privacy in the workplace. The common law remedies are limited to causes of action grounded in intrusion on seclusion, publicity to private life, false light, and appropriation of another's likeness. These common law causes of action provide some, but not comprehensive, protection of employee privacy in the workplace. As in the public workplace, privacy interests are circumscribed by societal views of what is a reasonable expectation of privacy, but also by the expectations that employers establish in their own workplaces. The patchwork of common law protections protects against abusive intrusions on privacy, and they do not typically protect employees from intrusions on their autonomy. States have enacted statutes to provide further protection of employee autonomy, as discussed in Lesson 22.

Lesson 17:
Privacy of Electronic Information and Communications

Objectives and Expected Learning Outcomes

In this Lesson, we consider an employee's privacy interest with regard to electronic information that may be generated during work time or while using employer devices. Employers may be held liable for intruding on the privacy interests of their employees, but the standard is generally high: the employee must have a reasonable expectation of privacy and the employer's intrusion must be highly offensive to a reasonable person under the circumstances.

In this era of rapidly changing technology, employers have many reasons to monitor the activities of their employees. First, employers concerned about productivity or employee job performance might want to discourage personal activity on the internet while at work. Second, monitoring might be necessary to protect trade secrets and confidential information from being shared or exposed. Third, monitoring might be used to detect improper employee behavior such as sexual harassment, fraud, theft, embezzlement, and data breaches. Employee misuse of company-provided devices and networks can expose the employer to liability. As you can see, employers have legitimate business reasons for monitoring employee activity and access to digital communications.

Employers now have many resources available to them to screen and monitor an employee's access to digital communications. Such mechanisms are in tension with an employee's fundamental interests in privacy. This is a specific application of the "intrusion upon seclusion" common law action for invasion of privacy, but the context of social media adds a different element, since the very purpose of social media is to share information.

1. Employee Expectation of Privacy on the Employer's E-mail System

Most workers presumably maintain an individual email account in addition to an e-mail account provided by their employer. Employees sometimes have difficulty making a sharp distinction between the two accounts as they may have social connections with co-workers and their private email account may sometimes be used for work purposes. Consider the issues raised by the following case.

SMYTH V. PILLSBURY CO.

914 F. Supp. 97 (E.D. Pa. 1996).

WEINER, J.

In this diversity action, plaintiff, an at-will employee, claims he was wrongfully discharged from his position as a regional operations manager by the defendant. Presently before the court is the motion of the defendant to dismiss pursuant to Rule 12(b)(6) of the Federal Rules of Civil Procedure. For the reasons which follow, the motion is granted.

. . . .

Defendant maintained an electronic mail communication system ("e-mail") in order to promote internal corporate communications between its employees. Defendant repeatedly assured its employees, including plaintiff, that all e-mail communications would remain confidential and privileged. Defendant further assured its employees, including plaintiff, that e-mail communications could not be intercepted and used by defendant against its employees as grounds for termination or reprimand.

In October 1994, plaintiff received certain e-mail communications from his supervisor over defendant's e-mail system on his computer at home. In reliance on defendant's assurances regarding defendant's e-mail system, plaintiff responded and exchanged e-mails with his supervisor. At some later date, contrary to the assurances of confidentiality made by defendant, defendant, acting through its agents, servants and employees, intercepted plaintiff's private e-mail messages made in October 1994. On January 17, 1995, defendant notified plaintiff that it was terminating his employment effective February 1, 1995, for transmitting what it deemed to be inappropriate and unprofessional comments over defendant's e-mail system in October, 1994.

As a general rule, Pennsylvania law does not provide a common law cause of action for the wrongful discharge of an at-will employee such as plaintiff. Pennsylvania is an employment at-will jurisdiction and an employer may discharge an employee with or without cause, at pleasure, unless restrained by some contract.

However, in the most limited of circumstances, exceptions have been recognized where discharge of an at-will employee threatens or violates a clear mandate of public policy. . . .

. . . .

Plaintiff claims that his termination was in violation of "public policy which precludes an employer from terminating an employee in violation of the employee's right to privacy as embodied in Pennsylvania common law."

. . . [O]ne of the torts which Pennsylvania recognizes as encompassing an action for invasion of privacy is the tort of "intrusion upon seclusion." As noted by the Court of Appeals, the Restatement (Second) of Torts defines the tort as follows:

> One who intentionally intrudes, physically or otherwise, upon the solitude or seclusion of another or his private affairs or concerns, is subject to liability to the other for invasion of his privacy, if the intrusion would be highly offensive to a reasonable person.

Restatement (Second) of Torts § 652B. Liability only attaches when the "intrusion is substantial and would be highly offensive to the 'ordinary reasonable person.' " . . .Applying the Restatement definition of the tort of intrusion upon seclusion to the facts and circumstances of the case *sub judice,* we find that plaintiff has failed to state a claim upon which relief can be granted. In the first instance, unlike urinalysis and personal property searches, we do not find a reasonable expectation of privacy in e-mail communications voluntarily made by an employee to his supervisor over the company e-mail system notwithstanding any assurances that such communications would not be intercepted by management. Once plaintiff communicated the alleged unprofessional comments to a second person (his supervisor) over an e-mail system which was apparently utilized by the entire company, any reasonable expectation of privacy was lost. Significantly, the defendant did not require plaintiff, as in the case of a urinalysis or personal property search to disclose any personal information about himself. Rather, plaintiff voluntarily communicated the alleged unprofessional comments over the company e-mail system. We find no privacy interests in such communications.

In the second instance, even if we found that an employee had a reasonable expectation of privacy in the contents of his e-mail communications over the company e-mail system, we do not find that a reasonable person would consider the defendant's interception of these communications to be a substantial and highly offensive invasion of his privacy. Again, we note that by intercepting such communications, the company is not, as in the case of urinalysis or personal property searches, requiring the employee to disclose any personal information about himself or invading the employee's person or personal effects. Moreover, the company's interest in preventing inappropriate and unprofessional comments or even illegal activity over its e-mail system outweighs any privacy interest the employee may have in those comments.

In sum, we find that the defendant's actions did not tortiously invade the plaintiff's privacy and, therefore, did not violate public policy. As a result, the motion to dismiss is granted.

QUESTIONS

1. Use of email was still new when the plaintiff corresponded with his supervisor on Pillsbury's system. Why does the court find that Pillsbury's assurances of confidentiality could not give rise to a reasonable expectation of privacy?
2. Today, most employers make clear that they can review an employee's work email account, eliminating any claim for a reasonable expectation of privacy. In the absence of such a warning, is there any basis for an employee to assert a right to privacy regarding emails on the company system that pertain to personal matters?

Problem 17-1

Sharon is fired by AJAX corporation. She learns that her former work email address is still active and accepting messages. She comes to you seeking advice after reading a blog about employee privacy rights. She believes that this practice invades her privacy in two ways. First, there is a chance that a social acquaintance might send an email to her work email inadvertently, and that AJAX would then have access to her private matters. If this happened during her employment, Sharon would immediately delete the email and advise the sender to use her private email address. Second, she believes that this practice of continuing her email address makes it appear that she is still employed there, and that AJAX is using her identity and likeness for its benefit without permission. Does Sharon have a potential case? What else do you need to know?

Does an employee have an expectation of privacy for messages generated on her private email account if she is accessing the account on her employer's computer and network during work time? The following case addresses this question in a particularly interesting context: the employee was using the employer's network to correspond with her attorney regarding the employer. This pits the employer's obvious interest in such uses of its equipment against the employee's privacy rights and the attorney client privilege.

Stengart v. Loving Care Agency, Inc.

201 N.J. 300 (2010).

Chief Justice Rabner delivered of the opinion of the Court.

In the past twenty years, businesses and private citizens alike have embraced the use of computers, electronic communication devices, the Internet, and e-mail. As those and other forms of technology evolve, the line separating business from personal activities can easily blur.

In the modern workplace, for example, occasional, personal use of the Internet is commonplace. Yet that simple act can raise complex issues about an employer's monitoring of the workplace and an employee's reasonable expectation of privacy.

This case presents novel questions about the extent to which an employee can expect privacy and confidentiality in personal e-mails with her attorney, which she accessed on a computer belonging to her employer. Marina Stengart used her company-issued laptop to exchange e-mails with her lawyer through her personal, password-protected, web-based e-mail account. She later filed an employment discrimination lawsuit against her employer, Loving Care Agency, Inc. (Loving Care), and others.

In anticipation of discovery, Loving Care hired a computer forensic expert to recover all files stored on the laptop including the e-mails, which had been automatically saved on the hard drive. Loving Care's attorneys reviewed the e-mails and used information culled from them in the course of discovery. In response, Stengart's lawyer demanded that communications between him and Stengart, which he considered privileged, be identified and returned. Opposing counsel disclosed the documents but maintained that the company had the right to review them. Stengart then sought relief in court.

The trial court ruled that, in light of the company's written policy on electronic communications, Stengart waived the attorney-client privilege by sending e-mails on a company computer. The Appellate Division reversed and found that Loving Care's counsel had violated [Rules of Professional Conduct] 4.4(b) by reading and using the privileged documents.

We hold that, under the circumstances, Stengart could reasonably expect that e-mail communications with her lawyer through her personal account would remain private, and that sending and receiving them via a company laptop did not eliminate the attorney-client privilege that protected them. By reading e-mails that were at least arguably privileged and failing to notify Stengart promptly about them, Loving Care's counsel breached RPC 4.4(b). We therefore modify and affirm the judgment of the Appellate Division and remand to the trial court to determine what, if any, sanctions should be imposed on counsel for Loving Care.

I.

. . . .

Loving Care provides home-care nursing and health services. Stengart began working for

Loving Care in 1994 and, over time, was promoted to Executive Director of Nursing. The company provided her with a laptop computer to conduct company business. From that laptop, Stengart could send e-mails using her company e-mail address; she could also access the Internet and visit websites through Loving Care's server. Unbeknownst to Stengart, certain browser software in place automatically made a copy of each web page she viewed, which was then saved on the computer's hard drive in a "cache" folder of temporary Internet files. Unless deleted and overwritten with new data, those temporary Internet files remained on the hard drive.

On several days in December 2007, Stengart used her laptop to access a personal, password-protected e-mail account on Yahoo's website, through which she communicated with her attorney about her situation at work. She never saved her Yahoo ID or password on the company laptop.

Not long after, Stengart left her employment with Loving Care and returned the laptop. On February 7, 2008, she filed the pending complaint.

In an effort to preserve electronic evidence for discovery, in or around April 2008, Loving Care hired experts to create a forensic image of the laptop's hard drive. Among the items retrieved were temporary Internet files containing the contents of seven or eight e-mails Stengart had exchanged with her lawyer via her Yahoo account.[1] Stengart's lawyers represented at oral argument that one e-mail was simply a communication he sent to her, to which she did not respond.

A legend appears at the bottom of the e-mails that Stengart's lawyer sent. It warns readers that

> THE INFORMATION CONTAINED IN THIS EMAIL COMMUNICATION IS INTENDED ONLY FOR THE PERSONAL AND CONFIDENTIAL USE OF THE DESIGNATED RECIPIENT NAMED ABOVE. This message may be an Attorney-Client communication, and as such is privileged and confidential. If the reader of this message is not the intended recipient, you are hereby notified that you have received this communication in error, and that your review, dissemination, distribution, or copying of the message is strictly prohibited. If you have received this transmission in error, please destroy this transmission and notify us immediately by telephone and/or reply email.

At least two attorneys from the law firm representing Loving Care, Sills Cummis (the "Firm"), reviewed the e-mail communications between Stengart and her attorney. The Firm did not advise opposing counsel about the e-mails until months later. In its October 21, 2008 reply to Stengart's first set of interrogatories, the Firm stated that it had obtained certain information from "e-mail correspondence"—between Stengart and her lawyer—

---

1 The record does not specify how many of the e-mails were sent or received during work hours. Loving Care asserts that the e-mails in question were exchanged during work hours through the company's server. However, counsel for Stengart represented at oral argument that four of the e-mails were transmitted or accessed during non-work hours—three on a weekend and one on a holiday. It is unclear, and ultimately not relevant, whether Stengart was at the office when she sent or reviewed them.

from Stengart's "office computer on December 12, 2007 at 2:25 p.m." In response, Stengart's attorney sent a letter demanding that the Firm identify and return all "attorney-client privileged communications" in its possession. The Firm identified and disclosed the e-mails but asserted that Stengart had no reasonable expectation of privacy in files on a company-owned computer in light of the company's policy on electronic communications.

Loving Care and its counsel relied on an Administrative and Office Staff Employee Handbook that they maintain contains the company's Electronic Communication policy (Policy). The record contains various versions of an electronic communications policy, and Stengart contends that none applied to her as a senior company official. Loving Care disagrees. We need not resolve that dispute and assume the Policy applies in addressing the issues on appeal.

The proffered Policy states, in relevant part:

> The company reserves and will exercise the right to review, audit, intercept, access, and disclose all matters on the company's media systems and services at any time, with or without notice.
>
> . . . .
>
> E-mail and voice mail messages, internet use and communication and computer files are considered part of the company's business and client records. Such communications are not to be considered private or personal to any individual employee.
>
> The principal purpose of electronic mail (*e-mail*) is for company business communications. Occasional personal use is permitted; however, the system should not be used to solicit for outside business ventures, charitable organizations, or for any political or religious purpose, unless authorized by the Director of Human Resources.

The Policy also specifically prohibits "[c]ertain uses of the e-mail system" including sending inappropriate sexual, discriminatory, or harassing messages, chain letters, "[m]essages in violation of government laws," or messages relating to job searches, business activities unrelated to Loving Care, or political activities. The Policy concludes with the following warning: "Abuse of the electronic communications system may result in disciplinary action up to and including separation of employment."

Stengart's attorney applied for an order to show cause seeking return of the e-mails and other relief. The trial court converted the application to a motion, which it later denied in a written opinion. The trial court concluded that the Firm did not breach the attorney-client privilege because the company's Policy placed Stengart on sufficient notice that her e-mails would be considered company property. Stengart's request to disqualify the Firm was therefore denied.

The Appellate Division granted Stengart's motion for leave to appeal. The panel reversed the trial court order and directed the Firm to turn over all copies of the e-mails and delete any record of them. Assuming that the Policy applied to Stengart, the panel found that "[a]n objective reader could reasonably conclude . . . that not all personal emails are necessarily company property." In other words, an employee could "retain an expectation of privacy" in personal e-mails sent on a company computer given the language of the Policy.

The panel balanced Loving Care's right to enforce reasonable rules for the workplace against the public policies underlying the attorney-client privilege. The court rejected the notion that "ownership of the computer [is] the sole determinative fact" at issue and instead explained that there must be a nexus between company policies and the employer's legitimate business interests. The panel concluded that society's important interest in shielding communications with an attorney from disclosure outweighed the company's interest in upholding the Policy. As a result, the panel found that the e-mails were protected by the attorney-client privilege and should be returned.

The Appellate Division also concluded that the Firm breached its obligations under RPC 4.4(b) by failing to alert Stengart's attorneys that it possessed the e-mails before reading them. The panel remanded for a hearing to determine whether disqualification of the Firm or some other sanction was appropriate.

We granted Loving Care's motion for leave to appeal and ordered a stay pending the outcome of this appeal.

II.

Loving Care argues that its employees have no expectation of privacy in their use of company computers based on the company's Policy. In its briefs before this Court, the company also asserts that by accessing e-mails on a personal account through Loving Care's computer and server, Stengart either prevented any attorney-client privilege from attaching or waived the privilege by voluntarily subjecting her e-mails to company scrutiny. Finally, Loving Care maintains that its counsel did not violate RPC 4.4(b) because the e-mails were left behind on Stengart's company computer—not "inadvertently sent," as per the Rule—and the Firm acted in the good faith belief that any privilege had been waived.

Stengart argues that she intended the e-mails with her lawyer to be confidential and that the Policy, even if it applied to her, failed to provide adequate warning that Loving Care would save on a hard drive, or monitor the contents of, e-mails sent from a personal account. Stengart also maintains that the communications with her lawyer were privileged. When the Firm encountered the arguably protected e-mails, Stengart contends it should have immediately returned them or sought judicial review as to whether the attorney-client privilege applied.

We granted amicus curiae status to the following organizations: the Employers Association of New Jersey (EANJ), the National Employment Lawyers Association of New Jersey (NELA-NJ), the Association of Criminal Defense Lawyers of New Jersey (ACDL-NJ), and the New Jersey State Bar Association (NJSBA).

EANJ calls for reversal of the Appellate Division decision. It notes the dramatic, recent increase in the use of non-business-related e-mails at work and submits that, by allowing occasional personal use of company property as a courtesy to employees, companies do not create a reasonable expectation of privacy in the use of their computer systems. EANJ also contends that the Appellate Division's analysis—particularly, its focus on whether workplace policies in the area of electronic communications further legitimate business interests—will unfairly burden employers and undermine their ability to protect corporate assets.

NELA-NJ and ACDL-NJ support the Appellate Division's ruling. NELA-NJ submits that an employee has a substantive right to privacy in her password-protected e-mails, even if accessed from an employer-owned computer, and that an employer's invasion of that privacy right must be narrowly tailored to the employer's legitimate business interests. ACDL-NJ adds that the need to shield private communications from disclosure is amplified when the attorney-client privilege is at stake.

NJSBA expresses concern about preserving the attorney-client privilege in the "increasingly technology-laden world" in which attorneys practice. NJSBA cautions against allowing inadvertent or casual waivers of the privilege. To analyze the competing interests presented in cases like this, NJSBA suggests various factors that courts should consider in deciding whether the privilege has been waived.

III.

Our analysis draws on two principal areas: the adequacy of the notice provided by the Policy and the important public policy concerns raised by the attorney-client privilege. Both inform the reasonableness of an employee's expectation of privacy in this matter. We address each area in turn.

A.

We start by examining the meaning and scope of the Policy itself. The Policy specifically reserves to Loving Care the right to review and access "all matters on the company's media systems and services at any time." In addition, e-mail messages are plainly "considered part of the company's business . . . records."

It is not clear from that language whether the use of personal, password-protected, web-based e-mail accounts via company equipment is covered. The Policy uses general language to refer to its "media systems and services" but does not define those terms. Elsewhere, the Policy prohibits certain uses of "the e-mail system," which appears to be a reference to company e-mail accounts. The Policy does not address personal accounts at all. In other words, employees do not have express notice that messages sent or received on a personal, web-based e-mail account are subject to monitoring if company equipment is used to access the account.

The Policy also does not warn employees that the contents of such e-mails are stored on a hard drive and can be forensically retrieved and read by Loving Care.

The Policy goes on to declare that e-mails "are not to be considered private or personal to any individual employee." In the very next point, the Policy acknowledges that "[o]ccasional personal use [of e-mail] is permitted." As written, the Policy creates ambiguity about whether personal e-mail use is company or private property.

The scope of the written Policy, therefore, is not entirely clear.

B.

The policies underlying the attorney-client privilege further animate this discussion. The venerable privilege is enshrined in history and practice. *Fellerman v. Bradley,* 99 *N.J.* 493, 498, 493 *A.*2d 1239 (1985) ("[T]he attorney-client privilege is recognized as one of 'the oldest of the privileges for confidential communications.' ") (quoting 8 J. Wigmore, *Evidence* § 2290, at 542 (McNaughton rev.1961)). Its primary rationale is to encourage "free and full disclosure of information from the client to the attorney." *Ibid.* That, in turn, benefits the public, which "is well served by sound legal counsel" based on full, candid, and confidential exchanges. *Id.* at 502, 493 A.2d 1239.

The privilege is codified at *N.J.S.A.* 2A:84A–20, and it appears in the *Rules of Evidence* as *N.J.R.E.* 504. Under the *Rule,* "[f]or a communication to be privileged it must initially be expressed by an individual in his capacity as a client in conjunction with seeking or receiving legal advice from the attorney in his capacity as such, with the expectation that its content remain confidential." *Fellerman, supra,* 99 *N.J.* at 499, 493 *A.*2d 1239 (citing *N.J.S.A.* 2A:84A–20(1) and (3)).

E-mail exchanges are covered by the privilege like any other form of communication. *See Seacoast Builders Corp. v. Rutgers,* 358 *N.J.Super.* 524, 553, 818 *A.*2d 455 (App.Div.2003) (finding e-mail from client to attorney "obviously protected by the attorney-client privilege as a communication with counsel in the course of a professional relationship and in confidence").

The e-mail communications between Stengart and her lawyers contain a standard warning that their contents are personal and confidential and may constitute attorney-client communications. The subject matter of those messages appears to relate to Stengart's working conditions and anticipated lawsuit against Loving Care.

IV.

Under the particular circumstances presented, how should a court evaluate whether Stengart had a reasonable expectation of privacy in the e-mails she exchanged with her attorney?

A.

Preliminarily, we note that the reasonable-expectation-of-privacy standard used by the parties derives from the common law and the Search and Seizure Clauses of both the Fourth Amendment and Article I, paragraph 7 of the New Jersey Constitution. The latter sources do not apply in this case, which involves conduct by private parties only.

The common law source is the tort of "intrusion on seclusion," which can be found in the Restatement (Second) of Torts § 652B (1977). That section provides that "[o]ne who intentionally intrudes, physically or otherwise, upon the solitude or seclusion of another or his private affairs or concerns, is subject to liability to the other for invasion of his privacy, if the intrusion would be highly offensive to a reasonable person." Restatement, supra, § 652B. A high threshold must be cleared to assert a cause of action based on that tort. *Hennessey, supra,* 129 *N.J.* at 116, 609 *A.*2d 11 (Pollock, J., concurring). A plaintiff must establish that the intrusion "would be highly offensive to the ordinary reasonable man, as the result of conduct to which the reasonable man would strongly object." Restatement, supra, § 652B cmt. d.

As is true in Fourth Amendment cases, the reasonableness of a claim for intrusion on seclusion has both a subjective and objective component. Moreover, whether an employee has a reasonable expectation of privacy in her particular work setting "must be addressed on a case-by-case basis." *O'Connor v. Ortega,* 480 *U.S.* 709, 718, 107 S.Ct. 1492, 1498, 94 L.Ed.2d 714, 723 (1987) (plurality opinion) (reviewing public sector employment).

B.

A number of courts have tested an employee's claim of privacy in files stored on company computers by evaluating the reasonableness of the employee's expectation. No reported decisions in New Jersey offer direct guidance for the facts of this case. . . .

. . . .

Certain decisions from outside New Jersey, which the parties also rely on, are more instructive. Among them, *National Economic Research Associates v. Evans,* 21 *Mass. L. Rptr.* No. 15, at 337, 2006 WL 2440008 (Mass.Super.Ct. Aug. 3, 2006), is most analogous to the facts here. In *Evans,* an employee used a company laptop to send and receive attorney-client communications by e-mail. In doing so, he used his personal, password-protected Yahoo account and not the company's e-mail address. The e-mails were automatically stored in a temporary Internet file on the computer's hard drive and were later retrieved by a computer forensic expert. The expert recovered various attorney-client e-mails; at the instruction of the company's lawyer, those e-mails were not reviewed pending guidance from the court.

A company manual governed the laptop's use. The manual permitted personal use of e-mail, to "be kept to a minimum," but warned that computer resources were the "property of the Company" and that e-mails were "not confidential" and could be read "during routine checks."

The court denied the company's application to allow disclosure of the e-mails that its expert possessed. The court reasoned,

> Based on the warnings furnished in the Manual, Evans [(the employee)] could not reasonably expect to communicate in confidence with his private attorney if Evans e-mailed his attorney using his NERA [(company)] e-mail address through the NERA Intranet, because the Manual plainly warned Evans that e-mails on the network could be read by NERA network administrators. The Manual, however, did not expressly declare that it would monitor the *content* of Internet communications. . . . Most importantly, the Manual did not expressly declare, or even implicitly suggest, that NERA would monitor the content of e-mail communications made from an employee's personal e-mail account via the Internet whenever those communications were viewed on a NERA-issued computer. Nor did NERA warn its employees that the content of such Internet e-mail communications is stored on the hard disk of a NERA-issued computer and therefore capable of being read by NERA.

As a result, the court found the employee's expectation of privacy in e-mails with his attorney to be reasonable.

In *Asia Global, supra,* the Bankruptcy Court for the Southern District of New York considered whether a bankruptcy trustee could force the production of e-mails sent by company employees to their personal attorneys on the *company's* e-mail system. The court developed a four-part test to "measure the employee's expectation of privacy in his computer files and e-mail":

> (1) does the corporation maintain a policy banning personal or other objectionable use, (2) does the company monitor the use of the employee's computer or e-mail, (3) do third parties have a right of access to the computer or e-mails, and (4) did the corporation notify the employee, or was the employee aware, of the use and monitoring policies?

Because the evidence was "equivocal" about the existence of a corporate policy banning personal use of e-mail and allowing monitoring, the court could not conclude that the employees' use of the company e-mail system eliminated any applicable attorney-client privilege.

Both *Evans* and *Asia Global* referenced a formal ethics opinion by the American Bar Association that noted "lawyers have a reasonable expectation of privacy when communicating by e-mail maintained by an [online service provider]." *See id.* at 256 (citing ABA Comm. on Ethics and Prof'l Responsibility, Formal Op. 413 (1999)); *Evans, supra,* 21 *Mass. L. Rptr.* No. 15, at 339 (same).

Other courts have measured the factors outlined in *Asia Global* among other considerations. In reviewing those cases, we are mindful of the fact-specific nature of the inquiry involved and the multitude of different facts that can affect the outcome in a given case. No one factor alone is necessarily dispositive.

According to some courts, employees appear to have a lesser expectation of privacy when they communicate with an attorney using a company e-mail system as compared to a personal, web-based account like the one used here. *See, e.g., Smyth v. Pillsbury Co.,* 914 *F.Supp.* 97, 100–01 (E.D.Pa.1996) (finding no reasonable expectation of privacy in unprofessional e-mails sent to supervisor through internal corporate e-mail system); *Scott v. Beth Israel Med. Ctr., Inc.,* 17 *Misc.*3d 934, 847 *N.Y.S.*2d 436, 441–43 (N.Y.Sup. Ct.2007) (finding no expectation of confidentiality when company e-mail used to send attorney-client messages). *But see Convertino v. U.S. Dep't of Justice,* 674 *F.Supp.2d* 97, 110 (D.D.C.2009) (finding reasonable expectation of privacy in attorney-client e-mails sent via employer's e-mail system). As a result, courts might treat e-mails transmitted via an employer's e-mail account differently than they would web-based e-mails sent on the same company computer.

Courts have also found that the existence of a clear company policy banning personal e-mails can also diminish the reasonableness of an employee's claim to privacy in e-mail messages with his or her attorney. *Compare Scott, supra,* 847 *N.Y.S.*2d at 441 (finding e-mails sent to attorney not privileged and noting that company's e-mail policy prohibiting personal use was "critical to the outcome"), *with Asia Global, supra,* 322 *B.R.* at 259–61 (declining to find e-mails to attorney were not privileged in light of unclear evidence as to existence of company policy banning personal e-mail use). We recognize that a zero-tolerance policy can be unworkable and unwelcome in today's dynamic and mobile workforce and do not seek to encourage that approach in any way.

The location of the company's computer may also be a relevant consideration. In *Curto v. Medical World Communications, Inc.,* 99 *Fair Empl. Prac. Cas.* (BNA) 298, 2006 WL 1318387 (E.D.N.Y. May 15, 2006), for example, an employee working from a home office sent e-mails to her attorney on a company laptop via her personal AOL account. *Id.* at 301. Those messages did not go through the company's servers but were nonetheless retrievable. Notwithstanding a company policy banning personal use, the trial court found that the e-mails were privileged. *Id.* at 305.

We realize that different concerns are implicated in cases that address the reasonableness of a privacy claim under the Fourth Amendment. . . . This case, however, involves no governmental action. Stengart's relationship with her private employer does not raise the specter of any government official unreasonably invading her rights.

V.

A.

H

Applying the above considerations to the facts before us, we find that Stengart had a reasonable expectation of privacy in the e-mails she exchanged with her attorney on Loving Care's laptop.

Stengart plainly took steps to protect the privacy of those e-mails and shield them from her employer. She used a personal, password-protected e-mail account instead of her company e-mail address and did not save the account's password on her computer. In other words, she had a subjective expectation of privacy in messages to and from her lawyer discussing the subject of a future lawsuit.

In light of the language of the Policy and the attorney-client nature of the communications, her expectation of privacy was also objectively reasonable. As noted earlier, the Policy does not address the use of personal, web-based e-mail accounts accessed through company equipment. It does not address personal accounts at all. Nor does it warn employees that the contents of e-mails sent via personal accounts can be forensically retrieved and read by the company. Indeed, in acknowledging that occasional personal use of e-mail is permitted, the Policy created doubt about whether those e-mails are company or private property.

Moreover, the e-mails are not illegal or inappropriate material stored on Loving Care's equipment, which might harm the company in some way. . . . They are conversations between a lawyer and client about confidential legal matters, which are historically cloaked in privacy. Our system strives to keep private the very type of conversations that took place here in order to foster probing and honest exchanges.

In addition, the e-mails bear a standard hallmark of attorney-client messages. They warn the reader directly that the e-mails are personal, confidential, and may be attorney-client communications. While a pro forma warning at the end of an e-mail might not, on its own, protect a communication, *see Scott, supra,* 847 *N.Y.S.*2d at 444, other facts present here raise additional privacy concerns.

Under all of the circumstances, we find that Stengart could reasonably expect that e-mails she exchanged with her attorney on her personal, password-protected, web-based e-mail account, accessed on a company laptop, would remain private.

It follows that the attorney-client privilege protects those e-mails. *See Asia Global, supra,* 322 *B.R.* at 258–59 (noting "close correlation between the objectively reasonable expectation of privacy and the objective reasonableness of the intent that a communication between a lawyer and a client was given in confidence"). In reaching that conclusion, we necessarily reject Loving Care's claim that the attorney-client privilege either did not attach or was waived. In its reply brief and at oral argument, Loving Care argued that the manner in which the e-mails were sent prevented the privilege from attaching. Specifically, Loving Care contends that Stengart effectively brought a third person into the conversation from the start—watching over her shoulder—and thereby forfeited any claim to confidentiality in her communications. We disagree.

Stengart has the right to prevent disclosures by third persons who learn of her communications "in a manner not reasonably to be anticipated." *See N.J.R.E.* 504(1)(c)(ii). That is what occurred here. The Policy did not give Stengart, or a reasonable person in her position, cause to anticipate that Loving Care would be peering over her shoulder as she opened e-mails from her lawyer on her personal, password-protected Yahoo account. *See Evans, supra,* 21 *Mass. L. Rptr.* No. 15, at 339. The language of the Policy, the method of transmittal that Stengart selected, and the warning on the e-mails themselves all support that conclusion.

Loving Care also argued in earlier submissions that Stengart waived the attorney-client privilege. For similar reasons, we again disagree.

A person waives the privilege if she, "without coercion and with knowledge of [her] right or privilege, made disclosure of any part of the privileged matter or consented to such a disclosure made by anyone." *N.J.R.E.* 530 (codifying *N.J.S.A.* 2A:84A–29). Because consent is not applicable here, we look to whether Stengart either knowingly disclosed the information contained in the e-mails or failed to "take reasonable steps to insure and maintain their confidentiality."

As discussed previously, Stengart took reasonable steps to keep discussions with her attorney confidential: she elected not to use the company e-mail system and relied on a personal, password-protected, web-based account instead. She also did not save the password on her laptop or share it in some other way with Loving Care.

As to whether Stengart knowingly disclosed the e-mails, she certified that she is unsophisticated in the use of computers and did not know that Loving Care could read communications sent on her Yahoo account. Use of a company laptop alone does not establish that knowledge. Nor does the Policy fill in that gap. Under the circumstances, we do not find either a knowing or reckless waiver.

B.

Our conclusion that Stengart had an expectation of privacy in e-mails with her lawyer does not mean that employers cannot monitor or regulate the use of workplace computers. Companies can adopt lawful policies relating to computer use to protect the assets, reputation, and productivity of a business and to ensure compliance with legitimate corporate policies. And employers can enforce such policies. They may discipline employees and, when appropriate, terminate them, for violating proper workplace rules that are not inconsistent with a clear mandate of public policy. For example, an employee who spends long stretches of the workday getting personal, confidential legal advice from a private lawyer may be disciplined for violating a policy permitting only occasional personal use of the Internet. But employers have no need or basis to read the specific *contents* of personal, privileged, attorney-client communications in order to enforce corporate policy. Because of the important public policy concerns underlying the attorney-client privilege, even a more clearly written company manual—that is, a policy that banned all personal computer use and provided unambiguous notice that an employer could retrieve and read an employee's attorney-client communications, if accessed on a personal, password-protected e-mail account using the company's computer system—would not be enforceable.

VI.

We next examine whether the Firm's review and use of the privileged e-mails violated RPC 4.4(b). The Rule provides that "[a] lawyer who receives a document and has reasonable cause to believe that the document was inadvertently sent shall not read the document or, if he or she has begun to do so, shall stop reading the document, promptly notify the sender, and return the document to the sender." According to the ABA Model Rules on which RPC 4.4(b) is patterned, the term " 'document' includes e-mail or other electronic modes of transmission subject to being read or put into readable form." Model Rules of Prof'l Conduct R. 4.4 cmt. 2 (2004).

Loving Care contends that the *Rule* does not apply because Stengart left the e-mails behind on her laptop and did not send them inadvertently. In actuality, the Firm retained a computer forensic expert to retrieve e-mails that were automatically saved on the laptop's hard drive in a "cache" folder of temporary Internet files. Without Stengart's knowledge, browser software made copies of each webpage she viewed. Under those circumstances, it is difficult to think of the e-mails as items that were simply left behind. We find that the Firm's review of privileged e-mails between Stengart and her lawyer, and use of the contents of at least one e-mail in responding to interrogatories, fell within the ambit of RPC 4.4(b) and violated that rule.

To be clear, the Firm did not hack into plaintiff's personal account or maliciously seek out attorney-client documents in a clandestine way. Nor did it rummage through an employee's personal files out of idle curiosity. Instead, it legitimately attempted to preserve evidence to defend a civil lawsuit. Its error was in not setting aside the arguably privileged messages once it realized they were attorney-client communications, and failing either to notify its adversary or seek court permission before reading further. There is nothing in the record before us to suggest any bad faith on the Firm's part in reading the Policy as it did. Nonetheless, the Firm should have promptly notified opposing counsel when it discovered the nature of the e-mails.

The Appellate Division remanded to the trial court to determine the appropriate remedy. It explained that a hearing was needed in that regard to consider

> the content of the emails, whether the information contained in the emails would have inevitably been divulged in discovery that would have occurred absent [the Firm's] knowledge of the emails' content, and the nature of the issues that have been or may in the future be pled in either this or the related Chancery action.

We agree. The forensically retrieved version of the e-mails submitted to the Court is not easy to read or fully understand in isolation, and no record has yet been developed about the e-mails' full use. For the same reason, we cannot determine how confidential or critical the messages are. In deciding what sanctions to impose, the trial court should evaluate the seriousness of the breach in light of the specific nature of the e-mails, the manner in which they were identified, reviewed, disseminated, and used, and other considerations noted by the Appellate Division. As to plaintiff's request for disqualification, the court should also "balance competing interests, weighing the 'need to maintain the highest standards of the profession' against 'a client's right freely to choose his counsel.' " *Dewey v. R.J. Reynolds Tobacco Co.,* 109 N.J. 201, 218, 536 A.2d 243 (1988) (quoting *Gov't of India v. Cook Indus., Inc.,* 569 F.2d 737, 739 (2d Cir.1978)).

We leave to the trial court to decide whether disqualification of the Firm, screening of attorneys, the imposition of costs, or some other remedy is appropriate. Under the circumstances, we do not believe a remand to the Chancery judge is required; the matter may proceed before the Law Division judge assigned to the case.

VII.

For the reasons set forth above, we modify and affirm the judgment of the Appellate Division and remand to the trial court for further proceedings.

QUESTION

1. What responsibilities should companies bear in managing the data accumulated from enhanced technology? Some companies have offered microchipping to their employees, which will allow them access to buildings and vending machines on company property. The microchips allow for storage of all types of scannable documents for the convenience of the individual. A driver's license can be stored on the employee's microchip, for example. Who owns the data on the microchip? Should the employer have access to the data once the microchip is in place? What happens when an employee leaves the employment? Does the microchip belong to the company? What about the information on the microchip?

Problem 17-2

Employees at an Amazon distribution warehouse are required to wear wristbands with GPS monitors on them during work. The devices track the location and hand movements of employees so that the company can determine the most efficient routes through the warehouse. Employees often forget to turn off their GPS devices after they leave work, which means that Amazon can continue to track their location once they leave the building. Amazon trackers collected data on employees that included Jan's visit to Olden Out, a labor-side employment law firm. Can Jan sue Amazon for privacy violations for tracking employee activities outside the distribution center when the tracking data meets no legitimate business-related purpose?

---

2. Intrusion upon an Employee's Social Media Privacy

In the modern era, many people find that a social media presence is an important part of their life. Because people are sharing information with each other, one might assume that there is no privacy interest at stake. However, social media sites often permit users wide latitude to control who can see activity on one's account, and employees may have a reasonable expectation that employers will not intrude on their private online lives.

Recently, some employers have resorted to asking prospective employees to access their social media sites during an interview so that the employer can review the site. California, for one, has outlawed this form of compelled relinquishment of one's privacy rights. The "Employer Use of Social Media" law prohibits an employer from requiring or requesting an employee or applicant for employment to disclose a username or password for the purpose of accessing personal social media, to access personal social media in the presence of the employer, or to divulge any personal social media. The Law also prohibits an employer from discharging, disciplining, threatening to discharge or discipline, or otherwise retaliating against an employee or applicant for not complying with a request or demand by the employer that violates these provisions. Cal. Labor Code § 980.

The following case describes the limits of privacy and the basis for the common admonition to assume that everything you post is available to the world. Having a federal district court judge with senior status explain how Facebook works is an added bonus.

Ehling v. Monmouth-Ocean Hosp. Srv. Corp.

961 F. Supp. 2d 659 (2013).

William J. Martini, U.S.D.J.

[P]laintiff was hired by MONOC in 2004 as a registered nurse and para-medic. . . . Plaintiff's claims in this case arise out of [a]n incident involving Plaintiff's Facebook account. . .The Court will summarize the pertinent facts relating to each issue.

A. The Facebook Incident

Facebook is a widely-used social-networking website. The website provides a digital medium that allows users to connect and communicate with each other. Every Facebook user must create a Profile Page, which is a webpage that is intended to convey information about the user. The Profile Page can include the user's contact information; pictures; biographical information, such as the user's birthday, hometown, educational background, work history, family members, and relationship status; and lists of places, musicians, movies, books, businesses, and products that the user likes. A Facebook user can connect with other users by adding them as "Facebook friends." Facebook users can have dozens, hundreds, or even thousands of Facebook friends. In addition to having a Profile Page, each user has a webpage called a News Feed. The News Feed aggregates information that has recently been shared by the user's Facebook friends. By default, Facebook pages are public. However, Facebook has customizable privacy settings that allow users to restrict access to their Facebook content. Access can be limited to the user's Facebook friends, to particular groups or individuals, or to just the user.

Facebook provides users with several means of communicating with one another. Users can send private messages to one or more users. Users can also communicate by posting information to their Facebook "wall," which is part of each user's Profile Page. A Facebook "wall post" can include written comments, photographs, digital images, videos, and content from other websites. To create a Facebook wall post, users upload data from their computers or mobile devices directly to the Facebook website. Facebook then saves that data onto its computers (called "servers"). New wall posts are typically distributed to a user's Facebook friends using the News Feed feature. Users' most recent wall posts also appear at the top of their Profile Pages. A user's Facebook friends can comment on the wall posts, indicate that they "like" the wall posts, or share the posts with other users. Facebook users typically do not post information to their Facebook walls with the intent to delete it later. Instead, Facebook designed its website so that its servers would save this data indefinitely. As more and more wall posts are added, earlier wall posts move lower and lower down on the user's Profile Page, and are eventually archived on separate pages that are accessible, but not displayed.

During the 2008–2009 timeframe, Plaintiff maintained a Facebook account and had approximately 300 Facebook friends. Plaintiff selected privacy settings for her account that limited access to her Facebook wall to only her Facebook friends. Plaintiff did not add any MONOC managers as Facebook friends. However, Plaintiff added many of her MONOC coworkers as friends, including a paramedic named Tim Ronco. Plaintiff posted on Ronco's Facebook wall, and Ronco had access to Plaintiff's Facebook wall. Unbeknownst to Plaintiff, Ronco was taking screenshots of Plaintiff's Facebook wall and printing them or emailing them to MONOC manager Andrew Caruso. Ronco and Caruso became friends while working together at a previous job, but Ronco never worked in Caruso's division at MONOC. The evidence reflects that Ronco independently came up with the idea to provide Plaintiff's Facebook posts to Caruso. Caruso never asked Ronco for any information about Plaintiff, and never requested that Ronco keep him apprised of Plaintiff's Facebook activity. In fact, Caruso was surprised that Ronco showed him Plaintiff's Facebook posts. Caruso never had the password to Ronco's Facebook account, Plaintiff's Facebook account, or any other employee's Facebook account. Once Caruso received copies of Plaintiff's Facebook posts, he passed them on to Quagliana, MONOC's Executive Director of Administration.

On June 8, 2009, Plaintiff posted the following statement to her Facebook wall:

> An 88 yr old sociopath white supremacist opened fire in the Wash D.C. Holocaust Museum this morning and killed an innocent guard (leaving children). Other guards opened fire. The 88 yr old was shot. He survived. I blame the DC paramedics. I want to say 2 things to the DC medics. 1. WHAT WERE YOU THINKING? and 2. This was your opportunity to really make a difference! WTF!!!! And to the other guards. . . .go to target practice.

Problematic Post

After MONOC management was alerted to the post, Plaintiff was temporarily suspended ***with*** pay, and received a memo stating that MONOC management was concerned that Plaintiff's comment reflected a "deliberate disregard for patient safety." In response, Plaintiff filed a complaint with the National Labor Relations Board ("NLRB"). After reviewing the evidence, the NLRB found that MONOC did not violate the National Labor Relations Act. The NLRB also found that there was no privacy violation because the post was sent, unsolicited, to MONOC management.

. . . .

PP

. . . .[P]laintiff asserts a claim for common law invasion of privacy. Plaintiff's claim is premised on Defendants' alleged unauthorized "accessing of her private Facebook postings" regarding the museum shooting. Defendants argue that they are entitled to summary judgment on the privacy claim because Plaintiff's friend "freely chose to share the information" with Defendants. The Court finds that summary judgment should be granted. . . .

Rules

A claim for invasion of privacy under New Jersey law will succeed if a plaintiff brings forth evidence showing that (1) there was an intentional intrusion "upon the solitude or seclusion of another or his private affairs," and that (2) this intrusion would highly offend the reasonable person. Under the first prong, a defendant must commit an intrusive act. "The converse of this principle is, however, of course, that there is no wrong where defendant did not actually delve into plaintiff's concerns." Plaintiff faces a high burden in asserting a cause of action based on intrusion of seclusion.

In this case, Plaintiff failed to show that there was an intentional intrusion by any of the Defendants. In the Amended Complaint, Plaintiff alleged that Defendants gained access to her Facebook page because a "member of upper management summoned a MONOC employee . . . into his office" and "threatened this employee into accessing his Facebook account." Now that discovery is complete, it is clear that there is no evidentiary support for these allegations. The evidence does not show that Defendants obtained access to Plaintiff's Facebook page by, say, logging into her account, logging into another employee's account, or asking another employee to log into Facebook. Instead, the evidence shows that Defendants were the passive recipients of information that they did not seek out or ask for. Plaintiff voluntarily gave information to her Facebook friend, and her Facebook friend voluntarily gave that information to someone else. . . .

This may have been a violation of trust, but it was not a violation of privacy.

Accordingly, the motion for summary judgment. . .is **GRANTED**.

QUESTIONS

1. Should employers be able to use information gleaned from social media sites to discipline employees? What employer interests are at stake?
2. Should states enact laws protecting employees from employer attempts to access employee social media accounts, such as California has done? If this case arose in California would the employee have a case?
3. Are privacy rights in social media better articulated through legislated rules or common law balancing?

Problem 17-3

The Big Hen, a chain restaurant specializing in chicken dishes, has a problem with employee morale. The wait staff at the Big Hen feel disrespected and underpaid. They believe the restaurant should pay them $15 per hour plus tips, even though neither federal nor state law require it. The wait staff started a private Facebook group as a way to vent frustrations about the daily insults they endure at the restaurant. One of the wait staff, Don, was recently promoted to shift supervisor. He immediately notified the restaurant owner of the existence of the private chat group, and gave her access to his password so that she could monitor the group's posts. The owner fired the members of the Facebook group for disparaging the company online. Do the members of the group have a viable invasion of privacy claim?

3. Federal and State Statutes Governing Electronic Communications

Congress has passed two statutes that may have relevance to the monitoring of electronic communications. The Electronic Communications Privacy Act ("ECPA") of 1986, amending the Federal Wiretap Act of 1968, regulates the monitoring of electronic communications, including e-mail. It imposes criminal and civil penalties against any person who intentionally intercepts an electronic communication. Electronic Communications Privacy Act of 1986, Pub. L. No. 99 508,100 Stat. 1848. Employer monitoring of its own equipment or of website addresses, however, will not likely meet the definition of "intercept" under the Act. ECPA also contains an ordinary course of business exception for employers who access employee emails on systems provided by the employer. An employer can, in the ordinary course of business, access employee emails sent on such a system. The statute allows for employer interceptions if it is "necessary incident to the rendition of the service or protection of the rights of [the provider's property] . . ." 18 U.S.C. § 2511(2)(a)(1) (2006).

Second, the Stored Communications Act ("SCA") prohibits intrusions on stored communications. This statute also has a "provider" exception that applies to employers who provide an electronic communication service. Under the SCA, an employer may access stored e-mails on servers the employer provides. This exception is broader than the ordinary course of business exception in the ECPA. However, the SCA does not provide similar protection for systems hosted by third-parties, e.g., web-based e-mail accounts stored on third party servers.

States have filled in some gaps in privacy protections with statutes that protect employees from employer requirements that might intrude on employee electronic privacy. For example, over twenty-five states have passed laws that prohibit an employer from requiring employees to share information such as passwords to social media accounts. The following is one example from California.

California Labor Code

§ 980. Employer Use of Social Media

(a) As used in this chapter, "social media" means an electronic service or account, or electronic content, including, but not limited to, videos, still photographs, blogs, video blogs, podcasts, instant and text messages, email, online services or accounts, or Internet Web site profiles or locations.

(b) An employer shall not require or request an employee or applicant for employment to do any of the following:

(1) Disclose a username or password for the purpose of accessing personal social media.

(2) Access personal social media in the presence of the employer.

(3) Divulge any personal social media, except as provided in subdivision (c).

(c) Nothing in this section shall affect an employer's existing rights and obligations to request an employee to divulge personal social media reasonably believed to be relevant to an investigation of allegations of employee misconduct or employee violation of applicable laws and regulations, provided that the social media is used solely for purposes of that investigation or a related proceeding.

(d) Nothing in this section precludes an employer from requiring or requesting an employee to disclose a username, password, or other method for the purpose of accessing an employer-issued electronic device.

(e) An employer shall not discharge, discipline, threaten to discharge or discipline, or otherwise retaliate against an employee or applicant for not complying with a request or demand by the employer that violates this section. However, this section does not prohibit an employer from terminating or otherwise taking an adverse action against an employee or applicant if otherwise permitted by law.

Mastery Problem 17-1

Sam and Marta work for IMart, a telemarketing company in Sacramento. Marta is a call center operator. Sam is an administrative assistant to Albert, one of the three call center managers, each of whom has hiring and firing authority over all staff in the office. Marta and Sam are secretly dating because IMart has a policy of not allowing co-workers to date. Although Marta and Sam are keeping their relationship hidden from their co-workers, their friends and family know about it. Sam and Marta went on a double date with Marta's sister, Gina. Forgetting that their relationship was a secret, Gina posted pictures of the evening on Facebook.

One night while scrolling through Facebook, Carla, one of the call center managers and a Facebook friend of Gina's, sees Gina's pictures of Marta and Sam smiling together, embracing and kissing. The next day, while having lunch with some of the telemarketers in the breakroom, Carla gossips to them about having seen the pictures of Sam and Marta on Facebook. Carla goes on to say that she thinks the company's policy is outdated and stupid, and she would not enforce it if she discovered co-workers in her department dating. She announces that she is sure they are romantically involved because she saw photos of them kissing.

Darlene, one of the telemarketers, does not like Marta. She goes straight to Albert, her boss, and tells him about Sam and Marta's relationship. Albert, knowing he must deal with the situation before it gets out of hand, decides to use this opportunity to fire Sam, Marta and Darlene. He calls them into his office and tells them they no longer have a job. He tells Sam and Marta that they are fired because they violated company policy, and he tells Darlene she's fired because he does not like snitches. On the same day, the company issues a memorandum reminding its employees of its policy against co-worker relationships. The memorandum names Marta and Sam specifically as employees who have been fired for violating the policy.

Independently, Marta, Sam and Darlene seek advice from your law firm about whether they have claims against IMart. Please advise each employee on the prospects of legal action.

During your investigation of Sam, Marta and Darlene's case, you interview several workers who have been fired because the company discovered their activities outside of work through Facebook, Twitter or Instagram posts. For example, IMart discovered a picture on Instagram of Jimmy, a sales representative, urinating in a public park at night. Jimmy was fired within a week. Please advise Jimmy about any claims that he might have against IMart.

Conclusion

In this Lesson, you have learned how the general torts as well as statutory remedies apply to privacy in electronic communications in the workplace. Employers can set out expectations for privacy in policies for use of electronic equipment, social media in the workplace and out of the workplace, and emerging technologies. State and federal statutes step into the breach to regulate in areas where common law privacy torts are silent.

Lesson 18:
Privacy and Testing

Objectives and Expected Learning Outcomes

In this Lesson, you will learn about privacy protections triggered when employers seek to test employees or screen them based on test results. You will learn to apply common law and statutory remedies in the workplace-testing context. You will learn the limits of privacy protections in this evolving field of employment relations.

Modern technology permits employers to learn a great deal about their employees. Genetic testing provides information about a person's heritage and might provide information about potential health issues. Drug testing can reveal substances that have been used by the employee and which may be affecting the employee on the job. Data scientists are able to take massive volumes of data and develop predictive algorithms that can assist the employer to ensure that the workplace is highly efficient. Finally, many employers have adopted wellness programs to reduce the costs that they incur when employees become sick or disabled.

We discuss all of these strategies and technologies in turn, asking whether the employee has a privacy interest that limits or precludes the employer's ability to use them.

1. Genetic Testing

DNA testing is now widely available through various commercial enterprises, although genetic testing generally is not conclusive regarding the health issues that will confront a person in the future. Employers might regard genetic testing of their employees to determine if they are hiring someone predisposed to certain diseases or conditions. The employer's motivation is to keep health care costs low and avoid absences due to illness. On the other hand, a genetic test is perhaps the most fundamental private information about a person. Congress resolved the conflict of these considerations at the early stage of the availability of affordable genetic testing by enacting the Genetic Information Nondiscrimination Act (GINA) in 2008.

GINA is similar to most nondiscrimination statutes in that it makes it unlawful for an employer to fail or refuse to hire, or to discharge, any employee, or otherwise to discriminate against any employee with respect to the compensation, terms, conditions, or privileges of employment of the employee, because of genetic information. The law also makes it illegal to limit, segregate, or classify the employee of the employer in any way that would deprive or tend to deprive any employee of employment opportunities or otherwise adversely affect the status of the employee as an employee, because of genetic information with respect to the employee. 42 U.S.C. § 2000ff–1(a).

There has been very little litigation surrounding GINA, as employers understand that they may not require employees to provide genetic information. One of the most important exceptions under GINA regulations makes clear that employers may not be found liable for using information that is "inadvertently acquired," usually because the employee has voluntarily shared the information.

Williams v. Graphic Packaging Int'l., Inc.

2018 WL 2118311 (M.D. Tenn. May 8, 2018).

William L. Campbell, Jr., United States District Judge.

Pending before the Court is Defendant's Motion for Summary Judgment. . . . For the reasons discussed below, Defendant's motion for summary judgment is GRANTED.

I. FACTUAL BACKGROUND

. . . .

Plaintiff was employed by Defendant as a department manager over cutting and gluing from September 2011 until December 2015. Plaintiff was 55 years old when Eddie Lee ("Lee") hired Plaintiff. During his tenure with the Defendant, Plaintiff consistently received positive performance evaluations for meeting and exceeding production goals. Plaintiff supervised four managers who reported directly to him: Tasha Pack ("Pack"), Sandy Williams ("Williams"), Jackie Miles ("Miles"), and Tony Sewell ("Sewell"). Plaintiff was "second in command" over operations at the facility, and the managers reported directly to him. Plaintiff was diagnosed with prostate cancer for the second time in September of 2015, and requested a leave of absence under Defendant's medical leave policy to undergo treatment.

Defendant granted Plaintiff's leave request and Plaintiff took medical leave from September 2015 until November 23, 2015. Pack assumed Plaintiff's duties while he was on leave.

> *[Editor's Note: Plaintiff was terminated after his four subordinates complained about his management practices during his leave. Plaintiff sued under a number of statutory provisions, including GINA.]*

. . . .

Plaintiff timely filed a charge of discrimination with the Equal Employment Opportunity Commission ("EEOC"), and filed his Complaint on November 21, 2016, within ninety (90) days of his receipt of the Notice of Rights to Sue Letter alleging that Defendant discriminated against him. (Doc. No. 1). In response, Defendant argues that Plaintiff was terminated for violating company policy by using fear, intimidation, and manipulation to manage his subordinates. (Doc. No. 24 at 1). Defendant denies discriminating, interfering, or retaliating against Plaintiff and seeks summary judgment on all claims.

. . . .

III. ANALYSIS

. . . .

E. PLAINTIFF'S GINA CLAIMS

An employer or labor organization is prohibited from discrimination on the basis of "genetic information." 42 U.S.C. §§ 2000ff–2. GINA defines "genetic information" as information about a "genetic test" or "the manifestation of a disease or disorder in family members." 42 U.S.C. § 2000ff(4)(A). A "genetic test" is further defined as "an analysis of human DNA, RNA, chromosomes, proteins, or metabolites that detects genotypes, mutations, or chromosomal changes." 42 U.S.C. § 2000ff(7)(A). Pursuant to GINA, "[i]t shall be an unlawful employment practice for an employment agency to request, require, or purchase genetic information with respect to an individual or a family member of the individual" unless an exception applies, such as an individual voluntarily providing the information or an employment agency inadvertently requests family medical history of the individual. 42 U.S.C. § 2000ff–2(b); *see also Punt v. Kelly Services*, 862 F.3d 1040 (10th

Cir. 2017) (holding evidence showed plaintiff told various individuals of her family history of breast cancer).

Defendant argues Plaintiff has no evidence to support his GINA claim because Defendant never required Plaintiff to provide any of his family genetic information, and Plaintiff voluntarily disclosed that cancer ran in his family. (Doc. No. 25 at 20–21). While Plaintiff argues Lee repeatedly questioned Plaintiff about his cancer, doctor's opinions, test results, and treatment options, Plaintiff's deposition states he voluntarily told three people, including Lee, that cancer ran in his family. (Doc. No. 30 at 26; Doc. No. 24–1, William Depo. at 223). Furthermore, Defendant never required or requested Plaintiff or his family to submit to a genetic test. (Doc. No. 24–1, William Depo. at 223–24).

Accordingly, the Court GRANTS Defendant's motion for summary judgment on Plaintiff's GINA discrimination claim, because Plaintiff voluntarily shared genetic information about his family, which is an exception under 42 U.S.C. § 2000ff–2(b).

. . . .

QUESTIONS

1. Should GINA's anti-discrimination protections be limited to cases in which the employer gathers information without employee consent? If an employer's discriminatory acts occur because of genetic information should it matter how the information was acquired?
2. Can an employer search through an employee's social media accounts for information related to family medical history?

Problem 18-1

Restful Acres, a nursing facility, hires nurse assistants on a regular basis. The facility's human resources manager makes offers pending a physical exam to ensure that assistants can carry out the responsibilities of the job, including some lifting and carrying objects heavier than thirty pounds. The facility sends its applicants to a third-party medical clinic for the physical exams. The medical clinic asks patients to fill out family medical history information as part of its protocol. Lisa Kline received an employment offer, went to the clinic for a physical, filled out the family medical history form, and was given an exam. The doctor discovered that Lisa had carpal tunnel syndrome, a condition that has nothing to do with Lisa's family medical history. Restful Acres rescinded Lisa's offer because the facility has a policy of not allowing assistants with carpal tunnel syndrome to lift heavy items. Can Lisa sue the facility for discrimination under GINA?

---

2. Drug Testing

The law of workplace drug testing can be separated into public and private employment. Public employees enjoy protection under the Fourth Amendment's prohibition on unreasonable searches and seizures. Constitutional challenges to public workplace drug testing in the 1980s and 1990s provided the framework for evaluating drug testing procedures for public employees. Generally, private employees have not been successful in challenging drug testing procedures.

Employers have an interest in regulating and surveilling their employees through workplace testing. Employees have a right to be free from wrongful intrusion upon their protected privacy interests. These considerations must be balanced when determining whether the employer's methods for screening and supervising the workplace are proper. Comment b to Restatement (Third) of Employment Law § 7.03 describes an employee's protected privacy interest into their physical person, personal physical functions, and personal possessions. Comment b states, "Under subsection (a), an employee has a protected privacy interest in the employee's physical person, private physical functions, and personal possessions. This includes the employee's body, bodily fluids, and other bodily by-products. An employer's job requirement that an employee provide a urine sample as part of a test for unlawful drug use is an intrusion into a protected privacy interest." However, most courts find that such intrusion is permissible because employees have no reasonable expectation of privacy and that this manner of testing is not "highly offensive."

Consider the following case involving public employees who work in a safety sensitive industry, and Justice Marshall's stinging dissent.

SKINNER v. RAILWAY LABOR EXECUTIVES' ASS'N

489 U.S. 602 (1989).

JUSTICE KENNEDY delivered the opinion of the Court.

The Federal Railroad Safety Act of 1970 authorizes the Secretary of Transportation to "prescribe, as necessary, appropriate rules, regulations, orders, and standards for all areas of railroad safety." Finding that alcohol and drug abuse by railroad employees poses a serious threat to safety, the Federal Railroad Administration (FRA) has promulgated regulations that mandate blood and urine tests of employees who are involved in certain train accidents. The FRA also has adopted regulations that do not require, but do authorize, railroads to administer breath and urine tests to employees who violate certain safety rules. The question presented by this case is whether these regulations violate the Fourth Amendment.

I

A

The problem of alcohol use on American railroads is as old as the industry itself, and efforts to deter it by carrier rules began at least a century ago. For many years, railroads have prohibited operating employees from possessing alcohol or being intoxicated while on duty and from consuming alcoholic beverages while subject to being called for duty. More recently, these proscriptions have been expanded to forbid possession or use of certain drugs. These restrictions are embodied in "Rule G," an industry-wide operating rule promulgated by the Association of American Railroads, and are enforced, in various formulations, by virtually every railroad in the country. The customary sanction for Rule G violations is dismissal.

In July 1983, the FRA expressed concern that these industry efforts were not adequate to curb alcohol and drug abuse by railroad employees. . . . In view of the obvious safety hazards of drug and alcohol use by railroad employees, the FRA announced in June 1984 its intention to promulgate federal regulations on the subject.

B

After reviewing further comments from representatives of the railroad industry, labor groups, and the general public, the FRA, in 1985, promulgated regulations addressing the problem of alcohol and drugs on the railroads.

The regulations prohibit covered employees from using or possessing alcohol or any controlled substance. To the extent pertinent here, . . . "Post-Accident Toxicological Testing," is mandatory. It provides that railroads "shall take all practicable steps to assure that all covered employees of the railroad directly involved . . . provide blood and urine samples for toxicological testing by FRA," upon the occurrence of certain specified events. . . .

. . . .

C

Respondents, the Railway Labor Executives' Association and various of its member labor organizations, brought the instant suit in the United States District Court for the Northern District of California, seeking to enjoin the FRA's regulations on various statutory and constitutional grounds. In a ruling from the bench, the District Court granted summary judgment in petitioners' favor. The court concluded that railroad employees "have a valid interest in the integrity of their own bodies" that deserved protection under the Fourth Amendment. The court held, however, that this interest was outweighed by the competing "public and governmental interest in the . . . promotion of . . . railway safety, safety for employees, and safety for the general public that is involved with the transportation." . . . .

A divided panel of the Court of Appeals for the Ninth Circuit reversed. . . .We granted the federal parties' petition for a writ of certiorari to consider whether the regulations invalidated by the Court of Appeals violate the Fourth Amendment. We now reverse.

II

The Fourth Amendment provides that "[t]he right of the people to be secure in their persons, houses, papers, and effects, against unreasonable searches and seizures, shall not be violated . . . ." The Amendment guarantees the privacy, dignity, and security of persons against certain arbitrary and invasive acts by officers of the Government or those acting at their direction. . . .

. . . .

Our precedents teach that where, as here, the Government seeks to obtain physical evidence from a person, the Fourth Amendment may be relevant at several levels. The initial detention necessary to procure the evidence may be a seizure of the person if the detention amounts to a meaningful interference with his freedom of movement. Obtaining and examining the evidence may also be a search, if doing so infringes an expectation of privacy that society is prepared to recognize as reasonable.

We have long recognized that a "compelled intrusio[n] into the body for blood to be analyzed for alcohol content" must be deemed a Fourth Amendment search. In light of our society's concern for the security of one's person, it is obvious that this physical intrusion, penetrating beneath the skin, infringes an expectation of privacy that society is prepared to recognize as reasonable. The ensuing chemical analysis of the sample to obtain physiological data is a further invasion of the tested employee's privacy interests. Much the same is true of the breath-testing procedures required under Subpart D of the regulations. Subjecting a person to a breathalyzer test, which generally requires the production of alveolar or "deep lung" breath for chemical analysis, implicates similar concerns about bodily integrity and, like the blood-alcohol test we considered in should also be deemed a search.

. . . .[T]he procedures prescribed by the FRA regulations for collecting and testing urine samples do not entail a surgical intrusion into the body. It is not disputed, however, that chemical analysis of urine, like that of blood, can reveal a host of private medical facts about an employee, including whether he or she is epileptic, pregnant, or diabetic. Nor can it be disputed that the process of collecting the sample to be tested, which may in some cases involve visual or aural monitoring of the act of urination, itself implicates privacy interests. As the Court of Appeals for the Fifth Circuit has stated:

> There are few activities in our society more personal or private than the passing of urine. Most people describe it by euphemisms if they talk about it at all. It is a function traditionally performed without public observation; indeed, its performance in public is generally prohibited by law as well as social custom.

Because it is clear that the collection and testing of urine intrudes upon expectations of privacy that society has long recognized as reasonable, the Federal Courts of Appeals have concluded unanimously, and we agree, that these intrusions must be deemed searches under the Fourth Amendment.

In view of our conclusion that the collection and subsequent analysis of the requisite biological samples must be deemed Fourth Amendment searches, we need not characterize the employer's antecedent interference with the employee's freedom of movement as an independent Fourth Amendment seizure. As our precedents indicate, not every governmental interference with an individual's freedom of movement raises such constitutional concerns that there is a seizure of the person. For present purposes, it suffices to note that any limitation on an employee's freedom of movement that is necessary to obtain the blood, urine, or breath samples contemplated by the regulations must be considered in assessing the intrusiveness of the searches effected by the Government's testing program.

III

A

To hold that the Fourth Amendment is applicable to the drug and alcohol testing prescribed by the FRA regulations is only to begin the inquiry into the standards governing such intrusions. For the Fourth Amendment does not proscribe all searches and seizures, but only those that are unreasonable. What is reasonable, of course, "depends on all of the circumstances surrounding the search or seizure and the nature of the search or seizure itself." [T]he permissibility of a particular practice "is judged by balancing its intrusion on the individual's Fourth Amendment interests against its promotion of legitimate governmental interests."

In most criminal cases, we strike this balance in favor of the procedures described by the Warrant Clause of the Fourth Amendment. Except in certain well-defined circumstances, a search or seizure in such a case is not reasonable unless it is accomplished pursuant to a judicial warrant issued upon probable cause. We have recognized exceptions to this rule, however, "when 'special needs, beyond the normal need for law enforcement, make the warrant and probable-cause requirement impracticable.' " When faced with such special needs, we have not hesitated to balance the governmental and privacy interests to assess the practicality of the warrant and probable-cause requirements in the particular context.

The Government's interest in regulating the conduct of railroad employees to ensure safety, like its supervision of probationers or regulated industries, or its operation of a government office, school, or prison, "likewise presents 'special needs' beyond normal law enforcement that may justify departures from the usual warrant and probable-cause requirements. "The hours of service employees covered by the FRA regulations include persons engaged in handling orders concerning train movements, operating crews, and those engaged in the maintenance and repair of signal systems. It is undisputed that these and other covered employees are engaged in safety-sensitive tasks. The FRA so found, and respondents conceded the point at oral argument. As we have recognized, the whole premise of the Hours of Service Act is that "[t]he length of hours of service has direct relation to the efficiency of the human agencies upon which protection [of] life and property necessarily depends."

The FRA has prescribed toxicological tests, not to assist in the prosecution of employees, but rather "to prevent accidents and casualties in railroad operations that result from impairment of employees by alcohol or drugs." This governmental interest in ensuring the safety of the traveling public and of the employees themselves plainly justifies prohibiting covered employees from using alcohol or drugs on duty, or while subject to being called for duty. This interest also "require[s] and justif[ies] the exercise of supervision to assure that the restrictions are in fact observed." The question that remains, then, is whether the Government's need to monitor compliance with these restrictions justifies the privacy intrusions at issue absent a warrant or individualized suspicion.

B

An essential purpose of a warrant requirement is to protect privacy interests by assuring citizens subject to a search or seizure that such intrusions are not the random or arbitrary acts of government agents. A warrant assures the citizen that the intrusion is authorized by law, and that it is narrowly limited in its objectives and scope. A warrant also provides the detached scrutiny of a neutral magistrate, and thus ensures an objective determination whether an intrusion is justified in any given case. In the present context, however, a warrant would do little to further these aims. Both the circumstances justifying toxicological testing and the permissible limits of such intrusions are defined narrowly and specifically in the regulations that authorize them, and doubtless are well known to covered employees. Indeed, in light of the standardized nature of the tests and the minimal discretion vested in those charged with administering the program, there are virtually no facts for a neutral magistrate to evaluate.

We have recognized, moreover, that the government's interest in dispensing with the warrant requirement is at its strongest when, as here, "the burden of obtaining a warrant is likely to frustrate the governmental purpose behind the search." As the FRA recognized, alcohol and other drugs are eliminated from the bloodstream at a constant rate and blood and breath samples taken to measure whether these substances were in the bloodstream when a triggering event occurred must be obtained as soon as possible. Although the metabolites of some drugs remain in the urine for longer periods of time and may enable the FRA to estimate whether the employee was impaired by those drugs at the time of a covered accident, incident, or rule violation, the delay necessary to procure a warrant nevertheless may result in the destruction of valuable evidence.

The Government's need to rely on private railroads to set the testing process in motion also indicates that insistence on a warrant requirement would impede the achievement of the Government's objective. Railroad supervisors, like school officials, and hospital administrators, are not in the business of investigating violations of the criminal laws or enforcing administrative codes, and otherwise have little occasion to become familiar with the intricacies of this Court's Fourth Amendment jurisprudence. "Imposing unwieldy warrant procedures . . . upon supervisors, who would otherwise have no reason to be familiar with such procedures, is simply unreasonable."

In sum, imposing a warrant requirement in the present context would add little to the assurances of certainty and regularity already afforded by the regulations, while significantly hindering, and in many cases frustrating, the objectives of the Government's testing program. We do not believe that a warrant is essential to render the intrusion here at issue reasonable under the Fourth Amendment.

. . . .

More importantly, the expectations of privacy of covered employees are diminished by reason of their participation in an industry that is regulated pervasively to ensure safety, a goal dependent, in substantial part, on the health and fitness of covered employees. . . .

We do not suggest, of course, that the interest in bodily security enjoyed by those employed in a regulated industry must always be considered minimal. Here, however, the covered employees have long been a principal focus of regulatory concern. As the dissenting judge below noted: "The reason is obvious. An idle locomotive, sitting in the round-house, is harmless. It becomes lethal when operated negligently by persons who are under the influence of alcohol or drugs." Though some of the privacy interests implicated by the toxicological testing at issue reasonably might be viewed as significant in other contexts, logic and history show that a diminished expectation of privacy attaches to information relating to the physical condition of covered employees and to this reasonable means of procuring such information. We conclude, therefore, that the testing procedures . . .pose only limited threats to the justifiable expectations of privacy of covered employees.

By contrast, the Government interest in testing without a showing of individualized suspicion is compelling. Employees subject to the tests discharge duties fraught with such risks of injury to others that even a momentary lapse of attention can have disastrous consequences. Much like persons who have routine access to dangerous nuclear power facilities, employees who are subject to testing under the FRA regulations can cause great human loss before any signs of impairment become noticeable to supervisors or others. . . .

While no procedure can identify all impaired employees with ease and perfect accuracy, the FRA regulations supply an effective means of deterring employees engaged in safety-sensitive tasks from using controlled substances or alcohol in the first place. The railroad industry's experience with Rule G persuasively shows, and common sense confirms, that the customary dismissal sanction that threatens employees who use drugs or alcohol while on duty cannot serve as an effective deterrent unless violators know that they are likely to be discovered. By ensuring that employees in safety-sensitive positions know they will be tested upon the occurrence of a triggering event, the timing of which no employee can predict with certainty, the regulations significantly increase the deterrent effect of the administrative penalties associated with the prohibited conduct, concomitantly increasing the likelihood that employees will forgo using drugs or alcohol while subject to being called for duty.

. . . .

. . . .In view of our conclusion that, on the present record, the toxicological testing contemplated by the regulations is not an undue infringement on the justifiable expectations of privacy of covered employees, the Government's compelling interests outweigh privacy concerns.

. . . .

JUSTICE MARSHALL, with whom JUSTICE BRENNAN joins, dissenting.

The issue in this case is not whether declaring a war on illegal drugs is good public policy. The importance of ridding our society of such drugs is, by now, apparent to all. Rather, the issue here is whether the Government's deployment in that war of a particularly Draconian weapon—the compulsory collection and chemical testing of railroad workers' blood and urine—comports with the Fourth Amendment. Precisely because the need for action against the drug scourge is manifest, the need for vigilance against unconstitutional excess is great. History teaches that grave threats to liberty often come in times of urgency, when constitutional rights seem too extravagant to endure. The World War II relocation-camp cases, *Hirabayashi v. United States,* 320 U.S. 81, 63 S.Ct. 1375, 87 L.Ed. 1774 (1943); *Korematsu v. United States,* 323 U.S. 214, 65 S.Ct. 193, 89 L.Ed. 194 (1944), and the Red scare and McCarthy-era internal subversion cases, *Schenck v. United States,* 249 U.S. 47, 39 S.Ct. 247, 63 L.Ed. 470 (1919); *Dennis v. United States,* 341 U.S. 494, 71 S.Ct. 857, 95 L.Ed. 1137 (1951), are only the most extreme reminders that when we allow fundamental freedoms to be sacrificed in the name of real or perceived exigency, we invariably come to regret it.

In permitting the Government to force entire railroad crews to submit to invasive blood and urine tests, even when it lacks any evidence of drug or alcohol use or other wrongdoing, the majority today joins those shortsighted courts which have allowed basic constitutional rights to fall prey to momentary emergencies. The majority holds that the need of the Federal Railroad Administration (FRA) to deter and diagnose train accidents outweighs any "minimal" intrusions on personal dignity and privacy posed by mass toxicological testing of persons who have given no indication whatsoever of impairment. In reaching this result, the majority ignores the text and doctrinal history of the Fourth Amendment, which require that highly intrusive searches of this type be based on probable cause, not on the evanescent cost-benefit calculations of agencies or judges. But the majority errs even under its own utilitarian standards, trivializing the raw intrusiveness of, and overlooking serious conceptual and operational flaws in, the FRA's testing program. These flaws cast grave doubts on whether that program, though born of good intentions, will do more than ineffectually symbolize the Government's opposition to drug use.

The majority purports to limit its decision to postaccident testing of workers in "safety-sensitive" jobs . . . But the damage done to the Fourth Amendment is not so easily cabined. The majority's acceptance of dragnet blood and urine testing ensures that the first, and worst, casualty of the war on drugs will be the precious liberties of our citizens. I therefore dissent.

. . . .

Consider how the issues addressed in *Skinner* translate to private employers. Most states have drug testing statutes that balance the employer's interest in having a "drug free workplace" with the employee's interest in not having intrusive testing. Generally, state statutes and regulations specify the circumstances under which an employer may require a drug test, procedures to be followed, and actions that may be taken in response. In California the state constitutional right of privacy is enforceable against employers, and so the courts must add a layer of analysis on top of the interpretation of drug testing laws.

KRASLAWSKY V. UPPER DECK CO.

56 Cal.App.4th 179 (1997).

HALLER, ASSOCIATE JUSTICE.

The Upper Deck Company terminated Janet Kraslawsky after Kraslawsky refused to take a urinalysis drug/alcohol test under Upper Deck's reasonable cause drug testing program. Kraslawsky sued Upper Deck, alleging Upper Deck violated her privacy rights under the California Constitution (Cal. Const. art. I, § 1), intentionally inflicted emotional distress, and wrongfully terminated her in violation of public policy. The trial court granted summary judgment in favor of Upper Deck on each of Kraslawsky's claims. Kraslawsky appeals.

Kraslawsky does not challenge the constitutionality of Upper Deck's suspicion-based testing program. Kraslawsky instead contends Upper Deck's demand that she submit to a urinalysis test violated her state constitutional right to privacy because Upper Deck did not have reasonable cause to believe she was intoxicated. Upper Deck counters that (1) the existence of reasonable cause is not relevant to the constitutional privacy analysis and (2) Kraslawsky did not proffer sufficient evidence to create a triable issue of fact on the reasonable cause issue.

. . . .

FACTUAL AND PROCEDURAL BACKGROUND

Upper Deck manufactures sports trading cards and sports memorabilia. In July 1991, Upper Deck interviewed Kraslawsky for an executive secretary position. Upper Deck notified Kraslawsky it would hire her if she underwent a medical examination and successfully completed a urine test for drugs and alcohol. During the ensuing medical examination, Kraslawsky voluntarily provided a urine sample and disclosed the prescription and non-prescription medications she was taking. The sample tested positive for a prescription medication. Kraslawsky later provided a doctor's note confirming the need for the medication.

Upper Deck then hired Kraslawsky as an executive secretary for company vice president and marketing director Anthony Loiacono. The personnel department gave Kraslawsky a copy of the Employee Handbook, which included a discussion of the company policy against alcohol and drug use in the workplace and the company's reasonable cause drug testing policy. The Handbook stated Upper Deck "may require an employee to submit to monitored tests whenever it has reasonable cause to believe that an employee is [under the influence of intoxicants]. . . . An employee's consent . . . to submission to tests is required as a condition of employment. An employee's refusal to consent when requested by [Upper Deck] may result in disciplinary action, including discharge, even for a first offense." Kraslawsky read the Handbook, and signed a form stating she agreed to abide by the stated policies.

Eight months later, on March 10, 1992 at approximately 4 p.m., an Upper Deck personnel employee requested that Kraslawsky drive to a medical facility and provide a urine sample for a drug test. Kraslawsky refused to take the test. Based on this refusal, Upper Deck terminated Kraslawsky.

On June 5, 1992, Kraslawsky brought an action against Upper Deck, alleging Upper Deck's demand that she submit to a drug test was made "without good cause or reason, and at random."

In March 1994, Upper Deck moved for summary judgment, relying on *Hill v. National Collegiate Athletic Assn.* (1994) 7 Cal.4th 1, 26 Cal.Rptr.2d 834, 865 P.2d 633. Upper Deck contended Kraslawsky could not recover on her privacy cause of action because Kraslawsky had no reasonable expectation of privacy, Kraslawsky consented to the "reasonable cause" drug test, and Upper Deck had a legitimate need to drug test its employees.

In support of its motion, Upper Deck proffered evidence showing that (1) Kraslawsky read and signed the Employee Handbook containing notice of the reasonable cause drug testing policy; (2) two Upper Deck managers personally observed Kraslawsky on March 10, 1992 and believed she was under the influence of intoxicants; (3) had Kraslawsky submitted to the test, her urination would not have been visually observed and the results would have been disclosed only to specified Upper Deck personnel; (4) Kraslawsky did not object to the preemployment urine test and at that time disclosed medications she was taking; and (5) Kraslawsky testified at a deposition that she did not believe the *procedure* involved in taking the test was intrusive.

Upper Deck also proffered the declaration of Brian Burr, an Upper Deck executive vice president of operations. Burr stated Upper Deck maintains a suspicion-based drug testing policy to (1) "further its interest in the efficient operation of its business and performance of its employees"; (2) reduce the risks of liability associated with employee drug or alcohol use; (3) ensure that its policies are "consistent with the drug and alcohol policies" of sporting organizations since "an image of being soft on drugs . . . would hinder its business in promoting competitive sports and sports stars"; (4) reduce the costs of health care premiums; and (5) ensure the health and safety of its employees. Burr stated Upper Deck does "not favor 'random' [drug] testing."

In opposition to the summary judgment motion, Kraslawsky contended she had a reasonable expectation of privacy and Upper Deck's asserted reasons for requiring the drug test were insufficient to overcome her privacy rights. Kraslawsky argued and presented evidence that Upper Deck did not have "reasonable cause" to believe she was under the influence of intoxicants. This evidence included Kraslawsky's declaration in which she denied that on March 10 she was intoxicated or acting as if she were intoxicated or that she exhibited the physical symptoms allegedly observed by the two Upper Deck managers. Kraslawsky also submitted deposition transcripts of the two managers who acknowledged they did not know what was wrong with Kraslawsky, never specifically believed she was under the influence of intoxicants, and had never received formal training on detecting substance abuse. Kraslawsky additionally proffered evidence that her job responsibilities were strictly secretarial and did not involve security or safety-related activities.

The court granted summary judgment in favor of Upper Deck. The court found the undisputed facts established Kraslawsky did not have a reasonable expectation of privacy because she "was on notice of the testing and consented to it" and Upper Deck's "testing procedures are suspicion-based and not random." The court also found the drug testing policy was not a "serious" invasion of Kraslawsky's privacy rights because the urine test was "unobserved" and "the results would be kept confidential." The court further determined Upper Deck's "legitimate and important countervailing interests in its drug testing policy outweigh any privacy interest plaintiff might have had . . . per the Burr Declaration." The court alternatively found Kraslawsky's consent to Upper Deck's reasonable cause drug testing policy was a "complete defense" to Kraslawsky's privacy claim. The court granted summary judgment on the wrongful termination and emotional distress claims because Kraslawsky could not establish an actionable invasion of privacy.

DISCUSSION

I. *Right of Privacy Under the State Constitution*

Kraslawsky contends the court erred in granting summary judgment on her claim that Upper Deck violated her privacy right under the California Constitution.

A. *Legal Principles*

Article I, section 1 of the California Constitution provides: "All people are by nature free and independent and have inalienable rights. Among these are enjoying and defending life and liberty, acquiring, possessing, and protecting property, and pursuing and obtaining safety, happiness, and *privacy.*" (Italics added.)

This provision "creates a right of action against private as well as government entities." (See *Hill v. National Collegiate Athletic Assn., supra,* 7 Cal.4th 1 (*Hill*).)

The California Supreme Court has recently addressed the validity of urinalysis drug testing under our state constitution in two decisions—*Loder v. City of Glendale* (1997) 14 Cal.4th 846, 59 Cal.Rptr.2d 696, 927 P.2d 1200 (*Loder*) and *Hill, supra,* 7 Cal.4th 1.

In *Hill,* the court articulated a test for evaluating whether a plaintiff has stated a cause of action for violation of privacy under the California Constitution. (*Hill, supra,* 7 Cal.4th at pp. 39–40.) The court stated a plaintiff has the burden to prove three elements: "(1) a legally protected privacy interest; (2) a reasonable expectation of privacy in the circumstances; and (3) conduct by defendant constituting a serious invasion of privacy." (*Ibid.*) A defendant may prevail by negating any of these three elements or by pleading and proving, as an affirmative defense, the invasion of privacy is justified because it substantively furthers one or more countervailing interests. (*Id.* at p. 40.)

The plaintiff in turn may rebut a defendant's assertion of countervailing interests by showing there are feasible and effective alternatives to defendant's conduct that have a lesser impact on privacy interests. (*Ibid.*)

Applying this analysis, *Hill* found the National Collegiate Athletic Association's (NCAA) visually monitored urinalysis testing program interferes with both autonomy privacy interests and informational privacy interests protected by the state constitution. (*Hill, supra,* 7 Cal.4th at pp. 40–41.) The court determined, however, that such interference was not unconstitutional, stressing that college athletes have substantially diminished expectations of privacy and the NCAA has legitimate and important interests in safeguarding the integrity of intercollegiate athletic competition and protecting the health and safety of student athletes. (*Id.* at pp. 41–54.)

Hill expressly declined to address the validity of drug testing conducted by an employer. (*Hill, supra,* 7 Cal.4th at p. 54.) Noting that "[e]mployment settings are diverse, complex, and very different from intercollegiate athletic competition," the court stated the "requirements . . . imposed on private employers by the California constitutional right to privacy will depend upon the application of the elements and considerations we have discussed to the employer's special interests and the employee's reasonable expectations prevailing in a particular employment setting." (*Id.* at pp. 54–55.)

Two years later, the California Supreme Court considered a facial challenge to a city employee drug testing program that tested job applicants and existing employees conditionally approved for a promotion. (*Loder, supra,* 14 Cal.4th 846.) The court issued five separate opinions . . . Although the justices expressed differing reasons for the conclusions, there was a majority for each of the results reached by the court—(1) five justices found the portion of the city drug testing program that tested *all job applicants conditionally approved for employment* was valid under the Fourth Amendment of the United States Constitution and under the California Constitution privacy clause and (2) four justices found the portion of the city drug testing program that tested *all existing employees conditionally approved for a promotion* was invalid under the Fourth Amendment of the United States Constitution. (See *id.* at p. 853, fn. 1.) The majority of the court reaffirmed the *Hill* test, but made clear that the primary focus of a state constitutional privacy claim in the employee drug testing context is a reasonableness balancing test—balancing the drug test's intrusion on the reasonable expectations of the employee against the drug test's promotion of the employer's legitimate interests. (*Loder, supra,* 14 Cal.4th at pp. 891–898; *id.* at p. 922 (conc. & dis. opn. of Chin, J.).)

II. *Analysis*

A. *The Existence of Reasonable Cause is Relevant to the Constitutional Analysis*

The thrust of Upper Deck's summary judgment and its appellate arguments is that its "*reasonable cause*" drug testing *program* is valid under the state constitutional privacy clause. However, as revealed in her complaint, Kraslawsky's invasion of privacy cause of action was not a facial challenge to Upper Deck's drug testing *program.* Rather, Kraslawsky claimed her privacy rights were violated by the manner in which the program was applied to her. Kraslawsky's complaint alleged "Upper Deck . . . *demanded without good cause or reason, and at random,* that plaintiff immediately submit to a drug test. . . . [S]uch action . . . constituted a violation of her constitutional rights to privacy." Consistent with this allegation, Kraslawsky sought to defeat Upper Deck's summary judgment motion by submitting evidence showing that Upper Deck had no reasonable cause for believing she was under the influence of drugs. Kraslawsky claimed that because reasonable cause did not exist, she was subjected to a random drug test, thereby violating her right of privacy.

Upper Deck does not attempt to argue that a *random* drug test would be consistent with the state constitution's privacy provision. Instead, Upper Deck maintains that the existence of reasonable cause is not relevant here because its reasonable cause *policy* was constitutional. Upper Deck thus contends that if an employer maintains a constitutionally valid suspicion-based testing policy, the fact that the suspicion did not actually exist does not matter.

We disagree. Under *Loder,* the constitutionality of a drug test under the California Constitution is evaluated by balancing the employee's reasonable expectation of privacy against the employer's legitimate interests in imposing the test. (*Loder, supra,* 14 Cal.4th at pp. 889–898.) In the absence of reasonable cause for a particular urinalysis request, the outcome of this balancing test may be different. If a drug test is not triggered by a reasonable belief the employee is intoxicated, the employee may have a stronger reason to expect to maintain his or her privacy and the employer may have less need to demand the test.

These principles apply with particular clarity in this case. Kraslawsky, an executive secretary whose job duties were neither safety nor security sensitive, had a substantial expectation that she would not be required to take a *random* drug test. As a condition of employment, she agreed to submit to suspicion-based testing; she was not asked and did not agree to random testing. In fact, Kraslawsky was given notice that such action would *not* occur. The Employee Handbook explicitly states that an employee may be asked to submit to a drug test based on "reasonable cause" to suspect the employee was violating the company's drug and alcohol policy. Based on the Handbook, Kraslawsky could reasonably infer that she would not be subjected to a random test. Further, there are no circumstances particular to Upper Deck's employment environment or Kraslawsky's job position that would have reduced Kraslawsky's expectations of privacy in the context of a random drug test.

By comparison, absent reasonable cause, Upper Deck's legitimate need to require the drug test was substantially reduced. Upper Deck's stated reasons for conducting employee drug tests were expressly premised on a reasonable cause program. Upper Deck admitted it did not use, nor favor, random testing. Additionally, there were other less intrusive ways Upper Deck could have satisfied its objective of ensuring a drug-free workplace, rather than imposing random drug tests on existing employees. (See *Loder, supra,* 14 Cal.4th at p. 883 ["[A]n employer generally need not resort to *suspicionless* drug testing to determine whether a current employee is likely to be absent from work or less productive or effective as a result of current drug or alcohol abuse. . . ."] (Italics added.).)

The Fourth Amendment decisions applying a similar balancing test do not support Upper Deck's position. In determining the constitutionality of a particular drug test demand (as opposed to a facial challenge), the federal courts regularly conduct a factual analysis as to the extent to which the employer had reasonable cause to require the test.

We are persuaded the issue of reasonable cause is relevant to determining the constitutionality of Upper Deck's drug test demand. A contrary holding would essentially give an employer with a constitutionally valid drug testing *policy* a free license to conduct random testing, regardless of the circumstances. This result would be inconsistent with the privacy rights protected by our state Constitution.

B. *Existence of Factual Issue as to Reasonable Cause*

Upper Deck argues alternatively that in moving for summary judgment it established the existence of reasonable cause and Kraslawsky's opposition failed to create a triable issue of fact on this issue. Reasonable cause connotes an objective standard. While the standard is not difficult to meet, it necessarily requires a showing of specific objective facts and rational inferences from those facts supporting the conclusion that an employee was under the influence of intoxicants. Thus, to prevail on its summary judgment motion, Upper Deck was required to establish undisputed facts creating an objective basis to believe Kraslawsky was under the influence of drugs or alcohol.

1. Summary Judgment Factual Record

To establish it had objectively reasonable cause to believe Kraslawsky was intoxicated, Upper Deck proffered evidence that two of its managers briefly observed Kraslawsky on the late afternoon of March 10 and suspected Kraslawsky was "under the influence of intoxicants." This evidence consisted of the deposition transcripts of Stephen E. Poludniak, an Upper Deck vice-president, and Sheri Clift, Upper Deck's personnel manager. These deposition transcripts established the following:

On the afternoon of March 10, 1992, Poludniak walked by Kraslawsky's desk and "saw her kind of slumped over" at a "45 degree angle" and "[k] ind of like with her elbows on her legs." Poludniak stood there for about 30 seconds, believing Kraslawsky was going to pick something up. When Kraslawsky did not sit back up, Poludniak asked whether everything was okay. Kraslawsky "kind of cranked her head to the right to look at [Poludniak] without moving up and said something again," without making eye contact. Poludniak could not understand what she said. Poludniak asked Kraslawsky where her boss was. Kraslawsky did not respond.

Poludniak then walked back into his office and called personnel director Clift. Poludniak told Clift he believed there was a "problem" with Kraslawsky. Poludniak was concerned Kraslawsky "may be having some sort of female problems and [he] wasn't exactly sure how to handle that." Poludniak said he didn't "know anything about medical stuff so I wasn't sure what I was actually seeing [but] at that time I kind of got this idea something was wrong physically with [Kraslawsky]."

Clift then spoke briefly with Kraslawsky. Clift observed that Kraslawsky's "speech was slurred, that her demeanor was lethargic, that she was swaying, that her eye contact was not there, that it seemed to be deliberate in the answers, it was very controlled and very deliberate." Kraslawsky denied drinking or being on medication. Clift said she "did not know what was wrong with [Kraslawsky] but I had a suspicion that there was something wrong, whether it was medication, whether it was alcohol, whatever, there was a suspicion that she was not acting like Jan Kraslawsky." When asked at her deposition whether she believed Kraslawsky was under the influence of alcohol, Clift responded "I did not know what influence she was under but I did have a suspicion that something was controlling her other than just being tired." Based on the foregoing, Clift and Poludniak made the decision to demand that Kraslawsky submit to a urinalysis drug test.

In opposing summary judgment, Kraslawsky refuted these facts by relying on her own declaration. Kraslawsky stated that when Poludniak first approached her on the afternoon of March 10, she was "sitting up in [her] chair reading some papers." In response to Poludniak's question, Kraslawsky told Poludniak her supervisor was in a meeting in the conference room and pointed to the room. Poludniak "nodded," and said " 'have him call me.' " Five minutes later, Clift told Kraslawsky to step into a nearby office and asked Kraslawsky a series of questions. Kraslawsky "answered all of the questions in [her] normal manner of speaking and indicated [she] felt fine." Five minutes later, at about 4 p.m., Clift's assistant told Kraslawsky to "go get a drug test and then come back to work." The drug lab was approximately ten to fifteen miles away. Kraslawsky was required to drive herself to the lab. Kraslawsky has never used illegal drugs, does not drink alcoholic beverages, was not under the influence of prescription medication or other drugs, and was not feeling ill or unusually tired.

Kraslawsky also submitted facts reflecting that Poludniak may have had ulterior motives in demanding the drug test. Approximately one week before he purportedly observed Kraslawsky "slumped over," Poludniak called a lunch meeting with all company executive secretaries. At the meeting, "Poludniak announced that all overtime pay for executive secretaries would cease immediately." Kraslawsky "spoke up in protest." Kraslawsky "said it was not fair that the company would require this of [her] and then not be willing to pay." Poludniak "did not respond, but became very red-faced and appeared upset." The next Monday, Kraslawsky stopped working overtime. Kraslawsky was terminated the next day.

Kraslawsky further relied on additional deposition transcripts of Poludniak and Clift, indicating that neither Clift nor Poludniak had formal training in detecting drug or alcohol use. In her deposition, Clift also admitted she never told Poludniak that she believed Kraslawsky was intoxicated or under the influence of drugs. Instead, after speaking with Kraslawsky, Clift "gave [Poludniak] [her] assessment of the situation and [she] came to the conclusion that [she] was concerned enough to want to find out what [the problem] was [by demanding that Kraslawsky submit to a drug test]."

2. Existence of Triable Issue of Fact

Upper Deck proffered evidence showing that Kraslawsky acted in an objectively intoxicated manner (Kraslawsky was bent over at her desk, her "speech was slurred," her demeanor was "lethargic," she was "swaying," "her eye contact was not there," and her speech was "very controlled and very deliberate"). In opposition, Kraslawsky submitted evidence that *directly contradicted these facts.* In her declaration, Kraslawsky expressly denied that she was bent over at her desk when Poludniak approached her. She said that when Poludniak "walked up to my work area and demanded to know the location of Mr. Loiacono[,] I was sitting up in my chair reading some papers. I looked up at Mr. Poludniak, motioned to a conference room and said '[h]e's in there.' " Kraslawsky also stated that she answered all of Clift's questions "in my normal manner of speaking and indicated I felt fine."

Upper Deck argues Kraslawsky's declaration is not "evidence of how others perceived her or how she appeared to others on March 10, 1992." (Italics deleted.) We disagree. Kraslawsky's description of her own conduct was competent to place the issue in dispute as to what occurred on the afternoon of March 10. If believed, Kraslawsky's statements negate the underlying facts used by Upper Deck to establish reasonable cause. While Kraslawsky's opposition would certainly have been stronger if she had proffered supporting evidence from other witnesses, a plaintiff need only create a material factual issue to defeat a summary judgment motion. Further, on the record before us, there was no evidence that anyone else saw Kraslawsky during the very brief period that Upper Deck contends she was acting intoxicated.

Contrary to Upper Deck's assertions, we are not suggesting that a plaintiff may defeat summary judgment merely by offering a declaration stating he or she was not in fact intoxicated. (See *Burton v. Security Pacific Nat. Bank* (1988) 197 Cal.App.3d 972, 979, 243 Cal.Rptr. 277.) Rather, the plaintiff must come forward with facts disputing that the employer had a reasonable basis to believe the employee was under the influence of drugs or alcohol. Kraslawsky's declaration created a factual issue as to whether there were any objective facts supporting Upper Deck's claims that Kraslawsky appeared intoxicated.

Further, Kraslawsky not only submitted her own declaration describing her conduct on the afternoon of March 10, but she also relied on additional facts supporting an inference that the objective circumstances did not establish reasonable cause to drug test. Kraslawsky proffered evidence of the recent executive secretary's meeting revealing a reason Poludniak would have wanted to create a pretext for terminating Kraslawsky. There was also evidence that neither Clift nor Poludniak believed Kraslawsky was intoxicated with drugs or alcohol. Poludniak thought Kraslawsky was having "female" or other unidentified "medical" problems; Clift vaguely thought "something was wrong" and believed a drug test would help identify what that was. The evidence also showed that Upper Deck had planned to permit Kraslawsky to drive alone to the medical facility and, when she refused to take the test, allowed Kraslawsky to drive 60 miles home. While such facts are not conclusive of the reasonable cause issue, they are relevant to the analysis and reasonably could support an inference that Upper Deck's drug test demand was random or pretextual, rather than based on objective individualized suspicion.

An employer must be given wide leeway in executing its reasonable cause drug testing policy. Such policy, however, cannot be used as a shield when there is credible evidence raising an inference that reasonable cause did not exist. Viewing the evidence in its entirety, we conclude a factual question exists as to whether Upper Deck had reasonable cause to believe Kraslawsky was under the influence of intoxicants. Accordingly, the evidence must be presented to a jury to determine (1) whether the objective factors Upper Deck contends existed did or did not exist; and (2) whether the objective factors found to exist constitute reasonable cause.

C. *Additional Arguments*

Upper Deck asserts a number of other reasons that Kraslawsky cannot prevail on her state constitutional privacy claim even if there was no reasonable cause for the drug test. We address these arguments briefly below.

Upper Deck first states that Kraslawsky had no reasonable expectation of privacy because the urinalysis test would not have been visually monitored.

Upper Deck argues that such "unobserved testing is not actionable under *Hill* because it is at most a slight, not serious, intrusion." (Italics deleted.) We do not read *Hill* so narrowly. Although *Hill* emphasized the NCAA's policy of direct observation of urination in finding that the invasion of privacy rights was "serious" (*Hill, supra,* 7 Cal.4th at p. 43), nothing in the opinion supports a blanket conclusion that a non-visually monitored drug test would be per se valid. In *Loder,* as here, the urinalysis test was monitored by a nurse listening for urination sounds outside the toilet area and employees were required to respond to a written inquiry concerning their current medications. (*Loder, supra,* 14 Cal.4th at pp. 854–855.) A majority of the justices found such monitoring sufficiently intruded on a nonsecurity/nonsafety-sensitive employee's privacy right so as to create an unconstitutional invasion of privacy under the Fourth Amendment. (See *Loder, supra,* at pp. 896–897; *id.* at p. 917, (conc. and dis. opn. of Mosk, J.); *id.* at p. 919 (conc. and dis. opn. of Kennard, J.).) We are not persuaded Upper Deck's testing procedure eliminates Kraslawsky's privacy claim under the California Constitution.

Upper Deck next argues Kraslawsky consented to the drug test. However, as explained above, this argument is supported only if there was reasonable cause for the test. There is no evidence Kraslawsky consented to a random drug test. Further, consent is generally viewed as a factor in the balancing analysis, and not as a complete defense to a privacy claim. (See *Loder, supra,* 14 Cal.4th at pp. 886–887, fn. 19; *American Federation of Labor v. Unemployment Ins. Appeals Bd.* (1994) 23 Cal.App.4th 51, 66, 28 Cal. Rptr.2d 210; but see *Loder, supra,* 14 Cal.4th at pp. 933–938 (conc. and dis. opn. of Brown, J.).)

Upper Deck additionally argues Kraslawsky had no reasonable expectation of privacy because she had already submitted to a preemployment drug test. This argument fails under *Loder.* A majority of the *Loder* court refused to hold an existing employee's prior applicant drug test was sufficient to eliminate the employee's reasonable expectations of privacy.

We additionally reject Upper Deck's argument that Kraslawsky agreed to continue to provide medical information to her employer. Upper Deck relies on portions of the Employee Handbook concerning the need for an employee to provide a doctor's note after a medical leave or illness and the procedures for a work-related injury. These provisions do not establish

Kraslawsky would have reasonably understood she had given up her privacy rights in connection with a drug test.

[Editor's Note: The Court held that the trial court properly granted summary judgment on the claim for intentional infliction of emotional distress, but that it erred in granting summary judgment on the wrongful termination claim.]

DISPOSITION

We reverse the summary judgment on Kraslawsky's state constitutional privacy and wrongful discharge claims . . .

QUESTIONS

1. At the time of the decision in *Kraslawsky* the Supreme Court of California had not determined whether random, suspicion-less drug testing of current employees violated the state constitutional right to privacy. Develop the arguments for both sides on the question.
2. After *Kraslawsky,* can an employee who is fired for refusing to take a drug test avoid summary judgment simply by signing an affidavit that says she was not under the influence of drugs at the time?

Class Exercise 18-1

The *Skinner* and *Kraslawsky* cases provide a constitutional analysis weighing the respective interests of the parties. Draw on these principles to develop a statutory scheme for a state that does not have a constitutional right of privacy, but which wants to balance the interests of the employer, employee and society.

A significant issue has arisen in states that have legalized medical cannabis. If an employer in the state were testing workers for off-site cannabis use and taking action in response, it would appear to interfere with the employee's medical care. Some states, such as California, have deferred to the employer's decision about employing medical cannabis patients. California Health and Safety Code § 11362.45 provides that the state legalization of marijuana does not affect the right of employers to maintain a drug-free workplace nor does it require employers to accommodate medical cannabis use by their employees on their own time. Other states have prohibited employers from discriminating against employees who use cannabis for medical purposes. For example, Connecticut Gen. Stat., Ch. 420f § 21A 408p (3) provides that an employer cannot refuse to hire, discharge, penalize or threaten a person based on their status as a qualified medical marijuana user. The provision does not prohibit an employer from prohibiting the use of intoxicating substances or from discharging an employee who is under the influence of cannabis or other drugs in the workplace.

3. Data Analytics

Employers have an interest in monitoring their employees' work activity and productivity levels. Employees have a lesser expectation of privacy concerning data analytics because employers are allowed to supervise their employees to make sure they are performing satisfactorily in the workplace. Data analytics is the process of refining data from a variety of sources, including social media, metadata, reviews, sales trends, and hiring trends, in a way that allows employers to make accurate predictions. In the workplace context, it can be used to make decisions around hiring and firing, retention, and training effectiveness.

Bank of America, for example, struggled to keep employees in its call centers because of the high-stress environment for center operators. The company analyzed data surrounding the environments at each of its call centers and discovered that low turnover coincided with interoffice collaboration. That is, the more people talked to each other, the lower the turnover rate. Bank of America used the information to change its break policy to allow teams to take breaks together and to overlap their lunches. This resulted in an increase in employee interactions, a boost in productivity, and a lower turnover rate.

Privacy concerns are raised, however, when the method for monitoring the factors that influence an employee's productivity becomes more invasive. For example, certain programs can measure the amount of keystrokes an employee uses on their keyboard during a given time period. These methods for gathering data for analytics purposes can become increasingly intrusive.

Opponents of data analytics in the workplace argue that they can have detrimental effects on employees such as lowering employee morale, and causing depression and anxiety. Moreover, such close monitoring has contributed to higher turnover rates of employment. Historically, employees being able to exert control over their own work has been crucial to an employee's sense of personal dignity.

Problem 18-2

The Bank of America example above demonstrates the advantages of data analytics. Develop a policy that informs employees of the company's use of data analytics in its productivity analyses.

---

4. Wellness Programs

Wellness programs are employer-sponsored programs that aim to improve the employee's health and well-being. These programs take many forms, including: company sponsored exercise, educational seminars, weight loss competitions, smoking cessation challenges, stress management, and other team exercises. Ideally, wellness programs will improve employee productivity and overall morale leading to a happier, healthier workforce. The health benefits of wellness programs may also affect operating costs as such programs may help lower insurance expenses. On the other hand, many employees may resent this intrusion on their privacy and the "big brother" aspect of the program.

Problem 18-3

Joe Castle, an employee at BigBox, a retail department store, had an accident after he crashed a small forklift into a wall in the store's warehouse. Joe went to the hospital and was placed on medical leave for two weeks. Immediately upon his return, the BigBox human resources department administered a post-accident drug test and found marijuana in his system. Joe said his doctors prescribed marijuana for pain, which was legal in the state. Joe was fired. He sued BigBox claiming invasion of privacy for administering the post-employment drug test and for firing him even though the marijuana was medically prescribed. Does Joe have a viable claim?

Mastery Problem 18-1

Several companies are marketing data analytics software for the health management of large populations. One such company is Advance Health Data (AHD), which uses data analytics to predict health plan costs based on plan participant profiles. AHD's product is so sophisticated it can make predictions about when certain health events, such as emergency room visits, are likely to occur and the nature of the health problem. It can also predict the likelihood of hospital admissions and re-admissions. The software analyzes data from claims, pharmacy and clinical sources, comparing it to real-world health data adjusted for comparable demographics, geography and industry of the employer. It can assign risk scores to employees, and identify those with elevated risk of health problems. The technology can also be used to help prevent or put off more adverse and expensive health events.

1. Can an employee be required to participate in the program?
2. Can an employer use the analytics program to encourage employee participation in return for lower health insurance costs, or to provide incentives that steer participants toward healthier behaviors or to get care sooner and less expensively?
3. Analyze the potential issues raised by implementing AHD's product in the workplace under common law privacy laws and GINA.

Conclusion

Balancing the employee's right to privacy and the employer's interest in maximizing the efficiency of its workplace is more difficult in the modern era, where technology has enabled unprecedented means of gathering data and motivating behavior. In this Lesson, you studied several discrete areas in which this conflict is manifest in order to reinforce the general themes. It is clear that these issues will continue to grow in importance in coming years.

B. Employee Expression

Key Concepts

- Most employees intuitively understand that the First Amendment stops at the factory gates for private employers, but public employers are bound by the First Amendment.
- Communications in the workplace intended to promote collective action may be protected by federal labor law.
- Communications that are intended to bring to light illegal activity are often protected by so-called "whistleblower" statutes.
- When employees speak in furtherance of a statutory purpose, such as by protesting violations of civil rights laws in the workplace, they are often protected from retaliation by courts even if the statutes do not grant a private right of action.

Lesson 19:
Employee Speech in the Public Workplace

Objective and Learning Outcomes

In this Lesson, you will learn how to identify and analyze claims based on the exercise of free speech rights in the workplace. Employees of a public employer have free speech rights under the First Amendment to the United States Constitution, and public employers may not take adverse actions based on the exercise of these rights. You will learn that only speech regarding a matter of public concern is protected. Finally, you will learn about the potential for protection of the exercise of free speech rights when the matters are unrelated to the public employee's employment.

Unlike private employers, public employers are prohibited from retaliating against employees who exercise their First Amendment right to speak on a matter of public concern. There is no general right to free speech in the workplace because the federal Constitution only forbids retaliation by government entities, not retaliation by private employers.

The public employee's right to speak without fear of retaliation is limited. First, the Constitution only protects employees from retaliation when they speak about matters of public concern, not matters that are only of private interest. As a refinement of this point, an employee speaking on a matter of public interest may not be protected by the Constitution if the employee is motivated in part by his or her personal interests. Moreover, even if the employee speaks out on a matter of public concern, courts will balance the employee's First Amendment rights with the governmental interest in effectively managing the governmental workplace. Finally, an employee is not protected from retaliation when the employee speaks as part of her job duties, even if the employee is speaking on a matter that concerns the public.

Courts impose liability when the public employer is motivated to limit public discourse. Thus, the employer will not be liable if it reasonably believes that the employee was speaking about personal matters rather than matters of public concern. On the other hand, this rule works to the employee's advantage if the public employer erroneously, but reasonably, believes that the employee engaged in protected speech/expression and then retaliated.

Finally, when a public employee speaks or writes on his own time on topics unrelated to his employment, the speech is protected against government retaliation absent some governmental justification far stronger than mere speculation of harm to the government. Nonetheless, there will be occasions when a governmental employer may impose certain restraints or take certain employment actions that will restrain the public employee's First Amendment rights, even when such actions would be unconstitutional if applied to a member of the general public.

These complex themes are explored in this Lesson by breaking down the elements of a public employee's claim to First Amendment protection.

1. Matters of Public Interest

A public employee's speech is constitutionally protected only if it relates to a matter of public concern. One way to think of this distinction is to ask if the employee is speaking in her capacity as a citizen, or merely as a self-interested employee talking about her workplace conditions. This requirement requires courts to carefully weigh a variety of factors to make the determination that the speech relates to a matter of public interest. You should first read the following three problems, and then read the cases that follow to develop the resources to respond to the problems.

Problem 19-1

A police officer posts a comment on his Facebook page criticizing what he views as a misguided general Department Policy of hiring police officers with minimal experience. A fellow officer comments on the post:

> Perfect example. . .and you know who I'm talking about . . .How can anyone look up to, or give respect to, a Sgt. on patrol with only one year of experience. . .It's a lawsuit waiting to happen. I'm a police vet who tried telling and warning the administration. . .that the young rookie was too inexperienced for that role. . .

Can the Police Department take action against this use of social media by the two officers?

Problem 19-2

A public employee does not believe that his employer is adhering to the City's workplace smoking ban. The City passed the ban because of its concerns that its citizens would inhale second hand smoke. The ban was controversial and generated substantial media coverage due to intense public interest. He is a jogger and does not like to inhale smoke. He complained to his supervisors and asked to be moved to a different office where he would not be exposed to second hand smoke. As a result, for the first time in his career, he was given several out-of-town assignments to remote parts of the state.

Has the City violated his free speech rights?

Problem 19-3

A police officer posts on his Facebook page that he believes his department is promoting "rookie" cops to supervisory positions too quickly, and that doing so endangers the lives of fellow police officers. He suggests that this practice is a function of a world that encourages instant gratification and adheres to political correctness. Two other officers "Liked" the post. Another officer chimed in that this practice of early promotions was a "lawsuit waiting to happen." He further stated that "the police department is only as good as its leaders", but "that it's hard to lead by example when there is no leader."

All officers were disciplined pursuant to a policy that stated, in part: "Negative comments regarding the internal operations of the police force, or specific conduct of supervisors or peers that impacts the public's perception of the department, is not protected by the First Amendment free speech clause, in accordance with established law." The policy goes on to state that officers may comment on matters of general or public concern provided that the comments do not lead to interference with working relationships or to the efficient conduct of work.

Does this policy survive challenge under the First Amendment?

Coomes v. Edmonds Sch. Dist. No. 15

816 F.3d 1255 (9th Cir. 2016).

O'Scannlain, Judge.

We must decide whether a public school teacher speaks as an employee or a private citizen when she voices concerns about the school's special education program to her supervisors and her students' parents.

I

Tristan Coomes worked for four years at Meadowdale Middle School ("Meadowdale"), in Edmonds School District ("District"), as the manager of the school's new Emotional/Behavioral Disorders ("EBD") program and the primary teacher for students in the program.

. . . .

In March 2010, Coomes sent Andi Nofziger, her union representative, and Debby Carter, a District human resources manager, an email complaining about treatment by Meadowdale administrators, including [the principal]. Coomes noted that she had expressed concerns that EBD students who were ready to move to mainstream classes were not moved or had moves delayed based on improper financial considerations. Coomes forwarded the email to a group of other Meadowdale teachers, and the email chain was then forwarded to [the Principal] in April 2010.

The Principal forwarded the email chain to District administrators, stating that it contained false accusations and that she hoped the District would "take a very strong position in stopping this behavior." . . . .

Then, during the next school year, the EBD program experienced a significant change. EBD students were placed in more "mainstream" academic classes than in past years as part of "a concerted effort to move the EBD program from a self-contained model to a more inclusive . . . model." Coomes objected to this change when it was originally proposed. She sent [the principal] an email stating that she thought that new students who had been in self-contained classrooms for sixth grade should start the year in her EBD classroom full time so she could get to know their needs and help them adjust to the new school setting.

. . . .

"[P]ublic employees do not surrender all their First Amendment rights by reason of their employment." *Garcetti v. Ceballos,* 547 U.S. 410, 417, 126 S.Ct. 1951, 164 L.Ed.2d 689 (2006). "Rather, the First Amendment protects a public employee's right, in certain circumstances, to speak as a citizen addressing matters of public concern." *Id.* While the protection of government employee speech serves both the individual's interest and "the public's interest in receiving the well-informed views of government employees engaging in civic discussion," the public interest is also served by "respect [ing] the needs of government employers attempting to perform their important public functions." *See id.* at 419–20, 126 S.Ct. 1951. As such, "while the First Amendment invests public employees with certain rights, it does not empower them to 'constitutionalize the employee grievance.' " *Id.* at 420 (quoting *Connick v. Myers,* 461 U.S. 138, 154, 103 S.Ct. 1684, 75 L.Ed.2d 708 (1983)).

Rules

. . . .

. . . .We are guided by ample precedent. The First Amendment does not protect speech by public employees that is made pursuant to their employment responsibilities—no matter how much a matter of public concern it might be. *See Garcetti,* 547 U.S. at 423–24, 126 S.Ct. 1951. In *Garcetti,* the Court explained "that when public employees make statements pursuant to their official duties, the employees are not speaking as citizens for First Amendment purposes, and the Constitution does not insulate their communications from employer discipline." *Id.* at 421. Consequently, "[r]estricting speech that owes its existence to a public employee's professional responsibilities does not infringe any liberties the employee might have enjoyed as a private citizen." *Id.* at 421–22.

The Supreme Court recently emphasized in *Lane v. Franks* that the "mere fact that a citizen's speech concerns information acquired by virtue of his public employment does not transform that speech into employee—rather than citizen—speech." 134 S.Ct. 2369, 2379, 189 L.Ed.2d 312 (2014). Instead, the "critical question under *Garcetti* is whether the speech at issue is itself ordinarily within the scope of an employee's duties, not whether it merely concerns those duties." *Id.* Thus, to the extent that Coomes's speech was within the scope of her employment duties, such speech is not protected by the First Amendment.

. . . .

Based on the job description and declaration, the district court concluded that "it was part of Coomes's job as the IEP manager and a member of the IEP team to point out failures to abide by IEPs" and that "it was part of Coomes's job as the EBD teacher to communicate with administrators and parents about her views on the placement and progress of EBD students and appropriate management of the EBD program." As discussed above, Coomes has not identified sufficient record evidence to demonstrate that an issue of fact exists with respect to the scope of her duties.

. . . .

Coomes also spoke to parents—clearly outside of her chain of command. However, communicating with parents about students' IEPs and their progress in the EBD program was part and parcel of Coomes's job. Coomes's own declaration repeatedly emphasizes that her responsibilities included collaborating with parents and encouraging parent involvement in the IEP process. Indeed, one of her complaints about the District's activity was that it interfered with the collaboration with parents that was part of her job. In an email from Coomes to Webster—relating Coomes's discussions with parents regarding their children's classroom placements—Coomes implied she did not agree with the placement choices being made, but also indicated that she believed communicating with parents regarding placement choices was part of her job. Coomes even stated in one of her emails to Avery that "[a]s case manager, *it is my role* to talk with parents about developments at school." (emphasis added). In her own self-assessment, Coomes stated that she believed she had been successful in fulfilling her responsibility to communicate with students' parents and guardians . . . .

. . . .

We therefore conclude that Coomes's speech to parents was within the scope of her duties and is not protected by the First Amendment.

MATTHEWS V. CITY OF NEW YORK

779 F.3d 167 (2d Cir. 2015).

WALKER, JUDGE.

Officer Craig Matthews brought suit alleging that the City of New York retaliated against him for speaking to his commanding officers about an arrest quota policy at his precinct of the New York City Police Department ("NYPD"). The United States District Court for the Southern District of New York (Paul A. Engelmayer, *Judge*) granted the defendants' motion for summary judgment, holding that Matthews spoke as a public employee, not as a citizen, and that his speech was thus not protected by the First Amendment. We conclude that because Matthews's comments on precinct policy did not fall within his official duties . . . he spoke as a citizen. Accordingly, we VACATE the district court's grant of summary judgment and REMAND for further proceedings consistent with this opinion.

BACKGROUND

I. Matthews's Speech about the Quota System

Since 1999, Craig Matthews, an NYPD police officer, has been assigned to the 42nd Precinct ("the Precinct") in the Bronx. He alleges that, starting in 2008, unnamed supervisors in the Precinct implemented a quota system mandating the number of arrests, summons, and stop-and-frisks that police officers must conduct. Matthews also alleges that Lieutenant Mark Sedran "refined the quota system" by creating a point system that awarded points to police officers for issuing what Sedran considered " 'good' summonses" and subtracted points for less desirable summonses. Compl. ¶ 18, Joint App'x 25. Matthews alleges that officers were under pressure to comply with the quota system.

In February 2009, Matthews, believing that the quota system was damaging to the NYPD's core mission, reported its existence to then-Captain Timothy Bugge, the Precinct's commanding officer at that time. In March and April of 2009, Matthews again reported the quota system's existence to Captain Bugge, and, in May 2009, Matthews reported the same to an unnamed Precinct executive officer.

In January 2011, Matthews met with then-Captain Jon Bloch, the Precinct's new commanding officer, and two other officers in Captain Bloch's office. Matthews told them about the quota system and stated that it was "causing unjustified stops, arrests, and summonses because police officers felt forced to abandon their discretion in order to meet their numbers," and that it "was having an adverse effect on the precinct's relationship with the community."

> *[Editor's Note: The alleged acts of retaliation for speaking about the quota system included punitive assignments, the denial of overtime and leave, separation from his career-long partner, negative evaluations, and abusive treatment.]*

. . . .

III. Matthews's Employment Duties

Matthews stated in an affidavit that the vast majority of his time as a police officer is spent:

> (1) going on radio runs, which are responses to 911 calls in the precinct, in addition to '311' requests, and requests that come through the station house telephone switchboard, (2) patrolling the streets and vertical patrolling of local housing, (3) filling out complaint reports and additional forms relating to criminal activity, lost property, and missing persons, including interviewing witnesses, (4) responding to traffic accidents, (5) transporting prisoners to and from the precinct house, courts, and hospitals, and (6) doing community visits with local businesses and organizations.

. . . .

DISCUSSION

. . . .

II. Legal Framework

A plaintiff asserting a First Amendment retaliation claim must establish that: "(1) his speech or conduct was protected by the First Amendment; (2) the defendant took an adverse action against him; and (3) there was a causal connection between this adverse action and the protected speech." *Cox v. Warwick Valley Cent. School Dist.*, 654 F.3d 267, 272 (2d Cir. 2011). The district court granted summary judgment to the defendants on the basis that Matthews's speech was not protected. We address only that issue.

A court conducts a two-step inquiry to determine whether a public employee's speech is protected: "The first requires determining whether the employee spoke as a citizen on a matter of public concern." *Garcetti v. Ceballos,* 547 U.S. 410, 418, 126 S.Ct. 1951, 164 L.Ed.2d 689 (2006) (citing *Pickering v. Bd. of Educ. of Twp. High Sch. Dist. 205, Will Cnty.*, 391 U.S. 563, 568, 88 S.Ct. 1731, 20 L.Ed.2d 811 (1968)). This step one inquiry in turn encompasses two separate subquestions: "(1) whether the subject of the employee's speech was a matter of public concern and (2) whether the employee spoke 'as a citizen' rather than solely as an employee." *Jackler v. Byrne,* 658 F.3d 225, 235 (2d Cir. 2011) (citing *Garcetti,* 547 U.S. at 420–22). If the answer to either question is no, that is the end of the matter. If, however, both questions are answered in the affirmative, the court then proceeds to the second step of the inquiry, commonly referred to as the *Pickering* analysis: whether the relevant government entity "had an adequate justification for treating the employee differently from any other member of the public based on the government's needs as an employer." *Lane v. Franks*, 134 S.Ct. 2369, 2380, 189 L.Ed.2d 312 (quoting *Garcetti,* 547 U.S. at 418); *see also Pickering,* 391 U.S. at 568.

. . . .

III. The Citizen/Employee Distinction

The Supreme Court has recognized a tension in public employment free speech cases between an employee's First Amendment rights and the "common sense realization that government offices could not function if every employment decision became a constitutional matter." *Connick v. Myers,* 461 U.S. 138, 143, 103 S.Ct. 1684, 75 L.Ed.2d 708 (1983). "The problem in any case is to arrive at a balance between the interests of the [employee], as a citizen, in commenting upon matters of public concern and the interest of the State, as an employer, in promoting the efficiency of the public services it performs through its employees." *Pickering,* 391 U.S. at 568.

Guided by the Supreme Court's decision in *Garcetti,* we ask two questions to determine whether a public employee speaks as a citizen: (A) did the speech fall outside of the employee's "official responsibilities," and (B) does a civilian analogue exist? *See Weintraub v. Bd. of Educ. of City Sch. Distr. of City of N.Y.,* 593 F.3d 196, 203–04 (2d Cir. 2010).

A. Official Duties

"[W]hen public employees make statements pursuant to their official duties, the employees are not speaking as citizens for First Amendment purposes." *Garcetti,* 547 U.S. at 421. Accordingly, we have held that speech is not protected if it is "part-and-parcel of [the employee's] concerns about his ability to properly execute his duties." *Weintraub,* 593 F.3d at 203 (internal quotation marks omitted).

In *Garcetti,* the Supreme Court adopted a functional approach toward evaluating an employee's job duties. There, a deputy district attorney alleged that he had been retaliated against for writing a memorandum recommending that a case be dismissed. The Supreme Court held that the prosecutor's memorandum to his superior was unprotected because it was "part of what [the speaker] . . . was employed to do." *Garcetti,* 547 U.S. at 421. The "controlling factor" in its decision, the Court noted, was that the employee's "expressions were made pursuant to his duties as a calendar deputy." *Id.* The Court counseled that the appropriate inquiry is a "practical one" directed to the regular duties of the employee. *Id.* at 424. While relevant to that inquiry, the Court cautioned, "[f]ormal job descriptions often bear little resemblance to the duties an employee actually is expected to perform" and "the listing of a given task in an employee's written job description is neither necessary nor sufficient to demonstrate that conducting the task is within the scope of the employee's professional duties for First Amendment purposes." *Id.* at 424–25.

. . . .

. . . .Captain Bugge also testified that Matthews neither met regularly with the Captains nor submitted regular reports to them. Apart from the occasions on which Matthews spoke to them about the quota system, he did not communicate with the Precinct's commanding officers beyond occasional hallway small talk. In sum, Matthews's actual, functional job responsibilities did not include reporting his opinions on precinct-wide quota systems to the Precinct commanders.

B. Civilian Analogue

. . . .

. . . .The channel Matthews chose to address concerns about the quota system [was available to all citizens, and] thus reinforces our conclusion that Matthews spoke as a citizen, not as a public employee. [Members of the community also spoke to the Precinct head about the quota system].

. . . .

QUESTIONS

1. What if Coomes made her comments at a PTA meeting and not solely to the parents of her students? What would you need to know to determine if protected speech is present?
2. The *Matthews* court talks in terms of "functional" job duties. Why? Shouldn't a job description be the best evidence of the employee's duties? Would the court need evidence of his job duties beyond what Matthews' testimony establishes?
3. Assume that you are representing Coomes before she gets into her tussle with her employer. How do you advise her with regard to framing her statement? What facts would need to be different for the statement by Coomes to be protected?

2. Protection for Speech That Is Unrelated to Employment

Public employees are also citizens and members of their communities. They have a civil right to engage in discourse relating to matters of public concern, especially if the communication is not directly related to their employment duties. Balancing these factors can be difficult, as the next case demonstrates.

San Diego v. Roe

543 U.S. 77 (2004).

Per Curiam.

The city of San Diego (City), a petitioner here, terminated a police officer, respondent, for selling videotapes he made and for related activity. The tapes showed respondent engaging in sexually explicit acts. Respondent brought suit alleging, among other things, that the termination violated his First and Fourteenth Amendment rights to freedom of speech. The United States District Court for the Southern District of California granted the City's motion to dismiss. The Court of Appeals for the Ninth Circuit reversed.

The petition for a writ of certiorari is granted, and the judgment of the Court of Appeals is reversed.

I

Facts

Respondent John Roe, a San Diego police officer, made a video showing himself stripping off a police uniform and masturbating. He sold the video on the adults-only section of eBay, the popular online auction site. His username was "Code3stud@aol.com," a wordplay on a high priority police radio call. The uniform apparently was not the specific uniform worn by the San Diego police, but it was clearly identifiable as a police uniform. Roe also sold custom videos, as well as police equipment, including official uniforms of the San Diego Police Department (SDPD), and various other items such as men's underwear. Roe's eBay user profile identified him as employed in the field of law enforcement.

Investigation

Roe's supervisor, a police sergeant, discovered Roe's activities when, while on eBay, he came across an official SDPD police uniform for sale offered by an individual with the username "Code3stud@aol.com." He searched for other items Code3stud offered and discovered listings for Roe's videos depicting the objectionable material. Recognizing Roe's picture, the sergeant printed images of certain of Roe's offerings and shared them with others in Roe's chain of command, including a police captain. The captain notified the SDPD's internal affairs department, which began an investigation. In response to a request by an undercover officer, Roe produced a custom video. It showed Roe, again in police uniform, issuing a traffic citation but revoking it after undoing the uniform and masturbating.

The investigation revealed that Roe's conduct violated specific SDPD policies, including conduct unbecoming of an officer, outside employment, and immoral conduct. When confronted, Roe admitted to selling the videos and police paraphernalia. The SDPD ordered Roe to "cease displaying, manufacturing, distributing or selling any sexually explicit materials or engaging in any similar behaviors, via the internet, U.S. Mail, commercial vendors or distributors, or any other medium available to the public." Although Roe removed some of the items he had offered for sale, he did not change his seller's profile, which described the first two videos he had produced and listed their prices as well as the prices for custom videos. After discovering Roe's failure to follow its orders, the SDPD-citing Roe for the added violation of disobedience of lawful orders-began termination proceedings. The proceedings resulted in Roe's dismissal from the police force.

. . . .

. . . .In granting the City's motion to dismiss, the District Court decided that Roe had not demonstrated that selling official police uniforms and producing, marketing, and selling sexually explicit videos for profit qualified as expression relating to a matter of "public concern" under this Court's decision in *Connick v. Myers*, 461 U.S. 138, 103 S.Ct. 1684, 75 L.Ed.2d 708 (1983).

In reversing, the Court of Appeals held Roe's conduct fell within the protected category of citizen commentary on matters of public concern. Central to the Court of Appeals' conclusion was that Roe's expression was not an internal workplace grievance, took place while he was off duty and away from his employer's premises, and was unrelated to his employment.

. . . .

The Court of Appeals noted the City conceded Roe's activities were "unrelated" to his employment. In the context of the pleadings and arguments, the proper interpretation of the City's statement is simply to underscore the obvious proposition that Roe's speech was not a comment on the workings or functioning of the SDPD. It is quite a different question whether the speech was detrimental to the SDPD. On that score the City's consistent position has been that the speech is contrary to its regulations and harmful to the proper functioning of the police force. The present case falls outside the protection afforded in *NTEU*. The authorities that instead control, and which are considered below, are this Court's decisions in *Pickering*, *supra*, *Connick*, and the decisions which follow them.

. . . .

Although the boundaries of the public concern test are not well defined, *Connick* provides some guidance. It directs courts to examine the "content, form, and context of a given statement, as revealed by the whole record" in assessing whether an employee's speech addresses a matter of public concern. *Id.*, at 146–147, 103 S.Ct. 1684. In addition, it notes that the standard for determining whether expression is of public concern is the same standard used to determine whether a common-law action for invasion of privacy is present. *Id.*, at 143, n. 5, 103 S.Ct. 1684. That standard is established by our decisions in *Cox Broadcasting Corp. v. Cohn*, 420 U.S. 469, 95 S.Ct. 1029, 43 L.Ed.2d 328 (1975), and *Time, Inc. v. Hill*, 385 U.S. 374, 387–388, 87 S.Ct. 534, 17 L.Ed.2d 456 (1967). These cases make clear that public concern is something that is a subject of legitimate news interest; that is, a subject of general interest and of value and concern to the public at the time of publication. The Court has also recognized that certain private remarks, such as negative comments about the President of the United States, touch on matters of public concern and should thus be subject to *Pickering* balancing. See *Rankin v. McPherson*, 483 U.S. 378, 107 S.Ct. 2891, 97 L.Ed.2d 315 (1987).

public concern standard

Applying these principles to the instant case, there is no difficulty in concluding that Roe's expression does not qualify as a matter of public concern under any view of the public concern test. He fails the threshold test and *Pickering* balancing does not come into play.

Connick is controlling precedent, but to show why this is not a close case it is instructive to note that even under the view expressed by the dissent in *Connick* from four Members of the Court, the speech here would not come within the definition of a matter of public concern. The dissent in *Connick* would have held that the entirety of the questionnaire circulated by the employee "discussed subjects that could reasonably be expected to be of interest to persons seeking to develop informed opinions about the manner in which . . . an elected official charged with managing a vital governmental agency, discharges his responsibilities." 461 U.S., at 163, 103 S.Ct. 1684 (opinion of Brennan, J.). No similar purpose could be attributed to the employee's speech in the present case. Roe's activities did nothing to inform the public about any aspect of the SDPD's functioning or operation. Nor were Roe's activities anything like the private remarks at issue in *Rankin*, where one co-worker commented to another co-worker on an item of political news.

Roe's expression was widely broadcast, linked to his official status as a police officer, and designed to exploit his employer's image.

The speech in question was detrimental to the mission and functions of the employer. There is no basis for finding that it was of concern to the community as the Court's cases have understood that term in the context of restrictions by governmental entities on the speech of their employees.

The judgment of the Court of Appeals is

Reversed.

Mastery Problem 19-1

Joe Smith is a firefighter. He is married to Lola Smith. In order to supplement his income, they started a website showing them engaged in sexual acts. To gain access to the website, it is necessary to subscribe and pay a fee. Joe and Lola sold videos through the mail, and also appeared at "meet and greet parties" where their subscribers could meet them. They did not use any firefighter equipment in their activities, nor did they suggest that Joe was a firefighter. Ultimately the Fire Department learned of these activities and ordered Joe to immediately stop. A short time later the news media learned of the website and began an investigation. Some firefighters expressed to management that the media attention was making it harder for them to do their jobs, and that morale was poor. As a general rule, however, there was no internal disruption of daily operations in the firehouse. However, the department received numerous emails and letters from citizens unhappy with their tax dollars being used for the salary of a moral degenerate such as Joe. Ultimately, Joe is terminated for violating a department rule prohibiting an employee from injuring the city's reputation.

Is this a violation of Joe's rights? Would your answer change if Joe was terminated because he lied to fire department investigators who were assigned to investigate his creation of the website? Is this case different from *Roe*? Do the factual differences make a legal difference in your analysis?

Mastery Problem 19-2

Five employees work at a counseling center that is part of a larger medical facility. The center and facility are state owned, and managed by Dr. Smith. The staff became dissatisfied with Dr. Smith's leadership. Dr. Adams filed a written complaint with the HR department complaining that she was being discriminated against because of race and age. Subsequently, Dr. Brim and Dr. Cain submitted a formal memorandum of concern to Dr. Smith's supervisor and delivered copies to that person's superior as well as the Office of Legal Affairs. They alleged that Dr. Smith's lack of leadership adversely impacted client care, and ultimately prevented medical staff from being effective employees. The memorandum also listed five areas of particular concern:

1. Dr. Smith's deficient knowledge of drug therapy
2. Dr. Smith's failure to maintain positive interpersonal relationships, which often required staff to intercede to smooth over work relationships
3. Dr. Smith's odd behavior, including emotional outbursts
4. Dr. Smith's suggestion that two staff members testify in a license revocation hearing in a manner that is favorable to the medical center
5. Dr. Smith's discrimination against staff members of color

The staff doctors asked for an investigation. The investigation found no offenses, and concluded that the staff resisted Dr. Smith's leadership because his style was autocratic while the former director's was collaborative. Two months after completion of the report, all staff members were terminated in a layoff.

Do the terminated staff members have a claim against the facility? Would it make a difference in the analysis if the report confirmed some or all of the allegations made?

Conclusion

The government is subject to First Amendment protections in its capacity as an employer with regard to speech by employees on a matter of public concern and not of a personal nature. Even when employee speech regards a matter of public concern, the courts balance the employee's right to speak with the government interest in managing the workplace.

Lesson 20:
Protected Concerted Activity in the Nonunion Workplace

Objectives and Expected Learning Outcomes

In this Lesson, you will study the right of employees—in both the public and private sector—to join together to speak out on shared concerns about working conditions. You will learn the elements of "concerted activity" that triggers protection under the National Labor Relations Act. In particular, you will develop an understanding of the rationale for protecting speech only when it addresses a shared concern. Finally, you will learn that communications that are malicious or defamatory are not protected under the law.

The National Labor Relations Act (NLRA) of 1935 was designed to protect the rights of employees to organize collectively to raise grievances and potentially to form a union. To make an informed decision about whether to unionize, employees must be free to discuss the merits of any such decision and to raise issues with their employer regarding their terms and conditions of employment. Consequently, the NLRA protects employees from retaliation for joining together to assert their collective rights. For employees to be protected from an adverse employment action they must engage in activity that is both concerted and protected.

"Concerted" simply means that more than one employee must engage in the discussions of the terms and conditions. This is accomplished through two or more employees raising their concerns or questions with management. Alternatively, one employee might inform management that the employee is speaking on behalf of fellow employees. The requirement that the communication be "protected" means that it must not be detrimentally disloyal to the employer or maliciously made in reckless disregard of the truth. The mere fact that an employee's statements are false, misleading, or inaccurate is insufficient to trigger the loss of the protection accorded to employees. Difficult cases arise when the statements by employees are made to the press or to customers of the employer. Finally, courts have recognized that protected activity might be implicated by general policies promulgated by the employer. The question in those circumstances is whether the policy "chills" the employees in the exercise of, or contemplation of exercising, the right to engage in protected concerted activity.

There is no private cause of action for employees who suffer an adverse employment action for exercising the right to engage in protected concerted activity. Any alleged violation can only be prosecuted by the National Labor Relations Board (NLRB) based on a charge of an unfair labor practice that is filed within six months of the alleged violation. The NLRB may order such relief as it finds necessary, including reinstatement of a terminated employee, with or without back pay.

1. The Statute

29 U.S.C. §§ 157, 158, 160

NLRA Section 7

Employees shall have the right to self-organization. To form, join or assist labor organizations to bargain collectively or to engage in other concerted activity for the purpose of mutual aid or protection.

NLRA Section 8

(a) It shall be an unlawful labor practice for an employer:

(1) To interfere, restrain, or to coerce employees in the exercise of rights protected in Section 7.

NLRA Section 10

(a) Powers of Board generally.

The Board is empowered, as hereinafter provided, to prevent any person from engaging in any unfair labor practice (listed in section 158 of this title) affecting commerce. . . .

(c) . . . Findings and Orders of the Board.

[Upon a finding of an unfair labor practice, the Board shall order the party] to take such affirmative action, including reinstatement of employees with or without back pay, as will effectuate the policies of this subchapter. . . . No order of the Board shall require the reinstatement of any individual as an employee . . . if such individual was suspended or discharged for cause."

Example 20-1

An employee believes that a supervisor is mistreating him and his co-workers by imposing unfair production quotas. She tells management,

"I believe that the supervisor is violating company policy by forcing us to manufacture 60 radios an hour." No mention is made of whether the employee is speaking on behalf of others or whether she has discussed the issue with coworkers. The employee is fired for her speech. There is no violation of the NLRA because there is no notice to the employer that the statement was made on behalf of multiple employees acting in concert.

Example 20-2

Two employees go to their supervisor's office and one of them says, "We do not like it when you use curse words while giving us instructions. It is unprofessional. Stop it!" The supervisor fires the employee who made the statement, and tells the other employee, "Let this be a lesson to you. Now get back to work." This action is a violation of the NLRA because even though only one employee spoke, the expression was concerted. Moreover, the expression was made in such a manner that it did not lose its status as speech in furtherance of protected activity. The NLRB may reinstate the fired employee and order back pay.

---

2. Section 7 and Concerted Activity

In the following case, the United States Supreme Court gave an expansive reading to Section 7 rights. As you read the case, weigh the competing interests of the employees and the employer and assess the Court's justification for coming down on the side of the employees.

N.L.R.B. v. Washington Aluminum Co.

370 U.S. 9 (1962).

Black, Justice.

. . . .

January 5, 1959, was an extraordinarily cold day for Baltimore, with unusually high winds and a low temperature of 11 degrees followed by a high of 22. When the employees on the day shift came to work that morning, they found the shop bitterly cold, due not only to the unusually harsh weather, but also to the fact that the large oil furnace had broken down the night before and had not as yet been put back into operation. As the workers gathered in the shop just before the starting hour of 7:30, one of them, a Mr. Caron, went into the office of Mr. Jarvis, the foreman, hoping to warm himself but, instead, found the foreman's quarters as uncomfortable as the rest of the shop. As Caron and Jarvis sat in Jarvis' office discussing how bitingly cold the building was, some of the other machinists walked by the office window 'huddled' together in a fashion that caused Jarvis to exclaim that '(i)f those fellows had any guts at all, they would go home.' When the starting buzzer sounded a few moments later, Caron walked back to his working place in the shop and found all the other machinists 'huddled there, shaking a little, cold.' Caron then said to these workers, 'Dave (Jarvis) told me if we had any guts, we would go home. I am going home, it is too damned cold to work.' Caron asked the other workers what they were going to do and, after some discussion among themselves, they decided to leave with him. One of these workers, testifying before the Board, summarized their entire discussion this way: 'And we had all got together and thought it would be a good idea to go home; maybe we could get some heat brought into the plant that way.' As they started to leave, Jarvis approached and persuaded one of the workers to remain at the job. But Caron and the other six workers on the day shift left practically in a body in a matter of minutes after the 7:30 buzzer.

When the company's general foreman arrived between 7:45 and 8 that morning, Jarvis promptly informed him that all but one of the employees had left because the shop was too cold. The company's president came in at approximately 8:20 a.m. and, upon learning of the walkout, immediately said to the foreman, 'if they have all gone, we are going to terminate them.' After discussion 'at great length' between the general foreman and the company president as to what might be the effect of the walkout on employee discipline and plant production, the president formalized his discharge of the workers who had walked out by giving orders at 9 a.m. that the affected workers should be notified about their discharge immediately, either by telephone, telegram or personally. This was done.

On these facts the Board found that the conduct of the workers was a concerted activity to protest the company's failure to supply adequate heat in its machine shop, that such conduct is protected under the provision of the National Labor Relations Act which guarantees that "Employees shall have the right to engage in concerted activities for the purpose of collective bargaining or other mutual aid or protection," and that the discharge of these workers by the company amounted to an unfair labor practice under § 8(a)(1) of the Act, which forbids employers "to interfere with, restrain, or coerce employees in the exercise of the rights guaranteed in section 7." Acting under the authority of § 10(c) of the Act, which provides that when an employer has been guilty of an unfair labor practice the Board can "take such affirmative action including reinstatement of employees with or without back pay, as will effectuate the policies of this Act," the Board then ordered the company to reinstate the discharged workers to their previous positions and to make them whole for losses resulting from what the Board found to have been the unlawful termination of their employment.

In denying enforcement of this order, the majority of the Court of Appeals took the position that because the workers simply "summarily left their place of employment" without affording the company an "opportunity to avoid the work stoppage by granting a concession to a demand," their walkout did not amount to a concerted activity protected by § 7 of the Act. On this basis, they held that there was no justification for the conduct of the workers in violating the established rules of the plant by leaving their jobs without permission and that the Board had therefore exceeded its power in issuing the order involved here because § 10(c) declares that the Board shall not require reinstatement or back pay for an employee whom an employer has suspended or discharged "for cause."

We cannot agree that employees necessarily lose their right to engage in concerted activities under § 7 merely because they do not present a specific demand upon their employer to remedy a condition they find objectionable. The language of § 7 is broad enough to protect concerted activities whether they take place before, after, or at the same time such a demand is made. To compel the Board to interpret and apply that language in the restricted fashion suggested by the respondent here would only tend to frustrate the policy of the Act to protect the right of workers to act together to better their working conditions. Indeed, as indicated by this very case, such an interpretation of § 7 might place burdens upon employees so great that it would effectively nullify the right to engage in concerted activities which that section protects. The seven employees here were part of a small group of employees who were wholly unorganized. They had no bargaining representative and, in fact, no representative of any kind to present their grievances to their employer. Under these circumstances, they had to speak for themselves as best they could. As pointed out above, prior to the day they left the shop, several of them had repeatedly complained to company officials about the cold working conditions in the shop. These had been more or less spontaneous individual pleas, unsupported by any threat of concerted protest, to which the company apparently gave little consideration and which it now says the Board should have treated as nothing more than 'the same sort of gripes as the gripes made about the heat in the summertime.' The bitter cold of January 5, however, finally brought these workers' individual complaints into concert so that some more effective action could be considered. Having no bargaining representative and no established procedure by which they could take full advantage of their unanimity of opinion in negotiations with the company, the men took the most direct course to let the company know that they wanted a warmer place in which to work. So, after talking among themselves, they walked out together in the hope that this action might spotlight their complaint and bring about some improvement in what they considered to be the 'miserable' conditions of their employment. This we think was enough to justify the Board's holding that they were not required to make any more specific demand than they did to be entitled to the protection of § 7.

. . . .

Nor can we accept the company's contention that because it admittedly had an established plant rule which forbade employees to leave their work without permission of the foreman, there was justifiable 'cause' for discharging these employees, wholly separate and apart from any concerted activities in which they engaged in protest against the poorly heated plant. Section 10(c) of the Act does authorize an employer to discharge employees for 'cause' and our cases have long recognized this right on the part of an employer. But this, of course, cannot mean that an employer is at liberty to punish a man by discharging him for engaging in concerted activities which § 7 of the Act protects. And the plant rule in question here purports to permit the company to do just that for it would prohibit even the most plainly protected kinds of concerted work stoppages until and unless the permission of the company's foreman was obtained.

. . . .

We hold therefore that the Board correctly interpreted and applied the Act to the circumstances of this case and it was error for the Court of Appeals to refuse to enforce its order. The judgment of the Court of Appeals is reversed and the cause is remanded to that court with directions to enforce the order in its entirety.

Reversed and remanded.

QUESTIONS

1. At what point did the conduct of the employees coalesce into activity protected by the NLRA?
2. Assume that Section 7 did not exist. What other rights would the employees have had? Consider the state of employment law when these events occurred.
3. Why did various courts of appeal require the employees to present a formalized complaint to the employer in order to invoke their Section 7 rights?
4. What circumstances would deprive employees of the protections of Section 7?
5. Would the Court's opinion be different if the employees were protesting an unsafe piece of machinery and staged a 12-hour sit-in? What if the employees were asked to leave the workplace but did not? Would it matter if the sit-in interfered with other aspects of production or access to the facility?
6. What if profanities were uttered when the employees voiced their concerns? Is that conduct sufficient to take the "protected" out of "protected concerted activity?"

MikLin Enterprises, Inc. v. NLRB

861 F.3d 812 (8th Cir. en banc, 2017).

Loken, Circuit Judge, with whom Smith, Chief Judge, Wollman, Riley, Gruender, and Shepherd, Circuit Judges, join.

MikLin Enterprises, Inc. ("MikLin") petitions for review of a National Labor Relations Board ("Board") Order holding that MikLin violated Sections 8(a)(1) and 8(a)(3) of the National Labor Relations Act ("NLRA" or "the Act"), 29 U.S.C. §§ 158(a)(1) and (3), when it (i) discharged and disciplined employees who publicly distributed posters suggesting that MikLin's "Jimmy John's" sandwiches posed a health risk to consumers . . . MikLin argues that the Board misapplied governing law and its decision is not supported by substantial evidence. The Board cross-petitions for enforcement of its Order.

A divided panel enforced the Order in its entirety. We granted rehearing en banc and vacated the panel decision. We now conclude that the means the disciplined employees used in their poster attack were so disloyal as to exceed their right to engage in concerted activities protected by the NLRA, as construed in a controlling Supreme Court precedent, *NLRB v. Local Union No. 1229, IBEW,* 346 U.S. 464, 74 S.Ct. 172, 98 L.Ed. 195 (1953) ("*Jefferson Standard*"). We therefore decline to enforce the determination that MikLin violated the Act by disciplining and discharging those employees . . . .

I. Background

A. The "Sick Day Posters" Campaign. MikLin is a family enterprise that owns and operates ten Jimmy John's sandwich-shop franchises in the Minneapolis-St. Paul area. Michael Mulligan is president and co-owner; Robert Mulligan, his son, is vice-president. In 2007, several MikLin workers began an organizing campaign seeking representation by the Industrial Workers of the World ("IWW") union. The IWW lost a Board-conducted election in October 2010, filed unfair labor practice charges and objections to the election with the Board, and continued its organizing campaign by urging MikLin to provide employees holiday pay in late 2010. On January 10, 2011, MikLin and the IWW settled the IWW's objections. MikLin admitted no wrongdoing but agreed to a Board-conducted rerun election if the IWW filed for the election after sixty days but not later than after eighteen months.

With the holiday season passed, the IWW decided its next "march on the boss" group action would be to demand paid sick leave. The IWW concluded that the approach of flu season was a good time to raise the issue. At this time, MikLin's handbook required any employee who would be absent from a shift to find a replacement and notify the store manager. Rule 11 of Jimmy John's Rules for Employment, which employees received when hired, stated: "Find your own replacement if you are not going to be at work. We do not allow people to simply call in sick! We require our employees and [managers] to find their own replacement! NO EXCEPTIONS!" Failure to follow this procedure resulted in termination. MikLin did not offer paid leave for sick employees, though an employee with sufficient tenure was entitled to paid leave to care for a sick child.

Organizers of the IWW sick leave campaign began their attack in late January and early February 2011 by designing and posting on community bulletin boards in MikLin stores posters that prominently featured two identical images of a Jimmy John's sandwich. Above the first image were the words, "YOUR SANDWICH MADE BY A HEALTHY JIMMY JOHN'S WORKER." The text above the second image said, "YOUR SANDWICH MADE BY A SICK JIMMY JOHN'S WORKER." "HEALTHY" and "SICK" were in red letters, larger than the surrounding text in white. Below the pictures, white text asked: "CAN'T TELL THE DIFFERENCE?" The response, in red and slightly smaller: "THAT'S TOO BAD BECAUSE JIMMY JOHN'S WORKERS DON'T GET PAID SICK DAYS. SHOOT, WE CAN'T EVEN CALL IN SICK." Below, in slightly smaller white text, was the warning, "WE HOPE YOUR IMMUNE SYSTEM IS READY BECAUSE YOU'RE ABOUT TO TAKE THE SANDWICH TEST." Text at the bottom of the poster asked readers to help the workers win paid sick days by going to their website.

MikLin managers quickly removed the posters from store bulletin boards. On the morning of March 10—the day before the IWW could request a rerun election—IWW supporters distributed a press release, letter, and the sandwich poster to more than one hundred media contacts, including local newspapers and major news outlets such as the Associated Press, Reuters, Bloomberg, and NBC News. The press release highlighted "unhealthy company behavior." Its second sentence framed the message: "As flu season continues, the sandwich makers at this 10-store franchise are sick and tired of putting their health and the health of their customers at risk." The release declared: "According to findings of a union survey, Jimmy John's workers have reported having to work with strep throat, colds and even the flu." The release ended with a threat: if Robert and Michael Mulligan would not talk with IWW supporters about their demands for paid sick leave, the supporters would proceed with "dramatic action" by "plastering the city with thousands of Sick Day posters."

Employees attached to the press release a "sick leave letter" to the Mulligans which asserted that health code violations occur at MikLin stores nearly every day. The employees complained: "By working sick, we are jeopardizing the entirety of [the company's] image and risking public safety." The letter accused MikLin of refusing to put customers first, risking customers' health, and "shoving [customers] to the bottom of the well of importance." Like the press release, the letter concluded with a threat: if the Mulligans would not meet the employees' demands, the campaign would "move forward with [its] Sick Day posters by posting them not only in stores, but on the University's Campus, in hospitals, on street corners, and any other place where postings are common, citywide."

Also on March 10, four organizers met with Robert Mulligan. They told Mulligan that MikLin's attendance policy and low wages pressured employees to work while sick. Mulligan said MikLin was in the process of reforming its policies. The organizers provided Mulligan a printed version of their letter and press release and warned that, unless MikLin took action to fix the sick day policy within ten days, employees would display sandwich posters throughout the area. Employees who attended felt they had achieved some "common ground."

MikLin posted a new sick leave policy in each store on March 16. The new policy provided a sliding scale of disciplinary points for absences. An employee who did not report but found a replacement would receive no points. An absent employee who could not find a replacement but notified the store manager at least one hour before shift start would receive one point. An absent employee without a replacement who called less than one hour prior to shift start would receive two points. An absent employee who did not call the manager and did not find a replacement would receive three points. An employee who received four disciplinary points within a twelve-month period would be terminated. The policy emphasized: "With regard to absenteeism due to flu like symptoms, Team Members are not allowed to work unless and until those symptoms have subsided for 24 hours." Between March 10 and March 20, MikLin posted a notice in its stores reminding workers: "[f]or those who 'don't feel good' we have a policy that expects them to find a replacement for their shift. . . . [T]he record clearly shows that we have demonstrated flexibility with regard to excusing those who cannot find replacements."

On March 20, IWW supporters implemented their threat to plaster the city with a new version of the Sick Day posters they had placed in MikLin stores in January and February. The bottom of the publicly distributed posters incorporated one change: rather than asking for support of the employees' request for paid sick leave, the public posters listed Robert Mulligan's personal telephone number and instructed customers to call him to "LET HIM KNOW YOU WANT HEALTHY WORKERS MAKING YOUR SANDWICH!" A copy of the publicly distributed posters appears as Appendix A to this opinion. Organizers placed posters in various locations near MikLin stores, including lampposts, trash cans, and mailboxes. Robert Mulligan testified that he was "bombarded by phone calls" for close to a month from people who thought it was unsafe to eat at Jimmy John's. Concerned about the effect on MikLin's business, Mulligan and some managers took down the public posters. On March 22, MikLin fired six employees who coordinated the attack and issued written warnings to three who assisted.

The IWW continued its sick leave attack. In a press release issued a day after the terminations, a discharged employee stated: "It just isn't safe—customers are getting their sandwiches made by people with the flu, and they have no idea. . . . [R]ather than safeguard public health and do the right thing for their employees and their customers, Jimmy John's owners Mike and Rob Mulligan are trying to silence us." On March 30, the IWW issued another press release stating that "[c]ustomers have a right to know that their sandwich could be filled with germs," that IWW members have a duty to speak out on this "public health issue," and that employees "blew the whistle by posting 3000 copies of a poster advising the public of health risks at the sandwich chain." The release quoted one employee as stating: "The unfettered greed of franchise owner Mike Mulligan and Jimmy John Liautaud himself jeopardizes the health of thousands of customers and workers almost every day. We will speak out until they realize that no one wants to eat a sandwich filled with cold and flu germs."

B. The NLRB Proceedings. Following a two-day evidentiary hearing, the Board's Administrative Law Judge ("ALJ") concluded that MikLin violated Sections 8(a)(1) and 8(a)(3) of the Act. Citing prior Board decisions, the ALJ ruled that "Section 7 [29 U.S.C. § 157] protects employee communications to the public that are part of and related to an ongoing labor dispute," such as the Sick Day posters and related press releases, unless they are "so disloyal, reckless, or maliciously untrue as to lose the Act's protections." To lose Section 7 protection, "an employee's public criticism . . . must evidence 'a malicious motive' " or be made with knowledge of the statements' falsity or with reckless disregard for their truth or falsity.

The ALJ found that the Sick Day posters were not maliciously untrue. While "it is not literally true that employees could not call in sick," the ALJ observed, employees "are subject to discipline if they call in sick without finding a replacement." Thus, the assertion, "SHOOT, WE CAN'T EVEN CALL IN SICK," was "protected hyperbole." The ALJ acknowledged record evidence that MikLin had served more than six million sandwiches over its ten-year existence and had been investigated by the Minnesota Department of Health only two times for food borne disease—once in 2006 and once in 2007, when the investigating sanitarian "noted overall compliance with food code requirements and no critical violations." The ALJ found, however, "it is at least arguable that [MikLin's] sick leave policy subjects the public to an increased risk of food borne disease," and MikLin "could have waged its own publicity campaign" to attract consumers. The ALJ made no mention of the false assertion in the open letter accompanying the IWW press release that health code violations occurred at MikLin stores nearly every day. Nor did the ALJ even attempt to analyze and apply the disloyalty principle of *Jefferson Standard*.

A divided panel of the Board affirmed the ALJ's findings and conclusions. *MikLin Enters., Inc.*, 361 N.L.R.B. No. 27, at *7 (2014). The majority concluded "that neither the posters nor the press release were shown to be so disloyal, reckless, or maliciously untrue as to lose the Act's protection." The public communications "were clearly related to the ongoing labor dispute concerning the employees' desire for paid sick leave. . . . Indeed, any person viewing the posters and press release would reasonably understand that the motive for the communications was to garner support for the campaign to improve the employees' terms and conditions of employment by obtaining paid sick leave rather than to disparage [MikLin] or its product." Nor were any of the statements maliciously untrue.

Turning to the question of disloyalty, the majority noted that "Board law has developed considerably in its approach to the question of employee disloyalty." "To lose the Act's protection as an act of disloyalty, an employee's public criticism of an employer must evidence a malicious motive," even if the public communication "raise[s] highly sensitive issues such as public safety." Accepting the majority's summary of prior Board decisions, the dissenting Member would nonetheless have held the Sick Day posters and press release unprotected, because "it is well established that employees lose the Act's protection if their means of protest are 'flagrantly disloyal, wholly incommensurate with any grievances which they may have, and manifested by public disparagement of the employer's product or undermining of its reputation,' " quoting *Five Star Transportation, Inc.*, 349 N.L.R.B. 42, 44–47 (2007), enforced, 522 F.3d 46 (1st Cir. 2008).

II. "Sick Day" Poster Issues

It is well established that an employer commits an unfair labor practice if it discharges employees for engaging in concerted activities that are protected by Section 7 of the NLRA, including communications to third parties or to the public that seek to "improve their lot as employees through channels outside the immediate employee-employer relationship." *Eastex, Inc. v. NLRB*, 437 U.S. 556, 565, 98 S.Ct. 2505, 57 L.Ed.2d 428 (1978). Section 10(c) of the Act, however, expressly limits the Board's broad authority to remedy unlawful employee discharges: "No order of the Board shall require the reinstatement of any individual as an employee . . . if such individual was suspended or discharged for cause." 29 U.S.C. § 160(c). The interplay between Section 7 and Section 10(c) was the critical question the Supreme Court addressed in *Jefferson Standard.*

A.

In *Jefferson Standard*, the Court upheld the Board's decision that a broadcasting station did not violate the Act when it fired technicians who distributed handbills "making a sharp, public, disparaging attack upon the quality of the company's product and its business policies, in a manner reasonably calculated to harm the company's reputation and reduce its income." 346 U.S. at 471. After bargaining negotiations broke down, employees first picketed the station for treating its employees unfairly. When this tactic failed, the employees distributed thousands of handbills, signed "WBT Technicians," criticizing the station's poor programming quality and asserting that Jefferson Standard did not value its customers and considered the local city to be a "second-class community." *Id.* at 468. The Board found the employee handbills unprotected because the technicians "deliberately undertook to alienate their employer's customers by impugning the technical quality of his product." *Jefferson Standard Broadcasting Co.*, 94 N.L.R.B. 1507, 1511 (1951). Though the technicians' purpose was "to extract a concession from the employer with respect to the terms of their employment," the Board found that they lost the Act's protection when they failed to disclose their interests as employees. *Id.* at 1511. The Board reasoned that the technicians lost the Act's protection because "the gist of [the technicians'] appeal to the public was that the employer ought to be boycotted because he offered a shoddy product to the consuming public—not because he was 'unfair' to the employees who worked on that product." *Id.* at 1512. The Board declined to decide whether the product disparagement in the handbills would justify discharge "had it been uttered in the context of a conventional appeal for support of the union in the labor dispute." *Id.* at 1512 n.18.

The Supreme Court, in affirming the Board, decided the case on broader grounds. After quoting the "for cause" language of Section 10(c), the Court declared that "[t]here is no more elemental cause for discharge of an employee than disloyalty to his employer." *Jefferson Standard*, 346 U.S. at 472. Congress in the NLRA "did not weaken the underlying contractual bonds and loyalties of employer and employee." *Id.* at 473. Absent a labor controversy, the technicians' conduct "unquestionably would have provided adequate cause for their disciplinary discharge within the meaning of § 10(c). . . . The fortuity of the coexistence of a labor dispute affords these technicians no substantial defense." *Id.* at 476. Thus, the handbill attack targeting "the quality of the company's product . . . was as adequate a cause for the discharge of its sponsors as if the labor controversy had not been pending." *Id.* at 477. Though the Court noted several times that the technicians failed to disclose a connection between their labor dispute and the handbill attack, the Court declined to remand for further consideration of whether the handbills were an "appeal for support in the pending dispute," rather than "a concerted separable attack," because the attack would be unprotected either way:

> Even if the attack were to be treated, as the Board has not treated it, as a concerted activity wholly or partly within the scope of those mentioned in § 7, the means used by the technicians in conducting the attack have deprived the attackers of the protection of that section, when read in the light and context of the purpose of the Act.

Id. at 477–78.

The Supreme Court's decision not to remand in *Jefferson Standard* made clear that the Court's disloyalty ruling includes communications that otherwise would fall within Section 7 protection, if those communications "mak[e] a sharp, public, disparaging attack upon the quality of the company's product and its business policies, in a manner reasonably calculated to harm the company's reputation and reduce its income." . . . Thus, we reject the dissent's suggestion that *Jefferson Standard* does not apply in this case because the employees' disparaging communications "expressly reference[d] ongoing labor disputes."

B.

Board decisions applying *Jefferson Standard* initially recognized that employers may protect their businesses from detrimental product disparagement whether or not an employee attack referenced a labor dispute. See *Patterson-Sargent Co.*, 115 N.L.R.B. 1627, 1630 (1956) (employees' handbill asserting replacement workers produced defective paint was unprotected "public disparagement of the quality of the employer's product"); *Coca Cola Bottling Works, Inc.*, 186 N.L.R.B. 1050, 1063–64 (1970) (employees' leaflet warning that inexperienced workers could leave objects such as roaches, bugs, and dead mice in the company's bottles was "the very type of [disparaging] conduct" held unprotected in *Jefferson Standard*).

. . . Although *Jefferson Standard* did not involve employee public communications that were reckless or maliciously untrue, we do not question the Board's view that such communications are not entitled to the protection of Section 7 as limited by Section 10(c). . . .

The issue in this case is the *Jefferson Standard* disloyalty principle—Section 10(c) permits an employer to fire an employee for "making a sharp, public, disparaging attack upon the quality of the company's product and its business policies, in a manner reasonably calculated to harm the company's reputation and reduce its income." On this issue, while always purporting to apply *Jefferson Standard*'s holding, the Board has migrated to a severely constrained interpretation of that decision. "To lose the Act's protection as an act of disloyalty, an employee's public criticism of an employer must evidence a malicious motive." *MikLin*, 361 N.L.R.B. No. 27, at *5 (quotation omitted). "[E]ven communications that raise highly sensitive issues such as public safety [are] protected where they are sufficiently linked to a legitimate labor dispute and are not maliciously motivated to harm the employer." *Id.* at *4–*5.

In our view, the Board fundamentally misconstrued *Jefferson Standard* in two ways. First, while an employee's subjective intent is of course relevant to the disloyalty inquiry—"sharp, public, disparaging attack" suggests an intent to harm—the *Jefferson Standard* principle includes an objective component that focuses, not on the employee's purpose, but on the means used—whether the disparaging attack was "reasonably calculated to harm the company's reputation and reduce its income," to such an extent that it was harmful, indefensible disparagement of the employer or its product. By holding that no act of employee disparagement is unprotected disloyalty unless it is "maliciously motivated to harm the employer," the Board has not interpreted *Jefferson Standard*—it has overruled it.

Second, the Board's definition of "malicious motive" for these purposes excludes from *Jefferson Standard*'s interpretation of Section 10(c) all employee disparagement that is part of or directly related to an ongoing labor dispute. While the employees "may have anticipated that some members of the public might choose not to patronize [MikLin's] restaurants after reading the posters or press release," the Board ruled, their public communications were protected activity because "there is no evidence that [their] purpose was to inflict harm on [MikLin]." Rather, "they were motivated by a sincere desire to improve their terms and conditions of employment." *MikLin*, 361 N.L.R.B. No. 27, at *6. In other words, the Board refuses to treat as "disloyal" any public communication intended to advance employees' aims in a labor dispute, regardless of the manner in which, and the extent to which, it harms the employer. As the Court held in *Jefferson Standard* that its disloyalty principle would apply even if the employees had explicitly related their public disparagement to their ongoing labor dispute, once again the Board has not interpreted *Jefferson Standard*—it has overruled it.

By requiring an employer to show that employees had a subjective intent to harm, and burdening that requirement with an overly restrictive need to show "malicious motive," the Board has effectively removed from the *Jefferson Standard* inquiry the central Section 10(c) issue as defined by the Supreme Court—whether the means used reflect indefensible employee disloyalty. This is an error of law. Our prior cases confirm that an employee's disloyal statements can lose Section 7 protection without a showing of actual malice....

Rather than employee motive, the critical question in the *Jefferson Standard* disloyalty inquiry is whether employee public communications reasonably targeted the employer's labor practices, or indefensibly disparaged the quality of the employer's product or services. The former furthers the policy of the NLRA; the latter does not. This distinction focuses on the type of harm employees' methods cause. When employees convince customers not to patronize an employer because its labor practices are unfair, subsequent settlement of the labor dispute brings the customers back, to the benefit of both employer and employee. By contrast, sharply disparaging the employer's product or services as unsafe, unhealthy, or of shoddy quality causes harm that outlasts the labor dispute, to the detriment of all employees as well as the employer. See *Diamond Walnut Growers, Inc. v. NLRB*, 113 F.3d 1259, 1267 (D.C. Cir. 1997) (en banc), cert. denied, 523 U.S. 1020, 118 S.Ct. 1299, 140 L.Ed.2d 466 (1998); compare *Montefiore*, 621 F.2d at 517 (efforts by striking doctors to discourage patients from entering the clinic were unprotected, although related to labor dispute, because they "appealed to patients to turn away not out of sympathy with the aims of the striking workers . . ., but in the belief that they could not obtain competent treatment there"), and *St. Luke's*, 268 F.3d at 580 (nurse's public statements relating to ongoing labor dispute were unprotected because she "disparaged the quality of patient care being provided by [her employer] in a way guaranteed to adversely affect the hospital's reputation with prospective patients and the public at large"), with *NLRB v. Greyhound Lines, Inc.*, 660 F.2d 354, 357 (8th Cir. 1981) (bus drivers' factual statements regarding anticipated service delays were not unprotected because they "did not contain any insults or negative insinuations about the Company's services or integrity with respect to its customers").

C.

[Editor's Note: The Court rejected the claim that it owed deference to the Board under the Chevron doctrine, because the courts had interpreted the relevant statutory language and the Board was striving to apply that interpretation.]

D.

[Editor's Note: The Court concluded that there was no substantial evidence supporting the finding of protected activity.]

. . . .

The attack was "sharp," proceeding "in a manner reasonably calculated to harm the company's reputation and reduce its income." *Id.* at 471. The posters, press releases, and letter were an effective campaign to convince customers that eating Jimmy John's sandwiches might cause them to become sick. The Sick Day poster warned that the reader was "about to take the sandwich test." Its enduring image was a MikLin-made Jimmy John's sandwich that, although appearing like any other, was filled with cold and flu germs. As in *Jefferson Standard*, the employees were not on strike, but continued to work and collect wages as they attempted to scare customers away from their employer and its products. "Nothing could be further from the purpose of the Act than to require an employer to finance such activities." *Jefferson Standard*, 346 U.S. at 476.

Allegations that a food industry employer is selling unhealthy food are likely to have a devastating impact on its business, what the D.C. Circuit called the "equivalent of a nuclear bomb" in a labor-relations dispute. *Diamond Walnut Growers*, 113 F.3d at 1267. MikLin's employees maximized this effect, choosing March as a "good time" to launch their attack "because it was flu season." The employees understood that MikLin's business was dependent on its "clean" public image, yet directly attacked that image. Like the technicians in *Jefferson Standard*, the MikLin employees accused their employer of not valuing its customers. *See Montefiore Hosp.*, 621 F.2d at 517; *Five Star*, 349 N.L.R.B. at 46. By targeting the food product itself, employees disparaged MikLin in a manner likely to outlive, and also unnecessary to aid, the labor dispute. Even if MikLin granted paid sick leave, the image of contaminated sandwiches made by employees who chose to work while sick was not one that would easily dissipate.

. . . .

Problem 20-1

An employee joins other employees on a private Facebook message group. The topic of discussion is organizing a social event. Ten people were in the group, seven of whom were current employees and three of whom were former employees. The discussion veered off into matters regarding the workplace when Aaron said that he had a disagreement with a supervisor earlier in the month and described the encounter by writing "(I) told him to back the freak off." Aaron continued: "They (the employer) are full of shit. . .They seem to be staying away from me, you know I don't bite my tongue anymore. F_CK. . .FIRE ME. . .Make my day. . ." Two hours later, another employee wrote that "it's getting bad (at the employer's workplace), it's annoying as hell. It's always some dumb shit going on." The next day the employer was informed about Aaron's comments and concluded that it was "obvious" that Aaron did not want to work there any longer. You are counsel to the company and are asked to determine if the company can terminate Aaron immediately.

Problem 20-2

A number of employees of a local bar communicated on a group Facebook page that was publicly available. A former employee posted that the owners of the bar had miscalculated tax withholding for their paychecks, resulting in them having to pay additional taxes out of their savings. Another former employee posted the following:

> "Maybe someone should do the owners of the bar a favor and buy it from them. They can't even do their own paperwork correctly!!!! Now I OWE money. WTF!!!! It's all Ralphs's {one of the owners} fault. He didn't do the paperwork right. I'm calling the Labor Board to look into it b/c he still owes me $2,000 in back pay."

At this juncture, one current employee clicked "like," and a second current employee posted in response: "I owe too. Ralph is such an ass." The owners were told about the "like" and the comment, and immediately fired both employees. The two employees claimed that they engaged in activity protected by Section 7 and that their terminations violated Section 8(a)(1). Describe the arguments that you would make on behalf of the employees and anticipate the arguments that will be made on behalf of the bar owners.

Mastery Problem 20-1

Bob worked at a loading dock. Bob believed that his supervisor mistreated him and his co-workers by failing to accord them with respect as required by the company handbook, because he repeatedly called them names such as "good for nothings" and "lazy bums." Additionally, Bob believed the supervisor was manipulating the hourly quota reports to claim that the employees were doing more loading than they actually were in order for the supervisor to increase his annual bonus. These manipulations did not affect the compensation of Bob's co-workers directly, but Bob believed that the supervisor was making them work off the clock on occasion in order to prove that the quotas were being exceeded. Bob spoke to his co-workers and they agreed that they should write a letter to management. Bob drafted the letter and wrote it in the plural, "We believe. . ." and all the co-workers signed it. Concerned that the co-workers might get in trouble, Bob retyped the letter exactly as it was, but took off their names. He then mailed it to management, which immediately conducted an investigation and concluded that none of the co-workers could support the factual allegations. Is Bob protected?

---

3. Workplace Rules as Violations of Section 7

Recent cases have focused on preventing employer policies that would interfere with the exercise of Section 7 rights. We will revisit the concept of protected speech in Lesson 21 regarding the anti-retaliation provisions of Title VII. As you read the following case, determine how workplace rules could purportedly "chill" an employee from exercising her rights under Section 7. In particular, consider whether the law requires the National Labor Relations Board to prove that the employer promulgated the rule in order to "chill" the exercise of Section 7.

T-Mobile USA, Inc. v. NLRB

865 F.3d 265 (5th Cir. 2017).

E. Grady Jolly, Circuit Judge:

In this appeal, the National Labor Relations Board ("NLRB" or "Board") challenges certain T-Mobile workplace rules, which it contends prohibit employees from exercising unionizing rights.

T-Mobile's employee handbook (1) encouraged employees to "maintain a positive work environment"; (2) prohibited "[a]rguing or fighting," "failing to treat others with respect," and "failing to demonstrate appropriate teamwork"; (3) prohibited all photography and audio or video recording in the workplace; and (4) prohibited access to electronic information by non-approved individuals. The Board determined that all four provisions violated the National Labor Relations Act because each of them discouraged unionizing or other concerted activity protected by the Act. T-Mobile resists and seeks review of the Board's order.

We hold that the Board erred in finding that a reasonable employee would construe policies (1), (2), and (4) to prohibit protected activity. However, we will not upset the Board's finding that a reasonable employee would construe policy (3) to prohibit protected activity. Accordingly, we grant in part and deny in part enforcement of the Board's order.

T-Mobile and MetroPCS are telecommunications companies that market cell phones and related services, with offices and retail locations located throughout the United States. In 2014, based on charges filed by the Communication Workers of America, the NLRB brought a complaint against T-Mobile alleging that several of the provisions of T-Mobile's employee handbook violated the National Labor Relations Act ("NLRA"), 29 U.S.C. § 151 et seq. This appeal concerns four provisions of the handbook that the NLRB determined were forbidden under the NLRA.

The "workplace conduct" policy is found under the "Standards of Conduct" heading in the employee handbook. The policy provides:

> [T-Mobile] expects all employees to behave in a professional manner that promotes efficiency, productivity, and cooperation. Employees are expected to maintain a positive work environment by communicating in a manner that is conducive to effective working relationships with internal and external customers, clients, co-workers, and management.

The "commitment-to-integrity" policy is found under the "Conducting Business" heading in the code of business conduct. The policy begins with the preface:

> At T-Mobile, we expect all employees, officers and directors to exercise integrity, common sense, good judgment, and to act in a professional manner. We do not tolerate inconsistent conduct. While we cannot anticipate every situation that might arise or list all possible violations, the acts listed below are unacceptable.

The commitment-to-integrity policy then lists seventeen non-inclusive examples of "unacceptable" acts, including, in relevant part:

> Arguing or fighting with co-workers, subordinates or supervisors; failing to treat others with respect; or failing to demonstrate appropriate teamwork.

The "recording" policy is found under the "Workplace Expectations" heading of the employee handbook. The policy provides:

> To prevent harassment, maintain individual privacy, encourage open communication, and protect confidential information employees are prohibited from recording people or confidential information using cameras, camera phones/devices, or recording devices (audio or video) in the workplace. Apart from customer calls that are recorded for quality purposes, employees may not tape or otherwise make sound recordings of work-related or workplace discussions. Exceptions may be granted when partici-

> pating in an authorized [T-Mobile] activity or with permission from an employee's Manager, HR Business Partner, or the Legal Department. If an exception is granted, employees may not take a picture, audiotape, or videotape others in the workplace without the prior notification of all participants.

Finally, the "acceptable use" policy is found under the "Security" heading of T-Mobile's "Acceptable Use Policy for Information and Communication Resources." The policy provides:

> Users may not permit non-approved individuals access to information or information resources, or any information transmitted by, received from, printed from, or stored in these resources, without prior written approval from an authorized T-Mobile representative.

. . . .

. . . .The Board . . .held that all four of the challenged policies violated the NLRA and issued an order to that effect.

. . . .

Section 7 of the NLRA provides a declaration of statutory policy: "[e]mployees shall have the right to self-organization, to form, join, or assist labor organizations, to bargain collectively through representatives of their own choosing, and to engage in other concerted activities for the purpose of collective bargaining or other mutual aid or protection." 29 U.S.C. § 157. Section 8(a)(1) of the Act in turn provides enforcement of that policy by stating that it shall be an "unfair labor practice" to "interfere with, restrain, or coerce employees in the exercise of the rights" protected by Section 7. 29 U.S.C. § 158(a)(1). Here, the "appropriate inquiry" is whether T-Mobile's rules for workplace conduct violate § 8(a)(1) by chilling a reasonable employee in the exercise of his or her Section 7 rights. . . . "[w]here the rules are likely to have a chilling effect, the Board may conclude that their maintenance is an unfair labor practice, even absent evidence of enforcement." *Id.* (quoting *Lafayette Park Hotel*, 326 NLRB 824, 825 (1998)) (ellipses omitted).

In order to determine whether a workplace rule violates Section 8(a)(1), this Court applies the two-part *Lutheran Heritage* framework. First, the Court decides "whether the rule *explicitly* restricts activities protected by Section 7." *Flex Frac*, 746 F.3d at 208–09 (quoting *Lutheran Heritage Village-Livonia*, 343 NLRB 646, 646 (2004)); . . . Second, even if the restriction is not explicit, the rule may still violate Section 8(a)(1) where "(1) employees would reasonably construe the language to prohibit Section 7 activity; (2) the rule was promulgated in response to union activity; or (3) the rule has been applied to restrict the exercise of Section 7 rights." *Id.* at 209 (quoting *Lutheran Heritage*, 343 NLRB at 647). When construing a work rule, the Board must "give the rule a reasonable reading." *Lutheran Heritage*, 343 NLRB at 646. Additionally, the Board "must refrain from reading particular phrases in isolation" and "must not presume improper interference with employee rights." *Id.* The appropriate, objective inquiry is not whether the rules "*could* conceivably be read to cover Section 7 activity, even though that reading is unreasonable," but rather whether "a reasonable employee reading the[ ] rules *would* . . . construe them to prohibit conduct protected by the Act." *Id.* at 647 (emphasis added).

The "reasonable employee," although not specifically defined in Lutheran Heritage or subsequent jurisprudence, refers to a hypothetical, objective standard analogous to the "reasonable person" in tort law. *Cf.* Restatement (Second) of Torts § 283 (1965) ("[T]he standard of conduct to which [an actor] must conform to avoid being negligent is that of a reasonable man under like circumstances."). In this case, where the record does not suggest that the rules have been applied in the context of union or collective activity, the "reasonable employee" is a T-Mobile employee aware of his legal rights but who also interprets work rules as they apply to the everydayness of his job. The reasonable employee does not view every employer policy through the prism of the NLRA. Indeed, "[the Board] must not presume improper interference with employee rights." *Lutheran Heritage*, 343 NLRB at 646. The question is whether a reasonable T-Mobile employee "would *reasonably construe* the language to prohibit Section 7 activity." *Lutheran Heritage*, 343 NLRB at 647 (emphasis added).

The Board's findings of fact are conclusive if supported by substantial evidence. 29 U.S.C. §§ 160(e)–(f); [we] defer to the Board's interpretation of the NLRA "so long as it is rational and consistent with the Act." *D.R. Horton, Inc. v. NLRB*, 737 F.3d 344, 349 (5th Cir. 2013) (citations and quotations omitted). "Our deference extends to our review of both the Board's findings of fact and its application of the law. It does not, however, extend to the Board's legal conclusions . . . which we review *de novo*." *J. Vallery Elec., Inc. v. NLRB*, 337 F.3d 446, 450 (5th Cir. 2003). Still, "[a]lthough we accord Board findings a measure of deference, our review is more than a mere rubber stamp of the decision." *Arkema*, 710 F.3d at 314 (citations and quotations omitted).

The NLRB found that each of the four policies at issue—the workplace conduct policy, the commitment-to-integrity policy, the recording policy, and the acceptable use policy—violated the Act because "employees would reasonably construe the language to prohibit Section 7 activity." *Lutheran Heritage*, 343 NLRB at 647. We address each policy in turn.

We first address the workplace conduct policy. The Board found that the workplace conduct policy, which encouraged employees to maintain a "positive work environment," violated the NLRA because a reasonable employee would read the language to discourage protected activity, including candid, potentially contentious discussions of unionizing. This finding is unreasonable.

To a "reasonable employee," context matters in the interpretation of these rules. The policy is titled "*Workplace* Conduct." The rule refers to a positive *work environment* and effective *working relationships* and requires employees to behave in a way that "promotes efficiency, productivity, and cooperation," with the obvious implication "with respect to work." In the context of the workplace presented in the record, this rule addresses a normal workplace, on a normal workday.

A reasonable employee of T-Mobile would interpret the policy as requiring professional manners, positive work environment, effective and courteous communications, getting along with everybody, common sense, and people skills. The reasonable T-Mobile employee would understand the rule to express a universally accepted guide for conduct in a responsible workplace. Indeed, the Board itself admonishes that these rules must be given a "reasonable reading." *Lutheran Heritage*, 343 NLRB at 646; *see also id.* ("[We] must not presume improper interference with employee rights."). In other words, the NLRB erred by interpreting the rule as to how the reasonable employee *could*, rather than *would*, interpret these policies—an analysis eschewed by the Board's own precedent. *See Lutheran Heritage*, 343 NLRB at 647.

This reading of these workplace rules is consistent with the only other circuit to have spoken on the matter. The DC Circuit in *Adtranz ABB Daimler-Benz Transportation, N.A., Inc. v. NLRB*, 253 F.3d 19 (D.C. Cir. 2001), addressed a policy similar to the ones at issue. There, asserting expected conduct from employees such as "[t]rust and respect for self and others," "[t]eamwork and cooperation," and "[e]ffective communication," the company prohibited "abusive or threatening language to anyone on company premises." *Id.* at 25. The NLRB had declared this rule in violation of the NLRA on the grounds that it prohibited an employee from engaging in heated labor discussions. *Id.* at 25–26. The DC Circuit did not buy in: "This position is not 'reasonably defensible.' It is not even close." *Id.* at 26. The court further rejected the NLRB's argument that the company's "effort to maintain a civil and decent workplace is an unfair labor practice that threatens the statutory rights of [its] employees under the NLRA." *Id.* at 25. The DC Circuit was in no mood for temporizing, saying that "it is preposterous that employees are incapable of organizing a union or exercising their other statutory rights under the NLRA without resort to abusive or threatening language." *Id.* at 25–26.

. . . .

In sum, we conclude that a reasonable employee would not construe a requirement to "maintain a positive work environment by communicating in a manner that is conducive to effective working relationships" to restrict Section 7 activity. We therefore deny enforcement of the Board's order as to the workplace conduct policy.

The Board also found that the commitment-to-integrity policy violated the NLRA because the policy would inhibit robust discussion of labor issues. The rule, like the workplace conduct rule, is on its face, only a common-sense civility guideline.

The policy, which prohibits "arguing or fighting," "failing to treat others with respect," and "failing to demonstrate appropriate teamwork," is prefaced by the conventional, common-sense admonition that T-Mobile expects its employees to "to exercise integrity, common sense, good judgment, and to act in a professional manner." These acts appear in a long, non-inclusive list of prohibited activity, including theft, fraud, dishonesty, and sleeping on the job. These examples that define the parameters of the rule address misconduct. As the DC Circuit noted in addressing such a rule, "[a]lthough [reasonable] employees are perhaps unlikely to know the term *ejusdem generis*, they no doubt grasp as well as anyone the concept it encapsulates." *Community Hospitals*, 335 F.3d at 1088.

Here, a reasonable employee would understand the language of the commitment-to-integrity policy to refer to similar misconduct. Furthermore, a reasonable employee would be fully capable of engaging in debate over union activity or working conditions, even vigorous or heated debate, without inappropriately "arguing or fighting," "failing to treat others with respect," or "failing to demonstrate appropriate teamwork." As the Board delineated in *Lutheran Heritage*, we view the rule from the perspective of the reasonable employee, not from the point of view of the exceptions to reasonableness. *See* 343 NLRB at 646–47.

Accordingly, we decline to enforce the Board's order as to the commitment-to-integrity policy.

The Board next found that T-Mobile's recording policy violates the NLRA because it would discourage workers from engaging in protected activity.

We are primarily concerned with the broad reach of the recording ban. The ban, by its plain language, encompasses any and all photography or recording on corporate premises at any time without permission from a supervisor. This ban is, by its own terms alone, stated so broadly that a reasonable employee, generally aware of employee rights, would interpret it to discourage protected concerted activity, such as even an off-duty employee photographing a wage schedule posted on a corporate bulletin board. *Cf. Flex Frac*, 746 F.3d at 208 ("A workplace rule that forbids the discussion of confidential wage information between employees patently violates section 8(a)(1)." (citations, quotations, alterations, and ellipses omitted)); *accord Whole Foods Mkt. Grp., Inc. v. NLRB*, 691 Fed.Appx. 49, 2017 WL 2374843, at *2 (2d Cir. June 1, 2017) (holding that where "no-recording policies prohibited all recording without management approval, employees would reasonably construe the language to prohibit recording protected by Section 7" (citations and quotations omitted)).

T-Mobile argues that the ban's stated purposes—"[t]o prevent harassment, maintain individual privacy, encourage open communication, and protect confidential information"—are legitimate business interests that ordinarily would justify the ban. But merely reciting such justifications does not alter the fact that the operative language of the rule on its face prohibits protected Section 7 activity, including Section 7 activity wholly unrelated to those stated interests.

Unlike the "workplace conduct" policy and the "commitment-to-integrity" policy, the recording policy forbids certain forms of clearly protected activity. We have earlier held that held those two policies would not be interpreted by a reasonable T-Mobile employee as forbidding protected activity. By contrast, a reasonable T-Mobile employee, aware of his legal rights, would read the language of the recording policy as plainly forbidding a means of engaging in protected activity.

Because a reasonable employee would construe the recording policy to prohibit forms of protected activity, we hold that the Board's determination that the recording policy violated the NLRA is supported by a reasonable interpretation of the record. Its order will be enforced in that respect.

Finally, the Board found that the acceptable use policy violated the NLRA because a reasonable employee would construe it to prohibit protected activity such as accessing and sharing wage and benefit information contained in his or her e-mail.

The NLRB's decision, however, disregards the context in which the acceptable use policy is to be read and understood. The "Scope" section of the acceptable use policy explicitly states that the policy "applies to all non-public T-Mobile information." Thus the policy only prohibits employees from sharing *non-public* information.

Where a company policy prohibits the disclosure of non-public information, courts presume that a reasonable employee would not construe the policy to prohibit the disclosure of information that may be properly used in protected activity, such as wage and benefit information, so long as the policy does not explicitly state that it encompasses such information. *See Lafayette Park Hotel*, 326 NLRB at 826 ("Although the term 'hotel-private' is not defined in the rule, employees in our view reasonably would understand that the rule is designed to protect that [proprietary business information] interest rather than to prohibit the discussion of their wages.") . . . Here, as in *Lafayette Park* and unlike in *Flex Frac*, the policy does not define "non-public T-Mobile information" in a way that would lead a reasonable worker to believe that it includes protected wage and benefit information. Instead, the policy only applies to the sort of proprietary business information that an employer may properly restrict its employees from sharing outside of the company. *See Lafayette Park Hotel*, 326 NLRB at 826 ("[B]usinesses have a substantial and legitimate interest in maintaining the confidentiality of private information, including . . . trade secrets, contracts with suppliers, and a range of other proprietary information.").

Thus the NLRB's finding that a reasonable worker would construe the acceptable use policy to discourage protected activity is unreasonable, and we deny enforcement as to that part of its order.

. . . .

Accordingly, T-Mobile's petition is GRANTED IN PART and DENIED IN PART and the NLRB's cross-application is correspondingly DENIED IN PART and GRANTED IN PART.

QUESTIONS

1. As a practical matter, do you believe that employees are aware of the legal rules that govern their collective activity? Do you think that they care? Should they care?
2. Is the Board impermissibly trying to manage an employer's workplace through the broad scope of Section 7?
3. How would one determine the validity of a rule promulgated by the Board? Do you agree with the Board's analysis?

Problem 20-3

You are an associate at a law firm that represents management. Consider the following workplace policies and determine whether the employer is exposed to a claim that any of these policies constitute a violation of the NLRA.

> Policy 1: "Employees are prohibited from discussing their compensation with other employees. Compensation is a private matter between the employee and the employer."
>
> Policy 2: "Sharing conversations that you have heard or overheard on the worksite with your co-workers, the public, or anyone outside of your immediate work group is strictly prohibited."
>
> Policy 3: "Unauthorized disclosure of business secrets or other confidential information is strictly prohibited."

> Policy 4: "No employee shall engage in rude or unprofessional behavior toward a customer or any member of the public who comes into contact with the company."
>
> Policy 5: "Each and every employee is expected to work in a cooperative manner with management, supervisors, co-workers, customers, and vendors."
>
> Policy 6: "Discuss work matters only with other employees who have a specific business reason to know about the matter, or who have access to the information . . ."
>
> Policy 7: "All employees are forbidden to send material that is fraudulent, harassing, embarrassing, sexually explicit, profane, defamatory or inappropriate through the company email server, or through use of company hardware or software."

Mastery Problem 20-2

Silvia is employed by McDaniels Trucking. McDaniels has a written Dispute Resolution Policy that is provided to every employee and signed by the employee. Under the Policy, McDaniels and the employees agree to resolve any employment disputes they have with one another through binding arbitration. The agreement further provides:

> Both parties waive their right to commence, be a party to, or act as a class member in any case or collective action in any court action against the other party relating to employment issues. Further, any group, class or collective action claim by or against (the employee) or the Company shall be heard without consolidation of such claim with any other person or entity's claim.

The policy further provides: "Notwithstanding the group, class or collective action waiver set forth in the preceding paragraph, employee and Company agree that employee is not waving his or her right under Section 7 of the (NLRA) to file a group, class or collective action waiver. . ."

Does this policy constitute a violation of Section 7?

Conclusion

The NLRA protects the right of all workers to engage in concerted activity regarding shared concerns about the workplace. However, this does not give workers license to act in a malicious or otherwise disloyal manner that causes harm to the employer. An employer who retaliates against employees for exercising this right is subject to a charge of an unfair labor practice by the National Labor Relations Board.

C. Employee Dignity

Key Concepts

- The at-will rule gives employers control over the workplace, but it does not permit the employer to ignore the dignity and personal autonomy of employees.
- Employers are held liable if they engage in extreme and outrageous behavior in the workplace that results in an employee suffering severe emotional distress.
- Employees have the right to personal autonomy when they are not working unless their activities conflict with the employer's legitimate business interests.

Lesson 21:
Emotional Distress

Objectives and Expected Learning Outcomes

In this Lesson, we consider how employees can use the tort of intentional infliction of emotional distress (IIED) to challenge abusive conditions in the workplace. The tort of IIED provides a remedy for employees who suffer severe emotional harm in response to extreme and outrageous behavior by the employer. We will discuss the high burdens of proof and specifically focus on the elements of "extreme and outrageous conduct," "severe emotional distress," and the various defenses available to an employer. This Lesson concerns the conditions in the workplace. In Lesson 35, we will discuss when the manner of termination may give rise to an IIED claim.

The at rule will sets the tone for employer control of the workplace. If the employer may fire employees for any reason or no reason at all, it is not surprising that the employer is generally accorded the flexibility to manage the workplace as it seems fit. However, the general rules of intentional tort provide some relief against an employer that creates or tolerates an abusive environment that causes harm to an employee. The traditional elements of this tort are provided by the Restatement.

Restatement (Third) Torts

§ 46. Intentional (or Reckless) Infliction of Emotional Harm

An actor who by extreme and outrageous conduct intentionally or recklessly causes severe emotional harm to another is subject to liability for that emotional harm and, if the emotional harm causes bodily harm, also for the bodily harm.

We will consider the principal elements in turn.

1. Extreme and Outrageous Conduct

To be held liable for IIED, an actor must do more than intentionally or recklessly cause emotional harm. The actor must act in a way that may reasonably be regarded as extreme and outrageous, a standard subject to interpretation by the courts and determined on a case-by-case basis. Courts commonly state that the behavior must be such as to exceed all bounds of civilized society. This standard is less than precise, but undoubtedly difficult to prove.

The nature of the employer's behavior must always be viewed in context. First, the employer is given wide leeway to manage the workplace. It may not be civilized to run up to a stranger on the street and begin to berate him, but if a supervisor uses harsh language to critique employees this may be considered an appropriate (even if counterproductive and misguided) exercise of authority over the workplace. On the other hand, the nature of "extreme and outrageous conduct" will be measured according to the employer's knowledge of the employee; what might simply be harsh treatment for most persons might be considered extreme and outrageous for a particular employee with known susceptibilities to emotional distress.

Example 21-1

A supervisor in a factory constantly berates employees to work harder and pits them against each other in production contests. The supervisor treats everyone equally, which is to say, disrespectfully. If an employee suffers severe emotional distress, it is unlikely that he will be able to recover because the employer will generally be regarded as not having acted in a manner that is extreme and outrageous.

Example 21-2

A supervisor knew that a maintenance employee had a severe phobia of heights. For the purpose of causing extreme fear, the supervisor made the employee use a 14-foot ladder to change the lightbulbs on the factory floor, even though this task was usually handled by another employee. After a few efforts, the employee broke down into tears and had to be hospitalized. Asking this particular employee to climb a ladder could be deemed extreme and outrageous behavior, given the context of the employee's susceptibility to emotional distress under those conditions.

The following case provides a classic discussion of what is required to establish extreme and outrageous behavior as opposed to merely harsh treatment that an employee may choose to endure as part of the job requirements. In this case, the classic mantra that the "customer is always right" is not too helpful to the employer, especially when the customer is also facing a suit for IIED by an employee because of the customer's extreme behavior.

Bodewig v. K-Mart, Inc.

635 P.2d 657 (Or. 1981).

Buttler, Presiding Judge.

In this tort action for outrageous conduct, plaintiff seeks damages against her former employer, K-Mart, and a K-Mart customer, Mrs. Golden. Both defendants moved for summary judgment, which the trial court granted. Plaintiff appeals from the resulting final judgments entered. We reverse and remand.

. . . On the evening of March 29, 1979, plaintiff was working as a part-time checker at K-Mart. Defendant Golden entered plaintiff's checkout lane and plaintiff began to ring up Golden's purchases on the cash register. When plaintiff called out the price on a package of curtains, Golden told plaintiff the price was incorrect because the curtains were on sale. Plaintiff called a domestics department clerk for a price check. That clerk told plaintiff the curtains in question were not on sale. Upon hearing this, Golden left her merchandise on plaintiff's counter and returned with the clerk to the domestic's department to find the "sale" curtains.

After Golden left, plaintiff moved Golden's merchandise to the service counter, voided the register slip containing the partial listing of Golden's items and began to check out other customers. Three to ten minutes later, Golden returned to plaintiff's check stand, where another customer was being served. Golden "looked around" that customer and asked what plaintiff had done with her money. When plaintiff replied, "What money?", Golden said that she had left four five-dollar bills on top of the merchandise she was purchasing before she left with the domestic's clerk. Plaintiff told Golden she had not seen any money. Golden continued in a loud, abrupt voice to demand her money from plaintiff and caused a general commotion. Customers and store personnel in the area began to look on curiously.

The K-Mart manager, who had been observing the incident from a nearby service desk, walked over to plaintiff's counter. After a short discussion with Golden, he walked up to plaintiff, pulled out her jacket pockets, looked inside and found nothing. Then he, plaintiff and two or three other store employees conducted a general search of the area for the money. When this effort proved fruitless, the manager explained there was nothing more he could do except check out plaintiff's register. Golden said, "Well, do it." The manager and an assistant manager locked plaintiff's register and took the till and the register receipt to the cash cage. While the register was being checked, Golden continued to glare at plaintiff while plaintiff checked out customers at another register. The register balanced perfectly. When the manager so advised Golden, Golden replied that she still believed plaintiff took her money and continued to "cause commotion" and glare at plaintiff. A further general search of the surrounding area was conducted without success. Golden still would not leave; another employee was trying to calm her down.

The manager then told plaintiff to accompany a female assistant manager into the women's public restroom for the purpose of disrobing in order to prove to Golden that she did not have the money. As plaintiff and the assistant manager walked to the restroom, the manager asked Golden if she wanted to watch the search; Golden replied: "You had better believe I do, it is my money." In the restroom, plaintiff took off all her clothes except her underwear while Golden and the assistant manager watched closely. When plaintiff asked Golden if she needed to take off more, Golden replied that it was not necessary because she could see through plaintiff's underwear anyway.

Plaintiff put on her clothes and started to leave the restroom when the assistant manager asked Golden how much money she had in her purse. Golden replied that she did not know the exact amount, but thought she had between five and six hundred dollars. She did not attempt to count it at that time.

Plaintiff then returned to her check stand. Golden followed plaintiff to the counter and continued to glare at her as she worked. Finally, the manager told Golden nothing more could be done for her, and after more loud protestations, Golden left the store.

Upon arriving home, Golden counted the money in her purse. She had $ 560. She called plaintiff's mother, whom she knew casually, and related the entire incident to her, stating that she had told K-Mart that plaintiff had taken her money. She described the strip search to plaintiff's mother and stated that when she was asked if she wanted to watch the strip, she responded, "Damn right." The mother expressed concern that plaintiff would lose her job; Golden said she would call the store and ask them not to let her go. Golden did make that call. After the conversation with Golden, plaintiff's mother, father and sister went to K-Mart to see if plaintiff was all right and to take her home.

Plaintiff returned to work the next day and was told that the keys to the cash register were lost and she was to work on a register with another employee. That procedure is known as "piggy-backing," and plaintiff had been told three months earlier that the store would no longer "piggy-back" checkers. Plaintiff believed the store was monitoring her by the "piggy-back" procedure; she quit at the end of her scheduled shift that day.

. . .

K-Mart contends that the trial court properly granted its motion, because the facts presented do not constitute outrageous conduct as a matter of law. Its principal argument is that plaintiff consented to the strip search, either expressly as its manager stated, or tacitly by not expressly objecting. Plaintiff stated, variously, that she was told or asked by the manager to disrobe, but, whether asked or told, she did not consider that she had a choice. She thought she would lose her job if she refused, and she needed the job. The issue of lack of consent to that search is an issue of fact, but whether it is an issue of material fact depends upon whether, assuming plaintiff's version to be true, the facts are sufficient to submit the case to the jury on the outrageous conduct theory.

The relatively short history and development of the tort of outrageous conduct, at least in Oregon, is summarized by the court in *Brewer v. Erwin*, 287 Or 435, 454–58, 600 P2d 398 (1979). As the court pointed out, the exact elements of the tort are still in process of clarification. There are at least two versions of the tort. One . . . involves intentional conduct, the very purpose of which is to inflict psychological and emotional distress on the plaintiff. The other is . . . where the wrongful purpose was lacking, but "the tortious element can be found in the breach of some obligation, statutory or otherwise, that attaches to defendant's relationship to plaintiff."

. . . Here, we are faced with the issue, unless there was the type of special relationship between plaintiff and K-Mart justifying recovery for emotional distress based on that defendant's conduct, which was not deliberately aimed at such distress but was reckless of the predictable effect of that conduct.

Neither the Supreme Court nor this court has been presented with the question of whether the employer-employee relationship falls into that special category. This court, however, has treated the landlord-tenant relationship as a "prime consideration" in evaluating the defendant's conduct. We reached that conclusion because landlords were in a position of authority with respect to tenants and could affect the tenants' interest in the quiet enjoyment of their leasehold. An employer has even more authority over an employee, who, by the nature of the relationship, is subject to the direction and control of the employer and may be discharged for any or no reason, absent an agreement restricting that authority. Clearly, that relationship is not an arm's length one between strangers. Accordingly, we conclude that the relationship between plaintiff and K-Mart was a special relationship, based on which liability may be imposed if K-Mart's conduct, though not deliberately aimed at causing emotional distress, was such that a jury might find it to be beyond the limits of social toleration and reckless of the conduct's predictable effects on plaintiff.

We conclude that a jury could find that the K-Mart manager, a 32-year-old male in charge of the entire store, after concluding that plaintiff did not take the customer's money, put her through the degrading and humiliating experience of submitting to a strip search in order to satisfy the customer, who was not only acting unreasonably, but was creating a commotion in the store; that the manager's conduct exceeded the bounds of social toleration and was in reckless disregard of its predictable effects on plaintiff.

Because there was no special relationship between plaintiff and Golden, the evidence must be such that a jury could find Golden's conduct not only socially intolerable, but that it was deliberately aimed at causing plaintiff emotional distress. Golden contends the evidence does not permit those findings, because she was merely trying to get her money back from plaintiff. To sustain that position, it would be necessary to resolve the disputed facts relating to Golden's conduct in her favor. As in the case against K-Mart, those factual issues are material only if, after resolving them in plaintiff's favor, the evidence would permit a jury to find for plaintiff.

We conclude that the facts, viewed most favorably to plaintiff, would permit a jury to find that Golden's entire course of conduct was intended to embarrass and humiliate plaintiff in order to coerce her into giving Golden $20, whether rightfully hers or not; that Golden did not know how much money she had in her purse, variously stated to be between $300 and $600, made no effort to determine if she was, in fact, missing four five dollar bills until she returned home, at which time she found she was mistaken; that Golden's insistence on a check of plaintiff's cash register, her insistence that plaintiff still had her money after the register checked out perfectly, her eager participation in the strip search of plaintiff and her continuing to stare angrily at plaintiff over an extended period, even after all efforts to find her money failed, would permit a jury to find Golden's conduct deliberately calculated to cause plaintiff emotional distress and exceeded the bounds of social toleration.

A jury could also find in Golden's favor, but the mere fact that her stated ultimate objective was to get her money back is not sufficient to defeat plaintiff's claim. . . . There are lawful (socially tolerable) ways to collect money from another, and there are unlawful (socially intolerable) ways to do so.

Common to her claims against both defendants is the requirement that plaintiff prove that she suffered severe emotional distress. If the facts presented are believed, plaintiff suffered shock, humiliation and embarrassment, suffering that was not merely transient. Plaintiff characterized herself as a shy, modest person, and said that she had two or three sleepless nights, cried a lot and still gets nervous and upset when she thinks about the incident. Concededly, this element of the tort has been, and still is, troublesome to courts. K-Mart contends there is no objective evidence of the distress, such as medical, economic or social problems. In *Rockhill v. Pollard, supra*, plaintiff became nervous and suffered from sleeplessness and a loss of appetite over a period of about two years. The court said "... Defendant belittles these symptoms, but it is the distress which must be severe, not the physical manifestations." 259 Or at 63.

Defendant Golden contends that the purpose of requiring proof of severe emotional distress is to guard against fraudulent or frivolous claims and that some degree of transient and trivial distress is a part of the price of living among people. Here, however, it is not unreasonable to expect that a shy, modest, young woman put in plaintiff's position would suffer the effects she claims to have suffered from the incident, and that her distress was more than that which a person might be reasonably expected to pay as the price of living among people.

We cannot say as a matter of law that plaintiff's evidence of severe emotional distress is insufficient to go to a jury. Because neither defendant was entitled to judgment as a matter of law, neither motion for summary judgment should have been granted. The judgment for each of the defendants is reversed. The case is remanded for trial.

QUESTIONS

1. What facts should the plaintiff show in this case to merit recovery?
2. The bounds of decency in a civilized society change over time, sometimes to great effect. How will the #MeToo movement change the discourse over boundaries in the workplace, and how will this affect IIED workplace claims?

In cases involving hostile work environment sexual harassment, employees sometimes will also allege IIED. Discriminatory treatment in the worksite may amount to extreme and outrageous conduct, but it is not necessarily the case that it will. Courts have found that discriminatory conduct alone does not give rise to a claim of IIED, because sexual harassment need not involve extreme and outrageous conduct. In *Meritor Savings Bank v. Vinson*, 477 U.S. 57, 67 (1986) the Supreme Court created the claim of hostile work environment sex harassment, but also made clear that an actionable harassment claim under Title VII does not depend on meeting the stricter test of the IIED tort.

Problem 21-1

James manages a farm for his employer, Dixon Chicken Farm. James and his family live on the chicken farm in a house owned by Dixon. James has two children with physical disabilities. James depends on the health insurance that Dixon provides its employees in order to pay for his children's health services. His supervisor knows that James is in a vulnerable position because of his children's health care needs. The supervisor becomes irritated with James and suddenly fires him with one week's notice, giving him only the week to vacate the house. Analyze whether James can succeed in a claim under IIED.

---

2. Severe Emotional Distress

Even if the employer engages in extreme and outrageous behavior, the employee can recover only if she has suffered "severe emotional distress." Consider the *K-Mart* case. The employer's behavior was reprehensible, but did the court fully explain the nature of the severe injury that resulted? Do you believe that courts might use a sliding scale, such that the worse the behavior is the less evidence of severe harm is necessary?

The following case involves abusive behavior that is less extreme than the behavior in the *K-Mart* case, but the behavior was constantly exhibited over time. Your focus should be on determining if the court adequately explains the criterion of compensating only for emotional distress that is severe.

GTE Southwest, Inc. v. Bruce

998 S.W.2d 605 (Tex. 1999).

In this case we determine whether three GTE Southwest, Incorporated employees may recover damages for intentional infliction of emotional distress based on the workplace conduct of their supervisor. The trial court rendered judgment for the employees on the jury verdict, and the court of appeals affirmed. We affirm the judgment of the court of appeals.

I. Facts

Three GTE employees, Rhonda Bruce, Linda Davis, and Joyce Poelstra, sued GTE for intentional infliction of emotional distress premised on the constant humiliating and abusive behavior of their supervisor, Morris Shields. Shields is a former U.S. Army supply sergeant who began working for GTE in 1971. Between 1981 and May 1991, Shields worked as a supervisor in GTE's supply department in Jacksonville, Arkansas. During his tenure there, four of Shields's subordinate employees (none of the employees involved in this case) filed formal grievances against Shields with GTE, alleging that Shields constantly harassed them. As a result of these complaints, GTE investigated Shields's conduct in 1988 and 1989, but took no formal disciplinary action against him.

In May 1991, GTE transferred Shields from Jacksonville to Nash, Texas, where he became the supply operations supervisor. The supply department at Nash was small, consisting of two offices and a store room. There were approximately eight employees other than Shields. Bruce, Davis, and Poelstra ("the employees") worked under Shields at the Nash facility. Like the GTE employees in Jacksonville, Bruce, Davis, and Poelstra complained to GTE of Shields's conduct, alleging that Shields constantly harassed and intimidated them. The employees complained about Shields's daily use of profanity, short temper, and his abusive and vulgar dictatorial manner. The employees complained that, among other offensive acts, Shields repeatedly yelled, screamed, cursed, and even "charged" at them. In addition, he intentionally humiliated and embarrassed the employees.

GTE investigated these complaints in April 1992, after which GTE issued Shields a "letter of reprimand." After the reprimand, Shields discontinued some of his egregious conduct, but did not end it completely.

Eventually, Bruce, Davis, and Poelstra sought medical treatment for emotional distress caused by Shields's conduct. In March 1994, the employees filed suit, alleging that GTE intentionally inflicted emotional distress on them through Shields. The employees asserted no causes of action other than intentional infliction of emotional distress. The jury awarded $100,000.00 plus prejudgment interest to Bruce, $100,000.00 plus interest to Davis, and $75,000.00 plus interest to Poelstra.

II

[Editor's Note: The Court first held that the Texas Workers' Compensation Act did not provide the exclusive remedy for the alleged behavior because the emotional injuries suffered do not flow from physical causes.]

III. Intentional Infliction of Emotional Distress

. . . .

GTE contests its liability for intentional infliction of emotional distress on several grounds. First, GTE argues that the alleged conduct does not rise to the level necessary to constitute extreme and outrageous conduct. Second, GTE argues that the employees did not prove that GTE, as opposed to Shields, had the requisite intent. And, third, GTE contends that the employees have not shown that they suffered severe emotional distress. We consider these arguments in turn.

A. Extreme and Outrageous Conduct

GTE first argues that Shields's conduct is not extreme and outrageous. To be extreme and outrageous, conduct must be "so outrageous in character, and so extreme in degree, as to go beyond all possible bounds of decency, and to be regarded as atrocious, and utterly intolerable in a civilized community." *Natividad v. Alexsis, Inc.,* 875 S.W.2d 695, 699 (Tex.1994) (quoting *Twyman v. Twyman,* 855 S.W.2d 619, 621 (Tex.1993)); Restatement (Second) of Torts § 46 cmt. d (1965). Generally, insensitive or even rude behavior does not constitute extreme and outrageous conduct. *Natividad,* 875 S.W.2d at 699. Similarly, mere insults, indignities, threats, annoyances, petty oppressions, or other trivialities do not rise to the level of extreme and outrageous conduct. *See Porterfield v. Galen Hosp. Corp.,* 948 S.W.2d 916, 920 (Tex.App.-San Antonio 1997, writ denied); Restatement (Second) of Torts § 46 cmt. d (1965).

In determining whether certain conduct is extreme and outrageous, courts consider the context and the relationship between the parties. . . . "The extreme and outrageous character of the conduct may arise from an abuse by the actor of a position, or a relation with the other, which gives him actual or apparent authority over the other, or power to affect his interests." restatement (Second) of Torts § 46 cmt. e (1965).

In the employment context, some courts have held that a plaintiff's status as an employee should entitle him to a greater degree of protection from insult and outrage by a supervisor with authority over him than if he were a stranger. . . . This approach is based partly on the rationale that, as opposed to most casual and temporary relationships, the workplace environment provides a captive victim and the opportunity for prolonged abuse.

In contrast, several courts, including Texas courts, have adopted a strict approach to intentional infliction of emotional distress claims arising in the workplace. . . . These courts rely on the fact that, to properly manage its business, an employer must be able to supervise, review, criticize, demote, transfer, and discipline employees. Although many of these acts are necessarily unpleasant for the employee, an employer must have latitude to exercise these rights in a permissible way, even though emotional distress results. We agree with the approach taken by these courts.

Given these considerations, Texas courts have held that a claim for intentional infliction of emotional distress does not lie for ordinary employment disputes. The range of behavior encompassed in "employment disputes" is broad, and includes at a minimum such things as criticism, lack of recognition, and low evaluations, which, although unpleasant and sometimes unfair, are ordinarily expected in the work environment. Thus, to establish a cause of action for intentional infliction of emotional distress in the workplace, an employee must prove the existence of some conduct that brings the dispute outside the scope of an ordinary employment dispute and into the realm of extreme and outrageous conduct. Such extreme conduct exists only in the most unusual of circumstances.

[Editor's Note: Shields repeatedly heaped abuse on workers by using vulgar words and sexual innuendo.]

More importantly, the employees testified that Shields repeatedly physically and verbally threatened and terrorized them. There was evidence that Shields was continuously in a rage, and that Shields would frequently assault each of the employees by physically charging at them. When doing so, Shields would bend his head down, put his arms straight down by his sides, ball his hands into fists, and walk quickly toward or "lunge" at the employees, stopping uncomfortably close to their faces while screaming and yelling. The employees were exceedingly frightened by this behavior, afraid that Shields might hit them. Linda Davis testified that Shields charged the employees with the intent to frighten them. At least once, another employee came between Shields and Poelstra to protect her from Shields's charge. A number of witnesses testified that Shields frequently yelled and screamed at the top of his voice, and pounded his fists when requesting the employees to do things. Bruce testified that Shields would "come up fast" and "get up over her"—causing her to lean back—and yell and scream in her face for her to get things for him. Shields included vulgar language in his yelling and screaming. Bruce stated that such conduct was not a part of any disciplinary action against her. Further, the incidents usually occurred in the open rather than in private. Bruce testified that, on one occasion, Shields began beating a banana on his desk, and when he jumped up and slammed the banana into the trash, Bruce thought he would hit her. Afterwards, Shields was shaking and said "I'm sick."

[Editor's Note: The employees testified to numerous instances of abusive behavior.]

As already noted, the employees demonstrated at trial that Shields engaged in a course of harassing conduct directed at each of them, the totality of which caused severe emotional distress. It is well recognized outside of the employment context that a course of harassing conduct may support liability for intentional infliction of emotional distress. In such cases, courts consider the totality of the conduct in determining whether it is extreme and outrageous.

Similarly, in the employment context, courts and commentators have almost unanimously recognized that liability may arise when one in a position of authority engages in repeated or ongoing harassment of an employee, if the cumulative quality and quantity of the harassment is extreme and outrageous.

When such repeated or ongoing harassment is alleged, the offensive conduct is evaluated as a whole.

. . . .

We agree with the overwhelming weight of authority in this state and around the country that when repeated or ongoing severe harassment is shown, the conduct should be evaluated as a whole in determining whether it is extreme and outrageous. Accordingly, we hold that the court of appeals did not err in doing so.

> *[Editor's Note: The Court held that the jury could reasonably have concluded that the conduct cumulatively amounted to extreme and outrageous behavior.]*

Occasional malicious and abusive incidents should not be condoned, but must often be tolerated in our society. But once conduct such as that shown here becomes a regular pattern of behavior and continues despite the victim's objection and attempts to remedy the situation, it can no longer be tolerated. It is the severity and regularity of Shields's abusive and threatening conduct that brings his behavior into the realm of extreme and outrageous conduct. Conduct such as being regularly assaulted, intimidated, and threatened is not typically encountered nor expected in the course of one's employment, nor should it be accepted in a civilized society. An employer certainly has much leeway in its chosen methods of supervising and disciplining employees, but terrorizing them is simply not acceptable. If GTE or Shields was dissatisfied with the employees' performance, GTE could have terminated them, disciplined them, or taken some other more appropriate approach to the problem instead of fostering the abuse, humiliation, and intimidation that was heaped on the employees. Accordingly, the trial court properly submitted the issue to the jury, and there was some evidence to support the jury's conclusion that Shields's conduct was extreme and outrageous.

B. Intent

> *[Editor's Note: The Court held that Shields' intent was imputed to the employer under* respondeat superior *because Shields was acting in the course and scope of his employment.]*

C. Severe Emotional Distress

GTE next contends that any distress the employees suffered was not severe. GTE argues that the employees' complaints of embarrassment, fear, stomach aches, loss of sleep, and headaches "are problems that are normally dealt with by each of us in everyday life."

Emotional distress includes all highly unpleasant mental reactions such as embarrassment, fright, horror, grief, shame, humiliation, and worry. Severe emotional distress is distress that is so severe that no reasonable person could be expected to endure it. The employees testified that, as a result of being exposed to Shields's outrageous conduct, they experienced a variety of emotional problems, including crying spells, emotional outbursts, nausea, stomach disorders, headaches, difficulty in sleeping and eating, stress, anxiety, and depression. The employees testified that they experienced anxiety and fear because of Shields's continuing harassment, especially his charges and rages. Each employee sought medical treatment for these problems, and all three plaintiffs were prescribed medication to alleviate the problems. An expert witness testified that each of them suffered from post-traumatic stress disorder. This evidence is legally sufficient to support the jury's finding that the employees suffered severe emotional distress.

. . . .

3. Defenses Based on Statutory Preclusion

Courts are split on whether a plaintiff can claim damages for infliction of emotional distress when the actionable behavior gives rise to claims for damages under a statutory scheme. We will see in Lesson 26 that workplace injuries typically are compensated exclusively through the Workers' Compensation Act, but that behavior that gives rise to injuries compensable under IIED is not likely to be within the exclusive scope of workers' compensation. However, many other workplace statutory remedies are not clearly exclusive, and so courts must determine if the employee may also recover under IIED. The following case illustrates this issue.

HOFFMAN-LAROCHE, INC. v. ZELTWANGER

144 S.W.3d 438 (Tex. 2004).

We must decide whether a plaintiff can recover damages on a claim for intentional infliction of emotional distress when the Legislature has created a statutory right to seek emotional damages for the same actions that form the basis of the intentional-infliction claim. The court of appeals concluded that the plaintiff could recover damages under both claims, electing mental anguish and punitive damages under her intentional-infliction claim while taking other compensatory damages and attorney's fees under her sexual harassment claim. We conclude that when the gravamen of the plaintiff's complaint is for sexual harassment, the plaintiff must proceed solely under a statutory claim unless there are additional facts, unrelated to sexual harassment, to support an independent tort claim for intentional infliction of emotional distress. We therefore reverse the judgment of the court of appeals and remand the cause to the trial court for rendition of judgment consistent with this opinion.

I

Joan Zeltwanger sued her former employer, Hoffmann La-Roche, Inc. ("Roche"), for sexual harassment under Texas Labor Code section 21.051, retaliation under Texas Labor Code section 21.055, and intentional infliction of emotional distress.

Except for the retaliation claim, Zeltwanger prevailed at trial on all of her claims against Roche . . . . On her sexual harassment claim against Roche, the jury awarded Zeltwanger $835,963 for front and back pay, $500,000 in compensatory damages, and an additional $8,000,000 in punitive damages. On the intentional infliction of emotional distress claim against Roche, the jury awarded $1,000,000 for mental anguish, $73,000 for past and future medical care, and another $8,000,000 in punitive damages.

Acknowledging potential double recovery and applicable statutory cap considerations with respect to the $500,000 in compensatory and the $8,000,000 in punitive damages of the harassment award, Zeltwanger moved to limit her harassment damages to front and back pay and attorney's fees while taking her mental anguish and punitive damages under her intentional-infliction claim. The trial court therefore rendered judgment awarding Zeltwanger $847,036 on her harassment claim, comprising front and back pay adjusted for disability payments and interest. Judgment on the intentional infliction of emotional distress claim against Roche, which at that time was not subject to a statutory cap, amounted to $9,504,706, adjusted for interest. The court of appeals affirmed these awards, and Roche appeals only the intentional infliction of emotional distress claim.

II

Zeltwanger began working in November 1990 as a sales representative for Roche, a pharmaceutical company. In this capacity, Zeltwanger worked out of her home, as did other Roche sales representatives. Roche, like many pharmaceutical sales companies, did not maintain regional offices, instead running its nationwide operations solely from its New Jersey corporate headquarters.

Until 1992, Zeltwanger worked under Dallas-based sales manager Betty Turicchi. When Turicchi became a Roche supervisor in another region, Webber, a Dallas-based division sales manager, became Zeltwanger's supervisor. Zeltwanger testified that Webber began telling dirty jokes in front of her in the last half of 1992, three or four months after Zeltwanger moved into his division, and went on to engage in other objectionable conduct.

Zeltwanger discussed Webber's behavior with Turicchi on several occasions. Turicchi, Zeltwanger says, gave her pointers on how to handle Webber and "document everything that was happening" but warned her that making a claim of sexual harassment within the company would jeopardize Zeltwanger's chances of advancement. Subsequently, Turicchi advised Zeltwanger that she would need to contact Roche human resources representative Betty DeVos in order to make a formal complaint.

Zeltwanger eventually did contact DeVos, and on August 19, 1994, she faxed a handwritten, five-page statement to her, which made the following complaints about Webber:

> 1. Last fall at Div Mtgs with Zore—during Rocephin game. I won a question & he delivered my $5 between his teeth to me stating & you've implied you've never been to those top-less bars in front of 2 work groups. Betty Turrichi witnessed this at meeting. Her division or group was there also.
>
> 2. At Dir Mtg last fall—told dirty jokes & talked about top-less dancers. I told him I do not like jokes like that & did not want to hear them.
>
> 3. Talked about his car name was in college & that they used to have sex or "do it" in the car.
>
> 4. Last summer field trip—continually tells dirty & inappropriate jokes—verbalized to me the sorority girls "he screwed" in college the couples they (him & his wife) still hang around & his goal to "do them" all while standing at the trunk of my car. I responded with "I don't want to hear this."
>
> 5. Had lunch last Summer/Spring with my Arl. Memorial Hospital Anesthesia & Jim made a comment to those physicians that I was not the typical homely Betty Turicchi hire & he thought it was a joke when I walked into Bennigans for a confirming interview. Their (the Drs.') reply was—what is a typical Betty Turicchi hire? Jim's reply was they don't have legs & a body like

that. I was standing outside of the room & heard this as I entered back into the room.

6. Told a Howard Stern panty (underwear) story from a concert his daughter attended—ask me if I was wearing panties. This story was told in one of my GI offices as I set up a teleconference last spring.

Despite my protest he continued as follows:

7. Last winter while on field trip Jim made inappropriate references to his body parts i.e. "his ding dong" & how when he was in school he whipped it out in class. I told him I did not want to hear it.

8. Last winter while on field trip Jim made reference to my having a bad hair day & flung my hair by touching it in front of one of my hospital pharmacists. Before this call I was lectured about going & "kicking some ass" with this RPH & telling him what a liar he is for publishing a newsletter at hospital. He continually disregards my credibility & work involved with the BID dosing problem at this hospital. To which the situation attempts have been with in converting BID to QID dosing of Rocephin.

9. Last month on field trips as on previous others he continually mentions & alludes to his sexual encounters & sex positions (on his back) while screwing this girl who lived in these apartments as we pass the apartments. I advised him at the time I don't want to hear this.

10. Last Dec. when Jim Webber came to my house to check samples I was in my office filling out a form. When I was finished I found him in my bedroom. When I ask him what he was doing & to get out of my bedroom he said he was trying to find my stereo.

There will be more to follow as I continue to compile a list.

On August 24, 1994, Webber conducted a regularly-scheduled performance review of Zeltwanger, which Zeltwanger and Turrichi attended. Zeltwanger testified that Webber "screamed and yelled" at her and repeatedly criticized her job performance during this review. Turicchi testified that the discussion at the review focused on Zeltwanger's job performance, particularly her sales skills, and that Zeltwanger disagreed with Webber's assessment of her performance. In his written evaluation based on the review, Webber gave Zeltwanger an "H" rating, a below average designation that signifies the employee is "meeting most" of the standards but needs to make improvements. Shortly after this review, Roche completed its investigation of Zeltwanger's complaint and terminated Webber because of his inappropriate behavior with Zeltwanger.

At the end of 1994, Zeltwanger received notification that Roche had fired her also. Shortly thereafter, she filed a complaint for sexual harassment against Roche with the Texas Commission on Human Rights. Under the section entitled "Discrimination Statement," she stated:

> I believe that I have been discriminated against, in violation of the Texas Commission on Human Rights Act, as amended, and Title VII of the Civil Rights Act of 1964, as amended, because of my sex, female (sexual harassment), inasmuch as:
>
> Background: Jim Webber's reflections and references to his sexual exploits, and matters of a sexual nature, became non-stop and always managed to get personal.
>
> Some examples of this intolerable behavior are:
>
>> —On a field trip in early Winter 1993, Mr. Webber made inappropriate remarks about his body parts, i.e., "his ding-dong" and remarked that in school, in class, he used to "whip it out". On the same trip, Mr. Webber belittled me by flinging my hair and referring to a "bad hair day" in front of my hospital pharmacists.
>>
>> —On a later trip, in December 1993, Mr. Webber described sexual encounters and his preferred position when "screwing this girl who lives in those apartments", as we passed an apartment complex.
>>
>> —Mr. Webber also invaded my privacy by entering my bedroom when he came to my home to inspect samples.
>>
>> —In early 1994, at several division meetings, Mr. Webber spoke of topless bars and told offensive, obscene jokes.

—In Spring 1994, Mr. Webber asked if I was wearing panties. This was also repeated to physicians in one of the offices while I set up for a teleconference.

—In spring/summer 1994, I overheard Mr. Webber telling physicians that I "was not the typical homely hire" and "they don't have legs and a body like that!"

—In mid summer 1994 on a field trip, Mr. Webber continually told lewd and smutty jokes. He mentioned the sorority girls "he screwed" in college. He also stated that his goal was to "do it" while standing at the trunk of his car.

A. I repeatedly rebuffed Mr. Webber for his behavior but this only made matters worse. My work environment was intolerable.

B. Due to Mr. Webber's hostility and vindictiveness, I requested that a third impartial party be present at my review in early August 1994. His behavior was unbearable and my review was unjustly negative. I was forced to seek counseling.

C. I am aware that an internal investigation of Mr. Webber's behavior found that the harassment allegations had "merit."

Zeltwanger's complaints have remained largely unchanged throughout this litigation, although at trial she added that she once caught Webber going through her underwear drawer, not merely that he had entered her bedroom without permission. Zeltwanger explained at trial that she maintained a home office and that it was standard procedure for her supervisor to come to her home to take an inventory of her pharmaceutical samples. During one such inventory, Webber wandered into her bedroom and went through her underwear drawer. Zeltwanger also offered medical testimony at trial that she experienced symptoms of depression and partial disability as a result of the alleged conduct.

III

To recover damages for intentional infliction of emotional distress, a plaintiff must establish that: (1) the defendant acted intentionally or recklessly; (2) the defendant's conduct was extreme and outrageous; (3) the defendant's actions caused the plaintiff emotional distress; and (4) the resulting emotional distress was severe. *Standard Fruit & Vegetable Co. v. Johnson*, 985 S.W.2d 62, 65 (Tex.1998). Extreme and outrageous conduct is conduct "'so outrageous in character, and so extreme in degree, as to go beyond all possible bounds of decency, and to be regarded as atrocious, and utterly intolerable in a civilized community.' " *Twyman v. Twyman*, 855 S.W.2d 619, 621 (Tex.1993) (quoting Restatement (Second) of Torts § 46 cmt 46 cmt. d (1965)). Liability does not extend to mere insults, indignities, threats, annoyances, petty oppressions, or other trivialities. *GTE Southwest, Inc. v. Bruce*, 998 S.W.2d 605, 612 (Tex.1999); Restatement (Second) of Torts § 46 cmt 46 cmt. d (1965). It is for the court to determine, in the first instance, whether a defendant's conduct was extreme and outrageous. . . . But when reasonable minds may differ, it is for the jury, subject to the court's control, to determine whether, in the particular case, the conduct was sufficiently extreme and outrageous to result in liability.

In addition to her common-law claim for intentional infliction of emotional distress, Zeltwanger sought damages for Roche's violation of the Texas Commission on Human Rights Act (CHRA). This statute prohibits an employer from discriminating against an individual because of race, color, disability, religion, sex, national origin or age. See Tex. Lab.Code § 46 cmt 21.051. Sexual harassment is one form of prohibited employment discrimination.

. . . .

In creating causes of action for discrimination, including sexual harassment, both Congress and the Texas Legislature have specified the types and amounts of damages that may be awarded. . . . The CHRA provides that a court may award compensatory damages upon finding that an employer has engaged in an unlawful intentional employment practice and may further award punitive damages when the discriminatory practice is with malice or reckless indifference. . . .The largest employers, like Roche, are subject to a maximum cap of $300,000. The compensatory damages which are capped specifically include, among other things, "emotional pain, suffering, inconvenience, mental anguish, loss of enjoyment of life, and other nonpecuniary losses." The cap does not apply to back pay, interest on back pay, and equitable relief.

As previously set out, the jury awarded Zeltwanger approximately $8.5 million in damages for mental anguish and punitive damages under her sexual harassment claim and about $9 million for mental anguish and punitive damages under her intentional-infliction claim. Because of the duplication in these awards, the trial court allowed Zeltwanger to take her mental anguish and punitive damages under the intentional-infliction claim, collecting only her front and back pay damages under the statutory claim. Zeltwanger's choice was understandable, as her statutory recovery for these damages was capped at $300,000, while her common-law damages were then uncapped. Thus, by electing to take part of her damages under her common law tort claim, Zeltwanger avoided the effect of the statutory cap.

IV

Roche complains that Zeltwanger has improperly used the intentional-infliction tort to circumvent the legal limitations on the amount of mental anguish and punitive damages recoverable in a sexual harassment suit. Roche submits that the intentional-infliction tort is a "gap-filler" that only applies under special circumstances when more established torts do not permit recovery. Because the CHRA provided a statutory remedy for essentially the same conduct, Roche submits there was no gap to be filled by the common law and hence no right to an award of further damages against it. Alternatively, Roche contends that if the tort of intentional infliction applies here, the evidence is legally insufficient to satisfy one or more of its elements.

Zeltwanger responds that her intentional infliction and sexual harassment claims were not based entirely upon the same conduct or the same facts. While the actions of Roche through Webber did include extreme and outrageous sexual harassment, Zeltwanger submits that they also included public humiliation, intimidating verbal abuse, threatening gestures, and invasions of Zeltwanger's privacy in her own home. Furthermore, Zeltwanger contends that Roche's "gap-filler" argument is an appellate afterthought that was neither raised nor preserved in the trial court. Finally, Zeltwanger concludes that the evidence fully supports the jury's finding that Roche intentionally or recklessly caused her severe emotional distress through extreme and outrageous conduct.

A

Roche's gap-filler argument is based on our decision in *Standard Fruit and Vegetable Co. v. Johnson,* 985 S.W.2d 62, 68 (Tex.1998). There we recognized that the intentional infliction of emotional distress was, first and foremost, a "gap-filler" tort, judicially created for the limited purpose of allowing recovery in those rare instances in which a defendant intentionally inflicts severe emotional distress in a manner so unusual that the victim has no other recognized theory of redress. *Id.* The tort's "clear purpose," we noted, was "to supplement existing forms of recovery by providing a cause of action for egregious conduct" that might otherwise go unremedied. *Id.* We cautioned, however, that the tort was "a 'gap-filler' tort that should not be extended to circumvent the limitations placed on the recovery of mental anguish damages under more established tort doctrines." *Id.*

Likewise, in this case, the tort should not be extended to thwart legislative limitations on statutory claims for mental anguish and punitive damages. By combining her sexual harassment claim with the intentional-infliction tort, Zeltwanger has circumvented, by more than thirty-fold, the legislative determination of the maximum amount that a defendant should pay for this type of conduct. In creating the new tort, we never intended that it be used to evade legislatively-imposed limitations on statutory claims or to supplant existing common law remedies. Properly cabined, the tort simply has no application when the "actor 'intends to invade some other legally protected interest,' even if emotional distress results." *Id.* at 67 (quoting Restatement (Second) of Torts § 46 cmt 47 cmt. a (1965)) . . . . Where the gravamen of a plaintiff's complaint is really another tort, intentional infliction of emotional distress should not be available. . . Thus, we need not decide whether, in the absence of a legislative remedy for sexual harassment, the evidence here would be sufficient to support a claim for intentional infliction of emotional distress.

In her concurring opinion, Justice O'Neill expresses concern that our gap-filler analysis may lead to unintended consequences such as a larger monetary recovery in tort for plaintiffs who cannot sustain their burden for sexual harassment. She asks: "Does the fact that the plaintiff did not sustain its evidentiary burden on an alternative claim create a gap that intentional-infliction was designed to fill?" She further worries that our analysis may lead to skewed trials in which defendants find it advantageous to confess liability for sexual harassment to avoid more onerous awards under the intentional-infliction tort. In answer to these concerns, we note that a plaintiff's failure to establish his or her claim for sexual harassment does not mean that the plaintiff has a claim for intentional infliction of emotional distress. If the gravamen of a plaintiff's complaint is the type of wrong that the statutory remedy was meant to cover, a plaintiff cannot maintain an intentional infliction claim regardless of whether he or she succeeds on, or even makes, a statutory claim.

B

Zeltwanger contends, however, that she can elect the higher recovery here because independent grounds, apart from sexual harassment, exist for the tort. She argues that there is evidence of additional egregious, but wholly non-sexual, conduct in this case involving public humiliation, verbal oppression, physical threats, invasion of privacy, abuse of power, and mistreatment of an employee known to have been rendered susceptible to emotional distress.

Roche responds that throughout this case Zeltwanger has consistently treated Webber's behavior as a cohesive set of actions that support both her sexual harassment and intentional-infliction claims. None of her mental anguish evidence at trial was separated into one claim or the other, and Roche submits that any such designation would have been artificial in any event. Sexual harassment, Roche points out, often devolves into other forms of abuse and bullying.

While the court of appeals did not differentiate between sexual and non-sexual conduct, it did find the following acts by Roche, taken together, sufficient to constitute extreme and outrageous conduct: (1) Roche "allowed" the development of a corporate culture that permitted vulgar joke-telling; (2) Turicchi failed initially to report to upper management Zeltwanger's discussions with her about Webber's conduct; (3) Roche subjected Zeltwanger to the August 1994 in-person review with Webber after she had formally complained about Webber's conduct and sent Turicchi only as an observer without authority to intervene when Webber verbally abused Zeltwanger during this session; (4) Roche terminated Zeltwanger and caused her to believe this termination was, in part, based on Webber's unfavorable evaluation of her at the August 1994 review; and (5) Roche allowed managers like Webber to function unsupervised in the field (including in cars and homes) with direct responsibility for female employees like *Zeltwanger.* 69 S.W.3d at 646–47. Even assuming that some or all of this conduct might be considered to be independent of Zeltwanger's sexual harassment claim, an assertion of which we are skeptical but need not decide, it does not rise to the level of extreme or outrageous conduct.

First, Zeltwanger's proof that Roche allowed a corporate culture of insensitive jokes relating to women and minorities falls short of constituting extreme and outrageous conduct. Zeltwanger's evidence showed only a handful of instances of off-color jokes being told among Roche employees over a period of several years in a company with 1,000 sales people. Such evidence is legally insufficient to show that Roche fostered a culture that encouraged extreme and outrageous conduct.

Second, we conclude that Turicchi's failure to report Zeltwanger's concerns about Webber to others within Roche was not extreme and outrageous. Zeltwanger does not claim that she attempted to file a formal complaint with Turicchi. Moreover, after Zeltwanger talked with Turicchi on several occasions about Webber's conduct, Turicchi told her about DeVos, the appropriate person with whom to file a formal complaint. Finally, Turicchi did not exercise authority over either Zeltwanger or Webber. In sum, Turicchi's failure to take more aggressive action in response to Zeltwanger's concerns about Webber is no evidence of extreme and outrageous conduct on the part of Roche.

Third, Zeltwanger's claim that Roche's conduct surrounding her August 1994 performance review with Webber was extreme and outrageous is without merit. Zeltwanger asserts that Roche itself caused her distress by telling Webber in advance that Turicchi would attend her review and by scheduling the review at Webber's home. Her complaint is not that Turicchi was present, but that Webber had several days to prepare for the review knowing that Zeltwanger would not be alone. We do not believe that such notice to a supervisor is in any way extreme or outrageous. Nor is the location of the review given the circumstance that Roche did not have physical offices in Texas. Zeltwanger does not assert that she felt physically imperiled by the prospect of going to Webber's home, especially with Turrichi present.

Fourth, Zeltwanger's charge that Roche led her to believe that Webber's performance evaluation of her after this review session was a factor in her termination is not extreme or outrageous. We have held that workplace and employment matters such as "criticism, lack of recognition, and low evaluations" are not actionable, even if they are unpleasant or unfair. . . . Nothing in this record indicates that Roche did anything more than make an honest error in telling her that the review would be a factor in whether she was retained or terminated.

Finally, Zeltwanger's claim that allowing managers to function unsupervised in the field (including in cars and homes) with direct responsibility for female employees is not extreme or outrageous. While it may well have been easier for Webber to engage in his objectionable conduct because he and Zeltwanger worked in the field rather than at a traditional business office, there is no evidence this management structure amounts to a corporate policy endorsing Webber's conduct. Thus, even assuming there is evidence of conduct by Roche which may be considered to be independent of the sexual harassment claim, we conclude that such conduct is not extreme or outrageous as a matter of law.

. . . .

In sum, we do not believe that Zeltwanger's intentional-infliction claim is independent of her sexual harassment claim. Because the CHRA provides a remedy for the same emotional damages caused by essentially the same actions, there is no remedial gap in this case and thus no support for the award of damages under the intentional-infliction claim. Moreover, even were we to consider only that conduct that might arguably form an independent basis for such a claim and indulge every reasonable inference and intendment in favor of such claim, it would still not be sufficient to raise a fact issue. Accordingly, the court of appeals erred in affirming that part of the trial court's judgment awarding damages under the tort theory. We reverse that judgment and remand the cause to the trial court for it to render judgment for the appropriate damages under Zeltwanger's sexual harassment claim.

. . . .

QUESTIONS

1. Should a plaintiff be able to recover damages for intentional infliction of emotional distress if she has already recovered damages for a statutory violation that resulted in emotional or mental injury?
2. Should a company be responsible for the ways in which its culture might facilitate bad behavior? Might blurring the line between work and non-work time in the age of remote employment sites contribute to a corporate culture that facilitates harassment?

Problem 21-2

Donna worked as a security guard for Acme International, a private security company that contracts with major airports across the country. Donna, who is African American, is one of two women who worked a guard shift with ten other men. Her co-workers were upset when a woman was hired, and they have tried several times to get her fired. They made her life difficult by refusing to relieve her of duty to take bathroom or other breaks; by leaving her out of discussions about scheduling and other work matters; by calling her lewd and demeaning names on a daily basis; and by threatening her family. One co-worker, Kevin, was the most consistent in his demeaning behavior towards Donna. When Donna complained to her shift supervisor, John, he told her that Kevin was like that with everyone, and that she had to toughen up if she wanted to be accepted by the rest of the shift guards. When Donna took her complaints to the human resources department, it failed to find evidence of problematic behavior by her co-workers. Donna had a nervous breakdown after six months and left the job. Can Donna recover for IIED against her co-worker, Kevin? Is John, the shift supervisor, also liable for IIED? Is the company liable for IIED?

Mastery Problem 21-1

The following news article describes the workplace harassment of Loretta Lee, who worked at Google. Read the following excerpt and analyze whether she might also be able to bring a claim for IIED against the company or any of her co-workers.

Ethan Baron, *'Bro-culture' at Google Led to Sexual Harassment and Violence, Lawsuit Alleges*

Mercury News (February 24, 2018).

Mountain View—As a young, female software engineer at male-dominated Google, Loretta Lee was slapped, groped and even had a co-worker pop up from beneath her desk one night and tell her she'd never know what he'd been doing under there, according to a lawsuit filed against the company.

The lawsuit comes as Silicon Valley's tech industry, dominated by white men, has been roiled by a series of sexual-misconduct scandals and gender-related upheavals as the #MeToo movement against sexual assault of women has prompted a nationwide cultural reckoning.

Google has been the focus of considerable gender-related controversy. It fired engineer James Damore over his memo claiming a biological basis for the gender gap in tech. It dismissed a transgender man who then sued the firm, claiming he was ousted for opposing bigotry in the workplace. And lawsuits by the U.S. Department of Labor and a former employee have accused the company of paying women less than men.

Now, Lee's lawsuit—filed in Santa Clara County Superior Court—alleges that the company did not protect her, saying, "Google's bro-culture contributed to (Lee's) suffering frequent sexual harassment and gender discrimination, for which Google failed to take corrective action."

She was fired in February 2016 for poor performance, according to the lawsuit.

Google said Friday that it has "strong policies against harassment in the workplace" and reviews every complaint it receives.

"We take action when we find violations, including termination of employment," a company spokesperson said.

Lee started at the company in 2008 in Los Angeles and later switched to the firm's Mountain View campus, according to the suit, which asserts that she "was considered a talented and rising star" who received consistently "excellent" performance reviews.

Lee claims that the "severe and pervasive" sexual harassment she experienced included daily abuse and egregious incidents. In addition to making lewd comments to her and ogling her "constantly," Lee's male co-workers spiked her drinks with whiskey and laughed about it; and shot Nerf balls and darts at her "almost every day," the suit alleges.

One male colleague sent her a text message asking if she wanted a "horizontal hug," while another showed up at her apartment with a bottle of liquor, offering to help her fix a problem with one of her devices, refusing to leave when she asked him to, she alleges.

At a holiday party, Lee "was slapped in the face by an intoxicated male co-worker for no apparent reason," according to the suit.

In January 2016, while working late one night, she was approaching her work space when she saw a male colleague with whom she had never spoken "on all fours, underneath her desk," she claims. When he saw her, the man "jumped up and shouted, 'You'll never know what I was doing!' " according to the suit.

"She was frightened by his comment and believed he may have installed some type of camera or similar device under her desk," the lawsuit states.

The next day, a co-worker grabbed the name badge hanging from a lanyard around her neck, asking her name and grazing her breasts with his hand, she claims.

Lee's superior and the firm's human resources department learned of that incident and repeatedly tried to persuade her to report the alleged groper, but she resisted out of fear of being ostracized as an "informer," she claims. After she was written up for being uncooperative, she relented and reported the man, but HR found her claims "unsubstantiated," according to the suit.

"This emboldened her colleagues to continue their inappropriate behavior," the suit says.

Her fear of being ostracized was realized, she claims, with co-workers refusing to approve her code in spite of her diligent work on it. Not getting her code approved led to her being "labeled as a 'poor performer,' " the suit says.

Lee also alleges that Google would not accommodate her after she suffered a disabling back injury from a car crash, with the company telling her she must get treatment and therapy on her own time.

Lee is seeking unspecified damages in excess of $25,000 for harassment, gender discrimination, failure to prevent sexual harassment, disability discrimination, wrongful termination and retaliation.

Conclusion

The at-will rule gives employers great flexibility in their treatment of workers, but the tort of intentional infliction of emotional distress provides recourse for truly abusive behavior in the workplace. To recover, an employee must establish that she was subjected to "extreme and outrageous" behavior that caused severe emotional distress. Given the nature of the tort, it is possible that the behavior may be outside the course and scope of employment, in which case the employer may not be subject to liability under *respondeat superior* principles.

Lesson 22:
Autonomy and Dignity

Objectives and Expected Learning Outcomes

In this Lesson, we consider the effect of statutes and common law principles in defining a zone of personal autonomy for the employee when she is not working. An employer is generally able to hire and fire at-will, but in many states the employer may not leverage that power to control an employee's political or civic activity or the employee's lawful use of free time. However, these protections tend to be narrowly defined against the backdrop of the at-will rule.

Employers have substantial authority over workplace conditions and their employees under the at-will rule, subject to statutory limits. However, a mixture of the common law, statutes, and contractual obligations under handbooks and similar employer means of communication have resulted in the recognition of the employee's interest in personal autonomy apart from the workplace. This autonomy interest is rooted in the respect for the dignity of persons who have interests and pursuits outside the workplace. The Restatement attempts to capture the protection of employee personal autonomy.

Restatement of Employment Law

§ 7.08. Protection of Employee Personal Autonomy

(a) Employees have protected interest in personal autonomy outside of the employment relationship. Such interests include:

(1) engaging in lawful conduct that occurs outside of the locations, hours, and responsibilities of employment and does not refer to or otherwise involve the employer or its business;

(2) adhering to political, moral, ethical, religious, or other personal beliefs or expressing such beliefs outside of the locations, hours, and responsibilities of employment in a manner that does not refer to or otherwise involve the employer or its business; or

(3) belonging to or participating in lawful associations when that membership or participation does not refer to or otherwise involve the employer or its business.

(b) Unless the employer and employee agree otherwise, an employer is subject to liability for intruding upon an employee's personal autonomy interests if the employer discharges the employee because the employee exercises a personal autonomy interest under § 7.08(a).

(c) The employer is not liable under § 7.08(b) if it can prove that it had a reasonable and good-faith belief that the employee's exercise of an autonomy interest interfered with the employer's legitimate business interests, including its orderly operations and reputation in the marketplace.

The Restatement summarizes the scope of the protection in Comment a: Conduct "outside of the employment relationship, including adhering to or expressing personal beliefs, or participating in lawful associations, when the conduct, beliefs, or participation does not refer to or otherwise involve the employer or its business. This Section recognizes a measure of legal protection for those interests while making clear that an employer has the right to terminate an employee in furtherance of its legitimate business interests."

However, § 7.08(b) makes clear that the protection of personal autonomy can be altered by agreement of the parties. As the Reporter explains:

> The premise of this Section is that the parties to every employment relationship implicitly agree to the level of protection stated in the Section. This implied understanding may be altered by the parties' express agreement. To change this default rule, the parties would have to agree that off-duty lawful conduct, adherence or expression of beliefs, or membership in lawful associations may be the subject of the employer's adverse personnel action.

Restatement of Employment Law, § 7.08 cmt. f.

Of course, if issues of personal autonomy are established by statute they may not be susceptible to the parties' agreement to waive those rights.

QUESTION

1. Is it proper to permit employees to agree to surrender personal autonomy rights? Would there ever be a limit to the conditions that an employer might demand as part of the employment bargain?

Problem 22-1

You are general counsel to Duffs, a major brewing company that produces a variety of mass-market beers. You have been asked by the CEO to develop language for a new policy that requires all employees to drink only Duffs products if they drink beer. The policy applies 24-7; it covers drinking in public but also drinking in one's home. The CEO wants to enforce the policy strictly as part of building strong brand loyalty. Will this agreement be enforceable under the Restatement rule? Would your analysis change if the policy stated that an employee who chooses to drink any kind of alcoholic drink, whether in public or private, must choose one of Duffs' beers?

---

1. Protecting Off-Site Legal Activity

Many states have enacted statutes that protect employees from retaliation by their employer for engaging in legal activity on their own time. Many of these statutes were actively promoted by the tobacco industry at a time when employers began considering whether to hire only non-smoking employees as a strategy to reduce absenteeism, health costs, and other costs attributed to smoking. However, the statutes were broadly worded and generally are phrased in terms of protecting all "legal" activity. Consider the potential scope of the following Colorado statute.

Colorado Rev. Stats.

§ 24–34–402.5. Unlawful prohibition of legal activities as a condition of employment

(1) It shall be a discriminatory or unfair employment practice for an employer to terminate the employment of any employee due to that employee's engaging in any lawful activity off the premises of the employer during nonworking hours unless such a restriction:

(a) Relates to a bona fide occupational requirement or is reasonably and rationally related to the employment activities and responsibilities of a particular employee or a particular group of employees, rather than to all employees of the employer; or

(b) Is necessary to avoid a conflict of interest with any responsibilities to the employer or the appearance of such a conflict of interest.

(2) (a) Notwithstanding any other provisions of this article, the sole remedy for any person claiming to be aggrieved by a discriminatory or unfair employment practice as defined in this section shall be as follows: He or she may bring a civil action for damages in any district court of competent jurisdiction and may sue for all wages and benefits that would have been due him or her up to and including the date of the judgment had the discriminatory or unfair employment practice not occurred; except that nothing in this section shall be construed to relieve the person from the obligation to mitigate his or her damages.

(b) (I) If the prevailing party in the civil action is the plaintiff, the court shall award the plaintiff court costs and a reasonable attorney fee. . . .

. . . .

Problem 22-2

How would your answer in Problem 22-1 change if the Duffs agreement will be governed by Colorado law?

Problem 22-3

Willie is employed at an insurance company in Denver, Colorado. Colorado law permits recreational use of cannabis by adults, and the state legislature has adopted a statute that indicates that the state has a strong public policy in favor of permitting adult use of cannabis. Cannabis remains listed as a Schedule 1 drug under the Controlled Substances Act, making it illegal under federal law for all purposes. Willie uses cannabis on his own time and has never come to work under the influence. Nevertheless, when Willie fails a drug test because it detected the use of cannabis, he is promptly fired. Can Willie prevail under the state statute?

---

2. Protecting Political Activity and Association

You will note that there is a strong connection with the common law cause of action for termination in violation of public policy. In some respects, it is in the public's interest for employees to be engaged in political, civic and social interests outside of the workplace, and so protecting these activities is not just a personal matter between employer and employee. Expressing this public policy, a number of states have enacted statutes that protect various activities from employer intrusion. Consider the following California statute.

California Labor Code

§ 1101. Political Activities of Employees; Prohibition of Prevention or Control by Employer

No employer shall make, adopt, or enforce any rule, regulation, or policy:

(a) Forbidding or preventing employees from engaging or participating in politics or from becoming candidates for public office.

(b) Controlling or directing, or tending to control or direct the political activities or affiliations of employees.

§ 1102. Coercion or Influence of Political Activities of Employees

No employer shall coerce or influence or attempt to coerce or influence his employees through or by means of threat of discharge or loss of employment to adopt or follow or refrain from adopting or following any particular course or line of political action or political activity.

The purpose of these statutes is clear, but defining the key terms quickly becomes difficult, as the following case demonstrates.

Smedley v. Capps, Staples, Ward, Hastings and Dodson

820 F. Supp. 1227 (N.D. Cal. 1993).

Caulfield, District Judge.

FACTS AND BACKGROUND

Plaintiff Lauren Smedley was hired by defendants Capps, Apps, Staples, Ward, Hastings & Dodson [and various individual partners as defendants ("the firm")] as an associate in the Spring of 1990 and started work on April 4, 1990. During the relevant time period, Ward was the partner at the firm in charge of associates. Defendants learned of plaintiff's sexual orientation shortly after she was hired and they admit that, to their knowledge, there had never been a gay or lesbian employee at the firm. Apparently while distributing paychecks, defendant Hollingshead noticed a heart-shaped picture frame containing a photograph of plaintiff and her companion, which Hollingshead showed to defendants Nossen and Allen. Plaintiff alleges that defendant Ward also saw the photograph and that he expressed the strongest opinions about employees bringing political and controversial issues into the office. Ward admits that he feels employees should refrain from bringing up controversial issues at social events. It is undisputed that on or about September 1990, during a meeting with plaintiff, Ward instructed her that he "did not think sexual preference was something that—the kind of discussion that should be initiated by members of the firm at the firm's social events." During deposition Ward clarified that he believed a person's sexual orientation is something that should be left at home.

On September 6, 1990, Ward wrote a note to plaintiff in which he stated:

> When I said your sexual preference should not be an issue, I meant that given our clientele it would not be appropriate to discuss lesbian rights, groups, activities, etc.

Plaintiff asserts that as a result of Ward's comments, she curtailed her activities with the Bay Area Lesbian Feminist Bar Association ("BALFBA"), of which she was a co-chair. She maintains that she felt she would have been fired if she discussed her lesbianism at firm social events, so she refrained from doing so. On March 4, 1991, an article in the Daily Journal about BALFBA identified plaintiff as an associate in defendant firm and quoted plaintiff as stating that "being out" at work would help other lesbian attorneys brave the threat of discrimination. On April 1, 1991, shortly after the article was published, plaintiff was terminated.[1]

DISCUSSION

I. *Plaintiff's Motion for Summary Judgment*

. . . .

B. Political Activities

In this case, the court is called upon to interpret California Labor Code § 1101 . . . The central, and most difficult, interpretive issue regarding the statute is which types of political actions and affiliations are protected against arbitrary action by a private employer which suppresses or directs employees' political activities. Another problematic issue is the meaning of the language of the statute, in this case, what is meant by "rule, regulation or policy."

Against a background of cases defining political activity in broad terms, the California Supreme Court concluded that the fight against discrimination on the basis of sexual preference was political in nature. "Measured by these standards, the struggle of the homosexual community for equal rights, particularly in the field of employment, must be recognized as a political activity." *Gay Law Students Assn. v. Pacific Tel. & Tel. Co.,* 24 Cal.3d 458, 488, 156 Cal.Rptr. 14, 595 P.2d 592 (1979). *Gay Law Students* interprets the statute as protecting those who identify themselves as "manifest homosexuals," who defend homosexuality, or who are identified with activist homosexual organizations. *Gay Law Students* also briefly discusses the political aspiration of the gay community for equal rights: "[o]ne important aspect of the struggle for equal rights is to induce homosexual individuals to come out of the closet, acknowledge their sexual preference, and to associate with others in working for equal rights." *Id.*

In the aftermath of *Gay Law Students,* there is no question that a cause of action exists under § 1101 when an employer makes, adopts or enforces any rule, regulation or policy that has as its purpose or succeeds in preventing or controlling the sexual preference-oriented political activities (aimed at achieving equal rights) of an employee. 69 Ops.Cal.Atty.Gen. 80 (1986). However, to grant plaintiff's motion for summary judgment would require

1 Plaintiff also points out that Ward admits asking Diane Tweedy, during an interview for an associate position at the firm, "whether she had a cause," and that he then "made reference to somebody else in the firm that had a cause which [he] thought was interfering with their ability to be a good attorney."

the court to accept plaintiff's personal interpretations of events without benefit of a trial and to draw clear inferences from ambiguous deposition testimony.

Plaintiff's motion is largely based on the deposition and written statements of defendant Ward. Specifically, she alleges that Ward instructed her not to initiate discussions about her sexual orientation at the firm's social events. In addition to Ward's deposition testimony, plaintiff offers a note sent to her by Ward in which he states (referring to the firm's social events), "Given the firm's clientele, it would not be appropriate to discuss lesbian rights groups activities, etc." Assuming *arguendo* that Ward's pronouncements constituted a "rule, regulation or policy forbidding plaintiff from participating in protected activity," it is still not clear that the activity in question—discussion of lesbianism at firm social events—satisfies the definition of "political activity" as propounded in *Gay Law Students. Gay Law Students* does not hold that any discussion of sexual preference in any forum is protected political activity. That case addressed an employer which did not employ any gay men or lesbians. The opinion is silent, as is the statute, about whether or not discussion of sexual preference by a lesbian at private firm functions (as compared to activities outside of work) is a political activity.

If, for example, plaintiff were prevented from discussing gay rights with other employees at firm gatherings, this might well be construed as an effort to prevent her from associating and communicating with or organizing other individuals in order to work for equal rights. Similarly, if plaintiff had been instructed to curtail her gay-oriented political activities outside the office, this would constitute a violation of § 1101. However, it is by no means certain that discussions of lesbianism with clients of her firm at firm social events are political activities as contemplated by the California Supreme Court in *Gay Law Students.*[3]

3 The courts have traditionally interpreted the statute as being intended to defend employees engaged in traditional political activity from reprisal by their employer. In *Lockheed Aircraft Corp. v. Superior Court*, 28 Cal.2d 481, 485, 171 P.2d 21 (1946), the California Supreme Court commented that the statute concerned activities related to or connected with the orderly conduct of government and the peaceful organization, regulation and administration of the government. Sections 1101 and 1102 protect the fundamental right of employees to engage in political activity without interference by employers. *Fort v. Civil Service Commission*, 61 Cal.2d 331, 335, 38 Cal.Rptr. 625, 392 P.2d 385 (1964); 69 Ops. Cal. Atty. Gen. 80 at 3. Yet no court has stated that the rights protected under §§ 1101 and 1102 are unlimited. Even under *Lockheed*, the proselytizing Republican described in the analogy might be lawfully terminated (the employer was not prevented from discharging an employee whose loyalty to the United States was not demonstrated to its satisfaction). More recently, *Mitchell v. International Ass'n of Machinists*, 196 Cal.App.2d 796, 16 Cal.Rptr. 813 (1961) contains the strong suggestion that an employer may use its power to curb an employee's advocacy of political views when the employee's political activities are patently in conflict with the employer's interests.

In furtherance of her motion for summary judgment under § 1101, plaintiff states that she was terminated from her employment with defendants shortly after an article on the BALFBA appeared in the San Francisco Daily Journal. The article identified plaintiff as an associate attorney at defendant firm and as co-chair of the BALFBA. The court is asked to infer the existence of a direct causal linkage between the appearance of the article and the termination by plaintiff's employer—that, in effect, defendants were ultimately motivated to fire her because of her participation in this particular political activity or association. Plaintiff offers no affidavits or other evidence in support of her allegation, nor does she provide incontrovertible facts or testimony. The connection between the article and her termination remains an unresolved issue of material fact that must be decided by a jury.

Essential issues of triable fact remain. The most significant among them is whether defendants, in violation of § 1101, made, adopted or enforced any rule, regulation or policy forbidding or preventing plaintiff from engaging or participating in politics or otherwise controlling, directing or coercing via pressure or threats of termination, plaintiff's political activities or affiliations.

Given the absence of clear and convincing evidence offered by plaintiff, the court, as matter of law, rules that several triable issues of fact exist as to plaintiff's third cause of action alleging defendants' violation of § 1101. Plaintiff will have the opportunity to present a case before the trier of fact.

. . . .

QUESTIONS

1. You are an associate with the firm representing the defendant law firm. The partner on the file has asked for your thoughts about how to proceed with discovery to avoid liability at trial. What is your theory of the case, and what is your discovery strategy?

2. Assume that Smedley is a lesbian activist who pickets outside churches and temples with signs that castigate the opposition to gay and lesbian rights by conservative elements of organized religion in harsh terms. For example, one sign read "Jesus hates you if you hate lesbians," while another said "Religion is the problem. Rights are the answer." A news story about a local protest indicates that Smedley is a lawyer at the firm, immediately causing a backlash among the firm's clients. Would her case survive summary judg-

ment if she had been terminated for negatively affecting the firm's reputation?

---

3. Legitimate Business Interests

The employer has an affirmative defense to a personal autonomy claim by an employee if the employer was acting in the good faith belief that the employee was interfering with a legitimate business interest. The scope of this defense, when read in the context of the underlying at-will rule, is broad.

> The at will rule . . . leaves undisturbed an employer's broad discretion to determine whether an employee's off-premises, after-work activity interferes with workplace responsibility or the company's reputation. The employer who acts in a reasonable good-faith belief that an employee's exercise of protected autonomy interests interferes with legitimate business interests is not subject to liability under this Section. This inquiry is necessarily contextual, taking into account the nature of the employee's activities, beliefs, or associations. Because smaller and more intense workplaces may magnify the effects of an employee's activities, beliefs, or associations, courts should take this into account.

Restatement of Employment Law, § 7.08 cmt. g. The following case provides an overview of the defenses.

MARSH v. DELTA AIR LINES, INC.

952 F.Supp. 1458 (D. Colo. 1997).

DANIEL, DISTRICT JUDGE.

I. Procedural and Factual Background

. . . .

The essential facts of this case are uncontroverted. Plaintiff was a Delta employee for 26 years. He was employed as a baggage handler (his official title was customer service agent) at the time of his termination. He was suspended, and later terminated, because he wrote a letter to the editor, criticizing Delta, that was published by the Denver Post. More specifically, in late November, 1994, Plaintiff wrote a letter to the editor of the Denver Post that strongly criticized Delta's decision to employ hourly contract workers to replace laid-off full-time employees. After composing the letter, he took the letter to work so that it could be photocopied. Thereafter, he mailed the letter and it was published by the Post on December 15, 1994. The letter, as published, stated:

> My trusted and faithful employer of more than 26 years has become infected with two of the latest industrial diseases going around—"re-engineering" and "cost-cutting."
>
> Delta Air Lines, a company which is renowned worldwide for its corporate family culture, enthusiastic and professional employees and superior service to customers, has decided to flush 60 years worth of care and paternalism down the executive washroom toilet, putting thousands of loyal Delta employees and their families on hold or in the street.
>
> The company is convinced it can continue to deliver its traditional high levels of customer service with $6 an hour help. The thinking here, apparently, is that what works for the fast-food industry should work for the airline business just as handily.
>
> Expenses and costs are so critical, we are told, that the company is spending $500 million to cut costs and enhance that sacred bottom line. Analysts, accountants, consultants and lawyers are hard at work, it would seem, destroying another fine American institution, and most of them probably have never had any practical experience in the world of airline complexities.
>
> In betraying the trust and loyalty of more than 60,000 dedicated employees, Delta has lost the very thing that made it so prosperous and efficient over six decades.
>
> And now has come the ultimate insult: Delta employees were called together and told that they would be responsible for training the cheap contract help that would be replacing them. This curious mandate speaks to corporate arrogance and ignorance of the first magnitude.
>
> MICHAEL A. MARSH
>
> Lakewood

As a result of the publication of this letter, on December 16, 1994, Plaintiff was summoned to a meeting where his supervisor, Dick Cassella, suspended Plaintiff indefinitely, without pay. On January 16, 1995, Plaintiff and Mr. Cassella had a second meeting where Mr. Cassella asked Plaintiff to resign. After Plaintiff refused to resign, Mr. Cassella fired Plaintiff "for conduct unbecoming a Delta employee." Mr. Marsh appealed his termination, and on January 31, 1995, flew to Atlanta to argue his case to two Delta managers. Approximately two weeks later, Plaintiff was informed by Mr. Cassella that his appeal had been denied.

. . . .

II. Cross-Motions for Summary Judgment—Analysis

. . . .

A. *Wrongful Discharge—Colo.Rev.Stat. § 24–34–402.5 (Cross-Motions)* (Claim 1)

Both parties argue that they are entitled to summary judgment on the wrongful discharge claim. Colo.Rev.Stat. § 24–34–402.5, which became effective on July 1, 1990, protects employees who are engaging in a legal activity from being punished by their employer. Specifically, the statute, in relevant part, provides:

> (1) It shall be discriminatory or unfair employment practice for an employer to terminate the employment of any employee due to that employee's engaging in any lawful activity off the premises of the employer during nonworking hours unless such a restriction:
>
> (a) Relates to a bona fide occupational requirement or is reasonably and rationally related to the employment activities and responsibilities of a particular employee or a particular group of employees, rather than to all employees of the employer; or
>
> (b) Is necessary to avoid a conflict of interest with any responsibilities to the employer or the appearance of such a conflict of interest.

In their briefs, and at the hearing on this matter, the parties agreed, and my independent research confirmed, that there exist no Colorado cases that interpret the substantive portions of this statute as they relate to the specific issues presented by this case. Moreover, the statute's legislative history is scant, and provides the Court with no illumination as to the meaning of the substantive portions of this statute.

Both parties agree that Plaintiff was engaged in a lawful activity when he wrote and sent the letter to the editor of the Denver Post. Plaintiff argues that he is entitled to summary judgment because Delta did not prohibit employees—in writing—from sending critical letters to the editor. Plaintiff also argues that none of the exceptions to the general rule—listed in the statute—apply. In contrast, Defendant argues that it is entitled to summary judgment because it was justified in firing the Plaintiff under the statute's following exceptions: 1) Plaintiff was terminated for engaging in an activity related to a bona fide occupational requirement; 2) the activity was rationally related to Plaintiff's particular job responsibilities; 3) publication of the letter led to a conflict—or the appearance of a conflict—of interest between Plaintiff and Defendant; and 4) a portion of the activity occurred on Delta property.

1. *PLAINTIFF'S MOTION FOR PARTIAL SUMMARY JUDGMENT*

I find that Plaintiff's claim that he is entitled to summary judgment because Defendant did not have a written policy prohibiting writing a letter to the editor is without merit and should be denied. In a recent case that was not selected for official publication, the Colorado Court of Appeals held that the wrongful discharge statute should be analyzed in two parts: first, did the employer terminate an employee for participation in a lawful activity; and second was there a statutory exception to justify that termination. *Gwin v. Chesrown Chevrolet, Inc.*, 931 P.2d 466, 470 (Colo.App.1996). The Court commented that "no specific restriction must be adopted by an employer as a predicate to violating the prohibition." *Id.* It logically follows, therefore, that if a specific prohibition does not need to be in effect for the statute to take effect, then a specific written prohibition does not need to be in place for the exceptions to the statute to apply. I conclude, therefore, that the language from *Gwin* dictates that the statute does not require an employer to adopt specific written restrictions for which it can terminate an employee, but merely requires that any restriction an employer is attempting to enforce must fall under the purview of the statute's exceptions.

2. *DEFENDANT'S MOTION FOR SUMMARY JUDGMENT*

Defendant's claim that it is entitled to summary judgment on the wrongful discharge claim must be analyzed under prong two of the *Gwin* analysis.

That is, the Court must determine whether Delta can justify its actions under the exceptions provided in the text of Colo.Rev.Stat. 24–34–402.5.

Delta first urges that there is an implied bona fide occupational requirement of loyalty owed by employees to their employer that Plaintiff breached by writing the critical letter to the Denver Post. Therefore, Delta argues that it was justified in terminating Plaintiff under the first exception contained in the wrongful discharge statute. Colo.Rev.Stat. § 24–34–402.5(1)(a). Because there is a paucity of Colorado case law on the issue, Defendant cites labor law cases where disloyalty was found to be an adequate cause for discharge. *NLRB v. Local Union No. 1229, International Brotherhood of Electrical Workers,* 346 U.S. 464, 475, 74 S.Ct. 172, 178, 98 L.Ed. 195 (1953); *George A. Hormel and Co. v. NLRB,* 962 F.2d 1061 (D.C.Cir.1992) (upholding termination for employee disloyalty). Defendant urges that these cases stand for the proposition that all employees owe an implied duty of loyalty to their employer. To determine the validity of Defendant's argument, I must examine the purpose of the statute.

The wrongful discharge statute, § 24–34–402.5, was created to protect employees in their "off-the-job-privacy." *Gwin,* at 469. More specifically, the law was meant to provide a shield to employees who engage in activities that are personally distasteful to their employer, but which activities are legal and unrelated to an employee's job duties. In application, this statute should protect the job security of homosexuals who would otherwise be fired by an employer who discriminates against gay people, members of Ross Perot's new political party who are employed by a fervent democrat, or even smokers who are employed by an employer with strong anti-tobacco feelings. *See Evans v. Romer,* 882 P.2d 1335, 1346–47 (Colo.1994). The one common thread that links all of these examples is that the statute shields employees who are engaging in private off-the-job activity, that is unrelated to the employees job duties, from termination for participation in the non-work related activities.

This statutory shield, however, is not absolute. The fact that the Colorado legislature provided three exceptions to the general rule reflects the fact that the legislature recognized that the policy of protecting an employee's off-the-job privacy must be balanced against the business needs of an employer. By providing exceptions to the statute's general rule, the legislature indicated that it did not intend this privacy statute to provide a sword to employees thereby allowing employees to strike indiscriminate public blows against the business reputation of their employer. Accordingly, I find that one of the bona fide occupational requirements encompassed within the scope of Colo.Rev.Stat. § 24–34–402.5(1)(a) is an implied duty of loyalty, with regard to public communications, that employees owe to their employers.

The issue thus becomes whether this implied duty of loyalty is applicable to the circumstances of this case. It is undisputed that the letter written by Plaintiff was harshly critical of Delta. However, at the hearing, Plaintiff's counsel argued that even if there is an implied duty of loyalty, Plaintiff should not be held to that duty because Plaintiff was in a position analogous to a whistle blower. That is, Plaintiff was reporting to the public that Delta was undermining safety by replacing long term employees with contract workers. If this claim were true, the implied duty of loyalty would be inapplicable to Plaintiff's actions. *See Martin Marietta Corp. v. Lorenz,* 823 P.2d 100, 108–110 (Colo.1992) (setting out elements for Colorado whistle blower claim, including protecting employees who are asked to forsake a public duty). However, the text of Plaintiff's letter makes clear that he could not be viewed as a whistle blower. Plaintiff was not exposing public safety concerns, instead he was a disgruntled worker venting his frustrations to his employer whom he felt betrayed him and his coworkers. The public concerns expressed in his letter relate to reduced customer service and not public safety. Further, it is undisputed that Plaintiff did not avail himself of the internal grievance policy that Delta provided its workers by taking his concerns to management. (*See* Help Preserve Delta's High Standards of Business Conduct, Exhibit G, Defendant's Opening Brief) (providing Delta employees with a toll-free telephone number where they could report internal grievances without repercussion on their employment status). For these reasons, I find that because Plaintiff was not attempting to inform the public of a safety concern, and because Plaintiff did not attempt to solve his grievance through Delta's grievance system, his actions breached the bona fide occupational requirements of an implied duty of loyalty encompassed in Colo.Rev.Stat. § 24–34–402.5(1)(a). Accordingly, Defendant's termination of Plaintiff was justified under this statutory exception.

Although I have found that Delta acted properly in terminating Plaintiff, because my interpretation of the state statute is one of first impression, I will analyze the other arguments made by Delta in support of its actions. Delta's second argument is that as a customer service agent (baggage handler), Plaintiff had the special job responsibility of promoting a positive image for Delta. Therefore, Defendant argues Plaintiff breached his duty to promote a positive Delta image, thereby allowing the airline to fire Defendant under the statutory exception that allows prohibition of activities that relate "to the employment activities and responsibilities of a *particular employee or a particular group of employees, rather than to all employees of the employer.*" § 24–34–402.5(1)(a) (emphasis added). This argument is unpersuasive. Delta cannot seriously contend that it is the unique function of a baggage handler to portray a positive image for Delta while other employees are not charged with that same responsibility. The fact is this portion of the statute was probably crafted to allow employers to require certain high profile members of their staff from foregoing involvement in activities that would call into question their competence. If this portion of the statute is expanded to include all members of the workforce, the exception would swallow the general rule. Promotion of a positive image for Delta is not the exclusive province of baggage handlers. Thus, this exception does not apply.

Delta's third argument is that the letter to the Denver Post resulted in a conflict, or appearance of a conflict, of interest between Plaintiff and Delta. § 24–34–402.5(1)(b). Delta relies on provisions of its standard practice manual (Exhibits D and F, Defendant's Opening Brief) to support its position that Plaintiff's letter constituted a conflict of interest. The first provision cited is 1002.2 which prohibits Delta employees from participation in various competing businesses. Plaintiff's letter clearly does not fall into this category. Delta also cites provision 1125 which deals with the control of information by Delta. Delta, however, cannot rely on this provision because Plaintiff was not fired for revealing business information, rather, he was fired because of the insubordinate nature of the letter published in the Denver Post. Finally, Delta argues that a conflict of interest does not have to be financial to allow termination, citing *Wild v. U.S. Dept. of Housing,* 692 F.2d 1129 (7th Cir.1982) (holding that HUD employee who moonlit as slumlord was properly terminated for a conflict of interest). However, when the government is involved, as in *Wild,* a conflict of interest cannot be financial because the government does not have a profit motive. In interpreting the plain meaning of the statute, the term conflict of interest should be given its generally understood meaning; that is, that it relates to "fiduciaries and their relationship to matters of private interest or gain to them" or a "situation in which regard for one duty tends to lead to disregard of another." *Black's Law Dictionary* 299 (6th ed. 1990). Plaintiff was not disregarding his duties in favor of personal gain by writing the Post. In fact, it cannot fairly be argued that Plaintiff sought any personal gain by writing the Post.

Therefore, under the generally understood meaning of the term, Plaintiff did not have any conflict of interest when writing to the Post.

Finally, Defendant argues that because Plaintiff made a photocopy of the letter—which Plaintiff retained for his own records—on Delta premises that the statute does not protect Plaintiff. Specifically, § 24–34–402.5(1) limits protections to "employee's engaging in any lawful activity off the premises of the employer. . . ." The Defendant, however, fails to demonstrate that the critical letter published in the Denver Post (the offense for which Plaintiff was fired) was written on Delta property. Although it may be true that Plaintiff broke a work rule by copying a personal letter on a Delta copying machine, it is disingenuous to suggest that the act for which Plaintiff was fired actually transpired on Delta property. Plaintiff drafted the letter away from Delta premises, on his own time, and sent the letter to the Denver Post where it was received, reviewed and published. Plaintiff's de minimis act of photocopying the letter on Delta property does not, by itself, vitiate the applicability of the statute.

For the foregoing reasons, I will GRANT Defendant's motion for summary judgment on the grounds that Plaintiff had a bona fide occupational duty to be loyal to Delta in his public communications regarding issues that do not implicate public safety. Because his letter to the editor was clearly critical of Delta, Defendant has an affirmative defense to Plaintiff's claim under § 24–34–402.5(1)(a).

. . . .

QUESTIONS

1. Assume that you represent Mr. Marsh and you are preparing to file an amended complaint. What other theories might you present on these facts?
2. The court concludes that the de minimis use of Delta's photocopier as part of his submission of the letter for publication was not enough to provide a defense. Why? Shouldn't the employer be able to enforce a zero-tolerance policy for using company assets to support personal interests outside of the workplace?

Problem 22-4

Jeff is employed by a tech firm in Silicon Valley. He has long been close friends with Samantha, who works for the chief competitor of Jeff's firm. Jeff and Samantha are consummate professionals. They never discuss confidential work matters with each other. Nevertheless, Jeff is fired when his employer learns that he regularly meets Samantha for social events, including meals, concerts, plays, etc. Develop the argument that Jeff can sue for interference with personal autonomy under the Restatement test.

Problem 22-5

Assume the facts in Problem 22-4, and also assume that a state statute protects "lawful activities outside of work." In particular, the statute specifically prohibits retaliation for:

> c. an individual's legal recreational activities outside work hours, off of the employer's premises, and without use of the employer's equipment or other property.

The statute defines "recreational activities" as:

> any lawful, leisure-time activity, for which the employee receives no compensation and which is generally engaged in for recreational purposes, including but not limited to sports, games, hobbies, exercise, reading, and the viewing of television, movies, and similar material.

Can Jeff prevail under this statute?

Problem 22-6

Return to Example 7-2, involving the Duke fan who was fired by her boss, a North Carolina fan. If the statute in Problem 22-5 applied to the case, could the Duke fan recover?

Conclusion

State courts and legislatures have defined a zone of personal autonomy that employers must respect. Although construed somewhat narrowly, this zone generally protects employees engaged in political or civic activities, and also the employee's pursuit of legal activities when outside the workplace.

7

Regulatory Structures

A. Compensation

Key Concepts

- The Fair Labor Standards Act ("FLSA") was enacted in 1938 to provide that workers receive a minimum wage for their hourly work and overtime compensation for hours worked in excess of 40 hours a week. The Supreme Court had refused to uphold the constitutionality of such laws enacted by states, reasoning that they were abridgements of the liberty interests of both the employer and the employee to agree upon the terms and conditions of employment. The FLSA commenced the modern era of employment law.
- The FLSA governs employers engaged in interstate commerce and applies to all employees, as opposed to independent contractors. Unlike most employment law statutes, the FLSA empowers employees to sue individual owners and managers for an FLSA violation, provided that they exercised control over the setting of wage and hour policies for the business entity.
- Significant exceptions to the FLSA exist for executive, administrative, or professional employees. The classification of employees exempt from the FLSA has given rise to extensive litigation.
- The FLSA protects employees who assert their rights under the statute, prohibiting retaliation by the employer.

Lesson 23:
The Fair Labor Standards Act

Objectives and Expected Learning Outcomes

In this Lesson, you will learn how to identify employees who are entitled to minimum wage and overtime pay under the FLSA. We will discuss the remedies for FLSA violations, including when owners and managers may be held personally liable. We will pay particular attention to the question of compensable time, which is particularly important in a 24/7 world connected by smart devices.

1. The FLSA as a Foundational Statute

The FLSA is a foundational statute of the modern workplace. It may seem, in hindsight, a foregone conclusion that all employees deserve a floor for how much they make an hour or that employees should receive additional compensation for working over 40 hours in a given work week. Not so. Prior to *West Coast Hotel*, which you will read below, the United States Supreme Court held that employers and employees had a liberty interest under the Constitution to determine for themselves the terms and conditions of employment. But, the growth of industry and the expansion of the American economy required that overarching mandates for minimum and overtime wages be put into place. The FLSA was enacted during the Great Depression and was designed in part to compel employers to provide more job opportunities for more individuals, the theory being that employers would be disinclined to pay overtime and thus would hire more workers to avoid payment of overtime. Despite these clear goals, significant interpretive issues arose early on.

The first step was to ensure that the FLSA would be constitutional. After the Great Depression started in 1929, the Roosevelt Administration enacted many relief measures at the federal level, and state governments followed suit. However, the Supreme Court found that these protections violated the "liberty" interests of the Due Process clause. President Roosevelt threatened to "pack the court" by expanding the number of Justices, and requiring retirement of Justices at age 70 in order to ensure that a majority of Justices would uphold his reform legislation. This triggered the famous "switch in time that saved nine," as the Court acknowledged the constitutionality of employment law protections. *West Coast Hotel* concerns a state minimum wage law limited to women and children, but its constitutional analysis supported the enactment of the FLSA the following year.

West Coast Hotel Co. v. Parrish

300 U.S. 379 (1937).

Hughes, J.

This case presents the question of the constitutional validity of the minimum wage law of the State of Washington.

The Act, entitled 'Minimum Wages for Women,' authorizes the fixing of minimum wages for women and minors. It provides:

> Section 1. The welfare of the State of Washington demands that women and minors be protected from conditions of labor which have a pernicious effect on their health and morals. The State of Washington, therefore, exercising herein its police and sovereign power declares that inadequate wages and unsanitary conditions of labor exert such pernicious effect.

. . . .

The appellant conducts a hotel. The appellee Elsie Parrish was employed as a chambermaid and (with her husband) brought this suit to recover the difference between the wages paid her and the minimum wage fixed pursuant to the state law. The minimum wage was $14.50 per week of 48 hours. The appellant challenged the act as repugnant to the due process clause of the Fourteenth Amendment of the Constitution of the United States. The Supreme Court of the state, reversing the trial court, sustained the statute and directed judgment for the plaintiffs. *Parrish v. West Coast Hotel Co.*, 185 Wash. 581, 55 P. (2d) 1083. The case is here on appeal.

. . . .

The principle which must control our decision is not in doubt. The constitutional provision invoked is the due process clause of the Fourteenth Amendment . . . . by those attacking minimum wage regulation for women [argue it] is deprivation of freedom of contract. What is this freedom? The Constitution does not speak of freedom of contract. It speaks of liberty and prohibits the deprivation of liberty without due process of law. In prohibiting that deprivation, the Constitution does not recognize an absolute and uncontrollable liberty. Liberty in each of its phases has its history and connotation. But the liberty safeguarded is liberty in a social organization which requires the protection of law against the evils which menace the health, safety, morals, and welfare of the people. Liberty under the Constitution is thus necessarily subject to the restraints of due process, and regulation which is reasonable in relation to its subject and is adopted in the interests of the community is due process.

. . . .

This essential limitation of liberty in general governs freedom of contract in particular. More than twenty-five years ago we set forth the applicable principle in these words, after referring to the cases where the liberty guaranteed by the Fourteenth Amendment had been broadly described.

> But it was recognized in [previous] cases . . . that freedom of contract is a qualified, and not an absolute, right. There is no absolute freedom to do as one wills or to contract as one chooses. The guaranty of liberty does not withdraw from legislative supervision that wide department of activity which consists of the making of contracts, or deny to government the power to provide restrictive safeguards. Liberty implies the absence of arbitrary restraint, not immunity from reasonable regulations and prohibitions imposed in the interests of the community.

Chicago, Burlington & Quincy R. Co. v. McGuire, 219 U.S. 549, 565.

. . . .

The Legislature of the state was clearly entitled to consider the situation of women in employment, the fact that they are in the class receiving the least pay, that their bargaining power is relatively weak, and that they are the ready victims of those who would take advantage of their necessitous circumstances. The Legislature was entitled to adopt measures to reduce the evils of the 'sweating system,' the exploiting of workers at wages so low as to be insufficient to meet the bare cost of living, thus making their very helplessness the occasion of a most injurious competition. The Legislature had the right to consider that its minimum wage requirements would be an important aid in carrying out its policy of protection. The adoption of similar requirements by many states evidences a deep seated conviction both as to the presence of the evil and as to the means adapted to check it . . . .

There is an additional and compelling consideration which recent economic experience has brought into a strong light. The exploitation of a class of workers who are in an unequal position with respect to bargaining power and are thus relatively defenseless against the denial of a living wage is not only detrimental to their health and well being, but casts a direct burden for their support upon the community. What these workers lose in wages the taxpayers are called upon to pay. The bare cost of living must be met. We may take judicial notice of the unparalleled demands for relief which arose during the recent period of depression and still continue to an alarming extent despite the degree of economic recovery which has been achieved. It is unnecessary to cite official statistics to establish what is of common knowledge through the length and breadth of the land. While in the instant case no factual brief has been presented, there is no reason to doubt that the state of Washington has encountered the same social problem that is present elsewhere. The community is not bound to provide what is in effect a subsidy for unconscionable employers. The community may direct its law-making power to correct the abuse which springs from their selfish disregard of the public interest.

. . . .

QUESTIONS

1. Was *West Coast Hotel* a decision that was driven to achieve the result? Why did the Court go out of its way to take judicial notice of the economic state of the country?
2. Do we still need statutes such as the FLSA? Are today's employers more enlightened such that they consider employees as true "human resources," and thus treat them accordingly? Would it now be better to allow workers and employers, especially in the Gig Economy, to determine the terms and conditions of employment?
3. Recent congressional efforts have sought to provide "comp", or compensatory, time in lieu of paid overtime. Do these proposals undermine the FLSA, or do they acknowledge that we have entered a more dynamic period with respect to compensation practices?
4. Consider a single mother who works 40 hours a week, which provides her with a living wage and also time to care for her child. If her employer decides that she must now work 50 hours per week, can she be fired for refusing?

The FLSA immediately posed significant interpretive questions because it did not define "work," "workweek," and other key terms. The courts accorded expansive definitions to effectuate the remedial purposes of the FLSA. Work was defined as "physical or mental exertion (whether burdensome or not) controlled or required by the employer and pursued necessarily for the benefit of the employer and his business." Workweek was defined to include "all time during which an employee is necessarily required to be on the employer's premises, on duty, or at a prescribed workplace." By 1946, the Court had applied these definitions to find that going to work from home or returning from work to home was compensable time.

These expansive definitions cascaded into numerous lawsuits in which nearly $6 billion in back pay and liquidated damages were sought. Declaring this situation to be an "emergency" that threatened many employers with financial ruin, Congress enacted the Portal-to-Portal Act as an amendment to the FLSA. The Act exempted employers from being required to compensate employees for time spent going to and from work as well as activities which were preliminary to work or post-preliminary to work. It would be almost another 60 years before the Court emphatically decided that pre and post-activities are compensable, but only if they are integral and indispensable to the performance of the job.

As a federal statute, the FLSA provides baseline protection for most employees in the country. However, the FLSA also contains exceptions to coverage and exemptions of certain employees. Some states, most notably California, have extended compensation laws well beyond the FLSA rules.

Before we turn to some modern problems in defining the scope of the FLSA, consider the following examples to guide you.

Example 23-1

Employees work in a warehouse in which they retrieve inventory and then pack it for shipment. The employer requires that employees undergo an anti-theft security screening at the end of their shift to ensure that they are not stealing any items from the warehouse. The time spent by the employees going through the screening is not compensable because the screening is not part of their job duties.

Example 23-2

Employees on a production line must put on protective gear and safety equipment before starting work and must take it off after completing their shift. The majority of courts consider the time spent donning and doffing gear and safety equipment to be integral to the performance of the job, and therefore compensable. A minority of courts recognize the time as compensable only when the employee must expend more than a *de minimis* amount of time in doing so.

---

2. Who Is Protected by the FLSA?

As you have seen, the designation of "employee" is critical for asserting coverage of many employment laws, and the FLSA is no different. The increase in the use of independent contractors has been driven in part by the desire of employers to avoid the record-keeping and financial obligations of employment law statutes. Perhaps more pertinent to most students, significant issues arise in connection with the offering of unpaid "internships." Is this a valuable educational benefit for students, or merely a failure to abide by minimum wage requirements?

Glatt v. Fox Searchlight Pictures, Inc.

811 F.3d 528 (2nd Cir. 2016).

John M. Walker, Jr., Circuit Judge:

Plaintiffs, who were hired as unpaid interns, claim compensation as employees under the Fair Labor Standards Act and New York Labor Law . . . Plaintiffs worked as unpaid interns either on the Fox Searchlight-distributed film Black Swan or at the Fox corporate offices in New York City. They contend that the defendants, Fox Searchlight and Fox Entertainment Group, violated the Fair Labor Standards Act (FLSA), 29 U.S.C. §§ 206–07, and New York Labor (NYLL), N.Y. Labor Law § 652, by failing to pay them as employees during their internships as required by the FLSA's and NYLL's minimum wage and overtime provisions.

Eric Glatt

Eric Glatt graduated with a degree in multimedia instructional design from New York University. Glatt was enrolled in a non-matriculated (non-degree) graduate program at NYU's School of Education when he started working on Black Swan. His graduate program did not offer him credit for his internship.

From December 2, 2009, through the end of February 2010, Glatt interned in Black Swan's accounting department under the supervision of Production Accountant Theodore Au. He worked from approximately 9:00 a.m. to 7:00 p.m. five days a week. As an accounting intern, Glatt's responsibilities included copying, scanning, and filing documents; tracking purchase orders; transporting paperwork and items to and from the Black Swan set; maintaining employee personnel files; and answering questions about the accounting department.

. . . .

Alexander Footman

Footman's responsibilities included picking up and setting up office furniture; arranging lodging for cast and crew; taking out the trash; taking lunch orders; answering phone calls; watermarking scripts; drafting daily call sheets; photocopying; making coffee; making deliveries to and from the film production set, rental houses, and the payroll office; accepting deliveries; admitting guests to the office; compiling lists of local vendors; breaking down, removing, and selling office furniture and supplies at the end of production; internet research; sending invitations to the wrap party; and other similar tasks and errands, including bringing tea to Aronofsky and dropping off a DVD of Black Swan footage at Aronofsky's apartment.

Eden Antalik

Eden Antalik worked as an unpaid publicity intern in Fox Searchlight's corporate office in New York from the beginning of May 2009 until the second week of August 2009. During her internship, Antalik was enrolled in a degree program at Duquesne University that required her to have an internship in order to graduate. Antalik was supposed to receive credit for her internship at Fox Searchlight, but, for reasons that are unclear from the record, she never actually received the credit.

Antalik began work each morning around 8:00 a.m. by assembling a brief, referred to as "the breaks," summarizing mentions of various Fox Searchlight films in the media. She also made travel arrangements, organized catering, shipped documents, and set up rooms for press events . . . . granted Antalik's motions to certify the class of New York interns and to conditionally certify the nationwide FLSA collective.

. . . .

The Supreme Court has yet to address the difference between unpaid interns and paid employees under the FLSA. In 1947, however, the Court recognized that unpaid railroad brakemen trainees should not be treated as employees, and thus that they were beyond the reach of the FLSA's minimum wage provision. *See Walling v. Portland Terminal Co.*, 330 U.S. 148, 67 S.Ct. 639, 91 L.Ed. 809 (1947). The Court adduced several facts. First, the brakemen-trainees at issue did not displace any regular employees, and their work did not expedite the employer's business. *Id.* at 149–50, 67 S. Ct. 639. Second, the brakemen-trainees did not expect to receive any compensation and would not necessarily be hired upon successful completion of the course. *See id.* at 150, 67 S.Ct. 639. Third, the training course was similar to one offered by a vocational school. *Id.* at 152, 67 S.Ct. 639. Finally, the employer received no immediate advantage from the work done by the trainees. *Id.* at 153, 67 S.Ct. 639.

In 2010, the DOL published . . . guidance for unpaid interns working in the for-profit private sector. This Intern Fact Sheet provides that an employment relationship does not exist if all of the following factors apply:

(1) The internship, even though it includes actual operation of the facilities of the employer, is similar to training which would be given in an educational environment;

(2) The internship experience is for the benefit of the intern;

(3) The intern does not displace regular employees, but works under close supervision of existing staff;

(4) The employer that provides the training derives no immediate advantage from the activities of the intern; and on occasion its operations may actually be impeded;

(5) The intern is not necessarily entitled to a job at the conclusion of the internship; and

(6) The employer and the intern understand that the intern is not entitled to wages for the time spent in the internship.

DOL, Wage & Hour Div., Fact Sheet # 71, Internship Programs Under The Fair Labor Standards Act (April 2010), available at http://www.dol.gov/whd/regs/compliance/whdfs71.pdf.

. . . .

The specific issue we face—when is an unpaid intern entitled to compensation as an employee under the FLSA?—is a matter of first impression in this Circuit. When properly designed, unpaid internship programs can greatly benefit interns. For this reason, internships are widely supported by educators and by employers looking to hire well-trained recent graduates. However, employers can also exploit unpaid interns by using their free labor without providing them with an appreciable benefit in education or experience. Recognizing this concern, all parties agree that there are circumstances in which someone who is labeled an unpaid intern is actually an employee entitled to compensation under the FLSA. All parties also agree that there are circumstances in which unpaid interns are not employees under the FLSA. They do not agree on what those circumstances are or what standard we should use to identify them.

The plaintiffs urge us to adopt a test whereby interns will be considered employees whenever the employer receives an immediate advantage from the interns' work. Plaintiffs argue that focusing on any immediate advantage that accrues to the employer is appropriate because, in their view, the Supreme Court in *Portland Terminal* rested its holding on the finding that the brakemen trainees provided no immediate advantage to the employer.

The defendants urge us to adopt a more nuanced primary beneficiary test. Under this standard, an employment relationship is not created when the tangible and intangible benefits provided to the intern are greater than the intern's contribution to the employer's operation. They argue that the primary beneficiary test best reflects the economic realities of the relationship between intern and employer. They further contend that a primary beneficiary test that considers the totality of the circumstances is in accordance with how we decide whether individuals are employees in other circumstances.

DOL, appearing as amicus curiae in support of the plaintiffs, defends the six factors enumerated in its Intern Fact Sheet and its requirement that every factor be present before the employer can escape its obligation to pay the worker. DOL argues (1) that its views on employee status are entitled to deference because it is the agency charged with administering the FLSA and (2) that we should use the six factors because they come directly from *Portland Terminal.*

We decline DOL's invitation to defer to the test laid out in the Intern Fact Sheet . . . .we do not find it persuasive, and we will not defer to it.

Instead, we agree with defendants that the proper question is whether the intern or the employer is the primary beneficiary of the relationship. The primary beneficiary test has three salient features. First, it focuses on what the intern receives in exchange for his work. *See Portland Terminal*, 330 U.S. at 152, 67 S.Ct. 639 (focusing on the trainee's interests). Second, it also accords courts the flexibility to examine the economic reality as it exists between the intern and the employer. *See Barfield v. N.Y.C. Health & Hosps. Corp.*, 537 F.3d 132, 141–42 (2d Cir. 2008) (employment for FLSA purposes is "a flexible concept to be determined on a case-by-case basis by review of the totality of the circumstances"). Third, it acknowledges that the intern-employer relationship should not be analyzed in the same manner as the standard employer-employee relationship because the intern enters into the relationship with the expectation of receiving educational or vocational benefits that are not necessarily expected with all forms of employment (though such benefits may be a product of experience on the job).

Although the flexibility of the primary beneficiary test is primarily a virtue, this virtue is not unalloyed. The defendants' conception of the primary beneficiary test requires courts to weigh a diverse set of benefits to the intern against an equally diverse set of benefits received by the employer without specifying the relevance of particular facts.

In somewhat analogous contexts, we have articulated a set of non-exhaustive factors to aid courts in determining whether a worker is an employee for purposes of the FLSA. (independent contractors). . . . In the context of unpaid internships, we think a non-exhaustive set of considerations should include:

(1) The extent to which the intern and the employer clearly understand that there is no expectation of compensation. Any promise of compensation, express or implied, suggests that the intern is an employee—and vice versa.

(2) The extent to which the internship provides training that would be similar to that which would be given in an educa-

tional environment, including the clinical and other hands-on training provided by educational institutions.

(3) The extent to which the internship is tied to the intern's formal education program by integrated coursework or the receipt of academic credit.

(4) The extent to which the internship accommodates the intern's academic commitments by corresponding to the academic calendar.

(5) The extent to which the internship's duration is limited to the period in which the internship provides the intern with beneficial learning.

(6) The extent to which the intern's work complements, rather than displaces, the work of paid employees while providing significant educational benefits to the intern.

(7) The extent to which the intern and the employer understand that the internship is conducted without entitlement to a paid job at the conclusion of the internship.

. . . .

The approach we adopt also reflects a central feature of the modern internship—the relationship between the internship and the intern's formal education—and is confined to internships and does not apply to training programs in other contexts. The purpose of a bona-fide internship is to integrate classroom learning with practical skill development in a real-world setting, and, unlike the brakemen at issue in *Portland Terminal*, all of the plaintiffs were enrolled in or had recently completed a formal course of post-secondary education. By focusing on the educational aspects of the internship, our approach better reflects the role of internships in today's economy than the DOL factors. . . .

QUESTIONS

1. What would the result be if the Court adopted the argument made by the plaintiffs?

2. Do these factors have any relevance to the question of independent contractor status?

Class Exercise 23-1

You are an Assistant General Counsel at a large corporation. The General Counsel asks you to draft a letter agreement that will be signed by all unpaid interns working in the General Counsel's office. The interns will all be current law students. They will assist in legal research, help prepare transaction documents, and interview employees in investigations of discrimination claims. Draft the letter agreement and prepare a cover memorandum for the General Counsel explaining why you drafted the letter in the manner you did.

The following case deals with a re-occurring issue in FLSA litigation. Can a worker properly be classified as an independent contractor, thereby removing her from the protections of the FLSA? The case that follows has unusual facts, but it applies traditional analysis. Because the FLSA does not cover independent contractors, many employers intentionally or unintentionally misclassify employees as independent contractors to cut costs and avoid liability. The Harvard Business Review recently discussed this issue. See David Weil, *Lots of Employees Get Misclassified as Contractors. Here's Why It Matters*, Harv. Bus. Rev. (2017). The article estimated that the use of independent contracting has risen almost 40% from 2005 to 2015. But, according to a 2009 report by the U.S. Government Accountability Office, a majority of these independent contractors are misclassified. The Honorable Edward M. Kennedy et al., Employee Misclassification: Improved Coordination, Outreach, and Targeting Could Better Ensure Detection and Prevention, (2009). In fact, about 1/3 of the construction workers in the U.S. South were estimated to be misclassified. Moreover, state-level data indicates that about 10% to 20% of employers misclassify at least one employee. Even more troubling, a study done for the U.S. Department of Labor found that up to 30% of audited employers misclassified their employees. *See* Lalith De Silva et al., Planmatics, Inc., Independent Contractors: Prevalence and Implications for Unemployment Insurance Programs iii (2000). This study determined that "[t]he number one reason employers use [independent contractors] and/or misclassify employees is the savings in not paying workers' compensation premiums and not being subject to workplace injury and disability-related disputes." *Id.* Another reason is to avoid the "costs associated with employee lawsuits against employers alleging discrimination, sexual harassment, and implementing regulations and reporting procedures that go along with having employees." *Id.*

What factors are at work in the employer's decision in the following case?

REICH V. CIRCLE C INVESTMENTS, INC.

998 F.2d 324 (5th Cir. 1993).

REAVLEY, CIRCUIT JUDGE:

The Secretary of Labor (Secretary) brought this action pursuant to § 17 of the Fair Labor Standards Act (FLSA), 29 U.S.C. §§ 201–219, to enjoin Circle C Investments, Inc. (Circle C), Beatrice Cranford, and Charles Cranford (collectively defendants) from violating the minimum wage, overtime, and record-keeping provisions of the FLSA and to restrain them from continuing to withhold back wages. . . .

Since October 1988, Circle C has operated the Crazy Horse Saloon, a nightclub featuring topless dancers. From 1988 to 1990, it also operated a similar nightclub, Lipstick. The Secretary alleges that, since October 1988, Circle C has improperly compensated its dancers, waitresses, disc jockeys, bartenders, doormen, and "house mothers" and has failed to keep accurate records of the hours worked by its employees. In addition to Circle C, the Secretary's complaint names Beatrice and Charles Cranford as defendants. Beatrice Cranford was the original owner of Circle C and served as its president from 1987 to 1991, but she had a minor role in the affairs of the corporation. The district court found Charles Cranford, Beatrice's husband, to be "the driving force behind . . . Circle C."

. . . [T]he district court determined that the topless dancers and the other workers are "employees" within the meaning of the FLSA. . . . The court enjoined the defendants from further violating the FLSA and restrained them from withholding $539,630 of back wages. Both sides appeal.

A. Employee Status of Topless Dancers

The dancers receive no compensation from Circle C. Their compensation is derived solely from tips they receive from customers for performing on stage and performing private "table dances" and "couch dances." At the end of each night, the dancers must pay Circle C a "tip-out," which at the time of trial was set at $20. The dancers are required to pay the "tip-out" regardless of how much they make in tips. The defendants characterize this "tip-out" as stage rental and argue that the dancers are merely "tenants." According to the defendants, the dancers are neither employees nor independent contractors, but are businesswomen renting space, stages, music, dressing rooms, and lights from Circle C.

To determine employee status under the FLSA, we focus on whether the alleged employee, as a matter of economic reality, is economically dependent upon the business to which she renders her services. . . . our focal inquiry in determining employee status is whether the individual is, as a matter of economic reality, in business for herself. To gauge the degree of the worker's dependency, we consider five factors:

(a) the degree of control exercised by the alleged employer;

(b) the extent of the relative investments of the worker and alleged employer;

(c) the degree to which the worker's opportunity for profit and loss is determined by the alleged employer;

(d) the skill and initiative required in performing the job; and

(e) the permanency of the relationship.

These factors are merely aids in determining the underlying question of dependency, and no single factor is determinative.

The district court found that Circle C exercises a great deal of control over the dancers. The dancers are required to comply with weekly work schedules, which Circle C compiles with input from the dancers as to the days that they wish to work. Circle C fines the dancers for absences and tardiness. Circle C instructs the dancers to charge at least $10 for table dances and $20 for couch dances. The dancers supply their own costumes, but the costumes must meet standards set by Circle C to promote the desired atmosphere. The dancers can express a preference for a certain type of music, but they do not have the final say in the matter. Several dancers testified that they were expected to mingle with customers when not dancing. Circle C has promulgated many other rules concerning the dancers' behavior; for example, no flat heels, no more than 15 minutes at one time in the dressing room, only one dancer in the restroom at a time, and all dancers must be "on the floor" at opening time. Circle C enforces these rules by fining infringers.

The defendants attempt to de-emphasize Circle C's control by arguing that most of the rules are directed at maintaining decorum or keeping the nightclub legal. The defendants explain that Circle C publishes the minimum charge for table and couch dances at the request of the dancers to prevent dancers from undercutting each others' prices. Finally, the defendants stress the fact that Circle C does not control the dancers' dance routines.

Despite the defendants' effort on appeal to downplay Circle C's control, the record fully supports the district court's finding of significant control.

2. Relative investment of worker and alleged employer

The district court found that a dancer's investment is limited to her costumes and a padlock. The amount spent on costumes varies from dancer to dancer and can be significant. (One dancer testified that she spends $600 per month on costumes, while another dancer testified that she spends approximately $40 per month on costumes.) The defendants contend that we should also consider as an investment each dancer's nightly "tip-out," which the defendants characterize as rent. The district court rejected the defendants' argument that the "tip-out" is rent, and so do we—it is the economic realities that control our determination of employee status.

A dancer's investment in costumes and a padlock is relatively minor to the considerable investment Circle C has in operating a nightclub. The fact that the district court did not make specific findings regarding Circle C's investment does not detract from our analysis given the obvious significant investment Circle C has in operating a nightclub. The record does not completely identify Circle C's investment, but it does reveal that Circle C owns the liquor license, owns the inventory of beverages and refreshments, leases fixtures for the nightclub (e.g., the stage and lights), owns sound equipment and music, maintains and renovates the facilities, and advertises extensively.

3. Degree to which employee's opportunity for profit and loss is determined by the alleged employer

The district court recognized that, once customers arrive at Circle C's nightclubs, a dancer's initiative, hustle, and costume significantly contribute to the amount of her tips. But Circle C has a significant role in drawing customers to its nightclubs. The district court recognized that Circle C is responsible for advertisement, location, business hours, maintenance of facilities, aesthetics, and inventory of beverages and food. . . Circle C exercises a high degree of control over a dancer's opportunity for "profit." The dancers "are far more closely akin to wage earners toiling for a living, than to independent entrepreneurs seeking a return on their risky capital investments."

. . . .

The parties do agree, and the district court found, that most dancers have short-term relationships with Circle C. Although not determinative, the impermanent relationship between the dancers and Circle C indicates non-employee status.

Despite the lack of permanency, on the balance, the five factors favor a determination of employee status. A dancer has no specialized skills and her only real investment is in her costumes. Circle C exercises significant control over a dancer's behavior and opportunity for "profit." The transient nature of the work force is not enough here to remove the dancers from the protections of the FLSA. In analyzing the five factors, we must not lose sight of economic reality. Here, the economic reality is that the dancers are not in business for themselves but are dependent upon finding employment in the business of others. We reject the defendants' creative argument that the dancers are mere tenants who rent stages, lights, dressing rooms, and music from Circle C.

. . . .

VACATED and REMANDED.

3. Who Is an "Employer" Liable Under the FLSA?

The FLSA is atypical, in that it imposes liability on individuals as well as the employer. This certainly will assist in motivating responsible company officials to ensure that the FLSA is fully followed. In the *Circle C* case, the court found that Charles Cranford was liable personally for the withheld wages.

Reich v. Circle C Investments, Inc.

998 F.2d 324 (5th Cir. 1993).

. . . .

Personal Liability

Charles Cranford does not have an ownership interest in Circle C and does not control the day-to-day operations of Circle C. His "consulting" agreement with Circle C purports to exclude personnel matters from his responsibilities. But the testimony at trial convinces us that Charles Cranford exercised control over the work situation: he was the driving force behind Circle C; he hired two of the dancers who testified at trial; several of the witnesses identified him as their supervisor and testified that he gave specific instructions to employees; when he was at the nightclubs, the dancers were required to dance to his favorite songs; he removed money from Circle C's safes; he signed employees' payroll checks; he ordered one employee to refrain from keeping records of the tip-outs; and he spoke for Circle C during the Secretary's investigation of possible FLSA violations. In addition to the above evidence, the Secretary introduced an inter-office memorandum that purports to be from Charles Cranford. The memorandum reports fines that had been assessed for rule infractions and warns of future fines if certain rules were not obeyed. Charles Cranford denies dictating or writing this memorandum. One of the Secretary's witnesses, however, testified that inter-office memoranda from Charles Cranford were common.

Compare this short analysis with the more expansive consideration in the next case.

Gray v. Powers

673 F.3d 352 (5th Cir. 2012).

Edith H. Jones, Chief Judge:

. . . .

BACKGROUND

In 2007, [Michael] Powers, Christian Bruckner, and Richard Stark formed PEG to run the Pasha Lounge as an investment in Houston, Texas. Stephen

Powers ("Stephen") and Kathleen Powers ("Kathleen") later joined the original members of PEG. Powers contributed about $100,000 and supervised remodeling of the nightclub. Stephen, Powers's brother, contributed as much as $80,000. A third member, Christian Bruckner, obtained the liquor license and personally guaranteed the lease of the building. PEG operated Pasha Lounge from April 2007 until the club closed in September 2008. Shortly after closing the nightclub, the members dissolved PEG.

After completion of the construction, Powers was not involved in the day-to-day operation of the Pasha Lounge. Powers only visited the club on five or six occasions during the seventeen months the club was open for business. He denies that he supervised any employee, defined employee job duties, controlled work schedules, or maintained employment records. During his rare trips to the lounge, the bartenders would tell him how much they made in tips. Powers was, however, a signatory on PEG's checking account, along with Kathleen and the club's general manager, and he occasionally signed several pages of pre-printed checks.

Other members, Kathleen in particular, were much more involved in the operation of the club. Kathleen kept the books, was a signatory on the accounts, received nightly numbers, and served as the point of contact for the general manager. The members of PEG collectively made significant business decisions such as hiring John W. Ritchey, Jr. as the first general manager. Ritchey's job duties included hiring and firing staff, handling promotions, setting operation hours, and supervising day-to-day operations. In Ritchey's words, he was "in charge of pretty much everything that went on at the club." Ritchey was later removed by the members of PEG because his salary was too expensive.

. . . .

The district court was not persuaded by Gray's argument that Powers was an FLSA "employer" and granted summary judgment. PEG suffered an adverse judgment when it failed to appear at trial. Gray now appeals the grant of summary judgment to Powers.

. . . .

DISCUSSION

. . . .

1. Power to Hire and Fire Employees

While it is undisputed that Powers neither hired Gray as a bartender nor supervised him directly, Gray argues that as a member and officer of PEG, Powers inherently had the power to fire him. Powers and the other members of PEG together hired (and terminated) the general manager of the club collectively, and the general manager hired and supervised the bartending staff. Gray argues that Powers's ability to act collectively in regard to club management included the power to fire Gray as a bartender.

. . . .

Lacking specific facts that Powers played a role in hiring or firing lower-level employees, Appellant asks this court to infer such authority based on Powers's position as a member and officer of PEG. Appellant cites several cases in which officers and shareholders of corporations have been held liable as FLSA employers. Each case, however, involves defendants who exerted actual operational control from which a fact finder could infer power to hire and fire. The common theme throughout these cases is that employer status may be appropriate where operational control coincides with one's position as a shareholder, officer, or owner. The cases do not suggest, however, that merely being an officer or shareholder subjects an individual to FLSA liability. Like the First Circuit, we recognize that "individuals ordinarily are shielded from personal liability when they do business in a corporate form, and . . . it should not lightly be inferred that Congress intended to disregard this shield in the context of the FLSA." *Baystate Alt. Staffing, Inc. v. Herman*, 163 F.3d 668, 677 (1st Cir. 1998). . . .

2. Supervision or Control of Employee Work Schedules or Conditions of Employment

The district court found that no reasonable jury could find that Powers supervised or controlled employee work schedules or conditions of employment. Appellant argues that because Powers and his fellow members of the L.L.C. hired the manager, they cannot escape duties they owe employees by delegating the duties to a manager. . . .

Gray . . . failed to offer any evidence of Powers's supervision and control over work schedules or employment conditions.

The only possible instances in which Powers "supervised" Gray occurred when Powers told Gray he was doing a "great job" and when he twice asked

Gray to serve specific individuals. In all three instances, however, Powers was present at the club socially. Moreover, Gray admitted that while he was a bartender he considered Ritchey to be his boss because Ritchey, not Powers, hired Gray and defined his job duties. These isolated events are too paltry to support an inference of control by Gray.

3. Determination of the Rate or Method of Payment

As the district court found, the evidence that Powers occasionally signed checks for the lounge and that bartenders casually told him how much money they made in tips during his rare trips to the club do not indicate that Powers determined the employees' rate or method of payment.

. . . .

CONCLUSION

Applying the economic reality test to Powers, we reaffirm the district court's conclusion that no reasonable jury could have found him to be an employer. The dominant theme in the case law is that those who have operating control over employees within companies may be individually liable for FLSA violations committed by the companies . . . . In this case, Powers was simply not sufficiently involved in the operation of the club to be an employer. The district court's judgment is AFFIRMED.

Problem 23-1

The owners and managers of Circle C come to you and ask you to prepare an independent contractor agreement that will hold up in court and insulate them from minimum wage and overtime obligations. Draft an agreement consistent with the client's objectives.

Problem 23-2

Your firm is defending an individual who owns part of a business in a lawsuit brought by an employee under FLSA. The deposition of the plaintiff is scheduled to take place in two weeks. The partner on the case asks you to prepare a list of questions that she should ask during the deposition regarding the worker's status as an employee and your client's potential liability. Drawing from the *Circle C* and *Gray* cases, draft the questions and explain their importance to the partner.

---

4. Compensable Time: The Problem of "On Call" Time

You might think that calculating compensable time would be a simple matter. An employee should be paid for all time spent working. There may be questions about pre and post-shift preparations as we discussed earlier, but these would seem to be relatively minor. However, significant issues arise in determining how to address "on call" time. The next case deals with this issue in 2000—long before our current workplace in which we are connected 24/7 to work. As you read this case describing the fundamental principles of analysis, think about its application to the work world as we now know it.

PABST V. OKLAHOMA

228 F.3d 1128 (10th Cir. 2000).

LUCERO, CIRCUIT JUDGE.

We again explore the question of when "on-call" time becomes sufficiently onerous to render it compensable under the Fair Labor Standards Act ("FLSA"). Surveying our precedents and applying them to the facts of this case, we conclude that plaintiffs' on-call duties requiring them to continually monitor automated alarms by pager and computer were compensable under the FLSA. In so holding, we reject the argument that on-call monitoring time is not compensable unless contemporaneously reported to the employer as overtime.

Plaintiffs are Electronic Technicians in Oklahoma Gas & Electric's ("OG&E") Facility Operations Department. Plaintiffs Pabst and Gilley were Electronic Technician I's ("Tech 1s") and plaintiff Barton was an Electronic Technician II ("Tech 2"). The three plaintiffs, along with two other employees, monitored automated heat, fire, and security systems in several OG&E buildings. Prior to an August 1994 reduction in force, these duties required twelve on-site employees working three eight-hour shifts.

Plaintiffs were on call to monitor OG&E building alarms weekdays from 4:30 p.m. to 7:30 a.m. and twenty-four hours a day on weekends. During these hours, alarms went to computers at Pabst's and Gilley's homes, as well as to pagers for all plaintiffs. After October 1994, Barton began to receive alarms at home via lap-top computer. Plaintiffs were required to respond to the alarms initially within ten minutes, then, after October 1996, within fifteen minutes. Failure to respond within the time limit was grounds for discipline. Each plaintiff was assigned, and required always to carry, an alpha-numeric pager. These pagers were only 70% reliable. The short response time, coupled with unreliable pagers, forced plaintiffs to remain at or near their homes while on call.

The district court found that plaintiffs received an average of three to five alarms per night, not including pages for security issues. Although not all alarms required plaintiffs to report to the office—it appears many could be fixed by remote computer—the district court found it took an average of forty-five minutes to respond to each alarm. Neither party disputes those findings on appeal.

At trial, the parties did dispute whether a rotational on-call schedule was ever proposed or implemented. Acknowledging the dispute, the district court found that "[c]ontrary to OG&E's contention, an examination of the overtime hours actually billed by plaintiffs does not demonstrate that a rotational schedule was ever in effect; rather, the records reveal significant overlap among the technicians, which indicates to the court that no rotational schedule was ever implemented prior to June 1997." The district court also found a rotational schedule would not have been feasible because of the frequency of alarms and plaintiffs' differing areas of expertise.

According to plaintiffs, their supervisor instructed them to report only on-call time spent responding to an alarm. OG&E paid plaintiffs for at least one hour for each alarm to which they responded, and two hours if they had to return to OG&E facilities. Plaintiffs apparently reported some, but not all, of the alarms they answered, but did not claim as overtime the remainder of their time spent on call.

Considerable testimony was presented regarding the extent to which monitoring interfered with plaintiffs' personal activities. Most significantly, an average of three to five alarms per night, each requiring on average forty-five minutes of work, severely disrupted plaintiffs' sleep habits; indeed, they testified to rarely experiencing more than five hours of uninterrupted sleep per night. In addition, even during waking hours, plaintiffs were unable to pursue many personal activities while on call because of the need to come into their homes to check their computers every fifteen minutes.

The district court found plaintiffs' on-call time compensable under the FLSA. . . .

OG&E argues that it did not know plaintiffs were working the entire time they were on call and thus did not "suffer or permit" them to work. 29 U.S.C. § 203(g). Its theory goes as follows: Plaintiffs were responsible for reporting their own overtime because they reported only time spent responding to calls (and apparently not even all of that), rather than all of their on-call time, OG&E lacked knowledge that they were working and therefore did not suffer or permit them to work. This argument misinterprets the nature of the on-call time inquiry and borders on the disingenuous.

As a factual matter, OG&E's purported lack of actual knowledge is dubious. Plaintiffs cite record testimony detailing a reprimand Pabst received for attempting to report the entire time spent monitoring systems as overtime. Although OG&E attempts to discount this testimony because the incident occurred after the cessation of the particular on-call monitoring system at issue here, the testimony nevertheless lends support to plaintiffs' assumption that it would have been futile—or even harmful—for plaintiffs if they had attempted to report all of their on-call time as overtime. More significantly, OG&E's policy informed plaintiffs they would be compensated only for on-call time spent responding to an alarm. The only logical inference was that they would not be compensated for time spent monitoring their computers and pagers, unless they took some specific action responding to an alarm. To claim, then, that OG&E did not know plaintiffs were working because they did not report every hour of their evenings and weekends as overtime is misleading. While OG&E arguably may have lacked knowledge of the legal proposition that the FLSA required compensating plaintiffs for their on-call time under the system at issue, OG&E certainly knew that plaintiffs were performing the duties they had been assigned.

. . . .

Although OG&E complains bitterly against having to compensate plaintiffs for working twenty-four hours a day, seven days a week, the cost to an employer of an "always on call" arrangement does not mean that such a system is not cognizable under the FLSA, so long as the on-call time qualifies as work under the relevant FLSA precedents. While one circuit has held that always being on call, while extremely burdensome, does not in and of itself make the on-call time compensable for FLSA purposes, *see Bright v. Houston Northwest Med. Ctr. Survivor, Inc.*, 934 F.2d 671, 678–79 (5th Cir. 1991) (en banc), another circuit found that requiring employees to monitor and respond all day, every day is a factor weighing in favor of compensability, *see Cross v. Arkansas Forestry Comm'n*, 938 F.2d 912, 916–17 (8th Cir. 1991) (holding that on-call time is compensable under the FLSA because employees were required to continuously monitor transmissions and respond within thirty minutes, and because they were subject to on-call status twenty-four hours per day for every day of a work period). We agree with both *Bright* and *Cross*: Although always being on call is not dispositive, such an added burden is relevant in assessing the extent to which all-the-time on-call duty deprives employees of the ability to engage in personal activities.

. . . .

QUESTION

1. The issue of on-call time being compensable engenders increasing debate and controversy given the advent of smart phone technology and the resulting 24/7 availability of workers to respond to messages. Consider the following scenarios in light of *Pabst* and ask yourself the extent to which on-call time can be restrictive and thus unpleasant should factor into whether the time spent is compensable.

   (a) Employees are firefighters. They worked from 8:00 am to 5:00 pm at the fire station. They are on call at the fire station and not permitted to leave from 5:00 pm until 8:00 am. They are then given 24 wholly unrestricted hours. The cycle is then repeated. At the fire station they can cook their meals, sleep, or entertain themselves with TV, pool, or books. Is their on-call time compensable?

   (b) An employee works from 7:30 am to 4:00 pm. She is then on-call from 4:00 pm to 7:30 am. The employee was permitted to go home but must be to be able to respond to a siren that sounded from the plant. Thus, she was free to do as she pleased but had to be within hearing distance of the siren at all times. Is the on-call time compensable?

5. Liquidated Damages and the Statute of Limitations

The FLSA seeks to ensure compliance in several ways. First, the statute of limitations for an action for unpaid wages is two years, but if the employer willfully violates its obligations under the FLSA the statute of limitations is extended to three years. In a similar vein, the FLSA provides that employers might have to pay double the damages awarded if they are found not to have acted in good faith. The following case describes the standard that must be satisfied for liquidated damages.

Reyes v. Aqua Life Corp.

632 F. App'x 552 (11th Cir. 2015).

Restani, Judge:

This matter arises out of several post-verdict motions filed by appellant Humberto Reyes ("Mr. Reyes") and appellee Aqua Life Corp. ("Aqua Life"), after a jury found in favor of Mr. Reyes in his suit to recover unpaid overtime wages under the Fair Labor Standards Act ("FLSA"). Mr. Reyes appeals the district court's omnibus order denying liquidated damages . . . we reverse the denial of liquidated damages . . . .

Mr. Reyes appeals the district court's order arguing that liquidated damages should have been awarded . . . .

DISCUSSION

I. Liquidated Damages

Under the FLSA, liquidated damages are mandatory absent a showing of good faith by the employer. *See* 29 U.S.C. § 216(b) (2012); *Joiner v. City of Macon*, 814 F.2d 1537, 1538–39 (11th Cir. 1987). Although liquidated damages are typically assessed at an equal amount of the wages lost due to the FLSA violation, they can be reduced to zero at the discretion of the court. If an employer shows to the satisfaction of the court that the act or omission giving rise to such action was in good faith and that he had reasonable grounds for believing that his act or omission was not a violation of the Fair Labor Standards Act . . . the court may, in its sound discretion, award no liquidated damages . . . . 29 U.S.C. § 260.

An employer who seeks to avoid liquidated damages bears the burden of proving to the court that its violation was "both in good faith and predicated upon such reasonable grounds that it would be unfair to impose upon him more than a compensatory verdict." "Before a district court may exercise its discretion to award less than the full amount of liquidated damages, it must explicitly find that the employer acted in good faith." *Joiner*, 814 F.2d at 1539.

The district court erred in denying liquidated damages on this record. Aqua Life had the burden of proving good faith and reasonable belief and failed to carry that burden. The only evidence of the alleged good faith was the testimony of its Vice President, Mr. Ibarra, who ostensibly researched [an] exception to the FLSA, concluding that Mr. Reyes did not need to be paid overtime hours for his work. Yet, Mr. Ibarra also admitted that he had never heard of the FLSA until legal action was taken by Mr. Reyes. Aqua Life thus did not make a sufficient factual showing upon which the district court could have reasonably relied to deny liquidated damages and the record does not support the district court's refusal to grant liquidated damages.

. . . .

QUESTIONS

1. A cellphone carrier hires workers to repair damage to cell towers after a category-five hurricane devastates the Gulf Coast. The carrier lacks internal capacity to cope with a disaster of this magnitude. It is estimated that repairs will take two years with crews working 50 hours a week. The client asks for your advice on how to classify the new workers. What factors should be considered? Ultimately, there will be approximately 100 workers retained to do this work.
2. You are a new lawyer at a firm. A client has been sued for violating the FLSA. The plaintiff alleges that she was an employee and not an independent contractor. Your client is a software developer who hired the plaintiff to write code. The client is new and used a different employment law firm previously. What questions do you ask the new client? What discovery questions do you propound of the plaintiff?
3. What could constitute "good faith" for purposes of liquidated damages? Can an employer establish good faith by showing that it had an "empty head" but "pure heart"? Or, does the avoidance of liquidated damages require more?
4. Why is a liquidated damages provision appropriate as an automatic award? Punitive damages for, say, race or gender discrimination are not automatic. Why should there be a difference?

5. A worker comes to your law office and complains that her employer knew she was working overtime because it gave her more work than could possibly be performed within 40 hours. Is this sufficient to establish employer knowledge? Does it matter that the employee works at the home office under supervision? What if she works at a remote, non supervised location?

6. Does a willful violation inevitably result in the imposition of liquidated damages?

Mastery Problem 23-1

A city police department issues Personal Assistant Devices (PADs) to detectives in the major crime unit. The PADs are to be used only for police business. Police officers often are required to work overtime. The Department requires that claims for overtime must be submitted in written form, called a slip. Not all police officers complete the slip. In response, the city circulates the following memo: "the City must carefully monitor the amount of overtime wages. Failure to properly report overtime on a slip means that you won't be paid overtime." Officers who requested overtime, but did not submit a slip, sued for unpaid overtime under the FLSA. They argue that The City can determine whether they were working overtime simply by checking the PDA records, which are incontrovertible as to what they were doing and when. The officers allege that the city's memo demonstrates animus toward complying with the FLSA. What other facts would you like to know?

Conclusion

The FLSA is a foundational statute of modern employment law. Some of the contemporary issues involve the treatment of interns, workers who are "on call," and the ubiquitous issue of drawing the line between employees covered by the FLSA and independent contractors who are not covered.

Lesson 24:
FLSA Exemptions

Objectives and Expected Learning Outcomes

In this Lesson, you will learn how to identify whether an employee is exempt from FLSA coverage. The exemption analysis is very fact intensive, but you will learn the key indicators. The FLSA exempts executive, administrative and professional employees from its scope, and you will study each category. We will particularly focus on the professional exemption and how it applies to licensed employees, including lawyers.

The FLSA exempts executive, administrative, and professional employees from the requirement that employers pay overtime wages. These exemptions are defined by regulations that are published in the Code of Federal Regulations. In addition to these general categories, the FLSA provides for specific exemptions of employees, such as certain retail, motor carrier, and agricultural employees. We will focus on the general exemptions, but a careful lawyer must always review all exemptions when counseling a client. Because the FLSA is a remedial statute, courts construe the exemptions narrowly, and thus rule in favor of the employee.

Litigation regarding the misclassification of nonexempt employees as exempt is common, because the stakes for employers are quite high. The FLSA provides a class action procedure (called "opt in") which permits misclassified employees to join a suit to create a strong plaintiff's class with significant damages for unpaid overtime. Additionally, recall that unpaid overtime is subject to an automatic doubling as liquidated damages, unless the employer can prove that it acted in both objective and subjective good faith when it classified the employees in question. Given the complexities of the law, a large employer can face substantial damage claims even if it did not intentionally violate the law by misclassification.

We will discuss the three general exemptions in turn. To provide a realistic experience, you will first read the detailed regulations and then learn how to apply the factors.

1. The Executive Exemption

The FLSA exempts an employee who is working in a "bona fide executive capacity." This makes obvious sense: a law designed to protect vulnerable workers would not be expected to cover executive employees. Additionally, executive compensation is much higher than standard wages, and so executive employees who work more than 40 hours per week presumably are already receiving a wage benefit for their work.

29 C.F.R. § 541.100. General Rule for Executive Employees

(a) The term "employee employed in a bona fide executive capacity" . . . shall mean any employee:

. . .

(2) Whose primary duty is management of the enterprise in which the employee is employed or of a customarily recognized department or subdepartment thereof;

(3) Who customarily and regularly directs the work of two or more other employees; and

(4) Who has the authority to hire or fire other employees or whose suggestions and recommendations as to the hiring, firing, advancement, promotion or any other change of status of other employees are given particular weight.

29 C.F.R. § 541.700. Primary Duty

(a) To qualify for exemption under this part, an employee's "primary duty" must be the performance of exempt work. The term "primary duty" means the principal, main, major or most important duty that the employee performs. Determination of an employee's primary duty must be based on all the facts in a particular case, with the major emphasis on the character of the employee's job as a whole. Factors to consider when determining the primary duty of an employee include, but are not limited to, the relative importance of the exempt duties as compared with other types of duties; the amount of time spent performing exempt work; the employee's relative freedom from direct supervision; and the relationship between the employee's salary and the wages paid to other employees for the kind of nonexempt work performed by the employee.

(b) The amount of time spent performing exempt work can be a useful guide in determining whether exempt work is the primary duty of an employee. Thus, employees who spend more than 50 percent of their time performing exempt work will generally satisfy the primary duty requirement. Time alone, however, is not the sole test, and nothing in this section requires that exempt employees spend more than 50 percent of their time performing exempt work. Employees who do not spend more than 50 percent of their time performing exempt duties may nonetheless meet the primary duty requirement if the other factors support such a conclusion.

(c) Thus, for example, assistant managers in a retail establishment who perform exempt executive work such as supervising and directing the work of other employees, ordering merchandise, managing the budget and authorizing payment of bills may have management as their primary duty even if the assistant managers spend more than 50 percent of the time performing nonexempt work such as running the cash register. However, if such assistant managers are closely supervised and earn little more than the nonexempt employees, the assistant managers generally would not satisfy the primary duty requirement.

QUESTIONS

1. Why does the regulation include language recognizing that the exemption applies if the employee is management in a "customarily recognized department or subdivision?"
2. Should the regulation be amended to provide that an employee is exempt if they have "a" primary duty to manage, among other duties? Would this be a more realistic way to assess the classification, or might this permit employers to exploit lower wage workers?
3. If you were an employer, would you be tempted to assign managerial titles and certain managerial duties to workers who often perform substantially blue collar work in order to avoid overtime? Other than a FLSA violation, what are the risks of doing so?

Mims v. Starbucks Corp.

2007 WL 10369 (S.D. Texas, Houston Division, 2007).

Ewing Werlein, Jr., United States District Judge.

Pending is Defendant Starbucks Corporation's Corrected Motion for Partial Summary Judgment with Respect to the Claims of Kevin Keevican and Michael Terrazas. . . .

I. Background

Plaintiffs Kevin Keevican ("Keevican") and Michael Terrazas ("Terrazas") (collectively, "Plaintiffs"), who are former Store Managers at Defendant Starbucks Corporation ("Defendant"), claim that they were improperly classified as exempt from the overtime requirements of the Fair Labor Standards Act ("FLSA"), 29 U.S.C. § 216(b). Plaintiffs assert that, despite their "store manager" titles, they were, in reality, "glorified baristas," and they primarily performed the job duties of these non-exempt, hourly employees. In addition to overtime wages, Plaintiffs seek liquidated damages, injunctive relief, attorneys' fees, and costs.

Defendant operates retail stores that sell coffee and related products. Keevican was hired as an entry-level barista in March, 2000. Keevican, who had prior management experience, was promoted to shift supervisor, assistant store manager, and then, in November, 2001, to store manager. According to Keevican, in his first Starbucks store manager position, he "improved [the] store substantially," and he won a retail sales award and improved pastry sales by 200 percent. Keevican was then "solicited" to work as manager for a larger Starbucks store, where he increased annual revenues from $500,000 to $1.4 million in "10 or 11 months" and again won a retail award. As a store manager, Keevican worked an average of 70 hours per week. His starting base salary as store manager was approximately $650 per week, and it increased to almost $800 per week (not including bonuses). Keevican reported to a district manager, who supervised from 9 to 13 different stores in the district. Keevican resigned from Starbucks in 2004.

Terrazas was hired as a Starbucks barista in December 2000, and he was promoted to shift supervisor, assistant store manager, and then to store manager in May, 2002. Terrazas worked as store manager for two different Starbucks stores, each of which generated between $1.2 and $1.4 million in annual revenue. Prior to October, 2002, Terrazas worked approximately

55 hours per week, and, after October, 2002, he worked an average of 65 hours per week. See Document No. 61 ex. D ¶ 3. Terrazas's starting base salary as store manager was approximately $615 per week, and it increased to approximately $750 per week. See Document No. 54 ex. C ¶ 4. Terrazas was terminated in 2005. See *id.* at 15, 279.

It is undisputed that Plaintiffs, as store managers, were the highest-ranking employees in their respective stores, and they "[s]upervised and motivated" staffs of six to 30 Starbucks employees, including entry-level baristas, shift supervisors, and, in certain stores, assistant managers. Plaintiffs testified that they were responsible for supervising store personnel, "driv[ing] sales" and developing strategies to increase revenues, control costs, and ensure compliance with Starbucks policies. They also oversaw customer service; prepared store reports and communications; processed employee time records, payroll, and inventory counts; ensured the safety of customers and employees; and implemented Starbucks policies and procedures. In short, as Terrazas testified during his deposition, Plaintiffs were responsible for "anything that was to go wrong in [their] store[s] and anything that was done correctly." See *id.* ex. B at 66.

Defendant now moves for summary judgment, arguing that Plaintiffs were executive employees who were exempt from the FLSA' s overtime provisions as a matter of law.

. . . .

III. Discussion

A. FLSA Standard

. . . As the employer, Defendant has the burden of establishing that Plaintiffs fall within one of these exemptions, all of which are to be narrowly construed against it.

New Department of Labor ("DOL") regulations governing exempt employees became effective in August, 2004. Under the new regulations, an employee qualifies for the executive exemption if: (1) he is paid a salary of not less than $455 per week; (2) he has management as his primary duty; (3) he regularly supervises two or more employees; and (4) he has "the authority to hire or fire other employees or [be someone] whose suggestions and recommendations as to hiring, firing, advancements, [or] promotion . . . are given particular weight." See 29 C.F.R. § 541.100(a)(1)–(4) (2005) (revised regulations). The parties are agreed that the only requirement at issue, under both the former and current regulations, is whether Plaintiffs' "primary duty" was one of management.

. . . .

Where an employee spends less than 50 percent of his time on management, as both Plaintiffs claim they did, management may still be the employee's primary duty if certain pertinent factors support such a conclusion. The four factors ordinarily considered are: (1) the relative importance of managerial duties compared to other duties; (2) the frequency with which the employee makes discretionary decisions; (3) the employee's relative freedom from supervision; and (4) the relationship between the employee's salary and the wages paid to employees who perform relevant non-exempt work. 29 C.F.R. § 541.700(a) (2005); *id.* § 541.103 (2004). Defendant argues that under these factors, each Plaintiff's primary duty was management, while Plaintiffs argue that the factors and the "sum total of [Plaintiffs'] duties" demonstrate that Plaintiffs' primary duty was "that of a barista, not a manager."

B. Consideration of the Four Factors

1. Relative Importance of the Managerial Duties

Assessing the importance of Plaintiffs' managerial tasks relative to non-managerial work requires one to consider "the significance of the managerial tasks to the success of the facility." It is uncontroverted that as store managers, Plaintiffs were the highest-ranking employees in their respective stores. Plaintiffs . . . acknowledged that they performed many management tasks, including: interviewing applicants and deciding whom to hire and promote for certain positions within their authority, training and supervising staff, evaluating staff performance, disciplining some infractions, creating weekly work schedules, assigning staff's day-to-day tasks, deciding the amount of products to order, overseeing their stores' financial performance, controlling costs, and ensuring compliance with Defendant's policies (ranging from "safety and security policies" to "drink and quality cleanliness standards"). In connection with these duties, Plaintiffs attended management meetings away from their stores and were responsible for relaying the information they learned to their numerous subordinates.

. . . Keevican acknowledged that he was "ultimately responsible" for his store's operation, analyzed profit and loss reports, adjusted inventory orders, and monitored labor costs. Keevican testified that he "substantially" improved the first store he ran, and he was later "solicited" to run a larger store, where he increased annual sales from $500,000 to $1.4 million in 10 or 11 months. Keevican started a catering business at his store to increase revenue, and he trained his staff to "treat the people that walk into our café right," because "making people happy brings in dollars." See *id.* at 173–74, 177–79. Terrazas testified that he and "my team" "successfully led the second largest [Starbucks] store in the United States . . . to exceed company expectations" in sales, customer service, "promotability," cash flow, and inventory control. Terrazas engineered a series of "themed" store promotions to increase sales and involved his store in community events. . . .

. . . .

[G]iving full credence to Plaintiffs' declarations [that managerial duties requires less than 40% of the job], no genuine issue of material fact has been raised regarding the critical importance of their managerial duties relative to their additional barista tasks. Although Plaintiffs now estimate that they spent 70 to 80 percent of their time performing non-exempt barista tasks, the Fifth Circuit has observed that an employee's "primary duty" is not determined "by applying a simple 'clock' standard that contrasts the amount of time each day an employee spends on exempt and nonexempt work." See *Dalheim*, 918 F.2d at 1227. Even so, Plaintiffs admittedly spent far larger proportions of their time on managerial tasks than did numerous other retail and restaurant managers who have been found to be exempt as a matter of law. (Citations omitted.) Moreover, the uncontroverted record establishes that even while performing barista tasks, Plaintiffs simultaneously also performed many of their management tasks. For instance, Terrazas testified that while working on the floor, he served as a "role model" for baristas and observed their performance for purposes of enforcing company standards, completing evaluations, giving feedback, and recommending promotions and terminations. Keevican testified that he "led by example" and served as a "role model" by modeling proper customer service while on the floor. He testified that he observed baristas "to make sure the[y] got the job done," and he gave his subordinates "positive feedback" and "constructive criticism" after observing their performance. . . .

. . . It is "irrelevant to the primary duty inquiry" that Plaintiffs, in their discretion, may have chosen to delegate some managerial tasks to their subordinates. Although Plaintiffs delegated some managerial tasks to their

delegation not important

subordinates, "such delegation does not render the duties any less 'managerial,' " nor does it "minimize the importance of the duties or render them non-exempt." *Moore*, 352 F.Supp.2d at 1276 In fact, as observed above . . . , Plaintiffs' bonuses were based in part on how well they trained prospective store managers, which obviously incentivised Plaintiffs to delegate selected managerial responsibilities to subordinates in order for Plaintiffs to achieve their own successes as managers who could well train others.

The uncontroverted summary judgment record establishes that Plaintiffs' significant managerial functions-such as ordering and controlling inventory; deciding whom to interview and hire for barista positions; training and scheduling employees; special marketing promotions; and monitoring labor costs-were critical to the successes of their respective stores. If Plaintiffs while each managing a store with annual sales exceeding $1 million were able to spend 70 or 80 percent of their time pouring coffee and performing other barista chores that six to 30 subordinates also performed, those activities of the manager quite obviously were of minor importance to Defendant when compared to the significant management responsibilities performed during the other 20 to 30 percent of their time, management responsibilities that directly influenced the ultimate commercial and financial success or failure of the store.

2. and 3. Frequency of Exercise of Discretion and Relative Freedom from Supervision

It is uncontroverted that Plaintiffs, as the highest-ranking employees in their stores, made decisions on matters such as deciding whom to interview and hire as a barista, whom to assign to train new hires, when to discipline employees, whom to deploy in certain positions, what promotions to run, and the amount of product to order for efficient inventory control. Plaintiffs argue, however, that they infrequently exercised discretion because they worked under the "ultimate managing authority" of their district managers, who had authority to hire more senior employees, approve changes to Plaintiffs' work schedules, set rates of pay for newly-hired employees if the pay exceeded Starbucks's guidelines, and establish guidelines for Plaintiffs when completing performance reviews. However, "the manager of a local store in a modern multi-store organization has management as his or her primary duty even though the discretion usually associated with management may be limited by the company's desire for standardization and uniformity." *Jones*, 69 Fed. Appx. at 638 (quoting Murray, 939 F.2d at 619). . . .

Uniformity of chains does not destroy discretion

Plaintiffs also contend that they were not relatively free from supervision because their district managers spent "substantial amounts of time" in Plaintiffs' stores. Keevican states in his Declaration that his district manager visited his store "3–4 times per week, staying, on average, a few hours to all day each visit," and she "issu[ed] directives" by phone and e-mail. Terrazas avers that his district managers visited the store "almost every day" or "every other day," and stayed in contact by e-mail and phone when not physically in the store. Plaintiffs aver that, during these visits, the district managers checked sales figures, repositioned products, observed and directed employees, and ensured that Starbucks's policies were being followed. Keevican admitted in his deposition that his manager generally supervised from 9 to 13 different urban stores spread over all of downtown Houston, parts of southwest Houston, and the Texas Medical Center, with some stores being located as much as a 30 minutes' drive from others. Terrazas recalled that his manager had approximately nine stores to supervise, which were located in a very large district with some stores being "extremely far apart." On the other hand, it is uncontroverted that each Plaintiff as store manager was the single highest-ranking employee in his particular store and was responsible on site for that store's day-to-day overall operations. . . .

4. Comparative Compensation

The final factor is the relationship between Plaintiffs' salary and the wages paid to non-exempt employees. . . . It is undisputed, however, that Plaintiffs received nearly twice the total annual compensation received by their highest-paid shift supervisors, . . . This marked disparity in pay and benefits between Plaintiffs and the non-exempt employees is a hallmark of exempt status.

. . . .

Defendant is therefore entitled to summary judgment on Plaintiffs' claims. . . .

QUESTION

1. The opinion states that the manager of a local store in a modern multi-state organization can have management as his or her primary duty even though the discretion usually associated with management may be sharply limited by the company's desire for standardization and uniformity. What does this mean? Can you reconcile the executive exemption with this language?

Problem 24-1

You are a corporate attorney working in-house at Starbucks. You have been asked to draft a job description for district managers that will establish that they are exempt executive employees. Working from the duties of a district manager as described in the Starbucks case, provide a draft of the job description.

2. The Administrative Exemption

The administrative exemption is the most misunderstood of the three general exemptions. Employers and courts both tend to treat it as a "catch-all" exemption for employees who are neither executives nor professionals, but who do not need the protections of the FLSA. Consider the difficulty in defining this exemption through regulations.

29 C.F.R. § 541.200. General Rule for Administrative Employees

(a) The term "employee employed in a bona fide administrative capacity" shall mean any employee:

(1) Whose primary duty is the performance of office or non-manual work directly related to the management or general business operations of the employer or the employer's customers; and

(2) Whose primary duty includes the exercise of discretion and independent judgment with respect to matters of significance.

This short excerpt is more complex than it may appear. To understand how this language is interpreted it is necessary to review how it was promulgated. The current regulation added that an employee is exempt if the employee's work relates to "general business operations" in addition to "management policies." Following this addition, workers with "servicing" duties such as purchasing, promoting sales, and planning and negotiating are now arguably within the scope of the exemption.

Originally, the proposed language would have exempted an employee who holds a "position of responsibility" and has a "high level of skill or training." The Department of Labor concluded that these standards were too vague and would invite endless litigation. Instead, "general business operations" was added to the regulation. The DOL stated that the addition of "general business operations" did not expand the exemption, citing to commentary from 1949 that the exemption applies to those who, while they may not be involved in the development or enforcement of policies, nonetheless carry out "major assignments" related to the business that may not involve management policies.

Given the complexities with (a), the true brake on a runaway administrative exemption is found in (b), which requires that the employee exercise discretion and independent judgment with respect to matters of significance. The discretion and independent judgment involved means making a considered choice between "x" and "y" and "z." The "matters of significance" test involves the importance of the task as well as the consequences flowing from doing the task well or poorly. In sum, the employee must make decisions that matter substantially. But this requires employers, if they want to avail themselves of the exemption, to empower employees to make decisions that could turn out to be poor decisions that harm the company.

Consider the details in the regulation regarding specific examples of jobs that fit within the administrative exemption.

29 C.F.R. § 541.203. Administrative Exemption Examples

(a) Insurance claims adjusters generally meet the duties requirements for the administrative exemption, whether they work for an insurance company or other type of company, if their duties include activities such as interviewing insureds, witnesses and physicians; inspecting property damage; reviewing factual information to prepare damage estimates; evaluating and making recommendations regarding coverage of claims; determining liability and total value of a claim; negotiating settlements; and making recommendations regarding litigation.

(b) Employees in the financial services industry generally meet the duties requirements for the administrative exemption if their duties include work such as collecting and analyzing information regarding the customer's income, assets, investments or debts; determining which financial products best meet the customer's needs and financial circumstances;

advising the customer regarding the advantages and disadvantages of different financial products; and marketing, servicing or promoting the employer's financial products. However, an employee whose primary duty is selling financial products does not qualify for the administrative exemption.

(c) An employee who leads a team of other employees assigned to complete major projects for the employer (such as purchasing, selling or closing all or part of the business, negotiating a real estate transaction or a collective bargaining agreement, or designing and implementing productivity improvements) generally meets the duties requirements for the administrative exemption, even if the employee does not have direct supervisory responsibility over the other employees on the team.

(d) An executive assistant or administrative assistant to a business owner or senior executive of a large business generally meets the duties requirements for the administrative exemption if such employee, without specific instructions or prescribed procedures, has been delegated authority regarding matters of significance.

(e) Human resources managers who formulate, interpret or implement employment policies and management consultants who study the operations of a business and propose changes in organization generally meet the duties requirements for the administrative exemption. However, personnel clerks who "screen" applicants to obtain data regarding their minimum qualifications and fitness for employment generally do not meet the duties requirements for the administrative exemption. Such personnel clerks typically will reject all applicants who do not meet minimum standards for the particular job or for employment by the company. The minimum standards are usually set by the exempt human resources manager or other company officials, and the decision to hire from the group of qualified applicants who do meet the minimum standards is similarly made by the exempt human resources manager or other company officials. Thus, when the interviewing and screening functions are performed by the human resources manager or personnel manager who makes the hiring decision or makes recommendations for hiring from the pool of qualified applicants, such duties constitute exempt work, even though routine, because this work is directly and closely related to the employee's exempt functions.

(f) . . .

(g) Ordinary inspection work generally does not meet the duties requirements for the administrative exemption. Inspectors normally perform specialized work along standardized lines involving well-established techniques and procedures which may have been catalogued and described in manuals or other sources. Such inspectors rely on techniques and skills acquired by special training or experience. They have some leeway in the performance of their work but only within closely prescribed limits.

(h) Employees usually called examiners or graders, such as employees that grade lumber, generally do not meet the duties requirements for the administrative exemption. Such employees usually perform work involving the comparison of products with established standards which are frequently catalogued. Often, after continued reference to the written standards, or through experience, the employee acquires sufficient knowledge so that reference to written standards is unnecessary. The substitution of the employee's memory for a manual of standards does not convert the character of the work performed to exempt work requiring the exercise of discretion and independent judgment.

(i) Comparison shopping performed by an employee of a retail store who merely reports to the buyer the prices at a competitor's store does not qualify for the administrative exemption. However, the buyer who evaluates such reports on competitor prices to set the employer's prices generally meets the duties requirements for the administrative exemption.

. . .

QUESTIONS

1. What are the continuing themes that appear in the examples of workers who are within the administrative exemption?
2. Using the regulation examples, can you describe the threshold questions that must be asked and answered in the positive in order to continue on an analysis of whether the exemption applies?
3. Is there a possibility of exploiting vulnerable employees by characterizing their duties as fitting within the administrative exemption? How would an employer do so?
4. List as many active verbs as you can that you could use in a job description to ensure that the employee would be exempt under the administrative exemption.

DEWAN v. M-I, L.L.C., DOING BUSINESS AS M-I SWACO

858 F.3d 331 (5th Cir. 2017).

[Editor's Note: the following case upended what appeared to be established law. Pay special attention to the dichotomy of production versus service positions. Is this dichotomy part of a bygone era?]

LESLIE H. SOUTHWICK, CIRCUIT JUDGE:

Two oilfield workers sued their employer for unpaid overtime wages. The district court granted summary judgment on the defendant's affirmative defense that the plaintiffs fell under the administrative exemption of the Fair Labor Standards Act. Finding there to be genuine disputes of material fact that affect whether the exemption applies, we REVERSE and REMAND.

FACTUAL AND PROCEDURAL BACKGROUND

Defendant M-I SWACO is an oilfield service company that specializes in engineering drilling-fluid systems and additives designed to improve performance for oil and gas well drilling operations. As part of its business, M-I employs Drilling Fluid Specialists, or "mud engineers," who work at M-I customer locations to manage the drilling-fluid system and interact directly with the customers by providing advice and other support.

The minimum educational requirement for a mud engineer is a high-school diploma. Once hired, mud engineers undergo an eight-week training program at M-I's office in Houston, Texas. During the program, trainees receive basic instruction on the functions of drilling fluids, their physical and chemical properties, mathematics, and training on the proper use of testing equipment and computer software.

A mud engineer works to ensure the properties of the drilling fluid, also known as drilling mud, are within designed specifications as set forth in the mud plan, which is created by a project engineer at M-I's headquarters and is based on historical drilling in the area. Both plaintiffs claimed that they did not have authority to deviate from the mud plan. Mud engineers perform their duties either by "sitting" on the customer's well (an extended, round-the-clock monitoring of one drill site) or doing a "drive-by" (quick visits to multiple drill sites).

To ensure the drilling mud is performing adequately and within its designated parameters, mud engineers test the mud's pH, rheology, weight, and viscosity.

The tests are generally conducted either in a lab trailer at the customer's site or on the tailgate of the mud engineer's assigned company vehicle. Plaintiff Dewan testified at his deposition that, after testing was complete, he would provide recommendations to the "company man." These recommendations were largely accepted without further inquiry. The plaintiffs were typically the only M-I employees or mud engineers on site.

. . . .

DISCUSSION

In 1938, Congress enacted the FLSA in an effort to ensure each employee covered by the Act would receive "[a] fair day's pay for a fair day's work and would be protected from the evil of overwork as well as underpay." *Barrentine v. Arkansas-Best Freight Sys., Inc.*, 450 U.S. 728, 739, 101 S.Ct. 1437, 67 L.Ed.2d 641 (1981). One way the FLSA effectuates these goals is through its overtime provision, which requires an employer to compensate any covered employee who works in excess of 40 hours in a workweek "at a rate not less than one and one-half times the [employee's] regular rate. . . ." 29 U.S.C. § 207(a)(1). Relevant here, the FLSA excludes from its overtime requirement those employees working "in a bona fide executive, administrative, or professional capacity. . . ." *Id.* § 213(a)(1).

. . . .

. . . As we note above, the first criterion of the administrative exemption, which concerns the plaintiffs' weekly earning, is clearly satisfied. Plaintiffs argue, however, that genuine issues of material fact exist as to the second and third criteria. Additionally, the plaintiffs argue the district court placed the burden on them to negate the affirmative defense while allowing M-I to rely on the absence of evidence of any element of the plaintiffs' case. We will address the two contested criteria separately. We conclude there is error as to both criteria and find it necessary to examine each individually to show the extent of the fact-finding still needed on remand.

I. Work "Directly Related" to "Management or General Business Operations"

To repeat, the administrative exemption requires the employee to have as his "primary duty . . . the performance of work directly related to the management or general business operations of the employer or the employer's customers." § 541.201(a). The regulations define an employee's "primary duty" as the "principal, main, major or most important duty that the employee performs." § 541.700(a). The "directly related" test is met by the employee's "assisting with the running or servicing of the business, as distinguished, for example, from working on a manufacturing production line or selling a product in a retail or service establishment." § 541.201(a). Under that inquiry, it is "the type of work performed by the employee" on which we must focus. *Id.*

The plaintiffs argue that their job duties—or the types of work they perform as mud engineers—are fundamentally different from the kinds of positions the regulations set out as examples. Examples of work "directly related to management or general business operations" include such functional areas as human resources, marketing, quality control, and safety and health. § 541.201(b). Another regulation entitled "Administrative exemption examples" includes insurance-claims adjusters, financial-services employees, and human-resource managers. § 541.203. The plaintiffs argue that their mud-engineer position is far removed from both sets of examples.

The plaintiffs also rely on a recent Texas district court decision that denied summary judgment to an employer on its affirmative defense that its manufacturing engineer was subject to the FLSA's administrative exemption. See *Elliott v. Dril-Quip, Inc.*, No. H–14–1743, 2015 WL 7302764 (S.D. Tex. Nov. 18, 2015). There, the district court stated that "it is the actual day-to-day activities of the employees that determine whether the employee is exempt, not the labels the employer or employee place on those duties." *Id.* at *6. The court found factual issues existed over the second criterion of whether a manufacturing engineer's primary duty was directly related to the management or general business operations of the employer or its customers. *Id.* at *6–*9. There were also factual uncertainties about the third criterion, namely, whether the plaintiff exercised the requisite discretion and independent judgment. *Id.* at *10–*11. At least for summary judgment, the employer failed to establish that the employee "falls plainly and unmistakably within the terms and spirit of the exemption." *Id.* at *11 (alteration omitted).

Relying on Elliott and the regulations, the plaintiffs argue the district court erred in concluding that they performed non-manual work for M-I or its customers. Instead, they contend mud engineers "produce those income-generating services" that are central to M-I's business model. The plaintiffs seek to align their work as mud engineers with that of oil-well drillers. There is support for that comparison, as the Labor Department included oil-well drillers in a list of "Blue-Collar Occupations That Are Most Likely Nonexempt" under the regulations. See Defining and Delimiting the Exemptions for Executive, Administrative, Professional, Outside Sales and Computer Employees, 69 Fed. Reg. 22,122, 22,242 (Apr. 23, 2004) (as codified at 29 C.F.R. pt. 541).

This court has addressed the needed analysis in a few opinions. Particularly relevant is a case in which we stated that the relevant distinction "is between those employees whose primary duty is administering the business affairs of the enterprise [and] those whose primary duty is producing the commodity or commodities, whether goods or services, that the enterprise exists to produce and market." *Dalheim v. KDFW-TV*, 918 F.2d 1220, 1230 (5th Cir. 1990). Other circuits have thought to label this distinction as the "administrative-production dichotomy, under which production employees (whose job it is to generate the product or service the business offers to the public) will not qualify for the exemption." *Foster v. Nationwide Mut. Ins. Co.*, 710 F.3d 640, 644 (6th Cir. 2013). Some courts, though, have doubted, saying such a distinction is more in keeping with the "industrial age" and not so much "the modern service-industry context." *Roe-Midgett v. CC Servs., Inc.*, 512 F.3d 865, 872 (7th Cir. 2008). Indeed, "[t]he line between administrative and production jobs is not a clear one, particularly given that the item being produced . . . is often an intangible service rather than a material good." *Davis v. J.P. Morgan Chase & Co.*, 587 F.3d 529, 532 (2d Cir. 2009).

Applying these concepts if not the analytical labels to our case, the undisputed evidence is that the plaintiffs' work requires continuous and regular contact with the company men at the drilling location where they are assigned. The plaintiffs provide recommendations, anticipate the customer's concerns with the drilling mud, then address those concerns on M-I's behalf. Based on this evidence, the district court found the plaintiffs performed work that "directly related to the general business operations of the employer or the employer's customers, which was their principal value to M-I and its business of supplying drilling fluid systems engineered to improve, even optimize, drilling performance to the oil industry while reducing costs."

It is true that Section 541.201(a) provides that the administrative exemption applies to work relating to the "general business operations" of an employer. What needs to be kept distinct, though, is that the exemption applies when the employee is involved with "administering the business affairs of the enterprise," not with "producing the commodity" of the business. *Dalheim*,

918 F.2d at 1230. Supplying the drilling-fluid systems seems more related to producing the commodities than the administering of M-I's business.

The district court also found that "nearly all of [the plaintiffs'] working time related directly to continually monitoring the mud for quality control, in compliance with 29 C.F.R. § 541.201(b). . . ." That section of the regulation identifies functional areas that are directly related to management and includes "quality control" in a list that also contains "areas such as tax; finance; accounting; budgeting; auditing; insurance; . . . purchasing; procurement;" and others. 29 C.F.R. § 541.201(b). The regulation's reference to "quality control," particularly considering the list of which it is a part, seems to mean the quality of the mud being provided to M-I's customers and not with monitoring and adding materials to the mud as it is being used in drilling wells to ensure that its properties stay within the specifications set forth in the mud plan developed by project engineers.

The district court also determined that the plaintiffs' work as mud engineers was "directly related to the general business operations" because the plaintiffs "acted as advisors or consultants to M-I's customers, in compliance with 29 C.F.R. § 541.201(c)." That regulation only sets forth two examples of the types of employees that may be exempt: tax experts and financial consultants. 29 C.F.R. § 541.201(c).

We find an opinion from another Circuit to be instructive on the type of work that an exempt advisor or consultant must perform. See *Bratt v. Cnty. of Los Angeles*, 912 F.2d 1066, 1070 (9th Cir. 1990). In determining whether probation officers fit within the regulation's concept of advisor, that court held this to be the test: "whether the activities are directly related to management policies or general business operations." *Id.* That is, the focus is not on a general concept of advice or consultancy but rather on "policy determinations [for] how a business should be run or run more efficiently. . . ." *Id.* Through that lens, the probation officers were not clearly "engaged in 'servicing' a business within the meaning of" the regulations. *Id.*

. . . .

There are significant distinctions between the work performed by these mud engineers and the Zannikos marine superintendents. The latter oversaw the work performed by the customers' employees, contractors, and equipment. *Id.* at 351. Mud engineers, on the other hand, neither assured compliance with health and safety standards nor engaged in tasks likely to qualify as the "general administrative work applicable to the running of any business." See *Davis*, 587 F.3d at 535. "[W]ork that [i]s primarily functional rather than conceptual" does not meet the standard. See *id.* We conclude that the district court erred in granting summary judgment on the issue of whether the plaintiffs' work could be classified as office or non-manual work directly related to the general business operations of M-I's customers.

II. Discretion and Independent Judgment in Matters of Significance

The final criterion for the administrative exemption requires that an employee's primary duty "include the exercise of discretion and independent judgment with respect to matters of significance." 29 C.F.R. § 541.202(a). The phrase "matters of significance" is defined to "refer[ ] to the level of importance or consequence of the work performed." *Id.* Additionally, the regulations require that the "exercise of discretion and independent judgment must be more than the use of skill in applying well-established techniques, procedures or specific standards described in manuals or other sources." § 541.202(e). Notably, "employees can exercise discretion and independent judgment even if their decisions or recommendations are reviewed at a higher level." § 541.202(c).

The regulations provide a non-exclusive list of factors relevant to this criterion. Included are "whether the employee has authority to formulate, affect, interpret, or implement management policies or operating practices; . . . whether the employee has authority to waive or deviate from established policies and procedures without prior approval; [and] whether the employee has authority to negotiate and bind the company on significant matters[.]" § 541.202(b). The employee's degree of discretion must be considered "in the light of all the facts involved in the particular employment situation in which the question arises." *Id.*

. . . .

There is little evidence that the plaintiffs were given "authority to formulate, affect, interpret, or implement management policies or operating practices[.]" 29 C.F.R. § 541.202(b) (factor one). Both Dewan and Casey testified that they lacked such authority. Dewan stated that he "didn't have the authority to change what was in the mud program." Instead, he could "make recommendations based on the drilling—the drilling procedures that were going on and all that, and then get approval if they wanted to change it." Casey agreed with the question that if he believed a change needed to be made in order to stay in compliance with the drilling plan, "you have to raise that to the people above you; right?"

A reasonable jury could credit this testimony and find that the plaintiffs exercised no discretion as mud engineers and merely "appl[ied] well-established techniques, procedures or specific standards described in manuals or other sources." See *id.* § 541.202(e). By regulation, there is no exemption if employees "simply apply well-established techniques or procedures described in manuals or other sources within closely prescribed limits. . . ." *Id.* § 541.704. Other Section 541.202(b) factors for which there was no evidence include whether the employees had the authority to commit M-I in matters that have significant financial impact, or negotiate and bind M-I on significant matters, or represent M-I in handling complaints, arbitrating disputes, or resolving grievances.

Moreover, a review of the plaintiffs' responsibilities suggests that their work involved little more than "the use of skill in applying well-established techniques, procedures or specific standards described in manuals or other sources," § 541.202(e), and that they primarily performed "inspector-type duties" consisting of "specialized work along standardized lines involving well-established techniques and procedures[,] which may have been catalogued and described in manuals or other sources," *Clark v. Centene Co. of Texas, L.P.*, 656 Fed.Appx. 688, 692 (5th Cir. 2016) (unpublished) (quoting § 541.203(g)).

. . . .

However, close the determination may be, M-I has not established its affirmative defense beyond peradventure.

We REVERSE and REMAND for further proceedings consistent with this opinion.

3. The Professional Exemption

Professionals such as lawyers and engineers are distinct because they are licensed and owe duties not just to their employer but also to the public. Professional employees tend to be highly compensated, and they are required to exercise independence to some degree by professional ethics codes and other standards. It should come as no surprise that professional employees are exempt employees, but that doesn't mean that the issues that arise are easily resolved.

29 C.F.R. § 541.300. General Rule for Professional Employees

(a) The term "employee employed in a bona fide professional capacity" in section 13(a)(1) of the Act shall mean any employee:

. . .

(2) Whose primary duty is the performance of work:

(i) Requiring knowledge of an advanced type in a field of science or learning customarily acquired by a prolonged course of specialized intellectual instruction; or

(ii) Requiring invention, imagination, originality or talent in a recognized field of artistic or creative endeavor.

29 C.F.R. § 541.301. Learned Professionals

(a) To qualify for the learned professional exemption, an employee's primary duty must be the performance of work requiring advanced knowledge in a field of science or learning customarily acquired by a prolonged course of specialized intellectual instruction. This primary duty test includes three elements:

(1) The employee must perform work requiring advanced knowledge;

(2) The advanced knowledge must be in a field of science or learning; and

(3) The advanced knowledge must be customarily acquired by a prolonged course of specialized intellectual instruction.

(b) The phrase "work requiring advanced knowledge" means work which is predominantly intellectual in character, and which includes work requiring the consistent exercise of discretion and judgment, as distinguished from performance of routine mental, manual, mechanical or physical work. An employee who performs work requiring advanced knowledge generally uses the advanced knowledge to analyze, interpret or make deductions from varying facts or circumstances. Advanced knowledge cannot be attained at the high school level.

(c) The phrase "field of science or learning" includes the traditional professions of law, medicine, theology, accounting, actuarial computation, engineering, architecture, teaching, various types of physical, chemical and biological sciences, pharmacy and other similar occupations that have a recognized professional status as distinguished from the mechanical arts or skilled trades where in some instances the knowledge is of a fairly advanced type, but is not in a field of science or learning.

(d) The phrase "customarily acquired by a prolonged course of specialized intellectual instruction" restricts the exemption to professions where specialized academic training is a standard prerequisite for entrance into the profession. The best prima facie evidence that an employee meets this requirement is possession of the appropriate academic degree. However, the word "customarily" means that the exemption is also available to employees in such professions who have substantially the same knowledge level and perform substantially the same work as the degreed employees, but who attained the advanced knowledge through a combination of work experience and intellectual instruction. Thus, for example, the learned professional exemption is available to the occasional lawyer who has not gone to law school, or the occasional chemist who is not the possessor of a degree in chemistry. However, the learned professional exemption is not available for occupations that customarily may be performed with only the general knowledge acquired by an academic degree in any field, with knowledge acquired through an apprenticeship, or with training in the performance of routine mental, manual, mechanical or physical processes. The learned professional exemption also does not apply to occupations in which most employees have acquired their skill by experience rather than by advanced specialized intellectual instruction.

(e)

(1) Registered or certified medical technologists. Registered or certified medical technologists who have successfully completed three academic years of pre-professional study in an accredited college or university plus a fourth year of professional course work in a school of medical technology approved by the Council of Medical Education of the American Medical Association generally meet the duties requirements for the learned professional exemption.

(2) Nurses. Registered nurses who are registered by the appropriate State examining board generally meet the duties requirements for the learned professional exemption. Licensed practical nurses and other similar health care employees, however, generally do not qualify as exempt learned professionals because possession of a

specialized advanced academic degree is not a standard prerequisite for entry into such occupations.

(3) Dental hygienists. Dental hygienists who have successfully completed four academic years of pre-professional and professional study in an accredited college or university approved by the Commission on Accreditation of Dental and Dental Auxiliary Educational Programs of the American Dental Association generally meet the duties requirements for the learned professional exemption.

(4) Physician assistants. Physician assistants who have successfully completed four academic years of pre-professional and professional study, including graduation from a physician assistant program accredited by the Accreditation Review Commission on Education for the Physician Assistant, and who are certified by the National Commission on Certification of Physician Assistants generally meet the duties requirements for the learned professional exemption.

(5) Accountants. Certified public accountants generally meet the duties requirements for the learned professional exemption. In addition, many other accountants who are not certified public accountants but perform similar job duties may qualify as exempt learned professionals. However, accounting clerks, bookkeepers and other employees who normally perform a great deal of routine work generally will not qualify as exempt professionals.

(6) Chefs. Chefs, such as executive chefs and sous chefs, who have attained a four-year specialized academic degree in a culinary arts program, generally meet the duties requirements for the learned professional exemption. The learned professional exemption is not available to cooks who perform predominantly routine mental, manual, mechanical or physical work.

(7) Paralegals. Paralegals and legal assistants generally do not qualify as exempt learned professionals because an advanced specialized academic degree is not a standard prerequisite for entry into the field. Although many paralegals possess general four-year advanced degrees, most specialized paralegal programs are two-year associate degree programs from a community college or equivalent institution. However, the learned professional exemption is available for paralegals who possess advanced specialized degrees in other professional fields and apply advanced knowledge in that field in the performance of their duties. For example, if a law firm hires an engineer as a paralegal to provide expert advice on product liability cases or to assist on patent matters, that engineer would qualify for exemption.

(8) Athletic trainers. Athletic trainers who have successfully completed four academic years of pre-professional and professional study in a specialized curriculum accredited by the Commission on Accreditation of Allied Health Education Programs and who are certified by the Board of Certification of the National Athletic Trainers Association Board of Certification generally meet the duties requirements for the learned professional exemption.

(9) Funeral directors or embalmers. Licensed funeral directors and embalmers who are licensed by and working in a state that requires successful completion of four academic years of pre-professional and professional study, including graduation from a college of mortuary science accredited by the American Board of Funeral Service Education, generally meet the duties requirements for the learned professional exemption.

(f) The areas in which the professional exemption may be available are expanding. As knowledge is developed, academic training is broadened and specialized degrees are offered in new and diverse fields, thus creating new specialists in particular fields of science or learning. When an advanced specialized degree has become a standard requirement for a particular occupation, that occupation may have acquired the characteristics of a learned profession. Accrediting and certifying organizations similar to those listed in paragraphs (e)(1), (e)(3), (e)(4), (e)(8) and (e)(9) of this section also may be created in the future. Such organizations may develop similar specialized curriculums and certification programs which, if a standard requirement for a particular occupation, may indicate that the occupation has acquired the characteristics of a learned profession.

Although lawyers ordinarily are considered the epitome of a professional for purposes of FLSA classification, the recent structural changes in the practice of law have raised new questions. A recent decision by the Second Circuit highlights these new questions.

Lola v. Skadden, Arps, Slate, Meagher & Flom LLP

620 Fed.Appx. 37 (2nd Cir. 2015).

Pooler, Circuit Judge:

David Lola, on behalf of himself and all others similarly situated, appeals from the September 16, 2014 opinion and order of the United States District Court for the Southern District of New York (Sullivan, J.) dismissing his putative collective action seeking damages from Skadden, Arps, Slate, Meagher & Flom LLP and Tower Legal Staffing, Inc. for violations of the overtime provision of the Fair Labor Standards Act, 29 U.S.C. §§ 201 et seq. ("FLSA"), arising out of Lola's work as a contract attorney in North Carolina. We agree with the district court's conclusion that: (1) state, not federal, law informs FLSA's definition of "practice of law;" and (2) North Carolina, as the place where Lola worked and lived, has the greatest interest in this litigation, and thus we look to North Carolina law to determine if Lola was practicing law within the meaning of FLSA. However, we disagree with the district court's conclusion, on a motion to dismiss, that by undertaking the document review Lola allegedly was hired to conduct, Lola was necessarily "practicing law" within the meaning of North Carolina law. We find that accepting the allegations as pleaded, Lola adequately alleged in his complaint that his document review was devoid of legal judgment such that he was not engaged in the practice of law, and remand for further proceedings.

BACKGROUND

Lola commenced this FLSA collective action against Skadden, Arps, Slate, Meagher & Flom LLP and Tower Legal Staffing Inc. In his first amended complaint, Lola alleged that Skadden, a Delaware limited liability partnership, is based in New York City. He alleges that Tower is a New York corporation that provides attorneys and paralegals on a contract basis to various law firms and corporate law departments. Lola alleges that Skadden and Tower (together, "Defendants") were joint employers within the meaning of FLSA.

Lola, a North Carolina resident, alleges that beginning in April 2012, he worked for Defendants for fifteen months in North Carolina. He conducted document review for Skadden in connection with a multi-district litigation pending in the United States District Court for the Northern District of Ohio. Lola is an attorney licensed to practice law in California, but he is not admitted to practice law in either North Carolina or the Northern District of Ohio.

Lola alleges that his work was closely supervised by the Defendants, and his "entire responsibility . . . consisted of (a) looking at documents to see what search terms, if any, appeared in the documents, (b) marking those documents into the categories predetermined by Defendants, and (c) at times drawing black boxes to redact portions of certain documents based on specific protocols that Defendants provided." App'x at 20 ¶ 28. Lola further alleges that Defendants provided him with the documents he reviewed, the search terms he was to use in connection with those documents, and the procedures he was to follow if the search terms appeared. Lola was paid $25 an hour for his work, and worked roughly forty-five to fifty-five hours a week. He was paid at the same rate for any hours he worked in excess of forty hours per week. Lola was told that he was an employee of Tower, but he was also told that he needed to follow any procedures set by Skadden attorneys, and he worked under the supervision of Skadden attorneys. Other attorneys employed to work on the same project performed similar work and were likewise paid hourly rates that remained the same for any hours worked in excess of forty hours per week.

Defendants moved to dismiss the complaint, arguing that Lola was exempt from FLSA's overtime rules because he was a licensed attorney engaged in the practice of law. The district court granted the motion, finding (1) state, not federal, standards applied in determining whether an attorney was practicing law under FLSA; (2) North Carolina had the greatest interest in the outcome of the litigation, thus North Carolina's law should apply; and (3) Lola was engaged in the practice of law as defined by North Carolina law, and was therefore an exempt employee under FLSA. *Lola v. Skadden, Arps, Slate, Meagher & Flom, LLP,* No. 13–cv–5008 (RJS), 2014 WL 4626228 (S.D.N.Y. Sept. 16, 2014). This appeal followed.

. . . .

III. Definition of "practice of law" under North Carolina law.

North Carolina defines the "practice of law" in its General Statutes, Section 84–2.1, which provides that:

> The phrase "practice law" as used in this Chapter is defined to be performing any legal service for any other person, firm or corporation, with or without compensation, specifically including . . . the

> preparation and filing of petitions for use in any court, including administrative tribunals and other judicial or quasi-judicial bodies, or assisting by advice, counsel, or otherwise in any legal work; and to advise or give opinion upon the legal rights of any person, firm or corporation. . . .N.C. Gen.Stat. § 84–2.1. North Carolina courts typically read Section 84–2.1 in conjunction with Section 84–4, which defines the unauthorized practice of law as follows:
>
> Except as otherwise permitted by law, . . . it shall be unlawful for any person or association of persons except active members of the Bar, for or without a fee or consideration, to give legal advice or counsel, [or] perform for or furnish to another legal services. . . .

Id. § 84–4; see *N.C. State Bar v. Lienguard, Inc.*, No. 11–cvs–7288, 2014 WL 1365418, at *6–7 (N.C.Super.Ct. Apr. 4, 2014).

The North Carolina General Statutes do not clarify whether "legal services" includes the performance of document review. Nevertheless, the North Carolina State Bar issued a formal ethics opinion shedding light on what is meant by "legal services." The question considered in the ethics opinion was: "May a lawyer ethically outsource legal support services abroad, if the individual providing the services is either a nonlawyer or a lawyer not admitted to practice in the United States (collectively 'foreign assistants')?" In its opinion, the Bar's Ethics Committee opined that:

> A lawyer may use foreign assistants for administrative support services such as document assembly, accounting, and clerical support. A lawyer may also use foreign assistants for limited legal support services such as reviewing documents; conducting due diligence; drafting contracts, pleadings, and memoranda of law; and conducting legal research. Foreign assistants may not exercise independent legal judgment in making decisions on behalf of a client. . . . The limitations on the type of legal services that can be outsourced, in conjunction with the selection and supervisory requirements associated with the use of foreign assistants, insures that the client is competently represented. See Rule 5.5(d). Nevertheless, when outsourcing legal support services, lawyers need to be mindful of the prohibitions on unauthorized practice of law in Chapter 84 of the General Statutes and on the prohibition on aiding the unauthorized practice of law in Rule 5.5(d).

N.C. State Bar Ethics Committee, 2007 Formal Ethics Op. 12 (Apr. 25, 2008).

The district court found that (1) under North Carolina law, document review is considered "legal support services," along with "drafting contracts, pleadings, and memoranda of law[,] and conducting legal research;" (2) the ethics opinion draws a clear line between legal support services, like document review, and "administrative support services," like "document assembly, accounting, and clerical support;" and (3) by emphasizing that only lawyers may undertake legal work, the ethics opinion makes clear that "document review, like other legal support services, constitutes the practice of law and may be lawfully performed by a non-lawyer only if that non-lawyer is supervised by a licensed attorney." *Lola*, 2014 WL 4626228, at *11–12 (alteration in the original). Thus, the district court concluded, any level of document review is considered the "practice of law" in North Carolina. *Id.* at 12. The district court also concluded that because FLSA's regulatory scheme carves doctors and lawyers out of the salary and duty analysis employed to discern if other types of employees fall within the professional exemption, a fact-intensive inquiry is at odds with FLSA's regulatory scheme. *Id.* at *13.

We disagree. The district court erred in concluding that engaging in document review per se constitutes practicing law in North Carolina. The ethics opinion does not delve into precisely what type of document review falls within the practice of law, but does note that while "reviewing documents" may be within the practice of law, "[f]oreign assistants may not exercise independent legal judgment in making decisions on behalf of a client." N.C. State Bar Ethics Committee, 2007 Formal Ethics Op. 12. The ethics opinion strongly suggests that inherent in the definition of "practice of law" in North Carolina is the exercise of at least a modicum of independent legal judgment.

. . . .

Moreover, many other states also consider the exercise of some legal judgment an essential element of the practice of law. See, e.g., *In re Discipline of Lerner*, 124 Nev. 1232, 197 P.3d 1067, 1069–70 (2008) ("exercise of legal judgment on a client's behalf" key to analysis of whether a person engaged in the unauthorized practice of law); *People v. Shell*, 148 P.3d 162, 174 (Colo.2006) ("[O]ne of the touchstones of Colorado's ban on the unauthorized practice of law is an unlicensed person offering advice or judgment about legal matters to another person for use in a specific legal setting");

Or. *State Bar v. Smith,* 149 Or.App. 171, 942 P.2d 793, 800 (1997) ("The 'practice of law' means the exercise of professional judgment in applying legal principles to address another person's individualized needs through analysis, advice, or other assistance."); *In re Discipio*, 163 Ill.2d 515, 206 Ill.Dec. 654, 645 N.E.2d 906, 910 (1994) ("The focus of the inquiry" into whether person engaged in unauthorized practice of law is, in fact, "whether the activity in question required legal knowledge and skill in order to apply legal principles and precedent."); *In re Rowe*, 80 N.Y.2d 336, 341–42, 590 N.Y.S.2d 179, 604 N.E.2d 728 (1992) (authoring an article on the legal rights of psychiatric patients who refuse treatment did not constitute the practice of law because "[t]he practice of law involves the rendering of legal advice and opinions directed to particular clients").

The gravamen of Lola's complaint is that he performed document review under such tight constraints that he exercised no legal judgment whatsoever—he alleges that he used criteria developed by others to simply sort documents into different categories. Accepting those allegations as true, as we must on a motion to dismiss, we find that Lola adequately alleged in his complaint that he failed to exercise any legal judgment in performing his duties for Defendants. A fair reading of the complaint in the light most favorable to Lola is that he provided services that a machine could have provided. The parties themselves agreed at oral argument that an individual who, in the course of reviewing discovery documents, undertakes tasks that could otherwise be performed entirely by a machine cannot be said to engage in the practice of law. We therefore vacate the judgment of the district court and remand for further proceedings consistent with this opinion.

Holding/ Rationale

CONCLUSION

For the reasons given above, the judgment of the district court is vacated, and this matter remanded.

Problem 24-2

A partner at your firm has asked you to prepare a memorandum on 29 C.F.R. 541.301(a). She specifically asks you to address the following questions:

(1) To qualify for the exemption must the employee exercise management authority?

(2) Does an employee qualify for the exemption if the employee is expected to follow established procedures and guidelines?

(3) What forms can the "application of advanced knowledge" take?

(4) What role, if any, do the standard operating procedures of the purported profession play in determining whether the employee is exercising judgment?

(5) What does it mean to engage in "a prolonged course of specialized intellectual study?"

(6) Can an entry level member of a profession qualify for the exemption?

(7) The partner is especially interested in answers to these questions as they pertain to an entry-level accountant (that is, a person who has been working as an accountant for less than two years).

Conclusion

The FLSA provides for numerous exemptions from the overtime requirements. The principal exemptions are for administrative, executive and professional employees. We have explored the complexities of these broad categories and the substantial exposure that employers face if they incorrectly categorize employees.

Lesson 25:
FLSA Protection Against Retaliation

Objectives and Expected Learning Outcomes

In this Lesson, we will discuss the purpose of the FLSA anti-retaliation provision. You will learn that courts interpreting a remedial statute such as the FLSA give the benefit of the doubt to the employee. However, this liberal reading of the statutory protections is tempered by the requirement that an employee's complaint must be specific enough to put the employer on notice that the complaint concerns a purported violation of the FLSA and take action to remedy it. We contrast this provision with similar provisions that protect employees from retaliation for opposing violations of Title VII (Lesson 37) and protections against public employees who exercise their rights under the First Amendment.

Like many remedial statutes, the FLSA protects an employee's ability to assert the substantive rights under the statute. It would obviously make little sense to say that employees are entitled to overtime pay, but that they may be fired for asserting that right. The employee must meet the requirements of the anti-retaliation provision, which requires the employee to claim a violation of the law and suffer an adverse employment action as a result. It is not necessary for the employee to use any particular words, but the gist of the employee's complaint must allege a violation of the employee's rights under the FLSA. The anti-retaliation provision extends to any employee, even if they are complaining about a violation of another employee's rights under the FLSA.

Because the statutory language is fairly general, a number of interpretive questions quickly arose regarding the elements of a sufficient complaint under the provisions. For example, the United States Supreme Court held that the complaint need not be in a formal writing, and that mere oral complaints can trigger protection. Read the statute carefully and think about the kinds of interpretive problems that courts will face in enforcing the provision.

29 U.S.C. § 215. Prohibited acts; prima facie evidence

(a) It shall be unlawful for any person—

. . .

(3) to discharge or in any other manner discriminate against any employee because such employee has filed any complaint or instituted or caused to be instituted any proceeding under or related to this chapter, or has testified or is about to testify in any such proceeding . . . .

QUESTIONS

1. You will learn in Lesson 37 that Title VII has an anti-retaliation provision that protects an employee from adverse employment actions if the employee "opposes" discriminatory practices that are not necessarily directed at the employee. Can the FLSA statutory language bear an interpretation that recognizes a cause of action for "opposition?"

2. What does it mean "to otherwise discriminate" against an employee? Does the term "discriminate" imply that a plaintiff must offer evidence that he or she was treated differently solely because of engaging in protected activity?

Example 25-1

An employee tells her supervisor that she does not want to work more than 40 hours in a given week. After refusing overtime hours several weeks in a row, the employee is fired. She has no viable claim of retaliation because she did not engage in protected activity. She is complaining about the scheduled work hours and not the employer's failure to pay overtime compensation. The FLSA does not protect employees from having to work overtime.

Example 25-2

During an argument, an employee tells his supervisor, "You work us to death here. Wages are lousy. We are not paid what we are worth and you know it." If the employee is disciplined he would have no action for retaliation because this is not protected activity regarding an alleged violation of the FLSA.

Example 25-3

An employee tells her supervisor that she is unable to log onto her work computer properly, with the result that her hours worked are not being accurately recorded. In particular, she claims that last week's paycheck incorrectly stated that she only worked 40 hours and did not pay her for a half hour of overtime. If the employee is later demoted, she can state a claim of retaliation because she engaged in protected activity that alerted the employer to noncompliance with the FLSA, for which she suffered an adverse employment action.

The following case begins with the Supreme Court determination that oral complaints are sufficient to trigger the FLSA anti-retaliation provision, and then addresses the unresolved issue of whether an employee, to engage in protected activity, must complain to a government official. This case is important for its doctrinal ruling, but for your purpose it is equally important as an example of how courts determine difficult issues of statutory interpretation to take full account of the text, legislative intent, purpose and public policy.

Greathouse v. JHS Security Inc.

784 F.3d 105 (2nd Cir. 2015).

Susan L. Carney, Circuit Judge:

In this appeal, we consider the effect of the Supreme Court's decision in *Kasten v. Saint-Gobain Performance Plastics Corp.*, ___ U.S. ___, 131 S.Ct. 1325, 179 L.Ed.2d 379 (2011), on our 1993 decision in *Lambert v. Genesee Hospital*, 10 F.3d 46 (2d Cir.1993), concerning what constitutes "fil[ing a] complaint" under the anti-retaliation provision of the Fair Labor Standards Act ("FLSA"), 29 U.S.C. § 215(a)(3).

Section 215(a) (3) makes it unlawful "to discharge or in any other manner discriminate against any employee because such employee has filed any complaint . . . related to" FLSA's provisions. In Lambert, we read section 215(a)(3) to require that an employee pursuing a claim for unlawful retaliation have done more than voice an equal pay complaint to a supervisor. 10 F.3d at 55–56. To serve as a predicate for an FLSA retaliation claim, we held, a complaint must be "formal[ly]" filed, see *id.*—a condition that we have subsequently interpreted to require (1) a written complaint, that is (2) filed with a government agency.

In its 2011 decision in *Kasten*, however, the Supreme Court held that the section's pivotal phrase—"filed any complaint"—encompasses oral as well as written complaints, so long as the complaint is "sufficiently clear and detailed for a reasonable employer to understand it, in light of both content and context, as an assertion of rights protected by the statute and a call for their protection." 131 S.Ct. at 1335. To the extent, then, that *Lambert* turned on the oral nature of the complaint made by the employee, *Kasten* rejected *Lambert*'s analysis. The *Kasten* Court refrained, however, from addressing the second factor on which the *Lambert* analysis hinged: that the complaint must be directed to a government agency, not merely to a supervisor in the ranks of the defendant employer. *Kasten*, 131 S.Ct. at 1336. Although *Kasten* itself arose in the context of an oral complaint made to an employer, not a government agency, the *Kasten* Court declined to address specifically whether retaliation for a complaint made to an employer is actionable. See *id.* at 1336.

Kasten overrules *Lambert*'s requirement that an employee seeking section 215(a)(3)'s protections file a written complaint. As we discuss below, *Kasten* also casts doubt on *Lambert*'s second requirement: that, for an employee's complaint to fall within the protections of section 215(a)(3), it be made to a government agency. Indeed, we not long ago characterized *Kasten* (albeit in a footnote) as effecting an "abrogation of our precedent in this area." *Kuebel v. Black & Decker Inc.*, 643 F.3d 352, 358 n.3 (2d Cir.2011). *Lambert*'s holding in this respect is at odds, moreover, with the weight of authority in our sister circuits, and with the consistently held position of the two authorities charged with section 215(a) (3)'s enforcement: the Secretary of Labor and the Equal Employment Opportunity Commission ("EEOC").

Therefore, today, we overrule *Lambert* to the extent it holds that section 215(a) (3) requires an employee to have filed a complaint with a government agency as a predicate for an FLSA retaliation claim. We conclude that an employee may premise a section 215(a)(3) retaliation action on an oral complaint made to an employer, so long as—pursuant to *Kasten*—the complaint is "sufficiently clear and detailed for a reasonable employer to

No requirement of complaint to gov

understand it, in light of both content and context, as an assertion of rights protected by the statute and a call for their protection." 131 S.Ct. at 1335. Accordingly, because the District Court denied Greathouse damages on his claim for retaliatory discharge based entirely on *Lambert*'s rule, we vacate the judgment insofar as it relied on Lambert and remand the cause for further proceedings consistent with this opinion.

FACTUAL AND PROCEDURAL BACKGROUND

We recite the facts as found by the Magistrate Judge in a report and recommendation that was adopted by the District Court. See *Greathouse v. JHS Sec., Inc.*, No. 11 Civ. 7845(PAE) (GWG), 2012 WL 3871523 (S.D.N.Y. Sept. 7, 2012), adopted by 2012 WL 5185591 (S.D.N.Y. Oct. 19, 2012). Because both defendants defaulted, the Magistrate Judge properly accepted as true the well-pleaded factual allegations of Greathouse's complaint regarding liability, and provided for further proceedings to determine the appropriate damage award. See *SEC v. Razmilovic*, 738 F.3d 14, 19 (2d Cir.2013).

From September 2006 through October 14, 2011, plaintiff Darnell Greathouse worked as a security guard for defendant JHS Security Inc. ("JHS"). *Greathouse* considered defendant Melvin Wilcox, the president and part-owner of JHS, to be his "boss." *Greathouse*, 2012 WL 3871523, at *2. During the course of his employment with JHS, Greathouse was the victim of a number of improper employment practices, including non-payment and late payment of wages, and improper payroll deductions. Although Wilcox repeatedly told Greathouse that he would receive his outstanding paychecks, those checks never arrived.

On October 14, 2011, Greathouse complained to Wilcox that he had not been paid in several months. Wilcox responded, "I'll pay you when I feel like it," and, without warning, drew a gun and pointed it at Greathouse. *Greathouse*, 2012 WL 3871523, at *2. Greathouse understood that response as ending his employment with JHS.

About two weeks later, Greathouse filed his complaint in the United States District Court for the Southern District of New York. In addition to various FLSA and New York Labor Law ("NYLL") claims related to his missing and improperly reduced wages, he alleged that Wilcox and JHS (through Wilcox) had effectively discharged him in retaliation for his October 14th complaint, thereby violating section 215(a)(3) and the NYLL.

Several months later, after neither defendant appeared or filed an answer, the clerk of court entered defaults against both. The District Court then referred the matter to a magistrate judge to evaluate Greathouse's claims for damages. The Magistrate Judge issued a Report and Recommendation in September 2012, recommending that the District Court enter a damages award in the total amount of $30,658.50, plus prejudgment interest, for Greathouse's claims for unpaid overtime, unpaid wages, improper deductions, and liquidated damages under the NYLL. *Greathouse*, 2012 WL 3871523, at *12.

As to the retaliation claim, however, the Magistrate Judge concluded that *Lambert* barred an award because Greathouse had not filed a complaint with any government agency or other prosecutorial authority, but had merely confronted his employer in person to demand his missing wages. The Magistrate Judge recognized that, under the Supreme Court's holding in *Kasten*, an oral complaint may serve as a predicate for an FLSA retaliation claim. The Magistrate Judge correctly acknowledged, however, that *Kasten* did not overturn *Lambert* insofar as we held there that a complaint made to a supervisor is not a complaint "filed" under section 215(a)(3).

Greathouse filed objections to the Magistrate Judge's report in the District Court, contesting, inter alia, the Magistrate Judge's finding that Greathouse was not entitled to damages for his FLSA retaliation claim. The District Court rejected Greathouse's objection on this issue, agreeing with the Magistrate Judge about the continued import of *Lambert.* The District Court subsequently adopted the Magistrate Judge's conclusions, subject only to two minor exceptions not relevant here, and the District Court entered default judgment.

On appeal, Greathouse argues primarily that, in light of *Kasten*, we should overrule what remains of *Lambert* and squarely hold that FLSA prohibits retaliation against employees who complain orally to their employers about perceived FLSA violations. Because defendants defaulted in the District Court and never filed an appearance in this Court, we appointed pro bono counsel to argue, as amicus curiae in support of defendants, that the Supreme Court's decision in *Kasten* did not abrogate our holding in *Lambert* and that the *Lambert* rule with respect to intra-company complaints should survive. The two administrative authorities charged with administering FLSA—the EEOC and the Secretary of Labor—filed amicus briefs in support of Greathouse's position.

DISCUSSION

Section 215(a)(3) forbids "any person" from "discharg[ing] or in any other manner discriminat[ing] against any employee because such employee has filed any complaint or instituted or caused to be instituted any proceeding under or related to this chapter. . . ." 29 U.S.C. § 215(a)(3) (emphasis added). As described above, the Supreme Court held in *Kasten* that FLSA's anti-retaliation provision "includes oral as well as written complaints." 131 S.Ct. at 1329. The Court overruled *Lambert* and our precedent following *Lambert* to the extent that *Lambert* required an employee to have filed a written complaint to claim FLSA's protections. *Id.* at 1330 (citing *Lambert* as a contrary decision). But the *Kasten* Court expressly declined to address the question whether an employer's retaliation for an intra-company complaint is actionable under FLSA. *Id.* at 1336.

It is difficult to ignore, however, that the complaint at issue in *Kasten* was lodged not with a government agency, but with an employer. See *id.* at 1340–41 (Scalia, J., dissenting). Although slightly different concerns animated the Court's discussion in Kasten, an interpretation that excludes clearly stated complaints from protection because they were made to the employer instead of a government agency would run counter to the broadly remedial purpose that the *Kasten* Court instructed FLSA serves. See *id.* at 1334. So, although we recognize that the Court has not yet ruled on this precise question, we conclude that its ruling in *Kasten* must be read as casting serious doubt on the second component of our ruling in *Lambert.*

A. Our Holding in Lambert

In *Lambert,* three female employees alleged that their employer, Genesee Hospital (the "Hospital"), retaliated against them in violation of the Equal Pay Act of 1963 ("EPA"), 29 U.S.C. § 206(d), a statute that amended FLSA. 10 F.3d at 50. Two of the plaintiffs, Janine Lambert and Eva Baker, alleged that they complained to their departmental supervisor and to a member of the Hospital's employee-affairs department about Baker's salary, which in their view was unfairly lower than that of a male employee in the department (Francis Dupre), whose responsibilities were substantially equivalent to Baker's. *Id.* at 51.

About one year after Lambert and Baker complained, the supervisor selected Dupre to manage the department. *Id.* Citing that incident and others, Lambert, Baker, and one of their female colleagues sued the Hospital, their supervisor, and Dupre, alleging that Dupre's promotion over Baker was made in retaliation for Lambert and Baker's complaints to their supervisor about Baker's unequal pay. *Id.* This, they contended, violated the EPA and section 215(a)(3).

The district court assumed that plaintiffs' allegations stated a retaliation claim under section 215(a)(3), *Lambert,* 10 F.3d at 56, and the case proceeded to trial, where a jury found for plaintiffs on their retaliation claim as well as on their equal pay claim, *id.* at 51–52. After trial, however, the district court granted defendants' motion for judgment notwithstanding the verdict. *Id.* at 52. Plaintiffs appealed the resulting dismissal.

On appeal, we held that the district court erred in granting judgment to defendants on plaintiffs' retaliation claim because defendants had waived their legal argument. *Id.* at 54. Nonetheless, we dismissed plaintiffs' section 215(a)(3) claim, on our own accord, for failure to state a claim. *Id.* at 56. We determined that the plain language of section 215(a)(3)—to "file[ ] any complaint"—"limits the cause of action to retaliation for filing formal complaints, instituting a proceeding, or testifying, but does not encompass complaints made to a supervisor." *Id.* at 55. Because plaintiffs premised their claim on "simply oral complaints to a supervisor," they had not stated a claim for retaliation under section 215(a)(3). *Id.* at 55–56.

The *Lambert* court's conclusion—that an employee pursuing a claim for unlawful retaliation must do more than voice an equal pay complaint to a supervisor to invoke section 215(a)(3)'s protections—is contrary to the weight of authority in our sister circuits, even more so now than when Lambert was decided. Indeed, the First, Fourth, Fifth, Seventh, Eighth, Ninth, Tenth, and Eleventh Circuits have all held that section 215(a)(3) protects employees from retaliation for their complaints made to employers, and the Sixth Circuit has assumed, without significant discussion, that complaints to an employer are covered by section 215(a)(3). The EEOC has long maintained the position that the Act protects employees who make such intra-company complaints.

B. The Supreme Court's Holding in Kasten

Nearly two decades after *Lambert* was decided, after these developments in other circuits and application of *Lambert* within our own, the Supreme Court granted certiorari in *Kasten* to resolve a "conflict among the Circuits as to whether an oral complaint is protected" by section 215(a)(3). 131 S.Ct.

at 1330. The question there arose from an employee's oral complaints to his shift supervisor and to other employees that their employer was violating FLSA by failing to compensate them for time spent donning and doffing their work-related protective gear. *Id.* at 1329–30. The Seventh Circuit had affirmed summary judgment for the employer, ruling that FLSA does not protect oral complaints. *Id.* at 1330.

Deciding that the statutory phrase "filed any complaint," read in isolation, is "open to competing interpretations," *id.* at 1330–31, the Supreme Court looked to FLSA's basic objectives for interpretive guidance. It also examined the range of meanings that the words "filed" and "complaint" and the phrase "filed any complaint" could bear and gave "a degree of weight" to the views of the agencies charged with enforcing FLSA—the Department of Labor and the EEOC, which argued for a broad reading of the section, one protective of employees. *Id.* at 1335.

The Court concluded that "only one interpretation is permissible": an oral complaint is protected by FLSA's anti-retaliation provision if the complaint is "sufficiently clear and detailed for a reasonable employer to understand it, in light of both content and context, as an assertion of rights protected by the statute and a call for their protection." *Id.* at 1331, 1335. Despite framing the inquiry by reference to what a "reasonable employer " would understand, *id.* at 1335 (emphasis added), the Court nevertheless expressly declined to address the logically prior question whether FLSA applies, in the first instance, to complaints made directly to employers, rather than to government agencies. *Id.* at 1336. It is to that question that we now turn.

C. Looking Anew at the Statutory Language: "Filed Any Complaint"

Both impelled and guided by *Kasten*, we now look anew at the statutory interpretation question that we addressed of our own accord in *Lambert*, but that the *Kasten* Court did not resolve: does section 215(a)(3) prohibit retaliation against employees for oral complaints made to employers?

1. The phrase "filed any complaint" admits of more than one meaning

A statute generally "should be enforced according to its plain and unambiguous meaning." *United States v. Livecchi*, 711 F.3d 345, 351 (2d Cir.2013). The "plainness or ambiguity of statutory language is determined by reference to the language itself, the specific context in which that language is used, and the broader context of the statute as a whole." *Robinson v. Shell Oil Co.*,

519 U.S. 337, 341, 117 S.Ct. 843, 136 L.Ed.2d 808 (1997). If we determine that a statutory provision is ambiguous, we then turn to canons of statutory construction for assistance in interpreting the statute. See *Daniel v. Am. Bd. of Emergency Med.*, 428 F.3d 408, 423 (2d Cir.2005).

In *Lambert*, we determined that the plain language of section 215(a)(3) prohibited only "retaliation for filing formal complaints, instituting a proceeding, or testifying." *Lambert*, 10 F.3d at 55 (emphasis added). But when we look again at section 215(a)(3), with the benefit of Kasten and the readings of our sister circuits, we now conclude that the statutory language is not as plain and unambiguous as it seemed when *Lambert* was decided. See *Kasten*, 131 S.Ct. at 1330–31 (stating that section 215(a)(3) "may be open to competing interpretations"). As the Supreme Court explained, "even if the word 'filed,' considered alone, might suggest a narrow interpretation limited to writings, the phrase 'any complaint' suggests a broad interpretation that would include an oral complaint." *Id.* at 1332.

Guided by this discussion, we must reevaluate the distinction drawn in *Lambert* and its progeny between "formal" complaints to government agencies and "informal" complaints to supervisors. First, we observe that the text of the statute does not provide that a complaint must be filed "formally," or exclude from its protections those complaints that are filed "informally." In short: it does not use either word. Nor does it expressly direct that, to be protected, a complaint must be filed with a government agency or any particular entity. Second, even if the word "filed," considered alone, might seem to contemplate lodging a complaint with a governmental body, the word's context counsels against a narrow reading: as the Supreme Court reasoned, the phrase "any complaint" suggests an expansive reading, one that could include complaints filed with or expressed to an employer.

Citing Justice Scalia's dissent in *Kasten*, 131 S.Ct. at 1337 (Scalia, J., dissenting), amicus curiae in support of defendants argues that the phrase "filed any complaint" clearly and unambiguously refers only to complaints made to government agencies, because every other use of the word "complaint" in FLSA refers to a governmental filing. See 29 U.S.C. § 216(b) (explaining that the right to bring certain actions "shall terminate upon the filing of a complaint by the Secretary of Labor"); *id.* § 216(c) (explaining that the statute of limitations for an action for unpaid wages commences "on the date when the complaint is filed"); *id.* § 218c(b) (setting forth the "Complaint procedure" by which one may "seek relief" by filing a complaint with the Department of Labor). Amicus also contends that the phrase "fil[ing a] complaint" is not commonly used to describe the act of complaining to an employer.

But, as our sister circuits have recognized, the phrase "filed any complaint" may also plausibly be interpreted to include intra-company complaints. The accepted definition of "to file," as the First Circuit has noted, may include an employee's submission of a written letter of complaint to an employer: the concept is "sufficiently elastic to encompass an internal complaint made to a private employer with the expectation the employer will place it on file among the employer's official records." *Valerio v. Putnam Assocs. Inc.*, 173 F.3d 35, 41–42 (1st Cir.1999) (Campbell, J.). And, filing work-related grievances with employers is a common practice in many workplaces. See, e.g., *Lambert v. Ackerley*, 180 F.3d 997, 1004 (9th Cir.1999) (en banc) (noting that "any complaint" is clearly broad enough to encompass complaints made to employers, and highlighting the widespread practice of "filing" grievances and complaints with unions and employers before commencing other internal or external proceedings). In addition, "filed any complaint" must be examined in context, contrasting it with the neighboring phrase, "instituted any proceeding": to avoid rendering one or the other surplusage, we may construe the first to contemplate a communication (such as an intra-company complaint seeking a change in company practice) that does not ordinarily trigger a "proceeding" (such as an adjudicatory process).

In light of these competing interpretations, we conclude that the statutory phrase "filed any complaint" is variable in meaning and does not unambiguously denote submission of complaints to government agencies alone. To interpret the language of the statute, then, we must apply traditional tools of statutory interpretation. These include looking to the purpose of FLSA, and affording some degree of weight to the interpretations of the agencies charged with enforcing it. See *Minor v. Bostwick Labs., Inc.*, 669 F.3d 428, 436 (4th Cir.2012) (concluding that " 'filed any complaint' is ambiguous as to whether intracompany complaints are protected activity under the FLSA," and "mov[ing] to other interpretive tools").

Not unambiguous

2. Statutory purpose

Congress declared its intention in FLSA "to correct and as rapidly as practicable to eliminate" labor conditions "detrimental to the maintenance of the minimum standard of living necessary for health, efficiency, and general well-being of workers," without substantially reducing employment or earning power. 29 U.S.C. § 202. To achieve this goal, FLSA sets forth minimum wage standards, *id.* § 206, and establishes certain payroll practice requirements, *id.* §§ 207, 211(c), among other mandates. Because the government cannot directly monitor every employer's payroll, FLSA also creates an enforcement mechanism that relies in significant part on employees' complaints. See *Mitchell v. Robert DeMario Jewelry, Inc.*, 361 U.S. 288, 292, 80 S.Ct. 332, 4 L.Ed.2d 323 (1960). Congress enacted section 215(a)(3) to "prevent[ ] fear of economic retaliation from inducing workers quietly to accept substandard conditions," *Kasten*, 131 S.Ct. at 1333 (internal quotation marks omitted), and to foster an atmosphere protective of employees who lodge such complaints.

We have repeatedly affirmed that "the remedial nature of the FLSA warrants an expansive interpretation of its provisions so that they will have the widest possible impact in the national economy." *Irizarry v. Catsimatidis*, 722 F.3d 99, 110 (2d Cir.2013) (internal quotation marks and alterations omitted); *Carter v. Dutchess Cmty. Coll.*, 735 F.2d 8, 12 (2d Cir.1984) (same); see also *Zheng v. Liberty Apparel Co.*, 355 F.3d 61, 66 (2d Cir.2003) (recognizing the "remedial purpose" of FLSA). FLSA's remedial goals counsel in favor of construing the phrase "filed any complaint" in section 215(a)(3) broadly, to include intra-company complaints to employers as well as complaints to government agencies. See, e.g., *Valerio*, 173 F.3d at 43 (concluding that the "remedial and humanitarian purposes of [FLSA] . . . would hardly be furthered by a narrow reading of § 215(a)(3)" (internal quotation marks and citations omitted)).

Prohibiting retaliation against employees who make internal complaints furthers the purposes of FLSA by encouraging speedier and more efficient resolution of employee grievances, and resolving FLSA-related issues before employees have lost significant wages or other benefits. As the Supreme Court cautioned in *Kasten*, limiting the protections of section 215(a)(3) to employees who make complaints to government agencies "would discourage the use of desirable informal workplace grievance procedures to secure compliance with the Act." 131 S.Ct. at 1334. Even before *Kasten*, the First Circuit opined that "[b]y protecting only those employees who kept secret their belief that they were being illegally treated until they filed a legal proceeding," a narrow interpretation of FLSA "would discourage prior discussion of the matter between employee and employer, and would have the bizarre effect both of discouraging early settlement attempts and creating an incentive for the employer to fire an employee as soon as possible after learning the employee believed he was being treated illegally." *Valerio*, 173 F.3d at 43.

The protective purpose of FLSA, recognized and acted on by the *Kasten* Court, counsels unmistakably in favor of adopting a reading of the statutory phrase "filed any complaint" that includes lodging an internal complaint with an employer.

3. Administrative interpretations

We next examine another factor relevant to our analysis: the views of the EEOC and the Secretary of Labor, as the authorities charged with enforcing FLSA. "The well-reasoned views of the agencies implementing a statute constitute a body of experience and informed judgment to which courts and litigants may properly resort for guidance. . . ." *United States v. Mead Corp.*, 533 U.S. 218, 227, 121 S.Ct. 2164, 150 L.Ed.2d 292 (2001) (internal quotation marks and brackets omitted). The weight appropriately afforded an agency interpretation that lacks the force of law—such as an agency manual or litigation document—depends upon "the thoroughness evident in its consideration, the validity of its reasoning, its consistency with earlier and later pronouncements, and all those factors which give it power to persuade, if lacking power to control." *Skidmore v. Swift & Co.*, 323 U.S. 134, 140, 65 S.Ct. 161, 89 L.Ed. 124 (1944). In *Kasten*, the Supreme Court ascribed "a degree of weight" to the views of the EEOC and the Secretary, finding them "reasonable" and "consistent with the Act," and explaining that "[t]he length of time the agencies have held them suggests that they reflect careful consideration, not 'post hoc rationalizatio[n].' " 131 S.Ct. at 1335 (quoting *Motor Vehicle Mfrs. Ass'n of United States, Inc. v. State Farm Mut. Automobile Ins. Co.*, 463 U.S. 29, 50, 103 S.Ct. 2856, 77 L.Ed.2d 443 (1983)).

Since no later than 1998, the EEOC Compliance Manual—a document intended, among other things, to "provide[ ] guidance and instructions for investigating and analyzing claims of retaliation under the statutes enforced by the EEOC"—has provided that employees are protected from retaliation "if an individual explicitly or implicitly communicates to his or her employer or other covered entity a belief that its activity" is unlawful. 2 EEOC Compliance Manual, Section 8: Retaliation § 8–II(B)(1) (May 20, 1998).

The agencies' litigation positions on this question have also been consistent for decades. Both the Secretary and the EEOC have filed numerous briefs in the various Courts of Appeals maintaining that section 215(a)(3) prohibits retaliation against employees who complain to their employers about FLSA violations. See *Minor*, 669 F.3d at 439 (noting that "although it is not determinative, because the Secretary and the EEOC have consistently advanced this reasonable and thoroughly considered position, it adds force to our conclusion" (internal quotation marks and alterations omitted)). We are advised that this litigation position dates back to at least 1989 for the EEOC and 1999 for the Secretary. See Brief for the EEOC as Amicus Curiae at 2; Brief for the Secretary of Labor as Amicus Curiae at 27.

For the reasons relied on by the Supreme Court in *Kasten* as to the question of oral complaints, then, we find that the agencies' longstanding, consistent interpretation provides additional support for the view that to "file[ ] any complaint" includes to submit a complaint to an employer.

D. To "File Any Complaint" Encompasses Intra-Company Complaints

Based on the foregoing analysis, we conclude that section 215(a)(3) does not restrict its protections to employees who file formal, written complaints with government agencies. Consistent with FLSA's text and remedial purpose, with the approach adopted in *Kasten*, and with Congressional design to encourage workers to report potential violations without fear of reprisal, we construe the phrase "file[ ] any complaint" as encompassing oral complaints made to employers in a context that makes the assertion of rights plain. Our reading derives support from the provision's consistent, longstanding interpretation by the agencies charged with its enforcement. It brings us in harmony, too, with the decisions of the other Courts of Appeals to have considered the issue.

Our reading is subject, however, to certain limitations. As observed in part by the *Kasten* Court, whether the "fil[ing of a] complaint"—especially an oral complaint delivered directly to an employer—constitutes an act protected by FLSA is a context-dependent inquiry. In some circumstances, an employer may find it difficult to recognize an oral complaint as one invoking rights protected by FLSA. It seems to us inconsistent with *Kasten* to elevate a grumble in the hallway about an employer's payroll practice to a complaint "filed" with the employer within the meaning of section 215(a)(3). Indeed, the Supreme Court observed in *Kasten* that "the phrase 'filed any complaint' contemplates some degree of formality," 131 S.Ct. at 1334 (emphasis added), but described the level of formality necessary in terms of the employer's interests in knowing when it need take care to avoid action that might be seen as retaliatory: "where the recipient has been given fair notice that a grievance has been lodged and does, or should, reasonably understand the matter as part of its business concerns." *Id.*

Recognizing the potential for ambiguity in oral communications, yet desiring not to impair the enforcement framework adopted in the statute, the *Kasten* Court explained that "a complaint is 'filed' [only] when a reasonable, objective person would have understood the employee to have put the employer on notice that the employee is asserting statutory rights under the Act." *Id.* at 1335 (internal quotation marks and alterations omitted). The employee need not invoke the Act by name, but, as the Court concluded, "[t]o fall within the scope of the anti-retaliation provision, a complaint must be sufficiently clear and detailed for a reasonable employer to understand it, in light of both content and context, as an assertion of rights protected by the statute and a call for their protection." *Id.* Defining the exact contours of that standard is beyond the scope of this opinion, but it would, for example, exclude from the concept of "fil[ing a] complaint" a mere passing comment. This limitation, applied with the statute's remedial purpose in mind, informs and cabins our holding today.

We decline, however, to address here the question whether Greathouse's complaint provided an adequate basis on which to enter a default judgment against his employer on his retaliation claim. The decision whether to enter default judgment is committed to the district court's discretion, see *City of New York v. Mickalis Pawn Shop, LLC,* 645 F.3d 114, 131 (2d Cir.2011), as is the decision whether to conduct a hearing before deciding the default judgment motion, see *Finkel v. Romanowicz,* 577 F.3d 79, 87 (2d Cir.2009). See also Fed.R.Civ.P. 55(b)(2) ("The court may conduct hearings or make referrals . . . when, to enter or effectuate judgment, it needs to . . . conduct an accounting; . . . determine the amount of damages; . . . establish the truth of any allegation by evidence; or . . . investigate any other matter."). We therefore remand the cause to the District Court for a ruling in the first instance on Greathouse's default judgment motion with respect to his claim for unlawful retaliation under FLSA.

CONCLUSION

In sum, we overrule what is left of our holding in *Lambert v. Genesee Hospital,* 10 F.3d 46 (2d Cir.1993), and conclude, in accordance with all of our sister circuits to have addressed the issue, that section 215(a)(3) prohibits retaliation against employees who orally complain to their employers, so long as their complaint is "sufficiently clear and detailed for a reasonable employer to understand it, in light of both content and context, as an assertion of rights protected by the statute and a call for their protection." *Kasten*, 131 S.Ct. at 1335. We therefore VACATE the District Court's judgment insofar as it relied on Lambert, and REMAND the cause to the District Court to determine, in the first instance, whether to grant Greathouse a default judgment on his retaliation claim under section 215(a)(3), and if so, what damages, if any, Greathouse is entitled to recover therefore.

QUESTION

1. Section 215 is written in the disjunctive. Why do you suppose the drafters use the disjunctive in five separate section of 215? What would the result be if they had not used the disjunctive?

Problem 25-1

Heather tells Tim, a co-employee, that the company is not paying them in accordance with the law. Specifically, she says that they should be paid overtime, but they are not. Heather constantly complains to Tim about her dissatisfaction with their employer's failure to pay overtime. Tim finally tells the manager that Heather is constantly complaining about not being paid overtime wages. The manager fires Heather for disruption in the workplace, but he tells Tim, "we're not going to fire you because we realize that your dissatisfaction was caused by Heather's constant complaining." Does Heather have a claim under section 215?

Problem 25-2

Hannah is the human resources manager at a firm. Several employees tell Hannah that they are not being paid overtime because they are misclassified as exempt employees. Hannah's investigation of the company's pay practices leads her to agree with the employees. She brings the employees' concerns, as well as the results of her investigation, to the attention of the operations manager. The next day, she is terminated. Does she have a claim under section 215?

Colvin v. Volusion, Inc.

___ F.3d ___, 2017 WL 2805010 (W.D. Tex. 2017).

Andrew W. Austin, United States Magistrate Judge.

Before the Court are Defendant's 12(b)(6) Partial Motion to Dismiss (Dkt. No. 4); Plaintiff's Response (Dkt. No. 8); Defendant's Reply (Dkt. No. 9); and Plaintiff's Sur-Reply (Dkt. No. 10). The District Court referred the motion to the undersigned Magistrate Judge for report and recommendation pursuant to 28 U.S.C. § 636(b) and Rule 1(c) of Appendix C of the Local Rules.

. . . .

III. ANALYSIS

B. FLSA Retaliation Claim

Colvin alleges that Volusion retaliated against him by firing him in violation of the FLSA, 29 U.S.C. § 215(a)(3), after he complained to his supervisor that Volusion's policies violated the FLSA. Specifically, Colvin alleges that after his supervisor informed him that he must begin using Paid Time Off ("PTO") for any future doctor's appointments "in spite of the fact that Mr. Colvin regularly worked additional hours in excess of the time he took off for his medical care and in excess of 40 hours per week without any additional compensation," he made a complaint to his supervisor that Volusion was violating the FLSA. Colvin alleges that he was fired five days later. The FLSA makes it illegal for an employer "to discharge or in any other manner discriminate against any employee because such employee has filed any complaint or instituted or caused to be instituted any proceeding under or related to [the FLSA]." 29 U.S.C. § 215(a)(3). In order to make out a prima facie case of retaliation under the FLSA, a plaintiff must allege (1) he participated in protected activity under the FLSA, (2) he experienced an adverse employment action, and (3) there is a causal link between the protected activity and the adverse employment action. *Hagan v. Echostar Satellite, L.L.C.*, 529 F.3d 617, 624 (5th Cir. 2008). Volusion argues that Colvin has failed to allege facts establishing a prima facie case of FLSA retaliation because he has failed to sufficiently allege he engaged in protected activity or that there was a causal link between his complaint and termination.

allegations

Elements

1. Protected Activity

To demonstrate that he participated in an FLSA protected activity, Colvin must first demonstrate that he filed a complaint. *Starnes v. Wallace,* 849 F.3d 627, 632 (5th Cir. 2017). In order for an employee's communication to constitute a complaint the

> employer must have fair notice that an employee is making a complaint that could subject the employer to a later claim of retaliation [and the] complaint must be sufficiently clear and detailed for a reasonable employer to understand it, in light of both content and context, as an assertion of rights protected by the [FLSA] and a call for their protection.

Kasten v. Saint-Gobain Performance Plastics Corp., 563 U.S. 1, 14 (2011). In addition, "such an assertion of rights requires that an employee step outside of his normal job role and assert a right adverse to the company." *Starnes,* 849 F.3d at 632. An informal oral complaint to the employer can satisfy this standard. *Kasten,* 563 U.S. at 14.

Colvin alleges that on October 23, 2015, he made a complaint to his supervisor "about what he reasonably in good faith believed were violations of the FLSA." Colvin contends that he filed the complaint after he "researched the issue, felt that he was being singled out, and believed that his supervisor's directive violated the FLSA." Colvin complains that

> Volusion classified Mr. Colvin as an "exempt" employee, he regularly worked hours in excess of 40 hours a week and hours that more than made up for any time missed at doctors' appointments without compensation, he had not before been required to take paid time off for such doctor's or medical appointments, and other salaried employees had not been required to use PTO time for such doctor's appointments.

Id. Volusion argues Colvin's allegations fail to allege he filed a protected complaint because "[n]o objectively reasonable person could believe the incredibly common practice of having exempt employees use PTO when they want to be away from work during business hours somehow violates the Fair Labor Standards Act." Dkt. No. 4 at 4. Volusion's argument is misplaced. "The FLSA does not require that a plaintiff successfully prove a claim for overtime under the FLSA, but merely that the plaintiff prove he was engaged in protected activity." *Little v. Technical Specialty Products, LLC,* 940 F. Supp.2d 460, 478 (E.D. Tex. 2013). See also, *Marcotte v. City of Rochester*, 2017 WL 392013, *2 (2nd Cir. 2017) ("It is possible to state an anti-retaliation claim under the FLSA without proving an actual violation of the FLSA.").

In addition, as noted above, the Fifth Circuit only requires that a complaint "be sufficiently clear and detailed for a reasonable employer to understand it, in light of both content and context, as an assertion of rights protected by the [FLSA] and a call for their protection." *Starnes*, 849 F.3d at 632. The Court finds that Colvin's allegations meet this standard. See *Little*, 940 F. Supp.2d at 478–79 (holding that plaintiff alleged prima facie case despite failing to show that overtime was illegal where she filed internal oral complaint complaining of policy); *Benge v. Highgate Holdings,* 2010 WL 2680113 at *2–3 (N.D. Tex. July 2, 2010) (finding that plaintiff alleged sufficient factual allegations to withstand motion to dismiss where she voiced concerns over possible illegality of her employer's actions). Moreover, the question at the motion to dismiss stage "is not whether a plaintiff will ultimately prevail but whether the claimant is entitled to offer evidence to support [his] claims." *Twombly*, 550 U.S. at 583.2 Colvin's allegations on this issue are sufficient to meet this standard.

2. Causal Link

Volusion argues that Colvin has failed to allege sufficient facts showing that there was a causal link between his complaint and his termination. It is incorrect. Colvin's Complaint alleges that "[l]ess than five days" after he complained to his supervisor regarding violations of the FLSA he was terminated. "In this Circuit, temporal proximity between protected activity and alleged retaliation is sometimes enough to establish causation at the prima facie stage." *Porter v. Houma Terrebonne Hous. Auth. Bd. of Comm'rs*, 810 F.3d 940, 948 (5th Cir. 2015). "[T]he protected act and the adverse employment action [must be] 'very close' in time" to establish causation by timing alone." *Id.* (quoting *Washburn v. Harvey*, 504 F.3d 505, 511 (5th Cir. 2007)). Thus, the Fifth Circuit has determined that a six-and-a-half-week timeframe between a plaintiff's protected activity and an adverse employment action is sufficient to satisfy the causation prong of a prima facie case, *Porter*, 810 F.3d at 949, while a two year period is insufficient to show a causal connection, *Washburn*, 504 F.3d at 511. Courts have found causation for three and four month gaps, and rejected claims with 20 month gaps.

E.g., *Clark County School Dist. v. Breeden*, 532 U.S. 268, 273–74 (2001) (noting that a three-month or four-month period may be close enough to make a prima facie showing of causation but holding that a twenty-month period was not). See also, *Guillory v. PF & B Mgmt., LP*, 2013 WL 1181439, at *6 (S.D. Tex. Feb. 27, 2013) (finding that a three-day period between the plaintiff filing the lawsuit and his termination was sufficient to raise a question of fact as to causation). Based upon the foregoing, Colvin has alleged sufficient facts to show a plausible causal link between the making of his complaint and his termination five days later. Accordingly, Volusion's Motion to Dismiss the FLSA retaliation claim should be denied.

QUESTION

1. *Colvin* considers the length of time between the protected activity and the adverse employment actions. This conclusion is obviously premised on the assumption that retaliation occurs generally on the heels of the protected activity. Is this correct? Is not revenge, as the saying goes, a "dish best served cold" rather than in the heat of the moment?

Problem 25-3

Consider whether the following statements would constitute protected activity and note what other facts you would need to know to make a complete assessment.

1. "I was promised I would be paid for my commute time. You are not honoring that promise."
2. "I checked on what other companies are paying for my position, and your company is way lower than them."
3. "I am not being paid all the money I am owed."
4. "What a lousy place to work. Start treating your employees fairly on their wages."

5. "The time clock is not working right. I am being shorted on the time I have been working."

Mastery Problem 25-1

Karen is the Director of Risk Management for a large retail company. Karen is good friends with two Hispanic employees who are married to each other. The husband, in addition to his 40-hour work week, is participating in training provided by the company that is designed to make him a more productive employee. He is not being paid overtime for this training, nor are the six other employees who are taking the training. In November 2018, Karen tells the company's Human Resources Director, "I am no expert on the law but I am pretty sure the failure to pay overtime for the extra hours violates the law." The Human Resources Director agrees and presents the problem to the CEO. After a number of months, the company starts paying overtime for training hours outside the normal workweek but does not pay employees for overtime for past training hours. Karen again raises the question with the Human Resources Director, and the company eventually negotiates a settlement with all seven employees. It pays a total of $100,000 in overtime backpay. Subsequently, Karen's official job duties are changed to include, "Report legal violations of any federal or state laws." In March 2020, Karen is fired as part of a reduction in force due to lagging sales. Karen argues that she was targeted for her complaints about the overtime, and that the reduction in force is not the genuine reason for her termination. Does Karen have a claim that will survive summary judgment?

Mastery Problem 25-2

You represent a client that the Department of Labor has found to be in flagrant disregard of the requirements of the FLSA. You decided to settle with the DOL. As part of the settlement, the DOL requires the client to draft and implement an anti-retaliation policy designed to ensure that employees understand their rights and are able to register their concerns and complaints without fear of retribution. Draft the policy.

Conclusion

FLSA protections would be hollow if employees were not protected from retaliation for asserting their rights. You have seen that the employee must effectively trigger the anti-retaliation provision with an appropriate complaint. Generalized workplace grievances are insufficient. On the other hand, there are no formal requirements regarding the complaint. An oral complaint to the employer is sufficient.

B. Safety

Key Concepts

- This subchapter covers regulatory structures that are designed to promote safety in the workplace or to compensate employees who suffer injury.
- We begin with workers' compensation statutes, which provide compensation to injured workers.
- The next two Lessons describe the regulatory structure of the Occupational Safety and Health Act, a complex federal statutory schemed designed to avoid injury by ensuring a safe workplace.

Lesson 26:
Workers' Compensation

Objectives and Expected Learning Outcomes

In this Lesson, we cover workers' compensation statutes that provide coverage to workers who suffer injury. In particular, you will learn the history of these statutes, when coverage under the statute is triggered, and how employers may manage the size of premiums or reduce exposure to personal injury suits.

Every state has a workers' compensation statutory scheme designed to compensate workers who suffer injury. Because each state has different rules and case law interpretations of the rules, we will discuss general principles. Workers' compensation statutes were enacted in response to the problems faced by employees who suffered serious injury without an easy remedy, and the risks that employers faced under general tort law for negligence that led to employee injury.

As a general matter, the statutes provide that injured employees are guaranteed certain benefits for lost wages and medical care. In exchange for this insurance, the employee relinquishes her right to sue the employer for negligently causing the injury. The payments are made on a "no fault" basis, with benefits awarded without any showing that the employer was negligent. Employers generally contract with an insurance company to cover this mandatory obligation. The insurance premiums are set, in part, based on the employer's loss experience. In exchange, the insurance company agrees to pay any benefits owed under the statute.

Not every injury suffered by an employee is compensable under workers' compensation statutes. Typically, the statutes require that the injury "arise out of employment"—incurred as part of performing work—and in the "course of employment"—related to the time, place, and circumstances of the work relationship. These requirements mean that a number of cases will not clearly fall within the scope of the statute. In uncertain cases, the employer may challenge a workers' compensation claim as a strategy for keeping its premiums lower. On the other hand, if the injuries are severe, the employer will be motivated to argue that workers' compensation provides the exclusive remedy for the employee, in order to avoid the possibility of a large damages award in a personal injury lawsuit. In the second instance, if an injured employee sues for his injuries the employer will assert workers' compensation as an affirmative defense to the personal injury suit.

In this Lesson, we briefly cover the history and development of workers' compensation statutes then discuss the general principles regarding their scope.

1. The History of Workers' Compensation Statutes

Workers' compensation benefits for workplace related injuries were first introduced more than a century ago, and the statutory schemes have continued to evolve. Under the common law, an employer had obligations to provide a safe workplace, but this duty was undercut by several legal doctrines. First, the "Fellow Servant Rule" provided that the employer was not liable for injuries caused by a fellow worker. Second, tort law at the beginning of the last century presented obstacles for plaintiffs. To begin, the injured employee had the burden of proving a negligent breach of duty by the employer. The doctrine of contributory negligence often meant that an employee who was negligent to any degree was precluded from recovering anything from the employer. The doctrine of assumption of the risk would hold an employer harmless if the injured employee voluntarily accepted the risks associated with the work. Although tort law has changed substantially since these times, the prospects for an effective recovery by an injured worker at the time were questionable.

At the same time, employers benefitted from the workers' compensation statutes because the remedies were limited (there is generally no payment for pain and suffering, punitive damages and other exemplary damages). This was the grand bargain struck by the statutes: employers would pay compensatory amounts to cover lost wages and medical bills without a showing of negligence, in exchange for these limited remedies being the exclusive recovery by the employee.

2. Elements of a Workers' Compensation Claim

Originally, workers' compensation benefits were awarded in narrowly circumscribed circumstances, such as an employee who is injured while operating a piece of machinery in the workplace. As cases accumulated, courts gradually developed a two-prong test to determine if benefits would be awarded to the injured employee. Every state requires, generally, that the injury is suffered in the course of employment and that the injury arise out of the employment relationship. We will discuss these two elements in turn.

A. In the Course of Employment

An injury occurs in the course of employment when the employee is performing a duty or task that the employee was employed to perform. The injury need not take place at the workplace. However, the employee is not acting in the course of employment if she deviated from her assigned task for personal reasons.

Example 26-1

Arvis is an employee of Goldberg's Furniture Company. Arvis was asked by his supervisor to load the truck with office furniture and deliver it to a local accounting firm. While in the Goldberg's warehouse, a fellow employee drops a file cabinet on Arvis's foot, causing injury. This injury was suffered in the course of Arvis's employment. Workers' compensation is designed for this scenario in which the employee is injured in the service of, and for the benefit of, the employer and so the bargain is appropriate. Arvis recovers his lost wages and reimbursement for medical care, and Goldberg's is freed of a potential personal injury lawsuit.

Example 26-2

Arvis is an employee of Goldberg's Furniture Company. Arvis was asked by his supervisor to load the truck with office furniture and to deliver it to a local accounting firm. Arvis loads the equipment and travels to the accounting firm office. While offloading the truck, Arvis drops a file cabinet on his foot, causing injury. This injury was suffered in the course of Arvis's employment. The fact that the injury occurs outside the Goldberg's workplace is irrelevant to that determination.

Example 26-3

Arvis is an employee of Goldberg's Furniture company. Arvis was asked by his supervisor to load the truck with office furniture and to deliver it to a local accounting firm. Arvis loads the truck and heads toward the accounting firm. While on his way, Arvis remembers that he needs cash, and so he drives two blocks over to his bank to withdrawal money from the ATM machine. As Arvis climbs out of the truck he twists his ankle severely. This injury was not suffered in the course of Arvis's employment. However, if the deviation from his course of employment is deemed *de minimus* it may be compensable under the workers' compensation statute.

Stroka v. United Airlines

835 A. 2d 1247 (N.J. App. Div. 2003).

Winkelstein, J.A.D.

facts

This case arises out of the tragic events of September 11, 2001. Petitioner is a flight attendant for United Airlines (United). She was scheduled to work Flight 93 from Newark to San Francisco on September 11, but several days earlier she had requested and received the day off [to attend to personal matters, including going bowling]. Consequently, she was not aboard the flight when it was attacked by terrorists and crashed in Shanksville, Pennsylvania. After learning of the crash, and the horrific way her fellow flight attendants died, petitioner developed post-traumatic stress syndrome, for which she sought and received medical and temporary total disability benefits. The workers' compensation judge also ordered United to pay petitioner's counsel fee. The judge stayed his order pending this appeal.

United concedes that petitioner's post-traumatic stress syndrome is directly related to the events of September 11, but argues that she does not qualify for worker's compensation benefits because her disability did not arise out of or in the course of her employment. Although petitioner presents a very sympathetic case, she does not qualify for workers' compensation benefits because her condition did not arise in the course of her employment. Accordingly, we reverse the decision of the workers' compensation court and remand for judgment to enter in favor of United.

Petitioner was hired as a flight attendant by United in 1984. She attended a training program that included safety issues, such as the evacuation of an aircraft under emergency circumstances. United did not provide her with training specific to hijackings; but, each year flight attendants were shown a security video which touched on the issue. In addition, United provided flight attendants with a Federal Aviation Administration (FAA) handbook that devoted a chapter to how flight attendants should handle a hijacking crisis, and what stressors flight attendants should expect as a result of their job. Petitioner read that chapter before September 11.

. . . .

Petitioner became aware of the terrorist attacks on the World Trade Center while at the bowling alley. She watched television after the first plane struck the North Tower, and realized after the second plane struck the South Tower that one of the jets was an American Airlines flight and the other a United flight. She also learned that a United flight crashed in Pennsylvania, but she did not know that the flight had originated in Newark.

While she was on route from the bowling alley to pick up her daughter, her husband called and told her that the plane that had crashed in Shanksville was Flight 93—the flight she was scheduled to be on board. Petitioner imm[illegible]ecame upset and emotionally distraught. She was sobbing and [illegible]useous, and began to have problems with her stools. She knew [illegible]ght attendants on Flight 93, and had flown with the pilots.

[illegible]ched the tragedy replayed on television over the next few [illegible], trembled and could not sleep. Initially, she was unable to [illegible]gan to binge.

[illegible]r 24, 2001, Dr. Stephen Clarfield, a psychologist, has treated [illegible]st-traumatic stress syndrome on a biweekly basis. Petitioner has been upset, forgetful and has had trouble sleeping. She has not returned to work. She remains afraid, having learned of the brutal way the hijackers murdered the flight attendants on the plane. She has panic attacks when she sees a runway. Petitioner is overwhelmed by guilt, knowing that her vacation day caused a co-employee to die. Her best friends were tortured and killed. The parties agree that petitioner is temporarily totally disabled as a result of her disorder, and requires ongoing psychiatric treatment.

To be entitled to compensation . . . an employee's accidental injury must "aris[e] out of and in the course of employment."

. . . .

We first address whether petitioner's disorder arose out of her employment. To qualify, her employment must have been a contributing cause of the injury, so that the risk of the occurrence was reasonably incidental to her employment. Although "[a]n employee does not have to be actually engaged in work for the employer at the time of an accident" for the disability to have arisen out of the employment, (citation omitted), the disorder must, however, "issue from or be contributed to by conditions which bear some essential relation to the work or its nature."

. . . .

Where we differ with petitioner's position, and with the conclusion of the workers' compensation judge, is whether petitioner's post-traumatic stress syndrome arose in the course of her employment. We hold that it did not.

An accident arises in the course of employment when "it occurs (a) within the period of the employment and (b) at a place where the employee may reasonably be, and (c) while he is reasonably fulfilling the duties of the employment, or doing something incidental thereto."

Here, when Flight 93 was attacked and crashed, petitioner was taking a day off without pay to care for her daughter and go bowling. She was not engaged in any activity that could conceivably constitute "a clear and substantial benefit to [her] employer."

Petitioner claims that the inherent risk of her job tied her disability to her work, even though she was not actually on the job at the time of the incident. She cites a line of cases for the proposition that it is not necessary that an injury actually occur during work to be compensable. These cases do not, however, support petitioner's position. Although the employees' injuries or disabilities arose while they were away from their places of employment and not engaged in an activity benefiting their employers, their injuries or disabilities originated, at least in part, while they were on the job at their places of employment.

That is not the case here. Petitioner's post-traumatic stress syndrome originated not while she was at work, but while she was taking a day off. Nothing happened while she was working which led to her current condition. She was not working at the time Flight 93 crashed, nor at the time she heard the news of the crash. In fact, her reaction to the event occurred because she was not working, not because she was working. If we were to accept petitioner's argument, off-duty police officers, firefighters, and others whose jobs are inherently risky could seek compensation benefits when a fellow employee was injured or killed while taking that employee's place. No authority exists to support that position.

To put it more simply, when Flight 93 was attacked and crashed, causing petitioner's post-traumatic stress syndrome, she was not reasonably fulfilling the duties of her employment, "or doing something intimate thereto." . . . Therefore, her disability did not arise in the course of her employment.

QUESTIONS

1. If you represented the plaintiff, how would you develop the facts to assert that the injury has a nexus to the requirements of the job?
2. What if United required its flight attendants to call in hourly to ascertain their availability to cover a flight? Would that be of sufficient "clear and substantial" benefit to the employer?

Richardson v. Fiedler Roofing, Inc.

67 N.Y.2d 246 (Ct. App. N.Y., 1986).

Simons, Judge.

Claimant's decedent, Norman Richardson, was employed by appellant, Fiedler Roofing, Inc. as a waterproofer and roofing mechanic. On January 20, 1981 he fell seven stories from the roof of a building near his jobsite sustaining head injuries which resulted in his death. Immediately before the accident, Richardson and a co-worker were at their work place on the roof waiting for material to arrive with no assigned work to do. While waiting, they moved some distance over the roof and across party walls to another part of the structure and removed some copper downspouts from the building to sell as salvage. While doing so, Richardson slipped on a patch of ice and fell to his death. Respondent Workers' Compensation Board affirmed a finding of the Administrative Law Judge that the accident occurred during the course of decedent's employment and that death was causally related to it and awarded benefits to decedent's five minor children. A divided Appellate Division affirmed the decision of the Board, and the employer and its insurer appeal. They claim that the employer should not be required to pay benefits because decedent was actually engaged in a theft at the time of his accident, and thus his death resulted not from his work duties, but from "decedent's purely personal act of stealing copper downspouts."

To be compensable, an injury must arise out of and in the course of employment. Activities which are purely personal pursuits are not within the scope of employment and compensation may not be recovered for injuries sustained while engaging in them. The test for determining whether specific activities are within the scope of employment or purely personal is whether the activities are both reasonable and sufficiently work related under the circumstances. It has been held that an employee directed to wait for a specified period of time until materials arrive, is not required to stand by idly but is free to engage in any reasonably related activity while waiting. Momentary deviation from the work routine for a customary and accepted purpose will not bar a claim for benefits. The determination of what is reasonable activity and what is unreasonable, and thus a deviation, is factual and the Board is afforded wide latitude in deciding whether the employee's conduct is disqualifying.

The Board found from the evidence in this case that it was common practice in the industry for roofers to remove copper downspouts and sell them for scrap. It further found that this employer not only knew of the practice but also frequently had been required to pay for or replace downspouts stolen by its employees. Despite this experience, the employer had never disciplined or discharged an employee for these thefts, and after it learned that decedent and his co-worker had been stealing downspouts on the day of the accident, it did not discipline or discharge the coemployee. Accordingly, the Board found that decedent's activities while waiting for necessary work materials to arrive did not constitute a deviation from, or an abandonment of, his employment and that the death arose out of and in the course of decedent's employment. These findings are supported by substantial evidence and thus are conclusive on the court.

Indeed, appellants do not now challenge the Appellate Division's finding that there was substantial evidence to support the award. They contend in this court, for the first time, that a claimant is excluded from compensation benefits, as a matter of law, if he is engaged in an illegal activity at the time of the accident. Normally, they would not be permitted to raise the issue when they challenged only the factual basis of the Administrative Law Judge's finding that decedent had not deviated from the scope of his employment before the Board. The argument raises solely a question of statutory interpretation, however, which we may address even though it was not presented below.

Appellants base their argument on policy grounds, urging that an employee who engages in illegal activity during his employment should not receive benefits. Appellants note that Workers' Compensation Law article 9, the disability benefits section, expressly precludes benefits for non-work-related injuries caused by a claimant's illegal acts (*see,* Workers' Compensation Law § 201[9] [A]; § 205[3]), and they contend that section 10 of the statute, the liability provision for work-related injuries, should be interpreted as containing a similar limitation.[1] The history and nature of these two clauses prove otherwise.

---

1 In 1981, when decedent died, Workers' Compensation Law § 10 provided: "Every employer subject to this chapter shall in accordance with this chapter, except as otherwise provided in section twenty-five-a hereof, secure compensation to his employees and pay or provide compensation for their disability or death from injury arising out of and in the course of the employment without regard to fault as a cause of the injury, except that there shall be no liability for compensation under this chapter when the injury has been solely occasioned by intoxication of the injured employee while on duty; or by wilful intention of the injured employee to bring about the injury or death of himself or another."

In 1913, the Bill of Rights of the 1894 New York State Constitution was amended to give the Legislature the power to enact workers' compensation legislation (*see,* 1894 N.Y. Const., art. I, § 19) and the next year the Legislature did so. The resulting statute provided that employees were to be compensated on a "no-fault" basis, regardless of any negligence on their own part, for all injuries "arising out of and in the course of" their employment (*see,* Workers' Compensation Law § 10). To further the claimant's ability to establish his right to benefits, the statute creates a presumption that the injuries are compensable (*see,* Workers' Compensation Law § 21). The statute was enacted for humanitarian purposes, framed, in the words of Chief Judge Cardozo, to insure that injured employees might "be saved from becoming one of the derelicts of society, a fragment of human wreckage" (*see, Surace v. Danna,* 248 N.Y. 18, 20–21, 161 N.E. 315 . . .). To further that purpose, we have held that the statutory obligation to compensate injuries sustained in the course of employment which are causally related to it does not depend on the equities of a particular case, nor may it be avoided because of the workers' fraud or wrongdoing: it is absolute.

The exceptions to this broad statutory liability are found in section 10, derived from the 1913 amendment to the Bill of Rights. They bar compensation when the injury has been occasioned solely by intoxication of the injured employee while on duty or by willful intention of the injured employee to bring about injury or death. Neither is applicable here.

The disability benefits provisions have an entirely different history and purpose. They were enacted in 1949 to expand the scope of the Workers' Compensation Law by providing short-term weekly benefits to employees for sickness or disability not arising "out of or in the course of" employment. We discussed the nature of article 9 in *Matter of Flo v. General Elec. Co.*, 7 N.Y.2d 96, 99, 195 N.Y.S.2d 652, 163 N.E.2d 876: "The Disability Benefits statute is broad in concept and general in terms. It was designed to assist the employee of the State who suffered disability by bridging the gap between the Workmen's Compensation Law and the Unemployment Insurance Law. Unlike the Workmen's Compensation Law, the Disability Benefits Law contains no requirement that the cause of a disability arise out of and in the course of employment. It contemplates a broad social coverage to protect the employee against the hazard of sickness and disability which interfere with and prevent his continuance in active employment and which can occur and do occur both within and outside of working hours."

Article 9 excludes benefits for several disabilities and disability periods and one of its provisions, section 205(3), provides that benefits shall not be paid for a disability occasioned by the "perpetration by the employee of an illegal act". That limitation is not duplicated in the provisions of the statute dealing with work-related injuries. Indeed, the only exception to liability that the disability benefits provisions and workers' compensation provisions have in common is the provision which bars recovery for injuries caused by the employee's willful intention to bring physical harm to himself or another (*compare,* Workers' Compensation Law §§ 10 and 205). It is not claimed that that provision has application to this case and there is nothing else in the text of the statute, its legislative history, or in our case law, that supports the appellants' claim that section 10 should be read to foreclose work-related death benefits in the same way that section 205 forecloses benefits for non-work-related injuries.

We have previously emphasized that the Workers' Compensation Law is remedial in nature and must be "construed liberally to accomplish the economic and humanitarian objects of the act" (*Matter of Holcomb v. Daily News,* 45 N.Y.2d 602, 607, 412 N.Y.S.2d 118, 384 N.E.2d 665). It is significant that although we have consistently interpreted the statute in this way, and the Legislature has amended and revised it repeatedly, the list of activities which will disqualify an employee from compensation for work-related injuries has remained unchanged for over 70 years. Indeed, despite this long history of liberal interpretation, when section 205(3) was subsequently enacted barring disability benefits for injuries resulting from illegal acts, there was no effort to change section 10 to include a similar exception for work-related injuries. It is reasonable to assume from all of this that the Legislature did not intend section 10 to be similarly limited. And there is good reason why it should not. It is one thing to disqualify a claimant for injuries he sustains during the course of an illegal activity pursued on his own time, an activity unknown to the employer and one which it cannot control. It is quite another to deprive dependents of benefits because the employee's death results from misconduct during the course of employment when the employer knows about the illegal activity and tolerates it (*compare, Matter of Chaffee v. Effron,* 1 A.D.2d 197, 198–199, 149 N.Y.S.2d 115).

Although the appellants' argument is based on moral grounds—the need to prevent parties from profiting from illegal acts—the suspicion is that the concern has more to do with dollars and cents than morality. The way for an employer to express dissatisfaction with its employees' acts and also avoid paying benefits for such claims, however, is not for the Board to disqualify innocent dependents but for the employer to make clear to its employees that illegal conduct on the job will not be tolerated.

Accordingly, the order of the Appellate Division should be affirmed, with costs.

TITONE, JUDGE (dissenting):

The majority holds that where an employer tolerates conduct blatantly in violation of the Penal Law, that conduct arises out of and in the course of employment within the meaning of Workers' Compensation Law § 10. Because I find that holding totally unacceptable, I must dissent.

Initially, where as here, the facts underlying the award of compensation are undisputed, only a question of law is presented. Therefore, the decision by the Board that decedent's activity was reasonable under the circumstances is fully reviewable by this court.

On the merits, the majority reasons that intoxication and intentional self-infliction of injury are the only exceptions to the broad statutory liability imposed in Workers' Compensation Law § 10. Such an analysis begs the very essence of the statute which endeavors to compensate workers for injuries, disabilities or deaths only "arising out of and in the course of employment". Thus, the threshold question to be decided in cases involving section 10, as here, is whether the employee's condition arose "out of and in the course of employment." In my view, it did not.

There is no dispute that where, as in this case, an employee is instructed to wait for materials, he is not obliged to stand idly by. An employee may " 'indulge in any *reasonable* activity at that place, and if he does so the risk inherent in such activity is an incident of his employment' " (*Matter of Capizzi v. Southern Dist. Reporters,* 61 N.Y.2d 50, 53, 471 N.Y.S.2d 554, 459 N.E.2d 847, quoting *Matter of Davis v. Newsweek Mag.,* 305 N.Y. 20, 28, 110 N.E.2d 406 [emphasis in original] . . .). For example, activities such as an associate editor of textbooks executing an exuberant dance step in an elevator, a live-in camp kitchen worker using recreational facilities for gymnastics during off hours, and a traveling employee bathing in a hotel have been held to be reasonable and the injuries sustained compensable. In addition, employee horseplay, given the nature of the materials at hand and the general habits of the employees, may give rise to compensable injury.

If the prevailing word "reasonable" is to have any meaning at all, however, I cannot condone compensation for an injury sustained during the perpetration of a larceny. There is no authority whatsoever nor definition of the word "reasonable" which would support the proposition that a reasonable activity includes a crime of moral turpitude during idle time. Such a dilution of the import of reasonableness, a standard imposed by our case law repeatedly for over 30 years is wholly unwarranted. When the decedent chose to steal—which by no stretch of the imagination can be deemed a "reasonable" activity in any civilized society—he removed himself from his employment and acted at his own peril.

Clearly, decedent was in a proper position to combine business with pleasure, as he was merely instructed to wait for materials. That he did so would not defeat his claim unless the accident resulted from risks produced by his unreasonable personal activities. Here, decedent not only strayed from the roof on which he was supposed to wait to a different one but also proceeded to engage in a theft and then a cover-up of his actions leading him to pretend to inspect the icy edge of the unrelated roof. This was a completely unreasonable personal, dangerous and illegal indulgence which substantially increased his risk of injury.

Moreover, that decedent's employer tolerated the criminal activity does not make him responsible for any injuries sustained during the larceny. The employer did not encourage the activity and certainly did not benefit from it. On the contrary, decedent's employer was put in a position of continually replacing downspouts. The decedent's conduct here does not even approach the equitable position of an employee who is injured while committing a relatively minor infraction which actually may further the employer's interest. More importantly, the employer is certainly empowered to waive its own rules by implied acquiescence in their habitual violation. Therefore, a violation of the employer's rules may not preclude compensation. The employer may not choose to ignore the mandates of the Penal Law, however, and the fact that a criminal statute is repeatedly violated cannot be construed as an implied permission on the part of the employer to allow such conduct.

The majority notes that it is the policy of this State to award compensation on a "no-fault" basis. It must also be recognized that this policy must be balanced with a strong policy against rewarding crime. I, too, sympathize with the plight of the innocent children who would suffer financially from the transgressions of their father. It is most unfortunate that children must bear the brunt of the nearsighted choices that their parents make. While it is true that we often disregard these "victims" of crime, this State has not seen fit to enact a workers' compensation law for the dependents of criminals who sustain injuries in the course of and arising out of their chosen "profession."

Accordingly, I would reverse the order of the Appellate Division and dismiss the claim.

Wachtler, C.J., and Kaye, Alexander and Hancock, JJ., concur with Simons, J. Titone, J., dissents and votes to reverse.

Problem 26-1

Criminal act may be w/in course

Joan is an employee at a call center. One evening Joan has a serious argument with her husband, Sean, that causes her to fear for her safety. Joan leaves their home with their three children and spends the night in a hotel. When Joan arrives at work the next day, she tells the security guard that she is having problems with her husband and that he should not be given entry to the building. Later that day, upon returning from the company cafeteria, Joan sees Sean at the entrance, calmly talking to the security guard. She approaches to ask him to leave, when Sean suddenly pulls out a gun, disarms the guard, and shoots Joan. Assess whether Joan is entitled to receive workers' compensation benefits.

Problem 26-2

George frequently travels for work and stays in hotels overnight. During one work trip, George meets a woman in the hotel bar. After a few drinks, they decide to go up to George's room to become intimate. While in the room, a fire breaks out in the hotel and George dies. Is George entitled to receive workers' compensation death benefits? Now assume that George engages an escort service to send a woman to his hotel room. The woman disables George with a taser, beats him, and steals all of his belongings. Is George entitled to receive workers' compensation benefits?

B. Arising out of the Employment Relationship

If employees were entitled to receive workers' compensation benefits for every injury suffered in the course of their employment, the bargain would be a strict liability scheme that would automatically pay an employee for any injury suffered while working. However, workers' compensation statutes add a requirement that there is a connection of some kind between the employment relationship and the injury. The second question—did the injury "arise out of the employment"—requires a causal connection such that the injury is somehow facilitated by the nature of the work performed, or a condition of the work that is imposed. Thus, the mere fact that the injury occurred in the workplace is insufficient to establish the claim.

Conversely, the workers' compensation statute reaches beyond the workplace. Even if the employee is offsite there may be a causal nexus to the employment relationship that establishes coverage. The issue is whether the employee has suffered the injury but for engaging in a task for which the employee was hired.

Example 26-4

Bernard is an employee of Literal Enterprises. While making a sales call on behalf of Literal, Bernard is attacked and injured by a mugger. Bernard is entitled to recover workers' compensation benefits for his injury.

Ezzy v. Workers' Comp. Appeals Bd.

146 Cal. App. 3d 252 (1983).

Smith, Associate Justice.

Petitioner, Marilyn Ezzy, sought and was granted a writ of review after the Workers' Compensation Appeals Board denied Ezzy's petition for reconsideration and affirmed the decision of the Workers' Compensation judge who found that petitioner's injury did not arise out of and in the course of her employment.

The sole issue before us is whether the injury to petitioner's finger, which occurred during a company-sponsored softball game, arises out of and in the course of her employment, and is therefore compensable.

Issue

Marilyn Ezzy (hereafter "Ezzy") at all relevant times was employed by the law firm of Gassett, Perry & Frank (hereafter "GPF") as a law clerk. On or about August 15, 1980 Ezzy participated in an employer-sponsored softball game, during which she injured the little finger on her right hand as she attempted to catch a fly ball.

The record of the WCAB hearing discloses that GPF participated in a softball league composed primarily of civil defense law firms. The rules of the league required that the teams be composed of both men and women, and required forfeiture if less than four women were present on each team.

John Burton, (hereafter "Burton") is a partner in GPF, and was the team coach. Burton stated that he did not have to recruit players; a sign up was conducted of all those who wanted to play. Burton testified that it was not a requirement that everyone play. Some of the older and less athletically inclined members of the firm did not play. Some, but not all, of the secretaries participated. Everyone in the GPF firm, player and non-player alike, was provided at the firm's expense a special teeshirt emblazoned with his or her GPF billing number. Burton testified that GPF paid for the balls, bats and post-game refreshments. A post-season awards banquet was provided by GPF to which all employees were invited. Burton stated that no one was ever reprimanded or fired for not playing.

Burton further testified that his secretary sent around memos reminding office personnel of games or practice. Burton stated that Administrative Director's Rule 9883, regarding [the lack of Worker's Compensation coverage for voluntary] off-duty recreational activities, was neither posted nor read to employees [as required by the regulation]. Burton testified that "the better players were more encouraged to be present than some of the ones that were not so good. That would also depend on how many men we had and how many women we had." Burton stated that his team had never forfeited a game, and that he always had the correct number of female players there. He further testified that he did have one or two problems making sure one of their key women would be present at the games. Burton admitted that, although no business was derived from the games, they were very good for office spirit.

Ezzy testified that she did not volunteer but was "drafted" to join the team. On the first day after she returned from vacation, Burton approached Ezzy, handed her a teeshirt, a schedule of games and practices, and said, "At the next one we'll see you there." Ezzy understood there was a coed requirement, and when there appeared to be a shortage of women, the female members were urged to get out and play. Ezzy felt there was a spirit of camaraderie that the firm was trying to create, and that the strong urgings to play and the concern over having an adequate number of females led her to believe that she should play softball. Ezzy stated that the firm paid for post-game pizza and other refreshments. Ezzy testified that on one occasion home movies of a softball game were shown in the conference room of GPF offices during working hours, and that she and others were called in to watch. At the awards banquet, Burton received a whip as a gag-gift because he was such a "hard driver."

In his "Opinion On Decision," the Workers' Compensation Judge stated that participation in the softball game, while encouraged, was not a requirement or a reasonable expectancy of petitioner's job. Petitioner contends that the Workers' Compensation Judge erred in concluding that petitioner's injury did not occur in the course of employment. We agree.

DISCUSSION

I

. . . .

In *Pacific Tel. & Tel. Co. v. Workers' Comp. Appeals Bd. (Brady)*, Ms. Brady, an employee of the phone company, was injured while playing softball on a team made up wholly of Pacific Telephone Co. employees. The team played other phone company teams comprising the league. The games were played off the employer's premises after working hours. Ms. Brady was not a regular team member, but participated on this occasion because the team would otherwise have had to forfeit for lack of sufficient players. Ms. Brady felt job pressure to play when asked to do so by team members who included Ms. Brady's supervisor. The management of the telephone company permitted league formation meetings to be conducted on the premises, and promulgated safety rules. The company photocopy machine was used in the dissemination of league and team information. Also, raffles to benefit the league were conducted on company premises during working hours. The WCAB judge relied upon (1) substantial employer involvement in creation and operation of the league, (2) benefit to the employer of improved employee morale, and (3) the job-related pressure upon Mr. Brady which led to her participation. The Court of Appeal denied a petition for writ of review.

In *California Highway Patrol v. Workers' Comp. Appeals Bd. (WCAB)* . . . Officer Loveless played on a softball team representing the Monterey area office of the CHP which participated in the Central Coast Counties Police League. Notices of games were posted in the locker room, play was encouraged by state and local CHP management. The WCAB judge concluded the softball activity was part and parcel of Loveless' job. The Court of Appeal denied CHP's petition for a writ of review.

Both the *Pacific Tel. & Tel.* and *California Highway Patrol* cases, in finding athletic injuries compensable . . . rely upon the more specific factors of employer involvement, benefit to employer, and job-related pressure to participate to find an activity within the course of employment (in determining whether benefits shall be awarded).

. . . .

Petitioner was a part-time law clerk in her second year of law school, a position which is low in the legal profession's hierarchy. As such, petitioner was more than usually vulnerable to pressure or suggestion that she join the law firm's softball team. Thus, when she was urged to play by one of the firm's partners, who was also the team coach, it was reasonable for petitioner to feel that she was expected to participate.

There was relatively more pressure on female employees to participate because of the league's requirement that four women be present on the field at all times.

A substantial benefit to the firm was generated by participation in the softball team by virtue of improved office cooperation, spirit, morale and camaraderie.

The law firm paid for all equipment, for tee-shirts for team members and other employees of the firm, as well as for post-game refreshments. The firm sponsored an awards banquet to which team members and other employees were invited.

. . . .

[We believe that the workers' compensation laws should] be liberally construed by the courts with the purpose of extending their benefits for the protection of persons injured in the course of their employment.

In the case at bar, the record shows that petitioner subjectively believed that her employer expected her to participate in the company sponsored baseball activities. Petitioner so stated under oath. We have determined that her subjective belief was objectively reasonable, and, therefore, conclude that petitioner's injury arose out of and in the course of her employment.

The decision of the Workers' Compensation Appeals Board is annulled and the cause is remanded to that board for proceedings consistent with the views expressed herein.

McKeever v. N.J. Bell Telephone Co.

179 N.J. Super. 29 (1981).

Fritz, P. J. A. D.

. . . .

The nature of the accident presents no problems. The decedent, a corporate attorney for New Jersey Bell Telephone Company, was driving home from work when he was involved in a three-car collision on McCarter Highway in Newark. He died as a result of injuries sustained in the accident. He was driving his own car and he was not reimbursed for traveling expenses. There is no suggestion that the locale of the accident represented any deviation from the most logical direct route between home and office, nor is there any hint of purpose other than one of returning home from work.

It is undisputed that decedent's briefcase, supplied to him by his employer and in the car at the time of the accident, held handwritten notes pertaining to a matter on which decedent was currently working for his employer, in addition to such things as bulletins and pamphlets containing general information relating to the Bell Telephone System.

In his oral opinion dismissing the claim petition, the judge of compensation said:

> The petitioner strongly urges the fact that her husband was carrying the briefcase with some company documents in it, apparently, to be reviewed by her husband at home, is sufficient to bring this case within one of the exceptions. She relies primarily on *Paige v. The City of Rahway* and *Sabat v. Fedders Corporation* to support her contention of compensability. She contends that her

> husband's work at home and "on call" status of the employees in both of the above cases are substantially similar. With that I cannot agree. Mr. McKeever was not on call at any time by New Jersey Bell Telephone Company. He brought material home with him to read, which he was not required to do at home, nor was he under any compulsion to report his activities, so that he could be found on a moment's notice. Doing work at home and being on call are not at all similar. The respondent well sets forth the test regarding work being done at home in *Sabat v. Fedders Corporation*, which states,
>
> "We note that Sabat's employment situation differs dramatically from that of employees who take work home out of a sense of self-imposed moral obligation or self-perceived necessity arising out of an inability to keep up with their work load during their normal workday. The benefits of such activities are predominantly personal with only incidental enhancement of the efficient functioning of the employer enterprise. In such case the work connection is, without more, too attenuated to justify the imposition of the cost of off-duty injury on the employer."

Dif. b/w on call + work from home

Furthermore, the mere fact that the decedent was carrying home material furnished by his employer is an insufficient basis upon which to award compensability. In *Morris v. Hermann Forwarding Company* the Court stated the plaintiff further contended that Morris was "in the course of his employment" because he was carrying home work materials furnished to him by his employer. The mere fact that a claimant while going to work or home carries with him "some of the paraphernalia of his employment" does not in itself convert the trip from personal to employment activity.

. . . .

We accept the proposition that the mere carrying home of "some of the paraphernalia of his employment" does not in and of itself render a commuting accident compensable, *Morris v. Hermann Forwarding Co* although we observe that that decision was 4–3 and has not escaped doubtful reference in a statement questioning the basis for the going and coming rule. We are also aware, from the dictum in *Sabat v. Fedders Corp.*, that "a sense of self-imposed moral obligation or self-perceived necessity arising out of an inability to cope with their workload during their normal workday" will not justify work at home as sufficiently essential to render the commuting an activity arising out of and in the course of the employment. The circumstances of decedent's employment in the matter before us make any further consideration of those principles unnecessary.

We are firmly persuaded that the testimony in this case is susceptible of no other finding than that it was essential for the decedent to work at home in order to live up to his employer's expectations; that the employer, through such agents as the decedent's immediate supervisors, encouraged such activity, and that the decedent undertook this obligation constantly with his employer's knowledge. Edward Evans, general attorney for the company, head of the general corporate section at New Jersey Bell Telephone Company and decedent's direct superior, testified that taking materials home was permitted by the company and that he knew decedent was doing this. He was then asked whether the practice was "actually encouraged." He responded:

> I don't recall any specific policy or practice that encouraged it. As I indicated to you before, you really had to read as much as you could *if you wanted to do your job professionally.* So, you took it on to take matters home and read them if you couldn't get them done during the course of the day. (Emphasis supplied)

His testimony clearly demonstrated that reading respecting "the legal developments and company things that were changing within the company" was necessary. He denied that it was necessary to take these home but only on the basis "that he could have stayed after hours and read them at work." It is beyond cavil that there simply was not enough time in the day during which the decedent had to be "at work" for him to do all of that which was required of him by his employer and the employment.

Indeed, Mr. Evans testified to his requiring—he said, "I wanted them to read it"; he was decedent's superior—reading of material even though "the attorneys in my section don't have responsibility for it and don't actively participate in these matters on a daily basis." It is clear that the decedent was required not only to perform the work assigned to him, but to keep abreast of company topics despite the fact that required reading "did not have any direct bearing on (decedent's) day-to-day work activity."

The evidence is equally clear that the decedent lived up to his employer's expectations in this regard. His hours at home were not at the expense of his hours at his other place of employment: Evans testified that not all of the attorneys under his supervision worked 50 hours a week at the place of employment, but decedent did. His brief case went home with him every night. Because of these extra-office requirements he had a desk in his bedroom and a small library. At the time of his death he was committed to a deadline on an antitrust matter and among the materials on that desk was a book entitled Antitrust Problems and Trade Practices.

The evidence permits no conclusion except that this was no mere carrying of "some paraphernalia" or "self-imposed moral obligation or self-perceived necessity." Our reading of the record convinces us this was a matter of continued professional survival at the New Jersey Bell Telephone Company.

Reversed and remanded for entry of judgment in favor of appellant.

QUESTION

1. What is the common thread between *Ezzy* and *McKeever*?

Problem 26-3

Draft a policy to be given to employees that will act as a defense to workers' compensation claims in situations such as *McKeever* and *Ezzy*.

---

3. Workers' Compensation as the Employee's Exclusive Remedy

In some cases, the employer will seek to have the injury fall within the scope of the workers' compensation statute because that coverage serves as a bar to personal injury lawsuits that may subject the employer to much more substantial damages. Consider the strategies at work in the following case.

Weiss v. City of Milwaukee

559 N. W. 2d 588 (Wisc. 1997).

Ann Walsh Bradley, Justice.

. . . .

The relevant facts are not in dispute. On July 31, 1990, Weiss obtained a temporary restraining order against her abusive husband, Osama Abughanim. Shortly thereafter, she commenced a divorce action. Abughanim, forced to vacate the marital residence, began a campaign of harassing telephone calls and personal visits during which he would threaten the lives of Weiss and their two children. In October 1990, Weiss vacated the residence and moved in with her parents in order to escape her husband's harassment. Abughanim persisted in making threatening telephone calls, both to Weiss's parents' residence and to her place of employment. The calls to Weiss's employer were of such frequency that they resulted in her termination in December 1990.

In February 1991, Weiss obtained employment with the City of Milwaukee as an engineering technician. As an employee, she was required to establish residence in Milwaukee within one month of hiring. She therefore moved from her parents' residence in Waukesha County to an apartment located in Milwaukee. At that time, Abughanim did not know Weiss's Milwaukee address or telephone number.

Weiss was instructed by her supervisor to provide her address and telephone number to the City's payroll department. She contacted the payroll department, explained that she had an abusive former husband, and expressed her desire that her residential information remain confidential. A City payroll clerk assured Weiss that the City had a policy prohibiting the disclosure of such employee information to private individuals. Relying on the clerk's assurance, Weiss provided her address and telephone number to the payroll department.

On July 10, 1991, Abughanim contacted the City's Department of Employee Relations and spoke with Sheila Bowle, an employee of the department. Abughanim falsely represented to Bowle that he was calling on behalf of a bank and needed to confirm Weiss's address and telephone number for credit purposes. Bowle relayed the bogus inquiry to her supervisor, Yvette Marchan, who, without attempting to verify Abughanim's claimed credentials, authorized Bowle to disclose Weiss's residential information.

By this ruse, Abughanim obtained Weiss's home address and telephone number. Thereafter, Abughanim regularly telephoned Weiss at work to inform her that he now knew her home address and telephone number, and that he would kill her and their two children. Her awareness that Abughanim knew her address, and her then existing financial inability to change her residence, caused Weiss severe emotional distress arising from fear for her safety and that of their two children.

We have repeatedly stated that the provisions of Chapter 102 must be liberally construed to effectuate the WCA's goal of compensating injured workers. *UFE Inc. v. LIRC* (citation omitted). However, courts must also exercise care to avoid upsetting the balance of interests achieved by the WCA. *County of La Crosse v. WERC* (citation omitted).

. . . .

It is well settled that when the . . . conditions of liability for worker's compensation are satisfied, the exclusive remedy provision . . . precludes an injured employee from maintaining a negligence action against his or her employer and fellow employees. See, e.g., County of La Crosse (exclusive remedy provision "was designed to supplant actions in tort by injured employees against their employers"); Jenson (plaintiff's "common law action is barred by the exclusivity provisions if she in all other respects is entitled to recovery under the Act"). Thus, Weiss's common law action against the City is barred if her alleged injuries are covered by [workers' compensation].

. . . .

The statutory clause "performing service growing out of and incidental to his or her employment" is used interchangeably with the phrase "course of employment." John D. Neal and Joseph Danas, Jr., Worker's Compensation Handbook § 3.7 (1996); Arthur Larson and Lex K. Larson, 1 The Law of Workmen's Compensation § 6.10 (1996) (hereinafter The Law of Workmen's Compensation). Both phrases refer to the "time, place, and circumstances" under which the injury occurred. *Goranson v. DILHR.*

An injury is said to arise in the course of the employment when it takes place within the period of the employment, at a place where the employee reasonably may be, and while he [or she] is fulfilling his [or her] duties or engaged in doing something incidental thereto.

There is no dispute that Weiss's alleged injury occurred within the time and place of her employment. The question is whether receiving a personal phone call at work constitutes a "circumstance" of employment. We conclude that it does. Under the liberal construction given to [our workers' compensation law], an employee acts within the course of employment when he or she is otherwise within the time and space limits of employment, and briefly turns away from his or her work to tend to matters "necessary or convenient to his [or her] own personal health or comfort." *American Motors Corp. v. Industrial Comm.* The personal comfort doctrine does not apply, and an employee is not within the course of employment, if the "extent of the departure is so great that an intent to abandon the job temporarily may be inferred, or . . . the method chosen is so unusual and unreasonable that the conduct cannot be considered an incident of the employment." *Id.* Applying the doctrine to the facts of this case, we conclude that regardless of the contents of a brief personal telephone call, the act of taking such a call at work constitutes a momentary departure from work duties to attend to a matter of personal comfort. Thus, when Weiss answered the personal telephone call from Abughanim, she was engaged in an activity incidental to employment, and was therefore within the course of employment.

Weiss cites several cases from foreign jurisdictions for the proposition that when purely private animosity manifests itself in a workplace attack, the employment connection to the injury is so minimal that worker's compensation should be denied. *Monahan v. United States Check Book*; *Ross v. Mark's, Inc.* In both *Monahan* and *Ross*, a non-employee attacked and killed an ex-spouse at the ex-spouse's place of employment. Worker's compensation was denied in both cases, on the ground that assaults do not arise out of employment when they involve private quarrels imported into the workplace. In neither case did the court find evidence that the employment contributed to or facilitated the attacks . . . .

We find unpersuasive the examples of worker's compensation denials cited by Weiss. . . we are of the view that in certain situations, "an injury from an admittedly private source should be compensable because it [is] facilitated or contributed to by the employment environment." 1 The Law of Workmen's Compensation § 11.23. For example, in *Carter v. Penney Tire & Recapping Co*, the claimant had previously quarreled with Crosby, a non-employee. On the date of the assault, Crosby threatened the claimant while the latter was engaged in repairing his employer's roof. Before returning to the roof, the claimant reported the threats to his employer, who responded that the claimant would be protected and should proceed with his work. Crosby later returned and shot the claimant, inflicting grievous injuries. The South Carolina Supreme Court determined that the claimant's injuries arose out of his employment, because:

> the employee was required to perform his duties under circumstances where he was endangered by a peril from a source outside of and unrelated to his actual work, which peril was known to the employer and against which the employer afforded no protection or relief.

In summary, Weiss has alleged an emotional injury which occurred in the course of employment and was caused by an accident arising out of that employment. Accordingly, we conclude that Weiss's complaint states a claim covered under [the worker's compensation statute]. Because the exclusive remedy provision of the [worker's compensation statute] bars Weiss's common law tort action against the City, the circuit court properly granted summary judgment dismissing the complaint, and the court of appeals correctly upheld the circuit court's decision.

The decision of the court of appeals is affirmed.

QUESTION

1. Does the result in this case seem unfair? Does the connection to the workplace seem too attenuated to trigger the affirmative defense of workers' compensation?

Problem 26-4

Sarah works as a custodial employee for a large university. While the university is on spring break recess, Sarah is assigned to clean the floors of a remote building on the sprawling campus. Sarah had broken up with her boyfriend, Arnold, two weeks earlier. Arnold knows her shift hours, but not where she is working. Arnold arrives at the university and persuades two custodial workers to tell him where Sarah is working that day, and to unlock an exterior door to the building where she is working. Arnold attacks Sarah, resulting in her death. Sarah's estate sues the university in negligence for wrongful death. Assess whether the university can raise the exclusivity of the workers' compensation system as an affirmative defense to the negligence action.

Conclusion

In this Lesson, you have learned about the emergence of workers' compensation statutory schemes that effectuate a grand bargain. In exchange for relatively certain payment of damages for injuries suffered in the course of, and arising out of, an employment relationship, employees are unable to pursue tort actions against their employer. Employers may try to characterize an injury as falling within the scope of the workers' compensation system to take advantage of the exclusive (limited) remedy provided.

Lesson 27:
The Occupational Safety and Health Act (OSHAct)

Objectives and Expected Learning Outcomes

In this Lesson, you will study the circumstances that led to the enactment of the Occupational Safety and Health Act (OSHAct) and the statutory tools Congress provided to the Agency to carry out its mission. You will also develop an understanding of employer defenses to the citations the Agency issues when it finds violations of the statute. Finally, you will gain a perspective on OSHAct and health and safety issues in a changed economy, one driven much less by manufacturing and physical labor and much more by the service industry and intellectual capital.

In the last Lesson, we discussed how states created workers' compensation statutes to mitigate losses after a workplace injury occurs. Although the employer is financially motivated to avoid workplace injuries because they raise the cost of workers' compensation insurance, this somewhat indirect cost proved insufficient to reduce injuries. In fact, workplace injuries continue to rise in number, leading many worker advocates to call for more emphasis on workplace safety. In this Lesson, we will review the enactment of the Occupational Safety and Health Act (OSHAct) and its general principles. In the next Lesson, we will review the exercise of regulatory authority by the Occupational Safety and Health Agency (OSHA).

1. The History of the OSHAct and OSHA

In the years leading up to the enactment of the OSHAct, over 14,500 workers were dying each year as a result of their jobs. Over two million workers each year were disabled by job-related accidents. The human cost of these statistics is obvious, but the economic impact was also substantial. Lost wages due to workplace injuries totaled $1.5 billion, and this translated to an annual loss to the Gross National Product of more than $8 billion. Congress finally took up the matter with a new regulatory agency created by the OSHAct. It created OSHA and armed it with two principal tools to create safer workplace.

The first tool is known as the General Duty clause. The sweeping and expansive mandate was stated directly: "Each employer (1) shall furnish to each of [its] employees employment and a place of employment which are free from recognized hazards that are causing or likely to cause death or serious physical harm to [its] employees." Quite literally, the Agency is charged with ensuring that workplaces are safe.

The second tool provided to OSHA is the power to develop and promulgate standards for industries or situations that have the force of law as regulations. For example, the Agency has promulgated detailed rules governing how trenches must be dug in order to ensure the safety of workers who go into the trench.

OSHA was placed within the Department of Labor. OSHA inspectors are empowered to investigate workplaces—sometimes, as we will see, after obtaining a warrant issued by a judge—to determine whether the General Duty clause or specific regulations are being violated. Upon finding a violation, the inspector will issue a citation that generally carries a very modest fine. An employer is entitled to contest the citation and seek an adjudicatory hearing before an Administrate Law Judge (ALJ). If the ALJ affirms the citation, the employer may petition for discretionary review by the Occupational Safety and Health Review Commission. After the Review Commission makes a determination it can be appealed to a federal court of appeals. The Court of Appeals ensures that the Review Commission's factual findings are supported by substantial evidence, and it determines whether the Commission's legal conclusions are arbitrary, capricious, an abuse of discretion, or otherwise not in accordance with the law.

Commentators have conflicting views about the success of the OSHAct. Fatalities had dropped from 14,500 per year to 4,800 per year by 2016. Additionally, some applaud the OSHAct for helping to build a culture of safety in the American workplace. On the other hand, some commentators find that the OSHAct has not accomplished its objectives. The total cost of occupational injuries and illnesses in the United States is at least $250 billion annually, and with workers' compensation paying only 21% of these costs there is a significant loss that can be mitigated only by prevention. Since 1970, OSHA has been able to promulgate only 37 major health and 55 major safety standards. Some regard this as a woefully low number, considering how long the statute has been on the books. Critics note, by way of example, that there still have not been any standards issued to address workplace violence.

The ability of OSHA to meet its mandate is hampered by lack of resources. In Fiscal Year 2015, OSHA was responsible for protecting workers in over eight million workplaces. However, in that same year OSHA had only 1,850 inspectors, and they were able to conduct only 35,385 inspections. Moreover, the average penalty for a serious violation of the Act—one that may cause death or serious bodily harm—was just $2,148. It may require more resources and legislative attention to increase workplace safety.

QUESTIONS

1. As we asked in Lesson 2 about laws banning discrimination, is there still a need for the OSHAct? Don't employers have a strong economic interest in having a healthy and safe work force, if only to avoid down time due to injuries and costs of replacing workers?
2. Does OSHA seek to do the impossible? Isn't it a fact of life that work can be dangerous and that there is an inherent risk associated with many jobs, especially in manufacturing settings?

---

2. Enforcing the General Duty Clause

The General Duty clause is simply stated and broadly worded. It was left to the courts to define its reach, particularly with regard to the employer's culpability. Should employers be strictly liable for injuries that are caused by hazards in the workplace? The following opinion by Judge Wright explores this issue in detail.

National Realty and Construction Co., Inc. v. Occupational Safety and Health Review Commission

489 F.2d 1257 (D.C. Cir. 1973).

J. Skelly Wright, Circuit Judge:

We review here an order of the Occupational Safety and Health Review Commission which found National Realty and Construction Company, Inc. to have committed a "serious violation" of the "general duty clause" of the Occupational Safety and Health Act of 1970, for which a civil fine of $300 was imposed. Unable to locate substantial evidence in the record to support the Commission's finding of a violation, we reverse. . . .

On September 24, 1971 the Secretary cited National Realty for serious breach of its general duty in that an employee was permitted to stand as a passenger on the running board of an Allis Chalmers 645 Front end loader while the loader was in motion.

After National Realty filed timely notice of contest, the Secretary entered a formal complaint charging that National Realty had permitted the existence of a condition which constituted a recognized hazard that was likely to cause death or serious physical harm to its employees. Said condition, which resulted in the death of foreman O. C. Smith, arose when Smith stood as a passenger on the running board of a piece of construction equipment which was in motion. . . .

On September 16, 1971, at a motel construction site operated by National Realty in Arlington, Virginia, O. C. Smith, a foreman with the company, rode the running board of a front-end loader driven by one of his subordinates, Clyde Williams. The loader suffered a stalled engine while going down an earthen ramp into an excavation and began to swerve off the ramp. Smith jumped from the loader, but was killed when it toppled off the ramp and fell on him. John Irwin, Smith's supervisor, testified that he had not seen the accident, that Smith's safety record had been very good, that the company had a 'policy' against equipment riding, and that he—Irwin—had stopped the '4 or 5' employees he had seen taking rides in the past two years. The loader's driver testified that he did not order Smith off the vehicle because Smith was his foreman; he further testified that loader riding was extremely rare at National Realty. Another company employee testified that it was contrary to company policy to ride on heavy equipment. A company supervisor said he had reprimanded violators of this policy and would fire second offenders should the occasion arise. Simms, the inspector, testified from personal experience that the Army Corps of Engineers has a policy against equipment riding. He stated he was unaware of other instances of equipment riding at National Realty and that the company had 'abated' its violation. Asked to define abatement, Simms said it would consist of orally instructing equipment drivers not to allow riding.

The hearing examiner dismissed the citation, finding that National Realty had not 'permitted' O. C. Smith to ride the loader, as charged in the citation and complaint. The examiner reasoned that a company did not 'permit' an activity which its safety policies prohibited unless the policies were 'not enforced or effective.' Such constructive permission could be found only if the hazardous activity were a 'practice' among employees, rather than—as here—a rare occurrence. Upon reviewing the hearing record, the Commission reversed its examiner by a 2–1 vote, each commissioner writing separately. Ruling for the Secretary, Commissioners Burch and Van Namee found inadequate implementation of National Realty's safety 'policy.' Rejecting the hearing examiner's factual findings in part, Commissioner Burch stated that it was 'incredible' that an oral safety policy could have reduced equipment riding to a rare occurrence. Commissioner Van Namee reasoned that the Smith incident and the '4 or 5' occurrences shown on the record 'put respondent on notice that more was required of it to obtain effective implementation of its safety policy.' The majority commissioners briefly suggested several improvements which National Realty might have effected in its safety policy: placing the policy in writing, posting no-riding signs, threatening riders with automatic discharge, and providing alternative means of transport at the construction site. In dissent, Commissioner Moran concluded that the Secretary had not proved his charge that National Realty had 'permitted' either equipment riding in general or the particular incident which caused Smith's death.

B. The Statutory Duty to Prevent Hazardous Conduct by employees

. . . .

Under the (General Duty) clause, the Secretary must prove (1) that the employer failed to render its workplace 'free' of a hazard which was (2) 'recognized' and (3) 'causing or likely to cause death or serious physical harm.' The hazard here was the dangerous activity of riding heavy equipment. The record clearly contains substantial evidence to support the Commission's finding that this hazard was 'recognized' and 'likely to cause death or serious physical harm.' The question then is whether National Realty rendered its construction site 'free' of the hazard. In this case of first impression, the meaning of that statutory term must be settled before the sufficiency of the evidence can be assessed.

Construing the term in the present context presents a dilemma. On the one hand, the adjective is unqualified and absolute: A workplace cannot be just 'reasonably free' of a hazard, or merely as free as the average workplace in the industry. On the other hand, Congress quite clearly did not intend the general duty clause to impose strict liability: The duty was to be an achievable one. Congress' language is consonant with its intent only where the 'recognized' hazard in question can be totally eliminated from a workplace. A hazard consisting of conduct by employees, such as equipment riding, cannot, however, be totally eliminated. A demented, suicidal, or willfully reckless employee may on occasion circumvent the best conceived and most vigorously enforced safety regime. This seeming dilemma is, however, soluble within the literal structure of the general duty clause. Congress intended to require elimination only of preventable hazards. It follows, we think, that Congress did not intend unpreventable hazards to be considered 'recognized' under the clause. Though a generic form of hazardous conduct, such as equipment riding, may be 'recognized,' unpreventable instances of it are not, and thus the possibility of their occurrence at a workplace is not inconsistent with the workplace being 'free' of recognized hazards.

Though resistant to precise definition, the criterion of preventability draws content from the informed judgment of safety experts. Hazardous conduct is not preventable if it is so idiosyncratic and implausible in motive or means that conscientious experts, familiar with the industry, would not take it into account in prescribing a safety program. Nor is misconduct preventable if its elimination would require methods of hiring, training, monitoring, or sanctioning workers which are either so untested or so expensive that safety experts would substantially concur in thinking the methods infeasible. All preventable forms and instances of hazardous conduct must, however, be entirely excluded from the workplace. To establish a violation of the general duty clause, hazardous conduct need not actually have occurred, for a safety program's feasibly curable inadequacies may sometimes be demonstrated before employees have acted dangerously. At the same time, however, actual occurrence of hazardous conduct is not, by itself, sufficient evidence of a violation, even when the conduct has led to injury. The record must additionally indicate that demonstrably feasible measures would have materially reduced the likelihood that such misconduct would have occurred.

. . . .

Only by requiring the Secretary, at the hearing, to formulate and defend his own theory of what a cited defendant should have done can the Commission and the courts assure evenhanded enforcement of the general duty clause. Because employers have a general duty to do virtually everything possible to prevent and repress hazardous conduct by employees, violations exist almost everywhere, and the Secretary has an awesomely broad discretion in selecting defendants and in proposing penalties. To assure that citations issue only upon careful deliberation, the Secretary must be constrained to specify the particular steps a cited employer should have taken to avoid citation, and to demonstrate the feasibility and likely utility of those measures.

Because the Secretary did not shoulder his burden of proof, the record lacks substantial evidence of a violation, and the Commission's decision and order are, therefore,

Reversed.

QUESTION

1. This seminal case developed the analytical structure under which subsequent citations have been reviewed. What is the key part of the holding? Are you persuaded by Judge Wright's determination that the OSHAct imposes a standard of foreseeability on employers rather than strict liability?

Consider the following example of a case that applies the standard established in *National Realty*. Is foreseeability a sufficient standard to guide review?

SAFEWAY, INC. v. OCCUPATIONAL SAFETY & HEALTH REVIEW COMMISSION

382 F.3d 1189 (10th Cir. 2004).

MURPHY, CIRCUIT JUDGE.

I. INTRODUCTION

After an accident involving a propane grill occurred at the petitioner's bread-baking plant, the Secretary of Labor conducted an inspection and issued a citation for a violation of the general duty clause of the Occupational Safety and Health Act of 1970 ("the Act"), 29 U.S.C. § 654(a)(1). The citation was later amended to allege, alternatively, a violation of 29 C.F.R. § 1910.101(b). Petitioner, Safeway, Inc., ("Safeway") contested the citation. After a hearing, the Administrative Law Judge ("ALJ") affirmed the violation of the general duty clause and Safeway filed a petition for discretionary review by the Occupational Safety and Health Review Commission ("the Commission"). The Commission granted review. When the two sitting Commissioners decided they could not agree on the appropriate resolution of the case, they vacated the decision to grant review and the ALJ's order became the final order of the Commission. Safeway filed a petition for review in this court. We have jurisdiction under 29 U.S.C. § 660(a) and affirm the ALJ's decision.

II. BACKGROUND

Safeway operates a bread-baking facility in Denver, Colorado. Safeway periodically holds company-sponsored outdoor barbecues for its employees. Safeway purchased a gas grill equipped with a twenty-pound propane tank for the barbecues. To ensure that the grill had sufficient gas for the barbecues, Safeway purchased a forty-pound tank. These larger tanks have a warning label which states they should not be used with a grill ordinarily equipped with a twenty-pound tank.

Safeway planned to hold an employee barbecue for July 17, 1998. The plant superintendent, Edward Boone, instructed the plant engineer, Jerry Lewis, to set up the grill for the barbecue. Upon being informed the grill was not adequately cooking the meat, the plant manager, Jim R. Kirk, again summoned Lewis. Lewis and the day-shift maintenance foreman, Fred Lake, attempted to improve the flow of gas to the grill by checking the regulator and repositioning the tank. While Lewis and Lake were working on the grill, fuel escaped and a "ball of fire" erupted. Lewis suffered severe burns to his hand and Lake's facial hair was singed.

After the accident, the Occupational Health and Safety Administration ("OSHA") investigated the accident and issued a citation. The citation alleged that Safeway had violated the general duty clause by exposing employees to "the release and ensuing fire of propane due to the improper use of a gas hose and regulator assembly in combination with a 40 pound cylinder."

. . . .

III. DISCUSSION

. . . .

D. The General Duty Clause Violation

The ALJ concluded that the use of a forty-pound tank with an ordinary grill was a violation of the general duty clause. To show a violation of the general duty clause, the Secretary must prove (1) that the employer failed to render its workplace free of an obvious and recognized hazard, (2) the hazard was causing or likely to cause death or serious physical harm, and (3) there was a feasible method by which the employer could have abated the hazard.

As the ALJ noted, the forty-pound tank itself included warnings against using such a tank with a grill designed for twenty-pound tanks. In addition, the instructions supplied with the grill indicate that the propane tank should be installed underneath the frame of the grill so that the "bottom ring [of the tank] rests in notches in the tank support strap." A Safeway supervisor authorized both the purchase of the tank and the purchase of the grill. Safeway supervisors were aware that the tank was too large to fit underneath the grill. Moreover, Safeway supervisors were aware that the tank could not be attached to the grill without a special adapter. Accordingly, there was substantial evidence to support the ALJ's finding that the use of the forty-pound tank was a recognized hazard and that Safeway was aware of the hazard.

Likewise, there is substantial evidence supporting the ALJ's conclusion that using the forty-pound tank was likely to cause serious injury. The forty-pound tank was difficult to connect to the grill. Because of the size of the tank, it had to be tipped against the frame of the grill to facilitate connection to the grill. In addition, a number of relevant safety standards recognize that failing to properly secure a tank creates a danger. Finally, it is clear that Safeway could have eliminated the hazard of using a forty-pound tank with the grill by simply using a twenty-pound tank. Accordingly, we conclude that the ALJ's decision was not arbitrary or capricious, an abuse of discretion, or otherwise not in accordance with the law.

IV. Conclusion

For the reasons stated above, we affirm the issuance of the citation.

QUESTIONS

1. Safeway also alleged that the cause of the accident was unforeseeable conduct by Lewis; namely, that he was working while under the influence of illegal drugs. Should this fact have any effect on whether the citation should be affirmed? Would it make a difference if the unforeseeable employee conduct directly led to the injury? Explain your answers.
2. Distinguish the *Safeway* and *National Realty* cases. Why was the employer able to defeat the citation in *National Reality* but not in *Safeway*? What are the key differences?

An employer acts through its agents. An employer is often held liable for behavior by its managers and supervisors acting on behalf of the employer, even if the supervisor is not following the employer's directions. The next case examines whether an employer can be held liable under the OSHAct when its supervisor fails to conform to the employer's safety rules. Should the supervisor's knowledge about the hazard automatically be imputed to the employer, or only under certain conditions? This case involves the failure to abide by governing regulations, rather than an action under the General Duty clause.

Dana Container, Inc. v. Secretary of Labor

847 F.3d 495 (7th Cir. 2017).

Wood, Chief Judge.

It is not hard to find people who complain about government regulations, but the regulations often exist because people do not take optimal precautions on a voluntary basis. This case illustrates that problem. It arose after toxic fumes in a large container knocked out a man who was working inside it. Fortunately, he was rescued by the local fire department, but his employer, Dana Container, wound up fighting citations from the Occupational Safety and Health Administration (OSHA). After an administrative law judge (ALJ) and the Occupational Safety and Health Review Commission upheld OSHA's actions, Dana turned to this Court. Because Dana has not provided a compelling reason to overturn the Commission's determinations, we deny its petition for review.

I

Dana operates a truck-tank washing facility near the Stevenson Expressway in Summit, Illinois. The tanks cleaned at Dana's facility are long metallic cylinders used to transport products such as ink and latex. After the tanks are emptied at their destination, truckers bring them to Dana's facility for a cleaning so that they can haul different products without adulteration. Before washing a tank, employees drain any residual product from it. They then insert a mechanical spinner that rotates scrubbers from one end of the tank to the other, simultaneously dousing it with soap or solvents (or both). They then give the tank a final rinse of water and blow it dry. Most of the time, this process suffices to clean the tank thoroughly. When it does not, however, employees enter the tank and manually clean out the remaining sludge or residue. Because the tank space is confined and may contain chemicals that are hazardous to health, OSHA has promulgated regulations that require companies to enforce certain safety precautions when their employees enter these "permit-required confined spaces (PRCSs)." 29 C.F.R. § 1910.146.

At Dana's facility in Summit, employees enter tanks to clean them approximately ten times per month. Before doing so, the employee must obtain an entry permit from a supervisor; the permit contains a checklist of required safety precautions. The employee then climbs onto a catwalk above the tank and hooks a full-body harness he is wearing to a mechanical retrieval device that can pull him out of the tank if he becomes incapacitated for any reason. He must also test the tank air for atmospheric hazards before going in. When he enters the tank, he is required to wear a respirator and to conduct continuous atmospheric testing. While an employee is in the tank, automatic blowers force fresh air into it. A fellow employee is required to be on standby outside the tank in order to assist in case of an emergency. OSHA regulations and Dana's safety rules prohibit employees from entering a "dirty" tank before it has been mechanically cleaned.

In the cold early morning hours of January 28, 2009, one of Dana's supervisors, Bobby Fox, was on the third shift along with former employee Cesar Jaimes. Fox was working on a trailer and encountered a problem with a clogged valve just as he was about to begin the mechanical cleaning process. Disregarding the safety rules, he entered the tank prior to cleaning it, without attaching himself to the retrieval device or following the entry permit procedures. After a short while, Jaimes looked inside, saw Fox unconscious in a pool of chemical sludge, and called the Summit Fire Department. The firefighters hoisted him out, rinsed off the chemical residue, and transported him to the hospital. Fox was diagnosed with "Syncope and Collapse, Toxic Effect of Unspecified Gas, Fume, or Vapor" (i.e., fainting). . . .

II

Dana attacks the Commission's decision in several ways. First, it asserts that it lacked the requisite knowledge to support the order and that it should be exonerated because the incident resulted from "unpreventable employee misconduct." It next argues that the Secretary did not prove the "willful" element of some of the items. Last, it contends that the Commission should have found that it satisfied the standard for alternate entry procedures.

A

The Occupational Safety and Health Act is not a strict liability statute. This means that the Secretary was required to prove that Dana knew about the problem in order to establish a "serious" violation. Under Commission precedent the Secretary can satisfy his burden without demonstrating any inadequacy or defect in the employer's safety program, if a supervisory employee has actual or constructive knowledge of the violation. In that case, the supervisor's knowledge can be imputed to the employer. Because Fox was a supervisor and had actual knowledge of his own misconduct, the Commission imputed his knowledge to Dana.

This path for imputing knowledge is common in employment law. When an employee is acting within the scope of her employment, her knowledge is typically imputed to the employer. *United States v. One Parcel of Land Located at 7326 Highway 45 North, Three Lakes, Oneida Cnty., Wis.*, 965 F.2d 311, 316 (7th Cir. 1992). Conduct is "within the scope of employment when [it is] 'actuated, at least in part, by a purpose to serve the [employer],' even if it is forbidden by the employer." *Burlington Indus., Inc. v. Ellerth*, 524 U.S. 742, 756, 118 S.Ct. 2257, 141 L.Ed.2d 633 (1998) (quoting Restatement (Second) of Agency §§ 228(1)(c), 230 (1957)). Here, Fox knew that he was violating the rules when he entered the dirty tank in order to kick loose a stuck valve so that he could then drain the tank. His act was in furtherance of Dana's tank cleaning business. We thus see no problem with the Commission's decision to impute Fox's knowledge to Dana.

Dana urges that the Third Circuit requires more than this, and that it has the better view. It requires the Secretary to prove that a supervisor's participation in misconduct was foreseeable by showing that the employer's safety program was inadequate. See *Pennsylvania Power & Light Co. v. OSHRC*, 737 F.2d 350, 354, 357–58 (3d Cir. 1984). In order to have an adequate safety program, that court says, the employer must have work rules designed to prevent the violation, adequately communicate those rules to its employees, take steps to discover violations, and effectively enforce the rules when it discovers violations. *Id.* at 358–59.

This argument would have more force if the Commission had ignored the Third Circuit's position. But it did not. At the time of its decision, it knew that the Third Circuit might hear this petition for review, because Dana's principal office is located in New Jersey. See 29 U.S.C. § 660(a). It therefore tested its conclusion under the standard of Pennsylvania Power & Light and found that Dana's safety program was indeed inadequate. That assessment finds sufficient support in the record. There was evidence showing that nearly all of the tank entry permits at Dana's Summit facility contained errors or omissions. Some indicated that the entries had exceeded the maximum duration of 20 minutes by over an hour. Others had other flaws: for example, they lacked the requisite air monitoring results; they failed to show the duration for which the permit was valid; they indicated that employees had not reviewed material safety data sheets (or had no information about review); and they failed to name either the entrant or the entry attendant. Whether these errors and omissions occurred because the employees were violating entry procedures or if they reflected only recording problems, there is no evidence that the Facility Manager followed up on the deficiencies. The Commission was therefore justified in concluding that there was a failure to enforce Dana's safety program.

Dana argues that the particular problems the Commission mentioned would not have allowed it to predict Fox's entry into a dirty tank. But this is asking for a higher degree of foreseeability than any court requires. The Commission was entitled to find that the uncorrected permit violations exhibited a pattern of disregard for the rules at Dana. Even in the face of a robust written program, lax disregard of the rules can send a message to employees that a company does not make safety a priority. In such an environment, conduct such as Fox's is reasonably foreseeable.

Written policy does not destroy foreseeability

Defense standard

Dana's effort to persuade us that the Commission erred by rejecting the "unpreventable employee misconduct" defense also falls short. To use the defense an employer must show that it took steps to discover violations of its safety rules and that it effectively enforced the rules when violations were discovered. See *Crowther Roofing & Sheet Metal of Florida v. Occupational Safety and Health Review Comm'n*, 454 Fed.Appx. 774, 776 (11th Cir. 2011). Here, the Commission agreed with the ALJ's conclusion that Dana failed to take these steps. It relied on the evidence of permit deficiencies and lack of disciplinary or follow-up action. We have no reason to set aside this conclusion. See *Howard Young*, 207 F.3d at 441.

B

While serious violations of 29 C.F.R. § 1910.146 each carry a maximum penalty of $7,000, willful violations are subject to stiffer monetary penalties—up to $70,000 for each one. 29 U.S.C. § 666(a)–(b). Though neither party disputes that Fox's behavior was willful, Dana argues that it established a good faith defense that should have precluded the Commission from imputing Fox's state of mind to the company. Dana cites a Commission case holding that an employer can demonstrate that the willful conduct of its supervisory personnel should not be imputed to the employer if the employer can demonstrate a good faith effort to comply with the standard. See, e.g., *Anderson Excavating & Wrecking Co.*, 17 BNA OSHC 1890 (No. 92–3684, 1997), aff'd, 131 F.3d 1254 (8th Cir. 1997).

Dana contends that it demonstrated this good faith effort in numerous ways: (1) it had rules prohibiting exactly what Fox did; (2) Dana employees did not usually violate the rules; (3) the record contained instances of discipline and a lack of recidivism; (4) Dana's wash process eliminated toxic atmospherics; (5) Dana had continuous testing and forced air ventilation in clean trailer tanks; (6) Dana's written program had previously been examined by OSHA and found acceptable; and (7) Dana had a good bilingual training program and no recordable injuries from tank injuries for years before the Fox incident. The Commission, however, was unpersuaded. It found that although, on the one hand, Dana had work rules that were communicated to its employees and had submitted evidence of three instances of disciplinary action, on the other hand the facility manager had never disciplined an employee for improperly completing permits or for the violations apparent on the face of the permits. The Commission concluded that Dana had therefore failed to take action when violations of safety rules were plain, as would have been required in a good faith effort.

. . . .

QUESTIONS

1. What is the most important point to take away from the *Dana* case?
2. Compare the approach in *Dana* with the approach in *Pennsylvania Power & Light,* which is discussed in *Dana*. Which case better effectuates the purpose of OSHA? Why?

Problem 27-1

You are the new assistant general counsel for a company that is engaged in an industry with hazards in the workplace. The company has been cited for a number of OSHA violations because of the conduct of its supervisors, as in the *Dana* case. The General Counsel requests that you assess how to reduce OSHA exposure. You divide your task into two parts: (1) what facts do you need to develop internally to carry out your charge; and (2) what policies and procedures do you suggest?

---

3. Workplace Safety: Challenges and Solutions

We have reviewed the general features of OSHA's authority to cite employers for hazards in the workplace. In this section we consider the complexity of workplace injury. Injuries don't occur just because an employee chooses not to follow a clearly articulated and enforced rule. Fatigue is one of the primary sources of poor decisionmaking that can result in injury, but it is difficult to think about how to effectively prevent fatigue in the workplace.

Sarah Trotto, *Fatigue and worker safety: Experts say employers play a role in tackling the issue*

195 Safety & Health 2 (February 26, 2017) (retrieved at safetyandhealthmagazine.com/articles/15271-fatigue-and-worker-safety).

Key points

—Risk factors for occupational fatigue include long work hours, a heavy workload, lack of sleep, environmental factors and medical conditions.

—Experts say employers can help combat fatigue by offering breaks, scheduling work when employees are most alert and promoting the importance of sleep.

—The National Safety Council has launched an initiative about fatigue, gathering data with the aim of identifying solutions and releasing a policy toolkit and other resources.

When his first daughter was born, Steve Marks was juggling two jobs.

From 10 a.m. to 6 p.m., Marks was a nurse manager at a casino medical unit. When his shift ended, he slept an hour or two before moving on to his other job as a hospital supervisor from 11 p.m. to 7 a.m. two nights a week. Afterward, he drove back to his first job, where he curled up under his desk for an hour-long nap.

"When you've got bills to pay and things that have to be done, children or parents or other things keeping you up, sleep is the last thing that gets paid attention to," he said. "It's like, 'All right, I can deal with this. Let me just close my eyes for a couple minutes and I'll get back to it.' That doesn't make up for the loss [of sleep]."

After two years, Marks decided to stop working two jobs. Now administrator of health and safety services at Viking Yachts in New Gretna, NJ, he shares his stories to educate people about occupational fatigue.

Kim Olszewski—vice president of Lewisburg, PA-based MidState Occupational Health Services—also understands fatigue after working the night shift in health care. She, alongside Marks, participates in presentations on occupational fatigue.

Employers are becoming increasingly aware that fatigue is a safety issue, Olszewski said, and they, along with workers, play a role in tackling the problem.

"The key is the proactive piece, driving it from the top down, talking about fatigue, how it can be managed, how can it impacts all aspects of life—not just work," she said.

Causes and effects

A 2012 guidance statement from the American College of Occupational and Environmental Medicine defines fatigue as the body's response to sleep deprivation or lengthy physical or mental hard work. Risk factors related to occupational fatigue include long work hours, a heavy workload, lack of sleep, environmental factors and medical conditions.

Even dealing with other people can result in fatigue, one researcher notes.

"You can be fatigued simply if you go to work and have really poor social interactions with your coworkers—it's not just about how much sleep you get," said Matthew Hallowell, associate professor of construction engineering at the University of Colorado Boulder.

Hallowell led a review of literature about causes and outcomes of occupational fatigue, which was published in the *Journal of Occupational and Environmental Medicine* in October.

Effects of fatigue can include slower reaction time, more errors and decreased cognitive ability. Fatigue can occur in all industries, but numerous studies have focused on its effects on shift workers, health care workers and drivers.

"The industries that are at highest risk would be those where people are working long hours, overtime, many days in a row, when they're exposed to harsh environmental conditions, like working outside in the rain, snow," Hallowell said. "Environmental conditions can include things like noise or vibration, really heavy mental task loads for long periods of time. You can extend to what industries that defines, like electrical transmission and distribution line workers, or people who drive snowplows."

In addition, many people work multiple jobs, leaving them vulnerable to fatigue. People who work several jobs get 40 minutes less sleep per day than those who work one job, according to David Lombardi, principal research scientist at the Center for Injury Epidemiology at the Liberty Mutual Research Institute for Safety in Hopkinton, MA. Lombardi presented this data during the Dec. 13 "Fatigue Blue Ribbon Panel" in Chicago, hosted by the National Safety Council.

"Fatigue is an increasing health and safety problem in our daily lives due to the 24-hour society with decreasing emphasis on sleep," Lombardi said.

Lombardi and researcher Simon Folkard, of the Université Paris Descartes, have published a risk index to estimate injury risk related to work schedules. Type of shift, number of consecutive shifts, hours worked per shift and rest breaks influence risk, Lombardi said. Risk was 31 percent higher among night shift workers than morning shift workers; by the fourth consecutive night shift, risk was 36 percent higher than on the first night, and risk nearly doubled by the 12th hour of work. However, injury risk decreased by nearly 50 percent after any length of rest break.

"An important message of our approach is that various features of a shift work schedule—beyond only working hours—need to be considered in combination when assessing the safety of a given work schedule," Lombardi said.

The estimated annual injury incidence rate per 100 workers is 7.89 for U.S. workers who usually sleep less than five hours per day, compared with 2.27 per 100 workers among those who tend to sleep between seven and eight hours, according to research from Lombardi and others, using data from the National Health Interview Survey.

Fatigue risk management systems

Medical and lifestyle interventions, as well as work organization factors, can help promote alertness, according to a 2012 American College of Occupational and Environmental Medicine guidance statement on fatigue risk management in the workplace. Organizations in which employees work long hours or at night—especially those with safety-sensitive jobs, such as in the energy, health care and transportation industries—can benefit from addressing fatigue.

ACOEM outlines the following key features of a fatigue risk management system:

—Supported by peer-reviewed science

—Decisions determined by data collection and analysis

—Designed by stakeholders

—System-wide use of tools, systems, policies and procedures

—Constructed into the corporate safety and health management systems

—Continuous improvement

—Budgeted

—Senior leaders take ownership

Other critical elements include a safety management policy, risk management, reporting, incident investigation, training and education, and auditing.

Key defenses of a fatigue risk management system are:

—Balancing workload and staffing

—Shift scheduling

—Training for employees on fatigue and managing sleep disorders

—Workplace design

—Monitoring of fatigue

Although workers are responsible for being well-rested, managers should provide information, motivation, and resources, ACOEM states.

In addition, workers should be educated about issues, such as fatigue-related hazards; sleep disorders; how to get adequate and quality sleep; how to recognize fatigue; the importance of diet, exercise and other health conditions; and alertness strategies, including designing workplaces with bright light, cool temperature, non-monotonous noise and low humidity.

Taking the initiative

In July, the National Safety Council launched an initiative on occupational fatigue. "Aside from just an increase in workplace risk, there's also long-term economic consequences," said Emily Whitcomb, senior program manager of the initiative. "NSC is tackling fatigue because as we're working toward eliminating preventable deaths, fatigue is one of the larger issues."

NSC has gathered research with the aim of identifying best practices; conducting a national survey; and releasing a cost calculator, policy toolkit and other educational resources.

The council's review of literature includes several findings:

—About 38 percent of U.S. workers sleep less than seven hours a night, according to a 2016 study from NIOSH.

—Several studies state that workers who have a sleeping disorder are more likely to be involved in a workplace safety incident.

—Fatigue-related productivity losses cost almost $2,000 per worker each year, according to estimates from a 2010 study conducted by Cupertino, CA-based Alertness Solutions.

"Fatigue has always been a problem—there's always been shift work, people have always not gotten their full night's rest," Whitcomb said. "It has started to come to light more in the past 20 years, when the research really started showing it was causing unsafe work practices, when it was increasing risk in the workplace.

"Probably in the last 10 years, as we've looked more at wellness in the workplace, it's gotten a lot more attention. A lot more employers are wanting to address fatigue in the workplace because they're starting to see those increased risks and lack of productivity from those employees who are fatigued."

Possible solutions

Although workers can help prevent fatigue through measures such as taking breaks and adopting better sleep habits, employers also can help combat the issue.

A November report from RAND Europe, part of the nonprofit research organization RAND Corp., concluded that lack of sleep results in a 13 percent increased risk of death and the loss of 1.2 million workdays per year in the United States. The report offers the following recommendations for employers:

—Understand the importance of sleep and promote it.

—Create brighter workplaces with settings for naps.

—Deter lengthy use of electronic devices after work.

According to a Liberty Mutual report, recommendations for scheduling include:

—Working during the day rather than at night

—Restricting consecutive day shifts to five or six days and night shifts to four days

—Ensuring workers have at least two consecutive days off

—Making schedules consistent

—Providing frequent breaks

Supervisors should be alert for signs of excessive fatigue among workers, such as yawning, head dropping, and difficulty remembering or concentrating, according to the statement from ACOEM.

Technology also can be used to monitor fatigue. For example, Chicago-based USG Corp., a manufacturer of construction materials, placed sensors in its trucks to monitor operators after one dozed off behind the wheel, resulting in the truck traveling up a berm and its load tipping over. The operator—who had worked more than 55 hours the previous week and was helping his family with another job—was uninjured, Justin Dugas, safety and health director at USG, said during the NSC panel. (USG is a member of the Campbell Institute at NSC.)

The sensor tracks an operator's eye movements and sends alerts through a loud buzzing or vibration of the seat when distracted driving or sleep is detected. Video footage is sent to a monitoring center for analysis.

During the initial months after the sensors were installed, two or three fatigue-related incidents occurred daily. They decreased to two or three per week, then one or two per month, Dugas said.

U.S. estimates of work-related all-cause injury incidence (per 100 workers) by usual daily sleep

Usual Hours Slept / Day	Number of Workers (NHIS 2004-08)	Percent of Workers	Number of est. Work-related Injuries Annually	Number of est. Workers Annually	Est. Annual Injury Incidence per 100 Workers[1]
≤ 4.99 h	1,431	1.9	83,730	1,061,759	7.89
5 - 5.99 h	4,407	5.9	172,462	3,310,950	5.21
6 - 6.99 h	17,251	22.9	469,756	12,988,074	3.62
7 - 7.99 h	25,950	34.5	448,458	19,774,245	2.27
8 - 8.99 h	22,604	30.0	413,942	16,571,317	2.50
9 - 9.99 h	2,361	3.1	39,101	1,759,342	2.22
> 10 h	1,267	1.7	41,694	883,551	4.72
Total	75,271	100.0	1,669,142	56,349,239	2.96

[1]Includes individuals reporting employment at a job or business and those who had reported usual sleep hours.

(Source: Lombardi DA, Folkard S, Willets JL, Smith GS. Daily sleep, weekly working hours, and risk of work-related injury: US National Health Interview Survey (2004-2008). Chronobiol Int. 2010 Jul; 27(5):1013-30.

15

From a presentation at the Fatigue Blue Ribbon Panel Meeting, December 13th, 2016

"[It's] significant improvement in terms of fatigue events, and this is now, as a result, part of our standard equipment specification for all our haulage units," he added.

In addition, a risk management system can help mitigate fatigue. (See "Fatigue risk management systems," above.) A risk management system can include reporting of fatigue-related incidents, investigation, training and auditing, Marks said, adding that "it would include things like making sure sleep disorders are covered on the insurance plan, and people are encouraged to get this evaluated."

Even if a company does not invest in a complex management system, it can share messages about fatigue, such as the importance of not consuming alcohol before bedtime.

"These are little things that can come out in toolbox safety talks, little five-minute lectures on a topic to pass on the information," Marks said.

Other ways to mitigate worker fatigue include moving safety-sensitive work to other employees or another time to take advantage of alertness, taking breaks, ingesting caffeine and changing environmental factors, according to ACOEM.

"Being cognizant of how the workplace is set up, how the work is handled, will help improve some of those issues," Marks said.

"The things that can help: Improving lighting, making sure the temperature is cooler—especially at night—minimizing humidity, noise, vibration. As employers are looking at reengineering workplaces or building new ones, these are things that can be put in place at the beginning or during retrofit to help minimize some of these situations."

Jia Tolentino, *The Gig Economy Celebrates Working Yourself to Death*

The New Yorker (Mar 22, 2017), https://www.newyorker.com/culture/jia-tolentino/the-gig-economy-celebrates-working-yourself-to-death.

Last September, a very twenty-first-century type of story appeared on the company blog of the ride-sharing app Lyft. "Long-time Lyft driver and mentor, Mary, was nine months pregnant when she picked up a passenger the night of July 21st," the post began. "About a week away from her due date, Mary decided to drive for a few hours after a day of mentoring." You can guess what happened next.

Mary, who was driving in Chicago, picked up a few riders, and then started having contractions. "Since she was still a week away from her due date," Lyft wrote, "she assumed they were simply a false alarm and continued driving." As the contractions continued, Mary decided to drive to the hospital. "Since she didn't believe she was going into labor yet," Lyft went on, "she stayed in driver mode, and sure enough—ping!—she received a ride request en route to the hospital."

"Luckily," as Lyft put it, the passenger requested a short trip. After completing it, Mary went to the hospital, where she was informed that she was in labor. She gave birth to a daughter, whose picture appears in the post. (She's wearing a "Little Miss Lyft" onesie.) The post concludes with a call for similar stories: "Do you have an exciting Lyft story you'd love to share? Tweet us your story at @lyft_CHI!"

Mary's story looks different to different people. Within the ghoulishly cheerful Lyft public-relations machinery, Mary is an exemplar of hard work and dedication—the latter being, perhaps, hard to come by in a company that refuses to classify its drivers as employees. Mary's entrepreneurial spirit—taking ride requests while she was in labor!—is an "exciting" example of how seamless and flexible app-based employment can be. Look at that hustle! You can make a quick buck with Lyft anytime, even when your cervix is dilating.

Lyft does not provide its drivers paid maternity leave or health insurance. (It offers to connect drivers with an insurance broker, and helpfully that "the Affordable Care Act offers many choices to make sure you're covered.") A third-party platform called SherpaShare, which some drivers use to track their earnings, found, in 2015, that Lyft drivers in Chicago net about 11 dollars per trip. Perhaps, as Lyft suggests, Mary kept accepting riders while experiencing contractions because "she was still a week away from her due date," or "she didn't believe she was going into labor yet." Or maybe Mary kept accepting riders because the gig economy has further normalized the circumstances in which earning an extra eleven dollars can feel more important than seeking out the urgent medical care that these quasi-employers do not sponsor. In the other version of Mary's story, she's an unprotected worker in precarious circumstances. "I can't pretend to know Mary's economic situation," Bryan Menegus at Gizmodo, when the story first appeared. "Maybe she's an heiress who happens to love the freedom of chauffeuring strangers from place to place on her own schedule. But that Lyft, for some reason, thought that this would reflect kindly on them is perhaps the most horrifying part."

It does require a fairly dystopian strain of doublethink for a company to celebrate how hard and how constantly its employees must work to make a living, given that these companies are themselves setting the terms. And yet this type of faux-inspirational tale has been appearing more lately, both in corporate advertising and in the news. Fiverr, an online freelance marketplace that promotes itself as being for "the lean entrepreneur"—as its name suggests, services advertised on Fiverr can be purchased for as low as five dollars—recently attracted ire for an ad campaign called "In Doers We Trust." One ad, prominently displayed on some New York City subway cars, features a woman staring at the camera with a look of blank determination. "You eat a coffee for lunch," the ad proclaims. "You follow through on your follow through. Sleep deprivation is your drug of choice. You might be a doer."

Fiverr, which had a hundred and ten million dollars in venture capital by November, 2015, has more about the "In Doers We Trust" campaign on its Web site. In one video, a peppy female voice-over urges "doers" to "always be available," to think about beating "the trust-fund kids," and to pitch themselves to everyone they see, including their dentist. A Fiverr press release about "In Doers We Trust" states, "The campaign positions Fiverr to seize today's emerging zeitgeist of entrepreneurial flexibility, rapid experimentation, and doing more with less. It pushes against bureaucratic overthinking, analysis-paralysis, and excessive whiteboarding." This is the jargon through which the essentially cannibalistic nature of the gig economy is dressed up as an aesthetic. No one wants to eat coffee for lunch or go on a bender of sleep deprivation—or answer a call from a client while having sex, as recommended in the video. It's a stretch to feel cheerful at all about the Fiverr marketplace, perusing the thousands of listings of people who will record any song, make any happy-birthday video, or design any book cover for five dollars. I'd guess that plenty of the people who advertise services on Fiverr would accept some "whiteboarding" in exchange for employer-sponsored health insurance.

At the root of this is the American obsession with self-reliance, which makes it more acceptable to applaud an individual for working himself to death than to argue that an individual working himself to death is evidence of a flawed economic system. The contrast between the gig economy's rhetoric (everyone is always connecting, having fun, and killing it!) and the conditions that allow it to exist (a lack of dependable employment that pays a living wage) makes this kink in our thinking especially clear. Human-interest stories about the beauty of some person standing up to the punishments of late capitalism are regular features in the news, too. I've come to detest the local-news set piece about the man who walks ten or eleven or twelve miles to work—a story that's been filed from Oxford, Alabama; from Detroit,

Michigan; from Plano, Texas. The story is always written as a tearjerker, with praise for the person's uncomplaining attitude; a car is usually donated to the subject in the end. Never mentioned or even implied is the shamefulness of a job that doesn't permit a worker to afford his own commute.

There's a painful distance between the chipper narratives surrounding labor and success in America and the lived experience of workers. A similar conflict drove Nathanael West, in 1934, to publish the novel "A Cool Million," which satirized the Horatio Alger bootstrap fables that remained popular into the Great Depression. "Alger is to America what Homer was to the Greeks," West once wrote. His protagonist in "A Cool Million," Lemuel Pitkin, is an innocent, energetic striver, tasked with saving his mother's house from foreclosure. A series of Algeresque plot twists ensue. But Pitkin, rather than triumphing, ends up losing his teeth, his eye, his leg, his scalp, and finally his thumb. Morris Dickstein, in his book "Dancing in the Dark: A Cultural History of the Great Depression," notes, "The novel ends with Lem as a vaudeville clown being beaten nightly until he simply falls apart." A former President named Shagpoke Whipple gives a speech valorizing Pitkin's fate, extolling "the right of every American boy to go into the world and . . . make his fortune by industry." Whipple describes Pitkin's dismemberment—"lovingly," Dickstein adds—and tells his audience that, through Pitkin's hard work and enthusiastic martyrdom, "America became again American."

QUESTIONS

1. Do employers expect employees to sacrifice their personal needs in favor of the company's interests despite negative impacts on the employee's own health and welfare?
2. Is there a culture (perhaps among the largest law firms, for example) where it is a badge of honor to exhaust oneself by working nonstop?
3. Will the much-discussed millennial generation place higher emphasis on health and wellbeing, leading to changes in employer expectations and worker practices?

Class Exercise 27-1

Fatigue is a serious problem in the workplace that results in injury. You will be charged with reducing the problem of fatigue. The class will divide into three groups. One group will be employers, one group will be employees, and one group will be staff members at OSHA. Each group will seek solutions to the problem of fatigue from its perspective.

Mastery Problem 27-1

You are an OSHA Inspector. You have been given a file to investigate, and your first task is to interview the company executives and employees. The partner has included the following summary memorandum with the file:

> The Company is in the business of digging trenches. In this instance, it was digging a trench alongside Interstate 5 at 2 pm on a Wednesday. The crew accidentally struck an underground cable while digging. Joe—one of the most experienced workers, with 19 years of service—walked across 3 lanes of Interstate traffic to the median, so he could check a junction box to determine if the crew had severed the cable connection. After his inspection, Joe walked back across the three lanes of Interstate traffic to return to the crew. He was killed when a car travelling 70 mph struck him. Please begin your preparation for an investigation by reading an email from the company and related documents that are in the file.

Inside the file you find the following email from the company to your boss, seeking to avoid an investigation of a potential OSHAct violation. The email reads:

> I don't understand why your agency is conducting an investigation. Isn't it obvious that no person should walk across multiple lanes of an active Interstate highway? Do we have to train our employees to use their common sense? Joe was a great person and a dedicated worker. He had a perfect safety record. We have rules that workers should use the company truck if they need to be on the highway, and that they are to pay attention to the traffic around them at all times. We have multiple signs on the site: "Watch out for cars!" "Drivers could be zoned out!" and "Know where you are at all times! Don't get careless and end up straying into an active lane of traffic!" Isn't it obvious that this is an

unfortunate and freak accident? I will plan to discuss this with your investigator on Tuesday.

Your boss also includes some of the Code of Federal Regulations in the folder:

29 C.F.R. § 1926. 20 (b): Accident prevention responsibilities.

(1) It shall be the responsibility of the employer to initiate and maintain such programs as may be necessary to comply with this part.

(2) Such programs shall provide for frequent and regular inspections of the job sites, materials, and equipment to be made by competent persons designated by the employers.

29 C.F.R. Section 1926.21 (b): Employer's duties.

(2): The employer shall instruct each employee in the recognition and avoidance of unsafe conditions and the regulations applicable to his work environment to control or eliminate any hazards or other exposure to illness or injury.

Prepare an outline of your strategy for interviewing the company's employees.

Conclusion

The OSHAct takes a preventative approach to workplace injuries by requiring employers to provide safe workplaces to their employees. In this Lesson, we have reviewed the circumstances leading to the enactment of the OSHAct and the general principles guiding OSHA's enforcement under the General Duty clause. In the next Lesson, we will consider more deeply OSHA's role in promulgating regulations.

Lesson 28:
OSHA Regulation

Objectives and Expected Learning Outcomes

In this Lesson, you will study the wide-ranging impact of OSHAct regulations. OSHA is empowered to promulgate health and safety standards that govern the workplace, but states continue to play a key role in workplace safety. You will learn how the OSHAct interacts with state law. First, we will consider whether the OSHAct preempts the effect of state law, and how state law can supplement the OSHAct. In particular, we will focus on whether states may impose criminal penalties for OSHA violations. Finally, you will study the OSHAct's anti-retaliation provision, which differs from the other anti-retaliation provisions we have studied.

In Lesson 27, we reviewed the enactment of the OSHAct and the general duty provision that requires employers to provide a safe workplace. It would not serve the interests of worker safety to only adjudge violations after the fact, and so OSHA is empowered by the OSHAct to promulgate health and safety standards that direct employer behavior in maintaining a safe work place. These standards have the legal authority of regulations, which means that they have the force and effect of a statute. As you might imagine, the standards can be quite detailed and complex. Consider the following standard relating to safety requirements for supporting the walls of a trench when employees are working in the trench.

29 C.F.R. § 1926. Safety and Health Regulations for Construction, Subpart P Excavations, "Aluminum Hydraulic Shoring for Trenches"

(a) Scope. This appendix contains information that can be used when aluminum hydraulic shoring is provided as a method of protection against cave-ins in trenches that do not exceed 20 feet (6.1m) in depth. This appendix must be used when design of the aluminum hydraulic protective system cannot be performed in accordance with 1926.652(c)(2).

(b) Soil Classification. In order to use data presented in this appendix, the soil type or types in which the excavation is made must first be determined using the soil classification method set forth in appendix A of subpart P of part 1926.

(c) Presentation of Information. Information is presented in several forms as follows:

(1) Information is presented in tabular form in Tables D-1.1, D-1.2, D-1.3 and D-1.4. Each table presents the maximum vertical and horizontal spacings that may be used with various aluminum member sizes and various hydraulic cylinder sizes. Each table contains data only for the particular soil type in which the excavation or portion of the excavation is made. Tables D-1.1 and D-1.2 are for vertical shores in Types A and B soil. Tables D-1.3 and D-1.4 are for horizontal waler systems in Types B and C soil.

(2) Information concerning the basis of the tabular data and the limitations of the data is presented in paragraph (d) of this appendix.

(3) Information explaining the use of the tabular data is presented in paragraph (e) of this appendix.

(4) Information illustrating the use of the tabular data is presented in paragraph (f) of this appendix.

(5) Miscellaneous notations (Footnotes) regarding Table D-1.1 through D-1.4 are presented in paragraph (g) of this appendix.

(6) Figures, illustrating typical installations of hydraulic shoring, are included just prior to the Tables. The illustrations page is entitled "Aluminum Hydraulic Shoring: Typical Installations."

(d) Basis and limitations of the data.

(1) Vertical shore rails and horizontal wales are those that meet the Section Modulus requirements in the D-1 Tables. Aluminum material is 6061-T6 or material of equivalent strength and properties.

(2) Hydraulic cylinders specifications.

(i) 2-inch cylinders shall be a minimum 2-inch inside diameter with a minimum safe working capacity of no less than 18,000 pounds axial compressive load at maximum extension. Maximum extension is to include full range of cylinder extensions as recommended by product manufacturer.

(ii) 3-inch cylinders shall be a minimum 3-inch inside diameter with a safe working capacity of not less than 30,000 pounds axial compressive load at extensions as recommended by product manufacturer.

(3) Limitation of application.

(i) It is not intended that the aluminum hydraulic specification apply to every situation that may be experienced in the field. These data were developed to apply to the situations that are most commonly experienced in current trenching practice. Shoring systems for use in situations that are not covered by the data in this appendix must be otherwise designed as specified in 1926.652(c).

(ii) When any of the following conditions are present, the members specified in the Tables are not considered adequate. In this case, an alternative aluminum hydraulic shoring system or other type of protective system must be designed in accordance with 1926.652.

(A) When vertical loads imposed on cross braces exceed a 100 Pound gravity load distributed on a one foot section of the center of the hydraulic cylinder.

(B) When surcharge loads are present from equipment weighing in excess of 20,000 pounds.

(C) When only the lower portion of a trench is shored and the remaining portion of the trench is sloped or benched unless: The sloped portion is sloped at an angle less steep than three horizontal to one vertical; or the members are selected from the tables for use at a depth which is determined from the top of the overall trench, and not from the toe of the sloped portion.

(e) Use of Tables D-1.1, D-1.2, D-1.3 and D-1.4. The members of the shoring system that are to be selected using this information are the hydraulic cylinders, and either the vertical shores or the horizontal wales. When a waler system is used the vertical timber sheeting to be used is also selected from these tables. The Tables D-1.1 and D-1.2 for vertical shores are used in Type A and B soils that do not require sheeting. Type B soils that may require sheeting, and Type C soils that always require sheeting, are found in the horizontal wale Tables D-1.3 and D-1.4. The soil type must first be determined in accordance with the soil classification system described in appendix A to subpart P of part 1926. Using the appropriate table, the selection of the size and spacing of the members is made. The selection is based on the depth and width of the trench where the members are to be installed. In these tables the vertical spacing is held constant at four feet on center. The tables show the maximum horizontal spacing of cylinders allowed for each size of wale in the waler system tables, and in the vertical shore tables, the hydraulic cylinder horizontal spacing is the same as the vertical shore spacing.

. . . .

This is just the first part of one regulation that addresses safety issues regarding trenches. As you might imagine, the employer can't review this language before every job, and so OSHA prepares guidance memoranda that summarize the requirements for ease of compliance. While seemingly complex, dense, and boring, we will focus on the human dimension behind such regulatory detail.

1. OSHA Enforcement and the Fourth Amendment

Our first topic is the ability of OSHA to police workplaces to ensure that employers are adhering to health and safety standards. The primary purpose of the OSHAct is to prevent injury and death, not to provide a response to those that occur. OSHA must adhere to the Fourth Amendment, which protects citizens from unreasonable search and seizure. The warrant requirements of the OSHAct were reviewed by the United States Supreme Court only eight years after its enactment. Note the facts which gave rise to the case. A small business owner in Idaho, as opposed to a large national corporation, brought the challenge that ended up before the Supreme Court. As you read the case, consider whether the appropriate balance was struck between OSHA's mandate to reduce injury and death (there were 14,000 workplace fatalities per year when the OSHAct was passed) and the Constitutional rights of business owners to be free from unreasonable intrusion.

Marshall v. Barlow's, Inc.

436 U.S. 307 (1978).

Mr. Justice White delivered the opinion of the Court.

Section 8(a) of the Occupational Safety and Health Act of 1970 (OSHA or Act) empowers agents of the Secretary of Labor (Secretary) to search the work area of any employment facility within the Act's jurisdiction. The purpose of the search is to inspect for safety hazards and violations of OSHA regulations. No search warrant or other process is expressly required under the Act.

On the morning of September 11, 1975, an OSHA inspector entered the customer service area of Barlow's, Inc., an electrical and plumbing installation business located in Pocatello, Idaho. The president and general manager, Ferrol G. "Bill" Barlow, was on hand; and the OSHA inspector, after showing his credentials, informed Mr. Barlow that he wished to conduct a search of the working areas of the business. Mr. Barlow inquired whether any complaint had been received about his company. The inspector answered no, but that Barlow's Inc., had simply turned up in the agency's selection process. The inspector again asked to enter the nonpublic area of the business; Mr. Barlow's response was to inquire whether the inspector had a search warrant. The inspector had none. Thereupon, Mr. Barlow refused the inspector admission to the employee area of his business. He said he was relying on his rights as guaranteed by the Fourth Amendment of the United States Constitution.

. . . .

I

The Secretary urges that warrantless inspections to enforce OSHA are reasonable within the meaning of the Fourth Amendment. Among other things, he relies on § 8(a) of the Act, 29 U.S.C. § 657(a), which authorizes inspection of business premises without a warrant and which the Secretary urges represents a congressional construction of the Fourth Amendment that the courts should not reject. Regrettably, we are unable to agree.

The Warrant Clause of the Fourth Amendment protects commercial buildings as well as private homes. To hold otherwise would belie the origin of that Amendment, and the American colonial experience. An important forerunner of the first 10 Amendments to the United States Constitution, the Virginia Bill of Rights, specifically opposed "general warrants, whereby an officer or messenger may be commanded to search suspected places without evidence of a fact committed." The general warrant was a recurring point of contention in the Colonies immediately preceding the Revolution. The particular offensiveness it engendered was acutely felt by the merchants and businessmen whose premises and products were inspected for compliance with the several parliamentary revenue measures that most irritated the colonists. "[T]he Fourth Amendment's commands grew in large measure out of the colonists' experience with the writs of assistance . . . [that] granted sweeping power to customs officials and other agents of the King to search at large for smuggled goods." *United States v. Chadwick*, 433 U.S. 1, 7–8,

97 S.Ct. 2476, 2481, 53 L.Ed.2d 538 (1977). See also *G. M. Leasing Corp. v. United States*, 429 U.S. 338, 355, 97 S.Ct. 619, 630, 50 L.Ed.2d 530 (1977). Against this background, it is untenable that the ban on warrantless searches was not intended to shield places of business as well as of residence.

This Court has already held that warrantless searches are generally unreasonable, and that this rule applies to commercial premises as well as homes. . . .

The critical fact in this case is that entry over Mr. Barlow's objection is being sought by a Government agent. Employees are not being prohibited from reporting OSHA violations. What they observe in their daily functions is undoubtedly beyond the employer's reasonable expectation of privacy. The Government inspector, however, is not an employee. Without a warrant he stands in no better position than a member of the public. What is observable by the public is observable, without a warrant, by the Government inspector as well. The owner of a business has not, by the necessary utilization of employees in his operation, thrown open the areas where employees alone are permitted to the warrantless scrutiny of Government agents. That an employee is free to report, and the Government is free to use, any evidence of noncompliance with OSHA that the employee observes furnishes no justification for federal agents to enter a place of business from which the public is restricted and to conduct their own warrantless search.

II

The Secretary nevertheless stoutly argues that the enforcement scheme of the Act requires warrantless searches, and that the restrictions on search discretion contained in the Act and its regulations already protect as much privacy as a warrant would. The Secretary thereby asserts the actual reasonableness of OSHA searches, whatever the general rule against warrantless searches might be. Because "reasonableness is still the ultimate standard," *Camara v. Municipal Court*, 387 U.S., at 539, 87 S.Ct., at 1736, the Secretary suggests that the Court decide whether a warrant is needed by arriving at a sensible balance between the administrative necessities of OSHA inspections and the incremental protection of privacy of business owners a warrant would afford. He suggests that only a decision exempting OSHA inspections from the Warrant Clause would give "full recognition to the competing public and private interests here at stake." *Ibid.*

The Secretary submits that warrantless inspections are essential to the proper enforcement of OSHA because they afford the opportunity to inspect without prior notice and hence to preserve the advantages of surprise. While the dangerous conditions outlawed by the Act include structural defects that cannot be quickly hidden or remedied, the Act also regulates a myriad of safety details that may be amenable to speedy alteration or disguise. The risk is that during the interval between an inspector's initial request to search a plant and his procuring a warrant following the owner's refusal of permission, violations of this latter type could be corrected and thus escape the inspector's notice. To the suggestion that warrants may be issued ex parte and executed without delay and without prior notice, thereby preserving the element of surprise, the Secretary expresses concern for the administrative strain that would be experienced by the inspection system, and by the courts, should ex parte warrants issued in advance become standard practice.

We are unconvinced, however, that requiring warrants to inspect will impose serious burdens on the inspection system or the courts, will prevent inspections necessary to enforce the statute, or will make them less effective. In the first place, the great majority of businessmen can be expected in normal course to consent to inspection without warrant; the Secretary has not brought to this Court's attention any widespread pattern of refusal. In those cases where an owner does insist on a warrant, the Secretary argues that inspection efficiency will be impeded by the advance notice and delay. The Act's penalty provisions for giving advance notice of a search, 29 U.S.C. § 666(f), and the Secretary's own regulations, 29 CFR § 1903.6 (1977), indicate that surprise searches are indeed contemplated. However, the Secretary has also promulgated a regulation providing that upon refusal to permit an inspector to enter the property or to complete his inspection, the inspector shall attempt to ascertain the reasons for the refusal and report to his superior, who shall "promptly take appropriate action, including compulsory process, if necessary." 29 CFR § 1903.4 (1977). The regulation represents a choice to proceed by process where entry is refused; and on the basis of evidence available from present practice, the Act's effectiveness has not been crippled by providing those owners who wish to refuse an initial requested entry with a time lapse while the inspector obtains the necessary process. Indeed, the kind of process sought in this case and apparently anticipated by the regulation provides notice to the business operator. If this safeguard endangers the efficient administration of OSHA, the Secretary should never have adopted it, particularly when the Act does not require it. Nor is it immediately apparent why the advantages of surprise would be lost if, after being refused entry, procedures were available for the Secretary to seek an ex parte warrant and to reappear at the premises without further notice to the establishment being inspected.

Whether the Secretary proceeds to secure a warrant or other process, with or without prior notice, his entitlement to inspect will not depend on his demonstrating probable cause to believe that conditions in violation of OSHA exist on the premises. Probable cause in the criminal law sense is not required. For purposes of an administrative search such as this, probable cause justifying the issuance of a warrant may be based not only on specific evidence of an existing violation but also on a showing that "reasonable legislative or administrative standards for conducting an . . . inspection are satisfied with respect to a particular [establishment]." *Camara v. Municipal Court*, 387 U.S., at 538, 87 S.Ct., at 1736. A warrant showing that a specific business has been chosen for an OSHA search on the basis of a general administrative plan for the enforcement of the Act derived from neutral sources such as, for example, dispersion of employees in various types of industries across a given area, and the desired frequency of searches in any of the lesser divisions of the area, would protect an employer's Fourth Amendment rights. We doubt that the consumption of enforcement energies in the obtaining of such warrants will exceed manageable proportions.

. . . .

III

We hold that Barlow's was entitled to a declaratory judgment that the Act is unconstitutional insofar as it purports to authorize inspections without warrant or its equivalent and to an injunction enjoining the Act's enforcement to that extent. The judgment of the District Court is therefore affirmed.

So ordered.

It is important to grasp the distinction between a criminal warrant and an administrative one. Recall that for a period of time after OSHA was enacted, an OSHA inspector, consistent with the language of the Act, could drop into a business location without a warrant and inspect the location for a possible OSHA violation. In 1967, the United States Supreme Court held in two cases that non-criminal regulatory inspections could not be conducted without a warrant being issued by a federal court. These holdings were applied in the OSHA context in Barlow. How are theses administrative warrants different from a criminal warrant? Well, both can be issued on a showing of probable cause; namely, that there is specific evidence of a crime or an OSHA violation occurring. But an OSHA warrant can also be issued on a lesser showing that the agency had a reasonable standard for selecting a location to be inspected; in other words, that OSHA is inspecting certain types of industries because of a high injury rate, and the companies are in that industry. The overriding concept is that there is some restraint on OSHA, and that the inspection is asked for based on a principled rationale. Two other distinctions: for an administrative warrant, an employer must raise a challenge before the Commission and can then appeal to a federal court of appeals. For a criminal warrant, a defendant can file a motion in district court attaching the basis of the warrant and ask that the evidence gathered be suppressed. Finally, the manner of execution of the warrant is different. For OSHA, if the employer refuses entry the normal course is for OSHA to initiate contempt proceedings against the employer. As the colorful Judge Posner described the difference: "(An administrative warrant differs from a criminal warrant because) with an honest-to-goodness criminal search warrant (the government will get) hold of a sledgehammer. . .and break down the door. . . Although moviegoers who remember the environmental police in the movie Ghostbusters will be surprised, the practice of allowing the target of an administrative warrant to forbid entry and thereby convert the warrant proceeding into a contempt proceeding is the standard method of enforcing (administrative) warrants." *In re Establishment Inspection of Skil Corp.*, 846 F.2d 1127, 1132 (7th Cir. 1988).

QUESTION

1. Rather than thinking about the facts and law when reading a Supreme Court case, it is often more productive and illuminating to ask: what problem was the Court trying to solve? Cases reach the Supreme Court not because that particular dispute needs to be resolved, but rather because a systemic problem requires an overarching answer. Considered in this way, how would you describe the problem addressed by the Court, its overarching answer, and the justification for that answer?

Problem 28-1

You are counsel to a manufacturing company. At 9:00 a.m., the President of the company calls you and says that an OSHA inspector has requested access to the entire workplace to determine if the company is in compliance. How do you advise your client? What additional information do you need to know?

---

2. Federal Preemption of State Law

Our second topic is the relationship between OSHA regulations and state safety regulations. The OSHAct permits states to enact their own safety and health standards governing the workplace, provided that the state first obtains OSHA's approval. States that establish their own safety regulations are known as "state-plan states." If there is an overlap between the subject matter of state regulation and federal regulation, the state rules must at least be as stringent as the corresponding federal provisions. If there is no corresponding federal provision, then a state is free to enact its own requirements in that federally unregulated area. Put simply, OSHA regulations establish a "floor" but not the "ceiling" for safety regulations.

The interplay of federal and state authority beyond safety regulations is determined by preemption analysis. The question is whether the OSHAct preempts or displaces general state laws, such as criminal negligence or whistleblower protections, when the issue generally falls within the scope of the OSHAct.

The following case adopts the majority view that the OSHAct does not preempt state laws that address criminally negligent homicide. As you read this case, consider the purposes for enacting the OSHAct and the purposes supporting state statutes that criminalize negligence leading to death.

Sabine Consolidated, Inc. v. Texas

806 S.W.2d 553 (Tex. Crim. App. 1991).

Baird, Judge.

The issue we consider in this case is whether the Occupational Safety and Health Act of 1970 (OSHA or the Act) (29 U.S.C. § 651 et seq. 1982), preempts Texas from prosecuting appellants for criminally negligent homicide under Tex. Penal Code Ann. § 19.07.

Appellant Tantillo was the president of appellant Sabine Consolidated, Inc. (Sabine). Both appellants pled nolo contendere to the offense of criminally negligent homicide. Sabine was fined $10,000.00, and Tantillo was sentenced to confinement for 180 days, probated for one year, and fined $2,000.00. The charges arose from an excavation trench cave-in on September 10, 1985, in which two employees of Sabine were killed when the walls of the trench collapsed, burying them.

The Court of Appeals reversed the convictions and ordered acquittals. The Court of Appeals held that the OSHA provisions reflect implied intent by Congress to usurp the entire field of occupational safety such that criminal prosecution, based upon the violation of state or local standards for working conditions, invades that area of occupational safety preempted by OSHA. We granted the State's petition for discretionary review to address the preemption issue.

. . . .

The informations alleged, in pertinent part, that appellants were criminally negligent by:

> fail[ing] to furnish and maintain a place of employment which was reasonably safe and healthful for the said [deceased], an employee of the said [appellant], and the said [appellant] did then and there fail to install and maintain and use such methods and processes and devices and safeguards as were reasonably necessary to protect the life and health and safety of the said [deceased], by then and there failing to provide an adequate shoring system for the wall of an excavation and by then and there failing to properly slope the wall of an excavation, thereby causing the wall of the said excavation to collapse, which caused the death of the said [deceased], when the said [appellant] had a duty to furnish and maintain a place of employment which was reasonably safe and healthful for the said [deceased] and the said [appellant] had a duty to install and maintain and use such methods and processes and devices and safeguards as were reasonably necessary to protect the life and health and safety of the said [deceased].

OSHA

The purpose and policy of OSHA is "to assure so far as possible every working man and woman in the nation safe and healthful working conditions and to preserve our human resources" 29 U.S.C. § 651(b). To further that purpose Congress authorized the creation of occupational safety and health standards and regulations for "businesses affecting interstate commerce," 29 U.S.C. § 651(b)(3), and enacted a general duty provision for such employers. 29 U.S.C. § 654.

The Act also provides for civil and criminal penalties for violations of the general duty provision or any standard, rule, order, or regulation promulgated pursuant to the Act. 29 U.S.C. § 666. Under this section the following penalties may be assessed: for a "willful or repeated violation" of specific OSHA standards or the general duty provision, a civil penalty of not more than $10,000.00 may be assessed for each violation; for a "serious violation", meaning there is a substantial probability that death or serious physical harm could result from a condition that exists or from practices or methods in place, a civil penalty of not more than $1,000.00 shall be assessed; for a violation determined not to be serious, a civil penalty of up to $1,000.00 may be assessed; for failure to correct a cited violation, a civil penalty of up to $1,000.00 a day until corrected; for a "willful violation" of OSHA standards which cause death, a criminal penalty of imprisonment for not more than 6 months and/or a fine of not more than $10,000.00 may be assessed; slightly stiffer penalties for one previously convicted of such violation(s); and finally, criminal penalties ranging from imprisonment for 6 months and a fine of between $1,000.00 and $10,000.00 may be assessed for giving advance notice of inspection or making false statements for information required under the Act.

Despite the availability of these penalties OSHA is primarily prophylactic in nature. *Whirlpool Corp. v. Marshall*, 445 U.S. 1, 12, 100 S.Ct. 883, 890, 63 L.Ed.2d 154, 164 (1980). The Act seeks to establish standards and regulations to prevent death or injury from occurring in the workplace.

PREEMPTION

The doctrine of preemption is based upon the supremacy clause of the United States Constitution, Article VI, cl. 2, which invalidates state laws that "interfere with, or are contrary to," federal law. *Gibbons v. Ogden*, 9 Wheat. 1, 211, 6 L.Ed. 23, 73 (1824). Federal law may supersede state law in three ways. First, Congress can expressly state that the particular federal law preempts state law. *Jones v. Rath Packing Co.*, 430 U.S. 519, 525, 97 S.Ct. 1305, 1309, 51 L.Ed.2d 604, 614 (1977). Second, Congressional intent to preempt can be implied from the scheme of federal regulation which is sufficiently comprehensive to make a reasonable inference that Congress left no room for the states to supplement it. *Rice v. Santa Fe Elevator Corp.*, 331

U.S. 218, 230, 67 S.Ct. 1146, 1152, 91 L.Ed. 1447, 1459 (1947). Implied intent can also be found where the federal interest in the field is so strong that it precludes state laws on the same subject. Third, federal law preempts state law when the state law conflicts with the federal law. This conflict occurs when compliance with federal and state laws is, in effect, a physical impossibility, *Florida Lime & Avocado Growers, Inc. v. Paul*, 373 U.S. 132, 142–143, 83 S.Ct. 1210, 1217–1218, 10 L.Ed.2d 248, 256–257 (1963), or when the state law is "an obstacle to the accomplishment and execution of the full purposes and objectives of Congress." *Hines v. Davidowitz*, 312 U.S. 52, 67, 61 S.Ct. 399, 404, 85 L.Ed. 581, 587 (1941).

OSHA permits states to preempt federal standards of occupational safety and health by adopting their own such standards and plan for enforcement, which must be approved by the Secretary of Labor. 29 U.S.C. § 667. The Act also specifies that states may assert "jurisdiction under State law over any occupational safety or health issue with respect to which no standard is in effect under section 6 [29 USC § 655]." 29 U.S.C. § 667(a). Finally, § 653(b)(4) states:

Nothing in this Act shall be construed to supersede or in any manner affect any workmen's compensation law or to enlarge or diminish or affect in any other manner the common law or statutory rights, duties, or liabilities of employers and employees under any law with respect to injuries, diseases, or death of employees arising out of, or in the course of, employment.

EXPRESS PREEMPTION

We will first address the express preemption issue.

Section 667 states, in part:

> Nothing in this Act shall prevent any State agency or court from asserting jurisdiction under State law over any occupational safety or health issue with respect to which no standard is in effect under section 6 [29 USC § 655].
>
> Any State which, at any time, desires to assume responsibility for development and enforcement therein of occupational safety and health standards relating to any occupational safety or health issue with respect to which a Federal standard has been promulgated under section 6 [29 USC § 655] shall submit a State plan for the development of such standards and their enforcement.

Under this section Congress clearly preempted state occupational safety and health laws and standards for "businesses affecting interstate commerce" unless the State takes steps to establish its own program in accord with OSHA requirements for substituting state standards. However, we do not believe that Congress intended that state criminal laws which affect or involve occupational safety and health be preempted. See and cf. *New York Dep't. of Social Services v. Dublino*, 413 U.S. 405, 415, 93 S.Ct. 2507, 2514, 37 L.Ed.2d 688, 696 (1973). There is no express language to that effect and other provisions indicate no such intent.

. . . .

In *People v. Chicago Magnet Wire Corp.*, 534 N.E.2d 962, cert. denied sub nom. *Asta v. Illinois*, 493 U.S. 809, 110 S.Ct. 52, 107 L.Ed.2d 21 (1989), the Illinois Supreme Court reversed an appellate court decision which had found state criminal law preempted by OSHA. In disposing of a claim of express preemption on the grounds that state criminal laws implicitly enforced occupational health and safety standards, the Court stated:

> Although the imposition of sanctions under State penal law may effect a regulation of behavior as OSHA safety standards do, regulation through deterrence, however, is not the sole purpose of criminal law. For example, it also serves to punish as a matter of retributive justice. Too, whereas OSHA standards apply only to specific hazards in the workplace, criminal law reaches to regulate conduct in society in general. In contrast, occupational health and safety standards are promulgated under OSHA primarily as a means of regulating conduct to prevent injuries in the workplace. *Id.* 128 Ill.Dec. at 521, 534 N.E.2d at 966. See also *People v. Hegedus*, 432 Mich. 598, 443 N.W.2d 127 (1989).

Nowhere in the Act is there language stating that Congress preempted any other laws or *all laws affecting* workplace safety and health. Section 653(b)(4) indicates the opposite as it specifically and broadly allows and does not "in any manner affect workmen's compensation law or . . . the common law or statutory rights, duties, or liabilities of employers and employees *under any law* with respect to injuries, diseases, or death of employees arising out of, or in the course of, employment." (Emphasis added).

. . . .

> The purpose of state criminal laws and criminally negligent homicide in particular, is not to set standards for workplace safety. The purpose is to punish one for an illegal act as defined [by Texas law] . . . .

So, what were the consequences of courts rejecting the preemption defense? The results were an increase in state criminal prosecutions and little activity by the United States Department of Justice in criminal prosecutions. Why? For there to be a criminal prosecution in federal court for an OSHA violation, the violation must be willful, a worker fatality must have occurred, and the violator must be an employer (which can include an individual, such as an officer or director of an entity). And, the consequences are minimal: a willful violation causing a worker's death is punishable by a fine of $250,000 for an individual defendant and up to 6 months incarceration and $500,000 for an entity. The numbers tell the story: on average 4,500 workers die on the job each year, but from 2006 to 2017 there were 78 referrals from OSHA to the Department of Justice for criminal prosecutions. According to the AFL-CIO only 110,000 months of jail time were served. In December 2015, "The Yates Memo" was issued by the Department of Justice to expand its role in criminal prosecutions and to assist local prosecutors in concurrent investigations. This effort started to take off but floundered with the changing of Administrations in 2018. By contrast, as we will see in the following material, state law prosecution for state law crimes, such as the involuntary manslaughter or reckless homicide, are made by local authorities. In light of criminal exposure for a client, an employment lawyer, pursuant to the ethical duty of competence, must ensure that lawyers with criminal law expertise are brought in to assist in representation. Moreover, the employment lawyers should have a high level of awareness that anything used in an OSHA defense can and will likely be used in a subsequent criminal investigation or indictment. Finally, employment lawyers should instruct their client, should there be any possible OSHA violation, but especially one involving serious injury or death, to preserve all evidence. If not, there can be prosecution for destruction of evidence.

*interplay of OSHA & state crim law

Eric J. Conn and Kate M. McMahon, *OSHA Criminal Cases on the Rise*

The OSHA Defense Report, OSHA Updates from Conn Maciel Carey's OSHA Practice Group (January 22, 2016).

In the forty plus years since Congress enacted the OSH Act, there have been more than 400,000 workplace fatalities, yet fewer than eighty total OSH Act criminal cases have been prosecuted—fewer than two per year—and only approximately a dozen have resulted in criminal convictions. Historically, the prosecutions typically have targeted cases in which the employers were alleged to have falsified documents and lied to OSHA in conjunction with underlying regulatory violations relating to an employee fatality. In other words, the "cover-up," so to speak, was worse than the crime. Chronic violators and employers who demonstrated a systematic rejection of worker safety laws also were more likely to face charges.

One primary reason that historically so few criminal cases have been pursued under the Occupational Safety and Health Act ("OSH Act") [citation omitted] is that it is challenging to prove a criminal violation under the Act. Combine that with the fact that, even with a conviction, the consequences are less significant than the consequences for many other white collar crimes and you end [up] with a situation where the criminal provision of the OSH Act is rarely employed.

Here is how it works. Section 17(e) states:

> Any employer who willfully violates any standard, rule, or order promulgated pursuant to Section 6 of this Act, or of any regulations proscribed pursuant to this Act, and that violation caused death to any employee, shall, upon conviction, be punished by a fine of not more than $10,000 or by imprisonment for not more than six months, or by both.

Pursuant to the Sentencing Reform Act of 1984, 18 U.S.C. § 3551 *et seq.*, [citation omitted] which standardized penalties and sentences for federal offenses, the criminal penalty for willful violations of the OSH Act causing loss of human life was amended to be punishable by fines up to $250,000 for individuals (18 U.S.C. Sec. 3574(b)(4)), and $500,000 for organizations (*id.* at Sec. 574(c)(4)).

Accordingly, if an employer's willful violation of an OSHA standard causes the death of an employee, Section 17(e) [citation omitted] of the OSH Act is implicated. However, violation of this provision is not a felony, but rather a "Class B" misdemeanor. And although Section 17(e) carries with it the possibility of a prison term, in practice, prison occurs only in the rare circumstances where a senior management official operates *de facto* as the company. Otherwise, practically, only criminal monetary fines are available for Section 17(e) criminal violations.

To obtain a conviction under Section 17(e), a prosecutor must establish *beyond a reasonable doubt* (unlike the lower civil standard for ordinary OSHA enforcement actions) that:

1. An OSHA regulatory standard was violated;
    a. A violation of OSHA's "General Duty Clause" (Sec. 5(a)(1)) may not serve as the basis for an OSH Act criminal charge.
2. The violation was committed [citation omitted] by the employer;
    a. Courts evaluating OSH Act criminal prosecutions distinguish between "employees" and "employers." Only in extremely rare circumstances are individuals considered to exert so much control over a corporate entity that the individual would be considered, for all intents and purposes, to be "the employer" for purposes of an OSH Act criminal charge. Although a corporate officer or director might in some circumstances be deemed to be the "employer." This is only in the case where "an officer's or director's role in a corporate entity (particularly a small one) may be so pervasive and total that the officer or director is in fact the corporation and is therefore an employer under § 666(e)." *U.S. v. Cusak*, 806 F. Supp. 47, 50 (D.N.J. 1992).
3. The violation of the standard was the direct cause of an employee's death;
    a. Prosecutors must prove beyond a reasonable doubt that the conduct which amounts to the violation of

an OSHA standard was both the "cause in fact" (i.e., the employer's conduct was the "but-for cause" of the accident) and the "legal cause" (the harm was a foreseeable and natural result of the conduct) of the injury.

4. The violation was committed [citation omitted] willfully by the employer.

   a. Courts are in substantial agreement that "willfully" under Section 17(e) refers to a deliberate action taken by the employer with knowledge of both the hazardous condition and the OSH Act's requirements (i.e., the employer knew the conduct was dangerous and unlawful).

. . . .

In addition to willful OSHA violations that caused an employee fatality, employers (and employees) can face criminal sanctions in the following circumstances:

1. **Falsifying OSHA documents.** Section 17(g) of the OSH Act provides for a criminal charge against anyone (not just employers) who 'knowingly makes any false statement, representation, or certification in any application, record, report, plan, or other document filed or required to be maintained pursuant to this Act . . . ."

2. **Advance notice of an OSHA inspection.** Section 17(f) of the OSH Act makes it a criminal act for "[a]ny person to give advance notice of any inspection to be conducted under this Act, without authority from the Secretary or his designees . . . ." (This provision generally applies to OSHA officials.)

3. **Perjury during OSHA proceedings.** 18 U.S.C. § 1001 provides felony penalties for false statements made in connection with any matter within the jurisdiction of the U.S. government, including any person who knowingly: (a) falsifies or conceals material facts; (b) makes materially false statements; or (c) presents any false document.

4. **State Criminal laws.** The OSH Act does not preempt prosecution under state criminal laws, such as manslaughter or negligent homicide for work related deaths and injuries.

5. **Environmental Statutes.** In addition to the criminal sanctions provided for under Section 17 of the OSH Act, employers with catastrophic events that also impact the environment could be subject to prosecution under the criminal provisions of numerous environmental statutes, such as, for instance, the Clean Water Act; the Clean Air Act; the Resource Conservation and Recovery Act (RCRA); the Emergency Planning and Community Right-to-Know Act (ERCRA) or the Hazardous Materials Transportation Act (HMTA). These statutes typically include broader criminal provisions than the OSH Act.

. . . .

In fact, we understand from several representatives within OSHA and the Department of Labor Solicitor's office (OSHA's lawyers) that, as a matter of informal policy, OSHA now makes a criminal referral to the Department of Justice in every case involving an employee fatality and a willful violation. Regardless of whether there is truly a 100 percent referral rate, the past few years certainly have seen a rise in the instances of criminal investigations of workplace accidents being initiated by the Department of Justice, and criminal charges being brought and/or significant plea deals being negotiated. Indeed, FY 2014 saw a record number of criminal referrals and prosecutions under the OSH Act.

3. A Case Study in Criminal Charges for Employee Deaths

The following materials relate to the collapse of a trench in Boston that tragically resulted in the death of two workers. OSHA investigated and found that the employer had committed safety violations, but it did not press criminal charges. However, the Commonwealth chose to issue indictments for criminally negligent homicide.

We begin with the accident itself, which was captured by a Boston Herald photographer who happened to walk by in the chaotic aftermath of the trench collapse.

Mark Garfinkel, *My Photos & Thoughts on the Deadly Boston Trench Collapse*

Picture Boston, Oct. 26, 2016, http://www.pictureboston.com/blog/2016/10/26/my-photos-thoughts-of-deadly-boston-trench-collapse.

While on the 7th hour of my Friday shift as a Boston Herald staff news photographer, I was summoned to Beacon Hill for photo coverage of the Herald's Home of the Week. I started that way from Melnea Cass Boulevard, near Northeastern University. While driving on Tremont St., approaching the traffic lights at Dartmouth St., I noticed the leading edge of what appeared to look like an ocean tide encroaching on a beach. This torrent of water, rolling down Dartmouth St., was quite strong. There was no audio from my police/fire radios regarding an event/emergency of this type, but I stopped anyway thinking this was newsworthy and might make for interesting photos. I parked, still thinking that I was going to photograph a short-lived apparent water main break. It was then that I heard police sirens. I started to take photos, but when I came upon the scene something seemed different. A police sergeant told me to leave the street, and the faces of workers, neighbors, police, and shortly thereafter Boston firefighters, told a story of anguish and deep concern. It was shortly thereafter that I learned that one, and then another worker was presumed trapped. Steve Smith, a construction laborer working close by, and who was on a break when he heard screaming, sprung into action as he tried to reach the trapped workers. He tried to enter the hole but dangerous conditions forced him back. I retreated to the sidewalk and watched, then photographed, as he was reaching into the water to attempt to find the street plates covering part of the trench. On his hands and knees he finally found part of the heavy plates where a chain can be affixed, to then lift with a backhoe. Smith seemed to pause for a split second, as exhaustion and grief overwhelmed him. Boston firefighters used sticks with hooks on the end to try and hook the workers, but to no avail. A very sad day. My photos appeared on page one and inside the October 22, 2016 issue of the Boston Herald.

Resident
Permit
Parking
Only

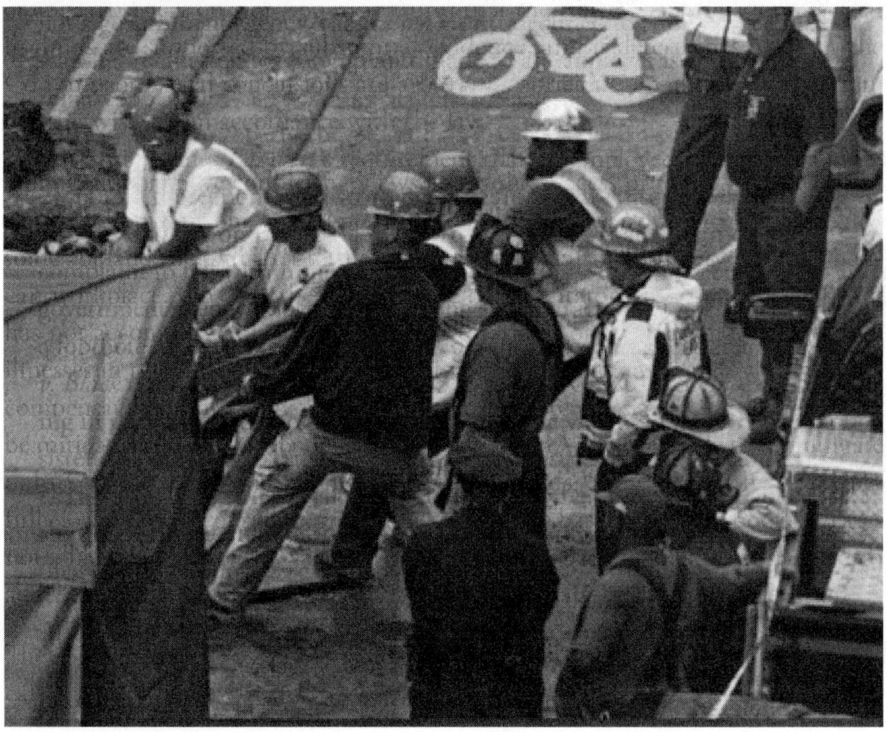

Mark Garfinkel, *My Photos & Thoughts on the Deadly Boston Trench Collapse*, Picture Boston, Oct. 26, 2016, http://www.pictureboston.com/blog/2016/10/26/my-photos-thoughts-of-deadly-boston-trench-collapse.

OSHA News Release - Region 1

U.S. Department of Labor

April 12, 2017 BOS 2017-028

Employer in fatal Boston trench collapse did not provide safety training and basic safeguards for employees, OSHA finds
Atlantic Drain Service Co. Inc. cited for 18 violations

BOSTON - Robert Higgins and Kelvin Mattocks died on Oct. 21, 2016, in Boston, when the approximately 12-foot deep trench in which they were working collapsed, breaking an adjacent fire hydrant supply line and filling the trench with water in a matter of seconds.

An investigation by the U.S. Department of Labor's Occupational Safety and Health Administration found that their employer, Atlantic Drain Service Co. Inc., failed to provide basic safeguards against collapse and did not train its employees - including Higgins and Mattocks - to recognize and avoid cave-in and other hazards.

"The deaths of these two men could have and should have been prevented. Their employer, which previously had been cited by OSHA for the same hazardous conditions, knew what safeguards were needed to protect its employees but chose to ignore that responsibility," said Galen Blanton, OSHA's New England regional administrator.

OSHA's inspection determined that Atlantic Drain and owner Kevin Otto, who oversaw the work on the day of the fatalities, did not:

- Install a support system to protect employees in an approximately 12-foot deep trench from a cave-in and prevent the adjacent fire hydrant from collapsing.
- Remove employees from the hazardous conditions in the trench.
- Train the workers in how to identify and address hazards associated with trenching and excavation work.
- Provide a ladder at all times so employees could exit the trench.
- Support structures next to the trench that posed overhead hazards.
- Provide employees with hardhats and eye protection.

As a result, OSHA has cited Atlantic Drain for a total of 18 willful, repeat, serious and other-than-serious violations of workplace safety standards and is proposing $1,475,813 in penalties for those violations. OSHA cited Atlantic Drain trenching worksites for similar hazards in 2007 and 2012. The full citations can be viewed here.

In February, a Suffolk County grand jury indicted Atlantic Drain and company owner, Kevin Otto, on two counts each of manslaughter and other charges in connection with the deaths. OSHA and the department's Regional Office of the Solicitor worked with the department's Office of the Inspector General, the Boston Police Department's Homicide Unit and the Suffolk County District Attorney's Office during the course of this investigation.

Atlantic Drain has 15 working days from receipt of the citations and proposed penalties to meet with OSHA's area director, and to contest the citations before the independent Occupational Safety and Health Review Commission, if it chooses to do so.

The walls of an unprotected trench can collapse suddenly and with great force, trapping and engulfing workers before they have a chance to react or escape. Protection against cave-in hazards may be provided through shoring of the trench walls, sloping the soil, or by using a protective trench box. Employers must ensure that workers enter trenches only after adequate protections are in place to address cave-in hazards. More information about protecting employees in trenches and excavations can be found here and here.

"We want to emphasize to all employers that trenching hazards can have catastrophic consequences if they are not addressed effectively before employees enter a trench," said Blanton.

To ask questions, obtain compliance assistance, file a complaint, or report amputations, eye loss, workplace hospitalizations, fatalities or situations posing imminent danger to workers, call OSHA's toll-free hotline at 800-321-OSHA (6742) or the nearest OSHA Area Office.

Under the Occupational Safety and Health Act of 1970, employers are responsible for providing safe and healthful working conditions for their employees. OSHA's role is to ensure these conditions for America's working men and women by setting and enforcing standards, and providing training, education and assistance. For more information, visit http://www.osha.gov.

###

Media Contacts:

Ted Fitzgerald, 617-565-2075, fitzgerald.edmund@dol.gov
James C. Lally, 617-565-2074, lally.james.c@dol.gov

Release Number: 17-413-BOS

SUFFOLK COUNTY
DISTRICT ATTORNEY
MASSACHUSETTS

DANIEL F. CONLEY

Trial Date Set for Business, Owner in Fatal Trench Collapse

BOSTON, Feb. 23, 2017—The individual and corporate defendants in the deaths of Robert Higgins and Kelvin Mattocks in a South End trench collapse were arraigned today and their trial has been scheduled for early next year, Suffolk County District Attorney Daniel F. Conley said.

The Boston-based ATLANTIC DRAIN SERVICES, INC., and its owner and sole officer, KEVIN OTTO (D.O.B. 3/17/74) of Blackstone, are scheduled for trial in Suffolk Superior Court on Feb. 5, 2018, on indictments charging them each with two counts of manslaughter, one count of misleading an investigator under the state's witness intimidation statute, and six counts of concealing a record under the evidence tampering statute. The Suffolk County Special Grand Jury returned the indictments Feb. 8 after an exhaustive probe by Suffolk prosecutors assisted by Boston Police homicide detectives and federal workplace safety investigators.

At arraignment today, Assistant District Attorney Lynn Feigenbaum of the DA's Senior Trial Unit recommended $1,000 bail for Otto, who walked into court, as well as an order that he surrender his passport. Suffolk Superior Court Clerk Magistrate Lisa Medeiros released Otto on his own recognizance but ordered him to surrender his passport and check in with probation officers once a week.

Feigenbaum told the court that Atlantic Drain Services had been hired last year to install new water and sewer lines at 12 Dartmouth St. On Oct. 21, after about five days of excavation, workers were inside the trench, which measured about five feet across by eight feet long by 12 feet deep, shoveling dirt and vacuuming it out, Feigenbaum said. Otto was present at the scene and maneuvering the vacuum truck.

"At no time during the excavation being done on Oct. 21, 2016, was any type of cave-in protection, either metal trench boxes or tongue-and-groove wooden planks, used in the trench," Feigenbaum told the court.

At about 12:30, she said, Higgins and Mattocks were working in the trench when dirt began to slough off the sides, burying the men up to their waists. At about this time, a fire hydrant at the side of the trench fell into the hole and water began to pour in. The trench was flooded within seconds and neither Higgins nor Mattocks was able to escape. Both died at the scene, and it would be almost six hours before their bodies could be recovered.

Prosecutors allege that Otto and Atlantic Drain Services were well aware of the extreme danger posed by a deep trench without cave-in protection because they had been cited twice by OSHA for failing to utilize them – first in 2007, when they were fined $15,000, and again in 2012, when they were fined $40,000. As a result, Atlantic Drain Services agreed to provide comprehensive training programs so workers understood the hazards to which they could be exposed while excavating.

In the course of the death investigation arising out of the Dartmouth Street fatalities, the Department of Labor's Occupational Safety and Health Administration and Conley's office served Atlantic Drain Services with subpoenas for certain records. In response, Atlantic Drain Services "submitted to OSHA various documents purporting to be sign-in sheets for excavating and trenching trainings, as well as documents regarding the receipt by workers of personal protective equipment," Feigenbaum said. But the individuals whose signatures appear on those documents told investigators that they did not sign them and did not authorize anyone else to sign them on their behalf.

Otto and Atlantic Drain Services allegedly misled OSHA investigators by providing those doctored records pursuant to the first subpoena, then concealed the records from the Suffolk County Grand Jury by failing to provide them pursuant to the second subpoena, prosecutors said.

Atlantic Drain Services, Inc., was represented today by attorney Camille Sarrouf, Jr., and Otto by attorney Maki Antzoulatos. The case returns to court on March 30.

QUESTIONS

1. Why would an employer fail to follow basic safety precautions that could avoid accidents like the one that occurred in Boston?
2. Explain why OSHA would choose not to file a criminal case, but the District Attorney would choose to indict? Is this case a good example of why the OSHAct should not preempt state criminal law, or is the case an example of conflicting signals that might make it more difficult for employers to understand their obligations and exposure to penalty?

---

4. OSHAct 11(c) and Retaliation

The anti-retaliation provision in the OSHAct is an odd hybrid. If an employee claims that she has suffered retaliation for asserting her rights under the OSHAct, the employee must file a complaint with OSHA within 30 days of suffering an adverse employment action. Only the Department of Labor is permitted to bring suit on behalf of an employee. Unlike other anti-retaliation statutes, the employee does not have a private right of action against the employer. On the other hand, because the OSHAct does not preempt state whistleblower statutes, employees may pursue such claims in their own name.

OSHAct

§ 11(c). Discrimination Against Employees

No person shall discharge or in any other manner discriminate against any employee because such employee has filed any complaint or instituted or caused to be instituted any proceeding under or related to this chapter or has testified or is about to testify in any such proceeding or because of the exercise by such employee on behalf of himself or others of any right afforded by this chapter. An employee who believes that he has been discharged or otherwise discriminated against by any person in violation of this subchapter may, within file a complaint within the 30 days after such violation occurs.

As with other anti-retaliation statutes we have studied, the employee needs to engage in protected activity. The activity may be written or oral, and it can consist of a direct protest regarding an occupational health or safety issue, or simply asking questions about health and safety matters, or even requesting copies of OSHA standards and regulations. The employee, in addition to asserting that he engaged in protected activity, must also allege that he suffered an unfavorable employment action as a result. That action can range from termination, to demotion, to a loss in compensation, to reassignment of job duties. The statute provides that the Secretary will report back to the employee within 90 days. There is no private right of action for retaliation; only the Secretary of Labor can bring a claim. These limitations have important consequences.

In Fiscal Year 2015, there were 6,297 complaints filed, a substantial increase from the 3,561 complaints filed in FY 2011. Two thirds of the complaints were screened out for failing to meet the time deadline or for failing to allege a protected activity. Of the 1,981 remaining complaints, 49% were dismissed, 23% were withdrawn, and only 27% settled in some manner. A mere 1% (17 complaints) were referred to the Solicitor of Labor for the filing of a civil suit. In all of FY 2015, total damages collected were $4,253,587 (with an average damage per case settled of $7,877 with only 42 cased settled with job reinstatement amounting to 7%).

QUESTIONS

1. What are the most important words used in 11(c)? Why are they key? Consider what other words could have been used by Congress and why those words were not chosen?
2. What conclusions do you draw from the above numbers? While the number of complaints filed in FY 2015 is an increase, the filings have not increased dramatically from an absolute standpoint. Why? If your client missed the limitations deadline, what other options are open to them?
3. A prospective client comes to see you and wants to file a claim for complaining and then being re-assigned to a less desirable shift? What do you tell her?
4. Why would Congress (as we will see below) not allow a private cause of action?
5. Do you believe corporations take into account how 11(c) operates in reality in making employment-related decisions?

Given the procedural limitations of 11(c) and the lack of a private right of action, employees may seek to recover under state law for retaliation. This again raises the question of preemption.

Schweiss v. Chrysler Motors Corp.

922 F.2d 473 (8th Cir. 1990).

Bowman, Circuit Judge.

Ann Schweiss appeals from the order of the District Court dismissing her wrongful discharge suit against Chrysler Motors Corporation. We reverse and remand.

I.

Schweiss was employed by Chrysler Motors Corporation ("Chrysler") from January 1984 to February 1989. Shortly before her discharge, Schweiss contacted the Occupational Safety and Health Administration about alleged violations of law occurring at the assembly plant where she worked. On February 8, 1989, Chrysler fired Schweiss, allegedly for excessive absenteeism. On April 13, 1989, Schweiss filed suit in Missouri state court against Chrysler and her immediate supervisor Perry Sigwerth, alleging that she had been wrongfully discharged for being a "whistle blower," a discharge that under Missouri law is an actionable tort. Chrysler and Sigwerth removed the suit to federal court on the grounds that the claim presented a question of federal law, and that Sigwerth fraudulently had been joined to defeat diversity jurisdiction.

Schweiss moved to remand the case to state court, while Sigwerth filed a motion to dismiss and Chrysler filed a motion for summary judgment, claiming that Schweiss's state law wrongful discharge action is pre-empted under both section 11(c) of the Occupational Safety and Health Act of 1970 ("OSHA"), 29 U.S.C. § 660(c) (1988), and section 301 of the Labor-Management Relations Act of 1947 ("LMRA"), 29 U.S.C. § 185 (1988). The District Court denied Schweiss's motion, granted Sigwerth's motion, and denied Chrysler's motion as moot. The District Court held that Schweiss's state law wrongful discharge claim is pre-empted by section 11(c) of OSHA, and dismissed the case with prejudice. The court did not decide the section 301 pre-emption issue.

On appeal, Schweiss claims the District Court erred in ruling that her wrongful discharge claim against Chrysler is pre-empted by section 11(c) of OSHA. She concedes that on remand it would be necessary for the District Court to address the question of pre-emption under section 301.

II.

Although Missouri is an at-will employment state, *Dake v. Tuell*, 687 S.W.2d 191, 192–93 (Mo.1985) (en banc), it does recognize a public policy exception to this rule. "[W]here an employer has discharged an at-will employee because that employee refused to violate the law or . . . because the employee reported . . . to public authorities serious misconduct that constitutes violations of the law . . . the employee has a cause of action in tort for damages for wrongful discharge." *Boyle v. Vista Eyewear, Inc.*, 700 S.W.2d 859, 878 (Mo.Ct.App.1985); see also *Loomstein v. Medicare Pharmacies, Inc.*, 750 S.W.2d 106, 112 (Mo.Ct.App.1988).

In her complaint, Schweiss alleges that she was discharged by Chrysler for reporting violations of federal law occurring at her place of employment to the Occupational Safety Health Administration. Joint Appendix at 8–9. She thus has alleged a cognizable claim based on Missouri law. The issue before us is whether this state law claim is pre-empted by federal law.

Pre-emption can occur in one of three ways: (1) federal law can expressly pre-empt state law; (2) federal law can occupy a field of law so completely that pre-emption may be inferred; or (3) federal law can conflict with state law, thereby pre-empting it. *English v. General Elec. Co.*, 496 U.S. 72, 110 S.Ct. 2270, 2275, 110 L.Ed.2d 65 (1990). The District Court did not hold that the OSHA legislation expressly pre-empts state law. Similarly, there is no claim that Congress intended to occupy this field of law in such a manner that pre-emption can be inferred. To the contrary, 29 U.S.C. § 667(a) expressly allows for state regulation in the occupational safety field of law. The District Court did hold, however, that "the ability of plaintiffs to pursue retaliatory discharge claims where available under state law [would] frustrate[ ] the remedial scheme provided for in [29 U.S.C.] § 660," *Schweiss v. Chrysler*, No. 89–943C (1), slip op. at 5 (E.D.Mo. Sept. 11, 1989), and thus such state law claims are pre-empted.

The decision of the District Court was issued on September 11, 1989. On June 4, 1990, the Supreme Court issued its ruling in *English v. General Electric*. That opinion dealt with the question of whether a state law tort claim is pre-empted by § 210 of the Energy Reorganization Act of 1974, 42 U.S.C. § 5851(a) (1988). . . .

The Court noted that "[o]rdinarily, the mere existence of a federal regulatory or enforcement scheme, even one as detailed as [42 U.S.C. § 5851], does not by itself imply pre-emption of state remedies." *English*, 110 S.Ct. at 2279. The Court held that the fact that the federal statute did not allow exemplary damages, while the state action did, was not sufficient to find pre-emption. "Absent some specific suggestion in the text or legislative history of [42 U.S.C. § 5851] . . . we cannot conclude that Congress intended to pre-empt all state actions that permit the recovery of exemplary damages." *English*, 110 S.Ct. at 2280.

Nor did the Court find convincing the argument that the "expeditious time frames provided by Congress for the processing of . . . claims" showed a conflict between the statute and the state action. *English*, 110 S.Ct. at 2280. The claim was made in *English* that "if a state-law remedy is available after the time for filing a [42 U.S.C. § 5851] claim has run," there will be less incentive to utilize the federal scheme. *English*, 110 S.Ct. at 2281. The Court rejected this argument, saying that they "do not believe that the problem is as great as respondent suggests." *Id.* "[W]e are not so sure as respondent seems to be that employees will forgo their [42 U.S.C. § 5851] options and rely solely on state remedies for retaliation. Such a prospect is simply too speculative a basis on which to rest a finding of pre-emption." *English*, 110 S.Ct. at 2281. The Court reiterated its rule that "pre-emption is ordinarily not to be implied absent an 'actual conflict.' " *Id.* (citation omitted). . . .

Applying the principles of English to this statute, we hold that its remedial scheme does not pre-empt Schweiss's state law wrongful discharge action. The District Court found that the action was pre-empted for two reasons. First, the court held that the congressional intent to have retaliatory discharge complaints administratively screened before proceeding in federal court would be frustrated by allowing state wrongful discharge actions. Second, the court held that the goal of involving the Secretary in the resultant lawsuit would be impeded. However, there is no evidence that "employees will forgo their [statutory] options and rely solely on state remedies for retaliation." *English*, 110 S.Ct. at 2281. Thus, the rationale relied upon by the District Court is "too speculative a basis on which to rest a finding of pre-emption." *Id.* . . .

As this case is indistinguishable from English in any material way, the decision of the District Court that Schweiss's claim is pre-empted by OSHA must be reversed.

. . . .

Mastery Problem 28-1

This problem requires you to use information from Lesson 27.

An OSHA assistant regional manager and her new spouse check into the honeymoon suite of XYZ Hotel. As she opens the drapes, she looks out at a building under construction across the street. She sees that two employees are working at a height of 90 feet without adequate safety cables. She calls the local OSHA office and speaks to an inspector, fills him in on what she has seen, and directs him to look into a possible violation. The investigator goes to the hotel manager and obtains permission to access the hotel roof. Once on the roof, the inspector videotapes the workers through a power camera lens for 50 minutes. The inspector then goes to the site, presents his credentials, and is allowed to interview the two workers, Smith and Jones. Smith is the leadsman (akin to a supervisor) and he admits to the inspector that he knew safety cables were required, but that the company did not have a sufficient number to cover the entire site. The inspector issues citations for safety violations. Should they be upheld?

Mastery Problem 28-2

Review the following language from an OSHA warrant. Are the paragraphs consistent with *Balow*?

(1) The desired inspection is part of an inspection and investigation program designed to assure compliance with OSHA in the steel fabrication industry. It is authorized by Section 8(a) of the Act.

(2) The desired inspection is also in response to an employee complaint that employees are required to climb on various products and crates, as high as possible, in order to perform various tasks in association with

their jobs. If true, employees are in danger of injury by falling because of this ad hoc method.

(3) Proper entry pursuant to section 8(a)(1) of the Act for the aforesaid purposes was attempted by duly authorized compliance officers of the Occupational Health Administration on XYZ date during a National-Local plan designed to achieve significant reduction in the high incidence of occupational injuries and illnesses found in the steel fabrication industry, but the right of entry was denied by the employer.

(4) There have been four prior inspections of the employer's workplace, each resulting in OSHA compliance officers response to employee complaints. In each case, the responding OSHA compliance officer(s) have found and cited the employer for alleged violations of the Act as a result of the inspections.

(5) You are authorized to enter into the premises during regular working hours or at other reasonable times, and to inspect and investigate, in a reasonable manner and to a reasonable extent (including but not limited to the taking of photographs and samples and the private questioning of any owner, operator, agent, employer of employee of the establishment), the workplace of the environment where work is performed by employees of the employer and all pertinent conditions, structures, machines (including records, files and papers) bearing on whether this employer is furnishing to its employees employment and a place of employment which are free from recognized hazards that are causing or likely to cause death or serious physical injuries to its employees, and whether this employer is complying with the occupational safety and health standards promulgated under the Act and the rules, regulations, and orders issued pursuant to the Act.

Conclusion

While OSHA deals with worker safety, its reach is much greater. The employment lawyer needs to understand OSHA's implication for possible criminal violations as well as civil lawsuits for employee injury or death. And while workers' compensation insurance, as we have discussed, almost always provides a defense to such civil suits, in certain instances a grossly negligent employer may be subject to direct suits for damages. Moreover, we see with OSHA what we have seen in other contexts, namely the interplay between state and federal laws. Thus, the wise employment lawyer will understand how OSHA impacts a possible whistleblower claim.

C. Benefits

Key Concepts

- In addition to compensation, employees often receive valuable benefits from their employer.
- We will learn about the protections offered to employees by the Employment Retirement Income Security Act (ERISA) with regard to pension and welfare benefit plans.
- Additionally, we will study the Family Medical Leave Act (FMLA) which ensures that employees cannot be summarily fired for attending to certain family needs.

Lesson 29:
Employee Retirement Income Security Act (ERISA)

Objectives and Expected Learning Outcomes

In this Lesson, you will develop a fundamental understanding of ERISA's protection of pensions and welfare benefits. We will focus on the standard of review for denial of benefits. Additionally, we will study the preemptive effect that ERISA has on state employment laws. ERISA will preempt—that is, displace—state law that may encroach on ERISA's purview. Finally, we will analyze ERISA's anti-retaliation provision and compare it with other anti-retaliation statutes that we have studied.

1. The Scope of ERISA Protections

All too often, employees would work for a firm for many years, only to find that the pension promised to them evaporated when the firm experienced financial distress. In the 1960s, numerous pension funds went bankrupt, leaving employees with little retirement savings. Typical "defined benefit" pension plans accepted payments from the employee, and sometimes the employer too, and managed these assets to build a fund for the employee's retirement. The plan had to be managed so that investments with current dollars would be able to pay promised pension benefits in the future. However, mismanagement was rampant. The famous bankruptcy of the Studebaker Car Company left thousands of employees without any retirement savings.

The Employee Retirement Security Act (ERISA) was enacted in 1974 in response to the massive number of pension funds that failed or were underfunded. ERISA first established strict vesting requirements to prevent the inequity of an employee working for years, only to lose the promised benefits under a pension plan because her employment was terminated. ERISA also imposed fiduciary duties on pension plan administrators to ensure the fiscal solvency of the plan. This was accomplished by imposing uniform national standards on the management of pension plans. Of particular importance was the imposition of a fiduciary duty upon plan administrators. The concept of a fiduciary duty was derived from trust law, which requires a person charged with administrating a trust to do so with prudence and absolute loyalty to the beneficiary.

The importance of ERISA's regulation of pension plans—the original impetus for the legislation—has faded dramatically. In 1983, 63% of all workers with retirement coverage had a defined benefit plan (pension plan). This number fell to 44% in 1992, 23% in 2011, and to 17% in 2013.[1]

Almost as an afterthought, Congress also decided to impose the fiduciary duties on administrators of employee welfare benefit plans. These benefits are now common in the workplace, but they were the exception in 1974. These benefits include: medical, disability, and life insurance benefits, and other benefits such as severance pay. The employer generally is free to change or adjust these benefits. In contrast to the decreasing importance of defined benefit pension plans, the importance of regulating welfare benefit plans has surged. ERISA does not require employers to offer these benefits. But, if they offer the benefits, the plan is regulated by ERISA. The same fiduciary duties owed to pension plan participants are owed to those enrolled in welfare benefit plans. The stakes can be very high, often touching on life and death issues and the basic quality of life, by presenting questions such as: "Does the medical plan have to cover a life-saving treatment?" "Does an employee who is unable to work qualify for long-term disability payments when unable to work?" and "Is a surviving spouse entitled to life insurance proceeds under the employer's plan?"

1 *See* Alicia Munnell, *401(k)/IRA Holdings in 2013: An Update From the SCF*, Center for Retirement Research Sept. 2014, at 3.

The following concurring opinion describes how ERISA may not be sufficient to protect employees in the modern workplace, but more importantly how ERISA's preemptive effect may preclude some efforts at the state level.

DIFELICE v. AETNA U.S. HEALTHCARE

346 F.3d 442 (3rd Cir. 2003).

BECKER, CIRCUIT JUDGE, concurring.

. . . .

ERISA was enacted in 1974 to address the increasingly-apparent insecurity of workers' vested pension funds, a problem that gained national recognition through such notorious events as the Studebaker plant shutdown in 1963, which caused approximately 4,400 workers to lose their pensions. . . . Prior to ERISA, workers were entitled only to the assets in the pension plan or to nominal pension benefits, whichever was lower; of course, it was entirely possible for a plan to have zero assets, as happened with some frequency when firms closed shop. ERISA contained a raft of provisions designed to protect plan participants against negligent or malfeasant plan managers. For example, it created the Pension Benefit Guarantee Corporation ("PBGC"), an insurer akin to the Federal Deposit Insurance Corporation, to protect against employer insolvency.

The "benefit plans" in need of protection, however, were of two distinct types—pension and welfare—and substantially different policy concerns animated Congress's reform in each area. Pension plans, to which employees contribute over the course of their careers and rely upon to provide retirement income, were thought to present far greater opportunity for mismanagement and underfunding. Unlike welfare benefit plans, pension plans accrue substantial funds that must be invested with prudence, and they must be able to survive continuously changing circumstances. Title 1 of ERISA therefore imposed on pension plan managers comprehensive reporting, disclosure, vesting, minimum funding, and fiduciary duty requirements.

Welfare benefit plans, which include medical, surgical, sickness, accident, disability, death, unemployment, and similar programs, posed a very different set of challenges. Unlike pension plans, welfare benefit plans operate on a "pay as you go" basis, and generally do not entail long-term financial commitments. ERISA's framers therefore saw no need to impose vesting requirements on such plans. Similarly, minimum funding requirements are intended to guard against plan default by the plan sponsor on its long-term commitments to plan beneficiaries, a minor concern where no substantial funds accrue. The framers thus exempted welfare benefit plans from ERISA's funding requirements as well.

The result is that welfare benefit plans are far less regulated than pension plans. They are subject to ERISA's reporting, disclosure, fiduciary, and remedial rules—those that govern procedure—but exempt from the substantive vesting and funding requirements, which are meant to guarantee a certain level of expected benefits. Congress's relative lack of concern with substantive regulation of welfare plans is clear from the Supreme Court's statement that "ERISA does not mandate that employers provide any particular benefits, and does not itself proscribe discrimination in the provision of employee benefits." *Shaw*, 463 U.S. at 91, 103 S.Ct. 2890. Indeed, courts have held that the absence of a vesting provision allows employers to amend their plans virtually at will, even in discriminatory fashion. See, e.g., *Confer v. Custom Engine Co.*, 952 F.2d 41, 43 (3d Cir.1991) (noting a plan sponsor may change benefits prospectively by formal written notice); *McGann v. H & H Music Co.*, 946 F.2d 401 (5th Cir.1991) (upholding an employer's amendment of its plan to exclude coverage for AIDS treatment).

Despite ERISA's relatively light regulation of welfare benefit plans, it is clear that the legislation provided substantially greater safeguards for both pension and welfare plan beneficiaries than had previously existed. But ERISA also contained a crucial concession to plan sponsors in the form of § 514(a), an express preemption provision mandating that Titles I and IV of ERISA, which impose the regulations discussed above, "shall supersede any and all State laws insofar as they may now or hereafter relate to any employee benefit plan." Although this section is subject to an important exception that allows states to impose laws regulating insurance, see § 514(b)(2)(A), its breadth is striking. The Supreme Court explains that Congress intended

> to ensure that plans and plan sponsors would be subject to a uniform body of benefits law; the goal was to minimize the administrative and financial burden of complying with conflicting directives among States or between States and the Federal Government . . ., [and to prevent] the potential for conflict in substantive law . . . requiring the tailoring of plans and employer conduct to the peculiarities of the law of each jurisdiction.

Ingersoll-Rand Co. v. McClendon, 498 U.S. 133, 142, 111 S.Ct. 478, 112 L.Ed.2d 474 (1990). This view is premised on the statement of Rep. John Dent, a sponsor of the Act in the House of Representatives, who declared that its purpose was to "eliminat[e] the threat of conflicting and inconsistent State and local regulation." 120 Cong. Reg. 29197 (1974).

. . . .

2. The Standard of Review in an Appeal from a Denial of Plan Benefits

A plan administrator of a Welfare Benefits plan is either the employer who is providing benefits under the Plan or the insurance company that has been engaged by the employer to fund and administer the Plan. When an employee applies for an award of benefits, the plan administrator determines whether the benefits are owed. If the benefit request is denied because the case does not fall within the terms of the policy, ERISA gives the employee the right to appeal to a federal court. The crucial legal question then becomes what standard of review a federal court must use in assessing the Plan Administrator's determination. De novo review requires a full-blown trial before a federal judge who issues an opinion on the question presented. In contrast, the court might defer to the Plan Administrator, which means that the denial will be affirmed by the district court, as long as there is some evidence to support the administrator's decision.

We begin with a flowchart that illustrates these two distinctive standards of review. To summarize, the court may defer to the Plan Administrator (leading to affirmance of the denial in most cases). Alternatively, the court may take up the question de novo, in effect giving the employee a second bite at the apple. After you review these two standards of review we will analyze when each is used.

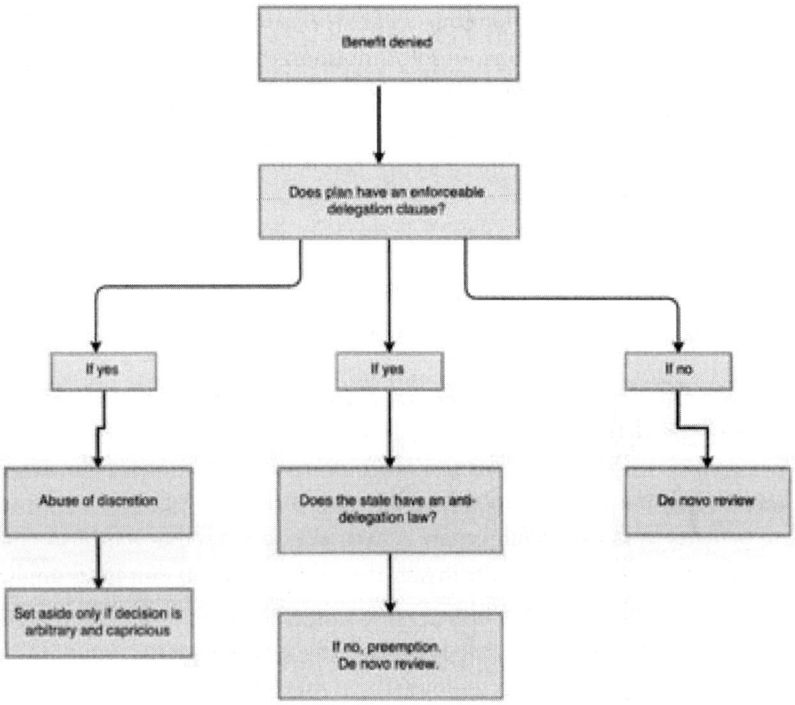

In 1989, the United States Supreme Court faced a dilemma. At issue was how a federal district court should review a decision by a plan administrator that denied a benefit to an employee. Reasons for denial can include the plan's provisions, or a dispute over whether the facts demonstrated that the employee was eligible under the plan. The problem is that the Plan Administrator has an inherent conflict of interest because the same entity that makes the eligibility decision also pays the benefits. One might fear that the Plan Administrator will seek to preserve assets by aggressively denying claims.

The Court was faced with two choices: de novo review or deference to the administrator's decision. On the one hand, allowing de novo review would permit a federal court to ensure that the correct decision was made on a benefit denial—a decision free from self-interest. But, de novo requires a lot of time and energy on the part of the courts and the administrators. And, after all, why should an employer offer the benefits in the first place if doing so means that they will be embroiled in litigation over every claim denial? On the other hand, a pure deference standard would essentially mean that the administrator's decision would be largely rubber-stamped and would invite possible abuse by self-interested administrators.

In *Firestone Tire & Rubber Co. v. Bruch*, 489 U.S. 101 (1989), the Court resolved the dilemma by creating a rule: If the Plan explicitly vested the Administrator with the discretion to make benefit determinations (called a "delegation clause"), then any such decision would be reviewed by a federal court for an abuse of discretion. In this circumstance, the court would set aside the denial only if the determination was arbitrary and capricious, which means that there is no evidence in the record to support the denial. The Court also held, however, that a federal court could consider any evidence of a conflict of interest. As you might expect, employers and insurance companies immediately inserted delegation clauses into their Plans to avoid successful court appeals of the Administrator's decision to deny benefits.

Example 29-1

Gerry files a claim for disability payments under the Plan administered by his employer. The Plan documents include a delegation clause that provides for the Administrator to exercise discretion. The administrative record shows that three doctors confirmed Gerry's disability, but a fourth doctor raised questions and determined that Gerry was probably not disabled. Because the Administrator had some basis for denying the benefit, the denial will not be overturned by the court on appeal because the court is required to defer to the administrator's factual determination.

QUESTIONS

1. If you were designing a welfare benefits plan and wanted to ensure maximum flexibility in the obligations under the plan, how would you structure the Plan?
2. Which of the following provisions creates an adequate delegation clause?
   (a) The Plan provides benefits in the event that you become disabled as defined by the terms of the Plan. Fickle Insurance Company administers the Plan and will make disability payments to you if you meet the appropriate definitions of disability. Fickle is solely responsible for paying benefits under the Plan. As Administrator, Fickle will make all decisions regarding claims and will review all denial of claims if challenged by you.
   (b) The responsibility for determinations of claims, of terms, of determinations of eligibility for benefits, of interpretations of claims, and appeals

of claims denied in whole or in part under the plan rests exclusively with the Plan Administrator.

States possess the primary authority for regulating insurance carriers. In response to the *Firestone* case and the effective elimination of appeals from denial of benefits, a majority of states responded with legislation or regulations that prohibited the use of delegation clauses in insurance policies. These include such diverse states as Alaska, Arkansas, California, Connecticut, South Dakota, Texas, and Wyoming. Consider the effect of the following Texas statute on the ERISA denial of benefits provision.

ERISA 29 U.S.C. § 1132. Civil Enforcement

(a) Persons empowered to bring a civil action

A civil action may be brought—

(1) by a participant or beneficiary—

. . . .

(B) to recover benefits due to him under the terms of his plan, to enforce his rights under the terms of the plan, or to clarify his rights to future benefits under the terms of the plan.

Texas Insurance Code

§ 1701.002. Applicability of Chapter to Forms of Certain Documents

This chapter applies to the form of the following document:

(1) a policy, contract, or certificate of:

(A) accident or health insurance, including group accident or health insurance;

(B) medical or surgical insurance, including group medical or surgical insurance;

(C) life or term insurance, including group life or term insurance;

(D) endowment insurance;

(E) industrial life insurance; or

(F) fraternal benefit insurance;

(2) an annuity or pure endowment contract, including a group annuity contract;

(3) an application attached or required to be attached to the policy, contract, or certificate; or

(4) a rider or endorsement to be attached to, printed on, or used in connection with the policy, contract, or certificate.

Texas Insurance Code

§ 1701.062. Discretionary Clauses Prohibited

(a) An insurer may not use a document described by Section 1701.002 in this state if the document contains a discretionary clause.

Was this action by states, which prohibited discretionary clauses, an impermissible intrusion into the ERISA scheme that should be preempted? Consider the following case which finds that ERISA does not preempt the action by the states, and which then addresses the practical consequences of a de novo review by a federal district court.

Orzechowski v. Boeing Co. Non-Union Long-Term Disability Plan

856 F.3d 686 (9th Cir. 2017).

Bybee, Circuit Judge:

Talana Orzechowski challenges Aetna Life Insurance Company's (Aetna) decision to terminate her long-term disability benefits under a plan created by her employer, The Boeing Company (Boeing). Under the Employee Retirement Income Security Act of 1974 (ERISA), we may review a denial of benefits. Where a plan grants discretion to an administrator to determine benefits, we ordinarily review for abuse of discretion. By statute, however, California has voided such provisions conferring discretionary authority to ERISA plan administrators such as Aetna. Cal. Ins. Code § 10110.6(a). The district court held that California's statute did not apply to Boeing's plan and upheld Aetna's denial of benefits to Orzechowski. We disagree and hold that § 10110.6(a) applies here. We reverse the district court's judgment and remand the case to the district court to review Aetna's decision de novo.

I. BACKGROUND

A. Boeing's ERISA Plan

The lawsuit arises from Aetna's termination of Orzechowski's benefits under a health and welfare benefits plan that Boeing offers to its non-union employees (the Plan), which is governed by ERISA. The principal plan document is The Boeing Company Master Welfare Plan (Master Plan). This document provides general information about the various benefit plans Boeing offers, but does not detail the various benefits payable through the Plan. The Master Plan has a broad grant of discretionary authority, which has been delegated to a service representative, Aetna. This grant includes the power to "determine all questions that may arise including all questions relating to the eligibility of Employees and Dependents to participate in the Plan and amount of benefits to which any Participant or Dependent may become entitled."

. . . .

B. Orzechowski Becomes Disabled

Talana Orzechowski worked at Boeing until February 27, 2009. In 2004, she was diagnosed with fibromyalgia and chronic fatigue syndrome. In January and February 2009, Orzechowski began suffering memory problems and increases in fatigue. Orzechowski suffered from a number of serious symptoms of largely unknown cause, including fatigue, loss of motor control, spinal and joint pain, and loss of cognitive functioning. Some of the symptoms appeared to be psychological in nature, including depression, obsessive compulsions, and suicidal thoughts. Other symptoms were more typical of physical illness, such as profuse sweating, muscle and nerve pains, and lung weakness. She also suffered from a wide range of other physical ailments, including fatigue, headaches, tiredness, extended periods of sleeping, asthma, decreasing muscle tone, and nausea.

Orzechowski saw numerous doctors to attempt to diagnose and address these issues. In February 2009, Orzechowski applied for short-term disability benefits under Boeing's employee benefits plan, which Aetna approved for the maximum duration of six months (26 weeks), until July 28, 2009.

Aetna then completed a long-term disability review, and approved long-term disability benefits under the "own occupation" definition of disability effective July 29, 2009. This benefits period would run through July 28, 2011.

In 2010, Aetna informed Orzechowski that the definition of disability would change from the "own occupation" to "any reasonable occupation" standard after her current benefit period ended. Aetna requested documentation to support her disability claim under the new standard.

Aetna received substantial medical records prepared by Orzechowski's physicians. It then sent Orzechowski's file to two physicians to review, a psychiatrist and a neurologist. Neither examined her. The psychiatrist agreed with Orzechowski's physicians that she could perform no work, including "even simple, routine and repetitive work duties reliably and safely." His conclusion was based on her psychiatric impairments, and the report noted that "potential physical impairment [was] outside the scope of [his] expertise." The neurologist acknowledged her extensive diagnoses, including "chronic fatigue, mood disorder, adrenal disorder and inflammatory polyarthropathy," and her symptoms of "fatigue, depression, memory impairment . . . loss of motor strength [and] deteriorating motor and cognitive skills," but he, however, concluded she had "[n]o functional limitations" on her ability to work and that she "can likely perform own occupation (light)" with "[n]o limitations or restrictions." Based on these reports, Aetna denied Orzechowski's claim.

In a response to Aetna's reviewers, Orzechowski's own treating physician wrote a letter formally disagreeing:

> It is concerning to me that a simple common sense review of the multiple historic findings detailed thoroughly in my monthly hour long evaluations of the patient would make it quite clear that this patient is not able to perform any level of work. She has not been able to care for herself without assistance and is unable to even administer her own medication. . . .

And while no specific neurological cause had been discovered for her condition, he noted that "if the patient has no neurological disorder, why has she remained so neurologically and functionally impaired? It is clear in this case that the absence of evidence does not constitute evidence of absence."

Aetna asked its outside reviewing neurologist to examine her file again. After a peer-to-peer conference with her doctors, he again concluded that Orzechowski's symptoms must be psychiatric in origin because there is no definite evidence of a neurologic diagnosis. In July 2011, Aetna terminated payment of Orzechowski's long-term disability benefits based on its determination that her disability is caused by a mental condition, more specifically depressive disorder and mood disorder, which falls under the Plan's 24-month mental health limitation. Aetna determined she was physically capable of "light work."

Orzechowski's attorney appealed Aetna's denial and provided additional documentation showing that "Orzechowski's depression and anxiety symptoms are clearly secondary to her medical conditions." Aetna referred Orzechowski's evidence to yet a third reviewer. He found that Ms. Orzechowski had "no functional impairment" that would preclude her ability to perform any reasonable occupation.

Orzechowski's primary physician sent another letter in disagreement and pointed out the problems with attempting to diagnose Orzechowski's medical condition based only on a paper review and suggested Aetna examine the patient in person:

> [B]asing your assessment solely on the "provided documentation" is as silly as trying to assess the quality of a meal at a restaurant by reading the menu's description without actually tasting the dish.

He also attacked Aetna's attempts to evaluate the severity of the chronic fatigue Orzechowski experienced, through objective evidence, when, by definition, there is no objective evidence of chronic fatigue.

In June 2012, Aetna upheld its decision to terminate Orzechowski's long-term disability benefits, stating that "there was insufficient medical evidence to support [Orzechowski's] continued disability for the period of July 29, 2011, and beyond based upon any physical conditions."

C. Orzechowski Appeals to the District Court

Orzechowski sought district court review under ERISA, 29 U.S.C. § 1132, of Aetna's determination that she fell into the mental health exception and was not totally disabled, as required for a continuation of benefits under Boeing's long term disability plan. Following a bench trial, the district court ruled in favor of Boeing.

The district court applied an abuse of discretion standard of review to Orzechowski's claim, rather than a de novo standard.

. . . .

III. DISCUSSION

A denial of ERISA benefits challenged under 29 U.S.C. § 1132 "is to be reviewed under a de novo standard unless the benefit plan gives the administrator or fiduciary discretionary authority to determine eligibility for benefits or to construe the terms of the plan." *Firestone Tire & Rubber Co. v. Bruch*, 489 U.S. 101, 115, 109 S.Ct. 948, 103 L.Ed.2d 80 (1989). If an insurance contract has a valid discretionary clause, the decisions of the insurance company are reviewed under an abuse of discretion standard.

We previously observed that discretionary clauses have been the subject of much controversy. Opponents believe such clauses lead to inappropriate claim practices, as insurers may use them as a shield to deny valid claims. Supporters, meanwhile, argue they keep insurance costs manageable. Resolving the merits of discretionary clauses is thankfully not before us; individual states make that policy determination for themselves. In response to a particularly notorious example of an insurer who had used discretionary clauses to boost its profits by intentionally denying valid claims, a number of states acted via statute, regulation, or administrative action to ban or limit discretionary clauses.

California Insurance Code § 10110.6 is one such example of state legislation limiting discretionary clauses. Section 10110.6 provides in relevant part:

> (a) If a policy, contract, certificate, or agreement offered, issued, delivered, or renewed, whether or not in California, that provides or funds life insurance or disability insurance coverage for any California resident contains a provision that reserves discretionary authority to the insurer, or an agent of the insurer, to determine eligibility for benefits or coverage, to interpret the terms of the policy, contract, certificate, or agreement, or to provide standards of interpretation or review that are inconsistent with the laws of this state, that provision is void and unenforceable.
>
> (b) For purposes of this section, "renewed" means continued in force on or after the policy's anniversary date.

. . . .

A. California Insurance Code § 10110.6 Is Saved from ERISA Preemption

ERISA preempts "any and all State laws insofar as they may now or hereafter relate to any employee benefit plan." 29 U.S.C. § 1144(a). Nevertheless, ERISA also has a saving clause that saves from preemption "any law of any State which regulates insurance, banking, or securities." *Id.* § 1144(b)(2)(A). So, although ERISA has broad preemptive force, its "saving clause then reclaims a substantial amount of ground." *Rush Prudential HMO, Inc. v. Moran*, 536 U.S. 355, 364, 122 S.Ct. 2151, 153 L.Ed.2d 375 (2002).

No one disputes that the California law comes within the broad terms of the preemption clause because it "relate[s] to any employee benefit plan." 29 U.S.C. § 1144(a). In order to take advantage of the saving clause in § 1144(b)(2)(A), California's statute must satisfy the two-part test set forth in *Kentucky Ass'n of Health Plans v. Miller*, 538 U.S. 329, 342, 123 S.Ct. 1471, 155 L.Ed.2d 468 (2003). [Most importantly], the law must be "specifically directed toward entities engaged in insurance," *Id.* at 342, 123 S.Ct. 1471.

1. The statute is directed toward entities engaged in insurance

. . . .

Our decision is consistent with holdings of other circuits. The Seventh Circuit recently addressed an Illinois statute similar to § 10110.6 in *Fontaine v. Metropolitan Life Insurance Co.*, 800 F.3d 883 (7th Cir. 2015). MetLife, the ERISA plan administrator for a law firm, denied long-term benefits to one of the firm's partners. As in this case, "[b]oth sides presented extensive medical evidence" and "[t]he standard of review [was] the pivotal issue." *Id.* at 885–86. MetLife argued that the Illinois statute was "not specifically directed toward entities engaged in insurance because it prohibits a plan sponsor . . . from delegating discretionary authority to the insurer of an employee benefit plan." *Id.* at 887. Applying *Miller* and citing our decision in *Morrison* with approval, the court held:

> While [the law firm] is not an insurer and is nevertheless affected by [the discretionary clause prohibition], that does not mean that [the law] is not specifically directed toward entities engaged in insurance. The Supreme Court rejected essentially the same too-clever argument in Miller. . . . Prohibitions on discretionary clauses, like any-willing-provider laws, have similarly inevitable

> effects on "entities outside the insurance industry. Just as in Miller, that does not change their character as insurance regulations.

Id. The court also rejected the argument that because "the discretionary clause in this case is not actually in an insurance policy but in an ERISA plan document," the statute was not a law specifically directed towards entities engaged in insurance. The Seventh Circuit termed it a "hyper-technical argument":

> Whether a provision for discretionary interpretation is placed in an insurance policy or in a different document is arbitrary and should make no legal difference. If MetLife's interpretation of ERISA's saving clause were correct, then states "would be powerless to alter the terms of the insurance relationship in ERISA plans; insurers could displace any state regulation simply by inserting a contrary term in plan documents. This interpretation would virtually 'read the saving clause out of ERISA.' "

Id. at 888 (quoting Ward, 526 U.S. at 376, 119 S.Ct. 1380); see also *Am. Council of Life Insurers v. Ross*, 558 F.3d 600, 602 (6th Cir. 2009) (holding that Michigan's regulation banning discretionary clauses was saved from preemption).

We too conclude that § 10110.6(a) regulates "entities engaged in insurance," *Miller*, 538 U.S. at 342, 123 S.Ct. 1471, even if they are not insurance companies. Section 10110.6 is directed at "insurance, not insurers," *id.* at 334, 123 S.Ct. 1471, because it covers "a policy, contract, certificate, or agreement . . . that provides or funds life insurance or disability insurance coverage," Cal. Ins. Code § 10110.6(a).

. . . .

IV. CONCLUSION

Because California Insurance Code § 10110.6 applies to Boeing's Master Plan and Summary Plan Description, the district court should have voided the discretionary clauses and reviewed Orzechowski's claim de novo. . . . We remand to the district court for review in accordance with this opinion.

REVERSED AND REMANDED.

QUESTION

1. Explain de novo review in your own words. What does it mean? What are the practical consequences for a lawyer representing an employee who was denied benefits? How should a lawyer for an employee develop the administrative record?

---

3. Anti-Retaliation Under ERISA

ERISA includes an anti-retaliation provision to protect beneficiaries who seek to secure their rights under ERISA. Consider how the provision is interpreted in the case that follows, keeping in mind that the case arose at the beginning of the AIDs epidemic.

ERISA 29 U.S.C. § 1140. Interference with Protected Rights

It shall be unlawful for any person to discharge, fine, suspend, expel, discipline, or discriminate against a participant or beneficiary for exercising any right to which he is entitled under the provisions of an employee benefit plan, this subchapter, section 1201 of this title, or the Welfare and Pension Plans Disclosure Act, or for the purpose of interfering with the attainment of any right to which such participant may become entitled under the plan, this subchapter, or the Welfare and Pension Plans Disclosure Act. It shall be unlawful for any person to discharge, fine, suspend, expel, or discriminate against any person because he has given information or has testified or is about to testify in any inquiry or proceeding relating to this chapter or the Welfare and Pension Plans Disclosure Act.

McGann v. H&H Music Co.

946 F.2d 401 (5th Cir. 1991).

Garwood, Circuit Judge:

Plaintiff-appellant John McGann (McGann) filed this suit under section 510 of the Employee Retirement Income Security Act of 1974, . . . (ERISA), against defendants-appellees H & H Music Company (H & H Music), Brook

Mays Music Company (Brook Mays) and General American Life Insurance Company (General American) (collectively defendants) claiming that they discriminated against McGann, an employee of H & H Music, by reducing benefits available to H & H Music's group medical plan beneficiaries for treatment for acquired immune deficiency syndrome (AIDS) and related illnesses. The district court granted defendants' motion for summary judgment on the ground that an employer has an absolute right to alter the terms of medical coverage available to plan beneficiaries. . . .We affirm.

FACTS AND PROCEEDINGS BELOW

McGann, an employee of H & H Music, discovered that he was afflicted with AIDS in December 1987. Soon thereafter, McGann submitted his first claims for reimbursement under H & H Music's group medical plan, provided through Brook Mays, the plan administrator, and issued by General American, the plan insurer, and informed his employer that he had AIDS. McGann met with officials of H & H Music in March 1988, at which time they discussed McGann's illness. Before the change in the terms of the plan, it provided for lifetime medical benefits of up to $1,000,000 to all employees.

In July 1988, H & H Music informed its employees that, effective August 1, 1988, changes would be made in their medical coverage. These changes included, but were not limited to, limitation of benefits payable for AIDS-related claims to a lifetime maximum of $5,000. No limitation was placed on any other catastrophic illness. H & H Music became self-insured under the new plan and General American became the plan's administrator. By January 1990, McGann had exhausted the $5,000 limit on coverage for his illness.

In August 1989, McGann sued H & H Music, Brook Mays and General American under section 510 of ERISA, . . .

He claimed that the provision limiting coverage for AIDS-related expenses was directed specifically at him in retaliation for exercising his rights under the medical plan and for the purpose of interfering with his attainment of a right to which he may become entitled under the plan.

Defendants, conceding the factual allegations of McGann's complaint, moved for summary judgment. These factual allegations include no assertion that the reduction of AIDS benefits was intended to deny benefits to McGann for any reason which would not be applicable to other beneficiaries who might then or thereafter have AIDS, but rather that the reduction was prompted by the knowledge of McGann's illness, and that McGann was the only beneficiary then known to have AIDS. On June 26, 1990, the district court granted defendants' motion on the ground that they had an absolute right to alter the terms of the plan, regardless of their intent in making the alterations. The district court also held that even if the issue of discriminatory motive were relevant, summary judgment would still be proper because the defendants' motive was to ensure the future existence of the plan and not specifically to retaliate against McGann or to interfere with his exercise of future rights under the plan.

DISCUSSION

McGann contends that defendants violated both clauses of section 510 by discriminating against him for two purposes: (1) "for exercising any right to which [the beneficiary] is entitled," and (2) "for the purpose of interfering with the attainment of any right to which such participant may become entitled." In order to preclude summary judgment in defendants' favor, McGann must make a showing sufficient to establish the existence of a genuine issue of material fact with respect to each material element on which he would carry the burden of proof at trial.

At trial, McGann would bear the burden of proving the existence of defendants' specific discriminatory intent as an essential element of either of his claims. *Kimbro v. Atlantic Richfield Co.*, 889 F.2d 869, 881 (9th Cir.1989) (employee must prove employer's specific intent to retaliate for employee's exercise of rights under plan), cert. denied, 498 U.S. 814, 111 S.Ct. 53, 112 L.Ed.2d 28 (1990). Thus, in order to survive summary judgment McGann must make a showing sufficient to establish that a genuine issue exists as to defendants' specific intent to retaliate against McGann for filing claims for AIDS-related treatment or to interfere with McGann's attainment of any right to which he may have become entitled.

Although we assume there was a connection between the benefits reduction and either McGann's filing of claims or his revelations about his illness, there is nothing in the record to suggest that defendants' motivation was other than as they asserted, namely to avoid the expense of paying for AIDS treatment (if not, indeed, also for other treatment), no more for McGann than for any other present or future plan beneficiary who might suffer from AIDS. McGann concedes that the reduction in AIDS benefits will apply equally to all employees filing AIDS-related claims and that the effect of the reduction will not necessarily be felt only by him. He fails to allege that the coverage reduction was otherwise specifically intended to deny him particularly medical coverage except "in effect." He does not challenge defendants' assertion that their purpose in reducing AIDS benefits was to reduce costs.

Furthermore, McGann has failed to adduce evidence of the existence of "any right to which [he] may become entitled under the plan." The right referred to in the second clause of section 510 is not simply any right to which an employee may conceivably become entitled, but rather any right to which an employee may become entitled pursuant to an existing, enforceable obligation assumed by the employer. "Congress viewed [section 510] as a crucial part of ERISA because, without it, employers would be able to circumvent the provision of promised benefits." *Ingersoll-Rand Co. v. McClendon*, 498 U.S. 133, 111 S.Ct. 478, 485, 112 L.Ed.2d 474 (1990).

McGann's allegations show no promised benefit, for there is nothing to indicate that defendants ever promised that the $1,000,000 coverage limit was permanent. The H & H Music plan expressly provides: "Termination or Amendment of Plan: The Plan Sponsor may terminate or amend the Plan at any time or terminate any benefit under the Plan at any time." There is no allegation or evidence that any oral or written representations were made to McGann that the $1,000,000 coverage limit would never be lowered. Defendants broke no promise to McGann. The continued availability of the $1,000,000 limit was not a right to which McGann may have become entitled for the purposes of section 510. To adopt McGann's contrary construction of this portion of section 510 would mean that an employer could not effectively reserve the right to amend a medical plan to reduce benefits respecting subsequently incurred medical expenses, as H & H Music did here, because such an amendment would obviously have as a purpose preventing participants from attaining the right to such future benefits as they otherwise might do under the existing plan absent the amendment. But this is plainly not the law, and ERISA does not require such "vesting" of the right to a continued level of the same medical benefits once those are ever included in a welfare plan.

. . . .

McGann effectively contends that section 510 was intended to prohibit any discrimination in the alteration of an employee benefits plan that results in an identifiable employee or group of employees being treated differently from other employees. The First Circuit rejected a somewhat similar contention in *Aronson v. Servus Rubber, Div. of Chromalloy*, 730 F.2d 12 (1st Cir.), cert. denied, 469 U.S. 1017, 105 S.Ct. 431, 83 L.Ed.2d 357 (1984). In *Aronson*, an employer eliminated a profit sharing plan with respect to employees at only one of two plants. The disenfranchised employees sued their employer under section 510, claiming that partial termination of the plan with respect to employees at one plant and not at the other constituted illegal discrimination. The court rejected the employees' discrimination claim, stating in part:

> [Section 510] relates to discriminatory conduct directed against individuals, not to actions involving the plan in general. The problem is with the word 'discriminate.' An overly literal interpretation of this section would make illegal any partial termination, since such terminations obviously interfere with the attainment of benefits by the terminated group, and, indeed, are expressly intended so to interfere.... This is not to say that a plan could not be discriminatorily modified, intentionally benefitting, or injuring, certain identified employees or a certain group of employees, but a partial termination cannot constitute discrimination per se. A termination that cuts along independently established lines-here separate divisions-and that has a readily apparent business justification, demonstrates no invidious intent.

Id. at 16 (citation omitted).

....

As persuasively explained by the Second Circuit, the policy of allowing employers freedom to amend or eliminate employee benefits is particularly compelling with respect to medical plans:

> With regard to an employer's right to change medical plans, Congress evidenced its recognition of the need for flexibility in rejecting the automatic vesting of welfare plans. Automatic vesting was rejected because the costs of such plans are subject to fluctuating and unpredictable variables. Actuarial decisions concerning fixed annuities are based on fairly stable data, and vesting is appropriate. In contrast, medical insurance must take account of inflation, changes in medical practice and technology, and increases in the costs of treatment independent of inflation.

> These unstable variables prevent accurate predictions of future needs and costs.

Moore v. Metropolitan Life Ins. Co., 856 F.2d 488, 492 (2d Cir. 1988) (Metropolitan Life).

. . . .

McGann's claim cannot be reconciled with the well-settled principle that Congress did not intend that ERISA circumscribe employers' control over the content of benefits plans they offered to their employees. McGann interprets section 510 to prevent an employer from reducing or eliminating coverage for a particular illness in response to the escalating costs of covering an employee suffering from that illness. Such an interpretation would, in effect, change the terms of H & H Music's plan. Instead of making the $1,000,000 limit available for medical expenses on an as-incurred basis only as long as the limit remained in effect, the policy would make the limit permanently available for all medical expenses as they might thereafter be incurred because of a single event, such as the contracting of AIDS. Under McGann's theory, defendants would be effectively proscribed from reducing coverage for AIDS once McGann had contracted that illness and filed claims for AIDS-related expenses. If a federal court could prevent an employer from reducing an employee's coverage limits for AIDS treatment once that employee contracted AIDS, the boundaries of judicial involvement in the creation, alteration or termination of ERISA plans would be sorely tested.

. . . .

Proof of defendants' specific intent to discriminate among plan beneficiaries on grounds not proscribed by section 510 does not enable McGann to avoid summary judgment. ERISA does not broadly prevent an employer from "discriminating" in the creation, alteration or termination of employee benefits plans; thus, evidence of such intentional discrimination cannot alone sustain a claim under section 510. That section does not prohibit welfare plan discrimination between or among categories of diseases. Section 510 does not mandate that if some, or most, or virtually all catastrophic illnesses are covered, AIDS (or any other particular catastrophic illness) must be among them. It does not prohibit an employer from electing not to cover or continue to cover AIDS, while covering or continuing to cover other catastrophic illnesses, even though the employer's decision in this respect may stem from some "prejudice" against AIDS or its victims generally. The same, of course, is true of any other disease and its victims. That sort of "discrimination" is simply not addressed by section 510. Under section 510, the asserted discrimination is illegal only if it is motivated by a desire to retaliate against an employee or to deprive an employee of an existing right to which he may become entitled. The district court's decision to grant summary judgment to defendants therefore was proper. Its judgment is accordingly

AFFIRMED.

Rule

H

QUESTIONS

1. Explain the distinction the court makes between the word "discriminate" in its common legal meaning and in its ERISA meaning.
2. This case seems to uphold an arbitrary and capricious decision by the Plan Administrator. If you advocated on behalf of equal rights for the LGBT community in the 1990s, how would you seek to ensure that this practice ended?

Problem 29-1

Joan works for a real estate company. Her employer provides health insurance. One day, her employer told her that it was changing her status from employee to independent contractor and gave her an agreement to sign to that effect. The new arrangement would not provide for health insurance. She refused and was terminated. Can she state a Section 510 claim?

Problem 29-2

Bill claims he was terminated from employment in violation of Section 510. He sues. The employer defends by arguing that he was already a participant in its benefit plans and, therefore, was not prevented from attaining rights in the plan. In short, the employer argues that once an employee has qualified for participation in a benefit plan, the employee can attain no increased right under the plan, and thus, termination of employment does not violate Section 510. You represent Bill. The court is holding a hearing on this argument. Draft your oral argument response.

The following case considers whether internal complaints are protected activity that can give rise to an ERISA claim.

EDWARDS V. A.H. CORNELL AND SON, INC.

610 F.3d 217 (3rd Cir. 2010).

FISHER, CIRCUIT JUDGE.

Shirley Edwards filed suit against her employer, A.H. Cornell and Son, Inc. ("A.H. Cornell"), and supervisors, Scott A. Cornell and Melissa J. Closterman, claiming that she was terminated in violation of Section 510 of the Employee Retirement Income Security Act of 1974 ("ERISA") and state common law after complaining to management about alleged ERISA violations. The defendants filed a Rule 12(b)(6) motion to dismiss, and the District Court granted the motion, holding that Edwards's complaints were not part of an "inquiry or proceeding" and thus not protected under Section 510. On appeal, we are presented with a single issue of first impression for this Court: whether the anti-retaliation provision of Section 510 of ERISA, 29 U.S.C. § 1140, protects an employee's unsolicited internal complaints to management. Four federal Courts of Appeals have ruled on this issue: the Fifth and Ninth Circuits have held in the affirmative, and the Second and Fourth Circuits have held in the negative. We agree with the latter, and hold that unsolicited internal complaints are not protected.

. . . .

Edwards claims that she discovered, during the last weeks of her employment, that A.H. Cornell was engaged in several ERISA violations: the company was allegedly administering the group health plan on a discriminatory basis, misrepresenting to some employees the cost of group health coverage in an effort to dissuade employees from opting into benefits, and enrolling non-citizens in its ERISA plans by providing false social security numbers and other fraudulent information to insurance carriers. Edwards alleges that she "objected to and/or complained to" A.H. Cornell's management about these ERISA violations and was terminated on or around February 11, 2009, as a result.

. . . .

III

The sole issue on appeal is whether the District Court erred in holding that unsolicited internal complaints are not protected activities under the anti-retaliation provision of Section 510 of ERISA, 29 U.S.C. § 1140. We will affirm.

. . . .

B. The Circuit Split

The federal Courts of Appeals are split on whether Section 510 encompasses unsolicited internal complaints. The Fifth and Ninth Circuits have held in the affirmative, see *Anderson v. Elec. Data Sys. Corp.*, 11 F.3d 1311 (5th Cir. 1994), and *Hashimoto v. Bank of Hawaii*, 999 F.2d 408 (9th Cir.1993), while the Second and Fourth Circuits have held in the negative, see *Nicolaou*, 402 F.3d 325, and *King v. Marriott Int'l Inc.*, 337 F.3d 421 (4th Cir. 2003).

. . . .

The sole federal Court of Appeals to address this issue in the context that we are presented with here—where an employee actually brings suit under Section 510 of ERISA itself—is the Second Circuit in *Nicolaou*. 402 F.3d at 327. Unlike the Fourth Circuit in *King*, the Second Circuit found that Section 510 of ERISA is "unambiguously broader in scope" than its counterpart in the FLSA. *Id.* at 328. Nevertheless, the court held that unsolicited internal complaints are not protected activities. First, the court explained that internal complaints could not fall under the term "proceeding" because "proceeding" "refers to the progression of a lawsuit or other business before a court, agency, or other official body[.]" *Id.* at 329. Second, the court held that, for an internal complaint to constitute an "inquiry," the employee would need to "demonstrate that she was contacted to meet with [management] in order to give information about the alleged [ERISA violation.]" *Id.* In other words, the employee's complaint would need to have been solicited.

C. The Plain Meaning of Section 510

We begin our analysis of ERISA's anti-retaliation provision "with an examination of ERISA's statutory language because 'absent a clearly expressed legislative intention to the contrary, that language must ordinarily be regarded as conclusive.' " *Wolk v. Unum Life Ins. of Am.*, 186 F.3d 352, 355 (3d Cir. 1999) (quoting *Kaiser Aluminum & Chem. Corp. v. Bonjorno*, 494

U.S. 827, 835, 110 S.Ct. 1570, 108 L.Ed.2d 842 (1990)). Therefore, "the first step is to determine whether [Section 510] has a plain and unambiguous meaning." *Dobrek v. Phelan*, 419 F.3d 259, 263 (3d Cir. 2005). Words or provisions are ambiguous when " 'they are reasonably susceptible of different interpretations.' " *Id.* at 264 (quoting *Nat'l R.R. Passenger Corp. v. Atchison Topeka & Santa Fe Ry. Co.*, 470 U.S. 451, 473 n. 27, 105 S.Ct. 1441, 84 L.Ed.2d 432 (1985)). If there is an ambiguity, we look to "the surrounding words and provisions and also to the words in context." *Id.*

. . . .

An "inquiry" is generally defined as "[a] request for information." Black's Law Dictionary 864 (9th ed.2009). Here, Edwards does not allege that anyone approached her requesting information regarding a potential ERISA violation. Rather, she made her complaint voluntarily, of her own accord. Under these circumstances, the information that Edwards relayed to management was not part of an inquiry under the term's plain meaning.

On appeal, Edwards argues that her objections and/or complaints were themselves the inquiry. We disagree. Edwards's complaints were statements regarding potential ERISA violations, not questions seeking information. Furthermore, because § 1140 protects employees that have "given information," not employees that have "received information," a plain reading of the provision indicates that "inquiry" includes only inquiries made of an employee, not inquiries made by an employee. The fact that Edwards's complaints may have eventually "culminat[ed]" in an inquiry, (see Secretary Br. at 17), underscores the fact that the complaints themselves, without more, do not constitute an inquiry.

Neither is Edwards's conduct encompassed by the term "proceeding." A "proceeding" is commonly defined as "[t]he regular and orderly progression of a lawsuit" or the "procedural means for seeking redress from a tribunal or agency." Black's Law Dictionary 1324 (9th ed. 2009). . . .

. . . [E]ven beyond the plain meaning of "inquiry" and "proceeding," the phrase "testified or is about to testify" implies that the phrase "inquiry or proceeding" is limited to more formal actions. Not all anti-retaliation statutes are so limited. In drafting § 1140, Congress could have used broad language similar to that present in the anti-retaliation provision in Section 704(a) of Title VII, which extends broad protection to employees that have "opposed any practice made an unlawful employment practice by [Title VII.]" 42 U.S.C. § 2000e–3(a). Congress declined to do so. . . .

Edwards and the Secretary argue that we should give Section 510 a broader reading because ERISA is a remedial statute. This connection is lacking. Although ERISA "should be liberally construed in favor of protecting the participants in employee benefit plans," see *IUE AFL-CIO Pension Fund v. Barker & Williamson, Inc.*, 788 F.2d 118, 127 (3d Cir. 1986), this does not entitle us to ignore clear statutory language. See *Wolk*, 186 F.3d at 355 ("[A]bsent a clearly expressed legislative intention to the contrary, [ERISA's statutory] language must ordinarily be regarded as conclusive." If Section 510 were ambiguous, we would construe the provision in favor of plan participants. However, as discussed above, we find the provision's plain meaning to be clear.

Likewise, Edwards and the Secretary argue that Section 510 deserves a broader reading because the failure to protect unsolicited internal complaints would undermine the provision's purpose, as "it would permit an employer to terminate an employee upon the employee first notifying the employer of the ERISA violation[.]" This contention must also fail. Presented as we are with clear statuary language, we do not need to speculate as to Congress's intent. It suffices to note that, had Congress been concerned with such a scenario, Congress could have used broad language mirroring the anti-retaliation provision of Title VII. Congress chose not to do so.

. . . .

Therefore, rather than base our holding on our prior case law regarding Section 507(a) of the CWA, we will ground our decision in the plain meaning of Section 510 of ERISA itself.

Affirmed.

Cowen, Circuit Judge, dissenting.

Unlike the Court, I conclude that ERISA's anti-retaliation provision does indeed protect "an employee's unsolicited internal complaints to management." Accordingly, I must respectfully dissent.

The majority is obviously correct that the statutory interpretation process must begin with the actual language of Section 510. Specifically, the statutory language at issue is generally regarded as conclusive, at least in the absence of a clearly expressed legislative intention to the contrary. See, e.g., *Wolk v. UNUM Life Ins. of Am.*, 186 F.3d 352, 355 (3d Cir. 1999). I further agree with the majority that "the first step is to determine whether [Section 510] has a plain and unambiguous meaning." *Dobrek v. Phelan*, 419 F.3d 259, 263 (3d Cir. 2005) (citing *Barnhart v. Sigmon Coal Co.*, 534 U.S. 438, 450, 122 S.Ct. 941, 151 L.Ed.2d 908 (2002)). I, however, believe that the statutory language used in this anti-retaliation provision is ambiguous. In fact, as explained below, I find it highly doubtful that Congress could have ever intended for its anti-retaliation provision to apply in the manner suggested by the majority, in particular because the majority's interpretation leaves totally unprotected a certain category of conduct (as well as the employees who may engage in such conduct) that this remedial statutory provision was enacted to protect in the first place. . . .

Initially, the majority does acknowledge at least some of the broad considerations underlying ERISA and its anti-retaliation provision, but it generally fails to give these various considerations the weight they deserve. Accordingly, the majority recognizes that ERISA, as a remedial statute, "should be liberally construed in favor of protecting the participants in employee benefit plans." *IUE AFL-CIO Pension Fund v. Barker & Williamson, Inc.*, 788 F.2d 118, 127 (3d Cir.1986). It likewise states that: (1) ERISA is a comprehensive statute designed to promote the interests of employees and their beneficiaries, see, e.g., *Shaw v. Delta Air Lines, Inc.*, 463 U.S. 85, 90, 103 S.Ct. 2890, 77 L.Ed.2d 490 (1983); (2) the statute imposes different standards and requirements with respect to the operation of the plans themselves; *id.* at 91, 103 S.Ct. 2890; (3) Congress similarly included various safeguards in order to deter abuse and " 'to completely secure the rights and expectations brought into being by this landmark reform legislation,' " *Ingersoll-Rand Co. v. McClendon*, 498 U.S. 133, 137, 111 S.Ct. 478, 112 L.Ed.2d 474 (1990) (quoting S.Rep. No. 93–127, at 36 (1973)); and (4) Section 510, designed to eliminate interference with the rights protected by ERISA, represents one of these critical statutory safeguards, *id.* I further note that "Congress viewed this section as a crucial part of ERISA because, without it, employers would be able to circumvent the provision of promised benefits." *Id.* at 143, 111 S.Ct. 478 (citing S.Rep. No. 93–127, at 35–36; H.R.Rep. No. 93–533, at 17 (1973)). In other words, this anti-retaliation provision plays a very important and even essential role in the proper implementation of the whole ERISA scheme because it actually " 'helps to make [ERISA's] promises credible.' " *Inter-Modal Rail Employees Ass'n v. Atchison, Topeka*

& Santa Fe Ry. Co., 520 U.S. 510, 515, 117 S.Ct. 1513, 137 L.Ed.2d 763 (1997) (quoting *Heath v. Varity Corp.*, 71 F.3d 256, 258 (7th Cir. 1995)).

Far from liberally construing this remedial legislation in favor of the very persons it was designed to protect, the majority adopts an ultimately unsustainable interpretation. At least at times, it appears to follow the very narrow approach adopted by the Fourth Circuit in *King v. Marriott International, Inc.*, 337 F.3d 421 (4th Cir. 2003), as opposed to the more moderate position taken by the Second Circuit in *Nicolaou v. Horizon Media, Inc.*, 402 F.3d 325 (2d Cir. 2005) (per curiam). However, even the Second Circuit disagreed with the Fourth Circuit's belief "that Congress's use of the phrase 'testify or about to testify' dictates" the conclusion "that Section 510 protects those who engage in 'something more formal than written or oral complaints made to a supervisor.' " *Id.* at 330 n. 3 (quoting *King*, 337 F.3d at 427). The *Nicolaou* court quite properly read this "reference to testimony" language as "wholly irrelevant to our understanding of the language 'given information . . . in any inquiry or proceeding.' " *Id.*

More broadly, I acknowledge that the Fifth Circuit did not examine this issue in any real detail in its ruling in *Anderson v. Electronic Data Systems Corp.*, 11 F.3d 1311 (5th Cir. 1994). On the other hand, the majority itself quotes the Ninth Circuit's reasonable and ultimately persuasive explanation for why it concluded in *Hashimoto v. Bank of Hawaii*, 999 F.2d 408 (9th Cir. 1993), that Section 510 does, in fact, encompass internal workplace complaints. It bears repeating here:

> . . . . The normal first step in giving information or testifying in any way that might tempt an employer to discharge one would be to present the problem first to the responsible managers of the ERISA plan. If one is then discharged for raising the problem, the process of giving information or testifying is interrupted at its start: the anticipatory discharge discourages the whistle blower before the whistle is blown.

Id. at 411. Like the Ninth Circuit, I find it difficult to believe that Congress could have ever intended to exclude from the protection of its remedial anti-retaliation provision employees who are terminated because they bring an ERISA-related problem to the attention of their superiors.

Likewise, the majority's narrow interpretation of the specific term "inquiry" appears questionable at best. In addition to leaving the crucial "first step" unprotected, the Second Circuit's whole "inquiry" standard could be difficult to apply and even unworkable in certain circumstances. Certain conduct may clearly constitute an "inquiry," such as the plaintiff's alleged activities in *Nicolaou* itself, which included contacting her employer's outside attorney regarding an alleged underfunding problem and then, after the lawyer conducted an inquiry of his own and evidently at the request of the lawyer, meeting with both him and the president of the company. *Nicolaou*, 402 F.3d at 326–27, 329–30. On the other hand, an internal workplace complaint would quite naturally constitute a preliminary step before a formal or informal inquiry is launched (and such a complaint may even have been necessary to trigger the investigation in the first place). However, where does one draw the line between such an initial step, which the Second Circuit and majority have held is not protected by the statutory provision, and otherwise "protected" statements purportedly made as part of some sort of inquiry? For instance, suppose an employee like Edwards complains to her superior, the superior asks some follow-up questions, and the employee responds to these questions. Are the informal responses to some impromptu questions to be regarded as protected because they evidently were made as part of an "inquiry?" In turn, why should such responses be protected while, at the same time, an employer is essentially permitted (and perhaps, in essence, encouraged) to fire an employee immediately after she makes an informal complaint instead of conducting an investigation of some sort?

. . . .

In the end, I am unable to agree with the majority's ruling here in light of the statutory language at issue, the expansive purposes and principles underpinning ERISA and its anti-retaliation provision, and (especially) prior decisions by this very Court broadly interpreting similar anti-retaliation statutes in other federal statutes. I accordingly would reverse the ruling of the District Court and remand for further proceedings.

Problem 29-3

The lawyer who knows the reason for a rule of law will always be at an advantage over a lawyer who just knows the rule. Prepare a summary analysis explaining the policy, practical, and legal rationales for the two competing interpretations in the preceding case.

Mastery Problem 29-1

Martha begins to experience severe back pain. She is treated by a physician who specializes in internal medicine and back pain. He concludes that her pain is caused by lumbar disk disease and arthritis, and she must have complete bedrest to obtain relief. Moreover, the doctor concluded that repeated transitions from standing to sitting and from sitting to standing would worsen her condition, as will walking and climbing stairs.

Because her work required a full range of activities, the doctor concluded that if Martha continued to work that she would aggravate her condition. The record also contains testimony by a different doctor who only reviewed the file and did not personally examine Martha. The second doctor concludes that Martha's obesity is the cause of her pain and that a weight loss plan would alleviate her medical issues. She also concludes that there is no objective evidence, such as an x-ray, of a disabling condition. Moreover, she concludes that the population as a whole suffers from Martha's conditions if they exceed a certain weight. She acknowledges that the condition is chronic, but it comes and goes and does not disqualify Martha from working.

The Plan Administrator, based on the second doctor's testimony, denied disability benefits for Martha. Martha then sued in federal court. You are a law clerk to the judge to whom the case has been assigned. She asks you for the following.

(a) What is the standard of review that she must follow? What information do you need to provide the answer?

(b) The judge also asks whether her review is limited to the record before the administrator, or whether she can allow additional record evidence? Also, is discovery permitted in the case? Prepare a memo on these questions based on your research.

Conclusion

ERISA was enacted primarily to address the failure of pension plans and the loss of retirement savings by workers. Today, ERISA is more significant for its regulation of welfare benefit plans. Although employers are not required to offer benefits, and can freely change or eliminate such benefits, they are bound to fiduciary duties in the administration of the plan. In this Lesson, we focused on how courts review a denial of benefits, the preemptory effect of ERISA, and the anti-retaliation provision of ERISA.

Lesson 30:
The Family and Medical Leave Act

Objectives and Expected Learning Outcomes

The Family and Medical Leave Act (FMLA) is the most complex statute we will study. In this Lesson, you will start to develop fluency in the language used and the concepts embodied in the regulations promulgated under the Act. More specifically, you will learn the various "threshold" requirements that must be satisfied by an employee to trigger FMLA entitlements and protections. We will discuss the FMLA's anti-retaliation provision, and also its "anti-interference" provision, which provides unique protections for an employee exercising a right under the Act. Because this modern statute is heavily dependent on regulations to provide detail, you will read excerpts from the Code of Federal Regulations and apply them to different scenarios. You should continually ask yourself if the law is accomplishing its original purpose or whether it needs modifications to do so.

The FMLA has been controversial since it was first proposed in 1983 and faced opposition by the administration of President Ronald Reagan. It was ultimately signed into law in 1993 by President Bill Clinton with the goal of ensuring more work/life balance for employees. The FMLA protects an employee's absence from work for the employee's own serious health condition ("self-care"); in order "to care for" a child or a parent with a serious health condition; or for the birth or adoption of a child. The employee is permitted a maximum of 12 weeks per year of unpaid leave, which may be taken in blocks of time or on an intermittent basis.

The FMLA contains several threshold requirements that must be met for an employee to be eligible under the "self-care" or "to care for" others coverage:

(1) the employer must have 50 or more employees in a 75-mile radius of the employee's worksite;

(2) the employee must have worked 1,250 hours in the preceding year of employment; and

(3) the absence must be triggered by a serious health condition (incapacity from work or school for more than three days, coupled with continuing

medical treatment generally two or more times in a 30-day period or a regime of continuous medical treatment).

Df for certain kinds of FMLA leave

However, the third requirement does not apply to those seeking FMLA leave due to pregnancy or prenatal care, for those seeking FMLA leave due to a chronic, serious health condition, and for the birth or adoption of a child.

In addition to prohibiting retaliation against those employees who engage in the protected activity of seeking or taking FMLA leave, the statute prohibits an employer from interfering with an employee taking such leave, either by discouraging the taking of leave or by interfering with an employee while the employee is on leave.

The FMLA is a complex statute with extensive regulations. We will address these general requirements in turn by applying the regulations to fact scenarios.

1. The FMLA: Origins, Mechanics, Results

This is the fourth statutory scheme we have studied that has a large impact on the day-to-day quality of an American worker's life. You have studied the FLSA (wages), ERISA (benefits), and OSHA (workplace safety), and we now turn to the FMLA (absences from work). It pays to recall the situation of workers before the enactment of the FMLA. An employer could discipline an employee, including summarily firing the employee, for being absent from work, even if the absence resulted from the employee having medically necessary surgery, placing a parent in hospice care, or staying at home with a sick child. When introduced in 1983, the FMLA languished, but gained traction a short time later when a federal judge struck down a California law that provided maternity leave for women but not paternity leave for men.

Proponents of maternity leave decided to lobby Congress for a gender-neutral bill, and two unlikely advocacy groups joined this effort. Groups who opposed abortion sought parental leave as a means of encouraging women to give birth without fear that they might lose their job. The second group was the American Association of Retired Persons (AARP), which recognized that an aging population would need to receive care from their children. As with all successful movements, a rally cry developed: "Employees shouldn't have to choose between the jobs they need and the families they love."[1] Despite these concerted efforts, President George H. W. Bush twice vetoed the FMLA, with the support of nearly half the country

1 Donna B. Lentoff and Lissa Bell, "Government Support for Working Families and for Communities: Family and Medical Leave Case Study," National Partnership for Women & Families.

according to polls. In 1993, a Democratic Congress passed the FMLA, and it was signed into law by President Bill Clinton.

Despite the public's apparent apathy when President Bush vetoed the FMLA, it has now become a fixture of the American workplace. On the 20th anniversary of the law's enactment, the Department of Labor issued a study stating that the FMLA has been used more than 100 million times by an estimated 35 million employees. The main reason was an employee's own illness. Around 50% of leave events lasted 10 days or less (likely due, in large part, to the unpaid nature of the FMLA). Only around 60% of workers were eligible for the law's protection, which is due to the legislative decision for a two-prong test to determine eligibility. Women, as with many other aspects of the workplace, are allegedly disadvantaged. As the National Partnership for Women & Families points out, despite the genesis of the FMLA, women are less likely to be eligible for FMLA coverage. Why? They tend to work for smaller employers, have shorter tenure in a job, and often work for several different employers, each on a part-time basis. All these factors short circuit a woman's ability to satisfy the eligibility prongs. Proponents had argued, ironically, that women particularly required help in maintaining a work-life balance. Finally, some question the utility of the FMLA. A parent cannot stay at home to care for an ill child or parent who does not meet the definition of "incapacitated." Additionally, important factors in work/life balance often involve issues less significant than a serious health condition. Finally, the unpaid character of the leave is problematic. A 2014 Pew Poll found that 30% of employees had no savings, and 36% of employees could only cover 6 months of leave or less without pay. Although paid leave is overwhelmingly favored by Americans (92% according to a 2105 Kaiser Family Poll for a new baby or a sick family member), the legislative will to impose this on employers is lacking, with no federal legislation on the horizon and with only 4 states mandating paid leave.[2]

Before beginning our study of the details of the FMLA, its complexity suggests the utility in providing a flow chart that reflects the requirements of an FMLA claim. Please note that the following claims do not need to satisfy the Level 4 analysis: (1) pregnancy-related absences and absences for prenatal care, (2) inpatient hospital care for at least one overnight stay, and (3) chronic conditions.

2 Maureen Hoch, *20 Years After FMLA, What's Changed and What Hasn't?*, Harv. Bus. Rev., Feb. 8, 2013.

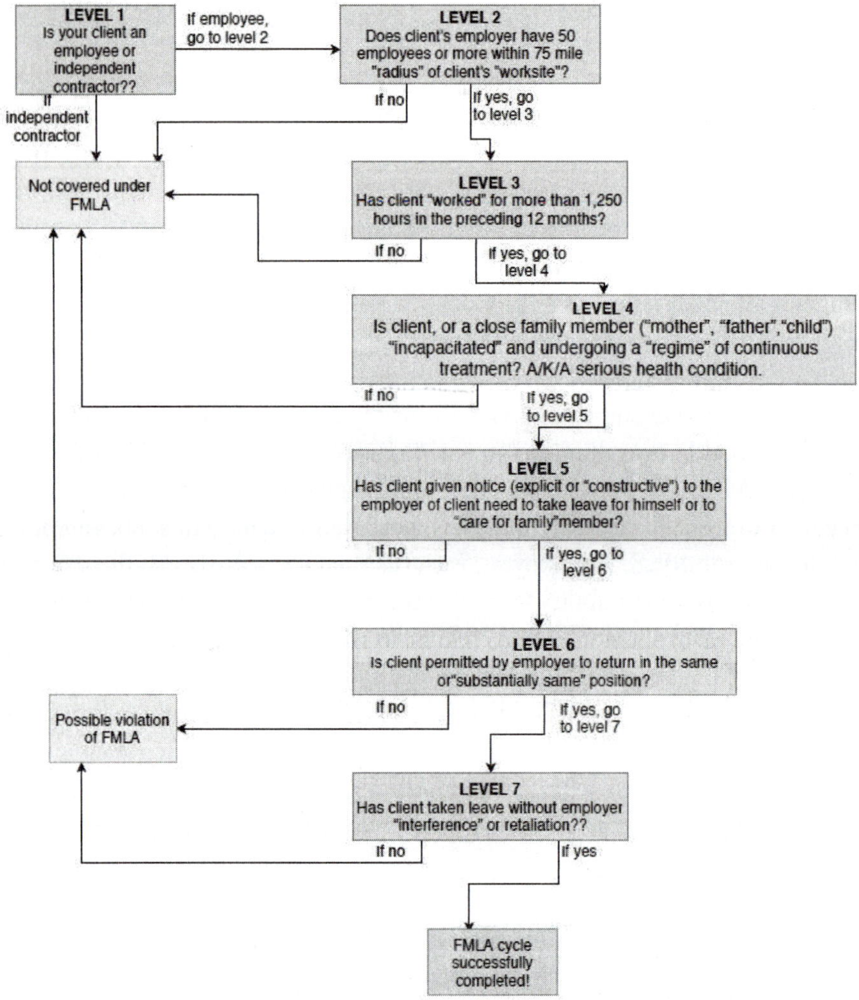

QUESTION

1. Look at the words in the chart with quotation marks around them. Do these terms have a plain meaning, or are they vague? Before reading the following excerpts from the CFR, think about how you believe the words should be construed. Provide definitions for expansive FMLA coverage and definitions for restricted coverage.

2. The Purpose of the FMLA

Most statutory schemes are more easily interpreted if you understand the purpose that the scheme is seeking to advance. We begin by focusing on the stated purposes of the FMLA and how that translates to specific rules.

29 C.F.R. § 825.101. Purpose of the Act

(a) The FMLA is intended to allow employees to balance their work and family life by taking reasonable unpaid leave for medical reasons, for the birth or adoption of a child, for the care of a child, spouse, or parent who has a serious health condition, for the care of a covered servicemember with a serious injury or illness, or because of a qualifying exigency arising out of the fact that the employee's spouse, son, daughter, or parent is a military member on covered active duty or call to covered active duty status. The Act is intended to balance the demands of the workplace with the needs of families, to promote the stability and economic security of families, and to promote national interests in preserving family integrity. It was intended that the Act accomplish these purposes in a manner that accommodates the legitimate interests of employers. . . .

(b) The FMLA was predicated on two fundamental concerns—the needs of the American workforce, and the development of high-performance organizations. Increasingly, America's children and elderly are dependent upon family members who must spend long hours at work. When a family emergency arises, requiring workers to attend to seriously-ill children or parents, or to newly-born or adopted infants, or even to their own serious illness, workers need reassurance that they will not be asked to choose between continuing their employment, and meeting their personal and family obligations or tending to vital needs at home.

(c) The FMLA is both intended and expected to benefit employers as well as their employees. A direct correlation exists between stability in the family and productivity in the workplace. FMLA will encourage the development of high-performance organizations. When workers can count on durable links to their workplace they are able to make their own full commitments to their jobs. The record of hearings on family and medical leave indicate the powerful productive advantages of stable workplace relationships, and the comparatively small costs of guaranteeing that those relationships will not be dissolved while workers attend to pressing family health obligations or their own serious illness.

QUESTIONS

1. The following questions are designed to trigger a discussion on the purposes of the FMLA as well as its effectiveness, after which you should pose the ultimate question: should the FMLA be expanded?
2. Have the goals of the FMLA been met? Consider your life and the lives of your friends and family. Have their lives been helped by the FMLA? Have their lives been adversely effected by not being FMLA eligible?
3. The initial goal of the FMLA was to encourage both males and females to avail themselves of time off for the birth or adoption of a child. Has that goal been achieved? Is there a stigma when males avail themselves of FMLA leave for these purposes?
4. What amendments would you make to the FMLA and why?
5. Would expanding the FMLA to cover smaller employers place too great a burden on them? Think about your own experiences with smaller employers, either as an employee or as a manager.

---

3. Scope of "Employee" Under the FMLA

29 C.F.R. § 825.110. Eligible Employee

(a) An eligible employee is an employee of a covered employer who:

(1) Has been employed by the employer for at least 12 months, and

(2) Has been employed for at least 1,250 hours of service during the 12-month period immediately preceding the commencement of the leave (see § 825.801 for special hours of service requirements for airline flight crew employees), and

(3) Is employed at a worksite where 50 or more employees are employed by the employer within 75 miles of that worksite. See § 825.105(b) regarding employees who work outside the U.S.

(b) The 12 months an employee must have been employed by the employer need not be consecutive months, provided

(1) Subject to the exceptions provided in paragraph (b)(2) of this section, employment periods prior to a break in service of seven years or more need not be counted in determining whether the employee has been employed by the employer for at least 12 months.

(2) Employment periods preceding a break in service of more than seven years must be counted in determining whether the employee has been employed by the employer for at least 12 months where:

(i) The employee's break in service is occasioned by the fulfillment of his or her Uniformed Services Employment and Reemployment Rights Act (USERRA), 38 U.S.C. 4301, et seq., covered service obligation. The period of absence from work due to or necessitated by USERRA-covered service must be also counted in determining whether the employee has been employed for at least 12 months by the employer. However, this section does not provide any greater entitlement to the employee than would be available under the USERRA; or

(ii) A written agreement, including a collective bargaining agreement, exists concerning the employer's intention to rehire the employee after the break in service (e.g., for purposes of the employee furthering his or her education or for childrearing purposes).

(3) If an employee is maintained on the payroll for any part of a week, including any periods of paid or unpaid leave (sick, vacation) during which other benefits or compensation are provided by the employer (e.g., workers' compensation, group health plan benefits, etc.), the week counts as a week of employment. For purposes of determining whether intermittent/occasional/casual employment qualifies as at least 12 months, 52 weeks is deemed to be equal to 12 months.

(4) Nothing in this section prevents employers from considering employment prior to a continuous break in service of more than seven years when determining whether an employee has met the 12-month employment requirement. However, if an employer chooses to recognize such prior employment, the employer must do so uniformly, with respect to all employees with similar breaks in service.

(c)

(1) Except as provided in paragraph (c)(2) of this section and in § 825.801 containing the special hours of service requirement for airline flight crew employees, whether an employee has worked the minimum 1,250 hours of service is determined according to the principles established under the Fair Labor Standards Act (FLSA) for determining compensable hours of work. See 29 CFR part 785. The determining factor is the number of hours an employee has worked for the employer within the meaning of the FLSA. The determination is not limited by methods of recordkeeping, or by compensation agreements that do not accurately reflect all of the hours an employee has worked for or been in service to the employer. Any accurate accounting of actual hours worked under FLSA's principles may be used.

(2) An employee returning from USERRA-covered service shall be credited with the hours of service that would have been performed but for the period of absence from work due to or necessitated by USERRA-covered service in determining the employee's eligibility for FMLA-qualifying leave. Accordingly, a person reemployed following USERRA-covered service has the hours that would have been worked for the employer added to any hours actually worked during the previous 12-month period to meet the hours of service requirement. In order to determine the hours that would have been worked during the period of absence from work due to or necessitated by USERRA-covered service, the employee's pre-service work schedule can generally be used for calculations. See § 825.801(c) for special rules applicable to airline flight crew employees.

(3) In the event an employer does not maintain an accurate record of hours worked by an employee, including for employees who are exempt from FLSA's requirement that a record be kept of their hours worked (e.g., bona fide executive, administrative, and professional employees as defined in FLSA Regulations, 29 CFR part 541), the employer has the burden of showing that the employee has not worked the requisite hours. An employer must be able to clearly demonstrate, for example, that full-time teachers (see § 825.102 for definition) of an elementary or secondary school system, or institution of higher education, or other educational establishment or institution (who often work outside the classroom or at their homes) did not work 1,250 hours during the previous 12 months in order to claim that the teachers are not eligible for FMLA leave. See § 825.801(d) for special rules applicable to airline flight crew employees.

Burden on ER to prove ≤ hours

(d) The determination of whether an employee meets the hours of service requirement and has been employed by the employer for a total of at least 12 months must be made as of the date the FMLA leave is to start. An employee may be on non-FMLA leave at the time he or she meets the 12-month eligibility requirement, and in that event, any portion of the leave taken for an FMLA-qualifying reason after the employee meets the eligibility requirement would be FMLA leave. See § 825.300(b) for rules governing the content of the eligibility notice given to employees.

(e) Whether 50 employees are employed within 75 miles to ascertain an employee's eligibility for FMLA benefits is determined when the employee gives notice of the need for leave. Whether the leave is to be taken at one time or on an intermittent or reduced leave schedule basis, once an employee is determined eligible in response to that notice of the need for leave, the employee's eligibility is not affected by any subsequent change in the number of employees employed at or within 75 miles of the employee's worksite, for that specific notice of the need for leave. Similarly, an employer may not terminate employee leave that has already started if the employee count drops below 50. For example, if an employer employs 60 employees in August, but expects that the number of employees will drop to 40 in December, the employer must grant FMLA benefits to an otherwise eligible employee who gives notice of the need for leave in August for a period of leave to begin in December.

Problem 30-1

A prospective client comes to see you about a potential FMLA case. He meets the 12-month requirement, but you are unsure about the 1,250 hours. Do you include in the working-hours requirement the time the employee was on vacation, which was a benefit that he accrued at the company?

Problem 30-2

In March, an employee tells her employer that, starting in August, she will need to take FMLA leave for a planned surgery. At the time that she tells her employer, she has not yet satisfied the threshold on length of service or work hours. But, at the end of July, she will have satisfied the requirement. She is terminated the following week. Does she have a retaliation claim?

Problem 30-3

An employee offers to work weekends. The employer thanks the employee for being willing to do so but declines the offer. Do the hours she is willing to work count towards the 1,250 threshold? What if the employee offered to work the hours but the employer said that the employee had to be "on call" as discussed in the FLSA chapter? Would the hours on call then count towards the threshold?

---

4. Qualifying Events Under the FMLA

29 C.F.R. § 825.113. Serious Health Condition

(a) For purposes of FMLA, serious health condition entitling an employee to FMLA leave means an illness, injury, impairment or physical or mental condition that involves inpatient care as defined in § 825.114 or continuing treatment by a health care provider as defined in § 825.115.

(b) The term incapacity means inability to work, attend school or perform other regular daily activities due to the serious health condition, treatment therefore, or recovery therefrom.

(c) The term treatment includes (but is not limited to) examinations to determine if a serious health condition exists and evaluations of the condition. Treatment does not include routine physical examinations, eye examinations, or dental examinations. A regimen of continuing treatment includes, for example, a course of prescription medication (e.g., an antibiotic) or therapy requiring special equipment to resolve or alleviate the health condition (e.g., oxygen). A regimen of continuing treatment that includes the taking of over-the-counter medications such as aspirin, antihistamines, or salves; or bed-rest, drinking fluids, exercise, and other similar activities that can be initiated without a visit to a health care provider, is not, by itself, sufficient to constitute a regimen of continuing treatment for purposes of FMLA leave.

(d) Conditions for which cosmetic treatments are administered (such as most treatments for acne or plastic surgery) are not serious health conditions unless inpatient hospital care is required or unless complications develop. Ordinarily, unless complications arise, the common cold, the flu, ear aches, upset stomach, minor ulcers, headaches other than migraine, routine dental or orthodontia problems, periodontal disease, etc., are examples of conditions that do not meet the definition of a serious health condition and do not qualify for FMLA leave. Restorative dental or plastic surgery after an injury or removal of cancerous growths are serious health conditions provided all the other conditions of this regulation are met. Mental illness or allergies may be serious health conditions, but only if all the conditions of this section are met.

Problem 30-4

An employee brings a note from her doctor that states that the employee should not be exposed to certain chemicals in the work place. The note states that daily exposure could cause respiratory tract disorders. The employer told her she had to remain on the job and she refused. She was fired. Does she have an FMLA claim?

---

29 C.F.R. § 825.114. Inpatient Care

Inpatient care means an overnight stay in a hospital, hospice, or residential medical care facility, including any period of incapacity as defined in § 825.113(b), or any subsequent treatment in connection with such inpatient care.

QUESTION

1. What is the most important phrase in this regulation? Why?

---

29 C.F.R. § 825.115. Continuing Treatment

A serious health condition involving continuing treatment by a health care provider includes any one or more of the following:

(a) Incapacity and treatment. A period of incapacity of more than three consecutive, full calendar days, and any subsequent treatment or period of incapacity relating to the same condition, that also involves:

(1) Treatment two or more times, within 30 days of the first day of incapacity, unless extenuating circumstances exist, by a health care provider, by a nurse under direct supervision of a health care provider, or by a provider of health care services (e.g., physical therapist) under orders of, or on referral by, a health care provider; or

(2) Treatment by a health care provider on at least one occasion, which results in a regimen of continuing treatment under the supervision of the health care provider.

(3) The requirement in paragraphs (a)(1) and (2) of this section for treatment by a health care provider means an in-person visit to a health care provider. The first (or only) in-person treatment visit must take place within seven days of the first day of incapacity.

(4) Whether additional treatment visits or a regimen of continuing treatment is necessary within the 30-day period shall be determined by the health care provider.

(5) The term extenuating circumstances in paragraph (a)(1) of this section means circumstances beyond the employee's control that prevent the follow-up visit from occurring as planned by the health care provider. Whether a given set of circumstances are extenuating depends on the facts. For example, extenuating circumstances exist if a health care provider determines that a second in-person visit is needed within the 30-day period, but the health care provider does not have any available appointments during that time period.

(b) Pregnancy or prenatal care. Any period of incapacity due to pregnancy, or for prenatal care. See also § 825.120.

. . . .

(f) Absences attributable to incapacity under paragraph (b) or (c) of this section qualify for FMLA leave even though the employee or the covered family member does not receive treatment from a health care provider during the absence, and even if the absence does not last more than three consecutive, full calendar days. For example, an employee with asthma may be unable to report for work due to the onset of an asthma attack or because the employee's health care provider has advised the employee to stay home when the pollen count exceeds a certain level. An employee who is pregnant may be unable to report to work because of severe morning sickness.

Problem 30-5

An employee injures her fingers when they get caught in a slamming car door. She goes to a hospital and receives multiple stitches. The doctor tells her she has a lifting restriction of no more than 10 pounds. She gives the note on the restrictions to her employer who says, "Don't come back to work until the restrictions are lifted." What questions would you ask on behalf of the employee, and why would you ask them?

---

29 C.F.R. § 825.119. Leave for Treatment of Substance Abuse

(a) Substance abuse may be a serious health condition if the conditions of §§ 825.113 through 825.115 are met. However, FMLA leave may only be taken for treatment for substance abuse by a health care provider or by a provider of health care services on referral by a health care provider. On the other hand, absence because of the employee's use of the substance, rather than for treatment, does not qualify for FMLA leave.

(b) Treatment for substance abuse does not prevent an employer from taking employment action against an employee. The employer may not take action against the employee because the employee has exercised his or her right to take FMLA leave for treatment. However, if the employer has an established policy, applied in a non-discriminatory manner that has been communicated to all employees, that provides under certain circumstances an employee may be terminated for substance abuse, pursuant to that policy the employee may be terminated whether or not the employee is presently taking FMLA leave. An employee may also take FMLA leave to care for a covered family member who is receiving treatment for substance abuse. The employer may not take action against an employee who is providing care for a covered family member receiving treatment for substance abuse.

Problem 30-6

An employee is using illegal drugs, which causes him to be absent from his job for three consecutive days before he admitted himself to a rehab facility. Upon successfully completing rehab, he was fired. The employee tells you that on the first day of his 3-day absence from work, his doctor told him that treatment for substance abuse starts with taking the "first step" by seeking help. Assuming he shows a serious health condition, are the three days FMLA protected leave?

---

29 C.F.R. § 825.120. Leave for Pregnancy or Birth

(a) General rules. Eligible employees are entitled to FMLA leave for pregnancy or birth of a child as follows:

(1) Both parents are entitled to FMLA leave for the birth of their child.

(2) Both parents are entitled to FMLA leave to be with the healthy newborn child (i.e., bonding time) during the 12-month period beginning on the date of birth. An employee's entitlement to FMLA leave for a birth expires at the end of the 12-month period beginning on the date of the birth. If state law allows, or the employer permits, bonding leave to be taken beyond this period, such leave will not qualify as FMLA leave. See § 825.701 regarding non-FMLA leave which may be available under applicable State laws. Under this section, both parents are entitled to FMLA leave even if the newborn does not have a serious health condition.

. . . .

(4) The expectant mother is entitled to FMLA leave for incapacity due to pregnancy, for prenatal care, or for her own serious health condition following the birth of the child. An expectant mother may take FMLA leave before the birth of the child for prenatal care or if her condition makes her unable to work. The mother is entitled to leave for incapacity due to pregnancy even though she does not receive treatment from a health care provider during the absence, and even if the absence does not last for more than three consecutive calendar days. The expectant mother is entitled to leave for incapacity due to pregnancy even though she does not receive treatment from a health care provider during the absence,

and even if the absence does not last for more than three consecutive calendar days.

(5) A spouse is entitled to FMLA leave if needed to care for a pregnant spouse who is incapacitated or if needed to care for her during her prenatal care, or if needed to care for her following the birth of a child if she has a serious health condition. See § 825.124.

Problem 30-7

A pregnant woman comes to you as a prospective client. She tells you that she has taken time off work to visit her doctor for treatment of chronic morning sickness. Her supervisor told her that she is not "incapacitated" and therefore is ineligible to claim time off under the FMLA. After several doctor visits she is fired for excessive absences. Does she have a claim?

---

29 C.F.R. § 825.124. Needed to Care for a Family Member or Covered Servicemember

(a) The medical certification provision that an employee is needed to care for a family member or covered servicemember encompasses both physical and psychological care. It includes situations where, for example, because of a serious health condition, the family member is unable to care for his or her own basic medical, hygienic, or nutritional needs or safety, or is unable to transport himself or herself to the doctor. The term also includes providing psychological comfort and reassurance which would be beneficial to a child, spouse or parent with a serious health condition who is receiving inpatient or home care.

(b) The term also includes situations where the employee may be needed to substitute for others who normally care for the family member or covered servicemember, or to make arrangements for changes in care, such as transfer to a nursing home. The employee need not be the only individual or family member available to care for the family member or covered servicemember.

Problem 30-8

An employee works for a company in St. Louis. Her mother is dying of cancer and has only three or four months to live. The woman visits her on a regular basis, helps cook her meals, bathes her, and administers her pain medication. The mother has a "bucket list" item: to visit Las Vegas to see the shows, eat at the restaurants, and enjoy the nightlife. The employee tells her employer the circumstances, but the employer refuses to grant an FMLA leave. When the employee takes off work for this trip, she is terminated. Does she have a claim?

Problem 30-9

A man and his wife are having a baby. She is close to delivery. They live in Sacramento. He is worried that their old clunker of a car will be unsafe to drive his wife and baby in, so he catches a ride to San Diego where he has a lead on a great car for a good price. His employer refused to excuse his absence for this trip. As he is driving the car back home, his wife goes into labor. He is on the phone with her constantly as he is driving, but when he is still an hour outside of Sacramento she gives birth. His employer fires him for the absence. Does he have a claim?

---

5. Leave Under the FMLA

29 C.F.R. § 825.202. Intermittent Leave or Reduced Leave Schedule

(a) Definition. FMLA leave may be taken intermittently or on a reduced leave schedule under certain circumstances. Intermittent leave is FMLA leave taken in separate blocks of time due to a single qualifying reason. A reduced leave schedule is a leave schedule that reduces an employee's usual number of working hours per workweek, or hours per workday. A reduced leave schedule is a change in the employee's schedule for a period of time, normally from full-time to part-time.

(b) Medical necessity. For intermittent leave or leave on a reduced leave schedule taken because of one's own serious health condition, to care for a spouse, parent, son, or daughter with a serious health condition, or to care for a covered servicemember with a serious injury or illness, there must be a medical need for leave and it must be that such medical need can be best accommodated through an intermittent or reduced leave schedule. The treatment regimen and other information described in the certification of a serious health condition and in the certification of a serious injury or illness, if required by the employer, addresses the medical necessity of intermittent leave or leave on a reduced leave schedule. See §§ 825.306, 825.310. Leave may be taken intermittently or on a reduced leave schedule when medically necessary for planned and/or unanticipated medical treatment of a serious health condition or of a covered servicemember's serious injury or illness, or for recovery from treatment or recovery from a serious health condition or a covered servicemember's serious injury or illness. It may also be taken to provide care or psychological comfort to a covered family member with a serious health condition or a covered servicemember with a serious injury or illness.

(1) Intermittent leave may be taken for a serious health condition of a spouse, parent, son, or daughter, for the employee's own serious health condition, or a serious injury or illness of a covered servicemember which requires treatment by a health care provider periodically, rather than for one continuous period of time, and may include leave of periods from an hour or more to several weeks. Examples of intermittent leave would include leave taken on an occasional basis for medical appointments, or leave taken several days at a time spread over a period of six months, such as for chemotherapy. A pregnant employee may take leave intermittently for prenatal examinations or for her own condition, such as for periods of severe morning sickness. An example of an employee taking leave on a reduced leave schedule is an employee who is recovering from a serious health condition and is not strong enough to work a full-time schedule.

. . . .

Problem 30-10

An employee is a diabetic. His employer is aware of the condition. He tells the employer that he may feel dizzy and woozy at times, and that he will, if so, need to eat something to regulate his levels of sugar in his blood. One day, when feeling dizzy, the employee leaves his work station as a customer service representative in a call center and goes to the company cafeteria to eat. He can't find his supervisor to tell him that he plans to do so. The supervisor sees his empty station and fires him. Does the employee have a claim?

---

6. Protected Right to Reinstatement

29 C.F.R. § 825.214. Employee Right to Reinstatement

General rule. On return from FMLA leave, an employee is entitled to be returned to the same position the employee held when leave commenced, or to an equivalent position with equivalent benefits, pay, and other terms and conditions of employment. An employee is entitled to such reinstatement even if the employee has been replaced or his or her position has been restructured to accommodate the employee's absence. See also § 825.106(e) for the obligations of joint employers.

29 C.F.R. § 825.215. Equivalent Position

(a) Equivalent position. An equivalent position is one that is virtually identical to the employee's former position in terms of pay, benefits and working conditions, including privileges, perquisites and status. It must involve the same or substantially similar duties and responsibilities, which must entail substantially equivalent skill, effort, responsibility, and authority.

(b) Conditions to qualify. If an employee is no longer qualified for the position because of the employee's inability to attend a necessary course, renew a license, fly a minimum number of hours, etc., as a result of the leave, the employee shall be given a reasonable opportunity to fulfill those conditions upon return to work.

(c) Equivalent pay.

. . . .

(2) Equivalent pay includes any bonus or payment, whether it is discretionary or non-discretionary, made to employees consistent with

the provisions of paragraph (c)(1) of this section. However, if a bonus or other payment is based on the achievement of a specified goal such as hours worked, products sold or perfect attendance, and the employee has not met the goal due to FMLA leave, then the payment may be denied, unless otherwise paid to employees on an equivalent leave status for a reason that does not qualify as FMLA leave. For example, if an employee who used paid vacation leave for a non-FMLA purpose would receive the payment, then the employee who used paid vacation leave for an FMLA-protected purpose also must receive the payment.

(d) Equivalent benefits. Benefits include all benefits provided or made available to employees by an employer, including group life insurance, health insurance, disability insurance, sick leave, annual leave, educational benefits, and pensions, regardless of whether such benefits are provided by a practice or written policy of an employer through an employee benefit plan as defined in Section 3(3) of the Employee Retirement Income Security Act of 1974, 29 U.S.C. 1002(3).

. . . .

(e) Equivalent terms and conditions of employment. An equivalent position must have substantially similar duties, conditions, responsibilities, privileges and status as the employee's original position.

(1) The employee must be reinstated to the same or a geographically proximate worksite (i.e., one that does not involve a significant increase in commuting time or distance) from where the employee had previously been employed. If the employee's original worksite has been closed, the employee is entitled to the same rights as if the employee had not been on leave when the worksite closed. For example, if an employer transfers all employees from a closed worksite to a new worksite in a different city, the employee on leave is also entitled to transfer under the same conditions as if he or she had continued to be employed.

(2) The employee is ordinarily entitled to return to the same shift or the same or an equivalent work schedule.

(3) The employee must have the same or an equivalent opportunity for bonuses, profit-sharing, and other similar discretionary and non-discretionary payments.

(4) FMLA does not prohibit an employer from accommodating an employee's request to be restored to a different shift, schedule, or position which better suits the employee's personal needs on return from leave, or to offer a promotion to a better position. However,

an employee cannot be induced by the employer to accept a different position against the employee's wishes.

(f) De minimis exception. The requirement that an employee be restored to the same or equivalent job with the same or equivalent pay, benefits, and terms and conditions of employment does not extend to de minimis, intangible, or unmeasurable aspects of the job.

QUESTIONS

1. If an employee takes FMLA leave and the employer comes to believe that prior to the leave the employee was ignoring her job duties, can the employee be placed on probation and investigatory status when she returns from her leave?
2. A police officer is injured while jogging after work. She takes FMLA leave from her position as a patrol officer. After twelve weeks, her doctor releases her only for light duty, and the only open position is dispatcher. The city refuses her request to return to work on light duty status as a dispatcher. What questions do you ask to determine if she has a claim?
3. A nurse working the day shift goes on FMLA leave. Upon his return from FMLA leave, his employer places him on the night shift. Compensation and benefits remain the same. Does the employee have a claim?
4. An employee returns from FMLA leave and is told that she will perform the same job, except that she will no longer have to travel. What questions would you ask to determine if she has a claim?

---

7. Protecting Employees from Retaliation or Interference

29 C.F.R. § 825.220. Protection for Employees Who Request Leave or Otherwise Assert FMLA Rights

(a) The FMLA prohibits interference with an employee's rights under the law, and with legal proceedings or inquiries relating to an employee's rights. More specifically, the law contains the following employee protections:

(1) An employer is prohibited from interfering with, restraining, or denying the exercise of (or attempts to exercise) any rights provided by the Act.

(2) An employer is prohibited from discharging or in any other way discriminating against any person (whether or not an employee) for opposing or complaining about any unlawful practice under the Act.

(3) All persons (whether or not employers) are prohibited from discharging or in any other way discriminating against any person (whether or not an employee) because that person has—

(i) Filed any charge, or has instituted (or caused to be instituted) any proceeding under or related to this Act;

(ii) Given, or is about to give, any information in connection with an inquiry or proceeding relating to a right under this Act;

(iii) Testified, or is about to testify, in any inquiry or proceeding relating to a right under this Act.

(b) Any violations of the Act or of these regulations constitute interfering with, restraining, or denying the exercise of rights provided by the Act. An employer may be liable for compensation and benefits lost by reason of the violation, for other actual monetary losses sustained as a direct result of the violation, and for appropriate equitable or other relief, including employment, reinstatement, promotion, or any other relief tailored to the harm suffered. See § 825.400(c). Interfering with the exercise of an employee's rights would include, for example, not only refusing to authorize FMLA leave, but discouraging an employee from using such leave. It would also include manipulation by a covered employer to avoid responsibilities under FMLA, for example:

(1) Transferring employees from one worksite to another for the purpose of reducing worksites, or to keep worksites, below the 50-employee threshold for employee eligibility under the Act;

(2) Changing the essential functions of the job in order to preclude the taking of leave;

(3) Reducing hours available to work in order to avoid employee eligibility.

(c) The Act's prohibition against interference prohibits an employer from discriminating or retaliating against an employee or prospective employee for having exercised or attempted to exercise FMLA rights. For example, if an employee on leave without pay would otherwise be entitled to full benefits (other than health benefits), the same benefits would be required to be provided to an employee on unpaid FMLA leave. By the same token, employers cannot use the taking of FMLA leave as a negative factor in employment actions, such as hiring, promotions or disciplinary actions; nor can FMLA leave be counted under no fault attendance policies. See § 825.215. . . .

QUESTIONS

1. An employee goes on FMLA leave without protest or interference from the employer. However, her boss calls several times a day to ask questions about work that the employee left uncompleted prior to taking the leave. Eventually, the employee decides to come back to work earlier than anticipated. Is there a claim under the FMLA?
2. What if the employer above only called once a week with a short question or two? If the employee takes all the leave afforded under the FMLA, does she have a claim?

---

8. Employee Obligations

29 C.F.R. § 825.302. Employee Notice Requirements for Foreseeable FMLA Leave

(a) Timing of notice. An employee must provide the employer at least 30 days advance notice before FMLA leave is to begin if the need for the leave is foreseeable based on an expected birth, placement for adoption or foster care, planned medical treatment for a serious health condition of the employee or of a family member, or the planned medical treatment for a serious injury or illness of a covered servicemember. If 30 days notice is not practicable, such as because of a lack of knowledge of approximately when leave will be required to begin, a change in circumstances, or a medical emergency, notice must be given as soon as practicable. For example, an employee's health condition may require leave to commence earlier than anticipated before the birth of a child. Similarly, little opportunity for notice may be given before placement for adoption. For foreseeable leave due to a qualifying exigency notice must be provided as soon as practicable, regardless of how far in advance such leave is foreseeable. Whether FMLA leave is to be continuous or is to be taken intermittently or on a reduced schedule basis, notice need only be given one time, but the employee shall advise the employer as soon as practicable if dates of scheduled leave change or are extended, or were initially unknown. In those cases where the employee is required to provide at least 30 days notice of foreseeable leave and does not do so, the employee shall explain the reasons why such notice was not practicable upon a request from the employer for such information.

(b) As soon as practicable means as soon as both possible and practical, taking into account all of the facts and circumstances in the individual case. When an employee becomes aware of a need for FMLA leave less than 30 days in advance, it should be practicable for the employee to provide notice of the need for leave either the same day or the next business day. In all cases, however, the determination of when an employee could practicably provide notice must take into account the individual facts and circumstances.

(c) Content of notice. An employee shall provide at least verbal notice sufficient to make the employer aware that the employee needs FMLA-qualifying leave, and the anticipated timing and duration of the leave. Depending on the situation, such information may include that a condition renders the employee unable to perform the functions of the job; that the employee is pregnant or has been hospitalized overnight; whether the employee or the employee's family member is under the continuing care of a health care provider; if the leave is due to a qualifying exigency, that a military member is on covered active duty or call to covered active duty status (or has been notified of an impending call or order to covered active duty), and that the requested leave is for one of the reasons listed in § 825.126(b); if the leave is for a family member, that the condition renders the family member unable to perform daily activities, or that the family member is a covered servicemember with a serious injury or illness; and the anticipated duration of the absence, if known. When an employee seeks leave for the first time for a FMLA-qualifying reason, the employee need not expressly assert rights under the FMLA or even mention the FMLA. When an employee seeks leave due to a FMLA-qualifying reason, for which the employer has previously provided FMLA-protected leave, the employee must specifically reference the qualifying reason for leave or the need for FMLA leave. In all cases, the employer should inquire further of the employee if it is necessary to have more information about whether FMLA leave is being sought by the employee, and obtain the necessary details of the leave to be taken. In the case of medical conditions, the employer may find it necessary to inquire further to determine if the leave is because of a serious health condition and may request medical certification to support the need for such leave. See § 825.305. An employer may also request certification to support the need for leave for a qualifying exigency or for military caregiver leave. See §§ 825.309, 825.310). When an employee has been previously certified for leave due to more than one FMLA-qualifying reason, the employer may need to inquire further to determine for which qualifying reason the leave is needed. An employee has an obligation to respond to an employer's questions designed to determine whether an absence is potentially FMLA-qualifying. Failure to respond to reasonable employer inquiries regarding the leave request may result in denial of FMLA protection if the employer is unable to determine whether the leave is FMLA-qualifying.

(d) Complying with employer policy. An employer may require an employee to comply with the employer's usual and customary notice and procedural requirements for requesting leave, absent unusual circumstances. For example, an employer may require that written notice set forth the reasons for the requested leave, the anticipated duration of the leave, and the anticipated start of the leave. An employee also may be required by an employer's policy to contact a specific individual. Unusual circumstances would include situations such as when an employee is unable to comply with the employer's policy that requests for leave should be made by contacting a specific number because on the day the employee needs to provide notice of his or her need for FMLA leave there is no one to answer the call-in number and the voice mail box is full. Where an employee does not comply with the employer's usual notice and procedural requirements, and no unusual circumstances justify the failure to comply, FMLA-protected leave may be delayed or denied. However, FMLA-protected leave may not be delayed or denied where the employer's policy requires notice to be given sooner than set forth in paragraph (a) of this section and the employee provides timely notice as set forth in paragraph (a) of this section.

(e) Scheduling planned medical treatment. When planning medical treatment, the employee must consult with the employer and make a reasonable effort to schedule the treatment so as not to disrupt unduly the employer's operations, subject to the approval of the health care provider. Employees are ordinarily expected to consult with their employers prior to the scheduling of treatment in order to work out a treatment schedule which best suits the needs of both the employer and the employee. For example, if an employee who provides notice of the need to take FMLA leave on an intermittent basis for planned medical treatment neglects to consult with the employer to make a reasonable effort to arrange the schedule of treatments so as not to unduly disrupt the employer's operations, the employer may initiate discussions with the employee and require the employee to attempt to make such arrangements, subject to the approval of the health care provider. See §§ 825.203 and 825.205.

(f) Intermittent leave or leave on a reduced leave schedule must be medically necessary due to a serious health condition or a serious injury or illness. An employee shall advise the employer, upon request, of the reasons why the intermittent/reduced leave schedule is necessary and of the schedule for treatment, if applicable. The employee and employer shall attempt to work out a schedule for such leave that meets the employee's needs without unduly disrupting the employer's operations, subject to the approval of the health care provider.

(g) An employer may waive employees' FMLA notice requirements. See § 825.304.

29 C.F.R. § 825.303. Employee Notice Requirements for Unforeseeable FMLA Leave

(a) Timing of notice. When the approximate timing of the need for leave is not foreseeable, an employee must provide notice to the employer as soon as practicable under the facts and circumstances of the particular case. It generally should be practicable for the employee to provide notice of leave that is unforeseeable within the time prescribed by the employer's usual and customary notice requirements applicable to such leave. See § 825.303(c). Notice may be given by the employee's spokesperson (e.g., spouse, adult family member, or other responsible party) if the employee is unable to do so personally. For example, if an employee's child has a severe asthma attack and the employee takes the child to the emergency room, the employee would not be required to leave his or her child in order to report the absence while the child is receiving emergency treatment. However, if the child's asthma attack required only the use of an inhaler at home followed by a period of rest, the employee would be expected to call the employer promptly after ensuring the child has used the inhaler.

(b) Content of notice. An employee shall provide sufficient information for an employer to reasonably determine whether the FMLA may apply to the leave request. Depending on the situation, such information may include that a condition renders the employee unable to perform the functions of the job; that the employee is pregnant or has been hospitalized overnight; whether the employee or the employee's family member is under the continuing care of a health care provider; if the leave is due to a qualifying exigency, that a military member is on covered active duty or call to covered active duty status (or has been notified of an impending call or order to covered active duty), that the requested leave is for one of the reasons listed in § 825.126(b), and the anticipated duration of the absence; or if the leave is for a family member that the condition renders the family member unable to perform daily activities or that the family member is a covered servicemember with a serious injury or illness; and the anticipated duration of the absence, if known. When an employee seeks leave for the first time for a FMLA-qualifying reason, the employee need not expressly assert rights under the FMLA or even mention the FMLA. When an employee seeks leave due to a qualifying reason, for which the employer has previously provided the employee FMLA-protected leave, the employee must specifically reference either the qualifying reason for leave or the need for FMLA leave. Calling in "sick" without providing more information will not be considered sufficient notice to trigger an employer's obligations under the Act. The employer will be expected to obtain any additional required information through informal means. An employee has an obligation to respond to an employer's questions designed to determine whether an absence is potentially FMLA-qualifying. Failure to respond to reasonable employer inquiries regarding the leave request may result in denial of FMLA protection if the employer is unable to determine whether the leave is FMLA-qualifying.

(c) Complying with employer policy. When the need for leave is not foreseeable, an employee must comply with the employer's usual and customary notice and procedural requirements for requesting leave, absent unusual circumstances. For example, an employer may require employees to call a designated number or a specific individual to request leave. However, if an employee requires emergency medical treatment, he or she would not be required to follow the call-in procedure until his or her condition is stabilized and he or she has access to, and is able to use, a phone. Similarly, in the case of an emergency requiring leave because of a FMLA-qualifying reason, written advance notice pursuant to an employer's internal rules and procedures may not be required when FMLA leave is involved. If an employee does not comply with the employer's usual notice and procedural requirements, and no unusual circumstances justify the failure to comply, FMLA-protected leave may be delayed or denied.

QUESTIONS

1. An employee works for a company for four years as a mechanic on the overnight shift. He has great performance reviews and is considered a very dependable employee. The employer learns that the employee is supposedly sleeping on the job, which is entirely out of character. The company installs cameras and films him sleeping. The supervisor calls him at home during the day to set up a meeting to discuss the issue. The employee mumbles gibberish, and his sister then gets on the phone and says that he is "very sick." The employee does not show up for work the next day and is fired for being absent. Later, after the termination, it is determined that the employee was suffering from a mental illness and was hospitalized for four days. Was the employer on notice for FMLA purposes?
2. A prospective client says, "I was at work. My sister called me and said that our dad was in the emergency room at the hospital and that I needed to come right away. So, I texted my supervisor and told him what my sister said and that I was going to swap my shift with another employee, which I did. Well, he fired me! Can you help? Isn't that against the law?" Did this employee meet her obligations under the FMLA?

Conclusion

This Lesson has been designed to help you develop a basic understanding of the FMLA and how it operates in practice. You have been exposed only to a taste of what is a much more complicated scheme with a great deal of nuance. Even experienced lawyers must constantly refer back to the statute and the regulations in counseling clients, and so this Lesson required you to do the same. Refer back to the chart, which summarizes the important threshold questions that must be resolved in determining whether a violation of the FMLA has occurred.

8

Terminating the Relationship

Key Concepts

- The employee has certain rights against discharge from employment.
- Once the employment relationship has been terminated, employees have certain protections.
- The employee also owes duties to the employer after termination of the relationship.
- Litigating employment cases requires special considerations.

A. Common Law Remedies for Discharge

Key Concepts

- Employees may recover if their termination was in violation of public policy.
- Employees may recover if their termination was in bad faith.
- Employees may recover under several common law theories in tort and contract.

Lesson 31:
Wrongful Discharge in Violation of Public Policy

Objectives and Expected Learning Outcomes

The first general challenge to the at-will rule targeted bad behavior by employers that had an effect beyond the employment relationship. Slowly, this cause of action was framed as providing the employee a right to recover if the termination of her employment was against public policy. In this Lesson, you will learn about the history of wrongful discharge and how the cause of action came to be narrowly defined.

Most state courts have held that an employer that discharges an employee for reasons that conflict with public policy may be held liable to the employee for tort damages. In some respects, this is not a surprising result. Although freedom of contract is a deeply respected norm in American law, a party may not enforce a contract that violates public policy. For example, if two persons enter a contract to injure a third party, courts will not enforce the agreement. In this same vein, courts have determined that an employer cannot use its right to discharge at-will in a manner that undermines important public policy. The cause of action is generally framed as a suit for "wrongful discharge in violation of public policy."

Although the cause of action is intended to promote public policy, the discharged employee who brings suit receives the damages. The employee recovers her losses related to the wrongful discharge, but the purpose of the tort is to incentivize employers to act in accordance with public policy. It should be no surprise that employers regarded this development in the common law as an assault on the at-will rule. In this Lesson, we examine the tort of wrongful discharge in violation of public policy by exploring the tensions between the accepted goals of promoting the public interest, protecting the employee from pressure to violate public policy, and ensuring that the employer has the flexibility to terminate employment at-will.

Restatement of Employment Law

§ 5.01. Wrongful Discharge in Violation of Public Policy

An employer that discharges an employee because the employee engages in activity protected by a well-established public policy as described in § 5.02 is subject to liability in tort for wrongful discharge in violation of public policy, unless the statute or other law forming the basis of the applicable public policy precludes tort liability or otherwise makes judicial recognition of a tort claim inappropriate.

This simple statement of blackletter law conceals a number of complex issues. In this Lesson, we cover the doctrinal basics. In the next Lesson, we explore deeper issues related to the cause of action.

1. The Emergence of the Tort of Wrongful Discharge

Employers have incredible leverage over their employees, given their ability to discharge an employee for any reason or no reason at all. Very few employees will have the fortitude to risk their job in order to meet their obligations as citizens or to assert their legal rights. Courts began to impose damages under the common law against employers who abused their power by firing employees in a manner that violated public policy. As with many common law developments in the employment arena, this cause of action varied widely between states and was subject to ebbs and flows.

Petermann v. Teamsters Local 396, 344 P.2d 25 (Cal. App. 1959) was a seminal case in the development of this cause of action. Petermann worked for a union. The union directed him to perjure himself before a state legislative committee, but he refused and was fired the following day. Given these extreme facts, the court provided relief to the employee. The court found that refusing to commit a crime was an important public policy, and that the common law should effectuate that public policy by denying "the employer his generally unlimited right to discharge an [at will] employee . . . when the reason for the dismissal is the employee's refusal to commit perjury." *Id.* at 27. *Petermann* provides an example of the most compelling case for granting the employee a right to sue. If an employer could terminate employees who refused to commit crimes at the direction of the employer, many employees would presumably choose to retain their jobs and acquiesce to their employer's criminal activities.

Other early cases expanded the reach of this new cause of action. For example, in *Frampton v. Central Indiana Gas Co.*, 297 N.E.2d 425 (Ind.1973), the court held that an employee who is fired for filing a workers' compensation claim for an injury suffered in the workplace can sue for wrongful discharge. The logic in this case is equally obvious. It would be a curious result if an employer could avoid its statutory obligations to injured workers by threatening their dismissal if they pursued their rights. Permitting a discharged employee to sue for damages supports the public policy embedded in workers' compensation statutory schemes.

While these core cases may make sense, it has proven difficult to articulate the contours of this cause of action. Initially, some courts articulated broad rules that favored the employee and the public interest while limiting the discretion of the employer. Other courts held firm to the at-will rule and refused to recognize a cause of action against employers for violating public policy. We consider these two extremes before focusing on the contemporary state of the doctrine.

A. *Monge v. Beebe Rubber Company*: The Public Policy Against Unfair Dismissal

One of the early cases to discuss a cause of action for discharge in violation of public policy shows the potentially radical implications that this cause of action held at its inception. Read the following case carefully and think about the lines of argument it opens for lawyers representing employees, as well as some of the limitations of the cause of action due to how the action was framed.

MONGE V. BEEBE RUBBER COMPANY

316 A.2d 549 (1974).

LAMPRON, JUSTICE.

[Editor's Note: Ms. Monge sued for breach of an oral contract. She alleged that she was promised that if she worked hard at Defendant's factory, she would be transferred to machines that offered a better hourly rate. Plaintiff claimed that her foreman told her that he would move her to a higher paying machine if she would be "nice" to him, but she refused and reminded him that she was married. She alleges that the foreman then disparaged her and refused to give her a raise, and that his hostility, condoned if not shared by Defendant's personnel manager, ultimately resulted in her being fired.]

Plaintiff sued for breach of an employment contract for an indefinite period of time. The employer has long ruled the workplace with an iron hand by reason of the prevailing common-law rule that such a hiring is presumed to be at will and terminable at any time by either party. . . . When asked to reexamine the long-standing common-law rule of property based on an ancient feudal system which fostered[,] in a tenancy at will[,] a relationship heavily weighted in favor of the landlord, this court did not hesitate to modify that rule to conform to modern circumstances. *Kline v. Burns*, 111 N.H. 87, 90, 276 A.2d 248, 250 (1971); *Sargent v. Ross*, 113 N.H. ___, ___, 308 A.2d 528 (1973).

The law governing the relations between employer and employee has similarly evolved over the years to reflect changing legal, social and economic conditions. Corbin, Contracts § 674 at 205, 206 (1960). In this area '(w)e are in the midst of a period in which the pot boils the hardest and in the process of change the fastest.' *Id.* Although many of these changes have resulted from the activity and influence of labor unions, the courts cannot ignore the new climate prevailing generally in the relationship of employer and employee. . . .

In all employment contracts, whether at will or for a definite term, the employer's interest in running his business as he sees fit must be balanced against the interest of the employee in maintaining his employment, and the public's interest in maintaining a proper balance between the two. Note, California's Controls On Employer Abuse of Employee Rights, 22 Stanford L.Rev. 1015 (1970). We hold that a termination by the employer of a contract of employment at will which is motivated by bad faith or malice or based on retaliation is not the best interest of the economic system or the public good and constitutes a breach of the employment contract. *Frampton v. Central Indiana Gas Co.*, 297 N.E.2d 425 (Ind.1973); see *Petermann v. International Brotherhood*, 174 Cal.App.2d 184, 189, 344 P.2d 25, 27 (1959); Blades, Employment At Will v. Individual Freedom: On Limiting the Abusive Exercise of Employer Power, 67 Colum.L.Rev. 1404, 1418, (1967). Such a rule affords the employee a certain stability of employment and does not interfere with the employer's normal exercise of his right to discharge, which is necessary to permit him to operate his business efficiently and profitably.

The sole question on appeal is whether there was sufficient evidence to support the jury's finding that defendant, through its agents, acted maliciously in terminating plaintiff's employment. It is the function of the jury to resolve conflicts in the testimony, *Kilfoyle v. Malatesta*, 101 N.H. 473, 475, 147 A.2d 111, 113 (1958); and the law is settled that a jury verdict will not be disturbed on appeal if there is evidence to support it. See *O'Brien v. Public Service Co.*, 95 N.H. 79, 58 A.2d 507 (1948); *Benoit v. Perkins*, 79 N.H. 11, 104 A. 254 (1918).

The jury could draw the not-so-subtle inference from the evidence before it that the hostility of defendant's foreman and connivance of the personnel manager resulted in the letter of August 13, 1969, and that that letter was in effect a discharge. See *Colorado Civil Rights Comm'n v. State School Dist. No. 1*, 30 Colo.App. 10, 488 P.2d 83, 86 (1971). The foreman's overtures and the capricious firing at 2:00 a.m., the seeming manipulation of job assignments, and the apparent connivance of the personnel manager in this course of events all support the jury's conclusion that the dismissal was maliciously motivated.

In our opinion, however, the verdict includes elements of damage not properly recoverable. The plaintiff lost 20 weeks employment at an average pay of $70.81 per week. This would account for $1,416.20 of the verdict, leaving $1,083.80 attributable to mental suffering. Such damages are not generally recoverable in a contract action. . . . They could not be found in this case to have resulted from the discharge. Defendant had been having difficulty with her husband and had been receiving annoying telephone calls which upset her. She presented no medical testimony. Although she alleged that her discharge caused her mental suffering, her difficulties all preceded the discharge. We therefore remand the case for a new trial unless the plaintiff consents to a reduction of the verdict by the amount of $1,083.80.

QUESTIONS

1. If the *Monge* case arose today, how would it be litigated? CRA 1964 Title VII sex harassment
2. What public policy did the *Monge* court vindicate? What is the source of this public policy?
3. Why did the court limit the damages available? How would you challenge this on behalf of Ms. Monge?

Despite the breadth of the *Monge* opinion, the New Hampshire Supreme Court eventually followed the lead of other jurisdictions by limiting the cause of action to cases in which the termination interfered directly with an important and independent public policy.

Howard v. Dorr Woolen Co.

120 N.H. 295 (1980).

Bois, Justice.

[Editor's Note: The plaintiff alleged termination of the deceased due to bad faith on the part of the employer, citing to the Monge *decision.]*

We also find the administrator's reliance upon *Monge v. Beebe Rubber Co.*, supra, for the proposition that a discharge due to age or sickness warrants recovery is misplaced. We construe *Monge* to apply only to a situation where an employee is discharged because he performed an act that public policy would encourage, or refused to do that which public policy would condemn .... A discharge due to sickness does not fall within this category, and is generally remedied by medical insurance or disability provisions in an employment contract. Nor does discharge because of age fall within this narrow category. The proper remedy for an action for unlawful age discrimination is provided for by statute. See RSA 354–A:8 I (Supp.1979); RSA 354–A:9; 29 U.S.C. § 623 (1976); 29 U.S.C. § 626 (1976). Accordingly, the administrator's claim must fail on the basis of his pleadings....

B. *Murphy* and *Weider*: The Case Against a Judicially Created Cause of Action for Wrongful Discharge

Some states have declined to create a cause of action on behalf of terminated employees in order to advance public policy. The New York Court of Appeals was the most prominent court to reject the trend. Recall *Murphy v. American Home Products*, in Lesson 7, in which the Court refused to temper the strict at-will rule by recognizing a cause of action for termination in violation of public policy. The plaintiff in *Murphy* claimed that he was fired because of his disclosure to senior management that corporate personnel had engaged in accounting improprieties. The Court concluded that creating an exception to the at-will rule was best left to the legislature, which could make the policy determination and also carefully define the elements of the cause of action.

Immediately after the *Murphy* decision was issued, the New York legislature responded to the court's call for a statutory solution by enacting protections for certain "whistleblowing" employees. That statute currently reads as follows:

N.Y. Labor Law

§ 740. Retaliatory Personnel Action by Employers; Prohibition

1. Definitions. For purposes of this section, unless the context specifically indicates otherwise:

   . . . .

   (e) "Retaliatory personnel action" means the discharge, suspension or demotion of an employee, or other adverse employment action taken against an employee in the terms and conditions of employment.

   . . . .

2. Prohibitions. An employer shall not take any retaliatory personnel action against an employer because such employee does any of the following:

   (a) discloses, or threatens to disclose to a supervisor or to a public body an activity, policy or practice of the employer that is in violation of law, rule or regulation which violation creates and presents a substantial and specific danger to the public health or safety . . . .

   (b) provides information to, or testifies before, any public body conducting an investigation, hearing or inquiry into any such violation of a law, rule or regulation by such employer; or

   (c) objects to, or refuses to participate in any such activity, policy or practice in violation of a law, rule or regulation.

   . . . .

5. Relief. In any action brought pursuant to . . . this section, the court may order relief as follows:

   (a) an injunction to restrain continued violation of this section;

   (b) the reinstatement of the employee to the same position held before the retaliatory personnel action, or to an equivalent position;

   (c) the reinstatement of full fringe benefits and seniority rights;

(d) the compensation for lost wages, benefits and other remuneration; and

(e) the payment by the employer of reasonable costs, disbursements, and attorney's fees.

6. Employer relief. A court, in its discretion, may also order that reasonable attorneys' fees and court costs and disbursements be awarded to an employer if the court determines that an action brought by an employee under this section was without basis in fact or law.

. . . .

QUESTIONS

1. If this statute was on the books at the time of the *Murphy* case, would Mr. Murphy have prevailed in his lawsuit? Develop critiques of this statute from the perspectives of both employers and employees.

2. The *Murphy* court noted that many remedial statutes affecting the employment relationship contain their own anti-retaliation provision to effectuate the underlying public policy of the particular statute. As you will learn in Lesson 37, Title VII of the Civil Rights Act of 1964 prohibits discrimination in the workplace and specifically prohibits retaliation against persons seeking to enforce the statutory protections. The anti-retaliation provision provides:

   > It shall be an unlawful employment practice for an employer to discriminate against any of [the employer's] employees or applicants . . . . because [the employee or applicant] has opposed any practice made an unlawful employment practice by this subchapter, or because [the employee or applicant] has made a charge, testified, assisted or participated in any manner in an investigation, proceeding or hearing under this subchapter.

   42 U.S.C. § 2000e–3(a). If an employer fires a woman employee because she has filed a claim for gender discrimination, she may recover under this provision for retaliation even if the employer prevails on the underlying discrimination complaint. This anti-retaliation provision has been interpreted broadly in order to effectuate the purpose of encouraging employees to vindicate their rights under the statute. *See, e.g., Thompson v. North American Stainless, LP*, 562 U.S. 179 (2011) (holding that an employee can sue after being fired because his fiancée co-employee filed a discrimination claim; the employee is within the zone of protection of the statute, which seeks to prevent employers from using their leverage to discourage the assertion of rights under the statute). Should courts imply an anti-retaliation provision in statutory schemes that are silent on the matter?

Consider the following New York case that rejected a cause of action for wrongful discharge, despite acknowledging the significant public policy interests at stake.

Weider v. Skala

609 N.E. 2d 105 (N.Y. Ct. App. 1992).

Hancock, Judge.

Plaintiff, a member of the Bar, has sued his former employer, a law firm. He claims he was wrongfully discharged as an associate because of his insistence that the firm comply with the governing disciplinary rules by reporting professional misconduct allegedly committed by another associate. The question presented is whether plaintiff has stated a claim for relief either for breach of contract or for the tort of wrongful discharge in violation of this State's public policy. The lower courts have dismissed both causes of action on motion as legally insufficient under CPLR 3211(a)(7) on the strength of New York's employment-at-will doctrine. For reasons which follow, we modify the order and reinstate plaintiff's cause of action for breach of contract.

I.

In the complaint, which must be accepted as true on a dismissal motion under CPLR 3211(a)(7), plaintiff alleges that he was a commercial litigation attorney associated with defendant law firm from June 16, 1986 until March 18, 1988. In early 1987, plaintiff requested that the law firm represent him in the purchase of a condominium apartment. The firm agreed and assigned a fellow associate (L.L.) "to do 'everything that needs to be done' ". For several months, L.L. neglected plaintiff's real estate transaction and, to conceal his neglect, made several "false and fraudulent material misrepresentations". In September 1987, when plaintiff learned of L.L.'s neglect and false statements, he advised two of the firm's senior partners. They conceded that the firm was aware "that [L.L.] was a pathological liar and that [L.L.] had previously lied to [members of the firm] regarding the status of other pending legal matters". When plaintiff confronted L.L., he acknowledged that he had lied about the real estate transaction and later admitted in writing that he had committed "several acts of legal malpractice and fraud and deceit upon plaintiff and several other clients of the firm".

The complaint further alleges that, after plaintiff asked the firm partners to report L.L.'s misconduct to the Appellate Division Disciplinary Committee as required under DR 1–103(A) of the Code of Professional Responsibility,[1] they declined to act. Later, in an effort to dissuade plaintiff from making the report himself, the partners told him that they would reimburse his losses. Plaintiff nonetheless met with the Committee "to discuss the entire matter". He withdrew his complaint, however, "because the [f]irm had indicated that it would fire plaintiff if he reported [L.L.'s] misconduct". Ultimately, in December 1987—as a result of plaintiff's insistence—the firm made a report concerning L.L.'s "numerous misrepresentations and [acts of] malpractice against clients of the [f]irm and acts of forgery of checks drawn on the [f]irm's account". Thereafter, two partners "continuously berated plaintiff for having caused them to report [the] misconduct". The firm nevertheless continued to employ plaintiff "because he was in charge of handling the most important litigation in the [f]irm". Plaintiff was fired in March 1988, a few days after he filed motion papers in that important case.

Plaintiff asserts that defendants wrongfully discharged him as a result of his insistence that L.L.'s misconduct be reported as required by DR 1–103(A). In his fourth cause of action, he alleges that the firm's termination constituted a breach of the employment relationship. In the fifth cause of action, he claims that his discharge was in violation of public policy and constituted a tort for which he seeks compensatory and punitive damages.

Defendants moved to dismiss the fourth and fifth causes of action as legally insufficient pursuant to CPLR 3211(a)(7). Supreme Court granted defendants' motion because his employment relationship was at will, holding:

> since [the] 'Whistleblowers Law' [Labor Law § 740] is not applicable to the facts of this case, and plaintiff has not pleaded facts to come within the exception set forth in *Weiner v. McGraw-Hill, Inc.,* 57 N.Y.2d 458, 457 N.Y.S.2d 193, 443 N.E.2d 441 (1982), the rules governing the causes of action for wrongful discharge are those set forth in *Murphy* [*v. American Home Prods. Corp.,* 58 N.Y.2d 293, 461 N.Y.S.2d 232, 448 N.E.2d 86]. Accordingly, since under the facts pleaded herein, the law firm had the right

1 DR 1–103(A) provides: "A lawyer possessing knowledge, not protected as a confidence or secret, of a violation of DR 1–103 that raises a substantial question as to another lawyer's honesty, trustworthiness or fitness in other respects as a lawyer shall report such knowledge to a tribunal or other authority empowered to investigate or act upon such violation."

to terminate plaintiff, the fourth and fifth causes of action are dismissed.

The Appellate Division affirmed, 167 A.D.2d 265, 562 N.Y.S.2d 930. It also concluded that plaintiff failed to state a cause of action because, as an at-will employee, the firm could terminate him without cause. This Court granted leave to appeal.

II.

We discuss first whether, notwithstanding our firmly established employment-at-will doctrine, plaintiff has stated a legal claim for breach of contract in the fourth cause of action. The answer requires a review of the three cases in which that doctrine is fully explained.

The employment-at-will doctrine is a judicially created common-law rule "that where an employment is for an indefinite term it is presumed to be a hiring at will which may be freely terminated by either party at any time for any reason or even for no reason" (*Murphy v. American Home Prods. Corp.*, 58 N.Y.2d 293, 300, 461 N.Y.S.2d 232, 448 N.E.2d 86, *supra* [citing *Martin v. New York Life Ins. Co.*, 148 N.Y. 117, 42 N.E. 416]). In *Murphy*, this Court dismissed the claim of an employee who alleged he had been discharged in bad faith in retaliation for his disclosure of accounting improprieties. In so doing, we expressly declined to follow other jurisdictions in adopting the tort-based abusive discharge cause of action for imposing "liability on employers where employees have been discharged for disclosing illegal activities on the part of their employers", being of the view "that such a significant change in our law is best left to the Legislature" (*id.*, 58 N.Y.2d at 301, 461 N.Y.S.2d 232, 448 N.E.2d 86).

With respect to the contract cause of action asserted in *Murphy*, the Court held that plaintiff had not shown evidence of any express agreement limiting the employer's unfettered right to fire the employee. For this reason, the Court distinguished *Weiner v. McGraw-Hill, Inc.*, 57 N.Y.2d 458, 457 N.Y.S.2d 193, 443 N.E.2d 441, *supra*, where such an express limitation had been found in language in the employer's personnel handbook. Finally, in *Murphy*, the Court rejected the argument that plaintiff's discharge for disclosing improprieties violated a legally implied obligation in the employment contract requiring the employer to deal fairly and in good faith with the employee, explaining:

> No New York case upholding any such broad proposition is cited to us by plaintiff (or identified by our dissenting colleague), and we know of none. New York does recognize that in appropriate circumstances an obligation of good faith and fair dealing on the part of a party to a contract may be implied and, if implied will be enforced (e.g., *Wood v. Duff-Gordon,* 222 N.Y. 88 [118 N.E. 214]; *Pernet v. Peabody Eng. Corp.,* 20 A.D.2d 781 [248 N.Y.S.2d 132]). *In such instances the implied obligation is in aid and furtherance of other terms of the agreement of the parties. No obligation can be implied, however, which would be inconsistent with other terms of the contractual relationship.* Thus, in the case now before us, plaintiff's employment was at will, a relationship in which the law accords the employer an unfettered right to terminate the employment at any time. In the context of such an employment it would be incongruous to say that an inference may be drawn that the employer impliedly agreed to a provision which would be destructive of his right of termination" (*id.,* 58 N.Y.2d at 304–305, 461 N.Y.S.2d 232, 448 N.E.2d 86 [emphasis added]).

Four years after *Murphy,* the Court decided *Sabetay v. Sterling Drug,* 69 N.Y.2d 329, 514 N.Y.S.2d 209, 506 N.E.2d 919. There, the Court dismissed the complaint of an employee who claimed he was fired for "blowing the whistle" and refusing to engage in improper and unethical activities. As in *Murphy,* the Court found no basis for an express limitation on the employer's right to discharge an at-will employee and, adhering to *Murphy* as a precedent, declined to base any such limitation on an implied-in-law obligation of dealing fairly and in good faith with its employee.

Not surprisingly, defendants' position here with respect to plaintiff's breach of contract cause of action is simple and direct, i.e., that: (1) as in *Murphy* and *Sabetay,* plaintiff has shown no factual basis for an express limitation on the right to terminate of the type upheld in *Weiner;* and (2) *Murphy* and *Sabetay* rule out any basis for contractual relief under an obligation implied-in-law. We agree that plaintiff's complaint does not contain allegations that could come within the *Weiner* exception for express contractual limitations (*see, Weiner v. McGraw-Hill, Inc., supra,* 57 N.Y.2d at 465, 457 N.Y.S.2d 193, 443 N.E.2d 441). As to an implied-in-law duty, however, a different analysis and other considerations pertain.

[Editor's Note: The Court found that an implied term of the employment relationship included an obligation to fully comport with legal ethics rules, because "in any hiring of an attorney as an associate to practice law with a firm there is implied an understanding so fundamental to the relationship and essential to its purpose as to require no expression: that both the associate and the firm in conducting the practice will do so in accordance with the ethical standards of the profession."]

From the foregoing, it is evident that both *Murphy* and *Sabetay* are markedly different. The defendants in those cases were large manufacturing concerns—not law firms engaged with their employee in a common professional enterprise, as here. In neither *Murphy* nor *Sabetay* was the plaintiff required to act in a way that subverted the core purpose of the employment. The company rules underlying the firing of *Murphy* and *Sabetay* were not, as in this case, general rules of conduct and ethical standards governing both plaintiff and defendants in carrying out the sole aim of their joint enterprise, the practice of their profession (*see,* Judiciary Law § 90[2]; *and see, e.g.,* Rules of App.Div., 1st Dept. [22 NYCRR] § 603.2). Unlike *Murphy* and *Sabetay,* giving effect to an implied understanding—that in their common endeavor of providing legal services plaintiff and the firm would comply with the governing rules and standards and that the firm would not act in any way to impede or discourage plaintiff's compliance—would be "in aid and furtherance of [the central purpose] of the agreement of the parties" (*Murphy v. American Home Prods. Corp., supra,* 58 N.Y.2d at 304, 461 N.Y.S.2d 232, 448 N.E.2d 86). Thus, the case is distinguishable from *Murphy* and *Sabetay* where giving effect to the implied obligation would have been "inconsistent with" and "destructive of" an elemental term in the agreement (*id.,* at 304–305, 461 N.Y.S.2d 232, 448 N.E.2d 86). We conclude, therefore, that plaintiff has stated a valid claim for breach of contract based on an implied-in-law obligation in his relationship with defendants.

III.

Plaintiff argues, moreover, citing our decision in *Cohen v. Lord, Day & Lord,*[3] 75 N.Y.2d 95, 101, 551 N.Y.S.2d 157, 550 N.E.2d 410, that the dictates of

3 In *Cohen*, the Court held that a term in a law firm partnership agreement which conditions payment of earned but uncollected partnership revenues upon a withdrawing partner's refraining from practicing law in competition with the firm restricts the practice of law in violation of DR 2–108(A) and is, therefore, unenforceable as against public policy.

public policy in DR 1–103(A) have such force as to warrant our recognition of the tort of abusive discharge pleaded in the fifth cause of action. While the arguments are persuasive and the circumstances here compelling, we have consistently held that "significant alteration of employment relationships, such as the plaintiff urges, is best left to the Legislature" (*Sabetay v. Sterling Drug, supra,* 69 N.Y.2d at 336, 514 N.Y.S.2d 209, 506 N.E.2d 919 [citing *Murphy v. American Home Prods. Corp., supra,* 58 N.Y.2d at 301–302, 461 N.Y.S.2d 232, 448 N.E.2d 86]). We believe that the same rationale applies here. In 1984, the Legislature enacted a "Whistleblower" statute (Labor Law § 740, added by L.1984, ch. 660, § 2). We have noted that, although the present "statute has been criticized by commentators for not affording sufficient safeguards against retaliatory discharge any additional protection must come from the Legislature" (*Remba v. Federation Empl. & Guidance Serv.,* 76 N.Y.2d 801, 803, 559 N.Y.S.2d 961, 559 N.E.2d 655).

Accordingly, the judgment appealed from and the order of the Appellate Division brought up for review should be modified, with costs to plaintiff, by denying defendant's motion to dismiss the fourth cause of action and, as so modified, affirmed.

QUESTIONS

1. Why did the allegations in *Weider* fall outside of Labor Law § 740 (the New York whistleblowing statute)?
2. Does the existence of Labor Law § 740 make it easier or more difficult for the New York Court of Appeals to recognize a common law cause of action that can provide relief to the plaintiff in *Weider*?

---

2. Contemporary Issues in Wrongful Discharge Litigation

Most courts permit some form of tort action for wrongful discharge in violation of public policy, but they also tend to define the tort narrowly so as to avoid unduly interfering with the employer's right to discharge at-will employees. The stark positions adopted in *Monge* and *Murphy* provide the paradigm arguments for employees and employers, but most cases have endorsed a compromise approach that falls somewhere in between.

We conclude this Lesson by considering the core elements of the claim of wrongful discharge in violation of public policy: the prohibited actions by the employer, and the protected activities by the employee.

A. Prohibited Actions by the Employer

As provided in § 5.01 of the Restatement, the employer is liable for "discharging" an employee in violation of public policy. Although the seminal cases involved termination of employment, courts have considered what actions by the employer should be prohibited. In Comment c, the Restatement concludes that the cases provide no uniform rule.

> *c. Constructive discharge.* While most tort claims of wrongful discharge in violation of public policy involve an actual discharge, § 5.01 also covers claims for constructive discharge. . . An employer constructively discharges an employee by creating working conditions so intolerable that a reasonable employee under the circumstances would be compelled to quit, and the employee in fact quits.
>
> . . . This restatement expresses no view on whether public-policy claims based on adverse employer actions falling short of discharge or constructive discharge (termed here "wrongful discipline") should be actionable. Relatively few courts have addressed the issue, largely because employees rarely sue their current employer and the smaller damages associated with such claims rarely warrant litigation. The few decisions on the subject are divided. Some courts have rejected wrongful-discipline claims on the ground that common-law courts should not, without a specific legislative directive, scrutinize and pass judgment on routine personnel decisions on pay, promotion, and the like. Other courts have recognized the cause of action, maintaining that discipline short of discharge can chill employee behavior in the public interest and noting that most statutory claims cover discipline short of discharge without creating special difficulties for the courts.

Mastery Problem 31-1

Jose García was hired by Rocket Mfg. in October 1990. From October 2007 to April 2010, García was a supervisor in Manufacturing Operations at the Rocket facility in San Diego, where Rocket fulfilled large government contracts with

NASA. As supervisor, García kept the time records for employees in his department, and he was responsible for charging each employee's time to the project the employee was working on. García mischarged the time of his employees to projects they were not working on, in order to shift billing to certain NASA contracts that were more profitable. In July 2009, García spoke to a representative of NASA's Inspector General's office. García told the representative that he had been ordered by his supervisor, Ron Ciotta, to mischarge his employees' time. Ciotta was the only person at Rocket who told García to mischarge his employee's time. García never discussed or verified Ciotta's alleged order to mischarge with any other person in Rocket's management. Ciotta categorically denied that he gave any such instructions. García knew that mischarging was illegal and unethical.

On November 6, 2009, García met with Rocket officials and told them he had spoken to an official from NASA in July 2009. García did not tell Rocket officials about his own mischarging activities at the November meeting. However, he did report that he had heard of mischarging on the Space Shuttle program by another supervisor, and that he had reported this wrongdoing to NASA.

On March 13, 2010, García again met with Rocket officials. At this meeting he signed a statement admitting he had personally engaged in mischarging. On March 17, García was placed on leave with pay, pending an investigation. Rocket then suspended him without pay on April 28. In July of 2010, García retained an attorney and brought suit for wrongful discharge. On October 10, Rocket offered to reinstate García to a nonsupervisory position with no reduction in pay at another Rocket facility that did not perform work for NASA. García returned to work at this new facility on October 28, 1980.

In his complaint, García alleged retaliatory disciplinary action by his employer, Rocket. In support of the summary judgment, Rocket contends a tort claim for damages for wrongful discharge arises only after a retaliatory firing or termination of employment. In the alternative, Rocket argues that the undisputed facts show it disciplined García for cause because he engaged in mischarging, not in retaliation for his revelations to NASA.

B. Protected Activities by the Employee

The Restatement describes five activities by an employee that trigger protection from discharge, plus a sixth general category.

Restatement of Employment Law

§ 5.02. Wrongful Discharge in Violation of Public Policy: Protected Activities

An employer is subject to liability in tort under § 5.01 for discharging an employee because the employee, acting in a reasonable manner:

(a) refuses to commit an act that the employee reasonably and in good faith believes violates a law or other well-established public policy, such as a professional or occupational code of conduct protective of the public interest;

(b) performs a public duty or obligation that the employee reasonably and in good faith believes the law imposes;

(c) files a charge or claims a benefit in good faith under an employment statute or law, whether or not the charge or claim is meritorious;

(d) refuses to waive a nonnegotiable or nonwaivable right when the employer's insistence on the waiver as a condition of employment, or the court's enforcement of the waiver, would violate well-established public policy;

(e) reports or inquires about conduct that the employee reasonably and in good faith believes violates a law or an established principle of a professional or occupational code of conduct protective of the public interests; or

(f) engages in other activity directly furthering a well-established public policy.

The Restatement provides a list of five protected activities, plus a general "catch-all" provision that permits courts to define the tort in specific circumstances. Is the Restatement too detailed, or not detailed enough? Consider the case and problems that follow.

ROTHROCK V. ROTHROCK MOTOR SALES, INC.

584 Pa. 297 (2005).

JUSTICE BAER.

We granted allowance of appeal to determine whether the Superior Court erred in extending a previously created exception to the at-will employment doctrine. For the reasons that follow, we affirm.

> *[Editor's Note: Rothrock Motor Sales was owned by Bruce Rothrock and his brother, Ted, was the body shop manager. Ted's son, Doug, worked as a body shop technician and reported directly to his father. Doug alleged that he suffered a workplace injury and reported it to the personnel office. Bruce was upset, because he believed that Doug actually was injured in a stock car race accident. Bruce contacted Ted to ask if Doug was planning to make a workers' compensation [WC] claim.]*

Bruce instructed Ted to have Doug sign a form releasing Motor Sales and thereby waiving Doug's WC benefits. As the Superior Court noted, Ted testified at trial that Bruce told him: "[I]f I [Ted] didn't do this, not one [presumably Doug] would be gone, two [presumably Doug and Ted] would be gone. Meaning that if I didn't get it done, not one [would be] fired, two are fired." Ted spoke to Doug sometime in June of 1992 about not pursuing his WC claim, explaining that if Doug did not sign the release abrogating his rights under the Workers' Compensation Act, Bruce would fire them both. Doug initially agreed to sign the release. Ted testified that Doug said, "Dad, to save your job, I will sign it." Ted evidently had a change of heart, and later told Doug that he need not sign the release. Doug presumably took his father's offer to heart, as he declined to execute the release. Notwithstanding his refusal to waive his benefits, Doug did not file a formal claim with the Bureau of WC during this time period.

On June 17, 1992, Doug underwent surgery for the removal of a herniated cervical disk. Dr. Yonas Zegeye performed the surgery, and subsequently proffered her expert opinion that Doug's injury was the result of his lifting of heavy computer equipment while at work. Approximately a month thereafter, on July 16, 1992, Bruce called a meeting and requested that his son, Bruce Jr., Ted, Doug, and Doug's wife attend. The purpose of the meeting was to attempt to coerce Doug into signing the release of his WC benefits. Again, as noted by the Superior Court, Ted's testimony during the trial of this case described the meeting as follows: "[Bruce] gave Doug a paper and he said, 'Doug I want this signed;' and Doug responded, 'Uncle Bruce, I can't sign this paper.' " Thereafter, Bruce and Doug got into an argument which escalated to the point where Bruce told Doug, "get the 'f' out of the shop, you're fired," causing Doug and his wife to exit the meeting. Bruce then turned his attention to Ted telling him: "remember what I told you." Ted took this to mean that he was also fired because he had not convinced Doug to sign the release. Ted gathered his personal belongings and left Motor Sales the same day.

On July 27, 1992, Doug finally filed a claim petition seeking WC compensation benefits. On September 13, 1992, Doug also filed a claim for unemployment compensation (UC) benefits with the Pennsylvania Department of Labor and Industry (DOL). The DOL asked Motor Sales to send information regarding Doug's termination from employment to permit evaluation of the UC claim. Motor Sales responded that Doug was on medical leave and as of September, 1992, had neither resigned nor been terminated from employment.

After reviewing the case, the DOL communicated its decision, by letter, finding that Doug reasonably believed he had been discharged during his verbal altercation with Bruce on July 16, 1992. Thus, Doug had not voluntarily terminated his employment. The DOL also determined that Doug's conduct prior to and during that incident did not constitute willful misconduct. Finally, the DOL determined that as of September 24, 1992, Doug's physician had released him only to engage in limited light duty work. On the basis of these premises, the DOL awarded Doug UC benefits.

Doug's father, Ted, also sought UC benefits. As in Doug's case, the DOL requested that Motor Sales provide information regarding Ted's termination, and Motor Sales responded asserting that Ted had been terminated for willful misconduct. The DOL determined that Motor Sales had failed to provide sufficient information to support this assertion. Accordingly, it also awarded Ted UC benefits. Motor Sales appealed that decision, but eventually withdrew the appeal. Accordingly, Ted was paid UC benefits.

Notwithstanding Doug's receipt of WC and UC benefits and Ted's receipt of UC benefits, on January 27, 1993, Doug and Ted filed a joint civil complaint against Motor Sales averring wrongful discharge from their employment. Seven years later, on September 6, 2000, the case went to trial. Doug proceeded upon the theory that he had been terminated for refusing to waive his WC benefits, in contravention of Pennsylvania law as articulated in *Shick v. Shirey,* 552 Pa. 590, 716 A.2d 1231 (1998). Ted proceeded on the theory that he had been terminated for refusing to coerce Doug into waiving such benefits, and that such a claim was cognizable as a logical corollary to *Shick.*

On September 11, 2000, a jury determined that Doug had not been wrongfully discharged, and, accordingly, entered a verdict in favor of Motor Sales and against Doug. The jury then determined that Motor Sales did terminate Ted because he refused to coerce Doug into waiving his workers' compensation claim. The jury awarded Ted compensatory damages totaling $192,000, but declined to award punitive damages. Motor Sales filed post-trial motions seeking remittitur and judgment *n.o.v.* The trial court denied those post-trial motions, and Motor Sales appealed to the Superior Court.

Before the Superior Court, Motor Sales argued, *inter alia,* that the trial court erred in permitting Ted, an at-will employee, to proceed on a claim for wrongful discharge based upon his refusal to interfere with a subordinate employee's pursuit of workers' compensation benefits. Motor Sales was well aware of our decision in *Shick,* where we determined that it violated Pennsylvania law to terminate an employee for seeking WC benefits, but, nevertheless, argued that such decision should not be extended to prohibit an employer from terminating a supervisory employee for refusing to attempt to dissuade a subordinate employee to not seek WC benefits.[9] The Superior Court rejected this contention, holding that our decision in *Shick* should be extended to prohibit Motor Sale's conduct in this case. It, therefore, affirmed the trial court, permitting the verdict against Motor Sales to stand.

Appellant filed a petition for allowance of appeal with this Court raising two issues for our review: (1) whether the Superior Court erred in creating a new exception to the at-will employment doctrine, and (2) whether the court erred in retroactively applying *Shick* to this matter. We granted allowance of appeal to consider these issues. We turn first to consideration of whether the Superior Court inappropriately established a new exception to the at-will employment doctrine.

. . . .

9 The facts of this case are unusual in that a father was the supervisory employee threatened with retaliation if he failed to dissuade his son, a subordinate employee, from filing for workers' compensation benefits. While the parties' relationship makes the case more compelling, it does not limit its holding. The precedent established herein is obviously applicable whenever an employer seeks to compel a supervisory employee to thwart a subordinate employee's unquestioned right to WC benefits.

The Superior Court's opinion below discusses *Lins v. Children's Discovery Centers of America, Inc.*, 95 Wash.App. 486, 976 P.2d 168 (1999), a decision from the state of Washington confronting the identical issue presented by this case. Washington, like Pennsylvania, recognizes an employer's essential right to terminate an at-will employee, absent statutory, regulatory, or contractual protection or some overarching public policy. However, the Washington legislature and its courts have been far less reluctant than Pennsylvania to create exceptions to the precept that an employer may fire an at-will employee for any reason. *See, Lins* at 171–172. This has necessitated the utilization by Washington courts of a four-prong test for determination of whether peculiar circumstances prohibit an employer from discharging an at-will employee. *Id.*

Our first inquiry is whether a clear public policy is implicated in Doug's termination by Motor Sales. In *Shick,* we held that an employee cannot be terminated for seeking WC benefits. Such decision would be a Pyrrhic victory for Doug and all other Pennsylvania employees, if it could be as easily circumvented as Motor Sales contends here. We believe it is self-evident that if public policy prohibits termination for seeking workers' compensation, it also prohibits termination for declining to compel a subordinate employee to not seek compensation. We, thus, have little difficulty in concluding that there is a clear public policy supporting the logical incremental extension of *Shick* to the facts of this case.

We next consider whether a policy prohibiting an employer's termination of a subordinate employee for seeking WC would be jeopardized unless we protect such employee's supervisor from an employer's demand that he coerce a subordinate employee into foregoing WC benefits or face termination. For the reasons just stated, we believe it clear that such supervisory employee requires our protection. Indeed, there is little doubt that the policy of protecting subordinate employees' rights to seek WC benefits will be well-nigh eliminated if employers can avoid the rule of *Shick* by pressuring and firing supervisors who do not or cannot coerce subordinate employees into foregoing their rights. Moreover, it would be equally repugnant for this Court to turn its back on such supervisors, who amount to innocent pawns in a conflict between employer and subordinate employee, and, nevertheless, would find themselves out of employment without cause or recourse absent this decision.

Third, we consider whether employers in general have an overriding justification for considering a supervisory employee's refusal to terminate a subordinate employee seeking WC benefits as a factor affecting the decision to discharge such supervisory employee. In the instant case, it appears from this record that Motor Sales has no justification, let alone one that overrides all, for terminating Ted because he refused to coerce Doug into foregoing his compensation benefits. Further, we agree with the Superior Court that an employer, such as Motor Sales, may not justify a supervisory employee's termination based on his or her refusal to perform a directive which is violative of public policy as enunciated in case law, such as the one at issue here.

Fourth and finally, we consider whether Ted's activity was a substantial factor in Motor Sales' decision to fire him. Initially, we note that the jury in this case entered its verdict through special interrogatories. It was asked: "Was the termination of plaintiff, Theodore C. Rothrock, due to the filing or pursuit of claim for workers' compensation by plaintiff, Douglas Rothrock?" It answered: "Yes." After the close of the trial, Motor Sales requested, *inter alia,* judgment *n.o.v.* Accordingly, as we now review this case, in substance we are being asked to grant judgment *n.o.v.,* and accordingly we may consider only the evidence supportive of the verdict, providing the verdict winner with the benefit of any doubt. *Degenhardt v. Dillon Company,* 543 Pa. 146, 669 A.2d 946, 950 (1996); *Moure v. The Raeuchle,* 529 Pa. 394, 604 A.2d 1003, 1007 (1992). In accord with that standard of review, we, without hesitation, conclude that the jury was free to believe that upon learning of Doug's injury, Bruce told Ted to force Doug to sign documents waiving compensation, or face personal termination. At the July 16, 1992 meeting, when Doug refused to waive his benefits, Bruce first told Doug he was fired and threw him out of the business, and then immediately turned to Ted and said remember what I told you, alluding to his prior threat that if Doug did not waive benefits, Ted would be fired. Thus, we find it self-evident that Ted's refusal to dissuade Doug from pursuing benefits was not only a substantial factor in Motor Sales' decision to fire Ted, but was the only factor.

On the basis of all the above, we hold, as a necessary corollary to the policy established in *Shick, supra,* that a Pennsylvania employer may not seek to have a supervisory employee dissuade a subordinate employee from seeking WC benefits. If an employer does so, the supervisory employee shall have a cause of action for wrongful discharge from employment.

Problem 31-1

An employee's child becomes seriously ill. The employee quickly exhausts all leave provided by the employer and mandated by family and medical leave laws. The employee tells the employer that he must continue to take time off for the care of his child. Does the employee have a cause of action for wrongful discharge if the employer terminates him?

Problem 31-2

An employee is injured in the workplace and is contemplating filing a workers' compensation claim. Before the employee can file, the employer fires her. Does the employee have a cause of action for wrongful discharge?

Problem 31-3

An employee drives an armored truck that delivers cash on behalf of legal marijuana companies. The employer has a strict policy that any employee who abandons the truck for any reason will be terminated immediately. The employee sees a bank robbery in progress during his route and briefly leaves the truck to assist bank customers who are escaping out the back door of the bank. When the employer learns of this through news accounts, the employer immediately fires the employee. Does the employee have a cause of action for wrongful discharge?

Conclusion

In this Lesson, you studied the development of the tort of wrongful discharge as an exception to the general rule of at-will employment. Although some early articulations of the tort action were broadly phrased and suggested a rethinking of the at-will rule entirely, the courts have narrowed the cause of action. In the next Lesson, you will delve more deeply into the nuances of wrongful discharge doctrine.

Lesson 32:
Sources of Public Policy

Objectives and Expected Learning Outcomes

As you learned in the previous Lesson, an at-will employee may have a cause of action for wrongful discharge if the employer terminates the employment for reasons that are contrary to public policy. In this Lesson, you will focus on the key element of this cause of action: how do courts define "public policy"? This question presents another instance in which courts struggle to articulate their role in the modern administrative state that is defined by statutes and regulations as the expressions of public policy. You will also consider the special considerations when an attorney seeks to recover for wrongful discharge.

Restatement of Employment Law

§ 5.03. Wrongful Discharge in Violation of Public Policy: Sources of Public Policy

Sources of public policy for the tort of wrongful discharge in violation of public policy under § 5.01 include:

(a) federal and state constitutions;

(b) federal, state and local statutes, ordinances and decisional law;

(c) federal, state, and local administrative regulations, decisions, and orders; and

(d) well-established principles in a professional or occupational code of conduct protective of the public interest.

As the Restatement makes clear, the primary sources of public policy supporting the tort of wrongful discharge are found in legislative and regulatory enactments. Although many courts originally referred to "public policy as expressed in statutes," when confronted with cases involving administrative regulations most courts agreed that regulatory law can also express the public policy of the state. *See, e.g., Green v. Ralee Eng. Co.*, 19 Cal. 4th 66 (1998).

The Restatement includes the term "decisional law" in the list of sources of public policy. The Reporter explains:

> Well-established judicial precedent in itself may be a useful guide. The central point will be that the public policy be well established . . . so that courts have a firm basis for recognizing the cause of action and employers and employees are put on notice as to the scope of activity that public policy protects. Whether the public policy is sufficiently established is usually a matter of law for the court to decide.

§ 5.03, comment a. Courts have been hesitant to use common law approaches to this tort for fear that it would amount to a judicial reversal of the at-will rule. Consequently, former employees seeking to recover for wrongful discharge should always cite to specific constitutional, statutory and/or regulatory sources as the public policy that is undermined by the employer's action.

1. The Public Interest and the De Minimus Exception

As you know from the previous Lesson, the *Petermann* case was one of the early instances in which a court accepted the tort of wrongful discharge in violation of public policy. As with most trend-setting cases, the facts were egregious. A union employee was threatened with termination if he did not lie under oath to an investigatory panel. Clearly, the public interest is not served by compelling an employee to commit the crime of perjury, particularly in a proceeding that was focused on governmental efficiency. However, not every allegation that an employee was terminated for acting in accordance with a statute or regulation will qualify as implicating a public policy for the purpose of the tort of wrongful discharge.

Example 32-1

A former employee of a trucking company filed suit against the trucking company for statutory and common law retaliatory discharge, alleging that his employment was terminated due to his refusal to violate a Tennessee Department of Safety regulation that required the truck to carry an original "cab card" evidencing the registration of the vehicle. The employer had directed the employee truck driver to deliver merchandise to a customer, but the original cab card for the truck could not be found. The employer gave the employee a photocopy of the valid and genuine cab card, but the employee refused to drive the truck with only a photocopy. Another truck could not be located to facilitate the delivery. The next day, the employee truck driver was fired. The truck driver sued the employer trucking company for retaliatory discharge, alleging that his employment was discharged for refusing to participate in an illegal activity. The former employee will not prevail, because the employee's refusal to perform the assigned work based on the regulation requiring the original cab card, as opposed to a photocopy, did not further important public policy concerns, and therefore does not support a claim of retaliatory discharge.

Example 32-2

A former employee refused to alter federal Department of Transportation records regarding the operation of a truck in violation of federal law and was fired. The federal rules have been adopted by the state legislature as governing intra-state trucking. The fact that state statutes provide criminal penalties for seeking to evade or defeat such regulations further evidences the degree of public interest. Finally, there is an express interest in the safety of persons and property on or near public highways, as expressed in several numerous statutes regulating almost every aspect of transportation and travel on the highways in an effort to promote safety. Because the former employee was faced with the dilemma of violating that public policy and risking imprisonment, or complying with the public policy and being fired from his employment, the facts give rise to a viable claim of wrongful discharge.

Problem 32-1

Rena Wilson works at a large department store in the downtown area of a major city. Her shift begins early in the morning before the store opens. On Election Day, she hears that lines at the polls were beginning to get exceptionally long, and were expected to be prohibitively long by the time that her shift ended. On a break, she clocked out of work and went to her polling place to ensure that she could vote. When she returned an hour later, her employer told her that "voting is a personal matter," and fired her for leaving work. Has the employer acted in violation of public policy?

Problem 32-2

Jack and Diane work at an accountant's office. There is a strict rule forbidding employees to date or be married to each other. After keeping their romance a secret, the employer finally discovered that Jack and Diane had married six weeks earlier. The employer fired them for violating company rules. Jack and Diane both sue, arguing that their termination is violative of the strong state public policy supporting marriage that is evidenced in numerous statutes. In particular, one statute declares that the state has a strong interest in the institution of marriage and that it is the policy of the state to promote family values. Do Jack and Diane have a viable cause of action?

---

2. The Authority of the Courts to Declare Public Policy Outside of Constitutional, Statutory, and Regulatory Provisions

As indicated in the Restatement, decisional law by courts may serve as a public policy basis for an action in wrongful discharge. However, the courts will seek to ensure that any such public policy is widely known in advance, such that a reasonable employer would know that terminating an employee under the circumstances would negatively affect the public interest.

To avoid having to make such decisions, some jurisdictions have determined that only constitutional, statutory, and regulatory law can serve as the basis for wrongful discharge. Consider the following case from California, and the vigorous dissent.

GANTT V. SENTRY INSURANCE

1 Cal. 4th 1083 (In Bank 1992).

ARABIAN, JUSTICE.

We granted review in this case to consider whether an employee who was terminated in retaliation for supporting a coworker's claim of sexual harassment may state a cause of action for tortious discharge against public policy and, if so, whether the exclusive remedy provisions of the Workers' Compensation Act bar the action. We hold that the claim is actionable under *Tameny v. Atlantic Richfield Co.* (1980) 27 Cal.3d 167, 164 Cal.Rptr. 839, 610 P.2d 1330 (*Tameny*), and is not preempted by the workers' compensation law.

I. PROCEDURAL BACKGROUND

Defendants, Sentry Insurance (Sentry), Frank Singer (Singer) and Caroline Fribance (Fribance) appealed from a judgment entered on a jury verdict of $1.34 million in favor of plaintiff, Vincent A. Gantt (hereafter plaintiff or Gantt) in his action for tortious discharge in violation of the covenant of good faith and fair dealing and in contravention of public policy (*Tameny* action), and intentional infliction of emotional distress.

The Court of Appeal reversed the judgment as to the individual defendants but affirmed in all other respects. As to the *Tameny* cause of action, the Court of Appeal noted that the allegation was predicated upon two distinct theories: the first, that plaintiff was constructively discharged in retaliation for supporting a coworker's claim of sexual harassment; and second, that Sentry attempted to induce plaintiff to give false information or to withhold information from the public agency investigating the sexual harassment charges. Although the Court of Appeal concluded that Gantt's first theory of recovery was preempted by the California Fair Employment and Housing Act (FEHA), it held that the FEHA did not preempt a *Tameny* claim premised on the second theory; that substantial evidence supported the jury's special verdict; and that the action was not barred by the exclusive remedy provisions of the Workers' Compensation Act.

Sentry petitioned this court for review, asserting that neither the facts nor the law supported a *Tameny* claim premised on plaintiff's second theory, and that the action was barred in any event by the workers' compensation law. After granting review, we requested additional briefing on the question whether a *Tameny* claim must be grounded in a violation of statute or constitutional provision.

For the reasons set forth below, we conclude that a termination in retaliation for testifying truthfully concerning a coworker's sexual harassment claim in the context of an administrative investigation is ACTIONABLE under *Tameny, supra,* 27 Cal.3d 167, 164 Cal.Rptr. 839, 610 P.2d 1330. We further conclude that neither the FEHA nor the Workers' Compensation Act preempts the claim. Accordingly, we shall affirm the decision of the Court of Appeal.

II. FACTS

Viewing the record most strongly in favor of the judgment, as we must, the following pertinent chronology of facts appears: In September 1979, Sentry hired Gantt to serve as the sales manager of its Sacramento office. His mission was to develop the Sacramento sales force. How successfully he performed this task was the subject of conflicting evidence at trial. However, as explained below, the record amply supports the jury's specific finding that his demotion and constructive discharge were the product of his support for another employee's sexual harassment claim rather than the result of any legally valid business reason.

. . . .

As noted earlier, the jury returned a special verdict in favor of Gantt, finding, inter alia, that Gantt had been constructively discharged; that Sentry lacked an "honest good faith belief the termination was warranted for legally valid business reasons"; that Gantt was discharged "in retaliation for his refusal to testify untruthfully or to withhold testimony"; that Gantt was further discharged in retaliation for his "actions or statements with respect to Joyce Bruno's sexual harassment allegations;" and that in committing these acts Sentry acted with malice, oppression or fraud.

III. DISCUSSION

A. *Sources of the Public Policy Exception*

This court first recognized a public policy exception to the at-will employment doctrine in *Tameny, supra,* 27 Cal.3d 167, 164 Cal.Rptr. 839, 610 P.2d 1330, and has since reaffirmed its commitment to that principle on several occasions. Indeed, following the seminal California decision in *Petermann v. International Brotherhood of Teamsters* (1959) 174 Cal.App.2d 184, 344 P.2d 25, the antecedent to our holding in *Tameny,* the vast majority of states have recognized that an at-will employee possesses a tort action when he or she is discharged for performing an act that public policy would encourage, or for refusing to do something that public policy would condemn.

Yet despite its broad acceptance, the principle underlying the public policy exception is more easily stated than applied. The difficulty, of course, lies in determining where and how to draw the line between claims that genuinely involve matters of public policy, and those that concern merely ordinary disputes between employer and employee. This determination depends in large part on whether the public policy alleged is sufficiently clear to provide the basis for such a potent remedy. In *Foley v. Interactive Data Corp., supra,* 47 Cal.3d 654, 254 Cal.Rptr. 211, 765 P.2d 373, we endeavored to provide some guidelines by noting that the policy in question must involve a matter that affects society at large rather than a purely personal or proprietary interest of the plaintiff or employer; in addition, the policy must be "fundamental," "substantial" and "well established" at the time of the discharge.

We declined in *Foley* to determine whether the violation of a statute or constitutional provision is invariably a prerequisite to the conclusion that a discharge violates public policy. A review of the pertinent case law in California and elsewhere, however, reveals that few courts have recognized a public policy claim absent a statute or constitutional provision evidencing the policy in question. Indeed, as courts and commentators alike have noted, the cases in which violations of public policy are found generally fall into four categories: (1) refusing to violate a statute (see, e.g., *Tameny, supra,* 27 Cal.3d 167, 164 Cal.Rptr. 839, 610 P.2d 1330 [employee discharged for refusing to participate in illegal price-fixing scheme]; *Petermann v. International Brotherhood of Teamsters, supra,* 174 Cal.App.2d 184, 344 P.2d 25 [employee terminated for refusing to perjure himself before state legislative committee]); (2) performing a statutory obligation (see, e.g., *Nees v. Hocks* (1975) 272 Or. 210, 536 P.2d 512 [performing jury duty]); (3) exercising a statutory right or privilege (*Wetherton v. Growers Farm Labor Assn.* (1969) 275 Cal.App.2d 168, 79 Cal.Rptr. 543 [engaging in union activities]); and (4) reporting an alleged violation of a statute of public importance (*Hentzel v. Singer Co.* (1982) 138 Cal.App.3d 290, 188 Cal.Rptr. 159; see generally Note, *Protecting Employees At Will Against Wrongful Discharge: The Public Policy Exception* (1983) 96 Harv.L.Rev.1931, 1936–1937; Rust et al., *Employee Termination At Will: A Principled Approach* (1982) 28 Vill.L.Rev. 1, 26–27.)

To be sure, those courts which have addressed the issue appear to be divided over the question whether nonlegislative sources may ever provide the basis of a public policy claim. *Pierce v. Ortho Pharmaceutical Corp.* (1980) 84 N.J. 58, 417 A.2d 505 is the leading case for a broad interpretation. As the New Jersey Supreme Court explained: "The sources of public policy [which may limit the employer's right of discharge] include legislation; administrative rules, regulations or decisions; and judicial decisions. In certain instances, a professional code of ethics may contain an expression of public policy." (*Id.,* 417 A.2d at p. 512.) Several other states have adopted similarly broad views of the public policy exception. (See *Parnar v. Americana Hotels, Inc.* (1982)

65 Haw. 370, 652 P.2d 625, 631 ["In determining whether a clear mandate of public policy is violated, courts should inquire whether the employer's conduct contravenes the letter or purpose of a constitutional, statutory, or regulatory provision or scheme. Prior judicial decisions may also establish the relevant public policy."]; *Palmateer v. International Harvester Co.* (1981) 85 Ill.2d 124, 52 Ill.Dec. 13, 15, 421 N.E.2d 876, 878 ["In general, it can be said that public policy concerns what is right and just and what affects the citizens of the State collectively. It is to be found in the State's constitution and statutes and, when they are silent, in its judicial decisions."]; *Boyle v. Vista Eyewear, Inc.* (Mo.Ct.App.1985) 700 S.W.2d 859, 871 [" 'Public policy' is that principle of law which holds that no one can lawfully do that which tends to be injurious to the public or against the public good. . . . It finds its sources in the state constitution, . . . in the letter and purpose of a constitutional, statutory or regulatory provision or scheme, . . . in the judicial decisions of the state and national courts, . . . in 'the constant practice of the government officials,' . . . and, in certain instances, in professional codes of ethics."]; *Phipps v. Clark Oil & Refining Corp., supra,* 396 N.W.2d 588, 593 ["A public policy exception can be reasonably defined by reference to clear mandates of legislative or judicially recognized public policy."]; *Cloutier v. Great Atlantic & Pac. Tea Co., supra,* 436 A.2d 1140, 1144 ["Public policy exceptions giving rise to wrongful discharge actions may also be based on non-statutory policies."]; *Wagenseller v. Scottsdale Memorial Hospital* (1985) 147 Ariz. 370, 710 P.2d 1025, 1034 ["reliance on prior judicial decisions, as part of the body of applicable common law, is appropriate . . ."]; *Yetter v. Ward Trucking Corp.* (1991) 401 Pa.Super. 467, 585 A.2d 1022, 1027 ["appellant has failed to point to any statutorily or judicially recognized public policy which was violated by appellee in terminating appellant"]; *Payne v. Rozendaal* (1986) 147 Vt. 488, 520 A.2d 586, 588 ["we necessarily reject . . . the holdings of some courts that the public policy exception to at will employment contracts must be legislatively defined."]; accord, *Burk v. K-Mart Corp.* (Okla.1989) 770 P.2d 24, 28; *Thompson v. St. Regis Paper Co.* (1984) 102 Wash.2d 219, 685 P.2d 1081, 1089; *Moore v. A.H. Riise Gift Shops* (D.V.I.1987) 659 F.Supp. 1417, 1423.)

Other courts have applied a stricter definition to public policy claims. The leading case is *Brockmeyer v. Dun & Bradstreet* (1983) 113 Wis.2d 561, 335 N.W.2d 834. There, the Wisconsin Supreme Court, while recognizing a public policy exception to the employment at-will doctrine, nevertheless limited plaintiffs to contract damages and confined such claims to statutory or constitutional violations. "Given the vagueness of the concept of public policy," the court explained, "it is necessary that we be more precise about the contours of the public policy exception. A wrongful discharge is actionable when the termination clearly contravenes the public welfare and gravely violates paramount requirements of public interest. The public policy must be evidenced by a constitutional or statutory provision." (*Id.*, 335 N.W.2d at p. 840.) Voicing similar concerns, the Kentucky Supreme Court adopted the *Brockmeyer* definition in *Firestone Textile Co. Div. v. Meadows* (Ky.1983) 666 S.W.2d 730: "Employers as a group have a legitimate interest to protect by having the cause of action for wrongful discharge clearly defined and suitably controlled. . . . [¶] When a discharged employee seeks to establish a cause of action for wrongful discharge, it is a question of law for the court to decide whether the reason for discharge is unlawful because of a constitutionally protected right or a right implicit in a statute." (*Id.* at p. 733.) Other courts have adopted similarly restrictive views of the contours of the public policy exception. (See *Sabine Pilot Service, Inc. v. Hauck* (Tex.1985) 687 S.W.2d 733, 735; *Adams v. George W. Cochran & Co., Inc.* (D.C.1991) 597 A.2d 28, 33–34; *Miller v. Fairfield Communities, Inc.* (Ct.App.1989) 299 S.C. 23, 382 S.E.2d 16, 19; *Merck v. Advanced Drainage Systems, Inc.* (4th Cir.1990) 921 F.2d 549, 554–555 [applying S.C. law].)

Turning from other jurisdictions to California law, one finds the courts similarly divided.

. . . .

Although we have not taken a position on this precise issue, it is true, as plaintiff notes, that this court has not previously confined itself to legislative enactments when determining the public policy of the state. We have, for example, long declined to enforce contracts inimical to law or the public interest, and long ago declared racial discrimination to be contrary to public policy under the common law duty of innkeepers and common carriers to furnish accommodations to all persons.[6]

The analogy to illegal contracts has particular force. For at root, the public policy exception rests on the recognition that in a civilized society the rights of each person are necessarily limited by the rights of others and of the pub-

6 As the Court of Appeal has stated: "It is primarily the prerogative of the legislature to declare what contracts and acts shall be unlawful; but courts, following the spirit and genius of the law, written and unwritten, of a state, may declare void as against public policy contracts which, though not in terms specifically forbidden by legislation, are clearly injurious to the interests of society." (*Maryland C. Co. v. Fidelity etc. Co.* (1925) 71 Cal.App. 492, 497, 236 P. 210 . . .

lic at large; this is the delicate balance which holds such societies together. Accordingly, while an at-will employee may be terminated for no reason, or for an arbitrary or irrational reason, there can be no right to terminate for an unlawful reason or a purpose that contravenes fundamental public policy. Any other conclusion would sanction lawlessness, which courts by their very nature are bound to oppose. (See *Morrill v. Nightingale* (1892) 93 Cal. 452, 458, 28 P. 1068 [" 'Courts owe it to public justice and to their own integrity to refuse to become parties to contracts essentially violating morality or public policy by entertaining actions upon them.' "].) It is a very short and logical step, therefore, from declining to enforce contracts inimical to law or the public interest, to refusing to sanction terminations in contravention of fundamental public policy. Indeed, we expressly acknowledged the analogy in *Foley,* noting, in the context of our *Tameny* discussion: "A comparison of the manner in which contracts for illegal purposes are treated is useful." (47 Cal.3d 654 at p. 667, fn. 7, 254 Cal.Rptr. 211, 765 P.2d 373; see also *Phipps v. Clark Oil & Refining Corp., supra,* 396 N.W.2d at p. 593.)

Def. of PP

Unfortunately, as we have also previously acknowledged, "[t]he term 'public policy' is inherently not subject to precise definition. . . . 'By "public policy" is intended that principle of law which holds that no citizen can lawfully do that which has a tendency to be injurious to the public or against the public good. . . .' " (*Safeway Stores v. Retail Clerks etc. Assn., supra,* 41 Cal.2d at p. 575, 261 P.2d 721.) It was this rather open-ended definition on which the court relied in *Petermann v. International Brotherhood of Teamsters, supra,* 174 Cal.App.2d 184, 188, 344 P.2d 25, the seminal decision articulating the public policy exception to the employment at-will doctrine.

Surveying the extensive and conflicting decisional law summarized above, several general observations are possible. First, notwithstanding the lively theoretical debate over the sources of public policy which may support a wrongful discharge claim, with few exceptions courts have, in practice, relied to some extent on statutory or constitutional expressions of public policy as a basis of the employee's claim. (See, e.g., *Dabbs v. Cardiopulmonary Management Services* (1987) 188 Cal.App.3d 1437, 1443, 234 Cal. Rptr. 129 ["We disagree with the . . . suggestion that the Legislature is the only source of policy determinations. . . . However, . . . in this case there is statutory support for plaintiff's assertion her discharge violated a substantial public policy principle."]; see also *Wagenseller v. Scottsdale Memorial Hosp., supra,* 710 P.2d at pp. 1033–1035; *Palmateer v. International Harvester Co., supra,* 52 Ill.Dec. at pp. 15–17, 421 N.E.2d at pp. 878–880; *Boyle v. Vista*

Eyewear, Inc., supra, 700 S.W.2d at pp. 871–872; *Cloutier v. Great Atlantic & Pac. Tea Co., supra,* 436 A.2d at pp. 1143–1145.)

Second, it is generally agreed that "public policy" as a concept is notoriously resistant to precise definition, and that courts should venture into this area, if at all, with great care and due deference to the judgment of the legislative branch, "lest they mistake their own predilections for public policy which deserves recognition at law." (*Hentzel v. Singer Co., supra,* 138 Cal.App.3d 290, 297, 188 Cal.Rptr. 159.) Indeed, one of the most frequently cited decisions favoring a broad interpretation, *Parnar v. Americana Hotels, Inc., supra,* 652 P.2d 625, observed that courts "should proceed cautiously" if called upon to declare public policy absent some prior legislative expression on the subject. (*Id.* at p. 631; accord *Wagenseller v. Scottsdale Memorial Hosp., supra,* 710 P.2d at p. 1034; *Burk v. K-Mart Corp., supra,* 770 P.2d at pp. 28–29; *Townsend v. L.W.M. Management, Inc., supra,* 494 A.2d at p. 242.)

These wise caveats against judicial policymaking are unnecessary if one recognizes that courts in *wrongful discharge actions* may not declare public policy without a basis in either the constitution or statutory provisions. A public policy exception carefully tethered to fundamental policies that are delineated in constitutional or statutory provisions strikes the proper balance among the interests of employers, employees and the public. The employer is bound, at a minimum, to know the fundamental public policies of the state and nation as expressed in their constitutions and statutes; so limited, the public policy exception presents no impediment to employers that operate within the bounds of law. Employees are protected against employer actions that contravene fundamental state policy. And society's interests are served through a more stable job market, in which its most important policies are safeguarded.

B. *Application of the Public Policy Exception*

Here, we are *not* being asked to declare public policy. The issue as framed by the pleadings and the parties is whether there exists a clear constitutional or legislative declaration of fundamental public policy forbidding plaintiff's discharge under the facts and circumstances presented.

[Editor's Note: The Court found that constitutional and statutory provisions clearly articulated a public policy supporting those who report sexual harassment against a co-worker. The Court also found

that the workers' compensation statute did not preclude an action for wrongful discharge.]

KENNARD, JUSTICE, concurring and dissenting.

. . . .

My second reason for writing separately is to respond to the majority's statement that a cause of action for wrongful termination in violation of public policy may be based only on public policies expressed in constitutional or statutory provisions. Plaintiff never attempted to articulate a public policy not grounded in a statute or a constitutional provision. Nevertheless, this court insisted that the parties brief the issue, and now purports to decide it. This purported decision is doubly misguided. The issue is not raised by the facts of the case or the contentions of the parties, so the majority's comments are purest dicta. And, "[a]s so often happens when a court reaches beyond the confines of the case before it to render a gratuitous advisory opinion, the majority decides the issue incorrectly." (*City of Sacramento v. State of California* (1990) 50 Cal.3d 51, 77, 266 Cal.Rptr. 139, 785 P.2d 522 [conc. & dis. opn. of Kaufman, J.].)

. . . .

The question whether an action for wrongful discharge may ever be based on a public policy not originating from statutory or constitutional provisions should await a case in which the public policy at issue has some nonstatutory and nonconstitutional basis. We should not decide this issue in a complete factual vacuum. Because the majority has chosen to address this issue and analyzed it in a faulty fashion, I feel compelled to respond.

. . . .

. . . Other legitimate sources of public policy, such as judicial decisions or codes of professional ethics, for instance, are readily available to employers or their counsel and thus provide no less "notice" than do statutes or constitutional provisions.

Implicit in the majority's objection to requiring employers to adhere to fundamental public policy set forth in published sources other than statutes or constitutional provisions is the notion that other sources express policies that are not "fundamental" or "substantial" enough. It may be somewhat easier to characterize as "fundamental" a public policy that is plainly based on the terms of a statute or constitutional provision than to so characterize one that is not so based. But it is a mistake to assume that only those policies based on statutes or constitutional provisions are firmly established and important.

An example is helpful. In *Verduzco v. General Dynamics, Convair Div.* (S.D.Cal.1990) 742 F.Supp. 559, the plaintiff, a production supervisor for a national defense project, alleged that he was terminated because he complained that workers without required security clearances had access to restricted documents, and that "security was so lax that workers at the plant could walk off with blueprints and other material," compromising the national security of the United States. (*Id.* at p. 560.)

The federal court found no statute that addressed this issue; it stated that "Verduzco is asking this court to recognize a public policy that is not based on or derived from a statute." (*Verduzco v. General Dynamics, Convair Div., supra,* 742 F.Supp. at p. 560.) Nevertheless, applying California law on wrongful termination, the court held that Verduzco had stated a cause of action for retaliatory dismissal in violation of "a fundamental public interest in preventing unauthorized persons from obtaining access to important technical data relating to military projects." (*Id.* at p. 562.)

Under the majority's approach, a plaintiff in Verduzco's position could be discharged without fear of consequences, because he could point to no statute or constitutional provision that was violated by his discharge. But the absence of a statute or constitutional provision should not prevent the recognition of a fundamental public policy in preserving national security that would be violated by the dismissal of an employee who complained that national security was compromised by lax procedures. Indeed, because the policy "inures to the benefit of the public at large rather than to a particular employer or employee," our cases demand its recognition. (*Foley v. Interactive Data Corp., supra,* 47 Cal.3d at p. 669, 254 Cal.Rptr. 211, 765 P.2d 373; accord, *Rojo v. Kliger* (1990) 52 Cal.3d 65, 90, 276 Cal.Rptr. 130, 801 P.2d 373.)

Other examples are no doubt available. But the point is plain. Courts should not be foreclosed from adjudicating wrongful discharge cases based on violations of public policy springing from nonstatutory and nonconstitutional sources. The majority's attempt to constrain the development of the law in a one-size-fits-all judicial straightjacket ignores the essential wisdom of the common law: law is best developed case by case, with attention to the facts of particular cases and the patterns of cases as they develop over time.

QUESTIONS

1. The at-will rule is generally a doctrine of the common law, although a number of states have restated the rule in their civil code. Why shouldn't courts articulate the contours of, and exceptions to, the at-will rule in a common law manner?

2. In a later decision, the Court extended its rationale to permit employees to ground a claim for wrongful discharge on the public policy established under federal statutory law and administrative regulations that implement statutory schemes. *See Green v. Ralee Eng. Co.*, 960 P. 2d 1046, 1059 (Cal. 1998). Does this clarification affect your assessment of whether principles of public policy could be grounded in the common law?

Problem 32-3

Hugh Beaumont receives a jury summons and tells his employer that he may be away from work for as long as four weeks. Hugh is fired and replaced when he reports for jury duty. The employer had warned Hugh that he couldn't afford to have Hugh absent from work that long. There is no statute that expressly protects employees from retaliation for performing jury service, but there are numerous indications in decisional law that jury service is the foundation of the justice system. Jury service is particularly important in the criminal setting where defendants are entitled to a speedy trial by a jury of their peers. Can Hugh establish a case for wrongful discharge?

---

3. Special Considerations When the Employee Is Acting as an Attorney

Many attorneys work as employees in corporations, effectively serving a single client. As a general rule, clients may dismiss their attorneys for any reason or no reason at all, subject only to the terms of the representation which may permit the attorney to recover earned fees. The following lengthy opinion considers the issues in detail.

General Dynamics Corp. v. Superior Court

7 Cal.4th 1164 (1994).

Arabian, Justice.

We granted review to consider an attorney's status as "in-house" counsel as it affects the right to pursue claims for damages following an allegedly wrongful termination of employment. Specifically, we are asked to decide whether an attorney's status as an employee bars the pursuit of implied-in-fact contract and retaliatory discharge tort causes of action against the employer that are commonly the subject of suits by *non*-attorney employees who assert the same claims.

We conclude that, because so-called "just cause" contractual claims are unlikely to implicate values central to the attorney-client relationship, there is no valid reason why an in-house attorney should not be permitted to pursue such a contract claim in the same way as the nonattorney employee. Our conclusion with respect to the tort cause of action is qualified; our holding seeks to accommodate two conflicting values, both of which arise from the nature of an attorney's professional role: the fiducial nature of the relationship with the client, on the one hand, and the duty to adhere to a handful of defining ethical norms, on the other. As will appear, we conclude that there is no reason inherent in the nature of an attorney's role as in-house counsel to a corporation that in itself precludes the maintenance of a retaliatory discharge claim, *provided* it can be established without breaching the attorney-client privilege or unduly endangering the values lying at the heart of the professional relationship.

Although the effect of the attorney-client relationship is to produce a remedy more limited than that available to the nonattorney employee, the similarities between the position of in-house attorneys and their non-attorney colleagues nevertheless justify an analogous cause of action. The complete economic dependence of in-house attorneys on their employers is indistinguishable from that of nonattorney employees who *are* entitled to pursue a retaliatory discharge remedy. Moreover, as we explain, the position of in-house counsel is especially sensitive to those fundamental ethical imperatives derived from an attorney's professional duties, as well as organizational pressures to ignore or subvert them. On balance, these considerations favor allowing a tort claim for discharges for reasons that contravene an attorney's mandatory ethical obligations or for which a *non*-attorney employee could maintain such a claim *and* a statute or ethical code provision permits the attorney to depart from the usual rule that client matters remain confidential.

The trial courts have at their disposal several measures to minimize or eliminate the potential untoward effects on both the attorney-client privilege and the interests of the client-employer resulting from the litigation of such wrongful termination claims by in-house counsel. Thus, we also hold that, in those instances where the attorney-employee's retaliatory discharge claim is incapable of complete resolution without breaching the attorney-client privilege, the suit may not proceed. That result, however, is rarely, if ever, appropriate where, as in this case, the litigation is still at the pleadings stage.

I

Andrew Rose, an attorney, began working for General Dynamics Corporation (hereafter General Dynamics) as a 27-year-old contract administrator at its Pomona plant in 1978. He progressed steadily within the organization, earning repeated commendations and, after 14 years with the company, was in line to become a division vice-president and general counsel. On June 24, 1991, he was fired, abruptly and wrongfully.

So Rose alleged in the complaint for damages that began this litigation. The complaint also alleged that although the stated reason for his discharge was a loss of the company's confidence in Rose's ability to represent vigorously its interests, the "real" reasons motivating his firing had more to do with an attempt by company officials to cover up widespread drug use among the General Dynamics work force, a refusal to investigate the mysterious "bugging" of the office of the company's chief of security, and the displeasure of company officials over certain legal advice Rose had given them, rather than any loss of confidence in his legal ability or commitment to the company's interests.

The complaint relied on two main theories of relief. First, it alleged that General Dynamics had, by its conduct and other assurances, impliedly represented to Rose over the years that he was subject to discharge only for "good cause," a condition that the complaint alleged was not present in the circumstances under which he was fired. Second, the complaint alleged that Rose was actually fired for cumulative reasons, all of which violated fundamental public policies: in part because he spearheaded an investigation into employee drug use at the Pomona plant (an investigation, the complaint alleged, that led to the termination of more than 60 General Dynamics employees), in part because he protested the company's failure to investigate the bugging of the office of the chief of security (allegedly a criminal offense and, since it involved a major defense contractor, a serious breach of national security), and in part as a result of advising General Dynamics officials that the company's salary policy with respect to the compensation paid a certain class of employees might be in violation of the federal Fair Labor Standards Act, possibly exposing the firm to several hundred million dollars in backpay claims.

General Dynamics filed a general demurrer to the complaint, asserting that Rose had failed to state a claim for relief. Because he had been employed as an in-house *attorney,* the company contended, Rose was subject to discharge at any time, "for any reason or for no reason." The trial court overruled the demurrer and the Court of Appeal denied General Dynamics's ensuing petition for a writ of mandate, ruling that, at least at the pleading stage, the complaint was sufficient to survive a general demurrer as to both theories of relief.

II

The last two decades have seen a marked rise in the number and professional stature of so-called in-house or corporate counsel. Increasingly, large corporations have turned inward for the acquisition of legal services, for a host of reasons ranging from cost incentives, to the increasing complexity of the regulatory environment, to the programmatic style characteristic of such organizations. According to a study conducted in the early 1980's, 50,000 lawyers were on corporate payrolls, a figure double that of 15 years earlier; a more recent survey indicates that more than 10 percent of all lawyers in the United States are employed in-house by corporations.

The growth in the number and role of in-house counsel has brought with it a widening recognition of the descriptive inadequacy of the nineteenth century model of the lawyer's place and role in society—one based predominantly on the small- to middle-sized firm of like-minded attorneys whose economic fortunes were not tethered to the good will of a single client—and of the social and legal consequences that have accompanied that transformation. Unlike the law firm partner, who typically possesses a significant measure of economic independence and professional distance derived from a multiple client base, the economic fate of in-house attorneys is tied directly to a single employer, at whose sufferance they serve. Thus, from an economic standpoint, the dependence of in-house counsel is indistinguishable from that of other corporate managers or senior executives who also owe their livelihoods, career goals and satisfaction to a single organizational employer.

Moreover, the professional relationship between the in-house attorney and the client is not the "one shot" undertaking—drafting a will, say, or handling a piece of litigation—characteristic of the outside law firm. Instead, the corporate attorney-employee, operating in a heavily regulated medium, often takes on a larger advisory and compliance role, anticipating potential legal problems, advising on possible solutions, and generally assisting the corporation in achieving its business aims while minimizing entanglement in the increasingly complex legal web that regulates organizational conduct in our society. This expansion in the scope and stature of in-house counsel's work, together with an inevitably close professional identification with the fortunes and objectives of the corporate employer, can easily subject the in-house attorney to unusual pressures to conform to organizational goals, pressures that are qualitatively different from those imposed on the outside lawyer. Even the most dedicated professionals, their economic and professional fate allied with that of the business organizations they serve, may be irresistibly tempted to cut corners by bending the ethical norms that regulate an attorney's professional conduct.

Indeed, the analogy of in-house counsel's position to that of his or her lay colleagues in the executive suite is inexact only because, as a licensed professional, an attorney labors under unique ethical imperatives that *exceed* those of the corporate executive who seeks, say, a tort remedy after being terminated for refusing to join a conspiracy to violate the antitrust laws. (See, e.g., *Tameny v. Atlantic Richfield Co.* (1980) 27 Cal.3d 167, 164 Cal. Rptr. 839, 610 P.2d 1330 [*Tameny*].) We turn, then, to a consideration of the effects of in-house counsel's professional role and ethical duties on access to judicial remedies for alleged wrongful termination that are available to the nonattorney colleague.

III

A

If there is a unifying theme in this conflict, it is the claim of General Dynamics that our opinion in *Fracasse v. Brent* (1972) 6 Cal.3d 784, 100 Cal.Rptr. 385, 494 P.2d 9 (*Fracasse*) is dispositive of *all* issues tendered against it by Rose in his complaint. Because *Fracasse* cloaks the client in an unfettered, absolute right to discharge an attorney at any time and for any reason, General Dynamics argues, the complaint cannot state a claim against the company that is judicially cognizable; the trial court should thus have sustained General Dynamics's demurrer without leave to amend.

In *Fracasse, supra,* 6 Cal.3d 784, 100 Cal.Rptr. 385, 494 P.2d 9, an attorney entered into a contingent fee contract with a client to represent her as a plaintiff in a personal injury lawsuit. Not long afterward—and before any recovery had been made on her behalf—the client decided to end the relationship. She discharged the attorney, and retained other counsel to pursue her claim. The former attorney then filed a declaratory relief action against her, alleging that he had been discharged without cause and in breach of the contingency fee agreement, and seeking a judgment that he was entitled to his one-third contingency fee as a percentage of any sum ultimately recovered by his former client. The trial court sustained the client's demurrer, ruling that the complaint failed to state a claim for relief.

Although the core proposition established by our opinion in *Fracasse, supra,* 6 Cal.3d at page 790, 100 Cal.Rptr. 385, 494 P.2d 9, affirming the trial court, undoubtedly remains valid—we concluded that "a client should have both the right and the power at any time to discharge his attorney with or without cause"—our holding in that case does not support the sweeping scope urged for it by General Dynamics. It should be evident to anyone reading our opinion in *Fracasse* that we confronted there one of the most common of the traditional forms of the lawyer-client relationship: the potential claimant who seeks redress by hiring an independent professional to prosecute her claim for personal injuries.

Our holdings in that case were expressly founded on the recognition that a client who retains an attorney to prosecute a personal injury action under a contingent fee agreement "may and often is very likely to be a person of limited means for whom the contingent fee arrangement offers the only realistic hope of establishing a legal claim." (*Fracasse, supra,* 6 Cal.3d at p.

792, 100 Cal.Rptr. 385, 494 P.2d 9.) We had such concerns in mind when we wrote that the contingent fee client " 'must rely almost entirely upon the good faith of the attorney who alone can make an informed estimate of the value of the client's legal right and of the expense and effort necessary to enforce it.' " (*Id.* at p. 789, 100 Cal.Rptr. 385, 494 P.2d 9, quoting *Salopek v. Schoemann* (1942) 20 Cal.2d 150, 157, 124 P.2d 21.) " 'The client,' " we observed, " 'may frequently be forced to choose between continuing the employment of an attorney in whom he has lost faith, or risking the payment of double contingency fees equal to the greater portion of any amount eventually recovered. . . .' " (*Ibid.*)

In stating that "the client's power to discharge an attorney, with or without cause, is absolute. . .," we relied on the provisions of Code of Civil Procedure section 284, permitting a change of attorneys in "an action or special proceeding." (*Fracasse, supra,* 6 Cal.3d at p. 790, 100 Cal.Rptr. 385, 494 P.2d 9; see also *Santa Clara County Counsel Attys. Assn. v. Woodside* (1994) 7 Cal.4th 525, 555, 28 Cal.Rptr.2d 617, 869 P.2d 1142.) In light of the specific hazards confronting the contingent fee plaintiff who has lost confidence in his or her attorney—notably the risk of guessing wrong whether cause for discharge existed and thereby losing "73 ⅓ percent of a recovered judgment"—we concluded that it "should be sufficient that the client has, for whatever reason, lost faith in the attorney, to establish 'cause' for discharging him." (*Fracasse, supra,* 6 Cal.3d at p. 790, 100 Cal.Rptr. 385, 494 P.2d 9.) Finally, we reasoned that, "since the attorney agreed initially to take his chances on recovering any fee whatever, we believe that the fact that the success of the litigation is no longer under his control is insufficient to justify imposing a new and more onerous burden on the client." (*Id.* at p. 792, 100 Cal.Rptr. 385, 494 P.2d 9.) "It follows," we concluded, "that the attorney will be denied compensation in the event such recovery is not obtained." (*Ibid.*)

Entwined with our concern for the specific risks facing the contingent-fee plaintiff who has lost faith in her attorney was an underlying perception that, whatever the circumstances, *no* client should be forced to suffer representation by an attorney in whom that confidence and trust lying at the heart of a fiduciary relationship has been lost. It is not surprising, given this chain of reasoning, that our opinion in *Fracasse, supra,* 6 Cal.3d 784, 100 Cal.Rptr. 385, 494 P.2d 9, should establish as bedrock law what remains probably *the* central value of the lawyer-client relationship—the primacy of fiducial values and its corollary: the unilateral right of the client to sever the professional relationship at any time and for any reason.

That rule, which we reaffirm today, some 22 years after our decision in *Fracasse, supra,* 6 Cal.3d 784, 100 Cal.Rptr. 385, 494 P.2d 9, does not mean, however, that the "absolute" right of the personal injury client to discharge unilaterally his attorney permits *all* clients to terminate the attorney-client relationship under *all* circumstances without consequence. The sources of contract and tort claims in wrongful termination cases are analytically distinct from the circumstances confronting the contingent-fee plaintiff that propelled our analysis in *Fracasse.* Given these disparate origins, it is unlikely that the client's undoubted power to discharge the attorney at will is one that can be invoked under all circumstances *without consequence.* Even in *Fracasse,* we recognized the requirement that the dissatisfied personal injury contingent fee client compensate discharged counsel, limiting that obligation, in light of the peculiar risks associated with contingent fee undertakings, to the reasonable value of any services provided in the event of a recovery.

Additionally, General Dynamics' claim of an unqualified immunity from any liability for terminating in-house counsel is inconsistent with the law in other areas, notably claims grounded in alleged violations of antidiscrimination laws and statutory rights to public collective bargaining. (See, e.g., *Hishon v. King & Spalding* (1984) 467 U.S. 69, 104 S.Ct. 2229, 81 L.Ed.2d 59 [federal civil rights laws apply to law firm partnership decisions]; *Golightly-Howell v. Oil, Chemical & Atomic Workers* (D.Colo.1992) 806 F.Supp. 921, 924 ["[B]ecause Title VII prohibits discrimination based on race or sex, it prohibits such discrimination against one employed as in-house counsel."]; *Santa Clara County Counsel Attys. Assn. v. Woodside, supra,* 7 Cal.4th 525, 28 Cal.Rptr.2d 617, 869 P.2d 1142 [Meyers-Milias-Brown Act creates an exception to the general rule that a client may discharge an attorney at-will].)

Indeed, General Dynamics's complete reliance on *Fracasse, supra,* 6 Cal.3d 784, 100 Cal.Rptr. 385, 494 P.2d 9, as dispositive of Rose's claims proves too much. If, as a matter of legal doctrine, the client's right of discharge can be invoked without consequence in all circumstances, it might easily produce unconscionable results. Suppose an attorney in New York responds to a professional advertisement seeking an assistant general counsel for a corporation headquartered in Los Angeles. A series of negotiations ensues and the parties execute a written contract under which the employer agrees to hire the attorney to perform legal work as a full time employee for an agreed salary. Suppose further that the agreement provides that the attorney can only be terminated for specified reasons. The newly hired lawyer-employee then sells his house, moves family and goods across the country, buys a new home, enrolls his children in local schools, and begins his new employment. Three months later, he is summarily fired by the company for reasons that are not among those stipulated in the employment contract. To insist in the face of such egregious circumstances that our opinion in *Fracasse, supra,* 6 Cal.3d 784, 100 Cal.Rptr. 385, 494 P.2d 9, immunizes the employer by providing an "absolute" right to discharge the employee with *complete* impunity, foreclosing suit on the contract terms, would compel us to embrace an intuitively unjust, even outrageous, result on the basis of a holding expressly shaped by the unique concerns confronting the contingent fee personal injury client who has lost faith in counsel.

. . . .

B

How does the fundamental rule of the client's unilateral power of discharge announced in *Fracasse, supra,* 6 Cal.3d 784, 100 Cal.Rptr. 385, 494 P.2d 9, apply in the circumstances of this case? First, Rose's complaint does not contest the right of General Dynamics to terminate a member of its corporate legal department at any time or for any reason, nor could it. It simply asserts that there is a cost to be paid for such an action under the circumstances alleged in the complaint—either in lost wages and related damages in the case of the implied-in-fact contract claim, or as tort damages in the case of the public policy tort claim. (Cf. *Howard v. Babcock* (1994) 6 Cal.4th 409, 419, 25 Cal.Rptr.2d 80, 863 P.2d 150 [law firm "non-compete" agreement "attaches an economic consequence to a departing partner's unrestricted choice to pursue a particular kind of practice."].) In neither case, however, is the client's power to rid itself of an attorney in whom it has lost confidence thwarted. To the extent that General Dynamics's claim that its "unfettered" right to discharge a member of its corporate legal department means that it may do so without liability of any kind under all circumstances, that is not, and never has been, the law of this state.

As a threshold matter, then, we do not feel constrained by our opinion in *Fracasse, supra,* 6 Cal.3d 784, 100 Cal.Rptr. 385, 494 P.2d 9, from considering the proposition that, under circumscribed conditions, an in-house attorney may pursue a wrongful discharge claim for damages against his corporate employer *even though* a judgment ordering his reinstatement is *not* an available remedy. We turn to a consideration of the merits of plaintiff's claims that his termination breached an implied-in-fact agreement with General Dynamics and violated fundamental public policies, as well as the possible limitations on the vitality of such claims when brought by in-house counsel.

IV

> *[Editor's Note: The Court held that an in-house attorney can state a claim for breach of an implied-in-fact contract, but also noted that in the case of confidential corporate employees, such as attorneys, the employer will have wider latitude in determining the circumstances under which it has just or good cause to terminate the relationship.]*

V

A

We turn next to an evaluation of Rose's claim that he was discharged for multiple reasons, each of which violated a "fundamental polic[y] that [is] delineated in constitutional or statutory provisions" of the law of this state. (*Gantt v. Sentry Insurance* (1992) 1 Cal.4th 1083, 1095, 4 Cal.Rptr.2d 874, 824 P.2d 680.) Unlike implied-in-fact contract claims, which, as discussed above, arise out of the conduct and expectations of the parties to the employment relationship, so-called public policy wrongful discharge claims are pure creatures of law.

. . . .

There is a third characteristic of such claims that warrants our attention, one that may, in the case of in-house counsel, be of surpassing significance. That characteristic is well stated in *Foley,* where we explained that "decisions recognizing a tort action for discharge in violation of public policy *seek to protect the public, by protecting the employee* who refuses to commit a crime [citations] . . ., who reports criminal activity to proper authorities [citations], or who discloses other illegal, unethical, or unsafe practices [citation]" italics added).

In other words, although the public policy served by the conduct of the aggrieved employee at issue may often be directly protective of the interest in employment itself, the doctrinal foundation of the public policy tort claim is not so much the *plaintiff's* continued interest in employment as the preservation of the *public* interest as it is expressed in multiple forms in the Constitution and statutory law. An employee who states a wrongful discharge claim for having refused to join a criminal conspiracy in violation of the antitrust laws (cf. *Tameny*), or for having resisted efforts to induce him to give false information in a public investigation of sexual harassment charges filed by a co-worker (cf. *Gantt*), is provided a remedy in tort *not only* to compensate the individual plaintiff for the loss of employment but as an indirect means of vindicating the underlying fundamental *public policy itself.*

B

This foundational *public* rationale is especially important in the case of the attorney-employee. Perhaps the defining feature of professionals as a class is the extent to which they embody a dual allegiance. On the one hand, an attorney's highest duty is to the welfare and interests of the client. This obligation is channeled, however, by a limiting and specifically *professional* qualification: attorneys are required to conduct themselves *as such,* meaning that they are bound at all events not to transgress a handful of professional ethical norms that distinguish their work from that of the nonattorney.

Some (but not all) of these professional norms incorporate important *public* values. Lawyers are given wide professional license in part because of ethical restraints on their discretion designed to further (or at least not endanger) the public weal. The minimal ethical standards that distinctively define the lawyer as a professional are, of course, those embodied in the codes of ethics, and, in California, in the Rules of Professional Conduct. These standards are in turn linked by their nature and goals to important values affecting the public interest at large. It is through this chain of ethical duty that lawyers and their work are affected with a public interest. Out of this duality of allegiance—for the interests of the client on the one hand, but within the bounds of ethical norms on the other—a genuine moral dilemma may arise.

This is especially so in the context of the large commercially driven corporation whose essential objectives are largely defined by the desire to maximize profitability. In such a business culture, the in-house professional may be trapped between a laudable desire to further the goals of the client-employer and restrictions on conduct imposed by the ethical norms prescribed by the Rules of Professional Conduct. Of course, the potential for such a dilemma is common to outside counsel as well. But, unlike their in-house counterparts, outside lawyers enjoy a measure of professional distance and economic independence that usually serves to lessen the pressure to bend or ignore professional norms. Here again, the distinguishing feature of the in-house attorney is a virtually complete dependence on the good will and confidence of a single employer to provide livelihood and career success.

The case for shielding the in-house attorney—among *all* corporate employees—from retaliation by the employer for either insisting on adhering to mandatory ethical norms of the profession or for refusing to violate them is thus clear. And because their professional work is by definition affected with a public interest, in-house attorneys are even more liable to conflicts between corporate goals and professional norms than their nonattorney colleagues. On this view, then, in-house counsel, forced to choose between the demands of the employer and the requirements of a professional code of ethics have, if anything, an *even more* powerful claim to judicial protection than their nonprofessional colleagues.

There is a substantial counterargument against permitting the pursuit of a retaliatory discharge *tort* claim by in-house counsel, one that also inheres in the essential nature of the attorney's professional role. Indeed, in the handful of reported cases dealing with the question, a majority of courts have refused to permit the maintenance of such suits on the ground that they pose *too great* a threat to the attorney-client relationship. This rationale is well illustrated in a trio of recent cases, each holding as a matter of law that retaliatory discharge suits by in-house counsel are not maintainable.

The leading opinion is perhaps *Balla v. Gambro, Inc.* (1991) 145 Ill.2d 492, 164 Ill.Dec. 892, 584 N.E.2d 104 (hereafter *Balla*), a case in which the general counsel of an Illinois distributor of German-made dialysis equipment sued his employer for wrongful discharge, complaining that he had learned internally of major defects in several dialysis machines shipped to his employer for distribution in the American market, defects which put users at serious risk of uremic poisoning. He advised his superiors to reject the machines as not in compliance with Food and Drug Administration (FDA) regulations and as potentially dangerous to consumers. On later learning that company officials had accepted delivery of the units for sale to a customer " 'who buys only on price,' " plaintiff confronted the company president and told him that he would "do whatever necessary to stop the sale of the dialyzers."

After being abruptly fired two weeks later, the lawyer-employee reported the equipment defects to FDA officials the following day; they seized the machines as "adulterated" within the meaning of the federal act and the employee filed a damage action for retaliatory discharge, contending that he was fired for reasons that contravened a fundamental public policy. The Illinois Supreme Court agreed that plaintiff's discharge "was in contravention of a clearly mandated public policy. . . . As we have stated before, '[t]here is no public policy more important or more fundamental than the one favoring the effective protection of the lives and property of citizens.' " The court declined, however, to permit the plaintiff to maintain a retaliatory discharge action because he "was not just an employee of [defendant], but also general counsel for [defendant]." Basing its decision "as much on the nature and purpose of the tort of retaliatory discharge, as on the effect on the attorney-client relationship that extending the tort would have," the court cited two reasons why such suits should not be maintainable.

First, "the public policy to be protected, that of protecting the lives and property of citizens, is adequately safeguarded without extending the tort of retaliatory discharge to in-house counsel. [Plaintiff] was required under the Rules of Professional Conduct to report [defendant's] intention to sell [the dialyzers]." Unlike other employees "[who] would be left with the difficult decision of choosing between whether to file a . . . claim and risk being fired, or retaining their jobs and losing their right to a remedy [citation], . . . [i]n-house counsel do not have a choice of whether to follow their ethical obligations as attorneys . . ., or follow the illegal and unethical demands of their clients. . . . [Plaintiff] had no choice but to report to the FDA Gambro's intention to sell . . . [the] dialyzers, and consequently to protect . . . public policy." Moreover, permitting such suits would "have an undesirable effect on the attorney-client relationship that exists between . . . employers and their in-house counsel. . . . [E]mployers might be less willing to be forthright and candid with their in-house counsel [and] might be hesitant to turn to their in-house counsel for advice regarding potentially questionable . . . conduct. . . ."

In its basic reasoning, the Illinois Supreme Court in *Balla* relied on a prior opinion of that state's intermediate appellate court in *Herbster v. North American Co.* (1986) 150 Ill.App.3d 21, 103 Ill.Dec. 322, 501 N.E.2d 343 (*Herbster*). There, the former chief legal officer and vice-president in charge of the corporate legal department for a life and health insurance underwriter alleged that he was fired after he protested being ordered to remove or destroy sensitive internal company documents subject to a discovery request in litigation brought by an insured then pending in an Alabama federal court. Such conduct, the plaintiff alleged, would have been a fraud on the

Alabama court and would have violated several provisions of the Illinois Code of Professional Responsibility.

The *Herbster* court agreed that public policy considerations supported one element of the retaliatory discharge cause of action, but concluded that was insufficient: "[W]e cannot," the court wrote, "separate plaintiff's role as an employee from his profession." "[U]nlike . . . employees in [other] retaliatory discharge cases, attorneys occupy a special position in our society," the court said. "The mutual trust, exchanges of confidence, reliance on judgment and personal nature of the attorney-client relationship demonstrate the unique position attorneys occupy in our society. . . . The attributes of the relationship are so important that we cannot permit this expansion of the [retaliatory discharge] exception which would have a serious impact on that relationship. . . ." (*Id.* at p. 327, 501 N.E.2d at p. 348; see also *Willy v. Coastal Corp.* (S.D.Tex.1986) 647 F.Supp. 116, 117–118, revd. in part on other grounds (5th Cir.1986) 855 F.2d 1160, affd. on other grounds 503 U.S. 131, 112 S.Ct. 1076, 117 L.Ed.2d 280 [hereafter *Willy*] [Granting employer's motion to dismiss complaint of plaintiff in-house counsel who alleged he was discharged for giving the company legal advice concerning "compliance with various federal and state environmental laws," on the ground that "[i]f an attorney believes that his client is intent upon pursuing an illegal act, the attorney's option is to voluntarily withdraw from employment. . . . The standard is the same for an in-house attorney."].)

Those courts that have declined to permit in-house counsel to pursue retaliatory discharge claims—in *Balla, Herbster,* and *Willy*—have rested their conclusion on two distinct grounds: First, because the fiducial qualities of their professional calling pervade the attorney-client relationship "lawyers are different." It is essential to the proper functioning of the lawyer's role that the client be assured that matters disclosed to counsel in confidence remain sacrosanct; to permit in-house attorneys to file suit against their clients can only harm that relationship. Second, to the extent that the retaliatory discharge tort rests on underpinnings designed to secure fundamental public policies, a tort remedy for in-house counsel is redundant—such attorneys are under an ethical obligation to sever their professional relationship with the erring client in any event—meaning, in the case of in-house counsel, resigning their employment.

D

There is no doubt that the Illinois courts in *Balla* and *Herbster* grappled conscientiously with the conflicting values presented by cases such as this one. If their reasoning and conclusions can be faulted, it is because one searches in vain for a principled link between the ethical duties of the in-house attorney and the courts' refusal to grant such an employee a tort remedy under conditions that directly implicate those professional obligations. As more than one critic of these opinions has pointed out, both cases appear to reflect not only an unspoken adherence to an anachronistic model of the attorney's place and role in contemporary society, but an inverted view of the consequences of the in-house attorney's essential professional role.

As one authoritative commentator on lawyers' ethics, criticizing the court's decision in *Balla* has written, "It is clear that there would have been a right of action had the employee not been a lawyer. It thus seems bizarre that a lawyer employee, who has affirmative duties concerning the administration of justice, should be denied redress for discharge resulting from trying to carry out those very duties. A good beginning point for analysis may well be the client's normal and broad right to discharge the lawyer, but that cannot be the ending point as well, for the lawyer-client relationship exists in a context of other law regulating both parties to that relationship, including the lawyer's duties to third persons, the courts, and the government." (1 Hazard & Hodes, The Law of Lawyering, *supra,* § 1.16.206 at p. 477, fns. omitted.)

Granted the priest-like license to receive the most intimate and damning disclosures of the client, granted the sanctity of the professional privilege, granted the uniquely influential position attorneys occupy in our society, it is precisely *because of* that role that attorneys should be accorded a retaliatory discharge remedy in those instances in which *mandatory ethical norms* embodied in the Rules of Professional Conduct *collide with illegitimate demands of the employer* and the attorney insists on *adhering to his or her clear professional duty.* It is, after all, the office of the retaliatory discharge tort to vindicate fundamental public policies by encouraging employees to act in ways that advance them. By providing the employee with a remedy in tort damages for resisting socially damaging organizational conduct, the courts mitigate the otherwise considerable economic and cultural pressures on the individual employee to silently conform.

Within their area of professional competence, in-house attorneys, more than other organizational employees, are imbued with ethical constraints on the direction their efforts may legitimately take. Among other strictures on their conduct, they may not be a party to the commission of a crime, destroy evidence or suborn perjury. They are forbidden to do these things by the very ethical codes that define their professional identity. It is a short step from this premise to the conclusion that in-house lawyers ought to have access to a judicial remedy in those instances in which their employment is terminated for adhering to the requirements of just such a mandatory professional duty, either by an *affirmative act* required by the ethical code or statute or by resisting a demand of the employer on the ground that it is unequivocally *barred* by the professional code.

. . . .

In addition, the emphasis by the *Balla, Herbster* and *Willy* courts on the "remedy" of the in-house attorney's duty of "withdrawal" strikes us as illusory. Courts do not require nonlawyer employees to quietly surrender their jobs rather than "go along" with an employer's unlawful demands. Indeed, the retaliatory discharge tort claim is designed to encourage and support precisely the *opposite* reaction. Why, then, did the courts in these three cases content themselves with the bland announcement that the only "choice" of an attorney confronted with an employer's demand that he violate his professional oath by committing, say, a criminal act, is to voluntarily withdraw from employment, a course fraught with the possibility of economic catastrophe and professional banishment?

Whatever the reason, the withdrawal "remedy" fails to confront seriously the extraordinarily high cost that resignation entails. More importantly, it is virtually certain that, without the prospect of limited judicial access, in-house attorneys—especially those in mid-career who occupy senior positions—confronted with the dilemma of choosing between adhering to professional ethical norms and surrendering to the employer's unethical demands will almost always find silence the better part of valor. Declining to provide a limited remedy under defined circumstances will thus almost certainly foster a degradation of in-house counsel's professional stature.

E

In addition to retaliatory discharge claims founded on allegations that an in-house attorney was terminated for refusing to violate a mandatory ethical duty embodied in the Rules of Professional Conduct, judicial access ought logically extend to those limited circumstances in which in-house counsel's *nonattorney* colleagues would be permitted to pursue a retaliatory discharge claim *and* governing professional rules or statutes expressly remove the requirement of attorney confidentiality. Thus, in determining whether an in-house attorney has a retaliatory discharge claim against his or her employer, a court must first ask whether the attorney was discharged for following a mandatory ethical obligation prescribed by professional rule or statute. If, for example, in-house counsel is asked to commit a crime, or to engage in an act of moral turpitude that would subject him to disbarment (see, e.g., Bus. & Prof.Code, §§ 6101, 6106 [providing, respectively, for disbarment on conviction of a felony or a misdemeanor involving moral turpitude, and for the "commission of any act involving moral turpitude, dishonesty or corruption"]), and is discharged for refusing to engage in such an act, counsel would have been discharged for adhering to a mandatory ethical obligation; under most circumstances, the attorney would have a retaliatory discharge cause of action against the employer.

If, on the other hand, the conduct in which the attorney has engaged is merely ethically *permissible,* but not *required* by statute or ethical code, then the inquiry facing the court is slightly more complex. Under these circumstances, a court must resolve *two* questions: First, whether the employer's conduct is of the kind that would give rise to a retaliatory discharge action by a *non*-attorney employee under *Gantt* and related cases; second, the court must determine whether some statute or ethical rule, such as the statutory exceptions to the attorney-client privilege codified in the Evidence Code (see *id.,* §§ 956–958) specifically permits the attorney to depart from the usual requirement of confidentiality with respect to the client-employer and engage in the "nonfiduciary" conduct for which he was terminated.

We emphasize the limited scope of our conclusion that in-house counsel may state a cause of action in tort for retaliatory discharge. The lawyer's high duty of fidelity to the interests of the client work against a tort remedy that is coextensive with that available to the nonattorney employee. Although claims by in-house attorneys are cognate to those we approved in *Foley* the underlying rationale differs somewhat, being grounded in the attorney's obligation to adhere to ethical norms specific to the profession. The cause of action is thus one designed to support in-house counsel in remaining faithful to those fundamental public policies reflected in the governing ethical code when carrying out professional assignments. Thus, in addition to the limitations on the scope of the retaliatory tort action mentioned above, the concerns expressed by the courts in *Balla* and *Herbster* for the integrity of the fiduciary aspects of the attorney-client relationship impose additional limitations.

First, those values that underlie the professional relationship—the fiduciary qualities of mutual trust and confidence—can be protected from the threat of damage by limiting judicial access to claims grounded in *explicit* and *unequivocal ethical norms* embodied in the Rules of Professional Responsibility and *statutes,* and claims which are maintainable by the *non*-attorney employee under our decision in *Gantt*, under circumstances in which the Legislature has manifested a judgment that the principle of professional confidentiality *does not apply.* See, e.g., Evid.Code, § 956.5 ["*There is no privilege* . . . if the lawyer reasonably believes that disclosure of any confidential communication . . . is necessary to prevent the client from committing a criminal act that the lawyer believes is likely to result in death or substantial bodily harm." [Italics added].]

Similarly, the in-house attorney who publicly exposes the client's secrets will usually find no sanctuary in the courts. Except in those rare instances when disclosure is explicitly permitted or mandated by an ethics code provision or statute, it is never the business of the lawyer to disclose publicly the secrets of the client. In any event, where the elements of a wrongful discharge in violation of fundamental public policy claim cannot, for reasons peculiar to the particular case, be fully established without breaching the attorney-client privilege, the suit must be dismissed in the interest of preserving the privilege. We underline the fact that such drastic action will seldom if ever be appropriate at the demurrer stage of litigation. Although General Dynamics argues that Rose's claims are barred from disclosure by the lawyer-client privilege, that is an issue that is incapable of resolution in a challenge to the facial sufficiency of the complaint. Indeed, in most wrongful termination suits brought by discharged in-house counsel, whether the attorney-client privilege precludes the plaintiff from recovery will not be resolvable at the demurrer stage. Rather, in the usual case, whether the privilege serves as a bar to the plaintiff's recovery will be litigated and determined in the context of motions for protective orders or to compel further discovery responses, as well as at the time of a motion for summary judgment.

Second, the contours of the statutory attorney-client privilege should continue to be strictly observed. We reject any suggestion that the scope of the privilege should be diluted in the context of in-house counsel and their corporate clients. Members of corporate legal departments are as fully subject to the demands of the privilege as their outside colleagues. It is likely, however, that many of the cases in which in-house counsel is faced with an ethical dilemma will lie outside the scope of the statutory privilege. Matters involving the commission of a crime or a fraud, or circumstances in which the attorney reasonably believes that disclosure is necessary to prevent the commission of a criminal act likely to result in death or substantial bodily harm, are statutory and well-recognized exceptions to the attorney-client privilege. As to them, "[t]he privilege takes flight if the relation is abused." (*Clark v. United States* (1933) 289 U.S. 1, 15, 53 S.Ct. 465, 469, 77 L.Ed. 993 (opinion of Cardozo, J.).) Although their revelation in the course of a retaliatory discharge suit may do lasting damage to the expectations of the corporate client (or, more likely, a corporate executive) that disclosures to counsel would remain inviolate, a concern for protecting the fiduciary aspects of the relationship in the case of a client who confides in counsel for the purpose of planning a crime or practicing a fraud is misplaced; such disclosures do not violate the privilege.

Moreover, the trial courts can and should apply an array of ad hoc measures from their equitable arsenal designed to permit the attorney plaintiff to attempt to make the necessary proof while protecting from disclosure client confidences subject to the privilege. The use of sealing and protective orders, limited admissibility of evidence, orders restricting the use of testimony in successive proceedings, and, where appropriate, in camera proceedings, are but some of a number of measures that might usefully be explored by the trial courts as circumstances warrant. We are confident that by taking an aggressive managerial role, judges can minimize the dangers to the legitimate privilege interests the trial of such cases may present.

Finally, a handful of subsidiary rules will effectively raise the ante on the in-house attorney contemplating a tort action, thus deterring the incidence of strike suits or claims filed in bad faith. The contested ethical requirement must be clearly established by the ethics code or statutory provision; disagreements over policy are *not* actionable. The plaintiff, of course, bears the burden of establishing the *unequivocal* requirements of the ethical norm at issue and that the employer's conduct was motivated by impermissible considerations under a "but for" standard of causation. The ethical norm at issue must be one that is intended for the protection of the public at large; measures designed solely for the benefit of the attorney or the client will not suffice to support a retaliatory discharge claim. Moreover, an attorney who unsuccessfully pursues a retaliatory discharge suit, and in doing so discloses privileged client confidences, may be subject to State Bar disciplinary proceedings. Finally, of course, the defendant employer is always free to challenge plaintiff's claim by demonstrating the discharge was motivated by reasons other than a demand that counsel engage in conduct amounting to a breach of professional ethical norms.

QUESTIONS

1. Develop an argument that attorneys are never really employees, but rather operate as independent professionals even in the in-house context.
2. Is it reasonable and practical to hold that the attorney-client privilege must apply strictly even in a suit for wrongful discharge by in-house counsel?

Problem 32-4

Julia is employed as a nurse at County Hospital. She was fired after refusing to administer kidney dialysis to a terminally ill patient for "moral, medical, and philosophical" reasons. Julia contended that the procedure did not respect the integrity of the patient, who had previously suffered cardiac arrest and severe internal bleeding after the procedure. Julia requested that another nurse be assigned to the patient for the procedure, which had been authorized by the family. County Hospital refused to consider her request and fired her for disobeying instructions.

The Code for Nurses, Section 1.4, provides, in part:

> The nurse's concern for human dignity and the provision of quality nursing care is not limited by personal attitudes or beliefs. If personally opposed to the delivery of care in a particular case because of the nature of the health problem or the procedures to be used, the nurse is justified in refusing to participate. Such refusal should be made known in advance and in time for other appropriate arrangements to be made for the client's nursing care. If the nurse must knowingly enter such a case under emergency circumstances or enters unknowingly, the obligation to provide the best possible care is observed. The

> nurse withdraws from this type of situation only when assured that alternative sources of nursing care are available to the client.

Can Julia successfully claim that her termination was in violation of public policy?

Conclusion

Courts define public policy that supports a cause of action for wrongful discharge by referring to constitutional, statutory, and regulatory law. Often, statutory schemes will include their own anti-retaliatory provision, but not all laws that articulate public policy have a private cause of action. There are special considerations when an attorney acting in her professional capacity as an in-house employee seeks to recover for wrongful discharge.

Lesson 33:
Good Faith and Fair Dealing

Objectives and Expected Learning Outcomes

Parties must perform their express duties under contracts, but courts also recognize an obligation of good faith and fair dealing to ensure that the reasonable expectations of the parties are met. In this Lesson, you will learn to apply this general principle of contract law to the employment law setting to protect an employee from losing an expected benefit due to a bad faith termination by the employer. The duty of good faith is a contract duty; courts have refused to interpret the duty in a way that undermines the at-will rule by requiring a "just cause" basis for termination.

The employment relationship is a contractual relationship, even if the contract is terminable at-will. It is a fundamental rule of contract law that the parties are obligated to adhere not only to the express terms of the contract, but also to act in good faith toward the other party. The "implied covenant of good faith and fair dealing" is treated as a term of the contract imposed by courts to respect the reasonable expectations of the parties. The justification for this judicial rule is that a party would not agree to be bound to another unless the other was pledging to carry out its contractual obligations in good faith. Consider two examples of this principle in areas other than employment law.

Example 33-1—The Insurance Context

Acme Insurance sells a liability insurance policy to Jennifer for her business. The policy limit is $250,000. A customer suffers a severe injury in her store, but it is unclear if the store is legally liable. Acme undertakes its duty to defend Jennifer under the policy and quickly learns that although there is only a 10% chance of a plaintiff's verdict, the damages would likely be $1 million. Acme decides not to offer to settle the case for the $250,000 policy limit because it stands a good chance of avoiding liability altogether. At trial, Jennifer is found liable for $1 million in damages. Acme tenders the policy limit of $250,000 and Jennifer is left uninsured for $750,000 of the verdict. Acme argues that it has completely fulfilled the terms of the insurance policy.

In these types of situations, courts have typically used the implied duty of good faith and fair dealing to hold insurance carriers liable for their actions in delaying or denying payment under the policy. Given the special vulnerability of insurance policy holders after a loss has occurred, courts in many states have developed a very robust principle of good faith to ensure that the reasonable expectations of the insured are respected. In a number of states, the insurer is held to tort liability for its bad faith treatment of its insured. In these instances, the implied duty of good faith appears to impose a much more substantive limitation on the insurance carrier's ability to avoid its reasonable obligations. See, e.g., *Communale v. Traders and General Ins. Co.*, 328 P.2d 198 (Cal. In Bank, 1958) (liability insurer that wrongfully refused to defend its insured and to settle the litigation against its insured within the policy limits is liable in tort for the full verdict amount, even if it exceeds the contractually agreed policy limit). As we learned in Lesson 7, courts refused to follow the insurance model of good faith, holding that it would eviscerate the at-will rule.

Example 33-2—Lender Liability

Acme Bank provides lines of credit to businesses to allow them the cash necessary to generate sales. In these arrangements, it is customary for banks extending a line of credit to insist that the terms of the loan include the absolute right of the lender to call for payment at any time and for any reason. As you can see, this express term essentially renders the relationship at-will. Acme had established a line of credit in the amount of $3.5 million for Jennifer's grocery store. Jennifer's store had very small margins of profit, and several times she had drawn down almost the entire line of credit. Acme was concerned about the account and had several conversations with Jennifer about its concerns. On October 1, Jennifer sought an advance of $800,000 which would have brought the balance to $3.45 million. Acme summarily refused to advance the funds, telling Jennifer that it did not believe that her business would survive. Jennifer's collateral (real estate, inventory, and receivables) was $4 million, and so Acme was not at risk in advancing the funds.

In response to some egregious cases such as this scenario, courts began a body of law known as "lender liability," which held that the implied covenant of good faith limited the express contract right to call the loan. Essentially, banks were held accountable if they called the line of credit in "bad faith." See, e.g., *K.M.C. Co., Inc. v. Irving Trust Co.*, 757 F.2d 752

(6th Cir. 1985) (lender's absolute power to demand repayment is qualified by the obligation to act in good faith, which in this case imposed a duty to provide notice before refusing to advance funds under the financing agreement). Eventually, there was a backlash by courts against permitting a judicially imposed term to alter the expressly agreed terms in the loan agreement. Additionally, states passed legislation to prevent evidence outside the loan agreement from establishing the contours of the good faith obligation. The ongoing conflicts in the lender liability cases have particular relevance to the development of good faith in the employment setting, because courts appear to want to enforce the reasonable expectations of the parties without undermining the fundamental at-will nature of the agreement.

In this Lesson, we consider the application of the implied covenant of good faith and fair dealing to the employment setting. Courts have determined that the employment relationship does not have a special nature, deserving of extra protection provided by the doctrine, and that the employment relationship is more like a typical commercial agreement in which courts are reluctant to undermine the express agreement of the parties under the doctrine of good faith.

The Restatement of Employment Law provides the doctrinal framework customarily used by courts to determine the application of the implied duty of good faith and fair dealing in the employment setting. The Restatement applies the same principles with regard to limiting the termination of employment (§ 2.07) and ensuring that the employee receives the promised compensation and benefits (§ 3.05).

Restatement of Employment Law

§ 2.07. Implied Duty of Good Faith and Fair Dealing (Termination)

(a) Each party to an employment relationship, including at-will employment, owes a nonwaivable duty of good faith and fair dealing to each other party, which includes a party's obligation not to hinder the other party's performance under, or to deprive the other party of the benefit of, their contractual relationship.

(b) The implied duty of good faith and fair dealing applies to at-will employment relationships in a manner consistent with the essential nature of such an at-will relationship.

(c) In any employment relationship, including at-will employment, the employer's implied duty of good faith and fair dealing includes the duty not to terminate or seek to terminate the employment relationship for the purpose of:

(1) preventing the vesting or accrual of an employee right or benefit; or

(2) retaliating against the employee for performing the employee's obligations under the employment contract or law.

QUESTIONS

1. What does it mean to recognize an implied duty of good faith and fair dealing in at-will employment relationship, but only in a manner that is consistent with the "essential nature" of the at-will relationship? Isn't an obligation of good faith fundamentally contradictory to the "essential nature" of at-will employment?

2. The Restatement does not resolve the conceptual tension, but the provision describes two situations in which an at-will relationship might be limited: using termination to preclude the vesting of a right, or in retaliation for the employee performing her contractual obligations in good faith. This "restated" rule is not accepted by all jurisdictions. For example, the New Mexico Supreme Court has held that "there is no contract of employment upon which the law can impose the stated duty to exercise good faith and fair dealing. Sanchez was an 'at-will' employee who could be dismissed for any or no reason." *Sanchez v. The New Mexican*, 106 N.M. 76, 738 P.2d 1321, 1324 (1987). Does it make more sense to say that the implied term of good faith can play no role when an employer is permitted to terminate for any reason, or no reason at all?

---

1. The Classic Application: Precluding the Vesting of a Benefit

The Restatement identifies the use of termination to prevent the vesting or accrual of a benefit as an example of the application of the doctrine of good faith. See § 2.07(c)(1). *Fortune* is one of the classic cases that established the applicability of the covenant of good faith in employment cases. Read the case and then develop a response to the Mastery Problem using both the *Fortune* case and the Restatement test.

Fortune v. National Cash Register Co.

364 N.E.2d 1251 (Mass. 1977).

[Editor's Note: Fortune was a salesman at NCR employed under a written contract that was terminable at-will on written notice. He earned commissions on sales of cash registers, and First National was one of his customers. In November 1968, First National purchased 2,000 new units. Fortune was listed as the salesman on the invoice, and the bonus credit shown on the order was $92,079.99. Under the terms of his contract, Fortune received commissions only when units were actually shipped, and only so long as he was employed at NCR at the time of shipment.

Immediately after the sale, Fortune's supervisor let him know that he was no longer valued as an employee and purported to fire him. Fortune was able to remain when he agreed to continue assisting with the First National account. Ultimately, Fortune was asked to retire, and when he refused he was fired in June. At that time, Fortune had received 75% of the bonus on the First National contract. NCR paid the final 25% of the First National bonus to another employee.]

The central issue on appeal is whether this "bad faith" termination constituted a breach of the employment at will contract. Traditionally, an employment contract which is "at will" may be terminated by either side without reason. Although the employment at will rule has been almost uniformly criticized, it has been widely followed.

The contract at issue is a classic terminable at will employment contract. It is clear that the contract itself reserved to the parties an explicit power to terminate the contract without cause on written notice. It is also clear that under the express terms of the contract Fortune has received all the bonus commissions to which he is entitled. Thus, NCR claims that it did not breach the contract, and that it has no further liability to Fortune. According to a literal reading of the contract, NCR is correct.

However, Fortune argues that, in spite of the literal wording of the contract, he is entitled to a jury determination on NCR's motives in terminating his services under the contract and in finally discharging him. We agree. We hold that NCR's written contract contains an implied covenant of good faith and fair dealing, and a termination not made in good faith constitutes a breach of the contract.

We do not question the general principles that an employer is entitled to be motivated by and to serve its own legitimate business interests; that an employer must have wide latitude in deciding whom it will employ in the face of the uncertainties of the business world; and that an employer needs flexibility in the face of changing circumstances. We recognize the employer's need for a large amount of control over its work force. However, we believe that where, as here, commissions are to be paid for work performed by the employee, the employer's decision to terminate its at will employee should be made in good faith. NCR's right to make decisions in its own interest is not, in our view, unduly hampered by a requirement of adherence to this standard.

On occasion some courts have avoided the rigidity of the "at will" rule by fashioning a remedy in tort *[Editor's Note: the court cites cases finding a wrongful discharge in violation of public policy].* We believe, however, that in this case there is remedy on the express contract. In so holding we are merely recognizing the general requirement in this Commonwealth that parties to contracts and commercial transactions must act in good faith toward one another. Good faith and fair dealing between parties are pervasive requirements in our law; it can be said fairly, that parties to contracts or commercial transactions are bound by this standard.

. . . .

Recent decisions in other jurisdictions lend support to the proposition that good faith is implied in contracts terminable at will. In a recent employment at will case, *Monge v. Beebe Rubber Co.*, 114 N.H. 130, 133, 316 A.2d 549, 552 (1974), the plaintiff alleged that her oral contract of employment had been terminated because she refused to date her foreman. The New Hampshire Supreme Court held that "(i)n all employment contracts, whether at will or for a definite term, the employer's interest in running his business as he sees fit must be balanced against the interest of the employee in maintaining his employment, and the public's interest in maintaining a proper balance between the two. . . . We hold that a termination by the employer of a contract of employment at will which is motivated by bad faith or malice . . . constitutes a breach of the employment contract. . . . Such a rule affords the employee a certain stability of employment and does not interfere with the employer's normal exercise of his right to discharge, which is necessary to permit him to operate his business efficiently and profitably."

. . . .

In the instant case, we need not pronounce our adherence to so broad a policy nor need we speculate as to whether the good faith requirement is implicit in every contract for employment at will. It is clear, however, that, on the facts before us, a finding is warranted that a breach of the contract occurred. Where the principal seeks to deprive the agent of all compensation by terminating the contractual relationship when the agent is on the brink of successfully completing the sale, the principal has acted in bad faith and the ensuing transaction between the principal and the buyer is to be regarded as having been accomplished by the agent. Restatement (Second) of Agency § 454, and Comment a (1958). The same result obtains where the principal attempts to deprive the agent of any portion of a commission due the agent. Courts have often applied this rule to prevent overreaching by employers and the forfeiture by employees of benefits almost earned by the rendering of substantial services. In our view, the Appeals Court erroneously focused only on literal compliance with payment provisions of the contract and failed to consider the issue of bad faith termination.

. . . .

. . . As we have said, the jury could have found that Fortune was stripped of his "salesman" designation in order to disqualify him for the remaining 25% of the commissions due on cash registers delivered prior to the date of his first termination. Similarly, the jury could have found that Fortune was fired so that NCR would avoid paying him any commissions on cash registers delivered after June, 1970.

Conversely, the jury could have found that Fortune was assigned by NCR to the First National account; that all he did in this case was arrange for a demonstration of the product; that he neither participated in obtaining the order nor did he assist NCR in closing the order; and that nevertheless NCR credited him with the sale. This, however, did not obligate the trial judge to direct a verdict. Where evidence is conflicting, the rule is clear: "If upon any reasonable view of the evidence there is found any combination of circumstances from which a rational inference may be drawn in favor of the plaintiff, then there was no error in the denial of the motion, even if there may be other and different circumstances disclosed in the evidence which, if accepted as true by the jury, would support a conclusion adverse to the plaintiff." *Howes v. Kelman*, 326 Mass. 696, 696–697, 96 N.E.2d 394, 395 (1951).

Holding

We think that NCR's conduct in June, 1970 permitted the jury to find bad faith.

Mastery Problem 33-1

Richard Pilar worked as an admissions representative for Career Education Corporation (CEC), recruiting students to enroll in CEC's for-profit culinary arts college. Until February 2011, Pilar and his fellow admissions representatives worked under a contract ("the Plan") that gave them a bonus for each student they recruited above a required minimum number, but only if the student completed a full academic program or a full year of study, whichever occurred first.

In October 2010, the U.S. Department of Education (ED) issued regulations prohibiting this kind of financial arrangement with admissions recruiters in the interest of protecting potential students from hard sales tactics. The new rules were scheduled to take effect in July 2011. CEC decided to advance the effective date of these new arrangements to February 2011, announcing to its admissions representatives that it would cease paying bonuses at the end of February 2011. It further stated that no bonuses would be regarded as earned by that date unless the student in question had completed the year of study or course by that time. The Plan reserved CEC's right to terminate the Plan itself at any time, for any reason:

> If CEC determines at any time that this Plan should be modified due to the requirements or standards of the U.S. Department of Education or any state agency or accrediting commission, then CEC may be obligated to modify this Plan. CEC reserves the right to terminate or amend the terms of this Plan at any time, for regulatory compliance purposes or for any other reason that CEC determines, in its sole discretion. Any interpretation of any provision of this Plan or of any regulatory authority may be made by CEC in its sole discretion.

The Plan also explained that if employment was terminated on any given day, the employee would be entitled only to bonuses for students who had completed a year or a full course of study before that day:

> An employee is considered to have "earned" supplemental compensation under this Plan for the evaluation period during which his/her employment ends if, as of the employee's termination date, the employee has

> exceeded his/her MPG Threshold for that evaluation period for students who have successfully completed either their academic program or one academic year of their program. The employee will only be entitled to supplemental compensation . . . based on those students who have successfully completed their academic program or one academic year of their program, whichever is shorter, as of the employee's termination date, and not for any students who successfully complete their academic program or one academic year of their program after the employee's termination date.

Pilar stood to earn $9,600 ($400 x 24) if all of those extra students completed their full program or one year of study. At the time the program was terminated on February 28, 2011, however, only one of the 24 extra students had completed either the full program or one year, and therefore CEC paid Pilar only $400 as a bonus. Pilar comes to your office, and argues that CEC owes him bonuses for his "pipeline" students—that is, those whom he had recruited and who were on target to complete a full course or year of study between March and June 2011. He asks, "Didn't I perform substantially until CEC interfered with my ability to earn the promised bonuses?"

If framed as a class action, this case could result in large verdicts given the scope of CEC's recruitment activities. Assess the strength of a case alleging that CEC breached the implied covenant of good faith and fair dealing.

---

2. Using Good Faith to Limit the Employer's At-Will Right to Discharge

In Lesson 7, you learned that in the watershed *Foley* case the California Supreme Court put an end to the development of caselaw that awarded tort damages for discharging an employee in bad faith. Many state courts concluded that a discharged employee could recover tort damages only when the wrongful discharge violated an independent public policy. Recall the *Dorr Woolen* opinion that narrowed the *Monge* case (excerpted in Lesson 32 and cited in *Fortune* above) by limiting tort recovery to cases that involve a wrongful discharge in violation of public policy. Even under the classic application of the doctrine of good faith when an employee is discharged to preclude the vesting of a benefit, most courts only award contract damages in the amount of the lost benefit and do not award damages for the economic effects of the discharge itself. See *Wakefield v. Northern Telecom, Inc.*,

769 F.2d 109, 112 (2nd Cir. 1985) (plaintiff can recover commissions but can't "recover for his termination *per se*.").

However, as provided in the Restatement, an employer that terminates an employee in retaliation for performing the employee's obligations under the contract or under law may be subject to an action for breach of contract regarding the implied duty to perform and enforce the contract in good faith. In Lesson 31, we explored the refusal of New York courts to embrace the tort of wrongful discharge in violation of public policy. Consider how you might use the implied contract term of good faith and fair dealing to address unfair terminations of employment by re-reading the *Wieder* case and applying it to the following problems.

Problem 33-1

Marsha was fired by NBC after complaining that the show for which she worked as a Producer was not adhering to NBC's written journalistic standards and refusing to continue the practices in question. She had been employed by NBC for 21 years and had won numerous journalistic awards. Marsha worked under a written agreement that required NBC to provide her with 28 days notice of termination, which it did. NBC argues that it fired Marsha as part of generalized cost-cutting. Marsha argues that her termination should be actionable under the *Wieder* precedent. Develop the arguments for NBC that there should be no liability under New York law.

Problem 33-2

Sheila was fired by The New York Times after she complained that Times employees asked her to turn over confidential medical files. Sheila is a physician whose primary duty at the Times was to determine if injuries suffered by employees were work-related, thus making them eligible for workers' compensation. She also provided on-site basic care to employees. When members of the HR department asked to review her medical files on employees claiming workplace-related injuries, she consulted with the New York Department of Health and the AMA. She was informed that sharing medical information without the patient's consent would violate provisions of state law and medical ethics. After refusing to share the patients' files, Sheila was fired as part of a restructuring of the Medical Department.

Sheila contends that her at-will relationship with the Times includes the implied fundamental understanding that a physician will conduct herself in accordance with all relevant ethical and legal guidelines. The Times argues that the *Wieder* precedent is inapt because the law firm employer in *Wieder* had the same obligations for reporting attorney misconduct, whereas the Times is not bound by any provisions of medical ethics. Develop the arguments for Sheila that the Times should be liable under New York law.

A. Bad Faith as Deceit and Misrepresentation

Employers who act irrationally, or even maliciously, may not be violating the implied covenant of good faith and fair dealing, given the strength of the at-will rule. However, when an employer actively uses misrepresentation in dealing with an employee, courts have found that the employer may be liable for bad faith. Consider the following case, which famously engaged in this analysis.

E.I. DuPont de Nemours & Co. v. Pressman

679 A.2d 436 (Del. 1996).

Veasey, Chief Justice:

In this appeal, we consider the scope of the employment-at-will doctrine (the "Doctrine") and the correlative application of the implied duty or covenant of good faith and fair dealing (the "Covenant") as a limitation on the Doctrine. We conclude that the scope of the Doctrine is broad. The Covenant is applicable here, but its scope is narrower than that articulated by the trial court. We reverse the judgment of the Superior Court on the ground that the jury instructions erroneously overstated the Covenant, and we direct that a new trial be ordered consistent with this Opinion.

The Doctrine generally permits the dismissal of employees without cause and regardless of motive. Nevertheless, we hold that the Covenant permits a cause of action against an employer for the deceitful acts of its agent in manufacturing materially false grounds to cause an employee's dismissal. Our holding here reinforces and reaffirms the breadth of the Doctrine and the narrow and carefully crafted nature of the Covenant.

. . . .

I. Procedural Posture

E.I. DuPont de Nemours and Company ("DuPont"), defendant below, appeals from a judgment entered upon a jury verdict in favor of Norman J. Pressman ("Pressman"). The jury verdict for Pressman, which was based on his claim that DuPont breached the Covenant, awarded Pressman $422,700 in compensatory damages for lost wages. The jury also awarded Pressman $25,000 for emotional distress and interest, and $75,000 in punitive damages on the breach of the Covenant claim.

The jury rendered a verdict for DuPont on a claim for breach of an implied-in-fact contract requiring good cause for a termination of employment and for David Pensak ("Pensak"), Pressman's former supervisor, on a claim for defamation. Claims against DuPont for defamation and negligent evaluation were dismissed prior to trial.

With respect to the Covenant, the Superior Court instructed the jury as follows:

> [U]nder Delaware law, DuPont owed plaintiff a duty of good faith and fair dealing. Plaintiff contends that DuPont breached this duty. *The duty of good faith and fair dealing is breached by [an] employer if it discharges an employee maliciously, that's as a result of hatred, ill will or intent to injure, or effects the discharge in bad faith, that is through acts of fraud, deceit or intentional misrepresentation.*
>
> What constitutes malice or bad faith depends on the intent of the persons effectuating the termination. One acts intentionally to cause a certain result. One acts maliciously if actions are [a result of] ill will or intent to injure.
>
> Bad faith implies the conscious doing of wrong because of dishonest purpose. It is not simply bad judgment or negligence. It contemplates a state of mind affirmatively operating with a furtive design or ill will.
>
> If you believe that by a preponderance of the evidence that Pensak or any other employee acted maliciously or in bad faith in terminating the plaintiff from his employment at DuPont, then you should find that DuPont violated its duty of good faith and fair dealing to Norman Pressman. If, however, Norman Pressman was terminated without malice or bad faith, or terminated

> for legitimate business reasons, then your verdict must be for the defendants.

(Emphasis supplied.) The jurors were also instructed that they could award punitive damages and damages for emotional distress if they found a breach of the duty of good faith and fair dealing. We find that the trial court's instructions to the jury erroneously overstated the Covenant and the allowable bases for awarding damages.

II. Facts

We view the evidence in the light most favorable to Pressman. Pressman presented evidence that his immediate supervisor, Pensak, engaged in a retaliatory campaign to persuade Pensak's superiors that Pressman should be fired. The campaign began after Pressman confronted Pensak with evidence that Pensak may have had a conflict of interest. DuPont presented evidence that Pressman was hired as a high level scientist and simply failed to meet the high expectations inherent in the position. The jury apparently credited Pressman's version of events and did not credit DuPont's.

....

Evidence was admitted at trial from which a rational jury could conclude that Pensak: (1) misrepresented Pressman's responsibilities to superiors so that it would appear that Pressman was not completing assigned tasks; (2) edited a progress report to superiors which would have had the effect of understating Pressman's accomplishments; and (3) failed to pass along the progress report showing some of Pressman's significant accomplishments during the critical time period in which Pressman's termination was decided.

....

IV. Good Faith and Fair Dealing in At-Will Employment

DuPont contends that the Covenant does not extend to the facts of this case. It points to the central importance of the Doctrine which "provides a heavy presumption that a contract for employment, unless otherwise expressly stated, is at-will in nature, with duration indefinite." *Merrill v. Crothall-American, Inc.,* Del.Supr., 606 A.2d 96, 102 (1992). The Doctrine has a long history in Delaware and the United States. The Covenant, perhaps in less robust form and by a different name, also has a long history. *See Blish v. Thompson Automatic Arms Corp.,* Del.Supr., 64 A.2d 581 (1948); *Wood v.*

Lucy, Lady Duff-Gordon, 222 N.Y. 88, 118 N.E. 214 (1917); *Heney v. Sutro & Co.,* 28 Cal.App. 698, 153 P. 972 (1915).

. . . .

C. The Narrow Application of the Covenant of Good Faith and Fair Dealing to the Facts of this Case

Courts have been reluctant to recognize a broad application of the Covenant out of a concern that the Covenant could thereby swallow the Doctrine and effectively end at-will employment. . . . The presumption of at-will employment is a fixture of American law, and continues to be followed in Delaware and in the vast majority of jurisdictions.

Although the Covenant is a generally acknowledged principle, its precise contours are not fixed. We begin with an analysis of various contexts where the concept of "good faith" is employed. Although both the Doctrine and the Covenant are products of decisional law and not statutory law, the Uniform Commercial Code ("UCC") is appropriate to consider by analogy. The UCC defines good faith as "honesty in fact in the conduct or transaction concerned," 6 *Del.C.* § 1–201(19), and "honesty in fact and the observance of reasonable commercial standards of fair dealing in the trade," 6 *Del.C.* § 2–103(1)(b). The *Restatement* comments:

> The phrase "good faith" is used in a variety of contexts, and its meaning varies somewhat with the context. Good faith performance or enforcement of a contract emphasizes faithfulness to an agreed common purpose and consistency with the justified expectations of the other party; it excludes a variety of types of conduct characterized as involving "bad faith" because they violate community standards of decency, fairness or reasonableness.

Restatement (Second) of Contracts § 205, cmt. a. (1979). *See also* Summers, *"Good Faith" in General Contract Law and the Sales Provisions of the Uniform Commercial Code,* 54 Va.L.Rev. 195, 201 (1968):

> [Good faith is] an excluder. It is a phrase without general meaning (or meanings) of its own and serves to exclude a wide range of heterogeneous forms of bad faith. In a particular context the phrase takes on specific meaning, but usually this is only by way of contrast with the specific form of bad faith actually or hypothetically excluded.

The Covenant is best understood as a way of "implying terms in the agreement." Farnsworth, *Good Faith Performance and Commercial Reasonableness under the Uniform Commercial Code,* 30 U.Chi.L.Rev. 666, 670 (1963). It is a way of "honoring the reasonable expectations created by the autonomous expressions of the contracting parties." *Tymshare, Inc. v. Covell,* D.C.Cir., 727 F.2d 1145, 1152 (1984); *accord Pierce v. International Ins. Co. of Ill.,* Del.Supr., 671 A.2d 1361, 1366 (1996).

The application of the Covenant here relates solely to an act or acts of the employer manifesting bad faith or unfair dealing achieved by deceit or misrepresentation in falsifying or manipulating a record to create fictitious grounds to terminate employment. Since an assurance of continued employment is antithetical to at-will employment, no legally cognizable harm arises solely from the termination itself. Here, the harm derives from Pensak's creation of false grounds and manufacturing a record in order to establish a fictitious basis for termination. The evidence viewed in the light most favorable to Pressman shows that Pensak set out on a campaign to discredit Pressman by creating fictitious negative information about Pressman's work and hiding positive information. Based on the distorted record he created, Pensak went to his superiors and caused Pressman to be terminated.

If the jury believed that Pensak did these acts, and did them intentionally, they amounted to a breach of the Covenant. But the trial court overstated the issue in its charge to the jury by permitting the jury to find in Pressman's favor if they found that DuPont discharged Pressman "maliciously, that is as a result of hatred, ill will *or* intent to injure, *or* effects the discharge in bad faith, that is through acts of fraud, deceit or intentional misrepresentation" (emphasis supplied).

Employment relationships are complex, ambiguous and, ultimately, personal. One commentator has described the peculiar features of employment:

> Employment agreements are intrinsically different from commercial contracts in many fundamental ways. Employment agreements create an ongoing personal relationship between employee and employer-or in larger companies, with the employer's managerial and supervisory agents-which transcends purely economic interests.

Leonard, 66 N.C.L.Rev. 631, 656 (1988). This aspect of employment relationships counsels caution about creating causes of action based solely on personal motivations. Employees and their supervisors work closely together and personality clashes have the potential to interfere seriously with the achievement of an organization's mission. Dislike, hatred or ill will, alone, cannot be the basis for a cause of action for termination of an at-will employment. The jury instruction here, which is expressed in the disjunctive, would permit a cause of action where an employee was discharged because of dislike, openly expressed. Here, if the jury believed that Pensak, not having authority unilaterally to fire Pressman, maliciously employed deceit and subterfuge to manufacture grounds for Pressman's dismissal at the hands of Pensak's superiors, Pensak went beyond the broad, permissible scope of the Doctrine and crossed into the limited zone of the Covenant. DuPont was made aware after the fact of this course of events and ratified Pensak's actions. Thus, DuPont can be held liable to Pressman on this claim based upon carefully limited instructions to the jury.

The precise problem with the trial court's instruction to the jury is that its disjunctive formulation did not tie the malice of Pensak toward Pressman to the intent to injure him by causing him to be terminated based on falsified grounds. The instruction would have permitted the jury, for example, to render a verdict for Pressman if they found he was terminated because Pensak "hated" him or harbored "ill will" toward him. The breadth of the jury charge therefore was inconsistent with the breadth of the Doctrine and the limited exception created by the Covenant.

VIII. Conclusion

The doctrine of employment at-will is well established and serves important social and economic goals. A significant erosion of the Doctrine could produce unacceptable costs in employment relationships. An implied covenant or duty of good faith and fair dealing is also a longstanding fixture of the common law of contracts. These two concepts can coexist if careful attention is paid to the objectively reasonable expectations of the parties to a contract of employment at-will. Since indefinite employment is not part of the bargain in an employment contract that does not explicitly so provide, neither party can point to the duty of good faith and fair dealing to support a requirement of good cause for termination. As in many other contracts, the Covenant limits, in a manner consistent with the terms of the contract, the ability of the parties to an at-will contract to exercise the freedom to terminate. In view of the importance of the personal dynamics of employment relationships, dislike or hatred as the sole basis for termination does not violate the Covenant. But fraud, deceit and misrepresentation, either in the inducement or in intentionally fictionalizing in a material way the employee's performance to cause dismissal, may be actionable as a breach of the Covenant.

QUESTIONS

1. Why is the employer responsible for the misrepresentations of Pensak, which seemed to be motivated by personal animosity toward Pressman?
2. How significant is the definition of "good faith" under the Uniform Commercial Code to the court? Does the UCC apply to this case?

B. Bad Faith as Unreasonableness: The Most Expansive Approach

The *DuPont* case found that using the covenant of good faith to police unreasonable terminations by employers would undermine the at-will rule. Consider the following case. Does the court make a persuasive distinction between the inability of the plaintiff to challenge the termination of his at-will termination of employment and the ability of the plaintiff to challenge the bad faith suspension?

LEUDTKE V. NABORS ALASKA DRILLING, INC.

834 P.2d 1220 (Ak., 1992).

COMPTON, JUSTICE.

Paul M. Luedtke was suspended and then terminated from his employment with Nabors Alaska Drilling, Inc. (Nabors) after testing positive for marijuana use in a urinalysis. This court upheld Nabors' *termination* of Luedtke in *Luedtke v. Nabors Alaska Drilling, Inc.*, 768 P.2d 1123 (Alaska 1989) (*Luedtke I*), but the case was remanded for a determination of whether Luedtke's *suspension* violated the covenant of good faith and fair dealing. On remand, the superior court found that Nabors did not violate the covenant of good faith and fair dealing when it suspended Luedtke. The court also imposed sanctions against Luedtke and his attorney pursuant to Alaska Civil Rules 11 and 95(a), and awarded attorney's fees pursuant to Alaska Civil Rule 82. Luedtke appeals the judgment in its entirety. We reverse.

. . . .

II. NABORS' SUSPENSION OF LUEDTKE VIOLATED THE COVENANT OF GOOD FAITH AND FAIR DEALING

. . . .

In finding that Luedtke's suspension did not violate the covenant, the superior court reasoned that "Nabors had no other alternative but to suspend Mr. Luedtke immediately." It stated that sending Luedtke to the work site would have compromised the safety of Nabors' employees and compromised Nabors in any litigation that resulted from an accident involving Luedtke. However, in reaching this conclusion, the superior court misapplied the covenant of good faith and fair dealing and misconstrued our instructions on remand.

B. The Covenant of Good Faith and Fair Dealing.

We have recognized a covenant of good faith and fair dealing in all at-will employment contracts. . .

. . . .

These cases, rather than focusing on the intent of the employer, indicate that the covenant of good faith and fair dealing also requires the parties to act in a manner which a reasonable person would regard as fair. Indeed, in *ARCO Alaska, Inc. v. Akers,* 753 P.2d 1150, 1156 (Alaska 1988), this court upheld a jury instruction in which the judge stressed that an employer's discretion must be "exercised *reasonably and* in good faith" and that the employer's decisions must be made "*fairly and* in good faith." (Emphasis added.) In *Klondike Indus. Corp. v. Gibson,* 741 P.2d 1161, 1168 (Alaska 1987), we cited with approval excerpts from the Restatement of Contracts:

> Subterfuges and evasions violate the obligation of good faith in performance even though the actor believes his conduct to be justified. But the obligation goes further: bad faith may be overt or may consist of inaction, and fair dealing may require more than honesty.

Restatement (Second) of Contracts § 205 comment d (1981).

Thus, our cases establish that the covenant of good faith and fair dealing includes multiple expectations about the behavior of the parties to a contract.

The Uniform Commercial Code's requirement of good faith and fair dealing in the case of merchants, contained in section 2–103, requires more than just absence of evil motive. " 'Good faith' in the case of a merchant means honesty in fact and the observance of reasonable commercial standards of fair dealing in the trade." U.C.C. § 2–103(1)(b). Courts and commentators which have addressed the issue say that this imposes an objective as well as a subjective standard.

C. Our Instructions on Remand.

In *Luedtke I,* we considered the issue of whether Nabors' decision to fire Paul Luedtke (and his brother Clarence) violated the covenant of good faith and fair dealing based on the claim that Nabors' drug tests intruded upon their privacy:

> We conclude that there is a public policy supporting the protection of employee privacy. Violation of that policy by an employer may rise to the level of a breach of the implied covenant of good faith and fair dealing. However, the competing public concern for employee safety present in the case at bar leads us to hold that Nabors' actions did not breach the implied covenant.

Luedtke I, 768 P.2d at 1130. We noted, however, that there are limits on the employer's right to invade the privacy of an employee, even if the employer has a legitimate concern for the health and safety of other workers. We held that a "drug test must be conducted at a time reasonably contemporaneous with the employee's work time" and that "an employee must receive notice of the adoption of a drug testing program." *Id.* at 1136–37.

In the case of Luedtke's *termination,* these considerations did not apply. Luedtke was fired after refusing to take a drug test for which he had ample notice and which would have been reasonably contemporaneous with his work schedule. However, in remanding the case for consideration of whether Luedtke's *suspension* violated the covenant of good faith and fair dealing, we suggested that the factors of timing and notice should have been taken into account by the superior court.

D. Luedtke's Suspension.

Nabors argues that Luedtke's suspension did not violate the covenant of good faith and fair dealing because breach of the covenant requires subjective bad faith on the part of the employer, and there is no evidence of subjective bad faith in the record with respect to the timing of or lack of notice prior to Luedtke's drug test. . . .

We agree that there is no evidence of subjective bad faith on Nabors' part, but as we have already stated, the covenant of good faith and fair dealing also requires that the employer be objectively fair. The superior court found that Luedtke was tested for drug use without prior notice, that no other employee was similarly tested, and that Nabors suspended Luedtke immediately upon learning of the results of the test. Nabors does not dispute these findings. We hold that as a matter of law, these facts constitute a violation of the covenant of good faith and fair dealing.

As we stated in *Luedtke I:*

> [a]n employee must receive notice of the adoption of a drug testing program. By requiring a test, an employer introduces an additional term of employment. An employee should have notice of the additional term so that he may contest it, refuse to accept it and quit, seek to negotiate its conditions, or prepare for the test so that he will not fail it and thereby suffer sanctions.

768 P.2d at 1137 (footnote omitted). There is evidence in the record that Luedtke might have followed at least one, if not more, of these alternative paths had he received notice of the new drug testing program. Nabors insists that Luedtke would have refused to take the test and quit. However, Luedtke presented evidence on remand to show that he has more recently taken several drug tests with negative results. Presumably, those were tests for which he had notice, and for which he prepared. Nabors' failure to give notice of the test was objectively unfair to Luedtke.

The superior court found that Luedtke did not have notice prior to being tested, and Nabors does not dispute this. Luedtke and Nabors agree that this testing was the cause of Luedtke's suspension. The superior court should have concluded, therefore, that in suspending Luedtke, Nabors breached the covenant of good faith and fair dealing.

E. Damages.

Breach of the covenant of good faith and fair dealing results in contract damages. *Akers,* 753 P.2d at 1154. "The goal of contract damages is to place the nonbreaching party in as good a position as if the contract had been fully performed." *Alyeska Pipeline Serv. Co. v. H.C. Price Co.,* 694 P.2d 782, 787

(Alaska 1985). In the case of wrongful discharge, this generally means that the employee "is entitled to the total amount of the agreed upon salary for the unexpired term of his employment, less what he could earn by making diligent efforts to obtain similar employment." *Skagway City School Bd. v. Davis,* 543 P.2d 218, 225 (Alaska 1975), *overruled on other grounds, Diedrich v. City of Ketchikan,* 805 P.2d 362, 366 (Alaska 1991). Where the employee is wrongfully suspended rather than discharged, the employee is still under contract to the employer and need not mitigate damages by seeking other employment. Thus, Luedtke may be entitled to back pay.

However, Luedtke was fired justifiably by Nabors for failing to take a drug test on November 30, 1982. *Luedtke I,* 768 P.2d at 1137. Any damages he may have suffered after that date were a result of his lawful termination and were caused by his own refusal to comply with reasonable company policy. Luedtke argues that he should be entitled to reinstatement as a remedy for the suspension apart from any remedies for his termination. This position, if adopted, would make it impossible for an employer to cure a wrongful act. Here Nabors impermissibly suspended Luedtke, but then attempted to cure the problem by offering Luedtke a legitimate retest. Nabors was, in a sense, mitigating its own damages. We decline to hold that an employer may never mitigate damages.

Luedtke may not recover for damages not caused by Nabors' breach of the covenant of good faith and fair dealing. Further, his damages may not exceed wages lost between November 5, 1982, the date of his suspension, and November 30, 1982, the date of his lawful termination, as well as any incidental damages he can prove. Because the superior court made no findings as to cause or damages, we must remand the case for a determination of these two issues.

Mastery Problem 33-2

Ariel is the financial controller of Xerxes, a software company. Ariel is an at-will employee, whose job duties include certifying tax filings and other financial documents. Ariel discovers that Xerxes appears to be violating several provisions of the tax code and other regulatory obligations. Ariel brings the matter to the attention of the Chief Financial Officer, who dismisses her concerns. She then advises the President of Xerxes of her concerns and is immediately terminated for insubordination and not following the proper chain of command.

Depending on the jurisdiction, this scenario may give rise to one or more causes of action. Describe these different options.

Conclusion

Employers and employees must perform their obligations in good faith, even if the relationship is at-will. However, courts have not permitted the implied obligation of good faith to undermine the at-will rule. In some instances, the termination of an at-will relationship may itself violate the obligation of good faith, but generally the cause of action concerns termination in a manner that prevents a benefit from accruing to the employee.

Lesson 34:
Employer Liability for Defamation

Objectives and Expected Learning Outcomes

In this Lesson, you will address how the law seeks to protect the reputation of employees with the tort of defamation, while balancing the public interest in having employers engage in truthful and candid communication with potential future employers. You will develop your analytical and problem-solving skills by addressing novel and complex fact patterns that relate to defining "defamatory meaning," "privilege" and "publication to third parties." You will also explore the overlapping protections provided by anti-blacklisting and "service letter" statutes.

When an employee leaves employment and seeks a new job, prospective employers will want to know how the employee has performed in the past and why the employee left previous jobs. This renders the employee vulnerable to negative comments made by a previous employer. The tort of defamation serves to protect employees from the harm caused by false statements by their previous employers. As with most torts, there is nuance in the elements of the cause of action. In response, employers are incentivized to say nothing about former employees, for fear of being sued for defamation. Silence about the employee's record and reason for separation can also inhibit the employee's search for a new job. A number of states require employers to speak, by mandating that they issue a "service letter" that describes the reason for the employee's separation from the employer. Finally, many states adopted "anti-blacklisting" statutes at the turn of the twentieth century in recognition of the harm caused when employers in a certain industry would ban labor union supporters from gaining any employment in the industry. You may be more familiar with blacklisting in the context of Hollywood's refusal to permit certain writers and other artists to work in the industry as a response to Senator Joseph McCarthy's campaign against alleged communists in the 1950s. These statutes are closely related to the use of tortious interference with prospective business relationships as a means to hold a former employer accountable for preventing a person from working. We take up these topics in turn.

1. Defamation of a Former Employee

An employer is liable if it defames a former employee, and the damages relate to the injury suffered by the employee because of the effect of the defamation on future employment opportunities. The Restatement sets forth the doctrinal framework.

Restatement of Employment Law

§ 6.01. Employer's Liability to Employee for Defamation

(a) Subject to the privilege stated in § 6.02 and other applicable privileges, an employer publishing a false and defamatory statement about an employee is subject to liability for the harm the publication causes.

(b) An employer publishes a statement about an employee when the employer makes the statement:

(1) to any third party, including prospective employers, regulatory authorities, or employment agencies;

(2) to employees or others within the employer's organization; or

(3) to the employee, if the employer knows or should know that the employee will have to disclose the statement to prospective employers or others, the employee asks the employer to promise not to disclose the statement to any third party, and the employer refuses to promise.

A. The "Employer" Must Make the Statement

The employer can defame a person only through the acts of its employees and agents. Because defamation is a tort, the employer is held liable under principles of *respondeat superior* that we discussed in Lesson 14. Consequently, the employer does not need to authorize the defamatory statement, either expressly or impliedly. Instead, the employer is liable for its employee's defamatory statement when the employee is acting within the scope of the employee's general authority in furtherance of the employee's business.

Example 34-1

Alicia is a supervisor at a department store who has engaged in embezzlement. Jorge is an assistant supervisor who reports to Alicia. Alicia informs management that Jorge has embezzled funds, and that she has fired him. Jorge sues, and establishes that Alicia fired him and made the allegations for the purpose of covering up her embezzlement. Jorge's claim for defamation against the employer is insufficient, because Alicia made the defamatory statements for her own purposes, and not within her course of employment with the store.

Example 34-2

Joe is a supervisor at a company that sells cleaning products through neighborhood representatives. Pat is a sales manager who reports to Joe, and who oversees fifteen salespersons. Joe receives complaints that Pat is engaged in excessively emotional and personal meetings to motivate her team, engaging in rituals and disclosures of personal matters. Joe investigates by interviewing some salespeople off-site and by conducting internet research into techniques for building a "cult" atmosphere. Joe terminates Pat's employment, stating that she appeared to be building a "cult" based on "Satanist" and "witch-like" principles. Pat may recover against the company for defamation, even if the manner of investigation by Joe was against company policy. Joe conducted the investigation within his authority and scope of employment, and for the benefit of his employer.

B. The Statement Must Be "False and Defamatory"

Not every negative statement about a person is defamatory. The line is generally between expressing a "negative opinion" and expressing a statement of "fact" which is false. If a former supervisor says that he never enjoyed working with an employee because she seemed to be a "loner" and "sneaky," there would not be a basis for alleging defamation in the absence of other facts. However, if a former supervisor says that he never enjoyed working with an employee because she stole supplies from the stock room for her personal use, this would clearly be actionable if the statement was false.

However, some "opinions" may be actionable if they imply certain factual allegations that support the opinion. For example, if a former supervisor were to say, "In my opinion, Sheila is a liar," there is an implication that the supervisor experienced situations in which Sheila lied during the course of her employment. In effect, this statement can be treated as the equivalent of saying "Sheila has lied to people." Similarly, a statement of facts that are true may imply other facts that may be defamatory if untrue.

Consider the analysis in the *Phelan* case and address the questions that follow.

Phelan v. May Dept. Stores Co.

443 Mass. 52 (2004).

Spina, J.

This case arises from a July 10, 1998, investigation by Filene's, a division of the May Department Stores Company (May), into allegations that Michael Phelan was attempting to hide significant accounting discrepancies from his superiors. Phelan brought an action against May, Michael Geraghty (Filene's chief financial officer), and Donald Lane (Filene's controller) (collectively, the defendants), alleging that their conduct during the investigation had constituted false imprisonment and defamation. A jury found in favor of Phelan on both claims and awarded him damages of $1,500 for false imprisonment and $75,000 for defamation. With respect to Phelan's defamation claim, the defendants moved for judgment notwithstanding the verdict (judgment n.o.v.), contending that Phelan had produced insufficient evidence on which a jury reasonably could have found either (1) the conduct alleged had defamatory significance to those witnessing it . . .

. . . .

Based on the testimony at trial, the jury could have found the following facts. Phelan was employed as assistant director of accounts payable for Filene's where, among other tasks, he was responsible for managing "vendor violations" and the related budget. Vendor violations occurred when vendors failed to comply with Filene's shipping or purchase order requirements, and Filene's imposed a charge on them to cover the additional costs. To challenge an imposed charge, a vendor would submit to Filene's a "vendor violations package," addressing why the charge was unjustified and requesting a refund. This package would be processed by Phelan's department, and if it was determined that the charge had been improperly assessed, the vendor would receive a repayment.

In 1997, Geraghty directed Phelan to pay "prior year invoices" (PYIs) from the vendor violations budget, notwithstanding the fact that severe fiscal problems had arisen in the past from this practice. Phelan and his direct supervisor, Catherine Rooney, warned Geraghty and Lane that this practice was ill advised because it hindered their ability to make timely repayments to deserving vendors and to meet budgetary goals. Nonetheless, Phelan was not instructed to stop this practice.

During this time, unbeknownst to Phelan, a backlog of vendor violations packages had begun to accumulate in the hands of Phelan's subordinate, Geoffrey Meade, who was in charge of evaluating these packages. In early July, 1998, Meade finally told Phelan about the backlog, indicating that the amount due to vendors was approximately $200,000. Phelan and Rooney promptly notified their supervisor, Michael Basler, who was Filene's assistant controller. As it turned out, the problem was significantly greater than Phelan had been led to believe; Meade reported to Basler that the backlogs and unpaid PYIs totaled $491,995. Meade attempted to shred his backlog of vendor violations packages, but the documents were ultimately retrieved.

At this juncture, Geraghty, Lane, and Basler decided to conduct an investigation and audit of the vendor violations program. On the morning of July 10, 1998, Lane interviewed Phelan as to alleged accounting irregularities and then directed him to Basler's office. Lane instructed a Filene's security officer, Johnny Guante, to guard Phelan, purportedly so that Phelan would not "influence" or "intimidate" his subordinates, who were being questioned as part of the investigation. Phelan was not permitted to use the telephone. Throughout the day, Guante relocated Phelan to various available offices and conference rooms, escorted him to the restroom, and accompanied him to the cafeteria. Coworkers did not speak with Phelan as he was moving about the building with Guante. Although Guante did not wear a badge or other insignia that identified him as a security guard, and did not carry a weapon or handcuffs, he did wear dark trousers, a shirt, a tie, and a blazer that Filene's had issued to him and that was similar to the clothing worn by other security guards in the store. Phelan felt embarrassed and humiliated because of his observation that, everywhere they went, coworkers were staring at him while he was in the company of security personnel. At the end of the day, Phelan was returned to Basler's office, was informed that he was being suspended, and was escorted out of the building by another Filene's executive. Phelan's employment with Filene's subsequently was terminated.

When considering a motion for judgment n.o.v., "the judge's task, 'taking into account all the evidence in its aspect most favorable to the plaintiff, [is] to determine whether, without weighing the credibility of the witnesses or otherwise considering the weight of the evidence, the jury reasonably could return a verdict for the plaintiff.' " *Tosti v. Ayik,* 394 Mass. 482, 494, 476 N.E.2d 928 (1985), quoting *Rubel v. Hayden, Harding & Buchanan, Inc.,* 15 Mass.App.Ct. 252, 254, 444 N.E.2d 1306 (1983). See *Cambridgeport Sav. Bank v. Boersner,* 413 Mass. 432, 438, 597 N.E.2d 1017 (1992). The judge will consider whether "anywhere in the evidence, from whatever source derived, any combination of circumstances could be found from which a reasonable inference could be drawn" in favor of the nonmoving party. *Poirier v. Plymouth,* 374 Mass. 206, 212, 372 N.E.2d 212 (1978), quoting *Raunela v. Hertz Corp.,* 361 Mass. 341, 343, 280 N.E.2d 179 (1972). To be reasonable, the inference "must be based on probabilities rather than possibilities and cannot be the result of mere speculation and conjecture." *McEvoy Travel Bur., Inc. v. Norton Co.,* 408 Mass. 704, 706–707 n. 3, 563 N.E.2d 188 (1990), quoting *McNamara v. Honeyman,* 406 Mass. 43, 45–46, 546 N.E.2d 139 (1989). When reviewing a judgment n.o.v., this court applies the same standard as the motion judge. See *Kattar v. Demoulas,* 433 Mass. 1, 8 n. 5, 739 N.E.2d 246 (2000).

To prevail on his defamation claim, Phelan had to establish that the defendants published a false statement about him to a third party that either caused him economic loss or was of the type that is actionable without proof of economic loss. See *White v. Blue Cross & Blue Shield of Mass., Inc.,* 442 Mass. 64, 66, 809 N.E.2d 1034 (2004); *Eyal v. Helen Broadcasting Corp.,* 411 Mass. 426, 429–430, 583 N.E.2d 228 (1991). See also Restatement (Second) of Torts § 558 (1977). A false statement that "would tend to hold the plaintiff up to scorn, hatred, ridicule or contempt, in the minds of any considerable and respectable segment in the community," would be considered defamatory, *Stone v. Essex County Newspapers, Inc.,* 367 Mass. 849, 853, 330 N.E.2d 161 (1975), and the imputation of a crime is defamatory per se, requiring no proof of special damages. See *Lynch v. Lyons,* 303 Mass. 116, 118–119, 20 N.E.2d 953 (1939). The element of publication is satisfied where the defamatory communication is transmitted to even one person other than the plaintiff. See *Brauer v. Globe Newspaper Co.,* 351 Mass. 53, 56, 217 N.E.2d 736 (1966); Restatement (Second) of Torts, *supra* at § 577. Contrast *Economopoulos v. A.G. Pollard Co.,* 218 Mass. 294, 297, 105 N.E. 896 (1914) (no publication where defamatory words, spoken in presence of others, uttered in foreign language and only understood by plaintiff).

The defendants contend that they were properly entitled to judgment n.o.v. on Phelan's defamation claim because their conduct did not convey a clear and unambiguous false statement about Phelan and, in the absence of evidence that an observer interpreted the defendants' conduct as conveying such a meaning, Phelan has failed to establish defamatory publication. We agree.

A threshold issue in a defamation action, whether a communication is reasonably susceptible of a defamatory meaning, is a question of law for the court. However, "[w]here the communication is susceptible of both a defamatory and nondefamatory meaning, a question of fact exists for the jury." *Jones v. Taibbi, supra* at 792, 512 N.E.2d 260. See Restatement (Second) of Torts, *supra* (jury decides "whether a communication, capable of a defamatory meaning, was so understood by its recipient"). In the context of determining whether articles published in a newspaper were defamatory to particular businesses, we stated that "an objective test—i.e., inquiry into a reasonable recipient's understanding of the words rather than the speaker's intent—has been used over the years to prove that words are defamatory" and that they concerned the plaintiff. *New England Tractor-Trailer Training of Conn., Inc. v. Globe Newspaper Co.,* 395 Mass. 471, 479–480, 480 N.E.2d 1005 (1985). Cf. *Economopoulos v. A.G. Pollard Co., supra* at 297, 105 N.E. 896.

When assessing the import of physical acts, which are at issue here, rather than written or spoken words, this objective test is equally applicable. Although not explicitly recognized in prior Massachusetts case law, we conclude that defamatory publication *may* result from the physical actions of a defendant, in the absence of written or spoken communication. See Restatement (Second) of Torts, *supra* at § 559 comment a, at 156 ("The word 'communication' is used to denote the fact that one person has brought an idea to the perception of another"); *id.* at § 563 comment a, at 162 (meaning of communication, "whether by written or spoken words or otherwise," is that which recipient understands it to convey); *id.* at § 565 comment a, at 170 (particular act may fall within definition of defamatory communication); *id.* at § 568 comment d, at 180 (publication of defamatory matter may be made by conduct and may be treated as libel, rather than slander). See also *Jorgensen v. Massachusetts Port Auth.,* 905 F.2d 515, 520 (1st Cir.1990) (defamation requires "a communication, defined as conduct that brings an idea to the perception of others"); *Jimenez-Nieves v. United States,* 682 F.2d 1, 6 (1st Cir.1982) (activity counts as "communication" if it conveys idea to third person); *Simas v. First Citizens' Fed. Credit Union,* 63 F.Supp.2d

110, 116 (D.Mass.1999) ("an individual's actions, separate from any written or spoken statements, may be sufficient grounds for a jury to find a cause of action [for defamation]"); *Petsch-Schmid v. Boston Edison Co.,* 914 F.Supp. 697, 705 (D.Mass.1996), aff'd, 108 F.3d 328 (1st Cir.1997) (where supervisor raised voice to employee while escorting her from building after suspension, "it is possible that the escort may have been conducted in such a manner as to communicate a defamatory statement to other employees about the plaintiff").

Even viewing the evidence in the light most favorable to Phelan, as we must, the defendants' conduct was ambiguous and open to various interpretations. The actions of Guante in escorting Phelan about the office on July 10, and in relocating him to various conference rooms, did not have a specific, obvious meaning and did not necessarily convey that Phelan had engaged in criminal wrongdoing. There was no chasing, grabbing, restraining, or searching such as would have conveyed a clear and commonly understood meaning. From the mere fact that he was being accompanied by a security guard, observers could have thought, for example, that the defendants were sequestering Phelan so that he could not communicate with others, or so that he could provide confidential assistance with their investigation. Where Guante's communication, through physical action, was ambiguous, it was for the jury to decide whether such communication was understood by Phelan's coworkers as having a defamatory meaning.

Phelan had the burden of proving that a reasonable third person observing Guante's conduct would have understood it to be defamatory. See *Leonard v. Allen,* 11 Cush. 241, 244–245, 65 Mass. 241, 1853 WL 5005 (1853). See also Restatement (Second) of Torts, *supra* at § 613 comments c and d, at 308 (plaintiff must convince jury that communication was understood as defamatory by third person). Cf. *Sharratt v. Housing Innovations, Inc.,* 365 Mass. 141, 144–145, 310 N.E.2d 343 (1974) (statement not defamatory on face may acquire defamatory meaning when audience presented with attendant circumstances). Contrast *Economopoulos v. A.G. Pollard Co., supra* at 297, 105 N.E. 896 (no publication, and thus no cause of action for defamation, where purported defamatory meaning only understood by plaintiff). Phelan presented no such evidence to satisfy his burden of proof. He testified that he was embarrassed and humiliated by the defendants because other employees stared at him in the company of Guante. However, Phelan's own belief that others viewed him in a defamatory light, without more, was insufficient to establish defamatory publication. In other words,

Phelan was not competent to testify as to his coworkers' interpretation of Guante's actions and whether, as a result of what they saw, they viewed Phelan with scorn, hatred, ridicule, or contempt. Publication to Phelan cannot be substituted for publication to a third party. Cf. *Economopoulos v. A.G. Pollard Co., supra.* To satisfy his burden of proof, Phelan needed to present testimony from at least one coworker who observed Guante's actions and interpreted such actions as defamatory. Cf. *Leonard v. Allen,* supra at 244, 1853 WL 5005 (where purported slander made by expressions and gestures, and not solely by words, it was necessary to inquire of witnesses what they understood defendant to mean both as to person intended and charge made against him). Because he failed to do so, we conclude that he did not establish the essential elements of defamation. Holding

. . . .

The judgment notwithstanding the verdict is affirmed.

QUESTIONS

1. If Phelan had introduced the testimony of one co-worker who understood the defendants' actions as defamatory, would he have prevailed on this appeal? If so, how can that be reconciled with the "objective" test that the court claims to use?

2. Assume that you have a client who works in a highly competitive sector of the tech industry. Your client has had to dismiss several employees for sharing industry secrets with competitors, and has had them escorted out of the building by armed security guards to ensure that they are unable to log in and do anything harmful after their termination. Having faced a few lawsuits for defamation, your client asks whether it makes sense to use armed guards to escort all employees who are leaving employment, so that there is no implication of wrongdoing with any particular employee. How would you advise your client?

Problem 34-1

After a construction site experienced a series of thefts, the general contractor hired an investigator to come to the site and determine who was stealing the materials. That afternoon, the employer posted a letter stating that five employees were no longer permitted on the work site, directing employees to immediately notify it if said employees were observed on the site. The general contractor argues that it had indeed banned the former employees from the site, so the statement was true. Additionally, it argues that the five former employees all worked at-will, so termination of their employment does not indicate any allegation of wrongdoing. Analyze the options for recovery by the five former employees for defamation and the employer's strategy for avoiding liability.

C. The Statement Must Be "Published"

The Restatement makes clear that an employer "publishes" the defamatory statement when it is made to any third party, to individuals within the employer's organization, or even to the plaintiff employee under the doctrine of "compelled self-publication." This broad definition of "publication" is offset by conferring a privilege in certain circumstances where public policy supports the dissemination of information about the employee.

Some jurisdictions do not consider certain communications within the employer's organization to be a "publication," in effect creating an absolute privilege for those intra-firm communications. For example, some jurisdictions would state that communications between executives of the employer are not "published" to a third person.

The most difficult issues revolve around determining the scope of the doctrine of compelled self-publication. Consider the following scenarios under the test set forth in Restatement § 6.01(3).

Problem 34-2

Amy works as a cashier at a food co-op. Her manager fires her, stating that he believes she has permitted her friends to leave the store without paying for all of their items. Amy later honestly recounts this conversation during a job interview when her prospective employer asks why she left the co-op. Amy is not hired as a result. Can Amy sue the co-op for defamation?

Problem 34-3

Assume that Amy's prospective employer does not ask her why she left the co-op, but she explains what happened anyway. Can Amy sue the co-op for defamation if the prospective employer does not hire her?

Problem 34-4

Assume that Amy's prospective employer asks her why she left the co-op, and Amy lies and says that she was interested in new opportunities. Can Amy sue the co-op for defamation for putting her in a situation where she needs to lie to avoid injury?

Problem 34-5

Assume that Amy requests that her manager at the co-op not disclose his suspicions of theft, and the manager promises not to disclose. Another cashier at the co-op reports to Amy that he overheard the manager assuring someone that Amy won't be able to get a job that requires honesty. Amy assumes that the manager will undermine her by telling prospective employers about his suspicions, and so she honestly responds to questions about why she left the co-op. Can Amy sue the co-op for defamation?

Even if a defamatory statement is published, it doesn't mean that the employer will be liable for damages. The plaintiff must prove that the publication of the statement caused a financial loss.

Arthaud v. Mutual of Omaha Ins. Co.

170 F.3d 860 (8th Cir. 1999).

Wollman, Circuit Judge.

[Editor's Note: Arthaud was general manager of the defendant's division office. At a managers' meeting he was told by his supervisor that his employment was terminated because of "inappropriate sales practices" and "violation of the company's conflict of interest policy." In the insurance and financial services industry, these are very serious claims. Arthaud demanded a "service letter" (see the next section of

this Lesson) and it repeated these ground for termination. Arthaud informed prospective employers of the content of his service letter, and he was turned down for several jobs before finding a new position. The jury found that the defendant was attempting to hide the fact that it was engaged in extensive downsizing, and it awarded Arthaud $50,000 in actual damages and $125,000 in punitive damages for defamation.]

To make out a claim of compelled self-defamation, Missouri law requires a plaintiff to show: (1) that the employer stated a false reason for termination; (2) that the employer knew the statement was false or had serious doubt about its truth when it was made; (3) that the employer intended or had reason to suppose that the statement would be disclosed to a third party; (4) that the statement tended to expose the employee to contempt within his profession; (5) that the statement was communicated to prospective employers; and (6) that the employee suffered actual damages to his reputation. . . . Mutual contends that Arthaud did not prove that he suffered any actual damages because he did not show that any prospective employers relied on Mutual's false statement in denying him employment. We agree.

Historically, defamation that harmed a person's trade or profession constituted defamation *per se,* which allowed for a presumption of damages. *Nazeri,* 860 S.W.2d at 311. Since *Nazeri,* however, Missouri courts require a showing of actual damages in all defamation cases. *See id.* at 313. To demonstrate actual damages, plaintiffs must show that defamatory statements caused a quantifiable professional or personal injury, such as interference with job performance, psychological or emotional distress, or depression. *See Jenkins v. Revolution Helicopter Corp.,* 925 S.W.2d 939, 942–43 (Mo.Ct.App.1996) (requiring plaintiffs to show monetary damages in defamation cases); *Taylor v. Chapman,* 927 S.W.2d 542, 544–45 (Mo.Ct.App.1996) (finding plaintiff's belief that her reputation was tarnished insufficient to demonstrate actual professional or personal injury); *Kennedy v. Jasper,* 928 S.W.2d 395, 400 (Mo.Ct.App.1996) (holding that the testimony of individuals who believed defamatory statements, and of a psychiatrist regarding plaintiff's mental distress, sufficiently demonstrated actual damages).

In the compelled self-defamation context, an employee must demonstrate a causal connection between the employer's false statement and a lost job opportunity to show actual professional damages. *See Herberholt,* 625 S.W.2d at 625; *Nazeri,* 860 S.W.2d at 314. Communication of the false statement to a prospective employer, without more, does not establish such a causal connection. A plaintiff must show that a prospective employer actually relied on the false statement in denying him employment. *See Jasperson v. Purolator Courier Corp.,* 765 F.2d 736, 741–42 (8th Cir.1985); *Kling v. Professional Care Ctr., Inc.,* 735 S.W.2d 168, 169 (Mo.Ct.App.1987); *Grasle v. Jenny Craig Weight Loss Centres, Inc.,* 167 F.R.D. 406, 413–14 (E.D.Mo.1996) (all holding that plaintiffs failed to show actual damages because they did not present evidence that prospective employers relied on false statements in service letters in denying them employment).

Arthaud informed prospective employers about the false statement in the service letter. At trial, he showed that a conflict of interest was a serious matter in the insurance industry and that many of his peers had learned that he was terminated for that reason. He also showed that he had difficulty obtaining a new position despite being highly qualified. Arthaud relied entirely on speculation, however, for his assertion that Mutual's false statement in the service letter actually caused his difficulty in finding a job. Arthaud offered no evidence that any prospective employers relied on, or even considered, the contents of the service letter. Arthaud simply inferred from his age and qualifications that he would have found employment sooner had Mutual not made the false statement in the service letter. As a matter of law, this is insufficient to establish a causal connection between Mutual's false statement and Arthaud's alleged professional injury. Thus, Mutual was entitled to judgment as a matter of law on Arthaud's compelled self-defamation claim, a holding that perforce requires that the award of damages also be set aside.

The judgment is reversed, and the case is remanded to the district court for entry of judgment in favor of Mutual.

D. The Statement Must Not Be "Privileged"

If employers could be held liable for every publication of a false statement about an employee, it would make it very difficult to maintain an effective workplace and to honestly appraise its employees. The common law addressed this problem by creating "privileges" that permit the employer to communicate with certain parties without fear of liability. The Restatement articulates this doctrine as a "qualified privilege to publish."

Restatement of Employment Law

§ 6.02. Employer Qualified Privilege to Publish Statements Concerning an Employee or Former Employee

(a) Unless denied under (b), an employer has a qualified privilege to publish statements about an employee to:

(1) prospective employers and employment agencies;

(2) public or private regulatory or licensing authorities; and

(3) the employer's own employees and agents.

(b) An employer is denied this privilege when the employer abuses it by publishing a statement, described in subsection (a), that the employer either (i) knows is false or acts with reckless disregard of its truth or falsity, or (ii) knows or should know that neither the employer nor the recipient has a legitimate interest in the recipient receiving the statement.

Consider the following circumstances and determine if the employer had a qualified privilege to publish the statement.

Problem 34-6

Ernest was employed as a mechanic at the Heisenberg factory. An office worker at Heisenberg received an obscene and crude phone message, and she reported that she believed it was from Ernest. Heisenberg investigated, and four co-workers familiar with Ernest identified his voice from the recording of the call. Heisenberg terminated Ernest, and when contacted for references it stated that Ernest was fired for making obscene phone calls in the workplace. Ernest later proves that the recorded voice on the message was not his, and sues Heisenberg for defamation. Is Heisenberg liable?

Problem 34-7

Assume that Ernest is told in his exit interview that Heisenberg plans to inform prospective employers of the reason for his discharge because of the severity of the matter. As a result, Ernest tells prospective employers about the reason for his termination when asked. Has Heisenberg published the statement? Is Heisenberg potentially liable for the statement?

Problem 34-8

Assume that the woman who received the phone call is worried about her safety and is speaking with her co-workers about the problem. Heisenberg's vice-president of H.R. gathers all the office workers together and reports that Ernest has been identified as the culprit and he has been terminated as a result. Is this communication privileged?

Mastery Problem 34-1

Florid is a florist shop with fifteen stores across the state. Luz is the sales coordinator for the Broadway store, Manny is the manager of that store, and Nadia works as a floral arranger in that store. Manny told Nadia that he was having an affair with Luz, who is married. Nadia confronted Luz, who denied the allegation. Nadia then called corporate H.R. and reported the situation, claiming that it was a hostile work environment for her. The Vice-President for H.R. came to the Broadway store and interviewed everyone. Manny claimed that he had kissed and hugged Luz on numerous occasions but denied that it was a "sexual relationship." Luz adamantly denied the allegation, saying that at most she had occasionally given Manny a friendly hug as a greeting. Florid decided to transfer Manny and Luz to different stores. At her new location, Luz's co-workers harassed her about "cheating on her husband to get ahead." Luz finally quit and sued Manny and Florid for defamation. You represent Florid. Can you protect the company from a verdict, even if Manny is found liable for defamation?

---

2. Service Letter Statutes

As you saw in the *Arthaud* case, some states require, under certain conditions, that employers provide a "service letter" to a former employee that describes the service provided by the employee and the cause for the employment relationship ending. These statutes were designed primarily to protect former employees by forcing the employer to provide a true account of their service.

Missouri Annot. Statute § 290.140

1. Whenever any employee of any corporation doing business in this state and which employs seven or more employees, who shall have been in the service of said corporation for a period of at least ninety days, shall be discharged or voluntarily quit the service of such corporation and who thereafter within a reasonable period of time, but not later than one year following the date the employee was discharged or voluntarily quit, requests in writing by certified mail to the superintendent, manager or registered agent of said corporation, with specific reference to the statute, it shall be the duty of the superintendent or manager of said corporation to issue to such employee, within forty-five days after the receipt of such request, a letter, duly signed by such superintendent or manager, setting forth the nature and character of service rendered by such employee to such corporation and the duration thereof, and truly stating for what cause, if any, such employee was discharged or voluntarily quit such service.
2. Any corporation which violates the provisions of subsection 1 of this section shall be liable for compensatory but not punitive damages but in the event that the evidence establishes that the employer did not issue the requested letter, said employer may be liable for nominal and punitive damages; but no award of punitive damages under this section shall be based upon the content of any such letter.

A federal Court of Appeals explained that the policies implemented by the Missouri statute extend beyond the goal of protecting former employees:

> The statute attempts to regulate the issuance of reference letters because the state recognized that straightforward letters would benefit prospective employers and potential employees alike. Missouri has decided that a corporate employer has no right to lie about a former employee's job history. Indeed, it has an affirmative duty to tell the truth as it perceives it, so that both the buyer and seller of labor have sufficient information to purchase and sell employment services in the job market. Missouri punishes deceit, misrepresentation or overreaching on the part of corporate employers by permitting the recovery of money damages for the employer's failure to comply with the statute.

Rimmer v. Colt Ind. Operating Co., 656 F. 2d 323, 328 (8th Cir. 1981). Caselaw has also established that it is insufficient for an employer to make vague statements about "unsatisfactory service." The courts interpret the statute to require that the former employer provide a full and fair accounting of the service of the former employee.

QUESTION

1. Does the statute effectively achieve the goals described by the *Rimmer* court? How could you revise the statute to be more effective?

---

3. Anti-Blacklisting Statutes

In the early days of the unionization effort, employees who supported forming a union were sometimes dismissed and then "blacklisted" by all employers in the industry in order to keep them from being in a position to work on behalf of unionization of the industry. This led many states to enact anti-blacklisting statutes, many of which carried criminal penalties. After the passage of the National Labor Relations Act, which we reviewed in Lesson 2, there are now direct causes of action against those engaging in unfair labor practices. However, other forms of blacklisting have arisen, most notably in Hollywood during the so-called "Red scare," when politicians were decrying the influence of communists on contemporary culture. A number of suspected communists were blacklisted in the movie industry, leading many writers to work anonymously through intermediaries.

Although these statutes are somewhat duplicative of the protections afforded by the tort of defamation and the tort of interference with prospective business advantage, there are important differences. An employee does not need to prove actual monetary loss to assert her rights under the statute, and the potential for criminal charges to be brought may be a disincentive for employers to sabotage their former employee's effort to find work.

Montana Code Annot. 39–2–803. Blacklisting Prohibited

If a company or corporation in this state authorizes or allows any of its agents to blacklist or if a person does blacklist any discharged employee or attempts by word or writing or any other means to prevent any discharged employee or any employee who may have voluntarily left the company's

> service from obtaining employment with another person, . . . the company, corporation, or person is liable in punitive damages to the employee prevented from obtaining employment, to be recovered in a civil action, and is also punishable [for a criminal misdemeanor].

Mastery Problem 34-2

Karl is a welder. He worked for Ajax Construction for eight years before resigning in order to teach welding at a local technical school. After Karl's resignation, his co-worker Fred reported that Karl and two other employees had been stealing supplies from construction sites where Ajax was working. Ajax conducted an investigation but could not find evidence connecting Karl to the thefts. Ajax fired Karl's two co-workers. A year later, Karl decided to leave his teaching post and return to the construction trade. He accepted a position with Beam Construction, a contractor that often was hired as a subcontractor by Ajax.

While working on a job, one of Karl's former supervisors saw him. Two weeks later, Karl was escorted off the jobsite by an employee of Ajax. Ajax then informed Beam that Karl could not work on any of Ajax's job sites. Subsequently, Beam fired Karl. Karl has had extreme difficulty finding work as a welder in the area.

You represent Karl. Analyze the discovery and research that you would conduct to determine if he can recover from any party for (i) defamation, (ii) tortious interference with contract, (iii) tortious interference with prospective business relations, and (iv) blacklisting.

Conclusion

Employees can use the tort of defamation to protect themselves against false statements made by a former employer. In some cases, the employee is considered to have been compelled to publish a defamatory statement made directly to the employee by the employer. Service Letter statutes protect employees from the employer remaining silent and leaving the implicit perception that the employee was terminated for cause. Anti-blacklisting statutes that were enacted in the early days of the labor movement might also protect employees from a former employer's interference with their ability to find future employment.

Lesson 35:
Other Common Law Protections

Objectives and Expected Learning Outcomes

In this Lesson, we consider how general tort actions may provide avenues of recovery for at-will employees who are misled by their employer in some way, or who are subjected to intolerable treatment in the manner in which they are terminated. You will learn how employees can use the torts of misrepresentation, false imprisonment, assault and battery, and intentional infliction of emotional distress to seek compensation for injuries suffered in connection with their termination of employment.

In light of the at-will rule, employees who are dismissed unfairly have no recourse as a general matter. However, it is possible that the events leading up to, or comprising, the termination of employment may be considered independently tortious. Employers are subject to the general law of torts no less than any other party. In this Lesson, we will consider the use of several torts by employees: negligent misrepresentation, false imprisonment, assault and battery, and intentional infliction of emotional distress. When employers overreach in terminating an employee these torts may provide some measure of relief.

As a matter of doctrine, the at-will rule regarding the duration of a contractual employment relationship should have no influence on the applicability of torts in the workplace. However, you will see that the at-will rule has an effect on how the elements of the torts are applied. If an employer fires a long time employee in a particularly callous and mean manner, it will be difficult to recover for the resulting "emotional distress," in light of the fact that the at-will rule permits the employer to fire the employee for any reason or no reason at all. Thus, although this Lesson will read as a grab bag of potential tort actions against the employer, you should pay attention to how the long shadow of the at-will rule shapes the interpretation of these torts in the employment context.

Finally, as you learned in Lesson 26, the workers' compensation system is designed to provide a no-fault source of recovery for employees who suffer injuries in the workplace. Suing an employer in tort for a workplace-related injury is generally precluded as part of the "grand bargain" of the no-fault workers' compensation program. As a consequence, these tort claims will be applicable only if they are deemed to reach injuries that are outside the scope of the workers' compensation system.

1. Negligent Misrepresentation

An employer may negligently provide information to a current or prospective employee that leads the employee to suffer a loss. Consider how this ordinary business tort has the opportunity to cut back on the scope of the at-will rule. Generally, this tort imposes a duty on employers to refrain from misleading current or prospective employees, and does not impose an affirmative duty of disclosure.

Restatement of Employment Law

§ 6.06. Employer's Negligent Provision of False Information to Employees

(a) An employer has a duty to a current or prospective employee to exercise reasonable care not to provide false information on a topic about which the employer has special knowledge and that the employee may reasonably rely on in deciding whether to enter into or maintain an employment relationship.

D'Ulisse-Cupo v. Bd. of Dir. of Notre Dame High School

520 A.2d 217 (Conn. 1987).

Peters, Chief Justice.

This case arises out of the failure of a school board to rehire a nontenured teacher despite representations that she would receive a new employment contract. The plaintiff, Maria D'Ulisse-Cupo, filed a three count complaint against the defendants, the board of directors of Notre Dame High School and the principal of the school, George Schmitz, seeking damages premised on liability for breach of contract and negligent misrepresentation. The trial court rendered judgment against her after granting the motion of the defendants to strike all three counts of her complaint for failure to state a cause of action. Upon appeal to the Appellate Court, that court found error and remanded the case for further trial court proceedings on all counts. We granted certification at the request of the defendants and now conclude that the Appellate Court's judgment must be reversed with respect to the plaintiff's contract counts, so that further trial court proceedings will be limited to the plaintiff's tort claim only.

. . . .

The plaintiff alleged the following facts in her complaint. From September, 1981, to June, 1983, she taught Spanish and Italian to ninth and tenth grade students at Notre Dame High School in West Haven. During that period, she was employed under an employment contract which expired in June, 1983. On or about March 21, 1983, the defendant Schmitz, the school principal, orally represented to the plaintiff, during a performance review, that "there would be no problem with her teaching certain courses and levels the following year, that everything looked fine for rehire for the next year, and that she should continue her planning for the exchange program" which she organized for the school. Shortly thereafter, during the week of April 11, 1983, Schmitz or his authorized representative posted a written notice on a bulletin board in the school stating: "All present faculty members will be offered contracts for next year." Upon her return from an exchange trip to Italy, the plaintiff was again informed that she would have a teaching contract for the following year. On or about May 4, 1983, however, the plaintiff was told by school officials that, due to staff cutbacks in various departments, her teaching contract would not be renewed.

The complaint further alleged that Schmitz interviewed the plaintiff for a position in the English department on or about May 27, 1983. Schmitz told the plaintiff and other teachers that the defendants would do everything possible to avoid discharging them. Subsequently, instead of hiring the plaintiff for the position available in the English department, the defendants hired an outside applicant for that position. Furthermore, the defendants allegedly failed to explore alternative job opportunities for the plaintiff or to offer her any substitute teaching positions for which she was qualified and available.

> *[Editor's Note: The plaintiff sued for wrongful discharge, promissory estoppel, and negligent misrepresentation. The Court of Appeals affirmed the dismissal of the wrongful discharge count because the plaintiff was not an at-will employee who was terminated, but instead a contract employee who was not renewed. The Court also affirmed the dismissal of the promissory estoppel count because the employer's statements were not definite enough to be a promise.]*

This court has long recognized liability for negligent misrepresentation. We have held that even an innocent misrepresentation of fact "may be actionable if the declarant has the means of knowing, ought to know, or has the duty of knowing the truth." *Richard v. A. Waldman & Sons, Inc.,* 155 Conn. 343, 346, 232 A.2d 307 (1967). The governing principles are set forth in similar terms in § 552 of the Restatement (Second) of Torts (1979): "One who, in the course of his business, profession or employment . . . supplies false information for the guidance of others in their business transactions, is subject to liability for pecuniary loss caused to them by their justifiable reliance upon the information, if he fails to exercise reasonable care or competence in obtaining or communicating the information."

The defendants argue, initially, that if they cannot be held liable in contract for their representations based on promissory estoppel, they likewise cannot be held liable in tort for negligent misrepresentation. For purposes of a cause of action for negligent misrepresentation, however, the plaintiff need not prove that the representations made by the defendants were promissory. It is sufficient to allege that the representations contained false information. The gravamen of the defendants' alleged negligence is that the defendants made unconditional representations of their plans to rehire the plaintiff, when in fact the defendants knew or should have known that hiring plans would be contingent upon student enrollment levels for the following year. The defendants ultimately relied on declining student enrollment levels as the justification for the staff cutbacks that resulted in the elimination of the plaintiff's teaching position. If the plaintiff's complaint otherwise contains the necessary elements of negligent misrepresentation, it survives a motion to strike even though the first and third counts grounded in promissory estoppel must fall.

> *[Editor's Note: The court found that the complaint stated a claim for negligent misrepresentation, even though it did not track the precise language of the Restatement.]*

In our view, the plaintiff's allegation that "the defendants negligently misrepresented the facts to the plaintiff" necessarily implied that the defendants did not exercise reasonable care or competence in communicating with the plaintiff about her prospects for reemployment. Although the complaint could have alleged the nature of the defendants' negligence more precisely, the lack of linguistic specificity does not warrant striking the second count. As the Appellate Court noted, under the rules of practice governing pleading, a party may plead legal effect as long as the pleading "fairly [apprises] the adverse party of the state of facts which it is intended to prove." Practice Book § 109; see Practice Book § 108. We agree with the Appellate Court that the facts alleged by the plaintiff in this case fairly apprised the defendants of her intent to pursue a claim for negligent misrepresentation. Moreover, if the defendants were in doubt as to the nature of this claim or the legal theory underlying it, they could "have sought a more particular description of the negligence charged" by filing a request to revise. *Scribner v. O'Brien, Inc.*, 169 Conn. 389, 399, 363 A.2d 160 (1975). The defendants in this case never filed such a request. We conclude, therefore, that the Appellate Court correctly determined that the plaintiff's allegation of negligent misrepresentation contained in the second count is sufficient to withstand a motion to strike. We affirm their holding that further proceedings are required on the second count.

QUESTIONS

1. Would Ms. D'Ulisse-Cupo prevail under the rule as articulated in the Restatement?
2. The Connecticut Supreme Court determined that Ms. D'Ulisse-Cupo had successfully pleaded a count of negligent misrepresentation. How would you develop a theory of the case for her trial?

Mastery Problem 35-1

Atianna Gomez is a third year law student who had an on-campus interview with a local law firm, Franks Law Group. Peggy Franks, the managing partner of the firm, conducted the on-campus interview. Atianna advised Peggy that she had an offer to join another firm, but that she really wanted to be part of the Franks Law Group. In her introductory remarks, Atianna said, "If you offer me an associate's position, I will accept." As the conversation continued, Peggy emphasized that she was nearly finished negotiating representation agreements with several large clients that would ensure the financial strength of Franks Law Group. One week later, Peggy called Atianna and offered her an associate position with the firm and Atianna accepted. Atianna advised the other firm that she had accepted another offer. Six months later, as Atianna was getting ready to begin work, Peggy called her and said that she was sorry, but that the firm could not sustain another associate at this time.

Atianna comes to your office and asks if she has any claims against Franks Law Group. She is now unable to find an associate position given the time of year, and is surviving by doing contract legal work for $25 per hour through a temp agency. Describe the avenues you would explore on behalf of Atianna and the kind of evidence you would seek in support of your theories of recovery.

2. False Imprisonment

It is tortious to restrain a person against her will without some manner of legal authority or justification. This tort is often invoked by employees who are detained by an employer for questioning an investigation of a workplace matter. The gravamen of the tort is the unjustified restraint of another. However, courts generally find that a threat to dismiss the employee unless the employee submits to questioning is not an unjustified "restraint" since the employee is free to choose to leave the premises, and the employer has the right to discharge the employee at-will.

Example 35-1

A grocery store manager suspects a cashier of stealing a $20 bill from the register. The manager and a security guard ask the employee to come to the manager's office. They ask her to sit down and the guard stands in front of the door. The manager accuses the employee of taking the money and demands a confession. When the employee stands up, the manager yells that she cannot leave the room until she makes her confession and that they will keep her there until the police arrive if she doesn't confess. The manager is likely exposed to liability for false imprisonment if the employee suffers injury, and the employer would be exposed to vicarious liability under the doctrine of *respondeat superior.*

Example 35-2

A grocery store manager suspects a cashier of stealing a $20 bill from the register. The manager and a security guard ask the employee to come to the manager's office for questioning about the theft. The employee says that she doesn't want to go to the office. The manager then says that she will either come to the office to discuss the theft, or she will be immediately fired. The manager is not exposed to liability for false imprisonment because the employer had the right to terminate the employee at-will and the employee was not "restrained."

Consider the following case in which the California Supreme Court determines that allegations of false imprisonment are always outside the workers' compensation bargain given the nature of the elements of this tort.

Fermino v. Fedco, Inc.

7 Cal.4th 701 (In Bank, 1994).

Mosk, Justice.

In this case we consider whether an employee subject to false imprisonment at the hands of her employer may sue that employer in a civil action, or whether such a suit is barred by the exclusivity provisions of the Workers' Compensation Act (Lab.Code, §§ 3600, 3602). We conclude that her suit would not be barred, because an employer that falsely imprisons its employee has stepped outside its proper role, and an injury resulting therefrom is beyond the scope of what we have termed the "compensation bargain."

I. Statement of Facts

The facts, as stated in plaintiff's second amended complaint, are as follows. Plaintiff Fermino was employed as a salesclerk in defendant's department store, working in the jewelry department. The store's personnel manager summoned her to a windowless room, and proceeded to interrogate her concerning her alleged theft of the proceeds of a $4.95 sale to a customer. The personnel manager was joined by the store's loss prevention manager and by two security agents. One of the security agents stated that a customer and an employee, who were waiting in the next room, had witnessed the theft. He then demanded that Fermino confess. He told her that the interrogation could be handled in two ways: the "Fedco way" or the "system way." The "Fedco way" was to award points each time she denied her guilt. When 14 points were reached, she would be handled the "system" way, i.e., handed over to the police. After each of plaintiff's repeated and vehement denials, the security agent said "one point." The loss prevention manager "hurled profanities" and demanded that Fermino confess.

Fermino's repeated requests to leave the room and to call her mother were denied. She was physically compelled to remain in the room for more than one hour. At one point Fermino rose out of her chair and walked toward the door of the interrogation room in an attempt to leave; however, as soon as she made a move toward the door, one of the security guards slid in front of the door, threw up a hand and gestured her to stop.

Finally, Fermino became hysterical, and broke down in tears. At this point her interrogators departed from the room. Upon returning, they admitted no employee or customer was waiting to testify against her. They further stated they believed her, and that she could leave.

As the result of this incident, Fermino sustained unspecified physical injury and "shock and injury to her nervous system and person," as well as "mental anguish and emotional distress." Fermino sued for false imprisonment, as well as intentional and negligent infliction of emotional distress. She claimed that the false imprisonment resulted from a method of interrogation that was approved company policy.

. . . .

II. Discussion

Labor Code section 3600, subdivision (a), provides that, subject to certain particular exceptions and conditions, workers' compensation liability, "in lieu of any other liability whatsoever" will exist "against an employer for any injury sustained by his or her employees arising out of and in the course of the employment." As we have recognized, the basis for the exclusivity rule in workers' compensation law is the "presumed 'compensation bargain,' pursuant to which the employer assumes liability for industrial personal injury or death without regard to fault in exchange for limitations on the amount of that liability. The employee is afforded relatively swift and certain payment of benefits to cure or relieve the effects of industrial injury without having to prove fault but, in exchange, gives up the wider range of damages potentially available in tort."

We recognized in *Shoemaker* and elsewhere, however, that certain types of injurious employer misconduct remain outside this bargain. There are some instances in which, although the injury arose in the course of employment, the employer engaging in that conduct " 'stepped out of [its] proper role[ ]' " or engaged in conduct of " ' "questionable" relationship to the employment.' "

. . . .

B. False Imprisonment and Workers' Compensation

The crime of false imprisonment is defined by Penal Code section 236 as the "unlawful violation of the personal liberty of another." The tort is identically defined. As we recently formulated it, the tort consists of the " 'nonconsensual, intentional confinement of a person, without lawful privilege, for an appreciable length of time, however short.' " That length of time can be as brief as 15 minutes. Restraint may be effectuated by means of physical force, threat of force or of arrest, confinement by physical barriers, or by means of any other form of unreasonable duress. (See Rest.2d Torts, § 40A.)

The only mental state required to be shown to prove false imprisonment is the intent to confine, or to create a similar intrusion. Thus, the intent element of false imprisonment does not entail an intent or motive to cause harm; indeed false imprisonments often appear to arise from initially legitimate motives.

Merchants who detain individuals whom they have probable cause to believe are about to injure their property are privileged against a false imprisonment action. The detention itself must be carried out for a reasonable time and in a reasonable manner. Thus, this court upheld a 20-minute detention of a department store customer who store personnel had probable cause to suspect was in the process of stealing merchandise, and who was being held until the police arrived. This common law privilege has been codified at Penal Code section 490.5, subdivision (f)(1): "A merchant may detain a person for a reasonable time for the purpose of conducting an investigation in a reasonable manner whenever the merchant has probable cause to believe the person to be detained is attempting to unlawfully take or has unlawfully taken merchandise from the merchant's premises." The Legislature made clear that the provisions of subdivision (f)(1) "do not constitute a change in, but are declaratory of, the existing law. . . ." (Stats.1976, ch. 1131, § 3, p. 5049.)

A case factually similar to the matter at hand illustrates the limits of the merchant's privilege. In *Moffat v. Buffums' Inc., supra,* 21 Cal.App.2d 371, 69 P.2d 424, plaintiff, an employee of defendant corporation, was suspected of stealing money from that corporation. She was detained for approximately five hours, while agents of the corporation attempted to coerce her into confessing. Defendant claimed the merchant's privilege, but the court disagreed, finding the detention unreasonable, as it was not done to stop a theft in progress or "for the purpose of investigation, but, on the contrary, . . . for the purpose of securing a confession to the theft of money at a prior time. The alleged offense had been completed and the manner of detention was unreasonable." (*Id.* at p. 375, 69 P.2d 424.)

The defendant also claimed that no false imprisonment had taken place because the employee had received her usual compensation for the time during which she was held in interrogation, and she was therefore merely performing an employment-related service during that time. The court rejected that contention, responding that the statutory and implied contractual provisions that require an employee to follow an employer's directions "do not authorize the employer to forcibly detain the person of an employee for the purpose of compelling a confession of a theft of the employer's property at some prior time." (*Moffat v. Buffums' Inc., supra,* 21 Cal.App.2d at pp. 374–375, 69 P.2d 424; accord, *Parrott v. Bank of America* (1950) 97 Cal. App.2d 14, 23–24, 217 P.2d 89 [upholding a false imprisonment verdict against an employer for an approximately three-hour detention of an innocent employee suspected of theft].)

. . . .

. . . Two more recent Court of Appeal cases have concluded that false imprisonment of an employee, in conjunction with assault and battery, was actionable at law. *Meyer v. Graphic Arts International Union, supra,* 88 Cal.App.3d 176, 151 Cal.Rptr. 597, concerned a female employee who had been forcibly confined and sexually assaulted on three occasions by fellow employees, despite complaints to her employer. The court concluded that her civil action was not barred, citing the dictum in *Magliulo v. Superior Court, supra,* 47 Cal.App.3d at pages 767–768, 121 Cal.Rptr. 621, that " ' "[i]ntentional injury inflicted by [an] employer . . . on his employee may be made the subject of a common-law action for damages on the theory that, in such an action, the employer will not be heard to say that his intentional act was an 'accidental' injury and so under . . . provisions of the compensation act . . ." [citations].' " (*Meyer v. Graphic Arts International Union, supra,* 88 Cal.App.3d at p. 178, 151 Cal.Rptr. 597, [hereafter *Meyer*].)

In *Iverson v. Atlas Pacific Engineering, supra,* 143 Cal.App.3d 219, 191 Cal. Rptr. 696 (hereafter *Iverson*), an employee was confined in a small space and forced to endure loud crashing noises from a large sledgehammer by a fellow employee, an action the employer ratified. The court, relying in large part on *Meyer,* held that the plaintiff had stated a cause of action for false imprisonment and assault not barred by the exclusivity rule. (*Id.* at p. 229, 191 Cal.Rptr. 696.)

Although the basis for *Meyer's* and *Iverson's* holdings appears to be overbroad, implying that all intentional torts are categorically excepted from the exclusivity rule, we find the results of these cases to be unassailable. Both cases concerned employer acts of assault, as well as false imprisonment. The case law in this state holding that an employer's assault is not protected by the exclusivity rule has been ratified by the Legislature in its 1982 amendment of section 3602, subdivision (b)(1), which explicitly permits civil actions based on "willful physical assault by the employer." But these cases and the 1982 amendments do not address explicitly the question before us: whether an employee action against an employer for false imprisonment alone, unalloyed with any allegations of assault, will be permitted under sections 3600 and 3602.

. . . .

It is true that whether a false imprisonment did indeed take place in this case is a closer question than that posed in the *Meyer, Iverson,* or *Moffat* cases cited above. The justification here for the confinement was arguably more substantial than in the former two cases, and the duration of the confinement was considerably shorter than in the third. We do not deny the right of an employer to reasonably detain an employee suspected of theft, and indeed to discharge an employee—consistent with the employee's contractual or other employment rights—if he or she refuses to cooperate with a reasonable investigation. But the question whether Fedco's actions were reasonable, justifiable, or privileged goes to the factual question *whether* its actions constituted false imprisonment—a question we cannot and do not resolve on the pleadings. Once it is determined, however, that a false imprisonment has indeed taken place, then such action cannot be said to be a normal aspect of the employment relationship, however legitimate its initial justification, any more than an assault on an employee can be brought within the scope of the exclusivity rule by claiming it was motivated by the need for employee discipline. (*See Miller v. Reed* (Ohio Ct.App.1986) 27 Ohio App.3d 70, 27 OBR 89, 499 N.E.2d 919, 922 [civil action permitted when supervisor "with force and violence, act[s] to discipline the plaintiff for disobedience of his directions. . . ."]) We conclude therefore that false imprisonment committed by an employer against an employee is always outside the scope of the compensation bargain.

Turning to the present case, we conclude that plaintiff has stated a cause of action for false imprisonment. Like the plaintiff in *Parrott v. Bank of America, supra,* 97 Cal.App.2d at page 22, 217 P.2d 89, plaintiff here has pleaded that she was held against her will by her employer for an appreciable time under threat of force and threat of arrest for an apparently ill-founded reason. As such, her cause of action for false imprisonment cannot be defeated on demurrer by raising the claim that it is barred by sections 3600 and 3602.

Mastery Problem 35-2

Juan Vargas works at an exclusive Peruvian restaurant as a waiter. The employees had been upset for some time regarding the calculation of hours, rest breaks and splitting of tips, and they sought the advice of an attorney. The attorney recommended that they exercise their rights of collective action and present their complaints to the owner, Ricardo Ramos. At 6:45 p.m. on Wednesday evening, Juan led a group of ten current and former employees into the restaurant, where they demanded to see Ricardo in order to present a letter describing their complaint. The manager refused to take the letter and advised the group that they should leave before she called the police. The group then walked out while clapping and chanting, "Solidarity!" The restaurant was filled with customers at the time.

Ricardo was enraged when he heard about this incident. He called a good friend on the police force, Sam, and asked him to come to the restaurant the following day to assist him in questioning the employees. When Juan arrived for work the next morning, Ricardo instructed him to come back to the office to discuss the previous evening. As Juan entered the office he was followed by Sam, who closed the door behind them and stood in front of the door. Sam was off-duty and wearing plain clothes, but he identified himself as a police officer and showed his badge.

Ricardo demanded to know the name of every person who collaborated in the incident or planned it. He told Juan that he would be heading to jail for trespass unless he fully cooperated. Sam remained standing in front of the door. Juan asked to go to his locker to retrieve his lawyer's business card so that he could call her, but Ricardo ignored the requests and continued to question Juan. Ricardo was asking questions such as, "Have you ever spent the night in a jail cell?" and "Do you know what it is like to be blackballed in the restaurant industry?" At one point, Juan stood and moved toward the door, but Sam stood still with his arms crossed and said, "Sit down." After another twenty minutes, Juan insisted that he be permitted to obtain his lawyer's business card, and at this point Ricardo said that he was finished with him and was calling 911.

When uniformed officers arrived, Juan advised them that this was all concerning a labor disturbance and he got his attorney on the phone. After an additional ten minutes of discussion in the office, the uniformed officers told Juan that he could leave and that no charges would be made.

May Juan recover for false imprisonment? What other avenue of recovery might he seek?

---

3. Assault and Battery

In the emotionally charged circumstances of a termination of employment, physical altercations may occur. An employer may be vicariously liable for actions that amount to an assault and battery against an employee, and it is highly unlikely that a state's workers' compensation scheme would be deemed the exclusive remedy for the injured employee.

Example 35-3

Edgar was a carpenter who worked for a construction firm. Edgar and his supervisor had a rocky relationship, and finally one day the arguments became so heated that the supervisor fired Edgar and ordered him to leave the worksite. After Edgar loaded his tools into his truck, he returned and requested information about his final paycheck. A loud and aggressive argument ensued. As Edgar turned and began walking to his car, the supervisor pushed him from behind, causing him to fall and sustain injuries. As a result of his injuries, Edgar was unable to work for nine months. Edgar may recover damages from the employer for the battery committed against him if the supervisor is deemed to have been acting in the course and scope of his employment during the altercation.

---

4. Intentional Infliction of Emotional Distress

When a party acts in an extreme and outrageous manner that causes another to suffer severe emotional distress, the injured party may recover for intentional infliction of emotional distress. In the at-will employment setting, the mere fact that an employer did not have good reason to terminate employment is insufficient to constitute extreme and outrageous behavior because the employer need not have any reason at all to fire an employee. Employees generally fail to state a claim based simply on the employer acting in an arbitrary or even callous manner, even after a long term employment relationship.

Consider *Rawson v. Sears Roebuck & Co.*, 530 F. Supp. 776, 780–81 (D. Colo. 1982), in which the plaintiff alleged that

> he had been an employee of the defendant for 33 years and the manager of defendant's Pueblo store for the last 14 years. He then alleges that the defendant "willfully, wantonly, and maliciously fired the (p)laintiff, . . . And would not allow him to resign with dignity," and that the defendant intended to cause the plaintiff severe emotional distress. The allegations do not state either a sufficiently outrageous pattern of conduct or a sufficiently outrageous isolated incident. Clearly there is not a sufficient recitation of facts to lead an average member of the community to exclaim, "outrageous."

One might wonder if the "average member of the community" would be so dismissive. The court explains that bar is set high for pleading a viable case. "In many, if not most, civil lawsuits the plaintiff believes that the defendant's conduct has been outrageous. Most lawsuits also cause the plaintiff (and often the defendant) emotional distress. Yet very few fact situations give rise to a cognizable claim for intentional infliction of emotional distress." *Id.* at 780.

Consider a typical explanation of the elements of a claim of intentional infliction of emotional distress in a workplace context.

> To recover for intentional infliction of emotional distress, a plaintiff must prove that (1) the defendant acted intentionally or recklessly; (2) the defendant's conduct was extreme and outrageous; (3) the defendant's actions caused the plaintiff emotional distress; and (4) the emotional distress suffered by the plaintiff was severe. [We adopt] the Restatement's formulation of the tort of intentional infliction of emotional distress, including the definition of extreme and outrageous conduct as conduct that is "so outrageous in character, and so extreme in degree, as to go

beyond all possible bounds of decency, and to be regarded as atrocious, and utterly intolerable in a civilized community."

Randall's Food Markets, Inc. v. Johnson, 891 S.W.2d 640, 644 (Tex. 1995). The court concluded that allegations of curt and pointed questioning of an employee regarding an alleged theft that caused the employee to cry were not sufficient to avoid summary judgment on a claim of intentional infliction of emotional distress.

Unfortunately, cases do exist where this high bar is met. Read the following case and determine whether this scenario amounts to an exception to the rule that an at-will employee can be terminated in an unreasonable manner without giving rise to liability.

ARCHER v. FARMER BROS. CO.

70 P.3d 495 (Colo. App. 2002).

Opinion by JUDGE DAILEY.

Defendants, Farmer Bros. Co., Al Henshaw, and Dennie Rawson, appeal from a judgment entered on jury verdicts awarding damages to plaintiff, Richard Archer, for intentional infliction of severe emotional distress (outrageous conduct). Archer cross-appeals an order denying him costs and awarding costs to Henshaw and Rawson. We affirm.

Farmer investigated Archer, whom it had employed for twenty-two years, for alleged misconduct. Later, on the order of Farmer's vice president of sales (VP), Archer's supervisors, Henshaw and Rawson, delivered notice of termination and a final paycheck to Archer while he lay in bed at his mother-in-law's home recuperating from a heart condition.

[Editor's Note: Archer filed a suit alleging a number of claims, but the jury awarded damages only for his claim of "outrageous conduct." The jury awarded Archer $30,500.00 in noneconomic damages and $30,500.00 in exemplary damages against Farmer, and $2,500.00 and $2,499.00 in noneconomic damages against Henshaw and Rawson, respectively.]

I.

Defendants contend that the trial court erred in not dismissing Archer's outrageous conduct claim as falling under the Colorado Workers' Compensation Act (Act). We disagree.

The Act is an employee's exclusive remedy against an employer or coworkers for personal injuries where, as pertinent here, "at the time of the injury, the employee is performing service *arising out of and in the course of* the employee's employment." Section 8–41–301(1)(b), C.R.S.2001 (emphasis supplied); *see* § 8–41–102, C.R.S.2001 (abolishing causes of action against employer).

"Arising out of" and "in the course of" employment are two separate requirements. *Triad Painting Co. v. Blair,* 812 P.2d 638, 641 (Colo.1991).

Here, while Henshaw and Rawson's delivery of the paycheck and notice of termination may have arisen out of Archer's employment, *see Horodyskyj v. Karanian,* 32 P.3d 470, 475–76 (Colo.2001), Archer's injury did not occur "in the course of" his employment.

. . . .

Here, Archer was on indefinite sick leave as a result of his heart condition when he was fired. Henshaw had previously reviewed and approved his sick leave, and Archer would not have been allowed to return to work without producing a doctor's release, which he did not have. Defendants did not give Archer advance notice of their visit, and, upon entering Archer's mother-in-law's home, Henshaw and Rawson went directly into the spare bedroom where Archer was lying partially undressed in bed and, without any further notice, delivered the news about his termination.

Although Henshaw and Rawson were engaged in work-related activity, Archer was not. Inasmuch as he was away from work on approved sick leave, the incident did not occur within the time or space parameters of his employment. . . .

II.

Defendants next contend that the trial court erred in denying their motions for directed verdict and judgment notwithstanding the verdict (JNOV) as to Archer's outrageous conduct claim. We disagree.

The elements of outrageous conduct are: (1) the defendant(s) engaged in extreme and outrageous conduct, (2) recklessly or with the intent of causing the plaintiff severe emotional distress, and (3) causing the plaintiff severe emotional distress. *See McCarty v. Kaiser-Hill Co.,* 15 P.3d 1122, 1126 (Colo.App.2000).

As to the first element, the level of outrageousness required to create liability is extremely high. Mere insults, indignities, threats, annoyances, petty oppressions, or other trivialities are insufficient; only conduct that is so outrageous in character, and so extreme in degree, as to go beyond all possible bounds of decency and be regarded as atrocious and utterly intolerable in a civilized community, will suffice. *Bob Blake Builders, Inc. v. Gramling,* 18 P.3d 859, 866 (Colo.App.2001). *See also Churchey v. Adolph Coors Co.,* 759 P.2d 1336, 1350 (Colo.1988)(facts must so arouse resentment in average members of the community against the defendant as to lead them to exclaim, "Outrageous!").

As a threshold matter, the trial court must determine whether the proof of outrageousness is sufficient as a matter of law. The claim should be submitted to the jury only if reasonable persons could differ on whether the defendant's conduct was sufficiently outrageous. *Coors Brewing Co. v. Floyd,* 978 P.2d 663, 665 (Colo.1999).

The same standard governs a trial court's rulings on motions for directed verdict and JNOV. Directed verdicts are appropriate only where the evidence compels the conclusion that reasonable persons could not disagree and that no evidence, or legitimate inference arising therefrom, has been presented on which the jury's verdict against the moving party could be sustained. Likewise, JNOV can be entered only if the evidence, viewed in the light most favorable to the nonmoving party, is such that no reasonable person could reach the same conclusion as that reached by the jury. *Jones v. Stevinson's Golden Ford,* 36 P.3d 129, 132 (Colo.App.2001).

Here, defendants challenge the sufficiency of the evidence only with respect to the outrageous conduct and mental culpability elements of the tort. The issue, then, is whether, viewing the evidence in the light most favorable to Archer, reasonable persons could disagree about whether the requisite level of outrageousness had been shown and whether defendants engaged in such conduct recklessly or with the intent to cause Archer severe emotional distress.

Although conflicting evidence was presented, the evidence, viewed in the light most favorable to Archer, revealed the following.

Farmer's VP, Henshaw, and Rawson all believed that Archer had suffered a heart attack just five days before the termination and were aware that Archer was out on indefinite sick leave. Although Archer had not missed a day of work in eight years, Henshaw and Rawson both knew he had been absent from work for four days before his termination.

Farmer's VP ordered Archer's termination from employment. When Henshaw initially demurred, Farmer's VP told him, "I don't give a shit if [Archer] is on his deathbed, if I tell you to fire him, that's what you will do, or I'll get somebody who will." Henshaw thereafter carried out his instructions, without inquiring further about the status of Archer's health, evaluating the possible medical consequences of delivering such news while Archer was ill, or discussing alternative means to deliver the news.

Instead, Henshaw and Rawson went in search of Archer, ending up at Archer's mother-in-law's home. In the twenty years Henshaw and Rawson had known Archer, they had never visited him or been invited to his home. Upon arrival at his mother-in-law's home, they entered uninvited.

Neither Henshaw nor Rawson announced the purpose of their visit or asked about Archer's health. Upon entering the spare bedroom, they found Archer lying in bed, not fully clothed. Without asking Archer whether he was fit to discuss work matters or when he intended to return to work, they peremptorily announced that they had his termination papers, which they needed him to initial.

Archer had a reputation as an accomplished branch manager, was fast approaching retirement, and, even though he was being investigated for alleged misconduct, had no reason to anticipate that he would be fired by Farmer. Consequently, news of his firing came as a shock to him.

Noticeably upset by the incident, Archer demanded that Henshaw and Rawson leave the premises. According to Archer's doctor, Archer's health was in such a delicate condition that the termination incident could have triggered a fatal heart attack. Archer attempted to commit suicide that evening.

From this evidence, we conclude that a reasonable person could find that defendants' conduct—barging into a relative's home and, without any prior notice or other consideration, abruptly firing a twenty-two-year employee while he lay in bed, partially undressed, recuperating from what five days earlier had appeared to be a heart attack, and was, in any event, a serious heart condition—so far exceeded the bounds of decency as to be atrocious and utterly intolerable in a civilized community.

Similarly, we conclude that the statement of Farmer's VP and the actions of Henshaw and Rawson, viewed in light of the information they had regarding Archer's condition, could support a determination by a reasonable person that defendants acted recklessly or with the intent of causing Archer severe emotional distress.

Defendants' reliance on various outrageous conduct cases involving physical assaults, threats of physical force, or overly coercive tactics is misplaced. None of those cases articulated a "physical force, threat, or coercion" requirement for recovery; they just happened to involve the application of outrageous conduct principles to those particular circumstances. In other cases, outrageous conduct has been found without such physical or coercive action. *See Rugg v. McCarty,* 173 Colo. 170, 476 P.2d 753 (1970)(harassment via telephone and mail and threats to garnish wages sufficient to support outrageous conduct claim); *Meiter v. Cavanaugh,* 40 Colo.App. 454, 457, 580 P.2d 399, 401 (1978)(outrageous conduct shown when attorney belligerently refused to vacate premises for subsequent tenant without regard for her poor medical condition and implied he had special influence in judicial proceedings); *Agis v. Howard Johnson Co.,* 371 Mass. 140, 141, 355 N.E.2d 315, 317 (1976)(firing waitresses in alphabetical order until one admitted theft sufficient to state a claim of outrageous conduct).

Consequently, the trial court properly denied defendants' motions for both directed verdict and JNOV.

III.

Farmer contends that the jury's award of exemplary damages is unsupported by the evidence. We disagree.

Pursuant to § 13–21–102(1)(a), C.R.S.2001, a person may recover reasonable exemplary damages in addition to, but not exceeding, the amount of actual damages awarded if the civil injury complained of is attended by circumstances of, among other things, willful and wanton conduct.

"Willful and wanton conduct" is defined in § 13–21–102(1)(b), C.R.S.2001, as "conduct purposefully committed which the actor must have realized as dangerous, done heedlessly and recklessly, without regard to consequences, or of the rights and safety of others, particularly the plaintiff."

This definition includes conduct that creates a substantial risk of harm to another and is purposefully performed with an awareness of the risk in disregard of the consequences. *Messler v. Phillips,* 867 P.2d 128, 134 (Colo. App.1993). *See also Boulder Meadows v. Saville,* 2 P.3d 131, 139 (Colo. App.2000) (exemplary damages awardable for conduct indicative of "a wanton and reckless disregard of the injured party's rights and feelings").

While an award of exemplary damages rests in the discretion of the trier of fact, the sufficiency of evidence to support such an award is a question of law for the court to decide. *Messler v. Phillips, supra,* 867 P.2d at 134.

Here, viewed in the light most favorable to Archer, the evidence showed that Henshaw and Rawson acted pursuant to the directions of Farmer's VP, who, despite being made aware of the seriousness of Archer's medical condition, ordered his immediate firing. This evidence, together with the VP's reported statement that he did not care if Archer was "on his death-bed," sufficed to support a reasonable conclusion that Farmer's agents acted purposefully with wanton and reckless disregard for Archer's feelings. Thus, the evidence was adequate to support an award of exemplary damages under § 13–21–102(1)(a).

. . . .

Accordingly, the judgment is affirmed.

Judge Roy dissenting.

I respectfully dissent.

I by no means condone the conduct or motive of the employer or its agents in this case. Nevertheless, all niceties and persuasive authorities to the contrary notwithstanding, in my view, a meeting called by an employer to discharge an employee inherently arises out of and is in the course of that employee's employment, regardless of the place of the meeting or the leave status of the employee at the time. Nothing is more inherent or inevitable in an employment relationship than its commencement and termination. Therefore, I would hold that employer's liability is limited to providing workers' compensation benefits under the statute.

QUESTIONS

1. Would the result change if the employer had a courier deliver a formal letter of termination to Archer's home address (on file with the company) advising him that he was fired effective immediately, if this then led Archer to attempt suicide that evening?
2. Why doesn't every viable claim of intentional infliction of emotional distress result in the possibility of punitive damages, since the tort requires "outrageous" behavior?

Even if the employer acts in an outrageous manner, the employee can recover damages only for extreme and severe emotional distress. The following case highlights issues relating to compensable harm and the damages recoverable.

MONIODIS V. COOK

64 Md. App. 1 (1985).

WEANT, JUDGE.

The appellees, Marguerite Cook, Dorothy Ebner, Diane Ruggiero Leicht, and Iris Torres, brought this action in the Circuit Court for Baltimore City against their former employer, appellant Rite-Aid of Maryland, Inc. (Rite-Aid), and certain Rite-Aid officers, including appellants Anthony Moniodis and James H. Spevock. The appellees alleged that Rite-Aid required groups of employees to submit to polygraph examinations regarding inventory shortages or "shrinkage" at certain Rite-Aid Stores, thereby violating Md.Ann. Code art. 100, § 95 (1979). They further claimed that Rite-Aid enforced this policy, acting through Spevock and Moniodis, among others, by firing recalcitrant employees outright or by creating working conditions calculated to force these employees to resign. The appellees sought compensatory and punitive damages under two theories, "abusive" or wrongful discharge and intentional infliction of emotional distress. Following trial in January, 1984, a jury found in favor of the appellee employees on both theories and awarded compensatory and punitive damages.

> *[Editor's Note: The Defendant appealed, arguing that the trial court erred in denying Appellants' motion for directed verdict on the intentional infliction of emotional distress counts because there was*

insufficient evidence of severe emotional distress and extreme and outrageous conduct. The Defendant also argued that the trial court erred when it denied Appellants' motion for directed verdicts as to Appellees' claims for punitive damages because there was insufficient evidence of malicious conduct.]

4.

In addition to wrongful discharge, the jury found the appellants liable for intentional infliction of emotional distress. In first recognizing such a tort, the Court of Appeals identified four elements which a plaintiff must prove:

(1) The conduct must be intentional or reckless;

(2) The conduct must be extreme and outrageous;

(3) There must be a causal connection between the wrongful conduct and the emotional distress;

(4) The emotional distress must be severe.

Harris v. Jones, 281 Md. 560, 566, 380 A.2d 611, 614 (1977). Appellants maintain that the above elements were not proven in the circuit court, requiring directed verdicts on the counts brought under *Harris.*

We shall first consider whether the appellees produced evidence to support a finding that they suffered extreme emotional distress. In the words of the *Harris* court, there must be a "*severely* disabling emotional response," so acute that ' "no reasonable man could be expected to endure it.' " 281 Md. at 570, 571, 380 A.2d at 616 (emphasis in original) (quoting in part Restatement (Second) of Torts § 46 comment j (1965)). Such severity is measured by factors including the intensity of the response as well as its duration. 281 Md. at 571, 380 A.2d at 616. Where extreme and outrageous conduct by the defendant is proven, this may be "important evidence that the distress existed." *Id.* Finally, the distress must be a reasonable response. A plaintiff's pre-existing susceptibility to emotional distress will not always preclude recovery. Where the plaintiff suffers "exaggerated and unreasonable" distress, however, the requirement is not satisfied, unless the defendant was aware of a particular sensitivity that caused the reaction. *Id.,* 281 Md. at 570 n. 2, 571, 380 A.2d at 616 & n. 2.

There was no evidence at trial from which the jury could properly have concluded that Ebner, Leicht, and Torres suffered the sort of emotional disablement described in *Harris.* Though each testified that she was upset after the terminations, and suffered symptoms such as increased smoking, lost sleep, and "hives," none indicated that she was emotionally unable, even temporarily, to carry on to some degree with the daily routine of her life. They produced no expert testimony to that effect. To the contrary, Ms. Torres, for example, said in letters to her husband that she was going through the worst times of her life during the period when Rite-Aid was forcing her out. She added that she was "disgusted." She revealed, however, that she was managing by herself an entire household including several children and her father-in-law, as well as tending to renovations to the family home. Similarly, Ebner and Leicht by their testimony disclosed that they were depressed and unhappy during the period in question but seemed quite capable of tending to necessary matters. Therefore, their claims should not have been submitted to the jury.

The reaction of Ms. Cook is another matter altogether. It appears that Cook took her duties at Rite-Aid quite seriously. When Moniodis told her she would be transferred, her hours diminished, and her store keys taken, she was deeply disturbed. Her husband found her at home crying and wringing her hands. There was evidence that she did suffer from a pre-existing nervous condition; her emotional state, however, deteriorated significantly after her termination. She took greater amounts of medication and began to sleep most of the time. She became a recluse, her husband testified, and did not "come out of it" for a year. Relatives came to the home to tend to household chores which Ms. Cook could no longer perform. She took pains to avoid contact with neighbors who might ask her why she no longer worked at Rite-Aid.

In our view, this evidence was more than enough to permit a jury finding that Ms. Cook was severely distressed. Even though there was evidence of some degree of pre-existing sensitivity on Ms. Cook's part, we do not believe her reaction was necessarily unreasonable. Her response was in part attributable to her laudable (though in retrospect misplaced) devotion to Rite-Aid. Further, the jury may properly have inferred that Moniodis was aware of her dedication when he chose the working conditions that would cause her to leave.

In addition to proving that she suffered severe distress, Ms. Cook was required to show that the appellants' actions were "extreme and outrageous." *Harris,* 281 Md. at 566, 380 A.2d at 614. The conduct must be " 'so outrageous in character, and so extreme in degree, as to go beyond all possible bounds of decency, and to be regarded as atrocious, and utterly intolerable in a civilized community' "; liability does not extend " 'to mere insults, indignities, threats, annoyances, petty oppressions, or other trivialities.' " *Id.*, 281 Md. at 567, 380 A.2d at 614 (quoting Restatement (Second) of Torts § 46 comment d). Finally, in determining whether a defendant's conduct amounted to "major outrage," factors to be considered include (a) " 'the actor's knowledge that the other is peculiarly susceptible to emotional distress,' " (b) the setting of the conduct, especially where an actor (such as an employer) is in a "peculiar position to harass the plaintiff," and (c) the "personality of the individual to whom the misconduct is directed." 281 Md. at 567–69, 380 A.2d at 615–16 (quoting in part Restatement, *supra,* § 46 comment f).

The circumstances surrounding Ms. Cook's departure from Rite-Aid present a veritable witches' brew of the factors described in *Harris,* so much so that the jury may quite justifiably have concluded that the conduct of Moniodis on Rite-Aid's behalf was extreme and outrageous. The actors in this case were an employer and a supervisor, and as such their conduct must be "carefully scrutinized." 281 Md. at 569, 380 A.2d at 615. Other significant ingredients are the testimony reflecting Ms. Cook's dedication to her work, her pre-existing nervousness, and the knowledge of these conditions attributable to Rite-Aid through its officers. Relevant too is the personality of Ms. Cook, a middle-aged lady who did not have the hardened character of a " 'Butte miner' " or a " 'United States marine.' " 281 Md. at 568, 380 A.2d at 615 (quoting Prosser, *Intentional Infliction of Mental Suffering: A New Tort,* 37 Mich.L.Rev. 874, 887 (1939)). Into the boiling kettle was cast the polygraph—by threatening its very use, Rite-Aid challenged the trustworthiness of Ms. Cook and her value as an employee. Rite-Aid through Moniodis aggravated the injury by attempting to force Ms. Cook to resign, rather than by firing her outright. Not satisfied with the mischief he had caused thus far, Moniodis testified against Ms. Cook in a hearing on whether Ms. Cook was eligible for unemployment insurance benefits, taking the position that Ms. Cook was responsible for her firing. Finally, stirring into this ugly mixture the fact that Rite-Aid's actions through Moniodis were willful violations of Ms. Cook's statutory rights made the "cauldron bubble."[5] The jury could properly conclude from this evidence that the appellants' conduct went far beyond the realm of "petty oppressions," and amounted to a complete denial of Ms. Cook's dignity as a person.

---

5 William Shakespeare, *Macbeth*, IV, i, 10.

We believe the actions against Ms. Cook to be substantially more extreme than the insulting language that was mainly present in *Continental Casualty Co. v. Mirabile,* 52 Md.App. 387, 449 A.2d 1176, *cert. denied,* 294 Md. 652 (1982), and the debt collector's threats of legal action that were at issue in *Dick v. Mercantile-Safe Deposit & Trust Co.,* 63 Md.App. 270, 274, 492 A.2d 674, 677 (1985). Moniodis's actions on behalf of Rite-Aid were more akin to those in *Agis v. Howard Johnson Co.,* 371 Mass. 140, 355 N.E.2d 315 (1976), where the plaintiff employee was summarily terminated pursuant to the defendant employer's announced intention of firing his waitresses in alphabetical order until he could determine who was stealing from his restaurant. The *Agis* court ruled that it was a jury question whether the employer's conduct was extreme and outrageous. We reach the same conclusion with regard to the conduct of Moniodis and Rite-Aid.

. . . .

Two questions remain with regard to Ms. Cook's claim under *Harris:* whether the elements of (1) intentional or reckless conduct, and (2) causation of the emotional distress were satisfied in the claims against Moniodis and Rite-Aid. The very nature of the above-described actions of Moniodis on Rite-Aid's behalf tends to show that they were undertaken intentionally. This inference is bolstered by the testimony of former Rite-Aid managers that Rite-Aid expressly intended to frustrate uncooperative employees. The evidence concerning the cause of Ms. Cook's distress is similarly unequivocal: her testimony and that of her husband revealed that she was affected immediately following and in direct response to her termination.

In sum, the circuit court properly denied the motions of Rite-Aid and Moniodis for directed verdicts on Ms. Cook's *Harris* claim. The court erred, however, in denying the motions as to all other claims under *Harris.*

5.

The fifth issue presented is whether there was sufficient evidence of malice to justify the punitive damage awards.

As this tort action arose out of the contractual relationship between Rite-Aid and the appellees, the trial court was correct in instructing the jury that it must find actual, rather than implied, malice in order to award punitive damages, at least with respect to Rite-Aid. *American Laundry Machinery Industries v. Horan,* 45 Md.App. 97, 117, 112–13, 412 A.2d 407, 417 (1980).

There are few cases upholding a finding of actual malice, which "has been characterized as the performance of an act without legal justification or excuse, but with an evil or rancorous motive influenced by hate, the purpose being to deliberately and willfully injure the plaintiff." *H & R Block, Inc. v. Testerman,* 275 Md. 36, 43, 338 A.2d 48, 52 (1975). Nevertheless, we find that the evidence here indicates a level of malice at least equivalent to that shown in *McClung-Logan Equipment Co. v. Thomas,* 226 Md. 136, 172 A.2d 494 (1961), where the court upheld a finding of actual malice on the part of the corporate defendant. In the case *sub judice,* uncontradicted evidence reflects that Rite-Aid through its officers was well aware of the appellees' rights under the statute but terminated the appellees in utter disregard for those rights. For example, one employee other than the appellees refused to submit to the test stating that the polygraph statute prohibited Rite-Aid from forcing her to take it. She was told that "Rite-Aid has its lawyers and that they would take care of that." Further, the jury may well have found that the requirement of "an evil motive or intent," *H & R Block,* 275 Md. at 46, 338 A.2d at 53, was proven by Rite-Aid's use of tactics calculated to frustrate and demoralize the defiant employees.

QUESTION

1. The Court determined that a statute prohibiting the use of lie detector tests as a condition of employment did not apply because it referred only to "applicants" and not to "employees." Subsequently, the lie detector statute was amended to provide a basis for employees to complain, and the court held that the administrative remedy of complaining to the Commissioner of Labor was the sole and exclusive remedy for employees. See *Wethersby v. Kentucky Fried Chicken Nat. Management Co,* 587 A.2d 569, 573–74 (Md. App. 1991). Who do you think promoted this statutory amendment, and how do you think it was described to the legislature?

Conclusion

The at-will rule means that employers are not liable for terminations that are unfounded, although the doctrines of good faith and wrongful discharge modify the strict at-will rule to some degree. However, the employer may act in a manner that is independently tortious when terminating employment, and the employee may be able to recover for the resulting injury. We have discussed application of the torts of negligent misrepresentation, false imprisonment, assault and battery, and intentional infliction of emotional distress.

B. Statutory Remedies for Discharge

Key Concepts

- Many states have adopted statutes to provide relief to employees who suffer retaliation because they are "blowing the whistle" on prohibited behavior by their employer.
- Title VII is the federal law protecting employees from discrimination, but it also protects other employees who "oppose" discriminatory activity without themselves being a target of discrimination.

Lesson 36:
Whistleblowing

Objectives and Expected Learning Outcomes

In this Lesson, you will study the different types of whistleblower statutes and will focus on assessing whether a worker has a colorable claim. You will also develop an appreciation for the special challenges involved in representing a whistleblower. Finally, we will discuss the special ethical and professional responsibility issues faced by in-house lawyers who are considering, or do in fact, blow the whistle on their employer.

True stories about whistleblowers literally provide the basis for hit movies. Consider *Serpico* (a story of a police officer exposing corruption in the New York City Police department) and *Silkwood* (the story of a woman who blows the whistle on safety issues at a nuclear power plant). But the reality of being a whistleblower is often very different than these movies. Whistleblowers are sometimes lauded for their efforts (those stories get made into movies), but more often they are punished by their employers for "harming" the company. One scholar has determined that 22% of whistleblowers suffer some form of retaliation. Nancy M. Modesitt, *Why Whistleblowers Lose: An Empirical and Qualitative Analysis of State Court Cases*, 62 U. Kan. L. Rev. 165, 167 (2013). It should be no surprise that studies have indicated that nearly half of all employees who know about wrongdoing in the workplace elect not to report it for fear of retaliation by their employer.

The extent and effect of retaliation against whistleblowers can be harsh. Consider this statement by a whistleblower: "I didn't just lose my job. I lost my house, and then I lost family. I don't even see my kids anymore. My ex-father-in-law said if I'd been a real whistleblower I'd have been on *60 Minutes*." C. Fred Alford, Whistleblowers: Broken Lives and Organizational Power 1 (2001). Alford's book chronicles a number of similar stories. Professor Modesitt explains that whistleblowers draw ire because often they expose wrongdoing not just at one employer, but throughout an entire industry. After reviewing the law of whistleblowing, we return to these special contextual concerns at the end of the Lesson.

1. Overview of Statutes Protecting Whistleblowers

In Lessons 31 and 32, we considered the development of the common law tort of wrongful discharge in violation of public policy. This tort often was the only recourse for whistleblowers who argued that their activity benefitted the public. However, some states did not accept the tort and called on the legislature to craft more definite rules. States that did accept the tort found that there were many details to work out in balancing the employer's flexibility with the public's interest. As a consequence, a number of states have enacted some manner of statute protecting whistleblowers.

Generally, there are two kinds of whistleblower statutes. The first may be called "topic related" statutes. For example, Rhode Island prohibits employers from retaliation for whistleblowing by appending an anti-retaliation clause to statutes regulating gaming, nursing homes, health-care facilities, nonprofit hospitals, insurance fraud, health maintenance organizations, and asbestos abatement. Federal whistleblower statutes follow the "topic related" model. In contrast, other states use a "catch all" statute to protect whistleblowers. For example, Minnesota has enacted a statute that protects employees who report an illegal activity, refuse to engage in illegal activity, or testify regarding illegal activity. These statutes are essentially broad-based anti-retaliation prohibitions. Finally, the statutory provisions might protect just private employees, just public employees, or both.

Problem 36-1

As a way to orient yourself to the different models of statutory protection, assume that you are an in-house attorney at a defense contracting firm that is considering building a new facility in Florida, Texas, or New Jersey. Because there have been some very high-profile whistleblowers at your company and in the industry, the General Counsel asks you to analyze the law of whistleblowers in each of these states. She specifically asks you to read the following statutes and to take note of similarities and differences with regard to the persons covered, the conduct protected, and the protections afforded.

Florida

§ 448.102. Prohibitions

An employer may not take any retaliatory personnel action against an employee because the employee has:

(1) Disclosed, or threatened to disclose, to any appropriate governmental agency, under oath, in writing, an activity, policy, or practice of the employer that is in violation of a law, rule, or regulation. However, this subsection does not apply unless the employee has, in writing, brought the activity, policy, or practice to the attention of a supervisor or the employer and has afforded the employer a reasonable opportunity to correct the activity, policy, or practice.

(2) Provided information to, or testified before, any appropriate governmental agency, person, or entity conducting an investigation, hearing, or inquiry into an alleged violation of a law, rule, or regulation by the employer.

(3) Objected to, or refused to participate in, any activity, policy, or practice of the employer which is in violation of a law, rule, or regulation.

public & private

Texas

§ 554.002. Retaliation Prohibited for Reporting Violation of Law

public

(a) A state or local governmental entity may not suspend or terminate the employment of, or take other adverse personnel action against, a public employee who in good faith reports a violation of law by the employing governmental entity or another public employee to an appropriate law enforcement authority.

(b) In this section, a report is made to an appropriate law enforcement authority if the authority is a part of a state or local governmental entity or of the federal government that the employee in good faith believes is authorized to:

(1) regulate under or enforce the law alleged to be violated in the report; or

(2) investigate or prosecute a violation of criminal law.

New Jersey

§ 34:19–3. Employer retaliatory action; protected employee actions

An employer shall not take any retaliatory action against an employee because the employee does any of the following:

a. Discloses, or threatens to disclose to a supervisor or to a public body an activity, policy or practice of the employer, or another employer, with whom there is a business relationship, that the employee reasonably believes:

(1) is in violation of a law, or a rule or regulation promulgated pursuant to law, including any violation involving deception of, or misrepresentation to, any shareholder, investor, client, patient, customer, employee, former employee, retiree or pensioner of the employer or any governmental entity, or, in the case of an employee who is a licensed or certified health care professional, reasonably believes constitutes improper quality of patient care; or

(2) is fraudulent or criminal, including any activity, policy or practice of deception or misrepresentation which the employee reasonably believes may defraud any shareholder, investor, client, patient, customer, employee, former employee, retiree or pensioner of the employer or any governmental entity;

b. Provides information to, or testifies before, any public body conducting an investigation, hearing or inquiry into any violation of law, or a rule or regulation promulgated pursuant to law by the employer, or another employer, with whom there is a business relationship, including any violation involving deception of, or misrepresentation to, any shareholder, investor, client, patient, customer, employee, former employee, retiree or pensioner of the employer or any governmental entity, or, in the case of an employee who is a licensed or certified health care professional, provides information to, or testifies before, any public body conducting an investigation, hearing or inquiry into the quality of patient care; or

c. Objects to, or refuses to participate in any activity, policy or practice which the employee reasonably believes:

(1) is in violation of a law, or a rule or regulation promulgated pursuant to law, including any violation involving deception of, or misrepresentation to, any shareholder, investor, client, patient, customer, employee, former employee, retiree or pensioner of the employer or any governmental entity, or, if the employee is a licensed or certified health care professional, constitutes improper quality of patient care;

(2) is fraudulent or criminal, including any activity, policy or practice of deception or misrepresentation which the employee reasonably believes may defraud any shareholder, investor, client, patient, customer, employee, former employee, retiree or pensioner of the employer or any governmental entity; or

(3) is incompatible with a clear mandate of public policy concerning the public health, safety or welfare or protection of the environment.

§ 34:19–12. Retaliatory action prohibited

No employer or employer's agent, representative or designee shall discharge, discipline or otherwise penalize or threaten to discharge, discipline or otherwise penalize any employee because the employee, or a person acting on behalf of the employee, makes a good faith report, verbally or in writing, of a violation or suspected violation of this act.

§ 34:19–13. Civil remedies

Any aggrieved employee may enforce the provisions of this act by means of a civil action brought no later than ninety days after the date of the alleged violation in a court of competent jurisdiction. The court shall award a prevailing employee all appropriate relief, including any of the following which are applicable to the violation:

a. A restraining order against any continuing violation;

b. The reinstatement of the employee to the employee's former position or an equivalent position and the reestablishment of any employee benefits and seniority rights;

c. The payment of any lost wages, benefits or other remuneration; and

d. The payment of reasonable attorneys' fees and costs of the action.

In addition, the court may award the prevailing employee punitive damages not greater than treble damages, or an assessment of a civil fine of not more than $1,000 for a first violation of the act and not more than $5,000 for each subsequent violation, which shall be paid to the State Treasurer for deposit in the General Fund.

§ 34:19–14. Effect of act on employee's right to bring action under common or contract law

Nothing in this act shall be construed to limit an employee's right to bring a common law cause of action against an employer for wrongful termination or to diminish or impair the rights of a person under any collective bargaining agreement.

2. Interpreting Whistleblower Statutes

We begin with an example of a court seeking to interpret the whistleblowing statute to determine its scope. As you read the *Linkletter* case, focus on the judge's careful attention to the statutory language, keeping in mind Mark Twain's quip that the difference between the right word and the almost right word is the difference between a lightning bug and a lightning bolt.

Linkletter v. Western & Southern Financial Group, Inc.

851 F.3d 632 (6th Cir. 2017).

Merritt, Circuit Judge.

In this Fair Housing Act case that was dismissed for failure to state a valid claim, the plaintiff, Gayle Linkletter, signed an online petition supporting a Cincinnati women's shelter, the Anna Louise Inn, after she had accepted a position with the defendant, Western & Southern. Western & Southern rescinded its employment agreement with Linkletter because she signed the petition while the company was engaged in a lengthy real estate dispute with the women's shelter over its location in the neighborhood. Residents of the shelter had previously sued Western & Southern in federal court under the Fair Housing Act, particularly 42 U.S.C. § 3617. As a result of that earlier litigation, Western & Southern reached a settlement with the shelter and purchased the property. After Linkletter's employment contract was rescinded she sued Western & Southern and its employee, Kim Chiodi, under § 3617 and the state analog in the Ohio Civil Rights Act. . . .

Specifically, Linkletter claims her petition-signing encouraged the residents of the women's shelter in their rights granted by § 3604, involving discrimination in the rental or sale of housing:

> [I]t shall be unlawful . . . (a) To refuse to sell or rent . . . or to refuse to negotiate for the sale or rental of, or otherwise make unavailable or deny, a dwelling to any person because of . . . sex. . . . (b) To discriminate . . . in the provision of services or facilities in connection therewith, because of . . . sex. . . . (c) To make, print, or publish . . . any notice, statement, or advertisement, with respect to the sale or rental of a dwelling that indicates any preference, limitation, or discrimination based on . . . sex. . . . (d) To represent to any person because of . . . sex . . . that any dwelling is not available for inspection, sale, or rental when such dwelling is in fact so available. . . . (e) For profit, to induce or attempt to induce any person to sell or rent any dwelling by representations regarding the entry or prospective entry into the neighborhood of a person or persons of a particular . . . sex. . . .

42 U.S.C. § 3604(a)–(e).

We conclude that Linkletter presents a plausible claim for relief. . . . Accordingly, the district court was in error when it granted the defendants' motion to dismiss, and we reverse the judgment.

I. Background

Western & Southern Financial Group, Inc. is an insurance company located in the Lytle Park neighborhood of Cincinnati, Ohio. Between 1997 and 2006, Linkletter worked as an employee of Western & Southern. The parties ended the first employment relationship amicably. In May 2014, Linkletter's former colleague at Western & Southern contacted her about a job opportunity at the company as a Senior Corporate Communications specialist. After several interviews, Linkletter accepted the position.

On September 8, 2014, before Linkletter began working, Western & Southern's Senior Vice President of Human Resources, Kim Chiodi, called Linkletter to notify her that Western & Southern had rescinded the employment offer. Linkletter claims that Chiodi justified the rescission due to Linkletter having taken "a position that was contrary to Western & Southern." Specifically, Chiodi mentioned Linkletter's support for the Anna Louise Inn.

Western & Southern had been in a controversial real estate dispute with the Anna Louise Inn women's shelter since 2011. See *Cooper v. Western & Southern Financial Group, Inc.*, 847 F.Supp.2d 1031, 1032–33 (S.D. Ohio 2012). The shelter, whose mission is "to provide women with safe, decent, and affordable housing, without regard to their economic condition, race, or lack of employment," was located in Lytle Park, the same neighborhood as Western & Southern. *Id.* at 1033. The residents of the shelter accused Western & Southern of violating the Fair Housing Act and the Ohio Civil Rights Act by attempting to illegally pressure them out of the neighborhood. The presence of the shelter interfered with Western & Southern's "master plan for [that] end of town," and the company was frustrated in attempting to buy the land where the shelter stood. In December 2010, the president of the company that controls Western & Southern's real estate holdings sent a letter to Cincinnati's mayor, arguing that the shelter was "not appropriate for the Lytle Park neighborhood" and objecting to "85 low-income permanent housing units for women" and "housing for up to 25 recovering prostitutes."

After the shelter refused to sell, Western & Southern engaged in a campaign to force a sale of the property and get the Anna Louise Inn out of the neighborhood, and the shelter's residents sued. When Western & Southern filed a motion to dismiss the complaint pursuant to Fed. R. Civ. P. 12(b)(6), the district court denied the motion, stating that the residents had sufficiently pled the elements of a § 3617 claim. *Cooper*, 847 F.Supp.2d at 1040 . . . . .

On February 21, 2012, while the dispute between the shelter and Western & Southern was ongoing, Linkletter signed a petition expressing support for the shelter. The petition was titled, "The Anna Louise Inn has my Support!" and the text stated, "I support the mission of the Anna Louise Inn, which has provided safe and affordable housing for women for 102 years in its current location." As a signor, Linkletter also stated that she appreciated "that women in Cincinnati have an option for permanent supportive housing," and that "[the] Anna Louise Inn should remain where it is and continue its mission of providing safe and affordable housing for single women." The Inn posted the petition online with the names of the signors, including Linkletter.

After the termination of her employment contract in 2014, Linkletter sued Western & Southern and its employee, Kim Chiodi. At the district court, Linkletter claimed that the rescission of her contract in response to her supporting the housing rights of the Inn's female residents violated § 3617 of the Fair Housing Act. Linkletter argued that by rescinding the contract, the defendants interfered with her employment because she encouraged the women of the Anna Louise Inn in the exercise of their rights under §§ 3603–06. Specifically Linkletter claimed she encouraged the rights in § 3604(a)–(e) pertaining to anti-discrimination in the rental or sale of housing. 42 U.S.C. § 3604. The provision Linkletter sued under, Section 3617, protects individuals who "aided or encouraged" the rights protected by § 3604. 42 U.S.C. § 3617.

The defendants moved to dismiss the complaint pursuant to Fed. R. Civ. P. 12(b)(6). The district court granted the motion, finding that Linkletter did not state a claim for relief. Without engaging in a trial or a fact-finding process, the district court agreed with the defendants that Linkletter did not "aid or encourage" the women of the Anna Louise Inn as contemplated by the statute, that the housing rights protected by § 3604 were not at issue, and that the defendants as "non-houser employers" did not fall within the scope of the statute. . . .

Linkletter now appeals.

. . . .

III. Fair Housing Act

The purpose of the Fair Housing Act is "to provide, within constitutional limitations, for fair housing throughout the United States." 42 U.S.C. § 3601. To that end, the Act prohibits discrimination against "any person because of race, color, religion, sex, familial status, or national origin" in the rental or sale of housing. 42 U.S.C. § 3604(a). In keeping with the law's overarching purpose, 42 U.S.C. § 3617 protects plaintiffs who "aided or encouraged" the housing rights enumerated in the statute. *Id.* Essentially, § 3617 allows a plaintiff to step into the shoes of the victims of certain types of housing discrimination when the plaintiff faces retribution for providing encouragement to the victims. As part of a remedial statute, the language of § 3617 should be broadly interpreted and applied with the Fair Housing Act's purpose in mind. . . . "The plain meaning of legislation should be conclusive, except in the 'rare cases [in which] the literal application of a statute will produce a result demonstrably at odds with the intentions of the drafters.' " . . . Linkletter claims that by signing a petition she "encouraged" women to pursue their right to be free from sex discrimination in the rental or sale of housing under § 3604, and that the defendants illegally retaliated by "interfering" with her employment. She does not accuse them of discriminating against her or illegally interfering with her housing rights. Rather, she claims that the defendants interfered with her employment because she aided or encouraged women in the exercise of their housing rights under § 3604.

A. "Interfere with"

The rescission of an employment contract can qualify as "interference" within the meaning of the statute. See *Walker v. City of Lakewood*, 272 F.3d 1114, 1128–30 (9th Cir. 2001) (explaining that interference refers to "hampering an activity or process" including frustrating the renewal of employment contracts). The complaint states that Linkletter and Western & Southern reached an employment agreement. After Linkletter accepted the job, Western & Southern's employee Chiodi terminated that employment agreement. It would be an understatement to say that the defendants' actions "hampered" Linkletter's employment process. See *id.* The defendants' interference left Linkletter with a distinct and palpable injury. . . .

The Department of Housing and Urban Development has also interpreted the Fair Housing Act in a manner consistent with the proposition that "interference" can refer to employment disputes. It is illegal to "[t]hreaten[ ] an employee or agent with dismissal or an adverse employment action, or [to] tak[e] such adverse employment action, for any effort to assist a person seeking access to the sale or rental of a dwelling or seeking access to any residential real estate-related transaction, because of the . . . sex . . . of that person. . . ." 24 C.F.R. § 100.400(c)(3).

Moreover, the language "interfere with" should be broadly interpreted to reach all practices which have the effect of interfering with housing rights. See *Babin*, 18 F.3d at 347 (citing *United States v. Am. Inst. of Real Estate Appraisers*, 442 F.Supp. 1072, 1079 (N.D. Ill. 1977)). Therefore the scope of the statute extends to employers who cancel contracts in retaliation for Fair Housing Act advocacy. See *Walker*, 272 F.3d at 1126. As the interference alleged in the present case fits this description, it appears to be covered by the statute.

B. "Aided or Encouraged"

To qualify for a § 3617 claim, a defendant's "interference" must still be in retaliation for a plaintiff having "aided or encouraged" another's enjoyment of the housing rights protected by §§ 3603–06. 42 U.S.C. § 3617. Linkletter's action, signing a petition, is seemingly innocuous. However, the language and timing of the petition demonstrate that it existed to encourage the women to remain in their residence in opposition to the alleged discrimination by Western & Southern. The defendants point out that the petition did not specifically mention Western & Southern. But while the petition did not explicitly mention the dispute with Western & Southern, the context suggests that the litigation with Western & Southern was the basis for the petition. The petition supported keeping the shelter at the "current location" in "Lytle Park," and that "[the] Anna Louise Inn should remain where it is and continue its mission of providing safe and affordable housing for single women." For purposes of analyzing the defendants' motion to dismiss, the court should assume that Linkletter signed the petition to "encourage" the women in their dispute with Western & Southern.

The district court noted that this act of encouragement by Linkletter is minor comparatively speaking. See *Linkletter*, 2016 WL 659136 at *5. However, the defendants fail to explain why a petition-signing is not encouragement beyond vague assertions that the action lacks "concreteness" or "directness." The allegations in the complaint show that the action was concrete and important enough to alert Linkletter's future employer to her public support, and result in her termination. If the encouragement is sufficiently concrete to lead to an individual's firing, it is sufficiently concrete to state a plausible claim.

Looking to the "structure, history, and purpose" of the statute, *Abramski v. United States*, ___ U.S. ___, 134 S.Ct. 2259, 2267, 189 L.Ed.2d 262 (2014), section 3617 was meant to protect assistance and advocacy for Fair Housing Act rights. A plain-meaning understanding of the word "encouraged" clearly covers the act of signing a petition advocating support for a women's shelter. Therefore, interpreting "encouraged" to include Linkletter's action is in keeping with both the plain meaning of the word and the overall purpose of the Fair Housing Act. See *Ron Pair Enters., Inc.*, 489 U.S. at 241–42, 109 S.Ct. 1026.

C. Nexus to 42 U.S.C. § 3604

Section 3617 requires a nexus with the rights protected by §§ 3603–06, without requiring an actual violation of the underlying provisions. See *Hidden Village, LLC v. City of Lakewood*, Ohio, 734 F.3d 519, 528 (6th Cir. 2013). In the present case, Linkletter claims her signing the petition implicated the rights of women against discrimination in the rental or sale of housing under § 3604. The litigation between the women's shelter and Western & Southern is well documented in the *Cooper* case, which described the housing dispute that motivated Linkletter's petition-signing. 847 F.Supp.2d at 1039–40. Just as the female residents of the Anna Louise Inn in the Cooper case stated a plausible § 3617 claim for relief based on their own § 3604 rights, so too Linkletter states a plausible claim for relief in facing retaliation for encouraging those rights. See *id.* at 1040 (finding the shelter's residents had "alleged facts from which the Court may plausibly infer that Western & Southern is in a position directly to disrupt [the residents'] federally-protected rights to reside at the Inn . . . and that Western & Southern ha[d] exercised its powers with a discriminatory animus.").

The defendants argue that even if they fired Linkletter because she signed the petition, Western & Southern's motivation in the underlying dispute with the women's shelter was motivated by economics rather than by sex discrimination. In the past the Sixth Circuit has required a showing of "discriminatory animus" for § 3617 claims. See *Babin*, 18 F.3d at 347. Discriminatory animus requires plaintiffs "to put forth 'some evidence of discriminatory effect or intent on the [defendant's] part.' " to survive summary judgment. *Campbell v. Robb, 162 Fed.Appx.* 460, 474 (6th Cir. 2006) (citing *Babin*, 18 F.3d at 347) (emphasis added).

Western & Southern's actions against the shelter as alleged in the complaint only affected one class of people—women. The defendants assert that the motivation for attempting to remove the shelter from the neighborhood was "economic," not "sex," and that financial motives exclude the case from the type of sex discrimination forbidden by the Fair Housing Act. But a violation of the Fair Housing Act can be shown either by proof of discriminatory animus or by proof of disparate impact or effect. See *Inclusive Cmtys. Project, Inc. v. Tex. Dept. of Hous. and Cmty. Affairs*, 747 F.3d 275, 280 (5th Cir. 2014). The existence of economic (or religious or moral) motivations does not protect the defendants from housing discrimination claims when their actions had a clear discriminatory effect. Economic motivation does not cleanse discrimination. The facts alleged by Linkletter, and detailed in the underlying Cooper case, are sufficient to state a valid claim that Western & Southern discriminated against the women of the shelter. See 847 F.Supp.2d at 1039–40.

. . . Section 3617 requires only that the plaintiff "encourage" a housing right protected by § 3604 and face retaliatory "interference" for the encouragement. See *Hidden Village, LLC*, 734 F.3d at 528–29 ("[Defendant] threatened [plaintiff] because [plaintiff] had encouraged [victim] to protect himself against discrimination relating to housing. The statute requires no more."). According to the complaint in the present case, the defendants sought to remove housing designated for a protected class from the neighborhood. As a non-houser that has allegedly denied housing rights to women, Western & Southern falls within the scope of the Fair Housing Act.

Taking the complaint in the light most favorable to the plaintiff, we do not agree with the district court that the petition-signing did not sufficiently implicate opposition to housing discrimination. . .

The judgment of the district court is REVERSED, and we REMAND the case for further proceedings.

QUESTIONS

1. How important is the law's status as a "remedial measure" in the judge's analysis?
2. How could you rewrite the statute to deprive Linkletter of a viable claim?

Problem 36-2

You work as a legislative aide for a state senator. The Senator wants to introduce a bill that will protect employees in the waste disposal business if they blow the whistle on their employers for skirting regulations promulgated by the State Department of Sanitation regarding permissible ways to dispose of waste. She asks you to draft a whistleblower protection provision to be added to the waste management statute. Develop a concise but carefully worded draft.

---

3. Elements of a Whistleblowing Claim

The primary question under a whistleblowing statute is whether the conduct of the employee is "protected activity." We have seen similar analysis when reviewing the concerted activity provision of the National Labor Relations Act and the effect of the First Amendment for public employees. There also must be some form of "adverse employment action" suffered and "causation" between the protected activity and the adverse employment action. The ADT case applies these elements.

Thibodeau v. ADT Security Service

2018 WL 637947 (S.D. Calif. 2018).

ORDER GRANTING IN PART AND DENYING IN PART DEFENDANT'S AMENDED MOTION FOR PARTIAL SUMMARY JUDGMENT

Hon. Gonzalo P. Curiel, United States District Judge.

Part I

Defendant ADT is a corporation that provides residential and business electronic security systems, fire protection, and other related alarm monitoring services. Cole Decl. ¶ 2. Plaintiff worked for Defendant as a Residential High Volume Sales Representative from September 9, 2014 through October 2, 2015. Thibodeau Decl. ¶ 2. Plaintiff was based out of ADT's San Diego Office, which had territorial responsibility for both San Diego and Imperial County. *Id.* ¶¶ 3, 125. High Volume Sales Representatives at ADT are tasked with securing new sales of portfolio package sales and upgrades to new ADT residential customers.

ADT had a written policy of issuing a sales quota to High Volume Sales Representatives. . . Plaintiff was required to sell 192 units a year with the expectation of selling 4 units weekly or 16 units per month, and was expected to perform at 100% of the quota. The quota of 192 units was contained within a written Sales Compensation Plan that Plaintiff was provided and signed upon his hiring on September 10, 2014. Plaintiff received a written warning on July 1, 2015 for failing to meet sales goals for the month of June. . On September 29, 2015, Plaintiff was given a written warning for failure to meet sales goals in August and September of 2015. Plaintiff resigned from employment with Defendant on October 2, 2016.

. . . .

B. Whistleblower Retaliation—Second Cause of Action

Plaintiff's second cause of action asserts a claim for whistleblower retaliation. California Labor Code Section 1102.5 is a whistleblower statute, the purpose of which is to encourage workplace whistle-blowers to report unlawful facts without fear of retaliation. The statute reflects a "broad public policy interest in encouraging workplace whistleblowers to report unlawful acts without fearing retaliation." *Green v. Ralee Eng. Co.*, 19 Cal. 4th 66, 77 (1998).

Courts analyzing claims under Section 1102.5 apply the *McDonnell-Douglas* burden shifting framework. . . . Under this framework, the plaintiff must first establish a prima facie case, which requires that plaintiff show that "(1) he or she engaged in a protected activity; (2) his employer subjected him to an adverse employment action; and (3) there is a causal link between the two." (citation omitted) If a plaintiff successfully establishes their prima facie case, the "burden of production, but not persuasion, shifts to the employer to articulate some legitimate, nondiscriminatory reason for the challenged action." (Citation omitted)

1. Protected Activity

Plaintiff alleges that he reported ADT wrongdoing to five separate persons above him. On July 22, 2015, Thibodeau sent a letter to Kurt Miller, Regional General Manager of California alerting him to management practices being practiced in San Diego that were "immoral, unethical, and unlawful." Tricia Cole completed a "Conversation Record" where she took notes regarding interviews she conducted with Plaintiff on July 28 and August 12, 2015.

Thibodeau challenges several allegedly illegal activities such as the (1) sales agent practice of crumpling paper over a telephone mouthpiece when the agent mentioned the name ADT; (2) the use of the "billboard approach" where ADT sales representatives would offer a free security system in exchange for placing an ADT sign in the homeowner's yards, and omitting any mention of the need to sign up for a two-year monitoring agreement to get the "free" security system; (3) an alleged ADT practice where ADT would provide ADT Dealers with Thibodeau's "leads." Mr. Thibodeau complained to Sales Manager Robert Harris about the use of the "billboard approach" and was granted permission to make corrections in his approach to "remove its illegal elements."

Defendant argues that Thibodeau has not established that he has engaged in a "protected activity" as he has never reported his complaints of illegal activity to any governmental agencies, filed any complaint in court, participated in company or governmental investigations, served as a witness, spoken to the government, or put into writing his complaints.

Section 1102.5(b) requires the disclosure of a violation of a state or federal regulation or local, state, or federal rule or regulation, not merely improper conduct. . .disclosure could be made to either a "government or law enforcement agency" or to "a person with authority over the employee" or "to another employee who has authority to investigate, discover, or correct the violation . . ." Plaintiff must demonstrate a "reasonably based suspicion of illegal activity."

Plaintiff has not adequately articulated how ADT's behaviors violated any local, state, or federal statutes. [The record] reveals that Plaintiff complained about a series of employment related grievances, but has never alleged any violations of particular local, state, or federal statutes.

Specifically, Thibodeau asserts that he complained about an instruction from Paul Singh to crumple paper while leaving a telephone message in order to increase call backs. . . . However, Plaintiff has failed to identify the superior to whom he complained about Singh's paper crumpling instruction. Moreover, Thibodeau has wholly failed to identify any federal or state law that was violated by this practice. Accordingly, this alleged complaint cannot be the basis of a protected activity claim.

Next, with regard to the use of the "billboard approach," Thibodeau describes this practice as one he learned at a Dealer Klatch as a way to "get in the door." The practice involved telling home owners that ADT would "give them a free security system if they would let us place an ADT sign in their yards, like a mini billboard." The salesperson would withhold the fact that the customer was required to sign-up for a two year monitoring agreement in order to get the "free" system. The two-year requirement was only revealed after the salesperson was already in the home where it was harder for customers to say no.

This unethical means to enter the house—which was reported to his Sales Manager Robert Harris—is one Thibodeau has pointed out as a potentially misleading sales technique, but he has not identified how this sales activity violated consumer protection statutes or other such laws. . . The Court observes that this technique, while initially misleading, provides pre-sales disclosures and ample room for consumer choice. Moreover, the statute requires that the plaintiff must have a legal foundation for a reasonable suspicion of illegal activity, not merely a suspicion of "improper conduct." See *Patten*, 134 Cal. App. 4th at 1384–85.

Finally, with regard to Mr. Singh providing company leads to dealers instead of his sales representatives, plaintiff has not identified how this employment grievance violated any laws . . . for example, even if the Court accepted the truth of Plaintiff's assertions, it is entirely possible that leads were provided to ADT dealers in an entirely legal manner. Because he has failed to provide a legal foundation for his suspicions of illegal activity, Plaintiff has failed to show that he reported a reasonably based suspicion of illegal activity sufficient to constitute a protected activity. See *Fitzgerald v. El Dorado Cty.*, 94 F. Supp. 3d 1155, 1172 (E.D. Cal. 2015) ("To have a reasonably based suspicion of illegal activity, the employee must be able to point to some legal foundation for his suspicion—some statute, rule or regulation which may have been violated by the conduct he disclosed.").

Accordingly, plaintiff has failed to meet his burden to show that he engaged in any protected activity, and thus has failed to establish a prima facie case of whistleblower discrimination

Part II

Adverse Employment Actions and Causation

Had plaintiff shown he engaged in a protected activity, plaintiff would be able to show both adverse employment actions and causation. In *Patten v. Grant Joint Union High School Dist.*, 134 Cal. App. 4th 1378, 1388 (2005), the Court of Appeal held that the definition of "adverse employment action" under FEHA *[Editor's Note: the California statute prohibiting employment discrimination]* as defined in *Yanowitz v. L'Oreal USA, Inc.*, 36 Cal. 4th 1028 (2005), should also apply in the context of Section 1102.5. Under that definition, an action is an "adverse employment action" when it "materially affects the terms and conditions of employment." This test encompasses not only "ultimate employment decisions," but also the "entire spectrum of employment actions that are reasonably likely to adversely and materially affect an employee's job performance or opportunity for advancement in his or her career." *Patten*, 134 Cal. App. 4th at 1387. However, "[m]inor or relatively trivial adverse actions by employers or fellow employees that, from an objective perspective, are reasonably likely to do no more than anger or upset an employee do not materially affect the terms or conditions of employment." *Id.*

Plaintiff argues that he was subjected to several forms of adverse employment actions, including that ADT retaliated against Plaintiff by (1) issuing a series of written warnings; (2) denying Plaintiff a promotion; (3) denying Plaintiff a transfer; (4) overwhelming Plaintiff with non-unit, non-SG, and non-commissionable activities; (5) assigning him low-yield appointments; (6) circumventing his resignation by delaying payment of monies owed and (7) singling Plaintiff out as pre-text for whistleblower retaliation. Under the *Patten* test, several of ADT's activities—such as the issuance of warnings, denial of promotions, denial of transfer, and denial of good work—likely constitute "adverse employment actions" because these actions could have "materially affect[ed]" plaintiff's "job performance or opportunity for advancement" in his career. *Patten*, 134 Cal. App. 4th at 1387.

Assuming arguendo that Plaintiff had established a protected activity, Plaintiff has arguably established a "causal link." Claims of whistleblower harassment and retaliatory termination may not succeed where a plaintiff "cannot demonstrate the required nexus between his reporting of alleged statutory violations and his allegedly adverse treatment by [the employer]." (citation omitted) The alleged adverse employment actions took place after Thibodeau revealed the dealer issues to Mr. Harris (June 2015) and after he complained about the Billboard approach (April 2015). For example, Thibodeau asserted that he received several warnings in July and September of 2015, a relatively short period of time after he would have reported wrongdoing. See *Morgan v. Regents of the University of California*, 88 Cal. App. 4th 52, 69 (2000) (causal link may be established by circumstantial evidence such as proximity in time between protected activity and alleged retaliation).

Nonetheless, the Court concludes that Thibodeau cannot show a prima facie case of whistleblower discrimination because he has not articulated facts indicating that he engaged in a protected activity.

3. Employer's Legitimate Nondiscriminatory Reason for the Challenged Action

While the Court need not reach the employer's legitimate nondiscriminatory reason for the challenged action, the Court observes that Defendant has presented adequate, non-pretextual reasons for some of its potential adverse employment actions. For example, Plaintiff was denied a transfer because he was not in good standing due to a written warning, and because he was regularly not meeting his quotas. Further, Plaintiff was denied a promotion because he was not qualified for the position, in comparison to the candidate ultimately hired. See *id.* at 258:21–259:23.

Plaintiff has not adequately demonstrated that these legitimate nondiscriminatory reasons are pretext. See *McRae v. Dep't of Corrections & Rehab.*, 142 Cal. App. 4th 377, 389 (2006) (Plaintiff must demonstrate "specific" and "substantial" evidence of pretext and cannot establish this burden by simply showing that ADT's actions were "wrong, mistaken, or unwise."). Mere repetition of the claim that these actions were pretext is not specific and substantial evidence of pretext. See, e.g., Opp. 10–14. Moreover, Plaintiff's own evidence suggests that other members of ADT's workforce—including James Brady—were denied transfers because of written warnings, suggesting that ADT's explanations are not pretext. See Brady Decl. ¶ 8 ("The Custom Home Division Sales Manager said he wanted me on his team. A few days after I applied for the position, I was issued a written warning and told that because of the written warning I could not transfer to the Custom Home Division.").

Accordingly, the Court will GRANT summary judgment as to Plaintiff's Second Cause of Action.

IT IS SO ORDERED.

QUESTIONS

1. Using the same analysis as ADT, could a judge find that an employee engaged in protected activity and yet did not have a viable claim? If the answer is "yes," is that a satisfactory resolution of a dispute?
2. There are numerous federal laws protecting whistleblowers that fall under the "topic related" type of statute. Research an example and create a flowchart to screen a potential client to determine if the requirements of the statute are met.

Problem 36-3

You are an associate at a law firm. Your supervising partner comes by your office and says, "I think there is money to be made with statutory whistleblower claims, based on a lunch CLE I attended last week. You took employment law, so prepare a flow chart to help us to assess potential cases." She is not big on a lot of dialogue, so this is all you have to go on. Draft a flowchart for use in screening clients.

---

4. Lawyers as Whistleblowers

Trzaska v. L'Oréal USA, Inc.

865 F.3d 155 (3rd Cir. 2017).

Ambro, Circuit Judge.

Steven J. Trzaska was an in-house patent attorney for L'Oréal USA, Inc. ("L'Oréal USA"), a cosmetics company. It fired him, he alleges, for his refusal to violate various ethical rules that govern the legal profession. He asserts that this action violated New Jersey employment law, as one cannot be fired for refusing to violate regulations or public policy at the instruction of his employer. The District Court dismissed Trzaska's claim without discovery. Because his allegations against the beauty-products corporation appear to be more than skin-deep, they plausibly pass muster at the motion-to-dismiss stage. Thus we reverse.

I. BACKGROUND

Beginning in 2004, Trzaska was employed as the head of L'Oréal USA's regional patent team in Clark, New Jersey, overseeing the process by which the latter would patent the company's newly developed products and inventions. The process would begin when an inventor submitted to the patent team an "invention disclosure" for a new product describing its potentially patentable subject matter. A patent attorney on the team then vetted the invention disclosure to determine the product's patentability by interviewing the inventor and searching L'Oréal USA's internal database to confirm that the subject matter of the product did not already exist. If the patent team determined that the product was patentable, an attorney prepared the necessary paperwork and submitted a patent application to the United States Patent and Trademark Office ("USPTO").

As with any legal practitioner, the attorneys on L'Oréal USA's patent team were required to follow various ethical standards known as Rules of Professional Conduct that guide and regulate the legal profession. Because he was admitted to practice law in Pennsylvania and before the USPTO, both the Rules of Professional conduct established by the Supreme Court of Pennsylvania and the professional rules promulgated by the USPTO (collectively, the "RPCs") governed Trzaska's conduct. In relevant part, these RPCs barred attorneys from filing frivolous or bad-faith patent applications or from knowingly making false statements before a tribunal. Violations of the RPCs could result in sanctions or disbarment.

L'Oréal, S.A.—the French parent company of L'Oréal USA (collectively, "L'Oréal")—established a global quota of patent applications that each regional office must file each year. In 2014, the annual quota for Trzaska's team was 40 patent applications. Management officials at L'Oréal told Trzaska and his team members that, if they failed to meet that quota, "there would be consequences which would negatively impact their careers and/or continued employment." J.A. at 32. At the same time, L'Oréal adopted an initiative to improve the quality of patent applications it filed with the USPTO. Adopting this company policy resulted in fewer invention disclosures submitted to the patent team for vetting.

With two competing company policies in place—one that required the patent team to meet an annual minimum of patent applications and one that effectively reduced the amount of invention disclosures that could be evaluated—Trzaska's team found itself in a predicament. According to several members of the team, there were very few patentable products submitted to it for vetting while L'Oréal continued to demand that the team meet the annual quota. Consequently, the patent team did not believe it was able to meet the mandatory quota for 2014 without filing patent applications for products that it did not in good faith believe were patentable. And, as L'Oréal had threatened, if the team did not meet that quota, the patent attorneys' job security would be in peril.

In the hope of resolving this professional Catch-22, Trzaska approached his superiors. He explained that neither he nor his team would be willing to file any patent applications for products that they in good faith believed were not patentable. He advised management that if any attorney on the patent team filed such a patent application, he or she would be in violation of the ethical standards—or RPCs—to which they were bound as licensed patent attorneys. Though Trzaska did not identify any offending patent application that he nonetheless was instructed to file, he informed his superiors that he would not do so should he come across one, even if that meant that the annual quota would not be met.

Apparently L'Oréal did not receive well Trzaska's protest. In the weeks following Trzaska's meeting with management, L'Oréal offered him two severance packages that he could accept so long as he left the company. If he chose not to leave, he was instructed to "go back to [his] office and get back to work." J.A. at 34. After he rejected both severance packages offered, L'Oréal fired Trzaska, stating that his position was no longer needed.

Trzaska brought suit in District Court against both L'Oréal entities for wrongful retaliatory discharge in violation of the New Jersey Conscientious Employee Protection Act ("CEPA"), N.J. Stat. Ann. § 34:19–1 et seq. Among other things, CEPA protects an employee from retaliatory termination following his disclosure of the employer's violation of law or his refusal to participate in illegal activity at the request of the employer, including a practice that the employee believes contravenes public policy. Trzaska alleged he was fired because he refused to participate in an illegal activity by filing frivolous or bad-faith patent applications that would violate the RPCs and his ethical obligations as a licensed patent attorney.

The District Court dismissed Trzaska's claims under Federal Rule of Civil Procedure 12(b)(6) because in its view the RPCs were an inadequate basis to maintain his CEPA claim. It reasoned that, because the RPCs do not govern any activities, ethical obligations, or business decisions of the L'Oréal entities, they did not violate any law on which a CEPA claim could be based. It further determined that Trzaska failed to show he had a reasonable belief that L'Oréal had violated a law or that a violation was imminent (which it deemed a necessary element for a CEPA claim). (Interestingly, the Court also dismissed Trzaska's claims against L'Oréal, S.A. for the same reasons even though it only sought a Rule 12(b)(5) dismissal for insufficient service of process.) This appeal followed. . . . .

III. ANALYSIS

A. RPCs and CEPA Violations

"CEPA . . . protect[s] employees from retaliatory actions by employers. . . ." *Blackburn v. United Parcel Serv., Inc.*, 179 F.3d 81, 91 (3d Cir. 1999) (quotations omitted). To that end, courts construe it flexibly. It provides in relevant part:

> An employer shall not take any retaliatory action against an employee because the employee does any of the following:
>
> . . . .
>
> (c) Objects to, or refuses to participate in any activity, policy or practice which the employee reasonably believes: (1) is in violation of a law, or a rule or regulation promulgated pursuant to law . . .; (2) is fraudulent or criminal . . .; or (3) is incompatible with a clear mandate of public policy concerning the public health, safety or welfare or protection of the environment.

N.J. Stat. Ann. § 34:19–3(c). Accordingly, a plaintiff must identify a law, rule, regulation, or clear mandate of public policy, that supports the basis of his CEPA claim as well as "unacceptable practices in the defendant employer's business" that contravene the identified authority.

Following these guidelines, an allegation that an employer instructed, coerced, or threatened its patent attorney employee to disregard the RPCs binding him violates a clear mandate of public policy within the meaning of CEPA. See N.J. Stat. Ann. § 34:19–3(c). Terminating that employee for refusing to follow such an instruction or its equivalent triggers CEPA protection for two reasons.

> *[Editor's Note: The court first noted that a patent, by its very nature, is affected with a public interest because patents are special privileges created to serve the public. As a result, attorneys are expected to uphold the highest degree of candor and good faith when dealing with the Patent Office.]*

Second, rules of professional conduct in general can underlay a CEPA violation. "In New Jersey, [the courts] are deeply committed to the principle that an employer's right to discharge an employee carries a correlative duty to protect his freedom to decline to perform an act that would constitute a violation of a clear mandate of public policy." See *Parker v. M&T Chemicals, Inc.*, 236 N.J.Super. 451, 566 A.2d 215, 219–20 (N.J. Super. Ct. App. Div. 1989) (in-house patent counsel's adherence to a state Supreme Court's ethical Rules of Professional Conduct constitutes a clear mandate of public policy that CEPA protects); see also *Weiss v. Carpenter, Bennett & Morrissey*, 143 N.J. 420, 672 A.2d 1132, 1144 (1996) (holding generally, in the arbitration context, that New Jersey "precedents demonstrate quite clearly that the Rules of Professional Conduct . . . express a clear mandate of public policy"); *Pierce v. Ortho Pharm. Corp.*, 84 N.J. 58, 417 A.2d 505, 512 (1980) (in a case giving rise to the passage of CEPA, the New Jersey Supreme Court determined that non-administrative Rules of Professional Conduct may contain expressions of public policy, and a request to violate them serves as a basis for wrongful termination). An employee cannot be terminated for refusing to violate or disregard ethical standards regulating his profession, as public policy in New Jersey requires that he follow them.

Given these two principles—that the abuse of the patent application system and the violation of Rules of Professional Conduct harm the public's interest—an employer's policy effecting the disregard of the RPCs contravenes clear mandates of public policy within the meaning of CEPA. Thus an allegation that an employer promulgates such a policy serves as an adequate basis to bring a CEPA claim

The District Court determined that the applicable RPCs could not serve as a basis for a CEPA violation because they do not regulate L'Oréal's business practices. That conclusion may be correct, but the basis of the CEPA claim here is not L'Oréal's violation of the RPCs; rather, it is the instruction to its employees that would result in the disregard of their RPC duties and hence violates a mandate of public policy. CEPA is clear: an employee cannot be terminated for refusing to participate in conduct that he reasonably believes violates public policy. This is especially so because we must construe the statute's protections liberally. . . .

B. Trzaska's Allegations

The District Court determined that, regardless whether an employer's instruction to an employee that would result in the disregard of the employee's professional ethical standards can be the basis of a CEPA claim, Trzaska failed to plead adequately such a claim. It found that Trzaska did not allege that L'Oréal had violated a law or public policy or that such a violation was imminent. His apparent failure to do so, the Court believed, was fatal to his CEPA claim. We disagree.

First, as stated above, professional ethical codes can serve as a basis to state a claim under CEPA when an employee is coerced to disregard them. In New Jersey

> the sensible meaning of CEPA is that the objecting employee must have an objectively reasonable belief, at the time of objection or refusal to participate in the employer's offensive activity, that such activity is . . . incompatible with a constitutional, statutory or regulatory provision, code of ethics, or other recognized source of public policy. Specific knowledge of the precise source of public policy is not required.

Mehlman v. Mobil Oil Corp., 153 N.J. 163, 707 A.2d 1000, 1015 (1998). Trzaska's allegations thereby come within the scope of CEPA protection, especially in light of the liberal construction afforded the statute. See *Blackburn*, 179 F.3d at 90.

Second, we disagree with the District Court that Trzaska's CEPA claim should be brushed away because his "pleadings contain no evidence that [L'Oréal] demanded or ordered that [he] or others relinquish their professional judgments or obligations." It misapplies the standard of review at the motion-to-dismiss stage. There a court must consider no more than whether the complaint establishes "enough facts to raise a reasonable expectation that discovery will reveal evidence of the necessary elements" of the cause of action. *Connelly v. Lane Constr. Corp.*, 809 F.3d 780, 789 (3d Cir. 2016) (quoting *Phillips v. Cty. of Allegheny*, 515 F.3d 224, 234 (3d Cir. 2008) (quotation and alteration omitted)). A plaintiff's allegations must be accepted as true and construed in the light most favorable to him when determining if his complaint should be dismissed.

Trzaska's complaint has met this threshold. It alleges there was a company policy of meeting the patent application quota regardless whether the applications submitted were for products that he did not believe were patentable. He also claimed that he and other colleagues were implicitly instructed to disregard the RPCs in order to meet the quota and that his supervisors expressly rejected his concern about violating the RPCs. And, to close the circle, L'Oréal threatened to terminate his employment if he did not meet the quota. J.A. at 32, 35–36. If these allegations are taken as true, which they must be for the purposes of deciding a motion to dismiss, Trzaska has alleged a colorable violation of CEPA. Whether he was in fact instructed to violate the RPCs is determined later in the litigation process.

IV. CONCLUSION

An instruction, coercion, or threat by an employer that would result in the disregard of obligatory ethical standards of one's profession violates a clear mandate of public policy within the meaning of CEPA. Under it, an employee cannot be terminated for refusing to engage in conduct in which he or she is prohibited from engaging. We therefore reverse the District Court's dismissal and remand the case for further proceedings without dismissing Trzaska's appeal as to L'Oréal, S.A.

CHAGARES, CIRCUIT JUDGE, concurring in part and dissenting in part.

I agree with my learned colleagues that rules of professional conduct ("RPCs") can serve as an adequate foundation for a claim under the New Jersey Conscientious Employee Protection Act ("CEPA"), N.J. Stat. Ann. § 34:19–1. I also agree with my colleagues' conclusion as to the motion to dismiss filed by L'Oréal, S.A., the parent company. I therefore join the majority's opinion as to section III, parts A and C. I disagree, however, that Trzaska pled a cognizable CEPA claim in the amended complaint or otherwise satisfied the heightened standard applying to him as an attorney proceeding on a CEPA claim. I therefore cannot join section III, part B and respectfully dissent from the majority as to its conclusion and judgment.

I.

The pertinent facts alleged in the amended complaint are as follows. Plaintiff Steven Trzaska was admitted to practice law in Pennsylvania in 1989 and admitted to practice before the United States Patent and Trademark Office in 1992. He began working for L'Oréal, USA, Inc. ("L'Oréal") in 2004. Since at least the start of Trzaska's employment at L'Oréal, L'Oréal's parent company "set a predetermined numerical quota of how many patent applications it was to file globally on an annual basis." Appendix ("App.") 27. The reason for the quota, according to Trzaska, "[was] to maintain and bolster the reputation of [L'Oréal] to financial analysts and shareholders following its stock, as innovative science-based players in the field of cosmetics." App. 28. The global quota was unchanged from at least 2012.

Working within the contours of this quota became objectionable to Trzaska as of October 2014, and that month he complained about the quota to the Global CFO of the Research and Innovation Organization of the parent company. Specifically, Trzaska "advised that neither he nor the patent attorneys who reported to him were willing to file patent applications that the attorneys believed were not patentable . . . ." App. 34. Thereafter, the head of Human Resources for Research in the United States offered Trzaska two options: a severance package if he would leave L'Oréal's employment or that he could "go back to [his] office and get back to work." App. 34. Trzaska received an offer for a more substantial severance package shortly thereafter but did not accept it. On December 8, 2014, L'Oréal terminated Trzaska.

Notwithstanding Trzaska's issues with the quota—which was the same as previous years—the amended complaint reveals that Trzaska's team had 87.5% of its Notice of Inventions, an abbreviated version of the invention disclosure, approved by October 2014. App. 30–31. Further, despite Trzaska's complaint about the patentability of certain applications, Trzaska acknowledged that in 2014, L'Oréal began "an internal initiative to improve the quality of patent applications being filed by L'Oréal." App. 33. Highlights of this 2014 initiative included "requiring inventors to provide examples evidencing that the proposed inventions performed as represented. . . ." App. 33. This initiative supplemented the already robust "vetting" process that was in place to ensure that "the subject matter of the invention is novel and unobvious" and to assist the reviewing patent attorney in making a "good faith determination whether the subject matter in an invention disclosure is potentially patentable." App. 32–33.

A.

To state a prima facie case under CEPA, a plaintiff must establish that:

> (1) he or she reasonably believed that his or her employer's conduct was violating either a law, rule, or regulation promulgated pursuant to law, or a clear mandate of public policy; (2) he or she performed a 'whistle-blowing' activity described in N.J.S.A. 34:19–3c; (3) an adverse employment action was taken against him or her; and (4) a causal connection exists between the whistle-blowing activity and the adverse employment action.

Dzwonar v. McDevitt, 177 N.J. 451, 828 A.2d 893, 900 (2003).

Trzaska's amended complaint fails to satisfy the first element of the CEPA prima facie case. This is because he has failed to meet the requirement that "a plaintiff must set forth facts that would support an objectively reasonable belief that a violation has occurred." *Id.* at 901.

. . . .

. . . Even taking the factual allegations in the light most favorable to him, Trzaska did not allege an objectively reasonable belief of past or imminent wrongdoing. Trzaska averred no facts suggesting that L'Oréal requested or demanded that he relinquish his professional obligations in evaluating or submitting patent applications. See Oral Arg. Tr. at 5 (Trzaska's counsel conceding that L'Oréal did not tell Trzaska to file "frivolous or unwarranted patent claims"); see generally *Johnson v. N.J. Higher Educ. Student Assistance Auth.*, No. A–3102–13T1, 2015 WL 6739525, at *6 (N.J. Super. Ct. App. Div. Nov. 5, 2015) (concluding the plaintiff's assertions were "patently insufficient" to support a CEPA claim when the plaintiff failed to allege that her employer "told her to fabricate facts, falsify documents, or falsely implicate others"). Nor did Trzaska allege that he informed his employer before September 2014 that he was displeased with the quality of invention disclosures or concerned about the quota policy. In this regard, the only specific notice that Trzaska alleges that he gave to his employer is that he advised the company "that neither he nor the patent attorneys who reported to him were willing to file patent applications that the attorneys believed were not patentable. . . ." App. 34. Yet, the amended complaint failed to identify even a single defective patent application that was submitted at any point during Trzaska's ten years of employment at L'Oréal—a period that entirely coincided with the existence of the global quota policy. See Oral Arg. Tr. at 5 (Trzaska's counsel responding in the negative to the question were any "frivolous or unwarranted patent claims . . . filed by Mr. Trzaska and/or his office?"). Such conclusory allegations fail to support the requirement that illegal activity was afoot or imminent. See *Blackburn*, 3 F.Supp.2d at 515.

Trzaska's allegations in the amended complaint actually refute rather than support his claims of wrongdoing. For instance, the amended complaint detailed at length the elaborate procedures used to "vet[ ]" an invention disclosure as well as the "internal initiative" L'Oréal adopted to improve overall quality in patent applications. App. 32–33. These detailed factual allegations undercut any suggestion that management encouraged the submission of frivolous patent applications. Any claim of wrongdoing on L'Oréal's part is further undermined by the fact that, at the time of his termination, Trzaska's team had nearly completed its annual quota requirement and seemingly had ample time to submit the remaining invention disclosures.

These facts, taken together, suggest that Trzaska at most alleged a policy disagreement with L'Oréal over the efficacy of the quota system. Such "routine dispute[s] in the workplace," however, are insufficient to state a viable CEPA claim. See *Hitesman*, 93 A.3d at 319; see also *Klein*, 871 A.2d at 690 (rejecting a CEPA claim when the plaintiff's concerns were essentially "disagreements with the internal procedures and priorities" of his employer). I would thus hold that Trzaska failed to state the first element of a prima facie CEPA claim.

III.

In sum, I do not believe that the District Court erred in concluding that Trzaska did not plead a viable CEPA claim because he failed to establish that L'Oréal had or would imminently violate a law, rule, regulation, or a clear mandate of public policy. I would also hold that Trzaska failed to satisfy the heightened standard applying to him as an attorney. Accordingly, I would affirm the District Court's dismissal of his CEPA claim for failure to state a claim. I respectfully dissent.

QUESTION

1. Does the majority or dissent have the better argument? Apply your civil procedure knowledge of Rule 12(b)(6) to make your case.

---

5. The Cost of Being a Whistleblower

The following article discusses some of the challenges an employee may encounter if she engages in whistleblowing. Although the audience for the article was composed of fraud examiners, it should provide you with insight into the dynamics of whistleblowing and how it affects the employee.

Patricia A. Patrick, *Be Prepared Before You Blow the Whistle: Protection Under State Whistle-blowing Laws*

Fraud Magazine 24, 28–31 (2010).

You might one day need to be a whistle-blower. Be forewarned: Your personal and professional lives will suffer. New research on state whistle-blower lawsuits shows it's likely you'll be fired and will lose your case. But then, doing the right thing never meant that right things would happen to you.

. . . .

Most Whistle-Blowers Are Fired

Seventy-four percent of the whistle-blowers in my review were terminated. Another 6 percent were suspended and 5 percent were transferred against their wishes. The remaining 15 percent were given poor evaluations, demoted or harassed. The results, summarized in Exhibit 1 (below), indicate that retaliation occurs, although this review can't determine how often.

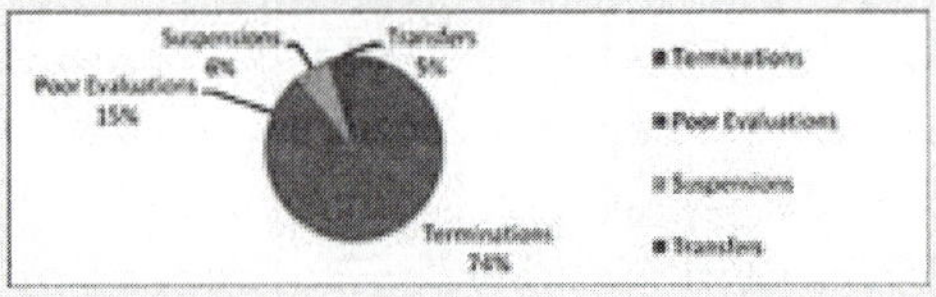

Approximately 60 percent of the lawsuits were filed in the past 10 years; however, it's impossible to say why employees are increasingly turning to the courts to solve their problems. Perhaps employees are reporting wrongful acts more frequently and filing more frivolous lawsuits. It's also possible that employers are committing more acts of wrongdoing and retaliating more often. Then again, it's possible the rise is due to the increasingly litigious nature of American society.

The whistle-blowers in this sample didn't fare well in their lawsuits. Fifty-five percent lost their cases. Fourteen percent lost because they failed to prove their cases. Eleven percent failed to prove a causal connection between the alleged retaliation and the whistle-blowing. Only 22 percent won their lawsuits. Of these, 2 percent were reinstated to their old jobs and 8 percent won damage awards. The remaining 23 percent of the cases were remanded for a new trial.

To prevail, employees will probably have to link their whistle-blowing to the retaliation. This can be difficult for employees having problems in the workplace because employers will claim their adverse personnel actions were based on the employees' poor performances—not the employees' decisions to blow the whistle. It's especially easy for employers to assert this claim if the person who conducted the retaliation claims no knowledge of the whistle-blowing.

Get Technicalities Correct

Twenty-two percent of the whistle-blowers lost because they didn't comply with some technicality in the laws. As discussed previously, the laws are very specific on how whistle-blowers must report the wrongdoing. Failing to comply with any aspect of the law will result in a loss of protection.

Six percent of the employees lost because they failed to exhaust all their internal remedies before reporting their concerns externally. Many laws require the employee to report internally first to give the employer an opportunity to correct the matter. This minimizes the potentially devastating impact that public reports can have on organizations when the claims don't have merit or could be handled more effectively internally. Internal reports can also allow the employer to conceal the unlawful activity, if they are so inclined.

Another 5 percent lost because they failed to report the act of wrongdoing correctly. Some laws require the witness to report the wrongdoing in writing within a certain period of time after it's discovered. Other laws require the whistle-blower to state the specific laws that were broken. The purpose of these requirements is to provide the employer with specificity so it can correct the problem.

Case in Point: A high-level officer, working for a government defense contractor, discovered that his employer was overbilling the government, supplying defective parts, and engaging in the unauthorized use of government equipment. He refused to participate in the activities and reported them to his employer's government liaison officer only to find himself terminated afterward. He sued under Florida's whistle-blower law and lost because he failed to first inform his employer of the alleged activity in writing.

. . . .

Finish this Lesson by working on the two mastery problems. Refer back to the statutes from Florida, New Jersey, and Texas at the beginning of the Lesson to identify statutory issues raised by the problems.

Mastery Problem 36-1

Lisa works for a company that makes parts for suspension bridges used above water. She reviews plans prepared by a construction firm and concludes that some of the parts that the firm plans to use for a suspension bridge project are highly likely to corrode because of proximity to salt water. Lisa presented her concerns to her supervisor, who tells her that her analysis is wrong. Lisa is upset. She decides to speak to the press and to contact her state representative to urge an investigation by the appropriate agency. Lisa's boss immediately fires her, telling her to find "another cross to carry." Does Lisa have a claim that can survive dismissal? Does it matter whether her analysis is correct or not?

Mastery Problem 36-2

Ginny is an experienced detective and administrator for the Smith County Sheriff's Department. When Sam was elected Sheriff, he appointed Ginny as Deputy Sheriff. Sam had a number of ideas for improving the productivity of the department. Sam suggested that the department appoint retired police officers to volunteer to guard the evidence lockers where crime evidence is stored. Ginny told Sam that she did not think this was a good idea because of the need to maintain a reliable record of the chain of custody for evidence, as well as the need to safeguard against leaked information. Sam's second idea was to implement a policy to rotate detectives out of their regular roles and into others, including returning them to street patrol. Ginny told the Sheriff that the rotation policy was a bad idea because most of the detectives were over forty years of age. Additionally, she noted that the rotation policy would move them from jobs that they had become used to into jobs that were more arduous and dangerous. After these responses, the Sheriff moved Ginny back to detective and then rotated her back to street patrol. Ginny sues as a whistleblower. Does she have a claim?

Conclusion

Whistleblowers face many difficulties for their disruptions of the employer's business practices. To encourage whistleblowers to come forward, many states protect them by statute, although the protections are not always sufficient. This Lesson has demonstrated again that most employment law is really a balancing of interests between the employer's business needs, the employee's need for security, and the public interest in the employment relationship not being used in ways that are detrimental to society.

Lesson 37:
Protection Against Retaliation

Objectives and Expected Learning Outcomes

In this Lesson, you will study the anti-retaliation provision of Title VII as an example of employee protections for those who oppose conduct that is illegal. The key determination is whether the opposition is protected conduct, as opposition can be expressed in a number of ways. Although we do not cover the anti-discrimination laws in this course, the anti-retaliation provisions operate as an employee protection that is not premised on discrimination against that particular employee. This is similar to protections for whistleblowers that we studied in the previous Lesson.

Title VII of the Civil Rights Act of 1964 put the force of federal law into the civil rights movement. The statute banned discrimination based upon race, sex, color, religion, or national origin. To ensure that the civil rights of workers would be respected, Congress prohibited employers from retaliating against any employees who protested against unlawful discriminatory practices or policies. Read literally, however, the anti-retaliation provision did not protect employees who opposed conduct that technically did not violate the law. The courts responded by extending protection if the employee "reasonably believed" that the conduct in question was unlawful discrimination. Of course, a "reasonable" belief held by someone who is not trained in the law is a difficult concept. Courts have continued to struggle to reconcile the express statutory language with the law's purpose of protecting employees from retaliation.

We begin with the statutory language and some blackletter basics. First, the conduct in question must be opposition to discrimination under Title VII. If the opposition is not protected activity under the anti-retaliation provision of Title VII, the employer might be able to retaliate against a complaining employee. Second, isolated comments about, for example, race or gender that evidence some unlawful animus are not, without more, actual violations of Title VII. However, courts sometimes find that an employee can be protected from reporting conduct that is reasonably viewed as an incipient violation of the law.

Title VII, Section 704(a)

It shall be an unlawful employment practice for an employer to discriminate against any of (its) employees or applicants for employment . . .because [that person] has opposed any practice made an unlawful employment practice by this subchapter. . .

1. Defining an Employee's "Reasonable Belief"

The employee must reasonably believe that she is opposing conduct that is illegal under Title VII in order to fall within the scope of the statutory protection. This element has been added to the statutory test by courts who seek to implement the purpose of the provision.

Example 37-1

An employee reports to human resources that her supervisor is rude to her, does not speak to her in the hallway, and writes her up simply because he dislikes her. The employee is fired the next day. The employee has no anti-retaliation claim under Title VII because she was not opposing an unlawful employment practice under Title VII.

Example 37-2

A female employee is told by a supervisor that he prefers that his wife stay home with the children and not work. He states that he believes women are better suited to a domestic life than a work-centered one. She tells him that this is a sexist belief. He never again mentions this belief or makes any sexist comment. The employee is later demoted by this manager. She likely has no claim under Title VII because no employee could reasonably believe that a single isolated comment could possibly be an unlawful employment practice under Title VII.

Consider one of the early cases to apply the "reasonable belief" standard to the anti-retaliation provision. The case presents a classic dilemma that courts encounter when interpreting statutory language.

Payne v. McLemore's Wholesale & Retail Stores

654 F.2d 1130 (5th Cir. 1981).

Johnson, Judge.

. . . .

In November 1970, plaintiff was once again laid off (from defendant) due to the seasonal business decline. Two other black employees and two white employees were laid off at the same time. About a month later, plaintiff became involved in the formation and organization of the Franklin Parish Improvement Organization, a nonprofit civil rights organization. The formation of the Improvement Organization was precipitated by an incident involving two black children who were turned away from a public swimming pool. The organization was interested in improving social conditions of blacks in Franklin Parish, and it focused especially on the need to get blacks hired in retail stores in money-handling and supervisory positions in order to improve the treatment that blacks received while shopping in stores. Shortly after its formation, the members of the organization decided to boycott several retail businesses, including those of defendant in Winnsboro. Plaintiff organized and implemented the boycott and was actively involved in picketing McLemore's Jitney Jungle Food Stores. Defendant knew of plaintiff's involvement in the boycott and picketing. Moreover, the boycott and picketing were effective and defendant's business suffered as a result.

In previous years when he had been laid off, plaintiff had always gone back to work for defendant when the work picked back up. In the year of the boycott, however, he was not recalled or rehired. In February 1971, plaintiff filed a charge of discrimination against McLemore's with the Equal Employment Opportunity Commission (EEOC).

. . . .

The opposition clause of section 704(a) of Title VII provides protection against retaliation for employees who oppose unlawful employment practices committed by an employer. (Section 704(a) also contains a participation clause that protects employees against retaliation for their participation in the procedures established by Title VII to enforce its provisions. . .)

. . . .

Defendant argues, however, that plaintiff failed to establish his prima facie case because he failed to prove that defendant had committed any unlawful employment practices. Plaintiff responds that he was not required to prove the actual existence of those unlawful employment practices; instead, he asserts that it was sufficient to establish a prima facie case if he had a reasonable belief that defendant had engaged in the unlawful employment practices. We agree with plaintiff and conclude that it was not fatal to plaintiff's section 704(a) case that he failed to prove, under the *McDonnell Douglas* criteria for proving an unlawful employment practice under section 703(a)(1), that McLemore's discriminated against blacks in retail store employment opportunities.

The Ninth Circuit was apparently the first appellate court to decide whether the opposition clause of section 704(a) required proof of actual discrimination. *Sias v. City Demonstration Agency*, 588 F.2d 692 (9th Cir. 1978). In *Sias*, the plaintiff alleged that he was discharged by the City Demonstration Agency (an agency of the City of Los Angeles) in retaliation for his opposition to acts of racial discrimination by the City of Los Angeles. The City did not deny that plaintiff "was discharged for writing a letter of grievance to the Regional Administrator of the Department of Housing and Urban Development (HUD). Rather, it contend(ed) that, inasmuch as the trial court made no finding of actual discrimination, it (could not) be held to have violated" section 704(a). *Id.* at 694. The Ninth Circuit concluded that "(s)uch a narrow interpretation . . . would not only chill the legitimate assertion of employee rights under Title VII but would tend to force employees to file formal charges rather than seek conciliation or informal adjustment of grievances." *Id.* at 695. The *Sias* court quoted extensively from *Hearth v. Metropolitan Transit Commission*, 436 F.Supp. 685 (D.Minn.1977), which held that "as long as the employee had a reasonable belief that what was being opposed constituted discrimination under Title VII, the claim of retaliation does not hinge upon a showing that the employer was in fact in violation of Title VII."

. . . .

To effectuate the policies of Title VII and to avoid the chilling effect that would otherwise arise, we are compelled to conclude that a plaintiff can establish a prima facie case of retaliatory discharge under the opposition clause of section 704(a) if he shows that he had a reasonable belief that the employer was engaged in unlawful employment practices. While the district court made no explicit finding that plaintiff's opposition was based upon a reasonable belief that McLemore's hiring and promotional policies violated Title VII, such a finding is implicit and is sufficiently supported by evidence in the record.

. . . .

AFFIRMED.

COLEMAN, JUDGE, dissenting.

. . . .

The gravamen of my concern is found in the concession of the majority opinion that "The Fifth Circuit has not heretofore directly addressed the issue whether proof of an actual unlawful employment practice is necessary under the opposition clause, or whether an employee is protected from retaliation under the opposition clause if the employee reasonably believes that the employer is engaged in unlawful employment practices".

The majority then proceeds to hold that reasonable belief is enough.

However, the statute, 2000e–3(a), stripped of its inapplicable verbiage, reads:

It shall be an unlawful practice for an employer to discriminate against [any employee or applicant] . . . because [that person] has opposed any practice made an unlawful employment practice by this subchapter.

The statute speaks in terms of practices not what someone "reasonably believes" to have been a practice when, in fact, the practice did not exist. I cannot believe that Congress intended (since it did not say so) to penalize employers for what an employee or applicant "believes" when, in fact, the employer is innocent. To hold otherwise is to deprive employers of their property rights in violation of the due process clause.

. . . .

QUESTIONS

1. Compare this case to the cases we discussed regarding protected concerted activity under the NLRA (National Labor Relations Act) and the First Amendment. Why is expressive conduct (picketing) entitled to the same protection

as verbal statements? Isn't verbal conduct more definitive and precise than expressive conduct?

2. Does the dissent have a valid point? Does the majority invite employees to make up claims that they reasonably believed they were opposing unlawful conduct? After all, the statute is clear: "oppose any practice made an unlawful employment practice. . ." Is there an element of common sense that enters the equation?

3. Does the law seem to require that an employee understand employment law? What if the employee reasonably believes that an employer is about to discriminate against another employee, but has not yet done so? Is anticipatory opposition protected? Should it be? If a reasonable person might have believed that the employer was engaged in unlawful employment practices, but the plaintiff actually did not in good faith hold such a belief, is the plaintiff's opposition conduct still protected?

Problem 37-1

Emilio is a male nurse who works at a facility for teenagers with developmental issues and behavioral problems. As part of his first day orientation, Emilio signed an acknowledgment that he had received a handbook which provides that any violent act against a patient is grounds for immediate termination, regardless of the reason for the act. After one of the male teenagers started acting in a sexualized manner toward a female nurse, Emilio asked for support from the administration to provide self-defense courses. The administration took no action. One day the resident placed his palms on the female nurse's breasts. Emilio immediately slapped the resident and pushed him away from his colleague. Does Emilio have a cause of action if he is fired for violence? Would the female nurse have a cause of action if she was fired for slapping the resident as an immediate response to the groping?

In the following case, the Supreme Court attempted to clarify the "reasonable belief" standard, but sidestepped the issue of whether "good faith" is also an element. Does the opinion provide clarity or leave too many questions open?

Clark County Sch. Dist. v. Breeden

532 U.S. 268 (2001).

Per Curiam.

. . . .

On October 21, 1994, respondent's male supervisor met with respondent and another male employee to review the psychological evaluation reports of four job applicants. The report for one of the applicants disclosed that the applicant had once commented to a co-worker, "I hear making love to you is like making love to the Grand Canyon." Brief in Opposition 3. At the meeting respondent's supervisor read the comment aloud, looked at respondent and stated, "I don't know what that means." *Ibid.* The other employee then said, "Well, I'll tell you later," and both men chuckled. *Ibid.* Respondent later complained about the comment to the offending employee, to Assistant Superintendent George Ann Rice, the employee's supervisor, and to another assistant superintendent of petitioner. Her first claim of retaliation asserts that she was punished for these complaints.

The Court of Appeals for the Ninth Circuit has applied § 2000e–3(a) to protect employee "oppos[ition]" not just to practices that are actually "made . . . unlawful" by Title VII, but also to practices that the employee could reasonably believe were unlawful. 2000 WL 991821, at *1 (stating that respondent's opposition was protected "if she had a reasonable, good faith belief that the incident involving the sexually explicit remark constituted unlawful sexual harassment"); *Trent v. Valley Electric Assn. Inc.*, 41 F.3d 524, 526 (C.A.9 1994). We have no occasion to rule on the propriety of this interpretation, because even assuming it is correct, no one could reasonably believe that the incident recounted above violated Title VII.

Title VII forbids actions taken on the basis of sex that "discriminate against any individual with respect to his compensation, terms, conditions, or privileges of employment." 42 U.S.C. § 2000e–2(a)(1). Just three Terms ago, we reiterated, what was plain from our previous decisions, that sexual harassment is actionable under Title VII only if it is "so 'severe or pervasive' as to 'alter the conditions of [the victim's] employment and create an abusive working environment.' " Workplace conduct is not measured in isolation; instead, "whether an environment is sufficiently hostile or abusive" must be judged "by 'looking at all the circumstances,' including the 'frequency of the discriminatory conduct; its severity; whether it is physically threatening or humiliating, or a mere offensive utterance; and whether it unreasonably interferes with an employee's work performance.' " Hence, "[a] recurring point in [our] opinions is that simple teasing, offhand comments, and isolated incidents (unless extremely serious) will not amount to discriminatory changes in the 'terms and conditions of employment.' "

No reasonable person could have believed that the single incident recounted above violated Title VII's standard. The ordinary terms and conditions of respondent's job required her to review the sexually explicit statement in the course of screening job applicants. Her co-workers who participated in the hiring process were subject to the same requirement, and indeed, in the District Court respondent "conceded that it did not bother or upset her" to read the statement in the file. Her supervisor's comment, made at a meeting to review the application, that he did not know what the statement meant; her co-worker's responding comment; and the chuckling of both are at worst an "isolated inciden[t]" that cannot remotely be considered "extremely serious," as our cases require. The holding of the Court of Appeals to the contrary must be reversed.

. . . .

QUESTION

1. In the wake of increased attention to sexual harassment epitomized by the #MeToo movement, is it still true that "offhand comments" are no longer regarded as problematic?

In the following case, the Fifth Circuit introduces two additional concepts for consideration. First, the court considers whether the opposition clause applies to "reactive" speech. Second, the court considers whether the definition of "reasonable" belief should be augmented by tacking on a "zone of conduct" requirement that extends anti-retaliation protection for employer actions that fall short of an actual Title VII violation but could reasonably be perceived by an employee as a violation. What began as a simply-worded statute has become increasingly complex.

EEOC v. Rite Way Serv.

819 F.3d 235 (5th Cir. 2016).

Costa, Judge.

It has long been the law in this and other circuits that a plaintiff contending that she was retaliated against for proactively reporting employment discrimination need not show that the discrimination rose to the level of a Title VII violation, but must at least show a reasonable belief that it did. See generally *Payne v. McLemore's Wholesale & Retail Stores*, 654 F.2d 1130, 1140 (5th Cir. Sept.1981). In this case, we address whether that same "reasonable belief" standard applies to a retaliation claim brought by a third party witness who was fired soon after answering questions in response to a company investigation into harassment allegations. See *Crawford v. Metro. Gov't of Nashville & Davidson Cty., Tenn.*, 555 U.S. 271, 277–78, 129 S.Ct. 846, 172 L.Ed.2d 650 (2009) (recognizing that a retaliation claim may be based on a complaint solicited by the employer).

. . . .

I

The Equal Employment Opportunity Commission brings this antiretaliation claim on behalf of Mekeva Tennort. Tennort was employed as a general cleaner for Rite Way Service, Inc., a janitorial services contractor with the Biloxi school system. She worked at Biloxi Junior High School for two full school years—2009–2010 and 2010–2011—and was rehired in August 2011 for the 2011–2012 school year. The breaks in that employment were not the result of any performance problems, but of the summer breaks from school when the Biloxi schools did not use Rite Way.

At the beginning of the 2011–2012 school year, Tennort's supervisor was let go and replaced by an interim supervisor, Willie Harris. Harris assumed this role on approximately August 5, 2011. Within one week, Tennort observed two interactions between Harris and another general cleaner, Linda Quarles, that troubled her. The first involved Harris pretending to smack Quarles's bottom and saying, "ooh wee." Tennort did not report the incident or speak to either Harris or Quarles about it, because she "didn't want to get involved."

Shortly thereafter, on August 11th, Tennort and Quarles were together on school property when Harris told Quarles that she should not have a cell phone in her back pocket pursuant to Rite Way policy. Tennort expressed surprise that Harris could tell what was in Quarles's pants pocket and stated that "somebody must be looking real hard at [Quarles's] behind." Harris responded that Quarles's pants were tight. Quarles took offense, pulling at her pants to show that they were not tight and telling Harris not to worry about how tight her pants were. Harris then said, "I'm a man, I'm gonna look." The comment visibly upset Quarles.

After this incident, Quarles complained to a police officer stationed at the junior high school and to Rite Way that Harris had sexually harassed her. She identified Tennort as an eye witness. Rite Way began investigating Quarles's complaint.

On the morning of August 18th, Alex McCullom—Rite Way's Project Manager for the Biloxi school system—came to the junior high school and questioned Tennort about the "I'm gonna look" incident. According to Tennort, McCullom tried to talk her out of reporting what she had seen, stating "you know what they do to people who do stuff like this" and that Quarles was "nothing but trouble." Despite these statements, Tennort wrote out her report and gave it to McCullom. As discussed in more depth below, the EEOC views the giving of her report as the protected activity against which Rite Way could not retaliate.

Approximately two days after this meeting, Rite Way decided to separate Harris and Quarles; Harris was transferred away from Biloxi Junior High School. Another Rite Way employee—oddly enough, Harris's brother-in-law—took over as Tennort's and Quarles's supervisor.

Tennort's tenure under her new supervisor was both eventful and short-lived. Over the next five weeks, she received two written warnings and up to two oral warnings for poor job performance. Her alleged infractions included not properly cleaning areas assigned to her, tardiness, and insubordination. These warnings were the first that Tennort had received since beginning her employment with Rite Way in 2009. As to both of the written warnings, Tennort disagreed that the criticism was justified and explained her position in writing on the warning itself.

II

The EEOC asserts that Tennort's purported performance issues were fabricated, and that Tennort was terminated as punishment for her decision to corroborate the "I'm gonna look" incident between Harris and Quarles. Rite Way moved for summary judgment on the claim, giving multiple reasons why it was entitled to judgment as a matter of law.

The district court granted summary judgment on the basis of Rite Way's first argument: that Tennort did not engage in protected conduct under Title VII's antiretaliation provision. It concluded that the requirement that a retaliation plaintiff have a "reasonable belief" that a Title VII violation occurred applies in the context of someone like Tennort, who was responding as a third party witness to a company inquiry. Applying that standard, and citing cases that rejected sexual harassment claims on summary judgment, it found that Tennort could not have reasonably believed that Harris's conduct violated Title VII.

III

Under Title VII's antiretaliation provision, protected activity can consist of either: (1) "oppos[ing] any practice made an unlawful employment practice by this subchapter" or (2) "ma[king] a charge, testif[ying], assist [ing], or participat[ing] in any manner in an investigation, proceeding, or hearing under this subchapter." 42 U.S.C. § 2000e–3(a). The first of these is known as the "opposition clause;" the second as the "participation clause."

On appeal, the EEOC argues only that Tennort's August 18th report was protected by the opposition clause. Its position finds support in *Crawford v. Metropolitan Government of Nashville and Davidson County, Tennessee,* 555 U.S. 271, 129 S.Ct. 846, 172 L.Ed.2d 650 (2009). Prior to *Crawford,* it was not clear that complaints solicited by the employer—as opposed to complaints initiated by the plaintiff employee—could amount to "opposition" under the statute. The *Crawford* decision settled that they could.

> [A] person can "oppose" by responding to someone else's question just as surely as by provoking the discussion, and nothing in the statute requires a freakish rule protecting an employee who reports discrimination on her own initiative but not one who reports the same discrimination in the same words when her boss asks a question.

Id. at 277–78, 129 S.Ct. 846.

Crawford thus confirms that solicited complaints like Tennort's constitute "opposition." But the opposition clause does not require opposition alone; it requires opposition *of a practice made unlawful by Title VII. See* 42 U.S.C. § 2000e–3(a). We have addressed this statutory language before, in *Payne v. McLemore's Wholesale & Retail Stores,* 654 F.2d 1130 (5th Cir. Unit A Sept.1981), a case involving affirmative rather than solicited opposition.

Payne addressed whether this "practice made unlawful" language requires the employee to prove that the employment practice he complained of was unlawful, or whether it was enough that he reasonably believed the employment practice to be unlawful. *See* 654 F.2d at 1137. We determined that the latter position was consistent with the text of the opposition clause and better-suited "[t]o effectuate the policies of Title VII and avoid the chilling effect that would otherwise arise. . . ." *See id.* at 1137–40.

We have since noted that *Payne*'s reasonable belief standard is "in tension with the plain text" of Section 704(a), "which appears to require that the employer's practice actually be unlawful." *Royal v. CCC & R Tres Arboles, L.L.C.,* 736 F.3d 396, 401 n. 2 (5th Cir.2013). Nonetheless, *Payne* remains good law. It is also in line with the law of every other circuit court. 2 Lex K. Larson, Employment Discrimination § 34.03[2], at 34–40 (2d ed. 2015) (describing how every circuit has adopted an objective "reasonable belief" requirement; most also include a subjective "good faith" requirement). The Supreme Court has not taken a position on the reasonable belief standard. *See Clark Cty. Sch. Dist. v. Breeden,* 532 U.S. 268, 270, 121 S.Ct. 1508, 149 L.Ed.2d 509 (2001) (per curiam) (stating that the Court has "no occasion to rule on the propriety" of the Ninth Circuit's interpretation that the opposition clause applies to "practices that the employee could reasonably believe were unlawful" because "no one could reasonably believe that the incident [opposed in this case] violated Title VII").

Despite the universal and longstanding application of this "reasonable belief" standard, the EEOC urges us to forego it in this retaliation case because Tennort did not affirmatively complain about Harris's conduct, but merely spoke up in response to questioning. The EEOC contends that this result would be consistent with *Crawford,* where no such reasonable belief standard was imposed.

The EEOC's argument makes too much of the absence of a discussion of reasonable belief in *Crawford*. That case presented a narrow issue: whether passive reporting could ever meet Section 704(a)'s requirement of "oppos[ing]" an employment practice. It did not grapple with whether the conduct opposed in that case was "an unlawful employment practice" as elsewhere required in the opposition clause. If anything, creating a lower threshold for reactive plaintiffs bringing retaliation claims would be at odds with *Crawford*'s reasoning that the language of the opposition clause does not permit courts to treat reactive opposition any differently than proactive opposition.

Nor are we persuaded to dispense with the reasonable belief standard for the policy reasons articulated by the EEOC. It argues that requiring reactive complainants to have a reasonable belief regarding the unlawfulness of the behavior they have witnessed would "frustrate the . . . function and purpose" of Title VII. But many of the points it makes have no greater force in the reactive context than in the proactive one. For example, the EEOC warns that "third party witnesses" will not "come forward in an internal investigation" out of uncertainty whether they "would be protected from retaliation," thus "deter[ring] the reporting of Title VII violations essential for the enforcement of the statute's antidiscrimination provision." This same argument can and has been made about proactive complainants. *See, e.g., Berg v. La Crosse Cooler Co.,* 612 F.2d 1041, 1045 (7th Cir.1980) (stating that a literal reading of the opposition clause would "undermine[ ] Title VII's central purpose, the elimination of employment discrimination by informal means" and "destroy[ ] one of the chief means of achieving that purpose, the frank and nondisruptive exchange of ideas between employers and employees"); *Sias v. City Demonstration Agency,* 588 F.2d 692, 695 (9th Cir.1978) (stating concern that requiring proof of illegality before an internal complaint is afforded protection against retaliation would "chill" the "resolution of [complaints of discrimination] without governmental prodding" and "force employees to file formal charges rather than seek conciliation or informal adjustment of grievances"). Indeed, the reasonable belief standard is itself a product of this concern—a compromise position struck by courts to avoid too parsimonious a grant of protection under the opposition clause yet still maintain a connection between what the plaintiff is "opposing" and the discriminatory conduct Title VII forbids.

Indeed, despite its attempt to do away with the reasonable belief standard in *Crawford* cases, the EEOC recognizes that the opposed conduct must have something to do with Title VII in order to support a retaliation claim.

We do not understand it to be arguing, for example, that an employee who believes she was fired for making statements about accounting fraud in response to an internal investigation would be able to bring a Title VII retaliation case. But the EEOC has not articulated a standard that would require some relationship between the opposition and a Title VII violation, albeit a showing less than a "reasonable belief" that Title VII was violated. We are reluctant to create yet another standard for assessing Title VII liability, as some confusion already exists concerning those that govern underlying violations and the one that governs reasonable belief in the retaliation context.

We are therefore not persuaded to establish a different standard for retaliation cases involving reactive opposition by third parties. The statute, case law, and interest in uniformity and ease of application support applying the "reasonable belief" standard to retaliation cases involving both proactive and reactive opposition.

IV

Although the reactive nature of Tennort's opposition does not support creating a different legal standard, the context in which she opposed her employer's conduct is one factor to consider in determining whether she had a reasonable belief that Title VII was being violated.

Everyone agrees that the harassment observed by Tennort was not "so severe or pervasive as to alter the conditions of . . . employment and create an abusive working environment." *Breeden,* 532 U.S. at 270, 121 S.Ct. 1508 (internal quotation marks and citation omitted). But the reasonable belief standard recognizes there is some zone of conduct that falls short of an actual violation but could be reasonably perceived to violate Title VII. The existence of this gray area between actual violation and perceived violation is best illustrated in cases where we have affirmed summary judgment on an employee's discrimination claim while simultaneously reversing summary judgment on his or her opposition clause claim. *See, e.g., Long v. Eastfield Coll.,* 88 F.3d 300, 305–09 (5th Cir.1996); *Parker v. State of La. Dep't of Educ. Special Sch. Dist.,* 323 Fed.Appx. 321, 329–30 (5th Cir.2009).

Could an employee like Tennort, not instructed on Title VII law as a jury would be, reasonably believe that she was providing information about a Title VII violation? The district court thought not, based on cases from this court and the Supreme Court in which retaliation claims were dismissed because the conduct opposed consisted of isolated remarks. In *Breeden,* a female employee complained that two male coworkers had chuckled at a sexually suggestive comment found within an application file that they and the plaintiff were reviewing as part of their job duties. *See* 532 U.S. at 269, 271, 121 S.Ct. 1508. In *Satterwhite v. City of Houston,* an employee complained of a coworker saying "Heil Hitler" in a work meeting. *See* 602 Fed.Appx. 585, 586 (5th Cir.2015) (per curiam). Both employees claimed that they were retaliated against for voicing their opposition to the conduct they observed. *Breeden,* 532 U.S. at 270, 121 S.Ct. 1508; *Satterwhite,* 602 Fed.Appx. at 588. Both claims ultimately failed on summary judgment because no reasonable person could have believed the isolated incidents complained of violated Title VII. *See Breeden,* 532 U.S. at 271, 121 S.Ct. 1508; *Satterwhite,* 602 Fed.Appx. at 588–89.

. . . .

But opposition clause claims grounded in isolated comments are not always doomed to summary judgment. In *Long v. Eastfield College,* a female plaintiff complained internally after a supervisor made an offensive joke about condoms in her presence. 88 F.3d 300, 309 (5th Cir.1996). She alleged that this initial grievance caused the supervisor to treat her differently than other employees—prompting her to lodge two other internal complaints—and eventually led to her termination. *Id.* at 305. We affirmed summary judgment on her sexual discrimination claim because "the alleged joke in this case is exactly the type of mere offensive utterance which should not, by itself, support a claim for hostile work environment." *Id.* at 309. But we reversed summary judgment on her retaliation claim. *Id.* Viewing the joke and the supervisor's alleged reactions to her internal complaints together, we found that the plaintiff had "presented sufficient evidence to create a fact issue as to her 'reasonable belief' that [the supervisor's] conduct violated Title VII." *Id.* at 305.

The conduct of which Tennort complained is closer to *Long* in which we concluded that the reasonable belief question should go to the jury. She heard Harris tell Quarles that he was looking at and admiring her rear end. Unlike *Breeden* and *Satterwhite,* this was conduct directed at a specific fellow employee. That it came from a person in a supervisory position is another important consideration. *Cf. Satterwhite,* 602 Fed.Appx. at 586 (stating that coworker who made offensive comment did not directly supervise the plaintiff).

We also consider the context in which the comment was made. Harris had been Tennort's and Quarles's supervisor for less than a week. Just days earlier, Tennort saw Harris pretend to slap Quarles on the bottom and exclaim "ooh wee." While Tennort did not report the earlier behavior to Rite Way, it is relevant to how she assessed the seriousness of Harris's later comment that he was "gonna look" at Quarles's rear end because he was a man: as a chance off-color comment or as repeated conduct, something more concerning. *Cf. Byers,* 209 F.3d at 428–29 (discussing information known to the complaining employee but not revealed in his complaint in analyzing the reasonableness of the employee's belief that the employer violated Title VII).

Finally, we consider the setting in which Tennort voiced her complaint. This is where the reactive nature of Tennort's complaint sets it apart from the more common proactive opposition case. Tennort was rehired at the beginning of the 2011–2012 school year. As part of the rehiring process, she received a pamphlet informing her that "sexual harassment"—including "unwelcomed sexual . . . comments" and "other verbal or physical conduct of a sexual nature that has the purpose or effect of . . . creating an intimidating, hostile, or offensive work environment"—is a type of workplace "discrimination" that Rite Way does not tolerate. Shortly thereafter, she saw a new supervisor make two sexually-fraught and unwelcome comments to a subordinate within the span of a week. And then she was asked about one of those incidents by a member of Rite Way's human resources department—using language strongly insinuating that Rite Way would rather Tennort *not* corroborate Quarles's sexual harassment complaint and would subject her to reprisal if she did. If Tennort had not yet reached a view that Harris violated federal employment law when he made offensive comments and gestures about Quarles's rear end, the circumstances surrounding her questioning may very well have caused her to do so. We thus conclude that there is a fact issue concerning whether Tennort could have reasonably believed that the conduct about which she chose to speak violated Title VII.

V

Rite Way asks us to affirm the district court on the basis of an alternative argument presented below, which focused on the sufficiency of the EEOC's causation evidence. It emphasizes certain customer complaints "concerning areas of the school for which Tennort was responsible," arguing that this evidence of Tennort's deficiencies is "uncontroverted." The customer complaints constitute strong evidence of a nonretaliatory justification for Tennort's termination.

But the EEOC has competing evidence that would allow a jury to find that the customer complaints were a pretextual reason for firing Tennort after she corroborated a sexual harassment claim made against her supervisor. This evidence includes the strong temporal proximity between her written report and her termination. *See Reeves v. Sanderson Plumbing Prods., Inc.,* 530 U.S. 133, 143, 148–49, 120 S.Ct. 2097, 147 L.Ed.2d 105 (2000) (noting that "the evidence establishing the plaintiff's prima facie case" remains relevant to pretext and that "the strength of the plaintiff's prima facie case" will factor into whether employer is entitled to judgment as a matter of law (citations omitted)). It includes the fact that Tennort's two-year employment record with Rite Way was unimpeached until she spoke out about Harris's actions and soon thereafter became a problem employee. *See, e.g., Evans v. City of Houston,* 246 F.3d 344, 354–56 (5th Cir.2001) (vacating summary judgment based on, among other evidence, "the close temporal proximity between [Plaintiff's] appearance at her co-worker's [race and age discrimination] grievance hearing and her demotion" and "the lack of *any* documentary evidence dated before her appearance or demotion that would tend to support a theory of disciplinary problems"). And it includes two cryptic statements from her supervisors from which a jury could infer retaliatory intent. First, the HR manager who took her statement warned "you know what they do to people who do stuff like this." Second, the supervisor who replaced Harris—Harris's own brother-in-law—told Tennort on the first day she began working under him that Mississippi is an "at will" state and that she would be denied unemployment benefits when she was fired. Statements such as these evincing the type of animus prohibited by Title VII can be considered at the pretext stage. *See Goudeau v. Nat'l Oilwell Varco, L.P.,* 793 F.3d 470, 478 (5th Cir.2015) (discussing how ageist comments, along with other evidence, could support a jury finding of discriminatory intent); *see also Wright v. Southland Corp.,* 187 F.3d 1287, 1305–06 (11th Cir.1999) (stating that a jury could find retaliatory intent on the basis of "[t]he threat of 'You will regret it,' made by a human resources director" to employee who had filed an EEOC complaint); *Rhoads v. FDIC,* 257 F.3d 373, 392–94 (4th Cir.2001) (reversing summary judgment because there was sufficient evidence of retaliatory intent, including a supervisor's statement that plaintiff "would regret" consulting with a lawyer about her American with Disabilities Act claim).

This is not to say that the evidence would not support Rite Way's more mundane version of events. But the difficult task of resolving this "conflict in substantial evidence" falls to the jury. *Long,* 88 F.3d at 308 (internal quotation marks and citation omitted). We REVERSE and REMAND for further proceedings.

QUESTIONS

1. Do you think that the plaintiff's job duties influenced the Court's holding in *Breeden*?
2. Would the result be different if the word used in *Breeden* was the "C" word or the "N" word? What additional information would you need to know to answer this question?
3. What do you think of the Fifth Circuit's efforts to establish a "zone of conduct" that falls short of an actual violation but could be reasonably perceived to violate Title VII? Is this an inevitable evolution of *Payne,* or does it change the rule? Wouldn't a "zone of conduct" approach require a detailed analysis and review of the facts of each individual case?
4. What is the distinction between the reasonableness of a plaintiff's belief and whether the plaintiff actually holds the belief? Should an employer, in its defense, attack both prongs?
5. What policy reasons motivated the court to extend protection to comments made in a "reactive" context? What if the employee was questioned and said, "Yes, it was a sexual joke and I liked it. Funny as all get out!"? Is it now unlawful to fire the employee for the comment?

Problem 37-2

Susan is an accountant at a business who normally works only during the day. One evening she goes to her office to retrieve some work papers that she meant to bring home. Her office is located off the main corridor in a relatively secluded spot. When she enters her office, she finds a supervisor and an employee having sex on her desk. She then learns that this has been going on for the last few months. Susan files a complaint with human resources, but she is told that she really shouldn't complain and that it is best if she just makes sure to "wash down" her desk each morning.

Susan protests vigorously, but eventually she leaves the meeting without any resolution. Susan is terminated a few weeks later. Her lawyer argues that her complaint was related to her opposition to a hostile work environment that amounted to sex discrimination. She alleges that she reasonably believed that she was opposing a practice made unlawful under Title VII. Can she prevail?

Problem 37-3

A female employee claims that a supervisor is making improper sexual comments to her. She tells him to stop. Is the request "opposing" unlawful conduct and thus considered protected activity? Take as a given that a single improper comment does not create an unlawful hostile environment based upon sex. Does this change your answer? Does your answer depend upon whether the supervisor does, in fact, stop making the comments? Is there such an idea as preemptive opposition that should be judicially grafted onto the language of the opposition clause? Consider these questions in light of the next case.

Does the following case provide a principled way to look at an employee who opposes one comment or action she reasonably believes may turn into an unlawful practice but is still inchoate? As you read the case, consider whether the opposition clause should protect premature opposition.

DeMasters v. Carilion Clinic

796 F.3d 409, 417 (4th Cir. 2015).

Krause, Judge.

Title VII's Opposition Clause, by its terms, prohibits retaliation against an employee who has "opposed any practice made an unlawful employment practice" by Title VII. 42 U.S.C. § 2000e–3(a). The Supreme Court has defined "oppose" in this context by looking to its ordinary meaning: "to resist or antagonize . . .; to contend against; to confront; resist; withstand, . . . to be hostile or adverse to, as in opinion." *Crawford v. Metro. Gov't of Nashville & Davidson Cnty., Tenn.*, 555 U.S. 271, 276, 129 S.Ct. 846, 172 L.Ed.2d 650 (2009) (internal citations omitted) (quoting Webster's New International Dictionary 1710 (2d ed.1958); Random House Dictionary of the English Language 1359 (2d ed.1987)). This broad definition led the Court to conclude that the threshold for oppositional conduct is not onerous. Instead, "[w]hen an employee communicates to her employer a belief that the employer has engaged in . . . a form of employment discrimination, that communication virtually always constitutes the employee's opposition to the activity." *Crawford*, 555 U.S. at 276, 129 S.Ct. 846 (internal quotation marks omitted) (citing 2 EEOC Compliance Manual §§ 8–II–B(1), (2), p. 614:0003 (Mar. 2003)).

This Circuit, as well as the other Courts of Appeals, also has articulated an expansive view of what constitutes oppositional conduct, recognizing that it "encompasses utilizing informal grievance procedures as well as staging informal protests and voicing one's opinions in order to bring attention to an employer's discriminatory activities."

And while the oppositional activity must be directed to "an unlawful employment practice" under Title VII, 42 U.S.C. § 2000e–3(a), this Circuit's recent en banc opinion in Boyer-Liberto made clear that we should also interpret "unlawful employment practice" broadly. 786 F.3d at 282. Thus, "an employee is protected when she opposes 'not only . . . employment actions actually unlawful under Title VII but also employment actions [she] reasonably believes to be unlawful,' " and the Title VII violation to which the oppositional communication is directed "may be complete, or it may be in progress."

In sum, nothing in the language of the Opposition Clause nor in its interpretation by the courts supports a myopic analysis under which an employee's opposition must be evaluated as a series of discrete acts. 42 U.S.C. § 2000e–3(a). On the contrary, as the Third Circuit has observed in a similar context, "[t]hese determinations depend on the totality of the circumstances, as [a] play cannot be understood on the basis of some of its scenes but only on its entire performance, and similarly, a discrimination analysis must concentrate not on individual incidents, but on the overall scenario." *Moore*, 461 F.3d at 346 (second alteration in original) (citations and internal quotation marks omitted). Likewise, in *Collazo*, where the plaintiff had arranged meetings with the HR department for a co-worker and then complained to HR about problems with his company's ongoing internal investigation of the co-worker's complaint, the First Circuit, reviewing the full range of the plaintiff's conduct, held that his "persistent efforts to help [the victim] initiate her sexual harassment complaint and urge Human Resources to act upon that complaint" constituted protected opposition activity. *Id.* at 43–44, 47.

. . . .

QUESTIONS

1. How can you square this case with the statutory language?
2. To what extent should the remedial purpose of Title VII play a role in the analysis?
3. Should courts extend protection to employees who oppose what they reasonably believe will become an unlawful practice but does not yet rise to that level? Should this be considered premature opposition, or opposition to an incipient violation?

Mastery Problem 37-1

Jocelyn is a bartender in a hotel lounge. She is African-American. When a customer asks her to prepare an unusual drink, she cuts through the kitchen to see another bartender in a different part of the hotel to determine how to make it. As she is walking through the kitchen, the kitchen manager yells at her in vulgar and racially derogatory terms, saying that he has told her to keep out of his kitchen. They have had altercations in the past. She immediately reports the comment to the hotel manager. Two days later she is terminated and she sues for a violation of Title VII. What significance for her case will the opposition clause have?

Mastery Problem 37-2

Leah works in a large office. She went to a general manager and reported that her supervisor has made a few inappropriate sexual comments to her, has repeatedly given her the "elevator look," and that as a result she feels uncomfortable in his presence. The general manager immediately went to the supervisor and instructed him to apologize. The supervisor gave a superficial and limited apology, telling Leah: "I did nothing wrong to you, but I am sorry if you took anything the wrong way."

The general manger then accompanied Leah to human resources where she made a formal complaint in detail under the company's policy. The general manager says nothing during the meeting. The general manager tells Leah that he will set up another meeting with human resources, but he is fired before the meeting takes place. The employer conducts an internal investigation that concludes there is no credible evidence that Leah was subjected to sexual harassment. Did the general manager engage in protected opposition?

Conclusion

Title VII protects employees who oppose illegal discriminatory conduct in the workplace, even if they are not targets of the discrimination themselves. The protection against retaliation is not triggered unless the underlying behavior is arguably a violation of Title VII. There is some movement toward recognizing that opposing conduct that opposes an incipient violation of Title VII is protected.

C. Remedies for Immigrant Workers

Key Concept

- This single Lesson section focuses on the complexities of awarding damages to immigrant workers who do not have work authorization but who suffer a violation of their employment law rights.

Lesson 38:
Immigration Law and Worker Protection

Objectives and Expected Learning Outcomes

In this Lesson, we return to the specific problems encountered by immigrants in the workplace. In Lesson 6, we learned that some undocumented immigrants might have work authorization, and even those who do not have authorization fall within the broad definition of "employee" under employment law statutes and caselaw. In this Lesson, you will consider the difficulty that immigrants will face in asserting employment law rights, since damages are often based on lost wages. Additionally, complex issues arise when state law seeks to extend protections to immigrant workers, but federal immigration law seeks to prevent them from being in the workforce.

In Lesson 6, we analyzed the various ways in which immigrants participate in the labor economy through various forms of work authorization. In this Lesson, we focus on the ability of immigrant workers to take advantage of employment law protections. In 1986, Congress expressly deepened the intersection between immigration and employment by making the workplace an important site of immigration enforcement. The Immigration Reform and Control Act (IRCA) established sanctions for employers who knowingly hire unauthorized workers but did not punish immigrant workers who were employed without authorization. Even though unauthorized work is not punished directly, the law had serious detrimental effects on the rights of immigrants working without authorization. For example, many statutory remedies for employer violations include the possibility of reinstatement of the injured employee, but this remedy is problematic when the undocumented worker cannot be employed legally. If reinstatement is not an available remedy, how can regulators ensure that the employer faces consequences for its violation of workplace laws? The following case was anticipated broadly as the first effort to begin answering these questions after the passage of the IRCA.

1. The *Hoffman Plastic* Case

Hoffman Plastic Compounds, Inc. v. National Labor Relations Board

535 U.S. 137 (2002).

Chief Justice Rehnquist delivered the opinion of the Court.

The National Labor Relations Board (Board) awarded backpay to an undocumented alien who has never been legally authorized to work in the United States. We hold that such relief is foreclosed by federal immigration policy, as expressed by Congress in the Immigration Reform and Control Act of 1986 (IRCA).

Petitioner Hoffman Plastic Compounds, Inc. (petitioner or Hoffman), custom-formulates chemical compounds for businesses that manufacture pharmaceutical, construction, and household products. In May 1988, petitioner hired Jose Castro to operate various blending machines that "mix and cook" the particular formulas per customer order. Before being hired for this position, Castro presented documents that appeared to verify his authorization to work in the United States. In December 1988, the United Rubber, Cork, Linoleum, and Plastic Workers of America, AFL-CIO, began a union-organizing campaign at petitioner's production plant. Castro and several other employees supported the organizing campaign and distributed authorization cards to co-workers. In January 1989, Hoffman laid off Castro and other employees engaged in these organizing activities.

Three years later, in January 1992, respondent Board found that Hoffman unlawfully selected four employees, including Castro, for layoff "in order to rid itself of known union supporters" in violation of § 8(a)(3) of the National Labor Relations Act (NLRA).To remedy this violation, the Board ordered that Hoffman (1) cease and desist from further violations of the NLRA, (2) post a detailed notice to its employees regarding the remedial order, and (3) offer reinstatement and backpay to the four affected employees. Hoffman entered into a stipulation with the Board's General Counsel and agreed to abide by the Board's order.

In June 1993, the parties proceeded to a compliance hearing before an Administrative Law Judge (ALJ) to determine the amount of backpay owed to each discriminatee. On the final day of the hearing, Castro testified that he was born in Mexico and that he had never been legally admitted to, or authorized to work in, the United States. He admitted gaining employment with Hoffman only after tendering a birth certificate belonging to a friend who was born in Texas. He also admitted that he used this birth certificate to fraudulently obtain a California driver's license and a Social Security card, and to fraudulently obtain employment following his layoff by Hoffman. Neither Castro nor the Board's General Counsel offered any evidence that Castro had applied or intended to apply for legal authorization to work in the United States. Based on this testimony, the ALJ found the Board precluded from awarding Castro backpay or reinstatement as such relief would be contrary to *Sure-Tan, Inc. v. NLRB*, 467 U.S. 883 (1984), and in conflict with IRCA, which makes it unlawful for employers knowingly to hire undocumented workers or for employees to use fraudulent documents to establish employment eligibility.

In September 1998 . . . the Board reversed with respect to backpay. Citing its earlier decision in A.P.R.A. Fuel Oil Buyers Group, Inc., 320 NLRB 408 (1995), the Board determined that "the most effective way to accommodate and further the immigration policies embodied in [IRCA] is to provide the protections and remedies of the [NLRA] to undocumented workers in the same manner as to other employees." The Board thus found that Castro was entitled to $66,951 of backpay, plus interest. . . .

We granted certiorari and now reverse. This case exemplifies the principle that the Board's discretion to select and fashion remedies for violations of the NLRA, though generally broad, is not unlimited. . . .

> [W]e have [ ] never deferred to the Board's remedial preferences where such preferences potentially trench upon federal statutes and policies unrelated to the NLRA. Thus, we have precluded the Board from enforcing orders found in conflict with the Bankruptcy Code, and precluded the Board from selecting remedies pursuant to its own interpretation of the Interstate Commerce Act. Our

> decision in *Sure-Tan* followed this line of cases and set aside an award closely analogous to the award challenged here. There we confronted for the first time a potential conflict between the NLRA and federal immigration policy, as then expressed in the Immigration and Nationality Act (INA). Two companies had unlawfully reported alien-employees to the Immigration and Naturalization Service (INS) in retaliation for union activity. Rather than face INS sanction, the employees voluntarily departed to Mexico. The Board investigated and found the companies acted in violation of §§ 8(a)(1) and (3) of the NLRA. The Board's ensuing order directed the companies to reinstate the affected workers and pay them six months' backpay.

We affirmed the Board's determination that the NLRA applied to undocumented workers, reasoning that the immigration laws "as presently written" expressed only a " 'peripheral concern' " with the employment of illegal aliens. "For whatever reason," Congress had not "made it a separate criminal offense" for employers to hire an illegal alien, or for an illegal alien "to accept employment after entering this country illegally." Therefore, we found "no reason to conclude that application of the NLRA to employment practices affecting such aliens would necessarily conflict with the terms of the INA."

With respect to the Board's selection of remedies, however, we found its authority limited by federal immigration policy. For example, the Board was prohibited from effectively rewarding a violation of the immigration laws by reinstating workers not authorized to reenter the United States. Thus, to avoid "a potential conflict with the INA," the Board's reinstatement order had to be conditioned upon proof of "the employees' legal reentry." "Similarly," with respect to backpay, we stated: "[T]he employees must be deemed 'unavailable' for work (and the accrual of backpay therefore tolled) during any period when they were not lawfully entitled to be present and employed in the United States." "[I]n light of the practical workings of the immigration laws," such remedial limitations were appropriate even if they led to "[t]he probable unavailability of the [NLRA's] more effective remedies."

. . . .

It is against this decisional background that we turn to the question presented here.

. . . .

The *Southern S. S. Co.* line of cases established that where the Board's chosen remedy trenches upon a federal statute or policy outside the Board's competence to administer, the Board's remedy may be required to yield. . . . In 1986, two years after *Sure-Tan,* Congress enacted IRCA, a comprehensive scheme prohibiting the employment of illegal aliens in the United States. As we have previously noted, IRCA "forcefully" made combating the employment of illegal aliens central to "[t]he policy of immigration law." It did so by establishing an extensive "employment verification system," § 1324a(a)(1), designed to deny employment to aliens who (a) are not lawfully present in the United States, or (b) are not lawfully authorized to work in the United States, § 1324a(h)(3). This verification system is critical to the IRCA regime. To enforce it, IRCA mandates that employers verify the identity and eligibility of all new hires by examining specified documents before they begin work. If an alien applicant is unable to present the required documentation, the unauthorized alien cannot be hired.

Similarly, if an employer unknowingly hires an unauthorized alien, or if the alien becomes unauthorized while employed, the employer is compelled to discharge the worker upon discovery of the worker's undocumented status. Employers who violate IRCA are punished by civil fines, and may be subject to criminal prosecution. IRCA also makes it a crime for an unauthorized alien to subvert the employer verification system by tendering fraudulent documents. It thus prohibits aliens from using or attempting to use "any forged, counterfeit, altered, or falsely made document" or "any document lawfully issued to or with respect to a person other than the possessor" for purposes of obtaining employment in the United States. Aliens who use or attempt to use such documents are subject to fines and criminal prosecution. There is no dispute that Castro's use of false documents to obtain employment with Hoffman violated these provisions.

Under the IRCA regime, it is impossible for an undocumented alien to obtain employment in the United States without some party directly contravening explicit congressional policies. Either the undocumented alien tenders fraudulent identification, which subverts the cornerstone of IRCA's enforcement mechanism, or the employer knowingly hires the undocumented alien in direct contradiction of its IRCA obligations. The Board asks that we overlook this fact and allow it to award backpay to an illegal alien for years of work not performed, for wages that could not lawfully have been earned, and for a job obtained in the first instance by a criminal fraud. We find, however, that awarding backpay to illegal aliens runs counter to policies underlying IRCA, policies the Board has no authority to enforce or administer. Therefore, as we have consistently held in like circumstances, the award lies beyond the bounds of the Board's remedial discretion.

The Board contends that awarding limited backpay to Castro "reasonably accommodates" IRCA, because, in the Board's view, such an award is not "inconsistent" with IRCA. The Board argues that because the backpay period was closed as of the date Hoffman learned of Castro's illegal status, Hoffman could have employed Castro during the backpay period without violating IRCA. The Board further argues that while IRCA criminalized the misuse of documents, "it did not make violators ineligible for back pay awards or other compensation flowing from employment secured by the misuse of such documents." This latter statement, of course, proves little: The mutiny statute in *Southern S. S. Co.,* and the INA in *Sure-Tan,* were likewise understandably silent with respect to such things as backpay awards under the NLRA. What matters here, and what sinks both of the Board's claims, is that Congress has expressly made it criminally punishable for an alien to obtain employment with false documents. There is no reason to think that Congress nonetheless intended to permit backpay where but for an employer's unfair labor practices, an alien-employee would have remained in the United States illegally, and continued to work illegally, all the while successfully evading apprehension by immigration authorities. Far from "accommodating" IRCA, the Board's position, recognizing employer misconduct but discounting the misconduct of illegal alien employees, subverts it.

Indeed, awarding backpay in a case like this not only trivializes the immigration laws, it also condones and encourages future violations. The Board admits that had the INS detained Castro, or had Castro obeyed the law and departed to Mexico, Castro would have lost his right to backpay. Castro thus qualifies for the Board's award only by remaining inside the United States illegally. Similarly, Castro cannot mitigate damages, a duty our cases require, without triggering new IRCA violations, either by tendering false documents to employers or by finding employers willing to ignore IRCA and hire illegal workers. The Board here has failed to even consider this tension.

We therefore conclude that allowing the Board to award backpay to illegal aliens would unduly trench upon explicit statutory prohibitions critical to federal immigration policy, as expressed in IRCA. It would encourage the successful evasion of apprehension by immigration authorities, condone prior violations of the immigration laws, and encourage future violations.

However broad the Board's discretion to fashion remedies when dealing only with the NLRA, it is not so unbounded as to authorize this sort of an award.

Lack of authority to award backpay does not mean that the employer gets off scot-free. The Board here has already imposed other significant sanctions against Hoffman—sanctions Hoffman does not challenge. These include orders that Hoffman cease and desist its violations of the NLRA, and that it conspicuously post a notice to employees setting forth their rights under the NLRA and detailing its prior unfair practices. Hoffman will be subject to contempt proceedings should it fail to comply with these orders. We have deemed such "traditional remedies" sufficient to effectuate national labor policy regardless of whether the "spur and catalyst" of backpay accompanies them. As we concluded in *Sure-Tan,* "in light of the practical workings of the immigration laws," any "perceived deficienc[y] in the NLRA's existing remedial arsenal" must be "addressed by congressional action," not the courts. In light of IRCA, this statement is even truer today.

The judgment of the Court of Appeals is reversed.

QUESTIONS

1. Should the policies underlying the Immigration and Nationality Act trump the policies underlying the National Labor Relations Act?
2. Should the *Hoffman* holding extend to other employment laws, such as the Fair Labor Standards Act or Title VII, the employment anti-discrimination statute? Do the values and norms underlying these statutes make for a stronger case for worker remedies regardless of immigration status?

---

2. Navigating the Post-*Hoffman* World

In response to *Hoffman*, states passed laws to ensure that all employees would receive full workplace protections regardless of their immigration status. Consider the following California statute:

> All protections, rights, and remedies available under state law, except any reinstatement remedy prohibited by federal law, are available to all

> individuals *regardless of immigration status* who have applied for employment, or who are or who have been employed, in this state.

California Labor Code § 1171.5. This statute is not necessarily at odds with federal law, but it certainly heightens the complexity of the intersection between immigration and employment law. In the following case, the California Supreme Court reviewed state authority to protect employees regardless of immigration status, given the preemptive effect of federal law.

SALAS V. SIERRA CHEMICAL CO.

327 P.3d 797 (Cal. 2014).

KENNARD, J.—

Plaintiff sued his former employer under the California Fair Employment and Housing Act (FEHA; Gov. Code, § 12900 et seq.), alleging that defendant employer failed to reasonably accommodate his physical disability and refused to rehire him in retaliation for plaintiff's having filed a workers' compensation claim. Thereafter, defendant learned of information suggesting that plaintiff, to gain employment with defendant, had used another man's Social Security number.

The trial court denied defendant employer's motion for summary judgment. When defendant sought a writ of mandate in the Court of Appeal, that court issued an alternative writ. In response, the trial court vacated its order denying defendant's motion for summary judgment, and it entered an order granting the motion. Plaintiff employee appealed from the ensuing judgment, which the Court of Appeal affirmed. It held that plaintiff's action was barred by the doctrines of after-acquired evidence and unclean hands (based on information defendant acquired during discovery showing wrongdoing by plaintiff), and that here application of those doctrines was not precluded by Senate Bill No. 1818. That state law declares: "All protections, rights, and remedies available under state law, except any reinstatement remedy prohibited by federal law, are available to all individuals *regardless of immigration status* who have applied for employment, or who are or who have been employed, in this state."

After we granted plaintiff employee's petition for review, we asked both parties for supplemental briefing on whether federal immigration law preempts California's Senate Bill No. 1818, an issue the parties had not raised before.

We conclude: (1) Senate Bill No. 1818, which extends state law employee protections and remedies to all workers "regardless of immigration status," is not preempted by federal immigration law except to the extent it authorizes an award of lost pay damages for any period after the employer's discovery of an employee's ineligibility to work in the United States, and (2) contrary to the Court of Appeal's holdings, the doctrines of after-acquired evidence and unclean hands are not complete defenses to a worker's claims under California's FEHA, although they do affect the availability of remedies. Accordingly, we reverse and remand the matter for further proceedings.

. . . Defendant Sierra Chemical Co. manufactures, packages, and distributes chemicals for treating water, including water in swimming pools. As the weather gets warmer in spring and summer, consumer demand for defendant's products increases, while in fall and winter demand decreases, which in turn results in defendant's seasonal layoffs of many production line employees. Those laid-off workers generally are recalled to work when consumer demand rises.

In April 2003, plaintiff Vicente Salas applied for a job with defendant, providing a Social Security number and a resident alien card. He completed and signed, under penalty of perjury, federal Immigration and Naturalization form I-9, in which he listed the same Social Security number he had given to defendant, and he attached to the form a copy of a Social Security card with that number. He also signed an employee's Internal Revenue Service withholding form W-4, which had the same Social Security number he had given defendant. In May 2003, plaintiff began working on defendant's production line.

In October 2003, plaintiff was laid off because of defendant's seasonal reduction of production line workers. In March 2004, when plaintiff was called back to work, he used the same Social Security number as before, and the same number again appeared on federal I-9 and W-4 forms he completed. In December 2004, plaintiff was again laid off. When he was recalled to work in March 2005, the federal W-4 form he signed had the same Social Security number he had provided earlier. Plaintiff was not laid off during the fall and winter of 2005.

In late 2004 or early 2005, plaintiff received a letter from the federal Social Security Administration stating that his name and Social Security number did not match the agency's records. Some of his coworkers received similar letters. Plaintiff asserts that a few days later defendant's production manager,

Leo Huizar, told the workers not to worry about discrepancies with Social Security numbers because as long as the company's president was satisfied with their work they would not be terminated.

In March 2006, plaintiff injured his back while stacking crates on defendant's production line, and he was taken to a hospital. The next day, plaintiff returned to work under a physician's restrictions that he was not to lift anything weighing more than 10 to 15 pounds; he was not to sit, stand, or walk for prolonged periods; and he was to limit bending, twisting, and stooping at the waist. Defendant employer modified plaintiff's work duties accordingly. On June 9, after giving defendant a doctor's release, plaintiff resumed full duties.

On August 16, 2006, plaintiff again injured his back while stacking crates and was taken to the hospital. That same day he returned to work, finishing his shift under the same work restrictions as before. Thereafter, plaintiff filed a workers' compensation claim for his workplace back injury. Plaintiff still came to work, performing modified duties, until December 15, 2006, when he was laid off during defendant's seasonal reduction of workers.

In either late January or early February of 2007, plaintiff started working for another company. According to plaintiff's declaration filed in opposition to defendant employer's motion for summary judgment, Leo Huizar, defendant's production manager, telephoned him in March 2007. Huizar asked plaintiff if he wanted to return to work and if he had fully recovered from his back injuries. When plaintiff said he was still seeing a doctor, Huizar responded that plaintiff could "not return to work like that," adding it would violate defendant employer's policies to do so.

On May 1, defendant sent plaintiff a letter stating that it was recalling laid-off employees and informing him to call or come to defendant's office to make arrangements to return to work. The letter also told him to bring "a copy of your doctor's release stating that you have been released to return to full duty."

According to Huizar's declaration in support of defendant's motion for summary judgment, plaintiff contacted Huizar on May 6, 2007, and said that he had not reported for work as he had not yet been released by his physician but that he had an appointment on June 12 to obtain the release. Huizar then agreed to hold the job open for plaintiff until plaintiff obtained the doctor's release, and Huizar told plaintiff to call him if plaintiff was unable to get the release. Huizar never heard from plaintiff again.

In August 2007, plaintiff sued defendant. Plaintiff alleged two causes of action. The first cause of action alleged that plaintiff was disabled and that defendant failed to provide reasonable accommodations for his disability, in violation of California's FEHA. The second cause of action alleged that defendant wrongfully denied plaintiff employment, in violation of the public policy expressed in the FEHA, by retaliating against him for filing a workers' compensation claim against defendant and for being disabled. Both causes of action sought to recover lost wages, compensatory damages for emotional distress, punitive damages, and attorney fees.

After trial was set for April 9, 2009, both parties filed motions in limine. In one of his motions, plaintiff employee acknowledged that it is a criminal offense under federal law (18 U.S.C. § 1546(b)(2)) and a felony under state law (Pen. Code, § 114) for a person to use false identification documents to conceal the person's true citizenship or resident alien status. Plaintiff stated that he would testify at trial and assert his privilege against self-incrimination under the Fifth Amendment to the United States Constitution if asked about his immigration status. He asked that he be allowed to assert the privilege outside the jury's presence and that the court and counsel not comment at trial on his assertion of the privilege. This information led defendant employer to investigate the authenticity of the documents plaintiff had given to defendant in connection with plaintiff's employment by defendant.

On July 24, 2009, defendant filed a motion for summary judgment, which is at issue here. Defendant sought a determination by the trial court that defendant was entitled to a judgment as a matter of law under the legal doctrines of after-acquired evidence and unclean hands, based on plaintiff's fraudulent use of another person's Social Security number and card to obtain employment with defendant. In support, defendant submitted a declaration from Kelly R. Tenney saying that he is a resident of North Carolina and has a certain Social Security number, which is the one plaintiff used when he applied for a job with defendant. Tenney said in his declaration that he did not know plaintiff and had given no one permission to use his Social Security number. Defendant also provided a declaration from its president, Stanley Kinder, stating that defendant has a long-standing policy of not hiring anyone who is prohibited by federal law from working in the United States, and that defendant would immediately discharge any employee upon defendant's discovery that the employee had given defendant false information or documents to establish work eligibility in the United States.

When the trial court denied defendant employer's motion for summary judgment, defendant sought a writ of mandate from the Court of Appeal. When that court issued an alternative writ, the trial court vacated its earlier order denying defendant's motion and entered a new order granting the motion. Plaintiff appealed from the ensuing judgment, which the Court of Appeal affirmed. The Court of Appeal concluded that plaintiff's claims were barred by both the doctrine of after-acquired evidence and the doctrine of unclean hands.

The Court of Appeal reasoned that the doctrine of after-acquired evidence barred plaintiff's causes of action because he had misrepresented to defendant employer his eligibility under federal law to work in the United States. It also held that plaintiff's claims were subject to the doctrine of unclean hands because he had falsely used another person's Social Security number in seeking employment with defendant, he was disqualified under federal law from working in the United States, and his conduct exposed defendant to penalties under federal law.

II

The threshold inquiry here is whether the federal Immigration Reform and Control Act of 1986 (8 U.S.C. § 1101 et seq.), also known as IRCA, preempts application of the antidiscrimination provisions of California's FEHA to workers who are unauthorized aliens. For the reasons given below, we conclude that the FEHA is generally not preempted by federal immigration law, but that federal preemption does bar an award of lost pay damages under the FEHA for any period of time *after* an employer's discovery of the employee's ineligibility under federal law to work in the United States.

Federal immigration law requires employers to verify the identity and work eligibility of new employees; upon an employer's discovery of a worker's unauthorized immigration status, termination is required. An *employer* who violates these federal law provisions is subject to civil fines and to criminal prosecution. A *worker* who uses false documents to gain employment is likewise subject to civil fines and criminal prosecution.

The California law at issue here is not only the FEHA, but also Senate Bill No. 1818, which added to California's statutory scheme four nearly identical provisions. . . Particularly pertinent here is Government Code section 7285, which states:

The Legislature finds and declares the following:

> (a) All protections, rights, and remedies available under state law, except any reinstatement remedy prohibited by federal law, are available to all individuals *regardless of immigration status* who have applied for employment, or who are or who have been employed, in this state.
>
> (b) For purposes of enforcing state labor, employment, civil rights, and employee housing laws, a person's immigration status is irrelevant to the issue of liability, and in proceedings or discovery undertaken to enforce those state laws no inquiry shall be permitted into a person's immigration status except where the person seeking to make the inquiry has shown by clear and convincing evidence that the inquiry is necessary in order to comply with federal immigration law.
>
> (c) The provisions of this section are declaratory of existing law.
>
> (d) The provisions of this section are severable. If any provision of this section or its application is held invalid, that invalidity shall not affect other provisions or applications that can be given effect without the invalid provision or application.

The California Legislature enacted Senate Bill No. 1818 in 2002 in response to the United States Supreme Court's decision earlier the same year in Hoffman Plastic Compounds v. NLRB, 535 U.S. 137 (2002) . . . .

Under the United States Constitution's supremacy clause (U.S. Const., art. VI, cl. 2), federal law can preempt or supersede state law. California law, as established by Senate Bill No. 1818, makes all state-provided worker protections, rights, and remedies (except reinstatement prohibited by federal law) "available to all individuals regardless of immigration status." . . . At issue here [ ] is whether federal immigration law preempts a *state* antidiscrimination law enforced through a *private action* for damages.

. . . California's FEHA, at issue here, differs significantly from the NLRA, at issue in *Hoffman.* In enacting the FEHA, California's Legislature sought to safeguard the rights of all persons to seek, obtain, and hold employment without discrimination on account of various characteristics, including race, national origin, physical disability, and medical condition. To combat invidious employment discrimination, the FEHA's remedial scheme depends heavily on private causes of action in which compensatory damages, including lost pay, may be awarded.

The federal NLRA, to achieve its goals, does not similarly rely on private causes of action or the remedy of lost pay damages. Rather, the NLRB can adequately enforce the NLRA's policies by issuing remedial orders enforceable through its contempt power. Because of this critical difference between California's FEHA and the federal NLRA, relating to the role played by lost pay awards in achieving California's remedial legislative goal, we do not consider the high court's decision in *Hoffman* controlling here.

. . . In addressing the issue of federal preemption, we note, preliminarily, that the federal Immigration Reform and Control Act of 1986 does not preempt all state laws relating to unauthorized aliens. In the words of the high court: "Power to regulate immigration is unquestionably exclusively a federal power. But the [United States Supreme] Court has never held that every state enactment which in any way deals with aliens is a regulation of immigration and thus *per se* pre-empted by this constitutional power, whether latent or exercised." The high court reaffirmed that observation recently in Arizona v. United States, 567 U.S. ___ (2012).

The high court in *Arizona v. U.S.* reiterated the three established types of federal law preemption. Federal law preempts a state law when: (1) Congress, acting within its authority, enacts an express provision requiring preemption; (2) the federal regulation's reach is so pervasive as to leave no room for state regulation, or the federal interest is so dominant that it will be assumed that federal law displaces any state law on the same subject; or (3) the state law conflicts with federal law, either because compliance with both laws is impossible or because the state law is an obstacle to accomplishing congressional objectives. Because "[f]ederalism, central to the constitutional design, adopts the principle that both the National and State Governments have elements of sovereignty the other is bound to respect", the presumption is *against* federal preemption of state law. In preemption analysis, therefore, "courts should assume that 'the historic police powers of the States' are not superseded 'unless that was the clear and manifest purpose of Congress.' "

We now apply these principles to the question here of whether federal immigration law (specifically, the federal Immigration Reform and Control Act of 1986) preempts California's Senate Bill No. 1818, which was enacted in 2002.

Turning to the *first* type of preemption—express preemption—we note that the federal Immigration Reform and Control Act of 1986 has an express preemption provision, which states: "The provisions of this section preempt any State or local law *imposing civil or criminal sanctions* (other than through licensing and similar laws) *upon those who employ . . . unauthorized aliens.*" We agree with plaintiff employee that this provision is inapplicable here. Rather than asserting any claim of employer wrongdoing in hiring unauthorized aliens, plaintiff seeks in this lawsuit to impose civil sanctions upon defendant employer for alleged violations of California's FEHA, which prohibits invidious employment discrimination. Accordingly, the relevant federal immigration law does not *expressly* preempt California's provisions, enacted by Senate Bill No. 1818, granting state employment law protections to all workers "regardless of immigration status."

. . . .

We now consider the *second* type of preemption—field preemption—which occurs *either* when the *federal regulation is so pervasive* as to leave no room for state regulation, or when the *federal interest is* " '*so dominant* that the federal system will be assumed to preclude enforcement of state laws on the same subject' ". Some years before its *Arizona* decision, the United States Supreme Court addressed the dominant federal interest aspect of field preemption in *De Canas*, supra, 424 U.S. 351. At issue there was the constitutionality of a former California law that prohibited employers from knowingly employing nonresident aliens if their employment adversely affected lawful resident workers. *De Canas* held that the federal interest in regulating employment of unauthorized aliens was not so dominant as to preclude state laws on the same subject, although the high court ultimately did not resolve the preemption issue, concluding that issues regarding the proper construction of the challenged state law needed to be resolved first by state courts. Plaintiff employee here relies on this statement by the high court in *De Canas:* "States possess broad authority under their police powers to regulate the employment relationship to protect workers within the State. Child labor laws, minimum and other wage laws, laws affecting occupational health and safety, and workmen's compensation laws are only a few examples." Because *De Canas* dealt only with the dominant federal interest aspect of field preemption, it did not address the federal regulation pervasiveness aspect, which is at issue here and which we explore below.

At the time of *De Canas,* federal immigration law expressed at best "a peripheral concern with employment of illegal entrants." That changed 10 years after the high court's 1976 *De Canas* decision, when Congress enacted the Immigration Reform and Control Act of 1986. That law, with its focus on employment of unauthorized aliens, " 'forcefully' made combating the employment of illegal aliens central to '[t]he policy of immigration law.' " The question before us: Has federal immigration regulation now become so pervasive as to leave no room for state employment laws that extend antidiscrimination protections with lost pay remedies to employees who are unauthorized aliens?

The high court has recently pointed out, as noted earlier, that the states' historic police powers are *not* preempted " 'unless that was the clear and manifest purpose of Congress' ", and it has acknowledged that regulation of the employment relationship is within the states' police powers. The parties here have not cited, nor has our research disclosed, evidence of a clear and manifest purpose by Congress to occupy the field of immigration regulation so completely as to preclude the states from applying to unauthorized aliens the states' own worker protection labor and employment laws. A conclusion that Congress has occupied the field would dramatically affect state laws such as those regulating workers' compensation, minimum wages, working hour limits, and worker safety. We therefore conclude that the federal regulation imposed by the Immigration Reform and Control Act of 1986 is not so pervasive as to leave no room for any state law on the same subject.

. . . .

We now address the *third* type of federal preemption—conflict preemption—which occurs when state law conflicts with federal law either because compliance with both laws is impossible or because state law is an obstacle to achieving the federal law's objectives. We first consider whether compliance with both federal and state laws is impossible. This inquiry requires us to distinguish here between (1) the period dating from the occurrence of the employer's alleged wrongful act until the employer's discovery of the employee's ineligibility under federal immigration law to work in the United States (the prediscovery period) and (2) the period *after* the employer's discovery of that ineligibility (the postdiscovery period). This distinction is called for because the federal Immigration Reform and Control Act of

1986 prohibits an employer from continuing to employ an unauthorized alien upon discovery of the worker's unauthorized status.

We first consider the postdiscovery period. Because under federal immigration law an employer may not continue to employ a worker known to be ineligible, any state law award that compensates an unauthorized alien worker for loss of employment during the postdiscovery period directly conflicts with the federal immigration law prohibition against continuing to employ workers whom the employer knows are unauthorized aliens. Such an award would impose liability on the employer for not performing an act (continuing to employ a worker known to be an unauthorized alien) expressly prohibited by federal law. Thus, federal law preempts state Senate Bill No. 1818 to the extent that it makes a California FEHA lost pay award available to an unauthorized alien worker for the postdiscovery period.

. . . .

We now turn to the prediscovery period. In allowing lost wages for that period, our state labor laws do not directly conflict with the federal Immigration Reform and Control Act of 1986 because compliance with both federal and state laws is not impossible, as we now explain. Although federal immigration law prohibits an unauthorized alien's use of any false document to get a job, that law does not prohibit an employer from paying, or an employee from receiving, wages earned during employment wrongfully obtained by false documents, so long as the employer remains unaware of the employee's unauthorized status. Thus, allowing recovery of lost wages for the prediscovery period does not produce an "inevitable collision between the two schemes of regulation."

. . . .

We now consider conflict preemption's remaining aspect—also known as obstacle preemption—which exists when the state regulation would frustrate the federal law's purpose. Whether there is obstacle preemption is determined by "examining the federal statute as a whole and identifying its purpose and intended effects." If the federal law's purpose cannot otherwise be achieved, " 'the state law must yield to the regulation of Congress within the sphere of its delegated power.' "

. . . .

The Immigration Reform and Control Act of 1986, at issue here, is "a comprehensive scheme prohibiting the employment of [unauthorized] aliens in the United States." To achieve the goal of eliminating employment of unauthorized aliens, federal law requires employers to verify that prospective employees are eligible to work in the United States prohibits employers from hiring those unable to provide documents establishing employment eligibility, and compels employers to immediately discharge any unauthorized alien worker upon discovery of the worker's unauthorized status. Employers violating these federal law provisions are subject to an escalating series of civil penalties, as well as potential criminal prosecution.

Far less stringent, however, is federal immigration law's approach to unauthorized alien workers. Although Congress made it a crime for an unauthorized alien to use false documents to obtain employment, Congress did not impose criminal sanctions on unauthorized aliens merely for seeking or engaging in unauthorized work. As the high court recently pointed out, "Congress made a deliberate choice not to impose criminal penalties on aliens who seek, or engage in, unauthorized employment," as this "would be inconsistent with federal policy and objectives."

. . . .

California's Senate Bill No. 1818 expressly makes the worker protection provisions of state employment and labor laws available to all workers "regardless of immigration status." The protections thus extend even to those unauthorized aliens who, in violation of federal immigration law, have used false documents to secure employment. Even if permitting those workers to obtain state remedies for violations of the state labor and employment laws provides an incentive for such federal law violations, the practical effect of such incentive is minimal because the typical unauthorized alien wage earner is not familiar with the state law remedies available for unlawful termination and because jobseekers rarely contemplate being terminated in violation of the law. Thus, it is highly unlikely that an unauthorized alien's decision to seek employment in this country would be based in any significant part on the availability of lost wages as a remedy for unlawful discharge. Any unauthorized aliens who did consider this remedy would also realize that by pursuing state law remedies after termination they would risk discovery of their unauthorized status, thereby exposing them to criminal prosecution under both federal law (18 U.S.C. § 1546(b)) and state law (Pen. Code, § 114) and to deportation.

. . . .

Furthermore, *not* allowing unauthorized workers to obtain state remedies for unlawful discharge, including prediscovery period lost wages, would effectively immunize *employers* that, in violation of fundamental state policy, discriminate against their workers on grounds such as disability or race, retaliate against workers who seek compensation for disabling workplace injuries, or fail to pay the wages that state law requires. The resulting lower employment costs would encourage employers to hire workers known or suspected to be unauthorized aliens, contrary to the federal law's purpose of eliminating employers' economic incentives to hire such workers by subjecting employers to civil as well as criminal penalties. It would frustrate rather than advance the policies underlying federal immigration law to leave unauthorized alien workers so bereft of state labor law protections that employers have a strong incentive to "look the other way" and exploit a black market for illegal labor. Accordingly, after comparing the likely effects of applying and not applying state labor and employment law protection to unauthorized alien workers, we conclude that Senate Bill No. 1818, insofar as it makes available to such workers the remedy of *prediscovery period* lost wages for unlawful termination in violation of the FEHA, does not frustrate the purpose of the federal Immigration Reform and Control Act of 1986, and thus is not preempted.

> *[Editor's Note: The Court determined that the doctrines of after-acquired evidence and unclean hands did not serve as complete defenses to the plaintiff's action.]*

<u>Disposition</u>

The judgment of the Court of Appeal is reversed, with directions to remand the matter to the trial court for further proceedings consistent with this opinion.

The Court's efforts to resolve the possible conflicts between state authority over workplace regulation and federal authority to regulate immigration introduces complexity and uncertainty. Consider the issues raised in the following excerpt of a law review article.

3. Worker Advocacy by States at the Intersection of Immigration and Employment Law

Leticia M. Saucedo, *States of Desire: How Immigration Law Allows States to Attract Desired Immigrants*

52 U.C. Davis L. Rev. 471 (2018).

[Editor's Note: For ease of reading, all footnotes have been omitted.]

. . . .

On October 5, 2017, the governor of California signed a collection of statutes that had the stated effect of making California a sanctuary state in opposition to the Trump administration's immigration policies and practices. News reports described this move as California's refusal to accede to federal policy determinations, despite the federal government's plenary authority over immigration. The plenary power doctrine is assumed to foreclose states playing a direct role in immigration regulation under our federal constitutional structure. This assumption is seemingly confirmed by *Arizona v. United States*, in which the Supreme Court held that the federal immigration system preempted state law, and that Arizona could not seek to frustrate the Obama administration's policy determinations about immigration enforcement. The Trump administration is also counting on the strength of the plenary power doctrine, and it sued California claiming its authority preempted California's legislation. When reading the news accounts of California's creation of a sanctuary state and the Trump lawsuit many might assume that the statutes will not survive court scrutiny, because the states cannot frustrate the Trump administrations exercise of plenary federal authority. However, in this case the many would be wrong.

The plenary power doctrine might foreclose much state action, but it does not foreclose Congress from granting some authority to the states. In fact, over the past 30 years, Congress increasingly has devolved considerable authority to states over decisions that affect immigration regulation. Congress has done so to effectuate public policy in the immigration area, and also to acknowledge the structuralist concerns for regulation that occurs at intersection of state police powers and immigration law. . . .

Although Congress has devolved power to the states in more than fifty provisions of the immigration statute, three areas of law—employment, family and criminal—demonstrate vividly how Congress has allowed states to actualize their differing preferences for immigrants. In each of these areas, Congress has left key definitions and terms under the immigration statute to the states. This is not due to inattention or unwillingness to prescribe federal standards. There are, after all, plenty of examples in the immigration statute demonstrating that Congress has exercised its federal prerogative. The plain effect is that Congress has invited states to create a body of regulation in consciously defined negative spaces of federal immigration law.

. . . .

In this environment, states increasingly are being very deliberate about how they operationalize this congressionally-delegated authority. In particular, this shared authority empowers states to define, and thereby to attract and keep, their own versions of desirable immigrants. Over the past decade, states that disagreed with what they saw as weak federal enforcement sought to counter the federal policy with restrictive immigration regimes under state law. These efforts ran aground on the shoals of plenary power and preemption arguments. However, states can more productively exploit the powers granted to them by Congress to shape the effect of immigration law within their borders, including efforts to protect immigrants within their jurisdictions from federal action. This use of the power was certainly not anticipated by Congress, and is best regarded as an unanticipated effect of seeking to incorporate state values, prejudices and biases into the immigration statute. Nevertheless, the power exists, and it is precisely this power that the state of California has wielded to create a sanctuary state.

. . . .

A. How Congressionally-Devolved Authority Produces Deliberate State Action

While many states are still careful to limit their roles in immigration regulation, in part because of the staying power of plenary power doctrine, others have become much more deliberate about entering the spaces that Congress has created for state involvement. States that deliberately seek to integrate their immigrant populations find much room to maneuver in the devolution of congressional authority. California is a current example. Its role is pro-active: the governor of California appointed a director of immigration integration to coordinate initiatives throughout the state. The state legislature has become a leader in establishing state-level protections for its immigrant residents. Importantly, California is not alone. States are finding, and the Supreme Court is acknowledging, that state trends should influence federal policy on issues such as criminal sanctions. This section analyzes two levels of power: the influence of a big state, and the influence of states acting as a majority voice.

A. California's Influential Pro-Active Efforts at the Intersections to Attract (and Protect) the Desired Immigrant

In response to the Trump administration's threats to destabilize the lives of immigrants, the state of California enacted a series of laws designed to demonstrate the state's commitment to its congressionally-enacted authority at the intersection of immigration regulation and its police powers. The legislature passed the California Values Act to—as Governor Jerry Brown put it—"protect public safety and people who come to California to work hard and make this state a better place." The media dubbed it a sanctuary state law. Through this law, the state has claimed its authority in the very spaces that Congress has devolved to the states. The law establishes the state's position on cooperation with federal immigration authorities in areas that Congress has left to the states. For example, when Congress implemented its U visa provisions facilitating visas for victims of crime, it declared that its purpose was to ensure that victims of crime would step forward to cooperate with law enforcement authorities. In enacting its California Values Act, the California legislature declared that "[a] relationship of trust between California's immigrant community and state and local agencies is central to the public safety of the people of California." To ensure the protection of crime victims, the law prohibits law enforcement agencies from providing information about immigration status to federal immigration authorities. The legislature characterized its measure as necessary to prevent entanglement with federal enforcement authority. Instead, the state drew upon its own police powers to ensure that immigrant community members would not fear "approaching police when they are victims of, and witnesses to, crimes, seeking basic health services, or attending school, to the detriment of public safety and the well-being of all Californians." The legislature emphasized that it was acting within its power "to ensure effective policing, to protect the safety, well-being, and constitutional rights of the people of California."

Specifically, the California Values Act declines congressional incentives to participate in immigration enforcement. It does so by prohibiting state and local law enforcement agencies from using state resources or personnel to "investigate, interrogate, detain, detect, or arrest persons for immigration enforcement purposes." The legislation expresses choices that Congress left to the states when it enacted section 287(g) of the immigration statute. Congress envisioned that cooperation from state and local law enforcement agencies would be voluntary, and it did not intend to commandeer the states' resources without state agreement. The California law ensures that, except in some extreme circumstances, state law enforcement agencies will not provide information about an individual's address, immigration status or release date; detain individuals based on immigration hold requests; arrest individuals based on civil immigration warrants; assist the federal government in section 287(g) activities, or perform the functions of an immigration officer. The law is also careful to ensure cooperation with federal authorities wherever it is required by federal statute, such as responding to requests for specific information about an individual's criminal history, sharing information necessary to certify crime victims for U or T visas, or participating in joint task forces with federal immigration agencies.

In response to the Trump administration's threats to deport immigrant workers, California enacted legislation prohibiting employers from giving federal immigration agents access to the non-public parts of their business property, or to employee records, without a judicial warrant. In addition, the law requires business owners to give their employees notice whenever federal immigration officers seek to inspect employee records. The legislature declared the sanctions law within its authority to regulate employment relations and to protect the state's economic conditions. More importantly, California enacted the legislation in the space that Congress left open for states to sanction businesses when it enacted employer sanctions provisions in the immigration statute. The law sanctions businesses with licensing penalties for violating its provisions. When Congress enacted employer sanctions, it gave sole authority to the states to impose licensing requirements as well as sanctions on licensed businesses for hiring undocumented workers. The California legislature had already passed laws protecting immigrants from unfair immigration-related employment practices in 2014. This legislation imposes further sanctions on public and private businesses that make their nonpublic areas accessible to federal immigration authorities. Also, in keeping with its authority to sanction licensed businesses, the legislation imposes sanctions on employers that re-verify the employment eligibility of a current employee at a time or in a manner not specified by federal law.

These two pieces of legislation are only the beginning. The governor signed nine more bills protecting immigrants from enforcement efforts on October 5, 2017. Protections include laws protecting the personal information of public university students; prohibiting landlords from inquiring about or disclosing a tenant's immigration status, unless required by law; prohibiting localities from requiring landlords to provide information about tenants' immigration status; providing in-state tuition to California's 36,000 refugee and special immigrant population; adding immigration status as a category protected from discrimination, and prohibiting public schools from collecting information regarding students' citizenship or immigration status; prohibiting public agencies from entering into contracts with the federal government to house or detain individuals in civil immigration custody; providing in-state tuition to all students (except nonimmigrants), regardless of immigration status, who have attended a California high school, community college, or university for three years; providing citizenship assistance to members of the military and the California National Guard who are California residents; and ensuring that students whose parents are removed from the state involuntarily, including through deportation, can maintain their residency status.

When it passed this series of laws, the state was responding, not by flouting federal immigration authority, but by inhabiting the spaces that Congress devolved to the states in the immigration statute. Congress created these spaces for the states both at the intersection of immigration law, and through incentives to cooperate with federal enforcement. Contrary to reports that California overstepped its state power and risks federal preemption, the state used the spaces for state shared sovereignty as its reasons for legislative actions. Importantly, California has established a federalism path that states can follow to deliberately fashion a set of laws that attract (and protect) desired immigrants, even in the face of hostile federal actors.

To be sure, the California legislature has also responded to a need to protect its immigrant population from parties seeking to exploit immigrants' vulnerabilities. In the past several years, the state created prohibitions against what the legislature termed, "unfair immigration-related employment practices." The legislature enacted several laws prohibiting employers and attorneys from retaliating against immigrant workers by disclosing their personal information to federal immigration authorities. These laws were enacted pursuant to the authority Congress devolved to states to control licensing issues and to regulate employment relations. The state has also set aside funds for legal assistance, healthcare, educational assistance to refugees, unaccompanied minors, immigrants seeking to regularize their status, and those facing deportation, all in the name of immigrant integration.

. . . .

In some cases, general workplace protections do not apply to immigrant workers if they lack work authorization. Consider the case of H2 workers, who may be hired under contract through a provision of immigration law that allows employers to recruit foreign workers when there are insufficient workers who are able, willing and available to take the open jobs. 8 U.S.C. § 1101(a)(15)(H). Immigrant workers under contract through the H2 program are in the United States temporarily to take low-skill jobs offered by a specific employer. They may not leave their employment and switch jobs without losing their immigration status. They are guaranteed a prevailing wage that is governed by the wages in the industry, as well as room and board during their stay. They are not, however, guaranteed full employment rights.

QUESTIONS

1. What forms of protection should H2 workers have, given that they are admitted to perform work for a single employer for a temporary period?
2. What law should govern the workplace relationship for these contracted workers? Are they more akin to independent contractors, employees, or some category of workers in between these basic categories?

Mastery Problem 38-1

You represent Stations Casinos and Resorts, Inc., a non-union hotel enterprise located in Las Vegas, Nevada. Stations is dealing with the aftermath of a number of employee terminations triggered by the employees' participation in a national day of protest against congressional inaction to enact comprehensive immigration reform. Several employees took sick days to participate in the Las Vegas march. They were arrested after they blocked Las Vegas Boulevard ("the strip") with signs that identified them as Stations Casinos employees. The signs read "Stations'

Back of the House Rules Need Reform," "Palace Station needs an Immigration Overhaul," and "Stations Casinos Can't Profit without its Immigrant Workers." When the employees returned to work, they were dismissed without explanation.

Other employees and the Hotel and Restaurant Employees union have raised concerns about their own political and civic activities outside the workplace. Stations Casinos, Inc. has hired a management-side labor firm to deal with the employer's obligations under federal labor law. In the meantime, the Stations Casino CEO has asked you to:

1. Determine whether Stations can discipline its workers without risking retaliation or speech claims from the immigrant workers.
2. Draft a fair policy that balances the interests of the employees and the company with respect to employee speech outside the workplace.

Mastery Problem 38-2

Jennifer worked for Ace Hardware in Sacramento for three years. She was fired last week after an altercation with her manager. Jennifer thought she and other workers should be paid overtime wages for opening and closing the store, and she had been arguing the point to her manager for months. The week before she was fired she had a long conversation with her manager, during which she accused the manager of discriminating against her because she is not a U.S. citizen. Her manager did not respond to the allegation, but did go back to check the I-9 in Jennifer's file and found that Jennifer had checked the box next to U.S. citizen on the form. Jennifer had signed the form under penalty of perjury. When the manager further investigated, she found that Jennifer's social security number was false. Jennifer was called into the manager's office and was fired on the spot. Jennifer believes that she was fired in retaliation for complaining about overtime wages.

Jennifer seeks your advice. You are trying to determine if Jennifer has a cause of action for wrongful discharge in violation of public policy, in light of the following statutes.

California AB 263

SECTION 1. The Legislature finds and declares all of the following:

. . . It is in the public policy interest of the State of California that workers be able to report concerns to their employers without fear of retaliation or discrimination.

. . . It is essential to the enforcement of this state's labor laws that we have broad, clear, and effective protections for workers engaging in conduct protected by law from all forms of employer retaliation, including prohibiting immigration-related threats.

California Labor Code

§ 1019. Unfair Immigration-Related Practices

(a) It shall be unlawful for an employer or any other person or entity to engage in, or to direct another person or entity to engage in, unfair immigration-related practices against any person for the purpose of, or with the intent of, retaliating against any person for exercising any right protected under this code or by any local ordinance applicable to employees.

. . . .

(b) (1) As used in this chapter, "unfair immigration-related practice" means any of the following practices, when undertaken for the retaliatory purposes prohibited by subdivision (a):

(A) Requesting more or different documents than are required under Section 1324a(b) of Title 8 of the United States Code, or a refusal to honor documents tendered pursuant to that section that on their face reasonably appear to be genuine.

(B) Using the federal E-Verify system to check the employment authorization status of a person at a time or in a manner not required under Section 1324a(b) of Title 8 of the United States Code, or not authorized under any memorandum of understanding governing the use of the federal E-Verify system.

(C) Threatening to file or the filing of a false police report.

(D) Threatening to contact or contacting immigration authorities.

(2) "Unfair immigration-related practice" does not include conduct undertaken at the express and specific direction or request of the federal government.

(c) Engaging in an unfair immigration-related practice against a person within 90 days of the person's exercise of rights protected under this code or local ordinance applicable to employees shall raise a rebuttable presumption of having done so in retaliation for the exercise of those rights.

(d) (1) An employee or other person who is the subject of an unfair immigration-related practice prohibited by this section, or a representative of that employee or person, may bring a civil action for equitable relief and any damages or penalties, in accordance with this section.

8 U.S.C. § 1324(a). Making Employment of Unauthorized Aliens Unlawful (INA § 274a)

(1) In general it is unlawful for a person or other entity—

(A) to hire, or to recruit or refer for a fee, for employment in the United States an alien knowing the alien is an unauthorized alien (as defined in subsection (h)(3) of this section) with respect to such employment . . .

Conclusion

In this Lesson, we focused on the rights of immigrants at the intersection of employment and immigration law. We also explored federal and state authority to regulate immigrant rights in the workplace. There are no easy and firm answers in this area of employment law.

Lesson 39:
Unemployment Compensation

Objectives and Expected Learning Outcomes

In this Lesson, we will study the unemployment compensation systems that arose during the New Deal to protect workers who lost their jobs. Employees who meet the requirements receive income replacement payments while they find another job, blunting the economic effects of being fired or laid off. You will learn that the system creates a category of "deserving" recipients: employees who are terminated rather than who quit; employees who are terminated for reasons other than misconduct; and employees who are seeking to find a new job and are available to accept work.

1. Overview of Unemployment Compensation Systems

The Great Depression was an economic disaster for millions of employees. The lack of a safety net for employees who lost their jobs resulted in great hardship. The Social Security Act of 1935, a cornerstone of the New Deal package of economic reforms, created a structure for the establishment of workers' compensation programs at the state level. The federal law authorized the initiative and set the baseline, but details and administration were left to individual states.

The goal of unemployment compensation programs is simple: to provide a source of replacement income on a temporary basis after an employee loses a job. This intervention serves a number of purposes. First, of course, it mitigates the economic distress caused by the loss of a job suffered by the employee and her family. Second, the potential for a cumulative effect on a community of large scale unemployment is also mitigated, as laid off employees can continue to shop for necessities. Finally, the program provides a disincentive to firing workers because it is funded by a tax premised on the employer's history. An employer who fires workers regularly pays more than those who do not, which is known as "experience rating."

As with many social programs in the United States, eligibility is often keyed to the idea of a "deserving" recipient. First, an employee must have an earnings history to qualify for coverage. A person just joining the workforce cannot apply for unemployment compensation if they are unable to find work. This requirement makes sense insofar as the program is designed to soften the effect of a sudden loss of income. Additionally, employees who quit a job are generally barred from receiving benefits, as their unemployment is deemed to be voluntary. Similarly, an employee who is fired for misconduct is not eligible because the termination of employment is deemed to be "deserved" to some extent. Finally, an employee who is fired may not simply sit back and collect payments: the employee must demonstrate that she is available to take a new job and is actively looking for one. We explore these details in turn.

2. The Employee Must Be Involuntarily Terminated

Unemployment compensation programs are designed to protect workers against unexpected loss of income, and so an employee is not eligible for benefits if the employee chooses to resign from a position. As you might expect, thorny problems arise when trying to define an "involuntary" separation from employment.

Wood v. Louisiana Dept. of Employment Security

632 So.2d 899 (Ct. App. La. 1994).

Norris, Judge.

Roy Wood appeals administrative and district court decisions that denied his claim for unemployment compensation. For the reasons expressed, we reverse and render.

For over nine years, Wood held two jobs. His full-time job was as a commissioned officer of the New Orleans Police Department. His part-time job, about 12 hours a week at $7.00 per hour, was as a security guard for Rue Parc Fontaine Apartments. Parc Fontaine's management agent, Mustang Management, used only off-duty commissioned police officers for security because these were permitted to carry a gun on private property. R. p. 34. According to Wood and his police supervisor, Sgt. Bass, Mustang had always used off-duty commissioned officers for security.

In late September 1991 the N.O.P.D. underwent some changes which were unfavorable to Wood. He therefore resigned his commission. According to Wood, Sgt. Bass then told him: "You know, I'll have to replace you on the [security] detail because . . . obviously you can't work here [at Parc Fontaine] if you're not a commissioned Police Officer." Sgt. Bass verified that he "advised him [Wood] that he no longer could work in a capacity

. . . with Mustang Management since he was no longer a commissioned Police Officer." Although Wood never explicitly testified that he quit the security detail, the department treated his claim as a "voluntary quit" and the adjudicator disqualified him. After a hearing, the ALJ also disqualified him, finding that "the claimant initiated his separation, and his leaving was not for good cause attributable to a substantial change made to the employment by the employer." La.R.S. 23:1601(1)(a). The Board of Review affirmed the ALJ without comment.

On judicial review, the district court disagreed with the agency's analysis of the record, ruling that Wood's separation from employment "came closer to being termination for lack of an important qualification than it did to a true layoff." Citing and relying on La.R.S. 23:1601(1)(a), the court further found that Mustang did not make a substantial change in Wood's employment, resulting in his separation. However, the court reasoned that an employer may adopt and enforce qualifications of employment, provided these are not discriminatory, against public morals, or in violation of regulation, ordinance or statute. In support the court cited *Cooper v. Doyal*, 205 So.2d 59 (La.App. 4th Cir.), *writ denied* 251 La. 755, 206 So.2d 97 (1968), and *Brown v. Southern Airways Inc.,* 170 So.2d 245 (La.App. 4th Cir.1964), *writ refused* 247 La. 361, 171 So.2d 478 (1965), which upheld disqualifications of airline stewardesses who got married contrary to company policy. Thus, even though Wood's separation was a termination at the employer's insistence, the court upheld the disqualification.

The distinction between a quit and a discharge is critical, as it affects the standard whereby the claimant is qualified for benefits. The statute, La.R.S. 23:1601, provides in pertinent part:

> § 1601. Disqualification for benefits
>
> An individual shall be disqualified for benefits:
>
> (1)(a) If the administrator finds that he has *left* his employment from a base period or subsequent employer without good cause attributable to a substantial change made to the employment by the employer. . . . (emphasis added)

This court has held that the word "left" in this subsection is intended to cover those situations where an employee quits, or voluntarily leaves or resigns, his employment. By contrast, a different standard applies to *discharges:*

> An individual shall be disqualified for benefits: . . .
>
> (2)(a) If the administrator finds that he has been discharged by a base period or subsequent employer for misconduct connected with his employment. Misconduct means mismanagement of a position of employment by action or inaction, neglect that places in jeopardy the lives or property of others, dishonesty, wrongdoing, violation of a law, or violation of a policy or rule adopted to insure orderly work or the safety of others. . . .

An element of intentional wrongdoing or wilful disregard of the employer's interests must be present for a *discharged* employee to be guilty of misconduct disqualifying him from receiving unemployment compensation benefits.

The unemployment compensation statute must be liberally construed to serve its remedial purpose. Thus "misconduct" under 23:1601(2)(a) must be construed in such a way as to favor coverage.

While the difference between a quit and a discharge may seem obvious, the courts have recognized that quits which are actually compelled by the employer are not voluntary at all. Such a quit is viewed as a "quit in lieu of discharge" or a "constructive discharge" and has been held, as a matter of law, to constitute good cause connected with the employment for leaving one's employment.

In our view, the department improperly characterized Wood's separation as a voluntary quit. The transcript of the hearing before the ALJ is abundantly clear that Wood was given no choice but to quit. The trial court was not plainly wrong to find, as a matter of law, that Wood's situation was tantamount to a discharge.

The trial court erred, however, in applying the wrong standard of qualification for benefits. In the event of a discharge, the claimant may be disqualified only on a finding of "misconduct connected with his employment." R.S. 23:1601(2)(a). On this record there is no allegation or hint of misconduct . . . Without such evidence, the trial court was plainly wrong to disqualify Wood.

The district court supported its result by citing the somewhat dated stewardess cases of *Brown* and *Cooper,* supra. Although factually similar, *Brown* is inapplicable because it involved a true resignation and thus a different standard of qualification. Further, we distinguish *Cooper;* there, the claimant was indeed guilty of some misconduct by intentionally making false statements in her re-employment request. There is simply no evidence of misconduct in the instant case. Further, the court in *Cooper* never mentioned R.S. 23:1601(2)(a).

The district court also rationalized its decision by saying that the employer may adopt and enforce reasonable qualifications of employment; if the employee fails to meet these, the employer may discharge him with the result that he is disqualified from benefits. While this analysis has a certain appeal, it does not conform to the statutory mandate that a *discharged* employee may be disqualified only on a finding of *misconduct* connected with employment. R.S. 23:1601(2)(a). Admittedly, an employee who is constructively discharged may also be guilty of intentional misconduct and therefore disqualified. In the absence of misconduct, however, an actual or constructive discharge is usually non-disqualifying.

The instant case is actually more comparable to situations in which an employee is fired because he is unable to perform the job for which he was hired. Such an employee obviously breaches the implicit "qualification of employment" that he be competent, but such a discharge is uniformly held to be non-disqualifying.

Finally, Wood's resignation from the N.O.P.D. was for good cause and non-disqualifying; with respect to the part-time job, it would be inconsistent to hold that this constructive discharge, which was simply a result of his resignation, was disqualifying. It was not.

. . . .

Reversed and rendered.

HIGHTOWER, JUDGE, concurring.

I concur in the result, but would observe that under certain circumstances, even in the absence of misconduct, an actually or "constructively" discharged employee may be denied unemployment benefits.

The actions of an employee who *voluntarily* disqualifies himself for continued employment, e.g., by *voluntarily* failing to renew a required chauffeur's license or by voluntarily resigning a required law enforcement commission, would be tantamount to "leaving" his employment. In such instances, his decision to "leave" should be evaluated for "good cause" under R.S. 23:1601(1)(a).

However, as shown by an exhibit in the present record, Mr. Wood reluctantly left the NOPD due to problems created by new working hours there, and only after he tried to obtain other shifts within the Department. Thus, he apparently found himself, in effect, forced to resign his commission. Under these facts, he should not be deprived of unemployment benefits.

Class Exercise 39-1

The concurring judge indicates that there may be some situations in which an employee loses a job as a result of voluntary actions and should not receive benefits. Work in small groups to develop a proposed regulation to the statutes in Louisiana to better define when disqualification is warranted.

Problem 39-1

Many states recognize that the loss of a job is not voluntary if one quits in order to follow a spouse who receives a new job in a different city. The states generally consider this "good cause" for quitting, which renders the unemployment "involuntary." How far should courts extend this doctrine of "good cause quit?" For example, should an employee who moves to be near a parent with a chronic illness be disqualified from receiving benefits? Develop a rule for determining when employees who move should be permitted to receive benefits.

3. Employee Must Not Be Fired for Misconduct

An employee may be disqualified from receiving unemployment compensation benefits if the involuntary termination was due to the employee's misconduct. This disqualification is premised on the assumption that an employee engaged in misconduct is not deserving of the benefits reserved for employees who lose their job through no fault of their own.

Braska v. Challenge Manufacturing Co.

307 Mich.App. 340 (2014).

Per Curiam.

[Editor's Note: The Court consolidated three appeals to consider whether an employee dismissed for testing positive for cannabis is disqualified from receiving workers' compensation benefits.]

I. BACKGROUND

A. *BRASKA v. CHALLENGE MANUFACTURING CO* (Docket No. 313932)

Braska began working for Challenge Manufacturing Company (Challenge) as a material handler and hi-lo operator in September 2009. On June 11, 2010, Braska injured his ankle and was sent to a medical center where he was required to take a drug test. Braska tested positive for marijuana and disclosed for the first time that he had obtained a medical marijuana card in May 2010 and regularly used medical marijuana for his chronic back pain. Challenge terminated Braska's employment for violation of the company's drug-free-workplace policy as set forth in the employee handbook.

Dr. Richard Rasmussen, certified as a medical review officer for drug tests, reviewed the "results verification record," which was a printout of the laboratory results that was given to him. He signed the record on June 15, 2010. The results verification record showed that Braska tested positive for marijuana. There were 225 nanograms per milliliter of blood, which, according to Rasmussen, was "higher than the average." According to Rasmussen and Dr. David Crocker, there are no objective standards to determine when someone is under the influence of marijuana.

Following his termination, Braska applied for unemployment benefits. On July 6, 2010, the Unemployment Insurance Agency (UIA) found that Braska was not fired for a deliberate disregard of his employer's interest. It concluded that Braska was not disqualified for unemployment benefits under MCL 421.29(1)(b) for engaging in misconduct. Challenge protested the determination, and the UIA modified its decision, finding that Braska was discharged for testing positive for marijuana. Although failing a drug test would ordinarily have disqualified Braska from receiving benefits under MCL 421.29(1)(m), the UIA determined that because Braska had a valid medical marijuana card, he was not disqualified for unemployment benefits under that provision.

Challenge appealed the redetermination, and a hearing was held before an administrative law judge (ALJ). At the hearing, the ALJ excluded from evidence the results verification record, as well as a "specimen result certification" that Rasmussen sent to Challenge, because of problems in the chain of custody of Braska's urine sample. At the conclusion of the hearing, the ALJ found that Braska was fired for testing positive for marijuana, not general misconduct. The ALJ noted that an employer is required to establish, as a foundational element to the admission of the results of a drug test, that the sample analyzed was the sample collected from the employee. In this case, Challenge failed to produce any witness to establish how the drug test was conducted and how the sample test was handled. According to the ALJ, in the absence of this foundational testimony, the test results were inadmissible hearsay, and disqualification from unemployment benefits could not be established without them.

Recognizing that there might be disagreement on the adequacy of the evidence presented by Challenge, the ALJ addressed the effect of Braska's possession of a medical marijuana card. The ALJ noted that it surpassed credulity to believe that Braska had the card but did not use medical marijuana and that Braska specifically did not ask for a retest when one was offered by Rasmussen. The ALJ found that there was no evidence that Braska had operated a hi-lo under the influence of marijuana. Therefore, the ALJ concluded that Braska was not disqualified from receiving unemployment benefits under § 29(1)(m).

Challenge appealed the ALJ's decision to the MCAC, and the MCAC reversed. The MCAC concluded that the only question governing the admission of a document in an administrative hearing is whether reasonable people would rely on the document. It found that all the documents offered by Challenge were reliable. The MCAC noted that the ALJ allowed Braska to collect unemployment benefits because he possessed a medical marijuana card. The MCAC concluded that this amounted to error, given that Challenge only needed to present evidence that Braska had tested positive on a drug test that was administered in a nondiscriminatory manner to disqualify Braska from receiving benefits. It ruled that the preponderance of the evidence established that Braska was disqualified from receiving benefits under § 29(1)(m).

Braska appealed the MCAC's decision in the circuit court, and the circuit court reversed on the ground that the MCAC's decision was not supported by competent, material, and substantial evidence. The court noted that the MCAC had failed to address the ALJ's interpretation and application of the MMMA and MESA, but the court declined to address those issues. This Court granted the Department's application for leave to appeal the circuit court's order.

B. *KEMP v. HAYES GREEN BEACH MEMORIAL HOSPITAL*
(Docket No. 315441)

Kemp worked for Hayes Green Memorial Hospital (HGB) as a CT technician. HGB had a zero-tolerance drug policy. Employees were tested for drugs upon hire and then upon reasonable suspicion. In May 2011, a patient complained about Kemp, claiming that Kemp had inserted an IV line in the patient without using gloves, discussed the patient's insurance coverage in a crowded area, and told the patient about her family's drug use, including that she ate "special brownies."

On June 2, 2011, following an investigation into the complaint, Jennifer Myers, the human resource manager for HGB, told Kemp that she needed to take a drug test. Kemp consented, and she wrote on the consent form that she used marijuana for medical reasons. At the meeting, Kemp showed no objective signs of intoxication. Kemp tested positive for marijuana and delta-9-tetrahydrocannabinol (THC). A second test confirmed the results. On June 8, 2011, Myers informed Kemp that she was terminated. The reason for the termination was the failed drug test.

Kemp suffered from lupus, neuropathy, and chronic pain in her hand. She obtained a medical marijuana card in December 2010 and it remained valid in May 2011, when she was terminated. According to Kemp, she was never under the influence of marijuana at work. She used marijuana between 6:00 p.m. and 7:00 p.m., and the effects were usually gone within two hours. Her shift at HGB was from 6:30 a.m. to 3:00 p.m.

Following her termination, Kemp applied for unemployment benefits. The UIA initially determined that, because Kemp was terminated for testing positive for an illegal substance, she was disqualified from receiving benefits under § 29(1)(m). The UIA reversed its decision after Kemp provided documentation that she possessed a medical marijuana card. HGB protested, and a hearing was held before an ALJ. The ALJ affirmed the UIA's redetermination that Kemp was not disqualified from receiving unemployment benefits. The ALJ explained that because marijuana was legally available to use for medical purposes, the issue whether Kemp's use of marijuana constituted misconduct or was illegal must include consideration of the MMMA. Because Kemp used marijuana for medical purposes, her use was lawful and, therefore, could not bar her receipt of benefits.

HGB appealed, and the MCAC reversed the ALJ's decision. The MCAC concluded that Kemp was disqualified from receiving unemployment benefits under § 29(1)(m). It reasoned that the MMMA only allows possession and consumption of marijuana; it does not regulate private employment or offer employment protection.

Kemp appealed in the Ingham Circuit Court, and the circuit court reversed the MCAC's decision. The circuit court noted that, although a federal court held that the MMMA did not prohibit a private employer from firing an employee who used medical marijuana, the present case involved state action. MESA, and specifically § 29, is enforced and interpreted by a state agency. Because there was state action, the MMMA was applicable and needed to be considered in determining whether Kemp was disqualified from receiving unemployment benefits. According to the circuit court, an employee who uses medical marijuana but is not intoxicated at work is not disqualified from receiving benefits under § 29(1)(m). It noted that the benefit interpretation by the UIA provided that an employee who uses medical marijuana should not be disqualified from benefits unless the employee is in possession of marijuana at work, is under the influence at work, or uses it at work. Specifically, regarding Kemp, the circuit court stated that Kemp did not fall under any of the three categories and that there was no evidence that she used medical marijuana other than as allowed by the MMMA. According to the circuit court, any disqualification from unemployment benefits would amount to a forfeiture of benefits that Kemp was otherwise qualified to receive, which constituted an impermissible penalty under the MMMA.

In reaching its conclusion, the circuit court rejected the Department's argument that Kemp tested positive for marijuana at work and that her discharge was akin to testing positive for any other intoxicating or illegal substance, such as Vicodin. It noted that the record did not show that Kemp tested positive for active marijuana. Rather, she tested positive for a metabolite of marijuana known as 11-carboxy-THC, which is not a Schedule 1 controlled substance and has no pharmacological effect on the body. Thus, according to the circuit court, the drug test simply demonstrated what Kemp had informed HGB of before the test—she used medical marijuana. This Court granted the Department's application for leave to appeal the circuit court's order.

C. *KUDZIA v. AVASI SERVICES INC* (Docket No. 318344)

Kudzia worked as an in-home service technician for Avasi Services, a corporate subsidiary of Art Van Furniture, Inc., whose employees repaired furniture for Art Van customers. Art Van required its employees to be drug-free, and it subjected the employees who drove an Art Van vehicle to random drug tests. On June 21, 2012, Daryl Smith, the service manager for Avasi Services, advised Kudzia that he had to report for a random drug test. Kudzia, who showed no signs of intoxication, said nothing in response. According to Dr. Stuart Hoffman, a medical review officer, Kudzia tested positive for "metabolized marijuana." On June 27, 2012, Smith met with Kudzia and informed him that he was discharged because of the failed test. Kudzia did not dispute the test results, and he informed Smith that he had a medical marijuana card.

In the past, Kudzia had undergone two surgeries on his knees. In July 2010, he received a medical marijuana card, which was valid through July 2012. After he received the card, Kudzia used a marijuana-infused cream on his knees.

The UIA found that Kudzia was discharged for testing positive on a drug test. It determined that he was not disqualified from receiving benefits under § 29(1)(m). Avasi Services appealed, and a hearing was held before an ALJ. The ALJ ruled that Kudzia was disqualified from receiving benefits under § 29(1)(b) (misconduct). The ALJ explained that no law prohibited an employer from having a policy that prohibited the use or possession of controlled substances. Kudzia acted in direct contravention of his employer's policy, as he did not request an exemption to use medical marijuana. However, the hearing referee also concluded that Kudzia was not disqualified from receiving benefits under § 29(1)(m). There was no evidence that Kudzia used medical marijuana in contravention of the MMMA.

Kudzia appealed, and the MCAC affirmed the ALJ's decision on different grounds. It reasoned that an employee who tests positive for a controlled substance is disqualified from receiving benefits under § 29(1)(m). Kudzia appealed the MCAC's decision in the Macomb Circuit Court, and the circuit court reversed. First, the circuit court ruled that, to the extent that provisions of the MMMA and MESA conflicted, the MMMA controlled. Second, it held that, although the MMMA does not impose restrictions on private employers, the MMMA applies to state action and the MCAC's decision to deny Kudzia benefits was an action by the state. The circuit court then held that Kudzia's use of medical marijuana implicated § 29(1)(m) because the MMMA did not legalize the use of marijuana. Nonetheless, the circuit court determined that the disqualification from benefits was contrary to the MMMA because it was a penalty or the denial of a right or privilege for the medical use of marijuana. The circuit court rejected the Department's argument that Kudzia's behavior was impermissible under the MMMA. It explained that Kudzia tested positive for marijuana metabolites and that it did not follow, from the presence of the metabolites, that Kudzia had ingested marijuana in the workplace or that he was under the influence of marijuana during work hours. This Court granted the Department's application for leave to appeal the circuit court's order.

II. STANDARD OF REVIEW

. . . .

These appeals involve issues of statutory interpretation, which are questions of law that we review de novo. *Id.* "The primary goal of statutory interpretation is to ascertain and give effect to the Legislature's intent as expressed by the language of the statute." [citation omitted] If the statutory language is clear and unambiguous, judicial construction is neither required nor permitted; the statute must be enforced as written. Regarding voter-initiated statutes such as the MMMA, the intent of the electors governs the interpretation of the statute. The statute's plain language is the most reliable evidence of the electors' intent.

III. ANALYSIS

A. MESA

When it enacted MESA, the Legislature declared that "[e]conomic insecurity due to unemployment is a serious menace" and that "[t]he systematic accumulation of funds during periods of employment to provide benefits for periods of unemployment by the setting aside of unemployment reserves to be used for the benefit of persons unemployed through no fault of their own . . . is for the public good, and the general welfare of the people of this state." MCL 421.2(1).

An individual must be eligible to receive unemployment benefits under MESA. Initially, an individual must meet certain threshold requirements set forth in MCL 421.28 such as, among other things, filing a claim for benefits and seeking employment. See MCL 421.28(1)(a), (b), and (c). In the event an individual meets the threshold requirements of § 28, he or she may nevertheless be disqualified from receiving benefits under MCL 421.29, which provides in pertinent part as follows:

> (1) Except as provided in subsection (5), an individual is disqualified from receiving benefits if he or she:
>
> . . . .
>
> (b) Was suspended or discharged for misconduct connected with the individual's work or for intoxication while at work.
>
> . . . .
>
> (m) Was discharged for illegally ingesting, injecting, inhaling, or possessing a controlled substance on the premises of the employer; refusing to submit to a drug test that was required to be administered in a nondiscriminatory manner; or testing positive on a drug test, if the test was administered in a nondiscriminatory manner. . . .

B. THE MMMA

The MMMA was approved by the state electors in November 2008. *People v. Kolanek,* 491 Mich. 382, 393, 817 N.W.2d 528 (2012). In approving the MMMA, the state electors found that, according to modern medical research, there were beneficial uses for marijuana in treating or alleviating the effects of a variety of debilitating medical conditions. MCL 333.26422 (a). "The purpose of the MMMA is to allow a limited class of individuals the medical use of marijuana. . . ." *Kolanek,* 491 Mich. at 393, 817 N.W.2d 528. However, the MMMA did not legalize the use or possession of marijuana in all contexts. *People v. Koon,* 494 Mich. 1, 5, 832 N.W.2d 724 (2013). Marijuana remains a Schedule 1 controlled substance. *Id.* "The MMMA does *not* create a general right for individuals to use and possess marijuana in Michigan. Possession, manufacture, and delivery of marijuana remain punishable offenses under Michigan law." *Kolanek,* 491 Mich. at 394, 817 N.W.2d 528.

The MMMA functions by granting immunity from arrest, prosecution, or penalty. *Koon,* 494 Mich. at 5, 832 N.W.2d 724. Section 4 of the MMMA provides, in pertinent part:

> A qualifying patient who has been issued and possesses a registry identification card *shall not be subject to arrest, prosecution, or penalty in any manner, or denied any right or privilege,* including but not limited to civil penalty or disciplinary action by a business or occupational or professional licensing board or bureau, for the medical use of marihuana in accordance with this act. . . . [MCL 333.26424(a) (emphasis added).]

The MMMA's immunity applies only if marijuana is used in accordance with the provisions of the MMMA. MCL 333.26427(a). The MMMA does not permit any person to "[u]ndertake any task under the influence of marihuana, when doing so would constitute negligence or professional malpractice" or to "[o]perate, navigate, or be in actual physical control of any motor vehicle, aircraft, or motorboat while under the influence of marihuana." MCL 333.26427(b)(1), (4). In addition, nothing in the MMMA may be construed to require an "employer to accommodate the ingestion of marihuana in any workplace or any employee working while under the influence of marihuana." MCL 333.26427(c)(2).

The MMMA also contains a broadly worded provision to ensure that qualifying individuals who adhere to the terms of the MMMA do not suffer penalties for their use of marijuana for medicinal purposes. Specifically, MCL 333.26427(e) provides "[a]ll other acts and parts of acts inconsistent with this act do not apply to the medical use of marihuana as provided for by this act." Thus, to the extent another law would penalize an individual for using medical marijuana in accordance with the MMMA, that law is superseded by the MMMA. *Koon,* 494 Mich. at 8–9, 832 N.W.2d 724.

C. APPLICATION

The central issue presented in these three appeals is whether an employee who has a medical marijuana card and is discharged after failing a drug test may be denied unemployment benefits. To resolve this issue, we must examine the interplay between MESA and the MMMA. Specifically, we must first determine (1) whether claimants met the threshold requirements for unemployment compensation under MESA, (2) whether claimants were nevertheless disqualified from receiving benefits under one of MESA's disqualification provisions, and (3), to the extent claimants were disqualified for testing positive for marijuana, whether the MMMA nevertheless provides immunity and supersedes MESA in this respect.

With respect to MESA, none of the parties disputes that claimants met the threshold requirements for unemployment benefits under MCL 421.28. The MCAC found claimants disqualified for benefits under § 29(1)(m). As set forth earlier, that statutory provision disqualifies an individual who was discharged for the following conduct:

> (1) "illegally ingesting, injecting, inhaling or possessing a controlled substance on the premises of the employer," (2) refusing to submit to a fairly administered drug test, and (3) for "testing positive on a drug test, if the test was administered in a nondiscriminatory manner."

MCL 421.29(1)(m). There is no evidence in the record that any of the three claimants ingested, injected, inhaled, or possessed marijuana on the premises of their respective employers. Furthermore, claimants' employers did not allege that claimants were under the influence of marijuana at any time during work hours. Similarly, claimants did not refuse to submit to a drug test. Thus, the first two disqualifiers under § 29(1)(m) are inapplicable in the present cases.

With respect to the third disqualifier, the MCAC determined that claimants were disqualified under that provision because they failed a drug test. However, although claimants failed their respective drug tests and ordinarily would have been disqualified for unemployment benefits under § 29(1)(m), we must determine whether claimants were nevertheless entitled to unemployment benefits under the MMMA provisions that grant immunity and supersede contrary laws.

As noted, the MMMA's immunity clause provides in relevant part as follows:

> A qualifying patient who has been issued and possesses a registry identification card *shall not be subject to* arrest, prosecution, or *penalty in any manner, or denied any right or privilege,* including but not limited to *civil penalty or disciplinary action* by a business or occupational or professional licensing board or bureau, for the medical use of marihuana in accordance with this act. . . . [MCL 333.26424(a) (emphasis added).]

The immunity provided under this section is broad. It prohibits the imposition of certain consequences on individuals who use medical marijuana in accordance with the MMMA. See *1031 Lapeer LLC v. Rice,* 290 Mich.App. 225, 231, 810 N.W.2d 293 (2010) (use of the phrase "shall not" designates a mandatory prohibition). Specifically, the statute provides that qualifying patients "shall not" (1) "be subject to arrest, prosecution, or penalty in any manner" or (2) be denied any "right" or "privilege," "*including but not limited to* civil penalty or disciplinary action by a business or occupational or professional licensing board or bureau. . . ." (Emphasis added).

In this case, none of the parties contends that claimants used medical marijuana in a manner that did not comply with the terms of the MMMA. Therefore, we must determine whether denial of unemployment benefits constitutes either imposition of a penalty or denial of a right or privilege.

The MMMA does not define the term "penalty." In *Ter Beek,* 495 Mich. at 20, 846 N.W.2d 531, in the context of the MMMA, our Supreme Court referred to a dictionary to define the term to mean "a 'punishment imposed or incurred for a violation of law or rule . . . something forfeited.' " *Id.,* quoting *Random House Webster's College Dictionary* (2000). Further, because the term "penalty" in MCL 333.26424(a) is modified by the phrase "in any manner," the immunity granted by the MMMA from penalties "is to be given the broadest application" and applies to both civil and criminal penalties. *Ter Beek v. Wyoming,* 297 Mich.App. 446, 455, 823 N.W.2d 864 (2012), aff'd 495 Mich. 1, 846 N.W.2d 531 (2014).

Applying this definition to the present case, we conclude that denial of unemployment benefits under § 29(1)(m) constitutes a "penalty" under the MMMA that was imposed upon claimants for their medical use of marijuana. As discussed earlier, none of the parties disputes that claimants met the threshold requirements for unemployment benefits under MCL 421.28. The only reason claimants were disqualified by the MCAC from receiving benefits was because they tested positive for marijuana. In other words, absent their medical use of marijuana—and there was no evidence that claimants, all of whom possessed a medical marijuana card, failed to abide by the MMMA's provisions in their use—claimants would not have been disqualified under § 29(1)(m). Thus, because claimants used medical marijuana, they were required to forfeit their unemployment benefits. For this reason, the decision by the MCAC to deny claimants unemployment benefits amounted to a penalty imposed for the medical use of marijuana contrary to MCL 333.26424(a). Accordingly, because the MMMA supersedes MESA in this respect, the MCAC erred by denying claimants unemployment benefits. See MCL 333.26427(e) ("All other acts and parts of acts inconsistent with [the MMMA] do not apply to the medical use of marihuana as provided for by this act.").

The Department argues that disqualification under § 29(1)(m) is not a "penalty." According to the Department, something cannot be forfeited unless one was entitled to it, and claimants were not entitled to unemployment benefits because MESA conditions the payment of benefits upon an individual's eligibility and qualification. We reject the Department's argument that, because claimants were disqualified under § 29(1)(m), they were not penalized. This argument ignores the salient fact that claimants met the threshold requirements for unemployment benefits and were disqualified only because of their use of medical marijuana.

In addition, the Department claims that, to the extent the denial of unemployment benefits constituted a penalty, the penalty was imposed not for the medical use of marijuana, but rather for failing a drug test. Essentially, the Department contends that we should distinguish the act of failing a drug test from claimants' medical use of marijuana. We decline the Department's invitation to ignore the basis for the positive drug tests and engage in linguistic gymnastics in an attempt to avoid the plain language of the MMMA. Claimants' use of medical marijuana and their subsequent positive drug tests are inextricably intertwined. Each claimant tested positive for marijuana. There was no dispute that each claimant possessed a medical marijuana card. No evidence was presented to suggest that the marijuana discovered in the drug tests was not from the medical use of marijuana or that claimants failed to use medical marijuana in accordance with the provisions of the MMMA. Stated simply, claimants would not have failed the drug test had they not used medical marijuana. The plain language of the MMMA's immunity clause states that claimants "*shall not*" suffer a penalty for their medical use of marijuana. In construing unambiguous language such as this, we will give the statutory words their plain meaning. See *Scalise v. Boy Scouts of America,* 265 Mich.App. 1, 26, 692 N.W.2d 858 (2005) ("When construing a statute, where the language is unambiguous, this Court gives the words their plain meaning."). But for claimants' use of medical marijuana, the MCAC would not have disqualified them for unemployment benefits. The disqualification clearly amounted to a penalty imposed on claimants for their medical use of marijuana that ran afoul of the MMMA's immunity clause. Because the MMMA supersedes conflicting provisions of MESA, the MCAC erred by concluding that claimants were disqualified for unemployment benefits.

The Department also argues that if we were to hold that the MMMA protects against the denial of unemployment benefits, we would disregard the MMMA's provision that employers are not required to accommodate the use of medical marijuana in the workplace. However, the Department reads the relevant provision of the MMMA, MCL 333.26427(c)(2), too broadly. The provision does not state that an employer is not required to accommodate the *medical use* of marijuana, which includes internal possession, MCL 333.26423(f). Rather, it states that nothing in the MMMA shall be construed to require "[a]n employer to accommodate the *ingestion* of marihuana *in any workplace* or any employee *working while under the influence* of marihuana." MCL 333.26427(c)(2) (emphasis added). There was no evidence that claimants ingested marijuana in the workplace or that they worked under the influence of marijuana. Thus, the Department's argument with respect to MCL 333.26427(c)(2) is misplaced.

In a related argument, the Department contends that awarding unemployment benefits in this case amounts to a penalty imposed on the employers because the employers ultimately will be required to pay increased contributions to the unemployment compensation fund. However, to the extent that applying the plain language of the MMMA results in employers being responsible for paying unemployment benefits, that is a matter of public policy. Our authority does not extend to setting public policy for the state. *Houston v. Governor,* 491 Mich. 876, 877, 810 N.W.2d 255 (2012). Rather, our concern is the plain language of the statute, which is the best indicator of the intent of the electorate in approving the medical marijuana initiative. *McQueen,* 493 Mich. at 147, 828 N.W.2d 644. Here, as discussed earlier, the denial of unemployment benefits conflicts with the plain language of the MMMA's immunity clause.

. . . .

Finally, the Department argues that even if the MMMA prevents claimants from being disqualified from receiving unemployment benefits under § 29(1)(m), they are still disqualified from receiving benefits under § 29(1)(b) of MESA. Under that provision, an individual is disqualified from receiving benefits if he or she was discharged for misconduct connected with the individual's work. MCL 421.29(1)(b). According to the Department, all three claimants engaged in misconduct because they acted in direct and knowing contravention of their employers' zero-tolerance drug policies.

Contrary to the Department's argument, § 29(1)(b) is not applicable in the present cases. "[I]t is a settled rule of statutory construction that where a statute contains a specific statutory provision and a related, but more general, provision, the specific one controls." *In re Haley,* 476 Mich. 180, 198, 720 N.W.2d 246 (2006). In these cases, the MCAC found that each claimant was discharged for testing positive on a drug test. Other than testing positive for marijuana, there was no misconduct that led to any claimant being discharged. MCL 421.29 contains a specific provision regarding disqualification when an individual tests positive on a drug test. Accordingly, under the settled rule of statutory interpretation set forth in *In re Haley,* claimants' disqualification from receiving unemployment benefits is governed by § 29(1)(m), the specific provision concerning testing positive on a drug test, rather than § 29(1)(b), a related, but more general, provision regarding misconduct.

In addition, even if § 29(1)(b) were applicable and the MCAC disqualified claimants from receiving unemployment benefits because they were discharged for misconduct, this would not affect our analysis with respect to the plain language of the MMMA's immunity clause. Claimants' misconduct involved testing positive for marijuana on a drug test, which violated their employers' zero-tolerance drug policies. However, the only reason that claimants tested positive on the drug tests was that they used medical marijuana. Absent their use of medical marijuana, claimants would not have been disqualified from receiving unemployment benefits. Thus, the denial of benefits as a result of disqualification under § 29(1)(b), like disqualification under § 29(1)(m), results in a "penalty in any manner" for the medical use of marijuana contrary to MCL 333.26424(a).

IV. CONCLUSION

Claimants tested positive for marijuana and would ordinarily have been disqualified for unemployment benefits under MESA, MCL 421.29(1)(m); however, because there was no evidence to suggest that the positive drug tests were caused by anything other than claimants' use of medical marijuana in accordance with the terms of the MMMA, the denial of the benefits constituted an improper penalty for the medical use of marijuana under the MMMA, MCL 333.26424(a). Because the MMMA supersedes conflicting provisions of MESA, the circuit courts did not err by reversing the MCAC's rulings that claimants were not entitled to unemployment compensation benefits.

Affirmed.

QUESTIONS

1. This case illustrates that employment-related statutes often must be interpreted in the context of other, non-employment-related, statutes and policies. Does the court provide a persuasive justification for its holding that the medical marijuana statute supersedes the provisions of the unemployment compensation program?
2. How would you respond on behalf of an employee if the employer argued that they "voluntarily" left employment by choosing to use cannabis products when the employer had a strict policy against ingesting drugs and enforced it with drug testing?

Problem 39-2

Mario was hired as a driver of a medicar, used to transport patients to and from hospitals and nursing homes, by Safe Transport. During his first two months with Safe Transport, Mario had four accidents in the medicar, all while backing up. One caused serious damage to the vehicle, and so he was fired for violating a company rule against negligent driving. Should Mario be entitled to receive unemployment compensation?

---

4. The Employee Must Be Available for Work and Seeking Employment

Unemployment compensation benefits are designed to provide temporary financial relief while an employee seeks a new job. It would frustrate the purpose of the program to permit workers who are terminated to simply sit back and collect payments until they expire. The following case explores some of the difficulties in determining whether an employee is seeking employment and is available to take a new job.

Glick v. Unemployment Insurance Appeals Bd.

591 P.2d 24 (Cal. 1979).

Tobriner, Acting, C. J.

This case presents the issue whether under section 1253, subdivision (c), of the Unemployment Insurance Code an applicant who is ready and willing to work, but whose status as a student necessarily curtails her availability for work, is eligible for unemployment benefits.[1] Section 1253, subdivision (c), provides that an unemployed individual is eligible to receive unemployment compensation benefits with respect to any week only if he is "able to work and available for work" for that week.

In the instant case, the California Unemployment Insurance Appeals Board concluded that the claimant satisfied this statutory requirement for eligibility by demonstrating her availability for work in a potential employment field. The trial court affirmed. The Director of the California Employment Development Department now seeks review of the board's decision, contending that because the restrictions which the claimant "voluntarily" imposed upon herself materially reduced the labor market available to her, she is ineligible for unemployment benefits. As we shall explain, however, we reject the director's contention.

Claimant Enid G. Ballantyne's testimony at an administrative hearing establishes the details of her extensive employment history. From 1968 to 1970 Ballantyne worked full time as a service representative. Thereafter, because she was caring for her three small children, Ballantyne restricted her employment to part-time and intermittent day and night work at a department store.

In 1973 Ballantyne began attending college full time after separating from her husband. Needing "more stable employment," she went to work at a

1 Section 1253 provides in full: "An unemployed individual is eligible to receive unemployment compensation benefits with respect to any week only if the director finds that:

"(a) A claim for benefits with respect to that week has been made in accordance with authorized regulations.

"(b) He has registered for work, and thereafter continued to report, at a public employment office or such other place as the director may approve. Either or both of the requirements of this subdivision may be waived or altered by authorized regulation as to partially employed individuals attached to regular jobs.

"(c) He was able to work and available for work for that week.

"(d) He has been unemployed for a waiting period of one week as defined in Section 1254.

"(e) He conducted a search for suitable work in accordance with specific and reasonable instructions of a public employment office."

movie theater as assistant manager and night cashier. Ballantyne worked an average of 30 hours per week, from 6 p.m. until 1 a.m., at the theater until it closed in April 1974. Meanwhile, in March 1974 Ballantyne began work for the Pasadena Unified School District administering and evaluating tests; Ballantyne worked 20 hours per week there for four months.

In July 1974 Ballantyne ceased working for the school district and accepted a secretarial job with the Los Angeles Times. She worked four days a week, approximately 25 to 30 hours per week, "from 6 in the morning until whenever I was let go." In March 1975 Ballantyne, through no fault of her own, lost this employment and began receiving unemployment insurance benefits.

In September 1975 Ballantyne entered law school at the University of California at Los Angeles. She attended classes Monday through Friday, at varying hours, and studied four hours each day. When her employment office asked her in a written questionnaire, "If offered work that conflicts with the hours you are attending school, what provisions could you make to take such work?" Ballantyne answered "none." The department thereupon found her "not available for work" and ineligible for continued benefits.

Ballantyne pursued an administrative appeal from this determination, and at the hearing testified as to the above stated facts of her employment history. At the time of the hearing itself Ballantyne was earning $5 an hour for two hours each week as a private tutor; moreover, she was preparing to begin weekend work as a credit checker. Ballantyne explained that although she would not be willing to forego schooling for a full-time job, she had been searching for work "in no special field," and had not limited her search to weekend or night work.

Aside from Ballantyne's own testimony, the only other evidence received at the hearing concerned the size of the potential market for labor within Ballantyne's time restrictions. A department representative testified that "The labor market is extremely small regardless of what she does for a living. There are just too many people out of work and there is very little night work now."

In affirming the department's denial of benefits, the administrative law judge declared that claimant had "restricted her availability to evening and weekend work" and thus "substantially removed herself from the labor market." Accordingly, the judge concluded that claimant was "not available for employment within the meaning of code Section 1253(c)."

On claimant's appeal, however, the board reversed the judge's decision. (Precedent Benefit Dec. P-B-313 (1976).) As the board stated, "Restric[t]ing acceptable work to part-time hours does not necessarily result in a finding that the claimant has withdrawn from the labor market and thus is not available for work. . . ." Moreover, the board pointed out, "the test of availability may not be predicated upon the lack of openings for a claimant, but rather must be based upon whether there is a potential employment field." Because the record demonstrated that a labor market, although small, did exist for Ballantyne, the board concluded that claimant had successfully overcome any inference of unavailability. The superior court upheld the board on the ground that "here the applicant continues to make herself available for precisely the work with which she earned her unemployment credits."

We recently examined the concept of availability for work in *Sanchez v. Unemployment Ins. Appeals Bd.* (1977) 20 Cal.3d 55 [141 Cal.Rptr. 146, 569 P.2d 740]. In that case, claimant Sanchez applied for unemployment insurance benefits when her employment as a restaurant waitress was terminated. She informed the department that she could not accept work on either Saturdays or Sundays because on those days she was required to care for her four-year-old son. Nevertheless, she was ready to accept either restaurant or factory work during the week when her sister-in-law was available to tend the child, and she imposed no time restrictions on such weekday work. The board concluded, however, that Sanchez was not "able to work and available for work" within the meaning of section 1253 of the code, in that her self-imposed exclusion from weekend employment eliminated a "major portion of her labor market" as a waitress, and therefore denied her benefits.

In our decision reversing the board's ruling, we recognized that the requirement of section 1253 was intimately related to the code's penalties for rejection of offers of "suitable work" without "good cause." "While the requirement that an applicant for unemployment benefits be 'able to work and available for work' establishes a prerequisite to eligibility for any benefits, the code also provides a temporary disqualification from eligibility for an individual who 'without good cause, refused to accept suitable employment when offered to him, or failed to apply for suitable employment when notified by a public employment office.' (§ 1257, subd. (b).)" (*Sanchez v. Unemployment Ins. Appeals Bd., supra*, 20 Cal.3d 55, 61.) We concluded that "[t]he combined effect of those sections is to allow a claimant to refuse, without risk of disqualification, work which is either unsuitable or which the claimant has other 'good cause' to refuse." (*Id.*, at p. 62.)

Nevertheless, we did not find the availability requirement satisfied "merely by a willingness to accept all such 'non-refusable' work." (20 Cal.3d at p. 65.) Rather, because the policy underlying availability "normally entails accessibility to work for which there is some social demand," we held that "a second element of the inquiry into availability consists of the determination whether, after a claimant has restricted his market to 'suitable work which he has no good cause for refusing,' he remains available for work for which there is a substantial field of potential employers." (*Id.*) Thus we concluded that " '[a]vailability for work' within the meaning of section 1253, subdivision (c), requires no more than (1) that an individual claimant be willing to accept suitable work which he has no good cause for refusing and (2) that the claimant thereby make himself available to a substantial field of employment." (Fn. omitted.) (*Id.*, at p. 67.)

Applying this availability standard to the facts before us we found in *Sanchez* that "a claimant who is a parent or guardian of a minor has 'good cause' for refusing employment which conflicts with parental activities reasonably necessary for the care or education of the minor if there exist no reasonable alternative means of discharging those responsibilities." (Fn. omitted.) (20 Cal.3d at p. 70.) Furthermore, we explained that by requiring claimant Sanchez to make herself available to a substantial field of employment we did not mean "to foreclose the possibility that even if an employment field is not large in absolute terms, it may nevertheless satisfy the availability requirement if it presents a substantial employment opportunity" for the claimant. (*Id.*, at p. 67, fn. 11.) In light of the board's failure to apply these correct criteria of availability, we remanded the case to the board for further proceedings.

Thus, *Sanchez* establishes the two-prong inquiry which we must follow in the present case to determine claimant Ballantyne's availability for work within the meaning of section 1253, subdivision (c). We turn first to the question whether claimant's status as a student provides good cause such that she may refuse suitable work during her school hours without risk of disqualification for unemployment insurance benefits.

1. *Claimant, a law student, has "good cause" for not accepting work which would conflict with the requirements of her schooling.*

In *Syrek v. California Unemployment Insurance Appeals Board* (1960) 54 Cal.2d 519, 529 [7 Cal.Rptr. 97, 354 P.2d 625], we asserted that "the term 'good cause' as used in the statute means an adequate cause, a cause that comports with the purposes of the Unemployment Insurance Code and with other laws." Thus, we held in *Sanchez* that the duties of parenthood provide "good cause" for refusing work which would conflict with the performance of those duties: "Because of the crucial importance of parental responsibility and supervision, it would be anomalous if the Legislature intended that the obligation of the prospective claimant of unemployment benefits to accept work be irreconcilable with the duties of parenthood." (20 Cal.3d 55, 69.)

In the present case claimant Ballantyne seeks unemployment benefits although she does not accept employment which would conflict with the requirements of a full-time law student. Given the "indispensable role which education plays in the modern industrial state" (*Serrano* v. *Priest* (1971) 5 Cal.3d 584, 605 [96 Cal.Rptr. 601, 487 P.2d 1241]), we cannot impose upon Ballantyne the Hobson's choice of the neglect of her professional education or the sacrifice of entitlement to benefits. Indeed, Ballantyne's full-time attendance at school comports ideally with the purposes of the Unemployment Insurance Code to provide benefits to persons unemployed through no fault of their own, and to reduce involuntary unemployment to a minimum (Unemp. Ins. Code, § 100). Ballantyne's training in law school will enable her most effectively to alleviate the hardships of involuntary unemployment, which she has suffered in the past, as well as to avoid the recurrence of such hardships in the future. We therefore affirm the trial court's holding that Ballantyne's status as a student, and the necessary curtailment of availability which that status entails, did not render claimant unavailable for work within the meaning of section 1253.

The director argues, however, that the effect of our ruling that Ballantyne can claim "good cause" for refusing to accept work which would conflict with the necessities of her school attendance is to subvert the unemployment compensation system by utilizing it to subsidize employees' education. The director's argument plainly disregards the explicit coverage of the Unemployment Insurance Code. Section 1253.8 provides that "[a]n unemployed individual shall not be disqualified for eligibility for unemployment compensation benefits solely on the basis that he or she is a student."

The legislative intent underlying this statute is evident: The same test of availability for work must be applied to students as is applied to other applicants for unemployment benefits. In providing that an unemployed individual should not be disqualified "solely on the basis that he or she is a student," the Legislature necessarily established that some limitation on availability does not negate the right to benefits. A student, of course, is not available for employment at all times, but only at such times as do not interfere with the student's studies. Thus, student claimants who can show that full-time study does not preclude their availability for work within the meaning of section 1253, subdivision (c), will be eligible to receive unemployment benefits. The present claimant is not entitled to recover *because* she seeks to gain a legal education, but, by the same token, *because* she seeks to gain a legal education she should not be denied benefits. Accordingly, proceeding to the second half of our two-step inquiry, we must determine whether Ballantyne has made herself available to a "substantial field of employment."

2. *Substantial evidence supports the board's finding that claimant made herself available to a substantial field of employment.*

In *Sanchez* we focused the second portion of our determination of availability on the question whether the claimant had made herself available to a "substantial field of employment." We explained that the availability requirement "is not satisfied merely by a willingness to accept all . . . 'non-refusable' work," but also entails "assuring that a claimant is 'attached to the labor market.' [Citations.]" (20 Cal.3d 55, 65.) Thus, we prescribed a second element of the inquiry into availability: after the claimant has restricted her market to "suitable work which she has no good cause for refusing," does she remain available for work for which there is a *substantial* field of potential employers?

. . . .

Claimant's own testimony at the hearing justifies the conclusion that she is available to a substantial number of potential employers in Los Angeles. As she stated, "I have been a student since 1973, and I have worked—let's see—as a cashier in a movie theater. I have worked for the Pasadena United School District. I have worked for Pasadena City College and then I went to work for the Los Angeles Times. All of this time, I was taking care of three children and attending school full time." She also testified that between 1970 and 1975 she worked at Bullocks department store between 9 a.m. and 9 p.m., or on weekends, depending on the store's needs. She was assistant manager and cashier at a movie theater from 6 p.m. to 1 a.m.

This evidence shows that claimant could indeed balance full-time law school attendance—which allowed her to leave school as early as 2 p.m. two days a week and arrive as late as 11 a.m. two other days—with a *substantial* array of suitable employment. Her movie theater work is obviously completely compatible with the restrictions imposed by the law school, and her longest job—working at Bullocks—could easily be arranged around a law school program. In light of this concrete evidence indicating claimant's availability to a substantial number of potential employers, the trial court correctly held that Ballantyne was available for work within the meaning of section 1253.

We conclude that claimant has established that she is available for work for which there is a substantial field of potential employers. She has adduced substantial evidence to sustain that proposition. We recognize that availability for a negligible, insignificant labor market will not suffice; the claimant, however, has shown in this case, and future claimants must show, availability for work in a substantial field of potential employers.

. . . .

The judgment is affirmed.

Clark, J.

I dissent.

Is a person who devotes 46 hours per week to law studies, keeps an irregular and inflexible schedule, maintains a home, and cares for three children "available for work" within the statutory definition? By answering yes, the majority reduce to a nullity the "availability for work" requirement of Unemployment Insurance Code section 1253, subdivision (c).

Although the majority set forth claimant's school requirements, they refuse to give full effect to them. During her first quarter of law school, she attended classes from 9 a.m. to 2 p.m. on Monday and Tuesday, 10 a.m. to 4 p.m. on Wednesday, and 11 a.m. to 4 p.m. on Thursday and Friday. She studied four hours a day. Her law school activities required more of her than the ordinary full-time worker spends on the job. In addition to her schooling, claimant has time burdens of transportation, caring for herself, and maintaining her three children. While claimant had worked part-time during undergraduate school, there is nothing to indicate the school time burdens were nearly so great as her present law school burdens.

The claimant stated that if offered a full-time job she would not be willing to forego her schooling in order to accept unless paid at least $1,000 per month. Obviously, claimants should not be able to remain eligible while rejecting all jobs paying less than $1,000 per month.

Given the claimant's responsibilities and undertakings apart from employment, it is obvious that accepting substantial employment would be a herculean undertaking. In the circumstances, there is no basis for a finding that she was "available for work" within the meaning of Unemployment Insurance Code section 1253, subdivision (c). The instant case differs substantially from *Sanchez v. Unemployment Ins. Appeals Bd.* (1977) 20 Cal.3d 55 [141 Cal.Rptr. 146, 569 P.2d 740], where the claimant's family duties rendered her unable to work on Saturdays and Sundays. There is substantial difference in the limited unavailability in *Sanchez* compared to the unavailability in the instant case.

Awarding benefits in the instant case and others like it means employers must effectively subsidize education. This is not the function of the Unemployment Compensation Act. The statue "is fundamentally designed to act as a buffer or hedge against the ravages of sudden and unexpected loss of one's livelihood." (*Zorrero v. Unemployment Ins. Appeals Bd.* (1975) 47 Cal. App.3d 434, 439, [120 Cal.Rptr. 855].) The program is not one funded out of general taxes but through compulsory contributions by employers.

In an attempt to minimize the employer subsidization of education, the majority assert that granting the present claim does not require equal treatment for the typical student worker whose summertime employment terminates each fall with the start of classes. Yet, if anything, just the opposite should ordinarily be true. The typical student is much more "available for work" than the present claimant. Relatively few students must set aside as much as 46 hours per week for study commitments. Few have undertaken the additional child care and home responsibilities the present claimant has. As such students who wish to work are far more "available for work" during the school term than the present claimant, fairness would seem to require they be eligible for benefits if claimant is.

Moreover, today's decision can only make it more difficult for students to secure part-time employment. Because employers are required to provide the benefits, they will be reluctant to hire either students or potential students. Faced with the choice between hiring students or others, employers can be expected to avoid the disproportionate exposure to increased unemployment insurance contributions.

I would reverse the judgment.

QUESTION

1. How would you respond to someone who says that paying unemployment compensation benefits to someone who decides to return to school full-time after being laid off is good policy, because it will permit the person to develop human capital and avoid future unemployment?

Problem 39-3

You represent nine farmworkers. Each of them maintains a permanent home in the lower Rio Grande Valley area of Texas. Each year for the past twenty years, the nine farmworkers have migrated to California to perform seasonal agricultural work from April through October. They return home to Texas in the fall, when the state migrant labor camps close and seasonal work becomes scarce. This year, the nine workers applied for unemployment insurance benefits. They asserted that they vigorously sought agricultural employment when they returned to Texas in the fall, but they were largely unsuccessful because the Texas employers had already hired local workers and generally preferred not to hire migrant laborers. The farmworkers were willing to accept nonagricultural work, but their previous work experience has been limited exclusively to farm labor.

The California Employment Development Department (CEDD) denied benefits to all nine farmworkers. The CEDD reasoned that the farmworkers had moved from California to an area where they were less likely to find employment, they were not "available for work" as required by statute. The California Unemployment Insurance Appeals Board (CUIAB) upheld the CEDD determinations.

Describe your strategy for appealing these adverse determinations to the court. What factual investigation would you undertake, and how you would interpret the "available for work" requirement?

Conclusion

Unemployment compensation programs provide temporary income replacement for employees who lose their job. To qualify for benefits, the employee must meet various statutory criteria designed to promote the underlying policy of the programs to provide benefits to those who lose their job involuntarily and are seeking to reenter the workforce.

D. Employee Obligations After Termination of the Relationship

Key Concepts

- Employees owe duties to their employers that survive termination of the relationship.
- Employees can contract with their employer promising not to compete with the employer after termination of the relationship.
- Federal and state statutes protect the employer's property interest in trade secrets. Employees may not misappropriate trade secrets when the relationship ends.
- Prior to leaving an employer, employees are bound by a duty of loyalty not to work against the employer's interests before they terminate the relationship.

Lesson 40:
Promises Not to Compete

Objectives and Expected Learning Outcomes

In this Lesson, you will explore how employers seek to protect their interests by having employees sign a contract promising not to compete with the employer after the relationship ends. Courts recognize the imbalance of power between employers and employees, and the public interest in competition in our economy. Consequently, courts will enforce only reasonable agreements. Some states do not permit employers and employees to sign a promise not to compete, and you will consider the policy rationales for rendering these promises unenforceable. Finally, you will learn to draft promises not to compete that can survive court scrutiny.

1. An Overview of Promises Not to Compete

A contract containing a promise not to compete with a former employer is generally referred to as a "covenant not to compete," a "restrictive covenant," or a "non-compete agreement." Essentially, an employee contractually promises not to enter into a similar profession or trade that is in competition with the employer. Employers use covenants not to compete to protect their business interests. Because they have the effect of restraining trade, courts generally disfavor them and interpret them narrowly. In some jurisdictions, such as California, they are unenforceable. See Calif. Bus. & Prof. Code § 16600. Moreover, professional codes may limit the ethical use of promises not to compete. The Model Rules of Professional Conduct generally prohibit attorneys from entering into restrictive covenants.

Rule

As a general rule, the covenant will be enforceable only if it is reasonably tailored to protect a legitimate business interest, is supported by adequate consideration, is reasonably tailored in scope, duration, and geographic boundary, and does not violate public policy.

Employers understand that an at-will employee may leave at any time and for any reason. If the employer fears that the employee will be able to divert business, a promise not to compete for a period of time after the relationship ends will protect the employer's interests. On the other hand, the employee must be free to earn a living in some manner, so courts balance these interests.

The Restatement of Employment Law provides the blackletter framework used by courts to determine whether a restrictive covenant is enforceable or whether it unreasonably restricts a former employee's working activities.

Restatement of Employment Law

§ 8.06. Enforcement of Restrictive Covenants in Employment Agreements

Except as otherwise provided by other law or applicable professional rules, a covenant in an agreement between an employer and a former employee restricting the former employee's working activities is enforceable only if it is reasonably tailored in scope, geography, and time to further a protectable interest of the employer, as defined in § 8.07, unless:

(a) the employer discharges the employee on a basis that makes enforcement of the covenant inequitable;

(b) the employer acted in bad faith in requiring or invoking the covenant;

(c) the employer materially breached the underlying employment agreement; or

(d) in the geographic region covered by the restriction, a great public need for the special skills and services of the former employee outweighs any legitimate interest of the employer in enforcing the covenant.

§ 8.07. Protectable Interests for Restrictive Covenants

(a) A restrictive covenant is enforceable only if the employer can demonstrate that the covenant furthers a legitimate interest of the employer.

(b) An employer has a legitimate interest in protecting, by means of a reasonably tailored restrictive covenant with its employee, the employer's:

1. trade secrets, as defined in § 8.02, and other protectable confidential information that does not meet the definition of trade secret;
2. customer relationships;
3. investment in the employee's reputation in the market; or
4. purchase of a business owned by the employee.

§ 8.08. Modification of Unreasonable Restrictive Covenant

A court may delete or modify provisions in an overbroad restrictive covenant in an employment agreement and then enforce the covenant as modified unless the agreement does not allow for modification or the employer lacked a reasonable and good-faith basis for believing the covenant was enforceable. Lack of a reasonable and good-faith basis for believing a covenant was enforceable may be manifested by its gross overbreadth alone, or by overbreadth coupled with other evidence that the employer sought to do more than protect its legitimate interests.

2. The Employer's Legitimate Business Interest

Promises not to compete are enforceable only if they protect an employer's legitimate business interest. Generally, an employer must show that the employee possesses special or unique skills or knowledge to justify enforcement of a restrictive covenant. Desire to simply prevent competition by former employees is not a protectable interest.

Example 40-1

Bill is a plumber for Mason Plumbing Service. Prior to his work with Mason Plumbing, Bill had never worked as a plumber. He learned everything about the trade on the job. When Bill began working at Mason Plumbing, he signed a non-competition agreement which stated that he could not work for any direct competitor of Mason Plumbing for six months after terminating his employment. In the small town where Bill lives, there are only two other plumbing companies. Seeking better working hours, Bill quits his position with Mason Plumbing and begins working for one of the other companies in town. Mason Plumbing's claim that Bill violated the non-competition clause in his employment contract would be unenforceable. Mason Plumbing does not have a legitimate business interest necessary for a valid covenant not to compete. The skills Bill learned while at Mason Plumbing were not specialized as a result of working there, but could have been learned at any plumbing company because general knowledge or skills of the trade are known throughout the plumbing industry.

Example 40-2

Marissa works for Fume, a tech startup located in Portland, Oregon. When she began working she signed a promise not to compete. As a computer engineer, she has access to all of Fume's product information. This information is a trade secret as defined by Restatement § 8.07(b)(1). Fume has a legitimate business interest in protecting its trade secrets and therefore, a reasonably tailored non-competition clause would be valid.

---

3. The Reasonableness Requirement: Scope, Duration, and Geographic Limits

If the employer establishes the threshold requirement that the promise not to compete serves to protect a legitimate business interest, the court will then test the reasonableness of the conditions imposed on the employee. Courts generally assess whether the promise not to compete is reasonably tailored in terms with regard to the scope of activities prohibited, the duration of the agreement, and the geographic area to which the agreement applies. The scope of the limits on activity imposed by the promise cannot be overly broad. For example, a software developer for a gaming company might be subject to a promise not to go to work as a developer for another gaming company, but could not prohibit the employee from engaging in other forms of software development unrelated to the employer's business interests. The duration of the promise is highly fact sensitive, and depends on the nature of the industry and the employer's business needs. It is possible that the promise would never expire, but it is also possible that the promise could be sharply limited in time given the fast-changing nature of the industry. In assessing the geographic limits imposed by a promise not to compete, courts look to the nature of the job and the relevant labor market to determine reasonableness.

The following case demonstrates the fact-specific inquiry into reasonableness when the industry in question is highly dynamic.

EarthWeb v. Schlack

71 F. Supp. 2d 299 (S.D.N.Y. 1999).

William H. Pauley, III, District Judge:

This diversity action involves claims of breach of contract and misappropriation of trade secrets in the fluid and ever-expanding world of the Internet. Plaintiff EarthWeb, Inc. ("EarthWeb") moves for preliminary injunctive relief enjoining defendant Mark Schlack ("Schlack"), a former EarthWeb vice president responsible for "content" on the company's websites, from: (1) commencing employment with International Data Group, Inc. ("IDG"), and (2) disclosing or revealing EarthWeb's trade secrets to IDG or any third parties. For the reasons discussed below, the motion is denied.

. . . .

Findings of Fact and Conclusions of Law

A. Background

EarthWeb, which was founded in 1994, provides online products and services to business professionals in the information technology ("IT") industry. IT professionals are individuals who manage and run computer systems, develop software and perform related tasks for the companies that employ them. EarthWeb employs approximately 230 individuals in offices located in New York City and around the country. Its stock is publicly traded.

EarthWeb operates through a family of websites offering IT professionals information, products and services to use for facilitating tasks and solving technology problems in a business setting. Some of EarthWeb's websites are free to the user, while others require a subscription fee. EarthWeb's websites contain, inter alia, (1) articles on subjects tailored to IT professionals that discuss and examine the implementation of technology in the corporate environment; (2) lists of articles, training materials, periodicals, books and downloads organized and indexed by subject matter; (3) compilations and aggregations of technical news; (4) a reference library of full-text versions of technical books; and (5) an online forum of discussion groups.

EarthWeb obtains this content primarily through licensing agreements with third parties. Advertising is EarthWeb's primary source of revenue. In 1998, the company generated approximately $ 3.3 million in revenue.

Schlack has worked in the publishing industry for the past 16 years. Prior to joining EarthWeb, Schlack had been employed as senior editor and/or editor-in-chief of several print magazines, such as BYTE and Web Builder.

Schlack began his employment with EarthWeb in its New York City office on October 19, 1998, and he remained with the company until his resignation on September 22, 1999. His title at EarthWeb was Vice President, Worldwide Content, and as the name suggests, Schlack was responsible for the content of all of EarthWeb's websites. Thus, as described in greater detail below, Schlack had overall editorial responsibility for what appeared on the websites.

Schlack permanently resides in Massachusetts. During his twelve-month tenure with EarthWeb, Schlack resided in a New York City hotel approximately two or three days per week at EarthWeb's expense. Schlack was one of ten vice presidents at EarthWeb. He served below two senior vice presidents, an executive vice president, and the chief executive officer.

On September 22, 1999, Schlack tendered to EarthWeb senior vice president William F. Gollan his letter of resignation. Upon inquiry by Gollan, Schlack revealed that he had accepted a position with ITworld.com, a subsidiary of IDG. According to EarthWeb, IDG is the world's leading provider of IT print-based information. The company generates over $ 1 billion in annual revenues and publishes more than 280 monthly periodicals. The position IDG offered Schlack is based in Massachusetts and would provide him a significant increase in compensation.

B. Schlack's Employment with EarthWeb

EarthWeb describes Schlack as one of its most important officers, while Schlack claims that EarthWeb has inflated the nature of his duties and responsibilities. Schlack also argues that the position waiting for him at IDG is so different that he would have no occasion to divulge any trade secrets belonging to EarthWeb. From those respective viewpoints, the parties have inundated the record with material concerning the extent to which Schlack had access to trade secrets and proprietary information. In particular, EarthWeb has produced copies of over 1,100 documents, a large percentage of which are intra-company e-mails, in order to show that Schlack reviewed and/or created this sensitive information. The trade secrets and other confidential information that EarthWeb claims are likely to be used and disclosed by Schlack to their detriment may be grouped into four broad categories: (1) strategic content planning; (2) licensing agreements and acquisitions; (3) advertising; and (4) technical knowledge. Each category is addressed below.

Strategic Content Planning

EarthWeb claims that Schlack's primary job responsibilities involved making all significant strategic decisions relating to content. The company also asserts that Schlack either authored or supervised the creation of the content plans for a number of EarthWeb websites launched within the last year. Thus, Schlack was involved in deciding what content EarthWeb licensed and how that content would be structured on its websites in order to reach specific types of IT professionals. Schlack was also involved in determining whether the users of a particular EarthWeb website should pay for access to the site, and if so, what the appropriate price should be. As a result, Schlack knows the specific target audience for each website, how EarthWeb aggregated content on those websites to reach the targeted audience, and how EarthWeb may intend to improve the content and delivery of particular websites.

Schlack does not dispute the extent of his editorial involvement with EarthWeb's websites. Instead, he claims that he had virtually no interaction with senior management and therefore knows little about EarthWeb's overall business goals. He also contends that whatever he knows about EarthWeb's strategic planning is likely to become obsolete rather quickly because the company's websites are constantly changing.

Licensing Agreements and Acquisitions

During his employment, Schlack was involved in negotiating at least two licensing agreements with third parties, and he was generally aware of the terms and conditions of other such agreements. Schlack also knows of companies whose content EarthWeb is interested in licensing. As vice president for content, Schlack often played a key role in determining whether particular content should be licensed, and if so, what the terms of the deal would be. With respect to acquisitions, Schlack analyzed and evaluated websites and companies that EarthWeb later acquired. Schlack also knows of at least four companies that EarthWeb continues to view as desirable acquisitions.

Schlack contends, and EarthWeb does not dispute, that the terms of EarthWeb's licensing agreements are frequently revealed by licensors as they continue to search for better deals. Schlack disputes the number of acquisitions in which he was actually involved, and claims that the mechanics of the deals were handled by a separate department at EarthWeb. Schlack also suggests that he analyzed prospective acquisitions simply by looking at their websites, but the record indicates that his research also included meetings with high-level managers of those companies.

It should be noted that EarthWeb does not allege that Schlack has retained copies of any licensing agreements or other sensitive documents concerning licensors. Schlack maintains that he does not remember the details of the licensing agreements which he worked on or approved.

Similarly, Schlack claims that he is unaware of the terms of any proposed or pending acquisitions. As the person ultimately responsible for deciding what content would be posted on EarthWeb's websites, Schlack asserts that his role was limited to evaluating the content to be licensed or acquired and determining whether a deal should be pursued.

Advertising

Schlack was also involved, albeit less directly, with EarthWeb's marketing and sales efforts. Schlack describes his role as "explaining EarthWeb's editorial focus and how [it] might relate to the advertiser's customer." On occasion, Schlack joined members of EarthWeb's sales and marketing departments on business development calls in order to solicit advertising and sponsorships on the company's websites. According to EarthWeb, Schlack's efforts in this area would have allowed him to gain some insights into the specific audiences that EarthWeb's advertisers were seeking to target. Schlack was also involved in the creation of custom publishing websites for EarthWeb's advertisers.

However, Schlack's main function with respect to advertising appears to have been one of internal coordination. Schlack, as vice president of content, met regularly with senior managers for the sales and marketing departments so that each department could make certain that it was coordinating its efforts with the others. Schlack received sales and marketing updates at those meetings and was consulted with respect to a number of particular products and initiatives. Here again, however, it should be noted that EarthWeb does not accuse Schlack of absconding with a list of advertisers or other confidential advertising information. EarthWeb's customer list was maintained in a special database which Schlack could not access.

Technical Knowledge

Schlack's job responsibilities required him to be familiar with the software and hardware infrastructure that supports EarthWeb's websites. Thus, Schlack has general knowledge of how EarthWeb customized and deployed the products of outside vendors and consultants in order to fit EarthWeb's programming needs. Schlack also gained an understanding of the technical problems that EarthWeb successfully tackled in order to make its websites operate efficiently.

However, Schlack had no access to EarthWeb's source codes or configuration files, so his knowledge of EarthWeb's proprietary software and infrastructure is necessarily limited. In addition, EarthWeb plans to revamp its software infrastructure in the near future, so any knowledge Schlack has may soon become obsolete.

EarthWeb's main concern is Schlack's awareness of the trial and error process that EarthWeb undertook in implementing the products and services of outside consultants. Armed with this knowledge, EarthWeb contends that Schlack would be able to solve similar technical problems if they arose at ITworld.com and thereby avoid the mistakes that EarthWeb made in the past. EarthWeb claims that such information constitutes a trade secret.

In summary, Schlack was primarily responsible for determining what content EarthWeb licensed or acquired for its websites. In that capacity, Schlack was privy to information concerning a wide range of matters. Schlack often worked collaboratively with other department heads and employees on technology issues, marketing and advertising. While such matters may have been handled principally by other departments, Schlack's decisions concerning content directly impacted these aspects of EarthWeb's business, and thus it is not surprising that Schlack's input and analysis would have been essential.

Nevertheless, Schlack had no access to EarthWeb's advertiser list, source codes or configuration files. Nor did Schlack have direct contact with EarthWeb's highest executive officers. He was not involved in developing or planning EarthWeb's overall business strategies and goals, and he had no access to company-wide financial reports or information. Thus, while the central nature of Schlack's position necessarily offered him a broad prospective over EarthWeb's day-to-day operations, in many important respects his access to highly confidential information was limited.

C. Schlack's Prospective Position with ITworld.com

At the moment, ITworld.com does not exist; the website is scheduled to be launched in January 2000. According to its president and CEO, William Reinstein, ITworld.com will consolidate four online publications of IDG—Computerworld, Network World, InfoWorld and CIO—and three additional wholly-owned websites. When operational, ITworld.com will be a single website for IT professionals that contains news, product information and editorial opinions written primarily by an internal staff of more than 275 journalists.

Thus, in contrast to EarthWeb's emphasis on obtaining the products and services of third parties through acquisitions and licensing agreements and then making those materials readily accessible on its websites, ITworld.com will rely on original content for over 70% of its website's material. Content such as product reviews and technical research will be created in-house by ITworld.com's staff.

Schlack contends that ITworld.com will also be distinguishable from EarthWeb in the type of audience it targets. While both EarthWeb and ITworld.com are intended to appeal to IT professionals, Schlack argues that the products and services offered by EarthWeb are aimed at programers and technicians, while ITworld.com will focus on upper level executives, such as technology managers and chief information officers. EarthWeb disputes this assertion, and claims that it offers "a wide range of technology-related content" tailored to, inter alia, IT managers and chief information officers. EarthWeb also claims that it is presently pursuing an acquisition that would expand its ability to reach this select audience. At the moment, however, EarthWeb's family of websites appears to offer a richer moraine of technical information while Computerworld.com concentrates on IT news in a magazine format.

Given the dynamics of the Internet, such comparisons may be ephemeral. This underscores the difficulty in assessing the characteristics of ITworld.

com, an embryonic business entity that will compete in a nascent industry which is evolving and re-inventing itself with breathtaking speed. Apart from the Reinstein affidavit, the only other description of what ITworld.com will ultimately do is contained in an undated memorandum submitted by defendant titled "Our Mission and the Opportunity." This four-page prolegomenon essentially extols the website's architecture, content and marketing strategy. While EarthWeb has dissected the document in an effort to identify potential similarities between EarthWeb and ITworld.com, the Court finds that exercise unpersuasive. The "mission" memorandum provides a visionary outline of what ITworld.com may eventually be, but fails to offer any meaningful description that transforms the idea into a perceptible reality.

D. The Employment Agreement

On October 13, 1998, EarthWeb and Schlack executed an "Employment Agreement" memorializing certain terms and conditions of Schlack's employment. The five-page agreement contains fourteen enumerated sections. Section one provides that Schlack's employment is "at-will." Section two addresses Schlack's compensation package and incorporates by reference an attached "offer letter." The letter, dated September 30, 1998, provides for an annual salary of $125,000, an annual performance-based bonus of $20,000, and the purchase of stock options. Section three provides a sweeping and encyclopedic definition of the term "inventions", which is incorporated by reference in the following provision concerning non-disclosure of "proprietary information."

Specifically, section four of the agreement, titled "Proprietary Information", provides in relevant part:

> (a) [Schlack] will not disclose or use, at any time either during or after the term of employment, except at the request of EarthWeb or an affiliate of EarthWeb, any Confidential Information (as herein defined). "Confidential Information shall mean all proprietary information, technical data, trade secrets, and know-how, including, without limitation, research, product plans, customer lists, markets, software, developments, inventions, discoveries, processes, formulas, algorithms, technology, designs, drawings, marketing and other plans, business strategies and financial data and information, including but not limited to Inventions, whether or not marked as "Confidential." " "Confidential Information" shall also mean information received by EarthWeb from custom-

> ers of EarthWeb or other third parties subject to a duty to keep confidential.

Section five of the employment agreement is titled "Limited Agreement Not To Compete." That section provides in relevant part:

> (c) For a period of twelve (12) months after the termination of Schlack's employment with EarthWeb, Schlack shall not, directly or indirectly:
>
>> (1) work as an employee, employer, consultant, agent, principal, partner, manager, officer, director, or in any other individual or representative capacity for any person or entity that directly competes with EarthWeb. For the purpose of this section, the term "directly competing" is defined as a person or entity or division on an entity that is
>>
>>> (i) an on-line service for Information Professionals whose primary business is to provide Information Technology Professionals with a directory of third party technology, software, and/or developer resources; and/or an online reference library, and or
>>>
>>> (ii) an on-line store, the primary purpose of which is to sell or distribute third party software or products used for Internet site or software development[.]

E. The Parties' Contentions

EarthWeb argues that under the "non-compete" provision of the employment agreement, Schlack should be enjoined from commencing employment with ITworld.com because that company will "directly compete" with EarthWeb, and because enforcement of the agreement is necessary to prevent the disclosure of EarthWeb's trade secrets. EarthWeb also contends that Schlack's services to EarthWeb are unique and extraordinary, thereby providing a further basis for enforcement of the non-compete provision. EarthWeb further asserts that under section four of the employment agreement barring the disclosure or use of "proprietary information", preliminary injunctive relief is necessary because Schlack will inevitably disclose EarthWeb's trade secrets during the course of his employment at ITworld.com. EarthWeb claims that since disclosure of trade secrets would be inevitable, Schlack may be enjoined from working for ITworld.com under this provision. Finally,

EarthWeb suggests that the doctrine of "inevitable disclosure" provides an independent basis upon which Schlack should be enjoined.

. . . .

Discussion

. . . .

B. Inevitable Disclosure of Trade Secrets as Irreparable Harm

The inevitable disclosure doctrine is not new. For example, in *Eastman Kodak Co. v. Powers Film Products*, 189 A.D. 556, 179 N.Y.S. 325 (4th Dep't 1919), the court enforced a non-compete covenant where the departing employee possessed information about Eastman Kodak's secret film manufacturing processes and formulas that he would have inevitably used in performing his new job duties for a competitor. However, more recent cases are notable because they have enjoined employees from working for competitors in the absence of an express non-compete agreement.

PepsiCo is a leading example. In that case the employee, Redmond, signed a confidentiality agreement at the outset of his employment, but he did not sign a non-compete agreement. Redmond worked within the highly competitive sports-drink industry, and he eventually became a general manager for a business unit that had annual revenues of over $500 million per year and accounted for twenty percent of PepsiCo's profit for all of the United States. *See PepsiCo*, 54 F.3d at 1264. Redmond's position made him privy to information such as PepsiCo's national and regional marketing strategies for the upcoming year. *Id.* at 1265–66. He was recruited for a similar, high level position with Quaker Oats, a direct competitor of PepsiCo in the sports drink industry. Under these circumstances, the court effectively converted Redmond's confidentiality agreement into a non-compete agreement by enjoining him from working for a direct competitor of PepsiCo for a sixth month period.

Doubleclick is also instructive. The defendants in *Doubleclick* were two senior executives for an Internet advertising company who were caught misappropriating trade secrets as they surreptitiously plotted to form their own company to compete directly with their former employer. Both defendants had signed confidentiality agreements and while one of them had also signed a non-compete agreement, although its applicability was disputed. Based on the evidence of actual misappropriation, which was "bolstered by . . . a high probability of 'inevitable disclosure' of trade secrets", the court enjoined the defendants from launching their company, or accepting employment with any competing company, for a period of six months. *Doubleclick*, 1997 WL 731413, at *5–6.

While *Doubleclick* appears to represent a high water mark for the inevitable disclosure doctrine in New York, its holding rests heavily on evidence of the defendants' overt theft of trade secrets and breaches of fiduciary duty. . . . However, in cases that do not involve the actual theft of trade secrets, the court is essentially asked to bind the employee to an implied-in-fact restrictive covenant based on a finding of inevitable disclosure. This runs counter to New York's strong public policy against such agreements and circumvents the strict judicial scrutiny they have traditionally required. Indeed, in post-employment disputes that do not involve trade secrets or tortious conduct on the part of the employee, restrictive covenants may not be implied.

Thus, in its purest form, the inevitable disclosure doctrine treads an exceedingly narrow path through judicially disfavored territory. Absent evidence of actual misappropriation by an employee, the doctrine should be applied in only the rarest of cases. Factors to consider in weighing the appropriateness of granting injunctive relief are whether: (1) the employers in question are direct competitors providing the same or very similar products or services; (2) the employee's new position is nearly identical to his old one, such that he could not reasonably be expected to fulfill his new job responsibilities without utilizing the trade secrets of his former employer; and (3) the trade secrets at issue are highly valuable to both employers. Other case-specific factors such as the nature of the industry and trade secrets should be considered as well.

While the inevitable disclosure doctrine may serve the salutary purpose of protecting a company's investment in its trade secrets, its application is fraught with hazards. Among these risks is the imperceptible shift in bargaining power that necessarily occurs upon the commencement of an employment relationship marked by the execution of a confidentiality agreement. When that relationship eventually ends, the parties' confidentiality agreement may be wielded as a restrictive covenant, depending on how the employer views the new job its former employee has accepted. This can be a powerful weapon in the hands of an employer; the risk of litigation alone may have a chilling effect on the employee. Such constraints should be the product of open negotiation.

Another drawback to the doctrine is that courts are left without a frame of reference because there is no express non-compete agreement to test for reasonableness. Instead, courts must grapple with a decidedly more nebulous standard of "inevitability." The absence of specific guideposts staked-out in a writing will only spawn such litigation, especially as the Internet becomes a primary medium for ideas and commerce. Clearly, a written agreement that contains a non-compete clause is the best way of promoting predictability during the employment relationship and afterwards.

Of course, that is precisely what Schlack got with Earthweb. Section five of the parties' employment agreement is a "limited" restrictive covenant in which Schlack agrees not to compete with EarthWeb in three narrow categories of employment: companies whose "primary business" is providing IT professionals with (1) "directory" of third party technology, (2) an "online reference library", or (3) an "online store." On the other hand, section four of the employment agreement contains extremely broad language concerning non-disclosure of "proprietary information."

Schlack viewed this distinction as critical and says he would not have knowingly agreed to a post-employment restraint on his ability to work in the field of IT journalism on the Internet. EarthWeb, however, appears to gloss over the distinctness of these provisions which it drafted. Under the banner of inevitable disclosure doctrine, EarthWeb contends that Schlack should be enjoined from working for any Internet company that targets IT professionals. Thus, at oral argument EarthWeb indicated that Schlack was free to work for an "organization that appealed to consumers that were interested in buying technology for themselves or people who are just plain consumers as opposed to [ ] IT professionals, which would be in the same area."

This Court declines to re-write the parties' employment agreement under the rubric of inevitable disclosure and thereby permit EarthWeb to broaden the sweep of its restrictive covenant. As discussed above, such retroactive alterations distort the terms of the employment relationship and upset the balance which courts have attempted to achieve in construing non-compete agreements.

The Court finds further support for a strict construction of the employment agreement based on its rather onerous terms. The agreement provided that Schlack's employment was at-will. While it contained a restrictive covenant, it made no provision for the payment of severance to Schlack in the event that EarthWeb terminated his employment. Moreover, EarthWeb purported to "reserve[ ] the right to modify the terms of this Agreement on a quarterly basis, subject to notice and acknowledgment by the Employee of such modifications." Read collectively, the effect of these provisions is to indenture the employee to EarthWeb. This Court will not allow EarthWeb to expand the agreement's confidentiality provision so that it potentially has that result. Nor can EarthWeb make an end-run around the agreement by asserting the doctrine of inevitable disclosure as an independent basis for relief.

Accordingly, EarthWeb's entitlement to a preliminary injunction enjoining Schlack's future employment must be found to rest, if at all, on the restrictive covenant it drafted, and not on a confidentiality provision conflated with the theory of inevitable disclosure. With this framework in mind, the Court turns to the specific terms of the employment agreement at issue here.

C. The Non-Compete Provision

By its terms, EarthWeb's non-compete provision only restricts Schlack from working for a company that is: "(i) an on-line service for Information Professionals whose primary business is to provide Information Technology Professionals with a directory of third party technology, software, and/or developer resources; and/or an online reference library, and or (ii) an online store, the primary purpose of which is to sell or distribute third party software or products used for Internet site or software development[.]" EarthWeb argues that ITworld.com will provide each of these services based on its interpretation of the "mission" memorandum and its review of the four IDG websites which Schlack is being hired to integrate.

Schlack responds that ITworld.com's primary business will not involve any of these activities. . . . Schlack argues that ITworld.com's primary focus will be to publish news, analysis and product information that is generated daily by its own editorial staff. . . . ITworld.com may, for example, offer some form of "directory of developer resources", but . . . this directory "will constitute not more than 2% of ITworld.com's offerings and revenues when we go online." Since EarthWeb's restrictive covenant only proscribes Schlack from working for companies whose "primary business" falls within a specified category, Schlack argues that such de minimis aspects of ITworld.com's content do not fall within the scope of the provision.

This Court agrees. EarthWeb has no probative basis for refuting . . . what ITworld.com intends to do. . . .

Even if the terms of EarthWeb's restrictive covenant reached Schlack's prospective employment at ITworld.com, EarthWeb would still have to establish that the restraint is reasonable and necessary to protect its legitimate interests. In New York, non-compete covenants will be enforced only if reasonably limited in scope and duration, and only "to the extent necessary (1) to prevent an employee's solicitation or disclosure of trade secrets, (2) to prevent an employee's release of confidential information regarding the employer's customers, or (3) in those cases where the employee's services to the employer are deemed special or unique." *Ticor Title Ins. Co. v. Cohen*, 173 F.3d 63, 70 (2d Cir. 1999). . . .

The policy underlying this strict approach rests on notions of employee mobility and free enterprise. "Once the term of an employment agreement has expired, the general public policy favoring robust and uninhibited competition should not give way merely because a particular employer wishes to insulate himself from competition." *American Broadcasting*, 52 N.Y.2d at 404, 438 N.Y.S.2d at 487. "Important, too, are the 'powerful considerations of public policy which militate against sanctioning the loss of a man's livelihood." *Id.*

Applying these principles here, EarthWeb's restrictive covenant would fail to pass muster even if Schlack's position at ITworld.com fell within the provision's relatively narrow parameters.

1. Duration

As a threshold matter, this Court finds that the one-year duration of EarthWeb's restrictive covenant is too long given the dynamic nature of this industry, its lack of geographical borders, and Schlack's former cutting-edge position with EarthWeb where his success depended on keeping abreast of daily changes in content on the Internet. . . . While courts may "blue pencil" such provisions to make them shorter and hence enforceable, see *Karpinski v. Ingrasci*, 28 N.Y.2d 45, 51–52, 320 N.Y.S.2d 1, 6–7, 268 N.E.2d 751 (1971), this Court would decline to exercise its discretion to do so in this case because, as discussed above, the employment agreement as a whole overreaches. See generally *Webcraft*, 674 F. Supp. at 1047.

2. Unique and Extraordinary Services

Contrary to EarthWeb's contention, Schlack's services are not "unique and extraordinary." Such characteristics have traditionally been associated with "various categories of employment where the services are dependent on an employee's special talents; such categories include musicians, professional athletes, actors and the like." *Ticor*, 173 F.3d at 70. However, in order to justify a [sic] enforcement of a restrictive covenant, more must . . . be shown to establish such a quality than that the employee excels at his work or that his performance is of high value to his employer. It must also appear that his services are of such character as to make his replacement impossible or that the loss of such services would cause the employer irreparable injury . . . EarthWeb has not shown that the nature of Schlack's services are unique or that he cultivated the type of special client relationships that the Second Circuit found worthy of protection in *Ticor.*

. . . .

F. Conclusion

For all these reasons, plaintiff's motion for a preliminary injunction is denied, and the temporary restraining order entered by this Court on September 28, 1999 and thereafter extended on October 12, 1999 is dissolved. . . .

SO ORDERED

Problem 40-1

Pixie, Inc. is an animation software company that produces technology for use in major motion pictures. Laura Ring was hired by Pixie to develop software and programming related to animation. Ring signed a non-compete agreement with Pixie that prohibited her from engaging in, or accepting employment with any entity engaged in, activities that are in competition with Pixie and its business during her employment, extending for a period of one year after her employment at Pixie ends. Pixie is headquartered in New York, does most of its business in Los Angeles, and has offices throughout the country. Ring worked in the company's Dallas office until it closed down; thereafter, she worked from her home in Dallas.

During her employment with Pixie, Ring started a side business to develop faster and more reliable lip-syncing capabilities for animation production. When Pixie discovered that Ring had a business on the side, it fired her and sued for breach of contract. Can Pixie enforce the promise not to compete against Ring?

4. The Requirement of Consideration

Promises not to compete are contracts; consequently they are enforceable only if they are supported by consideration. Most courts hold that a promise not to compete entered into prior to the commencement of employment is supported by consideration. In this case, the promise is part of the original agreement for employment.

Problems arise when an employer requires an employee to sign a promise not to compete during the course of employment. Courts are split as to whether agreeing to continue the employment relationship provides sufficient consideration, or if there must be new consideration such as an increase in salary, a bonus, or some other benefit. A number of states—including Connecticut, Minnesota, Montana, North Carolina, Pennsylvania, Washington, West Virginia, and Wyoming—require new consideration to support the enforcement of a promise not to compete.

5. Remedies: Modification and the Blue-Pencil Rule

Historically, courts would declare a promise not to compete unenforceable if it was unreasonable. Given the highly fact-sensitive assessment of reasonableness, this led employers to be cautious in drafting the terms of the non-compete agreement to ensure it would be enforceable. However, today a majority of courts follow the "blue-pencil" approach, in which the court will edit (metaphorically with a "blue pencil") the unreasonable parts of the non-compete agreement to render the agreement enforceable. Essentially, the court balances the interests of the employer and employee and revises the agreement to provide reasonable limitations on the employee.

Dean Van Horn Consulting Assocs., Inc., v. Wold

395 N.W. 2d. 405 (Minn. Ct. App. 1986).

Opinion by: Wozniak.

On appellant Dean Van Horn Consulting Associates, Inc.'s action to recover damages resulting from respondent Wold's breach of a restrictive covenant, Dean Van Horn appeals for the second time based upon the trial court's alleged error in hearing evidence on remand regarding the reasonableness of the restrictive covenant and the liquidated damages clause. The trial court found . . . the restrictive covenant clause overbroad, modifying the duration of the restrictive covenant clause from three years to one year. Dean Van Horn appeals. We affirm.

FACTS

In May of 1974, appellant Dean Van Horn Consulting Associates, Inc. hired respondent Charles Wold, then a college senior, to prepare tax returns and advise clients on tax and accounting matters. On June 11, 1975, Wold and Dean Van Horn, the president of Dean Van Horn Consulting Associates, signed an employment contract.

Section 13 of the employment agreement contained a restrictive covenant precluding Wold from soliciting or lending similar services to any customer he advised during his employment with Dean Van Horn. Section 14 of the employment contract contained a liquidated damages clause providing that, upon Wold's breach of the restrictive covenant, Dean Van Horn would be entitled to damages of 50% of Wold's billing to any client of Dean Van Horn for the first year, 30% for the second year, and 20% for the third year.

After working for Dean Van Horn for about 4 1/2 years, Wold submitted his resignation on January 22, 1980 and terminated his employment on February 28, 1980. When Wold left Dean Van Horn's employment, it owed him $1,296.68 in unpaid commissions.

Dean Van Horn personally took over the work previously performed by Wold and did not hire a new consultant. Dean Van Horn informed the clients with whom Wold had been working that Wold was leaving the company.

On January 20, 1980, Wold formed a corporation called Professional Consulting Group, Inc. (PCG). Wold became a consultant for PCG and advised former clients of Dean Van Horn.

Dean Van Horn instituted suit against Wold and PCG alleging breach of restrictive covenant and requesting damages in accordance with the liquidated damages clause of the employment contract. . . .

At the close of plaintiff's case, the trial court dismissed Dean Van Horn's claim against both defendants, stating Dean Van Horn was unable to prove actual damages against Wold, and that PCG was not a party to the employment contract. . . .

. . . .

On April 25, 1985, this court reversed the trial court in *Dean Van Horn Consulting Associates v. Wold*, 367 N.W.2d 556 (Minn. Ct. App. 1985). . . . With regard to the liquidated damages and restrictive covenant, this court stated:

> The contract here clearly contains a liquidated damages clause which will be applied since it is reasonable. Although restrictive covenants should generally be strictly construed, they will be enforced to the extent they are reasonable. * * * * This restrictive covenant and the liquidated damages clause were reasonably intended to protect Van Horn from loss of clients and profits. They will be applied. *Id.* at 560 (citation omitted).

. . . After remand, the trial court ordered both Dean Van Horn and Wold to try the issues of the reasonableness of the restrictive covenant and the liquidated damages clause. The trial court concluded:

> There was not adequate consideration to support the restrictive covenant as contained in Section 13 of the employment contract between plaintiff and defendant Wold. Rather this Court concludes that one year would be proper duration for the restrictive covenant to be in effect.

. . . .

ANALYSIS

. . . .

[T]he issue is whether the trial court was clearly erroneous in modifying the restrictive covenant based upon overbreadth.

In Minnesota, the reasonableness of the duration of a restrictive covenant may be tested under two alternative standards: 1) the length necessary to obliterate the identification between employer and employee in the minds of the employer's customers, and (2) the length of time necessary for an employee's replacement to obtain licenses and learn the fundamentals of the business. *Davies & Davies Agency, Inc. v. Davies*, 298 N.W.2d 127, 131 (Minn. 1980). The trial court applied those standards in this case.

The record on remand establishes that Dean Van Horn corresponded to each of the clients previously counseled by Wold, thus alerting the clients of the obliteration of the relationship between Wold and Dean Van Horn. With regard to the second *Davies* standard, the record indicates that Wold's training period was about one year. If Dean Van Horn had chosen to hire a replacement, which it did not, one year would have been a reasonable time for the restrictive covenant under the second *Davies* standard. The trial court was not clearly erroneous in finding the restriction overbroad.

After finding the restriction was overbroad, the trial court modified the restrictive covenant from a three-year period to a one-year period. Under the blue pencil doctrine as it has developed in Minnesota, a court can take an overly broad restriction and enforce it only to the extent that it is reasonable. The trial court's modification of the restrictive covenant was not clearly erroneous.

DECISION

The trial court correctly heard evidence on the reasonableness of the liquidated damages clause and the restrictive covenant. The trial court was not clearly erroneous in holding the restrictive covenant was overbroad and accordingly modifying the covenant to a one-year period.

Affirmed.

QUESTIONS

1. If Dean Van Horn had submitted evidence that the company consults with clients an average of once every three years, and that basic training in Wold's position does not amount to expertise on accounting matters, would the outcome of the case have changed?
2. Should an employer be able to use a liquidated damages clause in an employment contract?
3. What is the significance of the unpaid commissions Wold claims he was owed?

Problem 40-2

You are a lobbyist who works on behalf of organizations interested in employee rights. Your state has not adopted the "blue pencil" rule, but the legislature is considering enacting the rule by statute. Develop the arguments that employee rights organizations would make against this legislation.

---

6. Remedies for Breach of a Promise Not to Compete

A promise not to compete is a contract, and so the employer is entitled to contract damages if the employee breaches the terms of the agreement. Consider how those damages are assessed in the following case.

CLARK V. LIBERTY NAT'L LIFE INS. CO.

592 So. 2d 564 (Ala. 1992).

ALMON, JUSTICE.

Liberty National Life Insurance Company ("Liberty National") brought this action against its former insurance agent, Arthur Clark, for a declaratory judgment, an injunction, and damages arising out of Clark's alleged violations of a noncompetition clause in his employment contract with Liberty National. After hearing the evidence without a jury, the trial court entered a judgment declaring the noncompetition agreement valid and enforceable and awarding Liberty National damages in the amount of $ 14,819.61. Clark argues: (1) that the noncompetition agreement, which prohibited him from soliciting Liberty National's policyholders, violates § 8–1–1, Ala. Code 1975; (2) that the agreement was entered into under duress; and (3) that Liberty National did not carry its burden of proof as to damages.

When Clark began working for Liberty National as an insurance agent in November 1981, he was assigned an agency in an area of South Alabama that included parts of Houston, Henry, and Dale Counties. Clark was provided with a list of Liberty National policyholders and was responsible for collecting the premiums on his debit route. His duties also included soliciting and obtaining new policyholders and serving the customers in his area.

On April 1, 1985, Clark entered into a new agent's contract with Liberty National that included a covenant not to compete ("the covenant"). The contract was the same as his previous agent's contract, except for the covenant. The covenant provided, in pertinent part, that for a period of one year after the termination of his employment with Liberty National for whatever reason, Clark would not:

> Induce, promote, facilitate, bring about, solicit, quote rates for, receive, write, bind, broker, transfer or accept replacement or renewal insurance coverage or services for any insurance policy or service sold or serviced by you for the company, or for which you have been or were being compensated by the company, or the existence of which you learned of while in the employ of the company, nor shall you induce or seek to induce the discontinuance or lapse of such insurance policy or service.

Clark terminated his employment with Liberty National on March 4, 1988, and began working as an agent for Prudential Insurance Company. Clark stipulated that he violated the terms of the contract by quoting rates and facilitating and bringing about replacement coverage for Liberty National's policyholders. Clark maintains, however, that he did not solicit these policyholders, but, rather, that they contacted him. This contention does not defeat the application of the covenant, however, because the covenant prohibited Clark from receiving, writing, or accepting replacement or renewal coverage as well as from soliciting such coverage.

Alabama's public policy regarding contracts in restraint of trade is expressed in § 8–1–1, Ala. Code 1975. Contracts restraining employment are disfavored "because they tend not only to deprive the public of efficient service, but [also] . . . to impoverish the individual." *James S. Kemper & Co. v. Cox & Associates, Inc.*, 434 So. 2d 1380, 1384 (Ala. 1983), quoting *Robinson v. Computer Servicenters, Inc.*, 346 So. 2d 940, 943 (Ala. 1977).

Section 8–1–1, in pertinent part, states:

> (a) Every contract by which anyone is restrained from exercising a lawful profession, trade or business of any kind otherwise than is provided by this section is to that extent void.
>
> (b) One who sells the goodwill of a business may agree with the buyer and one who is employed as an agent, servant or employee

> may agree with his employer to refrain from carrying on or engaging in a similar business and from soliciting old customers of such employer within a specified county, city or part thereof so long as the buyer, or any person deriving title to the good will from him, or employer carries on a like business therein.

The courts will enforce a covenant not to compete that fits within the exception of § 8–1–1(b) only if:

> 1. the employer has a protectable interest;
>
> 2. the restriction is reasonably related to that interest;
>
> 3. the restriction is reasonable in time and place; [and]
>
> 4. the restriction imposes no undue hardship [on the employee].

DeVoe v. Cheatham, 413 So. 2d 1141, 1142 (Ala. 1982). An interest is a protectable interest when an employer possesses "a substantial right in its business sufficiently unique to warrant the type of protection contemplated by [a] noncompetition agreement." *DeVoe*, 413 So. 2d at 1142 (quoting *Cullman Broadcasting Co. v. Bosley*, 373 So. 2d 830, 836 (Ala. 1979)). A protectable interest may exist when an employee is "in a position to gain confidential information, [to gain] access to secret lists, or to develop a close relationship with clients." *DeVoe*, 413 So. 2d at 1143; see also *Restatement (Second) of Contracts* § 188, Comment B (1981).

There is ample evidence in the record to support a finding that Clark developed a close and special relationship with Liberty National's policyholders. Clark was Liberty National's sole contact with policyholders in the territory that he serviced. Clark had frequent and regular contact with many of the policyholders because he collected premiums at their houses each month. Clark knew which persons had Liberty National policies and knew the expiration dates of those polices. Liberty National's relationships with its customers were a valuable asset and it was important to its business to maintain these relationships. The customer acquaintances that Clark gained through his employment at Liberty National could easily be used to Liberty National's detriment by Clark in his subsequent job with Prudential. Clark's information regarding Liberty National's policyholders and the close relationships he developed with the policyholders in his agency clearly constituted protectable interests of Liberty National's. See *Calhoun v. Brendle, Inc.*, 502 So. 2d 689 (Ala. 1986); *James S. Kemper & Co. v. Cox & Associates, Inc.*, 434 So. 2d 1380 (Ala. 1983).

In *James S. Kemper & Co., supra*, a lumber industry casualty insurance agent signed a noncompetition agreement very similar to the agreement signed by Clark. In *Kemper* this Court held that the "restrictions in the covenant reasonably related to the protection of Kemper's interest in a narrow, identifiable group of clients with which [the agent] was involved." *Kemper, supra*, at 1384. We believe that this is also true for the noncompetition agreement signed by Clark. The covenant was necessary to protect Liberty National's customer relationship interests that had been developed by Clark.

As to the time and place of the restriction, the one-year limitation restricting Clark's solicitation, acceptance, etc., of Liberty National policyholders was reasonable and fair under the circumstances. The territory of a noncompetition agreement may "properly include part of Alabama, all of Alabama, or 'more territory than the State of Alabama,' depending on the circumstances." *Kemper, supra*, at 1385, quoting *Parker v. Ebsco Industries, Inc.*, 282 Ala. 98, 102, 209 So. 2d 383, 386 (1968). The Court in *Kemper* stated that "there can be no doubt that a two-year period for the [noncompetition] restriction is reasonable." *Id.* at 1384. The one-year restriction in Clark's contract was reasonable and was sufficiently limited to Liberty National's customers in Clark's territory.

The final consideration is whether the covenant not to compete places an undue hardship on Clark. We believe it does not. Clark was not prohibited from selling insurance, but only from soliciting or accepting replacement insurance from Liberty National's policyholders. See *Hoppe v. Preferred Risk Mutual Insurance Co.*, 470 So. 2d 1161 (Ala. 1985). Clark was not prohibited from engaging in the "only trade he [knew] and by which he [could] support himself." See *Chavers v. Copy Products Co.*, 519 So. 2d 942, 945 (Ala. 1988) (undue hardship placed on copier maintenance and repair person who signed noncompetition agreement prohibiting him from working in field for two years). Clark was free to sell insurance and to solicit new customers, except those customers for whom he had serviced policies or to whom he had sold policies while working for Liberty National. As stated in *Hill v. Rice*, 259 Ala. 587, 67 So. 2d 789 (1953), an undue hardship exists when a restriction "imposes on the employee [a] greater restraint than is reasonably necessary to secure to the business of the employer . . . such protection, regard being had to the injury which may result to the public from restraining the breach of the covenant, in the loss of the employee's service and skill and the danger of his becoming a charge on the public." *Hill*, 259 Ala. at 592–93, 67 So. 2d at 794. The restriction placed on Clark was reasonably necessary to protect Liberty National's interest and did not place an unreasonable burden on Clark's ability to earn a living selling insurance.

Clark also states an issue based on his contention that he entered into the agent's contract under duress. In his brief, however, he makes no argument on this issue except to cite a case listing the elements required for a prima facie case of economic duress.

Economic duress consists of: "(1) wrongful acts or threats; (2) financial distress caused by the wrongful acts or threats; [and] (3) the absence of any reasonable alternative to the terms presented by the wrongdoer." *International Paper Co. v. Whilden*, 469 So. 2d 560, 562 (Ala. 1985). The doctrine of economic duress applies only to "special, unusual, or extraordinary situations in which unjustified coercion is used to induce a contract, as where extortive measures are employed, or improper or unjustified demands are made, under such circumstances that the victim has little choice but to accede thereto." *International Paper*, 560 So. 2d at 563. "The entering into a contract with reluctance or even dissatisfaction with its terms because of economic necessity does not, of itself, constitute economic duress invalidating the contract. Unless unlawful or unconscionable pressure is applied by the other party to induce the entering into a contract, there is not economic compulsion amounting to duress." *International Paper*, 560 So. 2d at 563 (quoting *Chouinard v. Chouinard*, 568 F.2d 430 (5th Cir. 1978)).

The fact that Liberty National required Clark to sign the new contract in order to continue his employment at Liberty National does not amount to economic duress. Liberty National did not apply any unlawful or unconscionable pressure to force Clark to sign the contract. Clark was able to read the contract and ask any questions he had regarding its contents. There was sufficient and valid consideration for Clark's signing the contract. This consideration was his continued employment at Liberty National under the contract beyond April 1, 1985. We find no merit in Clark's argument that the agent's contract was signed under duress.

Clark's final argument is that Liberty National did not carry its burden of proof as to the damages it claimed as a result of Clark's breach of the covenant not to compete. In a breach of contract action, the ordinary measure of damages is "an amount sufficient to return the plaintiff to the position he would have occupied had the breach not occurred." *Aldridge v. Dolbeer*, 567 So. 2d 1267, 1269 (Ala. 1990). Liberty National bears the burden of proving the amount of damages it is entitled to as a result of the breaches by Clark. *James S. Kemper & Co. v. Cox & Associates, Inc.*, 434 So. 2d 1380 (Ala. 1983). The evidence produced by Liberty National must be sufficient evidence of its loss "to allow the factfinder to calculate the damages without operating from guesswork." *Aldridge*, 567 So. 2d at 1270.

The record clearly indicates that Clark breached the covenant on many occasions, causing many of Liberty National's policyholders to change their coverage from Liberty National to Prudential. Clark was compensated for each Liberty National policy he replaced with a Prudential policy.

At trial, Liberty National's actuary testified as to the amount of loss suffered by Liberty National as a result of Clark's breaches of the noncompetition agreement. In calculating the loss for each policy that was replaced by Clark during the one-year noncompetition period, Liberty National calculated its lost profit and multiplied this loss by a company-wide factor that approximated the loss due to the lapse of the policy. The lost profit consisted of underwriting income, investment income, and renewal commissions that Liberty National became entitled to when an agent left the company. Other factors that were considered in the calculation of damages included the length of time the policyholder had maintained the policy and Liberty National's persistency rate, reflecting the probability that a policyholder will remain with the company. Also, Liberty National's calculation of future payments was discounted by interest and a persistency factor.

The trial court, after hearing *ore tenus* evidence, awarded Liberty National damages totaling $ 14,819.61. The trial court properly excluded from its calculations certain policies for which Liberty National had claimed damages: policies that were not replaced, although initial steps to replace them had been taken; policies that were replaced beyond the one-year restriction; and policies belonging to Clark and his family.

After careful review of the record, we believe that Liberty National did carry its burden of proof as to damages. The formula used by Liberty National was reasonable and fair and reflected the loss suffered by Liberty National as a result of Clark's breaches of the covenant not to compete. Clark argues that when calculating damages Liberty National did not take into account such factors as a customer's loyalty to his agent, Clark's good relationship with his customers, and the fact that Clark's replacement did not have as good a relationship with the customers as Clark had. It is important to note that these are the very things that the noncompetition agreement protects Liberty National from and are not factors by which Clark is entitled to have the trier of fact decrease the amount of damages.

. . . .

AFFIRMED.

Mastery Problem 40-1

General Ed, Inc. hired Janice to produce content for its educational testing business. Janice supervised test question developers for standardized high school tests that General Ed sold to public school districts across the country. General Ed required Janice to sign a non-competition agreement that precluded Janice from working for any standardized educational testing business in any capacity for three years from the time of her termination with General Ed. Janice took the job supervising developers, even though her passion was in marketing and sales of educational products.

A year after Janice started working for General Ed, her dream job became available. Janice was offered a marketing management position with Home Test Ed, an educational resources company that targeted private schools and home schools. Although a portion of the Home Test Ed broad product line included standardized tests, the majority of its line included textbooks, school portfolio development, in-class program development, and extra-curricular activity book development. In her new position, Janice would oversee marketing for all of Home Test Ed's products.

Janice quit her job with General Ed and signed an agreement to work with Home Test Ed. Shortly before she started her work with Home Test Ed, General Ed sued her for breach of contract and sought an injunction to keep Janice from starting her work with General Ed. Does Janice's conduct fall within the scope of the non-competition agreement? Is a court likely to find that the non-competition agreement is reasonable with respect to scope, duration, and geography? If not, how should the court "blue pencil" the agreement? Finally, can General Ed obtain an injunction to keep Janice from starting her employment with Home Test Ed?

Conclusion

Employers can protect their investments in the training of employees and development of business practices by using promises not to compete. These non-competition agreements must be reasonably tailored with regard to scope, geography, and duration in order to protect a legitimate business interest without unduly burdening the employee. The touchstone of a valid promise not to compete is reasonableness.

Lesson 41:
Duty of Loyalty

Objectives and Expected Learning Outcomes

In this Lesson, you will explore the duty of loyalty owed by an employee to the employer. We will discuss the different types of loyalty owed, how these duties are defined, and how the employer can enforce the duty of loyalty.

Many employees owe a duty of loyalty to their employer. The scope of the duty depends on the nature of the relationship. Some employees may owe fiduciary duties to their employer, whereas others merely have an implied contractual term of loyalty. Employees who have substantial discretion in carrying out their work duties and employees who are not closely supervised in carrying out managerial, professional, or highly skilled work responsibilities are subject to a duty of loyalty. Generally, employees who are not granted substantial discretion in carrying out their work duties, and employees who are closely supervised, effectively do not have a duty of loyalty.

Restatement of Employment Law

§ 8.01. Employee Duty of Loyalty to Employer

(a) Employees in a position of trust and confidence with their employer owe a fiduciary duty of loyalty to the employer in matters related to their employment. Other employees who come into possession of the employer's trade secrets owe a *limited* fiduciary duty of loyalty with regard to those trade secrets. In addition, employees may, depending on the nature of the employment position, owe an *implied* contractual duty of loyalty to the employer in matters related to their employment.

(b) Employees breach their duty of loyalty to the employer by:

(1) disclosing or using the employer's trade secrets (as defined in § 8.02) for any purpose adverse to the employer's interest, including after termination of the employment relationship (§ 8.03);

(2) competing with the employer while employed by the employer (§ 8.04); or

(3) misappropriating the employer's property, whether tangible or intangible, or otherwise engaging in self-dealing through the use of the employee's position with the employer.

(c) The employee's duty of loyalty must be interpreted in a manner consistent with the employee's rights and responsibilities as set forth in Chapter 5 and under employment and other law, as well as with any right or privilege provided by law to cooperate with regulatory authorities.

As we will study in detail in Lesson 42, the duty of loyalty prevents employees from disclosing their employer's trade secrets. In this Lesson, we will focus on the duty of loyalty as preventing employees from: engaging in any dealings that negatively interfere with their employer's business opportunities, competing with their employer, and engaging in self-dealings that are detrimental to their employer's interest.

Remedies for breach of duty of loyalty include workforce discipline and termination of employment. An employee who breaches a *fiduciary* duty of loyalty may be subject to tort damages and other fiduciary remedies. An employee who breaches an *implied* contractual duty of loyalty is subject to contract damages (unless the behavior also constitutes an independent tort).

QUESTIONS

1. Should all employees have a duty of loyalty regardless of their title, occupation, and position?
2. How does the duty of loyalty square with the principle that forbids restraints of trade?

Problem 41-1

Lindsey Nguyen works at a brewing company called Five Mile Brewing Co. Lindsey has an entry level position at the company, is directly supervised by the floor manager, and does not have substantial discretion in carrying out her work tasks. During a meeting with her manager, Lindsey came across some papers on his desk labeled, "Confidential information." Lindsey opened the documents and discovered it included the company's secret ingredients to brew their best-selling beer. Does Lindsey owe a duty of loyalty to Five Mile Brewing not to divulge the information?

---

1. Competing with One's Current Employer as a Breach of the Duty of Loyalty

A central feature of the duty of loyalty is the duty of an employee not to compete with her current employer, without the consent of the employer. Implicit in the employment relationship is a commitment not to work against the employer's interests.

Restatement of Employment Law

§ 8.04. Competition by Current Employee with Current Employer

(a) Except as otherwise provided in subsections (b) and (c), an employee breaches the duty of loyalty to the employer if, without the employer's express or implied consent, the employee, while employed by the employer, works for a competitor or otherwise competes with the employer.

(b) Competition with the employer under subsection (a) includes solicitation of the employer's customers to divert their business to a competitor and recruitment of other employees to work for a competitor, but does not include reasonable preparation by an employee or group of employees to compete with the employer.

(c) Absent an agreement with their first employer to the contrary, employees, other than employees in a position of trust and confidence with their first employer under § 8.01(a), may work for a competitor of, or in competition with, the first employer as long as the work is not done during time committed to the first employer, does not involve the use or disclosure of the first employer's trade secrets, and does not injure the employer to any greater extent than would any other individual working for the competitor.

A current employee may not compete with her employer without consent, even if all work is done on her own time. However, the "moonlighting rule" of § 8.04(c) permits some manner of competition when there is no effect on the employer.

The following case explores the fact-intensive nature of these cases and the range of remedies available to an employer.

Cameco, Inc. v. Gedicke

724 A.2d 783 (N.J. 1999).

Pollock, J.

This appeal concerns the liability of an employee for a breach of the duty of loyalty owed to his employer. The primary issue is whether the employer may prove a *prima facie* case for an employee's breach of that duty by proving, not that the employee directly competed with the employer, but that the employee merely assisted the employer's competitor.

At the close of plaintiff's case, the Law Division dismissed the complaint, which asserted various claims in addition to the one alleging the employee's breach of his duty of loyalty. The Appellate Division affirmed the dismissal, except for the claims relating to the breach of the duty of loyalty. We granted Gedicke's petition for certification, and now affirm.

I.

This appeal arises from the dismissal of the complaint at the conclusion of plaintiff's case in a civil action tried by the court without a jury. In a non-jury action, the court, whether deciding the matter on a motion at the close of the plaintiff's case or the entire case, should support its decision with adequate findings of fact. . . .

In the present case, when dismissing the complaint, the trial court made only general factual findings. Because the dismissal occurred at the close of plaintiff's case, it invites a careful review of those findings. We reach this conclusion notwithstanding the fact that on plaintiff's case the trial court heard from the critical witnesses: Jerry Perl, president of plaintiff, Cameco, Inc. ("Cameco"); Scott Maier, a certified public accountant whom Cameco retained as an expert witness; and defendants Donald Gedicke and his wife, Priscilla Mueller. Accepting the truth of plaintiff's evidence and according it the benefit of all favorable inferences, the record supports the following factual findings.

Cameco employed Gedicke as a salaried traffic manager to arrange for the transportation of Cameco's food products, primarily tuna, ham, and poultry.

Unknown to Cameco, Gedicke and Mueller formed Newton Transport Service ("Newton"), through which they arranged for the transportation of goods for various companies, including two of Cameco's competitors.

In 1993, Cameco fired Gedicke for poor performance. To obtain the money he had paid into Cameco's pension fund, Gedicke signed an agreement not to compete with Cameco. Thereafter, when Cameco learned of Gedicke's activities with Newton, Cameco charged Gedicke with conversion, unjust enrichment, tortious interference with contractual rights and economic advantage, and breach of Gedicke's duty of loyalty as an employee.

As Cameco's traffic manager from March 1984 to January 1993, Gedicke was an employee at-will with a salary of approximately $38,000 per year. Gedicke's primary duty was arranging transportation of Cameco's food products to retail stores by common carrier. His duties included coordinating Cameco's shipping schedules, negotiating the lowest possible shipping rates, and supervising the warehouse employees who loaded the trucks. Cameco's shipping costs comprised fifteen to twenty percent of its operating expenses. Gedicke's duties also included inspecting Cameco's off-site warehouses for cleanliness and temperature maintenance. Because of his position, Gedicke became familiar with the identity of Cameco's suppliers, customers, and common carriers, as well as its delivery routes and rates, all of which Cameco considers to be confidential information.

In 1990, without telling Cameco, Gedicke and Mueller formed Newton, which they operated primarily from their home. Acting on behalf of distributors or truckers, Gedicke arranged for the transportation of food products to retailers. Typically, the shipper would pay Newton, which, after deducting its commission, would pay the trucker. Newton's net profits increased from $2536 in 1990 to $11,733 in 1992. In 1993, the year in which Cameco fired Gedicke, Newton earned $62,090 in net profits.

Sometimes, Newton acted for a particular trucker when communicating with distributors. On some of these occasions, the distributors paid the truckers directly. The truckers then paid Newton's commissions. Two of the distributors for which Newton arranged transportation, Atalanta Corporation ("Atalanta") and Kohler Delicatessen Meats, Inc. ("Kohler"), sold the same products as Cameco. The record is unclear, and the trial court did not make any findings, regarding the extent to which Gedicke, through Newton, assisted Atalanta or Kohler.

On over six hundred occasions, Gedicke arranged for a trucker transporting Cameco's goods also to transport goods for Newton's customers. Sometimes, the trucker would deliver goods to the same destination for both Cameco and the other distributors. Gedicke explained that "commingled" shipping is routine and that, even after the termination of his employment, goods brokered by Newton continued to be commingled with Cameco's goods. According to Gedicke, the addition of Newton's freight enabled him to negotiate lower rates for Cameco. In such situations, Cameco did not pay the per-pound, less-than-truckload rate or the full-truckload rate. By sharing space and costs with Newton's customers, Cameco paid a rate even lower than that for a full truckload. Thus, Cameco benefited from the commingling of goods.

Cameco claimed that occasionally when the same trucker was transporting both shipments, Gedicke would arrange for goods brokered by Newton to be delivered before Cameco's goods. Gedicke explained that because of the truck routes and the destination of the deliveries, this arrangement was practical and did not prejudice Cameco. Cameco also claimed that sometimes truckers would pick up Cameco's goods before picking up Newton's, thereby creating the risk that Newton's customers, some of whom competed with Cameco, would discover Cameco's product information.

When acting for Newton, Gedicke used the general knowledge he had acquired while working for Cameco and for prior employers. Although Mueller was primarily responsible for conducting Newton's business, she relied on Gedicke's superior knowledge. The trial court found that Mueller conducted most of Newton's business from home, and that Gedicke participated primarily during evenings and on weekends.

Gedicke acknowledged that he engaged in telephone conversations relating to Newton's business during his scheduled hours with Cameco. Because Gedicke used his personal credit card in making telephone calls for Newton, Cameco did not pay the toll charges. From day to day, the time that Gedicke spent on placing calls varied. An analysis produced by Gedicke, however, showed that he spent an average of 13.8 minutes per workday on these calls. Although Gedicke acknowledged receiving incoming calls, no record of the incoming calls was available. Occasionally, while truckers were on Cameco's premises, Gedicke would discuss Newton's business with them. The trial court concluded that Gedicke diverted no more than fifteen minutes per day to Newton's affairs.

In January 1993, Cameco became dissatisfied with Gedicke's job performance. Previously, Perl had reprimanded Gedicke for his failure regularly to inspect Cameco's off-site warehouses. According to Perl, he fired Gedicke for failing to conduct such inspections, failing to negotiate lower freight rates, and permitting excessive overtime in his department. Gedicke rejoined that the time he spent on Newton's business did not interfere with the discharge of his duties to Cameco. Additionally, Gedicke testified that he often worked overtime during evenings and weekends for no additional compensation.

The parties' testimony conflicted on several other issues, such as the significance of a rate reduction offered by truckers after Gedicke's termination. Perl claimed that the reduction showed generally that Gedicke had not negotiated the lowest possible rates for Cameco. According to Perl, the rate reduction demonstrated that Gedicke had not been securing the discount that Perl wanted whenever Cameco paid a full-truckload rate for a commingled shipment. Perl also claimed that the reduction demonstrated that Cameco had been paying for excess shipping capacity that Gedicke used for Newton's customers. Gedicke countered that the rate changes stemmed not from his involvement with Newton, but from market changes.

The parties also disagreed over the non-competition agreement that Perl required Gedicke to sign as a condition for receiving his pension funds after his discharge. Perl said the requirement was routine. The trial court, however, inferred from Cameco's failure to enforce the agreement that Newton never had competed with Cameco.

In dismissing the complaint, the trial court found that Gedicke's testimony was credible and that Perl's testimony was "exaggerated" and motivated by "vindictiveness." The court concluded that Gedicke had not breached his duty of loyalty, that he had not acted for anyone whose interests conflicted with those of Cameco, that Gedicke's actions were not detrimental to Cameco, that Newton had not competed directly with Cameco, and that Cameco had not suffered any damages.

Cameco appealed the dismissal of all claims except those asserting tortious interference with contractual rights and economic advantage. The Appellate Division affirmed the dismissal of Cameco's claims for conversion and unjust enrichment, but reversed and remanded for a new trial on the claim of breach of the duty of loyalty. It concluded that the trial court had erred in assessing the credibility of the witnesses and in weighing the evidence before ruling on defendants' motion for an involuntary dismissal. Instead, the trial court should have viewed the evidence in the light most favorable to Cameco and given Cameco the benefit of all inferences. According to the Appellate Division, Cameco had established a *prima facie* case of a breach of Gedicke's duty of loyalty to Cameco. *Ibid.* The Appellate Division held that the duty of loyalty may be breached by an employee whose actions do not rise to the level of "direct competition" with his employer; "mere assistance" to a competitor of the employer is enough if the employee's actions are contrary to his or her employer's interests.

Certain undisputed facts help to shape the legal analysis. Gedicke was not an officer, director, or shareholder of Cameco. Nor had Cameco, before dismissing Gedicke, required him to sign a covenant not to compete. Cameco, moreover, does not contend that Newton was a direct competitor. Cameco was not in the business of brokering shipments, and Newton was not a food distributor. Gedicke, however, was less than candid with Cameco. He never disclosed to Cameco that he was operating Newton or that he was conducting Newton's business on Cameco's premises during his regular work hours.

The case is not one in which an employee, while employed by one employer, advanced his interests by seeking other employment. Nor is it one in which the employee surreptitiously tried to capture the employer's business, disparage its products, or divert its business to another. Rather, the case is one in which a salaried employee, while working for his employer, supplemented his income by establishing a business that, although it did not compete directly with his employer, may have assisted certain of the employer's competitors. Hence, the question focuses on the level of assistance to a competitor that would justify a finding that an employee breached the duty of loyalty owed to his or her employer.

The trial court found that Cameco had not suffered any damage. Without explanation, the Appellate Division concluded that Cameco had presented a *prima facie* case on damages. It made this determination despite the fact that Cameco had not proved any specific compensatory damages such as lost sales, potential sales, profits, or customers.

II.

Having heard from Gedicke and Mueller, as well as from Cameco's president and accountant, the trial court proceeded at the conclusion of Cameco's case to assess the credibility of the witnesses. We need not question the accuracy of that assessment to conclude that it should have been deferred until after the close of the evidence.

As previously indicated, on a motion to dismiss at the close of a plaintiff's case, a trial court generally should accept the truth of the plaintiff's evidence and accord the plaintiff the benefit of all favorable inferences that the evidence supports. Assessment of the credibility of witnesses ordinarily awaits the close of the entire case. When dismissing at the close of a plaintiff's case, a trial court should accept the credibility of witnesses only when their testimony is so persuasive that no reasonable person could disbelieve it.

To some extent, the trial court's shortcut in assessing credibility at the close of plaintiff's case is understandable; the court had heard from the principal witnesses. Cameco nonetheless asserts that, although it presented Gedicke and Mueller on its own case as hostile witnesses, it was unable to cross-examine them. Gedicke and Mueller answer that they would not have testified further on their own behalf. Still, Gedicke and Mueller never rested their case. The record does not reveal whether the trial court explored these issues with the parties. In sum, we do not have sufficient confidence in the state of the record to endorse the trial court's assessment of the credibility of the witnesses at the close of Cameco's case.

III.

The procedural posture of the appeal and the absence of more complete factual findings prevent a definitive analysis of the dispositive rules of law. Also hampering the legal analysis is the fact-sensitive nature of cases involving an alleged breach of the duty of loyalty by employees. The contexts giving rise to claims of employee disloyalty are so varied that they preclude the mechanical application of abstract rules of law. In general, the adjudication of such claims summons rules of reason and fairness. Notwithstanding the need for flexibility when evaluating claims of employee disloyalty, certain principles emerge.

The scope of the duty of loyalty that an employee owes to an employer may vary with the nature of their relationship. Employees occupying a position of trust and confidence, for example, owe a higher duty than those performing low-level tasks. Assisting an employer's competitor can constitute a breach of the employee's duty of loyalty. Similarly, an employee's self-dealing may breach that duty.

A reality of contemporary life is that many families will consist of two wage earners, one wage earner with two jobs, or both. For some employees, particularly those earning low or modest incomes, second sources of income are an economic necessity. For them, a second job or "moonlighting" is the only way to make ends meet. Conversely, employers need the assurance that employees will not disserve them by furthering their own interests or those of competitors at the employers' expense.

To avoid the possibility of charges of disloyalty, employees generally should inform employers of their plans before establishing an independent business that might conflict with that of the employer. To an employee, the possibility of conflict with the employer's interest may seem remote; to the employer, the possibility may seem more immediate. The greater the possibility that another occupation will conflict with the employee's duties to the employer, the greater the need for the employee to alert the employer to that possibility.

The egregiousness of the employee's conduct may affect the determination of both the commission of a breach and the appropriate remedy. Whether an employee who has not obtained the employer's consent may engage in conduct that assists a competitor depends on the facts of each case. In some cases, the assistance may be so unintended or inconsequential that it will not result in a breach of the employee's duty of loyalty. In other cases, the assistance may be so substantial that the employee will be liable for a breach of that duty. Thus, slight assistance to a direct competitor could constitute a breach of the employee's duty of loyalty. When competition is indirect or minimal, however, the employer, to establish a breach, may be required to show that the employee rendered substantial assistance to the competitor. Employees also may breach their duty of loyalty by aiding an adverse party engaged in a transaction with their employer, or by aiding one whose interests conflict with those of their employer.

Depending on the facts of the case, an employee's breach of the duty of loyalty can give rise to either equitable or legal relief. Cameco does not demand such equitable relief as an injunction or accounting, but does seek disgorgement of Newton's profits and forfeiture of Gedicke's salary. It also requests compensatory money damages.

In an appropriate case, damages may include profits the employee earned in another enterprise while still employed, and compensation for a direct injury suffered by the employer as a result of the employee's breach. Thus, the Restatement (Second) of Agency states generally that "[a]n agent is subject to liability for loss caused to the principal by any breach of duty." Restatement (Second) of Agency, *supra,* § 401. If the employee usurped a corporate opportunity or secretly profited from a competitive activity, the employer may recover the value of the lost opportunity or the secret profit.

Generally, to recover money damages, the employer must establish that the employee's breach proximately caused the requested damages. In the present case, even under the generous standard applicable on a motion to dismiss, the record does not establish that Gedicke's alleged breach caused Cameco to suffer any money damages.

Finally, in addition to more traditional damages, an employer may seek forfeiture of its employee's compensation. As with other aspects of breach-of-duty cases, the facts color an employer's right to recoup compensation.

In *Joseph Toker, Inc. v. Cohen, 67 N.J.Super.* 68, 169 *A.*2d 838 (App.Div.1961), a fuel oil distributor sought to recover money paid to its former manager, who had received a salary plus a monthly draw as an advance payment of a percentage of profits. After leaving his employment, the employee established a competing company. The employer claimed part of the advances it had paid to him. In rejecting the employer's claim, the Appellate Division concluded that the advances constituted a guaranteed minimum that the employee need not return. The Appellate Division affirmed the trial court's finding that the employee had not breached his duty of loyalty and added: "In the absence of fraud, duress, mistake, or express or implied agreement to the contrary, a voluntary payment of wages may not be recovered from an employee, even though the latter's conduct subsequent to receipt of the payments would have disentitled him to receive them."

Recently, the Appellate Division revisited the issue of an employer's right to recover compensation paid to a disloyal employee. *Simulation Systems, supra,* 269 N.J.Super. 107, 634 A.2d 1034. In *Simulation Sys.,* the employee, a computer engineer, formed a company and for eleven months sold computer-related services in direct competition with his employer. The Chancery Division awarded the employer the employee's profits of $1711, but denied recovery of the compensation that had been paid to the employee. In affirming, the Appellate Division reasoned that the employer could recover the compensation it had paid during periods in which the employee had been disloyal. The court denied recovery, however, because the evidence failed to establish the pay periods in which disloyalty had occurred or the compensation paid for those periods.

Illinois and New York courts, in contrast, impose forfeiture on all compensation paid or owing an employee during a period of disloyalty. They do not permit set-off even for properly performed services in such a period.

Massachusetts courts have limited the employer's right of recovery to that part of compensation paid during disloyalty that exceeds the employee's value to the employer. For example, the Supreme Judicial Court of Massachusetts refused to require a disloyal employee to forfeit over seventy-five percent of his compensation when the disloyal conduct was a "practically harmless" act, and the employee's services otherwise were "wholly faithful and outstandingly successful." *Walsh v. Atlantic Research Assocs.,* 321 Mass. 57, 71 N.E.2d 580, 585 (1947).

In the *Restatement (Second) of Agency,* the American Law Institute has provided guidelines to govern employers' claims for damages. Section 469 states the general rule that "[a]n agent is entitled to no compensation for conduct which is disobedient or which is a breach of his duty of loyalty." The supporting rationale is that the compensation is part of the profit for which the disloyal employee must account. *Henderson v. Rep Tech, Inc.,* 162 A.D.2d 1028, 557 N.Y.S.2d 224, 225 (1990). Under the *Restatement,* an employer may recover compensation paid to a periodically paid employee for any periods during which the employee committed acts of disloyalty. *Simulation Sys., supra,* 269 N.J.Super. at 111–12, 634 A.2d 1034. Although the American Law Institute is drafting a new *Restatement of Agency,* it has not yet addressed the issue of an employer's right to recover compensation paid to a disloyal employee.

According to the current *Restatement,* when the employee's conduct is "willful and deliberate" or "serious," the employee may not set off the value of his or her services against the employer's claim to recoup compensation paid to the employee. *Restatement (Second) of Agency, supra,* § 469; *id.* § 469 comment b. Thus, the egregiousness of the employee's conduct may affect the employer's right to withhold or recoup the employee's compensation. If the employee directly competes with the employer, aids the employer's direct competitors or those with interests adverse to the employer's interests, participates in a plan to destroy the employer's business, or secretly deprives the employer of an economic opportunity, the employee may forfeit the right to compensation. In contrast, if the employee's breach is minor, involves only a minimal amount of time, or does not harm the employer, the employee may be entitled to all or substantially all of his or her compensation.

In sum, various considerations affect determination of the breach of an employee's duty of loyalty and the appropriate remedy for a breach, including forfeiture of the employee's compensation. One consideration is the possible existence of contractual provisions. A provision might permit an employee to seek a second source of income, whether through a second job or an independent business. Conversely, a non-competition covenant might limit an employee's economic activities both during and after employment. A second consideration is whether the employer knew of or agreed to its employee's secondary profit-seeking activities. An employee's disclosure of an intention to pursue a second source of income alerts the employer to potential problems and protects the employee from a charge of disloyalty. The third consideration concerns the status of the employee and his or her relationship to the employer. An officer, director, or key executive, for example, has a higher duty than an employee working on a production line. Fourth, the nature of the employee's second source of income and its effect on the employer are relevant. An employee's duty of loyalty to an employer generally precludes acts of direct competition. Employees should not engage in conduct that causes their employers to lose customers, sales, or potential sales. Nor should they take advantage of their employers by engaging in secret self-serving activities, such as accepting kickbacks from suppliers or usurping their employer's corporate opportunities. Employees who defraud their employers or engage in direct competition with them run the risk of discharge, forfeiture of the right to compensation, and other legal and equitable remedies. The extent to which the preceding considerations apply will vary from one case to another. Absent a governing contractual provision, the judicial task is to search for a fair and reasonable solution in light of the relevant considerations.

If, on remand, the trial court concludes that Gedicke breached his duty of loyalty to Cameco, the court must then consider the appropriate remedy. Two forms of relief might be appropriate for such a breach: forfeiture of part of Gedicke's salary or an award of part of Newton's profits. Of the two, forfeiture of part of Gedicke's salary seems more apt. Gedicke did not compete directly with Cameco, aided only marginally two of Cameco's competitors, and did not seek to destroy or injure Cameco's business.

Newton's profits during Gedicke's employment with Cameco were modest. The time that Gedicke spent on Newton's business during work hours with Cameco was minimal. Mueller, who was never employed by Cameco, may have contributed more than Gedicke to Newton's profits. Gedicke, however, spent some time during his workday on Newton's business. Even before learning of Newton's existence, Perl concluded that Gedicke was performing so unsatisfactorily that Perl fired him. One possible outcome is to limit Cameco's recovery to recoupment of part of the salary it paid to Gedicke during pay periods when Gedicke was advancing Newton's interests.

The limited record precludes a more definitive analysis of Cameco's right to recover. Among the facts supporting a recovery are that Gedicke never informed Perl that he had established an independent business as a truck broker; that Gedicke spent some time during his normal work hours engaged in Newton's business; that truck-brokerage put Gedicke in a position where he could assist, perhaps unintentionally, the truckers and Cameco's competitors.

Facts suggesting that Gedicke did not breach his duty of loyalty are that he was a low- or mid-level salaried employee; that during his employment, Gedicke was not subject to any contractual limitation preventing him from establishing an outside business; that he did not cause Cameco to lose any customers, sales, potential sales, or profits; and that he did not compete directly with Cameco or render substantial assistance to any of its competitors.

Viewing Cameco's evidence in the most favorable light, Cameco adduced sufficient evidence to survive Gedicke's motion to dismiss. Sitting as the ultimate fact finder, the trial court, however, might determine that Gedicke's "assistance" to Atalanta and Kohler was so insubstantial or that the competition between them and Cameco was so inconsequential that Gedicke's conduct did not harm Cameco. Similarly, the court could find that Gedicke did not act adversely to Cameco's interests concerning its customers or the truckers.

The judgment of the Appellate Division is affirmed as modified, and the matter is remanded to the Law Division.

2. Competing with One's Previous Employer

The duty not to compete with one's employer after leaving employment is much less stringent. In our economy, we prize competition between firms. Thus, as we saw in Lesson 11, competition is generally a defense against claims of interference with prospective business relationships. Employers are not left without options. As we learned in Lesson 40, an employer may protect itself from competition by having the employee agree to a promise not to compete, which is enforceable if it is reasonably tailored to the employer's interests. Absent a promise not to compete or a misappropriation of a trade secret, a former employee is generally entitled to compete with her former employer. *See Restatement of Employment Law, § 8.05 Competition by Former Employee with Former Employer.*

This analysis gets murky when an employee begins preparations to form a competing business while still employed. As a general rule, an employee may engage in reasonable preparations, such as leasing an office, obtaining financing, buying supplies, and hiring staff. As one court stated, ". . .an employee does not violate his duty of loyalty when he merely organizes a corporation during his employment to carry on a rival business after the expiration of his employment." *Fish v. Adams,* 401 So.2d 843, 845 (Fla.Dist.Ct.App. 1981). However, it is important that the employee not use company resources or begin preparing on company time.

Prior to termination, employees may announce their new business endeavor to the employer, customers, and coworkers, but they may not solicit the employer's customers or actively recruit their coworkers. More importantly, the employee may not recruit the employer's key employees, such as high ranking managerial staff. The general principal is that an employee cannot solicit customers or recruit employees in a way that would materially damage or threaten the employer's business.

Employees are free to agree to join the competitor so long as they don't recruit other employees to leave the employer with them. Employees are not liable for breach of the duty of loyalty if the other employees who leave are motivated by personal reasons, such as dissatisfaction with the employer because of a lack of opportunity for career growth. Because corporate officers and key executives play a unique role in their employer's businesses, they owe a special fiduciary duty to their employers not to seize business opportunities of the employer for their own benefit.

AUGAT, INC. V. AEGIS, INC.

565 N.E.2d 415 (Mass. 1991).

WILKINS, JUSTICE.

The plaintiff Isotronics, Inc. (Isotronics), a subsidiary of the plaintiff Augat, Inc. (Augat), manufactures high reliability metal microcircuit packages used to house electronic circuits. The individual defendant (Scherer) was one of three stockholders who sold Isotronics to Augat in 1975. He continued to work for Isotronics until 1980, served next as an Augat vice president, and

I, Augat ↓ Scherer + Augat

then acted as a consultant to Augat until April, 1983. In May 1984, one month after his agreement not to compete with Isotronics expired, Scherer formed the defendant Aegis, Inc., intending to manufacture high reliability metal and ceramic microcircuit packages.

Scherer then communicated with Jay Greenspan, who was vice president and general manager of Isotronics, offering him employment and an equity interest in Aegis. Greenspan held a position of trust and confidence in Isotronics and was primarily responsible for Isotronics's success in becoming the dominant force in the metal packaging industry. Greenspan was not happy at Isotronics. In 1983, he had explored the possibility of forming his own company, but had been unable to obtain financing. At that time, Greenspan had discussed his plan with four Isotronics employees who held important senior managerial positions. Greenspan told Scherer that these senior managers had been interested in Greenspan's 1983 plan. In May or June 1984, Greenspan and Scherer approached these four men, and over the next several months had meetings with them, separately and collectively, and on occasion also with prospective investors in Aegis. Three of these four men subsequently left Isotronics and went directly to work for Aegis. One major ground for the plaintiff's claims against the defendants is that, in secretly seeking to obtain the services of key Isotronics managers, they knowingly joined in Greenspan's breach of his duty to Isotronics. That breach, the plaintiffs assert, in time led to a disruption of Isotronics when all those managers left Isotronics within a period of approximately two months.

In the summer of 1984, Scherer devoted his efforts to obtaining financing for Aegis. Greenspan and three of the managers who had been on Greenspan's prospective list in 1983 were committed to work for Aegis, if Aegis could be funded. The existence of a prospective management team was the most important factor in the view of the venture capitalists. Scherer prepared a detailed business plan, describing Aegis's purposes; its potential competitors; the size and condition of the packaging market, including the fact that Isotronics controlled about two-thirds of that market; and, without naming the others, the experience and background of Aegis's anticipated management team. The other major ground for the plaintiff's claims in this case is that, in breach of his duty to maintain the confidentiality of Isotronic's gross sales figures, Greenspan disclosed precise figures to Scherer who was then able to include in his business plan information about the current size of the metal packaging market, information that Scherer would not otherwise have had and without which, it is claimed, venture capitalists would not have invested in Aegis.

Scherer sent his business plan to potential investors late in July, 1984. Greenspan delivered a letter of resignation on August 1, 1984, not stating any specific date for his departure. Greenspan left Isotronics on September 27. On October 9, Aegis received a commitment letter for an investment of $ 4,300,000. Aegis then entered the metal packaging business, not producing its first packages until May 1985.

Augat and Isotronics brought this action in April, 1985, advancing various claims against the defendants. In August, 1989, the judge filed his findings of fact and rulings of law. After a Justice of the Appeals Court, in October, 1989, allowed the defendants to take an interlocutory appeal, the judge filed amended and supplemental findings of fact and rulings of law. We transferred the defendants' interlocutory appeal here on our own motion.

The trial judge ruled in the plaintiffs' favor on only a portion of their theories of liability. He found for the defendants on the claim that various employees who went to Aegis had entered into noncompetition agreements with Isotronics. He found no appropriation of Isotronics's trade secrets, no solicitation by Aegis of customers while Greenspan worked for Isotronics, and no misappropriation of customer lists.

The judge concluded, however, that the defendants were liable for Greenspan's breach of his duty of loyalty to Isotronics in disclosing confidential information to Scherer about Isotronics's level of annual sales. We disagree with this ruling because information concerning Isotronics's general level of sales was not confidential and no specific information concerning that level of sales was required by prospective venture capitalists. The judge also ruled that Greenspan violated his duty of loyalty when, while still an Isotronics employee, he secretly solicited key managerial employees to join Aegis once it was funded. We uphold this ruling. He also ruled that other former Isotronics employees had violated their duty to Isotronics, a point we reject. Additionally, the judge found liability because of misrepresentations made to Isotronics and Augat and an intent of Greenspan and Scherer to cripple Isotronics. We reject these theories as independent bases of liability.

1. We reject the plaintiffs' theory of liability based on the fact that, as the judge found, Greenspan, while an employee of Isotronics, disclosed confidential information to Scherer concerning the precise level of Isotronics's

sales of metal packaging. The argument is that, armed with Isotronics's sales figures, Scherer was able to provide information to venture capitalists without which they would not have invested $ 4,300,000 in Aegis. Scherer did no disclose precise sales figures to potential investors, but he did state in a business plan sent to potential investors, late in July, 1984, that Isotronic's annual sales were between $30,000,000 and $32,000,000.

Potential investors would be interested, of course, in the approximate size of the market in which they would be investing their funds. We accept the conclusion, inherent in the judge's findings, that the people who invested in Aegis would not have done so without that information.

Isotronics held about two-thirds of the metal packaging market in 1984, a fact that was known to people knowledgeable about the industry, in part because Isotronics did not keep that fact confidential. This information suggests that the approximate volume of sales in the entire industry was known by people who knew the industry.

Although general business information and routine data of a particular company normally are not protectible as confidential, the gross sales of a corporation might properly be protectible as confidential in particular circumstances, although that information would not be a "trade secret" of the traditional kind. We shall assume that, in particular circumstances, the amount of Isotronics's gross annual sales of metal packages could be protectible, confidential information, and, if so, an employee would have a duty not to disclose that information.

In determining confidentiality, several factors are relevant, including "the extent to which the information is known outside of the business"; "the extent of measures taken by the employer to guard the secrecy of the information"; and "the ease or difficulty with which the information could be properly acquired . . . by others." *Jet Spray Cooler, Inc. v. Crampton*, 282 N.E.2d 921 (Mass 1972). By these tests, the plaintiffs' claim that the dollar volume of Isotronics's sales was entitled to protection as confidential information fails.

Isotronics did not consistently and diligently treat the level of its annual sales as a confidential corporate fact. Its acknowledgement and the acknowledgement of people interested in the industry that Isotronics had about two-thirds of the sales in the industry suggest strongly that the total annual sales of the industry were known in approximation by Isotronics and others. If the approximate volume of sales by Isotronics's competitors was generally known, as had to be the case for Isotronics to determine its market share, Isotronics's disclosure of its market share in effect disclosed its approximate annual sales volume. Moreover, the chairman of the board of directors of the plaintiff Augat met regularly with securities analysts who covered Augat and in effect provided them with estimates of the annual sales of Isotronics. In guiding securities analysts toward the approximate level of Isotronics's annual sales, the plaintiffs obviously did not "guard the secrecy of the information" and equally obviously made the information "known outside of the business" (i.e. outside of Augat and Isotronics). *Jet Spray, supra.*

In addition to disclosures by the plaintiffs that destroyed any confidentiality of Isotronics's annual sales figures, there was evidence that several analysts were able to arrive at approximations of Isotronics's annual sales volume from a study of generally available information. The judge made no findings on this evidence, perhaps because he concluded that the plaintiffs' unwillingness to disclose actual figures, as opposed to facilitating estimates, preserved the confidentiality of Isotronics's sales information. Because we conclude that the plaintiffs' own conduct belied the confidentiality of Isotronics's annual sales figures, we need not consider whether this unchallenged evidence that sales information was readily and independently discoverable provides an independent ground for denying confidentiality to Isotronics's sales figures.

The important point here is that, to make an investment decision, the people who invested funds in Aegis did not require or receive precise sales figures. They obtained only approximations, in circumstances not involving the disclosure of legally protected confidential information. Moreover, as a matter of law, the plaintiffs have failed to show that, but for Greenspan's disclosure of precise sales figures to Scherer, the financing of Aegis would not have been possible.

2. We agree with the plaintiffs that the defendants are liable for Greenspan's breach of his duty of loyalty to Isotronics in not protecting Isotronics's interests against the loss of key employees to Aegis. Greenspan, as a vice president and general manager of Isotronics from 1981 to September 27, 1984, ran all aspects of Isotronics under the general supervision of the president of Augat, who was also the president of Isotronics. Greenspan was responsible for staffing and for hiring necessary replacements for any employees who might leave Isotronics. He regarded his duties to include maintaining at least one "backup" employee for each managerial position.

While Greenspan was still general manager of Isotronics he and Scherer solicited several important Isotronics employees to join Aegis if and when it were to be financed. Among those solicited, who later left Isotronics and went directly to work at Aegis, were: the vice president for marketing and sales, who left Isotronics on November 11, 1984; the new product design manager, Isotronics's most experienced engineer in the technology of making metal packages, who left on November 30, 1984; the manufacturing manager for Isotronics, who left on January 7, 1985; and Isotronics's engineering manager, who left on January 4, 1985.

Employees who left

Scherer and Aegis make no serious argument that they are not liable if they participated with Greenspan (or any other Isotronics employee) in a violation of his duty of loyalty to Isotronics. . . .

It is important to define the limited basis for liability we recognize in this case. An at-will employee may properly plan to go into competition with his employer and may take active steps to do so while still employed. Such an employee has no general duty to disclose his plans to his employer, and generally he may secretly join other employees in the endeavor without violating any duty to his employer. The general policy considerations are that at-will employees should be allowed to change employers freely and competition should be encouraged. If an employer wishes to restrict the post-employment competitive activities of a key employee, it may seek that goal through a non-competition agreement. The plaintiffs did not do so in this case.

There are, however, certain limitations on the conduct of an employee who plans to compete with his employer. He may not appropriate his employer's trade secrets. He may not solicit his employer's customers while still working for his employer, and he may not carry away certain information, such as lists of customers. Of course, such a person may not act for his future interests at the expense of his employer by using the employer's funds or employees for personal gain or by a course of conduct designed to hurt the employer.

The special circumstance of this case, distinguishing it from the typical case of improper employee conduct leading to competition with a former employer, is that there is but one significant breach of duty. The defendants did not knowingly participate in any breach of duty by an Isotronics employee in any respect except in joining with Greenspan in soliciting the future employment of important employees. The employees other than Greenspan committed no breach of duty. There is no showing that the key employees who left Isotronics for Aegis joined together to destroy Isotronics. If Scherer and Aegis had solicited the employees of Isotronics without the involvement of Greenspan prior to his departure from Isotronics, there would be no liability here.

The principle that, before he terminates his employment, a top managerial employee may not solicit the departure of employees to work for a competitor has been applied in various situations. Although Greenspan's solicitation was directed only at certain key managerial personnel, his duty to maintain at least adequate managerial personnel forbade him, while still general manager of Isotronics, from seeking to draw key managers away to a competitor. The rule we express for the purposes of this case applies only to a general manager who, while still employed, secretly solicits key managerial employees to leave their employment to join the general manager in a competitive enterprise. Greenspan admitted that he put his loyalties to the people who were to go to Aegis ahead of his obligations as an officer of Isotronics.

The defendants argue that the plaintiffs failed to show that their wrongdoing caused any loss to the plaintiffs. In the liability portion of a bifurcated trial, the plaintiff must show that the defendant's breach of duty caused some harm for which the law provides redress because there can be no liability in the absence of causation. We have considered the evidence and conclude that the plaintiffs have shown that the departure of the key employees whom Greenspan solicited caused some disruption of Isotronics.

The plaintiff's damages relate to negative effects on operating results that would not have occurred but for the departure of the key managerial employees. Because there is not finding or showing that Aegis would not have been financed if these key employees were not to work for it, and Aegis did not sell any products until well into 1985, the plaintiffs' damages are not to be measure by Aegis's profits. The plaintiffs must prove that losses that Isotronics sustained would not have occurred but for Greenspan's breach of his duty of loyalty. These would be losses that were caused by problems arising from the departure to Aegis of key managerial employees who were approached by Greenspan while he and they were still employed by Isotronics, provided that the losses were caused by events occurring before Isotronics reasonably should have replaced the departed managerial employees with competent people.

3. We consider next other bases on which the judge concluded that the defendants were liable. We disagree with the judge's conclusions that Greenspan

and Scherer made actionable misrepresentations to Isotronics and that the evidence provides an independent ground for liability based on the theory that Greenspan and Scherer intended to destroy Isotronics. There is another relatively minor issue on which we agree with the judge that liability might be imposed on the defendant Aegis.

a. On August 1, 1984, Greenspan submitted a letter of resignation to the president of Augat, sending a copy to the chairman of Augat's board of directors. In that letter, Greenspan stated, "I do not presently have any other employment plans, and therefore can stay for a period of time." The judge found that this was an affirmative misrepresentation. It is correct in that, Aegis not yet having been funded, Greenspan had no assurance of employment by Aegis. He did, however, intend to join Aegis, if it were to be funded, under terms that had been established. In any event, Greenspan had no duty to disclose his tentative future employment plans in his letter of resignation. An employee who plans to work for a competitor of his employer has no duty to volunteer that fact, either before or after he submits his resignation. Greenspan's letter of August 1, 1984, provides no basis for the liability of the defendants.

b. The judge found that in 1984 Scherer had deliberately misrepresented his plans to reenter the packaging business to the president of Augat and to the chairman of the board of Augat, leading them to think that he was planning to enter the ceramics, rather than the metal, packaging business. Scherer had no duty to tell Augat what his plans were, nor did he have any duty not to mislead them. The evidence on which the judge's findings are based discloses no material misrepresentations on which Augat reasonably could have relied Scherer had revealed that he might be a prospective competitor of Augat and Isotronics. His comments and the circumstances, including Greenspan's disclosure to Augat that he might join Scherer, should have put Augat and Isotronics on guard rather than at ease.

c. We reject, as an independent basis for liability, the judge's conclusion that the defendants intended to cripple Isotronics in order to ease Aegis's entry into the market. There is no other significant respect in which the defendants may be held liable. They had an absolute right to compete with Isotronics. The possibility of crippling, or even destroying, a competitor is inherent in a competitive market. The defendants' state of mind in engaging in competition does not alone provide a basis for liability.

d. When Isotronics's engineering manager left in January, 1985, with full disclosure, he took a notebook that he had compiled containing certain information. He left copies behind at Isotronics. There is no evidence that the defendants knew about the notebook. The plaintiffs want the notebook and copies of it returned. The judge ruled that certain information in the notebook was confidential and that Aegis should return the notebook and copies. There is no evidence that Aegis's use of the notebook caused any harm to the plaintiffs or benefited the defendants in any significant way. A judgment directing Aegis to deliver the notebook and any copies to Isotronics should be entered.

4. The case is remanded to the Superior Court for proceedings consistent with this opinion.

So ordered.

QUESTIONS

1. In contemporary employment, the line between work and off-duty activity is increasingly blurred. How should courts determine whether an employee is using company time and resources to start a competing business?
2. How should employees shield themselves from breach of duty of loyalty claims when they seek to form a competing company?

Problem 41-2

Wilson Wau, an executive at a tire manufacturing company called Best Selling Tires, has decided to resign to start his own tire manufacturing company. His business will directly compete with his current employer. Before resigning, Wilson actively recruits several managers, supervisors, and regular employees and persuades them to join his new business. The employees all resign shortly after Wilson's departure and Wilson immediately hires all of them. Best Selling Tires was severely impacted by the loss of staff and production came to a halt for several weeks. Analyze whether Wilson has breached a duty of loyalty to his employer.

Problem 41-3

Dalton, an at-will employee at Millennial Communications, managed customer accounts and wrote columns for industry newsletters. Dalton edited, designed, and published the newsletter. He also handled payroll, bookkeeping, taxes, and account management. Dalton's responsibilities included personal contact with Millennial's representatives, including Boom Communications. Boom Communications plans to expand its business to develop communications strategies, including newsletter publishing for industry clients. As part of its growth strategy, Boom wooed Dalton away with a five-year contract and a significant salary raise. Analyze whether Millennial Communications has a valid claim against Dalton for breach of the duty of loyalty.

Mastery Problem 41-1

Enviroco, an environmental engineering firm specializing in federal, state, and local government contracts, employs 30 engineers, including Frances, Luz, and Oscar. The firm pays its engineers a salary plus yearly performance-based bonuses according to the company's written policies. Frances, Luz, and Oscar have been working very hard to prepare a bid for a federal project that must be submitted on June 30, the end of the fiscal year. They are also working very hard during their free time to build a partnership that will start their own boutique engineering firm, specializing in federal contracts. They each enjoy federal contract work and have become specialists in the field because of their work at Enviroco. They have formed relationships with several federal agency representatives, who have promised them the opportunity to compete in the future if they form their own firm. They have also talked to two of the firm's valued CAD assistants, who stated that they wanted to join the new firm. Frances, Luz, and Oscar anticipate that their current workload will prevent them from announcing their resignation and formation of their new firm until September.

On June 15, Frances, Luz, and Oscar are told by the director of the federal contracts unit that they will be terminated from employment on July 1, after the large federal bid is submitted. She explains that the company has discovered, through a routine review of company emails, that Frances, Luz, and Oscar are planning to resign and form a competing firm. Their last paycheck will cover work through June 30, and they will not receive a performance-based bonus.

Frances, Luz, and Oscar feel betrayed, both because the company has spied on them and because they worked quite hard to earn their bonuses. They immediately quit and the CAD assistants agree to go with them. Within a week, they have set up a temporary office. Working around the clock for two weeks, they manage to prepare and submit a competing bid for the federal government contract, which they are ultimately awarded.

The president of Enviroco has come to you seeking advice as to whether the company has claims against Frances, Luz, and Oscar for setting up a competing firm, and particularly whether they are liable for submitting the winning bid on the federal project. Advise her about the prospects in litigation.

Conclusion

Many employees have a duty of loyalty to their employer that is either fiduciary in nature or is implied in the relationship. Employees are strictly prohibited from competing against their current employer, but they may undertake preparations to form a competing business before resigning, as long as they do not violate any contract terms, misappropriate trade secrets, or solicit customers and co-employees.

Lesson 42:
Trade Secrets

Objectives and Expected Learning Outcomes

This Lesson covers the meaning and protection of an employer's trade secrets and confidential information. You will learn the meaning of "trade secret" in the employment context. We will discuss the ways in which employers seek to protect trade secrets through contract or tort doctrines. You will analyze federal and state attempts to help employers protect their secrets.

Trade secrets are highly confidential pieces of information that go to the essence of a company's brand. Easy examples include the secret recipes for Coca Cola and Kentucky Fried Chicken products. The scope of trade secrets is much broader, however, and can cover processes such as marketing and branding plans, and even customer lists, as long as the company acts to maintain the secrecy of this information. We begin this Lesson by defining "trade secret" and then analyze how the law protects the employer's interests in its trade secrets.

Trade secrets law originally was a matter of common law in each state. Subsequently, a Uniform Law has been adopted by most states in one form or another, bringing uniformity to the area of law. Additionally, Congress passed the Defend Trade Secrets Act of 2016 (DTSA), 130 Stat. 376, to give employers a private right of action and remedies against misappropriation of trade secrets in federal court. Although the DTSA provides remedies for employers in federal court, it does not preempt existing state trade secret laws.

1. Defining the Term "Trade Secret"

The Restatement succinctly captures the broad definition of a trade secret, as it is defined in the common law of most states:

Restatement of Employment Law

§ 8.02. Definition of Employer's Trade Secret

An employer's information is a trade secret under this Chapter if:

a) it derives independent economic value from being kept secret;

b) the employer has taken reasonable measures to keep it secret; and

c) the information is not

   1) generally known to the public or in the employer's industry;

   2) readily obtainable by others through proper means; or

   3) acquired by employees through their general experience, knowledge, training, or skills during the ordinary course of their employment.

The Uniform Trade Secrets Act (UTSA) sought to bring regularity to the disparate common law trade secret protections. Forty-seven states have adopted some version of the UTSA, and some courts interpret the UTSA as displacing common law causes of action for breach of duty of loyalty in cases involving the misappropriation of trade secret cases. In a jurisdiction where the UTSA has been adopted, an employer alleging improper disclosure of its trade secrets would bring a claim under the UTSA and not a common law action for breach of duty of loyalty.

Uniform Trade Secrets Act

§ 1. Definitions

. . .

(4) "Trade secret" means information, including a formula, pattern, compilation, program, device, method, technique, or process, that:

   (i) derives independent economic value, actual or potential, from not being generally known to, and not being readily ascertainable by proper means by, other persons who can obtain economic value from its disclosure or use, and maintain its secrecy; and

   (ii) is the subject of efforts that are reasonable under the circumstances to maintain its secrecy.

Examples of trade secrets include financial, business, scientific, technical, economic, or engineering information, including patterns, plans, compilations, program devices, formulas, designs, prototypes, methods, techniques, processes, procedures, programs, or codes. The information can be tangible or intangible, physical or electronic.

Courts use several factors to assess whether information qualifies as a trade secret, including:

[1] the extent to which the information is known outside of the owner's business;

[2] the extent to which it is known by employees and others involved in the owner's business;

[3] the extent of measures taken by the owner to guard the secrecy of the information;

[4] the value of the information to the owner and to his competitors;

[5] the amount of effort or money expended by the owner in developing the information; and

[6] the ease or difficulty with which the information could be properly acquired or duplicated by others.

Restatement of Torts, § 757 Liability for Disclosure or Use of Another's Trade Secret, cmt. b.

We now consider key aspects of the Restatement and UTSA definitions.

A. Economically Valuable Information

To qualify as a trade secret, the information must derive independent economic value from not being known to or readily ascertainable by another person through proper means. Courts require employers to show with specificity that the information they seek to protect gives them an edge over potential or actual competitors.

Example 42-1

Metcalf, Inc. produces vaccines for newly discovered diseases in Asia and Africa. Its processes are the most thorough, efficient, and least costly in the business. Danica, one of few scientists within Metcalf, Inc. who knows the process for producing the vaccines, has been hired by Metcalf's competitor, Meeq, Inc. If Metcalf can show it took steps to keep the process for vaccines a secret, it can claim that its processes for producing vaccines have economic value and are deserving of protection.

Example 42-2

Carpet King is a commercial carpet distributor. It seeks to stop a former sales executive, Ellen, from disclosing the names of its customers to her new employer, Carpet Queen. Carpet King maintains a website on which it lists its major customers. Because the customers can be identified independently, there is no economic value in its customer list. Therefore, the customer list is not subject to protection, and Ellen may disclose the list to Carpet Queen.

B. Reasonable Measures Undertaken to Keep the Information Secret

To qualify as a trade secret, an employer must also take reasonable measures to keep the information secret. Employers typically require employees to sign nondisclosure or confidentiality agreements. Alternatively, employers can show that they advised employees of the confidential nature of protected information by shielding it from the general population, by segregating or parsing out information among more than one person, or by using encryption or coding processes to keep information private.

Factors in assessing whether the employer took reasonable measures include:

a. Does the employer allow the protected information to be shared with everyone without justification, or do they restrict access to the information?

b. Does the employer require employees to keep the information secret while both on and off the clock?

c. Does the employer expressly require employees to sign a confidentiality agreement?

C. Not Generally Known and Readily Obtainable Through Proper Means

Information that is readily available and does not require substantial research investment to obtain is not a trade secret. For example, names and addresses of potential customers that are readily ascertainable will not be considered a trade secret. Matters or information that can be easily reverse engineered cannot be protected as trade secrets.

Trade secrets are protected regardless of the means used to obtain them. An employee who memorizes a trade secret, instead of obtaining a tangible or digital copy of it, is still subject to trade secret protection and may be liable for breach of loyalty for disclosing the information or using it to injure their employer.

Example 42-3

Life Long Battery Corporation designed and manufactured a solar powered cellphone battery. Samuel works as an engineer and has been employed by the corporation for 10 years. He knows the product design and how to manufacture the battery. Life Long Battery took substantial measures to keep the design and manufacturing process secret. The company keeps the information in a password protected computer that only engineers and top-level officials can access. Samuel quit and accepted a position with Solar Batteries Corporation, a competitor and rival of Life Long Battery. Life Long Battery's design and manufacturing process is commercially valuable because it is currently the only solar battery in the market. The product design and manufacturing process is protected as a trade secret.

D. What Type of Information Is Not a Trade Secret?

A trade secret does not include the subjective knowledge an employee acquires during employment, such as aptitude, skill, dexterity, and/or manual and mental ability. In other words, an employer cannot claim that the skills learned on the job amount to a trade secret. Trade secrets also do not include the employer's illegal activities, and it is against public policy for parties to agree not to disclose information related to alleged or potential violations of the law.

Problem 42-1

Jane has started a state-legal marijuana grow operation in Sacramento, California. Although permitted under state law, the federal government still classifies marijuana as an illegal drug under the Controlled Substances Act. Jane hired two key employees to help her develop a special strain of marijuana that will help users to deal with insomnia. The strain promises to give users a mellow high and induce sleepiness, but with no significant side effects the next morning. Can Jane assert that the new strain is a trade secret and prohibit her key employees from disclosing details about the strain to others? What public policy considerations would suggest that Jane should not be able to claim that the new strain is a trade secret?

Problem 42-2

Sensational Bakery Shop has a special recipe for coffee cake. The coffee cake is the best-selling item in the bakery and generates substantial economic value. The shop owners do not keep the recipe in a secured location and the recipe was once printed in a local newspaper, although the bakery would neither confirm nor deny that it was the correct recipe. Sam, the resident baker at Sensational, decides to start his own business, Sam's Sensations, and plans to feature the coffee cake on the menu under the name, "Sensational Bakery Coffee Cake." Does Sensational Bakery Shop have the right to claim the recipe as a protected trade secret?

Problem 42-3

Sacramento Auto Industry manufactures custom automobiles. They have a standard manufacturing process that is readily known in the industry. Karl Marc, a 10-year employee, leaves Sacramento Auto and starts his own business manufacturing automobiles. His manufacturing process follows the standard manufacturing process in the industry as it was implemented by Sacramento Auto. Can Sacramento Auto claim that its manufacturing process is a trade secret?

Problem 42-4

The National Aeronautics and Space Administration (NASA) hired Michael Milligan to serve as an astronaut for reusable rocket ships. NASA provides years of training and Michael becomes highly specialized in operating rocket ships. The Elon Corporation is developing a private space vehicle business based on the same type of rocket ship used by NASA. If Elon seeks to hire Michael, should Michael's training and experience be considered a trade secret?

---

2. The Duty of Loyalty Includes a Duty Not to Misappropriate or Reveal a Trade Secret

In Lesson 41, we discussed the contours of the general duty of loyalty owed by employees to employers. Restrictions on the employee's ability to misappropriate or reveal a trade secret is a particular manifestation of the duty of loyalty.

Restatement of Employment Law

§ 8.03. Disclosure or Use by Employee or Former Employee of Employer's Trade Secrets

(a) An employee or former employee breaches the duty of loyalty to the employer if, without the employer's consent, the employee discloses to a third party or uses for the employee's own benefit or a third party's benefit the employer's trade secrets, as that term is defined in § 8.02.

(b) The duty stated in subsection (a) is not breached if the employee acts under a legal duty, legal protection, or other legal permission in making the disclosure or use.

(c) The employee's obligation not to disclose or use the employer's trade secrets lasts as long as the information remains a trade secret under § 8.02, and continues beyond termination of the employment relationship regardless of the reason for termination.

A. Scope of the Duty of Loyalty to Preserve Trade Secrets

The duty not to disclose an employer's trade secrets applies during the course of employment and after termination of employment. When courts issue injunctions to protect against disclosure, the duration of the injunction varies depending on the facts of each case. For example, in one case the court emphasized that the duration of the injunction preserves commercial morality "by preventing one from wrongfully using secret information for a period of time no longer than that required to discover or reproduce that information by lawful means." *Ilg Indus. v. Scott,* 273 N.E.2d 393, 394 (Ill. 1971). Consequently, courts are reluctant to grant permanent injunctions, because such an approach would "subvert the public's interest in allowing technical employees to make full use of their knowledge and skill and in fostering research and development." *Winston Research Corp. v. 3M,* 350 F.2d 134, 142 (9th Cir. 1965).

Some courts are willing to grant indefinite injunctions, subject to a showing that the information has become public. For example, a Court of Appeals held that "an injunction issued to protect a right will be dissolved upon the extinguishment of that right." *Shellmar Prods. Co. v. Allen-Qualley Co.*, 87 F.2d 104, 107 (7th Cir. 1936).

B. Permissible Reasons to Disclose Trade Secrets

An employee who discloses a trade secret as part of performing a legal duty, such as cooperating in an investigation conducted by a law enforcement agency, does not violate the rule of § 8.03. Moreover, an employee does not violate this section if she shares the trade secret information with her legal counsel in the course of seeking legal advice. However, not all questions are easily answered.

Problem 42-5

Lorenzo Nuñez resigned from his position as a lawyer for Legal Assistance Law Firm, a non-profit firm devoted to advocacy litigation, and opened a solo law firm. One year later, Lorenzo was contacted by a local law enforcement agency and asked a series of questions in connection with a criminal investigation regarding the business practices of Legal Assistance. Lorenzo is aware that some of the information relates to the firm's processes for maintaining client confidentiality, and that the firm took extraordinary measures to ensure the confidentiality of these processes. Can Lorenzo disclose the processes without running afoul of trade secret principles?

Problem 42-6

Frank was fired from his position with Watson Marketing. During his employment, Frank learned one of Watson's trade-secrets (referred to as "operation double 'o' marketing.") Shortly after Frank's involuntary departure, "operation double 'o' marketing" lost its trade secret status because it became known in circles outside of Watson. One year later, Frank disclosed Watson's "operation double 'o' marketing" information to Watson's biggest competitor. Is Frank liable for misappropriating a protected trade secret?

C. Liability for Misappropriation of Trade Secrets

Determining whether an employee has "misappropriated" his employer's trade secrets can be difficult. Consider the definition in the UTSA.

Uniform Trade Secrets Act

§ 1. Definitions

(2) "Misappropriation" means:

(i) acquisition of a trade secret of another person who knows or has reason to know that the trade secret was acquired by improper means; or

(ii) disclosure or use of a trade secret of another without express or implied consent by a person who

(A) used improper means to acquire knowledge of the trade secret; or

(B) at the time of disclosure or use knew or had reason to know that his knowledge of the trade secret was

(I) derived from or through a person who has utilized improper means to acquire it;

(II) acquired under circumstances giving rise to a duty to maintain its secrecy or limit its use; or

(III) derived from or through a person who owed a duty to the person seeking relief to maintain its secrecy or limit its use; or

(C) before a material change of his position, knew or had reason to know that it was a trade secret and that knowledge of it had been acquired by accident or mistake.

The following case provides an example of a court finding the existence of a trade secret, its misappropriation by an employee, and the available remedies.

Saturn Sys. v. Militare

252 P.3d 516 (Ct. App. Colo. 2011).

Opinion by: Judge Loeb.

Defendant, Delbert J. Militare, appeals the judgment entered after a bench trial in favor of plaintiff, Saturn Systems, Inc., on its claims of misappropriation of trade secrets . . .We affirm . . . .

I. Background and Procedural History

Saturn is a debt collection agency that offers numerous types of debt collection services, including recovery of commercial, consumer, medical, government, and retail accounts, both domestically and abroad. According to testimony at trial, since its founding in 1997, Saturn has provided its services to over 1,600 clients, for whom it has processed and helped collect over 120,000 debts.

Evidence at trial showed that Saturn spent significant time and money to develop a proprietary website to provide its clients access to its database of client and debtor information. Thus, Saturn assigns each client a unique username and password that can be used to log in to the website and view real-time information related to that client's account. For example, a client can view a "status report" for its account, which summarizes Saturn's debt recovery to date and tells the client how many pre-purchased debt collection accounts it has available to designate to debtors in default so that Saturn can initiate collection activities. A client can also view the "debtor notes" for its debtors that have entered Saturn's "hardcore" collection phase. Saturn uses the "debtor notes" component of its website to record pending collection efforts, settlement negotiations, and all known personal information for a debtor, such as addresses, bank accounts, and employment history. Because of the confidential nature of the information that can be accessed via its website, Saturn only releases the usernames and passwords to the client and, if needed, to the sales agent assigned to that client's account.

On January 13, 2003, Saturn hired Militare for a sales agent position. The parties entered into a written sales agent agreement (Agreement) that outlined their respective roles. In that regard, Militare agreed to act as an independent contractor with the authority to sell Saturn's services, receive funds on Saturn's behalf, and make sales presentations to prospective clients. Additionally, Militare agreed to provide ongoing customer care to the clients that he signed up for Saturn's services. In return, Saturn agreed to pay Militare a commission on each sale that he made. . . .

As a Saturn sales agent, Militare was provided access to and was taught how to use the confidential database on the Saturn website.

Saturn terminated the Agreement with Militare approximately two years later by proper written notice. The effective date of the termination was January 18, 2005. Shortly thereafter, on January 31, 2005, Militare accepted a position with CB Solutions, LLC, a Texas-based company and a direct competitor of Saturn.

In March 2005, while working for CB Solutions, Militare personally visited Premier Members Federal Credit Union, a longtime Saturn client that still had unused pre-purchased debt collection accounts available with Saturn. Militare admitted at trial that he contacted Premier on behalf of CB Solutions to win the Premier account. Although the parties disputed the details of Militare's visit, the record indicates that Premier contacted Saturn shortly after the visit to request a new password for its Saturn account.

Upon learning of Militare's visit to Premier, in early April 2005, Saturn retained David Travis, a computer and website specialist, to investigate suspected unauthorized access of Saturn's website by Militare. Travis's investigation confirmed Saturn's suspicions. According to Travis, Militare repeatedly accessed fifteen client accounts, including the debtor notes associated with those accounts, subsequent to his termination from Saturn. Travis found that in doing so, Militare reviewed a total of seventy-two privileged and confidential Saturn web pages.

In March and April 2005, Saturn also sent cease and desist letters to Militare demanding that he stop using its confidential data and soliciting Saturn clients, in violation of the Agreement and Colorado's trade secret laws.

On May 6, 2005, Saturn filed its complaint in this action, alleging . . . misappropriation of trade secrets and . . .seeking damages and injunctive relief. The parties submitted cross-motions for summary judgment, which were denied, and the case was then tried. . . .

After the close of evidence, Militare stipulated to the injunctive relief requested by Saturn on its trade secrets claim, and the court entered a stipulated order for injunctive relief on October 1, 2007. . . .

On October 31, 2007, the court entered a written order of judgment in Saturn's favor, finding Militare liable for misappropriation of Saturn's trade secrets . . . The court awarded Saturn . . . damages . . . as well as attorney fees and costs under the fee-shifting provision of the Agreement. . . . Militare timely appealed from the court's. . . judgment . . . .

. . . .

III. Misappropriation of Trade Secrets

Militare contends the trial court erred by finding hat he misappropriated Saturn's trade secrets because there was insufficient evidence to show that (1) Saturn possessed valid trade secrets, and (2) Militare misappropriated Saturn's trade secrets. We reject these contentions in turn.

A. Trade Secrets Finding

First, Militare contends there is insufficient evidence to support the trial court's finding that the client and debtor information contained within Saturn's proprietary website database qualifies as trade secrets under Colorado law. We disagree.

What constitutes a trade secret is a question of fact for the trial court. Accordingly, if the court's trade secret determination is supported by the record, we will not disturb it on appeal.

The Colorado Uniform Trade Secrets Act (UTSA), sections 7–74–101 to –110, C.R.S. 2010, defines a trade secret as:

> The whole or any portion or phase of any scientific or technical information, design, process, procedure, formula, improvement, confidential business or financial information, listing of names, addresses, or telephone numbers, or other information relating to any business or profession which is secret and of value.

§ 7–74–102(4), C.R.S. 2010.

Colorado courts may consider several factors to make the factual determination of whether a trade secret exists under this statutory definition, including: (1) the extent to which the information is known outside the business; (2) the extent to which it is known to those inside the business, such as the employees; (3) the precautions taken by the holder of the trade secret to guard the secrecy of the information; (4) the savings effected and the value to the holder in having the information as against competitors; (5) the amount of effort or money expended in obtaining and developing the information; and (6) the amount of time and expense it would take for others to acquire and duplicate the information.

The UTSA further provides:

> To be a "trade secret" the owner thereof must have taken measures to prevent the secret from becoming available to persons other than those selected by the owner to have access thereto for limited purposes.

§ 7–74–102(4). Thus, prior divisions of this court have held that "the alleged secret must be the subject of efforts that are reasonable under the circumstances to maintain its secrecy," but that "[e]xtreme and unduly expensive procedures need not be taken." Reasonable efforts have been held to include advising employees of the existence of a trade secret, limiting access to a trade secret on a "need to know" basis, and controlling plant access.

Here, the trial court found that Saturn's client and debtor information stored within its proprietary database qualified as trade secrets under Colorado law because: (1) the information is confidential and not known outside of the business, either by competitors or the general public; (2) the real-time information is available only through the use of a client's username and password; (3) access to Saturn's database is strictly limited on a "need to know" basis; and (4) Saturn has taken reasonable efforts to maintain the secrecy of the information stored within its database.

The record supports the trial court's findings. Saturn's president testified that the specific information contained within its "status reports" and "debtor notes" is highly valuable to it and to competitors. For example, the testimony established that a competitor could use its knowledge of a client's available pre-purchased accounts and of the amount of debt recovered to date to develop a competitive marketing strategy exactly when that client was ripe for renewal with Saturn. Likewise, the testimony established that a competitor could use the highly detailed information contained within Saturn's debtor notes to usurp sales opportunities.

Further, Saturn's president described the security precautions that Saturn has taken to protect its proprietary information, including a password-protected and encrypted website and a policy of limited access. There was also testimony about the significant amount of money spent by Saturn to develop and maintain its database of information.

Accordingly, because there is substantial evidence in the record to support the trial court's finding that Saturn possessed valid trade secrets, we will not disturb that finding on appeal.

. . . .

B. Misappropriation Finding

Militare also contends there is insufficient evidence to support the trial court's finding that Militare misappropriated Saturn's trade secrets.

. . . .

2. Misappropriation

. . . We reject Militare's contention that the record does not support the trial court's finding that he misappropriated Saturn's trade secrets.

Under the UTSA, "misappropriation" is defined in pertinent part as the "[a]cquisition of a trade secret of another by a person who knows or has reason to know that the trade secret was acquired by improper means." " 'Improper means' includes theft, bribery, misrepresentation, breach or inducement of a breach of a duty to maintain secrecy, or espionage through electronic or other means." As a prior division of this court observed, "[t] here is no requirement in Colorado's [UTSA] that there be actual use or commercial implementation of the misappropriated trade secret for damages to accrue. Misappropriation consists only of the improper disclosure or acquisition of the trade secret."

Here, the trial court found that Militare "knowingly misappropriated numerous trade secrets belonging to Saturn" at the time of his termination and that "subsequent to that termination, [he] repeatedly accessed the Saturn website to review and update privileged information, without permission . . . caus[ing] injury to [Saturn]." The court further concluded that Militare "knowingly used improper means in order to use Saturn's trade secrets for his benefit."

The court's findings and conclusions are adequately supported by the record. Travis's expert report and testimony described specific instances of Militare's unauthorized access of Saturn's client accounts subsequent to his termination, and Militare himself confirmed at trial that he accessed confidential information on the Saturn website after the Agreement was terminated. At trial, Militare testified that he "viewed" the restricted areas of Saturn's website subsequent to his termination, but that he did not "utilize" or "print" any information. For the purposes of a misappropriation inquiry under the UTSA, it is irrelevant whether Militare actually used Saturn's client and debtor information to compete against Saturn, or actually disclosed the information to others. Thus, because there is ample evidence in the record that Militare knowingly acquired password-protected information by improper means, we will not disturb the court's misappropriation finding on appeal.

. . . .

On the other hand, how is it possible to segregate the information that an employee may have come in contact with during employment from other information gained independently? Some employers argue that trade secret information inside a former employee's head will inevitably be disclosed because an employee cannot compartmentalize the information that he or she acquired while employed with the former employer. The following case explores the doctrine of "inevitable disclosure."

PepsiCo v. Redmond

54 F. 3d 1262 (7th Cir. 1995).

Flaum, Circuit Judge.

Plaintiff PepsiCo, Inc., sought a preliminary injunction against defendants William Redmond and the Quaker Oats Company to prevent Redmond, a former PepsiCo employee, from divulging PepsiCo trade secrets and confidential information in his new job with Quaker and from assuming any duties with Quaker relating to beverage pricing, marketing, and distribution. The district court agreed with PepsiCo and granted the injunction. We now affirm that decision.

I.

The facts of this case lay against a backdrop of fierce beverage-industry competition between Quaker and PepsiCo, especially in "sports drinks" and "new age drinks." Quaker's sports drink, "Gatorade," is the dominant brand in its market niche. PepsiCo introduced its Gatorade rival, "All

Sport," in March and April of 1994, but sales of All Sport lag far behind those of Gatorade. Quaker also has the lead in the new-age-drink category. Although PepsiCo has entered the market through joint ventures with the Thomas J. Lipton Company and Ocean Spray Cranberries, Inc., Quaker purchased Snapple Beverage Corp., a large new-age-drink maker, in late 1994. PepsiCo's products have about half of Snapple's market share. Both companies see 1995 as an important year for their products: PepsiCo has developed extensive plans to increase its market presence, while Quaker is trying to solidify its lead by integrating Gatorade and Snapple distribution. Meanwhile, PepsiCo and Quaker each face strong competition from Coca Cola Co., which has its own sports drink, "PowerAde," and which introduced its own Snapple-rival, "Fruitopia," in 1994, as well as from independent beverage producers.

William Redmond, Jr., worked for PepsiCo in its Pepsi-Cola North America division ("PCNA") from 1984 to 1994. Redmond became the General Manager of the Northern California Business Unit in June, 1993, and was promoted one year later to General Manager of the business unit covering all of California, a unit having annual revenues of more than 500 million dollars and representing twenty percent of PCNA's profit for all of the United States.

Redmond's relatively high-level position at PCNA gave him access to inside information and trade secrets. Redmond, like other PepsiCo management employees, had signed a confidentiality agreement with PepsiCo. That agreement stated in relevant part that he

> would not disclose at any time, to anyone other than officers or employees of [PepsiCo], or make use of, confidential information relating to the business of [PepsiCo] . . . obtained while in the employ of [PepsiCo], which shall not be generally known or available to the public or recognized as standard practices.

Donald Uzzi, who had left PepsiCo in the beginning of 1994 to become the head of Quaker's Gatorade division, began courting Redmond for Quaker in May, 1994. Redmond met in Chicago with Quaker officers in August, 1994, and on October 20, 1994, Quaker, through Uzzi, offered Redmond the position of Vice President-On Premise Sales for Gatorade. Redmond did not then accept the offer but continued to negotiate for more money. Throughout this time,

Redmond kept his dealings with Quaker secret from his employers at PCNA.

On November 8, 1994, Uzzi extended Redmond a written offer for the position of Vice President-Field Operations for Gatorade and Redmond accepted. Later that same day, Redmond called William Bensyl, the Senior Vice President of Human Resources for PCNA, and told him that he had an offer from Quaker to become the Chief Operating Officer of the combined Gatorade and Snapple company but had not yet accepted it. Redmond also asked whether he should, in light of the offer, carry out his plans to make calls upon certain PCNA customers. Bensyl told Redmond to make the visits.

Redmond also misstated his situation to a number of his PCNA colleagues, including Craig Weatherup, PCNA's President and Chief Executive Officer, and Brenda Barnes, PCNA's Chief Operating Officer and Redmond's immediate superior. As with Bensyl, Redmond told them that he had been offered the position of Chief Operating Officer at Gatorade and that he was leaning "60/40" in favor of accepting the new position.

On November 10, 1994, Redmond met with Barnes and told her that he had decided to accept the Quaker offer and was resigning from PCNA. Barnes immediately took Redmond to Bensyl, who told Redmond that PepsiCo was considering legal action against him.

True to its word, PepsiCo filed this diversity suit on November 16, 1994, seeking a temporary restraining order to enjoin Redmond from assuming his duties at Quaker and to prevent him from disclosing trade secrets or confidential information to his new employer. The district court granted PepsiCo's request that same day but dissolved the order *sua sponte* two days later, after determining that PepsiCo had failed to meet its burden of establishing that it would suffer irreparable harm. The court found that PepsiCo's fears about Redmond were based upon a mistaken understanding of his new position at Quaker and that the likelihood that Redmond would improperly reveal any confidential information did not "rise above mere speculation."

From November 23, 1994, to December 1, 1994, the district court conducted a preliminary injunction hearing on the same matter. At the hearing, PepsiCo offered evidence of a number of trade secrets and confidential information it desired protected and to which Redmond was privy. First, it identified PCNA's "Strategic Plan," an annually revised document that contains PCNA's plans to compete, its financial goals, and its strategies for manufacturing, production, marketing, packaging, and distribution for the coming three years. Strategic Plans are developed by Weatherup and his staff with input from PCNA's general managers, including Redmond, and are considered highly confidential. The Strategic Plan derives much of its value from the fact that it is secret and competitors cannot anticipate PCNA's next moves. PCNA managers received the most recent Strategic Plan at a meeting in July, 1994, a meeting Redmond attended. PCNA also presented information at the meeting regarding its plans for Lipton ready-to-drink teas and for All Sport for 1995 and beyond, including new flavors and package sizes.

Second, PepsiCo pointed to PCNA's Annual Operating Plan ("AOP") as a trade secret. The AOP is a national plan for a given year and guides PCNA's financial goals, marketing plans, promotional event calendars, growth expectations, and operational changes in that year. The AOP, which is implemented by PCNA unit General Managers, including Redmond, contains specific information regarding all PCNA initiatives for the forthcoming year. The AOP bears a label that reads "Private and Confidential—Do Not Reproduce" and is considered highly confidential by PCNA managers.

In particular, the AOP contains important and sensitive information about "pricing architecture"—how PCNA prices its products in the marketplace. Pricing architecture covers both a national pricing approach and specific price points for given areas. Pricing architecture also encompasses PCNA's objectives for All Sport and its new age drinks with reference to trade channels, package sizes and other characteristics of both the products and the customers at which the products are aimed. Additionally, PCNA's pricing architecture outlines PCNA's customer development agreements. These agreements between PCNA and retailers provide for the retailer's participation in certain merchandising activities for PCNA products. As with other information contained in the AOP, pricing architecture is highly confidential and would be extremely valuable to a competitor. Knowing PCNA's pricing architecture would allow a competitor to anticipate PCNA's pricing moves and underbid PCNA strategically whenever and wherever the competitor so desired. PepsiCo introduced evidence that Redmond had detailed knowledge of PCNA's pricing architecture and that he was aware of and had been involved in preparing PCNA's customer development agreements with PCNA's California and California-based national customers. Indeed, PepsiCo showed that Redmond, as the General Manager for California, would have been responsible for implementing the pricing architecture guidelines for his business unit.

PepsiCo also showed that Redmond had intimate knowledge of PCNA "attack plans" for specific markets. Pursuant to these plans, PCNA dedicates extra funds to supporting its brands against other brands in selected markets. To use a hypothetical example, PCNA might budget an additional $ 500,000 to spend in Chicago at a particular time to help All Sport close its market gap with Gatorade. Testimony and documents demonstrated Redmond's awareness of these plans and his participation in drafting some of them.

Finally, PepsiCo offered evidence of PCNA trade secrets regarding innovations in its selling and delivery systems. Under this plan, PCNA is testing a new delivery system that could give PCNA an advantage over its competitors in negotiations with retailers over shelf space and merchandising. Redmond has knowledge of this secret because PCNA, which has invested over a million dollars in developing the system during the past two years, is testing the pilot program in California.

Having shown Redmond's intimate knowledge of PCNA's plans for 1995, PepsiCo argued that Redmond would inevitably disclose that information to Quaker in his new position, at which he would have substantial input as to Gatorade and Snapple pricing, costs, margins, distribution systems, products, packaging and marketing, and could give Quaker an unfair advantage in its upcoming skirmishes with PepsiCo. Redmond and Quaker countered that Redmond's primary initial duties at Quaker as Vice President-Field Operations would be to integrate Gatorade and Snapple distribution and then to manage that distribution as well as the promotion, marketing and sales of these products. Redmond asserted that the integration would be conducted according to a pre-existing plan and that his special knowledge of PCNA strategies would be irrelevant. This irrelevance would derive not only from the fact that Redmond would be implementing pre-existing plans but also from the fact that PCNA and Quaker distribute their products in entirely different ways: PCNA's distribution system is vertically integrated (i.e., PCNA owns the system) and delivers its product directly to retailers, while Quaker ships its product to wholesalers and customer warehouses and relies on independent distributors. The defendants also pointed out that Redmond had signed a confidentiality agreement with Quaker preventing him from disclosing "any confidential information belonging to others," as well as the Quaker Code of Ethics, which prohibits employees from engaging in "illegal or improper acts to acquire a competitor's trade secrets." Redmond additionally promised at the hearing that should he be faced with a situation at Quaker that might involve the use or disclosure of

PCNA information, he would seek advice from Quaker's in-house counsel and would refrain from making the decision.

PepsiCo responded to the defendants' representations by pointing out that the evidence did not show that Redmond would simply be implementing a business plan already in place. On the contrary, as of November, 1994, the plan to integrate Gatorade and Snapple distribution consisted of a single distributorship agreement and a two page "contract terms summary." Such a basic plan would not lend itself to widespread application among the over 300 independent Snapple distributors. Since the integration process would likely face resistance from Snapple distributors and Quaker had no scheme to deal with this probability, Redmond, as the person in charge of the integration, would likely have a great deal of influence on the process. PepsiCo further argued that Snapple's 1995 marketing and promotion plans had not necessarily been completed prior to Redmond's joining Quaker, that Uzzi disagreed with portions of the Snapple plans, and that the plans were open to re-evaluation. Uzzi testified that the plan for integrating Gatorade and Snapple distribution is something that would happen in the future. Redmond would therefore likely have input in remaking these plans, and if he did, he would inevitably be making decisions with PCNA's strategic plans and 1995 AOP in mind. Moreover, PepsiCo continued, diverging testimony made it difficult to know exactly what Redmond would be doing at Quaker. Redmond described his job as "managing the entire sales effort of Gatorade at the field level, possibly including strategic planning," and at least at one point considered his job to be equivalent to that of a Chief Operating Officer. Uzzi, on the other hand, characterized Redmond's position as "primarily and initially to restructure and integrate our—the distribution systems for Snapple and for Gatorade, as per our distribution plan" and then to "execute marketing, promotion and sales plans in the marketplace." Uzzi also denied having given Redmond detailed information about any business plans, while Redmond described such a plan in depth in an affidavit and said that he received the information from Uzzi. Thus, PepsiCo asserted, Redmond would have a high position in the Gatorade hierarchy, and PCNA trade secrets and confidential information would necessarily influence his decisions. Even if Redmond could somehow refrain from relying on this information, as he promised he would, his actions in leaving PCNA, Uzzi's actions in hiring Redmond, and the varying testimony regarding Redmond's new responsibilities, made Redmond's assurances to PepsiCo less than comforting.

On December 15, 1994, the district court issued an order enjoining Redmond from assuming his position at Quaker through May, 1995, and permanently from using or disclosing any PCNA trade secrets or confidential information. The court entered its findings of fact and conclusions of law on January 26, 1995, *nunc pro tunc* December 15, 1994. The court, which completely adopted PepsiCo's position, found that Redmond's new job posed a clear threat of misappropriation of trade secrets and confidential information that could be enjoined under Illinois statutory. . . The court also emphasized Redmond's lack of forthrightness both in his activities before accepting his job with Quaker and in his testimony as factors leading the court to believe the threat of misappropriation was real. This appeal followed.

II.

Both parties agree that the primary issue on appeal is whether the district court correctly concluded that PepsiCo had a reasonable likelihood of success on its various claims for trade secret misappropriation and breach of a confidentiality agreement. . . .

A.

The Illinois Trade Secrets Act ("ITSA"), which governs the trade secret issues in this case, provides that a court may enjoin the "actual or threatened misappropriation" of a trade secret. A party seeking an injunction must therefore prove both the existence of a trade secret and the misappropriation. The defendants' appeal focuses solely on misappropriation; although the defendants only reluctantly refer to PepsiCo's marketing and distribution plans as trade secrets, they do not seriously contest that this information falls under the ITSA.

The question of threatened or inevitable misappropriation in this case lies at the heart of a basic tension in trade secret law. Trade secret law serves to protect "standards of commercial morality" and "encourage invention and innovation" while maintaining "the public interest in having free and open competition in the manufacture and sale of unpatented goods." Yet that same law should not prevent workers from pursuing their livelihoods when they leave their current positions. . . .

This tension is particularly exacerbated when a plaintiff sues to prevent not the actual misappropriation of trade secrets but the mere threat that it will occur. While the ITSA plainly permits a court to enjoin the threat of misappropriation of trade secrets, there is little law in Illinois or in this circuit establishing what constitutes threatened or inevitable misappropriation. . . . Indeed, there are only two cases in this circuit that address the issue: *Teradyne, Inc. v. Clear Communications Corp.*, 707 F. Supp. 353 (N.D.Ill 1989), and *AMP Inc. v. Fleischhacker*, 823 F.2d 1199 (7th Cir. 1987).

In *Teradyne,* Teradyne alleged that a competitor, Clear Communications, had lured employees away from Teradyne and intended to employ them in the same field. In an insightful opinion, Judge Zagel observed that "threatened misappropriation can be enjoined under Illinois law" where there is a "high degree of probability of inevitable and immediate . . . use of . . . trade secrets." Judge Zagel held, however, that Teradyne's complaint failed to state a claim because Teradyne did not allege "that defendants have in fact threatened to use Teradyne's secrets or that they will inevitably do so." Teradyne's claims would have passed Rule 12(b)(6) muster had they properly alleged inevitable disclosure, including a statement that Clear intended to use Teradyne's trade secrets or that the former Teradyne employees had disavowed their confidentiality agreements with Teradyne, or an allegation that Clear could not operate without Teradyne's secrets.

. . . .

In *AMP,* we affirmed the denial of a preliminary injunction on the grounds that the plaintiff AMP had failed to show either the existence of any trade secrets or the likelihood that defendant Fleischhacker, a former AMP employee, would compromise those secrets or any other confidential business information. AMP, which produced electrical and electronic connection devices, argued that Fleishhacker's new position at AMP's competitor would inevitably lead him to compromise AMP's trade secrets regarding the manufacture of connectors. In rejecting that argument, we emphasized that the mere fact that a person assumed a similar position at a competitor does not, without more, make it "inevitable that he will use or disclose . . . trade secret information" so as to "demonstrate irreparable injury."

. . . .

The ITSA, *Teradyne,* and *AMP* lead to the same conclusion: a plaintiff may prove a claim of trade secret misappropriation by demonstrating that defendant's new employment will inevitably lead him to rely on the plaintiff's trade secrets. The defendants are incorrect that Illinois law does not allow a court to enjoin the "inevitable" disclosure of trade secrets. Questions remain, however, as to what constitutes inevitable misappropriation and whether PepsiCo's submissions rise above those of the *Teradyne* and *AMP* plaintiffs and meet that standard. We hold that they do.

PepsiCo presented substantial evidence at the preliminary injunction hearing that Redmond possessed extensive and intimate knowledge about PCNA's strategic goals for 1995 in sports drinks and new age drinks. The district court concluded on the basis of that presentation that unless Redmond possessed an uncanny ability to compartmentalize information, he would necessarily be making decisions about Gatorade and Snapple by relying on his knowledge of PCNA trade secrets. It is not the "general skills and knowledge acquired during his tenure with" PepsiCo that PepsiCo seeks to keep from falling into Quaker's hands, but rather "the particularized plans or processes developed by [PCNA] and disclosed to him while the employer-employee relationship existed, which are unknown to others in the industry and which give the employer an advantage over his competitors. The *Teradyne* and *AMP* plaintiffs could do nothing more than assert that skilled employees were taking their skills elsewhere; PepsiCo has done much more.

Admittedly, PepsiCo has not brought a traditional trade secret case, in which a former employee has knowledge of a special manufacturing process or customer list and can give a competitor an unfair advantage by transferring the technology or customers to that competitor. PepsiCo has not contended that Quaker has stolen the All Sport formula or its list of distributors. Rather PepsiCo has asserted that Redmond cannot help but rely on PCNA trade secrets as he help plots Gatorade and Snapple's new course, and that these secrets will enable Quaker to achieve a substantial advantage by knowing exactly how PCNA will price, distribute, and market its sports drinks and new age drinks and being able to respond strategically. This type of trade secret problem may arise less often, but it nevertheless falls within the realm of trade secret protection under the present circumstances.

Quaker and Redmond assert that they have not and do not intend to use whatever confidential information Redmond has by virtue of his former employment. They point out that Redmond has already signed an agreement with Quaker not to disclose any trade secrets or confidential information gleaned from his earlier employment. They also note with regard to distribution systems that even if Quaker wanted to steal information about

PCNA's distribution plans, they would be completely useless in attempting to integrate the Gatorade and Snapple beverage lines.

The defendants' arguments fall somewhat short of the mark. Again, the danger of misappropriation in the present case is not that Quaker threatens to use PCNA's secrets to create distribution systems or coopt PCNA's advertising and marketing ideas. Rather, PepsiCo believes that Quaker, unfairly armed with knowledge of PCNA's plans, will be able to anticipate its distribution, packaging, pricing, and marketing moves. Redmond and Quaker even concede that Redmond might be faced with a decision that could be influenced by certain confidential information that he obtained while at PepsiCo. In other words, PepsiCo finds itself in the position of a coach, one of whose players has left, playbook in hand, to join the opposing team before the big game. Quaker and Redmond's protestations that their distribution systems and plans are entirely different from PCNA's are thus not really responsive.

The district court also concluded from the evidence that Uzzi's actions in hiring Redmond and Redmond's actions in pursuing and accepting his new job demonstrated a lack of candor on their part and proof of their willingness to misuse PCNA trade secrets, findings Quaker and Redmond vigorously challenge. . . .

. . . .

The facts of the case do not ineluctably dictate the district court's conclusion. Redmond's ambiguous behavior toward his PepsiCo superiors might have been nothing more than an attempt to gain leverage in employment negotiations. The discrepancy between Redmond's and Uzzi's comprehension of what Redmond's job would entail may well have been a simple misunderstanding. The court also pointed out that Quaker, through Uzzi, seemed to express an unnatural interest in hiring PCNA employees: all three of the people interviewed for the position Redmond ultimately accepted worked at PCNA. Uzzi may well have focused on recruiting PCNA employees because he knew they were good and not because of their confidential knowledge. Nonetheless, the district court, after listening to the witnesses, determined otherwise. That conclusion was not an abuse of discretion.

. . . .

Thus, when we couple the demonstrated inevitability that Redmond would rely on PCNA trade secrets in his new job at Quaker with the district court's reluctance to believe that Redmond would refrain from disclosing these secrets in his new position . . ., we conclude that the district court correctly decided that PepsiCo demonstrated a likelihood of success on its statutory claim of trade secret misappropriation.

. . . .

C.

For the same reasons we concluded that the district court did not abuse its discretion in granting the preliminary injunction on the issue of trade secret misappropriation, we also agree with its decision on the likelihood of Redmond's breach of his confidentiality agreement should he begin working at Quaker. Because Redmond's position at Quaker would initially cause him to disclose trade secrets, it would necessarily force him to breach his agreement not to disclose confidential information acquired while employed in PCNA.

. . . .

III.

Finally, Redmond and Quaker have contended in the alternative that the injunction issued against them is overbroad. . . . A district court ordinarily has wide latitude in fashioning injunctive relief, and we will restrict the breadth of an injunction only where the district court has abused its discretion. Nonetheless, a court abuses its discretion where the scope of injunctive relief "exceeds the extent of the plaintiff's protectible rights."

While the defendants' arguments are not without some merit, the district court determined that the proposed integration would require Redmond to do more than execute a plan someone else had drafted. It also found that Redmond's knowledge of PCNA's trade secrets and confidential information would inevitably shape that integration and that Redmond could not be trusted to avoid that conflict of interest. If the injunction permanently enjoined Redmond from assuming these duties at Quaker, the defendants' argument would be stronger. However, the injunction against Redmond's immediate employment at Quaker extends no further than necessary and was well within the district court's discretion.

For the foregoing reasons, we affirm the district court's order enjoining Redmond from assuming his responsibilities at Quaker through May, 1995, and preventing him forever from disclosing PCNA trade secrets and confidential information.

AFFIRMED.

Mastery Problem 42-1

UberLaw is a new online platform for people who need the advice of a lawyer. UberLaw advertises itself as the place for affordable legal services of all kinds. Their advertising is specific: "If you need a will, UberLaw can provide the forms and the lawyer who will review them." Similarly, the site claims, "If you need to sign a contract, UberLaw will provide a lawyer who can review it in your state." Finally, the site proclaims, "If you need a visa, UberLaw can find you an immigration attorney."

UberLaw is headquartered in San Francisco, but it advertises its services throughout the country.

The UberLaw business model calls for the company to engage attorneys on contract throughout the country on a subcontractor basis. It also hires approximately 30 attorneys as full-time employees in its San Francisco office. The in-house attorneys oversee the work of the contract attorneys and ensure that UberLaw maintains a high level of quality legal services. The in-house attorneys monitor the work of the contract attorneys, provide technical assistance and conduct annual audits to ensure that contract attorneys are fulfilling their professional responsibilities to their UberLaw clients.

UberLaw has the following policies that apply to everyone, whether employees or independent contractors:

1. Employment with UberLaw is at-will, unless otherwise specified by written contract. You are free to resign at any time, for any reason, with or without notice. Likewise, UberLaw is free to end the employment relationship at any time, with or without cause, with or without notice.

2. In the course of employment with UberLaw, you may have access to confidential information, including, but not limited to: business

strategies, plans for the future, financial information, client information, personnel information, and information that UberLaw considers proprietary and confidential. You must protect the confidentiality of this information by using it only for business purposes and only when authorized to do so. This duty of confidentiality applies on- or off-duty and even at the end of your employment with the Company. If you establish a client relationship through UberLaw you are expected to maintain that relationship through UberLaw while you are employed with the company.

3. All desks, file drawers, cabinets, and equipment, (including computers, company-issued cellphones, email and voicemail) on the premises are property of the Company and intended for business use. Employees should have no expectation of privacy in company property or in anything stored or on company property. In addition, when the company deems appropriate, the company may search personal vehicles, parcels, purses, briefcases, lunchboxes, or any other possessions brought onto company property.

4. UberLaw reserves the right to access, monitor, and review electronic communications, blogs, "tweets," instant messages, email, and other digital communications to ensure that no violation of company policy or any law occurs.

Everyone must sign an acknowledgment of receipt and acceptance of UberLaw's policies upon hiring, which states in part: "I understand and agree that the policies described in the handbook are intended as a guide only and do not constitute a contract. The employment-at-will relationship may not be modified except by a specific written agreement between me and an authorized representative of the company."

Samantha is an employee of UberLaw who works in the San Francisco office. She audits and monitors the work of and provides technical assistance to attorneys working on employment disputes and contracts. She likes her job, especially its security and not having to worry about running her own business. Samantha did not sign a written contract with UberLaw. She did sign the employee policy acknowledgment form.

Recently, a rival company, LawJockey, approached Samantha. LawJockey wants to hire Samantha as its Vice President for Human Resources. Samantha likes Law-

Jockey's business model, which includes hiring everyone as employees as opposed to UberLaw's practice of classifying some attorneys as independent contractors.

UberLaw's IT department regularly monitors the company's electronic emails. An IT staff member flagged the emails between Samantha and LawJockey and forwarded them to UberLaw's VP for human resources, Kevin. Kevin directed IT to continue to monitor their electronic communications. A few days later, IT alerted Kevin that LawJockey was sending Samantha a draft contract by courier. Kevin intercepted it, opened the envelope and discovered that it was a draft employment contract.

Kevin immediately called Samantha into his office and fired her. He asked her to leave the premises and to return the next day for her belongings. The next day, UberLaw filed a claim in federal court under the DTSA, seeking an injunction keeping Samantha from starting at LawJockey under a theory of misappropriation of trade secrets.

1. Articulate UberLaw's inevitable disclosure claim.

2. Does UberLaw have a valid claim?

3. Should the judge issue an injunction?

4. What are the policy reasons for and against the grant of an injunction?

Conclusion

The law protects employers from employees who might learn their trade secrets and use them in a manner that harms the employer. Not all business practices are trade secrets, and so the employer must first establish that it has a legally protected interest. Additionally, when an employer's trade secrets are so woven into the employee's job, it may be difficult to determine where the employee's experience ends and the protected trade secret begins.

Lesson 43:
Professional Responsibility and Litigation Ethics

Objectives and Expected Learning Outcomes

By the end of the Lesson, you will have a working knowledge of the ethical rules that employment lawyers most frequently confront; understand when the rules are implicated; and you will develop a working framework on how to resolve ethical and professional challenges.

Lawyers are licensed at the state level, and so ethical requirements are also a matter of state law. The Model Rules of Professional Conduct promulgated by the American Bar Association have served as the basis for the ethical code in most states. The first sentence of the Preamble to the Model Rules succinctly states the multiple roles and corresponding duties undertaken by lawyers: "A lawyer, as a member of the legal profession, is a representative of clients, an officer of the legal system, and a public citizen having a special responsibility for the quality of justice."

The obligation to adhere to ethical rules is triggered by the formation of the attorney-client relationship, which is also governed by state law. The *Restatement Third: The Law Governing Lawyers* summarizes that the attorney client relationship may be formed explicitly (i.e., the lawyer and the person expressly agree to form the relationship) or implicitly (i.e., the lawyer's conduct is such that a person would reasonably believe that a relationship has been formed even though the lawyer has not expressly undertaken representation). Either way, upon creation of the relationship, the lawyer must act in accordance with the Rules. Several rules are particularly pertinent for employment lawyers. First, Rule 1.7 addresses the lawyer's duty of undivided loyalty and problems that arise in representing multiple persons. Second, Rule 1.9 addresses the lawyer's obligation not to gain an advantage in representing a client by using information gained in representing a former client. Third, Rule 1.6 requires the attorney to maintain the confidences of a client, with only a few narrow exceptions. Finally, a lawyer has a duty to be honest to the courts, to opposing parties, and to third parties (Rules 3.3, 4.1, and 8.4).

1. Ethical Dilemmas Arising with Multiple Representation

The following scenarios involve issues that arise out of multiple representation. First, we will discuss the situation where one lawyer or law firm represents multiple plaintiffs or defendants. Second, we will discuss one lawyer or law firm representing two parties that are adverse to one another in a different matter. We begin with the relevant rules from the Model Rules of Professional Conduct.

Rule 1.7. Conflict of Interest: Current Clients

(a) Except as provided in paragraph (b), a lawyer shall not represent a client if the representation involves a concurrent conflict of interest. A concurrent conflict of interest exists if:

(1) the representation of one client will be directly adverse to another client; or

(2) there is a significant risk that the representation of one or more clients will be materially limited by the lawyer's responsibilities to another client, a former client or a third person or by a personal interest of the lawyer.

(b) Notwithstanding the existence of a concurrent conflict of interest under paragraph (a), a lawyer may represent a client if:

(1) the lawyer reasonably believes that the lawyer will be able to provide competent and diligent representation to each affected client;

(2) the representation is not prohibited by law;

(3) the representation does not involve the assertion of a claim by one client against another client represented by the lawyer in the same litigation or other proceeding before a tribunal; and

(4) each affected client gives informed consent, confirmed in writing.

Comments:

. . . .

[2] Resolution of a conflict of interest problem under this Rule requires the lawyer to: 1) clearly identify the client or clients; 2) determine whether a conflict of interest exists; 3) decide whether the representation may be undertaken despite the existence of a conflict, i.e., whether the conflict is consentable; and 4) if so, consult with the clients affected under paragraph (a) and obtain their informed consent, confirmed in writing. The clients affected under paragraph (a) include both of the clients referred to in para-

graph (a) (1) and the one or more clients whose representation might be materially limited under paragraph (a) (2).

. . . .

Identifying Conflicts of Interest: Directly Adverse

. . . .

[6] Loyalty to a current client prohibits undertaking representation directly adverse to that client without that client's informed consent. Thus, absent consent, a lawyer may not act as an advocate in one matter against a person the lawyer represents in some other matter, even when the matters are wholly unrelated. The client as to whom the representation is directly adverse is likely to feel betrayed, and the resulting damage to the client-lawyer relationship is likely to impair the lawyer's ability to represent the client effectively. In addition, the client on whose behalf the adverse representation is undertaken reasonably may fear that the lawyer will pursue that client's case less effectively out of deference to the other client, i.e., that the representation may be materially limited by the lawyer's interest in retaining the current client. Similarly, a directly adverse conflict may arise when a lawyer is required to cross-examine a client who appears as a witness in a lawsuit involving another client, as when the testimony will be damaging to the client who is represented in the lawsuit. On the other hand, simultaneous representation in unrelated matters of clients whose interests are only economically adverse, such as representation of competing economic enterprises in unrelated litigation, does not ordinarily constitute a conflict of interest and thus may not require consent of the respective clients.

. . . .

Identifying Conflicts of Interest: Material Limitation

. . . .

[8] Even where there is no direct adverseness, a conflict of interest exists if there is a significant risk that a lawyer's ability to consider, recommend or carry out an appropriate course of action for the client will be materially limited as a result of the lawyer's other responsibilities or interests. For example, a lawyer asked to represent several individuals seeking to form a joint venture is likely to be materially limited in the lawyer's ability to recommend or advocate all possible positions that each might take because of the lawyer's duty of loyalty to the others. The conflict in effect forecloses alternatives that would otherwise be available to the client. The mere possibility of subsequent harm does not itself require disclosure and consent. The critical questions are the likelihood that a difference in interests will eventuate and, if it does, whether it will materially interfere with the lawyer's independent professional judgment in considering alternatives or

foreclose courses of action that reasonably should be pursued on behalf of the client.

. . . .

Interest of Person Paying for a Lawyer's Service

. . . .

[13] A lawyer may be paid from a source other than the client, including a co-client, if the client is informed of that fact and consents and the arrangement does not compromise the lawyer's duty of loyalty or independent judgment to the client. See Rule 1.8(f). If acceptance of the payment from any other source presents a significant risk that the lawyer's representation of the client will be materially limited by the lawyer's own interest in accommodating the person paying the lawyer's fee or by the lawyer's responsibilities to a payer who is also a co-client, then the lawyer must comply with the requirements of paragraph (b) before accepting the representation, including determining whether the conflict is consentable and, if so, that the client has adequate information about the material risks of the representation.

. . . .

[29] In considering whether to represent multiple clients in the same matter, a lawyer should be mindful that if the common representation fails because the potentially adverse interests cannot be reconciled, the result can be additional cost, embarrassment and recrimination. Ordinarily, the lawyer will be forced to withdraw from representing all of the clients if the common representation fails. In some situations, the risk of failure is so great that multiple representation is plainly impossible. For example, a lawyer cannot undertake common representation of clients where contentious litigation or negotiations between them are imminent or contemplated. Moreover, because the lawyer is required to be impartial between commonly represented clients, representation of multiple clients is improper when it is unlikely that impartiality can be maintained. Generally, if the relationship between the parties has already assumed antagonism, the possibility that the clients' interests can be adequately served by common representation is not very good. Other relevant factors are whether the lawyer subsequently will represent both parties on a continuing basis and whether the situation involves creating or terminating a relationship between the parties.

[30] A particularly important factor in determining the appropriateness of common representation is the effect on client-lawyer confidentiality and the attorney-client privilege. With regard to the attorney-client privilege, the prevailing rule is that, as between commonly represented clients, the privilege does not attach. Hence, it must be assumed that if litigation eventuates

between the clients, the privilege will not protect any such communications, and the clients should be so advised.

[31] As to the duty of confidentiality, continued common representation will almost certainly be inadequate if one client asks the lawyer not to disclose to the other client information relevant to the common representation. This is so because the lawyer has an equal duty of loyalty to each client, and each client has the right to be informed of anything bearing on the representation that might affect that client's interests and the right to expect that the lawyer will use that information to that client's benefit. See Rule 1.4. The lawyer should, at the outset of the common representation and as part of the process of obtaining each client's informed consent, advise each client that information will be shared and that the lawyer will have to withdraw if one client decides that some matter material to the representation should be kept from the other. In limited circumstances, it may be appropriate for the lawyer to proceed with the representation when the clients have agreed, after being properly informed, that the lawyer will keep certain information confidential. For example, the lawyer may reasonably conclude that failure to disclose one client's trade secrets to another client will not adversely affect representation involving a joint venture between the clients and agree to keep that information confidential with the informed consent of both clients.

Restatement Third, The Law Governing Lawyers

§ 128. Representing Clients with Conflicting Interests in Civil Litigation

Unless all affected clients consent to the representation under the limitations and conditions provided in § 122, a lawyer in civil litigation <u>may not</u>:

(1) represent two or more clients in a matter if there is a <u>substantial risk</u> that the lawyer's representation of one client would be <u>materially and adversely affected</u> by the lawyer's duties to another client in the matter; or

(2) represent one client to assert or defend a claim against or brought by another client currently represented by the lawyer, <u>even if the matters are not related.</u>

Problem 43-1

You practice employment law. Two employees from the same company come to you and say that their employer breached a promise in the employee handbook to only select the most qualified internal candidate for an open promotion. There was one position, they each applied, and each was rejected in favor of another candidate. You review the handbook and see that the clause the employees point to is phrased in mandatory language ("shall select") and that the handbook has a weak disclaimer that can be challenged. Analyze whether you can represent both employees.

Problem 43-2

You represent two employees who accuse their employer of race discrimination. The employer is small but has enough employees to be covered by Title VII. You have claimed damages of $100,000 on behalf of each employee. During discovery you learn that the employer has an employment-practices liability insurance policy that covers claims of discrimination. The coverage limit is $50,000 for all claims related to the same conduct. Analyze whether you can continue to represent both employees.

---

2. Ethical Dilemmas Involving Former Clients

Another type of potential conflict arises when a lawyer is considering adopting a position that is adverse to the interests of a former client. This situation is likely to arise if you practice in a small community, or in the case of a "migrating" lawyer who leaves one firm and its clients for another firm and a different set of clients.

Rule 1.9. Duties to Former Clients

(a) A lawyer who has formerly represented a client in a matter shall not thereafter represent another person in the same or a substantially related matter in which that person's interests are materially adverse to the interests of the former client unless the former client gives informed consent, confirmed in writing.

(b) A lawyer shall not knowingly represent a person in the same or a substantially related matter in which a firm with which the lawyer formerly was associated had previously represented a client

(1) whose interests are materially adverse to that person; and

(2) about whom the lawyer had acquired information protected by Rules 1.6 and 1.9(c) that is material to the matter; unless the former client gives informed consent, confirmed in writing.

(c) A lawyer who has formerly represented a client in a matter or whose present or former firm has formerly represented a client in a matter shall not thereafter:

(1) use information relating to the representation to the disadvantage of the former client except as these Rules would permit or require with respect to a client, or when the information has become generally known; or

(2) reveal information relating to the representation except as these Rules would permit or require with respect to a client.

Rule 1.10. Imputation Of Conflicts Of Interest: General Rule

(a) While lawyers are associated in a firm, none of them shall knowingly represent a client when any one of them practicing alone would be prohibited from doing so by Rules 1.7 or 1.9, unless

(1) the prohibition is based on a personal interest of the disqualified lawyer and does not present a significant risk of materially limiting the representation of the client by the remaining lawyers in the firm; or

(2) the prohibition is based upon Rule 1.9(a) or (b) and arises out of the disqualified lawyer's association with a prior firm, and

(i) the disqualified lawyer is timely screened from any participation in the matter and is apportioned no part of the fee therefrom;

(ii) written notice is promptly given to any affected former client to enable the former client to ascertain compliance with the provisions of this Rule, which shall include a description of the screening procedures employed; a statement of the firm's and of the screened lawyer's compliance with these Rules; a statement that review may be available before a tribunal; and an agreement by the firm to respond promptly to any written inquiries or objections by the former client about the screening procedures; and

(iii) certifications of compliance with these Rules and with the screening procedures are provided to the former client by the screened lawyer and by a partner of the firm, at reasonable intervals upon the former client's written request and upon termination of the screening procedures.

(b) When a lawyer has terminated an association with a firm, the firm is not prohibited from thereafter representing a person with interests materially adverse to those of a client represented by the formerly associated lawyer and not currently represented by the firm, unless:

(1) the matter is the same or substantially related to that in which the formerly associated lawyer represented the client; and

(2) any lawyer remaining in the firm has information protected by Rules 1.6 and 1.9(c) that is material to the matter.

(c) A disqualification prescribed by this rule may be waived by the affected client under the conditions stated in Rule 1.7.

(d) The disqualification of lawyers associated in a firm with former or current government lawyers is governed by Rule 1.11.

Problem 43-3

Jill works as a defense lawyer for a large law firm. She is defending an FLSA retaliation case for Mega Corp. Jill has conducted interviews, filed an answer, and deposed the plaintiff. The plaintiff's lawyer is Ed, who is a partner with a small plaintiff's employment firm. During a break in a deposition for the case, Ed takes Jill aside and says, "I like your style. I like it a lot. You could do so much good for wronged employees. Don't waste your talent with a big corporate firm. Come to my shop!" At this juncture, analyze the issues for Jill and how she should resolve them.

If Jill quits her job and joins Ed's firm, would she be disqualified from working on the FLSA lawsuit against Mega Corp.? Would Ed's firm be disqualified from continuing the representation of the plaintiffs? Provide justification for your answers.

3. Ethical Obligations in the Internet Era

Traditionally, a potential client would call a law office and make an appointment to come in and discuss a possible representation. The internet era provides a very different environment for the formation of attorney-client relationships. Case law governs the formation of the relationship, as summarized by the *Restatement of the Law Governing Lawyers*. Using modern technology to advertise and solicit business is governed by Rule 7.1.

Restatement Third, The Law Governing Lawyers

§ 14. Formation of a Client-Lawyer Relationship

A relationship of client and lawyer arise when:

(1) a person manifests to a lawyer the person's intent that the lawyer provide legal services for the person; and either

(a) the lawyer manifests to the person consent to do so; or

(b) the lawyer fails to manifest lack of consent to do so, and the lawyer knows or reasonably should know that the person reasonably relies on the lawyer to provide the services; or

(2) a tribunal with power to do so appoints the lawyer to provide the services.

Rule 7.1. Communications Concerning A Lawyer's Services

A lawyer shall not make a false or misleading communication about the lawyer or the lawyer's services. A communication is false or misleading if it contains a material misrepresentation of fact or law, or omits a fact necessary to make the statement considered as a whole not materially misleading.

Problem 43-4

You are partners with Linda and have just started an immigration law firm. You are working to develop a client base. Linda suggests that you join a chat room on the internet where you can have interactive conversations with potential clients. The chat room has the following disclaimer that all participants can see.

> Important Notice: . . . this chat room is for informational purposes only and is not intended to be used as a source of specific legal advice in any way, shape, or form. Participating in this chat room does not establish an attorney client relationship. For personal legal advice please consult your attorney.

You and Linda join the chat room. The following day, Linda reads the following question on the site.

> Q: I am in the US on a visa from the UK that expires in one month. I have been told by my abusive husband not to return to the UK. He has told US immigration officials about me and so if I go back to the UK I won't be able to re-enter the US. This is the only place I have a home!!!! Please help!?!"

Linda posts the following response in the chat room:

> It is difficult to change your status once the visa expires. You should consider applying for a nonimmigrant visa such as a student visa, known as an "F" visa. You most likely will have to go back to the UK to apply for it. Or, you should apply for a nonimmigrant, or perhaps an immigrant, work visa. I would need to know more facts. Call my toll-free number at xxx-xxx-xxxx. I offer a free 10-minute phone consultation.

Assume that this advice is not complete or sound based on the limited information posted in the chat room. Analyze whether Linda's post created an attorney-client relationship that might subject her to a malpractice claim. If it might create an attorney-client relationship, redraft the post to ensure that no relationship is created.

---

4. Reconciling Zealous Advocacy with the Rules of Professionalism

As we discussed in Lesson 1, and have seen in the subsequent Lessons, work is deeply significant for individuals. Consequently, employment disputes often arise out of emotional conflicts: the long-term employee who has been terminated; the dutiful manager who has been accused of unlawful discrimination; a business that finds a former employee is competing in violation of a non-compete agreement. Clients—both employees and employers—often feel betrayed, and this can lead them to ask their lawyers to aggressively litigate, to "pull no punches." Where does zealous advocacy end and unprofessional behavior begin?

Rule 1.1. Competence

A lawyer shall provide competent representation to a client. Competent representation requires the legal knowledge, skill, thoroughness and preparation reasonably necessary for the representation.

Rule 1.3. Diligence

A lawyer shall act with reasonable diligence and promptness in representing a client.

Rule 4.1. Truthfulness In Statements To Others

In the course of representing a client a lawyer shall not knowingly:

(a) make a false statement of material fact or law to a third person; or

(b) fail to disclose a material fact to a third person when disclosure is necessary to avoid assisting a criminal or fraudulent act by a client, unless disclosure is prohibited by Rule 1.6.

Rule 8.4. Misconduct

It is professional misconduct for a lawyer to:

(a) violate or attempt to violate the Rules of Professional Conduct, knowingly assist or induce another to do so, or do so through the acts of another;

(b) commit a criminal act that reflects adversely on the lawyer's honesty, trustworthiness or fitness as a lawyer in other respects;

(c) engage in conduct involving dishonesty, fraud, deceit or misrepresentation;

(d) engage in conduct that is prejudicial to the administration of justice;

(e) state or imply an ability to influence improperly a government agency or official or to achieve results by means that violate the Rules of Professional Conduct or other law;

(f) knowingly assist a judge or judicial officer in conduct that is a violation of applicable rules of judicial conduct or other law; or

(g) engage in conduct that the lawyer knows or reasonably should know is harassment or discrimination on the basis of race, sex, religion, national origin, ethnicity, disability, age, sexual orientation, gender identity, marital status or socioeconomic status in conduct related to the practice of law. This paragraph does not limit the ability of a lawyer to accept, decline or withdraw from a representation in accordance with Rule 1.16. This paragraph does not preclude legitimate advice or advocacy consistent with these Rules.

Problem 43-5

You are defending a sexual harassment lawsuit that turns on a conversation that is remembered differently by the parties. Your client claims that he said nothing improper, but the plaintiff vehemently claims that your client propositioned her. The parties agree that the conversation took place on August 25 at 4 pm. The parties agree to limit discovery to a deposition of each party. You are preparing to depose the plaintiff. You take a cassette box and label it in large and clear handwriting: "CONVERSATION of 8-25." During the deposition you take the cassette out of your briefcase and place it in plain view of the plaintiff. After the plaintiff answers a question in a manner that you honestly and in good faith believe is deceptive, you tap the cassette box and ask, "Are you sure?" The plaintiff then changes her testimony. Analyze whether you have violated the Model Rules.

---

5. The Foundational Rule: Confidentiality

Lawyers must hold confidences shared by their client confidential. The scope of Rule 1.6 is quite broad, requiring the lawyer to keep information confidential if it is provided to the lawyer and "relates" to the representation.

Rule 1.6. Confidentiality of Information

(a) A lawyer shall not reveal information relating to the representation of a client unless the client gives informed consent, the disclosure is impliedly authorized in order to carry out the representation or the disclosure is permitted by paragraph (b).

(b) A lawyer may reveal information relating to the representation of a client to the extent the lawyer reasonably believes necessary:

(1) to prevent reasonably certain death or substantial bodily harm;

(2) to prevent the client from committing a crime or fraud that is reasonably certain to result in substantial injury to the financial interests or property of another and in furtherance of which the client has used or is using the lawyer's services;

(3) to prevent, mitigate or rectify substantial injury to the financial interests or property of another that is reasonably certain to result or has resulted from the client's commission of a crime or fraud in furtherance of which the client has used the lawyer's services;

(4) to secure legal advice about the lawyer's compliance with these Rules;

(5) to establish a claim or defense on behalf of the lawyer in a controversy between the lawyer and the client, to establish a defense to a criminal charge or civil claim against the lawyer based upon conduct in which the client was involved, or to respond to allegations in any proceeding concerning the lawyer's representation of the client;

(6) to comply with other law or a court order; or

(7) to detect and resolve conflicts of interest arising from the lawyer's change of employment or from changes in the composition or ownership of a firm, but only if the revealed information would not compromise the attorney-client privilege or otherwise prejudice the client.

(c) A lawyer shall make reasonable efforts to prevent the inadvertent or unauthorized disclosure of, or unauthorized access to, information relating to the representation of a client.

Problem 43-6

You represented Joe in a personal injury lawsuit. He accepted a settlement that you negotiated as part of a mediation, but afterwards he complained that the settlement was too small and that you "sold him out." A few days later he writes a review of you on Yelp! that says, "Stay away from Chris. She is ineffective and will sell you down the river just to move her cases along. She promises a lot in order to get you to sign up as a client, but then she leaves you high and dry." In fact, you are a well-regarded lawyer, have won awards for your professionalism, and you have ample documentation that establishes your competent representation of Joe, including one in which you valued his case for less than you obtained in the negotiated settlement. The managing partner at your firms urges you to respond, recalling Mark Twain's witticism that "a lie can travel halfway around the world while the truth is still getting its pants on." Analyze what you can and cannot do in this situation.

6. The Tension Between Loyalty to the Client and Loyalty to the Legal System

Lawyers owe a duty of loyalty to their clients. However, the ethical rules recognize that lawyers have duties to other constituencies that can be in tension with their fealty to their clients. One such duty is the obligation to ensure the effective functioning of the legal system.

Rule 5.6. Restrictions On Right To Practice

A lawyer shall not participate in offering or making:

(a) a partnership, shareholders, operating, employment, or other similar type of agreement that restricts the right of a lawyer to practice after termination of the relationship, except an agreement concerning benefits upon retirement; or

(b) an agreement in which a restriction on the lawyer's right to practice is part of the settlement of a client controversy.

Rule 8.3. Reporting Professional Misconduct

(a) A lawyer who knows that another lawyer has committed a violation of the Rules of Professional Conduct that raises a substantial question as to that lawyer's honesty, trustworthiness or fitness as a lawyer in other respects, shall inform the appropriate professional authority.

(b) A lawyer who knows that a judge has committed a violation of applicable rules of judicial conduct that raises a substantial question as to the judge's fitness for office shall inform the appropriate authority.

(c) This Rule does not require disclosure of information otherwise protected by Rule 1.6 or information gained by a lawyer or judge while participating in an approved lawyers assistance program.

Problem 43-7

You are representing 35 plaintiffs in an FLSA class action (called an "opt in procedure" under the FLSA). You are sitting in your office when the lawyer for the employer calls and says, "Hey look, you have a pretty good case. My client misclassified lots of employees as exempt and then failed to pay proper overtime. We need help. We will settle this case for $1,000,000, which is pretty close to our total exposure. We then want you to advise us on cleaning up this mess. Name your price, but your consultant fee has to come out of the million." Analyze the basis for your response.

Mastery Problem 43-1

You are a new lawyer at a firm. A partner comes into your office, hands you a federal court complaint, and explains your assignment:

> This is a new lawsuit. The plaintiff is a former employee of our client, Mega Corporation. She is claiming a violation of Title VII and alleges that she was sexually harassed at work by the CEO. The client investigated and could not determine who was telling the truth. The plaintiff and CEO have different stories. The company reported the results of the investigation, and the plaintiff promptly quit. She then sued Mega Corp. under Title VII, and she also sued the CEO individually for assault and

battery and intentional infliction of emotional distress. We are going to represent both parties. Draft a retention agreement that will ensure that we are in full compliance with the rules of professional conduct.

Consider the following scenarios:

(a) What if the company and the CEO agree to joint representation but persuasive evidence later surfaces (perhaps a video or text message) that establishes that the CEO did engage in non-consensual touching. How should the joint-representation plan for this possibility?

(b) What if the joint representation agreement is entered into and you are now preparing the CEO for his deposition. He suddenly turns to you and says, "You're my lawyer right? What I tell you is protected from disclosure and you can't tell anyone else because of the attorney-client privilege stuff, right? Well, I did touch her a bit. I know I said I did not touch her during the investigation, but that's because I thought it was harmless. A pat on the back. An occasional side hug. And yes, I kissed her hand, like an old-fashioned gentleman. She giggled. I swear it was consensual. But you can't tell the Board of Directors or I will lose my job. I really didn't do anything wrong." How do you plan in the agreement for that possible contingency?

(c) How should you address other contingencies that may arise with respect to filing motions, payment of attorney's fees, and similar potential conflicting situations?

(d) Consider the role of "informed consent" in drafting and explaining the agreement.

In resolving this problem refer to MR 1.7 (posted earlier in the Lesson) as well as the commentary to the Rule and Restatement 128 and the comment to it of the *Restatement of The Law Third, The Law Governing Lawyers.* Also feel free to research the concept of a Joint Representation Agreement.

Conclusion

Ethical dilemmas permeate the practice of employment law. As we saw in this Lesson, a threshold issue is whether an attorney-client relationship has been formed. Once the relationship is formed, the lawyer is subject to the rules of professional conduct with regard to the client. The duty of loyalty is paramount, and the duty to preserve confidences relating to former clients is also a broad duty with narrow exceptions. Some of the rules benefit the public directly, such as duties of candor and truthfulness owed to the court. It is critical that you carefully review your state's ethical rules when you confront potential problems in practice.

E. Overview of Wrongful Discharge Law

Key Concepts

- In this single Lesson chapter, you will consider the advisability of resolving issues surrounding wrongful discharge claims with a comprehensive statutory scheme.
- We will use the Montana Wrongful Discharge from Employment Act as a model for consideration.

Lesson 44:
The Montana Wrongful Discharge from Employment Act

Objectives and Expected Learning Outcomes

In this Lesson, we will review much of the course material relating to wrongful discharge by comparing it with the statutory approach adopted in Montana. You will develop a sense of the uses and limits of statutory law for the employment field. You will learn how to present a public policy analysis.

In this course we have studied modern regulation of the employment relationship. Despite many qualifications and exceptions, the at-will rule continues to be the presumption from which courts and legislatures create exceptions. However, one state—Montana—has enacted a statutory regime that displaces the at-will rule. To conclude your study of employment regulation, work through the Montana Wrongful Discharge from Employment Act and determine whether such a comprehensive approach to regulation is desirable, and whether the statute strikes the appropriate balance between economic efficiency and workplace justice.

Montana Wrongful Discharge from Employment Act

39-2-901. Short title

This part may be cited as the "Wrongful Discharge from Employment Act."

39–2–902. Purpose

This part sets forth certain rights and remedies with respect to wrongful discharge. Except as provided in 39–2–912, this part provides the exclusive remedy for a wrongful discharge from employment.

39–2–903. Definitions

In this part, the following definitions apply:

(1) "Constructive discharge" means the voluntary termination of employment by an employee because of a situation created by an act or omission of the employer which an objective, reasonable person would find so intolerable that voluntary termination is the only reasonable alternative. Constructive discharge does not mean voluntary termination because of an employer's refusal to promote the employee or improve wages, responsibilities, or other terms and conditions of employment.

(2) "Discharge" includes a constructive discharge as defined in subsection (1) and any other termination of employment, including resignation, elimination of the job, layoff for lack of work, failure to recall or rehire, and any other cutback in the number of employees for a legitimate business reason.

(3) "Employee" means a person who works for another for hire. The term does not include a person who is an independent contractor.

(4) "Fringe benefits" means the value of any employer-paid vacation leave, sick leave, medical insurance plan, disability insurance plan, life insurance plan, and pension benefit plan in force on the date of the termination.

(5) "Good cause" means reasonable job-related grounds for dismissal based on a failure to satisfactorily perform job duties, disruption of the employer's operation, or other legitimate business reason. The legal use of a lawful product by an individual off the employer's premises during nonworking hours is not a legitimate business reason, unless the employer acts within the provisions of 39–2–313(3) or (4).

(6) "Lost wages" means the gross amount of wages that would have been reported to the internal revenue service as gross income on form W-2 and includes additional compensation deferred at the option of the employee.

(7) "Public policy" means a policy in effect at the time of the discharge concerning the public health, safety, or welfare established by constitutional provision, statute, or administrative rule.

39–2–904. Elements of wrongful discharge—presumptive probationary period

(1) A discharge is wrongful only if:

(a) it was in retaliation for the employee's refusal to violate public policy or for reporting a violation of public policy;

(b) the discharge was not for good cause and the employee had completed the employer's probationary period of employment; or

(c) the employer violated the express provisions of its own written personnel policy.

(2) (a) During a probationary period of employment, the employment may be terminated at the will of either the employer or the employee on notice to the other for any reason or for no reason.

(b) If an employer does not establish a specific probationary period or provide that there is no probationary period prior to or at the time of hire, there is a probationary period of 6 months from the date of hire.

39–2–905. Remedies

(1) If an employer has committed a wrongful discharge, the employee may be awarded lost wages and fringe benefits for a period not to exceed 4 years from the date of discharge, together with interest on the lost wages and fringe benefits. Interim earnings, including amounts the employee could have earned with reasonable diligence, must be deducted from the amount awarded for lost wages. Before interim earnings are deducted from lost wages, there must be deducted from the interim earnings any reasonable amounts expended by the employee in searching for, obtaining, or relocating to new employment.

(2) The employee may recover punitive damages otherwise allowed by law if it is established by clear and convincing evidence that the employer engaged in actual fraud or actual malice in the discharge of the employee in violation of 39–2–904(1)(a).

(3) There is no right under any legal theory to damages for wrongful discharge under this part for pain and suffering, emotional distress, compensatory damages, punitive damages, or any other form of damages, except as provided for in subsections (1) and (2).

39–2–911. Limitation of actions

(1) An action under this part must be filed within 1 year after the date of discharge.

(2) If an employer maintains written internal procedures, other than those specified in 39–2–912, under which an employee may appeal a discharge within the organizational structure of the employer, the employee shall first exhaust those procedures prior to filing an action under this part. The employee's failure to initiate or exhaust available internal procedures is a defense to an action brought under this part. If the employer's internal procedures are not completed within 90 days from the date the employee initiates the internal procedures, the employee may file an action under this part and for purposes of this subsection the employer's internal procedures are considered exhausted. The limitation period in subsection (1) is tolled until the procedures are exhausted. In no case may the provisions of the employer's internal procedures extend the limitation period in subsection (1) more than 120 days.

(3) If the employer maintains written internal procedures under which an employee may appeal a discharge within the organizational structure of the employer, the employer shall within 7 days of the date of the discharge notify the discharged employee of the existence of such procedures and shall supply the discharged employee with a copy of them. If the employer fails to comply with this subsection, the discharged employee need not comply with subsection (2).

39–2–912. Exemptions

This part does not apply to a discharge:

(1) that is subject to any other state or federal statute that provides a procedure or remedy for contesting the dispute. The statutes include those that prohibit discharge for filing complaints, charges, or claims with administrative bodies or that prohibit unlawful discrimination based on race, national origin, sex, age, disability, creed, religion, political belief, color, marital status, and other similar grounds.

(2) of an employee covered by a written collective bargaining agreement or a written contract of employment for a specific term.

39–2–913. Preemption of common-law remedies

Except as provided in this part, no claim for discharge may arise from tort or express or implied contract.

39–2–914. Arbitration

(1) A party may make a written offer to arbitrate a dispute that otherwise could be adjudicated under this part.

(2) An offer to arbitrate must be in writing and contain the following provisions:

(a) A neutral arbitrator must be selected by mutual agreement or, in the absence of agreement, as provided in 27–5–211.

(b) The arbitration must be governed by the Uniform Arbitration Act, Title 27, chapter 5. If there is a conflict between the Uniform Arbitration Act and this part, this part applies.

(c) The arbitrator is bound by this part.

(3) If a complaint is filed under this part, the offer to arbitrate must be made within 60 days after service of the complaint and must be accepted in writing within 30 days after the date the offer is made.

(4) A discharged employee who makes a valid offer to arbitrate that is accepted by the employer and who prevails in such arbitration is entitled to have the arbitrator's fee and all costs of arbitration paid by the employer.

(5) If a valid offer to arbitrate is made and accepted, arbitration is the exclusive remedy for the wrongful discharge dispute and there is no right to bring or continue a lawsuit under this part. The arbitrator's award is final and binding, subject to review of the arbitrator's decision under the provisions of the Uniform Arbitration Act.

39–2–915. Effect of rejection of offer to arbitrate

A party who makes a valid offer to arbitrate that is not accepted by the other party and who prevails in an action under this part is entitled as an element of costs to reasonable attorney fees incurred subsequent to the date of the offer.

Immediately after enactment, lawyers challenged the new statutory scheme by arguing that it unconstitutionally eliminated full recovery by injured employees. Read the following case carefully, and remember that the case arose in the 1980s, at the height of the development of common law remedies for wrongful discharge.

Meech v. Hillhaven West, Inc.

238 Mont. 21 (1989).

McDonough, Justice.

This opinion concerns questions certified to this Court by the United States District Court for the District of Montana, Great Falls Division, Honorable Paul G. Hatfield presiding. The questions are as follows:

> (1) Is the Montana Wrongful Discharge From Employment Act, §§ 39–2–901 to 39–2–914, MCA, unconstitutional in that it serves to wrongfully deprive an individual falling within the purview of the Act from his or her right to "full legal redress" within the meaning of Article II, § 16 of the Montana Constitution?
>
> (2) Are those provisions of the Montana Wrongful Discharge From Employment Act which expressly prohibit recovery of non-economic damages, and limit the recovery of punitive damages, violative of an individual's right to "full legal redress" within the meaning of Article II, § 16 of the Montana Constitution?

We answer "No" to both questions.

Petitioner Meech's action in the United States District Court claims damages for wrongful termination from employment, breach of the implied covenant of good faith and fair dealing, and intentional or negligent infliction of emotional distress. Meech also seeks punitive damages for allegedly oppressive, malicious, and unjustifiable conduct on the part of Meech's former employer, respondent Hillhaven. The claims grew from the alleged wrongful discharge of Meech by Hillhaven. Hillhaven moved to dismiss asserting that the Montana Wrongful Discharge From Employment Act (Act) precluded Meech's common-law claims. Meech responded to the motion by contending that the Act violated Article II, § 16 of the Montana Constitution. Certification of the questions presented here followed. Before fully answering the questions, a brief summary of the Act aids in understanding the issues.

The Act provides the exclusive remedy and procedure for actions formerly governed to a great extent by common-law requirements:

> *Preemption of common-law remedies:* Except as provided in this part, no claim for discharge may arise from tort or express or implied contract.

Section 39–2–913, MCA. The Act exempts from its provisions causes of action for discharge governed by other state or federal statutory procedures for contesting discharge disputes. For example, the Act exempts from its provisions, discriminatory discharges, and actions for wrongful discharge from employment covered by written collective bargaining agreements or controlled by a written contract for a specific term. For other wrongful discharge claims, however, the Act provides the exclusive procedure. Sections

39–2–912 to 9–2–913, MCA. The Act repeals Montana statutes which formerly granted to both employees and employers the right to terminate the employment relationship for fault on the part of the other party. Sections 39–2–504 to 39–2–505, MCA (1985). The Act's provisions on discharge also limit the operation of § 39–2–503, MCA, Montana's "at-will" statute. See § 39–2–902, MCA. In place of the prior governing statutes and the common-law causes of action it abrogates, the Act provides a statutorily defined cause of action for wrongful discharge.

. . . .

Meech in essence argues that the Act denies his fundamental right to full legal redress under Article II, § 16 of the Montana Constitution. Meech also contends that the Act violates equal protection by denying the fundamental right to full legal redress to a class of claimants without demonstrating that the classification furthers a compelling state interest. Hillhaven answers that the Act does not violate equal protection of the laws or infringe on a fundamental right to full legal redress because Article II, § 16 of the Montana Constitution guarantees only a right of access to courts to seek a remedy for wrongs recognized by common-law or statutory authority, and the legislature may alter common-law causes of action to promote a legitimate state interest. We agree with Hillhaven and overrule [previous cases] insofar as they hold that Article II, § 16 of the Montana Constitution guarantees a fundamental right to full legal redress.

I.

> *[Editor's Note: The Court first held that the Act does not violate the fundamental right of full legal redress because no such right is created by the Montana Constitution. The Constitution requires only that the courts provide the relief available under statutes and the common law, and does not upset the power of the legislature to change principles of the common law through statutory enactment. Judicial recognition of such a fundamental right would intrude on legislative powers and violate separation of powers.]*

The above cited examples of legislative and judicial limitations illustrate that the law, for a variety of policy reasons, refuses to provide a cause of action, remedy and redress for every injury. This proposition is expressed in Latin as *damnum absque injuria,* meaning a "loss which does not give rise to an action for damages against the person causing it." Black's Law Dictionary

345 (4th ed. 1979). The legislation at issue here similarly alters common-law rights and duties and arguably denies a cause of action, remedy, and redress for injuries recognized at common law. If Article II, § 16, guarantees a fundamental right to full legal redress as embodied in common-law causes of action, then a myriad of legislation altering common law in a restrictive manner, as well as the Act, denies this fundamental right . . .

. . . .

II.

[Editor's Note: The Court then held that the Act did not violate principles of equal protection because it is rationally related to a legitimate state interest.]

. . . .

Until recently, the fundamental body of law governing available damages in the employment area has been contract law. Courts, by virtue of their power to alter the common law, have expanded employers' liability by recognizing tort claims in the employment context. The legislature has now acted to reverse this trend by restricting damages for wrongful discharge. This decision to limit liability "emerges as a classic example of an economic regulation—a legislative effort to structure and accommodate 'the burdens and benefits of economic life.' " *Duke Power Co. v. Carolina Environmental Study Group* (1978), 438 U.S. 59, 83, 98 S.Ct. 2620, 2636, 57 L.Ed.2d 595, 617–18. A statutory "limitation on recovery is a classic economic regulation, . . . [which] must be upheld if it is reasonably related to a valid legislative purpose." *Boyd v. Bulala* (W.D.Va.1986), 647 F.Supp. 781, 786 (finding heightened scrutiny inappropriate for reviewing liability-limitation under requirements of Virginia's remedy guarantee).

. . . .

The legislative history of the Act demonstrates that lawmakers perceived an unreasonable financial threat to Montana employers from large judgments in common-law wrongful discharge claims. Testimony in legislative hearings also indicated to legislators that large judgments in common-law wrongful discharge cases could discourage employers from locating their businesses in Montana. The Act's limitation on damages is intended to alleviate these threats. Therefore, the Act passes muster on this leg of the test because promoting the financial interests of businesses in the State or potentially in the State to improve economic conditions in Montana constitutes a legitimate state goal.

We also conclude that the Act relates rationally to promoting Montana's economic interests. Some awards for common-law wrongful discharge have included wages which extend far into the claimant's employment future. The effect of the Act's limitations on damages to four years lost wages rationally relates to reducing this potential liability. Moreover, the limit itself is not irrational or so arbitrary that the classification it creates violates equal protection. As a matter of policy, the legislature determined that four years should be the maximum period for consideration of wage loss reasoning that claimants could generally be expected to find similar employment by the end of this period. The time period in any given claim is necessarily speculative. However, statistics before the legislature supported the conclusion that most wrongful discharge claimants with reasonable diligence will obtain other employment within the four year period. Therefore, judicial deference for the time period at issue is appropriate. The same sort of analysis applies to the Act's limitations on damages for pain and suffering and emotional distress; the restriction on recovery rationally relates to the legislature's legitimate purpose of limiting employers' liability for wrongful discharge.

It could be surmised too that this particular limitation relates rationally to another legitimate legislative aim, that is, it provides for greater certainty in defining an employer's duties by recalling a contract law limitation on damages for pain and suffering. As a corollary to this purpose, a greater certainty of the rights of employees also exists under the Act as a result of the "good cause" requirement.

. . . .

The differences in calculating personal injury damages and contract damages points out a problem with the emergence of tort claims in the employment relationship. Tort claims for at-will employees compensate for these workers' inability to control the term of their employment. Employers, however, are unable to plan for the extensive liability which may arise from damages available in these claims. Testimony in legislative hearings indicated that this is a source of great discontent in the Montana business community. The Act's limitation on noneconomic damages applies long-standing contract law in an attempt to solve this problem by dictating a more objective measure of damages. Under the Act, employers benefit because their potential liability is made more certain. Meanwhile, employees' control over the manner in which they are discharged remains, in part, as a result of the Act's "good employees' cause" requirement. The Act, in making this trade, is in no sense irrational. Therefore, classifications in the Act satisfy the requirements of the rational basis test.

. . . .

In conclusion, Montana's remedy clause seeks to guarantee equal access to courts to obtain remedies for injuries as provided by governing law. It does not, however, impart a definition of what the law considers a remedy or full legal redress. Nor does it empower this Court to exclude the legislature from defining what are legal injuries.

Finally, we make clear here that the proper test to apply to the Act's classifications burdening one class and not another, is the rational basis test. The classifications created under the Act at issue here survive scrutiny under this test, and even if Montana law required a *quid pro quo* for the old causes of actions, the Act provides a reasonable substitute. Thus, we answer "No" to both questions posed by the United States District Court.

TURNAGE, C.J., and GULBRANDSON and WEBER, JJ., concur.

SHEEHY, JUSTICE, dissenting:

This is the blackest judicial day in the eleven years that I have sat on this Court. Indeed it may be the blackest judicial day in the history of the state. Certainly this decision is more regressive than the ill-boded *Ashcraft v. Montana Power Company* (1971), 156 Mont. 368, 480 P.2d 812 case, which deprived injured workers of their full legal redress against third party tortfeasors. The decision today cleans the scalpel for the legislature to cut away unrestrainedly at the whole field of tort redress. Perhaps worse by this decision today, the Court throws in the sponge as a co-equal in our tripartite state government.

I.

For the reader to understand the drastic ramifications of the "Wrongful Discharge From Employment Act" the whole of the Act must be set out. . . .

The contraction of what was once in this state the tort of wrongful discharge is found principally in three sections of the Act, Section 4 [§ 39–2–904, MCA], Section 5 [§ 39–2–905, MCA] and Section 8 [§ 39–2–913, MCA].

Under Section 4 of the Act [§ 39–2–904, MCA] grounds for wrongful discharge are limited to three possibilities:

> (1) It was in retaliation for the employee's refusal to violate public policy or for reporting a violation of public policy;
>
> (2) The discharge was not for good cause and the employee had completed the employers probationary period of employment; [under the Act, a probationer has absolutely no right of recourse for a wrongful discharge] or
>
> (3) The employer violated the express provisions of its own written personnel policy.

The attorneys in this case supporting the Wrongful Discharge From Employment Act filed briefs claiming that it provided great new rights for discharged workers. Not true. Each of the elements listed above was established by this Court in decisions heretofore made and each was fully available to wrongfully discharged employees, *including probationers.*

. . . .

The elements of wrongful discharge, as found in the Act, therefore, are but restatements of cases based on some judicial policy heretofore promulgated by this Court. While perforce, the legislature had to recognize at least those three elements of wrongful discharge, it took care to provide that *no significant amount of damages could be recovered by a wrongfully discharged* employee even under those elements. A wronged employee's remedies are nearly emasculated under the Act.

Section 5 of the Act [§ 39–2–905, MCA] describes the recoverable remedies for a wrongfully discharged employee. He or she may recover no more than four years of lost wages and fringe benefits *from both of which are deducted* amounts the employees earned or could have earned with reasonable diligence during that period. Since Section 6 of the Act [§ 39–2–911, MCA] limits suits to one year from the date of discharge, the employee's loss is wholly speculative.

Section 5 of the Act completely wipes out any right of any discharged employee to damages for pain and suffering, emotional distress, compensatory damages or any other form of damages except the four years of mitigated lost wages and fringe benefits. These stricken elements of damages are traditionally allowed against tortfeasors, elements which we have supported in any number of cases, as proper items of recovery.

Finally, to make certain that a wronged employee would have to take his or her lumps without a legal basis for proper recovery, the legislature adopted Section 8 [§ 39–2–913, MCA] which states that no claim for discharge may arise from a tort or express or implied contract except as provided in the Act itself. The real purpose of Section 8 is to negate by elimination any possible employee claim of tort based upon an implied covenant of good faith and fair dealing in the employment contract. This provision takes Montana out of the mainstream of American legal thought.

. . . .

The approval by this Court in this case of the elimination by the legislature of the element of good faith and fair dealing in employment contracts has the effect of reversing all of the employment cases this Court has handed down in the last decade. The elimination has a profound effect on the recovery of punitive damages. Although the Act here in question provides [Section 5(2)] for punitive damages in case of actual fraud or actual malice on the part of the employer, unless an employee can show an implied covenant of good faith and fair dealing in his employment contract, he will find no basis upon which punitive damages can be awarded to him.

The legislature, in effect, has converted the tort of wrongful discharge into a sort of contract action by the adoption of the Wrongful Discharge From Employment Act. The legislature refused, nonetheless, to provide all the elements of the damages allowable for breach of contract which ordinarily would compensate the party aggrieved for *all* of the detriment proximately caused by the breach and in the ordinary course of things likely to result therefrom. Section 27–1–311, MCA.

. . . .

It is evident that the Wrongful Discharge From Employment Act adopted by the Montana legislature purporting to give a wronged employee some rights, instead, took away any possible right of meaningful recovery. The ominous implications of this Act for all employees not working under a union contract cannot be overstated. The longer the employee works for an employer, the greater reliance the employee places upon the employer's proffer of fringe benefits and retirement allowances, then the more the employee is at risk to be discharged, because the economic result of a wrongful discharge to the employer, even if the employee's suit under the Act should be successful, is nothing but paltry damages to the employee and possible profit to the employer. The lack of legislative clout of the unorganized workers, although they may comprise a majority of the workers in this state, is demonstrated in that this patently unfair legislation in 1987 passed the State Senate without a no vote on third reading, and with but 16 no votes out of 100 in the State House of Representatives.

II.

> When law can do no right [Then] it be lawful that law can bar no wrong.
>
> —William Shakespeare, *King John* (Magna Carta's John) Act III, Scene i.

Four centuries ago William Shakespeare stated in capsule the view of the majority of this Court in upholding the Act. The majority view is that the legislature can abolish any right of recovery and when it does courts are barred from awarding "full legal redress" under Art. II, Sec. 16, Montana State Constitution. . . .

. . . .

The final arbiter of what the state law in Montana shall be is this Court, under Art. II, Sec. 16, not the legislature. We are given that power, to be used judicially. The Justices in the majority do not seem to realize it, but in approving without objection or by inaction the Wrongful Discharge From Employment Act of 1987, they are making law. They have blessed what should be repugnant to a court—a savage curtailment of redress for wrongs, and they excuse their inaction by ceding overall power to the legislature. Though the State Constitution requires courts of justice (not the legislature) to afford a speedy remedy for *every* injury of person, of property, or of character, the majority have taken a detour from the road to remedy. They have declined to insist on not only a speedy remedy, but on full legal redress for wrongfully discharged employees. They have made law by being passive, and deserve no praise. A toothless court, when abstaining from its duty, is making law and is as great a threat to a just government as an unrestrained legislature.

This is not to say that this Court sits as a super legislature, governing by its discretion the policy, wisdom, and direction of legislative acts. When, however, the legislature acts invidiously to discriminate between persons similarly situated, as will be demonstrated below, Art. II, Sec. 16 imposes a duty upon this Court to make certain that right *and* justice are not denied.

III.

Having determined that Meech has no fundamental right to a full legal redress here, the majority sustain the equal protection implications of the Wrongful Discharge From Employment Act by applying the rational test. This leads the majority to the irrational result that it is rational to make the state safe for unscrupulous employers.

The legislature made no findings to accompany the Act, nor does the Act itself articulate its purpose. The statements by the majority as to the purpose of the Act are extrapolated from written statements of proponents submitted to the committees considering the Act, and not the whole legislature.

At its core, the Wrongful Discharge from Employment Act is nothing more than a cap on recoverable damages available to wronged employees. . . .

. . . .

It is not a legitimate state purpose to protect employers from their unscrupulous acts as against the traditional rights of individuals to earn their livelihood. Our state constitution includes among *inalienable* rights "pursuing life's basic necessities, enjoying and defending their lives and liberties, acquiring, possessing and protecting property, and seeking their safety, health and happiness in all lawful ways. In enjoying these rights, all persons recognize corresponding responsibilities." Art. II, § 3, 1972 Mont. Const.

Thus, no case can be made on a rational basis to sustain a law the principal purpose of which is to subsidize, protect or enhance the acts of wrongdoers.

Because of its manifest discrimination, because it serves no legitimate state purpose, and because it cannot survive a proper balancing test as between the rights of employers and of individuals to pursue life's basic necessities, the Wrongful Discharge from Employment Act of 1987 violates the Equal Protection Clause of the 1972 Montana Constitution, Art. II, § 4.

. . . .

It is usually a due process argument that an Act which limits the rights of recovery of injured parties must provide a reasonably adequate substitute, or *quid pro quo,* as the majority calls it. The majority, having adopted the irrational conclusion that the Wrongful Discharge From Employment Act was valid, is driven to a further irrationality in determining that the substitution of mitigated recovery provided to wronged employees in the Act was adequate. Not unlike Polonious in *Hamlet,* the majority can find in a cloud a camel's shape, a weasel's, or very like a whale.

In determining the adequacy of the substituted recovery in the Act, the majority confined itself to examination of the mitigated four years of damages as against what might be recovered for loss of wages or fringe benefits. The majority paid no attention in determining adequacy to the elimination of compensatory damages, damages for emotional or mental distress, and damages arising from the breach of the implied covenant of good faith and fair dealing. By so examining, the majority managed to escape the best indication of the inadequacy of the recoverable damages in the Act demonstrated by the cases that have come to this Court.... The Act simply does not survive an adequacy test when properly admeasured against the former law in Montana.

....

V.

If Art. II, § 16 of the Montana Constitution does anything, it imposes upon the judiciary the duty to guard the state constitution. In its decision today, this Court sidesteps that duty and reverses not only the cases mentioned in the majority opinion but a long line of cases in the past 15 years that have established solid boundaries for employers and employees, while adhering to the at-will principle declared in our statutes. In yielding our duty to the vagaries of the legislature, we have disadvantaged a large portion of the Montana labor market in the guise of a better business climate. The Wrongful Discharge From Employment Act of 1987 is economically and socially regressive. The majority opinion is legally regressive. Because of the unwillingness of the majority to act properly in a constitutional case, regressiveness is the order of the day.

I would hold the Wrongful Discharge From Employment Act of 1987 to be invalid on the basis that under an equal protection test it cannot meet even a rational scrutiny. The only basis for the Act that I can find is that as between business and the workers, the legislature discriminatingly prefers business. That is not a constitutional basis on which to found a statute.

HUNT, J., concurs.

QUESTIONS

1. At the time that *Meech* was decided, Montana common law decisions had established that bad faith terminations would give rise to tort damages (you will recall that the California Supreme Court later stemmed this tide in the *Foley* case). Is it appropriate for the legislature to cut back on recognized common law rights, or should the legislature have deferred to the judiciary to develop the law of wrongful discharge?

2. In 1996, Arizona enacted the Employment Protection Act, A.R.S. § 23–1501 et seq. The Arizona Supreme Court decided that the legislature properly exercised its authority to limit the damages available under the statutory cause of action, despite a state constitutional provision that prohibited the legislature from limiting remedies for common law violations. *See Cronin v. Sheldon*, 195 Ariz. 531 (*En Banc* 1999). The court concluded that the anti-abrogation clause of the constitution, which provides that a right of action to recover damages for injuries shall never be legislatively eliminated, applies only to tort causes of action that either existed at common law or evolved from rights recognized at common law. Was the Court correct to conclude that wrongful discharge actions did not meet this test, and that the rights of employees at issue were solely a creation of the Employment Protection Act?

Mastery Problem 44-1

Assume that your jurisdiction is considering adopting the Montana Act and that you are a legislative aid to a member of the state Senate. Prepare an analysis of the proposed law that includes a balanced assessment of the interests of employers, employees, and the public.

Public Policy analysts have adopted standard ways to assess legislation. Consider the following classic approach as a guide for organizing and structuring your analysis of the Montana Act.

Francis J. Mootz III, *A Summary of the Eightfold Path Guide for Policy Analysis Originally Developed by Eugene Bardach*[1]

I. Introduction

To provide effective policy analysis of proposed legislation, the analyst must be able to adopt multiple positions and to provide a balanced assessment to the client seeking the analysis. This requires as much art as science. This memorandum describes the "Eightfold Path" of policy analysis, which is comprised of the following steps:

1. Define the problem
2. Assemble the relevant evidence
3. Construct alternative approaches
4. Select criteria for judging the approaches
5. Project the likely outcomes of the proposed legislation
6. Confront the necessary tradeoffs
7. Decide on the recommended course of action
8. Provide a supporting narrative

It is critical to remember that this process is iterative; there is no end to policy analysis that can be final once and for all. However, at some point the conclusion must be drawn and defended.

II. The Eightfold Path

1. Define the Problem

This is a critical step: why should we care about the issue?

What private failure (market, moral, systemic, etc.) requires public intervention?

1 See Eugene Bardach and Eric M. Patashnik, A Practical Guide for Policy Analysis: The Eightfold Path to More Effective Problem Solving 1–82 (CQ Press, 5th ed. 2015).

Be proactive: do not assume the status quo.

2. Assemble the Relevant Evidence

This must be a thoughtful process, rather than just the hustling of data.

Be judicious about data: (i) does it help us to understand the solution to a problem; (ii) does it add more than a "best guess" approach; and (iii) does data really add value to confirming the hypothesis?

Use analogies to similar programs and their use of data and evidence.

Do not ignore those who disagree, or data that disconfirms a hypothesis.

3. Construct Alternative Approaches

Start with a comprehensive view, but end with a focused approach to the problem.

Simplify the list of alternatives (use a catchy phrase for each).

Bounce new alternatives off interested stakeholders to ensure creative thinking.

4. Select Criteria for Judging the Approaches

Use evaluative criteria that can generate a conclusion.

For example, one might seek to: maximize net social benefits, maximize the sum of individual benefits, maximize the welfare of the least advantaged, etc.

Assess the willingness of the public to pay for the proposal based upon current resources.

Assess cost effectiveness and equity issues as part of the analysis.

Legal constraints are real limits that must also be assessed.

5. Project the Likely Outcomes of the Proposed Legislation

It is difficult to project outcomes, but it is necessary.

Be realistic (avoid the temptation of optimism) and build on modeling and evidence.

Suggest the breakeven point (this bill will succeed if X number of individuals file under it).

What scenarios can cause the proposal to fail?

6. Confront the Necessary Trade-Offs

Compare the alternatives to the base status quo

Eliminate alternatives that clearly suffer from excessive tradeoffs.

7. Decide on the Recommended Course of Action

Pretend that you are the decision maker.

Convince yourself of the plausibility of your recommendation, before persuading others.

If your solution is such a great idea, why is it not already in place?

8. Tell Your Story

Know your audience, and speak to that audience.

Taxi driver test: can you persuade an average citizen in 15 minutes?

Provide a logical narrative in support of the recommendation.

Avoid a formulaic approach that pretends that the answer is easy and certain.

Avoid a qualified approach that has too many caveats to be persuasive.

III. Summary

Avoid excessive enthusiasm about new ideas, but at same time do not require more than "sufficient" evidence to implement necessary reforms.

Always attend to the importance of weighing risks and uncertainties.

Remember that when institutions are stuck in their ways, change can be a benefit in and of itself.

Conclusion

This Lesson provided you with the opportunity to take a broad view of employment law and to develop skills in public policy analysis. One of the central tensions in employment law is the allocation for decision-making between private parties (employer and employee), legislatures, administrative agencies, and courts. Analyzing the Montana statute brought these tensions into sharp relief.